Tashkent Modernism XX/XXI

Uzbekistan
Art and Culture
Development
Foundation

Edited by
Boris Chukhovich, Davide Del Curto, Ekaterina Golovatyuk

Lars Müller Publishers

This book was made possible thanks to Gayane Umerova, Chairperson of the Uzbekistan Art and Culture Development Foundation

Foreword:
Gayane Umerova
Preface:
Francesco Bandarin

Edited by:
Boris Chukhovich
Davide Del Curto
Ekaterina Golovatyuk

With essays by:
Sofia Celli, Research Fellow, Department of Architecture and Urban Studies, Politecnico di Milano
Boris Chukhovich
Davide Del Curto, Professor of Architectural Conservation, Department of Architecture and Urban Studies, Politecnico di Milano
Federica Deo, Research Fellow, Department of Architecture and Urban Studies, Politecnico di Milano
Ekaterina Golovatyuk
Nicola Russi, Professor of Architecture and Urban Studies, Department of Architecture and Urban Studies, Politecnico di Milano

Interview:
Rem Koolhaas

Visual essay:
Armin Linke

Tashkent Modernism XX/XXI Research:
GRACE
Ekaterina Golovatyuk
Giacomo Cantoni
Ksenia Bisti
Natalia Saltan
Riccardo Salomoni
Zhongjian Kee
Politecnico di Milano
Davide Del Curto
Andrea Gritti
Sofia Celli
Federica Deo
Boris Chukhovich
Laboratorio Permanente
Nicola Russi
Angelica Sylos Labini
Laine Lazda
Pietro Nobili Vitelleschi
Amedeo Noris
Novaya Labs
Ivan Kuryachiy
Maria Bobrinskaya
Kristina Emelianova
Olga Bazarova
Lina Filip
Kseniia Nikolaeva
Commonwealth Partnership
Nikolay Moroz
Anastasia Andruschak

Translations and copyediting:
Ruth Addison, Timur Zolotarev

Proofreading:
Rita Forbes, Deborah Cecere

Project coordination:
Hester van den Bold
(Lars Müller Publishers)

Image research and content coordination:
Ksenia Bisti (GRACE)

Design:
Hubertus Design
Jonas Voegeli
Kerstin Landis
Fabio Furlani

Lithography:
Gundula Seraphin,
Bad Münstereifel, Germany

Printing and binding:
DZA Druckerei zu Altenburg, Germany

Paper:
60 g/sm Prolight FSC,
100 g/sm MaxiGloss,
60 g/sm Holmen TRND 2.0

© 2025 Lars Müller Publishers, the Uzbekistan Art and Culture Development Foundation and the authors

No part of this book may be used or reproduced in any form or manner whatsoever without prior written permission, except in the case of brief quotations embedded in critical articles and reviews.

Lars Müller Publishers is supported by the Swiss Federal Office of Culture with a structural contribution for the years 2021–2025.

Lars Müller Publishers
Pfingstweidstrasse 6
CH-8005 Zürich
info@lars-muller.ch
lars-mueller-publishers.com
+41 44 274 37 40

Product safety producer:
Lars Müller Publishers
Responsible person in accordance with EU Regulation 2023/988 (GPSR):
Michael Klein, sales representative, Hub 1,
DE-84149 Velden
+49 8742 964 552 2
gpsr@lars-muller.ch

ISBN:
978-3-03778-751-9

Distributed in North America, Latin America and the Caribbean by ARTBOOK | D.A.P.
www.artbook.com

Printed in Germany

THE PROJECT TEAM WISHES TO THANK

Recommendations on the Cultural Trail:
Rustam Khusanov

Locating historical general plans of Tashkent:
Viliul' Gaziev

Consulting on the history of various buildings and their architects:
Rem Adylov
Valerii Akopdzhanian
Shukur Askarov
Mark Burlakov
Zlata Chebotareva
Aleksandr Kalislamov
Firuza Khairutdinova
Iurii Khaldeev
Aleksandr Kuranov
Anatolii Liss
Iurii Miroshnichenko
Ruslan Muradov
Vil' Muratov
Vladimir Narubanskii
Sergei Romanov
Vladislav Rusanov
Elena Sukhanova
Vladimir Sutiagin
Rafail Takhtaganov
Abdumannop Ziiaev

Providing materials from the archive of Farkhad Tursunov:
Shukhrat Abdullaev and Zaur Mansurov

Providing materials on the Zhemchug residential building:
Temur Karimov
Kamila Mukhamedieva
Diliara Saidumerova

Documents from family archives and family memoirs:
Ekaterina Berezina
Marina Ivanian
Firuza Khairutdinova
Rushena Seminogova
Karine Sutiagina
Niiara Zaidova

Documents from institutional archives:
Irina Bkharat and Igor' Rotanov
Vasila Faizieva
Zukhra Kasimova
Makhmudzhon Musaev
Shakirdzhan Pidaev
Gul'nara Rashidova
Takhir Sadykov

Help with organizing the photo shoot of Zhemchug:
Gul'nara Mansurova

Thermographic analysis, psychrometric analysis and microclimate studies on a selection of the buildings:
Luca Valisi,
Politecnico di Milano, LADC

Students from Politecnico di Milano who graduated with a thesis on Tashkent modernism:
Lavinia Bacci
Michela Barazzetti
Livia Bruno
Jingyuan Cheng
Laura Codilupi
Nicola Gianoli
Anette Jacob
Shivi Jindal
Elena Lauro
Bowei Li
Linmei Li
Gianluca Maggio
Cristina Meloni
Vanessa Meroni
Flavia Micelli
Karolina Pieniazek
Sara Puppi
Meixin Shao
Paawan Preet Singh
Meghna Srivastava

This book is dedicated to the memory of Jean-Louis Cohen

Tashkent Modernism XX/XXI

Research Essays

Investigating a Modernist Capital

Preserving a Modernist Capital

Gayane Umerova, Chairperson of the Uzbekistan Art and Culture Development Foundation

The preservation of Uzbekistan's cultural heritage is a key mission of the Art and Culture Development Foundation (ACDF). Our country serves as the custodian of some of the world's most remarkable architectural landmarks, ranging from the fortress complexes of ancient Khwarazm to the mosques, madrasas and sites of early scientific inquiry constructed by the Timurid Empire. However, modernist architecture, built from the 1960s to the 1990s, represents a historical urban phenomenon that has, until now, lacked both the broad appreciation and the preservation efforts it undeniably deserves.

Over the past three decades, large-scale transformations and redevelopment in Tashkent have threatened to disfigure or erase valuable features of the city's recent architectural past. In response to growing public interest and to spearhead preservation efforts, the ACDF initiated the Tashkent Modernism XX/XXI project to raise awareness of the value of this legacy, both domestically and internationally. The catalyst for this expansive, multi-year effort was the demolition of a well-known modernist landmark: the House of Cinema, designed by Rafael Khairutdinov and completed in 1982. Recognizing the urgent need for action and a consolidated effort to preserve cultural heritage under threat, a sizable team of historians, architects and other specialists, from inside Uzbekistan and overseas, gathered together. They convened around the shared mission of studying, preserving and recontextualizing Tashkent modernist architecture, both globally and within the existing urban narratives of the city itself.

As part of this undertaking, the ACDF has worked tirelessly, facilitating access to sites and spaces in the city for the preparation of documentation and

Lenin Museum, Tashkent, January 1974

Jean-Louis Cohen at the unofficial art exhibition in Moscow, September 1974

condition reports, which could become the basis for future development strategies and prevent further loss. Given the submerged histories of many of the buildings, much effort was expended in locating relevant archives and making contact with family members of the architects, engineers and administrators who brought the buildings into being. The administrative burden, which was not insignificant, was carried out against the pressure of time. Multiple districts were already being redeveloped, and the transformation of specific buildings, such as the State Museum of the History of Uzbekistan (originally the Lenin Museum) and the Palace of Aviation Constructors, was planned. Thankfully, these have now been spared.

The development of modernist architecture in Tashkent represents an exercise in twentieth-century city building unparalleled in scope and scale. After mass migration in the early twentieth century and the wake of World War II, Tashkent was the fourth-largest city in the Soviet Union, with ambitions of becoming the model of what a cosmopolitan, socialist city could be, at the crossroads of East and West. As such, it was supported with unprecedented vigor and investment. It became a laboratory for typological and technical innovation designed to mitigate the desert climate, to prepare for any future seismic activity and to incorporate the regional culture. It also integrated the values of modernism after the Khrushchëv Thaw, as part of its decolonial project. The earthquake that rocked Tashkent on April 26, 1966, brought both funding and manpower from across the Soviet Union. This provided a great opportunity for the fulfillment of ideas that had been circulating in both Tashkent and Moscow since the end of World War II.

Driven by interest in this unique architectural history that emerged during the three decades before the USSR's collapse, the Tashkent Modernism XX/XXI research project has taken on a variety of forms: exhibitions, publications, urban interventions, and the first international conference dedicated to the preservation and greater understanding of Tashkent's modernist legacy. The ACDF has successfully prevented further demolitions and continues to raise awareness of other sites, promoting their sensitive integration within the changing contemporary city.

The fact that ten examples of Tashkent modernist architecture are presently being evaluated by the UNESCO World Heritage Center is a clear validation of our progress to date. While the current list of buildings with heritage status contains many individual masterpieces, often by accepted giants of architecture from the Western canon, the criteria for serial listings are more exacting. They require not only "universal value" but also that the series, taken holistically, represent a "set of values pertaining to a phase of urban development of a city or region."

A key partner in this UNESCO nomination process has been the Politecnico di Milano. Working closely with the ACDF and the Agency of Cultural Heritage of Uzbekistan, Politecnico di Milano developed the management plan that addresses how these modernist buildings can be preserved in a way that enhances their outstanding universal value for decades to come. As part of this effort, a series of public sessions involved building owners and other stakeholders, ensuring everyone shares a unified vision for modernist heritage. Politecnico di Milano is now exploring further collaboration with universities in Uzbekistan to strengthen local education for preservation experts.

Most of the buildings included in the project have been nominated for heritage status, while monuments such as the State Museum of Arts and the French Institute for Central Asian Studies and Research Center for Art Restoration (originally the Republican House of Tourism) are already undergoing renovation. Perhaps most importantly, recent years have seen a noticeable shift in public opinion regarding the status and significance of the urban environment and its history. Government support was obtained by demonstrating that these buildings are not only essential to the city's identity but, crucially, that they can be revitalized and integrated as part of its future.

The former Republican House of Tourism (also referred to as the Cultural Information Center or KITs) stands as the ACDF's first major restoration initiative. Commissioned by the ACDF and developed by GRACE and Werner Sobek between 2019 and 2023, it will be transformed into the French Institute for Central Asian Studies, the Research Center for the Restoration of Cultural Heritage and Art Objects (under the ACDF), and a hub for the Aga Khan Foundation Training Program. Construction is set to begin soon, and this renovation will demonstrate how modernist structures can be successfully repurposed for cultural, academic and community-oriented use. This future center also lays the groundwork for a potential second French cultural center or French language center—further embedding international collaboration within Uzbekistan's modernist legacy.

The preservation of modernist architecture poses numerous questions and challenges, some of which were explored at the conference *Where in the World Is Tashkent* held in October 2023. This book is dedicated to the memory of architect and historian

Jean-Louis Cohen (1949–2023), who was an invaluable contributor through the first years of this project. His devotion to modern architecture and advocacy for its continued preservation and wider comprehension will continue to inspire and guide us in our endeavor.

The ACDF has significantly advanced the conversation around the preservation of Tashkent's architectural heritage; by bringing in global perspectives, experience and expertise, it fostered the convergence of ideas that would produce a comprehensive preservation strategy. In undertaking this major task, two distinct "waves" of demolition emerged as catalysts for greater awareness and action. The first wave occurred with the controversial demolition of the House of Cinema, a seminal modernist landmark. A second wave threatened other buildings soon after. In several cases, swift intervention by the ACDF and its partners halted or reevaluated proposed transformations, helping preserve iconic structures that would otherwise have been lost.

Tashkent Modernism XX / XXI, with its unparalleled scope, demonstrates the importance of systematically studying a city's recent history. It offers insights and methodologies that I hope will be applied not only in Central Asia but across the wider world.

Initiated and commissioned by the ACDF and the Tashkent Modernism XX / XXI project, this book is the culmination of extensive efforts by a large team of distinguished professional architects, historians, preservation experts and artists from around the world.

Preface

Francesco Bandarin

Francesco Bandarin was the director of the UNESCO World Heritage Center from 2000 to 2010 and the UNESCO Assistant Director-General for Culture from 2010 to 2018.

Tashkent architectural modernism represents a significant chapter in the history of twentieth-century urban development, showcasing how modernist principles were adapted and implemented within a specific cultural and geographical context. The city's architecture from this period stands as a testament to the ambitions and challenges of creating a modern urban environment under Soviet rule.

The development of Tashkent's architectural modernism, which began at the beginning of the sixties, was accelerated by a catastrophic earthquake on April 26, 1966, which caused extensive damage to the city. This disaster provided a unique opportunity to embrace modernist architectural principles and Soviet urban planning ideologies while adapting them to local architectural and artistic traditions. Consequently, Tashkent transformed into a beacon of contemporary design and construction methodologies of the era, exemplifying a remarkable regional adaptation of architectural modernism.

This book offers a comprehensive evaluation of what can be characterized as one of modern architecture and urbanism's most extraordinary ventures. It delivers an exhaustive and nuanced analysis of the architectural and urban design projects realized from the 1960s to the 1980s, examining their regional and international significance, assessing their current state of conservation and outlining their preservation challenges. This work serves not only as an indispensable compendium of this epoch of architectural ingenuity but also as a framework for understanding its impact on architectural culture and its contribution to global heritage.

The distinctiveness of Tashkent's architectural modernism is highlighted by several elements, starting with the expansive planning framework required for the creation of broad boulevards, public squares and green spaces. This vision of a spacious and orderly urban environment continued with the adoption of innovative construction methodologies and materials, including prefabricated components and large-panel system building techniques. These methods facilitated swift construction and allowed experimentation with contemporary architectural forms.

The substantial reconstruction endeavor resulted in a new modernist aesthetic that characterized the period's architecture, based on simplicity, functionality and the use of modern materials such as concrete, steel and glass.

Buildings frequently showcased clean lines, minimal ornamentation and a preference for geometric forms. Prominent examples include public buildings, residential complexes and cultural institutions, all designed to reflect the progressive ideals of the Soviet Union.

Significant emphasis was also placed on integrating modern architectural elements with the traditional styles of Uzbekistan. Architects attempted to incorporate traditional design elements, including decorative patterns, courtyards and water features, blending modernist principles with the local cultural and historical context.

As a result of this collective effort, Tashkent's modernist architectural heritage encompasses a range of buildings and structures that embody modernism's principles and merge local cultural motifs with pioneering design solutions.

This is evident in individual buildings such as the Uzbekistan Hotel and the State Museum of Arts, which stand as prominent examples of modern architecture in Tashkent, offering versatile settings for performances and exhibitions that integrate modernist principles, with clean lines and open spaces.

The architectural achievements of this creative period are numerous, ranging from the Panoramic Cinema to the Peoples' Friendship Palace. These buildings, along with others like the Circus and the Chorsu Bazaar, showcase engineering prowess comparable to the most advanced constructions of the time. In housing, innovative solutions were proposed, as exemplified by the striking Zhemchug residential building, a model of social architecture of international standing.

Tashkent modernism shares many characteristics with broader Soviet architectural practices of the same period while exhibiting unique features that reflect its regional context.

This era witnessed a transition across the Soviet Union from Stalinist neoclassical styles to more functional, modernist approaches, emphasizing simplicity, innovative material use and mass construction techniques. This transition varied regionally, leading to distinct variations that incorporated local cultural and historical elements.

In Tashkent, as in the wider Soviet Union, there was a discernible shift toward simple geometric forms, minimal ornamentation and new construction technologies, all focused on functionality and the social role of architecture. The use of prefabricated panels and large-scale, efficient construction methods aimed at swiftly providing architectural solutions is evident in Tashkent's residential areas and in other Soviet capitals.

Significant investments were made throughout the Soviet Union in constructing public buildings, including houses of culture, government buildings and metro stations, thereby creating architectural landmarks that showcased modernist aesthetics and engineering feats. These efforts are visible not only in Tashkent but also in other Central Asian cities such as Almaty, Ashgabat, Bishkek and Dushanbe, which exhibit a range of modernist influences and reflect diverse cultural, environmental and social landscapes.

The extensive urban planning efforts in Tashkent, necessitated as they were by the imperative to reconstruct after the 1966 earthquake, also emphasized creating a city resilient to seismic activity. This endeavor entailed adopting specialized construction techniques and urban layouts engineered to mitigate the risk of future seismic disturbances, a focus that, while not entirely unique, was particularly criti-cal in the context of Tashkent compared to other Soviet cities.

The realization of these significant technical and aesthetic outcomes was made possible through the contributions of a generation of architects and engineers from across the Soviet Union, collaboratively engaged in the monumental task of reconstruction.

The enduring legacy of the modernist tradition in Tashkent stands as a testament to the city's capacity to cultivate a unique identity through the synthesis of diverse architectural influences. It underscores the dynamic interplay between tradition and modernity, highlighting the crucial role of architectural heritage in shaping urban environments and cultural identities.

Today, the conservation of this remarkable urban and architectural ensemble presents a formidable challenge, particularly in the face of rapidly evolving urban landscapes and shifting cultural priorities.

Environmental conditions and the region's harsh climate have contributed to the degradation of many structures, exacerbated both by the incompatibility of post-earthquake building techniques and materials with the local context and by often neglected maintenance needs.

Moreover, the restoration of modernist buildings demands specialized expertise to accurately address the unique architectural features and construction techniques of their original designs.

The scarcity of craftspeople or construction firms equipped with the necessary skills and knowledge for such restorations has been a significant hurdle.

Following the dissolution of the Soviet Union, the appreciation and recognition of these architectural masterpieces by the public and by local governments diminished as new priorities emerged, including the pursuit of a national architectural style reflecting the visions of the newly independent republics.

Addressing these challenges necessitates raising public awareness regarding the value of modernist architecture. It also calls for developing policies and incentives for preservation, allocating resources for conservation projects and cultivating expertise in the restoration of modern buildings. Additionally, innovative solutions must be sought to adapt historic buildings to contemporary needs while honoring their architectural heritage.

These issues are pressing not only in Uzbekistan, but in other post-Soviet countries as well. The publication of this book emerges as a vital catalyst toward achieving these objectives, marking a period of renewed recognition of the international significance of the Tashkent modernist experience. It signifies a collective aspiration to safeguard these achievements as an enduring legacy for future generations.

Tashkent modernist architecture is gaining recognition as a unique artistic, cultural and social phenomenon that is best equipped to reveal the specific character of the modernization of Soviet Central Asia. More than just another peripheral case of multiple modernities or a point on the global map of twentieth-century architecture, Tashkent modernist architecture is relevant to the global cultural scene, reflecting the colonial, postcolonial and decolonial aspects of the Soviet social and cultural experiment.

Given its geographical location, developed resources and multiculturalism, Tashkent has been and continues to be one of the most important centers of Central Asia. Beginning in the Soviet era, numerous efforts were made to conserve and restore architectural monuments associated with the rich ancient and medieval history of the region. The modernist architecture of the 1960s to 1980s, which articulated the idea of a modern society and looked to the future, was never perceived as heritage. Following the independence of Uzbekistan in 1991, and with the arrival of the market economy, the architecture of the previous three decades, which was focused on social issues and economy of means, lost relevance. It risks being abandoned or destroyed under the pressure of rapid urban growth.

To address this risk, a road map for the preservation and adaptation of Tashkent's modernist architecture has been developed by the Art and Culture Development Foundation (ACDF) under the Cabinet of Ministers of the Republic of Uzbekistan and by the architecture studio GRACE, directed by Ekaterina Golovatyuk and Giacomo Cantoni, together with the Politecnico di Milano Department of Architecture and Urban Studies, represented by Davide Del Curto,

Sofia Celli, Andrea Gritti and Federica Deo; the studio Laboratorio Permanente, directed by Nicola Russi and Angelica Sylos Labini; and the historian Boris Chukhovich. The research was initiated in 2021 with the aim of establishing a methodology for preserving, reevaluating and including in the local and international agendas an important architectural layer of the city that was formed between the 1960s and the early 1990s.

The results of the research are varied and encompass protection instruments—such as building passports, the basic tool within Uzbekistan legislation on heritage preservation—and communication instruments—such as exhibitions and conferences that aim to make Tashkent architecture known and appreciated in Uzbekistan and beyond its borders. Another layer of the project is the actual preservation work on the buildings. Pilot projects are being developed for the former Republican House of Tourism (the future French Institute for Central Asian Studies and Research Center for Art Restoration) and for the State Museum of Arts. The Cultural Trail, a guide to modernist Tashkent for local and international visitors which already functions as an app, is an opportunity to rethink and improve the public space of Tashkent.

The publication *Tashkent Modernism XX/XXI* plays the role of a logbook and an archive which condenses the results of this multilayered research. It also aims to contribute to the global debate on the legacy of the twentieth century and the preservation of multiple modernities across the world.

The book consists of two related parts. Part one is a collection of visual and written essays, combining thematic and strategic reflections that emerged during the research. Part two consists of twelve condensed Monographs and Statements of Significance of individual buildings, which outline histories and architectural concepts of each architectural object, gather archival materials, document the present condition, describe the building's architectural and cultural value and, finally, assign levels of interest to various parts of the building. These levels of interest prescribe the extent both of changes allowed and of conservation activities required. Each Building Monograph concludes with a suggested preservation strategy.

The first section of essays, entitled "Investigating a Modernist Capital," lays out the context for a better understanding of the buildings described and analyzed in part two of the book. "Before Modernism: Historical and Architectural Notes" by Boris Chukhovich provides a brief overview of the history of Uzbekistan and Tashkent prior to the 1960s, with a focus on the concepts of national history and tradition instrumentalized by modernist architects who sought to make their projects more "local." In "Earthquake as Alibi: The 1966 Tashkent General Plan and the Construction of the Modernist Capital," Federica Deo analyzes the urban planning of the capital, describing the extent to which the urban logic has affected the architectural solutions and focusing on the relationship between the buildings and the green network of the city, as well as on the notion of ensemble. The third essay, "The Institutional History of the Architecture of Soviet Uzbekistan" by Boris Chukhovich, provides a critical overview of the education, readings, and professional contacts of Tashkent architects, as well as the specific agendas of the four most important project institutes that shaped the built environment of the city. In "Standardization and Hybrid Typologies," Boris Chukhovich and Ekaterina Golovatyuk compare the meaning of type/typology in European and Soviet practice, providing a new lens for understanding Soviet building types in relation to standardization and to programmatic and formal hybridization. As the fourth largest city of the former Soviet Union, many of Tashkent's public buildings provide emblematic case studies for this analysis. Boris Chukhovich's "Modernism as Orientalism" traces the intricate relationship between modernism and orientalism in Tashkent, where both the prescribed role of the "capital of the Soviet East" and the interventions of Moscow architects determined important features of the city's modernist architecture.

This section includes a timeline, which merges the events and buildings described in the book and a particular historical context focusing on Central Asia, the former Soviet Union and countries of North Africa, the Middle East and Asia. With only a few key events or buildings from the "West"—those that had more or less direct repercussions in Tashkent—punctuating the spreads, the timeline outlines a number of topics that may encourage the reader to explore this parallel history beyond the pages of this book.

The second group of essays, entitled "Preserving a Modernist Capital," lays out the methodological basis for the evaluation and formulation of preservation strategies for the selected modernist buildings in Tashkent. Davide Del Curto's "A Methodology for Preserving the Modernist Architecture of Tashkent" describes the theoretical premise of the entire effort, outlining the definition of the conservation management plan as a key tool for assessing cultural significance and ensuring protection of the twentieth-century heritage. In the following essay, Federica Deo and Sofia Celli explain key legislative principles of current preservation in Uzbekistan, underlining how modernist buildings deserve a place within national heritage legislation. After a historic outline of heritage listing and evaluation, "A Protection Inventory for Modernist Heritage" by Sofia Celli explains the key precedents that were used to structure the Monographs and the Statements of Significance, the documents that ultimately organized and summarized the research and analysis of each building.

Nicola Russi's "Modernist Palimpsest" cross-references the urban history of Tashkent's green spaces with the best-known urban experiments in the former Soviet Union and the American park movement. On a series of maps, Russi traces the green network that became the basis for the proposal of the Cultural Trail, a system of pedestrian paths through the green areas connecting the modernist buildings.

The final text, "Addressing the Future of Tashkent Modernism," reflects on the prospects for these efforts. Boris Chukhovich describes the actors at the citizen, municipal and republican levels that can guarantee the preservation of Tashkent modernism and take this work beyond mere communication and legislation. Ekaterina Golovatyuk explains the preservation and adaptation strategies that were developed individually for each building. These set out a vast repertoire of actions that can be undertaken to make the buildings suitable for the needs of contemporary Tashkent without affecting their architectural and cultural significance. Davide Del Curto describes the means for further enforcing protection of Tashkent's masterpieces by positioning them within global modernist heritage as one of the many faces of modernity, or one among diverse modernities, with Tashkent representing the unique geopolitical and cultural situation of Uzbekistan and Central Asia.

Part one concludes with a photographic sequence by Armin Linke, an immersive experience that forms a series of walks through the buildings, fixing their current condition and their contemporary value, at times intrinsic and at times acquired. Linke's images also reveal another important quality of these environments: the modernist architecture of Tashkent, with its sculptural volumes and elaborate surfaces, is like a set for staging larger social scripts.

In the second part of the book, the twelve condensed Monographs, each of which concludes with a Statement of Significance, are organized according to preservation logic, starting with cases that require little or no intervention and leading to those for which a more significant adaptation is suggested.

While this book was being prepared, all the buildings were listed within the register of national monuments thanks to the dedication and efforts of the Art and Culture Development Foundation.

This publication is an important—but not final—step in documenting the preservation process, and besides serving as a broadcasting tool to disseminate and discuss our work, we see it as a launchpad for a wider discussion on the preservation of the recent past.

Interview

Rem Koolhaas in conversation with Ekaterina Golovatyuk

The text that follows is built from a series of talks, public and private, held between April and December 2023

(Not) Being a Modernist

During the talk "Preserving Modernism" at Triennale Milano in 2023, Jean-Louis Cohen made an important comment regarding the word "modernism" (and particularly the term "Soviet modernism," coined by Feliks Novikov), suggesting that it is problematic. The controversial nature of this term is not explicitly articulated within our work, despite several internal team discussions.

Having said that, do you consider yourself a modernist? Has this evolved? Is it even possible to think in these terms today?

It's a very tricky question, of course. It totally depends on the definition of "modernist," but to me now the word "modernist" sounds too much like an ideological or an aesthetic category. Both definitions have always annoyed me, and I do not recognize myself in either. So, the aesthetic language of modernism is absolutely not mine and the ideology of modernism is also not mine at all. The only kind of comfortable relationship that I have with the word "modern" (and the only correct relationship) is that I am interested in modernization in architecture as a process that enables you to respond in an intelligent way to current conditions and current means and to have an interesting and creative balance between those two.

I think that, for instance, in the current crisis the word "modernism" is completely meaningless because it no longer defines an agenda. And it is clear that the agenda that we are facing now is, in a way, extraneous to our discipline. I feel that we all have to work on it by mobilizing the maximum intelligence of what is possible rather than entrusting a predetermined framework, language or ideology.

Would you have responded the same way in the 1980s or in the early 1990s?

I think not. In those first moments I was manifesting myself on the architectural stage. It was a really unique period because it was completely dominated by a groundswell of postmodernism and, at the same time, by a constant erosion of

any social potential in politics. So, in order to resist this combination, it was easy to confuse yourself or to be confused by others as modernist, but even then I had no interest in that kind of identification.

Continuity vs. Break

Preservation is an aspect of modernity, yet until recently modernity was not preoccupied with its own preservation, nor did it perceive itself as part of history. It saw itself as breaking away from history.

Now continuity with the past is sought on all levels: cultural, political, architectural... At what point do you think this changed? Is it related to the growth of neoliberalism?

Well, faintly...

The irony is that currently a lot is happening which is actually a real break from history, while at the same time we are trying to find comfort in the notion of continuity. The idea of a break has become almost obscene, because the word "break" indicates some kind of pain. For me this break has to do with the radical shift from the values of the French Revolution—liberty, equality, fraternity—to the values of comfort and security. We are now looking for comfort. This probably started with postmodernism, because postmodernism was exactly that comfort in telling ourselves that we were establishing continuity with the past, but I believe that if you actually look at what are we doing and how we are living, the continuity is inevitably less and less real. It can be seen in the protraction of "best practice" and absurd kinds of luxury and irrelevant details, while in fact we have to acknowledge that there has been a break.

Do you think it is more a narrative about continuity?

I would say it is a long-standing narrative where we tell ourselves to feel more comfortable even in the face of problems, and maybe this narrative is also a problem, because it is clear that what we need is not continuity but radical change.

Preservation and Change

In recent years the language of preservation (or, more correctly, conservation) has mutated. The latest version of the Burra Charter (2013) structures conservation practice through *a conservation management plan* rather than through *conservation policy* (1978), acknowledging that it is, among other things, about managing change.

More recently, in the article "Concrete Is One Hundred Years Old," Lucia Allais and Forrest Meggers review the nature of concrete, which used to be considered immutable but is now known to be impermanent.[1]

Can we translate these two considerations—of preservation as managing change and of the impermanence of concrete—into markers of a significant revision of the discipline and a blurring of the boundaries between preservation, architectural projects and other forms of intervention?

I think that "managing change" might be an opportunistic and slightly pessimistic new definition, because it is clear that you cannot really stop anything in its tracks. I feel that it is partly an abdication of ambition for certain preservation efforts. The word "management" is such an important ingredient of the rhetoric related to business, or even agriculture. I find it really strange that preservation has now adopted the same mantra. "Managing change" is lacking in depth as an ambition.

For me, the big enemy here, and the reason why "managing change" as a definition can only remotely be associated with preservation, is that currently, in almost every case, the possibility of preservation is inevitably connected to commercial feasibility. It is this connection that forces you to really redefine your goals. It is an interesting situation though.

1 Lucia Allais and Forrest Meggers, "Concrete Is One Hundred Years Old: The Carbonation Equation and Narratives of Anthropogenic Change," in *Writing Architectural History: Evidence and Narrative in the Twenty-First Century*, ed. Aggregate Architectural History Collaborative (Pittsburgh: University of Pittsburgh Press, 2021).

What I was implying is that if we extend the meanings of these definitions, it seems like preservation dissolves into working within an existing context, whether it is an urban condition or an existing building or a single room in which there is always a degree of something that can be changed.

What has been really exciting over the last couple of decades in terms of thinking about preservation is that the word "preservation" and the term "architectural project" can, for the first time, be combined rather than seen as opposites, and this for me is a genuine development. Maybe "managing change" is a faint echo of that radical transformation in terms of the definition. What is key to the entire rethinking of preservation for me is that it is not necessarily about stopping time but is another form of adjusting something to the times.

Undoing this contradiction in the past two decades produced the most creative situation, as it suspended an opposition and enabled both domains to be more curious and interested in each other.

The Ancient Monuments Protection Act of 1882, introduced by Sir John Lubbock, recognizes the need for governmental administration for the protection of ANCIENT MONUMENTS. The sixty-eight monuments listed are mostly unoccupied prehistoric structures such as dolmens, stones circles, barrows and pillars.

The Ancient Monuments Consolidation and Amendment Act expands the definition of the monument to "any structure, erection, or monument, of architectural or historic interest." It allows the inclusion of ROMANO-BRITISH AND MEDIEVAL MONUMENTS through the establishment of Royal Commissions.

The National Heritage Act establishes English Heritage as the government's lead advisor on the built environment. The Department of the Environment later removes the 1939 ceiling on listing buildings. It introduces the THIRTY YEAR RULE, by which any building older than this can be considered for listing.

The 2007 revision of the Planning and Policy Guidance of the Historic Environment defines NO LIKELY PERIODS OF INTEREST as absolute. Buildings less than thirty years old can be listed if they are of outstanding quality and under threat.

Prospective preservation predefines a building's status as monument, ensuring a building's longevity and protection even BEFORE IT IS PHYSICALLY MANIFESTED.

Prospective preservation diagram, from the *Cronocaos* exhibition (AMO) at the 2010 Venice Architecture Biennale

1882
The Ancient Monuments Protection Act

1712

1913
The Ancient Monuments Consolidation and Amendment Act

1953

1983
National Heritage Act, Dept. of the Environment Circular 8/87

2007

2007
Planning Policy Guidance Note 15: Planning and the Historic Environment

Prospective?

The Black Hole of Preservation

In the 2010 exhibition *Cronocaos*, you discussed the black hole of preservation, referring to the exclusion of modernism from the preservation agenda. Setting aside our project, do you think this is still the case?

When I became interested in preservation, I started looking at the interval between an object and its preservation—in other words, how much time people took to decide to preserve something. Initially, with regard to the eighteenth century the interval was 2,000 years, while in the nineteenth century it was reduced to about 200 years, and then to mere decades in the late twentieth and early twenty-first centuries. Now we can claim that you need to think about preservation not only as something in retrospect but also in prospect.

In the current situation there are three layers or reasons for the exclusion of modernism from the preservation agenda. One layer has to do with the shortening interval between construction and preservation. Modernism simply fell into a gap and did not trigger the kind of alarms that are triggered now. This was not a deliberate campaign against modernity but simply neglect and a lack of alertness to the fact that modernity, and particularly late modernity, also needed to be preserved.

The second layer is perhaps more recent. It is connected to the shortening of memory or a kind of historical dementia that is the consequence of neoliberal laissez-faire. If laissez-faire is the basic motivation of neoliberalism, it is very clear that preservation is outside that and is actually contrary to neoliberalism.

The third layer involves a strong sense of guilt about the signs of inequality, where we can no longer tolerate the kind of architecture that could be an antidote to inequality or that was able to articulate the value of equality in all its complexity.

But if you look at the tourism industry and how it relates to preservation, in reality preservation in the service of tourism is not so far outside of neoliberalism.

Yes, I was just making a super literal connection between laissez-faire and preservation, because laissez-faire means "let go," and preservation is the opposite of letting go. In a way you are right that neoliberalism and preservation can mutually reinforce each other. This is why I object somewhat to "managing change." It was actually an important UNESCO shift, and Francesco Bandarin was in part responsible for saying that we cannot stop time in its tracks, so we have to keep going. In all AMO's research we showed that there was a total parallel between neoliberalism and preservation, but very little of that is connected to the preservation of modernism.

In the case of modernism, I am suggesting not the absence of preservation but that there is a hostility that leads to destruction. Rather than a weak preservation impulse there is a strong destructive impulse to get rid of modernism, to remove it literally from our consciousness.

Palace of the Republic, Berlin, from the *Cronocaos* exhibition at the 2010 Venice Architecture Biennale

Now we can also claim that there is more temporal distance between the period when modernism was built and the present.

Yes, and obviously your efforts in Tashkent with the Uzbekistan Art and Culture Development Foundation have to do with a realization that interventions are necessary. I am particularly happy about the fact that you are dealing with a modernism which is not the old modernism but 1960s–1980s modernism. There are very interesting resonances and similarities between the architecture in Tashkent and, for instance, Team 10 and other internal revisions of modernism, rather than the polemical anti-modernism position that postmodernism represents. What I find beautiful in your research is that you see that modernists were struggling and addressing internal criticisms of modernism from modernists themselves. There was not a simplistic black-and-white division of the kind that dictated architectural polemics in America in the same period, but a really deep internal process of self-criticism with internal struggles, where you see that modernism can be reinvented and extended in very creative ways.

Freedom of Architects

Jean-Louis Cohen mentioned that Tashkent modernist architecture is a corpus of work that is "anxious" to find points of reference to both the West and to earlier Russian or Soviet developments. He claimed that Soviet architects had much more formal or creative freedom than their colleagues in the West.[2]

I endorse what Jean-Louis said. In addition to freedom, the architects also had a mandate and a purpose, and these three things can perhaps explain why many architects had the confidence to conduct official experiments without knowing what they would end up with. In Russia I have always found it quite difficult and often embarrassing to speak enthusiastically about the qualities of Soviet architecture. In Tashkent it is interesting that the architects made and officially embraced the attempt to create a local identity, and for this reason their architecture now appears less offensive than it may in Russia. The fact that not all modernist buildings in Tashkent were destroyed—and that they are, in fact, growing in popularity—may be the result of an official mandate to experiment with identity and other issues that we are still dealing with now.

Tashkent Modernism XX/XXI: Index (Milan, April 2023)
Left to right: Nicola Russi, Gayane Umerova, Jean-Louis Cohen, Ekaterina Golovatyuk, Rem Koolhaas and Davide Del Curto

2 In the talk "Preserving Modernism" at Triennale Milano in April 2023, Jean-Louis Cohen referred to the freedom of Soviet architects as a possibility of accessing without mediation the political leadership, which trusted the architects' professional expertise.

Views of Tashkent, taken by Jean-Louis Cohen in 1974

Soviet Generosity

What changes when you as an architect intervene on existing buildings, particularly Soviet ones?

It is one thing to talk about preservation in theoretical or ideological terms, but if you are involved in preservation as an architect, you realize very quickly that your activity is a combination of respect and disrespect, and to some extent of reconstruction and destruction. It is paradoxical that when you work on new buildings you aim to be very precise in terms of how events or relationships are established within them. When you work on an existing building, you declare its organization of different events null and void and try to insert yourself with new ideas in an existing physical structure. For me, this experience is interesting because it gives you every reason to be extremely modest about precision in architecture and it also forces you into a kind of ingenuity, since you have to abandon some of your instincts and be more meticulous in terms of fitting within the possibilities of what is there.

Soviet architecture was either extremely ornamented and charged with historical references or over dimensioned, suggesting an emancipatory condition. I was particularly interested in the over dimensioning of building elements. Many Soviet architects worked with strict functionalist principles, and this meant accommodating large numbers of people within public buildings in response to programmatic demands. They were also required by the government to dream about Renaissance palaces. Political ambition translated into a visual language can today be interpreted as a luxury, because neoliberalism does not invest in any over dimensioning which is not profit based. But this contradiction between functionalism and grandiosity leaves, particularly in Russian buildings, an enormous freedom or territory to reinvent them. In this sense, the experience of preserving buildings in

Europe and in the former USSR or Russia is fundamentally different, simply because of this political surplus, which, of course, no longer has any role and can be translated in terms of new ambitions.

This aspect fascinates me in your buildings in Tashkent, as well as in the Garage Museum of Contemporary Art or the New Tretyakov in Moscow.

Garage Museum of Contemporary Art, OMA
Moscow, Russia, 2015

How was this translated in your work?

The beauty of Garage is that it was planned as a restaurant for 1,200 people. We cannot even think about such a scale anymore. And it is exactly this kind of exaggerated proportion or interpretation of what is public that enabled us to insert a number of smaller-scale elements and benefit from the overall envelope and infrastructure that was implied by the building.

More recently the New Tretyakov building provided a similar experience, but on a much bigger scale, as the building is 700 meters long. It combines functionalism and dreams of the grandiose architecture of the past in a very explicit manner. Its architect, Nikolai Sukoian, a modernist, was inspired by the Doge's Palace in

Venice. The scale itself enabled him to insert an enormous number of unanticipated elements, but also it offered the opportunity to redefine what public means. My trauma regarding the disappearance of the public and its replacement by the private was in a way relieved in China and the former USSR, where the public, particularly in previous generations, was often translated into generosity rather than grandiosity. In a way OMA's projects for Garage and the Tretyakov cultivate this dimension.

Typologies and a Fair Society

The idea of standardization and prefabrication was usually associated with monotonous housing, although today this perception is changing. I know you are very interested in this topic and that you have also studied the ancient Roman system as an early example of standardization. Do you think these notions are acquiring new relevance today? And could this be seen as another form of sustainability?

I would like to talk about Palmyra. It is a Roman city in the center of the Syrian desert, and it seems inexplicable in that location. Its architecture reveals that standardization is the best method to bring out the uniqueness and specificity of a place. Seeing a Roman city there was an unbelievable revelation. Standard devices of Roman architecture proved incredibly eloquent in terms of exposing the peculiarity of light, topography and materials of that place, affirming a very complex connection between standardization and specificity. You could look at standard Soviet typologies in exactly same way. By putting the same elements in radically different conditions you get a tension of the repetition confronting unique conditions. Whether it has any relevance in terms of sustainability, I'm not sure.

Soviet typologies are unique in that they were, perhaps, the last inventory of a fair society. Whether the society was actually fair is, of course, a very dubious question, but at least there was a visible commitment to social functions like the marketplace, housing, the museum, and sports or youth palaces. Every single component of social life was articulated through architecture types. Maybe there is a certain model of sustainability in that, because it generated a repertoire beyond which you do not have to go and perhaps beyond which every further type of building seems like a waste. Standardization is also interesting as a form of economy of the imagination that clarifies where one's focus should go and limits the unfettered waste of imagination. Beyond that, I do not know.

I am not at all sure about the word "fair" in this context.

I think that is the dilemma for anyone who is interested in Soviet history. The architecture remains interesting and fascinating, but never convincing on the level of its official aim. It is obviously not really fair. At the same time, some of its ambitions and realizations remain very plausible.

In a way this shows my permanent struggle in being totally committed to libertarian ideas, but also able to deeply appreciate some authoritarian aesthetics and arguments. I do not know whether that is a bad thing or whether it is a kind of realism, or whether these are the two poles between which anyone with integrity has to move, or whether being susceptible to some aspects of authoritarianism is a condition that gives you the energy to avoid it. All these questions are totally justified, and this is actually one of the key things I am trying to write about now.

To sum up, Soviet building typologies to some extent offered an incredibly radical range of ingredients. Some of them were designed for a police state and others for its total opposite. Maybe rather than "fair" it is a weird and interesting form of balance.

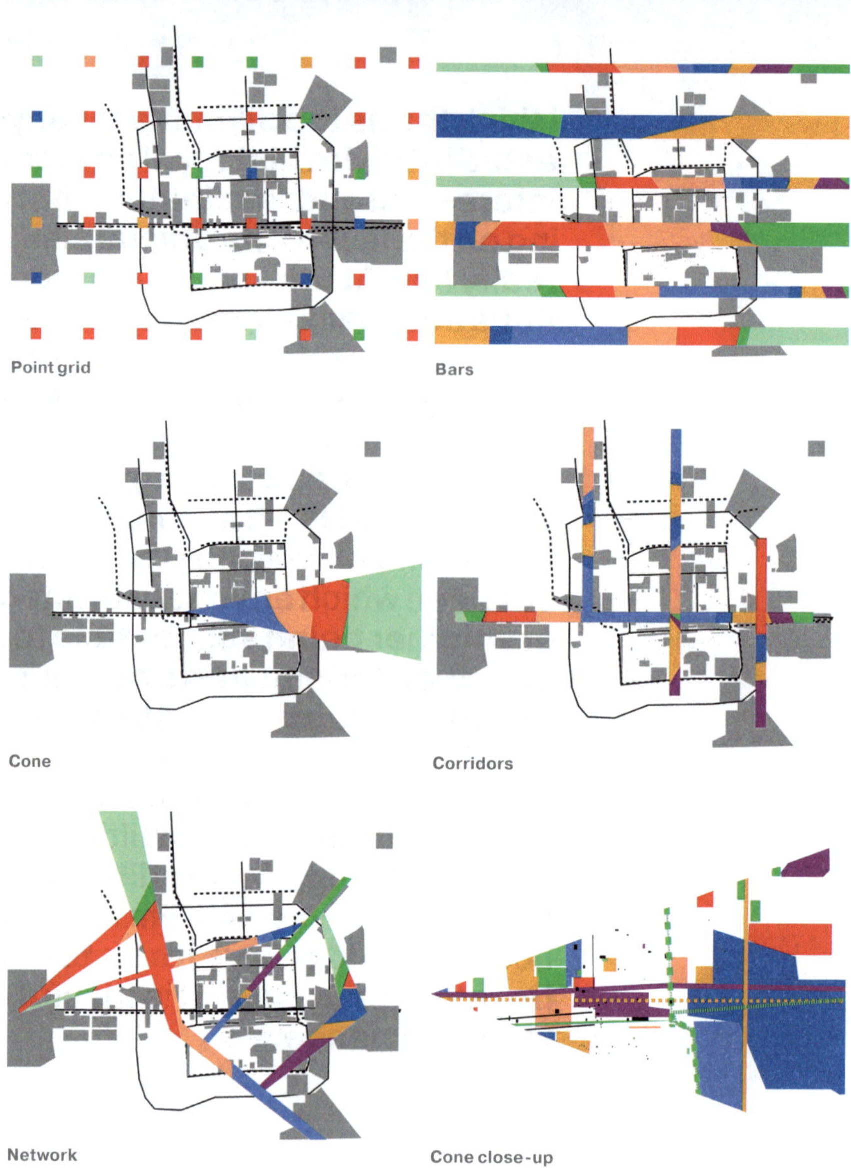

Preservation strategies for Beijing, OMA, 2003

Didactic Preservation

Your project for Beijing preservation shares the same scale of ambition as the project for Tashkent, although the logics of the two are quite different. We worked on individual buildings and made an overview chart showing a gradient of transformation/preservation. We also created a cultural trail that connects buildings by means of a green network, but we did not imagine different models of preservation, as you did in Beijing, that could act without aesthetic bias by means of sampling portions of the city, or include other categories of preservation that you list for Beijing: virtual, flexible, didactic, etc.

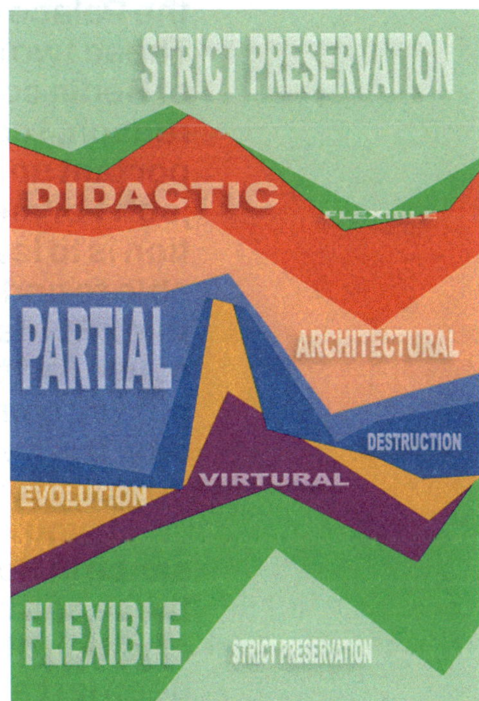

Beijing preservation project, OMA, 2003

Obviously, the Beijing project is more diagrammatic and includes a degree of provocation. It enabled you to articulate other scopes for preservation of buildings that are not only about saving something but also about conveying other messages or meanings. What opportunities do you see in this?

The word "didactic" has always fascinated me, and for me the interest in preservation became most acute when the Berlin Wall was eliminated very quickly after East and West Germany were unified again. Between 2006 and 2008 the Palace of the Republic was also demolished. These two interventions alone made the history of Berlin completely incomprehensible. For this reason, I considered the didactic impulse an important underlying impulse for the Beijing project. For me, the most relevant idea of preservation is to leave enough traces of history to be able to understand what happened. This is why I think Rome is such an incredible example, because relatively speaking there is not that much, but you completely understand the history of the city. It is not about layers but about leaving things in brutal form or transforming them brutally.

If you look at Roman antiquity, the Renaissance in Rome and the architecture of Mussolini, these can be seen as fantastic modes of preservation of classical architecture. The first has been left alone. The second recombined its elements and the third enhanced it and multiplied its aura, but in a very architectural way. There is very little direct connection to proper preservation. It is more about the preservation or reinvention of aura. For me, each of these modes is very didactic.

What is the fourth form or mode we are dealing with today?

Every historical moment in Rome is now exhausted to the maximum.

Yes, it is consumed by tourism and neoliberalism.

We have been asked to do something for the Mausoleum of Augustus. Originally it was a cylinder with many structural elements inside, entirely filled with earth. Later the building went through an incredible number of transformations. At various points it was a bullring and a nineteenth-century concert hall. Gradually, all the earth was removed and some of the building sections were used to introduce staircases or other architectural elements so visitors could access the center.

We have been asked to use the entire ring to show the history of its modifications. This project is definitely not about restoration, but about using the ruins as a tool to tell history rather than show history. Maybe that is what we are dealing with today: rhetorical approaches rather than physical; virtual, although not as in computer animation but by using the remaining elements pertaining to different historical moments to explain history. And with a rather low budget, which helps to make it totally virtual.

Mausoleum of Augustus, Rome, 2024

Research Essays

Investigating a Modernist Capital

Before Modernism: Historical and Architectural Notes

Boris Chukhovich

The description of Central Asia's past is usually tied to its position at the crossroads of civilizations: Chinese, Indian, Mongol, Iranian, Turkic, Russian and others. In speaking about ancient history and traditions, scholars, depending on their interests, may reference the ancient roots of Central Asian cultures that can be found in the past of Iran, the Parthian Empire, the Bactrian kingdom, the Kushan Empire, Margiana and Sogdia (to mention only the best-known states that included the territory of modern-day Uzbekistan within their borders). An examination of the peripeteia of the Middle Ages might bring under their microscope the interaction of nomadic and settled cultures, stories of splendid dynasties cut short by the Mongol conquest, Timur's empire, the Timurid and Shibanid states and the subsequent dynastic monarchies right up to the Russian conquest of the second half of the nineteenth century. At that point there were three states on the territory of the Central Asian land between two rivers (the Syr Darya and the Amu Darya): the Emirate of Bukhara, the Khanate of Khiva and the Khanate of Kokand. After the collapse of the Russian Empire and the founding of the USSR, in 1924 the Uzbek Soviet Socialist Republic, the direct forerunner of modern Uzbekistan, was created out of these three states, which had evolved during the tsarist period.

The gathering of these historical fragments into a unified narrative depends largely on the position of the researcher. At least two strategies formed. The first involved describing the historical metamorphoses of the region as an uninterrupted process which prefigured the emergence of independent Uzbekistan. In this approach Uzbekistan was the legal heir of the states and cultures that emerged on its territory and those of neighboring countries. In the second the history of Central Asia was a result of a series of events and cataclysms which led to the flourishing and decline of civilizations, on the remains of which new human populations, states and cultures appeared. The first strategy was mainly typical of researchers working in Uzbekistan and aiming to take an integral look at the history of the region, particularly its art and architecture.[1] The second was for those who examined separate fragments of the history of culture and did not aim to describe it in global terms. The difference in these strategies affects the study of Soviet modernism in Uzbekistan, which is difficult to define as the obvious result of one thousand years of tradition. Breaking with the classical heritage of Europe, the Modern Movement arose from the desire of European societies for the permanent reform and critical undermining of their own foundations. In studying its distribution in the non-Western world, researchers are tempted to see it as a Western implant in alien soil. In order to avoid this simplification where Uzbekistan is concerned, we need to understand contemporary architecture's link to local modernity and the contemporary social context. Of particular importance are contacts with the regional context, which local architects attempted to establish and even cultivate. In this way we will understand how modern architecture can (or cannot) be part of the cultural heritage of the republic.

On the Particularities of Uzbek Modernity

Both a symptom and a driver of the Modern Age, the Russian conquest of Central Asia was not peaceful. Moving deep into the Central Asian steppe and oases, the Russian army had a technological military advantage which enabled it to destroy both the fortifications of historic cities and its adversary's army. Today the history of the conquest can easily be seen in works by battle painters who were embedded with the Russian forces and reproduced not only the historical facts of war but

1 Galina Pugachenkova and Lazar' Rempel', *Istoriia iskusstv Uzbekistana s drevneishikh vremen do serediny deviatnadtsatogo veka* [*The History of the Arts of Uzbekistan from Ancient Times to the Mid-Nineteenth Century*] (Moscow: Iskusstvo, 1965); Shukur Askarov, *Genezis arkhitektury Uzbekistana* [*The Genesis of the Architecture of Uzbekistan*] (Tashkent: Izdatel'stvo San'at, 2014).

Maps of Central Asia, reflecting historical geographical knowledge and ideological views

Heinrich Karl Wilhelm Berghaus and Justus Perthes, *Iran und Turan: Persien, Afghanistan, Biludschistan, Turkestan: Eine geographische Skizze* (Gotha: Justus Perthes, 1835)

Abraham Ortelius and Jan Baptista Vrients, *Tartariae sive Magni Chami Regni týpus*

also the orientalist optic in which defeated peoples were usually depicted as uncivilized. Here, the discourse about the "blessings of civilization" brought to Central Asia by the Russian Empire was accompanied by representations of the legal right of "return" to the Central Asian steppe, to the foothills of the Pamir.[2]

In establishing political and economic domination on these lands, the Russian administration did not attempt to interfere in the life of the historic cities and tried to create new settlements outside the Muslim quarters. In particular, "New" Tashkent, which became the administrative capital of the Turkestan General Governorate (Turkestan Region from 1882), was built on the east side of the Ankhor Canal. The water formed a natural border between the Muslim city and the Russian military garrison, which settled first in the newly built fortress, and then in the new European residential areas that were arranged in a rectangular and later a radial/axial network of streets. The coexistence of two separate urban communities began. They were almost entirely isolated from each other spatially, judicially, culturally and linguistically, but were connected by relationships of political and economic rule and subordination.

Plan of Tashkent, 1890

Soviet Turkestan was formed almost immediately after the October Revolution. As the Bolsheviks took control of the local soviets and the Red Army re-established external control over the territory of the former Russian Empire, the preconditions appeared for a significant restructuring of the region. The Civil War resulted in the proclamation of the Soviet Union (1922) in Moscow, and two years later internal borders were defined in Central Asia, forming several new republics. A significant part of the territory of the Soviet republics of Bukhara and Khiva, which had earlier been formally independent of the USSR, along with

2 Nikolai Fedorov, "Vopros o bratstve, ili rodstve, o prichinakh nebratskogo, nerodstvennogo, t.e. nemirnogo, sostoianiia mira i o sredstvakh k vosstanovleniiu rodstva: Zapiska ot neuchenykh k uchenym, dukhovnym i svetskim, k veruiushchim i neveruiushchim [The Question of Brotherhood or Kinship, of the Reasons for the Unbrotherly, Unkindred or Unpeaceful State of the World, and of the Means for the Restoration of Kinship]," in Nikolai Federov, *Sochineniia* [*Writings*], vol. 4 (Moscow: Progress, 1995).

the former Khanate of Kokand, became part of the Uzbek Soviet Socialist Republic (UzSSR), the capital of which was Samarkand. Today two counter trends can be observed in the formation of Uzbekistan. On the one hand (and most contemporary researchers have written about this), the creation of the republic was closely controlled by the Moscow authorities. They had the final say not only on the configuration of the new borders of Central Asia but also in addressing a significant number of questions regarding the construction of the governmental and cultural institutions of the newly created republics.[3] This allowed many (not without foundation) to see what took place between the 1920s and the 1950s as a process of centralized "nation building" that answered to the current aims of the Soviet government and also reflected the Bolsheviks' strategy for their megaproject of constructing the New Society.[4] Against this background another opinion arose regarding the internal readiness of the urban intelligentsia of Khiva and Bukhara—the Jadids—to realize the national project and the building of contemporary nations using the administrative resources of the Bolsheviks.[5] Historians agree that at some point the interests and desires of the Jadids and the Bolsheviks coincided: both aimed to create national states on the territory of the former emirate and khanates, employing the support of the other side and seeing them as a temporary partner. It is also worth noting that while re-establishing strict centralism in the relationship between Moscow and the Central Asian republics, the Soviet government was, on a declarative level, developing a critique of "tsarist colonialism" and insisting on the need for a completely opposite national policy. Accordingly, in its actions and discourses colonialism, postcolonialism and decolonialism formed strange and changeable combinations depending on the questions and issues raised.

By 1938 this "partnership" had resulted in the destruction of the Jadids, almost all of whom disappeared in the camps. The nation-building project proposed by the Bolsheviks, based on Soviet socialist modernization, won out over the Jadids' project, with its dreams of a sovereign national state for Uzbeks. Nevertheless, the Bolsheviks appropriated some of the Jadids' ideas for nation building and put them into practice, which partly explains the stability of the direction taken and the active participation of the Uzbek population. The result of this contradictory process was the creation of Soviet Uzbek culture, particularly architecture.

3 Svetlana Gorshenina, *Asie centrale: L'invention des frontières et l'héritage russo-soviétique* (Paris: CNRS Éditions, 2012).

4 Olivier Roy, *La Nouvelle Asie centrale ou la Fabrication des nations* (Paris: Éditions du Seuil, 1997); Terry Martin, *The Affirmative Action Empire: Nations and Nationalism in the Soviet Union, 1923–1939* (Ithaca and London: Cornell University Press, 2001).

5 Arne Haugen, *The Establishment of National Republics in Soviet Central Asia* (New York: Palgrave Macmillan, 2003); Adeeb Khalid, *Making Uzbekistan: Nation, Empire, and Revolution in the Early USSR* (Ithaca and London: Cornell University Press, 2015).

Vasilii Rozhdestvenskii, *For the Soviet East! 10 Years of the Red Army* (Tashkent, 1928), propaganda poster

***Peasants and Workers! You Have Learned to Use a Rifle, Now Learn to Use a Pen!* (Tashkent, 1920s), propaganda poster**

Tashkent: Stages of Evolution

Even though by the mid-nineteenth century Tashkent exceeded the size and population of Kokand, Bukhara and Samarkand,[6] it was never the capital of any state until the conquest by the Russian Empire (1865). Located on the western edges of the Khanate of Kokand, the city was strategically important for the control of both the Fergana Valley and the oases of the Zarafshan River, where Samarkand, taken by Russian forces, and the Emirate of Bukhara, which had become a protectorate, were located. This prompted the tsarist administration to make Tashkent the center of "Russian Turkestan" and the main citadel of the Russian policies in the region. In the tsarist period the "European" part of the city was intensively developed, and the "Asian" part was placed in a situation of dependence. After the 1917 revolution in Petrograd Tashkent became the capital of the Turkestan Autonomous Soviet Republic, which inherited the borders of the Turkestan Region and formed part of the Russian Soviet Federation. However, this capital status was a subject of discussion during the delimiting of the borders of the Central Asian republics after the formation of the USSR. In addition, the inclusion of Tashkent within Uzbekistan was severely criticized by representatives of the future Kazakhstan and Kyrgyzstan, who believed that this large and ethnically international city, which was surrounded by a nomadic population of Kazakhs and Kyrgyz, should become their capital.[7] In the end, when the Uzbek SSR was created in 1924 the city was attached to Uzbekistan but ceded its capital functions to Samarkand. It was only in August 1930 that Tashkent was once again designated the capital.

The urban development of the city in the Soviet period took place in the following stages:

1. 1917–1929: The Separate Development of "Old" and "New" Tashkent

In the first decade of Soviet rule architecture and urbanism remained a local initiative par excellence. Unable to make large-scale changes, the city leadership acted selectively in various areas. In "new" Tashkent they tried to solve the problem of the city's slums, which had worsened during the Civil War. In line with the initial Soviet focus on creating suburban "garden cities," they proposed projects for building "Shumilov Town," "Workers' Town" and a cooperative town on the territory of "Tezikovka."[8] Only partly completed, these projects assumed that housing would be owned cooperatively by workers. For the "old city" the authorities proposed the symbolic Soviet reformatting of its center. A new park and a stadium with a square for political demonstrations were created near the historical nucleus of Chorsu. This required the demolition of the Beklyarbek Madrasah and the reprofiling of other buildings, such as the re-equipping of the Jami Mosque as a school (named after the Bolshevik Iakov Sverdlov).[9] Nearby the People's Theater and the Liberated Woman of the East House of Culture were constructed,[10] which radically changed the cultural picture of the "old city" without serious encroachments on its urban fabric. In administrative terms "old" and "new" Tashkent continued to live a detached life, with separate planning and management bodies.

6 See Vladimir Nil'sen, *U istokov sovremennogo gradostroitel'stva Uzbekistana (XIX – nachalo XX vekov)* [*The Sources of Contemporary Urban Construction of Uzbekistan (Nineteenth–Early Twentieth Century)*] (Tashkent: Izdatel'stvo literatury i iskusstva imeni Gafura Guliama, 1988).

7 Svetlana Gorshenina, *Asie centrale: L'invention des frontières et l'héritage russo-soviétique*, 267–269.

8 Abdumannop Ziiaev, *Tashkent: V trekh chastiakh; Chast' III, XX – nachalo XXI veka* [*Tashkent: In Three Parts; Part III, Twentieth–Early Twenty-First Century*] (Tashkent: Izdatel'stvo San'at, 2009), 9, 11, 16.

9 Ibid., 17.

10 Ibid.

Georgii Svarichevskii and Leonid Voronin, plan of "new" Tashkent, 1922–1925

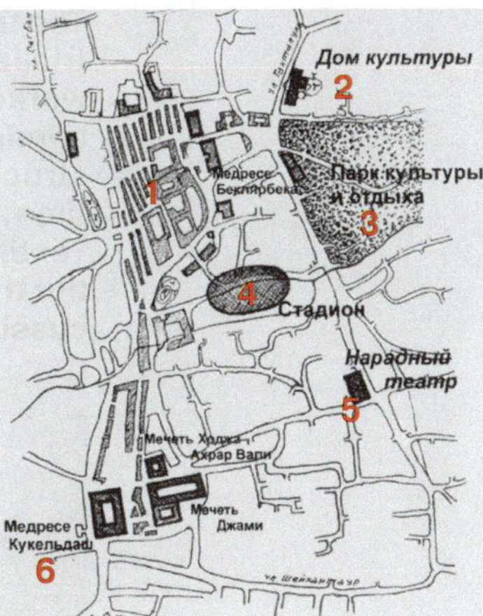

New construction in the core of the "old city" in the 1920s (according to Abdumannop Ziiaev):

1 Bazaar (old buildings)
2 House of Culture
3 Park of Culture and Leisure
4 Stadium
5 Theater
6 Madrasa (old building)

2. 1929–1941: The Unification of the City and the First Construction Plans

The context in which the administrative unification of the "Muslim" and "European" quarters of Tashkent took place in 1929[11] was prompted by the global turn of the USSR toward overcentralized management, rapid industrialization and "cultural revolution." In this year the Office for the Replanning of the Cities of Central Asia opened in Tashkent.[12] It was led by Aleksandr Sil'chenkov, a young VKhUTEMAS graduate and former student of Nikolai Ladovskii. The ideological aim involved an urban planning policy which opposed that of the former tsarist administration: the Soviet authorities planned a radical unification of the "Asian" and "European" parts of the city that had been subject to earlier division. Sil'chenkov proposed a very specific solution involving preserving the street layout of "European" Tashkent and drastically reconstructing the "old city," destroying not only architectural monuments and the traditional street system but also the city landscape and relief. He developed "European" Tashkent to the west in the spirit of "Ladovskii's parabola," setting out an absolutely symmetrical system of streets and placing a park zone with numerous public functions in the historic nucleus of "old" Tashkent. This idea was too utopian and abstract for the city administration. Specialists from Tashkent's Architecture and Planning Authority made several attempts to develop alternative versions for the unification of the two urban nuclei which were adapted to real conditions. Next came another proposal from Moscow. Taking into account the ideas of Tashkent architects, a team of planners from Moscow led by Aleksandr Kuznetsov developed a new, single general plan of Tashkent that involved the construction of new residential districts, green zones along the city canals and a united center with a main square. The key issue with all of these megalomaniac plans was their chronological indeterminacy.

11 Ibid., 24.
12 Shukur Askarov, "Pervyi proekt pereplanirovki Tashkenta [The First Project for Replanning Tashkent]," *Stroitel'stvo i arkhitektura Uzbekistana* [*Construction and Architecture of Uzbekistan*], no. 7, 1973, 33.

The true possibilities of the Soviet economy, with its priorities of industrialization and the construction of the cheapest housing possible for workers, limited the project to the laying of several central streets with administrative and residential buildings for the Soviet elite. The construction of standard mass housing for workers did not occur at that time, despite the initial experience of building a "social town" near the Textile Factory. The mismatch between plans and reality was obvious, but the policies of the state did not allow the possibility of openly discussing this contradiction.

Aleksandr Kuznetsov, masterplan of Tashkent, 1937–1938

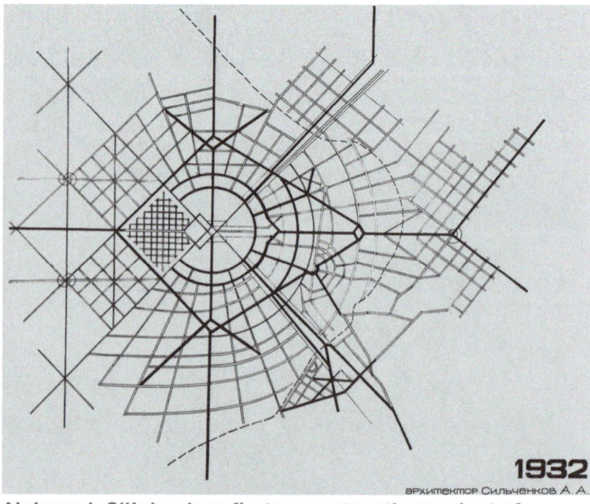

Aleksandr Sil'chenkov, first reconstruction project of Tashkent, 1929–1933

V. Zelikhov, *Navoi Street*, 1952

Unlike architects, artists allowed for the possibility of the harmonious coexistence of the "old" and "new" parts of the city: Nikolai Karakhan, *New Uzbekistan*, 1938

3. 1941–1955: The War Economy and Its Consequences

Regardless of the fact that there were 3,500 kilometers between the Uzbek capital and the western border of the USSR, from June 1941 life in Tashkent changed markedly. More than one hundred enterprises were evacuated to the city, including major production facilities such as the aviation factory, Rostsel'mash and Elektrokabel'. By the end of 1941 hundreds of thousands of people had been evacuated to Tashkent from Ukraine, Russia and Belarus, as had numerous higher education institutions, research centers and cultural organizations. The local economy was completely reorganized. According to *Tashkent: An Encyclopedia*, "whereas in 1940 81 percent [of the economy] was based on textiles, light industry and food production, in 1941 60 percent was made up of heavy industry, mainly machine building and metalworking."[13] At the same time, the war largely "justified" in the eyes of the authorities both the previous inertia regarding the grandiose urban development plans and the reactive measures of the authorities in a mobilized economy. The evacuated people and enterprises were housed chaotically, without any advance planning. However, since the infrastructure of the "old city" did not allow for heavy industry enterprises to be based there, they appeared in the north and east of the city, adjoining the "European" quarters. Accordingly, even though evacuated people were housed throughout the city, including in the traditional mahallas, "old" and "new" Tashkent were once more divided, and they developed differently. Around two million refugees passed through the city during the war,[14] and by its end the population was close to one million. At this point the urban fabric was almost ruined due to the enormous load and lack of any systemic actions to support it. In the immediate postwar years, the city's architects organized a series of discussions about this situation. In particular, they studied the applicability of Kuznetsov's 1937–1938 plan to the postwar development of the city. Opponents of this plan stated that it undervalued the quality of the "old city" quarters and the fact that they were adapted to the Tashkent climate and Uzbek culture. Supporters, including Kuznetsov himself, accused the opponents of not wishing to end the separation of "old" and "new" Tashkent and create for residents of traditional mahallas conditions befitting "modern life."[15] From 1952 to 1954 a new general plan was developed for the city,[16] but even so, construction followed prewar trends: the perimeter of new arterial roads such as Navoi Street, Beshagach Square, Shota Rustaveli Street and others were gradually built up with elite residences and public buildings designed as individual projects.

Aleksei Shchusev, Alisher Navoi Opera and Ballet Theater, 1947

13 *Tashkent: Entsiklopediia* [*Tashkent: An Encyclopedia*] (Tashkent: Glavnaia redaktsiia Uzbekskoi sovetskoi entsiklopedii, 1984), 11.
14 Paul Stronski, *Tashkent: Forging a Soviet City; 1930–1966* (Pittsburgh: University of Pittsburgh Press, 2010), 147.
15 Ibid., 156.
16 Mitkhat Bulatov, "Osobennosti i printsipy progressivnogo resheniia planirovki i zastroiki goroda Tashkenta [Features and Principles of Progressive Solutions for the Planning and Construction of the City of Tashkent]," in *Akademiia stroitel'stva i arkhitektury SSSR: Nauchno-issledovatel'skii institut raionnoi planirovki i gradostritel'stva* [*Academy of Construction and Architecture of the USSR: Scientific Research Institute for Regional Planning and Urban Planning*] (Moscow/Tashkent: Central State Archive, 1960), 4.

4. 1955–1966: Construction Reform and New Approaches to Urban Planning

The reform announced in 1954 by Nikita Khrushchëv rapidly and radically changed the aims and means of construction in cities in the USSR. Perhaps for the first time worldwide the aim was stated (and largely achieved) of quickly supplying cheap industrial housing for the entire population of the country, which had until that moment largely lived in barracks and communal apartments. To accomplish this, the construction industry needed to become unified and based on the assembling of factory-made elements. This completely changed the aesthetics of the buildings. Historical decorative elements made way for modernist minimalism and new building materials, such as concrete, metal and glass. These trends also concerned public buildings. The reform required the maximum distribution of typical or standard buildings to reduce project costs, and a minimalist design using factory-made, unified components even for unique buildings.

Mitkhat Bulatov, general plan of Tashkent, 1960
Monorails on the long-term development scheme of Tashkent (diagram)

The new general plan of Tashkent, on which work began in the late 1950s, was based on four structural levels. The first level constituted a residential unit for 1,500 to 2,500 people with a basic social block (a small store, a children's kitchen and so on). The second was the microdistrict, comprising three to five residential units with a developed center for shopping and services, a small park and a school. The third was a residential district of 40 to 50 hectares in which there were several microdistricts built around a park. The fourth was the so-called planning district, which encompassed several residential districts and had a large center for shopping, culture and services. Planning districts in Tashkent included Chilanzar, Karakamysh, Yunusabad and Sergeli. Reinforced concrete factories began to operate in the city and produced components for the construction of residential microdistricts under license from the French company Camus. Public transport was of particular significance in this universal system. Its development, including highways and metro lines, became an important element of the general plan. The final stage of this work was two All-Union competitions: for

the center of Tashkent, which was designated a special planning district (this competition was won by Tashkent architects from the Tashgiprogor Institute), and for the construction of Tashkent's main square (this competition was won by a team from Tashgiprogor and Moscow's TsNIIEP, or Central Scientific Research and Experimental Project Institute for Entertainment and Sport Facilities). The winning project for the center of Tashkent involved the creation of a green pedestrian esplanade linking the nuclei of the "new" and "old" cities—Revolution Square and Chorsu Square. It proposed placing on the space of the esplanade "free-floating," unique cultural and administrative buildings of republican and city significance.

Tashkent's chief architect, Aleksandr Iakushev, demonstrates to Sharaf Rashidov a model of the center of Tashkent with an esplanade connecting the cores of the "new" and "old" cities. Model made at Tashgiprogor, 1964

5. 1966–1991: From a City to an Urban Agglomeration

Objectively, the Tashkent earthquake of 1966 was not catastrophic in terms of its strength and consequences. It destroyed a number of buildings in the city center, but these mainly comprised dilapidated single-story housing. However, the fact of a political moment during which the new General Secretary of the Central Committee of the Communist Party of the Soviet Union, Leonid Brezhnev, needed to demonstrate the effectiveness of his leadership,[17] the positive dynamic in the economy and the internal readiness of the Uzbek authorities to radically restructure the city played their roles. The USSR and republican leadership decided to assign to Tashkent the necessary financial, human and technological resources for the rapid reconstruction of the city, which was, in essence, a process of structural reorganization. In demolishing historic districts in the "new" and then the "old" city, the government launched a mechanism for realizing the general plan for the creation of a new, modernist capital for Soviet Uzbekistan. The plan itself changed over time: in 1967 a new team led by Iurii Puretskii and Aleksandr Vanke proposed another version, the main innovation of which involved the inclusion of elements that defined Tashkent's agglomeration with large satellite cities such as Chirchik, Yangiyul and others.[18] Now the high-speed tangential arteries that had been designed to reduce traffic in the

17 Leonid Brezhnev replaced Nikita Khrushchëv as First Secretary of the Central Committee of the Communist Party of the Soviet Union in 1964, but for the first few years he attempted a collective style of leadership. By the Twenty-Third Congress of the CPSU he had managed to sideline all of his competitors. By decision of the congress, he received new powers and the title General Secretary of the Central Committee of the Communist Party of the Soviet Union. The congress closed in April 1966, eighteen days before the Tashkent earthquake. Brezhnev flew to the capital of Uzbekistan the following day. Tashkent was the first challenge that the new leader of the country had to tackle.

18 Aleksandr Vanke, Iurii Puretskii, A. Stazaeva and Aleksandr Iakushev, *Generalnyi plan razvitiia Tashkenta* [*General Plan for the Development of Tashkent*] (Tashkent: Izdatel'stvo TsK KP Uzbekistana, 1967).

city center matched the main transit flows between the various urban settlements. This formed the basis of "greater Tashkent," which included not only industrial but agrarian production in a unified system of functioning and management.

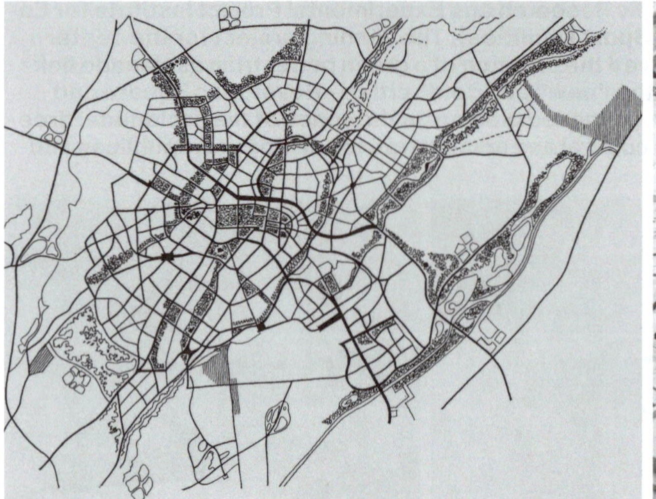
Iurii Puretskii, Aleksandr Vanke, city masterplan layout, 1967–1970

Model of the city center general plan, 1967

In the early 1970s the Central Committee of the Communist Party of Uzbekistan and the Council of Ministers of Uzbekistan issued a special decree regarding the demolition of the "old city" mahallas and the erection in their place of multistory housing.[19] This speeded up the discussion in the architectural community of appropriate principles for constructing new microdistricts within the "old city." Most of their ideas remained on paper,[20] and the "old city" gradually reduced in size, swallowed up by regular districts of four-, nine- and twelve-story buildings. In the meantime an urban planning problem became apparent which has not been solved even today. One of the main "arterial highways," 50 Years of UzSSR Avenue, would have cut in half the core of the "old city," the urban value of which architects and city authorities began to realize in the late 1970s and the 1980s.

Andrei Kosinskii et al., Kalkauz district (model), 1974–1978

19 Gennadii Korobovtsev, "Tashkent: 'Staryi' gorod, kakim tebe byt'? [Tashkent: 'Old' City, What Should You Be Like?]," *Stroitel'stvo i arkhitektura Uzbekistana* [*Construction and Architecture of Uzbekistan*], no. 10, 1971.

20 See Boris Chukhovich, "Architectural Modernism and 'Old Tashkent': The Long History of a Brief Encounter," in *Mahalla: Urban Rural Living*, exhibition catalogue of the Uzbekistan National Pavilion at the 17th Venice Architecture Biennale (Tashkent/Bolzano: Longo, 2021).

The 1960s and 1970s were a period of intense design and construction of modernist buildings. New museums, exhibition halls, restaurants, hotels, administrative buildings, cinemas and theaters were built in the city. In 1977 the first line of the Tashkent metro was launched. However, toward the end of this period and particularly from the early 1980s, the stagnation of the Soviet economy, the war in Afghanistan and a number of other factors once more created a gap between urban planning and reality. Construction of many buildings was halted midway, and others were canceled. The last large modernist buildings constructed in Tashkent were the Heliocomplex (1987), located in the mountains near Tashkent, and the Chorsu Bazaar (1990), which heralded a completely different epoch in construction, economics and social life in Uzbekistan. This milestone also marked the disappearance of the ideas and principles of Soviet modernism.

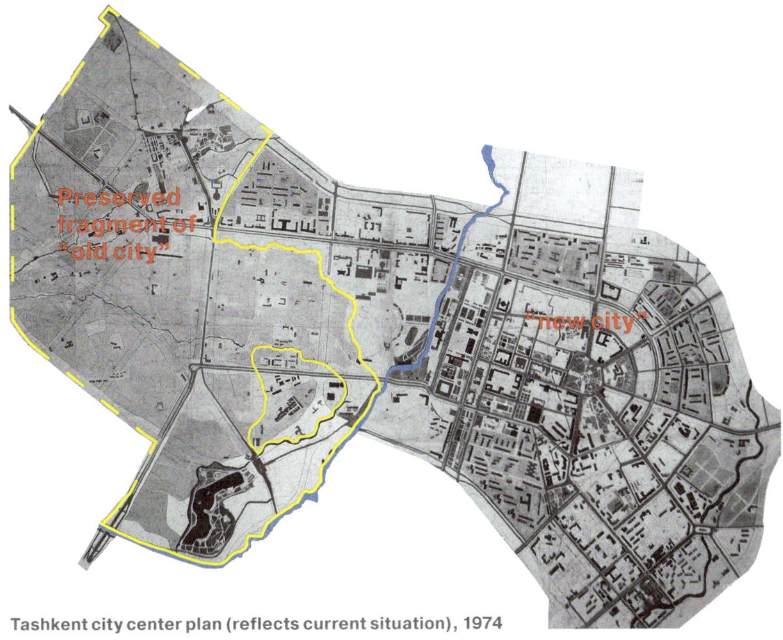

Tashkent city center plan (reflects current situation), 1974

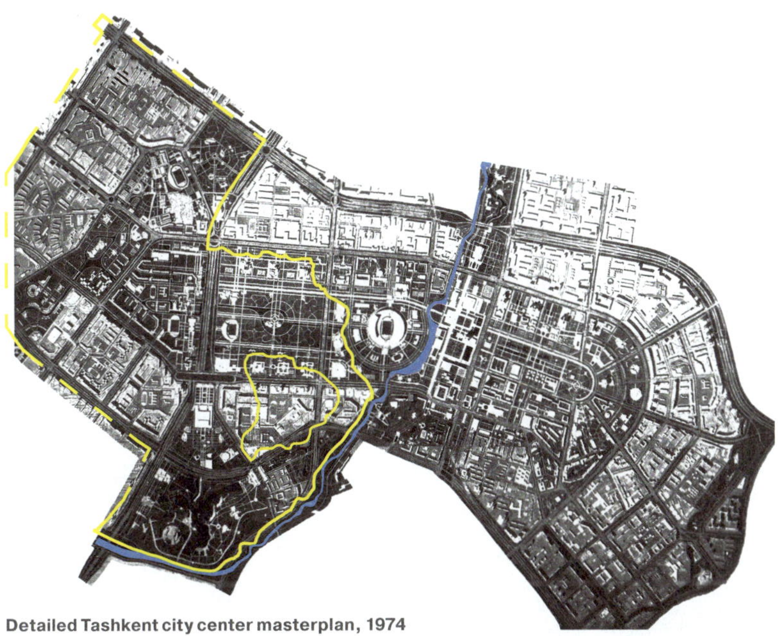

Detailed Tashkent city center masterplan, 1974

Earthquake as Alibi: The 1966 Tashkent General Plan and the Construction of the Modernist Capital

Federica Deo

"On the morning of April 26, 1966, an earthquake struck the capital of Uzbekistan. A few hours later, the General Secretary of the CPSU Central Committee, Comrade Leonid Brezhnev, and the Premier of the USSR Council of Ministers, Comrade A. N. Kosygin, arrived in Tashkent.... Unprecedented in the history of our State in its scope and scale, the Tashkent heroic episode of the Soviet peoples coming to the aid of the wounded capital of Uzbekistan began. More than three and a half years have passed.... From the ruins and ashes, the beautiful Tashkent has risen. Now it is rightly called not only a city of peace but also a city of courage and brotherhood of peoples."[1]

A New Day Dawning: An Introduction

As Arkhangel'skii recalls in an essay with the emblematic title *Tashkent, City of Brotherhood*, on April 26, 1966, at 5:23 a.m., Tashkent experienced a major earthquake measuring around 7.5 on the Richter scale, followed by several smaller ones throughout May.[2] The earthquake devastated much of the western part of the capital, the ancient city, claiming four lives,[3] injuring around 150 people, and leaving 78,000 families homeless. A significant amount of public infrastructure and facilities was irreversibly damaged. A few hours later, this news would reach every corner of the Soviet Union, rapidly disseminated not only through *Pravda Vostoka* (*Truth of the East*), the official newspaper of the Uzbek SSR, but also by the country's major newspapers,[4] and extending beyond the Iron Curtain.[5] This was one of the very first decisions effected by the Council of Ministers in its ambitious project to reconstruct the Uzbek capital: "Central and republican newspapers, journals, radio and television outlets to systematically report on the progress of the restoration and construction of the city of Tashkent."[6]

General Secretary Leonid Brezhnev and Prime Minister Aleksei Kosygin immediately rushed to the scene. After two intense days of inspections, discussions and meetings, they shared their priorities in a speech on April 28. At the top of the list was the housing problem, followed by measures to restore commerce and services, aiming to return to citizens the comforts of everyday life as quickly as possible. The second direction identified by the party aimed at strengthening the Uzbek construction sector. To this end, Brezhnev declared that Moscow, Leningrad and all Soviet republics would participate in the rapid and important reconstruction of the capital. "This marks the beginning of a new, more beautiful and stronger Tashkent that will be safe from earthquakes,"[7] Leonid Brezhnev stated in his speech, concluding with an image of optimism: "Within two years, we hope to see Tashkent in a new form, setting the architectural tone for a great city of the future."[8]

1 V. A. Arkhangel'skii, ed., *Tashkent – gorod bratstva* [*Tashkent, City of Brotherhood*] (Tashkent: Izd. TsK KP Uzbekistana, 1969), 7. Translations by the author, unless otherwise attributed.

2 Paul Stronski, *Tashkent: Forging a Soviet City, 1930–1966* (Pittsburgh: University of Pittsburgh Press, 2010), 251–252; Philipp Meuser, *Seismic Modernism: Architecture and Housing in Soviet Tashkent* (Berlin: DOM Publishers, 2016), 60–61.

3 The exact number of casualties is unclear; eight people died according to the Tashkent encyclopedia, 1984, 133.

4 Including *Pravda* [*Truth*] and *Stroitel'naia Gazeta* [*Construction Gazette*], which were among the newspapers with the largest circulation in the USSR. See Nigel Raab, "The Tashkent Earthquake of 1966: The Advantages and Disadvantages of a Natural Tragedy," *Jahrbücher für Geschichte Osteuropas* 62, no. 2, 2014, 273–294.

5 Through the cultural newspaper *Soviet Life*, disseminated in America by the Soviet government, but also the German newspaper *Neues Deutschland*.

6 Russian State Economic Archive, fund 339, list 3, file 2470, 1.31, transcript in Nigel Raab, "The Tashkent Earthquake of 1966," 274.

7 From Brezhnev's speech at the meeting of party activists of Uzbekistan on April 28, 1966, transcribed in V. A. Arkhangel'skii, ed., *Tashkent – gorod bratstva* [*Tashkent, City of Brotherhood*], 13.

8 Ibid., 15.

The Tashkent earthquake in the Soviet press

Poster by artist V. Dobrovol'skii

The Response to the Mobilization: Revisions to the 1966 General Plan

A few months before the earthquake, the Tashkent general plan had been approved, affirming the goal of transforming the capital of the Uzbek SSR into a major Soviet city that would rank among the largest in Central Asia. In 1960, during an official visit to India, Nikita Khrushchëv declared that the Soviet Union would exert every effort to unite the Asian peoples under socialism. Numerous cultural and sporting events were organized in Tashkent in the late 1950s and early 1960s to bring people from around the world to Central Asia and celebrate their differences, all united under the aegis of communism.[9] This intricate political project was rooted in a robust narrative palimpsest, designed to hide the less appealing side of the capital. The most evident manifestation of this was acknowledged in the supposedly disorderly, unclean and hazardous nature of the "old city," and in the relative division among various ethnic groups in the area. Instead, the emphasis was on showcasing the progress achieved through socialism.[10]

The dichotomy between the "old city" and the "new city" shifted in significance and importance over the decades, demanding resolution. In 1964, a call for submissions was issued for a new plan for the center of Tashkent, aimed at addressing the enduring divide between the two city centers. The winning design met the requirements of the call by developing a low-density ensemble of administrative and governmental buildings (Lenin Square) around green spaces that connected the two parts of the city. This proposal was incorporated into the general plan approved in 1966, a project that planners had been working on since 1960.[11] The explicit intention behind this endeavor was to bring uniformity to the city in terms of the relationships between the center and the suburbs.

The plan approved in early 1966, designed to meet new requirements, introduced heightened specificity in the planning of residential areas, differentiating the residential territory into planning zones and

9 See Paul Stronski, *Tashkent: Forging a Soviet City*, 242–243; Nigel Raab, "The Tashkent Earthquake of 1966," 274.

10 The urban plans drawn up by the Russians after 1865, and by the Soviets in the 1920s, tended to preserve the "old city" not in order to safeguard its cultural values but rather as a reminder of its supposed technological, social and administrative backwardness compared to the "new city."

11 Paul Stronski, *Tashkent: Forging a Soviet City*, 232.

microdistricts. It aimed to consolidate the city by integrating the center and the suburbs through a network of connecting infrastructure (metro and roads). This network was also intended to facilitate and reduce commuting times for workers. The plan set the housing density at 1.2 million inhabitants, imposing restrictions on migratory flows and prohibiting the establishment of new industries, except for those related to food and construction. It involved the demolition of old residential buildings and the construction of new complexes by the state. Percentage allocations for building construction were established relative to their heights: nine-story (49 percent), four-story (44 percent), one- to two-story (7 percent). The new threshold for public green space was set at 30 square meters per inhabitant, to be evenly distributed across the territory, with greater emphasis along waterways.[12]

The earthquake that occurred a few months after the approval of the 1966 general plan necessitated a revision to adapt it to the new emergency circumstances. Paradoxically, the aftermath of the earthquake, including the economic consequences, workforce availability and a clean slate, facilitated an accelerated modernization of the capital.

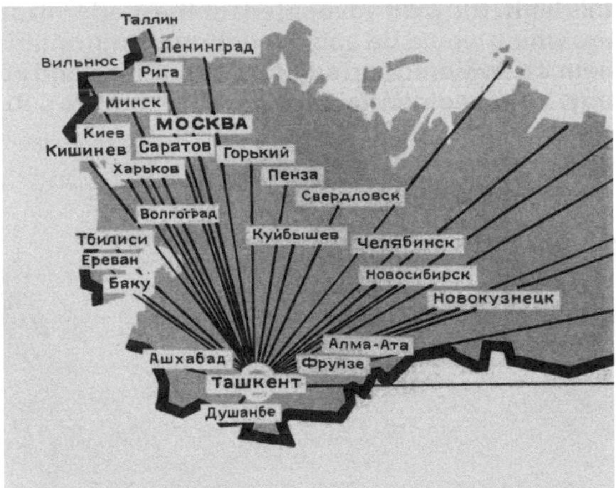

Map of the Soviet Union with cities which sent construction brigades to Tashkent after the earthquake

City center model prior to the earthquake

12 Philipp Meuser, *Seismic Modernism*, 69.

The Post-Earthquake Plan

The Tashkent-based project institute Tashgiprogor, along with specialized institutes such as Giprozem, Tashgiprotrans and Uzgosproekt, swiftly revised the general plan. It was approved by the USSR Council of Ministers in its resolution of February 21, 1967 "On the Fundamental Principles of the Tashkent General Development Plan." [13] Additionally, it received approval from the Central Committee of the Communist Party of Uzbekistan and the Council of Ministers of the Uzbek SSR in their resolution of April 10, 1967. [14]

The plan is presented in a volume published in 1967 that illustrates its strategies and aims. Notably, the key concept underlying the plan was to transform the capital into a garden city, as articulated by the authors: "Tashkent, a garden city, a city adorned with beautiful buildings surrounded by parks and gardens, intersected by a network of canals." [15] Around this central idea the planners outlined an expansive and ambitious vision to reconstruct Tashkent as one of the largest cities in the Soviet Union. A population limit was established, set at 1.4 million by 1980. Although industrial development was to be restricted to avoid exceeding this limit, the plan advocated for the modernization of existing enterprises, which would be achieved through automation of production, enhanced hygienic and sanitary conditions and advancements in technology. [16] The residential sector was to receive substantial investment.

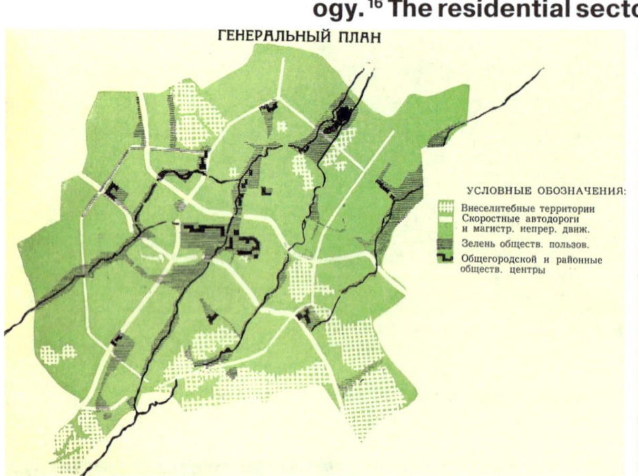

The 1967 general plan

Diagram of the Tashkent urban agglomeration

The plan prioritized housing, aiming for a high-quality solution despite the required speed of implementation. The per capita surface area was increased to 12 square meters by 1980 (15 square meters by 2000), with a shift in location away from the city center, which was considered geologically unsuitable, toward suburban areas. The height and number of stories for buildings underwent significant changes compared to pre-earthquake regulations: seven- to nine-story (10 percent), four-story (83 percent), two-story (7 percent). These adjustments stem from increased seismic requirements and the subsequent higher cost of tall buildings. The outlined provisions necessitated an expansion of land boundaries, with the plan identifying extensions in residential areas in

13 "Postanovlenie Soveta Ministrov SSSR 21 fevralia 1967 g: Ob osnovnykh printsipakh general'nogo plana razvitiia g. Tashkenta [Resolution of the Council of Ministers of the USSR of February 21, 1967: On the Fundamental Principles of the Tashkent General Development Plan]," http://docs.historyrussia.org/ru/nodes/355494-postanovlenie-soveta-ministrov-sssr-21-fevralya-1967-g-ob-osnovnyh-printsipah-generalnogo-plana-razvitiya-g-tashkenta#mode/inspect/page/3/zoom/4.

14 A. I. Vanke, Iu. P. Puretskii, et al., *General'nyi plan razvitiia Tashkenta* [*General Plan for the Development of Tashkent*] (Tashkent: Izdatel'stvo TsK KP Uzbekistana, 1967), 3.

15 Ibid., 17.

16 Ibid., 11.

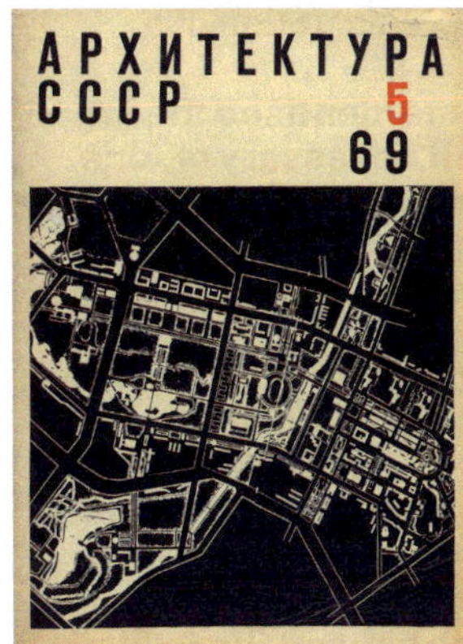

Cover of the journal *Architecture of the USSR*, depicting the 1967 general plan (no. 5, 1969)

the north-east and south-west zones, leading to an overall increase in the city area to 23,000 hectares by 1980, 2,000 more than in 1966. The expanded land area required the development of a new transportation network, a pivotal aspect of the updated proposal. This included a city road network, a railroad network, the construction of a new airport and the establishment of a tram, bus and metro network.[17]

The connections between residential and working areas were identified as the most critical aspect of the existing system. The plan proposed a series of measures to address the major issues: a new metro network with three lines ranging from 55 to 60 kilometers in length that would reduce the time required to traverse the city; the expansion of tram networks; the implementation of a railroad junction and urban road network system; and the construction of a new airport, larger than the existing one. Additionally, public green areas were to be expanded, especially in the city center. Another noteworthy aspect, emphasized by the authors, concerned the design of an urban center that would be representative of the city's growing political and social importance.

The plan established a prioritized sequence for interventions, distributing them across three time intervals. From 1966 to 1970 priority would be given to housing and cultural facilities, aiming for the construction of six million square meters of living space. The goal was to make housing available to city residents by 1971, with an increase in floor space to 7.5 square meters per capita. The construction of the first metro line was also included in this phase. From 1971 to 1980 the focus was on the reconstruction of city center districts and the completion of areas to the north. In this decade, the target was 12 square meters of living space per capita. Improvement of cultural and collective facilities, along with public services (transportation, sewerage and others), was also planned. From 1981 to 2000 the residential program would be completed, with an increase in the minimum area per person to 15 square meters, as would the development of public services.[18]

Model of the city center general plan

17 I. Tkachenko, "Rekonstruktsiia stolitsy Uzbekistana [Reconstruction of the Capital of Uzbekistan]," *Arkhitektura SSSR* [*Architecture of the USSR*], no. 5, 1969, 17–23.

18 A. I. Vanke, Iu. P. Puretskii, et al., *General'nyi plan razvitiia Tashkenta* [*General Plan for the Development of Tashkent*], 30–32.

The Center, the Park, the Ensembles: The Construction of a Grand Urban Project

The post-earthquake seismic zoning scheme identified the urban center as the area at higher risk. This data made it necessary or, one could say, possible to consider a different scenario from that previously planned. The authors presented this alternative proposal as a "new"[19] idea capable of "embracing the common interests of the entire Soviet population." The entire city, center and suburbs, would be structured around a green network of parks, gardens and boulders. The macropark area was delineated in accordance with the orography of the terrain and unfolded along two main directions. The first traversed the city diagonally from the south-west to the north-east, extending between the Boz-su and Burdzhar canals. It continued south-westward into Lenin Komsomol Park, established in the 1930s, and terminated in the north-east at the expansive postwar Victory Park, which housed the Exhibition of National Economic Achievements of Uzbekistan (VDNKh).[20] This park is the site of one of Tashkent's most iconic modernist landscape elements, the TV Tower, the design of which began in the late 1960s.[21] The second zone cut horizontally across the city, linking the "old" and "new" cities and coinciding with the heart of the city center. Tied to a broader network of parks and public green spaces, Tashkent's urban green project followed the course of the extensive canals that characterize the region, running parallel to the western border of the country, approximately twenty kilometers away.

The city center was conceived as a very low-density urban area, characterized by a network of parks and canals and dotted with public buildings, designed as urban ensembles, that made Tashkent a pioneering laboratory for urban planning. To be more precise, the authors stated that these buildings were specifically designed for the geographical, climatic and local cultural conditions[22] and were based on precise standards, with an agenda marked by three milestones (see Table A; values refer to the entire city). They affirmed that the landscape component of the plan was a key element for preserving the original morphology of the city.

The plan aimed to join the "old" and "new" cities through a well-structured urban grid on which many buildings worked like nodes. The green areas interwove with the grid as an urban and conceptual buffer, creating collective spaces and acting as a tool for climate mitigation. The buildings responded to the repertoire of new architectural typologies defined through architectural, social and urban research initiated in the Soviet Union after the revolution, and to the continual technological and aesthetic experimentation that took place at various Soviet project institutes until 1991.

19 Ibid., 17.

20 O. Legostaeva, "Proektirovanie kompleksa VDNKh Uzbekskoi SSR [Designing the VDNKh Complex of the Uzbek SSR]," *Arkhitektura i stroitel'stvo Uzbekistana* [*Architecture and Construction of Uzbekistan*], no. 3, 1974, 41; Iu. N. Egorov, "VDNKh: vchera, segodnia, zavtra: k 20-letiiu Vystavki dostizhenii narodnogo khoziaistva Uzbekskoi SSR [VDNKh: Yesterday, Today, Tomorrow; Twenty Years of the Exhibition of National Economic Achievements of the Uzbek SSR]," *Arkhitektura i stroitel'stvo Uzbekistana* [*Architecture and Construction of Uzbekistan*], no. 10, 1985, 18.

21 See V. Rusanov, "Novyi radioteletsentr [The New Radio and TV Center]," in *Arkhitektura Uzbekistana, Al'manakh* [*Architecture of Uzbekistan: An Almanac*] (Tashkent: Izdatel'stvo literatury i iskusstva imeni Gafura Guliama, 1989), 47.

22 A. I. Vanke, Iu. P. Puretskii, et al., *General'nyi plan razvitiia Tashkenta* [*General Plan for the Development of Tashkent*], 14.

Tashkent State Circus, construction site, 1975

The development of the urban center was planned as a system of ensembles along the two major urban axes. These ensembles were intended to form balanced groups of buildings within the urban context. Besides pure spatial and functional considerations, the urban logic was an important ingredient in defining each ensemble.

At the crossroads of the two axes delineating the directions of the green areas, the plan outlined the development of the administrative and governmental ensemble. Toward the east, the plan envisioned the establishment of commercial and educational zones, while to the west it foresaw the creation of sports and entertainment facilities.[23]

The masterplan in the 1967 publication included a number of buildings that would be inaugurated several years later, reinforcing key points of the plan.

In line with the urban development plan, in the western part of the city significant landmarks were built, including the Circus (1975),[24] the Peoples' Friendship Palace(1981),[25] the Moscow Hotel (later the Chorsu Hotel) (1982)[26] and the Chorsu Bazaar (1990).[27] Each of these structures played and still plays a crucial role in the city's layout. The Circus and the Peoples' Friendship Palace serve as prominent markers at opposite ends of Furkat Street, the major axis running north–south through the "old city" as envisioned in the plan.[28]

The Circus was placed at the intersection of Furkat Street and Navoi Street, a road axis designed to connect the two cities in the early Soviet period.[29] The mahalla[30] to the north of the plot was considerably

23 I. Tkachenko, "Rekonstruktsiia stolitsy Uzbekistana [Reconstruction of the Capital of Uzbekistan]"; T. F. Kadyrova, *Arkhitektura tsentra Tashkenta* [*The Architecture of the Center of Tashkent*] (Tashkent: Izdatel'stvo literatury i iskusstva imeni Gafura Guliama, 1976).

24 Inauguration year. See the Building Monograph for the Circus in this volume, p. 804.

25 Construction was completed in 1981, but we do not know the exact date of the inauguration. See E. P. Sukhanova and V. P. Krichevskii, "Dvorets Druzhby narodov SSSR im. V.I. Lenina v Tashkente [The V.I. Lenin Peoples' Friendship Palace in Tashkent]," *Arkhitektura i stroitel'stvo Uzbekistana* [*Architecture and Construction of Uzbekistan*], no. 8, 1981, 18–24.

26 V. Spivak, "Gostinitsa 'Moskva' v Tashkente [The Moscow Hotel in Tashkent]," *Arkhitektura i stroitel'stvo Uzbekistana* [*Architecture and Construction of Uzbekistan*], no. 2, 1983, 15–23.

27 According to the Building Monograph for the Chorsu Bazaar in this volume, p. 722.

28 Protocol No. 1, Tashkent, March 18, 1968. Creative Sections, Union of Architects of the Uzbek SSR. Materialy deiatel'nosti sektsii individual'nogo proektirovaniia i inter'erov. Nachato 1969 koncheno 1971. Na 12 listakh [Materials Concerning the Activities of the Section of Individual Design and Interiors. Begun 1969, completed 1971], Tashkent City Archive, fund 2532, list 2, item 89, 12 sheets.

29 Philipp Meuser, *Seismic Modernism*, 35–37.

30 Traditional residential neighborhood.

changed to create an urban park named after Pushkin.[31] The Peoples' Friendship Palace, completing the ensemble at the opposite end of Furkat Street, made its debut in the 1974 Detailed Plan (PDP)[32] and is Tashkent's biggest entertainment venue, having been one of the largest in the USSR.[33]

Two other significant modernist structures are situated to the west, the Moscow Hotel and the Chorsu Bazaar. The Moscow Hotel first appeared in the 1974 PDP, offering an efficient solution for a complex urban area.[34] The hotel, with its tall tower on a podium, was located on Akhunbabaev Square, with a commanding view of Navoi Street. This imposing building marks the conclusion of the street axis, directing attention toward the "old city". The giant building with an intricate podium, housing Tashkent's ancient bazaar, Chorsu, was conceived from 1981[35] onward in a location just west of where the market had previously thrived.

МИРМУХСИН,
главный редактор сатирического журнала «Муштум»

Рисунки Д. СИНИЦКОГО

ДРЕВНИЙ, НО ВЕЧНО ЮНЫЙ

Ташкенту — одному из древнейших городов Средней Азии — насчитывается около двух тысяч лет. Первые упоминания о нем датируются вторым веком до нашей эры. Однако известно, что еще во времена завоевательных походов персидского шаха Дария I, а точнее, в 519 году до нашей эры, воины проходили через поселения племен хоумаварги шак, которые находились вблизи Яксарта (Сыр-Дарьи) и у берегов Перрака (Чирчика).

В знаменитой поэме Фирдоуси «Шахнамэ» сказано, что Рустам-богатырь «взял в руки лук чачский». В «Шахнамэ» поэт, живший в десятом веке, описывал события, происходившие за тысячу лет до него. Великий караванный «шелковый путь» проходил тогда через Чач, позже Шош; так и стал называться город.

Шош превратился в Шаш, а потом получил окончание «кент», то есть «град», и в конце концов стал называться Ташкент. Словом, он не менее известен историкам, чем другие наши города: Самарканд, Бухара, Мерв,— хотя и несколько моложе их.

Мой город никогда не был столицей. Только после Октября он стал столицей и расцвел.

Если бы лет пятьдесят назад взобраться на самые высокие здания города — медресе Кукельтош или Беклярбеги, можно было бы увидеть невысокие плоские крыши, горбатые, потрескавшиеся глиняные дувалы, узкие, кривые улочки, непроходимые зимой и пыльные летом. И возвышавшийся над всем этим купол мечети Лайлак.

Сейчас все эти древности потерялись среди великолепных современных зданий.

Перед вами одна из прекрасных улиц Ташкента — проспект Алишера Навои. Эта улица начинается на востоке города и тянется далеко на запад. И солнце как бы поднимается над ней с одного конца, а садится на другом.

В начале улицы стоит медресе Кукельтош, которому уже четыре столетия (на рисунке — внизу слева). Его хорошо изобразил заслуженный деятель искусств нашей республики Д. Синицкий, который, кстати, выполнил этот рисунок, вдохновившись «портретами столиц» художника Г. Огородникова, публикуемыми в «Крокодиле».

Напротив Кукельтоша, на другой стороне улицы, вы видите памятник первому президенту нашей республики, аксакалу Юлдашу Ахунбабаеву.

Эта улица, самая красивая и оживленная, ведет к площади В. И. Ленина. Над ней возвышается монумент Владимиру Ильичу, дорогой сердцу каждого узбека.

Рядом с монументом находится здание, в котором происходила историческая встреча глав государств Индии и Пакистана. После этой встречи, организованной по инициативе Советского правительства, мир заговорил о «духе Ташкента». Наш древний город стал символом мира и взаимопонимания.

В нашем городе насчитывается более миллиона жителей. Почва под ним все еще вздрагивает, колеблется. Иной раз город подбрасывает, как крышку чайника, стоящего на огне. Землетрясение, начавшееся 26 апреля прошлого года, окончательно не успокоилось и до сих пор. Эпицентр — под городом. Старые, одноэтажные глиняные дома не выдержали (рисунок внизу). Но устояли основные здания — и современные и древние.

Выстояли и мы, ташкентцы. Хотя на долю Ташкента выпали тяжкие испытания, оказалось, что никакой напор стихии не страшен, если рядом верные друзья. С помощью всех братских республик, протянувших нам руку помощи, мы строим сейчас новый Ташкент — город, который будет столь же прочным, сколь и красивым. И мы уверены, что город наш пройдет еще через много тысячелетий.

По сторонам проспекта Навои тянутся зеленые аллеи, а в скверике, за которым взметнулась вверх ажурная башня антенны телевизионной студии,— памятник великому Алишеру Навои. Чуть поодаль — ребристый цилиндр Дворца искусств, прекрасное украшение Ташкента, с залом на три тысячи мест.

Теперь взгляните немного выше. Над крышей светлого здания, построенного в современном строгом стиле, реют два знамени: СССР и УзССР. Это административное здание на Узбекистанской улице — отличный подарок ташкентцам от наших замечательных строителей.

Чуть ниже — вместительная чаша самого крупного стадиона на Востоке. Это хорошо известный в стране (и, разумеется, в первую очередь болельщикам!) центральный стадион «Пахтакор». После реконструкции на его трибунах смогут расположиться сто тысяч зрителей. Невдалеке от стадиона несет свои прохладные, быстрые воды Урда-анхори — наша, так сказать, Москва-река. Берега ее скоро оденутся в гранит, а широкая полоса зелени протянется далеко по обоим берегам.

По левую сторону проспекта видны здания Центрального телеграфа, Министерства сельского хозяйства, других министерств и ведомств. Еще дальше вы видите Большой государственный театр оперы и балета имени Навои, ташкентские куранты, вокзал, аэропорт и, конечно же, краны. Стрелы башенных кранов в Ташкенте увидишь всюду, куда только ни посмотришь.

Если хвалить Ташкент, можно хвалить долго даже небольшую его часть, которую вы видите на рисунке. Но у нас говорят: лучше один раз увидеть, чем тысячу раз услышать. Приезжайте сами в Ташкент, в мой город хлебный, гостеприимный и мирный, мужественный и прекрасный.

Походите по его улицам, утопающим в зелени и цветах, отведайте сладких плодов наших. И будьте уверены, гостеприимные ташкентцы встретят вас душевно, сердечно, с широко распростертыми братскими объятиями!

Illustration from the Soviet magazine *Krokodil*, with Navoi Street in the foreground

In the intermediate area of the city center, a number of architectural ensembles are of great interest, exhibiting noteworthy features in both architectural and urban terms. The first cluster is situated within the confines of the "old city," to the south of Navoi Street. Here, three significant structures stand out: the Panoramic Cinema (1964),[36] the TV

31 In the 1930s. See Boris Chukhovich, "Urban History," in the Building Monograph for the Circus in this volume, p. 803.
32 The Detailed Plan (PDP) develops a specific area in detail in accordance with the general plan. In this case, the subject of the PDP is the urban center of Tashkent.
33 Designed to rival the Lenin Palace in Alma-Ata (1970), The Peoples' Friendship Palace has a seating capacity of 4,100 compared to 3,000 in the capital of Kazakhstan.
34 V. Spivak, "Gostinitsa 'Moskva' v Tashkente [The Moscow Hotel in Tashkent]," 15.
35 Tashgiprogor Technical Archive (refers to the dates of the historical drawings).
36 According to Sutiagin's notes, the building was constructed quickly in order to be inaugurated in 1964, the 40th anniversary of the founding of the Uzbek SSR. (Sergo Sutiagin, handwritten notes on the reconstruction of the Panoramic Cinema, 2020).

Наименование	Ед. изм.	На 1 янв. 1967 г.	К 1970 г.	К 1980 г.
1. Детские дошкольные учреждения	мест	39	58	100
2. Школы	"	118	160	190
3. Кинотеатры	"	15	25	50
4. Клубы	"	11	20	50
5. Больницы	коек	7	11,2	13,5
6. Поликлиники	посещен.	10	18	20
7. Магазины	раб. мест	3,5	6	10
8. Столовые	мест	22	32	100
9. Бани	"	2,5	3,4	5
10. Прачечные	кг. белья в смену	11,3	25	120
11. Гостиницы	мест	0,8	3,2	10

Table A: Milestones for the number of public buildings to be built per thousand inhabitants in 1967, 1970 and 1980, according to the 1967 general plan
1. Kindergartens
2. Schools
3. Cinemas
4. Clubs
5. Hospitals
6. Polyclinics
7. Shops
8. Canteens
9. Public baths
10. Laundries
11. Hotels

Center (1977),[37] and the House of Youth (1975).[38] The design of this architectural ensemble, incorporated into the 1966 general plan, took into account two preexisting structures with significant urban impact, Pakhtakor Stadium[39] and the Panoramic Cinema, both built before the earthquake, in order to ensure effective flow management between buildings and to establish a balanced composition. The cinema, boasting a capacity of 2,300 seats, was conceived as a multifunctional building, capable of hosting not only experimental film projections but also concerts, congresses and festivals.[40] The decision to set the cinema's façade back from Navoi Street was also coherent with urban planning that envisioned a series of indented squares facing the major road axis.

The earthquake of 1966 damaged the old TV Center, constructed in the 1950s close to the site of the cinema. This led to the decision to build a new TV Center[41] as a compact, rectangular building of considerable size, later adorned with precious mosaics by Moscow artist Evgenii Ablin.[42]

The third integral element of the ensemble is the building of the former House of Youth. The project, both functionally and planning-wise, is coherent with the post-earthquake general plan. This articulated structure, designed for a variety of cultural and entertainment functions for young people, is located on the last section of Pakhtakorskaia Street, before it ends at the stadium.

At the crossroads of the two urban green zones, the plan positioned the most emblematic architectural ensemble, Lenin Square, which featured three administrative and governmental buildings along with a grand celebratory fountain. This square served as the geographical and ideological focal point of the plan.[43] This location, just east of the Ankhor Canal, corresponds to the section of the city constructed after 1865, and its urban layout, rooted in Makarov's 1870 plan,[44] remained largely unchanged until the earthquake.

The 1967 masterplan introduced squares, parks, green spaces and several public buildings into this area. It was to serve as the cultural heart of the city, with notable establishments including the Navoi National Library, the Iskra Cinema, the Bakhor Concert Hall and, slightly south of Lenin Square, the Institute of Art Studies (1972).

37 The date refers to the end of the construction period, since we do not have precise information about the inauguration.

38 According to the Building Monograph for the House of Youth in this volume, p. 844.

39 See S. Sutiagin and A. Braslavskii, "Dvorets iskusstv v Tashkente [The Palace of Arts in Tashkent]," *Arkhitektura SSSR* [*Architecture of the USSR*], no. 11, 1965, 9.

40 "Programmnoe zadanie na proektirovanie Panoramnogo kinoteatra s universal'nym zalom na 2500 mest v gorode Tashkente: Stenogramma obsuzhdeniia proektov Panoramnogo kinoteatra pri Soiuze arkhitektorov UzSSR, 20 fevralia 1961 [Design Brief for a Panoramic Cinema with a Universal Auditorium with 2,500 Seats in Tashkent: Record of the Discussion of Projects for a Panoramic Cinema at the Union of Architects of the Uzbek SSR], State Archive of the Republic of Uzbekistan, fund 2532, list 1, item 258, 119 sheets, 107.

41 Iu. Ferdman, "Novye zdaniia i sooruzheniia televideniia i radio [New Buildings and Structures for Television and Radio]," *Arkhitektura SSSR* [*Architecture of the USSR*], no. 11, 1980, 46.

42 Although the first drafts have not been preserved, we can deduce the changes from the documents in the archive. See "Zakliuchenie ekspertnoi komissii po rassmotreniiu tekhnologicheskoi chasti Proektnogo zadaniia na stroitel'stvo Teletsentra v g. Tashkente, ot 22 oktiabria 1966 [Conclusion of the Expert Commission for the Assessment of the Technological Part of the Design Brief for the Construction of the Telecenter in Tashkent, October 22, 1966]," Tashkent City Archive, fund 36, list 1, item 1334. Protokoly zasedanii arkhitekturnoi komissii i ekspertnye zaklyuchenija po proektam i smetam stroitel'stva za n. 105–125 [Protocols of Meetings of the Architectural Commission and Expert Conclusions on Projects and Budgets for Construction, Numbers 105–125], 168 sheets, 156–159.

43 See A. I. Vanke, Iu. P. Puretskii, et al., *General'nyi plan razvitiia Tashkenta* [*General Plan for the Development of Tashkent*]; I. Tkachenko, "Rekonstruktsiia stolitsy Uzbekistana [Reconstruction of the Capital of Uzbekistan]"; T. F. Kadyrova, *Arkhitektura tsentra Tashkenta* [*The Architecture of the Center of Tashkent*].

44 G. C. Wolf, "Reproducing Tashkent: Reconceptualising Transition from the Socialist City to the Post-Socialist City" (Ph.D. diss., University of Manchester, 2019), 100.

Strategically positioned at specific points in the city, the modernist structures assumed vital roles within the green network. A little further south from Lenin Square on the east bank of the Ankhor Canal, the Central Committee of the Communist Party of Uzbekistan[45] was inaugurated in 1964. Further south along Samarkandskaia Street (renamed Lenin Avenue in 1970) was the Blue Domes Café (1970).[46] This hypostyle pavilion engaged in a dialogue with the surrounding park by blurring the boundaries between the interior and the exterior.

The avenue was designed to commemorate the centenary of Lenin's birth.[47] At its north-eastern end is one of the first modernist buildings in Tashkent, the Central Department Store (TsUM), which predated the plan, having been inaugurated in 1964.[48]

Administrative and governmental ensemble, 1972

The cultural, commercial, and educational functions that characterized this area, as outlined in the post-earthquake general plan, were reinforced through the construction of numerous other structures in subsequent decades, in line with the 1974 PDP and the 1980 general plan. Between 1968 and 1969 one of the architectural gems of Tashkent, the Lenin Museum (1970),[49] was designed for a site near Lenin Square, on

45 A.I. Fineleib, and E.F. Lenneshmidt, "Novoe administrativnoe zdanie stolitsy [A New Administrative Building in the Capital]," *Arkhitektura i stroitel'stvo Uzbekistana [Architecture and Construction of Uzbekistan]*, no. 3, 1965, 25.
46 See "1970s: Blue Domes Café," in *Tashkent: Corpus of Monuments*, n.p.
47 "Bul'var im. V. I. Lenina [V.I. Lenin Avenue]," *Arkhitektura i stroitel'stvo Uzbekistana [Architecture and Construction of Uzbekistan]*, no. 7, 1974, 11.
48 See "TsUM," in *Tashkent: Corpus of Monuments*, n.p.
49 E. Rozanov, "Muzei V. I. Lenin v Tashkente [The V.I. Lenin Museum in Tashkent]," *Arkhitektura i stroitel'stvo Uzbekistana [Architecture and Construction of Uzbekistan]*, no. 4, 1970, 24–33.

the elevated side of Lenin Avenue. To the east of the museum, the House of Publishers, a tall structure with an illuminated sign—the first functional LED strip in the city—completed the ensemble, forming what became the most popular postcard image of Tashkent.[50]

The 1974 PDP masterplan introduced several other modernist buildings strategically located at key points in the city center: the Union of Artists Exhibition Hall (1974), the State Museum of Arts (1974)[51] and the Turkestan Palace (1993). The Union of Artists Exhibition Hall is situated at the intersection of two crucial axes in the urban grid, Lenin Avenue and Uzbekistanskaia Street, overlooking Theater Square. The pavilion rises above the surrounding urban context, perched on a small artificial hill that acts as a podium and extends the exhibition space beyond the building. Like an open-air museum, the "green podium" features sculptures by contemporary artists of the period. The State Museum of Arts occupies a pivotal position, stitching together the western and the eastern areas of the "new city," the latter characterized by the radial grid of the 1870 plan. The plot is defined by Proletarskaia Street, which cuts across Revolution Square and extends northward through the city, and Shota Rustaveli Street, which traces the parabolic arm that outlines the perimeter of the former Russian part of the city. Lastly, the Turkestan Palace, designed to accommodate the Gor'kii Russian Drama Theater, is strategically located at the intersection of Navoi Street and Parade Avenue.

View of the House of Publishers and the Lenin Museum from the governmental ensemble

A Brief Closing Note on Storytelling

The post-earthquake plan both gave and shaped a "modernist identity" to the fourth-largest capital of the USSR, addressing long-standing issues that dated back to 1865. This was done in a specific way, by constructing "a showcase for socialism in the East," as outlined by Boris Chukhovich.[52]

50 R. V. Bleze, "Redaktsionno-izdatel'skii korpus kompleksa izdatel'stva TsK KP Uzbekistana [The Editing and Publishing Block of the Publishers' Complex of the Central Committee of the Communist Party of Uzbekistan," *Arkhitektura i stroitel'stvo Uzbekistana* [*Architecture and Construction of Uzbekistan*], no. 1, 1972, 20–22.

51 "Gosudarstvennyi muzei iskusstv Uzbekskoi SSR [The State Museum of Arts of the Uzbek SSR]," *Arkhitektura i stroitel'stvo Uzbekistana* [*Architecture and Construction of Uzbekistan*], no. 10, 1981, 18–23.

52 Boris Chukhovich, "Building the 'Living East,'" in *Soviet Modernism 1955–1991: Unknown History*, ed. Katharina Ritter, Ekaterina Shapiro-Obermair and Alexandra Wachter (Vienna: Park Books, 2012), 230.

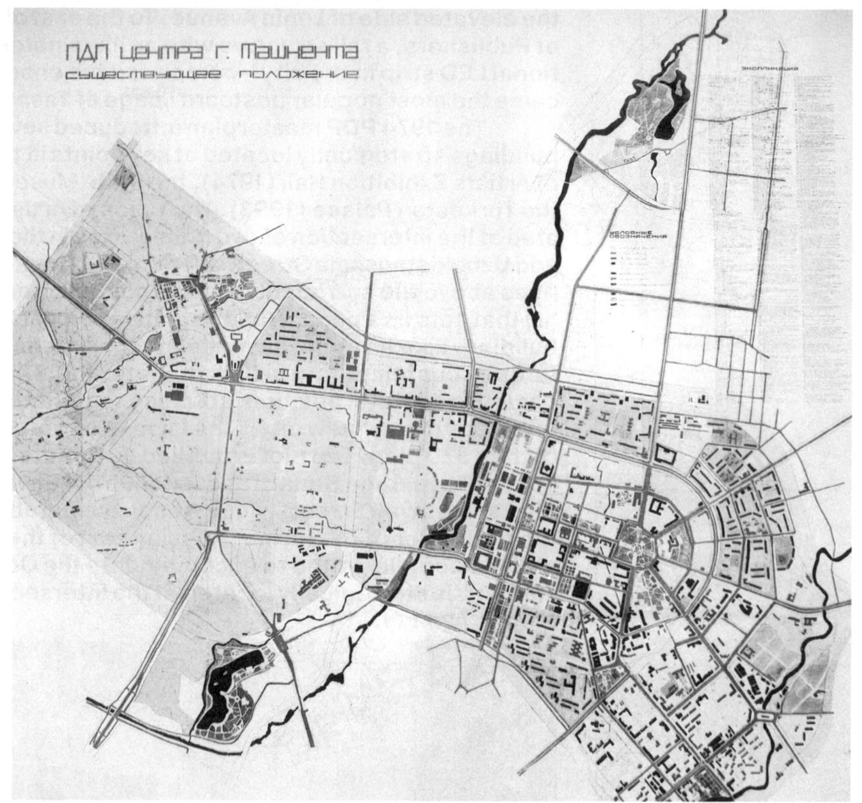

Tashkent city center, survey of the existing condition in 1974

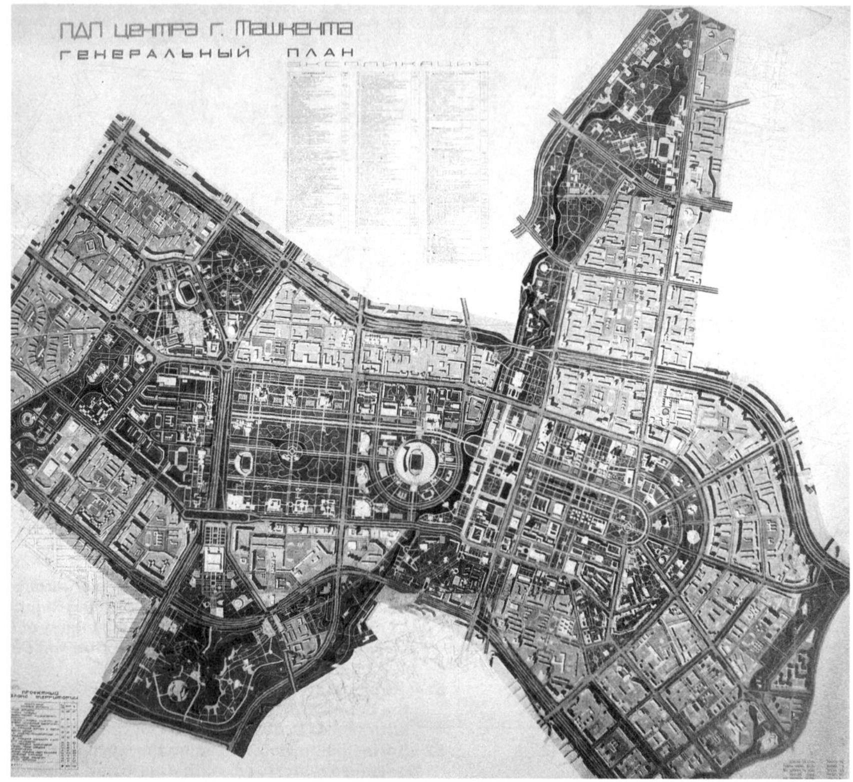

Detailed Plan (PDP) for the center of Tashkent, 1974

A closer examination of the urban planning history prompts a number of observations. The first concerns the pivotal concept of the plan that Tashkent should be rebuilt as a garden city, an idea declared "new" by the authors. However, this innovative idea for the capital can be traced back to the 1937–1939 general plan by Aleksandr Kuznetsov, an architect from Moscow's Mosoblproekt planning institute. The proposed network of green spaces was the key element in 1938 and this remained relevant, albeit to varying degrees, in the 1966 proposal. One of the purposes of this network was to cancel out the social and cultural differences between the "old" and "new" cities. Furthermore, within the framework of the 1974 PDP is yet another echo of the 1938 plan: Furkat Street, distinguished by splits at the southern and northern extremities, not only shapes the potential connections between the northern and southern sectors of the city but also underscores the subsequent significance assigned to the Circus and the Peoples' Friendship Palace.

As described by Boris Chukhovich, Kuznetsov's plan aimed to resolve the duality between the "old" and "new" cities by not preserving the architecture or the urban fabric of the former and connecting the two areas through a network of infrastructure and public spaces. When the postwar architectural debate regarding the possibility of adopting Kuznetsov's plan opened up, the public was divided: a sizable group opposed the destruction of the Uzbek part of the city and did not consider the plan to be in line with the "spirit of oriental architecture."[53] The 1967 plan utilized the alibi of the earthquake and damage to the "old city" to implement its erasure.

A second observation relates to the conceptualization of the city center as a system of architectural ensembles. The theme of constructing by ensemble was prominent in the architectural discourse of the 1930s. In the general plan devised for Moscow in 1935 by Vladimir Semenov, three design levels can be discerned, with one being oformlenie, or "shape making," which refers to the creation of a specific architectural-urban image for the "World Capital of the Proletariat."[54] The smallest unit of construction was the "ensemble,"[55] devised by the architectural design workshops under the supervision of Mossovet, the Moscow city administration.[56] Therefore, this aspect of the Tashkent plan is also based on a methodology developed in Moscow three decades earlier. However, it is important to emphasize that designing systems of ensembles also meant having a great deal of control over the territory, not only through urban space but also through the synoptic reduction of the masterplan on paper. Such control would be difficult in the chaotic and extremely dense urban fabric of the "old" city. Though facilitated by the earthquake's destruction, the ensemble proposals here took off late and, with a few exceptions, were not implemented until Uzbekistan's independence, which marked the end of the modernist project.

A final observation concerns the relationship between the urban plan and architecture. Many buildings described in this book have been identified as "players" in the urban plan formulated after the earthquake, but were actually designed before it. They include some of the

53 Boris Chukhovich, "Architectural Modernism and 'Old Tashkent': The Long History of a Brief Encounter," in *Mahalla: Urban Rural Living*, exhibition catalogue of the National Pavilion of Uzbekistan at the 17th Venice Architecture Biennale (Tashkent/Bolzano: Longo, 2021), 72.

54 A. De Magistris, *La costruzione della città totalitaria* (Milan: CittàStudiEdizioni, 1995).

55 On the concept of the ensemble as discussed in the 1930s, see M. Meriggi, "Affabulazione e montaggio: Il progetto dell'angelo e del diavolo nella città e nell'architettura russa e sovietica" (Ph.D. diss., Venice); Iu. Lotman, "Arkhitektura v kontkste kul'tury [Architecture in the Context of Culture]," in *Semiosfera* [*The Semiosphere*] (St. Petersburg: Iskusstvo SPb, 2010). See also F. Deo, "Sotsrealism: Architecture and Totalitarism in the Age of Stalin," *Eda Esempi di Architettura*, special issue, 2022, 43–56.

56 Defined in the first edition (1926–1947) of the Great Soviet Encyclopedia as "a unit of harmonious spatial composition of buildings, engineering structures [...], monumental paintings and sculptures, gardens and parks."

most iconic structures: the Circus, the Panoramic Cinema, the House of Youth, the House of Government, the Central Committee of the Communist Party and the Uzbekistan Hotel. These architectural landmarks have left a lasting imprint on the urban layout of the capital of Uzbekistan.

The earthquake gave the city the opportunity to finally implement projects with roots that went further back than expected. A brief look at the history of earthquakes and Soviet policies indicates that the strategies undertaken in Tashkent are markedly different from those implemented by the Soviets in response to the other two major earthquakes, in Crimea in 1927 and in Ashkhabad in 1948. An analysis of the Soviet and international press makes it clear that the project to recreate Tashkent as the largest Asian capital of the USSR and as the Soviet arena for contacts with developing countries runs in parallel with the global propaganda project.

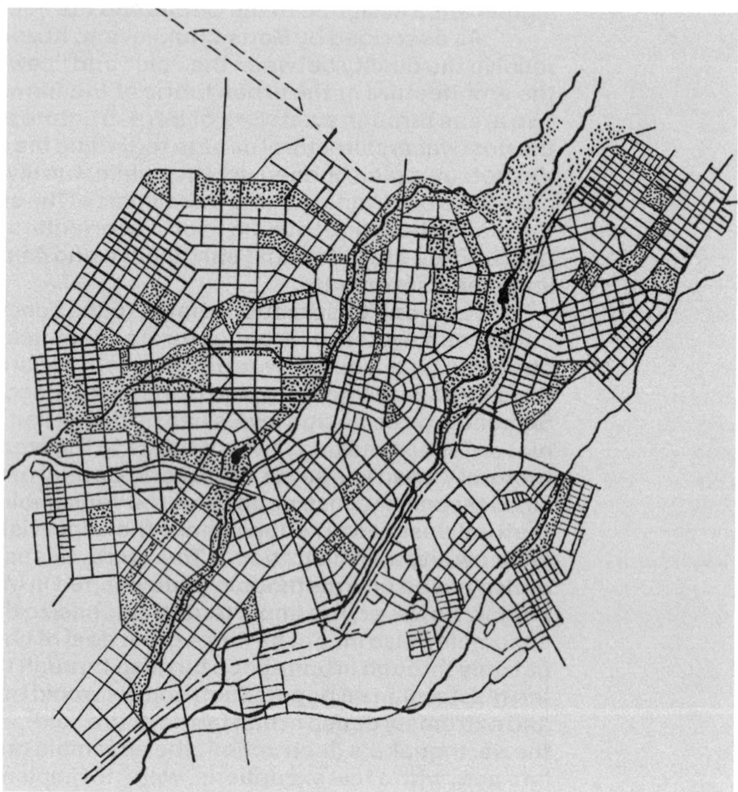

Aleksandr Kuznetsov, masterplan of Tashkent, 1937–1939

The Institutional History of the Architecture of Soviet Uzbekistan

Boris Chukhovich

In the early 1960s Tashkent was still considered to be divided into two parts: "old" and "new," so-called "Asian" and "European." This was an asymmetric two-language city. The majority of residents were native speakers of Uzbek, but by the 1960s they also spoke Russian to varying degrees, while the districts of the "new city" remained monolingual. The relationship between Tashkent and Moscow comprised another asymmetrical opposition. Moscow issued directives, maintained ideological control, regulated the financing of construction and influenced the aesthetic evolution of Tashkent's architecture. Tashkent was interested in attracting the maximum amount of funding from the federal Soviet budget, but it was also striving for greater autonomy in decision-making. The abundance of bipolar relationships made it tempting to interpret them in fictitious binary categories typical of the orientalist discourse. Tashkent was perceived as a "meeting place of East and West," a "dialogue of cultures," a transit point between Asia and Europe (see the essay "Modernism as Orientalism" in this volume, pp. 126–139). However, institutional history demonstrates that the architectural process involved numerous actors whose contradictory and multidirectional interests cannot be represented using simply binary oppositions.

Education

The initial situation appeared somewhat dualistic. In architecture the first decade of the Soviet Union was a time of two differently directed and practically unconnected processes. Firstly, the vernacular tradition of transferring construction knowledge and skills through artisans and workshops was slowly dying out. This was caused by the ban on construction of religious buildings and rapid contraction of the circle of wealthy private clients, whose requirements and tastes had previously been catered to by the builders' artels. Secondly, due to the absence of European-type educational institutions the architectural environment was formed largely by specialists of the tsarist epoch who had moved to the Turkestan Region from Russia (Georgii Svarichevskii) or Ukraine (Wilhelm Heinzelmann). The first Soviet general plan of Tashkent (1929–1933) was proposed by Muscovite Aleksandr Sil'chenkov, a former student of Nikolai Ladovskii's at VKhUTEMAS. Stefan Polupanov, who designed a number of Constructivist projects for Samarkand and Andijan and built the House of Government in Tashkent (1930–1931), was a graduate of Kharkiv Construction Institute in Ukraine.

III этап: 1945—1989 «Становление»

· САИИ · СазПИ · ТашПИ · СамГАСИ ·

ВЫСШЕМУ АРХИТЕКТУРНОМУ ОБРАЗОВАНИЮ УЗБЕКИСТАНА 60 ЛЕТ

A spread of the magazine *Architecture and Construction of Uzbekistan* (1990) on the history of architectural education in Uzbekistan

The Last Day of the Tower Epic: Special issue of the comic illustration from *For the Socialist Reconstruction of Tashkent* (cartoon), 1955. The caricature shows the shocked reaction of Tashkent architects to the government decree "On the Elimination of Excesses in Design and Construction" (November 4, 1955), which gave the green light to a new wave of modernist architecture. The government demanded that architects do away with the decorative use of forms of historical architecture and move to industrial construction defined by simplicity and economy of solutions. The cartoon is based on the famous painting *The Last Day of Pompeii* (1833) by Russian artist Karl Bryullov, depicting the demise of the Roman city after an earthquake and volcanic eruption. Tashkent architects are represented in Roman togas and tunics in the middle of the street, with collapsing buildings symbolizing the classical heritage: propylaea, towers with spires, arcades, colonnades, etc. In the foreground, the colonnade of Beshagach Square is being destroyed, and its author, Tashkent's chief architect, Mitkhat Bulatov, is running out from under it on the right. Nearby, architect Olga Gaazenkopf, the future author of the Institute of Pectoral Surgery, has fainted. In the left part of the picture, Irina Demchinskaia, the future author of many modernist buildings such as the House of Knowledge and the residential buildings on Bogdan Khmel'nitskii Street, is depicted as a woman with an infant fleeing from the lightning of the raging Jupiter-Khrushchëv. The teaching staff of the architectural department of SazPI is depicted on the left side of the cartoon, and one can also read dejection and confusion in their professors.

The history of modern architectural education in Uzbekistan began in 1929. Then the Central Asia Cotton Irrigation Polytechnic Institute (SAKhIPI) separated from Central Asia State University and opened an architecture department. Two years later the institute split into the Tashkent Institute of Irrigation and Agricultural Melioration (TIIMSKh) and the Central Asia Construction Institute (SASI), in which there were three faculties, including architecture. The main lecturers in this new institution were people from St. Petersburg/Leningrad professional circles.[1] The first small group of students graduated in 1934. In that year yet another reorganization of educational institutions took place, and they were brought together as part of the Central Asia Industrial Institute (SAII), where the construction faculty and architectural department merged.[2] From 1936 qualified architects began to graduate regularly from the institute. By 1941 there were around 150. The war resulted in a four-year gap. During the wartime evacuation of higher education institutions from Moscow and Leningrad to Tashkent, SASI merged with the Moscow Architectural Institute and was re-established with some difficulty only after the war ended in 1945. In 1949 it was restructured as the Central Asia Polytechnic Institute (SazPI) and then in 1961 renamed the Tashkent Polytechnic Institute (TashPI). An important aspect of the postwar situation was the increase in the authority of Tashkent specialists who had graduated from the city's institutions, judging by the fact that now they formed the backbone of the teaching staff. In 1963 an evening department opened, with places for one hundred people, and the overall number of students rose to 800.[3] This rapid growth led to the reorganization of the architectural department into an independent faculty. In the 1960s another architectural higher education institution appeared when in 1966 the Architecture and Construction Institute (SamGASI) opened in Samarkand. It had architecture and construction faculties and the first group graduated in 1972, with between fifty and seventy-six students joining each year. Together with TashPI graduates they produced an annual increase in architectural specialists of 250 people per year.[4]

The vast majority of Tashkent architects who created unique buildings in the city between the 1960s and the 1980s were graduates of TashPI. This refutes the stereotype that the "second Soviet modernism" was based entirely on the teaching activities of former VKhUTEMAS staff, who in the Stalinist period had settled in various Soviet higher education institutions and implicitly took up the baton of the 1920s avant-gardes. The genesis of education in Tashkent was in the prerevolutionary engineering schools of Russia and Ukraine, and contact between Tashkent students and post-VKhUTEMAS Moscow professors was limited to four years during the war, when it was impossible to broadcast the ideas of Constructivism. Of much greater significance was the informational environment in which architects were immersed from the late 1950s.

1 They were professors Georgii Svarichevskii, Leonid Voronin and Sergei Kolotov and docent Ivan Markevich (Konstantin Babievskii, Konstantin Kriukov and Khamza Ubaidullaev, "Arkhitekturnoe obrazovanie v Uzbekistane [Architectural Education in Uzbekistan]," *Stroitel'stvo i arkhitektura Uzbekistana* [*Construction and Architecture of Uzbekistan*], no. 12, 1972, 16).

2 Valentin Arkhangel'skii and Gennadii Korobovtsev, "I etap: 1929–1941; 'Zarozhdenie', SAKhIPI–SASI–SAII [I. Stage: 1929–1941; 'The Origin', SaKhIPI–SASI–SAII]," *Arkhitektura i stroitel'stvo Uzbekistana* [*Architecture and Construction of Uzbekistan*], no. 7, 1990, 2.

3 Konstantin Babievskii and Khamza Ubaidullaev, "Uzbekskaia arkhitekturnaia shkola [The Uzbek Architectural School]," *Stroitel'stvo i arkhitektura Uzbekistana* [*Construction and Architecture of Uzbekistan*], no. 12, 1979, 4. (According to other sources, the evening department began by accepting 75 people and the "overall number of entrants in 1963 was 125, later reaching 150–180." See Khamza Ubaidullaev and Valentin Arkhangel'skii, "III etap: 1945–1989; 'Stanovlenie,' SAII–SazPI–TashPI–SamGASI [III. Stage: 1945–1989; 'Formation,' SAII–SazPI–TashPI–SamGASI]," *Arkhitektura i stroitel'stvo Uzbekistana* [*Architecture and Construction of Uzbekistan*], no. 7, 1990, 9.)

4 Konstantin Babievskii, Konstantin Kriukov and Khamza Ubaidullaev, "Arkhitekturnoe obrazovanie v Uzbekistane [Architectural Education in Uzbekistan]," 17.

Channels of Information

Foreign Books and Journals

The main flow of foreign books and journals was into the Republican Scientific and Technical Library of the Academy of Sciences of Uzbekistan. Shukur Askarov recalled that the range of journals and books was almost as wide as in the foreign literature departments of the key libraries in Moscow and Leningrad. In particular, Tashkent received the main architectural journals from western European countries and North America. However, this literature was not accessible to everyone. Most architects, researchers and students did not have a sufficient command of foreign languages to read texts by their international colleagues. For this reason, materials were not so much read as leafed through, with the focus on images rather than texts. This was in line with Soviet trends. According to Aleksandr Kudriavtsev, "then architects usually rejected the analytical side of books on innovative contemporary architecture and focused on the pictures, since the texts were a priori critical of the experience of capitalist countries."[5]

From the early 1960s a number of translated Western journals began to be published in the USSR: *L'Architecture d'Aujourd'hui* (France), *Civil Engineering* (USA), *IndustrieBau* (Federal Republic of Germany) and *Construction Materials* (UK).[6] The latter three titles were aimed more at engineers and technologists, but *L'Architecture d'Aujourd'hui* was widely read. It was subscribed to by libraries of project institutes and by individual architects. And although the Russian version of the journal differed to some extent from the French original (for example, works of abstract art were edited out, as they were considered "bourgeois" and "decadent" in the USSR), the main contents of the journal were efficiently translated by Soviet specialists.

As well as journals, an important role in circulating the ideas of the Modern Movement was played by translations of books by foreign authors that were published in the USSR. The choice of authors for translation was largely ideological. In the USSR communist authors were readily published, as were architects with leftist views. Among the leaders of the Modern Movement, Oscar Niemeyer, who was a communist and winner of the international Lenin Peace Prize, had exceptional influence in the USSR. His books were published in the first half of the 1960s.[7] Translations of Le Corbusier,[8] Walter Gropius,[9] Kenzō Tange[10] and Alvar Aalto[11] followed. Particularly popular in Tashkent was communist Georges Candilis' book *Building Life*,[12] which shed light on the French experience in Casablanca, a subject of interest to Tashkent architects. However, in certain cases the translation of a book to Russian was based on scientific and technical aims rather than ideological ones. This explains

5 Quoted in Ol'ga Iakushenko, "Sovetskaia arkhitektura i Zapad: otkrytie i assimiliatsiia zapadnogo opyta v sovetskoi arkhitektury kontsa 1950-kh-1960-kh godov [Soviet Architecture and the West: The Discovery and Assimilation of Western Experience in Soviet Architecture of the Late 1950s and 1960s]," *Laboratorium* 8, no. 2, 2016, 85.

6 Ibid., 86.

7 Oscar Niemeyer, *Moi opyt stroitel'stva Braziliia* [*Minha experiência em Brasília*] (Moscow: Izdatel'stvo inostrannoi literatury, 1963); Oscar Niemeyer, *Arkhitektura i obshchestvo* [*Architecture and Society*] (Moscow: Progress, 1975).

8 Le Corbusier, *Arkhitektura XX veka* [*Architecture of the Twentieth Century*] (Moscow: Progress, 1970); Le Corbusier, *Modulor: MOD 1; MOD 2* [*The Modulor: Modulor 2*] (Moscow: Stroiizdat, 1976).

9 Walter Gropius, *Granitsy arkhitektury* [*The Scope of Total Architecture*] (Moscow: Iskusstvo, 1971).

10 Kenzō Tange, *Arkhitektura Iaponii* [*The Architecture of Japan*] (Moscow: Progress, 1978); Udo Kultermann, ed., *Kenzo Tange: 1949–1969* (Moscow: Stroiizdat, 1978).

11 Alvar Aalto, *Arkhitektura i gumanizm* [*Architecture and Humanism*] (Moscow: Progress, 1978). This is a collection of articles translated from Finnish, English, French and German.

12 Georges Candilis, *Stat' arkhitektorom* [*Becoming an Architect*] (Moscow: Stroiizdat, 1979).

A group of architectural students who graduated from SazPI in 1960 (including Sergo and Vladimir Sutiagin, Dmitrii Shuvaev, Richard Bleze, Iurii Miroshnichenko and Vil'Muratov)

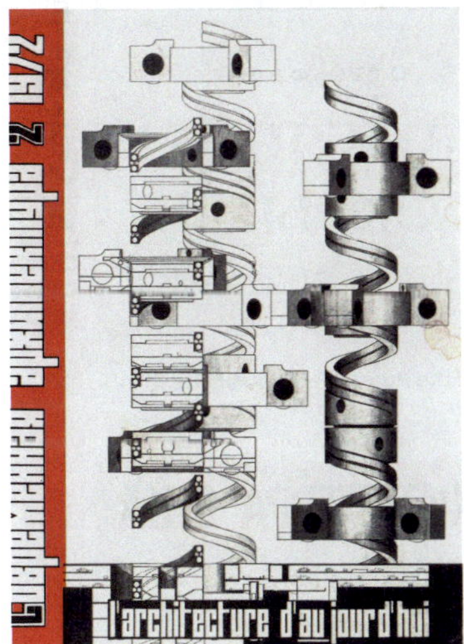

Cover of the Russian edition of *L'Architecture d'Aujourd'hui* (no. 2, 1972)

Cover of the Russian edition of Oscar Niemeyer's book *Minha experiência em Brasília*, 1963

Cover of the Russian edition of Le Corbusier's book *Architecture of the Twentieth Century*, 1970

Cover of the Russian edition of Frei Otto's book *Tensile Structures*, 1960

Cover of the Russian edition of Georges Candilis' book *Becoming an Architect*, 1979

Cover of the catalogue for the exhibition *Architecture of the USA*, shown in Minsk, Leningrad and Moscow in 1965

the publication of a book by Frei Otto,[13] who had been a Luftwaffe pilot during World War II. Also widely read was the catalogue of the exhibition *Architecture of the USA*, which took place in Leningrad, Minsk and Moscow in 1965.[14] Like any event in the Soviet-American exhibition duel of the 1960s and 1970s, it was an ideological shopwindow of the "American way of life," but even so was accessible thanks to being distributed free of charge and was popular. Such publications had clear consequences. In particular, Otto's book, according to Sergo Sutiagin, played a significant role in the plot tie of the design competition for the Panoramic Cinema in Tashkent, and the buildings in the catalogue of the American exhibition were at times "paraphrased" in Tashkent projects.

Soviet Literature

Texts by Soviet researchers were an important information channel regarding international practice. In discussing them we should focus on research by Moscow scientific institutes: the Institute of Art History of the Ministry of Culture of the USSR, the Scientific Research Institute for the Theory, History and Perspective Problems of Soviet Architecture (known as the Scientific Research Institute for the Theory of Architecture and Urban Planning from the 1980s), the Institute for the Study of Art of the Academy of Arts and others. The specificity of Soviet science presented the opportunity to bring together specialists for the publication of comprehensive research projects which claimed to systematically conceptualize processes taking place in various regions of the world and even in global architecture as a whole. Such projects included *A General History of Architecture* in twelve volumes (1966–1977) and *A General History of Art* in six volumes (1955–1966), which incorporated extensive chapters on the architecture of the peoples of the world. As well as these there was the comprehensive research project *Architecture of the West* (1972–1987)[15] and books about the contemporary architecture of Western countries.[16] Nevertheless, the concentration of research within several Moscow institutions seriously limited the diversity of views of Western architecture. Ideologically speaking, Soviet scholars were doomed to develop the idea of the impossibility of capitalism to solve problems of the contemporary development of cities, with the inevitable conclusion regarding the "superiority" of the Soviet system, which was at odds with the common practice among Soviet architects of borrowing ideas and forms from their Western colleagues.

Review articles about innovations in international architectural life and analytical texts on Western architecture were occasionally published

13 Frei Otto, *Visiachie pokrytiia: ikh formy i konstruktsii* [*Tensile Structures*] (Moscow: Gosizd. literatury po stroitel'stvu, arkhitektury i stroitel'nym materialam, 1960).

14 *Arkhitektura SShA* [*Architecture of the USA*], catalogue of the Seventh American Exhibition in the Soviet Union, 1965.

15 S. O. Khan-Magomedov, R. A. Katsnel'son and A. A. Strigalev, eds., *Arkhitektura Zapada: Kniga 1; Mastera i techeniia* [*Architecture of the West: Book 1; Masters and Trends*] Moscow: Stroiizdat, 1972); A. V. Ikonnikov et al., eds., *Arkhitektura Zapada: Kniga 2; Sotsial'nye i deologicheskie problemy* [*Architecture of the West: Book 2; Social and Ideological Problems*] (Moscow: Stroiizdat, 1975); D. K. Bernshtein et al., eds., *Arkhitektura Zapada: Kniga 3; Protivorechiia i poiski 60–70-kh godov* [*Architecture of the West: Book 3; Contradictions and Explorations of the 1960s and 1970s*] (Moscow: Stroiizdat, 1983); V. L. Khait, ed., *Arkhitektura Zapada: Kniga 4; Modernizm i postmodernizm, Kritika konteptsii* [*Architecture of the West: Book 4; Modernism and Postmodernism, A Critique of the Concept* (Moscow: Stroiizdat, 1987).

16 Andrei Ikonnikov, *Sovremennaia arkhitektura Anglii* [*The Contemporary Architecture of England*] (Leningrad: Gosizd. literatury po stroitel'stvu, arkhitektury i stroitel'nym materialam, 1958); Andrei Ikonnikov, *Novaia arkhitektura Finliandii* [*The New Architecture of Finland*] (Moscow: Stroiizdat, 1971); Andrei Ikonnikov, *Sovremennaia arkhitektura Shvetsii* [*The Contemporary Architecture of Sweden*] (Moscow: Stroiizdat, 1978); Andrei Ikonnikov, *Arkhitektura SShA: Arkhitektura v sisteme burzhuaznoi kul'tury* [*The Architecture of the USA: Architecture in the System of Bourgeois Culture*] (Moscow: Iskusstvo, 1979); N. K. Solov'ev et al., *Sovremennaia arkhitektura Frantsii* [*The Contemporary Architecture of France*] (Moscow: Stroiizdat, 1981); Raisa Katsnel'son, *Sovremennaia arkhitektura Italii* [*The Contemporary Architecture of Italy*] (Moscow: Stroiizdat, 1983).

in Soviet and Uzbek architectural journals. The Soviet journals had the opportunity to work with qualified experts, whereas *Arkhitektura i stroitel'stvo Uzbekistana* (*Architecture and Construction of Uzbekistan*) did not have this resource at its disposal. Its reviews of international practice were mostly presented by architects or functionaries who had been abroad or by researchers of narrow themes that included international experience (for example, low-rise, dense residential areas in countries with hot climates). Such articles were often the result of business trips to a particular country. For example, a member of a construction delegation from Uzbekistan that visited France to learn about industrial construction technologies using reinforced concrete standard elements wrote an article about French housing construction;[17] the Minister of Construction of Uzbekistan, after visiting Expo 67, presented the Uzbekistan public with an article about the residential and civil architecture of Canada and, after a visit to Japan, a text about anti-seismic methods in Japanese residential buildings;[18] and a working architect who had been part of a specialized group visit to England published a text about the transformation of the vernacular tradition in contemporary English architecture.[19] Regarding preferred themes, authors of Uzbekistan's architectural journal were particularly interested in the architecture of the Maghreb[20] and other countries with a majority Muslim population,[21] as well as architecture in the West.

Professional Contacts

Direct contacts between architects or groups of architects from socialist and capitalist countries and Tashkent were rare, and a result of particular circumstances. For example, in the late 1960s GDR and Czechoslovak journals published articles about Uzbekistan after their editorial boards visited Tashkent and talked to local architects. However, most contacts were mediated by Moscow and the Union of Architects of the USSR. It was through this creative union, which had a republican branch in Uzbekistan, that contacts developed between Uzbek architects and the outside world. In particular, the Union of Architects of the USSR was responsible for organizing the majority of professional familiarization visits.

During the 1960s visits abroad were rare. Only those who had passed a "test of ideological reliability" were allowed to go, which meant that delegations were largely made up of architectural functionaries.

17 E. Chepko, "Krupnopanel'noe domostroenie vo Frantsii [Large Panel House Building in France]," *Stroitel'stvo i arkhitektura Uzbekistana* [*Construction and Architecture of Uzbekistan*], no. 6, 1961.

18 S. Ibragimov, "Stroitel'stvo zhilykh i grazhdanskikh zdanii v Kanade, [Construction of Residential and Civil Buildings in Canada]," *Stroitel'stvo i arkhitektura Uzbekistana* [*Construction and Architecture of Uzbekistan*], no. 4, 1968; S. Ibragimov, "Stroitel'stvo v Iaponii [Construction in Japan]," *Stroitel'stvo i arkhitektura Uzbekistana* [*Construction and Architecture of Uzbekistan*], no. 3, 1967.

19 Svetlana Moiseeva, "Angliia: traditsii i sovremennost' [England: Traditions and Modernity]," *Stroitel'stvo i arkhitektura Uzbekistana* [*Construction and Architecture of Uzbekistan*], no. 11, 1965.

20 V. Voronina, "Iz istorii gorodov sovremennogo Alzhira [From the History of Cities of Contemporary Algeria]," *Stroitel'stvo i arkhitektura Uzbekistana* [*Construction and Architecture of Uzbekistan*], no. 8, 1977; V. Voronina, "Villy Severnoi Afriki [Villas of North Africa]," *Stroitel'stvo i arkhitektura Uzbekistana* [*Construction and Architecture of Uzbekistan*], no. 3, 1975; V. Voronina, "Klimat i arkhitektura Severnoi Afriki [The Climate and Architecture of North Africa]," *Stroitel'stvo i arkhitektura Uzbekistana* [*Construction and Architecture of Uzbekistan*], no. 8, 1966.

21 A. Azimov, "Zdanie Kairoskogo radio- i teletsentra [The Building of the Cairo Radio and TV Center]," *Stroitel'stvo i arkhitektura Uzbekistana* [*Construction and Architecture of Uzbekistan*], no. 7, 1969; A. Azimov, "Nekotorye tendentsii v sovremennom gradostroitel'stve Arabskoi respubliki Egipet [Some Trends in the Contemporary Urban Planning of the Arab Republic of Egypt]," *Stroitel'stvo i arkhitektura Uzbekistana* [*Construction and Architecture of Uzbekistan*], no. 10, 1972.

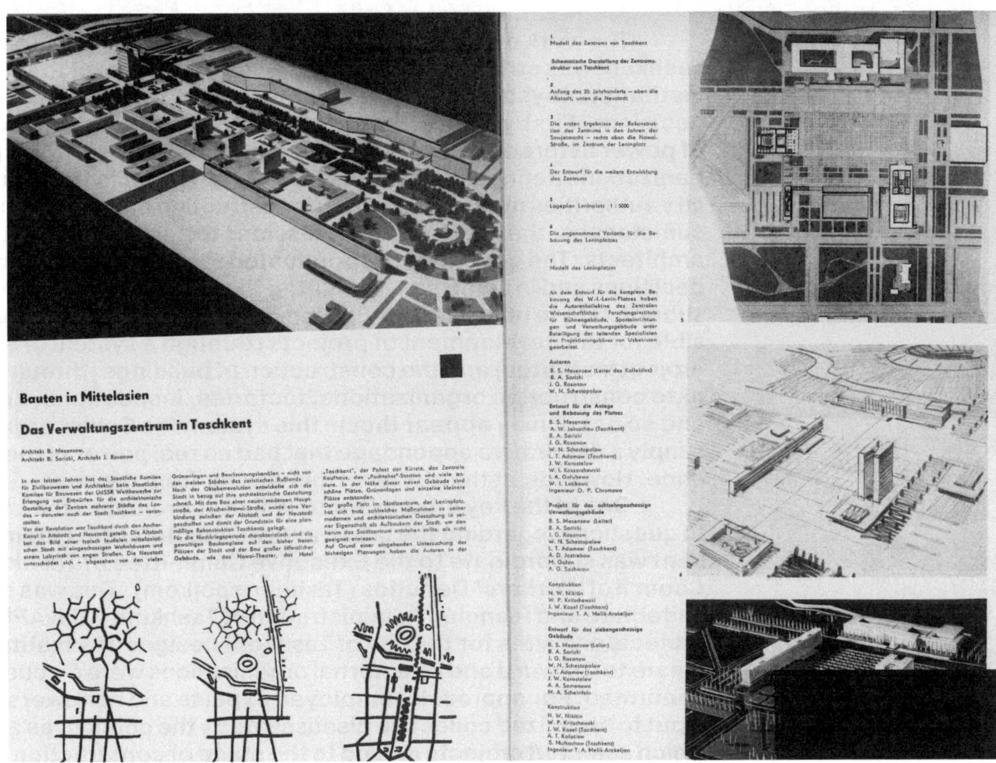

Bauten in Mittelasien

Das Verwaltungszentrum in Taschkent

Architekt B. Mesenzow,
Architekt B. Sorizki, Architekt J. Rosanow

In den letzten Jahren hat das Staatliche Komitee für Zivilbauwesen und Architektur beim Staatlichen Komitee für Bauwesen der UdSSR Wettbewerbe zur Erlangung von Entwürfen für die architektonische Gestaltung der Zentren mehrerer Städte des Landes – darunter auch der Stadt Taschkent – veranstaltet.

Vor der Revolution war Taschkent durch den Anchor-Kanal in Altstadt und Neustadt geteilt. Die Altstadt bot das Bild einer typisch feudalen mittelasiatischen Stadt mit eingeschossigen Wohnhäusern und einem Labyrinth von engen Straßen. Die Neustadt unterscheidet sich – abgesehen von den vielen Grünanlagen und Bewässerungskanälen – nicht von den meisten Städten des zaristischen Rußlands.

Nach der Oktoberrevolution entwickelte sich die Stadt in bezug auf ihre architektonische Gestaltung schnell. Mit dem Bau einer neuen modernen Hauptstraße, der Alischer-Nawoi-Straße, wurde eine Verbindung zwischen der Altstadt und der Neustadt geschaffen und damit der Grundstein für eine planmäßige Rekonstruktion Taschkents gelegt.

Für die Nachkriegsperiode charakteristisch sind die gewaltigen Baukomplexe auf den bisher freien Plätzen der Stadt und der Bau großer öffentlicher Gebäude, wie das Nawoi-Theater, das Hotel „Taschkent", der Palast der Künste, das Zentrale Kaufhaus, das „Pachtakor"-Stadion und viele andere. In der Nähe dieser neuen Gebäude sind schöne Plätze, Grünanlagen und einzelne kleinere Plätze entstanden.

Der große Platz im Stadtzentrum, der Leninplatz, hat sich trotz zahlreicher Maßnahmen zu seiner modernen und architektonischen Gestaltung in seiner Eigenschaft als Aufbaukern der Stadt, um den herum das Stadtzentrum entstehen sollte, als nicht geeignet erwiesen.

Auf Grund einer eingehenden Untersuchung der bisherigen Planungen haben die Autoren in der

1
Modell des Zentrums von Taschkent

Schematische Darstellung der Zentrumsstruktur von Taschkent

2
Anfang des 20. Jahrhunderts – oben die Altstadt, unten die Neustadt

3
Die ersten Ergebnisse der Rekonstruktion des Zentrums in den Jahren der Sowjetmacht – rechts oben die Nawoi-Straße, im Zentrum der Leninplatz

4
Der Entwurf für die weitere Entwicklung des Zentrums

5
Lageplan Leninplatz 1 : 5000

6
Die angenommene Variante für die Bebauung des Leninplatzes

7
Modell des Leninplatzes

An dem Entwurf für die komplexe Bebauung des W.-I.-Lenin-Platzes haben die Autorenkollektive des Zentralen Wissenschaftlichen Forschungsinstituts für Bühnengebäude, Sporteinrichtungen und Verwaltungsgebäude unter Beteiligung der leitenden Spezialisten der Projektierungsbüros von Usbekistan gearbeitet.

Autoren
B. S. Mesenzew (Leiter des Kollektivs)
B. A. Sorizki
J. G. Rosonow
W. N. Schestopalow

Entwurf für die Anlage und Bebauung des Platzes
B. S. Mesenzew
A. W. Jakuschew (Taschkent)
B. A. Sorizki
J. G. Rosonow
W. N. Schestopalow
L. T. Adamow (Taschkent)
J. W. Korostelow
W. I. Kossarshewski
I. A. Golubewa
W. I. Lutikowa
Ingenieur O. P. Chromowa

Projekt für das achtzehngeschossige Verwaltungsgebäude
B. S. Mesenzew (Leiter)
B. A. Sorizki
J. G. Rosonow
W. N. Schestopalow
L. T. Adamow (Taschkent)
A. D. Jastrebow
M. Galan
A. G. Sacharow

Konstruktion
N. W. Nikitin
W. P. Kritschewski
J. W. Kosel (Taschkent)
Ingenieur T. A. Melik-Arakeljan

Entwurf für das siebengeschossige Gebäude
B. S. Mesenzew (Leiter)
B. A. Sorizki
J. G. Rosonow
W. N. Schestopalow
L. T. Adamow (Taschkent)
J. W. Korostelew
A. A. Semenowa
M. A. Scheinfein

Konstruktion
N. W. Nikitin
W. P. Kritschewski
J. W. Kosel (Taschkent)
A. T. Kolotiew
S. Muftachow (Taschkent)
Ingenieur T. A. Melik-Arakeljan

Article in *Deutsche Architektur* (no. 3, 1966) about the project for the center of Tashkent designed by Tashgiprogor

A photo taken by Sergo Sutiagin while visiting Expo 67 in Montreal

Architectural Institutions

The work of institutions involved in producing architecture in Tashkent was strictly hierarchical, but this did not exclude diversity. The institutional system included several levels of making and executing decisions. Firstly, it was formed of party, government and Soviet organs of power at three levels: All-Union, republican and city. The party organizations defined the overall strategic aims, while the republican and city authorities made decisions on constructing buildings. In special circumstances, they awarded commissions to particular institutes or even architects. The government coordinated the implementation of party decisions and in some cases initiated them. Various ministries that were subordinate to union and republican councils of ministers were responsible for the development of projects (through a system of subordinate project institutes) and the construction of buildings (through subordinate construction organizations, factories, inspections, commissions and so on). It may appear that in this system the Soviet organs were simply a decorative appendage that had no real power or means of influence. However, at the city level this was far from the case.

One of the key organizations which coordinated the solutions to questions regarding the urban and architectural development of Tashkent was subordinate to the Executive Committee of Tashkent City Council of Workers' Deputies (Tashgorispolkom). This was the Main Architecture and Planning Administration of Tashkent (GlavAPU).[22] Here projects and sites for the city of Tashkent designed by institutes subordinate to GlavAPU and by external organizations were discussed and confirmed. For approvals, employed experts and reviewers gave their input to organized collective discussions by the council, as a result of which selected projects moved to the stage of construction documentation and comments by the council were given to the architects to be taken into account.

As well as the council of GlavAPU, public bodies played a key role in the architectural life of the city: these were mainly the Union of Architects of Uzbekistan and ancillary organizations such as the Society for the Protection of Historical and Material Culture Monuments of Uzbekistan and others. The Union of Architects could play both a consultative and an organizational role. There were not just public discussions deciding the fate of projects but also competitions organized by the Union, the best-known of which was that for the design of the Panoramic Cinema (1960). But perhaps the most obvious form of polyphony of architectural creativity in the city could be seen in the project institutes, each of which had not only their own image but also a particular mandate.

Project Institutes

Most project institutes in Uzbekistan were genealogically related to Uzstroiobedinenie, which was part of the Council of People's Commissars of the Uzbek SSR, created in 1925. From the late 1920s one branch of this institution reported directly to the republican authorities and the other to Tashkent. The institutes which were subordinate to the republican Council of People's Commissars were grouped under Uzgosproekt[23] and worked for all of the cities in Uzbekistan, including Tashkent. In 1951 Uzgosproekt was subordinated to Gosstroi of the Uzbek SSR and became the root institute from which many organizations emerged, including in particular the Tashkent Zonal Scientific Research Institute for

22 This institution had various names over the years: Architecture and Planning Authority (1933–1937); Architecture and Planning Department (1937–1939); Architecture and Planning Authority (1940–1944); Architecture Department (1944–1955); Construction and Architecture Department (1955–1960); Architecture and Planning Authority (1960–1966) (Tashkent City Archive, fund 36, list 1).

23 These included Uzzhilkomprogor, Uzplanproekt, Khlopkoproekt, Uzgiprolegprom, Uzpromproekt and other organizations.

Experimental and Standard Design (TashZNIIEP).[24] In 1972 Uzgosproekt was renamed UzNIIPgradostroitel'stva and a strong research department appeared there. In turn, a set of project institutes subordinate to the city and which worked only in Tashkent formed as part of GlavAPU. Tashgorproekt came into being there in 1939 and was later transformed into Tashgiprogor, from which Tashgenplan separated off in 1969. In 1976 Tashgenplan was renamed TashNIiPIgenplan and a research department was formed there, too.[25] These four institutions—Uzgosproekt (UzNIIPgradostroitel'stva), TashZNIIEP, Tashgiprogor and Tashgenplan (TashNIiPIgenplan)—largely formed the image of Tashkent from the 1960s to the 1980s.[26]

Tashgiprogor Institute wall newspaper (1976), depicting Andrei Kosinskii leading a cohort of his associates from the seventh studio to design the "old city"

Tashgiprogor Institute wall newspaper (1977), depicting scenes from the life of the first studio

The specific nature of all of these institutions was mainly connected to their mandate. Uzgosproekt was established to design standard and unique buildings, plan cities and city districts and research the climatic, social and cultural features of the architecture of Uzbekistan. Tashgiprogor was responsible for the massing of standard and unique buildings for Tashkent, the design of planning districts (and also, until 1969, the general detailed plan for the center of the city). The number of institutional studios depended on the number of city districts: it was assumed that the design of each district was "attached" to a concrete studio. This logic determined the creation of Tashgenplan. After a group of architects from Tashgiprogor won the All-Union competition for the center of Tashkent (1964), the question arose of the coherence and integrity of its construction, and the mandate of the new institute now not only included work on the general and detailed plans of the city center but also the design of unique buildings located there, as well as research

24 Isak Israilov, "Uzbekskii nauchno-isledovatel'skii i proektnyi institute po gradostroitel'stvu i ego razvitie [The Uzbek Scientific Research and Project Institute for Urban Planning and Its Development]," *Stroitel'stvo i arkhitektura Uzbekistana* [*Construction and Architecture of Uzbekistan*], no. 1, 1974, 35.

25 Leon Adamov, "TashNIiPIgenplanu – 20 let [TashNIiPIgenplan is 20]," *Arkhitektura i stroitel'stvo Uzbekistana* [*Architecture and Construction of Uzbekistan*], no. 9, 1989, 1.

26 Which does not lessen the significance of other institutes which had a narrower profile and mandate, such as Uzgiprotrans, Uzgiprotorg, the Tashkent studio of GiproNII and others.

into the development of the Tashkent agglomeration. The mandate of TashZNIIEP was the design of standard and unique buildings for the Central Asian zone and research into the climatic (in particular seismic), social and cultural aspects of construction in the republics of Central Asia. A strong stimulus for the scientific methodology advocated by the institute's staff was already present at its foundation, which occurred as a result of the merging of the department of standard design of Uzgosproekt with the Scientific Research Institute for Construction of the Academy of Construction and Architecture of the USSR in Tashkent. Accordingly, at the point when it was created there were already 314 employees, including eleven with Ph.D. degrees, in the research department of TashZNIIEP.[27]

A group of architects and engineers from Uzgosproekt who participated in the design of the Panoramic Cinema, 1964

As well as the mandate, the personality of the directors played a significant role in the forming of the creative credo of each institute. For example, the history of Uzgosproekt from the end of the 1950s was defined by the almost simultaneous arrival at the institute of Vladimir Berezin, Sergo Sutiagin, Richard Bleze and Dmitrii Shuvaev, who quickly became heads of the design studios. Having learned to cooperate when designing the main buildings of the early 1960s—the Central Committee of the Communist Party of the Uzbek SSR and the Panoramic Cinema—they had compatible views on architecture and formed collectives that shared their values. The oldest of them, Vladimir Berezin, who rapidly became the head architect at the institute, would define the staffing and creative policies for twenty-five years. As Sergo Sutiagin wrote, "at his creative peak Vladimir Vladimirovich agreed to become the head architect at the institute. This was a responsible and brave act by a creative personality who recognized what he was sacrificing and why. We persuaded him to take this important step for our institute, which was a personal sacrifice for him. We understood that any architect 'from outside' (this was also

27 Kh. Asamov, "Tvorcheskii put' TashZNIIEP za 10 let [The Creative Path of TashZNIIEP over 10 Years]," *Stroitel'stvo i arkhitektura Uzbekistana* [*Construction and Architecture of Uzbekistan*], no. 12, 1974, 1.

Four Apostles caricature (left to right: Sergo Sutiagin, Richard Bleze, Dmitrii Shuvaev, Aleksandr Braslavskii)

an option) may introduce dissonance into the established architectural and artistic style of our institute, 'the Uzgos school,' which had the most authority in the republic."[28] This example demonstrates that the head architect played an important role in defining the aesthetic orientations of his team.

An overview of the work of the four institutes allows us to conclude that the inclination to use historical quotations from earlier Central Asian architecture was mostly seen among the Tashgenplan architects and to a certain extent the specialists at Tashgiprogor, especially after Andrei Kosinskii joined the team from Moscow in 1966. The collectives of Uzgosproekt and in particular TashZNIIEP, in contrast, aimed for a stricter use of contemporary architectural techniques while maintaining the search for connections between their projects and the local climate, culture and genius loci.

As already stated, Moscow institutes also played a significant role in the design of Tashkent. A number of Tashkent higher education institutions, such as Tashkent State University (TashGU), Tashkent Institute of Irrigation and Agricultural Melioration (TIIMSKh) and several faculties at Tashkent Polytechnic Institute (TashPI) were designed by Moscow's Giprovuz; the Tashkent TV Tower by the TsNIIproektstal'konstruktsiia Institute; the TV Center by the project institute of the Ministry of Communications of the USSR; and so on. However, the most important architectural intervention in Tashkent by a Moscow institute was by the Central Scientific Research and Experimental Project Institute for Entertainment and Sport Facilities (TsNIIEP), the leadership of which, after the 1964 competition for Lenin Square in Tashkent, managed to establish a relationship with Sharaf Rashidov, who awarded the institute direct commissions for the design of the Lenin Museum and the Peoples' Friendship Palace. For the final Soviet decades, when the self-recognition of the Soviet republics was in its final phase, this type of reverence for Moscow was an atypical phenomenon that will be highlighted in the pages of book which explore individual buildings.

The First Secretary of the Central Committee of the Communist Party as an Institution

In 1994 Sharaf Rashidov was posthumously named an architectural winner of Uzbekistan's main award in the field of art and architecture, the Alisher Navoi Prize. In the accompanying presidential decree he was named as the "author of the idea and creative director of the construction" of the Peoples' Friendship Palace and Square.[29] This posthumous award was the first official admission of the role that Sharaf Rashidov played in defining the appearance of Tashkent's architecture from the 1960s to the 1980s. During his lifetime this theme was not covered by the national or professional press. In fact, the post of leader of the republic's party organization offered enormous opportunities, especially if that leader was keen on working with architects and artists. And Rashidov, who was a professional journalist and writer, was definitely keen. Today, documentary materials, memoirs and testimonies allow us to assess the evolution of his role in the architectural process.

After taking up the post of First Secretary of the Central Committee of the Communist Party of the Uzbek SSR, from 1959 to 1966 Rashidov remained in the shadows. During this period there were architectural competitions in which the Central Committee and Rashidov were either not involved at all or simply gave approval at the final stage. This was

28 Sergo Sutiagin, "Vladimir Vladimirovich Berezin (stranitsy tvorchestva) [Vladimir Vladimirovich Berezin (Pages of Creativity)]," *O'zbekiston Arxitektura va qurilishi*, no. 1, 2001, 59.

29 "Ukaz Prezidenta respubliki Uzbekistana 'O prisuzhdenii gosudarstvennoi premii respubliki Uzbekistan imeni Alishera Navoi v oblasti literatury, iskusstva i arkhitektury' [Decree of the President of the Republic of Uzbekistan 'On the Awarding of the Alisher Navoi State Prize of the Republic of Uzbekistan'], *Pravda Vostoka* [*Truth of the East*], February 5, 1994, 1.

Sharaf Rashidov (in the center) at the first Conference of Writers of Asian and African Countries, Tashkent, 1958

Sharaf Rashidov discussing architectural projects with heads of architectural and construction institutes, 1970s

the case with the competition for the Panoramic Cinema, which was run by the Union of Architects on the initiative of the Ministry of Culture. None of the documents related to this extremely important architectural event for Tashkent include any indication that the republic's leaders interfered in the discussions or the decision-making process. Even the project documents for the building of the Central Committee of the Communist Party of Uzbekistan (1962–1964) do not include Rashidov's name. All of the working correspondence was from the Deputy Head of the Central Committee Administration, B. Vygovskii, and during discussion and approval of the project the Central Committee was only the fourth approving body, after the Administration of Design of the Palace of the Soviets in Moscow, the Union of Architects of Uzbekistan and Gosstroi of the Uzbek SSR.

The situation began to change after the 1966 earthquake. Sharaf Rashidov played a key role in the organization of the campaign to rebuild the city and began to interact more closely with architects and builders, as shown by the fact that he often appears in their reminiscences regarding this period. In particular, Andrei Kosinskii recalled Rashidov's immediate reaction to the first sketch for the House of Creative Unions ("at last something that is 'ours' has appeared in architectural projects").[30] This episode demonstrates that by the second half of the 1960s it was important to Rashidov that Tashkent's modern architecture reflect Uzbekistan's specificity.

In the late 1960s and early 1970s we can trace the appearance of a new trend in decision-making for architectural competitions which may not have been devised by Sharaf Rashidov. This was the case for the 1969 competition for the building of the Supreme Soviet of the Uzbek SSR. The competition incorporated projects by a number of architectural teams, but the decision was taken not by a professional jury but by the direct client, Iadgar Nasriddinova, Chair of the Presidium of the Supreme Soviet of the Uzbek SSR. In future such decisions would also be taken by Sharaf Rashidov.[31] This also concerned the direct awarding of commissions. Elena Sukhanova recalls that Sharaf Rashidov took the strategic decision to commission the project for the Peoples' Friendship Palace from Moscow's Central Scientific Research and Experimental Project Institute for Entertainment and Sport Facilities (TsNIIEP) during a conversation with Evgenii Rozanov. During the 1970s and early 1980s such individual decisions were taken more than once. According to the reminiscences of many architects, "the trip to the sixth floor," or to Rashidov's office in the building of the Central Committee of the Communist Party of Uzbekistan, was a normal practice in architectural life. The leader of the republic knew the key architects very well, observed their careers and looked out for many of them. The relationship was often special. With some people Rashidov was respectful and stressed that their professionalism had priority over his "deeply personal" opinion,[32] and with others he expressed his ideas of how the building should look but did not discipline those who refused to take his recommendations into account.[33] In general, he appears in the reminiscences of Tashkent architects as a paternalistic figure whose positive characteristics are emphasized. Moscow architects tell a less homogeneous tale. Feliks Novikov, who was commissioned by the leader of Uzbekistan to design projects for the reconstruction of the centers of Samarkand and

30 "Arkhitektor Andrei Kosinskii: 'Ia do sikh por ne znaiu, chto takoe khoroshii vkus' (chast' III) [Architect Andrei Kosinskii: 'Even Now I Don't Know What Good Taste Is' (Part III)]," *Fergana News*, August 1, 2006, https://www.fergananews.com/articles/4524.

31 Sergo Sutiagin mentioned such an episode with regard to the selection of his version of the Cosmonauts Avenue metro station on several occasions.

32 This is how he is presented in the manuscript of Sergo Sutiagin's memoir, which was given to the author in 2018.

33 This type of episode was described by Iurii Miroshnichenko and relatives of the architect Richard Bleze.

Bukhara, recalled Rashidov with great respect as someone who did not insist on his own opinion or reject proposals.[34] Elena Sukhanova, who might be considered the main person behind the project for the Peoples' Friendship Palace, expressed a different view of Rashidov when looking back. She saw him as a client who knew what he wanted and tried to obtain his preferred solutions from project teams. Having observed Rashidov's evolution over a decade, Sukhanova suggested that even in the early 1960s he did not approve of modern architecture. According to her, it was because of Rashidov's insistence that the authors of the Peoples' Friendship Palace project were obliged to shift from their own professed principles of modern architecture to the decorative solution preferred by the leader of Uzbekistan, prompting a result that Sukhanova referred to heatedly as a "khan's palace."[35] Andrei Kosinskii provided a mostly negative description of Rashidov during the last period of his life. He recalled the leader of Uzbekistan as a ruler with no knowledge of architecture who, even so, permitted himself to "instruct" architects.[36] However, the emotional nature of Kosinskii's reminiscences is well known, as is the fact that he sometimes invented certain details that showed his point of view in a good light.

Sharaf Rashidov at the inauguration of the Tashkent metro, November 6, 1977

This characteristic of the institutional organization of Uzbekistan's architecture can be interpreted in various ways. Some scholars reject the significance of Soviet architecture in the international context and insist that Soviet architects "did not have the freedom" of their Western colleagues and, accordingly, their works were not so important or diverse. The opposing position was held by, for example, Jean-Louis Cohen, who suggested that Soviet architects had much more freedom than their Western counterparts thanks to the possibility of direct access to leaders of the country or individual republics, as a result of which the decision-making process was simplified and efficient realization of

34 From a discussion between Feliks Novikov and the author on October 23, 2013.

35 From a discussion between Ol'ga Kazakova, the author and Elena Sukhanova on February 2, 2020.

36 "Arkhitektor Andrei Kosinskii: 'Gody, provedennye v Tashkente, byli samym produktivnym i iarkim periodom v moei zhizni (chast' I) [Architect Andrei Kosinskii: 'The Years I Spent in Tashkent Were the Most Productive and Brilliant Period of My Life' (Part I)]," *Fergana News*, June 2, 2006, https://www.fergananews.com/articles/4430.

ideas was supported administratively.[37] In their own way each of these positions sheds light on the specific nature of the architectural process in Uzbekistan and bears witness to the importance of the personality of the First Secretary of the Central Committee in the hierarchy of the republic's architectural institutions.

Protagonists Real and Imagined

In discussing the "freedom of the Soviet architect" it is important to avoid any romanticization of the late Soviet period. The social organization of architecture placed numerous limitations on this freedom. Some were objectively linked to the functioning of Soviet project institutes and others were concealed within the subjective qualities of the ruling elite. If in international practice the heads of major design firms such as OMA and Herzog & de Meuron were indisputably acknowledged creative leaders who were responsible for the main creative and organizational decisions, those who produced Tashkent's architecture have not always been prominently listed among the authors. In reviewing the history of the capital of Uzbekistan's architecture in the late Soviet decades it is important to understand the following:

- *The initial idea for a project could belong to one author, be embodied in the construction documentation by another and built by yet another*. The directors of the institutes decided the team organization and any rearrangements. In identifying the main author we were led by the name of the lead architect on the document stamps, and where these were not present we took into consideration the sum total of publications and historic evidence. For example, the absence of documentation for buildings by TashZNIIEP made it difficult to identify the main authors of the Uzbekistan Hotel and the State Museum of Arts. It was only by comparing the extant archive documents and historical publications that we could understand who was the author of the idea and how it evolved.
- *In Tashkent at that time, the frequent occurrence of architects' names in lists of authors was not reliable evidence of their real input to the creative process*. Chief architect of Tashkent Sabir Adylov and his deputy Leon Adamov were at the top of the list of authors of many buildings, although their functions (fictitious in Adylov's case and somewhat more substantial when it came to Adamov) only involved placing the building within the city plan and discussing its inclusion in the urban context. The directors of the project institutes had similar administrative resources, but not all of them took advantage of this. The director and the main architect of UzNIIPgradostroitel'stva did not insert themselves into the list of authors of projects created by the institute, but the director of TashNIiPIgenplan was, in most cases, included in the list of authors of the institute's buildings (which was the subject of satirical sketches and epigrams among Tashkent architects).
- *In some cases the printed word reflected the real contribution of architects to the creative process, and in others it seriously exaggerated it*. For example, books were published about the two chief architects of Tashkent,[38] the famous practitioner and theorist Mitkhat Bulatov and the functionary Sabir Adylov, whose "authorship" of numerous buildings was privately disavowed by most practicing architects in Tashkent. At the same time another chief architect of Tashkent in the 1960s, Aleksandr Iakushev, who

37 Jean-Louis Cohen expressed this point of view in particular when discussing the project Tashkent Modernism XX/XXI in the talk "Preserving Modernism" at Triennale Milano on April 19, 2023.

38 Tulkinoi Kadyrova and Vladimir Strin'kovskii, *Zhit', chtoby sozidat'* [*Living to Create*] (Tashkent: Izdatel'stvo literatury i iskusstva imeni Gafura Guliama, 1978); Rustam Valiev, Tulkinoi Kadyrova and Abdulkhai Umarov, *Arkhitektor i vremia* [*The Architect and Time*] (Tashkent: Izdatel'stvo literatury i iskusstva imeni Gafura Guliama, 1982).

culptor Iakov Shapiro with
ne bust of Sharaf Rashidov,
pril 4, 2012

played a key role in making the most important urban planning decisions of Tashkent modernism, was far less fortunate. The only publication about him was a short article marking his birthday in the journal *Stroitel'stvo i arkhitektura Uzbekistana* (*Construction and Architecture of Uzbekistan*).[39]

- *Official titles and awards are not always relevant when determining the significance of an architect*. For example, city architect Sabir Adylov and director of TashNIiPIgenplan Farkhad Tursunov were, as well as being included in lists for various state prizes of Uzbekistan and the USSR, awarded rare ranks and titles. Adylov became a "people's architect of the USSR" and Tursunov was a corresponding member of the Academy of Arts of the USSR. The selection of recipients of state prizes was always primarily political, and for this reason authors who had made a significant contribution to the completion of a project could disappear from lists of laureates in favor of less significant or even nominal candidates. The list of laureates of the 1975 State Prize of the USSR for "the architecture of the center of Tashkent" did not include the majority of the authors (with the exception of Leon Adamov and Iurii Khaldeev) of the project that won the 1964 All-Union competition or the architects from UzNIIPgradostroitel'stva who were involved in creating such impressive buildings as the Panoramic Cinema, the Central Committee of the Communist Party of Uzbekistan, the House of Publishers and the House of Youth. The prize was awarded to the directors of Tashkent institutions and also numerous Moscow architects.

As can be seen, the system of institutional functioning of Soviet architecture limited the "freedom of the creator" in many respects, but left architects with an opportunity—where they had administrative support—to influence decision-making and shape urban planning and the architectural agenda. From the 1960s to the 1980s it was the institutional system rather than ideological impediments (which were considerable in the fields of visual art, literature or music, but much more flexible in the case of architecture) that sometimes blocked breakthrough solutions, while on other occasions it was quite effective in supporting the design and construction of unique buildings. In both cases, the main protagonists, who were responsible for developing the conceptual proposals and constructing the building on-site, remained the lead architects and project engineers, as well as the directors of the workshops at the project institutes.

39 E. Orlova, "Arkhitektor A. V. Iakushev: tvorcheskii portret [Architect A. V. Iakushev: A Creative Portrait]," *Stroitel'stvo i arkhitektura Uzbekistana* [*Construction and Architecture of Uzbekistan*], no. 7, 1978, 28–29.

Standardization and Hybrid Typologies

Boris Chukhovich, Ekaterina Golovatyuk

From the 1960s to the 1980s, Soviet modernity was part of the diversity of international modernities, yet at the same time had features that made it stand out. As far as Soviet Uzbekistan is concerned, its role can also be defined as both typical and special, and in some respects it was unique in the overall Soviet context. This was directly reflected in architecture. The architecture of Uzbekistan was part of Soviet architecture, but its history had special features. There were also direct links between the Uzbek SSR and the global context: Tashkent architects carefully observed international practice, especially what was built in countries with hot climates and populations historically linked to the traditions of Islam. These specific relationships of commonality and specificity are clearly readable in the architectural typologies that were developed in Tashkent. However, before discussing them in more detail, we should outline the terminology, since Western and Soviet architects' understanding of typologies did not always coincide.

Toward a Comparative History of Architectural Typologies

The Italian architect Aldo Rossi and the Soviet architectural historian Andrei Ikonnikov published books with the same title, *The Architecture of the City*, in 1966 and 1972 respectively.[1] As well as the title, the two texts had similar structures, although Rossi's book was not mentioned by Ikonnikov and was probably not known to him at the time of writing.[2] However, they were not completely aligned. In particular, Ikonnikov's book lacked the first and most frequently cited chapter of Rossi's book, which explored the issue of architectural types. This omission was not accidental.

Cover of *The Architecture of the City* by Aldo Rossi, 1966

Cover of *The Architecture of the City* by Andrei Ikonnikov, 1972

Architectural science strives to be objective and international. Nevertheless, in each country it developed in its own way and was largely dependent on the information to which researchers had access. Texts that played a key role in the development of a universal understanding of architectural typologies arrived in the Russian Empire and the USSR with a delay and not in their entirety. Thus, Vitruvius' treatises on architecture were first translated into Russian in the late eighteenth century (from French[3]), and the first translation of architectural texts by Leon Battista Alberti appeared in the USSR only in 1935 to 1937.[4] Even less

1 Aldo Rossi, *L'architettura della città* (Padua: Marsilio, 1966); Andrei Ikonnikov, *Arkhitektura goroda: esteticheskie problemy kompozitsii* [*The Architecture of the City: Aesthetic Problems of Composition*] (Moscow: Stroiizdat, 1972).

2 The footnotes in this book included texts in Russian, English, German and French, but no Italian sources were quoted.

3 Vitruvius' *Ten Books on Architecture* was translated from French by Fedor Karzhavin, with notes by Vasilii Bazhenov, and published in ten volumes in St. Petersburg from 1790 to 1797; Vitruve, *Les dix livres d'architecture, corrigez et traduits en françois avec des notes et des figures*, trans. Claude Perrault (Paris: Chez Jean Baptiste Coignard, 1673).

4 Leon Battista Alberti's *The Ten Books on Architecture* was translated into Russian by V. Zubov and published in two volumes in Moscow by the All-Union Academy of Architecture (1935–1937).

fortunate were French authors of the eighteenth and nineteenth centuries Marc-Antoine Laugier, Jean-Nicolas-Louis Durand and Antoine Quatremère de Quincy, who played a key role in the formation of ideas about architectural types in Europe. Their works were not translated into Russian at all. Of course, the intellectual borders were not impenetrable, and French was an integral part of educated Russian society of the time. In the late eighteenth and early nineteenth centuries, Laugier's concept of the primitive hut as the beginning of architectural history was retold in Russia as if it were their own idea by such famous authors as the historian Nikolai Karamzin and the writer Aleksandr Pisarev.[5] Durand's aspiration to classify architectural constructions of different epochs[6] was also accepted as an idea: the president of the Imperial Academy of Arts, Aleksei Olenin, personally recommended that academicians study his main work.[7] However, not everything was adopted and assimilated. In particular, Quatremère de Quincy's text on types, published in the *Encyclopédie méthodique* and later in his *Dictionnaire historique d'architecture*[8] had little influence in Russia. It seems that it was either not read or not considered important.

The approaches of Durand and Quatremère de Quincy were in many ways opposed. Durand derived typologies from the facts he knew, structuring historical experience. Quatremère de Quincy assumed the existence of certain types that nourish the development of architecture and inspire the architect to generate new forms. While Durand's notion of typology was embodied in a structured index of built objects, Quatremère de Quincy's types represented primary metaphorical ideas that emerged at the dawn of civilization and permanently stimulated the creation of new architecture. Durand's popularity in Imperial Russia reflected how Soviet architects would interpret architectural typologies from the 1960s to the 1980s.

The Modern Movement completely reinterpreted attitudes toward types and typologies. It was now pointless to be inspired by the past, as architecture had been virtually reinvented. However, the suppression of history led to the return of the suppressed in new forms. In his oft-cited article "On Typology," Rafael Moneo identified three forms of reintegration of types and typologies into Western architectural practice: through the "universal space" of Mies van der Rohe, mass industrial construction, and the functionalist approach.[9] In "universal space," a new modernist type of architecture— "space-form"—was established and began to vary endlessly. Mass industrial construction was doomed to the infinite repetition of the same building types. The functionalist approach made structures directly dependent on their social functions. As can easily be seen, it was thanks to Mies that the Neoplatonic idea, which gives rise to an infinite number of variations of the same form, found its place in the Modern Movement, which rejected any orientation toward the past. From the 1960s to the 1980s, the ideas of Quatremère de Quincy would inspire reflection on the architectural typologies of

5 Evgeniia Kirichenko, *Arkhitekturnye teorii XIX veka v Rossii* [*Nineteenth-Century Architectural Theories in Russia*] (Moscow: Iskusstvo, 1986), 15.

6 Jean-Nicolas-Louis Durand, *Recueil et parallèle des édifices de tout genre anciens et modernes, remarquables par leur beauté, par leur grandeur ou par leur singularité, et dessinés sur une même échelle* (Paris, 1801); Jean-Nicolas-Louis Durand, *Précis des leçons d'architecture données à l'École polytechnique* (Paris: Chez l'Auteur et Bernard, 1825).

7 M. V. Nashchokina, "Antichnoe nasledie v arkhitekture pozdnego russkogo klassitsizma [Antique Heritage in the Architecture of Late Russian Classicism]," in *Russkii klassitsizm vtoroi poloviny XVIII–nachala XIX veka* [*Russian Classicism of the Second Half of the Eighteenth and Early Nineteenth Centuries*] (Moscow: Izobrazitel'noe iskusstvo, 1994), 191.

8 Antoine Quatremère de Quincy, *Encyclopédie méthodique: Architecture*, vol. 3 (Paris: Chez Mme veuve Agasse, 1825), 543–545; Antoine Quatremère de Quincy, *Dictionnaire historique d'architecture: comprenant dans son plan les notions historiques, descriptives, archéologiques, théoriques, didactiques et pratiques de cet art* (Paris : Librairie d'Adrien le Clere et Cie, 1832).

9 Rafael Moneo, "On Typology," *Oppositions*, no. 13, Summer 1978, 22–45.

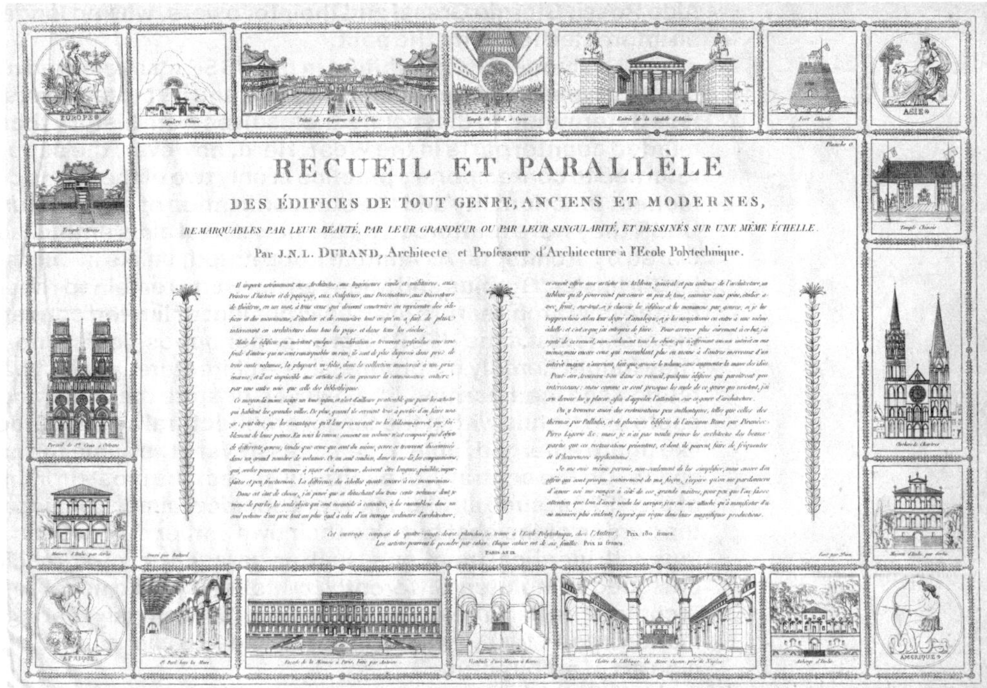

Cover of Jean-Nicolas-Louis Durand's book *Recueil et parallèle des édifices de tout genre anciens et modernes*, 1801

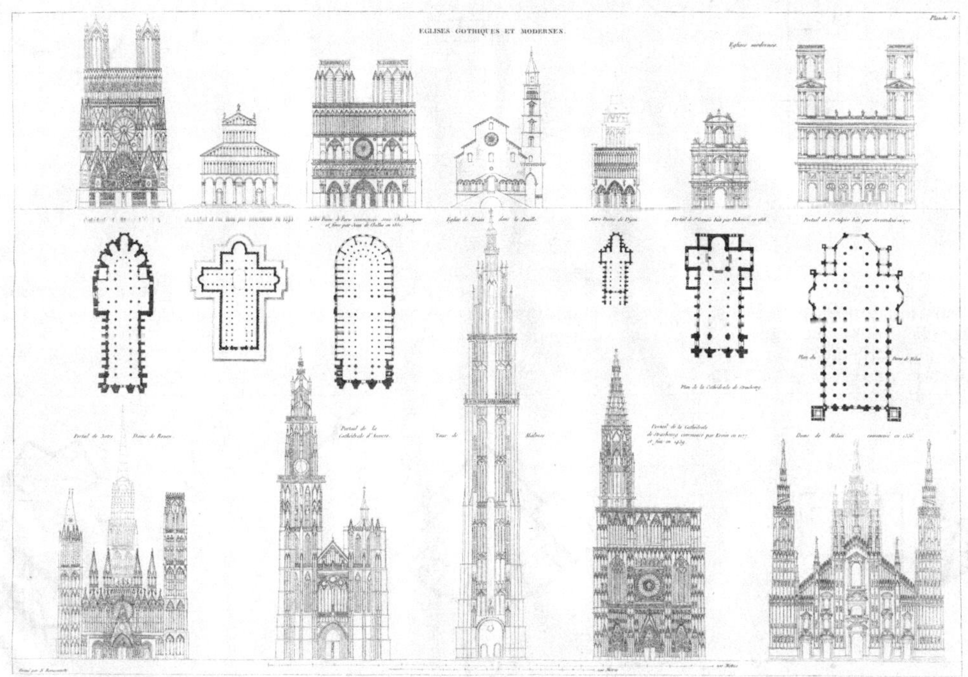

Jean-Nicolas-Louis Durand, *Recueil et parallèle des édifices de tout genre anciens et modernes*, 1801, plate 8.

Aldo Rossi, Giorgio Grassi and their followers, who no longer avoided an interested look into the past.

The modernist revolution in the USSR also rejected nineteenth-century types and typological thinking, and its protagonists were no less determined to dissociate themselves from history than their like-minded counterparts in the West. Here, however, the suppressed returned to contemporary practice in only two of the forms described by Moneo: functionality and the standardization of architecture. In the USSR they were reinforced by the new social aims enthusiastically declared by architects. As Anatole Kopp noted, unlike in Europe, where Le Corbusier, Gropius and Mies van der Rohe remained rebels, fighting for the new architecture in an environment of limited conservatism, the architects of the USSR "were neither oppositionists nor prophets. They fought fiercely for progressive architecture, against passéists, routine and mediocrities."[10] However, despite the wide range of concepts and trends within the Soviet architectural avant-garde, no Mies-like figure emerged, able to ceaselessly vary the same formal idea of space. On the contrary, in each new project the most prominent leaders of the 1920s, such as Mel'nikov or Leonidov, aimed to reject not only the burden of the past but also their own earlier discoveries. Even buildings with identical functions, such as garages or workers' clubs, were designed completely differently by Mel'nikov, who never repeated a technique he had already used, perhaps consciously fearing its transformation into a "type," which he perceived as a cliché unworthy of the high art of architecture.

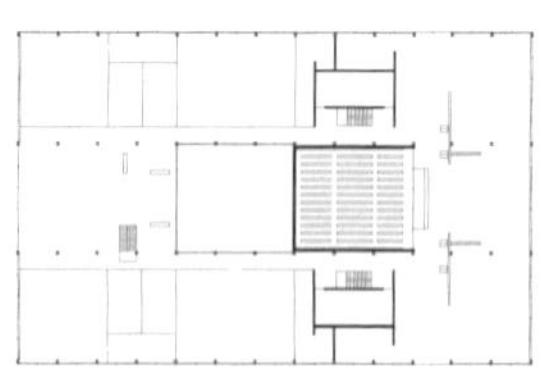

Ludwig Mies van der Rohe,
Illinois Institute of Technology,
library and administration
building proposal, floor plan
Chicago, designed 1939–1949

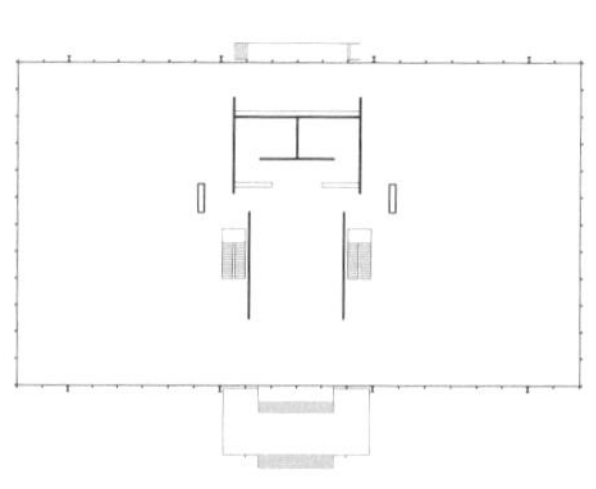

Ludwig Mies van der Rohe,
Illinois Institute of Technology,
Crown Hall, floor plan
Chicago, 1954

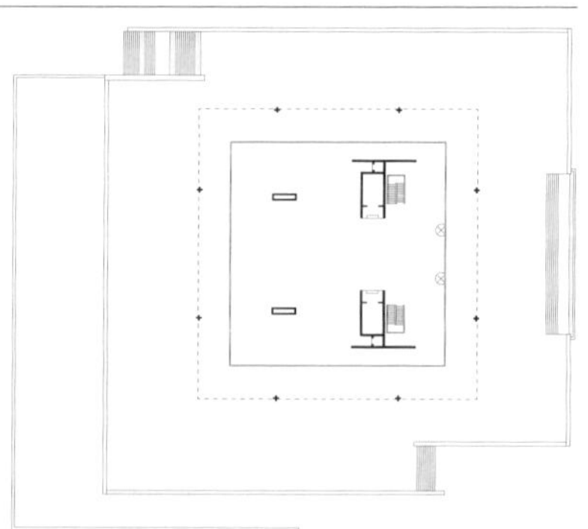

Ludwig Mies van der Rohe,
Neue Nationalgalerie, floor plan
Berlin, 1968

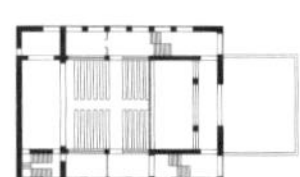

Konstantin Mel'nikov,
Club of the Union of Chemists of
the Mikhail Frunze Dorogomi-
lovsky Chemical Plant, floor plan
Moscow, 1929

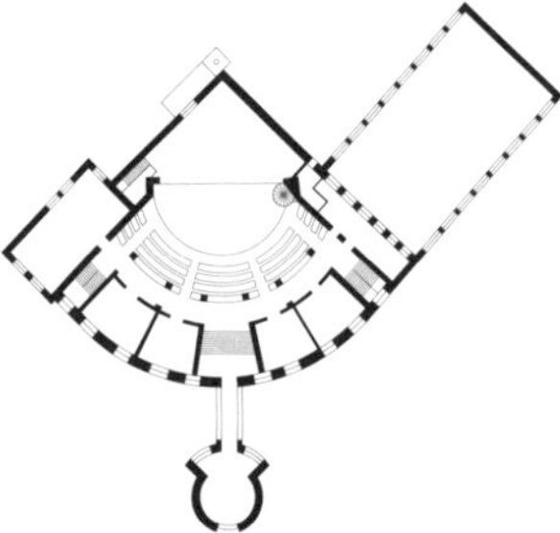

Konstantin Mel'nikov,
House of Culture of the Kauchuk
Factory, floor plan
Moscow, 1929

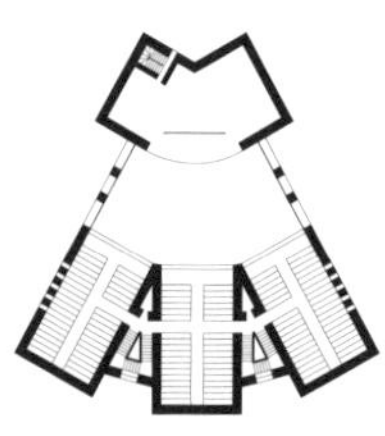

Konstantin Mel'nikov,
Rusakov House of Culture, floor plan
Moscow, 1929

10 Anatole Kopp, *Ville et révolution: architecture et urbanisme soviétiques des années vingt* (Paris: Édition Anthropos Paris, 1967), 18.

The theorists of Constructivism clearly postulated the reincarnation of the type through standardization and mass construction. "Today in our everyday vocabulary," wrote Aleksandr Pasternak, "three words have appeared that define our architectural line: NORM, STANDARD, TYPE."[11] The same was true of functionalism. As Moisei Ginzburg said at the first conference of the Organization of Contemporary Architects, "the functionalism of architecture, which leads to a dead end in the West, opens up new prospects for us—the creation of a new standardized architecture."[12] Simultaneously with "standard architecture," architects were developing new functional types of buildings reflecting the specifics of Soviet life: housing with spaces for collective use (kitchens, dining rooms, showers, etc.), factory kitchens, palaces of labor, workers' clubs, villages for settling nomads and so on. When we use the concept of type in relation to such new architectural structures, we refer primarily to their functional purpose. In this case the new type was a consequence of solving an actual social problem through architecture. The Constructivists acknowledged their connection with Greco-Roman antiquity, but it was the complete opposite of the idea of reproducing previously existing types. According to the Constructivists' idea, the types of Greek structures, such as the temple, theater or stadium, became an architectural response to the processes of the life of the polis, just as triumphal arches, circuses and baths were expressions of the social life of the Roman Republic and Empire. The journal *Contemporary Architecture* proclaimed: "We affirm that in the epoch of building socialism, the task of the architect is above all to 'invent' new social condensers of life, new types of architecture."[13]

Despite the conservative turn of the early 1930s, Soviet architecture continued to be dominated by functional typologies. The only changes were to the social tasks faced by architects, the formal language of architecture, which became classicist, and, accordingly, the types of buildings designed. Nor did this approach alter after the Khrushchëv reform. In a 1970s architecture textbook, the subsection "The Beginnings of Typology" first structures building types by activity (public, residential, industrial and agricultural buildings) and then outlines the internal typological structure of each group.[14] Books of this period about the architecture of individual republics are usually structured according to the function of buildings,[15] with separate sections on administrative buildings, theaters and cinemas, sports facilities, schools and kindergartens, residential architecture, industrial buildings and so on. The professional press actively published articles on special typologies (large-format cinemas, markets in hot climates, theaters with courtyards and so on) or elements of the urban environment (squares, esplanades, underground urban spaces) during this period.

At some point the typological discussion unfolding in the West came to the attention of scholars in the USSR, although they did not actively engage with it. For example, Aleksei Gutnov and Il'ia Lezhava recognized the existence of a limited number of "stereotypes in the architecture of the past," "each of which was formed over decades and

11 Aleksandr Pasternak, "Puti k standartu [Ways Toward a Standard]," *Sovremennaia arkhitektura* [*Contemporary Architecture*], no. 2, 1927, 54.

12 Moisei Ginzburg, "Konstruktivizm v arkhitekture [Constructivism in Architecture] (a speech)," *Sovremennaia arkhitektura* [*Contemporary Architecture*], no. 5, 1928, 144.

13 "Kritika konstruktivizma [A Critique of Constructivism]," *Sovremennaia arkhitektura* [*Contemporary Architecture*], no. 1, 1928, 2.

14 Aleksei Tits, ed., *Osnovy arkhitekturnoi kompozitsii i proektirovaniia* [*The Foundations of Architectural Composition and Design*] (Kyiv: Vishcha shkola, 1978), 211.

15 Particular reference is made to books about the architecture of Uzbekistan: Tulkinoi Kadyrova, Konstantin Babievskii and Farkhad Tursunov, *Arkhitektura sovetskogo Uzbekistana* [*Architecture of Soviet Uzbekistan*] (Moscow: Stroiizdat, 1972); Tulkinoi Kadyrova, *Sovremennaia arkhitektura Uzbekistana* [*Contemporary Architecture of Uzbekistan*] (Tashkent: Izdatel'stvo literatury i iskusstva imeni Gafura Guliama, 1974); Tulkinoi Kadyrova, *Arkhitektura sovetskogo Uzbekistana* [*Architecture of Soviet Uzbekistan*] (Moscow: Stroiizdat, 1978) and others.

even hundreds of years, with the most successful models selected from generation to generation."[16] However, this theoretical recognition in the spirit of Rossi entailed practical conclusions aimed at a more flexible compliance of buildings to an evolving society. Moscow urbanists felt that after the International Style one should think not about reconsidering the attitude to former "stereotypes" but about the possibility of dynamically adapting buildings to the new requirements of the time.

Since Soviet architectural theory invariably made questions of form and style dependent on the social tasks of architecture, we would like firstly to examine the typological specificity of modernist buildings in Tashkent in terms of their function. We will then try to test the applicability to Tashkent architecture of the concept of architectural types proposed by Quatremère de Quincy, followed by those of the architect-theorists of the second half of the twentieth century.

Specifics of the Typology of Public Buildings in Tashkent

Selected types of buildings oriented toward the private client were always significantly more developed in the West than in the socialist countries. This was particularly true of residential architecture, which was maximally standardized in the USSR. However, despite the differences in the nature of ownership, certain types of housing in capitalist and socialist countries had typologically related features. This broad topic is beyond the scope of the project Tashkent Modernism XX/XXI, which focuses on revealing the specific nature of Tashkent's unique public buildings. For a typology of industrial housing, the reader can refer to the books of the German researcher Philipp Meuser[17] and the work of Swiss architects Emanuel Christ, Christoph Gantenbein and Victoria Easton, which is soon to be published.[18] Also, certain Soviet public buildings had some similarities to those in capitalist countries. Structures that were functionally similar to their Western counterparts included university campuses, hotels, airports, railroad stations and sports facilities. However, the differences in the political, social and cultural life of the USSR conditioned the formation of special types of buildings and architectural spaces.

16 Aleksei Gutnov and Il'ia Lezhava, "Estetika goroda (predposylki sovershenstvovaniia khudozhestvennogo oblika sovremennykh gorodov) [Aesthetics of the City (Preconditions for the Improvement of the Artistic Image of Contemporary Cities)]," *Zodchestvo* [*Architecture*], no. 2 (21).

17 Philipp Meuser, Jörn Börner and Caroline Uhlig, *Die Ästhetik der Platte: Wohnungsbau in der Sowjetunion zwischen Stalin und Glasnost* (Berlin: DOM Publishers, 2014); Philipp Meuser and Dimitrij Zadorin, *Towards a Typology of Soviet Mass Housing: Prefabrication in the USSR, 1955–1991* (Berlin: DOM Publishers, 2015); Philipp Meuser, *Seismic Modernism: Architecture and Housing in Soviet Tashkent* (Berlin: DOM Publishers, 2016).

18 Emanuel Christ et al., eds., *Typology: Tashkent, Genoa, Tbilisi, Casablanca*, Review no. IV (Zurich: Park Books, forthcoming).

Cheremushinskii Market, Moscow, 1961

Zhdanovskii Market, Moscow, 1963

Central Market, Novosibirsk, 1966

Kuibyshevskii Market, Simferopol', 1974

Central Market, Belgorod, 1975

Komarovskii Market, Minsk, 1979

Central Market, Cherkasy, 1970

Zaliznychyi Market, Kyiv, 1973

Central Market, Rivne, 1979

Saltov Market, Kharkiv, 1980

Anzhi Bazaar, Makhachkala, 1982

Pecherskii Market, Kyiv, 1983

A Typological Tale of Administrative and Cultural/Entertainment Buildings

In 1964 in Tashkent there was a competition for the design of the main square of the republic, Lenin Square. The winning project involved the construction of two administrative buildings—one vertical and one horizontal—the direct prototype of which was Oscar Niemeyer's government complex in Brasília.

National Congress of Brazil, Brasília, 1960
Architect: Oscar Niemeyer

Ministries Building, Tashkent, 1972
Architects: Boris Mezentsev, Boris Zaritskii, Evgenii Rozanov, Vladislav Shestopalov

The replica that was built allows us to make some comparative observations. The main square in Brasília was named the Square of the Three Powers, as it housed the parliament, the presidential palace and the supreme court building. Ministries Esplanade, where the main executive institutions of the state were located, led to the square. Thus, the urban planning situation predetermined the subordination of ministries in relation to the three branches of political power: legislative, executive and judicial. The situation in Tashkent was radically different. Both buildings on Lenin Square belonged to the executive branch: the horizontal block of the Council of Ministers was complemented by the vertical Ministries Building.

Palace of Agriculture, São Paulo, 1956
Architect: Oscar Niemeyer

Council of Ministers, Tashkent, 1967
Architects: Boris Zaritskii, Evgenii Rozanov, Vladislav Shestopalov, Leon Adamov

The construction of anything even remotely resembling the supreme courts of Brasília or Chandigarh was never envisaged here. As for the Supreme Soviet, the story was somewhat more complicated.

The USSR was initially proclaimed a "state of the Soviets," i.e. of representative organs of power with functions and authority that evolved over time. Many historians, however, believe that their role was always decorative. As Mikhail Voslensky wrote, "The Supreme Soviets began to be proudly called 'Soviet parliaments,' although, in truth, they did not deserve such a title. This was done despite the fact that Lenin loudly mocked 'parliamentary cretinism' and for a long time the word 'parliament' was a pejorative term in the USSR."[19] The two competitions for a Palace of the Soviets in Moscow (1931–1933 and 1957–1959) clearly demonstrated a paradoxical situation: they were held with great pomp, displaying the symbolic importance of the Soviets, but the construction of the gigantic building never took place, as there was no practical need for it. Meanwhile, from the late 1920s and early 1930s, Houses of Government were erected in many Soviet republics to accommodate the urgent needs of the executive branch.

As for the Supreme Soviet of the Uzbek SSR, from the 1930s it was located in the northern annex of the House of Government in Tashkent. From the late 1960s to the late 1980s, the Uzbek authorities organized several competitions for the building of the Supreme Soviet, but despite an abundance of proposals and options, it was never constructed. Moreover, since by the end of the 1960s there were two official conference halls in Tashkent (at the Central Committee of the Communist Party of Uzbekistan and the Council of Ministers), the Supreme Soviet conference hall, built in 1931 to a design by Stefan Polupanov and reconstructed by him using the forms of Stalinist architecture in 1940, was allocated to the city philharmonic and the Bakhor dance ensemble. A political space was handed over to cultural workers. More significant, however, was the reverse trend.

Unlike European parliaments, the supreme councils of the Soviet republics met twice a year to vote unanimously in favor of bills that had already been drafted. The Communist Party functioned in a similar way. Major party decisions were made by a narrow circle of top leaders and communicated to the Politburo of the Central Committee and the bureaus of the Communist Party Central Committees of the union republics. The decisions were then approved by the plenums of the Central Committee of the CPSU and the Central Committees of the Communist Party of the union republics. The highest form of their legitimization was the party congress, which was held every five years. These congresses were attended by several thousand delegates and in order to organize them a specific type of building was created in the USSR. Its model was the Kremlin Palace of Congresses with its 6,000-seat auditorium, a banquet hall for elite celebrations, a wide stage that could accommodate the presidium of the congress with invited foreign guests, and state-of-the-art facilities (a transformable stage, an orchestra pit, dressing rooms and auxiliary theater spaces). The theatrical setup of the Palace had a dual role. Official concerts and plays could be staged here between party congresses, meaning that the building would not lie empty. Plus, the functioning of the party machine was deeply theatrical: the leaders on stage and the obedient audience in the auditorium at congresses demonstrated the "triumph of communist democracy."

Tashkent's first modernist structure designed for party congresses was the Panoramic Cinema. Its typology was profoundly hybrid. It was partly conditioned by the worldwide fashion for immersive, widescreen cinema and also by the need to provide for party and Soviet congresses a suitable space for thousands of delegates and crowded presidiums on stage. From the Kremlin Palace of Congresses, the Panoramic Cinema "inherited" a well-developed performative block: an orchestra pit, storage for scenery and dressing rooms for artists. The cinema was inaugurated in November 1964, and from day one it was actively used as a place for major public events. In between it was a cinema with an unusually large, 2,300-seat auditorium. In 1968 it became the main hub of the Tashkent International Film Festival of Asia and Africa. In some respects, however, the Panoramic Cinema remained different from the Palace of Congresses, and above all it was too accessible and

19 Michael Voslensky, *Nomenklatura: The Ruling Class in the Soviet Union*, trans. E. Mosbacher, second revised and expanded edition (London: Overseas Publications Interchange Ltd, 1990), 382.

democratic for a "Palace." Perhaps this is why, in the early 1970s, the Uzbek authorities commissioned the design of a new structure—the Lenin Peoples' Friendship Palace with 4,100 seats—which typologically matched the Kremlin Palace of Congresses and similar buildings in other Soviet republics (the Lenin Palace in Alma-Ata, the Lenin Palace in Baku and so on). Declaratively, the new building was presented to city residents as a "cinema-concert hall," but it was never used for film screenings[20] and extremely rarely for concerts. Its exceptionally expensive decoration and set of spaces (a generous foyer, a conference hall, a banquet hall, etc.) indicated the governmental and administrative nature of the building, although the media vaunted its ability to enrich the cultural life of Tashkent.

Right up to its collapse, the Soviet Union did not produce the type of modernist parliament[21] in which different parties would discuss political issues and reach consensus in decision-making. Perestroika, which provoked the first public disagreements between different social groups since the 1920s, demonstrated with comic clarity the lack of readiness of "palaces of congresses" to be a space for political debate. The auditoria, designed for the silent majority to listen to political leaders, turned out to be extremely inconvenient for the work of political factions, while voting mechanisms which could result in a decision put before the deputies being rejected actually had to be improvised. Soviet architecture did not foresee such pluralism of opinions, much less encourage it. The USSR built many unusually large cinemas and concert halls, the gigantomania of which is now perceived as an enigmatic feature of the distant Soviet past.

The Unequal Marriage of Architectural Typology and Cultural Policy

Although architectural clients in the Soviet Union were few in number and almost all of them were associated with the state, the typology of public buildings was by no means monotonous and included buildings that had no direct analogues in Western practice. Most of them were a direct consequence of the cultural policies of the last Soviet decades. Each republic could select what it considered relevant from the arsenal of Soviet architectural typology. As a result, Soviet capitals came to be characterized by their own set of unique buildings. Somewhere there was a modernist opera house and a "wedding palace," but no circus or representative building for congresses and concerts (Vilnius); somewhere there was an opera house, concert hall and circus but no "wedding palace" (Kishinev); somewhere there was a modernist Lenin museum (Tashkent, Kyiv); somewhere there was an art museum (Tashkent, Alma-Ata, Frunze) and so on. Mixed and special types also appeared. Concert and sport complexes were popular mixed types (Yerevan, Baku). Special types included the "chess palaces" that appeared in Tbilisi and Yerevan after the success of representatives of these republics in the international chess arena.[22] The abovementioned "wedding palaces" can also be considered a special Soviet type not found in Western Europe and North America: they appeared due to the struggle against "vestiges of religion" and the desire to create a new type "Soviet rite."

20 However, in the 1980s the Peoples' Friendship Palace became the venue for the opening and closing ceremonies of Tashkent's international film festivals.
21 The exceptions were the Supreme Soviets of the Lithuanian SSR and the Azerbaijan SSR.
22 In 1962 Georgian chess player Nona Gaprindashvili became women's world champion, and in 1963 Armenian chess player Tigran Petrosian became men's world champion.

Wedding Palace, Tbilisi, 1985
Architects: Viktor Dzhorbenadze and Vazha Orbeladze

Wedding Palace, Belgorod, 1981
Architect: Vladimir Vishnevskii

Wedding Palace, Kyiv, 1982
Architects: Vadym Hrechyna, Iryna Hrechyna and Vadym Hopkalo

Wedding Palace, Samara, 1983
Architects: Aleksei Gerasimov and Vagan Karkar'yan

The capital of Uzbekistan also saw the emergence of structures that were a direct consequence of Soviet cultural policy. Let us consider a few examples.

The resounding performance of Soviet circus performers at the World Festival of Youth and Students in 1955 demonstrated that they were even more effective than the famous Soviet ballet in wowing international audiences. In 1956 the Moscow Circus made a triumphant tour of Belgium and France and then toured almost all Western countries and Japan, attracting the press, celebrities and even politicians. For example, the Queen of England attended many performances, and the American press noted that "if the Bolshoi Theater won our hearts, the Moscow Circus stole them away."[23] The furore in the West around the Soviet circus stimulated the systematic development of circus infrastructure within the USSR, including the construction of new circuses throughout the country. However, Soviet architects had nothing to guide them: there were no modernist circuses anywhere in the world, and artists performed either in traditional circuses or in sports halls. Four new circus types, oriented toward the various regions of the USSR, were developed in the early 1960s by Giproteatr and the Central Scientific Research and Experimental Project Institute for Entertainment and Sport

23 Quoted in Feodosii Bardian, *Sovetskii tsirk na piati kontinentakh* [*The Soviet Circus on Five Continents*] (Moscow: Iskusstvo, 1977), 194.

Education and Research | **Administration and Public** | **Sports and Health** | **Hospitality and Commercial**

School

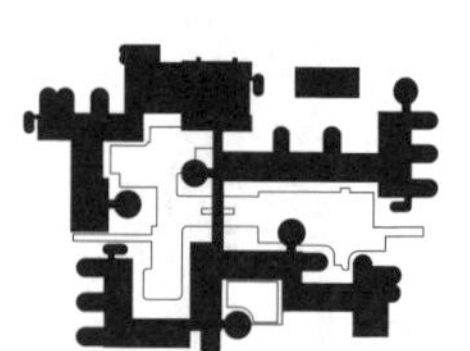

Administration

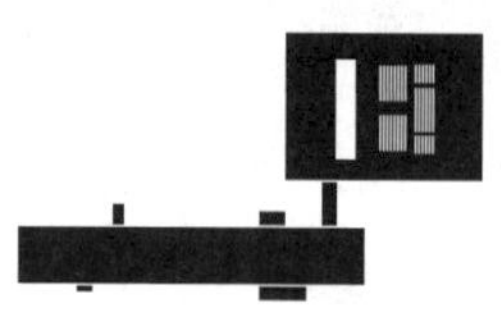

Sports palace

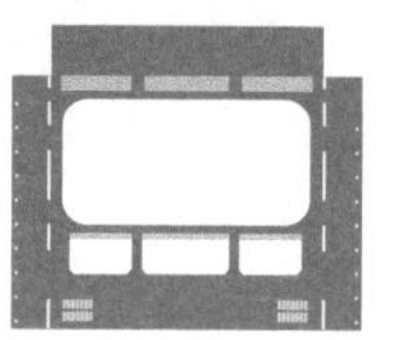

Hotel

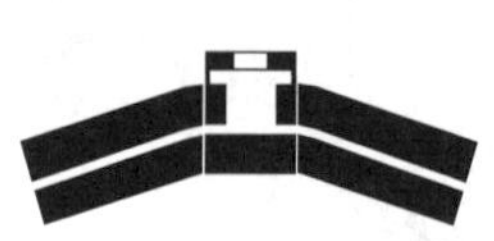

University

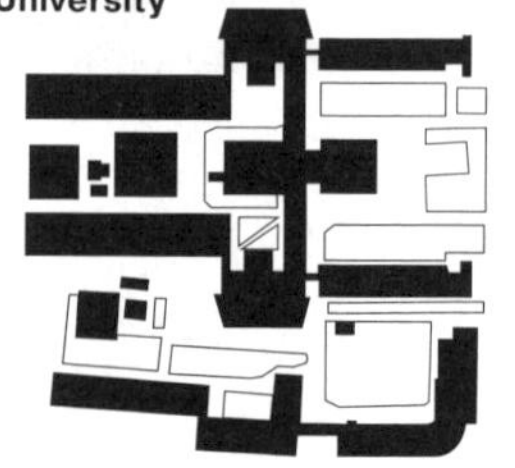

Congress hall

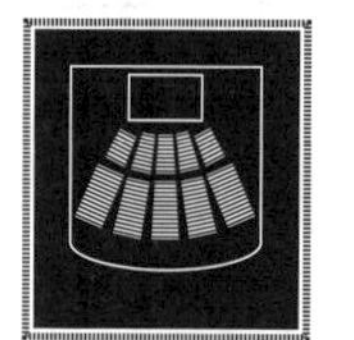

Hospital

Restaurant

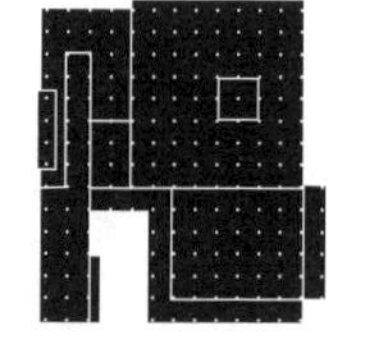

Research institute

Wedding palace

Steam bath

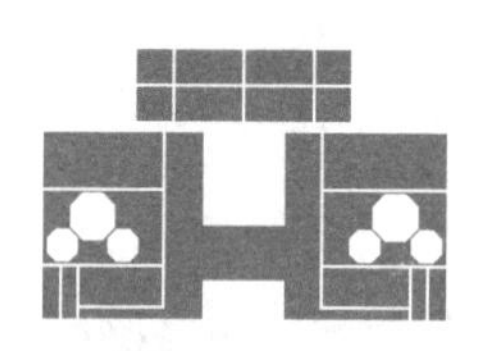

Department store

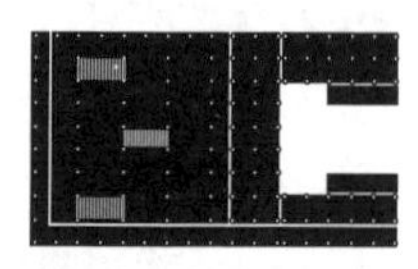

Covered market

House of youth

- ■ **Modernist functional building types in Tashkent**
- ■ **Modernist functional building types in Tashkent (demol-ished)**
- □ **Non-modernist functional building types in Tashkent**

Infrastructure

Train station

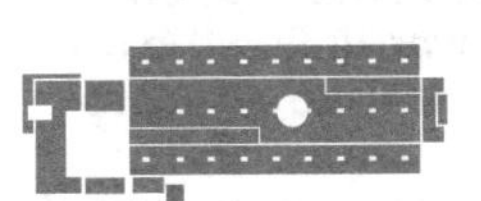

Airport

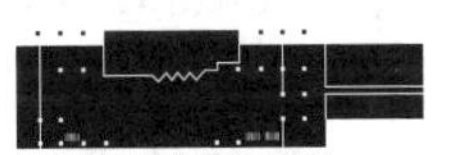

TV tower

Metro

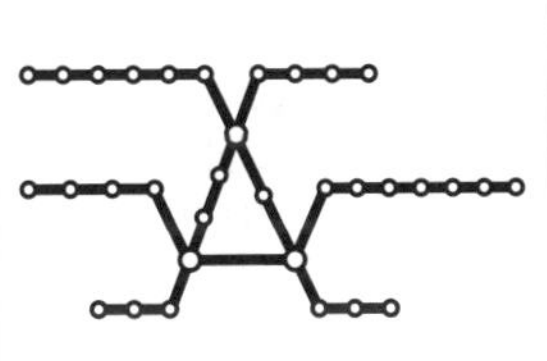

Culture and Performance

House of culture

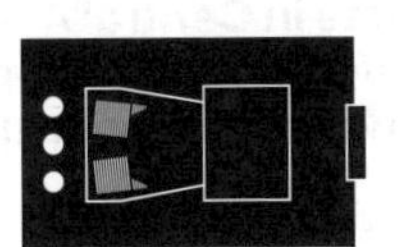

House of pioneers

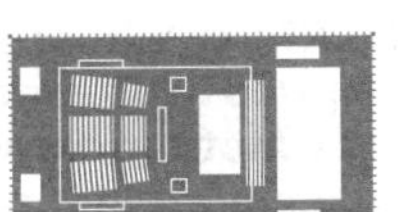

Theater

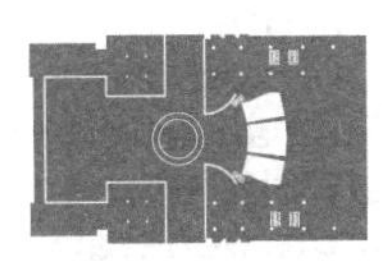

Cinema

Circus

Library

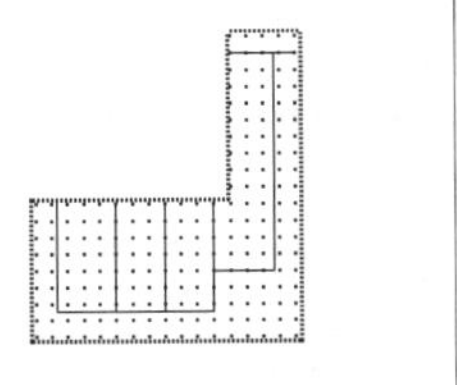

Visual Culture

Lenin museum

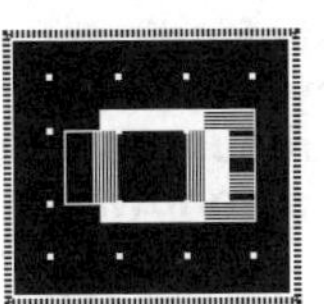

Museum

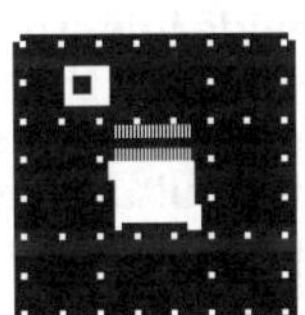

Residential

Housing

Facilities (TsNIIEP),[24] after which standard circuses began to appear in dozens of cities across the USSR. However, Tashkent won the right to build a circus based on an individual project, something facilitated by two circumstances. Firstly, the city was the fourth largest in the USSR in terms of population and could not be satisfied by a standard 2,000-seat circus, and secondly, the long (in fact, millennial) history of the development of indigenous circus arts in Central Asia allowed the republic to lobby for the construction of a special facility that was unlike the others. As a result, Tashkent became home to a structure that had no prototypes worldwide.

The specific features of Soviet cultural policy also determined the appearance of the Tashkent House of Youth. It cannot be said that "houses of youth" were completely absent from global practice. The idea was likely borrowed from France, where since 1950s there had been Maisons des Jeunes et de la Culture, a special type of state institution designed to provide leisure activities and education to the population. They were in contrast to the houses of culture, whose mandate, according to Minister of Culture André Malraux, was to provide all citizens with access to national cultural heritage. Such institutions were a priority in "red municipalities," which aimed to attract marginalized urban youth to study, education and sport. If houses of culture were, in Malraux's words, to become "modern cathedrals,"[25] the youth and cultural centers were fundamentally anti-elitist. Soviet houses of youth, unlike their French prototypes, were not intended for the inhabitants of small towns. The ulterior motive behind the creation of such complexes in the USSR was the state's desire to maintain control of youth initiatives and the international contacts of creative youth groups. Houses of youth functioned under the wing of the republican and regional committees of the Komsomol, which cooperated closely with the security agencies. These institutions were designed not for the general public but for the elite youth of the largest cities of the USSR. This conditioned, in particular, their external appearance with its inherent modernist "palace-like" character. However, this type of building also had an internal logic, sometimes counter to that of the state. For example, the House of Youth in Tashkent in 1976 housed the Studio of Creative Youth, which soon transformed into the Ilkhom Theater, the first non-state theater in the USSR, which for several decades was the center of the cultural underground in Uzbekistan.

The "urban restaurant" was a curious example of Soviet architectural typology. In capitalist countries, restaurants were a purely private affair and often grew out of a family business. This differentiated restaurants, the main advantages of which were always coziness and intimacy, from works canteens or buffets. The roots of Soviet "public catering" were radically different. The first Soviet decades gave rise to numerous proposals for the construction of new types of facilities in which food would be prepared and distributed in an industrialized manner. In particular, a "factory kitchen" was built in Tashkent (architect: S. Cherniavskii, 1932). Although the transition to Stalinist architecture seemed to put an end to such experiments, in the 1960s architects returned to some of them. After the 1959 party decree "On the Further Development and Improvement of Public Catering," cafés and restaurants began to be built more frequently and, most importantly, they were designed not only for the party elite or foreign tourists but also for ordinary citizens. The decree noted that traditional food preparation in canteens, cafés and restaurants was economically unproductive. In order to reach the population more widely, it was decided to "shift

24 I. Chipiga, "Tsirki [Circuses]," *Arkhitektura SSSR* [*Architecture of the USSR*], no. 7, 1972, 28–29; V. G. Ivanov, *Arkhitektura, vdokhnovlennaia kosmosom: Obraz budushchego v pozdnesovetskoi arkhitekture* [*Architecture Inspired by Space: The Image of the Future in Late Soviet Architecture*] (St. Petersburg: Borei Art, 2017), 101–108.

25 From André Malraux's speech to the French National Assembly, 1966.

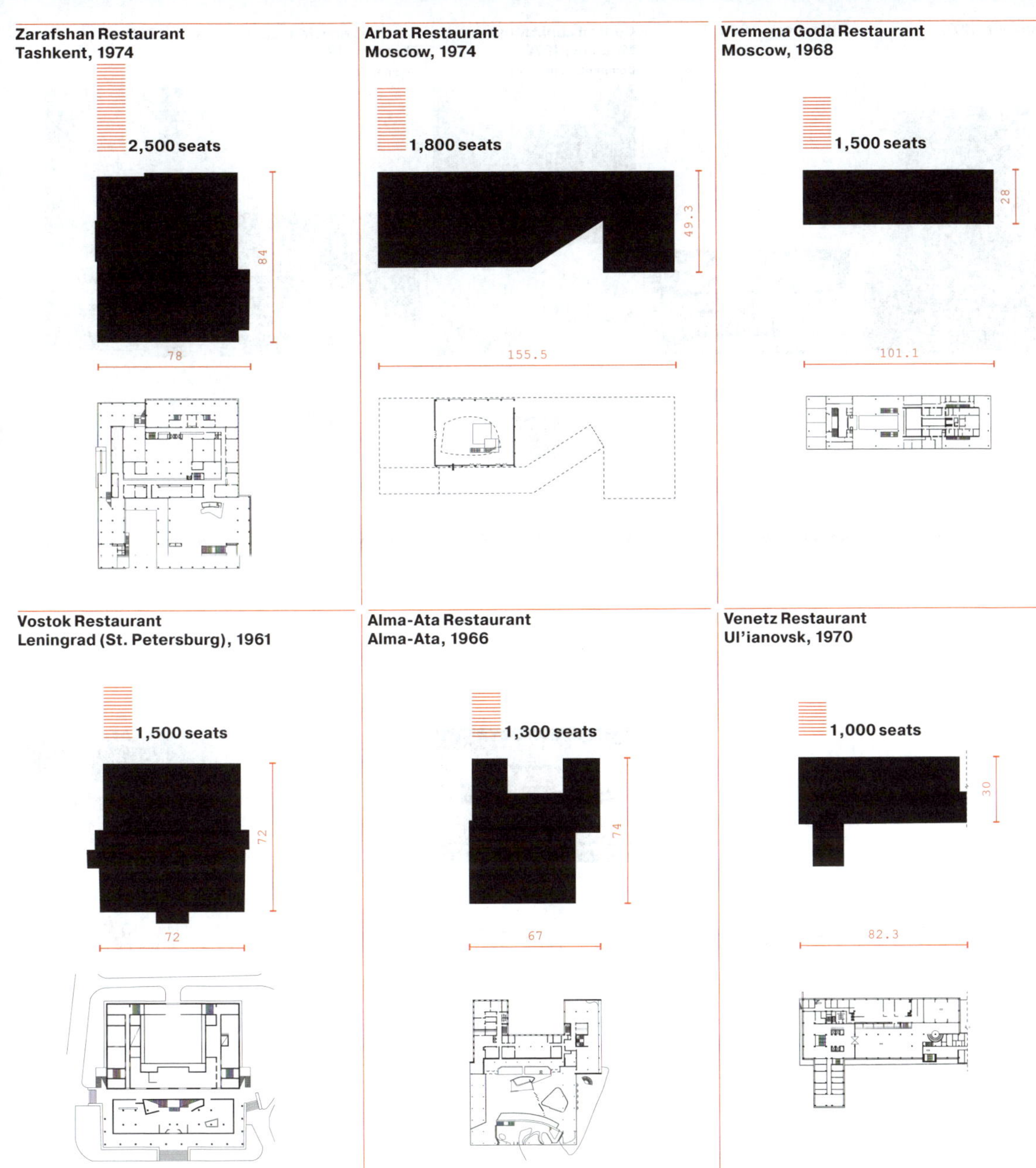
Zarafshan Restaurant
Tashkent, 1974
2,500 seats
84
78
Arbat Restaurant
Moscow, 1974
1,800 seats
49.3
155.5
Vremena Goda Restaurant
Moscow, 1968
1,500 seats
28
101.1
Vostok Restaurant
Leningrad (St. Petersburg), 1961
1,500 seats
72
72
Alma-Ata Restaurant
Alma-Ata, 1966
1,300 seats
74
67
Venetz Restaurant
Ul'ianovsk, 1970
1,000 seats
30
82.3

Tashkent, 1970

Ul'ianovsk, 1970

Central Lenin Museum, Moscow, 1970
Competition Round 1

Central Lenin Museum, Moscow, 1972
Competition Open Round

Kyiv, 1982

Frunze (Bishkek), 1984

Kazan', 1987

Gorki Leninskie, 1987

Krasnoyarsk, 1987

Samara (Kuibyshev), 1989

Comparison of Lenin Museum Atriums

canteens, teahouses, cafés and snack bars to working with semiprepared food, which it is more expedient to make in specially organized workshops, factory kitchens or enterprises of the meat/milk and food industries."[26] According to the new urban planning norms, cultural and residential centers of large urban districts had to include "public catering enterprises." As a result, the Gulistan Restaurant (1967) appeared in the center of the Oktiabr'skii district and the Chilanzar Restaurant (1972) in the Chilanzar district. These impressive buildings, designed from 1964 to 1965, before the Tashkent earthquake, had hundreds of seats. The city center was to be the location of the "main restaurant of the city" with 2,500 seats, which would become the Zarafshan Restaurant (1966–1974). It occupied a whole city block and implemented many ideas that had emerged in the 1920s. For example, there was a kitchen making semifinished products which could be purchased in the restaurant shop, and dishes for its several halls were prepared in a centralized kitchen core, from where they were delivered by automated means to the serving areas located on two floors. Typologically, the Tashkent "megarestaurant" was similar to a number of buildings in other cities of the USSR, such as the Alma-Ata Restaurant (1966) in Alma-Ata, Vremena Goda (1968) and Arbat (1974) in Moscow and Venetz in Ul'ianovsk (1970), but it had its own distinctive functional features. If the Moscow and Alma-Ata "megarestaurants," whose plan represented a continuous open space with endless rows of tables for visitors, literally reproduced the idea of an architectural eating machine, the Tashkent restaurant complex was divided into numerous independent spaces. Accordingly, the technological process implying the flow principle of the "factory kitchen" was complemented by the architects' attempts to create a comfortable atmosphere for visitors and, in particular, to include several halls of national cuisine.

From Greek Temples to Mosques: Historical Roots of Soviet Typologies

Although functional typologies dominated Soviet practices, they were not the only ones. Typologies varied according to natural factors (seismic and solar conditions, topography, humidity, winds, etc.), cultural traditions and construction techniques. At the same time, we can state that the original architectural "types" which came into the field of view of architectural historians thanks to Quatremère de Quincy were also present in the modernist architecture of Tashkent, even if this was not theoretically postulated or commented on by architects.

Nor were historical prototypes completely bypassed. However, whereas Quatremère de Quincy related his ideas only to Greco-Roman classics, Soviet, and hence Tashkent, architecture varied the primary types, producing hybrid crossovers. The interior of the Lenin Museum, which formed the first manifesto of modernist architecture in Tashkent, was clearly inspired by the naos of a Greek temple, with overhead light pouring down on a statue of a glorified deity, while on the exterior its entire volume was decorated with a geometric pattern that clearly correlated with the continuous ornamentation of blank walls in historical Islamic architecture.

The Peoples' Friendship Palace was created as an Uzbekistan version of the Kremlin Palace of Congresses and therefore reproduced the theme of the "modernist peripter" that was evident in the Moscow building. Situated on an elevated position and open to the city square from various angles, this "peripter" was devoid of an obvious front and back.

26 "Postanovlenie TsK KPSS i Soveta Ministrov SSSR 'O dal'neishem razvitii i uluchshenii obshchestvennogo pitaniia' [Decree of the Central Committee of the CPSU and the Council of Ministers of the USSR 'On the Further Development and Improvement of Public Catering']," *Sobranie postanovlenii pravitel'stva SSSR za 1959 g.* [*Collection of Decrees of the Government of the USSR for 1959*], nos. 1–20 (Moscow: Gosiurizdat, no year), 66.

Kremlin Palace of Congresses, Moscow, 1961
Architects: Mikhail Posokhin, Ashot Mndoiants, Evgenii Stamo, Pavel Shteller

Peoples' Friendship Palace, Tashkent, 1981
Architects: Evgenii Rozanov, Elena Sukhanova, Vladislav Shestopalov et al.

Parthenon, Athens, 438 BC
Architects: Ictinus and Callicrates

In the interior, however, the naos was replaced by a theatrical amphitheater, one typology crossed with another. However, in the capital of Soviet Uzbekistan Greek references could not be the only ones, and they were complemented by the "Islamic ornamentation" of the façade and the abundant decoration of the interiors. Post-factum, another prototype was seen in the finished building, the early medieval fortress structure, or qala, of Khorezm, the main rectangular volume of which was concealed by walls with honeycomb "loopholes."

Hybridization became an important characteristic of Tashkent building types. The State Museum of Arts played with the abstract forms of the Modern Movement, the cube and the square. Its interior was an enclosed atrium with clear Roman roots but could also be associated with the almost cubic Kaaba, within which there was a perimeter gallery. The exterior of the Union of Artists Exhibition Hall featured an arcade reminiscent of the squares of Isfahan or Tabriz, but in Iran these arcades encircled the interior of a square, bazaar or courtyard, whereas the arcade of the Exhibition Hall faced the city like a Venetian palazzo. At the same time, its sunken atrium beneath skylights was an obvious replica of the Roman impluvium. The auditorium of the Tashkent Circus, like any circus building, could not escape the form of the ancient Roman arena, although these were not covered with a dome. When comparing the domes of Central Asian circuses, one can see their link to local motifs. If in Alma-Ata the dome was associated with the yurt, i.e. the dwelling of nomads, the squat outlines of the Tashkent dome, especially noticeable

Transcultural variation of impluvium that migrated to the folk architecture of Central Asia: covered courtyard, or "kashgarcha," in Margelan, mid-19th century

Roman impluvium

against the background of the high dome of the Chorsu Bazaar, evoked less obvious associations with the roofs of Bukhara's bazaars.

To summarize, we can confirm that Quatremère de Quincy's generative types also penetrated Tashkent architectural practice. In many respects this is not accidental, above all because the creators of Tashkent modernism received a traditional architectural education that drew on many of the principles of the École des Beaux-Arts. During their four years of study, they took a full academic course in drawing and painting, from plaster casts to life classes. The history of architecture as taught in the architecture faculty at Tashkent Polytechnic Institute consisted of academic courses on European architecture from Greece to neoclassicism and rather scattered information on non-Western and modern architecture. The only exception was Central Asia, as some professors were engaged in the systematic study of the region. This is probably why the types that emerged in the work of Tashkent architects were "decentralized" and represented a hybrid field of intersections. They reflected the specific nature of the cultures of Soviet Central Asia, which absorbed various civilizational influences between the late 1950s and the 1980s, and which once again found themselves at the crossroads of international life after the lifting of the Iron Curtain.

Modernism as Orientalism

Boris Chukhovich

At first glance the ideas of the Modern Movement seem to be incompatible with orientalism. The Modern Movement aspired to being inclusive and universal, whereas orientalism related only to some countries and cultures. The Modern Movement was focused on innovation and the future, and orientalism was a bearer of established stereotypes. The Modern Movement used a language of its own invention, while orientalism was inspired by an aesthetic inherited from the nineteenth century. Accordingly, there is nothing surprising about the fact that historians of academic orientalism end its chronology in the early twentieth century and historians of modern architecture do not as a rule pay attention to its orientalist modes.

Lenin Museum

The radical turn in the understanding of the phenomenon of orientalism produced by Edward Said and postcolonial studies did not lead to a significant shift in the study of the manifestation of orientalism in architecture. Today one can identify only individual attempts to apply the expanded understanding of orientalism formed in the social sciences to the study of architecture.[1] Such exceptions include the special edition of *Revue du monde musulman et de la Méditerranée* in which the authors considered as varieties of orientalism not only the formal influence of Islamic architecture on architectural processes in Europe but also the "East" constructed in situ by European architects, Jorge Liernur's consideration of orientalism and modern architecture and so on. I will try to present a condensed view of this problem with regard to the study of the architecture of Tashkent from the 1960s to the 1980s, based on hypotheses that have partly already been included in my articles on this theme.[2]

1 "Figures de l'orientalisme en architecture." Special issue, *Revue du monde musulman et de la Méditerranée*, nos. 73–74, 1994; Tom Avermaete, Serhat Karakayali and Marion von Osten, eds., *Colonial Modern: Aesthetics of the Past, Rebellions for the Future* (London: Black Dog Publishing, 2010); Jorge Liernur, "Orientalism and Modern Architecture: The Debate on the Flat Roof," *Ra. Revista de Arquitectura*, June 2010, 61–78.

2 Boris Chukhovich, "Building the 'Living East,'" in *Soviet Modernism 1955–1991: Unknown History*, ed. Katharina Ritter, et al. (Vienna: Park Books, 2012), 214–231; Chukhovich, "Local Modernism and Global Orientalism: Building the 'Soviet Orient,'" in "19th Vienna Architecture Congress: Soviet Modernism 1955–1991; Unknown Stories," special issue, *Hintergrund* 54, 2013, 31–39.; Boris Chukhovich, "Orientalist Modes of Modernism in Architecture: Colonial/Postcolonial/Soviet," in *Orientalism from the Margins: Perspectives from India and Russia*, ed. Svetlana Gorshenina and Philippe Bornet (Lausanne: PUL, 2014), 263–293.

In one way or another, architects who worked for Tashkent aimed to create buildings that were specific to the city. Their comments on this subject focused on the originality of the natural, political and cultural features of the capital of Uzbekistan. Consideration of natural factors such as the sharply continental climate and seismic risk did not require a departure from the means of modern architecture. This is clearly demonstrated in Tashkent buildings of the early 1960s such as the Central Department Store (TsUM), the Central Committee of the Communist Party of Uzbekistan, the Panoramic Cinema, the Chilanzar Shopping Center and others, which survived the 1966 earthquake unscathed and became popular in the city thanks both to their exceptional planning and to their sculptural and social solutions. In adapting projects to the Tashkent climate, architects used the orientation of the building, sun protection, the natural cooling of water features and landscaping, shaded internal spaces and cooling ventilation, the effect of which was known by the medieval architects of the Middle East. Until the mid-1960s the architectural community assumed that these techniques were sufficient for integrating new architecture into the local context. However, in the late 1960s the expressive language began to change: functional techniques that suited the natural conditions were now accompanied by symbolic images, the connotations of which were consonant with the orientalist discourse.

Building of the Central Committee of the Communist Party of the UzSSR

Life of the Peoples of the Soviet East and the East of Capitalist Countries, poster, 1920s

Tashkent, "the Star of the East"

The refrain of a song by Moscow authors that was popular in the USSR depicted Tashkent as "the star of the East" and "the capital of friendship and warmth." These epithets revealed a new social role delegated by Moscow to the capital of Uzbekistan as far back as the late 1950s, when the Soviet Union began to open the Iron Curtain. After the collapse of the global colonial system and at the height of the Cold War, the two main global blocs were seeking new allies. In 1955 the Bandung Conference in Indonesia preceded the creation of the Non-Aligned Movement. It formulated ten principles for peaceful coexistence which became known as "the spirit of Bandung." Soon the leadership of the USSR initiated the first Conference of Writers of Asian and African Countries in Tashkent (1958), proposing a new expression—"the spirit of Tashkent." As a counterweight to the "spirit of Bandung," which was based on ideas of sovereignty, national independence and noninterference in the internal affairs of the new countries, the "spirit of Tashkent" stressed "brotherhood," "mutual assistance," and the "friendship of peoples." These slogans promised potential satellites from the Non-Aligned Movement material resources and the political support of the socialist bloc.

Throughout the 1960s and 1970s Tashkent was used effectively as a shopwindow for the rapid modernization of Central Asia. From the beginning of this period Uzbek newspapers were full of articles about the visits of politicians, trade unionists and artists from dozens of countries in Asia, Africa and Latin America. Delegations from the socialist bloc and Western Europe were also frequent visitors. The capital of Uzbekistan showed its foreign guests examples of sweeping industrialization, intensive social construction, housing reform, mass free education and multilevel medical services. For many visitors the shopwindow looked good. "We are in a country that is somehow similar to Algeria," wrote journalists from the French newspaper *Libération*, "but this Algieria is liberated and independent, a country whose people irrigated their land and made it fertile [. . .], a country that uses atomic energy produced by modern power plants."[3]

The political mandate gave birth to a new mythology and even a new topography. The popular Uzbek poet Gafur Guliam defined it in the following way:

You, my Tashkent, are the gates to the East
And Moscow, our mother, is the focus of the universe.
She gave us peace, and so we carry
The banner of peace and sacred friendship to all.[4]

As emerges from this worldview, Tashkent was not located at the center of the imaginary East but at its border. For this reason, its image differed significantly in comparison to the references of classical orientalism such as Baghdad, Istanbul or Cairo. As a counterweight to the "ancient," "dormant" and "mystical" Orient, Tashkent needed to present a dynamic, progressive and open East. Only this type of city could effectively translate the doctrinal ideas of "mother Moscow" to the former colonies that had achieved independence. Paradoxically, this is precisely the kind of Europe—dynamic, progressive, open—that appeared in Edward Said's binary descriptions. Therefore, in Tashkent it was necessary to create a modernized "European city" that had an "oriental look." On entering the city guests should sense an "Eastern" aroma, and on leaving a "European" emancipatedness.

A clearer metaphor for this dichotomy may be found in the design for Bogdan Khmel'nitskii Street (1970–1973) by Andrei Kosinskii, who arrived in Tashkent from Moscow to help rebuild the city after the 1966 earthquake. The urban planning significance of this street was to connect the airport and the city center. Whereas all of the buildings constructed in Tashkent in the early 1960s featured a white/gray monochrome, this street greeted visitors with an explosion of ornamental polychromy: after all, the Orient was supposed to be florid and covered with arabesques. In addition, the façades of the nine-story residential buildings were decorated with stylized "oriental" arches and "stalactites" in the form of wittily situated balconies on the upper floors. The architect compared the unusual bends of some of the walls with the duvol walls of streets in the "old city." However, this "oriental" decoration had a "European" flip side in at least two senses. Firstly, Kosinskii noted on more than one occasion that when developing the composition of the streets he was inspired by the structure and perspectives of Nevskii Avenue in St. Petersburg, the main street of the Russian Empire and of the most European city in Russia.[5] Its straightforward "organized irregularity" did not, of course, have anything in common with the historic streets of Central Asian cities. Secondly, Bogdan Khmel'nitskii Street was not only the first image of the capital of Uzbekistan on entering the city but also the last on leaving, and the architects believed that the last impression should not match the first. On the end of one of the walls that guests saw when leaving Tashkent Kosinskii planned to place a bas-relief by Ernst Neizvestnyi, one of the best-known modernist sculptors in the USSR. This bas-relief depicted a child against the background of a rainbow and an industrial landscape with elements of historic architecture and cotton plantations. In this way, the "oriental" connotations that met tourists on entry would be supplemented on exit by images of the dynamic present and future of Uzbekistan. The constructed version, however, turned

3 "Parizhane o Tashkente [Parisians on Tashkent]," *Pravda Vostoka* [*Truth of the East*], February 2, 1960, 4.
4 Gafur Guliam, "Slava Leninu, Partii slavu poiu [Glory to Lenin, Glory to the Party I Sing]," *Ogonëk* [*Little Flame*], no. 9, February 27, 1959, 4.
5 Andrei Kosinskii, "Poisk obraza magistrali (zastroika ul. Bogdana Khmel'nitskogo) [The Search for an Image of the Arterial Road (The Construction of Bogdan Khmel'nitskii Street)]," *Stroitel'stvo i arkhitektura Uzbekistana* [*Construction and Architecture of Uzbekistan*], no. 3, 1974, 28.

Alisher Mirzaev, *Tashkent, City of Peace, Friendship and Brotherhood* (triptych), 1984
Oil on canvas (200 × 200 cm, 200 × 260 cm, 200 × 200 cm)

Andrei Kosinskii (project lead), Iurii Miroshnichenko, Irina Demchinskaia, et al., perspective of Bogdan Khmel'nitskii (Bobur) Street, 1970–1972
Watercolor, pencil, ink on paper

Andrei Kosinskii (project lead), Iurii Miroshnichenko, Irina Demchinskaia, et al., perspective of Bogdan Khmel'nitskii (Bobur) Street, 1970–1972
Ink, gouache, pencil, color pencil on paper

out to be ultimately less dualistic. Andrei Kosinskii associated buildings with a long, curved façade with a duvol, the wall of a traditional Uzbek house in the "old city," and the mosaic which departing tourists saw was dedicated to the "eternal East," depicting a medieval astronomer against the background of a tree with strong roots.

The Orientalism of "National Form"

A particular feature of the French translation of Edward Said's *Orientalism* was its expressive subtitle, "The Orient Created by the Occident."[6] The description of "the Orient" as a Western fiction completely matched the representative function of "the beacon of socialism in the East" that was delegated to Tashkent by Moscow. However, as well as the external political aim there was also a cultural imperative which required the creation in Tashkent of a special architecture that differed from everything that appeared in the center of the USSR and in other Soviet republics. This imperative was shared and stimulated by the Moscow and Tashkent authorities, who were guided by official Soviet aesthetics, but it was so completely interiorized by architects that it allowed them to talk about an "Orient created in the East."

The specific nature of Tashkent's architecture was mainly defined by means of the concept of "national architecture." The use of this concept in the USSR was closely connected to official "Marxist-Leninist" aesthetics, which arose from the Stalinist slogan about a culture "proletarian in content and national in form," as stated in 1925 at a meeting with students of the Communist University for Workers of the East. Each generation of Soviet artists and architects interpreted the vague concept of "national form" in their own way, but they were obliged to refer to it. The link between the concepts of "national form" and "national architecture" and the orientalist discourse is not studied. Nevertheless, it definitely existed.

In 1968 the main official newspaper of Uzbekistan's communists, *Pravda Vostoka* (*Truth of the East*), published an appeal by influential historians, cultural figures, politicians and architects of Tashkent. It was directed at the lack of "artistic originality" in Tashkent's contemporary architecture. The authors stressed that they did "not in any way reject the means of contemporary architecture" and were "not calling for a return to historical styles, the antique order or Eastern domes and minarets." However, they stated that "architecture should reflect the culture of the people, its best traditions and its innovations," its "national principles." The text did not contain a new formula for "national architecture," and in essence it returned to orientalist presumptions: "How would we like the center of Tashkent to be? We imagine a freely spreading garden city with colorful, oriental architectural ensembles...."[7] The collective imagination of the signatories (among them influential historians such as Galina Pugachenkova, Lazar' Rempel' and Mikhail Masson) reflected the at that time undisputed perception of Uzbekistan as part of the East. But did the scholars who studied the "East" and the architects who created the "national architecture" of Uzbekistan consider themselves part of it?

6 Edward W. Said, *L'orientalisme: L'Orient créé par l'Occident* (Paris: Éditions du Seuil, 1980).

7 "Kakim byt' tsentru Tashkenta? [How Should the Center of Tashkent Be?]," *Pravda Vostoka* [*Truth of the East*], May 19, 1968, 1.

Peoples' Friendship Palace,
skylight in the main hall, 2022
Architects: Evgenii Rozanov (project lead),
Elena Sukhanova, et al., 1981

Peoples' Friendship Palace,
façade detail, 2022
Architects: Evgenii Rozanov (project lead),
Elena Sukhanova, et al., 1981

In the late 1960s and 1970s Moscow architects had a significant influence on the transformation of Tashkent's architecture. As well as Andrei Kosinskii, who moved to Tashkent, the designers of Moscow's Central Scientific Research and Experimental Project Institute for Entertainment and Sport Facilities (TsNIIEP) made a particularly important contribution to the formation of a new architectural language. Oddly, their solutions were imbued with a more direct and insistent desire to create something that could be literally perceived as "Eastern" or "national" than Tashkent architects' works. The famous Soviet architectural historian Selim Khan-Magomedov noted this phenomenon in the 1970s: "Paradoxically, 'national features' are easier to see (and to use) when analyzing the architecture of a given people outside'—in other words, when comparing it with the architecture of another people. Might this be the explanation for the lightness with which, in the recent past, many Moscow and Leningrad architects created projects in 'oriental style' for the republics of Central Asia? They could clearly see the exotic 'differences' between the traditional architecture of these republics and Russian architecture. Yet these architects sincerely believed that in their projects they were revealing the national features of the architecture of one or another republic."[8] But whereas for an astute historian the translation of generic images—the exotic and "oriental"—into something specifically "national" was obvious, the republican authorities turned out to be sensitive to the literal and visual differences thanks to which the architecture of Tashkent appeared to be a unique phenomenon and one which they believed was limited to Uzbekistan. The reaction of the leader of the Communist Party of the republic, Sharaf Rashidov, to the design for the House of Creative Unions presented to him by Andrei Kosinskii was revealing: "At last something that is 'ours' has appeared in architectural

8 Selim Khan-Magomedov, "Natsional'noe i internatsional'noe v sovremennoi arkhitekture [The National and International in Modern Architecture]," in *Internatsional'noe i natsional'noe v iskusstve* [*The International and National in Art*] (Moscow: Nauka, 1974), 222.

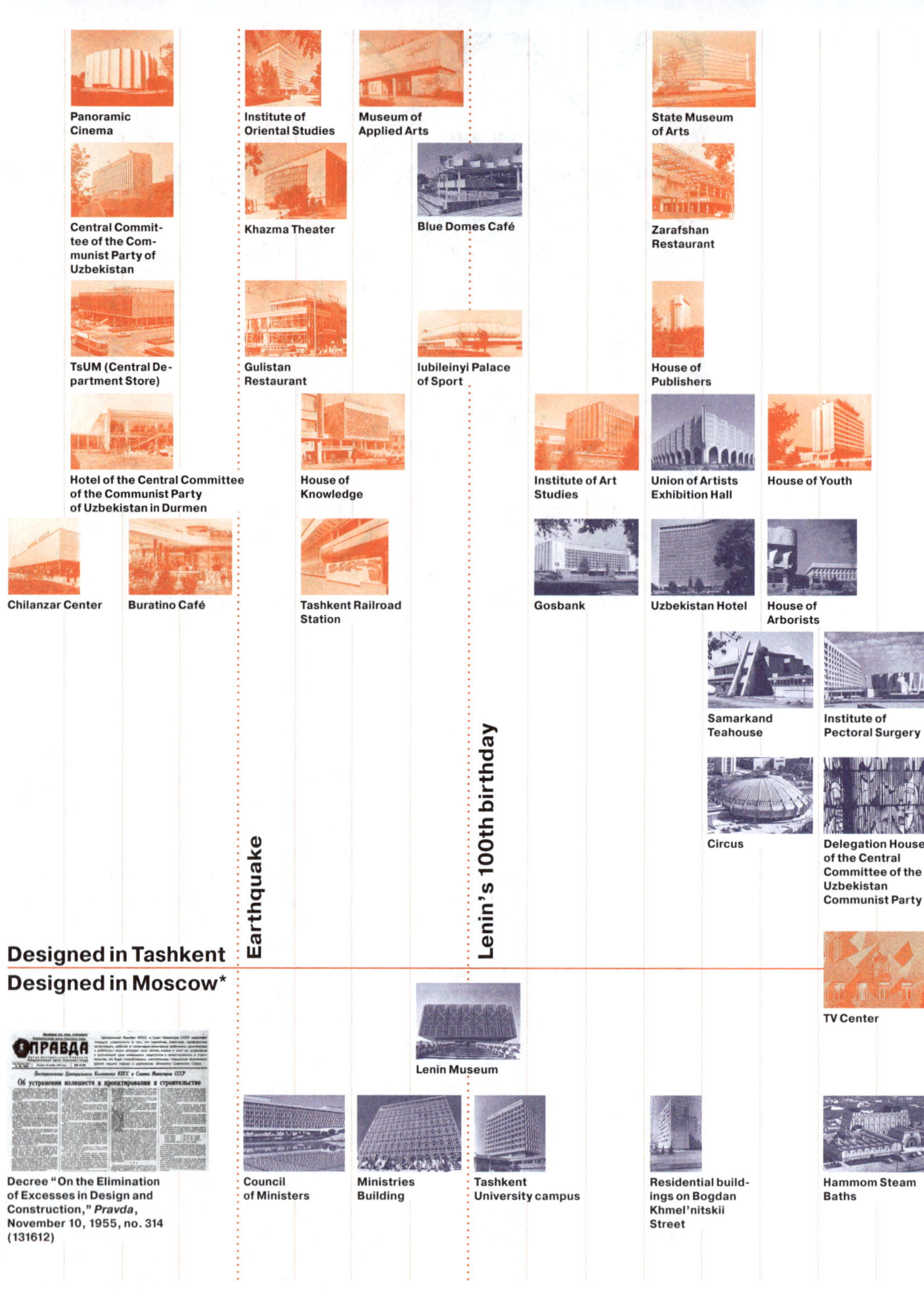

1963 1964 1965 1966 1967 1968 1969 1970 1971 1972 1973 1974 1975 1976 1977

Modernism
Mix of modernism and orientalism
* or designed by Moscow architects

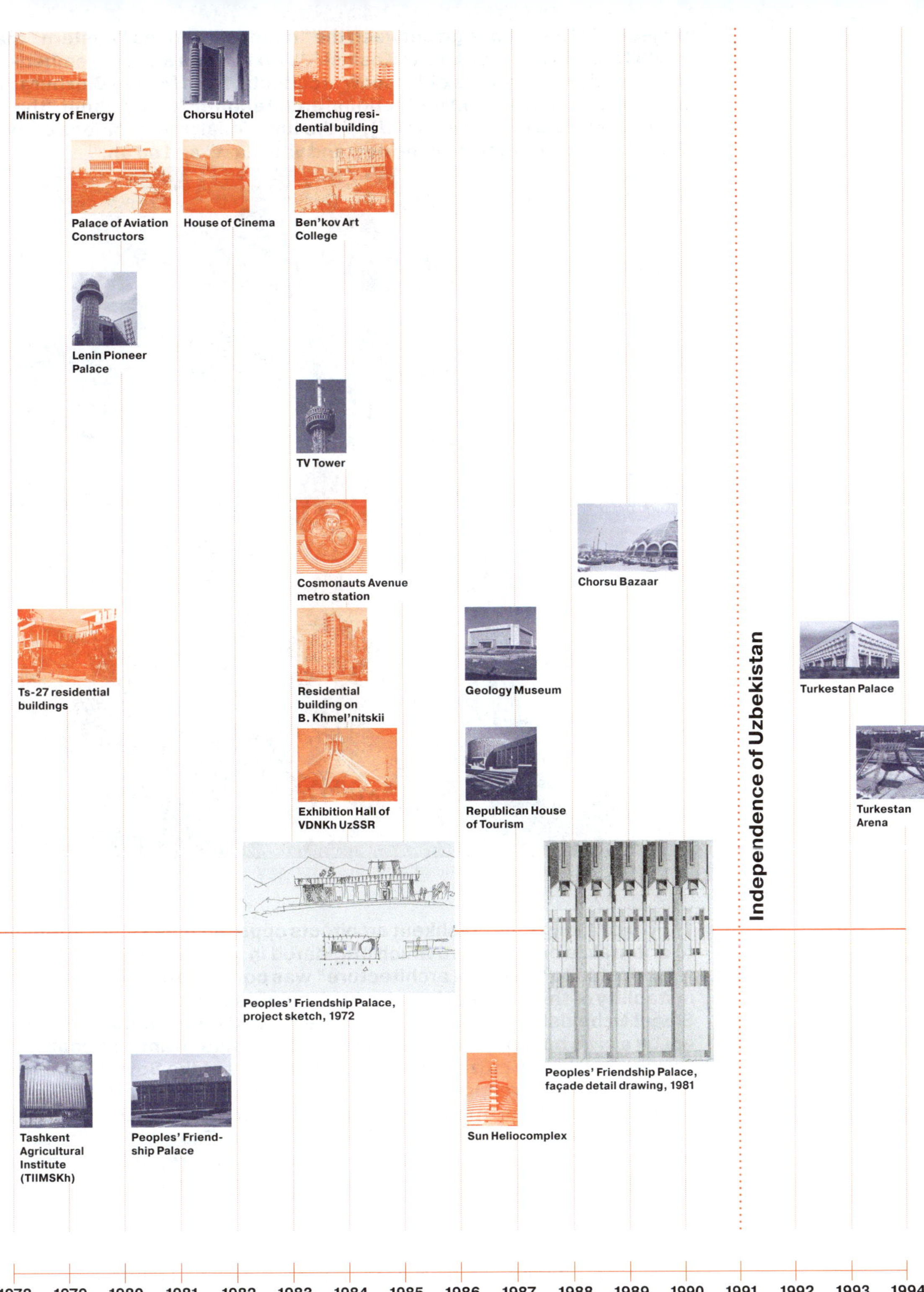

Ministry of Energy
Chorsu Hotel
Zhemchug residential building
Palace of Aviation Constructors
House of Cinema
Ben'kov Art College
Lenin Pioneer Palace
TV Tower
Cosmonauts Avenue metro station
Chorsu Bazaar
Ts-27 residential buildings
Residential building on B. Khmel'nitskii
Geology Museum
Independence of Uzbekistan
Turkestan Palace
Exhibition Hall of VDNKh UzSSR
Republican House of Tourism
Turkestan Arena
Peoples' Friendship Palace, project sketch, 1972
Peoples' Friendship Palace, façade detail drawing, 1981
Tashkent Agricultural Institute (TIIMSKh)
Peoples' Friendship Palace
Sun Heliocomplex
1978
1979
1980
1981
1982
1983
1984
1985
1986
1987
1988
1989
1990
1991
1992
1993
1994

projects."[9] The equal sign between the "national" and the "Eastern" that could found in many of Andrei Kosinskii's texts[10] was a deeply embedded tradition in the texts of Moscow architects. Even Moisei Ginzburg, in his main conceptual text on "national architecture," wrote about "the national culture of the East [*sic!*]," "the functional preconditions of the East," the "architecture of the new and vital East" and so on.[11]

Plasterers, SU-2 Brigade of Communist Labor, in front of residential building on Bogdan Khmel'nitskii (Bobur) Street, 1971

For a long time, Tashkent architects opposed these blunt attempts to orientalize architecture which originated in Moscow, but their own relationship to "national architecture" was complicated not only by the instability of this concept but also by the ambiguity of their identity in Soviet Uzbekistan. The USSR authorities based their "nation building" not on a civic but on an ethnic understanding of nation and nationality. Consequently, the citizenship of the inhabitants of the Soviet republics did not always correspond to their ethnic origin as noted in their passports. This led to an ethnic connotation of such terms as the "national culture" or "national architecture" of Uzbekistan. They implied the culture and architecture of the Uzbek people, while the republic was home to people of various backgrounds and cultural horizons.

9 "Arkhitektor Andrei Kosinskii: 'Ia do sikh por ne znaiu, chto takoe khoroshii vkus, (chast' III) [Architect Andrei Kosinskii: 'Even Now I Don't Know What Good Taste Is' (Part III)]," *Fergana News*, August 1, 2006, https://www.fergananews.com/articles/4524.

10 See, for example, Andrei Kosinskii, "V chem zhe Pravda arkhitektury? [What Is the Truth of Architecture?]," *Dekorativnoe iskusstvo* [*Decorative Art*], no. 6, 1979.

11 Moisei Ginzburg, "Natsional'naia arkhitektura narodov SSSR [The National Architecture of the Peoples of the USSR]," *Sovremennaia arkhitektura* [*Modern Architecture*], nos. 5–6, 1926, 113.

Vil' Muratov, sketch of the Blue Domes Café, eastern façade, 1969
Pencil, watercolor, ink on tracing paper

In addition, regardless of the fact that the republic was mainly made up of residents of Uzbek origin, there were few of them among the best-known Tashkent modernists of the 1960s and 1970s. This is largely explained by the fact that until the early 1970s the architecture faculty at Tashkent Polytechnic Institute taught in Russian, which gave an advantage to those who knew the language well.

In terms of other arts, such as music or visual art, the possibility of direct expression of the "national spirit" by non-Uzbek artists was questioned. Artist Mikhail Kurzin noted that "Uzbeks should have their own national visual art. And we Russian artists should help them with that."[12] When academic Uzbek music and the opera theater came into being, creative tandems appeared—Sergei Vasilenko and Mukhtar Ashrafi, Reingol'd Glier and Talib Sadykov—in which each had a separate role: composers of Russian or Ukrainian origin developed scores using the melodic intonations of their Uzbek colleagues.

North façade of the Exhibition Hall of the Union of Artists, 2023
Architects: Rafael' Khairutdinov and Farkhad Tursunov, 1974

12 Quoted in T. Kuriazov, *Chelovek s utonchennym golosom [A Person with a Refined Voice]* (Tashkent: Turon-Iqbol, 2015), 54–55.

Architects were never subject to direct messages that it was necessary to be an ethnic Uzbek to create "national architecture." The architectural community found a discursive solution to this situation: whereas artists and composers should *express* the national culture, it was sufficient for architects to *reflect* it. Stefan Polupanov wrote: "The architect who works creatively cannot but take into account the deep desire of the people to see in architecture a reflection of their national culture and everyday life."[13] However, the reflection and development of the culture of *Others* created the preconditions for the orientalist imagination: the construction of the new *Other* was based on old presumptions. Considering the mental division of Tashkent into "old" and "new" parts in which "Asian" and "European" populations lived, the binary categories of orientalism implicitly appeared in many plastic images.

This notwithstanding, the orientalist element did not entirely disrupt the path of Tashkent's modernist architecture. Alongside buildings that constructed "national architecture," in the final three Soviet decades quite a few appeared that avoided orientalist clichés, such as the House of Youth, the House of Publishers, the Palace of Aviation Constructors, the Sun Heliocomplex and others. Also important was the fact that, regardless of the political, economic and cultural dependence of Tashkent on Moscow, Soviet reality paradoxically combined colonial, postcolonial and decolonial features. The first could be seen in Tashkent's tangible dependence on Moscow for key questions on the political and economic agendas and also in the serious role of scientific, cultural and artistic institutions of the communist metropole in the formation of the culture of Soviet Uzbekistan across the entire Soviet period. Even so, the policy of the Soviet authorities was always critical of tsarist colonialism and declared values and aims that were directly opposed to it (where tsarism preferred urbanist segregation, the Soviets proclaimed a policy of merging the "Asian" and "European" districts of historic cities). This policy was based on imperatives that were simultaneously postcolonial and decolonial: postcolonial in terms of the transformation of tsarist colonialism into a more complex relationship between the authorities and subordinates, which was typical of the Soviet period, and decolonial in terms of the emancipatory declarations and internationalist slogans of the Soviet project.

Andrei Kosinskii (project lead), Gennadii Korobovtsev, et al., Kalkauz project, 1974–1978
Watercolor, pencil, ink on paper

As a consequence of these complexities, various types of Uzbek subjectivity characterized the architectural process. The leaders of the Communist Party and other governing organs in Uzbekistan who commissioned architecture were mostly of the titular nation. Architectural education was open to everyone and through the 1960s and 1970s and particularly the 1980s an increasing number of creative individuals of Uzbek origin became not only architects but also architectural scholars, critics and historians.

13 Stefan Polupanov, "Zal zasedanii Verkhovnogo soveta Uzbekskoi SSR [The Conference Hall of the Supreme Soviet of the Uzbek SSR]," *Arkhitektura SSSR* [*Architecture of the USSR*], no. 12, 1940, 50.

Due to the abovementioned discursive multiplicity, Uzbekistan's architecture was shaped by numerous groups of people with divergent interests and values. Consequently, it would be an extreme and counterproductive oversimplification to interpret the modernist architecture built in the Uzbek capital as the outcome of a binary confrontation between Tashkent and Moscow. The design approaches of Moscow architects working in Tashkent were far from uniform, just as the reception of these approaches in Uzbekistan was highly diverse—not to mention the fact that some buildings were designed in cities like Kyiv or Ashkhabad, and were at times heavily orientalized and richly decorated, at times minimalist and austere. Tashkent architects themselves also adopted different creative approaches. Therefore, rather than defining Tashkent modernism as orientalism, it is more correct to distinguish in Tashkent's modernist buildings the variable presence (or absence) of orientalist expressions and nuances.

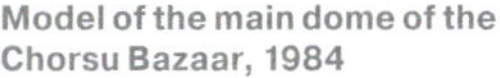

Model of the main dome of the Chorsu Bazaar, 1984

Chorsu Bazaar dome, 2021
Architects: Vladimir Azimov, et al., 1990

Outlining the Context
A Timeline by ACDF, GRACE and Boris Chukhovich

The timeline merges the events and buildings described in the book with various historical contexts, including their political, social, cultural, intellectual and architectural dimensions. The primary emphasis is on Tashkent, followed by Uzbekistan, Central Asia and the Soviet Union, as well as various countries in North Africa, the Middle East and Southeast Asia that either interacted with Uzbekistan or experienced similar historical developments. With only a few key events or buildings from the "West"—those that had more or less direct repercussions in Tashkent— punctuating the spreads, the timeline outlines several topics that may encourage the reader to explore this parallel history beyond the pages of this book.

Political events
Cultural events related to buildings (film festivals, exhibitions, concerts, etc.)
Reflections on orientalism
Ordinances related to town planning, seismic regulations, housing construction, public buildings (markets, museums, circuses, etc.)
Preservation of heritage
Protagonists, institutions, conferences and competitions
International references, precedents, publications
● Modernist buildings in Tashkent

1954

Nikita Khrushchëv's speech at the All-Union Meeting of Builders. The beginning of construction reform.

May 14: The USSR and the socialist countries of Europe sign the "Warsaw Pact" on "friendship, cooperation and mutual assistance."

June 27: The world's first nuclear power plant is launched in Obninsk, in the USSR.

Walter Gropius, The Architects Collaborative (TAC) and Hisham A. Munir begin designing the University of Baghdad campus.

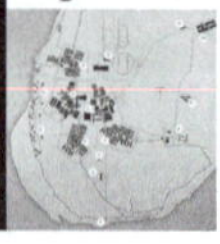

1955

Indian Prime Minister Jawaharlal Nehru and Indira Gandhi visit Tashkent.

April 18–24: A conference of 29 Asian and African countries on developing principles of peaceful coexistence is held in Bandung (Indonesia).

U 109-55
"Guidelines for the Use of Prefabricated Structures in the Construction of Buildings and Structures in Seismic Regions" (Gosstroi USSR).

November 4: Resolution of the Central Committee of the Communist Party of the Soviet Union (CPSU) and the Council of Ministers of the USSR "On Elimination of Excesses in Design and Construction."

ПРАВДА

Постановление Центрального Комитета КПСС и Совета Министров СССР

Об устранении излишеств в проектировании и строительстве

In the mid-1950s, architectural historians specializing in the protection of monuments are assigned to historic cities in Uzbekistan.

The main capitol buildings designed by Le Corbusier for Chandigarh (India) are completed.

The covered market in Sidi Bel Abbès (Algeria), designed by Marcel Mauri, is completed.

Gordon Bunshaft and Sedat Hakkı Eldem build the Hilton Istanbul Bosphorus Hotel.

The Sanskar Kendra Museum by Le Corbusier is inaugurated in Ahmedabad (India).

1956

February 25: Nikita Khrushchëv in a secret report to the 20th Congress of the CPSU exposes the personality cult of Stalin.

June 30: Shah of Iran Mohammad Reza Pahlavi visits Tashkent.

September 5–6: Indonesian President Sukarno visits Tashkent.

November 4: Hungarian uprising.

The monthly illustrated magazine *America* begins publishing again in the USSR without restrictions.

- Pakhtakor Stadium is completed.

1957

January 19: Chinese Premier Zhou Enlai visits Tashkent.

February 13–14: At the plenum of the CPSU Central Committee, Nikita Khrushchëv initiates reform of the economy based on the idea of decentralization.

July 31: King of Afghanistan Mohammad Zahir Shah visits Tashkent.

October 4: The USSR launches the first artificial satellite into orbit.

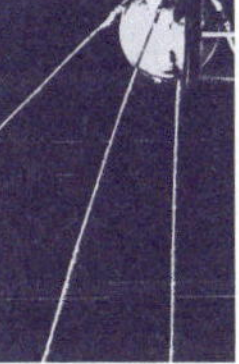

December 26: Sharaf Rashidov leads the Soviet delegation at the Conference of Solidarity of the Peoples of Asia and Africa.

July 28: The 6th World Festival of Youth and Students opens in Moscow.

SN-8-57
"Norms and Regulations for Construction in Seismic Regions" (Gosstroi USSR).

August 30: By Decree of the Government of Uzbekistan No. 557, the Committee for the Protection of Monuments of Material Culture is created. The council formed under the committee functions from 1957 to 1961.

The Climat de France residential complex is built by Fernand Pouillon as one of the largest attempts to construct modernist housing for the Muslim population of Algeria.

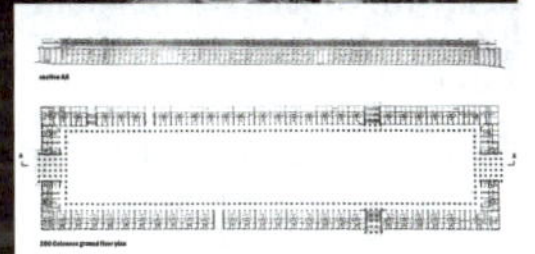

1958

May 16: Visit to Tashkent by Egyptian President Gamal Abdel Nasser.

1st Tashkent Film Festival of Asian and African Countries.

October 7–13: 1st Conference of Writers of Asian and African Countries.

Frank Lloyd Wright proposes a design for an opera house based on the spirit of traditional architecture for Baghdad. The project, adorned by a 92-meter gold statue of Harun al-Rashid and images of camels, remains unrealized.

From December 1, 1958, the rules and regulations for city planning and construction in Uzbekistan require urban planning projects to include a special section on the protection of cultural monuments, which must be approved by the relevant protection authorities.

From 1953 to 1958, buffer zones for architectural monuments listed in the republican register in Uzbekistan are determined.

A contract is signed allowing the French company Camus to construct house-building plants in Baku and Tashkent.

1959

January 2: Fidel Castro comes to power in Cuba.

January 27–February 5: 21st Congress of the Communist Party of the Soviet Union.

March 15: Sharaf Rashidov takes over as First Secretary of the Central Committee of the Communist Party of the Uzbek SSR.

September 13: Soviet interplanetary station lands on the moon for the first time.

September 15: Nikita Khrushchëv visits the USA.

July 24–September 5: *American National Exhibition* held in Sokolniki Park, Moscow. Beginning of the so-called "Kitchen Debates" between Khrushchëv and Nixon.

Edward Durell Stone completes construction of the US Embassy in Delhi.

The Museum of Western Art in Tokyo is built by Le Corbusier.

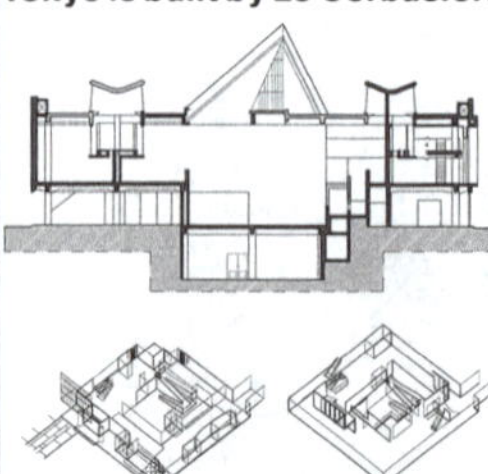

1960

March 3: President of India Rajendra Prasad visits Tashkent.

A group from Gosstroi UzSSR is sent to France to study precedents of industrial housing construction.

The magazine *Construction and Architecture of Uzbekistan* begins to be published in Tashkent.

The main buildings of the administrative complex in Brazil, designed by Oscar Niemeyer, are completed.

Constantinos A. Doxiadis designs the masterplan for Islamabad, capital of Pakistan.

Walter Gropius, TAC and Hisham A. Munir propose two options for the University of Baghdad mosque.

1961

February 12: The USSR launches *Venera-1*, the first spacecraft to study Venus.

April 12: The USSR sends the first human, Iurii Gagarin, into space.

July 18: Ghanaian President Kwame Nkrumah visits Tashkent.

September 1–6: The Belgrade Conference decides to establish the Non-Aligned Movement.

October 17–31: The 22nd Congress of the Communist Party of the Soviet Union adopts a program promising to build communism by 1980.

October 31: Stalin's body is removed from the mausoleum and reburied at the Kremlin wall.

L'Architecture d'aujourd'hui starts publishing in Russian.

October 17: The Kremlin Palace of Congresses (architect: Mikhail Posokhin) in Moscow opens.

In Chandigarh, Aditya Prakash builds the Tagore Theatre.

1962

In June, Sharaf Rashidov visits Cuba.

October 22–28: Cuban Missile Crisis.

The New York Times.

U.S. IMPOSES ARMS BLOCKADE ON CUBA ON FINDING OFFENSIVE-MISSILE SITES; KENNEDY READY FOR SOVIET SHOWDOWN

November 1: The USSR launches *Mars-1*, the first spacecraft to explore Mars.

Aleksandr Iakushev succeeds Mitkhat Bulatov as chief architect of Tashkent.

Sverre Fehn builds the Nordic Pavilion, an example of pronounced "regional modernism," in Giardini, Venice.

1963

May 10: Fidel Castro visits Uzbekistan.

June 5: Arrest in Iran of Qom Ruhollah Khomeini, who opposed the pro-American Shah Mohammad Reza Pahlavi. In November 1964, Khomeini will be arrested and expelled from the country.

July 15: First Secretary of the Central Committee of the Hungarian Socialist Workers Party Janos Kadar arrives in Tashkent.

SNiP II-A, 12-62 "Construction in Seismic Areas: Design Standards" (Gosstroi USSR).

TashZNIIEP is established out of the department of standard design of Uzgosproekt.

The Beinecke Rare Book and Manuscript Library at Yale University, designed by Gordon Bunshaft, is built.

The Amon Carter Museum of Western Art is built in Texas by Philip Johnson.

Kenzō Tange creates a new masterplan for the city of Skopje, three quarters of which was destroyed by a catastrophic earthquake.

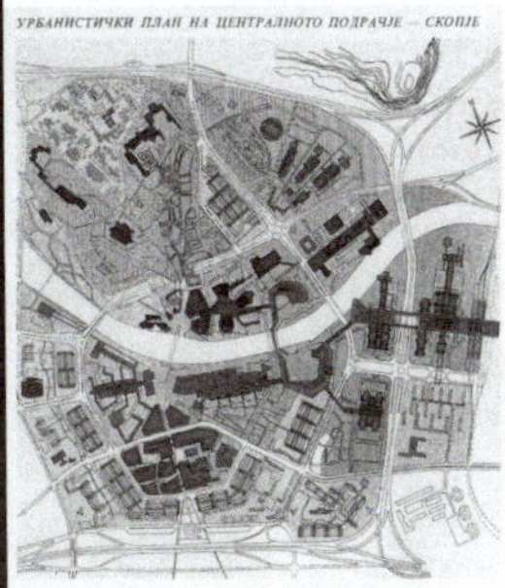

In Ankara, Altuğ Çinici and Behruz Çinici build the Middle East Technical University.

Mahatma Gandhi Sangrahalaya (Gandhi Memorial Institution), designed by Charles Correa, is inaugurated in Ahmedabad (India).

1964

Under Mohammad Zahir Shah, a new constitution makes Afghanistan a constitutional monarchy with a parliament and a government responsible to it.

January 17: Construction of the first stage of the world's largest gas pipeline, Bukhara–Ural, is completed.

April 28: Algerian President Ahmed Ben Bella arrives in Tashkent.

October 14: Leonid Brezhnev is appointed First Secretary of the Central Committee. For two years he headed a group plotting to overthrow Khrushchëv.

November 20: In the presence of Leonid Brezhnev and other leaders of the USSR and Uzbekistan, an event marking the 40th anniversary of the USSR and the CPSU is held at the Panoramic Cinema.

ТОРЖЕСТВО ЛЕНИНСКИХ ИДЕЙ

ПРАВДА ВОСТОКА

РЕЧЬ ТОВАРИЩА Л. И. БРЕЖНЕВА

ПРОЦВЕТАЙ, УЗБЕКИСТАН!

The Venice Charter for the Conservation and Restoration of Monuments and Sites is drawn up.

Projects by Tashgiprogor and TsNIIEP (Central Scientific Research and Experimental Project Institute for Entertainment and Sport Facilities) win the competition for Lenin Square.

Tashgiprogor's project wins the All-Union competition for the center of Tashkent.

Villa Namazee, by Gio Ponti, is built in Tehran, Iran.

● The Central Department Store (TsUM) is completed.

● The Panoramic Cinema Large Hall is completed.

● The Central Committee of the Communist Party of Uzbekistan building is completed.

● The Chilanzar Shopping Center is completed.

1965

June 3: Norwegian Prime Minister Einar Gerhardsen arrives in Tashkent.

September 29: The September plenum of the CPSU Central Committee launches economic reforms that will last until the late 1960s.

The Panoramic Cinema and the building of the Central Committee of the Communist Party of the UzSSR receive awards for quality construction at the All-Union competition.

Vladimir Berezin becomes the chief architect of Uzgosproekt.

The exhibition *Architecture of the USA* is held in Leningrad, Minsk and Moscow.

A competition is announced in Armenia for a memorial to the victims of the 1915 genocide. Despite the theme of national trauma, all competition proposals are radically modernist in nature.

1966

January 10: The signing of the Tashkent Declaration marks the beginning of the normalization of relations between India and Pakistan after the war of 1965 between them.

March 29–April 8: The 23rd Congress of the CPSU elects Brezhnev as General Secretary of the CPSU Central Committee.

April 26: Earthquake in Tashkent.

April 27: Leonid Brezhnev and Aleksei Kosygin arrive in Tashkent and take a decision on the reconstruction of the city.

October 25: Yugoslav President Josip Broz Tito visits Tashkent.

Moscow architect Andrei Kosinskii comes to work in Tashkent.

An Uzbek delegation visits Japan to learn about construction techniques in seismic areas.

The Samarkand State Architecture and Construction Institute (SamGASI) opens.

1967

June 5–10: Six-Day War (Third Arab-Israeli War) between Israel and a coalition of Arab states (Egypt, Syria, Jordan).

September 23: Visit of Turkish Prime Minister Süleyman Demirel to Tashkent.

November 7: The USSR celebrates its 50th anniversary.

The architecture exhibition *Tashkent 1980* is held in the foyer of the conference hall of the Central Committee of the Communist Party of Uzbekistan.

December 30: The Council of Ministers of the UzSSR approves the masterplan of the center of Tashkent.

March 27: The Society for the Protection of Historical and Material Culture Monuments of Uzbekistan is established by the decision of the UzSSR Council of Ministers.

December 25: The results of one of the largest architectural competitions in Tashkent, for an Art Square behind the Uzbekistan Hotel, are announced.

April 27: The international exhibition Expo-67 opens in Montreal.

Habitat 67, by architect Moshe Safdie, is completed as part of the Expo.

The Palace of Art Exhibitions is built in Vilnius (Lithuania) by Vytautas Čekanauskas.

1968

January 5–August 21: Prague Spring.

May 2–June 23: Student and worker protests in France and Europe.

October 21: The 1st Tashkent International Film Festival of Asia and Africa opens at the Panoramic Cinema.

May 19: An article by scholars and cultural figures, "How Should the Center of Tashkent Be?," demands that new architecture be oriental.

The UzSSR Supreme Council adopts the law "On the Protection of Cultural Monuments," in accordance with which the Council of Ministers of the UzSSR approves the "Regulations on the Procedure for the Application of the Law on the Protection of Cultural Monuments," the "Regulations on the Protection Zones of Material Cultural Monuments and Development Zones around Them" and the "Regulations on the Procedure for the Design and Construction of Monuments."

The Museum of Art by Lina Bo Bardi opens in São Paulo.

The Sardarapat memorial complex, built by Rafael Israelian, opens in Armenia.

The Neue Nationalgalerie, designed by Mies van der Rohe, opens in Berlin (Germany).

In Tus (Iran), the Ferdowsi Museum is built by Houshang Seyhoun.

In Chandigarh the Government Museum and Art Gallery, designed by Le Corbusier, opens.

In Baghdad, Mustansiriyah University is built by Qahtan Awni.

● The House of Knowledge is completed.

● The Institute of Oriental Studies is completed.

1969

June 5: The International Meeting of Communist and Workers' Parties in Moscow gathers representatives of 75 countries.

July 20: Neil Amstrong sets foot on the surface of the moon.

September 9: A series of concerts and exhibitions of the culture and arts of the Kirghiz SSR opens at the Panoramic Cinema.

The USSR Council of Ministers approves the design brief for the construction of the Tashkent metro.

ОНИ ПОСТРОЯТ МЕТРО

The Tashgenplan Institute is established by resolution of the Central Committee of the Communist Party and the Council of Ministers of the UzSSR.

The competition for the building of the UzSSR Supreme Soviet is won by Iurii Khaldeev's team with the project "Red Square."

Alvar Aalto designs a museum of modern art for Shiraz (Iran), but the project remains unrealized.

● The Museum of Applied Arts is completed.

● The Council of Ministers building is completed.

1970

Numerous "jubilee buildings" are constructed in the USSR to mark 100 years since Lenin's birth.

Soviet physicist Andrei Sakharov and other scientists write a letter to USSR leaders demanding the democratization of Soviet society.

October 8: Aleksandr Solzhenitsyn is awarded the Nobel Prize in Literature.

October 10: Visit of French President Georges Pompidou to Tashkent.

SNiP II-A, 12-69 "Construction in Seismic Areas: Design Standards" (Gosstroi USSR).

Aleksandr Iakushev is replaced by Sabir Adylov as chief architect of Tashkent.

The authors of the Central Committee of the Communist Party of Uzbekistan building and the Panoramic Cinema are awarded the Hamza Prize.

The Lenin Palace is built in Alma-Ata, the capital of Kazakhstan (architect: Nikolai Ripinskii and others).

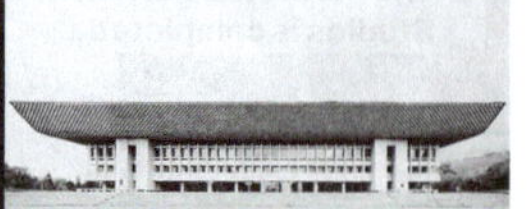

The Lenin Memorial Complex in Ul'ianovsk opens, designed by Boris Mezentsev, Mikhail Konstantinov, Geral'd Isakovich and Viktor Shul'rikhter.

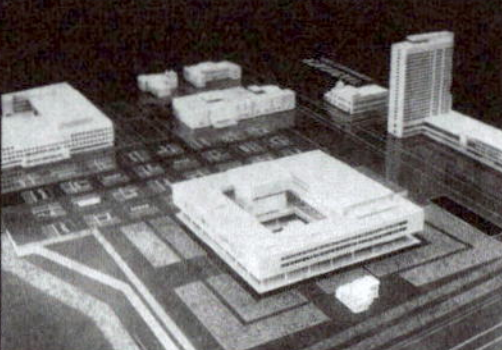

● The Lenin Museum is completed.

● The Tashkent University campus is completed.

● The Blue Domes Café is completed.

1971

February 24–March 4: The 24th CPSU Congress completes winding down of economic reform.

April 19: The USSR launches the world's first orbital station into space.

February: The Lenin Museum presents the exhibition *Leniniana in Philately*.

Construction and Architecture of Uzbekistan publishes an article by Valentina Manakova criticizing the "exoticism" of the Blue Domes Café.

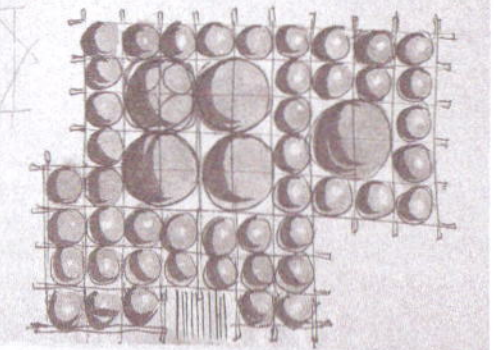

Iosif Notkin and I. Gordeeva produce "Temporary Instructions for the Development of Historical Cities" as part of the activities of the Urban Planning Department of TashZNIIEP.

The Central Committee of the Communist Party and the Council of Ministers of the UzSSR adopt a program for the reconstruction of the "old city."

The order for the design of the Peoples' Friendship Palace is transferred to Moscow's Central Scientific Research and Experimental Project Institute for Entertainment and Sport Facilities (TsNIIEP)

Azadi Tower, by Houssein Amanat, is completed in Tehran.

The Intercontinental Teheran Hotel by Rader Mileto Associates (Neal Prince) is completed.

1972

March 5: Bangladesh Prime Minister Sheikh Mujibur Rahman visits Tashkent.

July 20: UN Secretary General Kurt Waldheim visits Tashkent.

October 3: The USSR and the USA sign the Strategic Arms Limitation Treaty (SALT).

U.S.	NUCLEAR LIMITS	U.S.S.R.
200	ABM	200
1,054	ICBM	1,550
5,700 (MIRV)	WARHEADS	5,700 (MRV)
41	NUCLEAR SUBS	42

May 24–June 2: The 2nd Tashkent International Film Festival of Asia and Africa takes place at the Panoramic Cinema.

Construction and Architecture of Uzbekistan publishes two articles criticizing "faux-oriental exotica."

The Department of History and Theory of Architecture of the Faculty of Architecture at Tashkent Polytechnic Institute produces its first graduates in the field of restoration of monuments. The department's specialists compile a "program and guidelines for drawing up diploma projects on the restoration of monuments."

● The Institute of Art Studies is completed.

● The Gosbank building is completed.

● The Ministries Building is completed.

● The first nine-story residential building on Bogdan Khmel'nitskii Street is completed.

1973

July 17: King Mohammad Zahir Shah's cousin, Mohammad Daoud Khan, stages a coup and establishes a one-party regime in Afghanistan.

February: The Panoramic Cinema screens Sergei Gerasimov's film *The Love of Mankind* about young architects.

Law of the USSR "On the Protection and Use of Historical and Cultural Monuments."

A number of institutions in Uzbekistan (Institute of Archeology, Institute of History and Institute of Art Studies) begin work on the "Code of Historical and Cultural Monuments of the USSR."

The nearly 20-year construction of Shahid Bahonar University of Kerman, Iran, begins.

1974

The UzSSR celebrates its 50th anniversary, in connection with which a number of "jubilee buildings" are constructed in Tashkent.

The 1973 crisis is followed by an oil boom that causes severe inflation in Iran. Tens of thousands of foreign specialists are invited to the country to introduce American oil production equipment.

May 20: The 3rd Tashkent International Film Festival of Asia and Africa opens in the Panoramic Cinema.

The Republican Conference on Earthquake-Resistant Construction in the UzSSR is held in Tashkent.

In Ashkhabad, the construction of the Karl Marx Library is completed by Abdula Akhmedov.

The Indian Institute of Management, designed by Louis Kahn, is built in Ahmedabad.

● The Zarafshan Restaurant is completed.

● The State Museum of Arts is completed.

● The Exhibition Hall of the Union of Artists is completed.

● The Uzbekistan Hotel is completed.

● The House of Publishers is completed.

● The Ts-27 residential buildings are completed.

1975

January 15: The USSR denounces the disarmament treaty with the USA.

April 13: The Lebanon Civil War begins.

July 17: The *Soyuz* (USSR) and *Apollo* (USA) spacecraft dock in orbit.

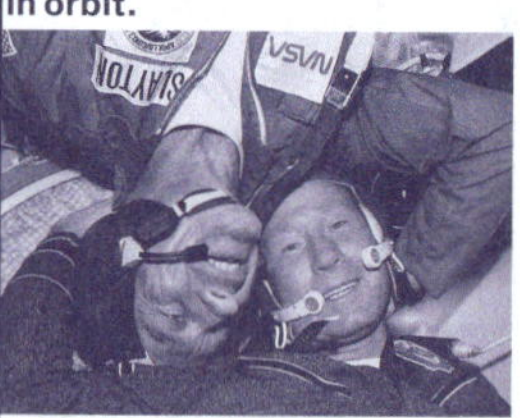

In Tashkent, architectural historians raise the issue of including eleven buildings from the 1920s and early 1930s in the "Code of Historical and Cultural Monuments of the USSR."

A group of authors is awarded the State Prize of the USSR for the architecture of the center of Tashkent.

Sharif University of Technology (SUT), by Houssein Amanat, is built in Tehran.

In Algiers (Algeria), the Hôtel El Aurassi is built by Luigi Moretti.

● The Institute of Pectoral Surgery main building is completed.

● The Delegation House of the Central Committee of the Uzbekistan Communist Party is completed.

● The Circus is completed.

● The Tashkent Institute of Irrigation and Agricultural Melioration (TIIMSKh) is completed.

● The House of Youth is completed.

1976

February 24–March 5: The 25th CPSU Congress ignores the economic slowdown of the USSR. Among other decisions, the Congress resolves to start work on diverting the flows of Siberian rivers to Central Asia.

Mark Weil, founder of the Ilkhom Theater, stages his first street theater performance.

May 19–29: The 4th Tashkent International Film Festival of Asia, Africa and Latin America opens at the Panoramic Cinema. Participants are accommodated in the Uzbekistan Hotel.

September: The State Museum of Arts presents the exhibition *Ten Centuries of Iranian Art*.

October 29: Law of the USSR "On the Protection and Use of Historical and Cultural Monuments."

Moshe Safdie designs Habitat Tehran, which remains unbuilt.

The Palast der Republik, by Heinz Graffunder, is inaugurated in Berlin. It hosts the Volkskammer, the parliament of East Germany, from 1976 to 1990.

● The Ministry of Energy is completed.

● The Samarkand Teahouse is completed.

1977

June 16: Leonid Brezhnev begins to combine the posts of General Secretary of the CPSU Central Committee and Chairman of the USSR Supreme Soviet.

July 10: A new USSR constitution is adopted. The USSR celebrates the 60th anniversary of the October Revolution.

The Ilkhom Creative Youth Studio is established at the House of Youth, where the basement and foyer are remodeled to accommodate the studio.

January: An exhibition of works on paper by Uzbekistan artists is held in the Exhibition Hall of the Union of Artists.

March: An exhibition of Bakhodyr Dzhalalov's work is held at the Ilkhom Theater exhibition hall.

April 29: The exhibition *Women of Uzbekistan Are Active Participants in Communist Construction* opens at the Lenin Museum.

June: An exhibition of works by Aleksei Isupov takes place at the State Museum of Arts.

October: An exhibition of People's Artist of the UzSSR Vladimir Kaidalov is held in the Exhibition Hall of the Union of Artists.

The first metro line is commissioned as the main "jubilee" object in Tashkent.

The Tehran Museum of Contemporary Art, by Kamran Diba, is completed.

- The Hammom Steam Baths, designed by Andrei Kosinskii, are completed.
- The TV Center is completed.

- The addition of the Small Hall to the Panoramic Cinema is completed.

1978

January 10–16: The Uzbek cosmonaut Vladimir Dzhanibekov makes the first of his five space flights.

April 30: The Democratic Republic of Afghanistan is proclaimed, with President Nur Mohammad Taraki launching a program of socialist construction.

May 23–June 1: The 5th Tashkent International Film Festival of Asia, Africa and Latin America opens at the Panoramic Cinema. Participants are accommodated at the Uzbekistan Hotel.

October 17–21: The IUPAC International Symposium on Macromolecular Chemistry is held at the Panoramic Cinema, which underwent emergency reconstruction due to a major fire that destroyed the main hall and part of the lobby three months earlier. The symposium is attended by over 2,500 scientists from 28 countries.

December: The State Museum of Arts hosts an exhibition of works by Aleksandr Nikolaev (Usto Mumin).

December: The Ilkhom Theater stages the play *Duck Hunt* about conformism and its conflicts.

Edward Said's *Orientalism* is published in New York. There is no mention of him in the texts of the protagonists of Tashkent architecture.

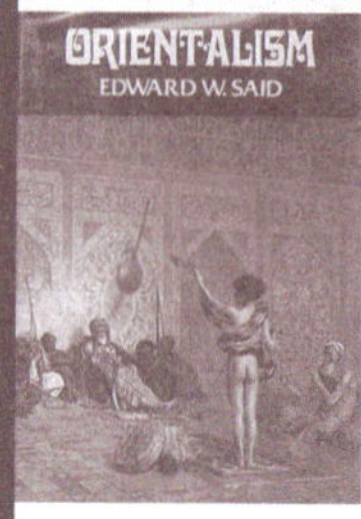

The 3rd plenum of the Society for the Protection of Historical and Material Cultural Monuments of Uzbekistan is held in Tashkent, focusing on urban planning aspects of the protection of monuments.

By Decree of the Council of Ministers of the UzSSR, the Uzbek Special Scientific and Restoration Project Workshop (UzSNRPM) is transformed into the Uzbek Research and Project Institute of Conservation and Restoration of Cultural Monuments (UzNIIP-Irestavratsii).

The 5th General Assembly, on "The Protection of Historical Cities and Historical Quarters in the Framework of Urban Development," is held in Moscow.

1979

February 11: The Islamic Revolution succeeds in Iran.

June 17: The USSR and the USA sign the SALT II strategic arms limitation treaty.

July 3: The United States finds it necessary in the current situation to provide military assistance to the rebels in Afghanistan via Pakistan. President Jimmy Carter signs the first directive on secret aid to opponents of the pro-Soviet regime in Kabul. His security adviser, Zbigniew Brzezinski, predicts that this will lead to Soviet military intervention.

December 25: The USSR sends troops to Afghanistan. President Hafizullah Amin is assassinated on December 27.

May: An exhibition of works by Ural Tansykbaev is held at the State Museum of Arts.

May: An exhibition of works by Vladimir Burmakin is held at the Institute of Art Studies.

December: An exhibition of works by Pavel Ben'kov is held at the State Museum of Arts.

Bertolt Brecht's *The Bourgeois Wedding* is staged at the Ilkhom Theater.

February 24: Resolution No. 149 of the Uzbek SSR "On Measures to Further Improve the Management of the Protection and Restoration of Monuments of Tangible Cultural Significance of the Republic."

August 19: The Burra Charter is signed in Burra, Australia.

The Main Scientific and Production Directorate for the protection, restoration and use of cultural monuments, fine arts, construction and repair of monuments is created (GlavNPU of cultural monuments of the Ministry of Culture of the UzSSR).

The 4th Congress of the Society for the Protection of Historical and Cultural Monuments of Uzbekistan is held.

Habitat East-Village "prototype," by Justus Dahinden and Associates, is built in Amirabad, Iran.

1980

July 19–August 3: Over 60 countries boycott the Moscow Olympics.

January: The State Museum of Arts presents an exhibition of works by Nikolai and Sviatoslav Roerich.

May 20–30: The 6th Tashkent International Film Festival of Asia, Africa and Latin America opens at the Panoramic Cinema. Participants are accommodated at the Uzbekistan Hotel.

December: The All-Union Exhibition of Young Artists is shown at the Exhibition Hall of the Union of Artists.

December: The Ilkhom Theater presents *Magomed, Mamed, Mamish*, about corruption among the Soviet elite.

April: The 11th Congress of Architects of Uzbekistan is held in Tashkent.

Andrei Kosinskii leaves Tashkent.

December: Joint plenum of the board of the Union of Architects of Uzbekistan and the UzSSR Council of Arts, "Problems of Synthesis of Architecture and Monumental Art."

● The Institute of Pectoral Surgery conference hall is completed.

● The Palace of Aviation Constructors is completed.

1981

February 3: The 20th Congress of the Communist Party of the USSR opens in the Peoples' Friendship Palace.

April 12: First flight of the US Space Shuttle program.

December 13: Polish Council of Ministers Chairman Wojciech Jaruzelski declares martial law in the country.

March: The Ilkhom Theater presents the play *Scenes at the Fountain*, described by an official critic as "a model of social pessimism."

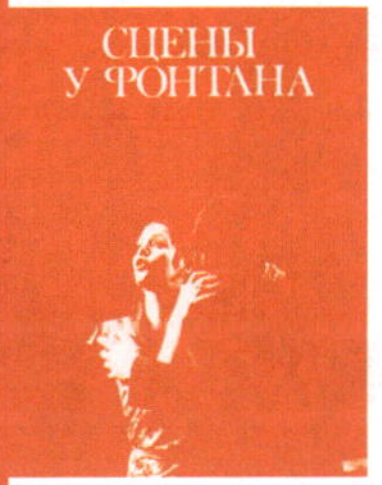

● The Peoples' Friendship Palace is completed.

1982

November 10: Leonid Brezhnev dies.

November 12: Iurii Andropov becomes General Secretary of the CPSU Central Committee.

December: The Consulate-General of Afghanistan opens in Tashkent in the presence of Foreign Minister Shah Mohammad Dost.

May 25: The 7th Tashkent International Film Festival of Asia, Africa and Latin America opens at the Peoples' Friendship Palace.

September 11: The 1st All-Union Golden Autumn Festival Tashkent opens at the Peoples' Friendship Palace.

September 11: Evgenii Shvarts' 1943 play *The Dragon: A Fairytale*, which exposes the links between totalitarian societies of the twentieth century, is staged at the Ilkhom Theater.

SNiP II-7-81 "Construction in Seismic Areas" (Gosstroi USSR).

January: Visiting plenum in Bukhara of the board of the Union of Architects of Uzbekistan, "The Problem of Heritage Development in the Modern Architecture of Uzbekistan."

October 22: In Tashkent the expanded presidium of the board of the Union of Architects of Uzbekistan hears Sergo Sutiagin's report "On the Problems of Originality in the Architecture of Uzbekistan."

- The Chorsu Hotel is completed.

- The House of Cinema is completed.

1983

April: First detentions are made in the so-called "cotton case," about corruption in the UzSSR government.

August 1: The USSR Council of Ministers creates a Commission for Economic Experiments.

September 5: The 4th session of the Intergovernmental Council of the UNESCO Communication Development Program is held in Tashkent.

October 31: Sharaf Rashidov dies.

ПРАВДА ВОСТОКА

ГЛУБОКОЕ СОБОЛЕЗНОВАНИЯ

November 3: Inamzhon Usmankhodzhaev (an architect by training) is elected First Secretary of the Central Committee of the Communist Party of Uzbekistan.

January: The State Museum of Arts presents an exhibition of works from the collection of the Nukus Museum.

September 6: An exhibition of Japanese art opens at the State Museum of Arts.

September 6: The exhibition *Tashkent: City of Peace and Friendship* opens in the Exhibition Hall of the Union of Artists.

September 9: An event at the Peoples' Friendship Palace marks the 2,000th anniversary of Tashkent.

September: The 2nd All-Union Golden Autumn Festival Tashkent is held.

September 21: Law No. 1002-X of the USSR "On the Protection and Use of Historical and Cultural Monuments."

ЗАБОТА О СОХРАНЕНИИ ИСТОРИЧЕСКИХ И ДРУГИХ КУЛЬТУРНЫХ ЦЕННОСТЕЙ — ДОЛГ И ОБЯЗАННОСТЬ ГРАЖДАН СССР

The Union of Architects of Uzbekistan holds an architectural competition for a memorial dedicated to the 2,000th anniversary of Tashkent.

February: The Inter-republican Zonal Conference of the Central Asian Regional Group of ICOMOS is held in Tashkent.

April 29: The Union of Architects of Uzbekistan holds a meeting with members of the bureau of the Department of Architecture and Monumental Art of the Academy of Arts of the USSR, dedicated to the problem of national identity in the modern architecture and monumental art of Uzbekistan.

September: The House of Architects presents the exhibition *Tashkent Yesterday, Today, Tomorrow* to mark the 2,000th anniversary of Tashkent.

1984

February 9: Iurii Andropov dies.

February 13: Konstantin Chernenko succeeds Andropov as General Secretary of the CPSU Central Committee.

Revelations and detentions in the so-called "cotton case" continue; Sharaf Rashidov's leadership methods are criticized.

May: The 8th Tashkent International Film Festival of Asia, Africa and Latin America opens at the Peoples' Friendship Palace.

September: The 3rd All-Union Golden Autumn Festival Tashkent is held.

June: The plenum of the Union of Architects of Uzbekistan, "Traditions and Modernity of Uzbek Soviet Architecture," is held in Tashkent.

● The Cosmonauts Avenue metro station is completed.

1985

March 10: Konstantin Chernenko dies and is succeeded as General Secretary of the CPSU Central Committee by Mikhail Gorbachev.

April 23: The plenum of the CPSU Central Committee announces a course for "acceleration" (of economic development).

August: The exhibition *Showing Young Artists* takes place at the Union of Artists Exhibition Hall.

September 10: The 4th All Union Golden Autumn Festival Tashkent opens at the Peoples' Friendship Palace.

● The TV Tower is completed.

● The Zhemchug residential building is completed.

1986

January 28: The space shuttle *Challenger* is lost.

February 25–March 6: The 27th Congress of the CPSU.

April 26: Accident at the Chernobyl nuclear power plant.

December 16: Riots in Kazakhstan after the resignation of First Secretary Dzhinmukhammed Kunaev.

May: The 9th Tashkent International Film Festival of Asia, Africa and Latin America opens at the Peoples' Friendship Palace.

An exhibition at the State Museum of Arts marks the centenary of Aleksandr Volkov.

Ragtime for Clowns, a performance based on pantomime, is staged at the Ilkhom Theater.

An exhibition of Andrei Krikis' works is held at the Ilkhom Theater.

Charter of the Society for the Protection of Historical and Material Cultural Monuments of Uzbekistan.

March 19–21: The 12th Congress of Architects of Uzbekistan takes place in Tashkent.

April 14–23: The 7th International Meeting of National Committees of the Working Group of Socialist Countries on Restoration of Monuments of History, Culture and Museum Values takes place in Tashkent.

August: The exhibition *Iraq Today* is shown in the hall of the Union of Architects of Uzbekistan.

The Pakistani parliament building, designed by Edward Durell Stone, is completed in Islamabad.

● Ben'kov Art College is completed.

1987

January 27: The plenum of the CPSU Central Committee sets the course for perestroika, which includes democratization of power, decentralization of the economy and a policy of glasnost (openness).

June 28: The 19th All-Union Conference of the CPSU adopts a draft constitutional reform introducing Congresses of People's Deputies and the post of President of the USSR.

The exhibition *Rehabilitation of Opportunities* is held at the Ilkhom Theater.

Gayatri Chakravorty Spivak publishes the essay "Can the Subaltern Speak?"

Richard Bleze's team (UzNIIP-gradostroitel'stva) is awarded first prize in the Union of Architects competition for the Tashkent city center.

The jury of the competition of the State Construction Committee and the Union of Architects of Uzbekistan for the building of the Supreme Soviet does not select a winner.

1981–1987: The Arab World Institute is built in Paris by Jean Nouvel.

● The sixteen-story residential building on Bogdan Khmel'nitskii Street is completed.

● The Republican House of Tourism is completed.

● The Sun Heliocomplex is completed.

1988

January 12: Inamzhon Usmankhodzhaev is removed as First Secretary of the Central Committee of the Communist Party of the Uzbek SSR due to accusations in the so-called "cotton case." His post is taken by Rafik Nishanov.

May 15: The USSR begins withdrawal of troops from Afghanistan. The last troops will be withdrawn on February 15, 1989.

January: Days of Architecture of Uzbekistan takes place in Tashkent, with exhibitions at the Panoramic Cinema, the hall of the Union of Architects of Uzbekistan, the City Executive Committee and other venues.

February 25: The American exhibition *Informatics in the USA* opens at the All-Union Exhibition Center.

May 24–30: The 10th Tashkent International Film Festival of Asia, Africa and Latin America opens at the Peoples' Friendship Palace.

September: An exhibition of works by young artists from Central Asia and Kazakhstan is presented in the Exhibition Hall of the Union of Artists.

September 14: Prime Minister of Finland Harri Holkeri, during a trip to Tashkent, visits the Peoples' Friendship Palace and the Khamid Olimjon metro station.

The new club "Friends of Cinema" organizes sessions of "non-commercial films" at the Republican House of Tourism.

TashZNIIEP develops the "Recommendations on Modernization, Reconstruction and Anti-seismic Reinforcement of Residential Buildings."

A visiting meeting of the editors in chief of the USSR construction magazines is held in Tashkent on the topic of "Mass Housing in Hot Climate Conditions."

1989

Abrupt political changes and revolutions take place in Eastern Europe. Soviet republics such as Lithuania, Latvia, Armenia and Azerbaijan begin to reinstate national languages and declare independence.

April: The Afghan Civil War, which began in 1989, ends. Afghan political parties sign the Peshawar Accord, which creates the Islamic State of Afghanistan and proclaims Sibghatullah Mojadded its interim president.

June 23: Rafik Nishanov resigns as First Secretary of the Central Committee of the Communist Party of the Uzbek SSR and Islam Karimov is appointed in his place.

December 27: Inamzhon Usmankhodzhaev is sentenced to twelve years in jail on corruption charges. He is released in 1990.

March 16: An Evening of International Friendship between Cuba, Uzbekistan and Tajikistan is held at the House of Youth.

March 30: The Congress of Agrarians of Uzbekistan is held at the Peoples' Friendship Palace.

April 10: An exhibition of works by Lutfulla Abdullaev is held at the Union of Artists.

April 13: An exhibition from the Irkutsk Arts Museum, of Russian portraits from the eighteenth to the early twentieth century, opens at the State Museum of Arts.

May 17: The international forum "Women for Peace and Peace for Women" opens at the Republican House of Tourism.

May 29: Tashkent-89, a meeting of twin cities of the USSR and the USA, opens at the Intourist Culture and Information Center and the Uzbekistan Hotel, including an exhibition at the Intourist Center of works by artists from Tashkent and Seattle.

May 29: An exhibition marking the 50th anniversary of the Union of Artists takes place in the Exhibition Hall.

June 29–July 7: Days of Architecture of Uzbekistan takes place in Tashkent, with thematic exhibitions in the hall of the Union of Architects of Uzbekistan and at the project institutes.

August 14: The Tanovar traditional Uzbek dance ensemble performs at the Museum of Applied Arts.

February–March: The Union of Architects of Uzbekistan hosts an exhibition of diploma works of graduates of Tashkent Polytechnic Institute and Samarkand State Architecture and Construction Institute, marking the 60th anniversary of architectural education in Uzbekistan.

The Union of Architects of Uzbekistan receives the Secretary General of the Aga Khan Foundation, Said Ibrahim Zulfiqar (Egypt).

1981–1989: I.M. Pei conceives and implements the construction of the Louvre Pyramid.

1990

National conflicts unfold in the South Caucasus and Central Asia.

February 26: The Congress of People's Deputies of the USSR adopts a law on various forms of ownership.

March 15: Mikhail Gorbachev becomes President of the USSR.

ИЗВЕСТИЯ

М. ГОРБАЧЕВ—ПРЕЗИДЕНТ СССР

March 24: Islam Karimov is elected President of the Uzbek SSR, retaining the post of First Secretary of the Central Committee of the Communist Party of Uzbekistan.

June 12: The Russian Soviet Federative Socialist Republic (RSFSR) declares state sovereignty.

June 14: The last Congress of the Communist Party of the Uzbek SSR opens at the Panoramic Cinema.

June 20: Uzbekistan declares state sovereignty.

July 2–13: The 28th and last Congress of the CPSU is held in Moscow.

1991

From 1992 on, all events are related to Uzbekistan.

December 7: The second stage of the 22nd Congress of the Communist Party of the UzSSR opens at the Panoramic Cinema.

March 20: The Congress of Agrarians of Uzbekistan is held at the Peoples' Friendship Palace.

May 13: The newspaper *Truth of the East* reports on preparations for an exhibition of works by the Russian avant-garde at the State Museum of Arts.

September 14: The Uzbekistan Hotel hosts participants of the World Islamic Conference "The Spiritual Heritage of At-Termezi and Modernity."

October 26: The exhibition *Iranian Art from the Fifteenth to the Twentieth Century* opens at the State Museum of Arts.

October 29: An exhibition of works by Indian artists opens at the State Museum of Arts.

June 20: An exhibition of works by ceramist-monumentalist Aleksandr Kedrin opens in the hall of the Union of Architects of Uzbekistan.

● The Chorsu Bazaar is completed.

March 17: In the referendum on the preservation of the USSR, the majority, including the citizens of Uzbekistan (93.7%), give an affirmative answer (six republics boycott the referendum).

August 19–21: The failed August Coup leads to a sharp weakening of Gorbachev's power.

November 1: Founding Congress of the People's Democratic Party of Uzbekistan, which elects Islam Karimov as party chairman.

December 25: Mikhail Gorbachev announces his resignation from the presidency. The USSR is officially dissolved.

The New York Times

GORBACHEV, LAST SOVIET LEADER, RESIGNS; U.S. RECOGNIZES REPUBLICS' INDEPENDENCE

Communist Flag Is Removed; Yeltsin Gets Nuclear Control

The Soviet State, Born of a Dream, Dies

December 29: Islam Karimov wins the presidential election in Uzbekistan (98% of citizens are in favor of state independence).

December: Islam Karimov pardons all those convicted in the "cotton case." The rehabilitation of Sharaf Rashidov begins.

March 23: The Congress of Agrarians of Uzbekistan is held at the Peoples' Friendship Palace.

March 27: The 4th republican sculpture exhibition opens at the State Museum of Arts.

April 15: An alley is created and trees are planted at the Tashkent Circus, dedicated to the 125th anniversary of the birth of Tashkenbai Egamberdiev, founder of the Tashkenbaev dynasty of circus performers.

May 5: Opening of an exhibition of works by Syrian calligrapher Mohammad Ghannoum at the State Museum of Arts.

May 16: An exhibition of Russian porcelain from the eighteenth to the twentieth century opens at the State Museum of Arts.

May 29: An event marking the 85th birthday of the Uzbek actress Tamara Khanum is held at the Peoples' Friendship Palace.

July: An exhibition of works by graphic artists Sergei Abaturov, Vladimir Liss and Igor Shipovskii takes place at the House of Youth.

October: An exhibition of works by Ruza Chariev is held at the State Museum of Arts.

October: An exhibition dedicated to Alisher Navoi is held at the Exhibition Hall of the Union of Artists.

November: An exhibition of works by Markos Karpuzas takes place at the Ilkhom Theater.

November 1: The Founding Congress of the People's Democratic Party of Uzbekistan is held at the Panoramic Cinema.

1992

January 2: Diplomatic relations are established between Uzbekistan and China (later in the year diplomatic relations are established with dozens of other countries).

May 15: In Tashkent, the newly independent countries of Armenia, Kazakhstan, Kyrgyzstan, Russia, Tajikistan and Uzbekistan sign the Collective Security Treaty ("Tashkent Treaty").

October 16: The Tashkent International Film Festival closes.

The Ilkhom Theater presents *Happy Beggars* (based on a play by Carlo Gozzi), which centers on a tyrant, the secret police and the residents of Samarkand, who dream of emigration.

February 28: The Congress of Architects of Uzbekistan opens.

July: Three Tashkent architects—Sergo Sutiagin, Iosif Notkin and Mitkhat Bulatov—are elected to the Moscow branch of the International Academy of Architecture.

September 19: The Aga Khan Award in the field of architecture is presented at Registan Square in Samarkand.

1993

January 4: A meeting of the presidents of Kazakhstan, Kyrgyzstan, Tajikistan, Turkmenistan and Uzbekistan is held at the Peoples' Friendship Palace.

February 2: President Karimov signs the "Decree on Private Land Ownership."

April 5: Negotiations between the presidents of Uzbekistan and Turkey are held at the Peoples' Friendship Palace.

September 2: Uzbekistan announces the replacement of the Cyrillic alphabet with the Latin alphabet by 2000.

November 15: Uzbekistan introduces the "Sum-Kupon" monetary unit.

January: The State Museum of the History of Uzbekistan presents the exhibition *Uyghur Contemporary Art*.

January 27: The Exhibition Hall of the Union of Artists presents an exhibition of works by Karakalpak artists.

April 18: An evening at the Circus marks the 50th anniversary of the troupe.

June 29–July 7: Days of Architecture of Uzbekistan takes place in Tashkent, with thematic exhibitions in the hall of the Union of Architects of Uzbekistan and at the project institutes.

September 1: An exhibition about Uzbekistan's independence opens at the Exhibition Hall of the Union of Artists.

November: The Exhibition Hall of the Union of Artists presents an international exhibition of eleven galleries from Kazakhstan, Turkmenistan and Kyrgyzstan.

April 3: The Union of Architects of Uzbekistan discusses creating the International Union of Architects of Uzbekistan, Turkey, Tajikistan, Kyrgyzstan, Turkmenistan and Azerbaijan.

● The Turkestan Palace is completed.

1994

April 20: The "Tashkent Treaty" comes into force.

April 27: Negotiations between the presidents of Uzbekistan and France are held at the Peoples' Friendship Palace.

July 1: A new national currency, the Sum, is introduced in Uzbekistan.

October 10: Negotiations between the presidents of Uzbekistan and Tajikistan are held at the Peoples' Friendship Palace.

December 22: Negotiations between the presidents of Uzbekistan and Belarus are held at the Peoples' Friendship Palace.

January: An exhibition-sale is held at the State Museum of Arts, several paintings of which end up in the museum's collection.

March 1: The art group Association 23 shows in the Exhibition Hall of the Union of Artists.

July 18: A presentation of the German Konrad Adenauer Foundation takes place at the Peoples' Friendship Palace.

August 22: The gala concert of the Festival of Creativity of the Peoples of Uzbekistan is held at the Peoples' Friendship Palace.

September 28: A CSCE (Conference on Security and Cooperation in Europe) seminar is held at the Peoples' Friendship Palace, concluding a series of meetings organized by CSCE in Central Asian capitals.

October 13: An international conference marking the 600th anniversary of the birth of Samarkand astronomer and statesman Mirzo Ulugbek opens at the Peoples' Friendship Palace.

December 9: An exhibition of works by the People's Artist of Uzbekistan, ceramist Muhiddin Rakhimov, opens at the State Museum of Arts.

December 23: The Cabinet of Ministers of Uzbekistan adopts a resolution on improving the activities of museums, according to which the State Museum of Arts is slated for reconstruction.

The Uzneftegazstroi building, unfinished in the 1980s, is decorated with aluminum and tinted glass.

● April: A joint venture with foreign funding is formed to reconstruct the Uzbekistan Hotel.

● The Turkestan Arena is completed.

1995

March 26: A referendum extends Islam Karimov's presidential term until 2000.

1996

KMK 2.01.03-96 Construction in Seismic Areas: Design Standards (Goskomarkhitektstroi RUz).

December 6: The law of the Republic of Uzbekistan on architecture and planning is published.

Mark Weil directs *End of the Century: Tashkent*, a film exploring the city's cultural evolution throughout the twentieth century.

● May 15: The Ardus supermarket begins operating at the Zarafshan Restaurant (the first reconstruction of the building using alucobond).

● Reconstruction of the House of Youth (Shodlik Hotel).

1999

February 16: The building of the Cabinet of Ministers of the Republic (originally the Council of Ministers) is seriously damaged by an explosion. The government makes the decision to rebuild it, changing its forms and materials.

● The Hammom Steam Baths, designed by Andrei Kosinskii, are demolished.

2000

● Reconstruction of the Panoramic Cinema begins.

● Reconstruction of the Lenin Museum (State Museum of the History of Uzbekistan).

● Reconstruction of the Uzbekistan Hotel.

● Reconstruction of the State Museum of Arts.

2001

October: The 1st Tashkent Biennale of Contemporary Art, organized by the Academy of Arts, is held in the Exhibition Hall of the Union of Artists.

August 30: Law No. 269-II of the Republic of Uzbekistan "On the Protection and Use of Objects of Cultural Heritage."

● Reconstruction of the Uzbekistan Hotel.

2002

February 27: As a result of a referendum, the presidential term is extended from 5 to 7 years.

July 29: Regulation No. 269 of the Republic of Uzbekistan "On Measures to Enhance the Protection and Use of Cultural Heritage Objects."

● Reconstruction of the façade of the State Museum of Arts, radically changing the building's appearance.

2003

October: The 2nd Tashkent Biennale of Contemporary Art, organized by the Academy of Arts of Uzbekistan and the Tashkent Khokimiyat, is held in the Exhibition Hall of the Union of Artists.

2005

October 3–6: The 3rd Tashkent Biennale, "East and West: Myth and Beauty," organized by the Forum of Culture and Art of Uzbekistan Foundation and the Academy of Arts of Uzbekistan, is held in the Exhibition Hall of the Union of Artists.

Mark Weil stages the play *Radiance with Pomegranate*, dedicated to a fantasy interpretation of the life and work of the artist Aleksandr Nikolaev (Usto Mumin), at the Ilkhom Theater.

● Reconstruction of the Lenin Museum (State Museum of the History of Uzbekistan).

● Radical reconstruction of the Ministries Building on Lenin Square, with changes to the number of floors, façades and plans of the complex.

2006

Mark Weil stages the theater's most poignant political play, *Flights of Mashrab*, on the stage of the Ilkhom Theater.

2007

December 23: Islam Karimov wins the presidential election.

October 2–9: The 4th Tashkent International Biennale of Contemporary Art, "New: Illusions and Reality," organized by the Forum of Culture and Art of Uzbekistan Foundation and the Tashkent Khokimiyat, is held in the Exhibition Hall of the Union of Artists.

September 7: Mark Weil's death.

2008

● The former Gosplan building, by Richard Bleze, is radically rebuilt, resulting in the loss of its modernist appearance.

2009

October 15–22: The 5th Tashkent Biennale of Contemporary Art, "Philosophy of the City: Anthropological Landscape," organized by the Forum of Culture and Art of Uzbekistan Foundation, the Academy of Arts of the Republic of Uzbekistan and the UNESCO office in Uzbekistan, is held in the Exhibition Hall of the Union of Artists.

October 13: Law No. ORQ-229 of the Republic of Uzbekistan "On the Protection and Use of Archeological Heritage Objects."

- The former Zarafshan Restaurant is radically rebuilt, resulting in the loss of its modernist appearance.

- The former Samarkand Teahouse is radically rebuilt, resulting in the loss of its modernist appearance.

2010

- Reconstruction of the Institute of Art Studies.

- Reconstruction of the Exhibition Hall of the Union of Artists.

- Reconstruction of the House of Publishers.

2011

October 23–29: The 6th Tashkent Biennale of Contemporary Art, "Contemporary Art: Territory of the Artist and Society," organized by the Forum of Art and Culture of Uzbekistan Foundation, opens in various locations, including the Exhibition Hall of the Union of Artists.

February 23: Resolution No. 47 of the Cabinet of Ministers of the Republic of Uzbekistan "On the Approval of Regulatory Documents for the Protection of Intangible Cultural Heritage."

- Reconstruction of the Institute of Art Studies.

2013

- The former building of Uzbekbrlyashu (Academy of Public Administration under the President of the Republic of Uzbekistan) is completely rebuilt, resulting in the loss of its modernist appearance.

2014

July 21: Decision No. 200 of the Cabinet of Ministers of Uzbekistan "On Additional Measures to Further Improve the Protection and Use of Objects of Tangible Cultural and Archeological Heritage."

2015

March 29: Islam Karimov wins the presidential election for his 4th presidential term.

2016

September 2: Islam Karimov dies.

December 14: Shavkat Mirziyoyev is elected President of the Republic of Uzbekistan.

● The conference hall of the former building of the Central Committee of the Communist Party of Uzbekistan (now the Office of the President of the Republic of Uzbekistan) is completely rebuilt, resulting in the loss of its modernist appearance.

2017

● Due to the announcement of the construction of the Tashkent City district, four modernist buildings are demolished: the House of Cinema, the House of Forestry Workers, the Pioneer Palace and the Geology Museum.

2018

January 16: Decree No. F-5181 of the President of the Republic of Uzbekistan.

December 19: Decision No. PQ-4068 of the President of the Republic of Uzbekistan "On Measures to Improve Activity in the Field of Protection of Objects of Tangible Cultural and Archeological Heritage and Improving Their Use."

● Reconstruction of the Peoples' Friendship Palace.

● The modernist building of the Central Bank is rebuilt.

2019

March 30: Resolution No. 265 of the Republic of Uzbekistan "On the Approval of the Regulations on the Use and Protection of Objects of Tangible Cultural Heritage and the Organization of the Activities of the Department of Cultural Heritage under the Ministry of Culture of Uzbekistan."

July 17: Decision No. 598 of the Cabinet of Ministers of Uzbekistan "On the Organization of the Activity of the Scientific Research Center for the Restoration of Cultural Heritage Objects and Art Objects under the Uzbekistan Art and Culture Development Foundation."

August 30: Law No. ORQ-560 of the Republic of Uzbekistan "On Amendments and Additions to Certain Legislative Documents of the Republic of Uzbekistan with Respect to Strengthening the Protection of Tangible Cultural Heritage Objects."

October 4: Resolution No. 846 of the Cabinet of Ministers of the Republic of Uzbekistan "On the Approval of the National List of Real Estate Objects of Tangible Cultural Heritage."

October 11: The new law of the Republic of Uzbekistan "On Patronage" regulates relations in the field of patronage.

October 18: Decision No. 881 of the Court of Ministers of the Republic of Uzbekistan "On the Approval of the Regulations Regarding the Use of Tangible Cultural Heritage Objects."

December 20: Decision No. 1021 of the Cabinet of Ministers of the Republic of Uzbekistan.

● The modernist building of the former Tashkent City Committee and Regional Committee of the Communist Party (now the Ministry of Foreign Affairs of the Republic of Uzbekistan) is rebuilt.

2020

December 29: Resolution No. 814 of the Cabinet of Ministers of the Republic of Uzbekistan "On Organizing the Activities of the Cultural Heritage Research Institute under the Ministry of Culture of the Republic of Uzbekistan."

2021

May 22–November 21: Uzbekistan takes part in the Venice Biennale of Architecture for the first time, with a national pavilion entitled *Mahalla: Urban Rural Living*.

October 15: Launch of the Tashkent Modernism XX/XXI project, initiated by the Uzbekistan Art and Culture Development Foundation.

March 3: Decision No. 119 of the Court of Ministers of the Republic of Uzbekistan.

April 6: Decree No. UP-6199 of the Republic of Uzbekistan "On Measures to Further Improve the Public Administration System in the Fields of Tourism, Sports and Cultural Heritage."

June 19: Resolution No. PP-5150 of the Republic of Uzbekistan "On Measures for the Organization of Activities of the Agency of Cultural Heritage Under the Ministry of Tourism and Sport of the Republic of Uzbekistan, and also to Innovative Development of the Field."

October 15: Resolution No. 649 of the Cabinet of Ministers of the Republic of Uzbekistan "On Approval of the Regulations of the Agency for Cultural Heritage under the Ministry of Tourism and Sport of the Republic of Uzbekistan: On Measures to Strengthen Protection of Tangible Cultural Heritage of Sites and Territories Included in the UNESCO World Heritage List."

● The modernist building of the former Tashkent City Committee and Regional Committee of the Communist Party (now the Ministry of Foreign Affairs of the Republic of Uzbekistan) is rebuilt.

● March: The reconstruction of the VodGeo Institute is completed. It results in the loss of the building's modernist appearance.

● Reconstruction of the Panoramic Cinema.

2022

The national pavilion of Uzbekistan debuts at the Venice Biennale of Art with the exhibition *Dixit Algorizmi: The Garden of Knowledge*, commissioned by the Art and Culture Development Foundation.

October 24–28: The 9th Tashkent Biennale of Contemporary Art, "Artist and Society: Concepts of Art of the Future," organized by the Academy of Arts of Uzbekistan, is held in the Exhibition Hall of the Union of Artists.

February 18: Decision No. PQ-135 of the President of the Republic of Uzbekistan "On Organizing the Activities of the Ministry of Tourism and Cultural Heritage."

April 23: Resolution No. 209.

● The Chilanzar Shopping Center is radically rebuilt, resulting in the loss of its modernist appearance.

2023

July 9: Shavkat Mirziyoyev is re-elected as President of Uzbekistan.

April 17: The exhibition *Tashkent Modernism: Index*, initiated and commissioned by the Uzbekistan Art and Culture Development Foundation, opens at Triennale Milano.

October 18–19: The State Museum of Arts of Uzbekistan hosts the international conference *Where in the World Is Tashkent*, which coincides with the exhibition *Tashkent Modernism: Index*, dedicated to the Tashkent Modernism XX/XXI project. It is initiated and commissioned by the Uzbekistan Art and Culture Development Foundation.

2024

March 25: 157 mosaics in Tashkent and other cities of the republic are included in the register of cultural heritage.

April 22: With the passage of Resolution No. 227 of the Cabinet of Ministers of the Republic of Uzbekistan "On Introducing Amendments and Additions to the National Register of Intangible Property of Tangible Cultural Heritage," 11 modernist buildings are added to the register of cultural heritage.

Preserving a Modernist Capital

A Methodology for Preserving the Modernist Architecture of Tashkent

Davide Del Curto

What Is Preservation?

Preservation deals with the challenge of conserving and passing on to future generations tangible and intangible traces from the past that are valued and cherished by society.[1] This brief sentence contains the keywords to help us define a highly complex activity that contributed to the rise of the nineteenth-century concept of modernity in Europe. In all advanced countries this concept continued to grow in terms of importance and social recognition throughout the twentieth century, and especially since the 1970s and the so-called "cultural turn."

Preservation is a challenge because the set of activities it encompasses aims to counteract the effects of time on matter. Sooner or later, just like all human activities, it is doomed to succumb to the inevitable passing of time. Yet it is precisely this certain defeat that has given preservation a romantic, even heroic, character ever since its nineteenth-century dawn and across its multiple semantic and lexical transfers, including literature, figurative arts and the progress of science.

Preservation deals with what we currently call heritage—that is, the remnants of the past. Heritage comprises both tangible and intangible traces, continuously intertwining with each other. According to one of the most globally accepted definitions, heritage is the link between the past (i.e., the time in which we have not lived and from which we inherited), the present (i.e., the time we live in and which we must manage) and the future (i.e., the time in which we will not live, but future generations will). Preservation hence implies individual responsibility for managing a historically relevant asset, like any other property. Our present duty is to conserve what we inherit, manage it wisely and pass it on to those who will come after us, following the modern concept of history as a continuum. Of course, not everything is heritage and not everything can be preserved. Thus, preservation has had to address more and more in depth the question of defining which are the traces of the past that are valued and cherished by society—that is, how to assess the value and the social role of remnants of the past.

Architectural Preservation and the Management of History

The preservation and management of historic heritage have contributed significantly to the construction of modern European society. After the French Revolution and the fall of the empires, the newborn nations needed to build a set of values and collective identities to replace the former structure based on social classes and on the divine right of the ruling families. In this process, history served as a reservoir to select the most suitable values on which to lay the basis of the new society of nations, founded on the Enlightenment's ideals of freedom, equality and brotherhood. The choice fell on the Middle Ages, a time of peace, relative wellbeing and freedom, where power was shared rather than held by a few elite people, as would happen starting from the sixteenth century. Such an idealized view of the Middle Ages offered the perfect support for fostering peace and consensus in nineteenth-century European nation building. The so-called exoticization process made it possible to see the past as a foreign country, a place that is different, often idealized and better than the present people lived in.[2] Since architecture and the city are the locus of collective memory,[3] through a careful selection of past traces buildings came to play a fundamental role in the process of managing this. Thanks to its solid, reassuring brick walls, throughout Europe medieval architecture was taken as a model for both restoring heritage

1 François Mairesse and Renata F. Peters, eds., *What Is the Essence of Conservation? Materials for a Discussion: Papers from the ICOM-CC and ICOFOM Session at the 25th General Conference held in Kyoto, 4 September 2019* (Paris: ICOFOM, 2019), 12–13.

2 David Lowenthal, *The Past Is a Foreign Country* (Cambridge: Cambridge University Press, 1985).

3 Aldo Rossi, *The Architecture of the City* (Cambridge: MIT Press, 1982), 15.

assets and designing new buildings. The main outcome was the Gothic Revival, a unifying symbol of the new-old brotherhood among nations. The work of architects such as Karl Friedrich Schinkel (Prussia), Eugène Emmanuel Viollet-le-Duc (France), Luca Beltrami (Italy), Otto Wagner (Austria), Augustus Pugin (England) and many others testifies to that search for a collective identity through a historicist figurative language and a national style. Results went far beyond the national borders they intended to represent, and scholars later highlighted how the long period of the Gothic Revival produced an early and largely involuntary international style.[4] Something similar happened in Uzbekistan with the celebration of the Timurid era as a Renaissance and the resulting process of "Timuridization" of national memory and cultural heritage, which was deliberately restored in tsarist and Soviet times so as to make aesthetically appropriate references to that idealized period.

A century and a half later, the national pavilion of Uzbekistan at the 2023 Venice Biennale of Architecture, *Unbuild Together: Archaism vs. Modernity*, attempted to replicate the same nineteenth-century attitude toward built heritage, using it as a tool for the narrative of national history. The installation, curated by Studio KO in collaboration with students and teachers from Ajou University in Tashkent, represented the past as a labyrinth of solid bricks enveloped by darkness. The metaphor alludes to the obscurity of history, accepting that it is mostly unknown and challenging to grasp. The brick labyrinth also refers to qala architecture, that of the ancient fortresses of the Karakalpakstan region and the Khorezm civilization. Having to select an architecture with which to identify itself, Uzbekistan retraced its history and chose the strength and safeness of bricks from an archaic past, thus repeating what the new society of nations did in Europe at the end of the nineteenth century. Walking through the maze, visitors quickly travel across time, jumping from antiquity to the twentieth century, here represented by Tashkent's State Museum of Arts (1974), which is the subject of the final video installation. The presence of ceramist Abdulvahid Bukhorii, one of the few artisans still using the Blue Bukhara technique, shows how craftsmanship can help intertwine the tangible and intangible sides of heritage. The installation suggests that the future is just as uncertain as the past, but that it relies on the will of the people of the new Uzbekistan, who can therefore trust in the future. Once again, and not without a certain naivety, heritage is the means to state a brand-new national identity through a thoughtful choice of fragments from the past and to affirm "who we are" through the narrative of "who we were" or "who we wish we had been."

The Recent Past

The recent past is often difficult to manage within the narrative of national history, because temporal proximity brings up vivid memories of both the positive and negative aspects of yesterday's events. History passed very quickly during the twentieth century, which was an extremely eventful period. The inclusion of twentieth-century architecture in heritage protection lists is thus often controversial.

It took Italy half a century to separate the historical-political judgment of fascism from the historical-architectural assessment of architecture of the 1920s and 1930s. While the historical judgment of the fascist regime that led the country to the tragedy of World War II consolidated, the history of architecture began to consider those buildings from a more balanced historiographical perspective. Their extraordinary value[5] was finally acknowledged, and the correct place in the global history of twentieth-century architecture was assigned to

4 Georg Germann, *Gothic Revival in Europe and Britain: Sources, Influences and Ideas* (London: Lund Humphries, 1972).

5 Paolo Nicoloso, *Mussolini, Architect: Propaganda and Urban Landscape in Fascist Italy*, trans. Sylvia Notini (Toronto: University of Toronto Press, 2022).

absolute masterpieces such as Casa del Fascio by Giuseppe Terragni in Como or Curzio Malaparte's house by Adalberto Libera on Capri. Also, innovative research from both inside[6] and outside national borders helped overcome unavoidable stereotypes and stimulated an open debate among people with differing historiographic views.[7]

Similarly, a progressive refinement of the perspective on the recent past occurred in Germany, where the elaboration of the sense of guilt for twentieth-century crimes was the main historiographical issue for over sixty years, with consequences also for the history of architecture.[8] Winfried Speitkamp, former director of Weimar University and expert in postcolonial studies, brilliantly defined the conservation of historic buildings as "the management of history," meaning that by conserving or not conserving a building of the past, we decide what should be remembered and what can be forgotten. By retaining some buildings, i.e., the tangible evidence of the past, and abandoning others, we choose which aspects of the past we want to remember and which ones we prefer to forget. This is the history we wish to tell.[9]

How to manage the legacy of the recent past is a widespread problem in every country of the former USSR. Thirty years after independence they are now experiencing an exciting historical phase, where temporal distance makes it possible to formulate a more balanced historiographical assessment of the history and architecture of the second half of the twentieth century. The time has come to recognize that modernist architecture from the 1970s and 1980s is part of the national heritage, because the cultural values it embodies bear witness to a completed historical phase, even though it dates to the recent past.

Building Archeology

The fact that modernist architecture can and, therefore, should be preserved[10] was already clear at the beginning of the 1990s. The novelty of this issue seemed to call for a theoretical revision of the discipline of conservation toward a simplified idea of figurative restoration. However, as soon as the twentieth century was identified as a self-concluded historical phase from the historiographical point of view, its architecture became the object of inexhaustible research, which greatly contributed to the updating of the contemporary theory of preservation rather than refuting its fundamentals.[11] This renewal affected the material aspects, the reasons and regulatory means for protection and the tools for managing such a specific and extensive heritage.[12]

Alongside theoretical discussion, the conservation of twentieth-century architecture rapidly aligned with the principles of modern conservation with reference to the method of material history of built heritage (histoire matérielle du patrimoine bâti), one of the "microstories" or "particular stories" which form the history of material civilization in the wake of what Jacques Le Goff and Pierre Nora called *nouvelle histoire*, or "new history." The material history of the built environment differs from the history of architecture derived from the history of art, which identifies and traces a succession of periods dominated by a

6 Carmen Belmonte, *A Difficult Heritage: The Afterlives of Fascist-Era Art and Architecture* (Cinisello Balsamo: Silvana Editoriale, 2023).

7 Kay Bea Jones and Stephanie Pilat, eds., *The Routledge Companion to Italian Fascist Architecture: Reception and Legacy* (London: Routledge, 2021).

8 Werner Durth and Winfried Nerdinger, *Nicht vergessen... Architektur und Städtebau der 30er/40er Jahre: Ergebnisse der Fachtagung in München, 26.–28. November 1993* (Bonn: Deutsches Nationalkomitee für Denkmalschutz, 1994).

9 Winfried Speitkamp, *Die Verwaltung der Geschichte: Denkmalpflege und Staat in Deutschland 1871–1933* (Göttingen: Vandenhoeck & Ruprecht, 1996).

10 Wessel Reinik, "Altern und ewige Jugend: Restauration und Authentizität," *Daidalos*, no. 56, June 1995, 96–106.

11 Giovanni Carbonara, "Il restauro come problema di metodo," *Parametro*, no. 266, 2006, 21–55.

12 Susan Macdonald, "Conserving the Modern in the Twenty-First Century," in *Modern Architectures: The Rise of a Heritage*, ed. Maristella Casciato and Emilie d'Orgeix (Wavre: Mardaga, 2012), 149–156.

movement of ideas, a formal style, a school or a single master. Such history is, in fact, insufficient to support conservation activity, which is the goal of any research into architectural heritage. On the contrary, the material history of the built environment combines the methods of historical-archival analysis with Bauforschung, which is postclassical archeology applied to the built environment. The latter assumes that the investigation of as-built architecture is the primary source of information, alongside archive documents and previous research. The design and construction of any building typically follows a logical order: (1) client needs or political program; (2) architectural design; (3) authorization process; (4) construction; (5) as-built drawings; (6) decay, repairs, transformations. When preserving/restoring a building, this order is reversed; the building is already there, and the research needs to investigate the past going backwards: (1) decay, repairs, transformations; (2) as-built drawings; (3) construction; (4) authorization process; (5) architectural design; (6) client needs or political program. While this method is not a novelty for pre-industrial buildings, it is rather new for twentieth-century architecture, which due to its young age has rarely been studied using this approach.

This disciplinary update has undoubtedly been accomplished for the iconic buildings of modern architecture. Their restorations have in fact become laboratories for experimenting with investigation methodologies and intervention techniques, as in the cases of the former Zonnestraal sanatorium in Hilversum, the Netherlands, the Pirelli skyscraper in Milan, the experimental district Cité Satellite du Lignon in Geneva, the Narkomfin building in Moscow and numerous others. The restoration of these masterpieces was a training ground where many architects applied the archeology of the built environment to twentieth-century buildings, investigating industrial materials and techniques using the same methods already successfully tested for pre-industrial buildings. Sometimes, when historical information and archival documentation were insufficient, researchers dismantled and reassembled the building or some parts (the façade, a window, a floor) to fully understand how it was made. Thanks to such conscious disassembling, practical conservation activity has contributed significantly to a better understanding of the buildings of the past and demonstrated that in architecture, preservation is not a mere consequence of history and criticism but that, on the contrary, the two activities of architecture and preservation feed on each other continuously.[13]

However, alongside these renowned icons, there still are many twentieth-century buildings waiting to be adequately investigated, preserved and valorized. In particular, the intervention into so-called "controversial heritage" in countries of the former USSR calls for a specific sensitivity in conservation, where it is not simply a technical exercise seeking balance between figurative restoration and preservation of material authenticity, but a formidable opportunity to contribute to the process of reconciliation between communities and recent history through the heritage itself.

Elements of Architecture

More than new theory, preserving twentieth-century architecture requires specific operational tools for directly acquiring knowledge of the buildings and their components and tracing the history of construction, which can be seen as an extreme expression of industrial production in terms of materials and organization of the construction site. The material history of the built environment therefore focuses on the architecture of the industrial era, investigating the development of the

13 Paul Meurs and Maria Theresia Antoinette van Thoor, eds., *Sanatorium Zonnestraal: History and Restoration of a Modern Monument* (Rotterdam: Nai Publishers, 2010).

design phase, the history of the construction site and the history of the production of materials and assembly techniques. The innovative and experimental character of production determined modernist architecture's style and expression and laid the foundations for the subsequent degradation processes.[14] Even though the first break with tradition was made by historicism—when proto-industrial materials specifically developed for industry[15] contaminated the building sector—the Modern Movement radically innovated the way of designing buildings. The construction techniques and the physical properties of the materials made modernist architecture radically innovative in comparison to pre-industrial architecture. At the same time, they also determined the continuity between the two periods, because in both cases expression depended on materials and techniques—that is, the "elements of architecture."[16] Consequently, curtain walls, iron windows, stairs, elevators, roofings, technological systems and all the other features that are typical of twentieth-century architecture are today being studied and catalogued according to the method of building archeology, which is already commonly used to investigate pre-industrial buildings. Moreover, twentieth-century buildings were constructed using innovative, highly experimental, and often untested techniques and materials. Modernist architects focused on designing highly creative forms rather than on controlling individual details, and many decisions were taken directly on the building site. For this reason, when investigating twentieth-century architecture with the Bauforschung method, researchers often encounter significant incoherence between the as-built situation and the information offered by the drawings of the original design, or even by the narratives of the architects.[17]

Assessing the Value of Modern Architecture

Studying modern architecture through building archeology means adopting a scientific approach based on the dialectic between hypothesis and model and on experimental data, which can only derive from the investigation of as-built architecture. Assuming that the value assessment of any work of the past is relative, contemporary conservation aims to retain all parts of a heritage building because they could potentially bear several values and meanings. They only partially reveal themselves, based on the viewer's sensitivity and what Alois Riegl referred to as the Kunstwollen of our time. But they may reveal themselves fully in the future, if the conditions are right. Contemporary conservation therefore aims to preserve the inherent polysemy of every fragment of the past, to enable everyone to decipher possible meanings and values. For this reason, conservation involves protecting the physical matter, making it available for different interpretative readings and multiple narratives of the past.

To this end, the introduction of the conservation management plan (CMP) methodology has recently contributed to the conservation of twentieth-century architecture. Defined by the Burra Charter in 2013,[18] a CMP is not a restoration project—a specialized architectural project which intends to maintain authorship, even when oriented toward

14 Franz Graf and Giulia Marino, "Concerning the Research 'Material History of the Built Environment and the Conservation Project' (2008–2020), Methodology and Results," in *History of Construction Cultures: Proceedings of the 7th International Congress on Construction History (7ICCH), Lisbon, Portugal, 12–16 July 2021*, ed. João Mascarenhas-Mateus et al. (Abingdon: Taylor & Francis Group, 2021), 780–786.

15 Peter Collins, *Changing Ideals in Modern Architecture, 1750–1950*, 2nd edition (Montreal: McGill-Queen's University Press, 1998).

16 Rem Koolhaas et al., *Elements of Architecture* (Cologne: Taschen, 2018).

17 Davide Del Curto and Sofia Celli, "The Treachery of Images: Redefining the Structural System of Havana's National Art Schools," *Sustainability* 13, no. 7 (2021): 3767–3801.

18 *The Burra Charter: The Australia ICOMOS Charter for Places of Cultural Significance*, 2013.

pure conservation. Although they share a large number of objectives, a CMP is not even a conservation project, which aims to document the historic building and preserve its material authenticity:

"A conservation management plan is a document which sets out the significance of a heritage asset, and how that significance will be retained in any future use, management, alteration or repair. It is based on a very simple thinking process which starts with describing what is there, why it matters, what is happening to it and the principles by which you will manage it and then sets more detailed work programmes for maintenance, management, access, use or other issues. A plan helps you care for a site by making sure you understand what matters and why before you take major decisions. The approach can be used for any type of heritage asset, site or place."[19]

One of the most important steps in the CMP process is thus to assess the cultural significance of the site through a brief written statement. The latter is not a history or a description of the building or site but a concise paragraph summarizing its main features and values, which can be either tangible or intangible. To this end it is essential to develop a comprehensive understanding of the object, considering all relevant aspects, including history, use, transformations, etc. In accordance with this statement of significance, the CMP then outlines the overall conservation and management strategy of the asset and provides a sequence of operations to be carried out. This entails an in-depth analysis of the building/site and its context, aimed at highlighting possible risks, constraints and opportunities. Considerations about appropriate use should be developed at this time. Once exhaustive information has been collected, it is possible to further articulate the management plan by setting specific actions based on priorities, resources and timing. Through these actions the CMP aims to ensure that any possible transformation of the asset will be consistent with its original values, and hence that its cultural significance will remain intact.[20]

Building Passports and Denkmaltopographie

In line with the Burra Charter's recommendations, the research for the Tashkent Modernism XX/XXI project has involved a thorough study of the most relevant modernist buildings in Tashkent, with the objective of assessing their cultural significance and, subsequently, ensuring their protection. Data collected throughout this process were catalogued and recorded in a set of monographic dossiers—one for each selected building—thus creating an inventory of the modernist architecture of Tashkent. Each Monograph offers a detailed description of the building, encompassing historical, typological, formal and technical aspects. Given the strong connection between Tashkent modernist architecture and the post-earthquake masterplan which generated it, the Monographs consider different scales, exploring the role of individual buildings within the urban design of the capital, as well as their reciprocal relationships.[21] Information in the opening section of each Monograph supports the Statement of Significance that follows. Besides stating the main characteristics and values of the building, the Statement of Significance helps assess its authenticity and integrity. Moreover, each building's Monograph provides general measures of preservation by defining three different levels of significance and corresponding intervention strategies.[22]

19 *Conservation Management Plans: A Guide* (London: Heritage Lottery Fund, 2002).

20 James Semple Kerr, *The Conservation Plan*, 7th edition (Sydney: Australia ICOMOS, 2013).

21 In this regard see Federica Deo's essay "Earthquake as Alibi: The 1966 Tashkent General Plan and the Construction of the Modernist Capital" in this book, pp. 72–87.

22 The structure and contents of the Monographs are illustrated in Sofia Celli's essay "A Protection Inventory for Modernist Heritage" in this book, pp. 186–203.

The Monographs are not meant to be static documents, and over time they should be fed new information in order to be up-to-date and able to inform conservation policies. The current set of Monographs is an open series that can be continuously expanded to include other buildings. The inventory of Tashkent's modernist architecture contributes to the larger effort of producing the city's urban catalogue of buildings and sites of historical and cultural interest, which is no different from an inventory listing the artworks in a museum collection. Just like Tashkent's State Museum of Arts houses a collection that includes ancient, medieval and modern art, the city of Tashkent is made up of buildings of historical and artistic interest dating back to different epochs. Tashkent's Denkmaltopographie[23] now has the most recent layer, from the second half of the twentieth century.

Finally, when the Tashkent Modernism XX/XXI research started in 2021, only a few buildings were listed as National Heritage objects. Three years later, on April 22, 2024, Resolution 227 of the Cabinet of Ministers of the Republic of Uzbekistan added eleven Tashkent Modernist buildings to the National Register of Tangible Cultural Heritage. Resolution 227 adopted the Monographs as the respective buildings' passports, which, according to the national law of Uzbekistan "On the Protection and Use of Objects of Cultural Heritage,"[24] must provide the essential information about any object or building included in the Register of Tangible Cultural Heritage and determine the basis for its preservation.[25]

23 Jens Werner Jordan, Hans-Rudolf Meier and Thomas Will, eds., *Baudenkmale in Taschkent: Beiträge zu einer Denkmaltopographie* (Dresden: Thelem, 2022).
24 Law No. 269-II, August 30, 2001.
25 See Sofia Celli and Federica Deo's essay "An Overview of National Legislation for the Protection of Cultural Heritage in Uzbekistan: From the Late Soviet Period to the Present Day" in this book, pp. 176–185.

An Overview of National Legislation for the Protection of Cultural Heritage in Uzbekistan: From the Late Soviet Period to the Present Day

Sofia Celli, Federica Deo

An Introductory Note

Recognizing the value of cultural heritage assets is not enough to guarantee their preservation. Conservation principles and management tools must be incorporated into the legal and procedural frameworks guiding every nation.[1] Therefore, understanding the legal framework for the protection of cultural heritage is a fundamental step in the development of a conservation plan. On the one hand, awareness of the legal framework holds clear operative value, as is also emphasized by the Burra Charter.[2] On the other, it helps analyze and clarify the meaning of "cultural heritage" in the specific historical and cultural context.

Since gaining independence, Uzbekistan's policy has aimed to preserve its cultural heritage. To this end, besides creating a national list of protection, several historical and cultural sites have obtained recognition beyond national borders, being included in the UNESCO World Heritage List.[3] Nonetheless, so far the scientific literature on Uzbekistan's cultural heritage[4] has mainly focused on ancient times, paying little attention to twentieth-century architecture, which is just starting to find its place among objects of the past worth protecting.[5] In fact, Soviet modernist architecture shares the same fate as the worldwide heritage of modernism, the recognition of the value of which has produced a decades-long debate among international associations and institutions.[6] Due to this delay, some of Tashkent's modernist buildings have already been compromised or lost.

Against this backdrop, it might seem surprising to observe that in Uzbekistan the issue of modernist architecture started to be considered in 1990, at an extremely delicate time for the Soviet Union.[7] At that time,

1 This fundamental concept has guided interesting research by James K. Reap, Ryan M. Rowberry and Andrew P. Gamble, who have critically analyzed the cultural heritage legislation currently in force in five Central Asian countries—namely, Kazakhstan, Kyrgyzstan, Tajikistan, Turkmenistan and Uzbekistan. See James K. Reap, et al., *Preserving the Silk Road: Cultural Heritage Legislation in 5 Central Asian Countries* (Samarkand: International Institute for Central Asian Studies, 2024), 7.

2 *The Burra Charter: The Australia ICOMOS Charter for Places of Cultural Significance*, 2013.

3 To date, the World Heritage List includes seven properties located in Uzbekistan. Another thirty-two sites are on the UNESCO Tentative List. See "Uzbekistan," UNESCO World Heritage Convention, https://whc.unesco.org/en/statesparties/uz.

4 On the scientific literature about preservation of cultural heritage in Uzbekistan, see E. Baydarov, "Analysis of the Preservation of Historical and Cultural Heritage in Uzbekistan," *Eurasian Research Institute weekly e-bulletin*, no. 98, January 10–17, 2017; Sindorkul Khalikov, Azimjon Kahhorov and Nemat Abdusamatov, "The Problem of Protection and Use of Architectural Reserves of Historical Cities of Uzbekistan," *IJDIAS* 1, no. 5, 2021; O. Vileikis, E. Escalante Carrillo, S. Allayarov and A. Feyzulayev, "Documentation for Preservation: Methodology and a GIS Database of Three World Heritage Cities in Uzbekistan," in *ICOMOS/ISPRS International Scientific Committee on Heritage Documentation (CIPA): 26th International CIPA Symposium – Digital Workflows for Heritage Conservation*, ed. J. Hayes, C. Ouimet, M. Santana Quintero, S. Fai and L. Smith, 311–318; *The Workshop 2008 for Protection of Cultural Heritage at Tashkent in Uzbekistan*, Cultural Heritage Protection Cooperation Office, Asia/Pacific Cultural Centre for UNESCO, 2009; C. Shaw, "The Gur-i Amir Mausoleum and the Soviet Politics of Preservation," *Future Anterior: Journal of Historic Preservation, History, Theory, and Criticism*, vol. 8, no. 1, 2011, 43–63.

5 A first batch of modernist buildings was included in the National List of Real Estate Objects of Tangible Cultural Heritage in 2019 (Resolution of the Cabinet of Ministers of the Republic of Uzbekistan No. 846 of October 4, 2019). Further twentieth-century buildings were added to the list in 2024, together with 157 modernist mosaics (Resolutions of the Cabinet of Ministers of the Republic of Uzbekistan No. 227 of April 22, 2024, and No. 154 of March 25, 2024).

6 Among the main ones: ICOMOS (International Council on Monuments and Sites), DOCOMOMO (Working Party for the Documentation and Conservation of Buildings, Sites and Neighborhoods of the Modern Movement) and the Getty Conservation Institute. Thanks to the cooperation of a large number of associations, in April 2006 the international conference *Heritage at Risk: Preservation of Twentieth Century Architecture and World Heritage* took place in Moscow (see https://whc.unesco.org/en/events/297/).

7 The year 1990 was the climax of nationalist turmoil. At that time, thanks to the first true parliamentary elections, Lithuania, Moldova, Estonia, Latvia, Armenia and Georgia gained independence. See D. R. Marples, *The Collapse of the Soviet Union, 1985–1991* (London: Routledge, 2004); M. R. Beissinger, "Nationalism and the Collapse of Soviet Communism," *Contemporary European History*, vol. 18, no. 3, 2009, 331–347.

the leading journal in the field of architecture and construction (*Stroitel'stvo i arkhitektura Uzbekistana*) published an interesting article[8] discussing the historical value of monuments in relation to the 1976 Soviet law "On the Protection and Use of Historical and Cultural Monuments."[9] The author, Vladimir Artem'ev, raised two significant questions. The first investigated the possibility of considering the so-called *khrushchevka*[10] a "Monument of the Epoch." Indeed, despite the material and moral failure of the experiment, this building typology symbolizes an important project in socialist history, which, according to the author, argued for its preservation. The second point concerned the conservation of pre-Soviet toponymy. In this regard, referring to the case of St. Petersburg/Leningrad, the author stated that regardless of the apparent politicization of this debate, "historical truth and historical memory come first!"[11] Thirty years later, these issues are still the subject of debate. When a "cancel culture" attitude prevails, Artem'ev's discourse on the historical instance reminds us that a monument is also a document, a valuable support for both memory and knowledge.

However, the acknowledgment of the importance of Soviet modern architecture began in the second decade of the twenty-first century, thanks to a series of initiatives such as the exhibition *Soviet Modernism 1955–1991* held in 2012 at the Architekturzentrum Wien. A pioneering role in Central Asia was played by the international observatory Alerte Héritage, founded by Boris Chukhovich and Svetlana Gorshenina to raise awareness about endangered modernist heritage in Uzbekistan.[12] In the wake of these events, the Uzbekistan Art and Culture Development Foundation initiated and commissioned several research projects, making an essential contribution to the knowledge, promotion and protection of Tashkent's twentieth-century buildings. The Tashkent Modernism XX/XXI research, the *Tashkent Modernism: Index* exhibition, the international conference *Where in the World is Tashkent*, and the Tashkent Modernism app and Instagram page, together with the present volume and the book *Tashkent: A Modernist Capital*, are just a few of them.

The most relevant outcome is, however, the recent inclusion of some of Tashkent's modernist buildings in the National List of Real Estate Objects of Tangible Cultural Heritage. In particular, the Resolutions of the Cabinet of Ministers of the Republic of Uzbekistan No. 846 of October 4, 2019,[13] and No. 227 of April 22, 2024,[14] confirmed the addition of twenty-one modernist buildings to the national list of cultural heritage. Resolution No. 154 of March 25, 2024, also extended the list by including 157 mosaics dating back to the second half of the twentieth century.

8 V. Artem'ev, "Pamiatnik epokhi v sovremennoij zastroike [A Historical Monument in a Contemporary Neighborhood]," *Stroitel'stvo i arkhitektura Uzbekistana* [*Construction and Architecture of Uzbekistan*], no. 4, 1990.

9 Law of the USSR "Ob okhrane i ispol'zovanii pamiatnikov istorii i kul'tury [On the Protection and Use of Historical and Cultural Monuments]," October 29, 1976. In 1990, Law of the USSR No. 1002-X (September 21, 1983), which updated the 1976 law, was also in force.

10 The term refers to a type of low-cost prefabricated building that became widespread in the Soviet Union under Khrushchëv's leadership. These buildings were constructed as part of the efforts to quickly and affordably address the severe housing shortage in urban areas.

11 V. Artem'ev, "Pamiatnik epokhi v sovremennoij zastroike [A Historical Monument in a Contemporary Neighborhood]," 28.

12 See https://archalert.net/.

13 Resolution No. 846 of October 4, 2019, confirmed the addition of the following buildings to the national list of protection: Zhemchug residential building, Panoramic Cinema, Circus, Peoples' Friendship Palace, Museum of the History of Uzbekistan (originally Lenin Museum), TV Tower, Museum of Applied Arts, Blue Domes Café, Union of Artists Exhibition Hall, Central Committee of the Communist Party of Uzbekistan.

14 Resolution No. 227 of April 22, 2024, confirmed the addition of the following buildings to the national list of protection: Sun Heliocomplex, Uzbekistan Hotel, State Museum of Arts, TV Center, Chorsu Bazaar, Shodlik Hotel and Ilkhom Theater (originally House of Youth), Republican Specialized Scientific and Practical Medical Center for Surgery (originally Institute of Pectoral Surgery), Cosmonauts Avenue metro station, Palace of Aviation Constructors, Turkestan Arena, Delegation House of the Central Committee of the Uzbekistan Communist Party.

As the process of recognition and preservation of this recent heritage has officially begun, the aim of this contribution is to outline the national legal framework for the protection of the cultural heritage of Uzbekistan and to illustrate to what extent twentieth-century modernist architecture is represented within this regulatory framework.

On the Legislation in Force: Structure and Operational Process

The legislation protecting the cultural heritage of Uzbekistan comprises various laws and resolutions, which offer both a general framework and specific instructions on how to deal with different typologies of cultural heritage, such as archeological sites, monuments, objects of artistic value and intangible heritage.

Two laws emerge as key statutory texts. The most comprehensive law on the matter is No. 269-II "On the Protection and Use of Objects of Cultural Heritage,"[15] which was enacted in 2001, ten years after the fall of the Soviet Union. The second fundamental legislative text is Resolution No. 265 "On the Approval of the Regulations on the Use and Protection of Tangible Cultural Heritage and the Organization of the Activities of the Department of Cultural Heritage under the Ministry of Culture of Uzbekistan," issued on March 30, 2019.[16]

The two aforementioned laws are somewhat complementary. Law No. 269-II/2001 aims to "regulate relations in the field of protection and use of objects of cultural heritage, which are the national heritage of the people of Uzbekistan" (art. 1). To this end it offers definitions and describes different types of interventions and protection measures. Resolution No. 265/2019 focuses on operational processes, clarifying who is in charge of the protection of cultural heritage and illustrating the tools and resources available.[17] Note that Law No. 269-II/2001 already addressed these topics, as in part II it describes the roles and responsibilities of the public administration toward cultural heritage. Cabinet reshuffles which occurred in the last twenty years changed the organizational setup, leading to the updates provided by Resolution No. 265/2019, which, above all, established the Department of Cultural Heritage of the Republic of Uzbekistan, a new institution for the protection of tangible cultural heritage and archeological heritage sites. Three years later, according to Resolution No. 209 of April 23, 2022, the Department of Cultural Heritage was replaced by the Agency of Cultural Heritage (*O'zbekiston Respublikasi Madaniy meros agentligi,* hereinafter the Agency).

According to Law No. 269-II/2001 (and subsequent amendments), cultural heritage encompasses both tangible and intangible objects. The former includes ensembles,[18] sites[19] and monuments[20] of historical,

15 Zakon Respubliki Uzbekistan, ot 30.08.2001 g. No. 269–II.

16 Postanovlenie Kabineta Ministrov Respubliki Uzbekistan, ot 30.03.2019 g. No. 265.

17 Note that, due to cabinet reshuffles, this resolution was amended by the following documents: Decree No. PP-5150 (June 19, 2021), Resolution No. 209 (April 23, 2022) and Resolution No. 295 (May 20, 2024).

18 "Clearly localized groups within historically developed territories consisting of isolated or combined monuments, buildings, and structures of public, administrative, religious, scientific, educational, fortification, palace, residential, commercial, industrial and other purposes. These are associated with works of painting, sculpture, decorative and applied arts and architecture, whose unity or connection with the landscape represents historical, archeological, architectural, aesthetic or socio-cultural value. They also include fragments of historical layouts and settlements, works of landscape architecture and garden-park art (gardens, parks, squares, boulevards)."—Law No. 269-II/2001, art. 3.

19 "Joint creations of humans and nature, as well as territories of historical, archeological, urban planning, aesthetic, ethnological or anthropological value. These include places where folk crafts are practiced, centers of historical settlements or urban layouts and buildings, memorial sites, natural landscapes associated with historical (including military) events, monuments and the lives of outstanding historical figures, as well as cultural layers, remains of ancient city buildings, settlements, camps and ritual sites."—Law No. 269-II/2001, art. 3.

20 "Individual buildings, structures and edifices associated with works of painting, sculpture and decorative and applied arts, and their historically established territories. This category also includes "memorial houses" of historical figures;

scientific, artistic or other cultural value. Objects of tangible cultural heritage can either be categorized as of national significance or of local significance, according to their relevance (art. 4). Consequently, their management will be appointed to the state administration or to the competent regional administration.

State protection of cultural heritage (part III, art. 10–19) is assured for the objects included in the National List of Real Estate Objects of Tangible Cultural Heritage (*Gosudarstvennyj kadastr ob"ektov kul'turnogo naslediia,* hereinafter National List) or in the List of Intangible Cultural Heritage Objects (*Spisok ob"ektov material'nogo kul'turnogo naslediia*). Resolution No. 269 of July 29, 2002 ("On Measures to Enhance the Protection and Use of Cultural Heritage Objects"),[21] defines the National List as "a system of updated information and documents on the geographical location, legal status, quantitative and qualitative characteristics and assessment of cultural heritage objects" (art. 2).

The decision to list or to exclude a property from the National List is driven by its historical and cultural relevance, which is assessed by the Scientific and Expert Council of the Agency. Such evaluation not only determines the object's eligibility but also establishes the specific category to which the object belongs (according to Resolution No. 265/2019). While the Agency oversees the maintenance and monitoring of the National List—and thus participates in the process for the inclusion of new objects—the Ministry of Culture holds decision-making power. However, once an object is listed in the National List, the Agency has to fulfill tasks such as "monitoring, protecting and maintaining the state of the object, as well as identifying factors that may lead to its destruction, demolition, damage and misuse, and possibly respond with measures to address these situations."[22] Furthermore, each item included in the National List is accompanied by a document referred to as a "passport" (*pasport*). This contains essential information about the object, highlighting those features that are particularly significant and thus laying the basis for their preservation. The contents and management of the National List of Cultural Heritage Objects are regulated by the Resolution of the Cabinet of Ministers No. 269/2002. Protection measures also include the creation of a buffer zone, which is an area surrounding the listed property that is subject to specific restrictions on use and development, as well as the development of scientific and technical-scientific research on objects of cultural heritage.

Law No. 269-II/2001 also describes the possible interventions to be performed on objects of tangible cultural heritage. Article 20[23] provides definitions of Preservation (*konservatsia*), Refurbishment (*remont*), Restoration (*restavratsiia*) and Adaptation (*prisposoblenie*) to contemporary use. Article 21 even envisions the remote possibility of the complete Reconstruction (*vossozdanie*) of a lost cultural heritage site, which makes it even more surprising to find no explicit mention of maintenance or other preventive measures (e.g. routine inspections). In the last twenty years there has been a shift in conservation policies, which have moved from a reactive to a proactive approach. This means that rather than focusing on repairs, current practices aim to prevent

apartments; necropolises, mausoleums and individual burials; works of monumental art; objects of science and technology (including military); materials of anthropology, ethnography, numismatics, epigraphy and cartography; photography, films, audio and video recordings and recordings on other media; literary and artistic works; archival, manuscript and graphic documents; book manuscripts, incunabula and antique and rare editions; musical scores; relics and items of memorial significance; stone sculptures, rock paintings and archeological monuments that represent historical, scientific, artistic or other cultural value."—Law No. 269-II/2001, art. 3.

21 Postanovlenie Kabineta Ministrov Respubliki Uzbekistan, ot 29.07.2002 g. No. 269.

22 Resolution of the Cabinet of Ministers No. 265 of March 30, 2019, appendix 8, art. 5.

23 This article was partially modified by Law of the Republic of Uzbekistan No. ZRU 288 of October 10, 2009, "On the Protection and Use of Cultural Heritage Objects."

damage from happening thanks to risk management. This concept, referred to as preventive conservation, began to take root in the 1990s, and in several countries it has already been absorbed by national laws for the protection of cultural heritage.[24] In 2008 the term was officially adopted by ICOM-CC (Committee for Conservation of the International Council of Museums), which states that preventive conservation involves "all measures and actions aimed at avoiding and minimizing future deterioration or loss. They are carried out within the context [of] or on the surroundings of an item, but more often a group of items, whatever their age and condition. These measures and actions are indirect—they do not interfere with the materials and structures of the items. They do not modify their appearance."[25]

Prevention is currently the founding principle of any conservation plan, and this most certainly includes twentieth-century architecture.[26] The purpose of a conservation plan is to manage change—thus preventing unsuitable interventions—rather than to blindly avoid any transformation, possibly condemning the building to underuse or progressive abandonment. This approach stresses the importance of the aforementioned "passport." By clearly stating which are the valuable features of a building (or object) of cultural heritage, this document becomes the main tool for preserving the building's significance while also fostering its use, bearing in mind that use is the main guarantee of the preservation of a building.

What is the Place of Modernist Architecture in This Legislative Context?

Although the categories of objects comprising cultural heritage are identified by Law No. 269-II/2001, to get a clearer idea of the value that is currently attributed to Soviet modernist architecture we must refer to an appendix of Resolution No. 265/2019. This appendix, titled "Calculation of the Amount of Material Damage to Immovable Property Objects of Tangible Cultural Heritage," has a specific operational purpose, as it allows one to quantify the value of an object. Through a simple equation[27] it is possible to establish the economic damage of a specific object: $M = B \times U \times V \times E + A$,

where:
M = amount of damage
B = damage score
U = object coefficient
V = volume of damage caused
E = base calculation amount for the territory of the Republic of Uzbekistan
A = amount of damage to the most important artistic decorations, patterns, tiles, images and other important aspects of the object

The damage score (B) is determined by summing the points associated with seven specific criteria. The first criterion regards the Type of Object. It is interesting to note that the Architectural Monument type is assigned the highest score (10 points), followed by Archeological

24 The Italian Code of Cultural Heritage and Landscape lists prevention among the conservation measures and defines it as "the set of activities capable of limiting situations of risk connected to the cultural property within its context" – Legislative Decree No. 42 of January 22, 2004.
25 "Terminology to Characterize the Conservation of Tangible Cultural Heritage," a resolution adopted by the ICOM-CC membership at the Fifteenth Triennial Conference, New Delhi, September 22–26, 2008.
26 For instance, the Getty Foundation's Keeping It Modern initiative has offered seventy-seven grants for the development of conservation management plans for modernist buildings of outstanding architectural significance around the world.
27 Resolution No. 265 of March 30, 2019, "Appendix to the Regulation on the Procedure for Implementation of State Control over the Protection, Preservation and Use of Immovable Property Objects of Tangible Cultural Heritage."

Monument (8 points), Art Monument (7 points) and Attraction (6 points). The second criterion is the most relevant when addressing the question of modernist architecture, as it concerns the Age of the Object. In this case, twentieth-century architecture ranks last with a mere 5 points, which is a significantly low score if compared to the 40 points allocated to pre-ninth-century objects. This should not come as a surprise, as the scoring system simply applies the most basic market principle, which values the least available goods the most. The subtext is the assumption that objects from ancient times are far more rare (and thus more valuable) than objects produced less than a century ago. The remaining criteria refer to the Level of Complexity of the Object, the Integrity of the Object, the Possibility of Restoring the Object (which is evaluated based on the existence of sources documenting the original setting of the building), the Level of Importance of the Object (local/national) and the Use of the Object.

The abovementioned equation reveals an aspect of continuity with Soviet times. Although there is no direct evidence of it in the legislative compendium, the adoption of a comparable methodology for assessing the value of a monument was a subject of discussion among specialists.[28]

Even though the low score awarded to twentieth-century architecture by the equation seems to undermine the relevance of modernist architecture, the inclusion of a significant number of twentieth-century objects in the National List proves otherwise. Resolution No. 846 of October 4, 2019 (the same year in which the calculation formula was issued) added 354 objects to the list, of which 206 originate in the twentieth and twenty-first centuries and 91 date to the post-1950 period.[29] This apparent contrast testifies to the (worldwide) slow process of acknowledgment of modernist heritage, although it is increasingly recognized. This is also confirmed by the recent addition of further modernist buildings and artifacts to the National List of Protection[30] and the inclusion of sixteen of Tashkent's modernist buildings in the UNESCO tentative list.

A Comparison with Soviet Legislation on Protection

The legislation for the protection of cultural heritage in Uzbekistan derives from the laws that regulated the subject in the former Soviet Union. A comparative examination highlights the similarities between the two regulatory frameworks, as well as the existing differences, which indicate a changed attitude toward the concepts of history, memory and heritage.

The first significant aspect of continuity between the Soviet period and the current legislation of the Republic of Uzbekistan on cultural heritage protection is the National List of Real Estate Objects of Tangible Cultural Heritage. It was established by Law No. 4692-IX/1976 "On the Protection and Use of Historic and Cultural Monuments" (art. 10, 11 and 12) and it still is an essential tool for conservation activities in the Republic of Uzbekistan.

Law No. 4692-IX (approved in 1976 and amended in 1983) was founded on a specific concept of history that began forming as far back as the October Revolution and continued to do so throughout the process of nation building and the development of socialism and Soviet society.[31] Monuments and objects of historical value were protected

28 V. Artem'ev, "Pamiatnik epokhi v sovremennoij zastroike [A Historical Monument in a Contemporary Neighborhood]," 28–30.

29 See Postanovlenie Kabineta Ministrov Respubliki Uzbekistan, ot 04.10.2019 g. No. 846 "Ob utverzhdenii natsional'nogo perechnia ob"ektov nedvizhimosti material'nogo kul'turnogo naslediia" [Resolution of the Cabinet of Ministers of the Republic of Uzbekistan "On Approval of the National List of Real Estate Objects of Tangible Cultural Heritage," No. 846, 10.04.2019].

30 The reference is to Resolutions No. 227 of April 22, 2024 (eleven modernist buildings), and No. 154 of March 25, 2024 (157 modern mosaics).

31 See for example "Law of Georgia: Freedom Charter," https://matsne.gov.ge/ru/document/download/1381526/8/en/pdf.

if (and to the extent that) they contributed to the preservation of the memory of events and protagonists of that history.

Article 1 states: "Historic and cultural monuments are structures, memorable places and objects connected with historic events in the life of the people, the development of society and the State, works of material and spiritual creation that are of historical, scientific, artistic or other cultural value."

Article 5 goes on: "Historic monuments, buildings, structures, memorable places and objects connected with major historic events in the life of the people, the development of society and the State, the revolutionary movement, the Great October Socialist Revolution, the Civil War and the Great Patriotic War, the building of socialism and communism, the strengthening of international solidarity; also with the development of the science, technology, culture and life of the peoples, with the lives of outstanding political figures, statesmen, military leaders, national heroes and men of science, literature, and art."

This idea of cultural heritage as a support to national history can be found in the laws enacted by the Uzbek SSR, in particular Law No. 149 of February 24, 1979, "On Measures to Further Improve the Management of the Protection and Restoration of Monuments of Tangible Cultural Significance of the Republic," and in the 1986 "Charter of the Society for the Protection of Historical and Cultural Monuments of Uzbekistan."

However, in the first law on the protection of cultural heritage enacted by the Republic of Uzbekistan (Law No. 269-II/2001 "On the Protection and Use of Objects of Cultural Heritage"), the adjective "historical" is not mentioned in the title or in article 3, where the categories of protected objects are defined. This appears to reflect the newborn Republic's intention to consider the legacy of the past not only for its memorial value but also for other types of cultural and artistic value. Moreover, compared to the Soviet Law No. 4692-IX/1976 (art. 5), Law No. 269-II/2001 considerably increases the categories of objects to be regarded as cultural heritage, including ancient art and architecture as well as archeological ensembles. Within this broadening of cultural heritage boundaries, we can detect an analogy with the 1948 resolution "Instructions for the Identification, Registration, Maintenance and Restoration of Architectural Monuments under State Protection."[32] This resolution was the means by which Stalin's USSR aimed to reconstruct national identity, adopting an extremely inclusive approach toward heritage that also included religious buildings.

It is interesting to note that both the current and the Soviet legislation show good alignment with the international debate on the conservation of tangible cultural heritage. The 1948 "Instructions" envisioned three categories of intervention on tangible cultural heritage: maintenance, repair and restoration. The law exhaustively describes each one of them, demonstrating full awareness of the founding principles of the 1931 Athens Charter, such as the importance of careful and constant maintenance (art. 2), intended as a primary conservation tool. On the other hand, within the third section, dealing with the "Repair and Restoration of Architectural Monuments," article 89 seems to recall the principles of scientific restoration promoted by Camillo Boito and Gustavo Giovannoni, stating that "In the partial recreation of a monument, as a general rule, newly constructed portions should correspond to the portions authentically preserved, creating a unified whole. Newly created portions, however, are to be marked and identified in some way."

Unlike the 1948 "Instructions," Law No. 4692-IX/1976 does not define the concepts of restoration, conservation and repair. Nonetheless, the international debate on the progressive broadening of the

32 Richard Anderson, "The USSR's 1948 Instructions for the Identification, Registration, Maintenance, and Restoration of Architectural Monuments under State Protection," *Future Anterior: Journal of Historic Preservation, History, Theory, and Criticism* 5, no. 1, 2008, 64–72.

concept of cultural heritage, which led to the drafting of the Venice Charter and the creation of ICOMOS, found its way into architectural journals in Uzbekistan in the 1970s and 1980s. This proves familiar how foundational concepts such as "protection zones" and "cultural landscapes" were to Tashkent's architects and conservators.[33]

Concluding Remarks

The current geopolitical scenario poses questions that have arisen in recent years and are now taking on a more urgent tone. The protection of Soviet architectural heritage is one of the most controversial issues. In this context, several former Soviet republics pursued a policy of de-Sovietization while searching for a new national identity. Such policies have been partly translated into legislation which, instead of protecting the heritage in question, has often compromised its integrity. This is the case in Georgia, where in 2011 the approval of the Freedom Charter (Law No. 1867 of December 25, 2013) established a requirement for preventive measures against the principles of communist ideologies and to remove the symbols and names of cult buildings, memorials, monuments, bas-reliefs, inscriptions, streets, squares, villages and settlements of communist rule (art. 1).[34] In many other countries legislative measures for the demolition or the removal of Soviet symbols have been approved.[35] The policy adopted in Uzbekistan differs, as demonstrated by the rich architectural heritage that we can still appreciate today.

In 2021, the Art and Culture Development Foundation (ACDF) under the Cabinet of Ministers of the Republic of Uzbekistan spearheaded a project aimed at preserving the most significant Soviet modernist buildings of Tashkent.[36] The Tashkent Modernism XX/XXI research pro-

33 See Pulat Zakhidov, "Organizatsii okhrannykh pamiatnikov Uzbekistana [Organization of Protected Monuments of Uzbekistan]," *Arkhitektura i stroitel'stvo Uzbekistana* [*Architecture and Construction of Uzbekistan*], no. 10, 1968, 29–30; Aleksei Asanov, "Pamiatnik arkhitektury i ego okhrannaia zona [The Heritage Building and Its Protected Zone]," *Arkhitektura i stroitel'stvo Uzbekistana* [*Architecture and Construction of Uzbekistan*], no. 3, 1969, 20–23; Liia Man'kovskaia, "O rabote sektsii istorii arkhitektury, restavratsii i okhrany pamiatnikov (1967–1971 gg.) [On the Work of the Section of the History of Architecture, Restoration and Protection of Monuments (1967–1971)]," *Arkhitektura i stroitel'stvo Uzbekistana* [*Architecture and Construction of Uzbekistan*], no. 8, 1971, 20–21; Pulat Zakhidov, "Nekotorye voprosy okhrany pamiatnikov Uzbekistana [Some Questions on the Protection of Uzbekistan's Monuments]," *Arkhitektura i stroitel'stvo Uzbekistana* [*Architecture and Construction of Uzbekistan*], no. 11, 1971, 28–31; Shukur Askarov, "Okhrana pamiatnikov – na uroven' sovremennykh gradostroitel'nykh trebovanii [The Protection of Monuments – According to Modern Urban Planning Requirements]," *Arkhitektura i stroitel'stvo Uzbekistana* [*Architecture and Construction of Uzbekistan*], no. 11, 1975, 30–32; N. Machanov, "Okhrana i restavratsiia pamiatnikov istorii i kul'tury – na nauchnuiu osnovu [Protection and Restoration of Monuments of History and Culture on a Scientific Basis]," *Arkhitektura i stroitel'stvo Uzbekistana* [*Architecture and Construction of Uzbekistan*], no. 1, 1978, 1–4; Pulat Zakhidov, "Okhrana pamiatnikov – zadacha gradostroitel'naia [Protection of Monuments is an Urban Planning Task]," *Arkhitektura i stroitel'stvo Uzbekistana* [*Architecture and Construction of Uzbekistan*], no. 11, 1978, 1–3; Galina Pugachenkova, "K sozdaniiu regional'noi initsiativnoi gruppy respublik Srednei Azii Sovetskogo komiteta ICOMOSa [On Creating a Regional Initiative Group of the Republics of Central Asia within the Soviet ICOMOS Committee]," *Arkhitektura i stroitel'stvo Uzbekistana* [*Architecture and Construction of Uzbekistan*], no. 6, 1982, 31–33; Galina Pugachenkova and Liia Man'kovskaia, "Mezhrespublikanaskaia zonal'naia konferentsiia sredneaziatskoi regional'noj gruppy Komiteta ICOMOSa [An Interrepublican Zonal Conference of the Central Asian Regional Group of ICOMOS]," *Arkhitektura i stroitel'stvo Uzbekistana* [*Architecture and Construction of Uzbekistan*], no. 5, 1984, 1–10; Irina Kirilova, "Istoriko-arkhitekturnoe nasledie v sovremennoi gorodskoi srede [Historical and Architectural Heritage in the Contemporary Urban Environment]," *Arkhitektura i stroitel'stvo Uzbekistana* [*Architecture and Construction of Uzbekistan*], no. 9, 1989, 15–16.

34 "Law of Georgia: Freedom Charter," https://matsne.gov.ge/ru/document/download/1381526/8/en/pdf.

35 For example, this happened in Latvia, where a law prohibiting the exhibition of objects glorifying Soviet rule was approved in June 2022 (https://likumi.lv/ta/en/en/id/333439). Similar measures were also discussed by the Lithuanian, Estonian and Romanian governments.

36 Note that the research did not consider mass housing, as it mostly focused on unique buildings.

ject initiated an extensive process of knowledge acquisition, study and analysis of these buildings, opening up the possibility of reinterpreting through new and different lenses the urban and architectural history of Uzbekistan's capital city. The outcome so far has been the inclusion of numerous objects from the Soviet period in the National List, among which are eleven modernist buildings (in addition to ten that were already listed). The preservation of these buildings, along with up-to-date, debated and shared scientific research, can now contribute to redefining the boundaries of the cultural heritage of the country, finally taking into account the legacy of the recent past. The legal framework will need to adapt, possibly aligning with renewed international practices by embracing the principles of preventive conservation.

This essay is the result of collaborative research between the two authors. The sections "An Introductory Note," "A Comparison with Soviet Legislation on Protection" and "Concluding Remarks" were written by Federica Deo. The sections "On the Legislation in Force: Structure and Operational Process" and "What Is the Place of Modernist Architecture in This Legislative Context?" were written by Sofia Celli.

A Protection Inventory for Modernist Heritage

Sofia Celli

Inventories: An Ancient Practice

The practice of making inventories is a rather old one. It is in fact the most effective and immediate way to identify and describe assets, be they commercial goods, artworks or architectures. In the construction sector, for centuries inventories were made on the occasion of deeds of sale: buildings were described room by room to define their selling price. When the modern concept of cultural heritage developed, inventories also became the main tool for conservation. The first cataloguing experiences recorded in Europe can be traced back to the eighteenth century.[1] At that time, many European states took action to limit the increasing and unregulated circulation of artworks.[2] Creating a list of worthy items (either movable or immovable) guaranteed better control over them, reducing the risk of their dispersion and possible destruction. The French Revolution and the subsequent Napoleonic looting of art fostered this process by introducing the idea that protecting the legacy of the past meant safeguarding the national identity.[3] Among other outcomes, this equation led to the opening of the first public museums, such as the Musei Capitolini in Rome, the Uffizi in Florence, the British Museum in London and the Louvre in Paris. In line with the founding principles of the revolution (liberté, égalité, fraternité), art and culture were no longer a privilege of the aristocracy, but a right of the whole population, a tool for the community to learn about its roots.[4]

Theodor Josef Hubert Hoffbauer, *Exposition des produits de l'industrie française, dans la cour du Louvre*, 1801

Most importantly, the revolutionary events pushed European countries to focus their attention on protection and to formulate some kind of conservation policies. This situation boosted the role of inventories, which soon became more organic, comprehensive and structured.

1 Among others: the inventory attempts by François-Roger de Gaignières and Bernard de Montfaucon in France at the end of the seventeenth century (Carlo Manfredi, ed., *Le politiche di tutela del patrimonio costruito: Modelli a confronto in Europa* [Milan: Mimesis, 2017], 44–45); the *Museum florentinum*, a catalogue of the Medici antiquities and artistic objects drawn up in the first half of the eighteenth century (ibid., 19); the catalogue of Venetian paintings compiled by Anton Maria Zanetti, starting in 1773 (Mario Speroni, *La tutela dei beni culturali negli stati italiani preunitari* [Milan: Giuffrè, 1988]).

2 Note that the Papal States had had rudimentary protection regulations from the sixteenth century. Elena Cagiano de Azevedo and Roberta Geremia Nucci, *Riflessioni sulla tutela: Temi, problemi, esperienze* (Florence: Polistampa, 2010), 12ff.; Édouard Pommier, *L'invenzione dell'arte nell'Italia del Rinascimento* (Turin: Einaudi, 2007), 175–210.

3 Carlo Manfredi, ed., *Le politiche di tutela del patrimonio costruito: Modelli a confronto in Europa*, 16.

4 On the birth of the public museum, see Karsten Schubert, *Museo: Storia di un'idea; dalla Rivoluzione Francese a oggi* (Milan: il Saggiatore, 2004).

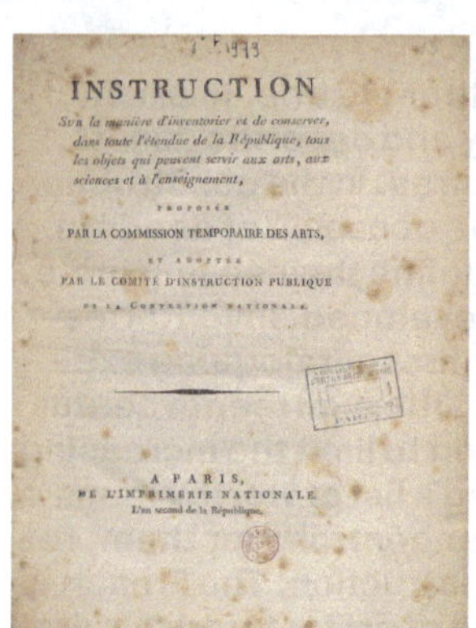

Title page of Félix Vicq d'Azyr's treatise *Instruction sur la manière d'inventorier et de conserver dans toute l'étendue de la République, tous les objets qui peuvent servir aux arts, aux sciences et à l'enseignement*, 1794

In 1794 Félix Vicq d'Azyr published the *Instruction sur la manière d'inventorier et de conserver dans toute l'étendue de la République, tous les objets qui peuvent servir aux arts, aux sciences et à l'enseignement*, which provided a methodology for the compilation of the first inventory at a national scale, comprising both movable artworks and monuments.[5] A few years later, similar experiences were recorded in Germany[6] and Austria.[7] Although most pre-union states had already started the inventorying process, Italy found a new impulse after unification in 1861. In particular, a royal decree enacted in 1876 established provincial committees for the conservation of monuments, antiquities and fine arts,[8] whose primary duty was to compile a catalogue of all the valuable items to be found in the territory of their respective territories. Once again, this action had a twofold purpose: it had the ambition of preserving the legacy of the past and it aimed at forging a new national identity, seeking common roots in the rich cultural heritage of the country. However, it was not until 1923 that Italy received a unified and consistent inventory that extended across the entire nation. A new royal decree[9] urged the creation of a catalogue for the protection of monuments, also providing general information about its structure. In particular, it explained that the catalogue should contain a descriptive spread for each listed item, possibly enriched with photographs. Indeed, when dealing with cultural heritage, creating a catalogue of objects worth preserving implies acknowledging their value and getting to know them, at least at a preliminary level. We can therefore state that inventories are a tool for knowledge, as well as the founding premise of any further protection activity.

Throughout the nineteenth and twentieth centuries, while continuing to feed and update inventories, European countries developed and implemented protection laws. In the meantime, restoration theories began to flourish and together with them the need arose for an international debate to discuss the best approaches to addressing the issue of conservation. The resulting resolutions were collected in restoration charters, starting in 1931 with the Athens Charter for the Restoration of Historic Monuments.[10]

If until then the process had been quite linear, the disruptive events brought about by World War II raised new questions. The extensive damage caused by aerial bombardments shifted attention away from single objects to groups of them. In fact, entire neighborhoods and city centers were destroyed, which called for new measures in the reconstruction phase that followed. The aftermath of the war led to the drafting of new guidelines, gathered in the 1964 International Charter for the Conservation and Restoration of Monuments and Sites, also known as the Venice Charter. The latter introduced some important and novel ideas, such as the need to take into consideration both the monument and its environment, rather than focusing solely on the monument, as well as

5 Carlo Manfredi, ed., *Le politiche di tutela del patrimonio costruito: Modelli a confronto in Europa*, 32.
6 The reference is to *Die Grundsätze zur Erhaltung alter Denkmäler und Altertümer in unserem Lande*, a catalogue drafted in 1815 by Karl Friedrich Schinkel (Carlo Manfredi, ed., *Le politiche di tutela del patrimonio costruito: Modelli a confronto in Europa*, 32).
7 In the first half of the nineteenth century several historical associations (*Altertumsvereine*) were founded in Austria with the purpose of preserving and describing monuments (Carlo Manfredi, ed., *Le politiche di tutela del patrimonio costruito: Modelli a confronto in Europa*, 32).
8 Royal Decree, March 5, 1875, no. 3028, *Gazzetta Ufficiale*, no. 81, April 6, 1876.
9 Royal Decree, June 14, 1923, no. 1889, *Gazzetta Ufficiale*, no. 213, September 10, 1923. A previous attempt in this direction was made through law no. 185 of June 12, 1902.
10 For a comprehensive overview of restoration charters and resolutions see Ruggero Boschi and Pietro Segala, *Codici per la conservazione del patrimonio storico: Cento anni di riflessioni, "grida" e carte* (Florence: Nardini Editore, 2006) and "Carte ed altri testi dottrinali," ICOMOS Italia, https://www.icomositalia.com/carte-e-testi-dottrinali.

the acknowledgment that not only great artworks but even modest works of the past could be of cultural significance.[11]

Piero Gazzola, chairman of the committee that drafted the Charter, believed in those ideas and shaped his work around them. In particular, he was firmly convinced of the importance of inventories, which he considered to be an indispensable premise to heritage protection and to play a strategic role in territorial planning.[12] At the request of the Council of Europe, in 1965 he participated in the development of a unified protection catalogue for the knowledge and preservation of European cultural heritage (IPCE). The inventory was composed of standard forms which provided the same data for each monument or site, namely the basic information to identify the object, a plan and at least one photograph.[13]

Dresden after the bombings of World War II

Gazzola also advocated the recognition of historical centers as cultural heritage and thus objects of protection. Due to his influential roles as the president of the International Council on Monuments and Sites (ICOMOS) and a UNESCO consultant, he was able to shed light on this issue at an international level. Soon after, several European countries introduced new laws to make it possible to preserve entire urban sectors.[14] Among them was France, which, in 1962, introduced the secteurs sauveguardés,[15] becoming a role model for many European countries.[16]

As for the setting of standards for cataloguing activities, measures have been taken both at national and international levels. In Italy a

11 "The concept of a historic monument embraces not only the single architectural work but also the urban or rural setting in which is found the evidence of a particular civilization, a significant development, or a historic event. This applies not only to great works of art but also to more modest works of the past which have acquired cultural significance with the passing of time." Venice Charter, 1964, Art. 1.

12 Piero Gazzola and Loris A. Fontana, *Analisi culturale del territorio: Il centro storico urbano* (Padua: Marsilio, 1973), 23; Piero Gazzola, "La responsabilità dello storico di fronte ai problemi della tutela del volto delle antiche città," *Bulletin C.I.H.A.*, II, April–September 1967, 4.

13 Piero Gazzola, *L'inventario di protezione del patrimonio culturale: Settore dei beni immobili; IPCE scopo e norme di esecuzione* (Verona, 1970), 7.

14 Leonardo Benevolo, *Storia dell'Architettura Moderna* (Bari: Laterza, 2010), 936–937.

15 Law of August 4, 1962, also known as the "Malraux Law."

16 Claudia Aveta, "Piero Gazzola: Restauro dei monumenti e conservazione dei centri storici e del paesaggio" (Ph.D. diss., Università degli Studi di Napoli Federico II, 2005), 171.

designated office for cataloguing standards was created in 1969. Originally established as the Catalogue Office, in 1975 it converged into the Central Institute for the Catalogue and Documentation (ICCD). While inventorying is carried out by local, regional and state bodies, the ICCD guarantees coherence and homogeneity in the national inventory. Today the Italian catalogue of cultural heritage comprises 2,983,677 objects in nine different categories.[17]

The Council of Europe plays a similar role at the European level, as it has worked toward the harmonization of inventory and documentation processes since the 1960s. In 2009 it published a book[18] which offers guidelines for inventorying cultural heritage, based on best practices of member states. After centuries of existence, "[inventories of historic buildings] are fundamental in enabling us to order information and so come to an understanding of our past. They provide a mechanism for enabling us to identify and evaluate those artefacts from the past, which we then may wish to protect and celebrate as indispensable evidence of the history which has shaped us as individuals and societies."[19]

Heritage: An Evolving Concept

The evolution of inventories of protection has not only involved their structure or the sort of information they collect. Most of all, inventories have changed and expanded in line with the continuous deepening and broadening of the concept of heritage. If until the first half of the twentieth century there was a tendency to identify cultural heritage with unique historic monuments or works of art, by the end of the century it came to include items from a more recent and more ordinary past. As mentioned, an early step in this direction was taken by the Venice Charter,[20] which fostered the inclusion of urban ensembles in protection inventories. The 1975 Declaration of Amsterdam took a further step by introducing the idea that even modern architecture should be considered cultural heritage.[21] The statement "new buildings of today will be the heritage of tomorrow"[22] is of the essence, as it confirms the occurrence of a paradigm shift from exemplary to representative and, more importantly, from change to historical continuity. Each stage of history—including the present day—has contributed to shaping the world and society we live in today and is therefore a heritage in the strict sense of the word.

The acknowledgment of the significance of modern architecture had, however, begun decades before. In the 1950s and 1960s, the demolition of important buildings such as the Larkin Administration Building[23] or the Maison du Peuple[24] provoked an outcry at local and international levels.

17 See the online database "Catalogo generale dei Beni Culturali," https://catalogo.beniculturali.it/.
18 *Guidance on Inventory and Documentation of the Cultural Heritage* (Strasbourg: Council of Europe, 2009).
19 Ibid., 15.
20 See footnote 11.
21 "Protection is needed today for historic towns, the old quarters of cities, and towns and villages with a traditional character as well as historic parks and gardens. The conservation of these architectural complexes can only be conceived in a wide perspective, embracing all buildings of cultural value, from the greatest to the humblest—not forgetting those of our own day together with their surroundings. This overall protection will complement the piecemeal protection of individual and isolated monuments and sites." Declaration of Amsterdam, 1975.
22 Ibid.
23 Located in Buffalo (New York), it was built between 1904 and 1906 to a design by Frank Lloyd Wright. In 1950, seven years after its closure, the building was demolished.
24 Built in Brussels (Belgium) in 1897 to a design by Victor Horta, it was demolished in 1965.

The Larkin Administration Building, designed by Frank Lloyd Wright in 1904 and photographed in 1906. The building was demolished in 1950.

The Maison du Peuple of the P.O.B. (Belgian Workers Party), built in 1897 to a design by Victor Horta. The building was demolished in 1965.

In 1949, in an attempt to save the Larkin Building from destruction, architect J. Stanley Sharp wrote to the *New York Herald Tribune* that "the Larkin Building [...] should be regarded not as an outmoded utilitarian structure but as a monument [...]. Hopefully, in the future we will consider the value of a significant building such as this, and work to preserve it."[25] Similarly, the demolition of the Maison du Peuple was often referred to as an "architectural crime," but, nonetheless, many other modernist buildings met the same fate. Some, however, were saved. The most relevant case is that of the Zonnestraal sanatorium in the Netherlands. Designed in 1926 by Johannes Duiker and Bernard Bijvoet, the building was soon hailed as a noteworthy example of modern architecture.[26] In 1982, after decades of abandonment, the sanatorium was restored by architects Hubert-Jan Henket and Wessel de Jonge at the request of the Dutch government.

View of the former Zonnestraal Sanatorium, 2009

25 Jerry Malloy, "The Larkin Administration Building: A 'Wright' of Passage in Buffalo," *The Buffalo History Gazette*, October 4, 2011, https://www.buffalohistorygazette.net/2011/10/.

26 "Then, Now and Later: Rich History and Inspired Stories," Zonnestraal Hilversum, https://zonnestraal.nl/en/then-now/.

This experience had a twofold outcome: it set a good example of how to preserve modern buildings and it led to the establishment of DOCOMOMO International. Since 1988, DOCOMOMO has encouraged the documentation and conservation of buildings, sites and neighborhoods of the Modern Movement.[27] To achieve these goals, the organization has developed an inventory of modern architecture which includes both outstanding individual buildings and everyday examples. Today DOCOMOMO is an international reference point and has branches in seventy-nine countries and regions. Its diffusion has made it possible to create a web-based platform (MoMove) that serves as a worldwide inventory of modern architecture, which so far encompasses 4,388 sites.[28] This experience is of primary importance, as it reveals the newly emerged need to implement cataloguing standards on a global scale.[29] This necessity is also underlined by the Council of Europe[30] and has been a target for other important organizations in charge of cataloguing activities. The UNESCO World Heritage List (and tentative list) addresses the same challenges. The 1,199 sites currently on the list are described using a standard form. This facilitates information retrieval, as well as possible comparisons between sites or architectures.

An interesting aspect of the UNESCO proposal is its inclusiveness. In line with the evolving concept of cultural heritage, in 1994 the World Heritage Committee launched the *Global Strategy for a Representative, Balanced and Credible World Heritage List*. The aim is to fill in the gaps in the list by including properties from categories or geographical areas that are currently underrepresented,[31] including modern architecture. A similar role is played by organizations such as the World Monuments Fund, which promotes the preservation of the world's diverse cultural heritage in the broad sense. Several modernist buildings have been included in World Monuments Watch since its launch in 1996.[32]

Another important actor in the conservation of twentieth-century heritage is the Getty Foundation. In recent decades, it has implemented more than one initiative relating to this topic. In 2012 the Getty Conservation Institute launched the Conserving Modern Architecture Initiative, which aims to improve conservation practices for modern architecture through research and knowledge distribution.[33] Two years later, in 2014, the Keeping It Modern initiative was launched to fund practical conservation experiences internationally. Although those two projects did not involve any cataloguing activities in the strict sense, they have provided an extensive library of specific publications and case studies to support the preservation of the legacy of the Modern Movement.

Programs were also set up at a local level. For example, in 2002 the Italian Ministry of Culture started mapping significant contemporary

27 "About," DOCOMOMO International, https://docomomo.com/organization/.
28 Ana Tostões, Zara Ferreira and Joana Gouveia Alves, "MoMove: The Docomomo Virtual Exhibition," *Docomomo Journal*, no. 54, January 2016, 86–88, https://docomomojournal.com/index.php/journal/article/view/394/142.
29 Meriç Altintaş Kaptan et al., "Connecting the Dots: A Global Exploration of Local Docomomo Inventories," *Docomomo Journal* 69, no. 2, 2023, 76–85.
30 "Now with the possibilities that information technology offers for contact and information sharing, the benefits of creating cultural heritage information networks are clear. These include the enabling of common access to inventories created and managed by diverse organizations. Common access can be achieved, however, only if documentation standards are developed to ensure compatibility between the databases that constitute the network." *Guidance on Inventory and Documentation of the Cultural Heritage*, 12.
31 "This new vision goes beyond the narrow definitions of heritage and strives to recognize and protect sites that are outstanding demonstrations of human coexistence with the land as well as human interactions, cultural coexistence, spirituality and creative expression." https:/whc.unesco.org/en/globalstrategy/.
32 "World Monuments Watch," World Monuments Fund, https://www.wmf.org/watch.
33 Susan Macdonald, "Conserving Modern Heritage: The Work of the J. Paul Getty Trust," in *Conserving 20th-Century Architecture*, ed. Maria Paola Borgarino and Davide Del Curto (Switzerland: Springer Nature, 2023), 31.

architecture built across Italy since 1945.[34] The initiative features an online repository, where each building is described using a standard form. As of October 2022, the inventory included 4,958 entries.[35] The project is constantly being expanded and updated, including by means of side events such as the conference *Ereditare il presente* (*Inheriting the Present*) organized in Rome in 2022, which focused on the topic of knowledge, protection and enhancement of contemporary architecture. Similarly, in 2020, ICOMOS Nepal published the *Inventory of 19th and 20th Century Architectural and Industrial Heritage of Nepal*,[36] which aimed to stop the indiscriminate demolition of important monuments that are not protected by law because of their "young" age.[37] These attempts once again confirm the importance of inventories, even for those buildings that are not currently protected by law. To quote Gazzola, "[the inventory] of all the objects constituting the heritage of the history, culture and traditional physiognomy of the country is the only means to regulate protection. [...] It is self-evident that it is not possible to respect and safeguard what is unknown and does not rightfully exist: the register of monumental heritage is the first step in achieving this essential knowledge."[38]

An Inventory for Tashkent Modernism

While this essay focuses on protection inventories, not all architecture inventories have the purpose of ensuring preservation of buildings. Guidebooks[39] are de facto inventories aimed at promoting visits and tourism. Thematic architectural photography catalogues are also inventories, but are mostly intended as artistic statements. Many other target-specific inventories have been developed across the world. They might refer to a particular architectural typology or function, to the work of a single architect, to a certain geographical area or to a limited period. The latter is the case for Novikov and Belogolovskii's work *Soviet Modernism 1955–1985*[40] and Frédéric Chaubin's *CCCP: Cosmic Communist Constructions Photographed*.[41] Both books offer a photographic overview of representative Soviet architecture built throughout a well-defined period, 1955 to 1985 and 1970 to 1990 respectively. The *Soviet Modernism 1955–1991* exhibition[42] held in 2012 at the Architekturzentrum Wien follows the same concept and created the first online

Cover of Frédéric Chaubin's book *CCCP: Cosmic Communist Constructions Photographed*, 2011

Cover of the exhibition catalogue *Soviet Modernism 1955–1991: Unknown History*, 2012

34 "Censimento delle architetture italiane dal 1945 ad oggi," Direzione Generale Creatività Contemporanea, https://censimentoarchitetturecontemporanee.cultura.gov.it/.

35 Maria Vittoria Marini Clarelli, "Il censimento oggi," oral presentation delivered at the conference *Ereditare il presente: Conoscenza, tutela e valorizzazione dell'architettura italiana dal 1945 ad oggi*, Rome, October 11–12, 2022.

36 Kai Weise et al., eds., *Inventory of 19th and 20th Century Architectural and Industrial Heritage of Nepal* (ICOMOS Nepal, 2020) (can be downloaded at: https://icomosnepal.wordpress.com/publication/).

37 Nepalese legislation, in particular the Ancient Monument Preservation Act, states that to be included in the national heritage list, buildings must be at least one hundred years old. See Kai Weise et al., eds., *Inventory of 19th and 20th Century Architectural and Industrial Heritage of Nepal.*

38 Translation by the author. Original text: "[L'inventario] di tutto quanto costituisce il patrimonio della storia, della cultura e della fisionomia tradizionale del Paese è solo il mezzo per disciplinare la tutela. [...] E' lapalissiano che non si può rispettare e difendere ciò che non si conosce e che di diritto non esiste: l'anagrafe del patrimonio monumentale è il primo passo per raggiungere questa imprescindibile conoscenza." Piero Gazzola, "La responsabilità dello storico di fronte ai problemi della tutela del volto delle antiche città," 4.

39 Sticking to modern architecture, we could mention (among others): Anna Bronovitskaya, Nikolay Malinin and Yuri Palmin, *Moscow: A Guide to Soviet Modernist Architecture 1955–1991* (Prague: Artguide Editions, 2019); Manuel Gausa et al., *Barcelona: Modern Architecture Guide* (Barcelona: Actar Publishers, 2013) or Eduardo Luis Rodríguez, *The Havana Guide: Modern Architecture 1925–1965* (Princeton: Princeton Architectural Press, 2000).

40 Feliks Novikov and Vladimir Belogolovskii, *Soviet Modernism 1955–1985* (Yekaterinburg: Izdatel'stvo TATLIN, 2010).

41 Frédéric Chaubin, *CCCP: Cosmic Communist Constructions Photographed* (Cologne: Taschen, 2011).

42 Katharina Ritter et al., eds., *Soviet Modernism 1955–1991: Unknown History* (Vienna: Park Books, 2012).

1968 2022

House of Knowledge
Architects: G. Aleksandrovich, Iu. Miroshnichenko, I. Demchinskaia

1974 2023

Zarafshan Restaurant
Architects: V. Spivak, R. Memetov

1974 2023

State Museum of Arts
Architects: S. Rozenblium, I. Abdulov, A. Nikiforov

1975 2023

Samarkand Teahouse
Architect: S. Sutiagin

1980 2022

Palace of Aviation Constructors
Architects: A. Onischenko, M. Vakhidov, R. Takhtaganov

1985 2022

Zhemchug (The Pearl) residential building
Architect: O. Aidinova

Unlike in the early 1990s, when all architectural modernity was perceived as an explicit reminder of the problematic Soviet past, today Tashkent's inhabitants consider this an inherent and valuable part of the city, contributing to its texture and its iconicity. At times disfigured and deprived of their modernist essence by the spontaneous appropriations of the owners, these buildings absorb and reflect new tastes and economic possibilities.

Another mechanism is producing pressure on architecture as well. Since 2016, Uzbekistan, and Tashkent in particular, has been undergoing rapid urban growth and development. The opening of the country to international investments has made possible the transformation of large portions of the city. And, as elsewhere in the world, economic concerns often rank higher than the historic layers of the city, especially when it comes to the legacy of the recent past, the management of which implies dealing with multiple complex issues.

Panoramic Cinema, 1964
Listed 2019

CCCP of Uzbekistan, 1964
Listed 2019

TsUM, 1964

Institute of Oriental Studies, 1968

House of Knowledge, 1968

Museum of Applied Arts, 1969
Listed 2019

Council of Ministers, 1969

Lenin Museum, 1970
Listed 2019

Blue Domes Café, 1970
Listed 2019

Tashkent University campus, 1970

Iubileinyi Palace of Sport, 1970

9-story residential buildings, B. Khmel'nitskii Street, 1970s

Institute of Art Studies, 1972

Gosbank, 1972

Ministries Building, 1972

House of Publishers, 1974

Zarafshan Restaurant, 1974

State Museum of Arts, 1974
Listed 2024

Union of Artists Exhibition Hall, 1974 Listed 2019

Uzbekistan Hotel, 1974
Listed 2024

Ts-27 residential buildings, 1974

The Circus, 1975
Listed 2019

Institute of Pectoral Surgery, 1975 Listed 2024

Delegation House of CCCP UzSSR, 1975 Listed 2024

House of Youth, 1975
Listed 2024

Samarkand Teahouse, 1976

House of Arborists, 1976

Ministry of Energy, 1976

Agricultural Institute (TIIMSKh), 1977

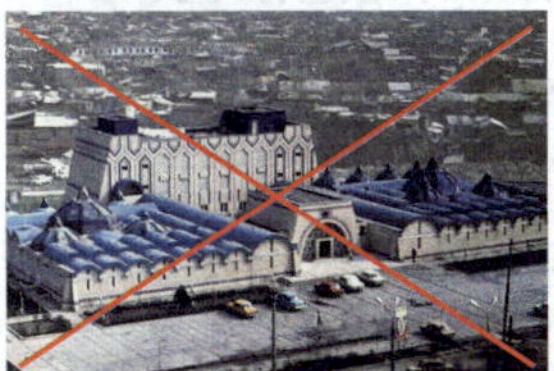
Hammom Public Baths, 1977

TV Center, 1977
Listed 2024

Palace of Aviation Constructors, 1980 Listed 2024

Lenin Pioneer Palace, 1980

Peoples' Friendship Palace, 1981 Listed 2019

Chorsu Hotel, 1982

House of Cinema, 1982

Cosmonauts Avenue metro station, 1984 Listed 2024

Exhibition Hall of VDNKh, 1984

TV Tower, 1985
Listed 2019

Zhemchug residential building, 1985 Listed 2019

Ben'kov Art College, 1986

16-story residential building, B. Khmel'nitskii Street, 1987

Geology Museum, 1987

Republican House of Tourism, 1987

Sun Heliocomplex, 1987
Listed 2024

Chorsu Bazaar, 1990
Listed 2024

Turkestan Palace, 1993

Turkestan Arena, 1994
Listed 2024

Tashkent was the fourth-most-populated city in the Soviet Union, after Moscow, Leningrad and Kyiv. Beginning in the 1930s, it was a testing ground for technical, social, cultural and urban experiments in Central Asia, generating prototypes for other republican capitals. The aspiration to make Tashkent a model capital and a showcase of socialism in the East gained new momentum in the early 1960s, with the authorities opening influential scientific centers, developing high-tech production facilities and stimulating new forms of art and culture.

This experimental attitude was very quickly translated into visible urban and built layers. The 1966 earthquake—the epicenter of which was right under the city center—accelerated the rapid (re)construction process, transforming Tashkent into a laboratory of modern architecture which was extensively documented in the trade press.

After Uzbekistan gained independence in 1991, however, the exceptional and innovative character of the urban fabric did not prevent it from becoming a target of significant alteration, and at times even destruction.

To prevent further losses, an inventory of Tashkent's modernist heritage has been created, identifying qualities and values of each building, assessing levels of authenticity and integrity, and evaluating risks. This inventory functions as a protection list, finally recognizing Tashkent's modernist architecture as a relevant heritage demanding specific measures of preservation.

Demolished

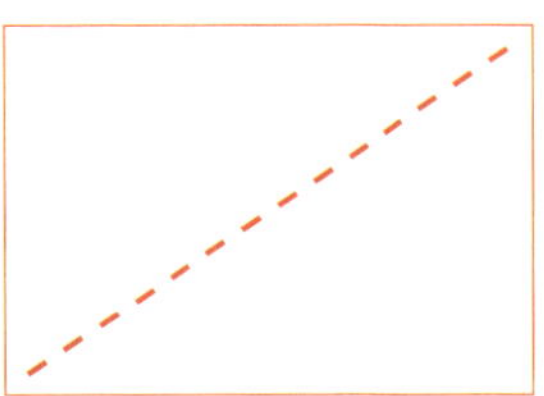
Significantly changed or at risk

inventory of Soviet modernist architecture.[43] The event succeeded in raising awareness of the importance and endangerment of such buildings.[44] This acknowledgment further enlarged the boundaries of the concept of cultural heritage, finally overcoming the idea of a standardized Soviet architecture.

Despite the new international interest in Soviet modernism, the legal and methodological tools for the preservation of this heritage are still relatively new and mostly refer to individual case studies. Indeed, while reinforced concrete was "invented" as a building material at the end of the nineteenth century, the issue of its conservation only arose a few decades ago. The experimental nature of and the novelties introduced by modern architecture pose specific conservation challenges that need to be addressed on a case-by-case basis.

The research illustrated in this book—specifically focused on Tashkent—was designed to acquire the knowledge that is the foundation of any protection activity and to provide a concrete contribution to the conservation practices for this type of heritage. It began with the identification and cataloguing of the most relevant modernist buildings of the city. A preliminary survey identified forty buildings, which were then narrowed down to twenty-five according to multiple criteria, taking into account tangible and intangible values. The initial evaluation was based on architectural and urban qualities, which were then compared with the original design in order to assess the authenticity and integrity of the buildings. Studying the history of these buildings also offered the possibility to understand their relevance and representativeness within the specific socio-political context that generated them. Great importance was also assigned to the perceptions of the local community: tailored surveys were conducted in Tashkent (targeting different categories of users) to capture the point of view of the population and whether—and to what extent—they felt connected to Tashkent's modernist architecture. The availability of information and willingness of building owners to collaborate inevitably affected the whole process, which, on the bright side, involved the participation of local authorities and scholars, who offered an indispensable contribution to the definition of the final short list.

Each building was then thoroughly examined following the Burra Charter Process,[45] with the ultimate objective of implementing individual conservation and management plans.[46] In order to analyze the collected data, a standard form was developed. While drawing inspiration from existing inventories, the form was tailor-made to suit the purposes of the research.

First, due to the large amount of available information, the inventory has been conceived as a "box set" of monographic booklets dedicated to single buildings. The reference is to the Swiss architecture inventory INSA,[47] which comprises ten volumes recounting the rapid growth of forty Swiss towns. The INSA catalogue also integrates the urban and architectural scales, which is very important in the case of Tashkent[48] and is addressed in a specific section of the form.

43 "Soviet Modernism 1955–1991," Architekturzentrum Wien, http://wiki.azw.at/sovietmodernism_database/home.php.

44 In this regard it is also worth mentioning the work of Alerte Héritage, established in 2016, which focuses on Central Asian heritage. https://archalert.net/

45 *The Burra Charter: The Australia ICOMOS Charter for Places of Cultural Significance*, 2013.

46 See Davide Del Curto's essay "A Methodology for Preserving the Modernist Architecture of Tashkent" in this book, pp. 168–175.

47 Inventario Svizzero di Architettura (INSA), available at https://www.gsk.ch/it/insa.html.

48 The relationship between individual buildings and urban planning in Tashkent is well described in Federica Deo's essay "Earthquake as Alibi: The 1966 Tashkent General Plan and the Construction of the Modernist Capital" in this book, pp. 72–87.

Another distinctive characteristic of the Tashkent Monographs is their internal subdivision, which includes an "overview" and a "description." The aim is to provide both a ready-to-use summary for quick consultation and extensive texts offering comprehensive reports, to fulfill the needs of different categories of users. This approach was borrowed from DOCOMOMO, which suggests two types of standard forms, one being the "Full Documentation Fiche" and the other the "Minimum Documentation Fiche." Both fiches feature the same categories of information,[49] but the former has more subcategories, and its compilation requires a deeper knowledge of the building. Similarly, the "overview" in the Tashkent Monographs displays most of the fields that are further detailed in the "description" section. The DOCOMOMO fiches were also useful in defining the contents of the Monographs: many of the subcategories from the fiches were maintained, with others dismissed, slightly modified or added from scratch.

Finally, the last section of the Tashkent Monographs comprises the "Statement of Significance," which aims to highlight the main qualities and values of the building. While somewhat present in the DOCOMOMO fiches (section 4, "Evaluation"), this section has been modeled on the UNESCO World Heritage Site form, in which the Justification of Outstanding Universal Value is made up of an extensive descriptive text followed by a statement of authenticity and integrity. This solution appeared well suited to Tashkent's modernist architecture and was redeveloped accordingly.

Piecing together all these suggestions, the full Building Monographs contain four main sections, articulated as follows:

- The "overview" acts as a ready-to-use summary providing core data. It includes a city map showing the "building position" and a "brief description of the building" organized in bullet points. The latter offers basic information concerning the ownership, typology, construction history, actors, main dimensions and use of the building.
- The "description" provides an in-depth and multifaceted portrait of the building, starting from the urban scale and reaching a detailed scale. The first four subsections, namely "Urban Context and Development," "Architecture of the Building and Its History," "Protagonists" and "Institutional Framework," depict the historical, cultural, and political context within which the architecture was conceived, built and used. The subsequent subsections, titled "Functional Analysis," "Additional Drawings," "Historical Drawings" and "Photographic Survey," collect all of the architectural drawings required for a thorough understanding of the building (plans, sections, elevations and axonometries), diagrams describing the use of the building, and pictures documenting its current and past states. These subsections also include a systematic comparison between the current situation and the original design. This process allows for a better understanding of changes that have occurred over time (intended or unintended; due to normal aging or human intervention) and aids in assessing the authenticity and integrity of the building. Finally, the remaining subsections dive into more technical issues by describing the "Structural System" of the building, assessing its overall "State of Repair" and reporting the results of any "Instrumental Analysis" performed on-site.
- The "Statement of Significance" is possibly the most important section of the Monograph. Rather than adding further "objective" data, it proposes a critical and protection-oriented interpretation

49 Namely, (1) identity of the building, (2) history of the building, (3) description, (4) evaluation, (5) documentation, (6) fiche report examination by ISC/R. https://docomomo-nytri.org/about/documentation.

of the information contained in the "description." In particular, the "Highlights" subsection outlines the main qualities of the building and the reasons it should be preserved, either entirely or in part. The "State of Repair," "Integrity" and "Authenticity" subsections evaluate the extent of the transformations that a building may have undergone since its construction. To this end, the "Before/After Comparison" made using current and historical photographs provides essential support. Finally, the subsections concerning "Levels of Interest" offer concrete indications to guide the development of a preservation strategy. Three different categories have been identified. The first one ("Level 1 – Maximum level of interest") refers to the most representative and valuable features of the building, calling for attentive conservation measures and forbidding any transformation. The second level of interest ("Level 2 – Medium level of interest") includes elements that can be moderately transformed following approval by a designated committee. Both levels of interest consider three different scales: the urban scale, the architectural scale and the detail scale. A third category, "Hidden modernist features," identifies those modernist characteristics of the building which have been concealed but still exist and can be reinstated, contributing to a better reading of the original design.

- The "Bibliography" is the last section and collects all of the sources that were used to draft the Monograph.

Depending on the information available, the Monographs can be filled in completely or partly. They can be revised and fed new data, so that they are always up-to-date, reliable and able to efficiently support conservation activities.

The second part of this book contains condensed versions of the Monographs of twelve of Tashkent's most outstanding or representative modernist buildings—namely, the Panoramic Cinema, Cosmonauts Avenue metro station, the Peoples' Friendship Palace, the State Museum of the History of Uzbekistan (originally the Lenin Museum), the Exhibition Hall of the Union of Artists, the Sun Heliocomplex, the Zhemchug residential building, the Chorsu Bazaar, the State Museum of Arts, the Circus, the complex comprising the Shodlik Hotel and Ilkhom Theater (originally the House of Youth), and the Uzbekistan Hotel. These Monographs also contain preservation and adaptation strategies.

At the beginning of this research, only ten of the buildings included in the inventory were listed in the National List of Real Estate Objects of Tangible Cultural Heritage. Since April 2024, the other eleven buildings have been added to the national protection list.[50] Although this event marks an important turning point, it should be considered a beginning rather than an end. The most significant modernist buildings in Tashkent are finally safe from demolition and irreversible transformations, and the next and most important step is to actively guarantee their preservation by developing and implementing the necessary conservation measures.

50 See Resolution No. 227 of the Cabinet of Ministers of the Republic of Uzbekistan, April 22, 2024. (Postanovlenie Kabineta Ministrov Respubliki Uzbekistan ot 22 aprelia 2024 goda.)

Example table of contents of the Monographs developed for the inventory of Tashkent modernist architecture

	Panoramic Cinema	Uzbekistan Hotel	State Museum of Arts	Lenin Museum	Exhibition Hall of the Union of Artists	Museum of Applied Arts	House of Youth	Sun Heliocomplex	Zhemchug residential building	Chorsu Bazaar	Circus	Delegation House of the CCCP UzSSR*	Peoples' Friendship Palace	Cosmonauts Avenue metro station	Turkestan Arena*	Republican House of Tourism
State of Repair	3	3	3	3	3	3	2	2	2	3	2	3	4	4	3	2
Integrity																
Exterior	2	2	1	4	4	2	2	3	4	4	3	1	4			2
Interior	2	1	3	2	3	3	1	2	3	4	3	1	4	4		1
Authenticity																
Exterior	2	2	1	4	4	3	3	4	3	3	3	1	4		4	2
Interior	2	1	3	2	3	3	1	3	2	4	3	1	4	4		2

*** Additional research required**

Assessment and comparison of the state of repair, authenticity and integrity of the main modernist buildings in Tashkent

State of Repair

Definition

The "state of repair" describes the physical condition of the building and the functioning of its parts or elements.

(1 = poor state of repair; 4 = good state of repair)

Integrity

Definition

In the framework of UNESCO's Operational Guidelines for the Implementation of the World Heritage Convention (2024), "integrity" is understood as the wholeness and intactness of a heritage site and its defining attributes. A site's integrity is determined by the extent to which it includes the essential elements that convey its Outstanding Universal Value (OUV); has a size that adequately reflects its significance; and has been compromised by major adverse effects from development and/or neglect.

(1 = poor level of integrity; 4 = high level of integrity)

Authenticity

Definition

Based on the Nara Document on Authenticity (1994), "authenticity" is understood as the ability of a cultural heritage site or object to truthfully and credibly express its value and meaning, reflecting its cultural and historical significance. This expression can be demonstrated through various attributes, including form and design, materials and substance, use and function, traditions and techniques, location and setting, and spirit and feeling.

(1 = poor level of authenticity; 4 = high level of authenticity)

Modernist Palimpsest

Nicola Russi

It is not a frequent situation in which a collection of modernist buildings, diverse in type, form and function, can be read as an archipelago of architectures, coherently and simultaneously immersed in an equally cohesive and congruent urban landscape. But this is the case in Tashkent.

The best-known examples, such as Brasília or Chandigarh, have buildings conceived and constructed in unison with their cities, where the long period of time that usually elapses between urban planning and architectural design is condensed in the hands of individual architects. Tashkent is equally significant, but different for many reasons. It cannot be considered a purely planned city. Since the late nineteenth century, its modern part has been built close to, and partially within, a preexisting historical fabric. Tashkent's development process through multiple plans is attributable to five main phases: the Turkestan period, the Soviet architectural avant-garde (until the early 1930s), the Stalinist period (until the 1950s), the modernist period (until 1991), during which the 1966 earthquake occurred, and contemporary development. Unlike planned cities, which are a result of the implementation of a single project by a few authors, the complexity that modernist Tashkent expresses is that of an urban palimpsest written in a time frame sufficiently short to retain coherence and sufficiently dilated to allow for different interpretations of the same design culture.

The different plans that succeeded one another have left different legacies, some of which are immediately recognizable in the major infrastructure and general functional arrangements. Others, which are seemingly more concealed but no less significant, take the form of weak networks of open spaces capable of tying together the major modernist buildings that dot the city.

This reticular structure of a void that relies on preexisting water and environmental systems is one of the most significant physical manifestations of an urban design culture that, in other historical and geographical contexts, has yet to be applied as extensively and pervasively as in Tashkent. Principles already present in the culture of the American park movement of the mid-nineteenth century resonate in its continuous networks of open spaces and concretize those established by early-twentieth-century Soviet Disurbanism. However, unlike other significant planned urban realities, Tashkent is distinguished by the completeness of this reticular layout of the void and the fact that it has survived almost intact.

The relationship between the figure and the ground that Tashkent's modernist architecture establishes with the existing system of voids produces two different but not opposing outcomes: the system of voids assigns buildings a monumentality that makes them protagonists within the urban landscape, while at the same time enforcing their role of social infrastructure, the functional programs of which resonate within the broader framework of the open spaces that surround them. This system acquires even more complexity in its interaction with the historic urban fabric, which can collide and bend or, in some cases, prevail, generating unprecedented conditions that characterize this city's specificity.

In this context of recurrence and variation, each modernist building defines a particular relationship with the urban void, some encompassing the void within the building either horizontally or vertically, some artificially shaping the ground by creating artificial bumps and hills and others simply extending their plan geometry to the outer space around them. At a time in history marked by significant climate change and the emergence of new cultural paradigms, this continuous system of interconnected open spaces and modernist architecture may have great environmental potential and be a powerful identity resource for the city. However, Tashkent's rapid real estate development of the past decade is jeopardizing the continuity of this network, and thus its functioning, by incrementally eroding significant portions of its open spaces and green surfaces.

Protecting this heritage may mean building an appropriate system of urban regulations to be enforced within precisely identified boundaries to preserve its environmental, landscape and architectural structure. While at first glance, preservation through a regulatory apparatus may seem the path of best protection, over a short period a simple regulatory system can easily be subject to varying degrees of reversibility triggered by cultural, social, and economic changes that are difficult to foresee today. As an alternative or in addition to this mode, it is possible to take a more ambitious but more robust path: to recognize the existing network of buildings and open spaces as the support for a new environmental and cultural enhancement project for the city. We called this project the Cultural Trail. A design rewrite of the architecture and urban spaces that comprise this palimpsest can enable the elaboration of a new urban vision capable of expressing contemporary values while preserving the essence of the modernist city.

If the most potent form of preservation implies the broadest communication of importance of a place or artifact, it is through a design gaze that this awareness can be generated. The project is the most effective tool for revealing the potential of a historic artifact to the society that inherited it and lives within it, assigning values, urgencies and visions of its contemporary relevance.

Gardens and Canals as Subjects of Earlier Masterplanning

Until the Industrial Revolution, gardens and parks were mainly a stage for upper-class leisure and representative practices.[1] However, with the growth of industrial zones and related hygiene issues, by the end of the nineteenth century the idea of the public park had spread. British parliamentary legislation regarding the sanitary conditions of the working class quickly reached growing industrialized urban centers in France and Germany, directing urban planning practices in favor of the Volkspark, a public park to treat ailments of body and mind.[2] The first available maps from prerevolutionary Tashkent portray a comparable story of urban development that holistically considered public gardens and urban blocks.

The plan for the construction of the eastern (new) part of the city between the Ankhor and Chauli canals was drafted by the military engineer Kolesnikov.[3] The settlement was designed in an orthogonal way according to the urban planning canons of the time, such as the schemes of Alma-Ata drawn in 1858 by engineer Leonard Aleksandrovskii.[4] The grid structure of newly founded Russian Tashkent was defined and contained by preexisting artifacts of an Asian city, such as the Urda military fortress and the old Tashkent wall, the naturally hilly topography, and the Ankhor and Chauli canals.

However, as late nineteenth-century maps illustrate, the rigid system of the orthogonal grid of tsarist-era Russian Tashkent did not interfere with the shape of the water, instead organizing parks and gardens along the course of the rivers, canals and streams that supplied the city.

Comparing the map of 1870 with that of 1872, where the project for Konstaninovskii Square (now Amir Temur Square) and the powerful system of radial streets that derive from it is depicted, it is clear that no

1 Denis E. Cosgrove, *Social Formation and Symbolic Landscape* (London: Croom Helm, 1984).
2 Stefanie Hennecke, "Der Volkspark für die Gesundung von Geist und Körper – Das ideologische Spannungsfeld einer bürgerlichen Reformbewegung zwischen Emanzipation und Disziplinierung des Volkes," in *Gärten und Parks als Lebens- und Erlebnisraum: Funktions- und nutzungsgeschichtliche Aspekte der Gartenkunst in Früher Neuzeit und Moderne*, ed. Stefan Schweizer (Worms: Wernersche Verlagsanstalt, 2008), 151–164.
3 Paul Stronski, *Tashkent: Forging a Soviet City, 1930–1966* (Pittsburgh: University of Pittsburgh Press), 2011.
4 See "Historic Maps of Verny, Alma-Ata, and Almaty," https://www.walkingalmaty.com/post/historic-maps-of-verny-alma-ata-and-almaty.

modification was made to the shape of the stream that separates the square from the city center to the east. Along this waterway and the short stretch of the Ankhor Canal represented on the map, green surfaces comparable to those of the flower beds inside the square and the gardens of the "new city" are organized. The relationship established between the water system and the public green system is a theme that would recur in subsequent urban projects developed for the Uzbek capital.

First visible traces of Konstantinovskii Square (now Amir Temur Square), Ensign Vasil'ev's map, 1870

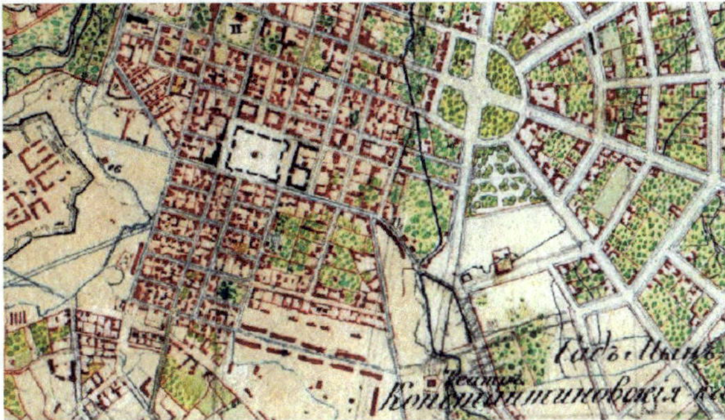
Formation of Konstantinovskii Square (now Amir Temur Square), 1872

Intermezzo 1: Moscow Planning References

The plans developed for Tashkent between 1929 and 1938 must be read in the wider context of the international urban studies and the heated political and cultural debate in Moscow among the Constructivists, who later divided into Urbanists and Disurbanists during the postrevolutionary reconstruction.

Among the main themes that sparked discussion between the two groups about the city, then commonly understood as a new social organism and condenser, were the different forms of relationship it established with its surrounding context. While this aspect immediately emerges in the design of planned cities and the natural environment, the new sociopolitical conditions also forced a radical rethinking of existing cities, raising questions about how new forms of urban development related to the historical fabric. However, the radical transformation of the existing context is separate from its destruction and reduction to a tabula rasa. The projects developed for Moscow in that brief and fertile moment of urban rethinking of the city, characterized by approaches that were sometimes in opposition, are connected by an attempt to reconcile the utopian impetus of superimposed forms on the existing urban fabric with proposals for the reuse of the existing historical landscape, particularly its heritage aspects. Such proposals involve all scales: maintaining the city's main buildings and public spaces as monumentalized and representational spaces, but also studying architectural types appropriate to the new society, replacing previous ones and developing proposals for new development patterns at the urban scale that structurally alter the original layout of the city.

The radical visions that were drawn up for Moscow in the short period of the late 1920s and early 1930s were never actually applied in the capital, although they stimulated a cultural debate that reverberated in different forms in the production of plans for other cities in the Soviet Union. Two plans, by Nikolai Kolli and Sergei Kirov in 1929 and Moisei Ginzburg in 1931, clearly impacted the urban visions produced in that period for Tashkent, notably the 1938 plan. The two visions for Moscow show similarities in the use of greenery and both proposals utilize the figurative power of the void, not intended solely as a background but as a structuring figure of the city. However, this new "urban material" was interpreted using different principles.

Kolli and Kirov designed a system of concentric rings for Moscow, repurposing the Howardian vision of a green belt around the city. A continuous circular park, the shape of which recalls El Lissitzky's Suprematist aesthetic, is the pivotal infrastructure on which the new cultural and leisure facilities rest. However, it also represents a clear desire to demarcate the city from its natural context.

In 1931, Moisei Ginzburg proposed a "Park System of Moscow" as part of his competition entry for the Central Park of Culture and Leisure in Moscow. Ginzburg's park system replaces Kolli and Kirov's form with a reticular system of open spaces. Here, the green spaces, recognized as the structuring materials of a new urban condition, connect existing natural environments, run in the grooves of the city's historical structure and rely on the influential geographical figure of the water system. Ginzburg, considered one of the most radical representatives of Disurbanist thought, admitted moving away from geometric principles and abstract patterns. The use of pure geometric forms, derived from the Constructivist artistic movement, had a purely diagrammatic value that required adaptation to the project context: "As far as the principle of linear settlement is concerned, it is necessary to remember how the straight line adopted in the abstract must assume an entirely free, unprefigured course in practice. This line must follow the same trends as nature, setting itself the goal of bringing man as close as possible to the environment."[5]

Another plan drawn up in that period, Nikolai Ladovskii's dynamo-parabolic vision of New Moscow (1932), fitted within a debate involving two opposing models: conservative architects oriented toward a centripetal urban vision in contrast to proposals for a linear city. For Ladovskii, the parabola form was the way to "develop the idea of the linear city within the traditional concept of urban centrality."[6] His design recognized Moscow's historical centrality. However, it broke its circular system in the northwestern sector of the city, providing an opportunity to grow freely from the center in the direction of Leningrad.

In its attempt to mediate between two opposing approaches, this figure, unprecedented in the history of urban design, took the shape of a formal solution rather than a new urban model. The diagrammatic power of the proposal did not correspond to an equally innovative study of the quality and mode of operation of the urban habitats it proposed.

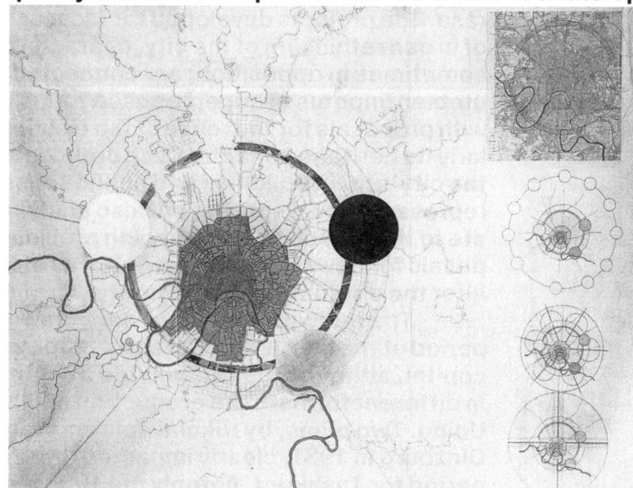

Nikolai Kolli and Sergei Kirov's map of the city, 1929

5 Moisei Ginzburg and Mikhail Barshch, "La città verde," in *La costruzione della città sovietica 1929–31*, ed. Paolo Ceccarelli (Padua: Marsilio, 1970), 192–193. English translation by the author.

6 Alessandra Latour, *Mosca 1890–2000* (Rome: Edizioni Kappa, 2008), 55. English translation by the author.

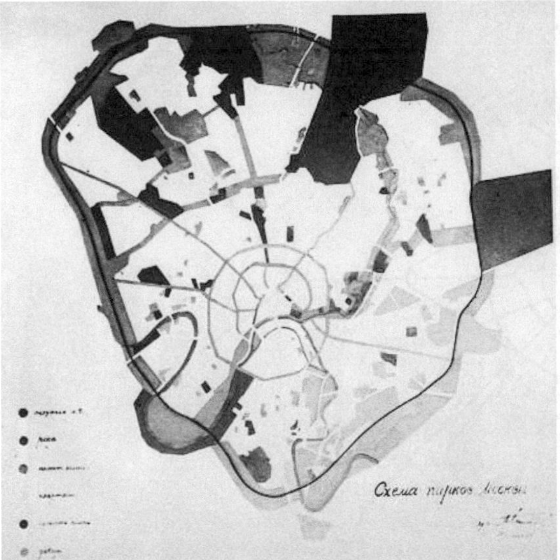

Moisei Ginzburg, Park System of Moscow, 1931

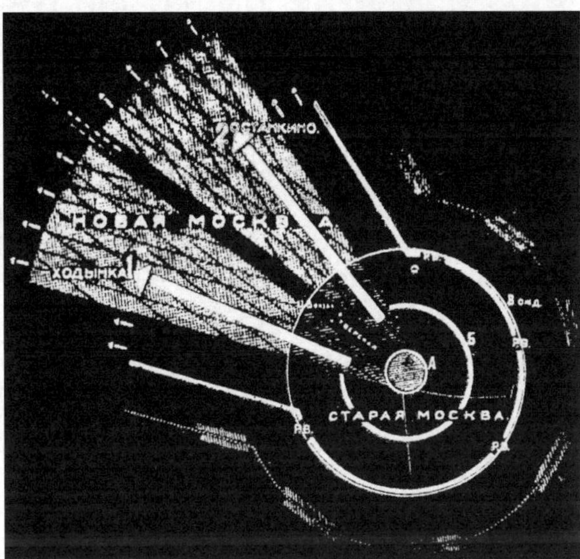

Nikolai Ladovskii, Dynamo-parabolic vision of New Moscow, 1932

Tabula Rasa: Unification of the Binary City

In 1929 the Bureau for the Redevelopment of the Cities of Central Asia was set up in Tashkent as a consequence of the administrative unification of the Asian and European quarters, which was a result of the accelerated speed of cultural and industrial revolution in the Soviet Union.[7] For the first time, a masterplan unifying two poles into a single union could be developed.

The Soviet urban vision at the time was strongly influenced by two architects teaching in Moscow: Moisei Ginzburg and Nikolai Ladovskii. They had very different understandings of the formational elements of the city. While Ginzburg in his 1931 project for a park system for Moscow[8] traced a structural network of green as a fundamental design ingredient of the settlement, for Ladovskii nature was designed as a container surrounding the city center. The masterplan scheme produced by Aleksandr Sil'chenkov, a former pupil of Nikolai Ladovskii's, took the tabula rasa approach, using the reticular geometries of infrastructure as design tools for overcoming and erasing preexisting urban figures in the city. The new geometric layout in the spirit of the "Ladovskii parabola" that was popular at the time[9] spared the European quarters but proposed erasing the preexisting urban fabric of the historical Asian city with its complex topography and medieval monuments. The use of pure, almost primitive geometries corresponds to a clear, re-foundational intention of the society for its host territory, without indulging its historical and environmental preexistences.

Although Sil'chenkov rejected Ginzburg's continuity of the green system, he borrowed the concept of the public park as a powerful cultural complex where public, administrative, physical and cultural institutions for the masses are placed.

7 See Boris Chukhovich, "Zapovednik (k arkheologii muzeeifitsirovaniia v gradostroitel'stve Uzbekistana) [The Cultural Reserve (Toward an Archeology of Museification in the Urban Planning of Uzbekistan)]," 2019, https://www.caa-network.org/archives/14980.

8 Alla Vronskaya, "The Utopia of Personality: Moisei Ginzburg's Project for the Moscow Park of Culture and Leisure," *Quaestio Rossica*, no. 4, 2015, 40–56.

9 Elena Ovsyannikova and Vladimir Shukhov, "Phenomenon of the Russian Avant-Garde: Moscow Architectural School of the 1920s," *Docomomo Journal*, no. 49, 2013, 22–27.

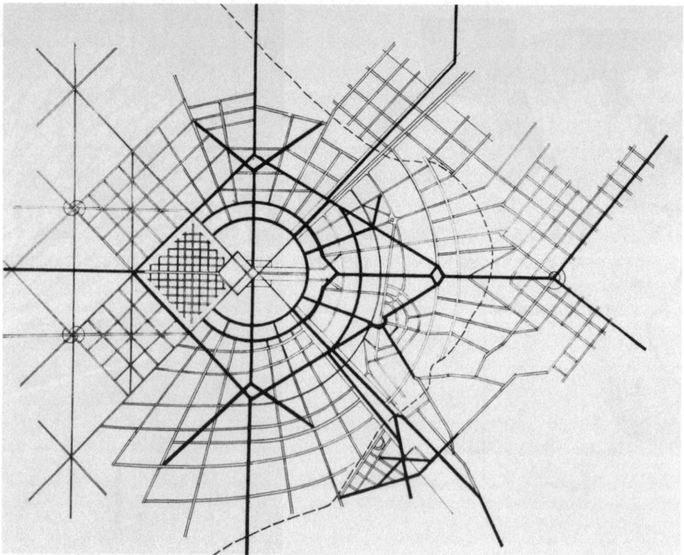

Aleksandr Sil'chenkov, first reconstruction project of Tashkent, 1929–1933 (not approved)

Green Network: A Structural Element of the Masterplan of Tashkent

Affinities with Moisei Ginzburg's continuous green system are visible in the first plan approved for the reconstruction of modern Tashkent, developed under the supervision of architect Aleksandr Kuznetsov from 1937 to 1939. This concept later reverberated in the masterplan of 1954 developed by Tashgiprogor and in the general plan of 1966. According to a document prepared by the Tashkent City Committee of the Communist Party of Uzbekistan,[10] the 1954 masterplan foresaw the construction of new boulevards and parks along the main canals as well as expansion of the existing ones to support more pleasant and hygienic pedestrian mobility and access to services. In contrast to Sil'chenkov's scheme, a preexisting green network around the canals was recognized as an element that reinforced the objectives of the Soviet modernist planners and could easily overlap with the grid of urban blocks and transport infrastructure, thus establishing an instantly recognizable backbone for the masterplan.

The radical nature of this proposal does not lie in the abstract power of a geometric figure dropped from above, as in the case of Ladovskii's Moscow masterplan, but, like in the plans by Kolli/Kirov and Ginzburg, rests on the figurative power of emptiness as the structuring element of the "new city." In contrast to the latter two plans, Kuznetsov's relies on the morphology of the geographic context without abruptly interrupting the green belt marked as a boundary between the city and its surrounding territory. This network of subtle and sinuous paths, equally distributed throughout the city's neighborhoods, overcomes the classic dichotomy between center and periphery, between city and territory, without erasing the variety of the geographical context it fits. However, Kuznetsov's plan creates a significant transformation of the historic fabric, especially in the city's western sector. He retained a few original infrastructural paths by correcting them, but most of the existing neighborhoods were erased by repurposing already-present infrastructural grids in the eastern part of the city. It is worth noting that the plan does not specify any buildings, and the proposed infrastructural grid is secondary to the green corridor system.

10 Philipp Meuser, *Seismic Modernism: Architecture and Housing in Soviet Tashkent* (Berlin: DOM Publishers, 2016).

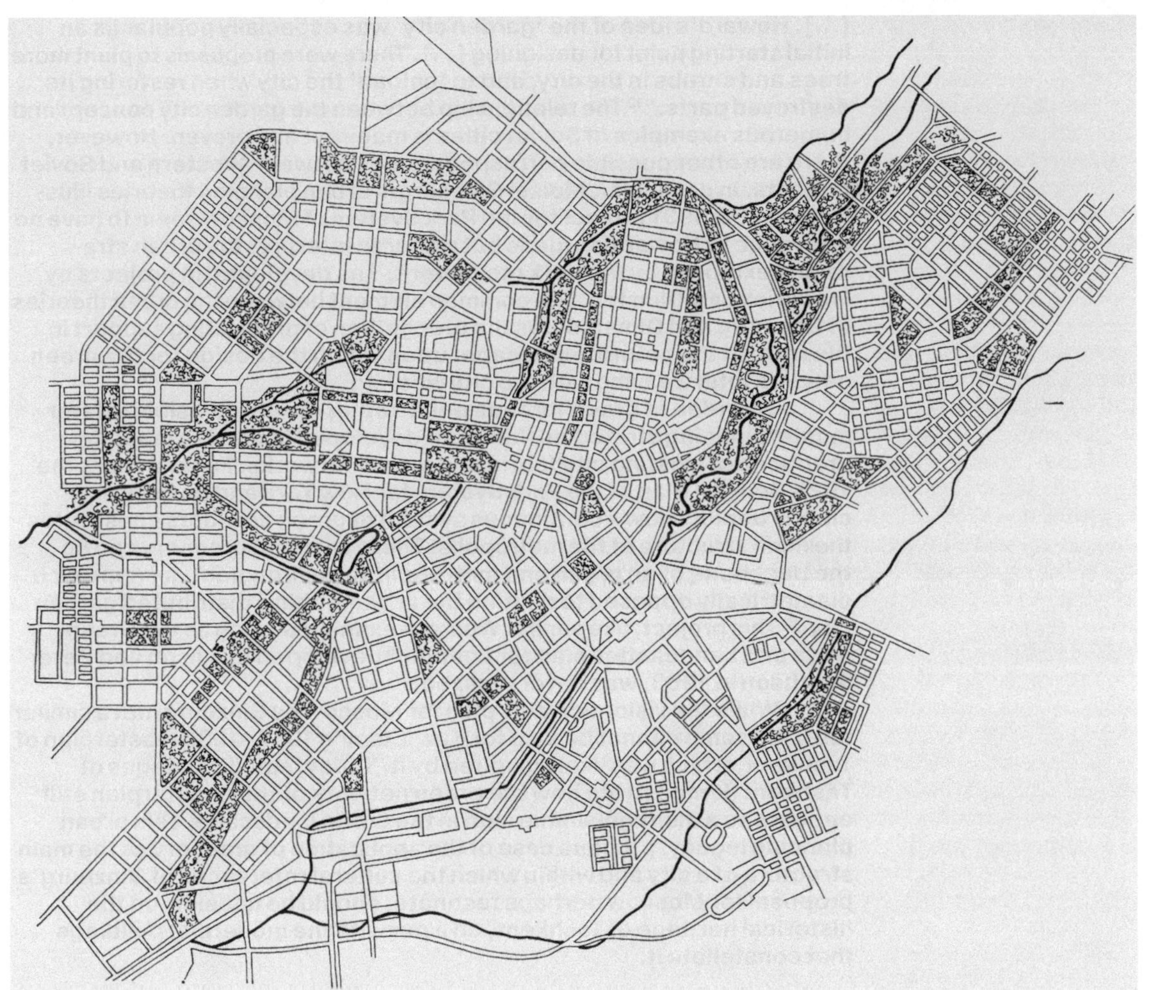

Aleksandr Kuznetsov, masterplan of Tashkent, 1937–1939

Intermezzo 2: Western Green Planning References

It is well known that there was a close connection between Western and Soviet designers after the 1917 revolution. Hannes Meyer, Ernst May, Mart Stam and Le Corbusier all had direct relationships with Moscow and saw in the birth of the Soviet Union the opportunity to implement their urban theories fully. As Anatole Kopp later wrote, "The conditions of the new socialist city in Russia between the 1920s and 1930s, when the country was confronted, even before the West, with the realization of new planned cities and the adaptation of old cities to the new political thinking, were fertile ground for the boldest experiments."[11]

In addition to the influence of modern architects in both the pre- and postrevolutionary periods, Western urban planning theories such as Ebenezer Howard's garden city (1898), Arturo Soria y Mata's linear city (1882) and Tony Garnier's cité industrielle (1905) progressively influenced the development of the Soviet city, including its expansionist dimension and its aspects of social control.

Tatyana Budantseva explained in her Ph.D. dissertation that the introduction in the 1920s of a "new planned economy and the abolition of private ownership of land opened up new paths for Soviet town building

11 Anatole Kopp, *Città e Rivoluzione: Architettura e urbanistica sovietiche degli anni Venti* (Milan: Feltrinelli, 1987), 179. English translation by the author.

[...]. Howard's idea of the 'garden city' was especially popular as an initial starting point for designing [...]. There were proposals to plant more trees and shrubs in the city, and to 'unload' the city when restoring its destroyed parts."[12] The relationship between the garden city concept and numerous examples of Soviet cities is manifest and proven. However, there are other possible correspondences between Western and Soviet projects. In particular, Moisei Ginzburg's urban planning theories illustrated in the 1931 project for the Park System of Moscow seem to have no relevance to Howardian ideas but rather to interpret the urban strategies explored by the park movement,[13] as developed in projects by Frederick Law Olmsted. The common element between the urban theories of Ginzburg and Olmsted was the recognition of preexisting support in the form of the natural landscape, upon which the design for the green network interweaving with the city was laid.

This idea of green threads penetrating the city is visible in later masterplanning strategies that were developed in precise mapping practices of existing city fabric and green networks. For instance, the 1928 General Plan of the Park System for New York and Its Environs[14] clearly depicts how a continuous system of green corridors constitutes the main structure of the metropolis. The idea is that greenery can be the backbone of an urban and metropolitan environment, an approach diametrically opposed to diluting the urban within a distributed garden city.[15] This project, like similar Western examples, such as the Greenways and Landcastles plan for London[16] developed by Alison and Peter Smithson in 1963, was never realized.

While the visionary 1931 plan for Moscow by Ginzburg met a similar fate, the same cannot be said for Kuznetsov's 1937–1939 masterplan of Tashkent, which was likely inspired by it. Today, satellite images of Tashkent demonstrate how the green network of that masterplan still appears as a distinguishable sign in the urban landscape. This urban planning legacy, a unique case of the application of greenery as the main structure of a city and within which the cultural references of Ginzburg's proposal for Moscow perhaps resonate, should be considered the historical heritage of Tashkent, on a par with the modernist buildings that constellate it.

12 Tatyana Budantseva, "Avant-Garde Between East and West: Modern Architecture and Town Planning in the Urals 1920–1930s," (Ph.D. diss., TU Delft, 2007), 32.

13 In the mid-nineteenth century, the upper middle class sought to respond to the challenges of city life through the creation of public urban parks in a territorial scale project that has been termed the "park movement." The park movement involved not only the design and development of parks but also extensive writing, including work by Frederick Law Olmsted and Ralph Waldo Emerson and even a novel by Sylvester Judd that centered on public park design. See John Evelev, *Picturesque Literature and the Transformation of the American Landscape: 1835–1874* (Oxford: Oxford University Press, 2021).

14 See "1911–1929: From Chicago to NYC; The Creation of Regional Plan Association," https://rpa.org/work/reports/regional-plan-associations-100-year-history-in-nyc#1911-1929-from-chicago-to-nyc-the-creation-of-regional-plan-association.

15 It can be argued that Frederick Law Olmsted was less influenced by the Romantic idealism of the English garden, which denied the man-made in favor of the natural, and was more concerned with the integration of the two. For him the natural landscape was intended to be a conveyor of the unexpected and a place of action for all human activity, be it social, political or natural. See Timothy D. Martin, "Robert Smithson and the Anglo-American Picturesque," in *Anglo-American Exchange in Postwar Sculpture: 1945–1975*, ed. Rebecca Peabody (Los Angeles: J. Paul Getty Museum, 2011), 164–174; Robert Smithson, "Frederick Law Olmsted and the Dialectical Landscape," *Art Forum*, no. 11, 1973, 62–68, https://www.artforum.com/print/197302/frederick-law-olmsted-and-the-dialectical-landscape-36282.

16 Alison Smithson and Peter Smithson, *The Charged Void: Urbanism* (New York: Monacelli Press, 2005), 351.

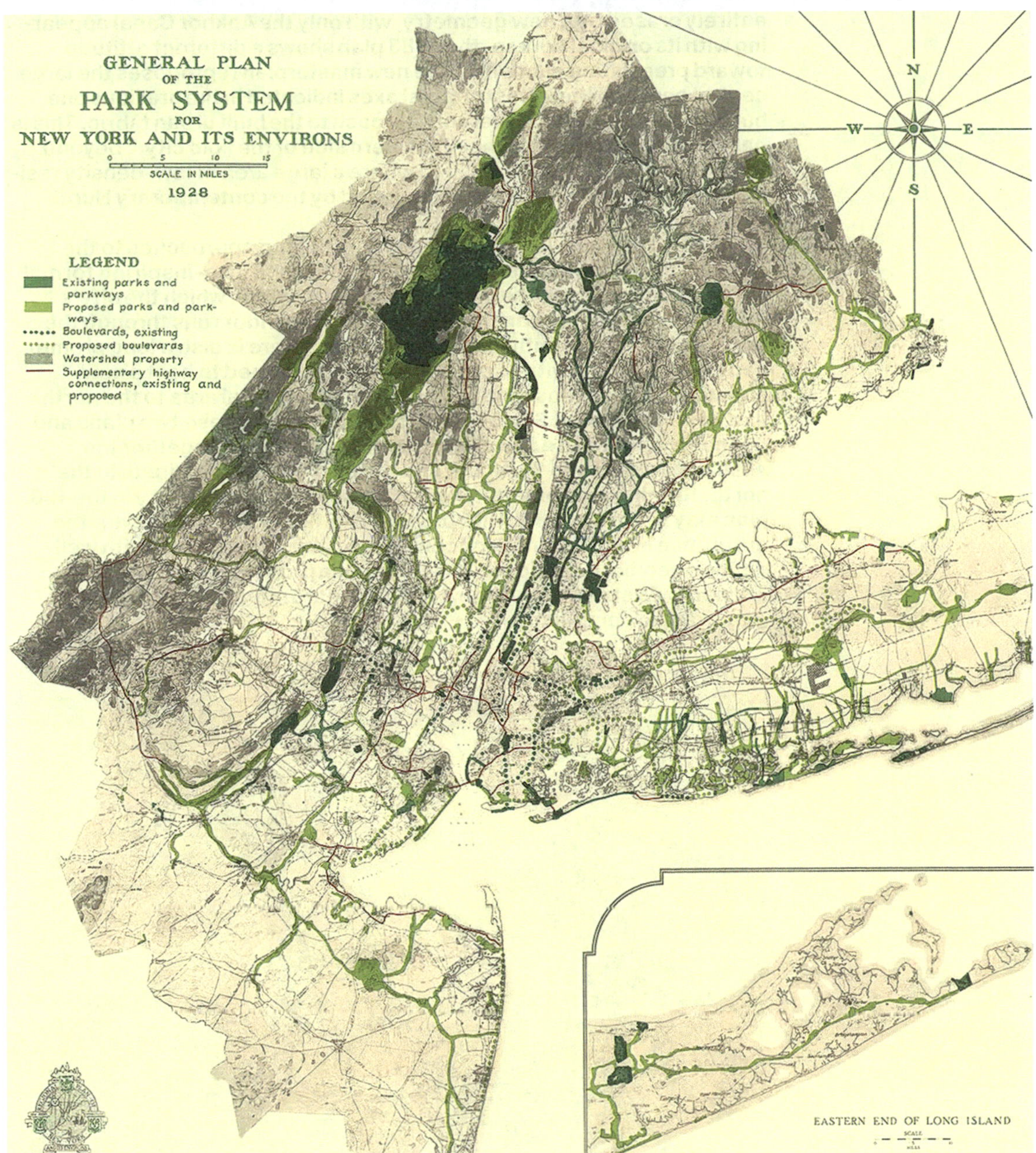

General Plan of the Park System for New York and Its Environs, 1928

Formal Green

In contrast to previous maps of Tashkent, in the masterplan of 1974 the urban block had changed from the perimetral construction of the Stalin period to freestanding objects immersed in a continuous public park, following the typical socialist city layout of urban planning at the time. The park, which reunites the "old" and "new" cities through uniform geometry, is surrounded by clusters characterized by slab buildings and interior courtyards. The new clusters almost replace the mahalla's historic fabric with new architectural types. Only around the Chorsu Bazaar area can a preserved fragment of the historic fabric be recognized, surrounded by new buildings and green areas. While the 1974 map depicts the original topography of the historic parts of Tashkent as

entirely erased by a new geometry, with only the Ankhor Canal appearing with its original course, the 1983 plan shows a different attitude toward preexisting elements. The new masterplan reproposes the large central park and the infrastructural axes indicated in the previous one but it takes a markedly different approach to the built urban fabric. This is particularly evident in the northwestern side of the "old city," beyond the Circus and the park behind it, where a large area of low-density residential fabric is preserved and encircled by the contemporary Nurafshon Street.

The 1974 and 1983 plans have contrasting approaches to the existing framework, but they share a sizable and awe-inspiring formal garden that serves as the city's green heart, within which the city's major public buildings are located. A green corridor runs through the park from north to south, along the Ankhor. There is also a long promenade with a large central space, originally designed to host a new highway, which almost entirely encloses the central area to the north and east. The Furkat Street axis is taking shape in these two plans and defines the western edge of the central park. It joins together the Alisher Navoi Park to the south and the park behind the Circus to the north, forming an elongated hourglass shape. The greenery in the 1983 plan may seem similar to that proposed in 1937–1939. However, the difference lies in how it is concentrated in the central area, with well-defined geometric shapes. This sets these proposals apart from Kuznetsov's structural vision, which appears more fluid and open to topographic complexity.

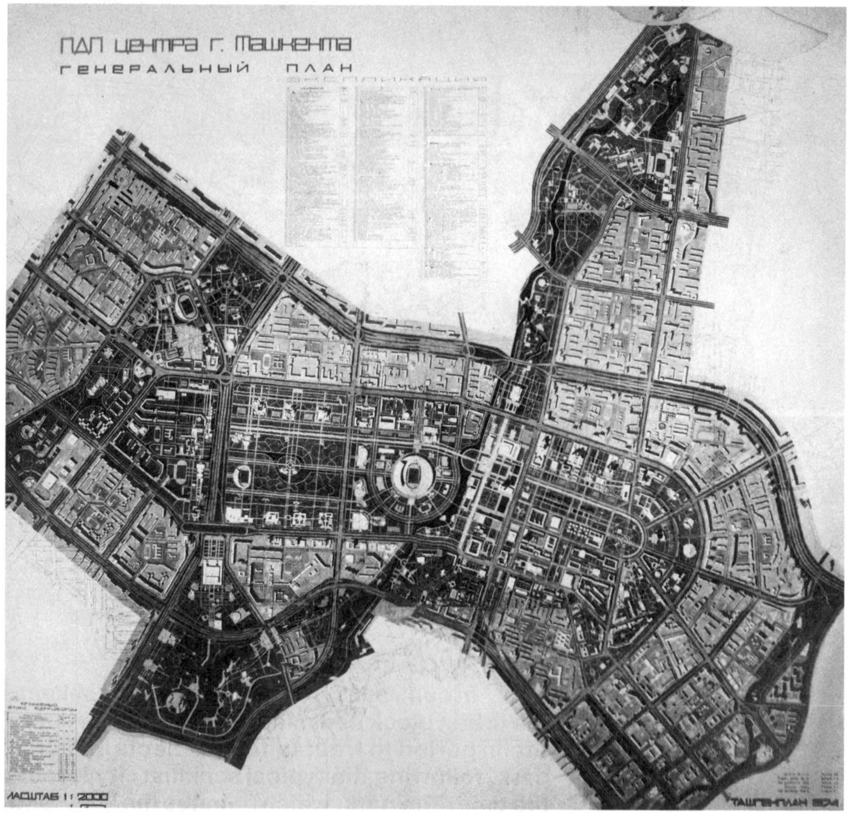

Detailed Tashkent city center masterplan, Tashgenplan, 1974

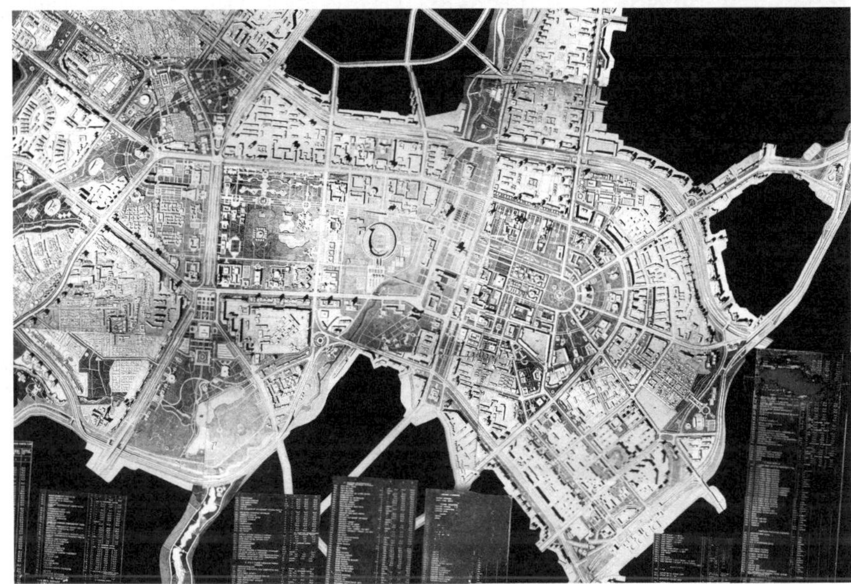

Detailed Tashkent city center masterplan (project), Tashgenplan, 1983

Green Legacies

A profound understanding of the city's urban composition is unveiled through a meticulous comparison of historical maps from various epochs and contemporary satellite images of Tashkent. This comprehensive approach allows us to trace the evolution of the city's layout and appreciate the intricate interplay between its past and present.

Upon examining the structure of the urban voids, satellite images reveal how some of the formal green figures suggested in the 1974 and 1983 masterplans are still visible. The green heart is evident on the center's east side, while the recently constructed interventions on the west side adhere to the Cartesian geometry dictated by the street infrastructure, without reproducing the continuous green-city idea promoted by the modernist masterplans, with buildings immersed in vegetation. Here, Western-style courtyard blocks and large commercial buildings frame a square-shaped park. The elongated hourglass shape of the Furkat axis with the two parks and the fragment of the promenade north of the center are also clearly distinguishable. The current structure of green voids, one of the city's most prominent features, is the result of overlapping projects that were sometimes only partially implemented and have succeeded one another throughout history. The contemporary situation is reminiscent of the green network of the 1937–1939 masterplan.

When we compare the modernist buildings relevant to the Tashkent Modernism XX/XXI research with these green spaces, we can observe that they mainly coincide. The correlation between modernist architecture and the green structure of Tashkent is not just a coincidence, but a unique and significant legacy of the city. This distinctive feature sets Tashkent apart from other cities and is a testament to its rich modernist culture. To disregard or eliminate this interconnection between modernist architecture and green spaces would mean to lose one of the most distinctive features of its modernist culture. This unique landscape, characterized by the interplay of architecture and open spaces, is further enriched by its relationship with the historic fabric of the traditional mahalla that mostly surrounds it in the western part of the city.

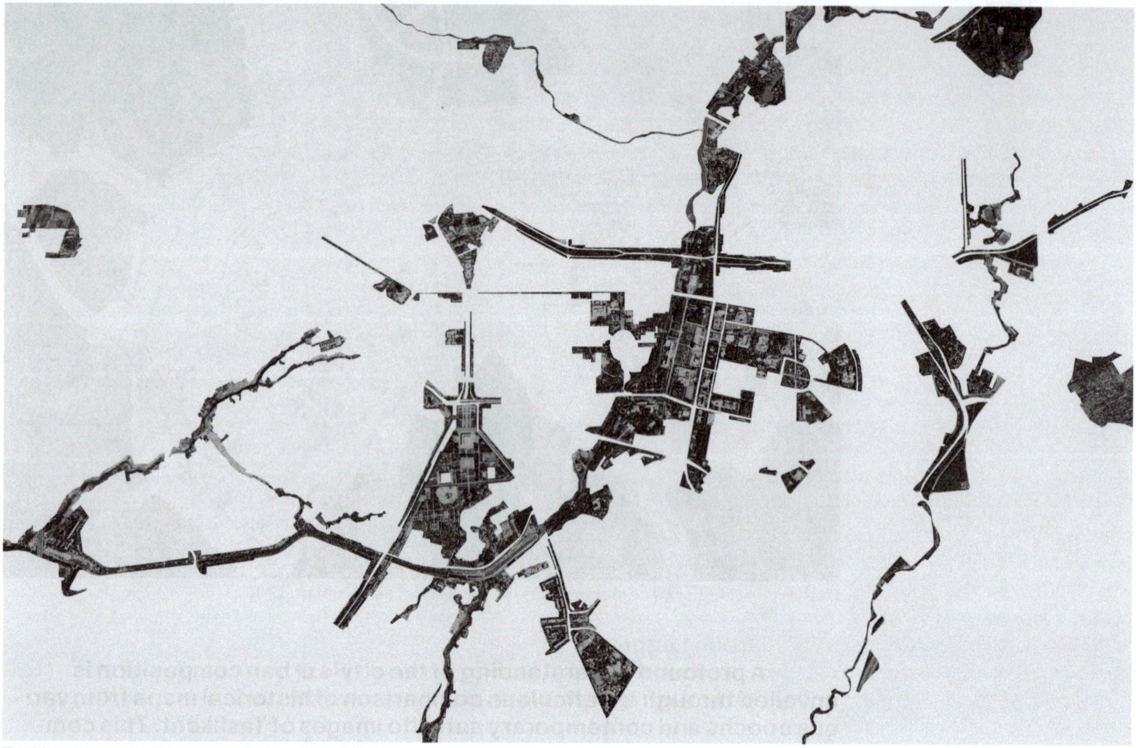

Tashkent green voids, current situation, 2020

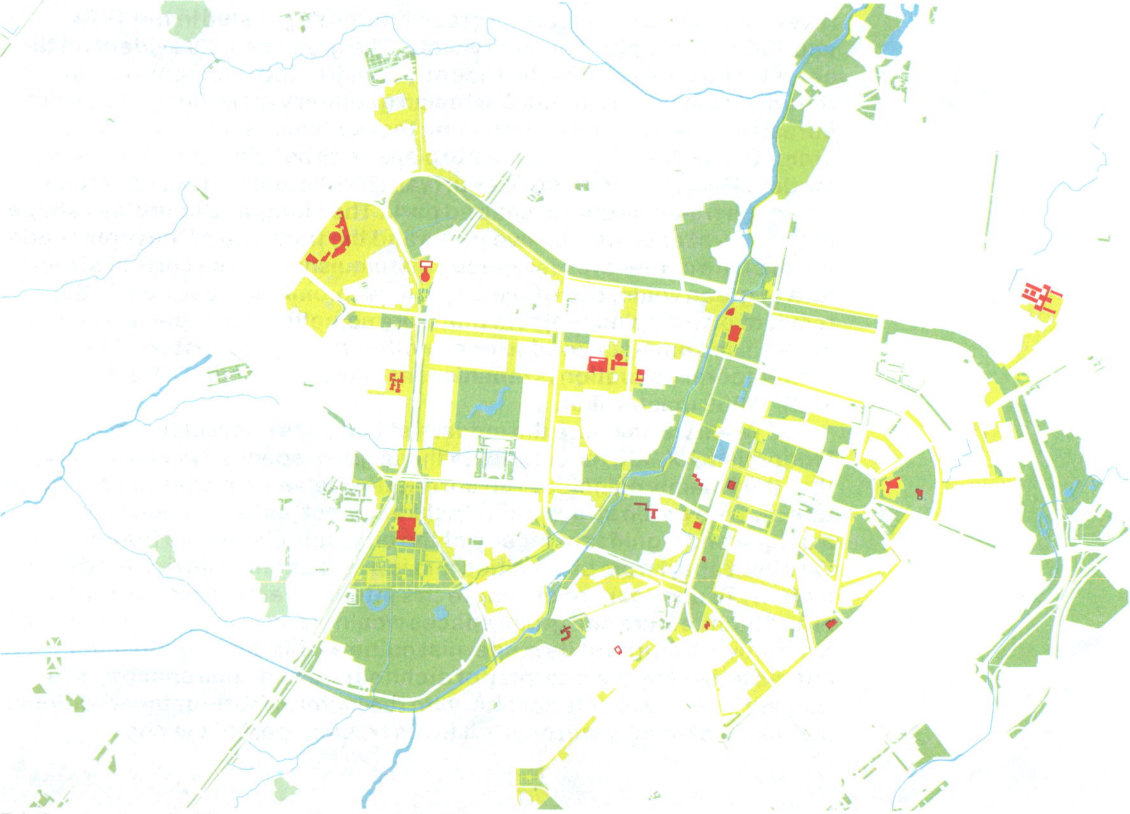

Existing structure of public spaces with modernist buildings selected by the research project, Tashkent, 2020
Yellow: predominantly pedestrian public space, green: public green space, red: selected modernist buildings

Cultural Trails as a Protection and Enhancement Project

The correspondence between modernist architecture built since the 1960s and the reticular system of voids derived from the 1938 plan and subsequent plans is visible and still forms the main structure of the public and collective spaces in Tashkent. This grand urban design is not the outcome of a single hand. It is the product of the sedimentation of an architectural and urban culture that has lasted almost half a century. Modernist architecture has interpreted its role within a unitary vision without bending to compositional conformism and the reiteration of already practiced typological solutions.

The Cultural Trail[17] identified as part of the research project Tashkent Modernism XX/XXI links together most of the significant modernist buildings along the existing traces of the masterplans. Rather than being a single loop or uniform green network, the project uncovers the image of a complex system of urban environments: modernist monumental clusters and residential quarters, together with historical patterns and collective spaces such as parks, riverbanks and squares are described in a more revealing way with the Cultural Trail as a mediator. Six variations of the Cultural Trail emerged through physical and online dérives in a microcosm of maps, historical documents, photographs and paintings (some of which are described below). Each of the trails was given a name that describes its predominant characteristics and use of collective space.

The trail named "Esplanade" retraces the paths suggested by modernist masterplans of 1974 and 1983 to connect the two centers of Tashkent by passing through a series of large collective spaces, such as Amir Temur Square, Independence Square and Pakhtakor Stadium. As well as the immense squares, the trail connects modernist buildings that assume a different posture in relation to the void that surrounds them: the slightly bent blade volume of the Uzbekistan Hotel (1974) builds an architectural backdrop to Amir Temur Square and marks the end point of the axis to the east with its verticality. As one ventures past the bustling commercial axis of Sayilgoh Street and Independence Square and crosses the Ankhor Canal, the trail leads to the Panoramic Cinema building (1964), its monumental cylinder piercing the lush greenery that envelops it. At its base, a sleek, glazed linear volume seamlessly blends into a sprawling public space, maintaining its visual harmony. The cinema is part of a cluster of modernist masterpieces that includes the House of Youth (1975), which extends the city's space within it through a sophisticated system of ramps and levels, and the TV Center (1977), which relates to urban space with a multicolored mosaic façade on which the moving shadows of the linear planted trees it faces reverberate. The architecture's value is distinct from the current state of the public spaces, which are predominantly used as parking lots. However, a small section of the linear park, leading to the Alisher Navoi metro station, harks back to the grander green axis proposed in the 1974 and 1983 masterplans. Continuing to the domes of the Circus (1975) and the busy Chorsu Bazaar (1990), the trail passes through the new neighborhood built around Tashkent City Park, the square shape of which definitively nullifies the ambition of modernist plans to unite the two parts of the city through a continuous green system.

The "Monumental Mile" trail, running north–south orthogonally to the "Esplanade" trail, explores the densest ensemble of modernist buildings and the monumental landscaping surrounding them. Saidulla Abdullaev's painting *Calm Evening* (1982) gives a precise impression of the vast modernist Independence Square in front of the Council of Ministers, defined by large fountains flowing under the crowns of trees

17 The Cultural Trail project is part of the research project Tashkent Modernism XX/XXI. The Laboratorio Permanente team responsible for the project is made up of Nicola Russi, Angelica Sylos Labini, Laine Lazda, Pietro Nobili Vitelleschi and Amedeo Noris.

covered in blossoms. Along this trail, monumental buildings alternate with large areas of pavement and greenery, like a checkerboard. The land, treated as an integral part of the architectural design, adds a layer of complexity to this part of the city. For instance, the Union of Artists Exhibition Hall (1974) is slightly elevated above the urban landscape by a green podium, raising its horizontal plate in comparison to the surrounding green surfaces. A short distance away, the State Museum of the History of Uzbekistan (originally the Lenin Museum, 1970) ascends above the ground through public staircases leading to a spacious terrace. Along with a well-articulated system of green spaces, the museum stands as a central garden monument. Importantly, it also fulfills a civic function, configuring itself as an open infrastructure for the city.

The "Monumental Mile" trail ends at the southern boundary of the green rectangle of Park V Tashkente, where the Zhemchug residential building (1985) stands. This significant architectural landmark marks the intersection with the "Modernist Neighborhoods" trail, which crosses diverse housing districts, uncovering the domestic life of residential zones constructed in various periods. The trail reveals the internal life of courtyards, playgrounds and small squares lined with multistory buildings, blurring the boundary between public and private realms. In this context, the Zhemchug residential building establishes a particular relationship between architecture and the urban void, addressing this theme at two scales. Inside, an overlay of vertically developed collective loggias mimics the rarefied system of the voids of the mahalla's domestic courtyards. This building expresses in the most emblematic form how Uzbek modernism was able to interpret its history, not only from a stylistic point of view but also through a reinterpretation of its spatial conditions.

The Chorsu Bazaar, with its complex articulation of domes and horizontal vaulted volumes, fits within the mahalla, encompassing the porous dimension of labyrinthine streets and courtyards within its floor plan. The interpenetration of large modernist buildings, Soviet-style residential fabric and the mahalla is unique to the western part of the city of Tashkent. In Pavel Ben'kov's *Girlfriends* (1945), the image of the girls sitting beneath a timber structure covered with vines recalls a drawing of a two-story residential building project in the C-5 microdistrict, where the public square is decorated with a pergola like the one in the painting. A similar scene of walkways surrounded by gardens and lined with pergolas and latticework supporting climbing plants is evident along the "Garden Line" trail. The path connecting the Circus and the Peoples' Friendship Palace (1981) provides a quiet pedestrian alternative to busy Furkat Street, traversing an intact Soviet residential neighborhood that is nestled in a world of small gardens and narrow walkways and then meets the porous fabric of the mahalla.

The "Boulevard" trail has a very different character. It follows a promenade in the middle of Abdulla Qodiriy Street that modernist urban planners envisioned as a highway, but which was never built. Their unrealized utopia of high-speed infrastructure has become a modern promenade, a free space for the contemporary ideal of metropolitan public space. Here, the mosaic façades of modernist residential buildings form a harmonious sequence, echoing the precise geometric rhythm of the rigid Soviet-style urban layout. No significant buildings emerge along this trail, but the strength of a unified urban design prevails, making it possible to imagine a comprehensive project to redevelop its green and pedestrian areas.

The "Water Trail" explores urban nature in Tashkent by following the Ankhor Canal from the Peoples' Friendship Palace gardens to the TV Tower (1985). This watercourse, accompanied by a varied system of parks and open spaces for its whole length, is the dominant figure in the system of urban voids and has remained present in all plans over the years. Manon Saidov's *Family* (1969) depicts a family cycling along the canal, the image conveying slices of life in nature, and conditions such as the flickering of light off water and the miraculous multitude of colors are still present in the heart of the big city. Today this natural landscape, which was preserved by each historical masterplan, is being assaulted by urban development projects that are gradually eroding the greenery along the banks and irreparably transforming this unique fragment of nature into a conventional urban canal.

The six routes of the Cultural Trail act as mediators, revealing through their itineraries the complexity of an urban palimpsest in which urban spaces and architecture are deeply interlaced. They aim to stimulate a new awareness of an existing fragile heritage that requires protection, but also reveal new opportunities through projects of physical transformation of public spaces along the routes and near significant buildings. A design rewrite of the architecture and urban spaces as a single whole that comprises this palimpsest can elaborate a new urban vision capable of expressing contemporary values and preserving the most relevant values of modernism.

This design approach holds the potential for simple yet effective interventions to pave the way for new practices in using public space, while enhancing the city's architectural heritage. The redesign of the misused urban voids along the trail can not only "mean freeing space from impediments, even immaterial ones," as I wrote in an earlier work, "but it can also correspond to the definition of new borders and frames so that the different potentials of the use of the city are uncovered."[18] How can we clear some public surfaces of cars and return them to the city? What new uses can we imagine for these spaces? What would it mean for citizens to have wider, safe and livable sidewalks? Which gates can we remove to create new urban pathways? How can we enforce construction restrictions near water? Finally, how can all these actions build a network of quality spaces around modernist architecture?

By reusing existing spaces in a simple yet sophisticated way, Tashkent can tackle the challenges of the modern city without losing the unity between architecture, urban design and green spaces that is probably the most interesting characteristic of its modernist legacy.

M. Nuritdinov, *City Landscape*, 1983
Oil on canvas

18 Nicola Russi, *Background: Il progetto del vuoto* (Macerata: Quodlibet, 2019), 10. English translation by the author.

Cultural Trail

- Esplanade, 5 km
- Garden Line, 3 km
- Monumental Mile, 2 km
- Boulevard, 5 km
- Modernist Neighborhoods, 6 km
- Water Trail, 8 km
- Alternative route

Significant Modernist Buildings

1. Panoramic Cinema (1964)
2. Former CCCP of Uzbekistan (1964)
3. TV Center (1977)
4. Museum of Applied Arts (1969)
5. State Museum of the History of Uzbekistan (1970)
6. Blue Domes Café (1970)
7. Institute of Art Studies (1972)
8. Museum of Arts (1974)
9. Union of Artists (1974)
10. Circus (1975)
11. Institute of Pectoral Surgery (1975), not shown on map
12. Ilkhom Theater and Shodlik Hotel (1975)
13. Uzbekistan Hotel (1974)
14. Palace of Aviation Constructors (1980), not shown on map
15. Peoples' Friendship Palace (1981)
16. TV Tower (1985), not shown on map
17. Zhemchug residential building (1985)
18. Ben'kov Art College (1986)
19. Former Republican House of Tourism (1987)
20. Sun Heliocomplex (1987), not shown on map
21. Chorsu Bazaar (1990)
22. Turkestan Palace (1993)
23. Turkestan Arena (1994)
24. Former Delegation House of CCCP UzSSR (1975)
25. Tashkent Agricultural Institute (TIIMSKh) (1975)
26. Cosmonauts Avenue metro station (1984)

Additional Points of Interest

1. Amir Temur Square
2. "Broadway" Promenade (since 1870s)
3. Former Zarafshan Restaurant (1974)
4. Independence Square
5. Pakhtakor Stadium (1956)
6. Tashkent City Park (since 2017)
7. Abror Khidoyatov Uzbek Drama Theater (1928)
8. Dzhuma Mosque (rebuilt 2003)
9. Former Chorsu Hotel (1982)
10. Soviet mosaics
11. Residential building, Sebzar Street (1960s)
12. Soviet mosaics
13. Uzbekistan Youth State Theater
14. Shayhantaur Memorial Complex
15. Microbiology Institute (1970s)
16. Architecture Faculty, TAQU (1979)
17. Soviet mosaics
18. Former Museum of Olympic Glory (1996)
19. Tashkent Financial Institute (1976–1982)
20. Rashidov's childhood home
21. Former Prerevolutionary Russian Quarter
22. Khamid Alimdjan Square
23. "Triple House" (1969)
24. Bauhaus residential building (1932)
25. Bakhor Restaurant (1958)
26. House of Photography (1934)
27. The Center for Contemporary Art
28. Soviet mosaics on School Nr. 110 (1969)
29. Karatash Quarter
30. Former City Committee of the Communist Party (1971)
31. Former TsUM (1964)
32. Former Typographies Building (1974)
33. Former House of Knowledge (1968)
34. Residence Park Hotel (1960s)
35. Ex-Brewery
36. Hydroelectric Station (1933)
37. Former House of Specialists (1931)
38. Beshagach Square (1950s)
39. Mukimiy Uzbek State Music Theater (1943)
40. Pavilion with Soviet mosaics (1980)

- Public swimming areas
- M Modernist metro stations

GAFUR GULOM
CHORSU
BUNYODKOR
MILLIY BOG

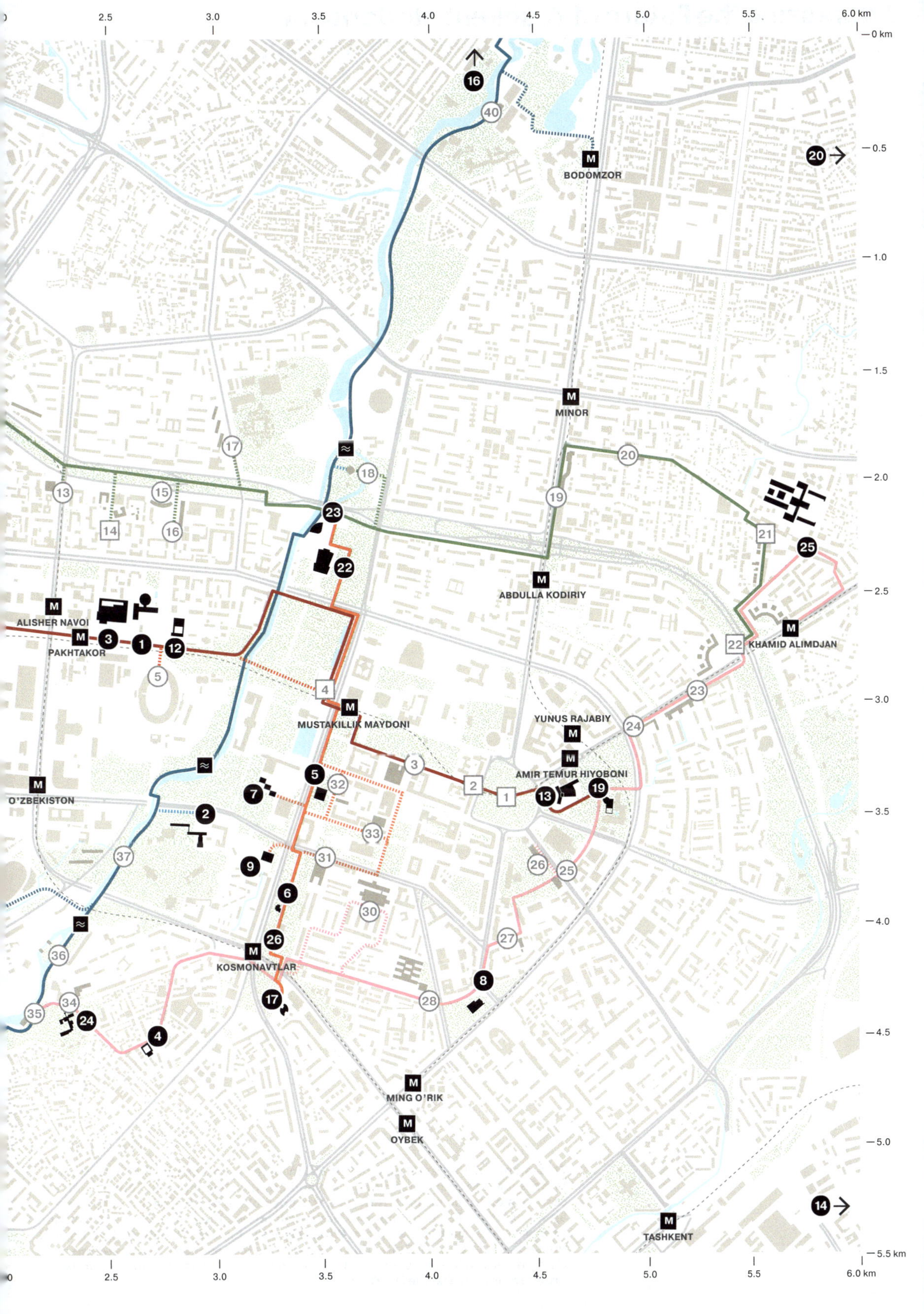

BODOMZOR
MINOR
ABDULLA KODIRIY
ALISHER NAVOI
PAKHTAKOR
MUSTAKILLIK MAYDONI
YUNUS RAJABIY
AMIR TEMUR HIYOBONI
KHAMID ALIMDJAN
O'ZBEKISTON
KOSMONAVTLAR
MING O'RIK
OYBEK
TASHKENT
0 km
0.5
1.0
1.5
2.0
2.5
3.0
3.5
4.0
4.5
5.0
5.5 km
6.0 km

Addressing the Future of Tashkent Modernism

Gayane Umerova, Boris Chukhovich, Davide Del Curto, Ekaterina Golovatyuk

This chapter is the result of joint reflection on the research results by the three editors and the chairperson of the Art and Culture Development Foundation, who commissioned the project. However, it is possible to attribute with reasonable approximation the introduction to Gayane Umerova, the first section, "Actors in Preserving Tashkent Modernism: What Might We Expect?," to Boris Chukhovich, the second section, "A Collection of Strategies for Tashkent," to Ekaterina Golovatyuk and the last section, "More Than One Modernism: Tashkent Modernist Architecture," to Davide Del Curto.

Preserving the modernist architecture of Tashkent is an ambitious and multifaceted process that involves several interconnected components: legislative framework, effective tools for communication, and multiple operational strategies. We understand that safeguarding Tashkent modernism is not a task that can be accomplished overnight. It will take years of persistent work to achieve tangible results.

The first important step is to build an engaged community comprised of property owners and a new generation of local experts and stakeholders. Local expertise is currently scarce, and developing a robust network of professionals and government experts is essential for effectively addressing the challenges of twentieth-century architectural preservation.

The pilot building projects will serve as pivotal case studies, demonstrating how modernist architecture can be adapted to contemporary needs while respecting its original ethos. By showcasing these transformations, we can cultivate broader societal understanding and acceptance of this architectural legacy. The Cultural Trail project further underscores the relationship between Tashkent's modernist architecture and its urban public spaces. By connecting key landmarks through a curated route, this initiative can revitalize these spaces, introduce contemporary uses for existing buildings, and highlight their social significance.

Finally, communicating information about our project both in Uzbekistan and worldwide is crucial in order to gain international visibility and to exchange ideas and expertise with cities that maintain similar initiatives.

Therefore, this essay deals with the larger agenda for preservation of Tashkent modernism. Our team's efforts to document and interpret the modernist architecture of Tashkent contributed to its public recognition and protection by state legislation. We now feel that it is important to focus on three important aspects in order to address the future of these efforts.

Firstly, we delineate the different actors responsible for protecting Tashkent modernist architecture at the national and local levels, as well as the other players who may contribute worldwide. Secondly, we outline the logic behind the intervention strategies that have been developed as part of the project to accompany the Statements of Significance. They are not projects to execute literally, but rather design investigations exploring the possibility of adapting modernist buildings to current needs without losing their authenticity and their historical and cultural value. Finally, we describe the necessity of positioning Tashkent modernist architecture among other world modernisms and sustaining the significance of this architecture internationally through the process of nomination to the UNESCO World Heritage List.

Cover of *Tashkent: A Modernist Capital*, 2024

Actors in Preserving Tashkent Modernism: What Might We Expect?

Tashkent Modernism XX/XXI is a long-term initiative, and its success relies on the collaborative efforts of various stakeholders involved in preserving cultural heritage. In today's Uzbekistan, this responsibility can be shared not only by government institutions but also by international and local donors, NGOs, activist communities, individuals interested in protecting modern architecture and the media, each playing a vital role in highlighting current issues related to these monuments.

The role of the Uzbekistan state as a custodian of cultural heritage preservation is crucial. The government has included the monuments to which our project is dedicated in the national historical and cultural monuments list. We believe that this crucial step will be complemented by additional measures that will prevent the type of problems that have arisen in the past. We recall that in the first decade of the twenty-first century some monuments that were once included in the category of municipal cultural heritage were easily removed from the list if the owners required improper reconstruction. Another issue was the lack of funds for the owners to correctly maintain monuments in proper condition. It is our understanding that today the government of Uzbekistan sees these dangers and is trying to respond flexibly to current challenges. Perhaps the adoption of legislative measures that toughen responsibility for mistreatment of cultural heritage sites and the facilitation of grants and tax breaks for the maintenance of buildings would help to resolve the situation systemically. Given that municipalities make the most important urban decisions, it would be useful for their work to be more supported by the expertise of the Agency of Cultural Heritage of the Republic of Uzbekistan, because proactive work in preventing possible threats to monuments is always more effective than crisis management.

In addition to physical preservation, urban regulation, which implies tracing protection buffer zones, is an essential tool for conserving monuments. These zones could become fundamental operating documents for city and district municipalities. In October 2019, the Senate of the Republic of Uzbekistan approved a law on patronage aimed, among other objectives, at encouraging nongovernmental institutions and private individuals to contribute to the preservation of cultural heritage. This law aligns with global practices and has already helped to sustain many cultural initiatives. Hence, there is hope for a gradual increase in philanthropic support for restoring and reconstructing architectural monuments.

After 2016, changes in Uzbekistan's political climate affected the activities of foreign and local media and NGOs working in Uzbekistan. Throughout our work, we were pleased to observe that many media outlets and influencers competed to communicate information about monument preservation issues to their audiences faster and more accurately. This gives hope that influential local NGOs will emerge in the republic, bringing together people interested in heritage protection and assisting the state with information and actions to monitor the wellbeing of monuments. On the other hand, the practice of recent years, characterized by fluctuation between preservation, destruction and rebuilding, shows that heritage protection is a process, not an outcome, and that much needs to be done in the coming years to consolidate those social forces interested in preserving cultural memory.

A Collection of Strategies for Tashkent

Architecture embodies the memory of the past more evidently than many other cultural objects. Besides the original design concepts, authorship, social functions and technological innovation, many buildings are worth preserving because of the histories that happened in them. Every time an architect intervenes in an existing building, they have to choose what is to be kept, what can be forgotten and changed, and how to position the newly added layer in relation to those already in place.

The same choice arises in dealing with modernist buildings, despite their relatively short histories. They embody numerous and at times controversial memories of the recent past. Therefore, as (preservation) architects, we must ask ourselves which traces of time should be preserved as relevant testimonies of past values and events and how much transformation is appropriate. This decision can be translated into a repertoire of interventions, balanced and nuanced to make sure the valuable aspects of the historical artifact are emphasized and not lost in the process. Rather than seeing the architectural project and the preservation project as mutually exclusive or as opposite choices, we see their combination as a cultural and design decision that is tailored to each specific building case.

As part of the Tashkent Modernism XX/XXI initiative, the project team developed strategies of preservation and adaptation for fifteen

State Museum of Arts

The strategy is to remove the added façade layer and to insert a new material that provides a present-day reading of what has been lost: the stevite. The façade will be studied for added value depending on sun exposure—for example, the possibility to communicate, gain transparency or collect energy. The ground level is redesigned to be more open and connected to the city.

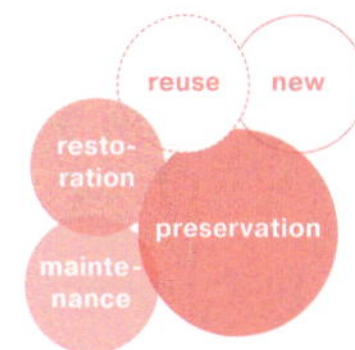

House of Youth (Shodlik Hotel and Ilkhom Theater)

The main ambition of the proposal is to recreate the architectural and programmatic unity the building once had. Rather than being two distinct parts, as today (hotel and theater in a semi-abandoned block), it should resume its function as a single entity. The medium-/long-term stay hotel and coworking space for creative disciplines complement the existing program.

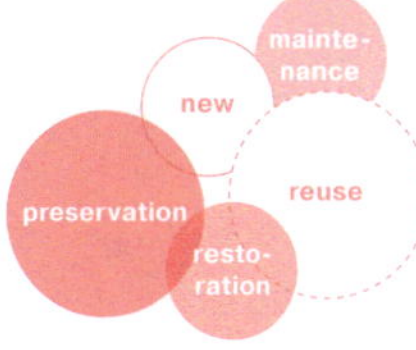

Circus

The main goal of the preservation strategy of the dome is to balance out the relationship between the inside and outside, lost after recent interventions to gain foyer space. The façade, designed as a cooling device consisting of an ornate filter, reminiscent of a traditional panjara, and glazing, must be restored. The glazing should revert to its original position, detached from the panjara, to create a cool exterior walkway and to make the façade perform as originally conceived.

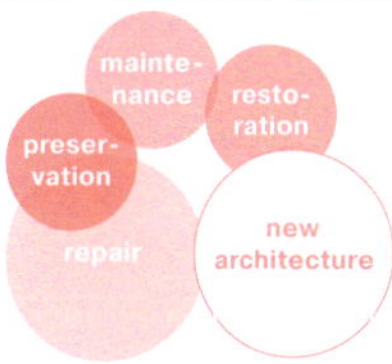

Uzbekistan Hotel

The main action is to preserve the existing building, particularly the upper volume, with partial restoration of the façade. The new plinth is another very important component of the strategy, designed as a new architectural element that bears the memory of the original public courtyard at the base of the hotel.

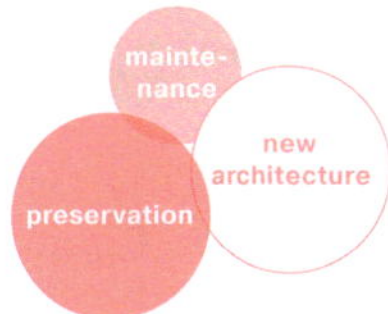

Chorsu Bazaar

An important aspect of the strategy is to consider the main dome as part of a larger urban whole: not only the vast underground plinth which connects all systems of retail around the market but also the urban block, including the adjacent mahalla, the madrasa and the mosque. This is a rich urban ecosystem that requires strategic rethinking and different levels of preservation/transformation.

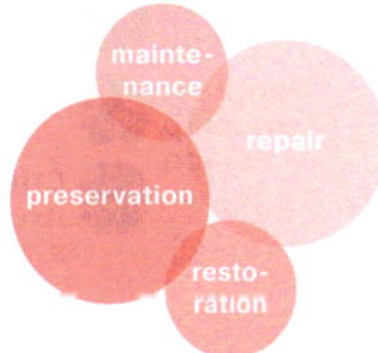

Sun Heliocomplex

We propose focusing mainly on the preservation of the artistic and landscape components of the complex, leaving the rest to the scientists. The only proposed transformation regards the separation of flows of scientists and tourists, whose experience can be built around the perimeter of the compound in order not to interfere with scientific work.

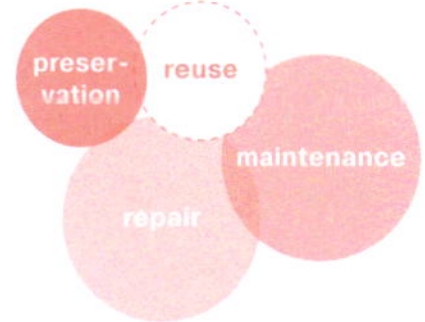

Lenin Museum (State Museum of the History of Uzbekistan)

The main action is to preserve the existing building, particularly the upper volume, with partial restoration of the façade to recover the lost transparency. The ground level is redesigned to be more open and connected to the city.

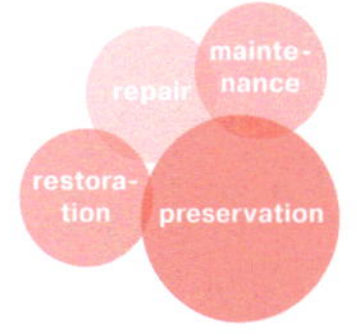

Panoramic Cinema

This building is the most unique 1960s modernist ensemble in Tashkent. It is treated as a monument. Hence, the preservation proposal is the most conservative, aiming to preserve—and reinstate, where possible—the original condition, in particular the transparent façade of the foyer, which has been compromised by a recent insertion of new screening halls.

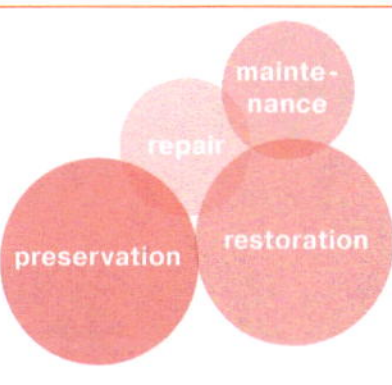

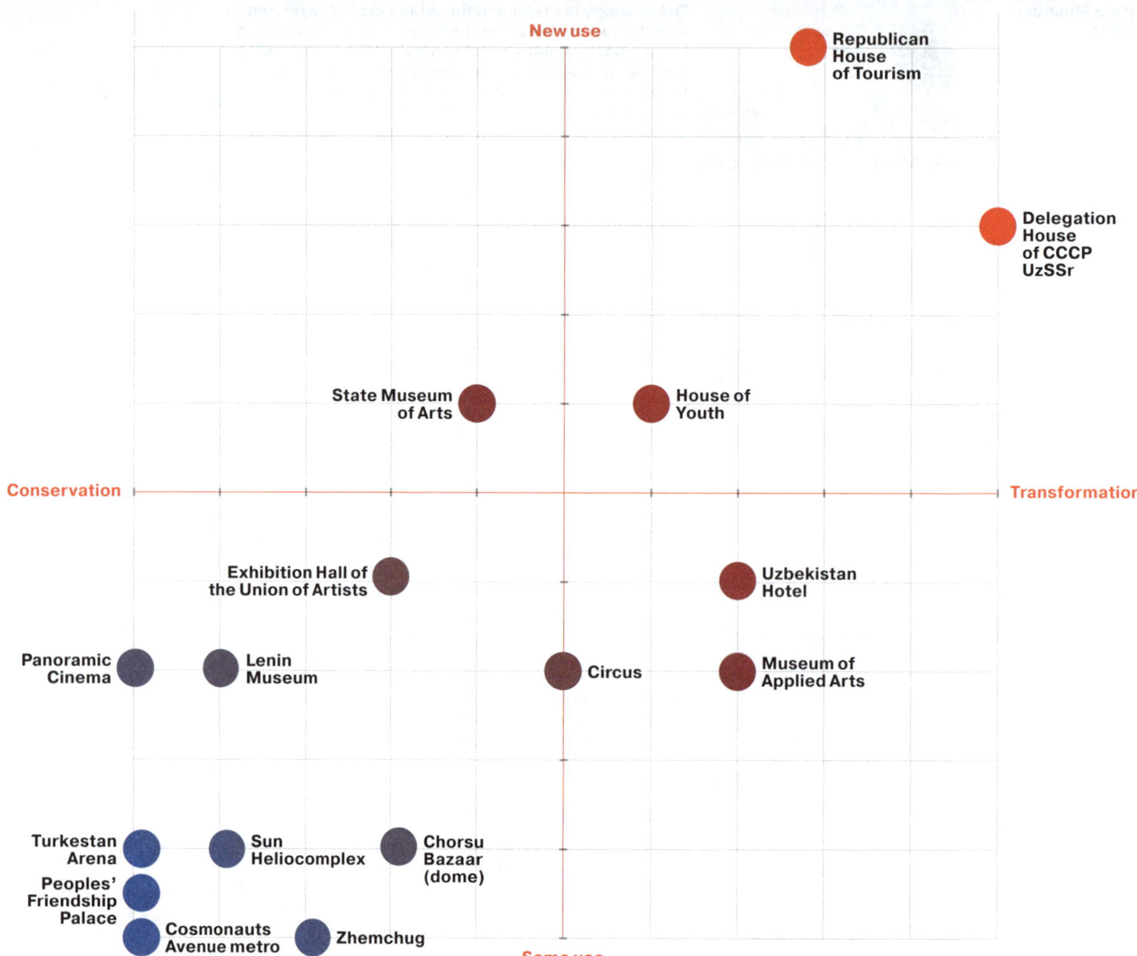

Preservation chart illustrating the relative positions of individual preservation strategies, based on two parameters: the nature of the physical transformation (conservation versus transformation) and use (continuity or change of function)

buildings out of the twenty-four selected with the Art and Culture Development Foundation for which Statements of Significance were written. These strategies are not yet projects to execute but rather case studies illustrating how the preservation of modernist architecture can coexist with adaptation to actual uses, allowing this layer to be part of the city's growth. We aimed to provide the owners with examples of potential modernization of their buildings that are compatible with the Statements of Significance and coherent with current or potential use. The idea is to make these buildings more livable and more sustainable. The strategies range from simple maintenance, as in the case of the Peoples' Friendship Palace and the Cosmonauts Avenue metro station, to adaptation with a certain amount of change, as in the case of the Uzbekistan Hotel and the State Museum of Arts. The amount of suggested changes depends on the building's state of repair, its level of integrity and authenticity and its suitability for the actual use.

Each intervention strategy results from a careful investigation and a comparative analysis among the buildings in this selection. The strategies do not aim to preserve the found condition and keep every trace of time and each subsequent modification. Nor do they have the ambition of fully restoring these structures to their presumed original state. Each strategy defines a set of actions specific to each building to preserve its architectural, spatial and material qualities, its historical and cultural significance and also the stratifications that have modified the original form over time when these have added value to the building.

Each strategy consists of a combination of interventions that may include preservation, restoration, addition of new architectural elements, repair, maintenance and change of use, applied in different degrees to various parts of each building. The Preservation Chart on page 226 illustrates the relative positions of individual strategies along two axes, representing two parameters: the nature of the physical transformation (preservation vs. innovation) and use (continuity or change of function).

Some buildings are enriched by the individual or group interpretations of their inhabitants, such as the Zhemchug residential building, where the residents have expanded their apartments toward the suspended courtyards, making them look much more like the mahalla neighborhood that inspired architect Ofeliia Aidinova than her original design. We do not know whether Aidinova would appreciate this result today. Even so, we would like to think that these spontaneous transformations confirm the validity of her design and the quasi-anthropological reference to mahallas. The building has proven capable of changing its appearance and metabolizing the additions. The integrity of the original design has been exchanged for sustaining community life and the longevity of the building. Here, our strategy suggests repainting the exterior façade in white (as in the building's original condition) and leaving the suspended courtyards as spaces for spontaneous adaptations. Zhemchug makes us reflect on how much this architecture has the right to change over the years, recording the traces of time. Indeed, the right to age has been recognized for every architecture of the past, but not sufficiently for the architecture of the twentieth century. How willing are we to accept that the perfect design from the photographs of the sixties and seventies is today compromised by the addition of new decorations, technical volumes or ways of reuse that can modify the modernist building radically? To what extent are these additions acceptable, and when do they increase the value of the building?

We are probably willing to accept that the Chorsu Bazaar has a backdrop of colorful stalls, tents and kiosks populating the empty space around the large ceramic dome. Similarly to Zhemchug, we see these spontaneous structures as coherent with the original concept of the building. Hence, the sporadic transformations of its parts are seen not as a sacrifice, but rather as an intrinsic and vital ingredient of its functioning.

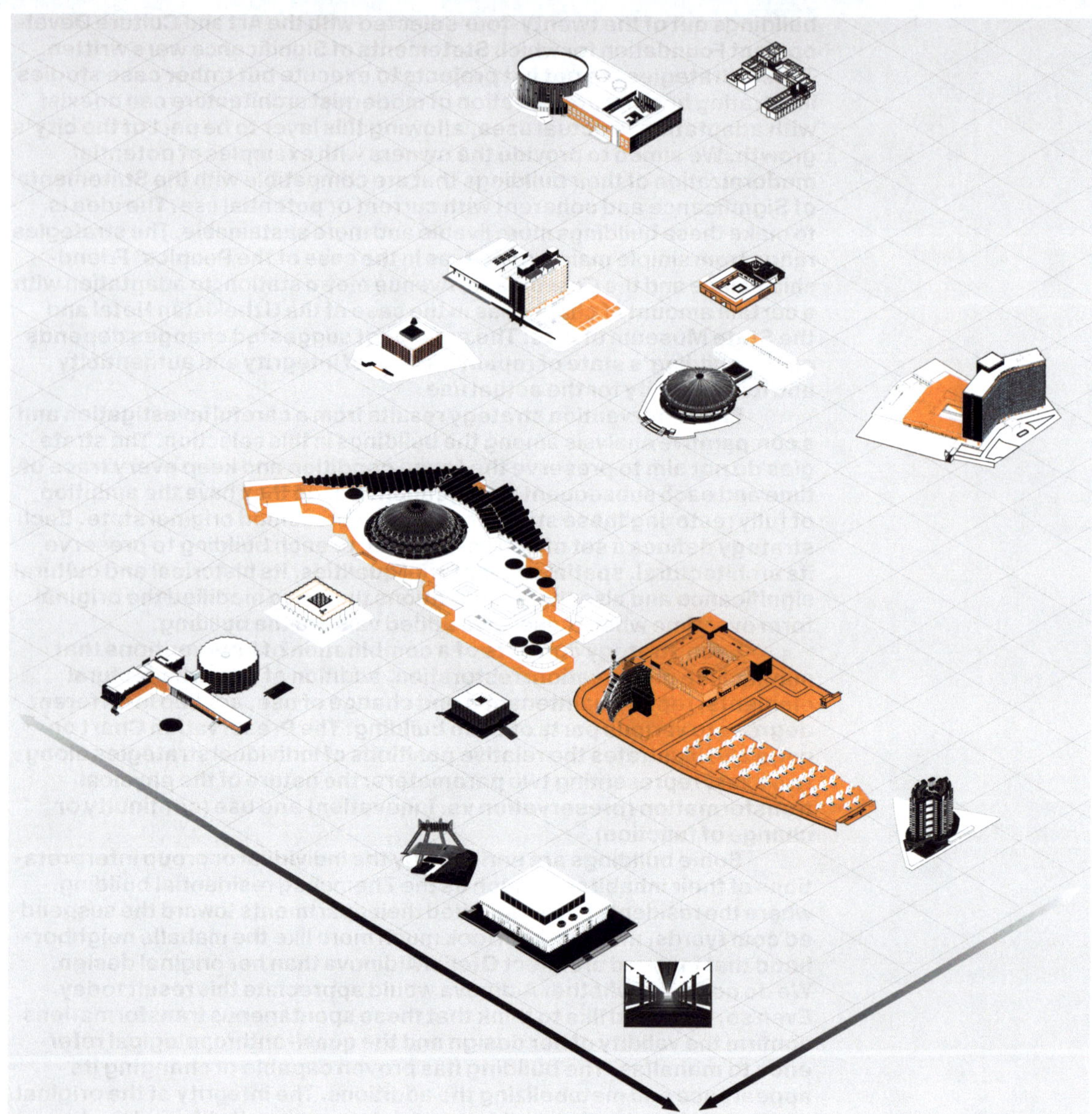

Map illustrating the recommended actions for each modernist building, balancing transformations and the preservation of its cultural significance:
Black = maximum preservation
White = transformation possible
Orange = hidden modernist features to be exposed

The preservation and adaptation strategy here suggests rethinking the invisible underground plinth as an important infrastructural ingredient that organizes the flow logistics of the market and ensures its safety and hygiene.

In contrast, we are unwilling to accept the gigantic advertising screens covering the Panoramic Cinema's rectilinear foyer volume, which also testify to the vitality of this building and its ability to adapt its original function to contemporary needs. However, these large LED screens impact Sergo Sutiagin's modernist architecture much more severely than the abovementioned cases.

Similarly, the current layout of the State Museum of the History of Uzbekistan presents interesting vitrines and a didactic narration of national history. However, such a layout has totally compromised the architectural quality of the former Lenin Museum, which, like the Panoramic Cinema, was based on the concept of transparency and the political will to maintain a continuous visual dialogue between the interior of the museum, the narrative of history, and the contemporary city's present-day life. For this building our strategy focuses primarily on recovering key elements of the original proposal, while adapting to the standards of the contemporary public museum.

As a final example, the main ambition for the State Museum of Arts is to uncover the original façade, hidden by a new layer of glass and alucobond in the early 2000s, in order to reinstate the geometry and materiality of Rozenblium's floating volume on the top of the hill. The spaces below the hill can be slightly rearranged to create more open, public and contemporary museum conditions. This means combining preservation of the original interior elements, restoration of the façade, localized new architecture at the ground level and repair and maintenance of everything that concerns administrative and building services. All proposals for adaptation are made with the aim of valorizing the original architecture and locally adjusting it to upgrade to the current use and technology.

The fifteen proposals are thought of as a palette or as a brief that can be expanded and reinterpreted by a variety of architects with different backgrounds when called to intervene in each building. The project and the book speak to this flexibility of thought and to this kind of attention toward the past. And this is one of our messages for the future of Tashkent. The way we work with the past significantly defines our present and future.

More Than One Modernism: Tashkent Modernist Architecture

This book testifies to the global effort to advance the conservation of twentieth-century built heritage in recognition of the aging of essential works of the Modern Movement and of the need to tackle the specific conservation challenges presented by the innovative construction techniques and materials that are features of modernist buildings. Our research provided comprehensive documentation as the basis for state protection of such fragile heritage against the multiple risks it faces within the current scenario of rapid economic growth and social shifts in Central Asia, where the pressure of urban speculation seriously threatens modernist heritage. We also drafted a detailed strategy for preservation and adaptation, preparing a case-by-case list of measures tailored to every single building. Also, by investigating the case of Tashkent, this research addressed the theoretical issues twentieth-century architecture raises since it has been promoted to heritage status and the methodological progress that has occurred in architectural preservation due to the conservation challenges such recent heritage faces worldwide. Our research aimed to contribute to the broadening recognition of the diverse ways modernism has manifested itself globally. It stimulated a conceptual rethinking of modernism's cultural and geographical roots and the way and places it arose and flourished worldwide.

Twentieth-century architecture has achieved significant recognition in recent decades and numerous efforts have been made to protect the most renowned masterpieces of the last century. Twentieth-century architecture is increasingly represented in the UNESCO WHL, as confirmed by the launch of the Modern Heritage Program in 2001, following the Global Strategy for a Representative, Balanced and Credible World Heritage List (1994–2004), which aimed to focus attention on less represented areas and heritage most at risk. Many inscriptions focus on a single building and its distinctive role in the history of twentieth-century architecture and society—for example, Schröder House (2000), Villa Tugendhat (2001), Sydney Opera House (2007) and Van Nelle Fabriek in Rotterdam (2014). Parallel to modernist icons, serial nominations consider a series of modernist buildings instead of a single masterpiece, where they represent a set of values pertaining to a phase of urban development of a city or region—for example, White City of Tel Aviv – the Modern Movement (2003), Berlin Modernism Housing Estates (2006) and Ivrea, Industrial City of the 20th Century (2018). In other cases, the WHL recognized the outstanding universal value of a set of buildings designed by a single master who thus left their footprint on social and urban development—for example, works of Antoni Gaudí (1984), Le Havre, the city rebuilt by Auguste Perret (2005) and the works of Jože Plečnik in Ljubljana – Human Centered Urban Design (2021). The serial sites dedicated to the work of Le Corbusier (2016) and Frank Lloyd Wright (2019) show how the great masters contributed to the global spread of the Modern Movement's ideals. Many other candidacies focusing on twentieth-century architecture have lately populated the UNESCO Tentative List and demonstrate the extent to which modernism has achieved global heritage status.

Despite these efforts, most of the inscriptions belong to Europe and the United States. Asia, Africa and the rest of the world remain largely underrepresented in the list, with the paradox that preservation efforts are concentrated where the legal framework is already fit, leaving vulnerable that heritage belonging to areas or nations where legal protection is still fragile. This lack of representativeness includes Soviet modernism, which, equally to that of Europe and the United States, made a significant contribution to the history of modernization during the twentieth century and left its footprint across the entire territory of the former USSR, covering nearly one-sixth of the Earth's surface. As in Tashkent, many vital testimonies to modernist architecture, directly or indirectly influenced by the late Soviet period, remain in these areas and face numerous risks due to rapid and uncontrolled economic growth and the pressure of urban speculation, the weakness of safeguarding measures, the fragile political framework and social or armed conflicts.

However, contemporary conservation has already identified the need for enlarging the idea of heritage beyond the Europe-centered. Following the Venice Charter (1964) and the Declaration of Amsterdam (1975), the Nara Document on Authenticity (1994) was the first such document signed outside of Europe, demonstrating the move toward a global rethinking of heritage by tackling the core concept of any conservation activity, i.e., what is authenticity and how can it be retained in any conservation process. The history of architecture has been investigating modernity beyond Europe and the United States since the first decade of the twenty-first century, after the concept of global history became widely accepted in the architectural field. The ICOMOS International Specialist Committee for Twentieth Century Heritage (ISC20C) was established in 2001 and began working with the Getty Conservation Institute to enlarge the boundaries of modernism in preservation. DOCOMOMO International has expanded its area of investigation since its 2006 biennial conference, *"Other" Modernisms*, held in Ankara, Turkey. The Cape Town Document on Modern Heritage resulted from the launch (in 2020) of the Modern Heritage of Africa program, which aims to raise international awareness of modern heritage in Africa, build conservation capacities and reduce the imbalance in the World Heritage List for the African continent. Nongovernmental agencies such as the Arab Center for Architecture and the Association of Southeast Asian Nations study modern architecture by widening the attention to numerous heritage places, authors and typologies. Government heritage agencies in the United Arab Emirates and across South and Southeast Asia have already understood modern architecture as part of a heritage worth protecting and contribute to enriching the understanding of the modern era by reflecting upon their specific microhistory. More recently, social media has played an essential role in the international development of modern heritage, promoting a rise in global awareness of many important but forgotten modernist buildings. The Bucharest-based Socialist Modernism Instagram profile has over 440,000 followers and is actively documenting the buildings of the socialist period of Eastern Europe, advocating for their protection. Our research on Tashkent modernist architecture aims to be part of the global rising interest in modern heritage and the effort to expand the definition of modernism toward the idea of multiple modernities that are time- and place-specific and ask for a deeper understanding of the variety of twentieth-century heritage.

The reasons for promoting this broadening of the investigative perspective are not limited to historical and scientific research. On the contrary, the tragic events that have already occurred in this initial glimpse of the twenty-first century are of global concern and suggest the need to insist on building multicultural dialogue scenarios and promoting a multivoiced discussion on the recent past. One recalls George Orwell's 1940 essay "Inside the Whale," in which he warned us to pay close attention to the risk of falling for simplified narratives such as the spy hunt, distrust of others, the unilateral narrative of the sins and atrocities committed by "enemies," the idea of irreconcilable ethnic and cultural differences in which we are (and always will be) the "good guys," while they are (and always will be) the "bad guys," all of which have proven to be fertile ground for war to proliferate throughout modern history. Rather than hiding behind this simplified rhetoric, research must continue to deepen the analysis of reality and promote dialectics among cultures and different points of view on recent history. This way, research confirms its role in overcoming preconceived ideas and stimulating the scientific approach to critical thinking. By turning to comparative history and building archeology, we can avoid damaging one-sided descriptions. As a scientific method of investigation, building archeology and modern history objectively apply to any past period, including the most recent one. Tashkent's architecture is evidence of an authentic search for modernity in the second half of the twentieth century. However, what yesterday appeared to be modern, positive, and disruptive today belongs to historic heritage and deserves to be scientifically analyzed and critically assessed. As Manfredo Tafuri put it, "Those who seem to negate history produce historically motivated work. Those who try not to cut their links with it run into the shoals of ambiguity."

Social Scripts (Tashkent Sequences) Armin Linke

Armin Linke's visual essay is conceived as an immersive journey through Tashkent's modernist buildings. Scanning the city from east to west, the narration meanders across the spaces of science, culture and social infrastructure, across the "new" city and the "old."

Armin Linke's work avoids the clichés formed in the last fifteen years by publications on Soviet and East European modernism, whereby modernist buildings are glorified as remnants of an exotic, remote and extinguished culture. Rather than immortalizing the passing beauty of Tashkent architecture, Linke's photographs aim to highlight its contemporary value and to reveal another important quality that is crucial to his oeuvre: this architecture, with its sculptural volumes and elaborate surfaces, is the scenography for staging the larger social scripts.

Like most of Linke's narrations, the essay poses a larger question of the nature of images. Today, when photography has become much more than a mere representation of reality and has an ambiguous reality of its own, these pages incorporate a sub-narration that has a critical attitude toward the image. Oscillating between wide shots and details, and sometimes sequencing nearly identical frames on the same page, the images are laid out as notes for film location scouting and leave generous portions of empty space for the reader's thoughts and annotations.

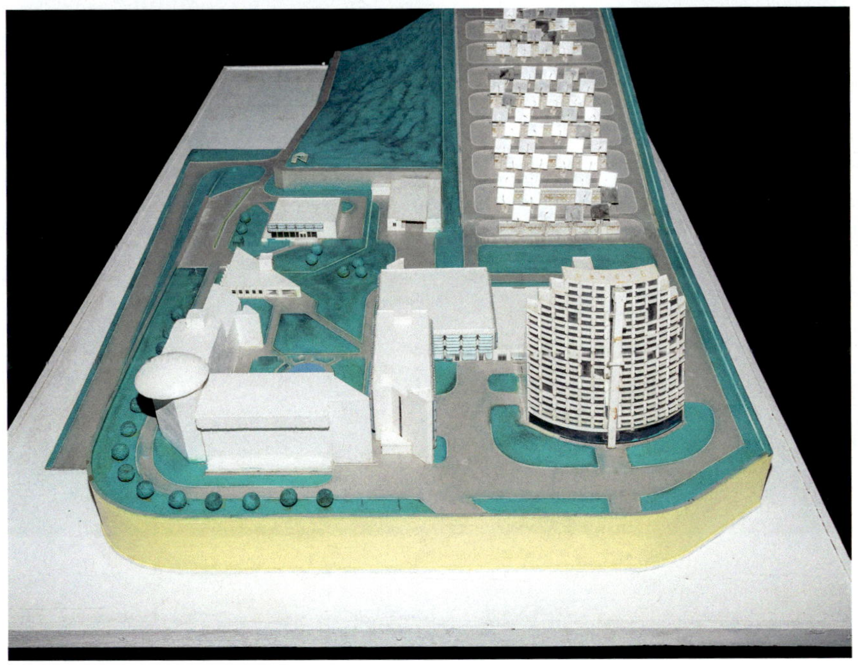

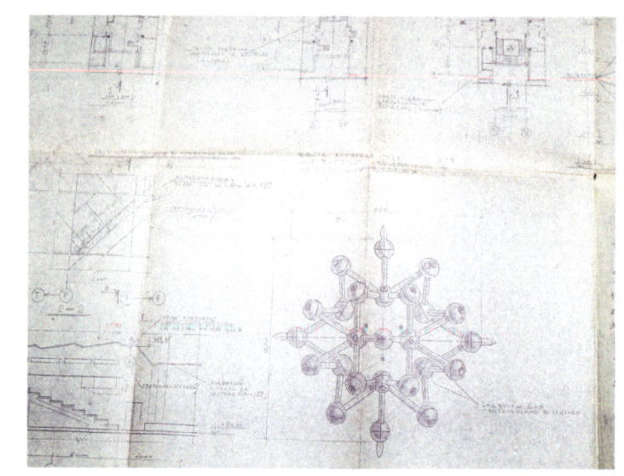

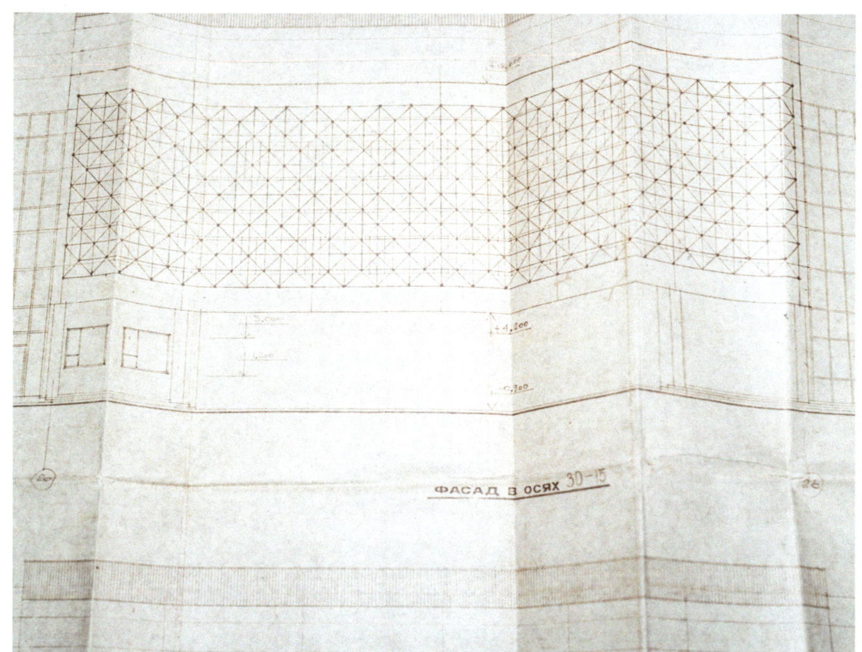
ФАСАД В ОСЯХ 30-15

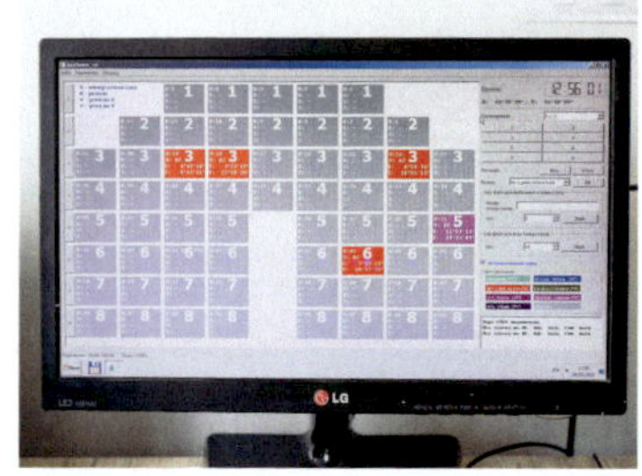
LG

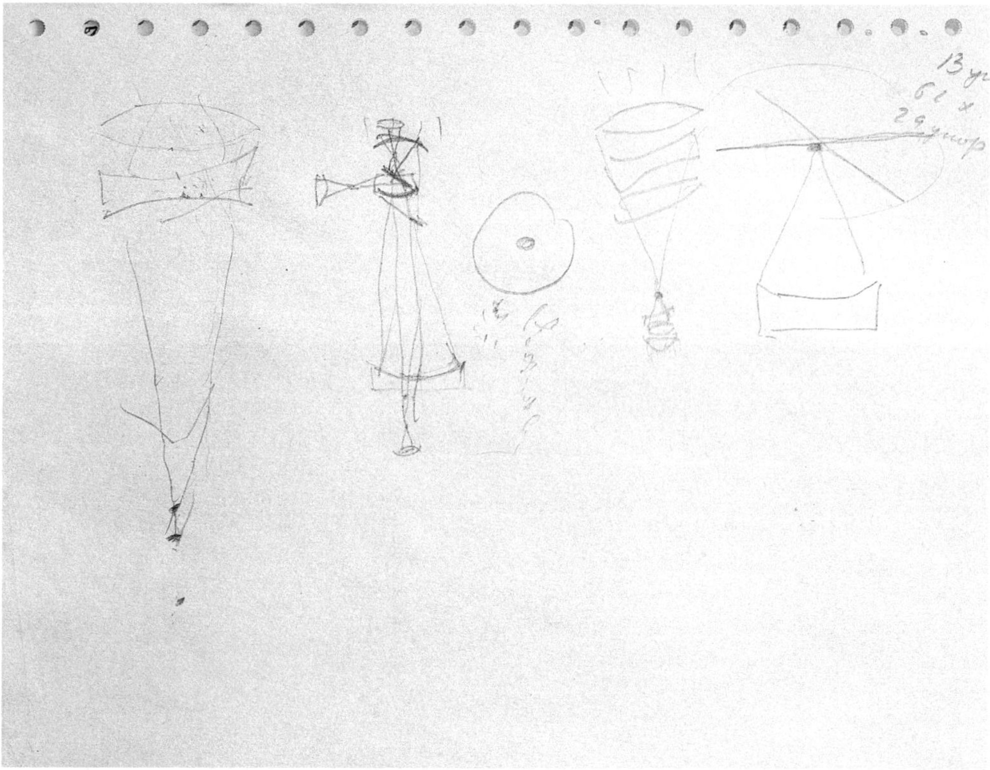

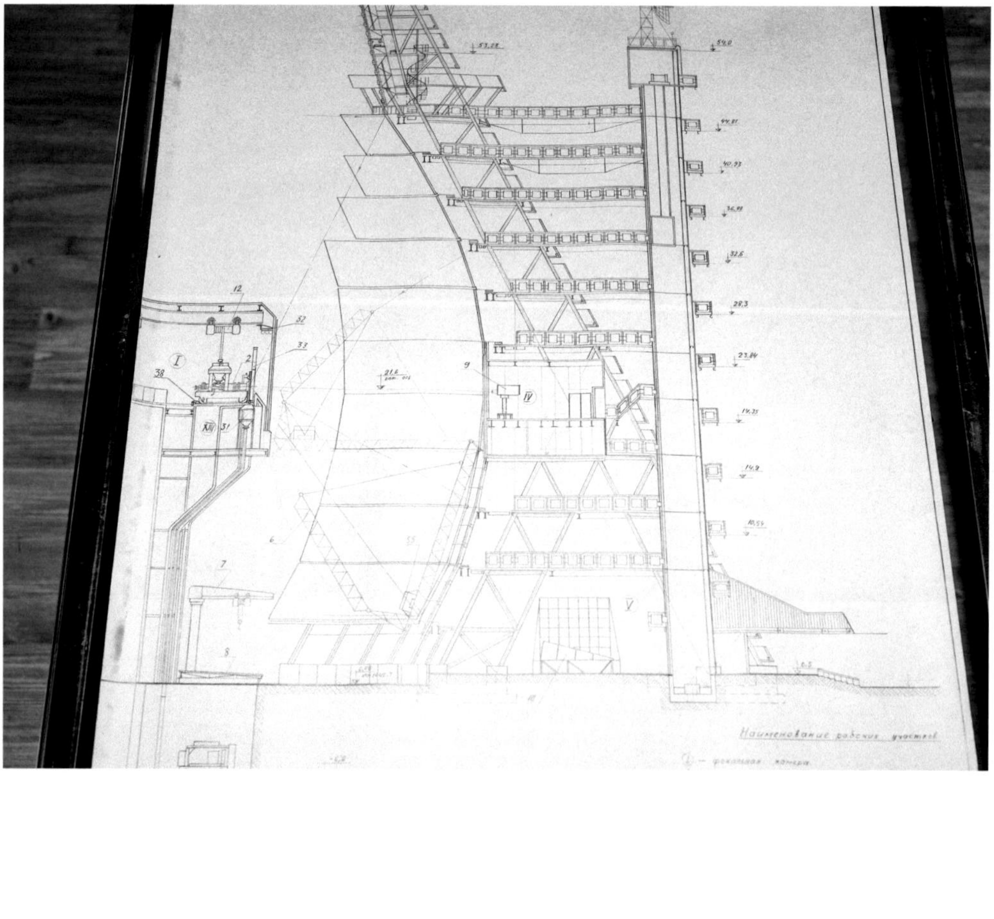
Наименование рабочих участков

"TIQXMMI" MILLIY TADQIQOT UNIVERSITETI
2022-ГОД
ОБЕСПЕЧЕНИЯ
ИНТЕРЕСОВ
ЧЕЛОВЕКА И
РАЗВИТИЯ
МАХАЛЛИ

12 45
TEATR
SADO

TASHKENT TV-TOWER

Residential buildings on Bogdan Khmel'nitskii Street

Uzbekistan Hotel

В.А. ДЖАНИБЕКОВ

Cosmonauts Avenue metro station

СОЮЗ - АПОЛЛОН

Ю.А. ГАГАРИН - ПЕРВЫЙ В МИРЕ КОСМОНАВТ
К О С

Cosmonauts Avenue metro station

SHIVA

SHIVAKI

The world is vast, there are
countries, but our Uzbekistan is
This wonderful and sacred land
created for us. This thought
inspire all our hearts and provide
reason for our lives.

Daqiqani abadiyatdan ayri holda tasavvur qilib bo`lmaganidek, Sharof Rashidovning hayotini ham o`zbek xalqining tarixidan, hayotidan ayri tasavvur qilib bo`lmaydi.
I.KARIMOV
Toshkent metropoliteni qurilishida, ayniqsa, Sharof aka Rashidovning hissasi beqiyos bo'lgan. U Moskvadagi amaldorlarni shu ishga rozilik berishga ko'ndira olgan. Yangi stansiyalarni ko'zdan kechirar ekanman, avvalo, bu ishlarni boshlab bergan ana shu insonning zahmati-yu g'ayrati yodimga tushdi.
I. Karimov
XALQNING BUNYODKORLIK QUDRATI
50-80-yillarda O`zbekiston xalqning yaratuvchilik qudrati tufayli rivojlanishning yangi pog`onalariga ko`tarildi. 1985-yilda respublikada issiqlik energetika, metallurgiya, mashinasozlik, kimyo, yengil va agrosanoat majmualariga mansub bo`lgan 1549 ta korxona faoliyat ko`rsatdi. Sanoat yalpi mahsulotlarining ishlab chiqarilishi bu vaqtga kelib 1940-yilga nisbatan 21 martadan ko`proqqa ortdi.
O`ZBEKISTON FASHIZMGA QARSHI URUSH YILLARIDA (1941-1945 - yy.)
II Jahon urushi davrida O`zbekistondan frontga 1 mln. 433320 kishi yuborilgan. Jang maydonlarida 400 mingga yaqin o`zbekistonliklar qolgan, 132670 kishi bedarak yo`qolgan, 60542 o`zbekistonlik jangchi esa nogiron bo`lib qaytgan.
URUSH YILLARIDA O`ZBEKISTONGA BIR MILLIONGA YAQIN AHOLI, SHU JUMLADAN 300 MING YAHUDIY, 100 MINGDAN ORTIQ UKRAIN VA BOSHQA MILLAT VAKILLARI EVAKUATSIYA QILINDI.
ОБОРОННЫЙ КОНЦЕ

O'lkamizda bolsheviklar tomonidan o'rnatilgan tuzumning xalq xo'jaligi va iqtisodiyotni davlat tasarrufiga o'tkazish, halokatli oziq-ovqat razvertkasi siyosatini joriy qilish va keng ko'lamda harbiy harakat olib borishdan iborat tadbirlari oqibatida 1917-1923 - yillarda dahshatli ommaviy qahatchilik kelib chiqdi. Buning natijasida Farg'ona vodiysida 1 milliondan ziyod, Turkiston o'lkasi bo'yicha esa aholining yarmiga yaqini (2,5 mln kishi) aziyat chekdi.

State Museum of the History of Uzbekistan (Lenin Museum)

Shodlik Hotel and Ilkhom Theater (House of Youth)

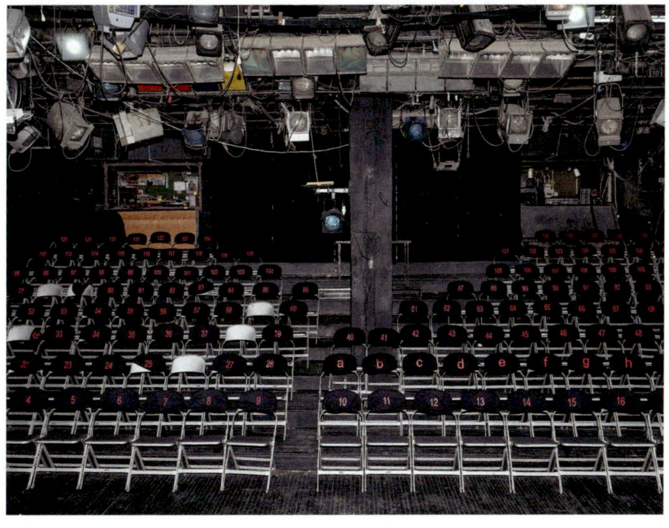

Shodlik Hotel and Ilkhom Theater (House of Youth)

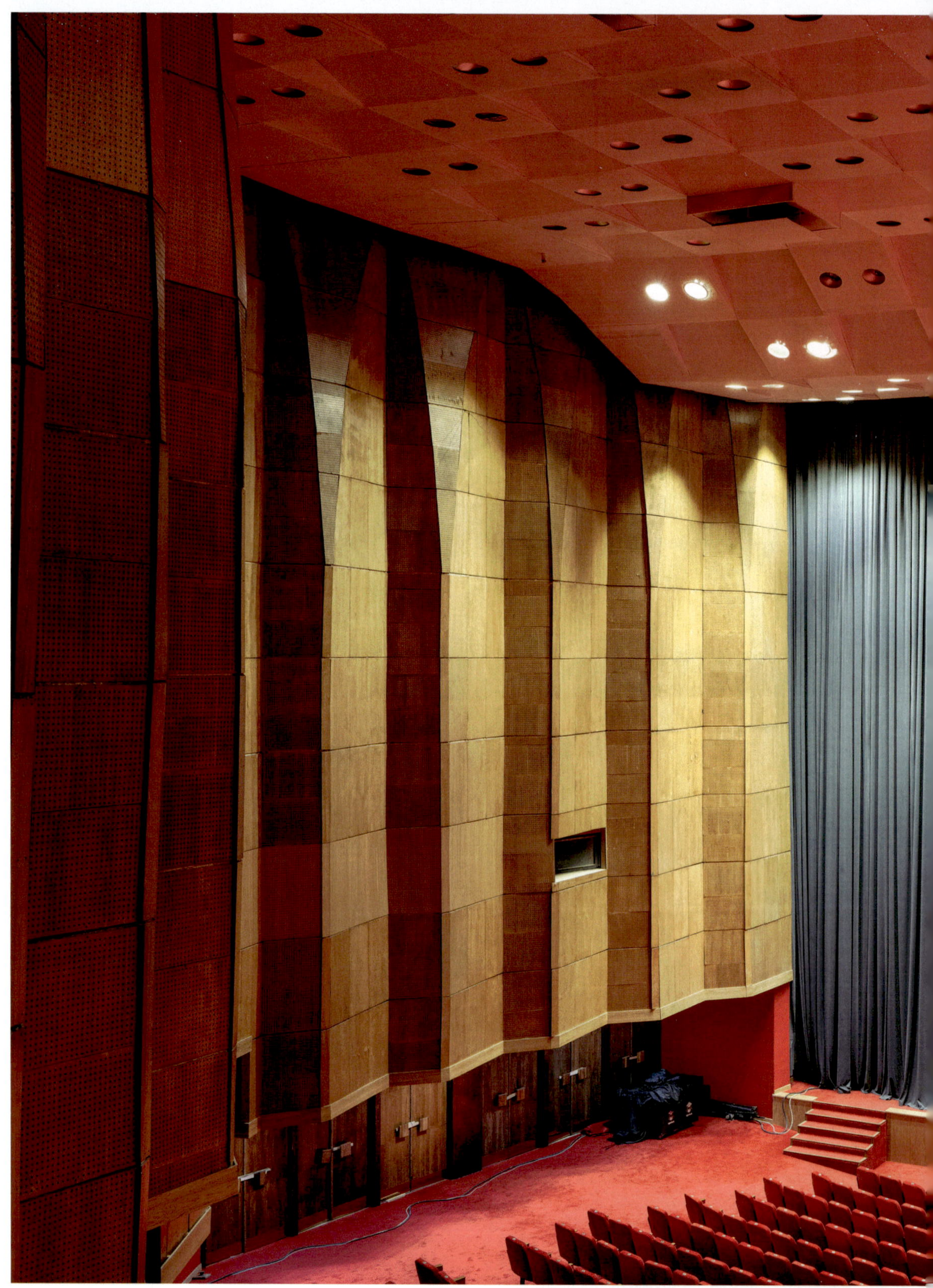

2023

Спутник кино фестиваля
III МЕЖДУНАРОДНЫЙ КИНОФЕСТИВАЛЬ
СТРАН
в ТАШКЕНТЕ
ПРИГЛАШЕНИЕ
КАТАЛОГ

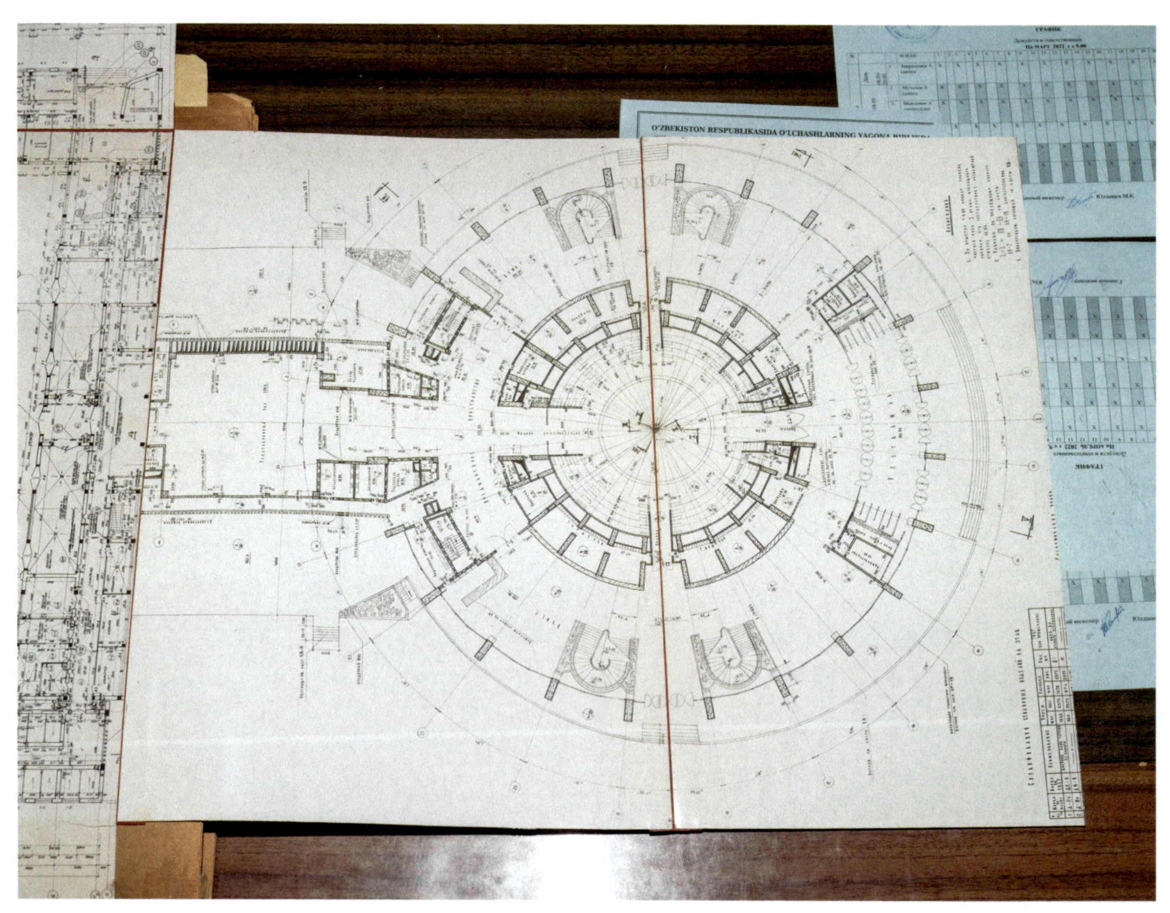
ГРАФИК
O'ZBEKISTON RESPUBLIKASIDA O'LCHASHLARNING YAGONA

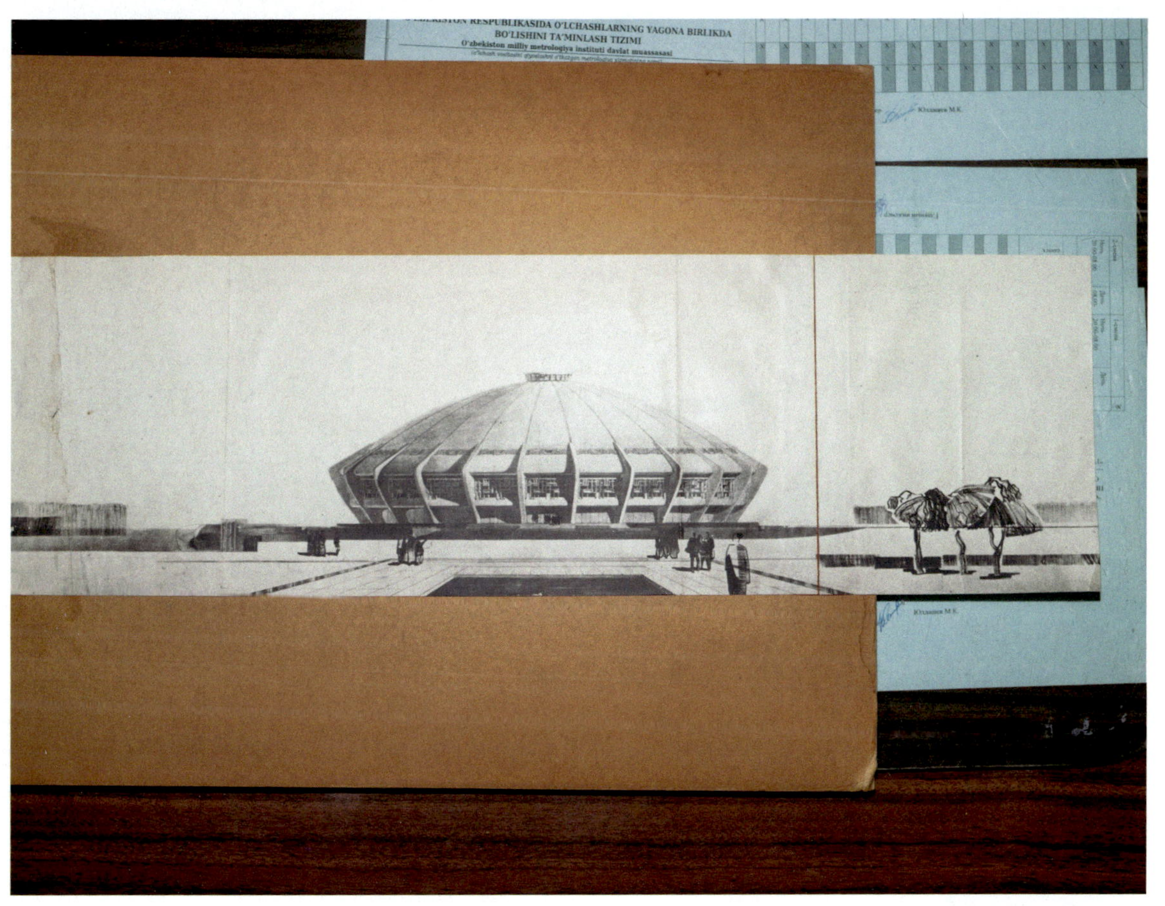
RESPUBLIKASIDA O'LCHASHLARNING YAGONA BIRLIKDA
BO'LISHINI TA'MINLASH TIZIMI
O'zbekiston milliy metrologiya instituti davlat muassasasi

IRK

ZARHAL

YANGI O'ZBEKISTON

Building Monographs

This part of the book consists of twelve condensed Monographs which retrace the history and architectural concept of each building, bring together archival materials and document the present condition. Each Monograph concludes with a Statement of Significance, which outlines the architectural and cultural value and assigns different levels of interest to each artefact, and a suggested preservation strategy. These documents form the basis of building "passports," which every national monument in Uzbekistan should possess and which prescribe the significance of cultural heritage.

As a result of our research, on April 22, 2024, a selection of modernist buildings was awarded national heritage status, with the passports forming the legal basis for their protection. In the book the most representative cases are organized according to preservation logic, starting with buildings that require less intervention and ending with those for which the proposed amount of change is more significant. The aim of this logic is to shift the focus from the historical narrative toward more operative considerations of how to work with this heritage today.

While these pages represent a united effort, certain contributions should be highlighted. Boris Chukhovich wrote the texts describing the history and concept of each building and also drew up brief information about the architects and project institutes. Together with the Art and Culture Development Foundation team, he was in charge of gathering all the archival documents from Tashkent's private and public archives. The Politecnico di Milano team outlined the methodology, structured the Monographs, Statements of Significance and preservation strategies, and wrote these with support from GRACE. The GRACE team produced the graphic, 3D and analytical materials that describe the buildings and clarify the Statements. Finally, GRACE, with support from Politecnico di Milano, developed the adaptation strategies.

GRADING SCALE FOR THE STATEMENTS OF SIGNIFICANCE

STATE OF REPAIR

(1 = poor state of repair; 4 = good state of repair)

- 1 – The building is in a complete state of disarray, possibly impacting the load-bearing structure, and is not usable
- 2 – The building shows severe localized damage and/or diffused and extended deterioration patterns. It is, however, still possible to use it.
- 3 – The building shows localized deterioration patterns which do not affect its stability
- 4 – The building is in perfect (or near perfect) condition

INTEGRITY

(1 = poor level of integrity; 4 = high level of integrity)

- 1 – The building has lost most of the elements necessary to express its significance
- 2 – Transformations to the building and its surroundings have caused the loss of some of the elements necessary to express its significance
- 3 – The building has retained all the elements necessary to express its significance but is in a poor state of repair
- 4 – The building has retained all the elements necessary to express its significance and is in a good state of repair

AUTHENTICITY

(1 = poor level of authenticity; 4 = high level of authenticity)

- 1 – The building has been subjected to major interventions which resulted in an overall transformation
- 2 – The building has been subjected to localized but significant modifications
- 3 – The building has been subjected to slight changes and replacements
- 4 – Only minor repairs and conservation activities have been carried out on the building

Panoramic Cinema

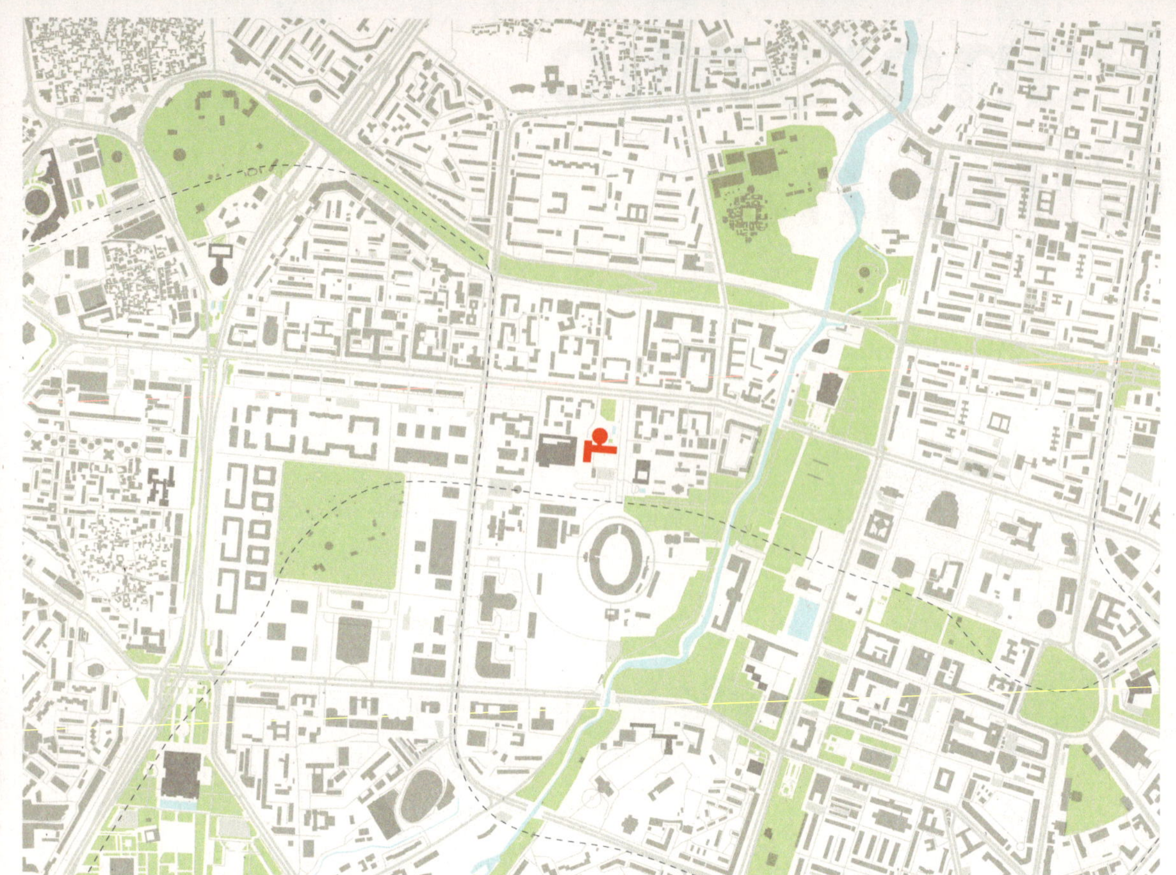

Building position and address: 15 Navoi Street, Tashkent

0 0.5 1km

The site on which the complex was built was within the historical boundaries of "old" Tashkent, to the south of the historical Sheikhantaur ensemble, with several medieval buildings. The tsarist administration made very few urban planning interventions in this district, although immediately after the conquest of Tashkent it destroyed the Urda medieval fortress, which was a little to the east. In the 1930s the site of the former fortress was connected to the street that was later named after poet Alisher Navoi and to Khadra Square, which was at the heart of the "old city." By 1960 administrative and residential buildings in typical Stalinist style had been constructed along the perimeter of Navoi Street and were an eclectic mix of European architecture and stylized elements of "Eastern" architecture. In 1956 Pakhtakor Stadium, designed by Mitkhat Bulatov, was built to the south of the site. Pakhtakorskaia Street was constructed from the stadium to Navoi Street. Accordingly, the primary urban axes that needed to be considered when the complex was constructed were Navoi Street and Pakhtakorskaia Street. For decades Navoi Street was the main transport and pedestrian artery connecting the "old and new" cities. In the 1960s there was very little traffic on Pakhtakorskaia Street, but on days when there were football matches it became a transit route for around 35,000 people who walked to the stadium and then back. This urban planning context determined the planning of the cinema and the landscaping around it. Firstly, between Navoi Street and the cinema the architects had to establish the necessary buffer zone for viewers to gather while waiting for a screening or leaving the building. Secondly, it was extremely important to split the flows of people who might be exiting the stadium and the cinema at the same time. The two main vantage points, from the stadium and from Navoi Street, defined the free planning of the building, which did not have "main" and "secondary" façades. The architects also took into account that the traditional single-story mahallas that adjoined the site from the south-west would sooner or later be replaced by a park zone, which had been a feature of general plans of Tashkent since 1937. All of these urban planning factors had a serious influence on the competition decision of 1960.

After a 1964 competition a third axis to the center of Tashkent appeared by the cinema. This was the northern perimeter of a green esplanade along which modernist buildings—the House of Youth and the TV Center—began to be constructed in the 1960s. The idea of the esplanade was prompted by the siting of large buildings in the park zone and the need for residents to be able to circulate freely around them. Accordingly, it was assumed that each building would be accessible, both to enter and to walk past. For this reason, the space in front of the TV Center and between the TV Center and the Palace of Arts was left open to pedestrians until 1991. After the fall of the USSR the urban space was divided between government bodies and private organizations. The square in front of the TV Center was fenced off and the passage between it and the Palace of Arts became difficult to access.

Main dimensions of the Panoramic Cinema
General axonometric view

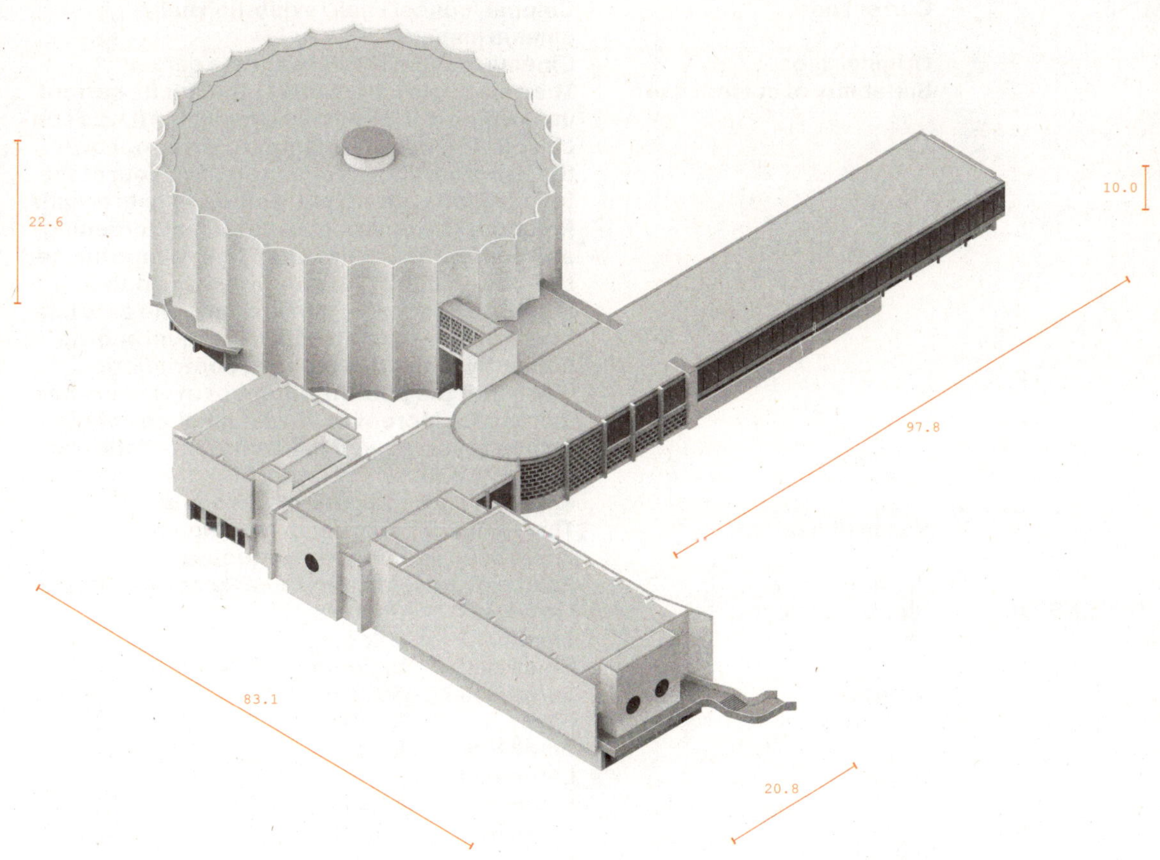

ACTORS	**Architects:**	**Vladimir Berezin, Sergo Sutiagin, Iurii Khaldeev, Dmitrii Shuvaev, with Ol'ga Legostaeva**
	Engineers:	**Aleksandr Braslavskii, David Antman, A. Prigozhin**
	Artists:	**Arnol'd Gan, Viktor Gan, Aleksandr Kedrin, R. Avakian**
	Institute:	**Uzgosproekt/UzNIIPgradostroitel'stva**
DATES	**Design period:**	**1960–1964**
	Construction period:	**1962–1964**
	Inauguration date:	**1964**
	Addition of Small Hall:	**1977 (Architects: Sergo Sutiagin, with D. Mursalimova, A. Vinokurov, P. Sagalaev, A. Tokhtaev; Engineers: Alexandr Braslavskii, with Vitalii Shterenshis, G. Tarasov, I. Leont'eva, I. Kazanskaia, N. Isaevich)**
	Later interventions:	**1978:** **The building was seriously damaged by fire (the fire affected the main Large Hall and the foyer, without touching the Small Hall) and subsequently repaired within three and a half months.** **2000s (first decade):** **The Panoramic Cinema was renovated and additional cinema halls were created within the foyer volume.**

		2021: Renovation of the Panoramic Cinema and modernization of the technical systems.
USE	**Current use:**	Cinema/concert hall/exhibition hall/cinema museum
	Original use:	Cinema/concert hall/congress center
	Suitability of current use:	The building is only partly suited for its current use, which is the same use for which it was conceived. The transformations carried out over the years drastically changed the layout of the foyer volume, completely modifying its original function. The creation of additional screening and conference halls within this volume caused the loss of important amenities and public facilities (e.g. café, cloakroom). The café has been relocated to the entrance level and significantly resized, which is a contradiction given that the potential number of viewers has increased. Moreover, the linear shape of the former foyer, as well as its characteristic transparency, is ill-suited for the new uses of a cinema museum and projection rooms.
	Space utilization:	The building is fully used. No unused/underused spaces were detected.
	Previous names:	Palace of Arts, Alisher Navoi Palace of Cinema
DIMENSIONS	**Number of floors:**	Large Hall 3 floors Foyer 2 floors Small Hall basement + 3 floors
	Length:	Large Hall 58.3 m Foyer 97.8 m Small Hall 81.5 m
	Width:	Large Hall 55.0 m Foyer 17.0 m Small Hall 20.8 m
	Height:	Large Hall 22.6 m Foyer 10.0 m Small Hall 13.0 m
	Gross floor area (first floor):	Large Hall 2,070.0 m² Foyer 1,580.0 m² Small Hall 1,885.0 m²
	Gross floor area (total):	13,652.0 m²

Panoramic Cinema (Palace of Arts/Alisher Navoi Palace of Cinema)

There are a wide range of documents on which the description of this building is based. In the archive at O'zshaharsozlik LITI (Uzbekistan Urban Planning Research Institute) there is an extensive dossier on the design and construction of the cinema. The research also incorporated materials from the National Archive of Uzbekistan containing the expert assessment and transcriptions of discussions of the competition projects, three personal archives of project architects and numerous historical publications of the 1960s and 1970s.

The Design Contexts

The history of the Panoramic Cinema in Tashkent emerges out of three contexts: international, Soviet and Uzbek.

The international context of the 1950s and 1960s primarily involved an experimental revolution of cinematic technology. In the search for the spectacular, the film industry invented new camera formats, new types of film stock and new projectors, which enabled cinemas to create the illusion of immersive experience for the viewer. This was mainly achieved through increasing the width and curve of the screen so that it exceeded the natural viewing angle of the human eye. In 1952 the Cinerama system was developed in the USA. It was based on filming using three cameras and simultaneous projection of three projectors on semicircular screens. Later, other innovative systems were quickly launched: Cinemiracle, CinemaScope, VistaVision, Technirama, Super Technirama70, Todd-AO, Dimension-150, Ultra Panavision 70, Superpanorama 70 and others. This intensive experimental period largely came to an end in 1970 with the appearance of the IMAX format, which is still used to show wide-screen films today. As a result, panoramic cinemas began to appear in the New and Old Worlds. At first, they were installed in existing buildings (Le Kinopanorama, Paris, 1959), but, sensing a demand for a new type of building, architects began to design them (Cooper Theater, Denver, Colorado, and others).

In the USSR, where, in the 1920s, cinema was seen as the "most important of the arts," the idea of panoramic film screenings was quickly accepted and developed. Soviet film engineers created their own technology, NIKFI (1956), for wide-format shoots and screenings, which was demonstrated at Brussels EXPO 58 and later installed in Le Kinopanorama in Paris. The first Soviet panoramic cinemas, Mir (Moscow, 1958) and Leningrad (Leningrad, 1959), were also installed in adapted nineteenth-century buildings, but in the late 1950s and early 1960s panoramic cinemas were constructed in many cities in the USSR: Kyiv (1958), Rostov-on-Don (1959), Frunze (1963), Alma-Ata (1964), Tallinn (1964) and others. However, even at the end of the 1950s, the rapidly changing situation in the world of cinematographic technologies forced Soviet architects to consider creating universal auditoria for showing panoramic, wide-format and ordinary films.[1] This type of universal auditorium was to be built in Tashkent.

The demand for constructing the new complex was prompted by politics as well as new technologies. After the Twentieth Congress of the Communist Party, and in the context of Khrushchëv's reform of the construction industry, which put an end to the neoclassicist and neobaroque architectural trends of previous decades, Soviet leaders at all levels found themselves in a new situation: the most important events in public life took place in buildings that were aesthetically alien to the new party doctrine. This dissonance was not a feature of the Stalinist era. Then, such events normally took place in major theaters: the Bol'shoi Theater in Moscow, the Opera and Ballet Theater in Tashkent and so on. From the mid-1950s, a new type of public building developed, one which could be used for meetings and congresses of the party, trade unions and professional bodies. During the design and construction of the Kremlin Palace of Congresses (1958–1961) in Moscow the authorities in each Soviet republic began to consider the question of suitable buildings for local party forums. Simultaneously, the architectural agenda now included the creation of large, representational cinema and concert halls which could be used for film screenings, concerts, conferences, festivals and other public and cultural events. The October Concert Hall in Leningrad (1959–1967) and the October Cinema in Moscow (1967) were examples of this type of building that were completed after the construction of the Panoramic Cinema. In Tashkent there were insufficient funds to erect three large buildings—a palace of congresses, a concert hall and a cinema for several thousand people—so the Panoramic Cinema had to combine these functions. According to the program brief, "a cinema with seats [was required] to be designed with an auditorium for universal use, where the following could be organized:

a) film screenings with various types of projection: panoramic, wide-format, wide-screen with stereophonic sound;
b) symphony orchestra and choir concerts;

1 V. Bykov and Iu. Khripunov, "Tipy kinoteatrov s universal'noi proektsiei [Types of Cinemas with Universal Projection]," *Arkhitektura SSSR* [*Architecture of the USSR*], no. 9, 1959, 24–37.

c) performances by dance ensembles;
d) public and political events."[2]

This predetermined the presence in the building of a spacious foyer where viewers and participants of public and political forums could gather, a universal auditorium with a stage and an orchestra pit and auxiliary spaces for concert performers.

The Competition and Working Design

The initial design commission was awarded to Savelii Rozenblium in 1960. His institute colleagues considered the first versions professionally rendered but conceptually unoriginal[3] and requested that the Ministry of Culture of the Uzbek SSR organize a competition. The Ministry agreed, Savelii Rozenblium devised the competition program, and by mid-January 1961 the administration of the Union of Architects of the Uzbek SSR had received five projects for evaluation. Projects 1 and 2 were by a team led by Rozenblium, Projects A and B by a team of young architects from Uzgosproekt led by Iurii Khaldeev and Vladimir Berezin, and another, named in the documents "Version with Stage," was by architect Voitsekhovskii from the project and estimates office of the Ministry of Culture. The expert committee unanimously rejected the latter project, as it exceeded the design brief and proposed a developed stage with the necessary floor mechanisms and a stage volume.

Design for the Cinema Theater (2,500 seats) by Lenproekt Institute (Leningrad) in 1959, adapted by Savelii Rozenblium

In both Rozenblium projects the idea involved a trapezoidal auditorium with an adjacent glass foyer facing Navoi Street. The experts noted the lack of a memorable aesthetic vision and a number of town planning weaknesses. Firstly, as it was to be constructed right out to Navoi, the building did not have the buffer zone required for 2,500 viewers to exit to the street after a screening, and secondly, it completely ignored the existence of Pakhtakor Stadium, which was behind the cinema and attracted tens of thousands of people for sporting events. The experts also noted the positive sides of the project: the fact that it was compact and economical, its convenient facilities for performers and so on. Opponents insisted that the trapezoidal form of the auditorium meant that there were too many seats with a poor view, meaning viewers could not experience the effect of being immersed in the panoramic image. As a result, Projects 1 and 2 were rejected.

According to the competition documents, the team that produced Projects A and B was led by Iurii Khaldeev. However, he admitted that he developed Project A and his colleagues, led by Vladimir Berezin, worked on Project B. Nevertheless, the plans of Project A also include the names of Sergo Sutiagin, Vladimir Berezin, Dmitrii Shuvaev, Leon Adamov and Vil' Muratov, for which reason they should be considered co-authors. Projects A and B were significantly different from each other but were marked by two very similar solutions. Firstly, in both cases the main auditorium, or large hall, was oval. This choice was based on comparative geometric construction drawings by Iurii Gnedovskii and M. Savchenko published in 1959,[4] which showed that of circular, oval and trapezoidal auditoria, the latter provided space for fewer seats in the zone that was best for panoramic screenings. Secondly, both versions used tensile structures for the roof of the main viewing hall. Sergo Sutiagin recalled that in 1960 he read Frei Otto's book about tensile structures.[5] Having agreed to take part in the competition, he suggested that Iurii Khaldeev read the text. As a result, the team's competition proposals were based not only on a preference for tensile structures but were also likely inspired by examples from Otto's book.

The expressive possibilities of tensile structures were mainly revealed in Project A. Here the ellipsoidal auditorium in the right part of the building was adjacent to a curved wall 100 meters long and 22–26 meters high, from

2 See "Programmnoe zadanie na proektirovanie panoramnogo kinoteatra s universal'nym zalom na 2500 mest v gorode Tashkente [Program Brief for the Design of a Panoramic Cinema with a Universal Auditorium with 2,500 Seats in the City of Tashkent]," Stenogramma obsuzhdeniia proektov panoramnogo kinoteatra pri Soiuze arkhitektorov UzSSR, 20 fevralia 1961 [Transcription of a Discussion of Designs for a Panoramic Cinema at the Union of Architects of the Uzbek SSR, February 20, 1961], National Archive of the Republic of Uzbekistan, fund 2352, list 1, item 258, 119 sheets, 107.

3 As Sergo Sutiagin put it, "a beautifully drawn standard design." "Dvorets iskusstv [The Palace of Arts]" (manuscript of memoirs), personal archive of Karine Sutiagina, 20 sheets, 3.

4 V. Bykov and Iu. Khripunov, "Tipy kinoteatrov s universal'noi proektsiei [Types of Cinemas with Universal Projection]," 24–25.

5 Frei Otto, *Visiachie pokrytiia: ikh formy i konstruktsii* [*Tensile Structures*] (Moscow: State Publisher of Literature on Construction, Architecture and Construction Materials, 1960).

which the ceiling membranes descended, resulting in a form reminiscent of a snail shell. The most striking part of the building was the spiral foyer, where a ramp took viewers up from the entrance area facing Navoi Street to the auditorium. The prototype of this concept may have been the design for a concert hall on the bank of the Lietzensee lake in Berlin (1951) which was included in Otto's book. That building also incorporated a bow-shaped wall that was the support for the tensile structures of the main auditorium. However, the Tashkent experts saw many problems in this version. In particular, they doubted the functionality and hypertrophied dimensions of the base wall, especially as the supports for the tensile structure extended beyond its perimeter and were vulnerable to external temperatures and humidity. They also criticized the positioning of the building, as the striking form of the auditorium could hardly be seen from Navoi Street. The authors did not agree with this criticism, stating that the gradual opening up of the complex volume and the consideration of all points of view, including from Pakhtakor Stadium, were virtues of their version rather than shortcomings. Nevertheless, the expert committee, having first noted the original nature of the design, asked the architects to rework a number of elements. After the second reading it rejected this version. The older generation of architectural historians and critics agreed with the jury. In particular, Vladimir Nil'sen and Viktor Dmitriev wrote: "The young Tashkent architect Iu. A. Khaldeev created an extremely odd design for a cinema, the highlight of which was to be an enormous curved wall, on one side of which was the auditorium and on the other the entrance area. In plan the building took the form of a dissected snail. Although this clearly formalist design was heavily criticized by the Union of Soviet Architects of Uzbekistan, there were also those who insistently supported this absurd idea."[6]

Project B, which was developed by almost the same group (Berezin, Khaldeev, Sutiagin, Shuvaev),[7] appeared simpler. It combined two volumes: the horizontal parallelepiped of the two-story foyer, which included ticket desks, and the elliptical cylinder of the main auditorium with a parabolic tensile roof. The architects achieved a contrasting effect. The horizontal block with ribbon windows was completely transparent, and the cylindrical block had solid walls with "fluting." The latter created a visual association with a section of a Doric column, since the volume of the main auditorium appeared circular from the outside and its oval form could only be seen from above. Project B offered a good solution to urban planning issues. Firstly, it was set back from Navoi Street, which created a small square with good sight lines, secondly, the south façade acknowledged the neighboring Pakhtakor Stadium, and thirdly, it successfully separated flows of people in cases when the stadium and the cinema emptied simultaneously. In this version the performers' and administrative spaces were situated in the cylindrical volume under the main auditorium. Some experts were critical, stating that performers needed natural light. Others liked this arrangement, since it limited the cubic capacity of the building and construction costs.[8] The experts considered the most controversial element of Project B to be the tensile roof, which created a dynamic silhouette for the building. The basic construction was also similar to examples from Otto's book, such as the Swiss Pavilion at the Berlin Industrial Exhibition of 1952 (Hans Stettbacher) or the Schwarzwaldhalle in Karlsruhe. However, the expert committee decided that, given the seismic conditions in Tashkent, the main volume should be more static and the roof construction based on more familiar trusses. The authors of Project B accepted this conclusion. They first replaced the tensile structure with radial steel half trusses with a central drum, and then made the upper section of the cylindrical space strictly horizontal. They discovered that by focusing the load-bearing reinforcement on the ends rather than along the perimeter of the walls, this "allowed for the complete assembly of the walls and significantly simplified their production at the factory."[9] As well as providing an extremely stable structure, this solution turned out to be more balanced aesthetically. Both the rectangular and cylindrical blocks remained static, and their joins and transitions provided the composition with dynamism and plasticity. The interior of the main auditorium became more spectacular, impressing the viewer with its volume and forms, in contrast to the extended single-story foyer on the first floor. The height of the auditorium was visually raised by the development of the walls, which featured the rhythm of rising elements with conical tips, similar to elongated, almost

6 Viktor Dmitriev and Vladimir Nil'sen, "O napravlennosti v sovremennoi arkhitektury Uzbekistana [On the Direction of Uzbekistan's Modern Architecture]," *Obshchestvennye nauki v Uzbekistane* [*Social Sciences in Uzbekistan*], no. 12, 1962, 16.

7 The description of this group of architects often included the phrase "with the participation of Ol'ga Legostaeva."

8 Post factum we can state that throughout the twentieth century the building was used almost exclusively as a cinema, and the occasional concerts would not have justified the inclusion of spaces for performers in the visible part.

9 Sergo Sutiagin and Aleksandr Braslavskii, "Dvorets iskusstv v Tashkente [The Palace of Arts in Tashkent]," *Arkhitektura SSSR* [*Architecture of the USSR*], no. 11, 1965, 9.

Façade drawing of the Panoramic Cinema, competition project proposal, Project A, 1960

Façade drawing of the Panoramic Cinema, competition project proposal, Project B, 1960

Panoramic Cinema, project development of Project B (competition winner, 1960), façade drawing, 1961

Panoramic Cinema, project development of Project B (competition winner, 1960), façade drawing, 1961

Gothic sails. The jury accepted the adjustments to Project B and approved it for construction.

After the competition result was decided, development of the construction drawings began in late 1961. Until mid-1963 the lead architect was Vladimir Berezin, but various building details were developed by Sergo Sutiagin, Ol'ga Legostaeva and others. In mid-1963, when Berezin took charge of the design of the building for the Central Committee of the Communist Party of Uzbekistan, Sergo Sutiagin became lead architect for the Panoramic Cinema. He was responsible for supervision of construction and revealed an ability to work inventively with the builders in the context of Uzbekistan's poorly developed construction industry.

As far as project metamorphoses during the design and construction phases are concerned, something should be said about the refinement of the plans and façades, the selection of materials, and the search for suitable monumental art for installation in the building. The main idea was to reduce expressive means and discover more subtle solutions. One of the options for regulating the outflow of viewers after a film screening was two-level evacuation, with the construction of staircases to the second level at both sides of the auditorium, which would shorten the exit route for viewers in the back rows, but in the end the architects created exits from the west and east sides of the main auditorium at street level. In Sergo Sutiagin's documents there is a version of the plastic development of the "fluting" using rising linear steps decorated with figurative-like compositions, but this was replaced with textured monotone horizontal lines along the entire façade. The selection of materials was less minimalist. As well as concrete, they included brick and broken marble tiles with chipped edges, with wood, aluminum and ceramic panels in the interior.

Monumental Art

The monumental art that was so abundant in the sketches was transformed during the design and construction phases, and this helps us to determine the aesthetic evolution of the project. In Project A the monumental counter-reliefs covered the entire perimeter of the external wall and also the interior walls. Sergo Sutiagin invited Arnol'd Gan, a graduate of the Mukhina Higher School of Art and Industrial Design in Leningrad who had spent his childhood and youth in Tashkent, to make the sketches. The theme of the counter-reliefs was typical for the Thaw period. The background featured space motifs in the form of planetary orbits and at the center of the composition, surrounded by an aura, were a young woman and man reminiscent of characters in Maksim Gor'kii's early works, with their Nietzschean expectation of the superhuman. Behind this Promethean couple, in a less extravagant but still celebratory register, was a group of young people with the gifts of nature from a good harvest, and to the right was a smaller couple presenting the world with a baby. Accordingly, the main themes of the monumental art in Project A were youth, humankind's heroic deeds and the fertility of nature (as the architects wrote in the explanatory note, the image symbolized "peace, labor, abundance, love, space.")[10]

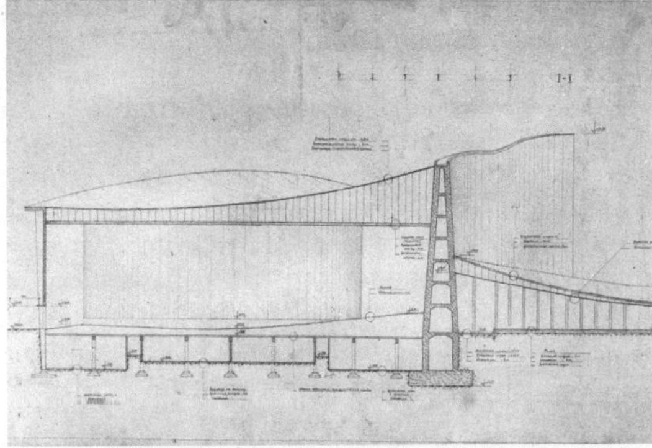

Top: Section of the Panoramic Cinema, competition project proposal, Project A, 1960
Bottom: Swiss Pavilion at the German Industrial Exhibition, Berlin, 1952, arch. Hans Stettbacher

For Project B, Gan produced a figurative bas-relief for the external east end of the foyer, but during the design process the architects left this wall blank so as not to interrupt the play of plastic volumes and dynamic shadows on the "fluting" of the main auditorium. Arnol'd Gan's primary area of work was transferred to the

10 Valentin Arkhangel'skii, "Otzyv o proekte kinokontsertnogo zala na 2500 mest. Proekt gruppy molodykh arkhitektorov 'Uzgosproekta.' Variant 'A' [Review of the Design for a Cinema and Concert Hall with 2,500 Seats by a Group of Young Architects from Uzgosproekt, Version A]," Stenogramma obsuzhdeniia proektov panoramnogo kinoteatra pri Soiuze arkhitektorov UzSSR, 20 fevralia 1961 [Transcription of a Discussion of Designs for a Panoramic Cinema at the Union of Architects of the Uzbek SSR, February 20, 1961], National Archive of the Republic of Uzbekistan, fund 2352, list 1, item 258, 119 sheets, 66.

interior. The theme of Project A changed the appearance of the finished building. Having removed the subjects of space and Promethean heroics, the artist focused on depicting youth, abundance and the friendship of peoples. The fresco that was named *The Birth of Dance*[11] depicted a garden in bloom that was a place for girls dressed in khan-atlas dresses and Russian/Ukrainian sarafans, which for Tashkent embodied inter-ethnic harmony and creative collaboration. The theme of choreography only partly correlated with the typology of the building. Although also designed for concerts by dance ensembles and choirs, it was mainly intended for use as a panoramic and wide-format cinema. This may be why the architects spent considerable time trying to supplement the fresco with images more suited to its purpose.

They suggested at least three versions of monumental art for the external walls of the auditorium. Sculpture-like works appeared on two of them, at the join of the "fluting" facing Navoi Street. One depicted a human face and had elements recognizable as brushes and other attributes of artistic professions (by the end of the construction period the Panoramic Cinema had been given a different official name, the Palace of Arts).[12] The other appeared to depict a figure that was either half-human, half-bird or a dancing couple. However, the correlation of both images with the cinema and concert hall was vague, and their figurative character contradicted the elegant play of semicircular forms on the façade. In another sketch the architects attempted to encrust the "fluting" with a stepped pattern of small semifigurative and symbolic images. However, this ornamentation also lost out aesthetically to the existing elegant form. Accordingly, the main volume remained free from monumental forms.

For the interior, on the right side of the main auditorium, the architects also tried to imagine a monumental panel. This time the idea involved a linear bas-relief that was separated from the wall and depicted an Uzbek dutar player and, yet again, a girl dancing to his tune. This time the work was based on Persian miniatures. It was never made, but the basic concept, which involved orientalizing the interior of the building, would form the basis of later ideas. The wall of the buffet in the foyer was faced with carved beech with an accentuated oriental pattern,[13] and Aleksandr Kedrin's decorative objects in the buffet and bar had similar connotations.

However, the most interesting development of the theme of links to the local culture could be found on one of the façade walls in the west part of the building, in a place between the auditorium and the staff staircase that was less visible to the public. In fact, it could only be seen by staff of the Panoramic Cinema and the occasional passerby who entered the complex from the nearby mahalla. This wall was carefully designed and well made. It can be seen in the construction drawings of December 1961. The material was ocher-terra-cotta decorative brick in various formats, including narrow tiles, which were similar in size to modules used in the historic architecture of Central Asia. Knowing the construction practices of the early 1960s, one can state that such bricks were produced as a special order, i.e. they were not used for new buildings but for restoration work in the medieval cities of Uzbekistan. The surface of the wall was designed to be both decorative and figurative: alongside the traditional scattered figures of modernist language, such as the circle and its derivatives, an incomplete pointed arch was laid on the horizontal masonry. This motif was not characteristic of the modernist language of this building or of Tashkent architecture of the early 1960s as a whole. On the reverse of the photograph of this wall, Vladimir Berezin wrote: "Detail of 'Brick wall with motifs from local antiquity.' The past and the old gives way to the new architecture."[14] As a result, history played a cruel trick on the building and the architects. The brick wall symbolizing the "defeat" of the old architecture, which went unnoticed by contemporaries, became the main theme of the second phase of the Panoramic Cinema in the mid-1970s. A renewed "old" returned, rising alongside a mature "new."

The Completion of Construction and a New Design Stage

The cinema opened in October 1964. As well as daily screenings there were also major public events, such as party congresses, professional meetings and conferences. From the mid-1960s the complex was named the Palace of Arts, and in 1968 it became the hub for the Tashkent International Film Festival of Asia and Africa. Meanwhile, buildings with individual functions would soon be preferred to the multifunctional use of space in Soviet practice.

11 Sergo Sutiagin, "Dvorets iskusstv v Tashkente [The Palace of Arts in Tashkent]," *Stroitel'stvo i arkhitektura Uzbekistana* [Construction and Architecture of Uzbekistan], no. 6, 1977, 24.

12 The reverse of the photograph of this sketch from Sergo Sutiagin's archive gives the date 1962–1963, which is evidence that the search for forms of monumental art continued after construction began, simultaneously with the production of construction drawings.

13 According to Larisa Simukova, Sergo Sutiagin told her that the interior of the bar and the bar counter were designed by Ol'ga Legostaeva (from correspondence between Boris Chukhovich and Larisa Simukova, July 22, 2022).

14 From the personal archive of Ekaterina Berezina.

Large Hall of the Panoramic Cinema, project development of Project B (competition winner, 1960), 1961

Panoramic Cinema, 1966

Panoramic Cinema, new block inaugurated in 1977

Several years after the completion of the Panoramic Cinema in Tashkent, design began on "palaces of congresses" for the capitals of Kazakhstan and Azerbaijan: the Lenin Palace in Alma-Ata (1970) and the Lenin Palace in Baku (1972). As a result, the authorities in Uzbekistan announced the need for a similar specialized building in Tashkent. In 1971 they commissioned the Mezentsev Central Scientific Research and Experimental Project Institute for Entertainment and Sport Facilities (TsNIIEP) in Moscow to design the future Peoples' Friendship Palace, which was not intended for film screenings. Following a decree of the Council of Ministers of the Uzbek SSR of August 1, 1973, redesign of the Palace of Arts began with the addition of the adjoining Small Hall. The main purpose of the planned reconstruction was hosting the Nineteenth Congress of the Communist Party of Uzbekistan. It was assumed that the Small Hall would become "an auditorium for film chronicles and repeat films."[15]

The reconstruction was required for objective as well as ideological reasons. The construction of the cinema in the early 1960s was associated with numerous restrictions on the use of more durable but more expensive materials and equipment, as a result of which a significant number of elements had worn out and required replacement after ten years. The numerous commissions made particular note of the building's failure to meet fire safety standards. The key issue was the main auditorium, the walls of which had been constructed using wooden panels that produced good acoustics but were flammable. Their replacement with suitable panels was long discussed at a number of levels.[16] The electrical and technical equipment that had been installed originally was also out-of-date by 1970.[17]

15 Richard Bleze, "Ekspertnoe zakliuchenie na proekt kompleksnoi rekonstruktsii kinokontsertnogo zala Dvortsa iskusstv v g. Tashkente [Export Opinion on the Project for the Complex Reconstruction of the Cinema and Concert Hall of the Palace of Arts in Tashkent]," 1 (March 4, 1974), O'zshaharsozlik LITI Archive, file 1397.

16 "Protokol soveshchaniia pri Zamestitele Predsedatelia Gosstroia UzSSR tov. Sarkisovoi R. A., ot 10 sentiabria 1974; po voprosu kapital'nogo remonta i rekonstruktsii Dvortsa iskusstv v g. Tashkente, Pis'mo UzNIIPgradostroitel'stva – UPO UVD Tashgorispolkoma za No.ASO-4-180 ot 29 iiulia 1974 goda, Pis'ma MVD UzSSR i UzNIIPgradostroitel'stva ot 16 marta 1972 goda, 25 i 29 marta 1975 goda, 18 iiunia1975; UzNIIPgradostroitel'stva – Gosstroiu UzSSR ot 20 marta 1975 goda; i dr. [Protocol of a Meeting with the Vice Chairman of Gosstroi of the Uzbek SSR Comrade Sarkisova R. A. of September 10, 1974; On the Question of Major Renovation and Reconstruction of the Palace of Arts in Tashkent, Letter from UzNIIPgradostroitel'stva to UPO UVD Tashgorispolkoma, No.ASO-4-180, July 29, 1974, Letters of the Ministry of Internal Affairs of the Uzbek SSR and UzNIIPgradostroitel'stva, March 16, 1972, March 25 and 29, 1975, June 18, 1975; From UzNIIPgradostroitel'stva to Gosstroi of the Uzbek SSR, March 30, 1975; etc.]," O'zshaharsozlik LITI Archive, file 1397.

Unlike the first stage of construction, a competition was not organized for the second stage. The design was assigned to Sergo Sutiagin, who had been responsible for completing the construction documentation and for architectural supervision of construction of the cinema from 1962 to 1964. By the 1970s he was an experienced architect who had designed major buildings such as the Samarkand Teahouse and a cinema and concert complex in Dushanbe. Commissioning him also solved the problem of authorship and copyright. Even though the situation with attribution of authorship of architecture in the USSR was unclear, during the production process the question occasionally came up, and an attempt was made to assign the transformation of the building to the original designer.

The aesthetic benchmarks of the 1970s were notably different from those of the 1960s, when the Panoramic Cinema was built. Initially the building—a result of the Thaw and the last Soviet generation to construct images of the future—had a futuristic feel. It was no accident that the themes of youth and the future dominated in both the original sketches and the main fresco in the foyer. However, against a background of growing social confusion and fatigue, an opposing trend appeared: a search for lost roots, an interest in "the ghosts of forgotten ancestors," an immersion in the past, the clear outlines of which began to prevail over images of the future that were vacillating and fading into the background. Many buildings designed in the 1960s and constructed in the 1970s seriously changed their appearance. The Palace of Arts differed from them because the building evolved thanks to the addition of a new volume, adjacent to the main part, which preserved the original look.

The lead architect, who had moved away from the aesthetic of the early 1960s, had a conceptual choice to make. He could design the new block by developing or reproducing the formal language of the existing building, even if it was an attribute of a past era, or he could risk the aesthetic integrity and construct something completely new. Sutiagin chose the latter. The hinge between the old and new blocks was an experimental brick wall that had been constructed in 1961. Hence, carefully developed volumes made of brick combined with travertine surfaces became the key motif of the main part of the building.

17 "Pis'mo direktora Dvortsa iskusstv N. Vaslieva glavnomu inzheneru Uzenergosbyta Akhmedovu [Letter from N. Vasliev, Director of the Palace of Arts, to Akhmedov, Chief Engineer of Uzenergosbyt]," O'zshaharsozlik LITI Archive, file 1397.

Geometrically the new block correlated with the old one only in terms of the width of the foyer and the length of the extension of the new auditorium to the south, which was equal to the distance between the intersection of the old and new parts and the marble pylon that separated the staircase space of the foyer from the café. This use of proportion was important for the most problematic joint between the two buildings, which could be seen from the south-eastern, park side. The heterogeneity of styles and materials in this segment of the building was obvious, but the geometric proportions gave it a feeling of integrity. The architect also attempted to level out the problem of heterogeneity of materials through a complete lack of details on the east façade of the new block. Its travertine wall was the background for the meticulously developed two-story 1960s foyer. Opposite, viewed from the TV Center, the detailed south-west wall of the new block screened the old volumes. The south part of the Small Hall was perceived more as a plastic introduction to the space in front of the park and sculpture, rather than part of a volume hidden behind the park. In contrast, in the interior the new and old aesthetics clashed more tangibly, as if percolating into each other without mixing and still retaining their own meanings. The connecting element here was not only the shared transit space and the staircase in the foyer but also the materials, including the same wooden handrails and surfaces textured with the chipped edges of marble tiles. In the old foyer they covered the pylons, and in the new one the load-bearing columns.

It may be that a clearer difference between the two spaces was marked out by monumental art. From the 1960s foyer with its figurative fresco by Gan, the viewer could see a circular, abstract stained glass window.[18] This theme at the end of the high space had connotations of church architecture, and its abstract design gave the space the grandness of a "temple of arts."

At the dawn of its existence, the Modern Movement was based on a desire for the homogenization and reduction of means of expression. However, the Panoramic Cinema, which was built in 1964, already contained the opposition of two different elements: the solid volume and the transparent foyer. The reconstruction for the Palace of Arts of 1974–1977 gave this heterogeneity both a spatial and a historical dimension. The contrast of the concrete cylinder and the glass parallelepiped remained a symbol of the attempt by the Tashkent architects to be part of the cosmopolitan world without borders, to insert themselves in the outlines of the International Style. The second block of the Palace of Arts was an obvious antithesis: it opposed universalism with regionalism, isolation from context with rootedness in it, dreams of the future with metaphysical meditation. Even so, the plastic language of the new block remained modernist. The texture of the façade walls was developed with the help of the scattered figures of the twentieth-century avant-garde: the rhythm of straight and extended rectangles accented with circles. Unlike the staff wall of the 1960s, it contained no direct historical citations. The monumental art was more radical from the point of view of modernist aims, having lost its former figurativeness and moved toward abstraction, which was not typical of the art of Soviet Uzbekistan. Also innovative was the means of joining the two historical strata. Without mixing, they set each other off and created a new whole.

The Fire of 1978 and the Transformation of the Building

Construction began in winter 1974, in parallel with preparation of the construction drawings, and was completed in 1977. The Palace was to have been the venue for a number of important forums, including, in October 1978, the International Symposium on Macromolecular Chemistry, which would involve more than 2,500 participants from twenty-eight countries. However, three and a half months before the opening of the symposium, which was scheduled for October 17, there was a catastrophic fire. Information about it was kept secret, and today the only source regarding what happened is two manuscripts by Sergo Sutiagin.[19] According to the architect's notes, in the main auditorium the entire wall cladding, the aluminum structures of the ceiling, the seats and the floor supports caught fire, as did all of the sound and electrical equipment. In addition, there was a real threat to the entire roof; it was saved by the central drum, which the flames burned through up to the outside without melting the structure to the extent that it was no longer load-bearing. The flames also spread to the foyer, which led to all of the façade glazing being smashed and damage to the fresco, among other things. However, the Soviet authorities allocated the necessary funds for emergency repair of the building. Over a period of three and a half months it was reconstructed, with the damaged electrics and equipment replaced, new, Hungarian-made seats installed and new floors and windows in the foyer. Arnol'd Gan repainted the fresco, which took on more orientalist forms and lost

18 Sutiagin planned to commission Irena Lipene for the stained glass composition, but she was not in Tashkent at the time, and the architect passed this work to Viktor Gan.

19 Sutiagin sent Boris Chukhovich the first in 2017, and Chukhovich found the second in Sutiagin's personal archive in 2022, after the architect's death.

the turquoise and red color scheme that had linked it to the stained glass tondo.

In the years around 2020, regardless of its protected status, the owner of the Palace subjected it to uncontrolled reconstruction. In that period four additional auditoria were created in the second-floor foyer and the same type of room also appeared in the first-floor foyer and at the basement level.

New plans for reconstruction appeared after ownership of the Palace was transferred to the Uzbekkino National Agency. Its spontaneous actions were stopped with the help of a public campaign. For a time, the transformation project was supervised by Sergo Sutiagin, but since his death in July 2021 the question of a suitable approach to the preservation of the leading example of Tashkent modernism remains open.

Top: Panoramic cinema, interior of the new block inaugurated in 1977
Bottom: Interior of the Small Hall, inaugurated in 1977

ARCHITECT
VLADIMIR BEREZIN

Place and year of birth:
Tashkent, 1931
Place and year of death:
Tashkent, 2007
Education:
1949–1955, Architecture Department of Central Asia Polytechnic Institute (SazPI)

In Uzgosproekt since 1956, until 1960 he designed residential settlements in the Hungry Steppe and worked in the department of standard design.

In 1961 he was a member of the creative team that won the competition for the Panoramic Cinema. Until June 1962 he was the chief architect of the Panoramic Cinema project. According to Sergo Sutiagin, the competition team for the Panoramic Cinema was headed by Vladimir Berezin and Iurii Khaldeev, and judging by the fact that Berezin was appointed the chief architect, he played a major role in decision-making.

In mid-1962, he began work on the project of the building of the Central Committee of the Communist Party of Uzbekistan as GAP, supervising the development of the idea and working drawings, as well as author's supervision of construction, as head of the department of Uzgosproekt. The successful completion of both projects—the Panoramic Cinema and the Central Committee of the Communist Party of the UzSSR—in 1964 put him among the most experienced and notable architects in Tashkent.

From 1965 to 1991 he worked as the chief architect of Uzgosproekt/UzNIIPgradostroitel'stva. Sergo Sutiagin characterized Berezin's transition to administrative work as follows: "At the very height of his creativity, Vladimir Vladimirovich agreed to become the chief architect of the Institute. It was a responsible and courageous act of a creative person who realizes what he sacrifices and why. We ourselves persuaded him to make this important step for our institute, first of all, a sacrifice for him personally. We realized that any architect 'from the outside' (there was also such an option) could bring dissonance to the already established architectural and artistic style of our institute, the 'Uzgos school,' which had the highest authority in the republic." (Among other things, these words testify to the legitimacy of the institutional approach to the consideration of the creative biographies of Tashkent architects).

In the 1970s, three drama theaters were built according to Vladimir Berezin's designs: in Urgench (1972, together with Yulia Zakirova), Karshi (1975, together with A. Kozlova) and Nukus (1974, together with Yulia Zakirova).

CREATIVE ORIENTATIONS

Free planning. None of the architect's buildings were symmetrical, nor were any of his façades, including the side façades. This did not exclude elements of symmetry integrated into the overall composition: symmetrical halls of all his constructions (the Panoramic Cinema, the conference hall of the Central Committee of the Communist Party of the UzSSR and the auditoria of three theaters), entrance blocks, etc.

Spatial division of functions. The office block and the conference hall with a canteen (CC), as well as the foyer and the auditorium, (Panoramic Cinema) are separated into different volumes; the theater foyer, the audience courtyard, the auditorium, the stage box, the service building and the actors' courtyard, being united by one horizontal belt, are distinguished as different volumes thanks to the transparency of the foyer and the entrance block, which makes it possible to distinguish from the outside the internal structure of the individual parts of the building.

The rhythmic development of the façades with monotonous vertical elements and the allocation of the entrance blocks. Development of cubic, parallelepipedic and circular forms.

Refusal of façade ornamentation (exception: decorated façade of the stage box of the theater in Nukus).

ARCHITECT
SERGO SUTIAGIN

Place and year of birth:
Moscow, 1937
Place and year of death:
Tashkent, 2021
Education:
1955–1960, Architecture Department of Central Asia Polytechnic Institute (SazPI)

Worked at Uzgosproekt from 1960 and in 1961 became part of the creative team (V. Berezin, Iu. Khaldeev, D. Shuvaev) that won the competition for the Panoramic Cinema. From 1962, Sutiagin led the construction documentation and construction phases of the Panoramic Cinema. At completion of construction he was twenty-seven years old.

Sergo Sutiagin was better integrated than other architects of his generation into the creative and administrative elite of Uzbekistan.

He developed a more metaphysical language within his later work, as can be seen in his projects for the Brutalist and symbolically loaded Samarkand Teahouse (1968–1976), the cinema and concert hall in Dushanbe (1965–1985), the Navoi Library in Tashkent (design 1970–1978) and other buildings. From the mid-1970s to the early 2000s he moved away from minimalist concrete Brutalism, preferring the play of the plastic qualities of brick and natural stone (Small Hall of the Panoramic Cinema, the theater and the literary museum in Kokand, the museum in Nukus), ceramics, metal, glass and other materials (Cosmonauts Avenue metro station).

See full biography in Cosmonauts Avenue metro station monograph, page 482

INSTITUTIONAL FRAMEWORK

Uzgosproekt/
UzNIIPgradostroitel'stva

CADRE

The history of Uzgosproekt since the early 1960s was defined by the arrival of Vladimir Berezin, Sergo Sutiagin, Richard Bleze and Dmitrii Shuvaev, who quickly became the heads of the design studios. Having learned to cooperate in designing the major projects of the first half of the 1960s—building of the Central Committee of the Communist Party of Uzbekistan and the Panoramic Cinema—they had compatible views on architecture and formed architectural groups that shared their values.

PRIORITIES

Use of techniques and vocabulary of modern architecture, rejection of historicism and formal quotations, evolution from simple and transparent volumes in the 1960s to more complex Brutalist forms in the 1970s and 1980s, functionalism of the plan which determined the volume solution. Representative buildings: Central Committee of Communist Party of Uzbekistan, Panoramic Cinema, House of Publishers, Navoi Library (not built), Computing Center (not completed), State Planning Committee, Music and Drama Theater and Literature Museum in Kokand, Cosmonauts Avenue metro station, theaters in Nukus, Karshi and Urgench, Namangan and Bukhara Party Committees.

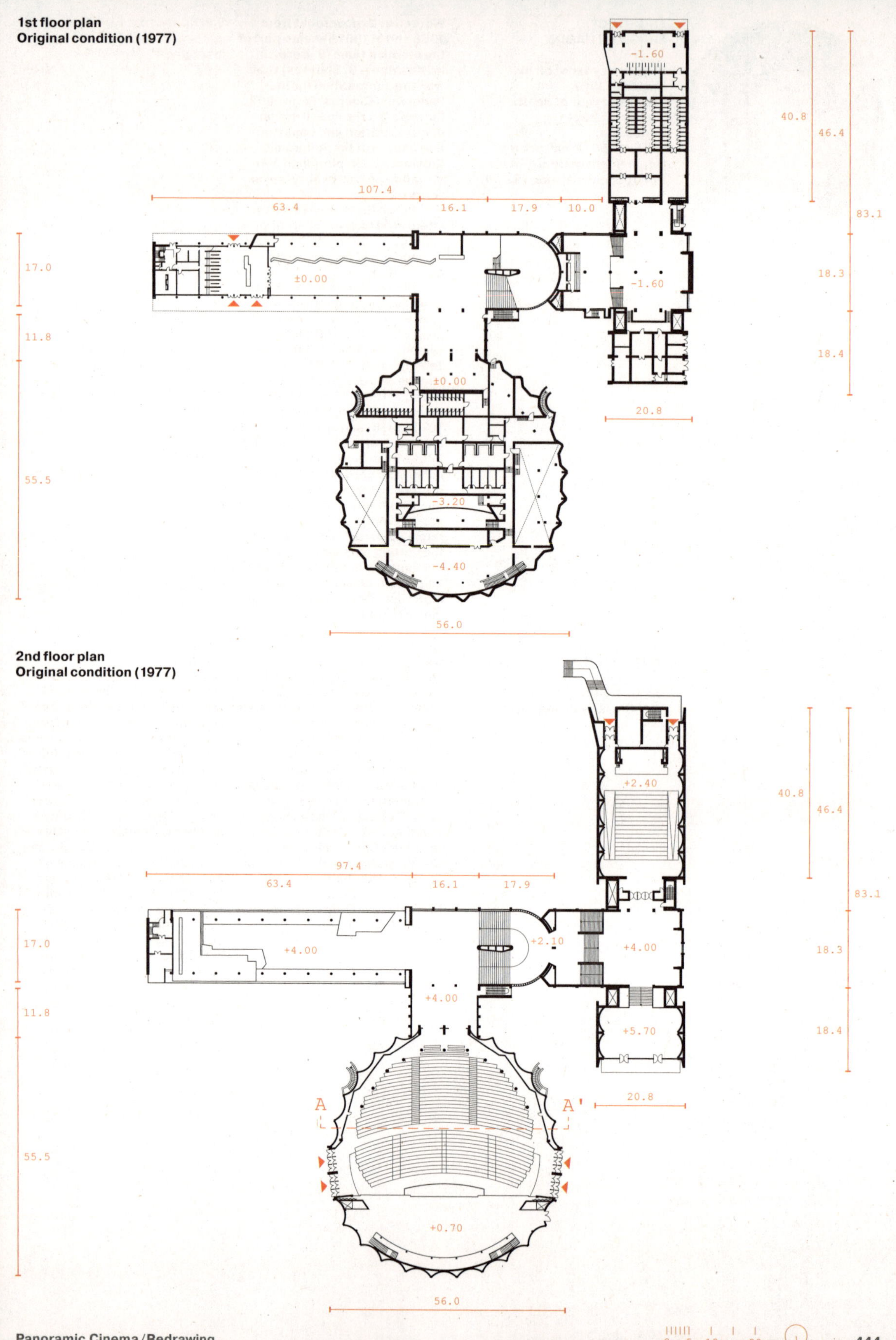
1st floor plan
Original condition (1977)
107.4
63.4
16.1
17.9
10.0
40.8
46.4
83.1
-1.60
17.0
±0.00
18.3
11.8
18.4
±0.00
20.8
55.5
-3.20
-4.40
56.0
2nd floor plan
Original condition (1977)
40.8
46.4
+2.40
97.4
63.4
16.1
17.9
83.1
17.0
+4.00
+2.10
+4.00
18.3
+4.00
11.8
+5.70
18.4
A
A'
20.8
55.5
+0.70
56.0
0
5
10
20m

East elevation
Original condition (1977)

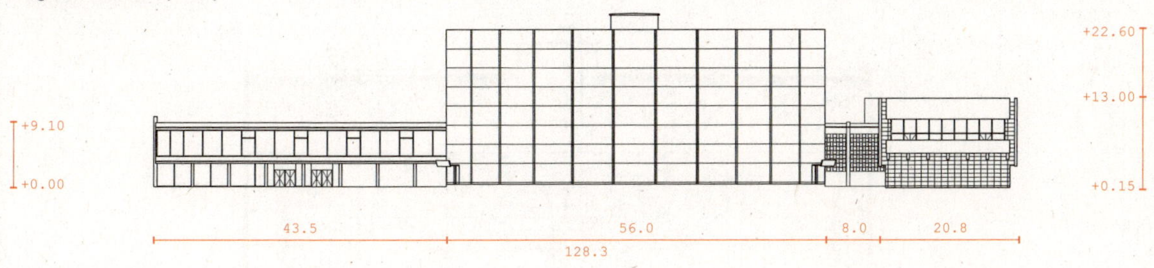

South elevation
Original condition (1977)

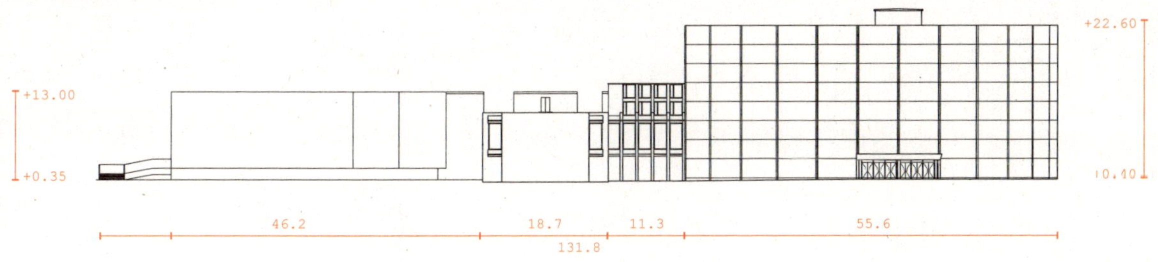

West elevation
Original condition (1977)

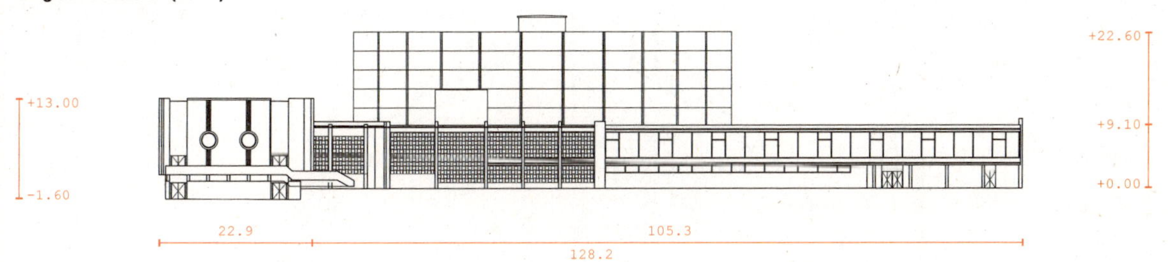

North elevation
Original condition (1977)

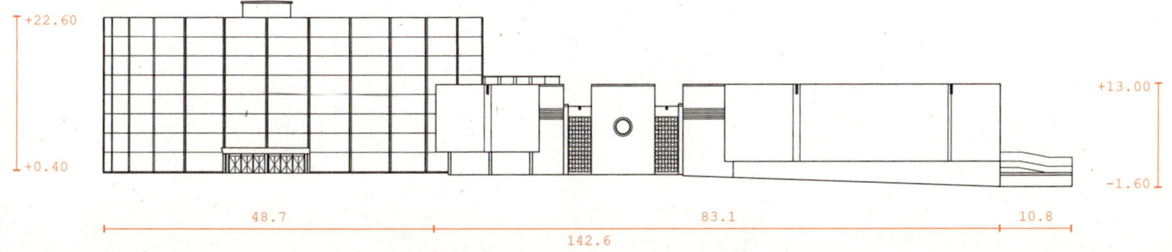

0 5 10 20m

Section AA'
Original condition (1977)

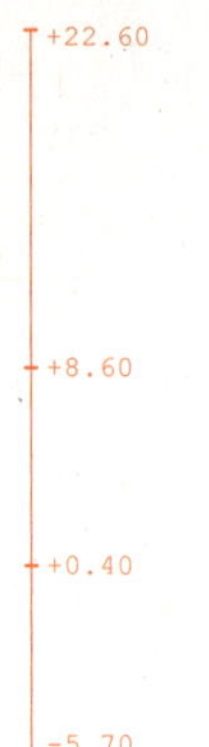

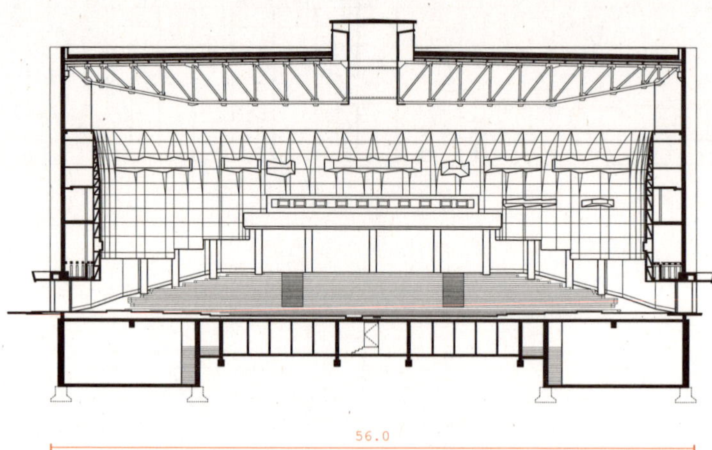

2nd floor plan, Large Hall
Original condition (1977)

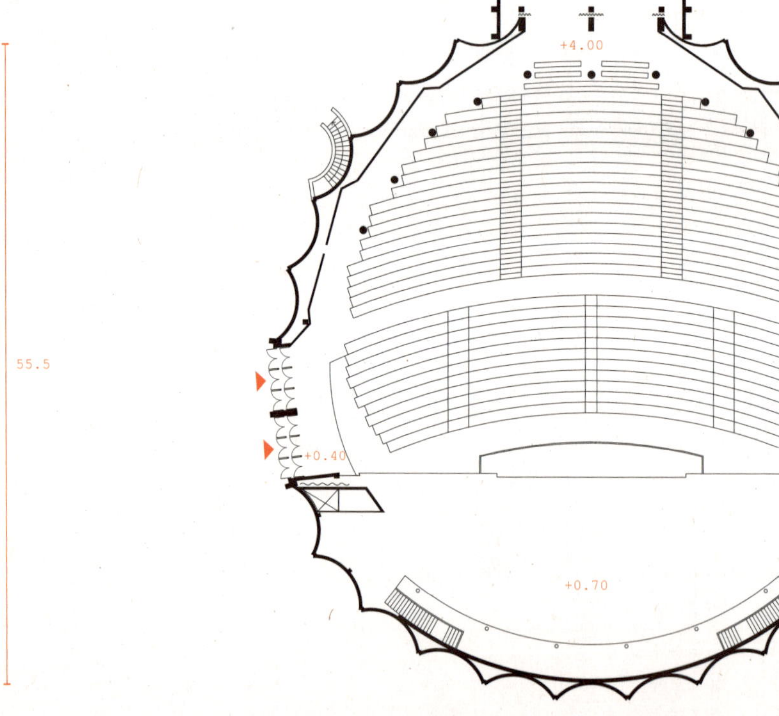

South-west axonometric view
Original condition (1977)

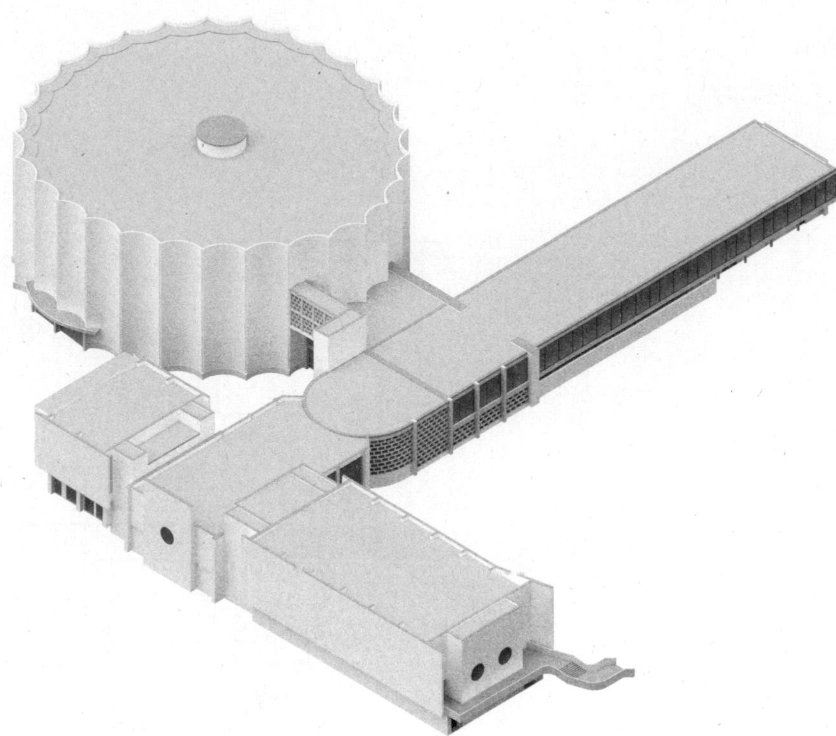

North-east axonometric view
Original condition (1977)

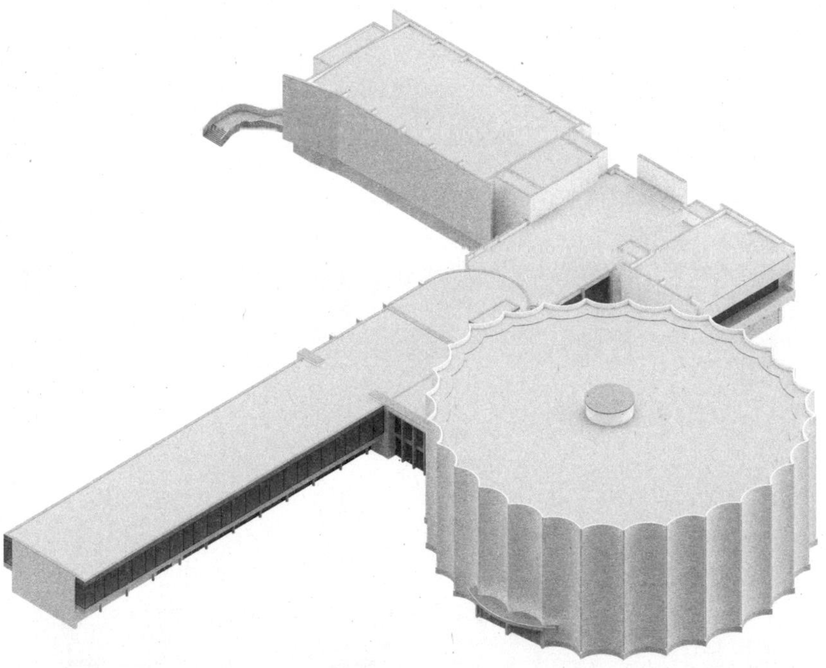

1964/1977

1st floor plan
Original condition

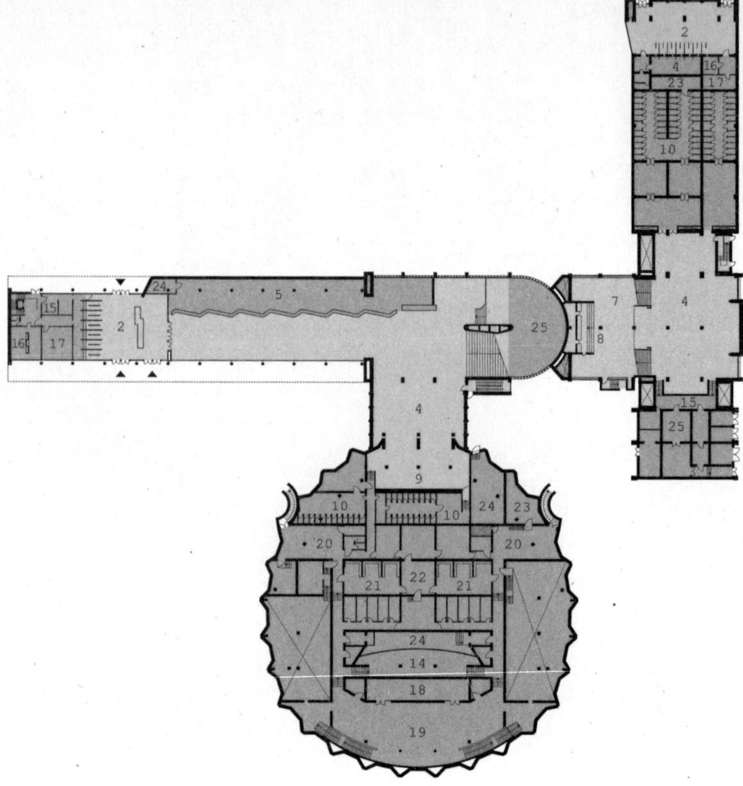

2nd floor plan
Original condition

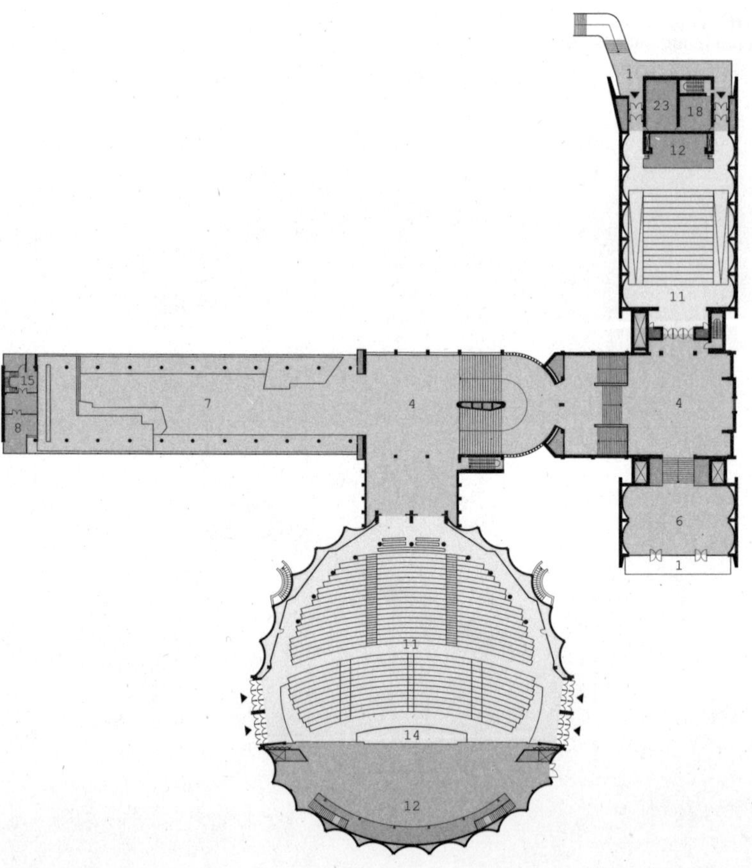

Cinema halls
Public
Service and technical
Change of function

2022

1st floor plan
Current condition

2nd floor plan
Current condition

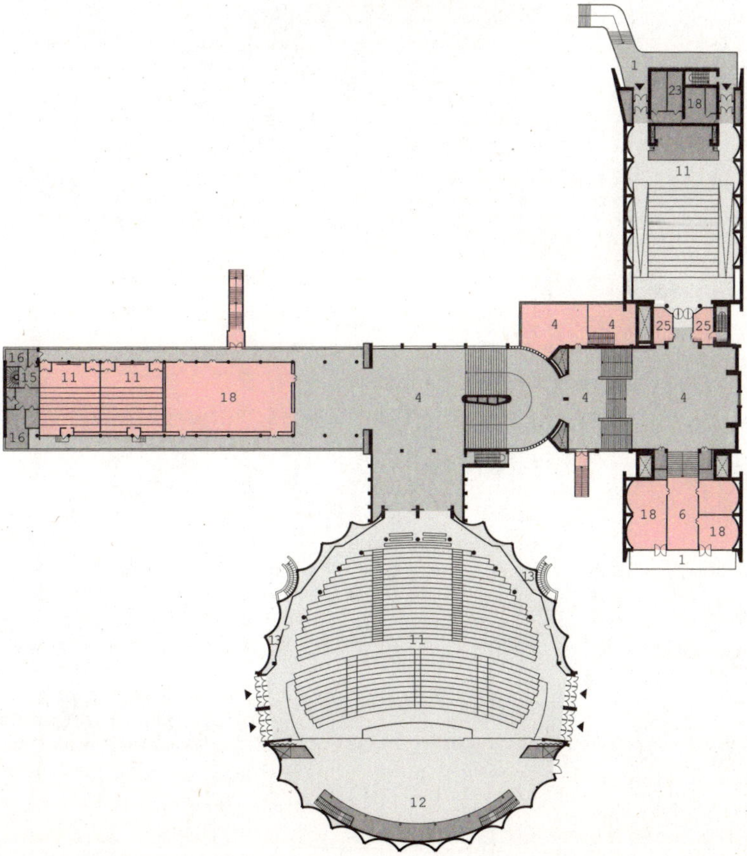

1 Terrace
2 Entrance vestibule
3 Ticket office
4 Vestibule
5 Cloakroom
6 Exhibition vestibule
7 Café
8 Café service rooms
9 Smoking room
10 Restroom
11 Concert/cinema hall
12 Stage
13 Technical stage
14 Orchestra pit
15 Circulation, workers
16 Administration
17 Staff room
18 Meeting room
19 Rehearsal room
20 Artists' vestibule with cloakroom
21 Artists' changing room
22 Dressing room
23 Service room
24 Storage
25 Technical area

0 5 10 20m

Construction of the foyer

Views of public spaces surrounding the building before construction of the TV Center, 1967

View of the wing connecting the Large Hall to the foyer

Panoramic Cinema team, 1964

View of the east façade of the Panoramic Cinema

Cloakroom on the first floor of the foyer block

Café on the second floor of the foyer block

Café on the second floor of the foyer block

View of the Large Hall with the connection between it and the former foyer, 2022

View of the Large Hall and foyer block, 2022

Large Hall façade detail, 2023

View of the south façade of the Panoramic Cinema, 2022

Foyer of the Small Hall, stained glass by Viktor Gan, 2023

Decorative tiles on the first floor of the foyer, 2023

Interior of the Large Hall, 2021

Fresco wall supporting the stairs, 2021

Interior of the Large Hall, 2021

Model of a development of Project B after the competition, 1962

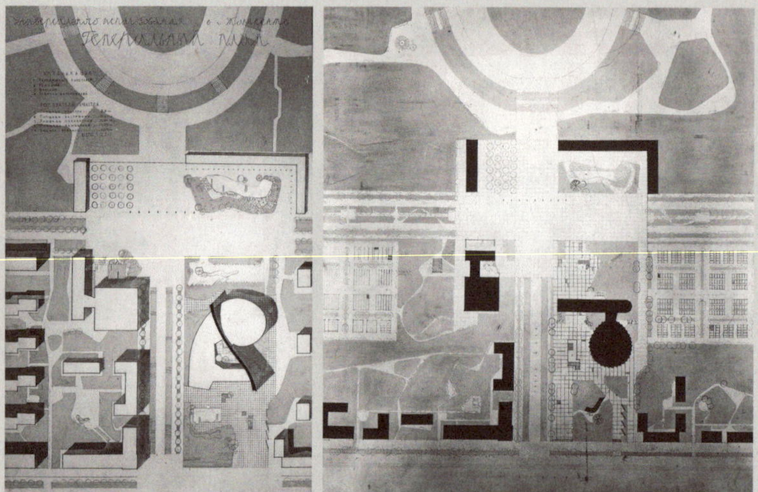
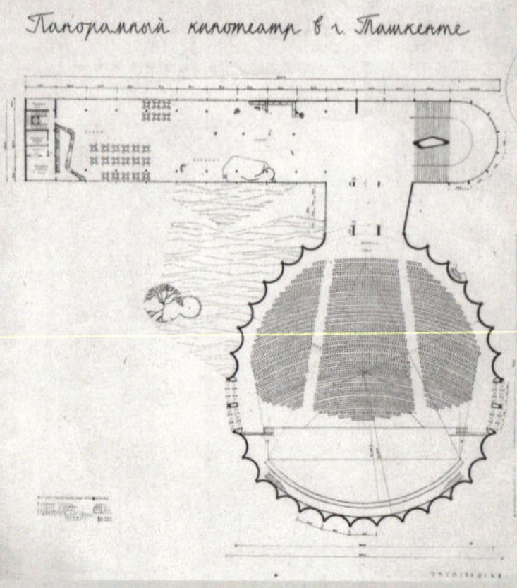

Left: Masterplan of the area around the Panoramic Cinema, proposal, Project A, 1960
Middle: Masterplan of the area around the Panoramic Cinema, proposal, Project B, 1960
Right: Plan of the Panoramic Cinema auditorium, proposal, Project B, 1960

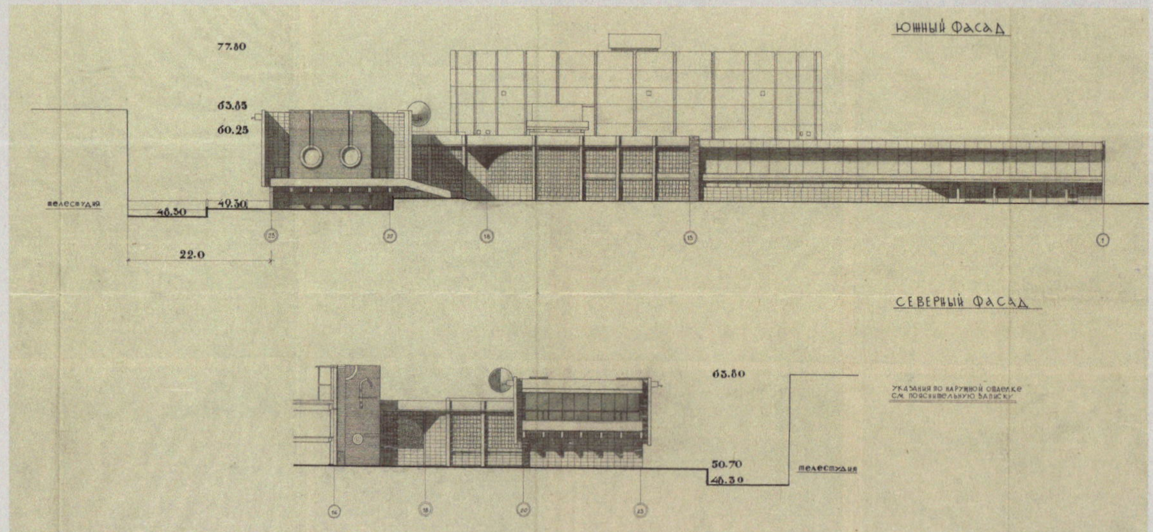

Reconstruction of the Panoramic Cinema, including the Small Hall, west and south façades, 1974

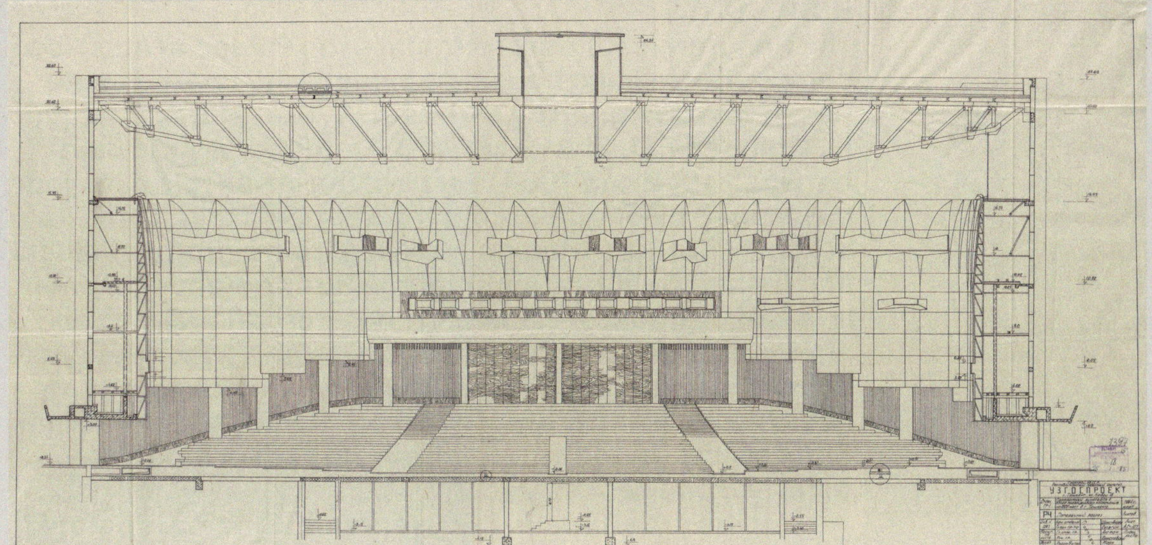

Panoramic Cinema, cross section of the Large Hall, 1964

Sketch of the Large Hall of the Panoramic Cinema, 1963

HIGHLIGHTS

The Panoramic Cinema (originally the Palace of Arts) is a composite building housing a cinema and related facilities. It was designed by architects V. Berezin, S. Sutiagin, Iu. Khaldeev, D. Shuvaev and O. Legostaeva, and built between 1962 and 1964. For both the urban role it played in the post-earthquake construction of Tashkent and its original and iconic design, deriving from cultural, political and technological requirements, the Panoramic Cinema is one of the most outstanding and internationally known modernist buildings in Tashkent and a perfect representation of the spirit of the Thaw. Given its overall integrity, it deserves to be entirely preserved. Some modernist features remain hidden under the most recent modifications and can be restored.

At the urban scale, the Panoramic Cinema is part of an urban modernist ensemble placed between Navoi Street and a pedestrian axis tracing the unrealized esplanade project of 1960s, together with the TV Center and the former House of Youth (now the Shodlik Hotel and Ilkhom Theater). The buildings are part of a vast public space, a buffer area that separates the large flows of crowds attending events at the Cinema and Pakhtakor Stadium, which is located behind the ensemble.

The architects pushed the Panoramic Cinema back from the main façade line of Navoi Street for two reasons. One was, as mentioned above, to give sufficient space for the crowd exiting film screenings. The second concerned the logic of urban composition along Navoi, whereby a system of small side squares along both sides of the street created a rhythm of compression and expansion of public space. The abundance of open space made the cinema visible from different angles, valorizing its iconic shape. Indeed, the architectural concept of the Panoramic Cinema relies on the elegant combination of a massive concrete cylinder, housing the main 2,300-seat auditorium and resembling the drum of a giant Doric column, and a transparent glass parallelepiped where the foyer and café originally were. In the 1970s Sergo Sutiagin designed an expansion of the cinema, adding a smaller hall for 550 viewers to the original foyer. This addition became a coherent and valuable part of the composition of the building.

Today, the concrete block retains its original solid appearance, while a large LED screen has replaced the ribbon windows on the north façade of the former foyer. The south façade has recently been renovated, with the original frames and glazing replaced.

Sergo Sutiagin's volume has been completely obscured by low sheds on the east side, obstructing the visibility of the complex.

The Panoramic Cinema exemplifies both a unique architectural concept shaped by progress in cinmatographic technology and a typical Soviet multifunctional building for representational events. Generated by the political and cultural agenda of the 1960s, such buildings combined social, representational and leisure functions in a single space.

As well as party congresses, for twenty years, starting in 1968, the cinema hosted the Tashkent International Film Festival of Asia and Africa, which was one of the most significant international cultural events in the region.

STATE OF REPAIR
SCORE:
EXTERIOR

- Overall: 3 – The building shows localized deterioration patterns which do not affect its stability
- Large Hall: 4 – The building is in perfect (or near perfect) condition
- Foyer: 4 – The building is in perfect (or near perfect) condition
- Small Hall (1977 Sutiagin extension): 3 – The building shows localized deterioration patterns which do not affect its stability

INTERIOR

- Overall: 3 – The building shows localized patterns of deterioration
- Large Hall: 3 – The building shows localized deterioration patterns
- Foyer: 4 – The building is in perfect (or near perfect) condition
- Small Hall (1977 Sutiagin extension): 4 – The building is in perfect (or near perfect) condition

Protection status:	The building is listed and protected according to Decision No. 846 of the Cabinet of Ministers, October 4, 2019.
Main criticalities:	Despite the large number of viewers the building can accommodate, there is no space for visitor amenities (café, food court, cloakroom, proper toilets, etc.). The new use of the former foyer has completely transformed the building, overriding its original and characteristic transparency.
Possible risks:	Further modifications by the operator.

INTEGRITY SCORE:

- Exterior: 2 – Transformations to the building and its surroundings have caused the loss of some of the elements necessary to express its significance
- Interior: 2 – Transformations to the building and its surroundings have caused the loss of some of the elements necessary to express its significance

Although the three main blocks composing the Panoramic Cinema are still in place, the integrity of the building has been seriously affected by renovations that took place over the years.

The renovations of the first decade of the twenty-first century and 2021–2022 have changed the functioning of the building, as well as the internal relationship between its components. The function of the former foyer was altered by creating screening and conference rooms enclosed by multiple opaque walls, obstructing the original transparency of this volume. Despite these significant changes, the Panoramic Cinema has retained its urban integrity and still represents an important hinge point within the area.

AUTHENTICITY SCORE:

EXTERIOR

- Overall: 2 – The building has been subjected to localized but significant modifications
- Large Hall: 4 – Only minor repairs and conservation activities have been carried out on the building
- Foyer: 2 – The building has been subjected to localized but significant modifications
- Small Hall (1977 Sutiagin addition): 2 – The building has been subjected to localized but significant modifications

INTERIOR

- Overall: 2 – The building has been subjected to localized but significant modifications
- Large Hall: 4 – Only minor repairs and conservation activities have been carried out on the building
- Foyer: 1 – The building has been subjected to major interventions which resulted in an overall transformation
- Small Hall (1977 Sutiagin extension): 1 – The building has been subjected to major interventions which resulted in an overall transformation

Due to the numerous renovations carried out in the building since its construction, the overall level of authenticity of the Panoramic Cinema is rather poor. This is particularly true of the former foyer, which has been heavily transformed and lost most of its characteristic features.

The original design concept of the Panoramic Cinema aimed to create a strong contrast between the massive and material block of the Large Hall and the light, transparent volume of the foyer. Interventions made in the first decade of the twenty-first century and in 2021–2022 to add more halls to the cinema complex erased this contrast, drastically reducing, if not completely overriding, the transparency of the foyer.

The interior of the Small Hall has also been largely transformed, whereas within the Large Hall changes have been minimal. The latter is thus the most authentic block within the Panoramic Cinema.

1964

2022

Connection between the foyer and the Large Hall, 1964

Connection between the foyer and the Large Hall, 2022
The glazing on the north façade of the foyer has been completely covered up.

View of the south façade of the foyer, 1964

View of the south façade of the foyer, 2022
The second floor has lost its transparency. Window frames and other finishings have been replaced.

Main staircase located at the west end of the foyer, 1964

Main staircase located at the west end of the foyer, 2022
The original sunshade elements have been replaced with plain windows.

1977

2022

View of the masonry back staircase at the connection between the foyer and the Large Hall, 1977

View of the masonry back staircase at the connection between the foyer and the Large Hall, 2022
The original sunshade elements on the west end of the foyer have been removed.

Cloakroom on the first floor of the foyer, 1977

First floor of the foyer, 2021
This floor has lost its transparency.

LEVEL 1 – MAXIMUM LEVEL OF INTEREST
(No transformations allowed; conservation activities required)

URBAN LEVEL

The Panoramic Cinema plays a relevant role within the urban context of Tashkent. Its design took into consideration the surrounding context, in particular Navoi Street and Pakhtakor Stadium. In order to avoid congestion due to simultaneous arrival and egress of visitors from the cinema and the adjacent stadium, a large public square was planned all around the building. In order to retain the composition of solids and voids and the spatial relationship between the building and its surroundings, the following requirements should be met:

- no new buildings or volumes are to be added within the block of the Panoramic Cinema;
- the volume, eave height and shape of the buildings within the block of the Panoramic Cinema should remain unaltered;
- the eave height of the buildings on Pakhtakorskaia Street should remain unaltered.

ARCHITECTURAL LEVEL

EXTERIOR

Despite numerous changes, the building has (mostly) retained its original proportions. The volume, height and shape of the building (including the 1977 addition) should thus be maintained as is.

The block containing the Large Hall should retain its massive and plain appearance. No openings are therefore to be added on the façade.

The block connecting the foyer to the Large Hall has mostly retained its original features and should be preserved as is, with reference to its transparency.

Due to use requirements the 1977 block is mostly enclosed by a solid façade. This feature should be retained, and no new windows or doors should be opened on the building's façades.

INTERIOR

The Large Hall should retain its spatial quality, avoiding the introduction of vertical and horizontal partitions.

Within the Large Hall, the suspended gallery facing the stage should remain unchanged as it is an important compositional element that adds dynamism to the space's geometry.

The spatial features of the main staircase leading to the second floor should be preserved.

The spatial features of the Small Hall should be preserved.

LEVEL 2 – MEDIUM LEVEL OF INTEREST

(Elements included in the second level can be moderately transformed, pending approval by a designated preservation committee[1])

URBAN LEVEL

Any changes regarding the layout of the public space surrounding the building should be submitted to and subject to approval by the designated committee.

Any changes concerning the façades of the buildings on Pakhtakorskaia Street should be submitted for preliminary approval.

ARCHITECTURAL LEVEL

INTERIOR

Any changes concerning the first floor of the Large Hall should be submitted for approval.

Any changes within the former foyer volume and the main staircase should be subject to approval by the designated committee.

Any changes within the 1977 block should be subject to approval by the designated committee.

DETAIL LEVEL

EXTERIOR

Any replacements or changes concerning finishes, doors and windows of the former foyer, the connection volume, and the main cylindrical volume should be submitted for approval.

INTERIOR

Changes to finishes, technical systems, lighting and seating could have a significant impact on the appearance and quality of the Large Hall. Such changes should therefore be subject to approval by the designated committee.

HIDDEN MODERNIST FEATURES

The original transparency of the façade of the foyer block can be restored by eliminating the newly added halls and decorations on the first- and second-floor levels. Similarly, the overall composition on the south side would benefit if the volumes recently added to the 1977 Sutiagin block were removed.

1 An international committee of heritage preservation experts to be appointed.

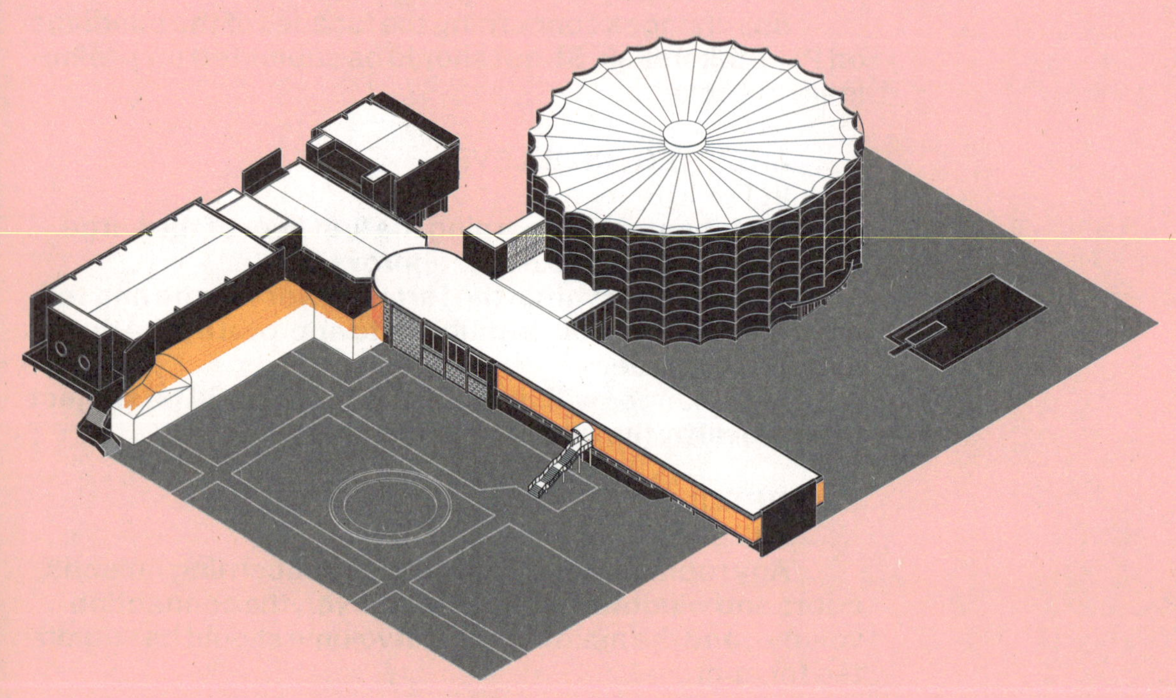

Preservation Level 1
Maximum Level of Interest
Materials and elements to be preserved

Preservation Level 2
Medium Level of Interest
Materials and elements to be preserved

Hidden Modernist Features
Materials and elements to be preserved

Transformation allowed

Preservation Strategy

The Panoramic Cinema is undoubtedly one of the most outstanding and internationally renowned modernist buildings in Tashkent. Inaugurated in 1964, the Palace of Arts, as it was named at the time, was well positioned in relation to the urban masterplan and perfectly embodied the "spirit of the age," combining technical and formal experimentation. The strength of the design lay in the contrast between the two blocks composing the volume: a massive concrete cylinder resembling a fragment of a Doric column and a light, transparent glass parallelepiped. In 1977, in order to provide an additional and smaller cinema hall, a third block was added to the composition. Although it used a different language, the addition blended in quite well.

Unfortunately, while the main auditorium appears well preserved and mostly unchanged, the transparent foyer has been significantly transformed due to new programmatic requirements. The need to add additional and smaller cinema halls led to the construction of partitions inside the foyer and the loss of its characteristic transparency. The glazing on the north façade has been covered up completely and the façade is currently opaque. The glazing on the south façade, although replaced, is still visible, but transparency is denied by a plasterboard wall located right behind it.

The main objective of the preservation strategy is to restore the original design of this iconic building, reducing the changes to a minimum. Because of the great architectural and cultural relevance of the building a decision was taken to treat it as a true monument, embracing a strict philological approach. Particular attention will be paid to the former foyer, where the lost transparency will be reinstated, bringing back the contrast that characterized the 1960s design concept and highlighting its modernist background.

To this end, four main preservation actions will be implemented.

The first action will focus on the former foyer and will aim to return its original transparency. This implies the demolition of the internal partitions on the first and second floors (and the subsequent relocation of the three existing halls), the removal of the panels covering the north façade and the all-round replacement of the glazing to make its appearance closer to the original in terms of glass and frame color and profile.

The second action will involve the demolition of the most recent additions, which are inconsistent with the original design and of poor architectural quality. In particular, the elements to be removed are: the external stairs located on the south side of the former foyer and the sheds that were built against the east façade of the Sutiagin building, concealing it.

A third action will entail maintenance activities, such as local repairs and cleaning of the façades, with particular reference to the main auditorium and to the 1977 Sergo Sutiagin building. These simple actions, especially if repeated over time, will guarantee longer conservation of those original features that have persisted until now.

Finally, it is advisable to verify whether the few original sunshades that remain are made of asbestos, as suggested by archival documents. If this is the case, the sunshades should be removed (taking the required precautions) and replaced with new ones that, while maintaining the original shape, are made of a different material.

Additional important actions concern the preservation of the main auditorium, which is in relatively good (and authentic) condition, but needs some localized maintenance and repair.

The technology of the building needs to be examined and eventually upgraded. This includes the mechanical, electrical and plumbing systems.

In order to implement the proposed preservation strategy a few aspects will need to be clarified and/or further developed. The very first step will be to acquire a full understanding of the national regulations concerning architectural heritage protection. Although the building has already been included in the national list of cultural heritage sites, its mandatory "passport" seems to be missing. Once the organization and contents of the passport are clarified, it will be possible to collect any further information needed.

It would be useful to conduct a series of surveys in order to better assess the state of repair of the building and obtain a chemical and physical characterization of the main building materials. This will enable an evaluation of the compatibility between the building materials and the materials to be used during conservation interventions. A general inspection of the roof and of the technical systems is also recommended, with particular reference to the main auditorium, which was never renovated.

According to historical documents, asbestos was used in the construction of the Panoramic Cinema and, in particular, in the sun lattice blocks. Although the latter were mostly removed in the 1970s, it is advisable to remove the remaining blocks and to check the whole building to identify any further presence of toxic materials.

Once all the information is obtained, it will be possible to develop a more detailed and comprehensive project, which could be tested on a limited portion of the building (pilot site). During the pilot phase different materials and techniques will be tried out with the aim of identifying the most suitable ones. At this point it will finally be possible to make the last adjustments to the project and to execute it.

Panoramic Cinema, night view, November 1964

Panoramic Cinema hall, night view
Strategy visualization

Adaptation Strategy

The goal of the adaptation strategy is to transform the Panoramic Cinema into a contemporary cultural and cinema venue, while preserving its original architecture and symbolic value. Currently, the building is underused, notwithstanding its potential to become an incredibly relevant and lively location in Tashkent.

Since the main function of the venue is film screenings, we recommend adding smaller halls in order to maximize the commercial viability of the complex. The smaller halls will allow an increase in the turnover of visitors, diversify the programming and cater to a wider audience.

Besides regular screenings, the Panoramic Cinema can function as a cultural space for movie premieres, international film festivals, thematic lectures, temporary exhibitions and special events, taking advantage of its spectacular main auditorium. We would also like to suggest the archive of Uzbekfilm (closed a number of years ago) be relocated to the Cinema and made accessible to the public.

In terms of spatial organization, we suggest allocating amenities for visitors (including ticketing, a café and a bookshop) and the exhibition space at the ground level of the main foyer, with the upper level combining an event space (potentially separated by a curtain) and a good-quality restaurant (that can be leased to an external operator).

In the "Sutiagin wing," additional small halls (70–100 seats) will be added at the first-floor level, replacing the outdated technical zones. On the upper level, the original Sutiagin hall will be preserved. This wing has an autonomous entrance facing Pakhtakor Stadium, which is convenient for separating visitor flows. We propose transforming the existing conference room into a space containing the Uzbekfilm archive.

As an option for a more significant expansion, building additional screening halls under the southern square has been taken into consideration, although a more compact version is preferred.

Now

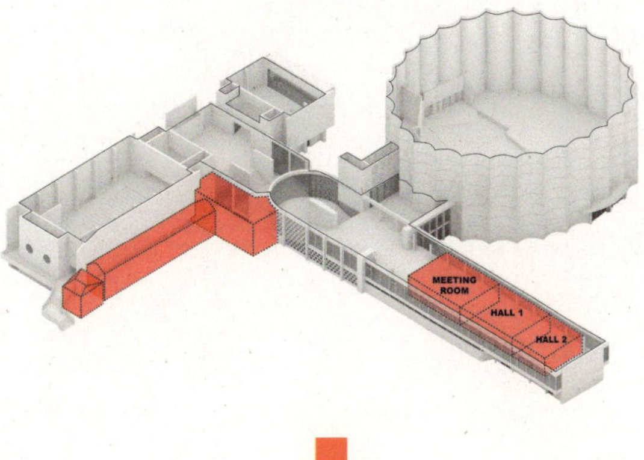

Potential

Option 1

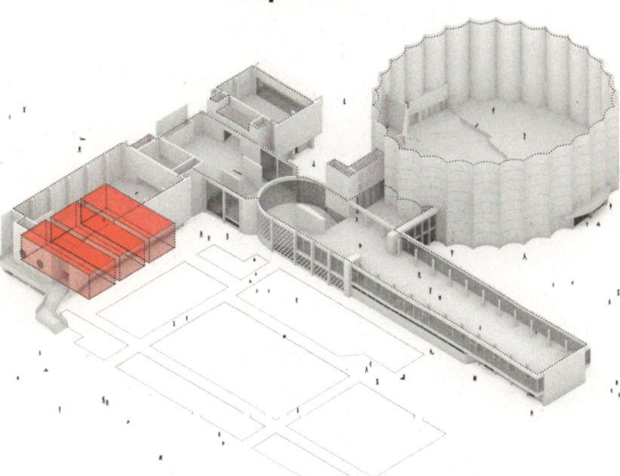

Option 2

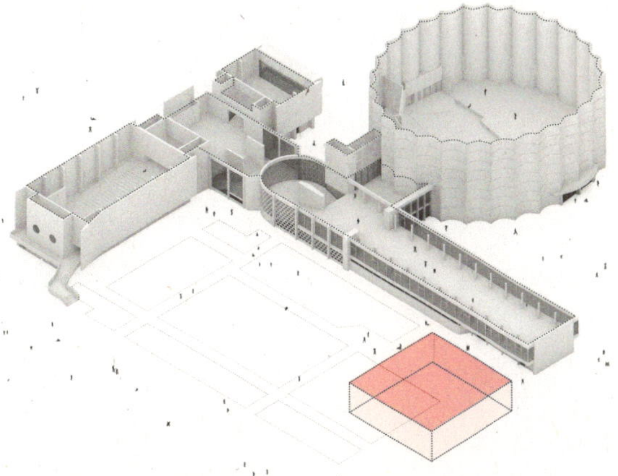

Cosmonauts Avenue Metro Station

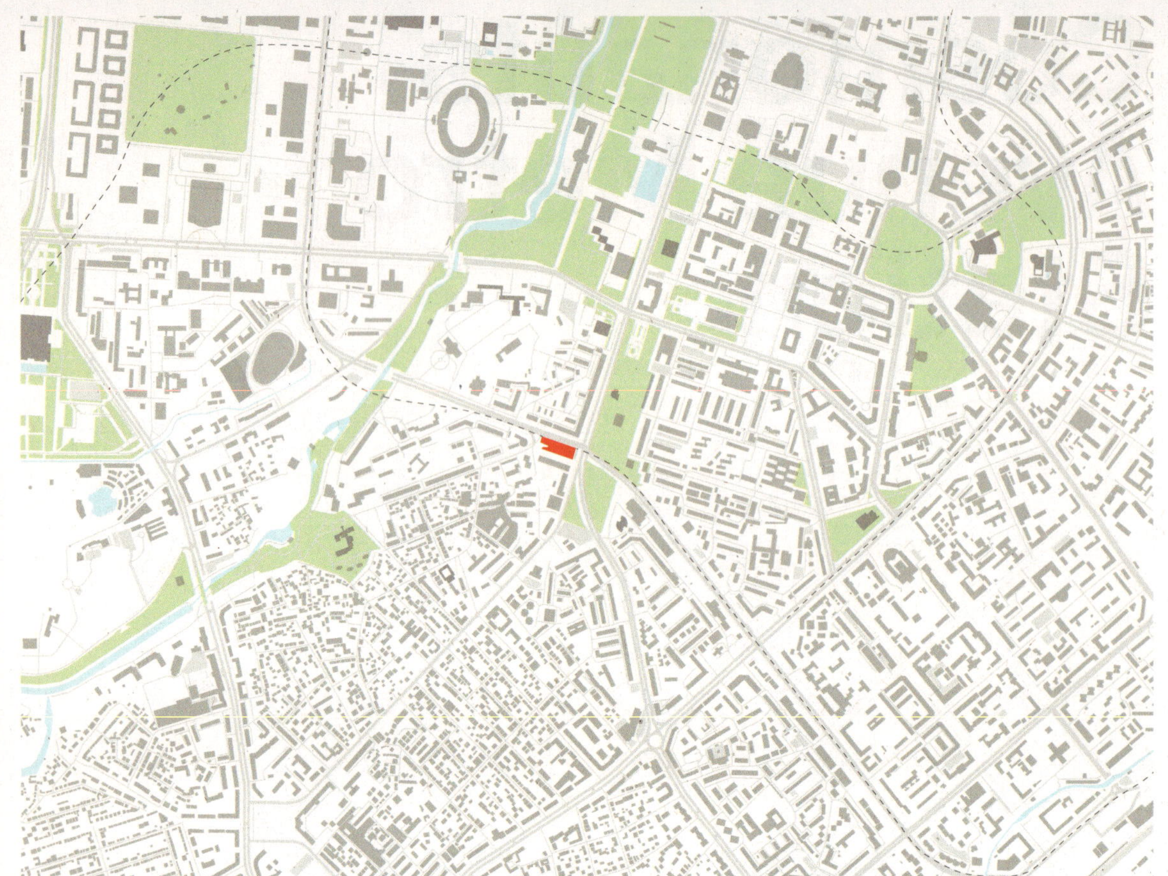

Building position and address: Afrosiyob Street, intersection with Sharaf Rashidov Avenue and Mirobod Street, Tashkent

0 0.5 1km

The station is situated in the historical district of the "Turkmen market," which appeared a little to the south of the site in the late nineteenth century on a square at the intersection of several roads. During the Thaw a residential cluster for the party and state elite began to form not far from here on German Lopatin Street, and this rapidly raised the status of the area. After Lenin Boulevard was constructed between the building at 40 Lenin Avenue (Sharaf Rashidov Avenue) and the Ministry of Internal Affairs in 1970, a square began to form, which was supplemented by the circular House of Shoes by architect Rafael' Khairutdinov. While the station was being designed, the square was transformed into Cosmonauts Square. It was the site of a bronze bust of the first Uzbek cosmonaut, Vladimir Dzhanibekov, behind which was a monument to the conquerors of space by architect Iurii Miroshnichenko and sculptor Iakov Shapiro. The square and station were designed together and conceived as a unified whole.

Cosmonauts Avenue metro station

ACTORS	**Architects:**	**Sergo Sutiagin, Sergei Sokolov, R. Niiazolieva, B. Bekbaev**
	Artists:	**Arnol'd Gan, Viktor Gan, Aleksandr Kedrin**
	Institute:	**Uzgosproekt/UzNIIPgradostroitel'stva**
DATES	**Design period:**	**1981–1982**
	Construction period:	**1982–1984**
	Inauguration date:	**December 8, 1984**
USE	**Current use:**	**Metro station**
	Original use:	**Metro station**
	Suitability of current use:	**The architectural layout of the station is perfectly suited for its use.**
	Space utilization:	**The building is fully used. No unused / underused spaces were detected.**

Cosmonauts Avenue Metro Station

The documentary material on which this research is based comes mainly from the personal archive of the lead architect of the metro station, Sergo Sutiagin, and also from the personal archive of architect Sergei Polozov, who worked in Sutiagin's studio. Unfortunately, the archive of UzNIIPgradostroitel'stva (O'zshaharsozlik LITI) has not retained any project materials. Nor are there many historical professional publications about the station. This lacuna is partly filled by the description of the station in the corpus of heritage buildings compiled for publication by the Tashkent Institute of Art History in the mid-1980s. Finally, the reminiscences of the project team are important, particularly those of Sergo Sutiagin, who gave a number of wide-ranging interviews about his work on the project.

Questions of Typology

The Soviet metro is a special theme, and anyone who comes into contact with it, whether they are a researcher or a passenger, realizes this. The main features that distinguished the Soviet metro from other subway systems were its ideological character and strategic military purpose. The metro was built not only for the quick and comfortable movement of people but also to demonstrate the "advantages of the socialist way of life" and to fulfill secret aims of so-called "civil defense." This led to a well-known paradox: all stations were conceived as "underground palaces," but it was forbidden to take photographs of them. Of course, the general stylistic trends of Soviet architecture influenced the development of the metro. The excessive baroque decorativeness of the Moscow Metro's Circle Line, which was built in the Stalin years, differed from the more severe modernist stations of Moscow, Leningrad and Kyiv that were constructed during the Thaw.

Tashkent bore witness to the reverse process, where baroque decorativism returned to modernist metro stations. Even in 1969 one of the organizers of construction wrote: "Our metro will be beautiful. The architecture of the stations will reflect the rich revolutionary and working traditions of the city; it will employ national motifs and the progressive traditions of Uzbek architecture. It will make extensive use of monumental propaganda. For example, the design of Sabir Rakhimov station will reflect the participation of the Uzbek people in the Great Patriotic War [World War II] and the design of Tinchlik station will show the desire of Soviet people for peace, joy and constructive labor. The design of Dustlik station will show the unbreakable friendship of the peoples of our country, their brotherhood and internationalism, the unselfish help of all of the peoples of the Soviet Union for Tashkent, which suffered during the earthquake."[1] This approach, which took shape in the late 1960s and early 1970s, was the main focus of subsequent design.

Tashkent architects did not consider the possibility of a utilitarian design solution for all metro lines, with a unified visuality. On the contrary, the design was to be based on a variety of architectural and monumental solutions. Due to the limitations of standardized production, only two types of station were possible—with columns or vaulted—so the architects had to develop creative ways of decorating either a vault or walls with columns and a ceiling. Tashkent's architects made a sober assessment of the limited and obligatory nature of such an approach. Architectural historian Shukur Askarov wrote: "The palace-like Moscow stations, the ethically unacceptable pop style of a recent Belgian station, the spectacularly naked rock formations of the Scandinavian metro, impossible in Central Asian underground systems, and the technologically unattainable effects of coarse concrete of the North American stations all sank into oblivion. In reality, there was a choice between single- and triple-nave stations with strictly defined parameters. The architect's work now depended on the treatment of predetermined surfaces. Just the material, its structure, texture and color. Miserly plasticity. That was it. You can call it a lack of opportunity to reveal the spatial conceptuality of the architectural intent, the reduction of the task to decoration. But this is reality."[2] It clearly follows from this statement that decorativism as an aesthetic solution for the Tashkent Metro was accepted by the architectural community of Tashkent due to the archaic nature of the construction industry.

However, there were internal gradations in decoration. Sergei Sokolov, one of the architects of Cosmonauts Avenue station, noted the dual connection between the design of the stations and their names. Some stations had formal decoration that was in no way connected with their names. Others featured plastic associations with the theme of the station. On the design solution for his own station, he wrote, "At Cosmonauts Avenue station in Tashkent there is a different approach: a tangible relationship to space exploration and the creation of associations with the infinite nature of the universe, space flight and the starry twinkle of galaxies in contrast to the sunny, earth-related design of

1 M. Korovin, "Tashkentskii metropolitan [The Tashkent Metro]," *Stroitel'stvo i arkhitektura Uzbekistana* [*Construction and Architecture of Uzbekistan*], no. 9, 1969, 4.

2 Shukur Askarov, "Krizis khudozhestvennogo [Crisis of the Artistic]," *Arkhitektura i stroitel'stvo Uzbekistana* [*Architecture and Construction of Uzbekistan*], no. 2, 1988, 12.

the vestibules."[3] In other words, the focus was the unbreakable link between the artistic design of the station and its theme, predetermined by the name. The virtues of this approach, which seemed logical and justified at the point when Sokolov wrote his text, turned out to be weaknesses after 1991, when many metro stations were renamed (during which process it became clear that it was easier for Hamza station,[4] with its formal geometric play of lights on the ceiling, to become Novza[5] than for Revolution Square,[6] with its communist-themed reliefs, to become Amir Temur Square[7]).

Cosmonauts Avenue station was part of the second line of the Tashkent metro, which opened on December 8, 1984. The exact date of the beginning of the design process is not clear, but based on the fact that in May 1982 the journal *Arkhitektura i stroitel'stvo Uzbekistana* (*Architecture and Construction of Uzbekistan*) published sketches that had already been selected for construction, it was probably in 1981. This year was connected to a specific event which prompted interest in the space theme in Tashkent. From March 22 to March 30 Vladimir Dzhanibekov, the first Uzbek cosmonaut, who was from Tashkent Region, made his second flight into space. According to established practice, after each space flight Soviet cosmonauts were awarded the title Hero of the Soviet Union, and for those who received this title twice a bronze bust was erected in the region where they were born. Accordingly, the Main Architecture and Planning Administration of Tashkent (GlavAPU) decided to establish Cosmonauts Square in the center of the city. The new high-speed artery near the square was named Cosmonauts Avenue, which determined the metro station's name.

3 Sergei Sokolov, "O problemakh proektirovaniia metropolitena [On the Problems of Designing the Metro]," *Arkhitektura i stroitel'stvo Uzbekistana* [*Architecture and Construction of Uzbekistan*], no. 2, 1988, 16.

4 Hamza station was named after cultural figure Hamza Hakimzade Niyazi (1889–1929), the founder of Uzbek Soviet drama, poetry, music and theater, who was murdered by Islamic fundamentalists for his attempts to emancipate the women of Uzbekistan.

5 Novza is the historical toponym of the place where the station is situated.

6 Revolution Square station was dedicated to the sixtieth anniversary of the October Revolution and contained several bas-reliefs about the establishment of Soviet power in Russia and Central Asia.

7 Amir Temur Square station is named after the medieval conqueror and founder of an extensive empire stretching from Damascus to India, with its capital at Samarkand (late fourteenth–early fifteenth century).

Competition Projects

The project was executed as part of a competition, which means that there was not a great deal of time to develop the initial concept, since architectural competitions usually ran for no longer than a few months. It took place in the second half of 1981 or in early 1982. The only accessible source that allows us to make a judgment on this competition is Sergo Sutiagin's testimony, which varies. It states that fifteen projects were considered (of which five were designed by the chief architect of the city, Sabir Adylov) and the choice was made by Sharaf Rashidov after all the versions were presented to him by Adylov. This episode testifies to serious changes in the behavior of Uzbekistan's leader. Having remained in the background during the 1960s competitions and paid close attention to the opinion of the professional community in the 1970s, toward the end of his life he set convention aside and considered it acceptable to substitute his own opinion in place of the collective discussions of juries. Nor is it clear whether a jury was actually formed or whether the competition was so informal that the decision was delegated to Rashidov from the beginning. In addition, today it is not known which version of the design was submitted by Sutiagin's team. Based on the architect's recollections, the detailed design of the project mainly took place on-site, and for this reason none of the preparatory sketches match the finished station.

Based on the technical conditions, Cosmonauts Avenue should have been a type of station with columns. Today we have images of five different sketches of the main space of the station, and a number of the vestibule. We have no information about how the sketch design process took place or who was the author of particular ideas, but the sequence of sketches demonstrates that they were linked. One can surmise that work flowed in the same way as in any large studio with a clear leader: first the master and his young colleagues made individual sketches, and then he continued working with those architects whose ideas he liked in order to condense the concept. We will look in detail at the extant versions.

Version 1 was a space with a fresco extending across the suspended vaulted plafond that united the space of three "naves." The architect made the following comments on his version:

- [...] This station should, in our view, become an original monument (hymn) to the historical stage of the exploration of space.
- "The poetry of the cosmos," "cosmic music," the human dream of flight, the launch of exploration and the infinite nature of space are the themes of the ceiling fresco which is the main element of the interior. The close-

ness of the points of perception allows for a reading of the second scale of the main, global theme that is perceived in its entirety as a colored, dynamic symphony of humans' associative idea of the cosmos.

- The polished metal of the frames of the supports, combined with the mirrored surface of the crystal light fittings, reinforces the musicality of the space and promotes an impression of the vertical movement of a multitude of specks of light (rays) and the dynamism of the space as a whole. The bench lamps supplement the interpretation of the image of space exploration.
- The second version of this project proposes concentrating the fresco in the central "gap" of the plafond. The illusion of "cosmic space" is strengthened by the backlighting of the upper part of the side walls of the tunnel along the entire platform. The suspended surface is made up of prefabricated panels of aluminum sheets painted matte white.[8]

Several elements from this sketch were included in the final project: attempts to widen the space using mirrored surfaces and specks of light on polished metal, a figurative fresco about the exploration of space, ornamental development of the floor using outlines of black squares on the central axis of the nave, and columns framed with metal tubular surfaces (such columns shift from this sketch to the vestibule of the finished station). The most problematic aspects of this sketch were the gigantic fresco that was five times larger than the Sistine Chapel ceiling[9] and the installation of lighting on the plafond. Situated between the columns, the light fittings blocked the view of the fresco and the light from them would have blinded those looking up. However, there was little choice. Second-level arches, as in the Sistine Chapel, were unsuitable for the metro and lamps fixed to the columns with light directed upward would have introduced a completely different and, likely, alien theme to the aesthetics of the station. It is no surprise that the authors rejected this version, the success of which was entirely dependent on the painter and the failure of which would have been the responsibility of the architects.

Version 2 combined two new elements not included in Version 1: the central nave was in an industrial style, made up of metallic elements of various outlines extending along the ceiling the length of the station, and the side naves were based on circles that served as lamps to direct the overhead artificial light. In describing this version, the authors wrote:

- The idea of dynamic continuousness, of infinity within the space, of speed and technical precision is expressed using simple, typically industrial means. The combination of several types of linear profile fittings with hidden lights will create the effect of a floating, rapid linear structure with complex relationships of light and shadow. The rhythm of the lit columns clad with slabs of cast, smoky glass, which "flow" freely into this suspended structure, will reinforce the theme of dynamic development.[10]

This sketch is also echoed in the final design. In particular, it articulated the idea of the illuminated thread on the ceiling of the central nave, which encouraged passengers to move into the depths of the station. Here the theme of circles also first appeared, which combined much more clearly with the theme of space stations than industrial channels and corners of various configurations, engendering an association with a row of portholes and giving the space a look of the *Solaris* film set.[11] This version also had problems. They included the disproportionate distribution of light. The main sources distributed light to where it was needed less, such as on the rails and on the roof of arriving trains, meaning that the central space was only illuminated with reflected light directed at the ceiling from the metal elements beneath it. The square columns combined successfully with the channels, but were a poor match for the interplanetary aesthetic, which required more sloping and rounded surfaces. Finally, the team's initial efforts to express the essence of the theme directly in the visual solution for the station were strained in this version. Its industrial aesthetic was more associated with other themes on this metro line, such as the aircraft factory, the railroad station or the Tashsel'mash agricultural machinery factory.

Version 3 developed the ceiling of the central nave as an endless sequence of constellations. The stars (spherical light fittings) were threaded onto a metallic construction that was stretched between two "wings" of the plafonds and was reminiscent of the overhead baggage compartment on an airplane (in a video interview with Ramiz Bakhtiiarov, architect Sergo Sutiagin admitted that he wanted "the ceiling to be like the aluminum structure of the inside of an

8 The sketch with text is located in the Sutiagin family archive.
9 Judging by the dimensions on the sketches, the length of the station exceeds 100 m and is around 25 m wide, meaning the space is 2,500 m^2. The Sistine Chapel ceiling is 500 m^2.
10 The sketch with text is located in the Sutiagin family archive.
11 In our correspondence, architect Sergei Romanov mentioned *Solaris* several times, underlining, however, that this was his own personal association and not a theme that the architects insisted on when working on the project.

airplane"[12]). Between the suspended plafonds a black space was revealed that was associated with infinity. In the explanatory note the authors wrote:

- Thanks to the boundless nature and depth of the theme of space exploration and taking into account the limited structural possibilities of its standard post and beam structural scheme, the visual solution for Cosmonauts Avenue metro station requires something completely unusual and integral, i.e. a large-scale, global approach rather than something addressed locally.
- In this project the theme is expressed using nonfigurative means. The interpretation of the suspended rod structure with crystal spherical light fittings is conventional; it is associated with part of the structure of the universe, the galaxy, the planetary system and also, perhaps, with the system of satellites that strike out into the "infinite space" thanks to its significant length, the repetition of elements and the effect of the longitudinal aperture above it. The "winged" form of the suspended ceiling and the effect of its isolation from the supports sharpen the illusion of movement of this illuminated structure of "the universe."[13]

This sketch was also reflected in the final version. It mostly concerned the space of the central nave, which was formed using suspended "wings" between which a row of illuminated "planets" extended. In the finished building they would be replaced by the "Milky Way," which was created using other means but had the same semantic meaning. The remaining elements of the station were designed rather schematically and could not easily be associated with the theme of space. In particular, the heavy square section columns were totally unrelated, and it is unsurprising that they were replaced in the final version. Meanwhile, the lighting was designed in optimal fashion: the nave and platforms were illuminated evenly and sufficiently.

Final Versions and Evolution during Construction

We do not know which version Sharaf Rashidov selected. However, the last sketch versions of the project that we are aware of,[14] which we will call Version 4, are similar to each other and to what was built on-site. Unfortunately, we do not have the architects' explanatory notes on this version. However, since it accumulated ideas explicitly recorded in the versions described above, it is not difficult to decode the semantic meanings invested in each element by the authors. The "wings" of the plafond left free space in the upper part of the central nave for the illuminated "Milky Way," a strip that extended along the entire station. The circular lamps, which in Version 2 were poorly positioned in the side naves and lit the rails, were inserted as cylindrical recesses in the "wings," successfully arranged around the columns. Initially, the section of these columns remained square,[15] which contradicted the cylindrical recess. This contradiction was removed when the columns were given cylindrical form. Thus, the problem of the distribution of light was solved: the focus of the lamps was now on the platforms and passenger passageways.

Simultaneously, the theme of portholes was reproduced on the side walls of the station. To ensure that no one could doubt the cosmic features of this image, the architects incorporated into the tondi figurative images reflecting the history of humankind's space journey, from early myths to the manned spaceflight of the twentieth century. At first the tondi were designed as convex portholes, which produced a telescopic effect. However, there were technical difficulties,[16] since the convex surfaces could have become dangerous as a result of the vibration of the carriages. The decision was made to use concave surfaces, and the "portholes" became more like the Uzbek liagan, or traditional plate. According to Sergo Sutiagin initially these were planned to be ceramic, as a logical continuation of the ceramic ceiling surface, but the production of ceramic figurative images required considerably more time due to the delicate nature of the technology and the artists suggested a compromise to the architect. The ceramic was replaced by frescoes, of which the main author was the artist Arnol'd Gan, who had worked with Sutiagin on a number of buildings. He was helped by his brother, Viktor. Sutiagin states that he personally suggested the twelve symbolic subjects for the frescoes.[17] They started with mythology. Icarus (portrayed with local, Central Asian features) was depicted on one of the tondi and on another was a symbolic image with the caption "Human-Reason-Universe." Next

12 Published on *uz.sputniknews.ru*, April 12, 2021, https://ok.ru/videoembed/2550897183470.
13 The sketch with text is located in the Sutiagin family archive.
14 One of them is preserved in the personal archive of Sergei Romanov and the other was published in Tashmetroproekt architects R. Faizullaev and Ia. Mansurov's article "Tashkentskii metropolitan im. V.I. Lenina [The Tashkent V.I. Lenin Metro]," *Arkhitektura i stroitel'stvo Uzbekistana* [*Architecture and Construction of Uzbekistan*], no. 5, 1982, 19.
15 See the sketch from the archive of Sergei Romanov.
16 The sketch and the information about it are drawn from Boris Chukhovich's correspondence with Sergei Romanov.
17 Video interview with Sergo Sutiagin by Ramiz Bakhtiiarov, 2020.

Proposal for Cosmonauts Avenue metro station, Version 1

Proposal for Cosmonauts Avenue metro station, Version 2

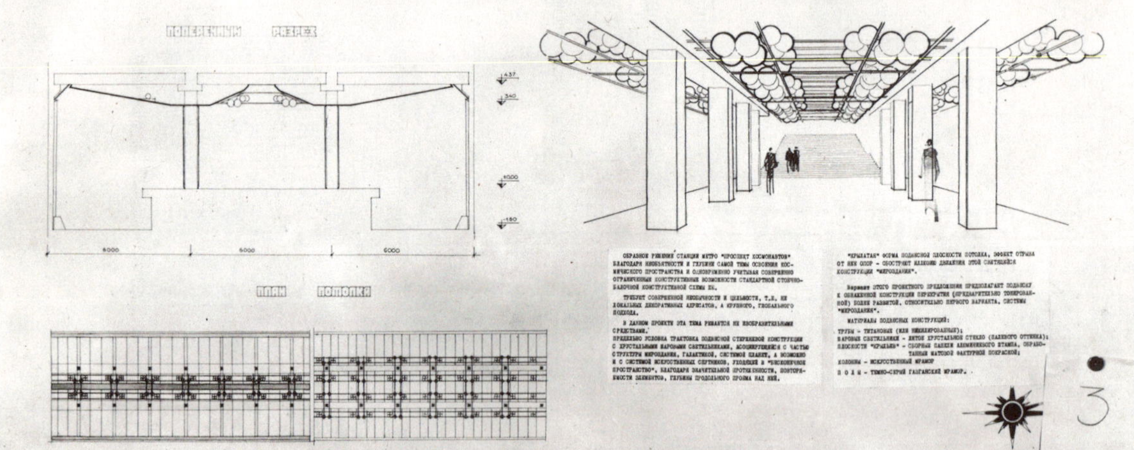

Proposal for Cosmonauts Avenue metro station, Version 3

Cosmonauts Avenue metro station, drawing, Version 4

came a prehistory of cosmonautics which began chronologically with ruler of Samarkand and astronomer Mirzo Ulugbek, followed by theorist of spaceflight Konstantin Tsiolkovskii and chief spacecraft engineer Sergei Korolëv. Next, predictably, came the first cosmonaut, Iurii Gagarin; the first woman in space, Valentina Tereshkova; the first person to conduct a space walk, Aleksei Leonov; and, finally, the person to whom the station was latently dedicated, Uzbekistan's first cosmonaut, Vladimir Dzhanibekov. The picture gallery ended with events rather than people. One tondo depicted the first lunar rover, the next the American-Soviet project Apollo-Soiuz and the third the Intercosmos program, which brought cosmonauts from socialist countries and later from others to the Soviet space stations Mir and Saliut. In discussion, Sergo Sutiagin stated that the choice was the result of lengthy study of the history of cosmonautics. However, the carefully politically balanced selection of names for the "cosmic pantheon" placed Soviet figures at the center and found a place for local history, but did not include the US moon program or the Space Shuttle, which was first launched in the year that design of the metro station began. This selectivity leads us to assume that the subjects of the frescoes must at the very least have been coordinated with the republican party leader, and some may even have been suggested by him.

The next and probably most original feature of the station is the mosaic cladding of the walls, made from specially produced elements with an individual profile. The horizontal rows of these elements comprise a colored strip that begins with white and ends with a dark shade of ultramarine. Thanks to an obvious (and often remarked upon by Sergo Sutiagin) association, this strip was intended to give the impression of the endless cosmos dissolving into darkness. From the point of view of composition, the circles incorporated in the horizontally textured surface were a feature of Sutiagin's creative work starting with the design of the second phase of the Panoramic Cinema (1974–1977) and referenced classic works of high modernism from Louis Kahn to Kenzō Tange. In order to produce the ceramic elements, artist Aleksandr Kedrin required an industrial ceramic press. A suitable press was found in a Tashkent factory and transported to the ceramic manufactory, where the industrial technology for molding, decorating and firing the elements, which were required in quantities unusually large for monumental decoration, was fine-tuned. An error was made during production. The circular elements that framed the perimeter of the tondo were made in reverse color gradient and did not match the background. However, this produced an unexpectedly aesthetic effect, and the random nature of this mistake resulted in a more lively and organic relief surface.

Other recollections by Sutiagin also confirm the concept of an illusory "widening of the space." The architects planned to place mirrors in the cylindrical recesses of the "wings" in order to give the impression that the columns stretched back endlessly. In reality, they could only achieve infinity by creating a mirrored floor, which would have been unsuitable for those wearing skirts and posed a slip hazard for passengers in a hurry. As a result, the mirrors were not installed, even at ceiling height. If damaged during an earthquake the glass could injure passengers, and in Tashkent of the early 1980s architects could only dream of metal surfaces with a high-quality mirror finish. For the same reason it was not possible to install a mirrored surface in the vestibule above the staircase down to the platforms: the architects replaced the mirror wall designed as a background for Aleksandr Kedrin's circular ceramic composition with travertine.

Another trick used to amplify the space involved increasing the standard height of the station by 60 cm, which offered the opportunity to make the "Milky Way" more three-dimensional and convincing. This visual expansion was also achieved by narrowing the load-bearing columns, which was possible thanks to engineer Aleksandr Braslavskii's calculations. Made from sparkling, dark glass, they almost lost their materiality, and the mass hanging above appeared to float and be weightless. The pressed aluminum used to create the "wings" of the plafond did not produce an ideally even form, as it was an extremely soft material. However, the architects found a way to transform this shortcoming into a virtue, spraying the surfaces with a solution that produced a small-scale, organic texture, the dispersed nature of which expanded the space.

A Thaw Theme at a Time of Crisis

There were, however, other visual features of the project which were not expressed and may not even have been acknowledged by the authors. The use of the cosmic theme occurred for an unusual reason: in fact, the idea was not to anticipate the future but to memorialize the past. Accordingly, regardless of the declared bombastic aims, which were similar to the discourses of the Soviet boomers of the 1960s ("humankind's striving for perfection," "the human dream of flight," "cosmic music"), the station was significantly different from the Soviet constructions of the dynamic epoch of the 1960s, when space was a synonym for a leap toward the future, technological progress, the subjugation of nature, the appearance of the "new man," and building "a new type of society." Cosmonauts

Avenue metro station is completely free of the buoyant utopianism of the Thaw. Its metaphysical cosmos is melancholy and full of reminiscences. It is directed not to the future but to the past, and the museified narrative of cosmonautics "from Icarus to today," as in any pantheon, forces the past to dominate the present and make the future less significant against a background of the founding acts of the history of space conquest. The use of building materials is demonstrative of this. In the sketches described above there was an obvious preference for contemporary materials: stainless steel, special light fittings, molded aluminum, etc. In the finished building these were replaced by organic materials: mainly numerous types of carefully selected marble and granite and also the warm travertine of the vestibule. The most striking element of the building, the wall structured as an illuminated "cosmic" strip, has its own material metaphysics that is connected to the past. In Uzbekistan dark blue and ultramarine glazed ceramic is inevitably associated with the local architectural tradition and Persian-language poetry, in which images of clay and ceramic wares are symbols of the frailty of earthly existence. At the dawn of the Swinging Sixties, Sergo Sutiagin was a member of the design team for the futuristic concrete and glass Panoramic Cinema, one of the less noticeable pylons of which was clad in brick and called the "wall of memory." In the early 1980s meditative melancholy became dominant.

Detail of ceramic cladding covering the walls, medallion of A.A.Leonov's space walk, 2021

When contemporaries criticized the finished station for "grimness" they likely did not realize that this was not an omission or shortcoming but an internal intention, whether conscious or not. Gul'sara Babadzhanova defined it as an error by the architects: "[...] the individual shortcomings [of the station] are disappointing. In particular, and almost all passengers notice this, insufficient lighting creates a sense of the ceiling pressing down, which is intensified by the ceramic wall because of the positioning of light tones below and dark ones above."[18] However, forty years later we can state without bias that the architects' design more accurately reflected the changing values of Soviet society than their explanatory notes.

When speaking about possible contradictions between declared and hidden connotations of the station, we can use as an example the authors' perception of the vestibule. Sergei Sokolov traced a clear contrasting line between the cold, "celestial shining of galaxies" on the lower level of the station and the "sunny, earthly solution of the vestibules." Meanwhile, it was the vestibule that opened up the theme of museification and memoriality. Here, the names of every Soviet cosmonaut who had traveled to space by the time the station was opened were arranged on an eloquent black stone ledge on the end wall. The warm travertine and illuminated ceiling made the space light, but this physical illumination did not remove the symbolic meanings linked to the archival repository of heroes living and dead. The memorial list was the first thing people saw when entering the metro and the last thing when leaving.

Another virtually unnoticed feature of the station is the original, rhythmic marking of the wall surfaces which frames the descent from street level to the underground corridor that leads to the station entrance. It is created using a combination of dark and light vertical stripes. The surface begins with an extended rectangle in a dark tone which is interrupted by an increasingly rapid rhythm of light verticals that are initially slim and gradually widen. According to two sources,[19] Sergei Sokolov conceived this marking using proportions based on the Fibonacci sequence. Despite the careful conception and execution of this detail, the authors never explained the motifs behind it. It may make sense to seek a link with the expression of the principles of geometric proportionality, which was more common in the architectural theory of the

18 Gul'sara Babadzhanova, "Khudozhnik i metro [The Artist and the Metro]," *Arkhitektura i stroitel'stvo Uzbekistana* [*Architecture and Construction of Uzbekistan*], no. 6, 1985, 18.

19 Evsei Slonim, who taught at the architectural faculty of Tashkent Polytechnic Institute, told me about this in the early 1980s, and Sergei Romanov confirmed it in 2022.

Central Asian region. Regardless, this degree of attention to abstract details that were outside the passenger's field of vision adds complexity and intellectual content to the architectural concept of the station.

Occasional critical voices notwithstanding, from the moment it opened the station was an "architectural hit" in the city and was highly rated by specialists. Their collective opinion was clearly expressed in sociological research published by the journal *Arkhitektura i stroitel'stvo Uzbekistana* (*Architecture and Construction of Uzbekistan*) in 1988. The expert respondents were lecturers and students from the architectural faculty of Tashkent Polytechnic Institute plus historians, archeologists and journalists. Cosmonauts Avenue station was way ahead of other competitors, receiving the most votes as "Excellent" and with no one awarding it the lowest rating, "Poor" (it was the only station that completely avoided this rating).[20] When foreign architects began visiting Tashkent after Uzbekistan's independence, the station often featured in professional publications, which stressed its strict modernist look in relation to the eclectic overall background.

20 Gennadii Korobovtsev, "Arkhitektura Tashkentskogo metropolitena: obratnaia sviaz' [The Architecture of the Tashkent Metro: Feedback]," *Arkhitektura i stroitel'stvo Uzbekistana* [*Architecture and Construction of Uzbekistan*], no. 2, 1988, 7.

ARCHITECT SERGO SUTIAGIN

Place and year of birth:
Moscow, 1937 (evacuated to Uzbekistan in 1941)

Place and year of death:
Tashkent, 2021

Education:
1955–1960, Architecture Department of Central Asia Polytechnic Institute (SazPI)

Worked at Uzgosproekt from 1960 and in 1961 became part of the creative team (V. Berezin, Iu. Khaldeev, D. Shuvaev) that won the competition for the Panoramic Cinema. The team submitted three versions for the competition and the one with the circular auditorium was selected. In a 2015 interview Sutiagin admitted that he did not like this version. The team leaders, as Sutiagin noted in another interview, were V. Berezin and Iu. Khaldeev, who were more experienced. However, from 1962, after they were reassigned to other buildings, Sutiagin led the construction documentation and construction phases of the Panoramic Cinema. At completion of construction he was twenty-seven years old and already had very good experience of working on a unique building.

Sergo Sutiagin was better integrated than other architects of his generation into the creative and administrative elite of Uzbekistan. Moscow institutions also preferred to deal with him as a representative of Uzbekistan during trips, conferences and other events organized by the Union of Architects of the USSR, Gosstroi and others. Accordingly, his creative circle was broad, and the group of architects from Uzgosproekt/UzNIIPgradostroitel'stva and representatives of union republics met regularly in Moscow. Among Moscow architects he was friends with Feliks Novikov, Iurii Platonov and Vladilen Krasil'nikov, and his closest friends from the union republics were Dzhim Torosian from Yerevan and Abdula Akhmedov from Ashkhabad, two architects who had quickly rejected an average International Style in favor of exploring the metaphysical connection between their buildings and the local context. Sutiagin also developed in this direction, as can be seen in his projects for the Brutalist and symbolically loaded Samarkand Teahouse (1968–1976), the cinema and concert hall in Dushanbe (1965–1985), the Navoi Library in Tashkent (design 1970–1978, two versions) and other buildings.

From the mid-1970s to the early 2000s he moved away from minimalist concrete Brutalism, preferring the play of the plastic qualities of brick and natural stone (Small Hall of the Panoramic Cinema, the theater and the literary museum in Kokand, the museum in Nukus), ceramics, metal, glass and other materials (Cosmonauts Avenue metro station).

CREATIVE ORIENTATIONS

"The main thing is the milieu, the environment, the need for mutual subordination."

"But there is always architectural constructiveness in a sculptural approach (even to a functional space), almost always experimentation focused on development (of tradition, structure, the construction industry and so on)."

"I consider it important that the author has passion and confidence, professionalism and a particularly sensitive understanding of the land on which they are building and the people for whom they are building."

"Since my first major work—the Palace of Arts complex in Tashkent, which we began in 1960 and which can be traced in all of the following works—we learned from our predecessors how to master the possibilities of the construction materials and structures of the time, inventiveness and innovation (especially in the interpretation of traditions), a feeling for the environment, form and color. And the main thing was to incorporate organically, to uniquely supplement and develop the space, creating for it a new quality, independent of whether an existing building was being completed or something was being created anew."

From these postulates, formed by the architect himself (Sergo Sutiagin, *Arkhitektura SSSR* [*Architecture of the USSR*], no. 12, 1983), we can extract the principles he adhered to:

- rejection of historical citations but use of historical Central Asian experience in terms of work with space and integrating a new building into the existing context;
- a particular "sculptural" plasticity of architecture while using minimalist forms;
- an effort to structure the functions of buildings clearly with the framework of a "sculptural" approach to the organization of space.

INFLUENCES

GENERAL
International Style, Brutalism

PERSONAL
The projects and buildings of Abdula Akhmedov and Dzhim Torosian (possibly also Rafael Israelian)

INSTITUTIONAL FRAMEWORK

Uzgosproekt / UzNIIPgradostroitel'stva

CADRE
The history of Uzgosproekt since the early 1960s was defined by the arrival of Vladimir Berezin, Sergo Sutiagin, Richard Bleze and Dmitrii Shuvaev, who quickly became the heads of the design studios. Having learned to cooperate in designing the major projects of the first half of the 1960s—building of the Central Committee of the Communist Party of Uzbekistan and the Panoramic Cinema—they had compatible views on architecture and formed architectural groups that shared their values.

PRIORITIES
Use of techniques and vocabulary of modern architecture, rejection of historicism and formal quotations, evolution from simple and transparent volumes in the 1960s to more complex Brutalist forms in the 1970s and 1980s, functionalism of the plan which determined the volume solution. Representative buildings: Central Committee of Communist Party of Uzbekistan, Panoramic Cinema, House of Publishers, Navoi Library (not built), Computing Center (not completed), State Planning Committee, Music and Drama Theater and Literature Museum in Kokand, Cosmonauts Avenue metro station, theaters in Nukus, Karshi and Urgench, Namangan and Bukhara Party Committees.

Construction of the Tashkent metro, 1977

Decorative medallion of Icarus

Sergo Sutiagin and Sergei Sokolov on the platform of Cosmonauts Avenue metro station, 1984

Decorative medallion of Sergei Korolëv

Entrance hall of Cosmonauts Avenue metro station

Entrance hall of Cosmonauts Avenue metro station, 2019

Stairs leading to the platforms, 2022

Interior of the station, 2021

Detail of ceramic cladding covering the walls, medallion of Aleksei Leonov's space walk, 2021

Column detail, 2022

Detail of the lighting and glass decorations running the entire length of the ceiling, 2022

Detail of ceramic cladding covering the walls, medallion of Apollo-Soiuz, 2021

Platform of Cosmonauts Avenue metro station, medallion of Valentina Tereshkova, the world's first female cosmonaut, 2021

Cosmonauts Avenue metro station, entrance hall 1

Cosmonauts Avenue metro station, entrance hall 2

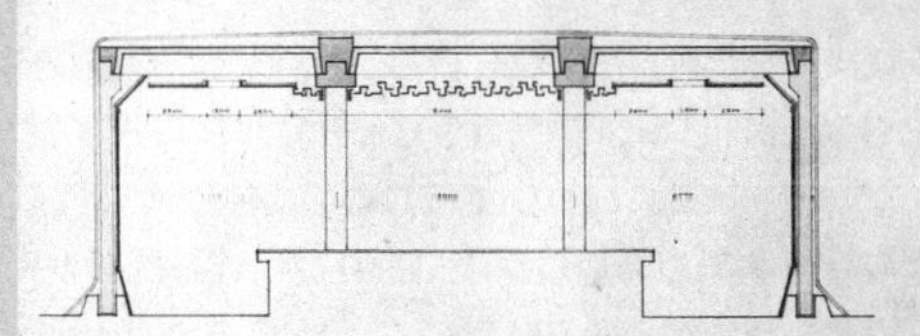

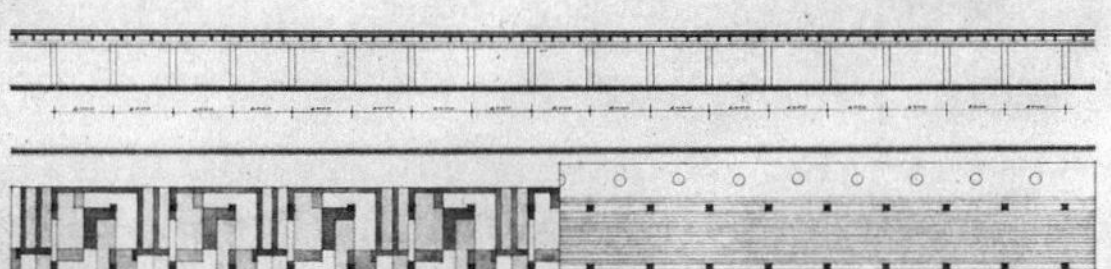

Cosmonauts Avenue metro station, design proposal, Version 2

Cosmonauts Avenue metro station, perspective drawing

HIGHLIGHTS

Tashkent's metro, built in 1972 and operating since 1977, was the first in Central Asia. Cosmonauts Avenue (now Kosmonavtlar) is a metro station designed by Sergo Sutiagin and Sergei Sokolov, with the participation of R. Niiazolieva and B. Bekbaev. It was inaugurated in 1984 as a part of the O'zbekiston metro line.

The station is well connected to many points of interest in the "new city," being at the intersection of three primary urban axes: Sharaf Rashidov Avenue, Mirobod Street and Afrosiyob Street.

At the urban scale, Tashkent's subway represented a very important step in the modernization of the city. The metro was seen as more than a transportation system. It had not only strategic defensive but also ideological functions, testifying to the country's history and identity by means of the architecture of the stations. Each station was designed with a specific celebratory theme, often revealed by its name. This is the case with Cosmonauts Avenue station, which commemorated the Soviet heroes of the time, the cosmonauts.

A team of architects supervised by Sergo Sutiagin designed the station, pursuing a high level of architectural and spatial quality and fine finishes that included numerous works of monumental art. While the turnstile hall has a commemorative function, the platform level addresses the cosmos and its exploration by humankind. The walls along the entire length of the platform are covered with ceramic tiles that gradually shift from light blue (below) to dark blue (above), reminiscent of the Earth's atmosphere. These walls are marked by regularly placed frescoed tondi created by Arnol'd and Viktor Gan, which trace the history of human flight and space conquest from Icarus to Gagarin and to the Uzbek astronaut Vladimir Dzhanibekov. The glass clad columns supporting the ceiling terminate with a backlit opening instead of a traditional capital and, together with the glass "Milky Way" on the ceiling, further augment the effect of spatial expansion. The station lobbies are extensively decorated with glass, metal, granite and marble.

Cosmonauts Avenue station is the most iconic modernist metro station in Tashkent. Considering the high level of integrity and authenticity, it deserves to be carefully preserved.

STATE OF REPAIR
SCORE:

4 – The building is in perfect (or near perfect) condition

Protection status: The building is listed according to the Resolution of the Cabinet of Ministers of the Republic of Uzbekistan no. 227 dated April 22, 2024, "On introducing amendments and additions to the National Register of Intangible Property of Tangible Cultural Heritage."

Main criticalities: Neon tubes have been added to the original lighting. Although not evident, this solution is not well integrated into the design and, in general, is not particularly suitable.

INTEGRITY
SCORE:

Interior: 4 – The building has retained all the elements necessary to express its significance and is in a good state of repair

Cosmonauts Avenue metro station fully retains its integrity. Indeed, while no relevant changes have occurred since the inauguration of the station, its good state of repair suggests that upkeep has been constant.

Therefore, today the station is for the most part as the architects Sutiagin and Sokolov designed and constructed it.

AUTHENTICITY
SCORE:

Interior: 4 – Only minor repairs and conservation activities have been carried out on the building

No major interventions have been carried out at Cosmonauts Avenue metro station since its construction. The level of authenticity is therefore very good.

The station has not faced substantial transformations since its construction. The current layout and appearance of the station are thus authentic and coherent with the original design concept.

A slight modification in the lighting system occurred to improve the original design's lights. Neon tubes were installed on the ceiling of the platform tunnel to illuminate the station more satisfactorily. Such an intervention is not particularly invasive and is indisputably reversible. However, it does not integrate well with the overall concept of the station and therefore a more suitable solution should be designed.

Platform, Cosmonauts Avenue metro station, 1984

Entrance hall with turnstiles, 1984

2024

Platform, Cosmonauts Avenue metro station, 2021

Entrance hall with turnstiles, 2024

LEVEL 1 – MAXIMUM LEVEL OF INTEREST
(No transformations allowed; conservation activities required)

ARCHITECTURAL LEVEL

EXTERIOR

The Cosmonaut monument located on the street level at the entrance of the station was designed and built as a whole with the subway station. The monument introduces subway passengers to the theme of the cosmonauts and should be maintained.

INTERIOR

The platform area should retain its spatial organization and continuity. No partitions are to be added and the width, height and length of the tunnel should remain unaltered.

The hall where the turnstiles are located is also interesting and shows good architectural quality. This space should also remain as is, avoiding the addition of partitions and maintaining the current dimensions.

DETAIL LEVEL

Within the platform tunnel all the finishes and artworks should be carefully preserved. Namely:

- the blue ceramic cladding on the vertical walls;
- the shimmering glass on the columns;
- the gray granite and black Ukrainian labradorite pavement;
- the glass pendants of the skylight, simulating the Milky Way;
- the medallions (tondi).

The round cuts in the ceiling above the columns should be kept as they are.

Within the turnstiles hall the following items should be retained:

- the marble cladding (of pavement and walls);
- the columns featuring mirrors on the four faces and metallic profiles on the corners;
- the decorated metal foil of the false ceiling;
- the commemorative engraved plaque.

Any artworks located within the subway station should be retained.

LEVEL 2 – MEDIUM LEVEL OF INTEREST
(Elements included in the second level can be moderately transformed following approval by a designated committee[1])

ARCHITECTURAL LEVEL
EXTERIOR

Any changes to the Cosmonauts monument should be submitted to the designated committee for approval.

1 An international committee of heritage preservation experts to be appointed.

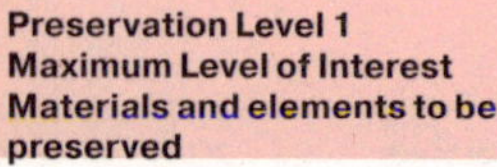

Preservation Level 1
Maximum Level of Interest
Materials and elements to be preserved

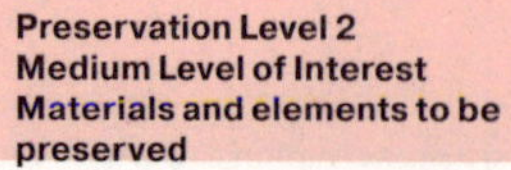

Preservation Level 2
Medium Level of Interest
Materials and elements to be preserved

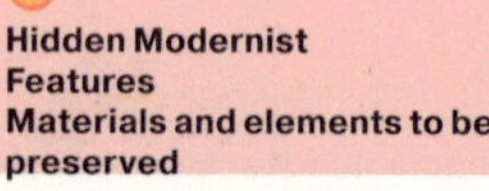

Hidden Modernist Features
Materials and elements to be preserved

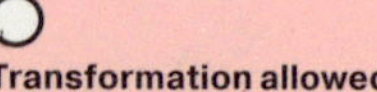

Transformation allowed

Preservation Strategy

Cosmonauts Avenue metro station, inaugurated in 1984, is one of the most iconic modernist metro stations in Tashkent. It is part of Tashkent's first metro line, O'zbekiston, which opened to the public in 1972. The metro was designed by the architects Sergo Sutiagin, Sergei Sokolov, R. Niiazolieva and B. Bekbaev, with the artists Arnol'd Gan, Viktor Gan and Aleksandr Kedrin, who participated in the concept phase. In addition to fulfilling transportation and defensive functions, the station celebrated Soviet achievements in space.

Since the station has not undergone any substantial transformations since its opening, its state of integrity is very high (maximum). The state of conservation of the building is also very high due to constant maintenance. Accordingly, the main objective of the preservation strategy is to guarantee the conservation of this outstanding structure while keeping changes to a minimum.

The preservation strategy aims at conserving the building through a maintenance plan because of its great historical and artistic relevance. To this end, three main preservation actions will be implemented.

The first action concerns the general maintenance of the building, which implies cleaning operations and local repairs for the most relevant parts of the platform tunnel: the blue ceramic cladding on the vertical walls, the shimmering glass covering the columns, the gray granite and black Ukrainian labradorite pavement, the glass pendants of the skylight and the ceramic medallions. In the turnstile hall this includes the marble cladding of the floor and walls, the columns featuring mirrors on all four faces and metallic profiles on the corners, and the decorated metal foil of the false ceiling.

The second action concerns lighting. The original lighting, designed by the architects, created a more subdued and mysterious atmosphere. The lighting was contained in the circular niches around the columns and in the central strip. A few years after the opening, additional light fittings were added between the columns, significantly altering the perception of space. This was done because the station appeared insufficiently lit. Given the advanced possibilities of contemporary light fittings (in terms of safety, duration, ability to direct diffused light), we believe it is possible to return to the original lighting strategy, while improving its performance (i.e. the amount of light).

The third action concerns the maintenance of the technical systems.

Peoples' Friendship Palace

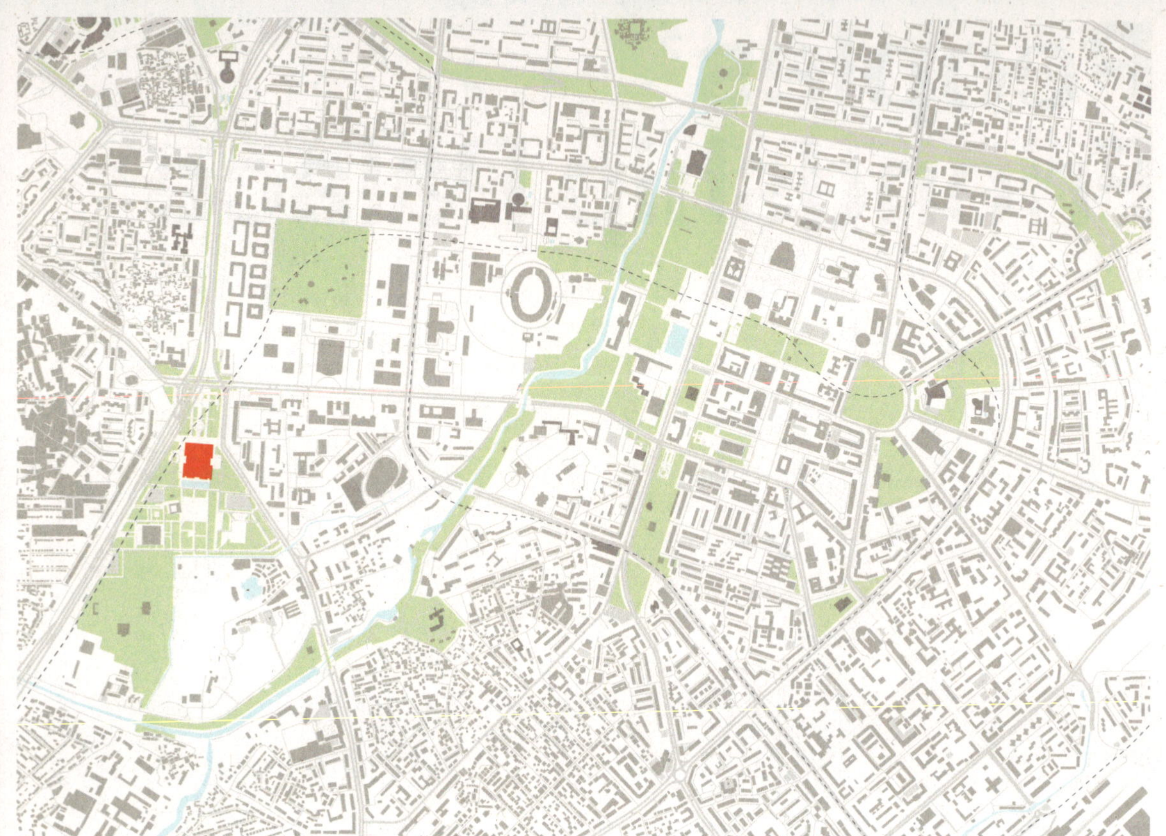
Building position and address: 3 Furkat Street, Tashkent

0 0.5 1km

Historically the place where the Peoples' Friendship Palace was built was in the former "old city" in the Beshagach Dakha district. The intensive integration of European architectural forms into this district began in the 1930s, when the largest park in the city (Lenin Komsomol Park), with Komsomol Lake at its center, was laid out in an area to the south of the future site of the Palace. In the early 1950s Beshagach Square (architect: Mitkhat Bulatov) was built by the central entrance to the park. In the early 1960s a huge residential area, Chilanzar, began to be constructed on the western outskirts of Tashkent. Peoples' Friendship Avenue was designed as the main transport artery linking Chilanzar with the city center. Simultaneously, a project for the detailed planning of the center of Tashkent was approved (1964–1965), according to which the southern boundary of the city center nucleus was Uzbekistanskaia Street (Islam Karimov Street). This is how a large square came about in the south-east of the city, which became Peoples' Friendship Square. From the north side a complex of administrative buildings was formed, including in particular the Institute of the History of the Communist Party and the Party Archive, and on the north-east corner was the entrance pavilion to the Peoples' Friendship metro station. From the direction of the microdistrict of Almazar and the opposite side of Peoples' Friendship Avenue, standard nine-story buildings adapted for the square were constructed, with balconies decorated with sun-protection elements in the form of triangular arches. These extended buildings formed a backdrop against which the large structures—the Peoples' Friendship Palace and the high-rise hotel located in the western part of the square, at the end of Uzbekistanskaia Street—would look good.

The square in front of the Palace was equipped with grand stairs rising up the relief, granite and marble slabs, and small areas of grass. This urban planning solution was subject to criticism in the second half of the 1980s, as during the summer the square over-heated to critical temperatures, which made crossing it a real struggle. In 1982 a sculptural group was erected at the center of the square in honor of the Shamakhmudov family, who adopted fifteen children who were evacuated to Tashkent without their parents during World War II. In 2008 the monument was dismantled and moved to the outskirts of Tashkent, and Peoples' Friendship Square and the Palace were renamed Istiklol (Independence); however, ten years later the original names were reinstated and the sculpture was reinstalled.

Main dimensions of the Peoples' Friendship Palace
General axonometric view

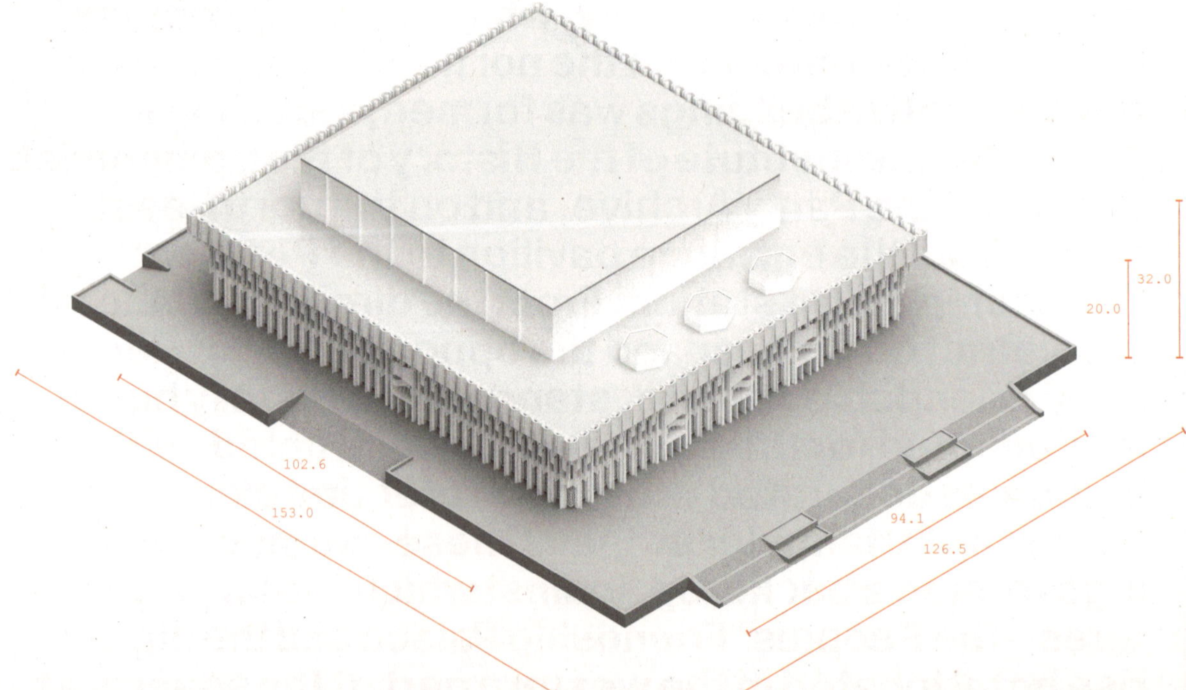

ACTORS	**Architects:**	**Evgenii Rozanov, Vladislav Shestopalov, E. Shumov, Elena Sukhanova, L. Berezovskaia**
	Engineers:	**V. Krichevskii, I. Lentochnikov, N. Korobova**
	Artists:	**Aleksandr Kedrin, Bakhodyr Jalalov, A. Il'khomov, Kh. Jalilov, D. Faizullaev, Kadyrjan Khaidarov, Rufa Nemirovskii, Vladimir Burmakin, Abdumalik Bukharbaev**
	Institute:	**Central Scientific Research and Experimental Project Institute for Entertainment and Sport Facilities (TsNIIEP)**
DATES	**Design period:**	**1971–?**
	Construction period:	**Second half of 1970s–1981**
	Inauguration date:	**1981**
	Later interventions:	**2018: Renovation intervention focusing on Bunyodkor Square and the Palace façades. 2021–2022: Minor interior upgrade.**
USE	**Current use:**	**Concert hall**
	Original use:	**Concert hall, party meetings and congresses**
	Suitability of current use:	**The Peoples' Friendship Palace is well suited for its current use. A few aspects could be improved, with particular reference to the foyer signage, auditorium lighting and upholstery.**
	Space utilization:	**The building is fully used. No unused / underused spaces were detected.**
DIMENSIONS	**Number of floors:**	**2 basement floors + 5 floors + 2 technical mezzanines**
	Length:	**102.6 m**
	Width:	**94.1 m**
	Height:	**20.0 m**
	Gross floor area (first floor):	**8,579.0 m²**
	Gross floor area (total):	**55,066.0 m²**

Peoples' Friendship Palace

The main sources for the description of this building were manuscripts in the archive of the Institute of Art History in Tashkent, historical publications in the journals Arkhitektura SSSR (Architecture of the USSR) *and* Arkhitektura i stroitel'stvo Uzbekistana (Architecture and Construction of Uzbekistan)*, books on the history of Soviet architecture in Uzbekistan and newspaper articles from the construction period. Of additional value for the research was a discussion with one of the lead architects of the project, Elena Sukhanova, who headed work on the construction documentation phase after the team, led by Evgenii Rozanov, had consolidated the main artistic and planning solutions.*

The Decision to Build

A year after the opening of the Lenin Museum in Tashkent (1970) the Central Scientific Research and Experimental Project Institute for Entertainment and Sport Facilities (TsNIIEP) received another prestigious commission for the construction of a large cinema and concert complex in Tashkent. The client's motivation was not obvious. An existing contemporary cinema and concert hall, the Palace of Arts (Panoramic Cinema), fulfilled similar functions. However, the city lacked contemporary spaces for two academic dramatic theaters, there were no chamber concert halls, and the philharmonic was operating in a prerevolutionary circus building that was poorly equipped for concerts. In this context, the construction of a new, gigantic complex that was typologically similar to the Palace of Arts seemed an unnecessary excess. The fate of the new palace, which was rarely used during the final Soviet decade, did not clarify the situation, instead reinforcing doubts that the declared aims of the design matched reality.

The latent competition in the Soviet arena between the leaders of Kazakhstan and Uzbekistan, Dzhinmukhammed Kunaev and Sharaf Rashidov, suggests that the idea behind the construction of this complex for party and government forums on Peoples' Friendship Square was a reaction from Rashidov to the appearance of a new building in Alma-Ata, the Lenin Palace. It opened in 1970, like the Lenin Museum in Tashkent. There was no official announcement of the fact that Rashidov demanded the architects surpass the Alma-Ata palace, but the tone of Uzbek newspapers, which commented enthusiastically on TsNIIEP's new project in Tashkent, left no doubt regarding its competitive spirit. In the article "The Largest in Central Asia," *Pravda Vostoka* (*Truth of the East*) grandly announced "the construction of the largest cinema and concert hall in Central Asia, with 4,000 seats."[1] This was repeated by *Vechernii Tashkent* (*Evening Tashkent*): "A cinema and concert hall, the largest entertainment complex in the city, will be erected on the same spatial axis as the circus, on Khadra Square. In terms of its parameters, artistic design and technical equipment it is surpassed only by the Kremlin Palace of Congresses and Leningrad's October Concert Hall."[2] If we take the completion of construction of the Lenin Palace in Alma-Ata as the trigger for the Peoples' Friendship Palace in Tashkent, the typological characteristics of the latter become clearer. In terms of profile the Kazakh building was close to Moscow's Palace of Congresses. It included an enormous multistory foyer and an unusually broad auditorium with a stage. Such a stage was convenient not only for placing a tribune with wide rows for a presidium but also for hosting government concerts, with several collectives the size of the Alexandrov Ensemble (formerly known as the Red Army Choir) fitting simultaneously. The Alma-Ata building was considerably less well suited for film screenings, since it exceeded the comfortable angles from which the performance was visible to a large part of the audience. The unusual width of the stage and the colossal auditorium were even less suitable for theater productions. Even the Kremlin Palace of Congresses hosted opera and ballet productions from time to time to ensure that this grandiose complex did not stand empty, but they were attended by a wider public that wished to visit the center of the Kremlin. Inveterate theatergoers preferred the Bolshoi.

In Tashkent party congresses and state concerts took place at the Navoi Theater from 1947, and after 1967 at the Palace of Arts. However, the latter, which had been built in the spirit of the Thaw, did not have the necessary party and nomenklatura luster. Immediately after construction was completed it began being used systematically as a "people's cinema," attracting up to ten thousand visitors a day. The foyer of the "Panorama" was spacious and elegant, but expensive materials had not been used for fitting it out and, as far as the party top brass was concerned, this made it an insufficient representative space. The extended glass parallelepiped was accessible and open to the street, differing significant from Mikhail Posokhin's modernist keep, hidden behind the Kremlin walls, and the Alma-Ata palace, which was set back into a wide square. It is not difficult to imagine that in preparing for new party congresses

1 A. Tankhel'son, "Samyi bol'shoi v Srednei Azii [The Largest in Central Asia]," *Pravda Vostoka* [*Truth of the East*], no. 13, January 16, 1977.
2 A. Azimov, "Simvol druzhby narodov [A Symbol of Peoples' Friendship]," *Vechernii Tashkent* [*Evening Tashkent*], no. 106, May 12, 1978.

and international forums the republican authorities wished to acquire a more isolated and imposing building suitable not only for mass, thousands-strong meetings but also for intimate gatherings and plenary meetings, press conferences, banquets and so on.

Unlike in the case of the Panoramic Cinema, the decision to construct a gigantic new building in Tashkent was taken without competitions and collective discussions. The reminiscences of Moscow architect Elena Sukhanova are particularly valuable for understanding this decision and the circumstances behind the design. Elena Sukhanova began working at Moscow's Central Scientific Research and Experimental Project Institute for Entertainment and Sport Facilities (TsNIIEP) in 1970, when it was led by Evgenii Rozanov. She believes that Rozanov personally persuaded Sharaf Rashidov to commission TsNIIEP. By this time the project institute had completed the construction of the Lenin Museum in Tashkent and the administrative buildings for the main city square. The new commission was evidence that the client was satisfied. However, another theme arises from Elena Sukhanova's recollections: the commission was delegated to the Moscow team because, in their efforts to satisfy the client's demand for more "Eastern" architecture, they showed greater flexibility than Tashkent architects. Sensing the Muscovites' inclination to create buildings in Tashkent that had a clearly accentuated Central Asian appearance, Sharaf Rashidov could talk more openly with them about their preferred stylistic solutions. Looking back, Sukhanova was extremely critical and scrupulous in her view of her Tashkent brainchild. She believes it is incorrect to refer to the Peoples' Friendship Palace as a work of contemporary architecture, since the architects had a traditional remake using modernist means thrust upon them.[3] This view from the person who bore the brunt of the practical design and supervision for the entire decade-long epic of design and construction of the building helps us to re-establish the logic of the evolution and completion of the project.

Stages of the Design

Design began in 1971 and took place in three stages. During the first stage the architects, in the spirit of the 1960s, saw the building as asymmetrical.[4] It was suggested that the palace could incorporate a banqueting hall and a cinema and concert complex. Since they varied in terms of function, these blocks had differing volumetric interpretations. However, this solution was soon rejected. According to research carried out by Elena Sarkisiants in the 1970s, the asymmetry was scrapped because the rectangular site required a symmetrical parallelepiped building. It is difficult to agree with this conclusion, since the site was not a given and was created by planners based on their changing tastes. Tastes were evolving toward the rapid monumentalization of official buildings, which was expressed in the 1970s through greater staticity and pomposity. Fifteen years later, Elena Sarkisiants (Kriukova) would be franker. Firstly, the initial versions were rejected by the authorities and not by the architects, and secondly, the reason was "the limited capacity of the auditorium and so on."[5] This indirectly confirms that the Tashkent building had to be larger than the one in Alma-Ata, and the first version was rejected because it did not meet this requirement.

At the next stage of design, the palace had already become symmetrical and combined three functions: the cinema-concert and banqueting blocks were supplemented with an exhibition hall.[6] However, the authors could not find a coherent layout for this concept. The banqueting hall required catering facilities and the exhibition hall needed special equipment and lighting. Having excluded the exhibition space and catering block, the architects produced a traditional symmetrical volume, in the center of which was an auditorium for 3,100 people, surrounded on three sides by a spacious foyer. By refining this version, the authors were able to increase the capacity to 4,000, having constructed it like an amphitheater with a tier of high balconies under which the projection room was located. Spaces for a small banqueting hall and a presidium hall were included in order to accommodate small-scale official functions. Nominally the complex remained a "cinema and

3 In a discussion between Elena Sukhanova, Ol'ga Kazakova and Boris Chukhovich which took place in Moscow on February 2, 2020, Sukhanova said, "We did not want to do that... But then we understood that if this was the commission then we had to internalize it. [...] Architects are unprincipled, they do what you tell them. And that's how we worked. Without principles."

4 Elena Sarkisiants, "Tvorcheskie poiski i slozhenie obraza kinokontsertnogo zala v Tashkente [Creative Explorations and the Coming Together of the Image of the Cinema and Concert Hall in Tashkent]," *Stroitel'stvo i arkhitektura Uzbekistana [Construction and Architecture of Uzbekistan]*, no. 10, 1977, 19.

5 Elena Kriukova, *Arkhitektura obshchestvennykh zdanii Uzbekistana (1970–1995) [Architecture of Public Buildings of Uzbekistan (1970–1995)]*, manuscript, 1996, Archive of the Institute of Art History of the Academy of Sciences of the Republic of Uzbekistan, IA (M), K-95, no. 1398, 60.

6 Elena Sarkisiants, "Tvorcheskie poiski i slozhenie obraza kinokontsertnogo zala v Tashkente [Creative Explorations and the Coming Together of the Image of the Cinema and Concert Hall in Tashkent]."

Sketch of the Peoples' Friendship Palace, unbuilt design

South façade of the Peoples' Friendship Palace, 1988–1989

concert hall," but the evolution of its functions clearly demonstrated that it was intended primarily for important political events.

The plan of the palace was simple. An auditorium for 4,100 people, surrounded from the north, west and east by a grand multilevel foyer with a vestibule and buffet, was incorporated into a rectangular outline (102 × 93 m). From the south side the auditorium was framed by spaces for artists, administrators, technical services and service personnel. The ticket desks were on the first floor, while in the basement there were ventilation chambers and an underground parking lot. Visitors entering the building could distribute through the foyer and go up to the second floor to the auditorium. There, staircases adjoining the west and east cores led to a gallery on the third floor where there were stairs to the balconies within five towers. From a construction point of view, the building had a metal structure, while the internal walls and pylons were made of brick and clad with various materials which require a detailed description.

The Visual Solution

The most important structures in Tashkent were named after Lenin, but the grandiose palace was planned for a square that was dedicated to the friendship of peoples. The ideological theme of "proletarian internationalism" was a priority in the city. In the field of foreign relations, the capital of Uzbekistan played the role of a vitrine on the "Soviet East," and its image within the union was based on having received evacuees from Nazi-occupied territory and on the reconstruction of the city after the 1966 earthquake, in which most Soviet republics participated. As a result, the building was given a dual name, the V.I. Lenin Peoples' Friendship Palace. One might assume that this name forced the designers to incorporate the themes of internationalism, Soviet multiculturalism and Leninism as a universal ideological doctrine into the appearance of the building, however, images of "peoples' friendship," like the International Style of the previous decade, were not reflected in the aesthetic concept of the palace. The Moscow architects, based on their experience of designing the "national Lenin Museum," focused their efforts on seeking means of expression that correlated with the historical architecture of Uzbekistan. "For the building," they wrote, "it was necessary to find an architectural appearance that answered to the national traditions of the culture of Uzbekistan."[7] A gap formed between the internationalist theme and an aesthetic solution focused on "national traditions."

Since the authorities had a positive perception of the sun-protection panjara grilles on the Lenin Museum and the Ministries Building, the architects decided to develop this successful approach by decorating the entire perimeter of the Peoples' Friendship Palace with a similar reinforced concrete lattice. As it was placed on a stylobate, it looked more traditional than the grilles on previous buildings, which were suspended on load-bearing structures. However, on this occasion one element linked to local tradition was insufficient: according to the authors (or the client), this would result in the façades of the gigantic building looking too monotone. So, the panjara was supplemented by a cornice with whimsically designed hanging elements. Their structure was vaguely reminiscent of muqarnas stalactite vaulting borrowed from the vocabulary of "Islamic architecture." However, the similarity was only external. Muqarnas was traditionally connected with the structure of vaults or load-bearing columns. It either had a structural purpose or visually illustrated the way the structure performed. In the Peoples' Friendship Palace the vertical elements of the cornice with reinforced concrete "wings"[8] and the cell-like structures above them were to be fixed to the load-bearing constructions. Despite the authors' insistence, their sun-protection function was largely fictional since even the north façade, which was always in the shade, was "protected" from the sun in the same way as the others. A decorative and intertextual function remained: by playing with muqarnas forms on the façade of the new palace the Moscow architects marked their building as "national." However, they did not wish to reproduce the tradition literally. "When developing the form of the façades and interiors," they wrote, "we aimed to create our own aesthetic line that would offer the possibility of recognizing traditional techniques through complex associations, not direct repetition."[9]

But "complex associations" are not always predictable. For many the vertical elements of the cornice, a bristling mass hanging over the square, were reminiscent of fortress merlons. This association was reinforced by slits that looked like loopholes. If the merlons and loopholes were associated with a fortress parapet, the monolithic concrete parallelepiped of the main auditorium which rose above them could be

7 Elena Sukhanova and Vladimir Krichevskii, "Dvorets Druzhby narodov SSSR im. V.I. Lenina v Tashkente [The V.I. Lenin Peoples' Friendship Palace in Tashkent]," *Stroitel'stvo i arkhitektura Uzbekistana* [*Construction and Architecture of Uzbekistan*], no. 8, 1981, 18.

8 According to Elena Sukhanova, the idea of the "wings" was also taken from muqarnas forms, reproducing a stylized version of one of the elements of a stalactite vault.

9 Elena Sukhanova and Vladimir Krichevskii, "Dvorets Druzhby narodov SSSR im. V.I. Lenina v Tashkente [The V. I. Lenin Peoples' Friendship Palace in Tashkent]," 24.

visually compared to a keep. This connotatively transformed the palace into a fortress, with its inherent inaccessibility. Paradoxically, this composition, which combines a fortress wall and a minimalist modernist volume, brought the Peoples' Friendship Palace closer to the Palace of Congresses behind the Kremlin wall. The Moscow model was modified in Tashkent and presented as traditionally Uzbek. A Moscow critic wrote in the journal *Arkhitektura SSSR* (*Architecture of the USSR*) that "the broad acceptance of the new Palace of Friendship" was defined by "a sense of being local, 'Uzbek' architecture."[10] Note that the word "Uzbek" was in eloquent quotation marks.

Unexpectedly, after the collapse of the USSR many authors began to associate the Peoples' Friendship Palace with Central Asian buildings of the pre-Islamic period. The following thought was repeated in various versions across the internet: "The unique architectural form of the building is similar to the archeological discoveries at Varakhsha and Kampirkala. The basis of the construction is a square and all four walls have the same finish and decoration."[11] The architects of the Palace did not mention this, but their insistence on "complex associations" allowed for free interpretation. It so happens that in ancient Central Asian architecture there were a number of examples of castles with a square plan and fortress walls.

Monumental Art and the Interior

The entrance area in the north part of the façade represented a conscious step away from stylized elements of "Islamic architecture." Here, marking the entrance doors from a distance, were three concrete reliefs on musical themes (sculptor: Rufa Nemirovskii, artist: Vladimir Burmakin). The composition of the left-hand relief was constructed around an image of an Uzbek karnay trumpet, the right-hand relief was of a European muse and a violin, and the central one depicted a stylized image of a human face, probably a musician. In terms of style the reliefs referred to Cubism and, through it, to African masks. These references had their own discursive logic. The pre-Islamic civilizations of Central Asia had their own "primitives," but the design of the reliefs gravitated toward modernist appropriations of African art and appeared eclectic among the stylized panjara and muqarnas.

In the early 1980s the systemic economic crisis was deepening, forcing the gradual reduction of nonessential construction expenses. However, the palace appears not to have been subject to such limitations and its interior decoration was incredibly luxurious. The plafonds of the north part of the foyer were decorated with three skylights with chandeliers inside them that were reminiscent of bunches of grapes or illuminated pearls.[12] The ceilings were composed of three-dimensional plaster panels of various configurations. The staircases featured gilding, the floors were made of figurative parquet and there was extensive use of Nurata and Gazgan marble, reinforced plaster, special Austrian plaster and tinted glass.[13] The gigantic wall surfaces that separated the foyer from the auditorium were clad with dark blue ceramic with elements of gilding. According to Sukhanova, she borrowed this combination of dark blue and gold sparkles from standard Soviet teapots that were produced in Uzbekistan, which had an ultramarine background and gold-colored drawings. When Rashidov, who was happy with the work, asked the architect how he could reward her, she asked him for 300 grams of gold. Rashidov was surprised by the request, but after Sukhanova's explanation he requested his subordinates make the necessary quantity of the precious metal available for construction. In order to produce the blue ceramic cladding tiles in almost industrial quantities they had to add a special technological production line at the factory.

Monumental works were placed against this already saturated background. They comprised three Florentine mosaics—*Peoples' Friendship*, *Holiday* and *Blossoming Land*—created in the vestibule by A. Bukharbaev and ceramic panels by Aleksandr Kedrin on the walls of the buffet and the banqueting hall. Kedrin's *Gulinaf*, which symbolized spring, was made in emerald-green tones, and *Gulichakh* symbolized fall and featured reddish terra-cotta shades. The teams of local craftsmen, Kh. Dzhalilov, A. Ilkhomov, K. Khaidarov and D. Faizullaev, also took part in the decoration of the internal spaces.

The presidium hall was decorated with a tapestry based on a design by Bakhodyr Dzhalalov. It showed a happy family unit—a man, a woman and two children—against a background of Aphrodite, geometric patterns, rings of fire and "symbols of knowledge" (books, a cosmonaut, stars). Across the tapestry ran the inscription "Glory to Man the Creator and His Constructive Activity in the Name of Peace and Progress!"

10 "Dvorets Druzhby narodov imeni V.I.Lenina v Tashkente [The V. I. Lenin Peoples' Friendship Palace in Tashkent]," *Arkhitektura SSSR* [*Architecture of the USSR*], nos. 3–4, 1983, 86.

11 https://ru.wikipedia.org/wiki/Дворец_«Дружбы_народов».

12 The chandeliers were made in Czechoslovakia based on designs by Elena Sukhanova.

13 Elena Sukhanova and Vladimir Krichevskii, "Dvorets Druzhby narodov SSSR im. V.I. Lenina v Tashkente [The V.I. Lenin Peoples' Friendship Palace in Tashkent]," 18.

The Main Auditorium

According to Sukhanova, this space was her design ("the auditorium is my favorite creation; it turned out completely contemporary. They left me to get on with it"). The auditorium was integrated into a 63-meter square. The architect's main aim was to find a configuration in which 4,100 people could be as close as possible to the stage. This is why the decision was made to raise a significant part of it to form boxes and balconies that hung over half of the amphitheater. The stage was unusually wide and, at 500 square meters, could compete with the Alma-Ata version.

One of the main technical problems the architects faced was the acoustics. They were specially calculated by experts from the Leningrad branch of Giprokino, the state cinema design body, led by E.B. Galkin, who created an acoustic model of the auditorium. The main role in the even distribution of sound was played by a system of wooden elements installed above the stage, which could be transformed based on the nature of the sound. There were three aims: it was necessary to create a system of sound amplification that would have a configuration for public events (conferences, party congresses), another configuration for concerts that used electric instruments and microphones and, finally, a setup to reproduce the acoustics of a philharmonic hall, with natural sound for classical instruments. Testing of the various regimes of the system took place in the auditorium with musicians of different genres, from symphony orchestras to variety performers, and, according to the authors, it demonstrated its effectiveness. They wrote: "We were able to create an acoustic shell that simultaneously performs the function of a mobile stage portal and, when transformed, creates a small stage for a symphony orchestra."[14]

Like the foyer ceiling, the plafond of the auditorium was made from three-dimensional plaster elements, but here they combined decorative and functional roles. Firstly, these elements served to distribute the sound, which improved the acoustics, and secondly, they incorporated lights directed at the stage that were concealed from viewers. The architect came across the form of the elements accidentally. Having seen musicians with karnay trumpets on the street, Sukhanova realized that the conical tip of this folk instrument was an ideal form for the plastic arrangement of the auditorium ceiling since it was modernist and connotative of traditional music. In fact, the rhythmic play of a number of karnay trumpets was employed by many artists from Uzbekistan, from Aleksandr Volkov and Nikolai Karakhan to Dzhavlon Umarbekov. Moving into architecture and ceasing to be figurative, this technique took on new echoes: the modernist theme now had local connotations. However, this solution was not completely pure. The gaps between the protruding half cones featured images of a pointed Islamic arch, which was a decorative and nonessential element in the functional play of plastic volumes conceived for the light fittings.

Other notable architectural elements include the form of the walls, which were clad with various plaster elements with an industrial aesthetic (this almost baroque excess also helped to distribute sound) and the floor, which was covered with fire-retardant red fabric. Such material was not produced in the USSR, and Sukhanova recalls that it was imported from Denmark. The auditorium was equipped for film screenings (the projection rooms were incorporated in the gap between the balcony and the amphitheater) and for international conferences, with simultaneous translation into eight languages. The translators' booths were above the balcony, as were the recording studios, control rooms and other staff areas.

The grand opening of the palace took place in 1981. The building turned out to be so expensive that it was almost always used for exclusive purposes. Since there was no plan to allow in ordinary people on a daily basis, it was never used as an ordinary cinema. In the 1980s, congresses, state concerts and other official events took place here, but they were infrequent. This practice had analogues in other parts of the USSR. The October Concert Hall in Leningrad, which was of similar scale and purpose to the Peoples' Friendship Palace, was also announced as a "cinema and concert" hall during the design stage. The latest imported cinema equipment was acquired for it. However, as Anna Bronovitskaia and Nikolai Malinin wrote, later "it was decided not to reduce the status of the hall to an unnecessarily democratic cinema, plus the imported equipment needed to be protected. For this reason, there were never any film screenings in the Large Concert Hall and the word 'cinema' disappeared from its name (although initially this universality was a source of pride)."[15] The Peoples' Friendship Palace, which could seat 4,000 people, was unsuitable for philharmonic concerts since the audience did not even fill the front rows of the parterre. Touring theater productions were also a rarity. The opening and closing ceremonies of the

14 Ibid., 23.

15 Anna Bronovitskaia and Nikolai Malinin, *Leningrad: Arkhitektura sovetskogo modernizma 1955–1991* [*Leningrad: Soviet Modernist Architecture 1955–1991*] (Moscow: Garage Museum of Contemporary Art, 2021), 142.

Relief on the north façade of the Peoples' Friendship Palace, 1988–1989

Tashkent International Film Festival of Asia, Africa and Latin America took place only biennially, and in 1988 the festival was organized for the last time. As a result, this fortress-like building mostly stood empty, an original monument to the era of stagnation with its dissonance between words and reality and the noncorrelation of architectural decorations and real social processes.

The Architectural Community's Perceptions

The reflection of the Peoples' Friendship Palace in the mirror of professional architectural criticism is also part of the biography of the building. Two opposing perceptions collided—those of apologists and critics—between which there was a spectrum of transitional opinions and analytical statements. The official perception was entirely positive but not homogeneous. It quickly became clear that everyone could find something in the building that matched their values, meaning that the statement reflected the speaker more than the building. Those praising it focused mainly on the link between the palace and historical tradition. For example, A. Azimov wrote: "The progressive traditions of oriental architecture have been used for the external appearance of the cinema and concert hall. The building's perimeter is surrounded by a panjara, a closed grille that links the interior to the outdoor green environment. [...] Along the perimeter of the building there are portals that once again reproduce elements of oriental classical architecture."[16] When preparing materials for the *Corpus of Monuments*, researchers from the Tashkent Institute of Art Studies focused on the contemporary appearance of the building. "The Peoples' Friendship Palace," they wrote, "is a universal entertainment building [...]. It is one of the largest of its type in the country. It is distinguished by its precision and laconic architectural form [...]. The building is a leading work of Soviet architecture of the 1970s, a concentration of its technical achievements and contemporary aesthetic ideals."[17] Another group of authors summarized the official view as follows: "The architects were given the task of creating a large entertainment complex for public and political events, film festivals and concerts; a venue that would reflect the best achievements of Soviet architecture, rich national traditions and meet the latest requirements of cinema technology. We can state that they were successful in completing the task."[18] At the other extreme was a complete lack of acceptance. Toward the end of the era of stagnation this view could not appear in published texts, but Elena Sukhanova recalled with emotion: "They wanted to do the project themselves. Why did they need these Muscovites? They were contemporary architects and of course they didn't like us. I understand them. They wanted to work themselves and to create something contemporary. Just imagine, they live in their city, they're smart, talented, contemporary and suddenly they get *this*!"

Alongside these polarized views there were intermediate opinions. Architect Richard Bleze, who had criticized Lenin Square, built by architects from TsNIIEP, wrote: "There are relatively successful buildings within the practice of this team of architects. They are the branch of the Central Lenin Museum and the Peoples' Friendship Palace. However, where the museum integrated organically into the group of memorable figurative buildings, the cinema and concert hall on a hypertrophied square did not form an ensemble with surrounding buildings, leading to contradictory opinions about the quality of the work."[19] The review by theorist and architectural historian Iosif Notkin was equally complex: "I consider the Peoples' Friendship Palace and the Moscow Hotel to be among the more interesting buildings of recent years. They have been discussed in detail by the architectural community and alongside their merits (the intricate appearance, the inventive interiors) they have shortcomings (mostly in terms of urban planning; the unconvincing nature of the plastic interpretation, which is either banal or extravagant, and the simplified nature of the building's integration in the environment), which unfortunately deprive these important works of capital-city architecture of the view that they are ideas with a future."[20] Architect Sergo Sutiagin, speaking about the palace, diplomatically stressed that he "liked some of the interiors."[21] Based on these statements, which come from various texts and which are eloquent in terms of what was said and left unsaid, we can imagine the complex emotions of Tashkent architects when they saw an expensive building which had led to the

16 A. Azimov, "Simvol druzhby narodov [A Symbol of Peoples' Friendship]," *Vechernii Tashkent* [*Evening Tashkent*].

17 "Dvorets druzhby narodov imeni Lenina [The Lenin Peoples' Friendship Palace]," *Svod pamiatnikov istorii i kul'tury Uzbekistana [Corpus of Monuments of History and Culture of Uzbekistan]*, vol. 2, *Tashkent: Pamiatniki khudozhestvennoi kul'tury (arkhitektury i monumental'nogo iskusstva) Tashkenta [Tashkent: Monuments of Artistic Culture (Architecture and Monumental Art) of Tashkent]*, Archive of the Institute of Art Studies of the Academy of Sciences of the Republic of Uzbekistan, IA. S48, no. 1253.

18 Rustam Valiev, Tulkinoi Kadyrova and Abdulkhai Umarov, *Arkhitektor i vremia* [*The Architect and Time*] (Tashkent: Izdatel'stvo literatury i iskusstva imeni Gafura Guliama, 1982), 53.

19 Richard Bleze, "Nash gorod [Our City]," *Arkhitektura i stroitel'stvo Uzbekistana* [*Architecture and Construction of Uzbekistan*], no. 9, 1987, 4.

20 "Nasha anketa [Our Questionnaire]," *Arkhitektura i stroitel'stvo Uzbekistana* [*Architecture and Construction of Uzbekistan*], nos. 2–3, 1986, 6.

21 Ibid., 8.

freezing or cancellation of many of their own ideas and projects, and which was at odds with their own aesthetic ideas.

In the first post-Soviet decade architectural critics continued to settle scores with the building, since it embodied a past epoch and was considered to be verbose, eclectic and, in compositional terms, archaic. In 1996 Elena Kriukova (Sukhanova) described the building as follows: "The demonstrative luxury of the interiors led to an overload when works of monumental and decorative art and design were added, each of which was of high artistic quality, but which did not always harmonize with each other and with the architecture."[22] However, she also noted that in the Palace there was "originality and scale" and "free interpretation of both ancient and deeply contemporary motifs" and that "the skill of the architects cannot be denied, allowing them, despite the questionable nature of the architectural interpretations, to make this building one of the leading works of the Soviet period."[23]

The perception of the Palace by the architectural community and the city as a whole changed over time. This was helped by the fact that the grandiose complex, which was built in the name of "the friendship of Soviet peoples" and which stood idle through the era of stagnation and perestroika, began to revive after the collapse of the USSR. Initially it continued to be used as a place for official international events. For example, on May 15, 1992, the Collective Security Treaty, which was the origin of the Collective Security Treaty Organization (CSTO), was signed in the Peoples' Friendship Palace by leaders of Commonwealth of Independent States (CIS) countries.[24] Here concerts by performers from Uzbekistan and the CIS began to be organized. After the closure of the philharmonic Sverdlov Hall, the Palace became the main variety theater in the city, alongside the Turkestan Concert Hall. The situation changed gradually. Even five years after the collapse of the USSR it was noted that "in Tashkent many large entertainment complexes (the Peoples' Friendship Palace, the Turkestan Cinema and Concert Hall) are only used occasionally."[25]

Abdumannop Ziiaev drew attention to the fact that the Palace created a new urban planning situation, allowing the creation in the first decade of the twenty-first century of Navoi Park, which featured a sculpture of the poet in a domed rotunda.[26] But most importantly, the thorough development of the details, the lack of literal historical quotations and the particular refinement of the façades and interiors of the Palace became obvious when compared to new buildings of the 1990s and early 2000s. In summing up her thoughts on the place of the Palace in the history of Tashkent's architecture, Elena Kriukova found an expressive metaphor: the Peoples' Friendship Palace was the Navoi Theater of the 1970s and 1980s. "Like Shchusev's theater, the new cinema and concert hall incorporated in its appearance the sum of ideas of contemporaries regarding a particular type of architecture, based on conceptualizing in new materials and structures the traditional motifs and forms and typical decorative techniques of Uzbekistan of the time."[27]

Main auditorium of the Peoples' Friendship Palace

Gigantism

The historical understanding of the origin and ideas of a significant building is undoubtedly important, but changing contexts and times produce new meanings. If the monumentality and symmetry of the Palace façades continue even today to call to mind associations with a church or a fortress, the interior of the building is perceived more as baroque. If on the outside the rigid forms of the ribs dominate, on the inside the plasticity that extends the "Euclidean space" attracts attention. This distortion, which disavows physical heaviness and transforms the forms of the building into weightless decoration, occurs as a result of two optical effects. The first can be associated with Pavel Filonov's analytical method. It is the endless splitting up of form, the collapse of blocks and surfaces into a multitude of fragments inside which new volumes, cavities, elements and details can be ob-

22 Elena Kriukova, *Arkhitektura obshchestvennykh zdanii Uzbekistana (1970–1995)* [*Architecture of Public Buildings of Uzbekistan (1970–1995)*], 61–62.
23 Ibid.
24 Despite the fact that this was unofficially known as the "Tashkent Pact" or "Tashkent Treaty," Uzbekistan would later leave the organization.
25 Elena Kriukova, *Arkhitektura obshchestvennykh zdanii Uzbekistana (1970–1995)* [*Architecture of Public Buildings of Uzbekistan (1970–1995)*], 39.
26 Abdumannop Ziiaev, *Tashkent, chast' III. XX–nachalo XXI vv.* [*Tashkent, Part III, 20th–Early 21st Century*] (Tashkent: San"at, 2009).
27 Elena Kriukova, *Arkhitektura obshchestvennykh zdanii Uzbekistana (1970–1995)* [*Architecture of Public Buildings of Uzbekistan (1970–1995)*], 59.

served. Reflections and highlights play an important role in this dematerialization, filling the volumes of the foyer and complicating the perception of its polished, shiny, semitransparent and transparent materials: stone, glass, metal, ceramic. The second is the effect of the endless expansion of the boundaries of the picture surface, which comes from the classical art of China and from American painting of the late nineteenth century, and which would later become part of the arsenal of contemporary filmmakers working with the panoramic format. The essence of the effect is explained not only by the fact that the space of the foyer is enormous. As well as its physical dimensions it has particular proportions. The plan gives a false sense of the disproportionately narrow depth and huge width of the entrance space. This makes the frontal view of the ceramic wall of the foyer immersive, like the opposite view of the city from the interior of the Palace, i.e. the natural angle of human vision is significantly narrower than the boundaries of the architectural views. Accordingly, these perspectives take on the character of panoscopic reality: the space continues to extend in places where it should be closing in, like the endlessly expanding perspectives in the film *Avatar*. As in *Avatar*, vertical movements take on a particular role, distorting forms and volumes. If from below the plastic elements of the foyer ceiling seem to be proportional and elegant, on ascending to the gallery levels they expand telescopically in size and acquire an industrial look. The staircases and parapets below, in contrast, telescopically contract into an image with tiny details.

In his well-known essay on bigness Rem Koolhaas wrote about the particular features of architecture that outgrow our familiar ideas of "large." His thoughts include the following: "In Bigness, the distance between core and envelope increases to the point where the façade can no longer reveal what happens inside."[28] This idea seems completely justified in relation to the Palace. Its façade is a dry, formal system based on the classicist typology of staticity and symmetry. The foyer and auditorium have a completely different aesthetic; they are baroque and full of optical effects. However, Koolhaas noted the incomparability of the external scales of the gigantic building and the ordinary functionality of its interiors. The skyscraper amazes with its excessive height, but inside it is full of ordinary offices. In the Peoples' Friendship Palace gigantism is turned inside-out. From the outside it is an impressive but tangible building, the dimensions of which can be encompassed and assessed with the gaze. The foyer, on the other hand, is an endlessly unfolding and slippery space, the size of which does not fit within the usual categories. Externally the Palace is constructed according to a comprehensible if stylized architectural principle: columns, order, muqarnas, roof. Inside the visitor sees only volumes that escape the analytical eye. The move into this space signifies the switching off of the routine world and entry into ephemerality and artificiality, which can be a suitable prelude to the perception of an artistic event.

Regardless of all of the discussions, the Palace is unquestionably an important building architecturally and culturally for Uzbek society and it is one of the few modernist constructions included in the national list of cultural heritage sites in 2019. It was renovated and changed hands on a number of occasions. Initially it belonged to the hokimiyat (municipality) of Tashkent and then to the Ministry of Culture, but thanks to its irregular use and a construction quality rare for the 1970s it remains one of the few important 1980s buildings that retains its initial appearance.

28 Rem Koolhaas, "Bigness, or the Problem of Large," in Rem Koolhaas and Bruce Mau, *S, M, L, XL* (New York: Monacelli Press, 1997), 494–517.

ARCHITECT
EVGENII ROZANOV

Place and year of birth:
Moscow, 1925
Place and year of death:
Moscow, 2006
Education:
1945–1952, Moscow Architectural Institute

Evgenii Rozanov was one of the most awarded Soviet and Russian architects. He graduated in 1951 from Moscow Architectural Institute. He worked at the Central Scientific Research Institute for Standard and Experimental Design of Entertainment and Sport Facilities from its foundation in 1964 until 1985. He designed numerous buildings in various cities of the USSR, and, in Tashkent, as well as designing the Lenin Museum, he led the architectural team for the complex on Lenin Square and the Peoples' Friendship Palace.

See full biography in Lenin Museum monograph, page 552

ARCHITECT
ELENA SUKHANOVA

Place and year of birth:
Moscow, 1938
Education:
1955–1961, Moscow Architectural Institute

Elena Sukhanova graduated from Moscow Architectural Institute in 1961 as one of the urbanist conceptualists that designed the New Unit of Settlement (NER). Group members were Aleksei Gutnov, Andrei Baburov, Natal'ia Gladkova, Andrei Zvezdin, Nikita Kostrikin, Il'ia Lezhava, Slava Sadovskii, Elena Sukhanova and Zoia Kharitonova. The group was part of a conceptual futurist trend in Soviet urban planning of the 1960s. After graduating, Sukhanova worked with architect Aleksandr Vlasov, who was the secretary of the administration of the Union of Architects of the USSR. In 1970 she moved to Evgenii Rozanov's studio at TsNIIEP. After the completion of the concept design for the Peoples' Friendship Palace she played a leading role in the development of the project and the supervision of construction. She also designed a government center in Luanda (Angola), a club block in Essentuki, the Russian Drama Theater in Ulan-Ude, a hotel complex in Sochi and many other buildings.

INSTITUTIONAL FRAMEWORK

Central Scientific Research and Experimental Project Institute for Entertainment and Sport Facilities (TsNIIEP)

PRIORITIES

Initially the profile of this Moscow institute, which focused on sport and entertainment, did not include offices. TsNIIEP was founded in 1964, immediately before the commission to design the buildings on Lenin Square in Tashkent, and therefore, unlike Tashkent project institutes, did not have practical experience of designing administrative buildings. And although in Moscow in the 1960s there really were "head institutes" that specialized in designing particular types of building for the whole USSR (Giprovuz for higher education, Giproteatr for theaters, TsNIIEP Residential and others), their remit did not usually include the main government complexes for Soviet republics. The construction of such complexes was a question of honor for the republican elite, since they were considered the main shop window of national identity.

Lenin Square (Mustaqillik Square since 1991), after 1974

Basement (-7.60m) floor plan
Original condition

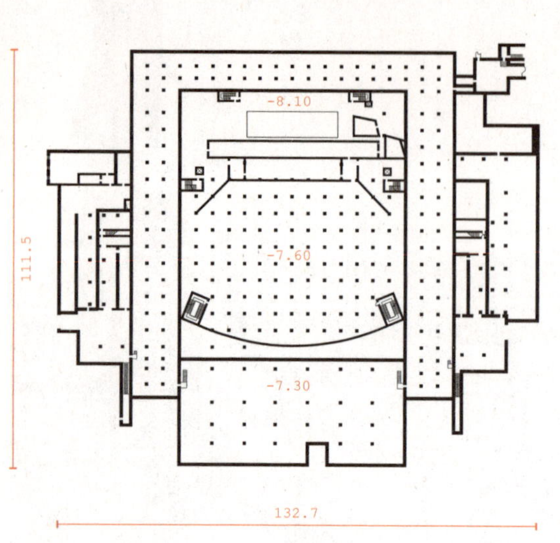

Basement (-5.30m) floor plan
Original condition

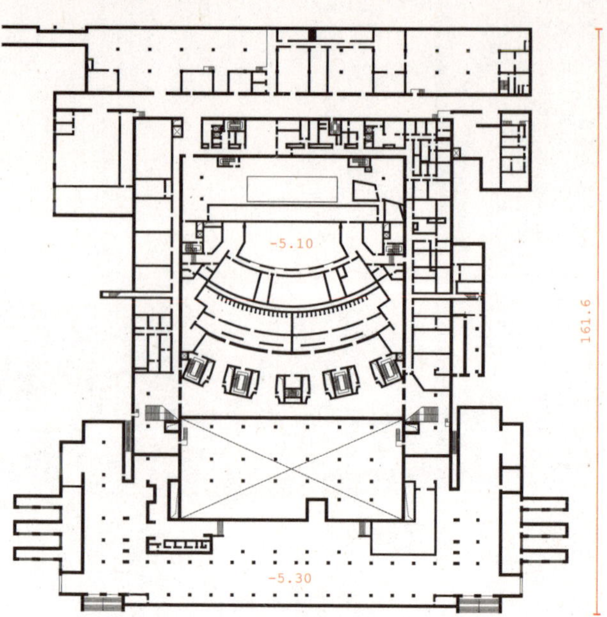

1st floor plan
Original condition

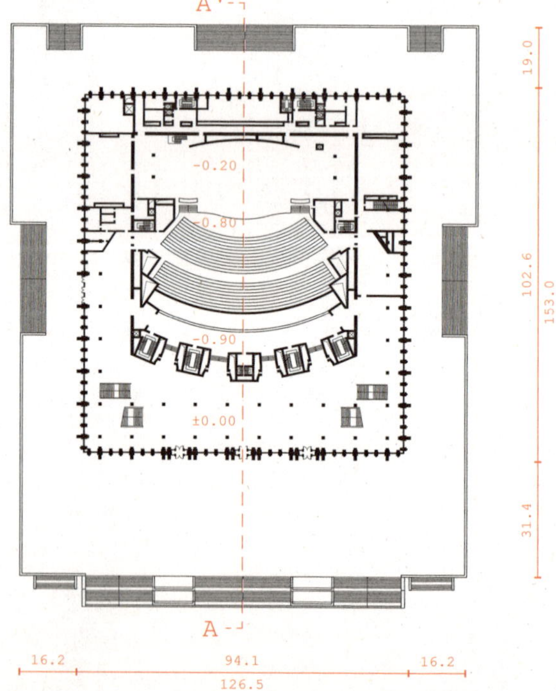

2nd floor plan
Original condition

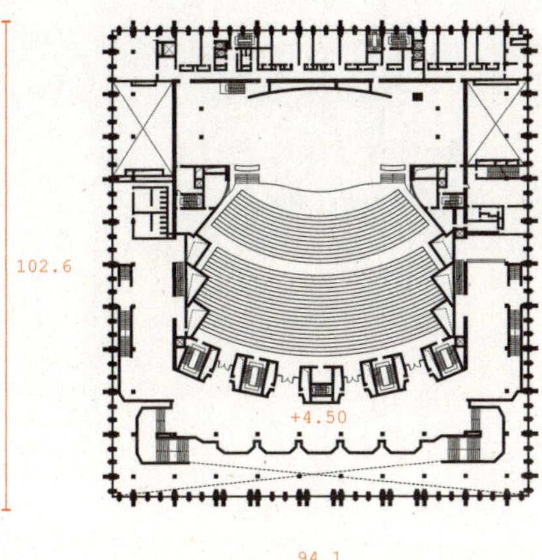

3rd floor plan
Original condition

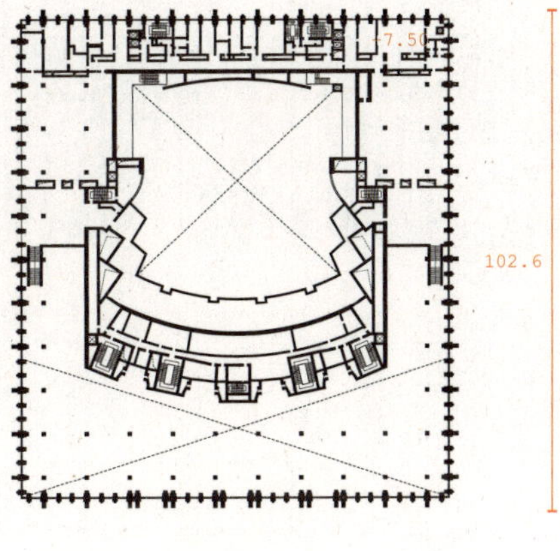

4th floor plan
Original condition

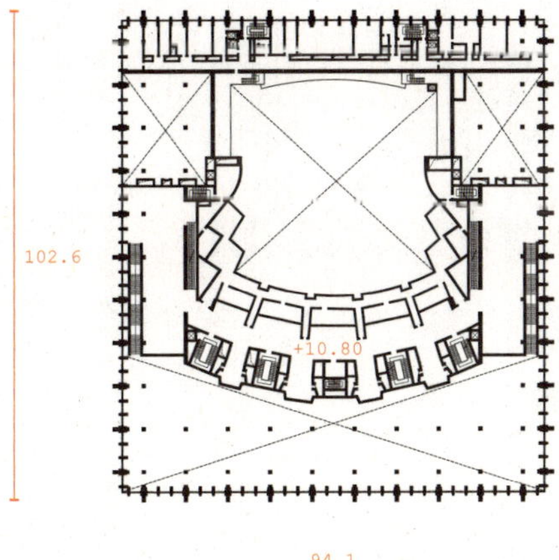

0 5 10 20m

North elevation
Original condition

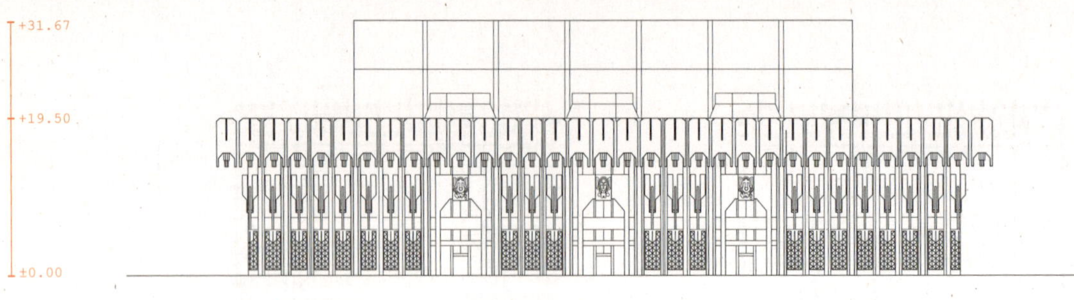

South elevation
Original condition

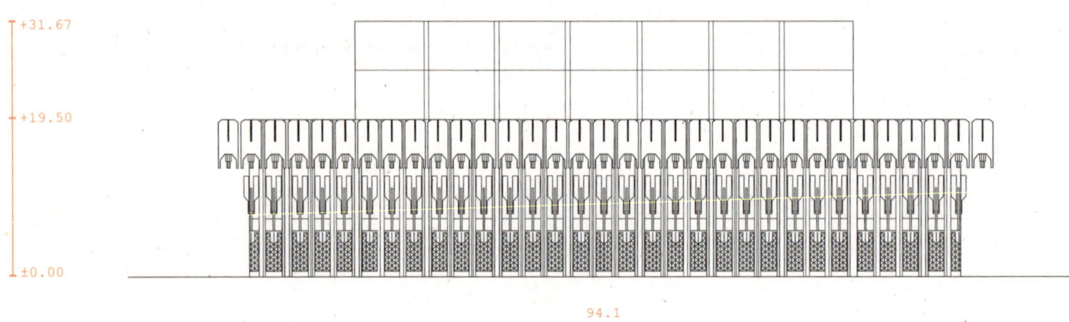

East elevation
Original condition

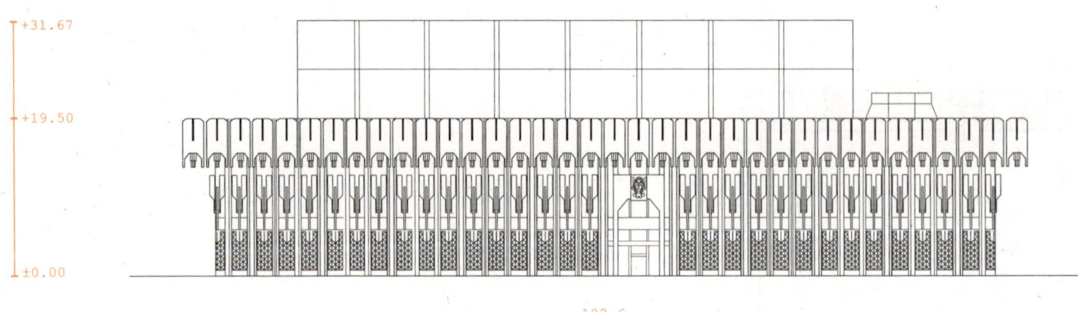

West elevation
Original condition

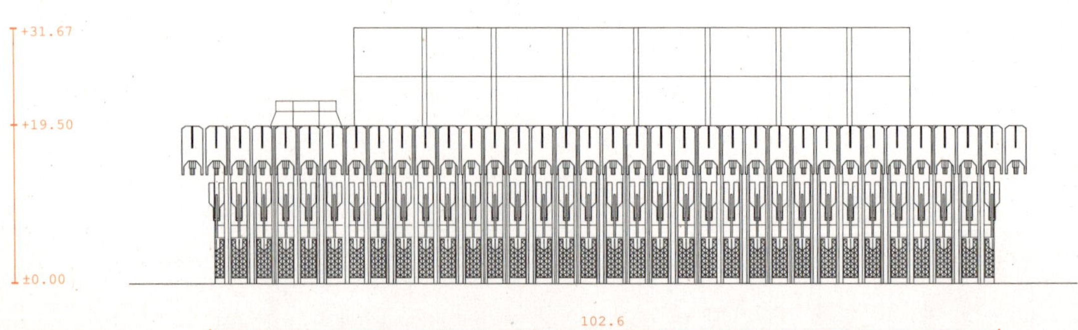

0 5 10 20m

Section AA'
Original condition

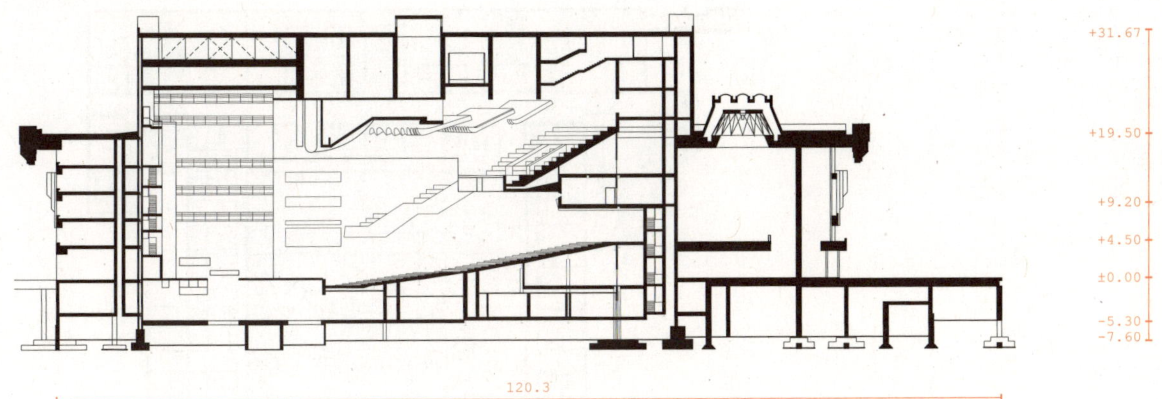

North façade, perspective view
Original condition

Perspective view
Original condition

0 5 15m

1981/2022

Basement (-5.30 m) floor plan
Original/current condition

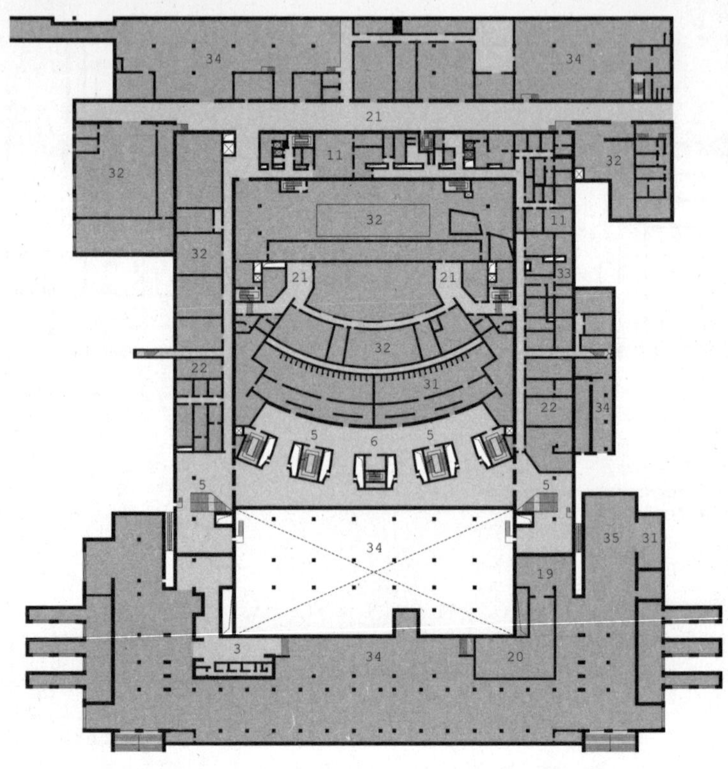

1st floor plan
Original/current condition

1	Entrance vestibule
2	Vestibule
3	Ticket office
4	Cloakroom
5	Circulation, visitors
6	Foyer
7	Special complex
8	VIP room
9	Banquet hall
10	Café
11	Kitchen & service
12	Concert hall
13	Stage
14	Balcony
15	Control room
16	Stage service
17	Radio & TV
18	Actors' room
19	Actors' changing and dressing room
20	Rehearsal room
21	Circulation, workers
22	Workers' room
23	Administration
24	Staff room
25	Workshop
26	Studio
27	Translators' room
28	Archive
29	Photo lab
30	Security room
31	Restroom
32	Warehouse & storage
33	Service room
34	Technical area
35	Empty space

1981/2022

2nd floor plan
Original/current condition

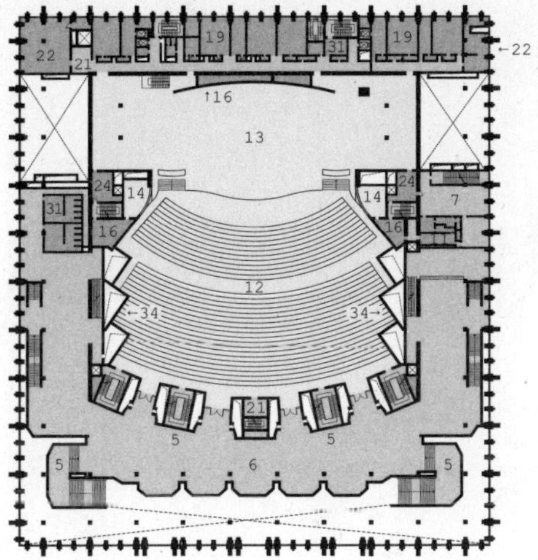

3rd floor plan
Original/current condition

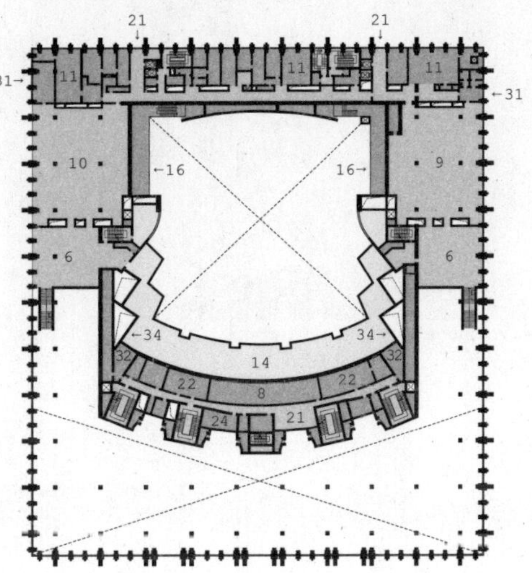

4th floor plan
Original/current condition

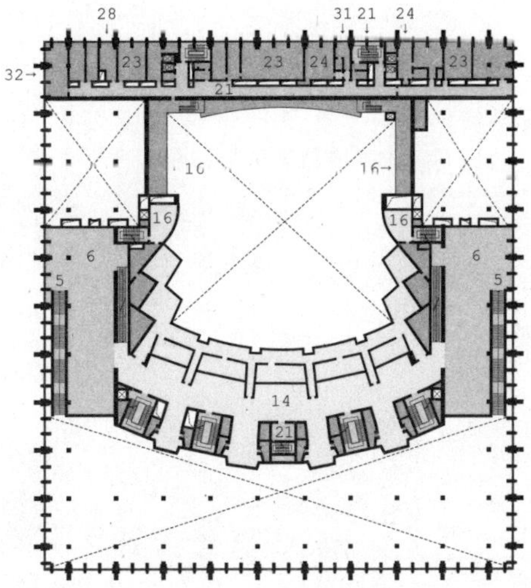

	Theater hall
	Public
	Service and technical
	Change of function

0 5 10 20m

Peoples' Friendship Palace during construction

Peoples' Friendship Palace during construction

Peoples' Friendship Palace during construction, installing ceiling panels

Peoples' Friendship Palace and its surroundings, 1983

View of the east façade, 1982

View of west façade, 1982

Views of the foyer mezzanine

Views of the main auditorium

Main façade of the Peoples' Friendship Palace, 2022

Façade views, 2022

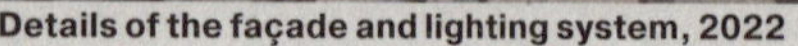

Details of the façade and lighting system, 2022

Foyer mezzanine, 2022

Foyer, view toward the façade, 2022

Façade details, view from the interior, 2022

Banquet hall with ceramic decorations by Aleksandr Kedrin, 2022

Main auditorium, 2021

Model of an unbuilt design proposal

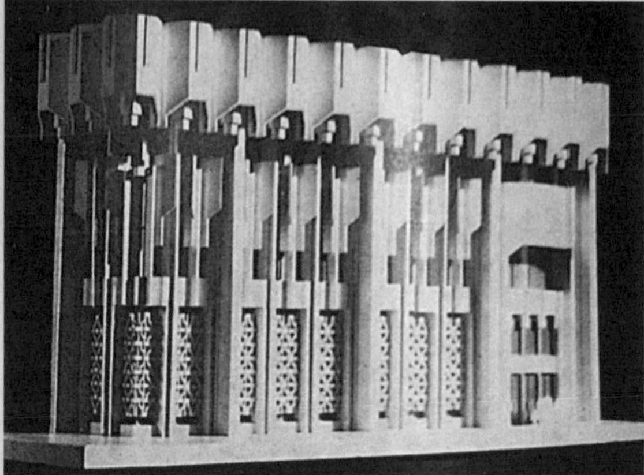

Model of the façade

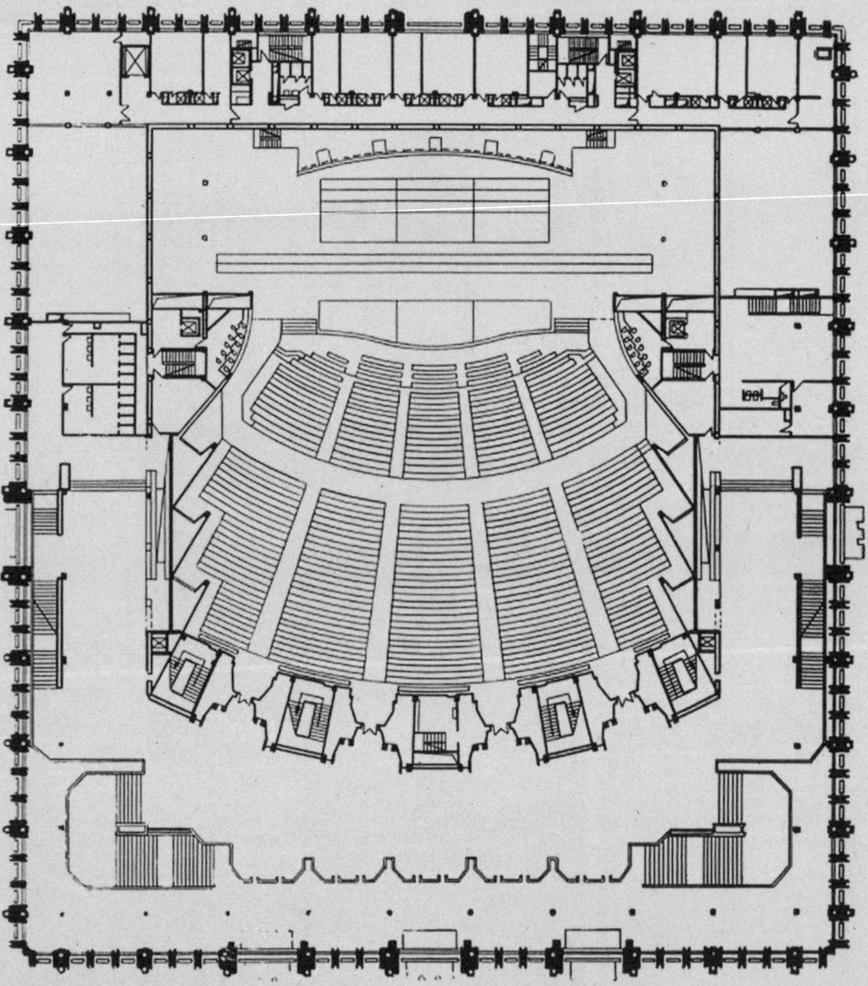

Plan of the Peoples' Friendship Palace

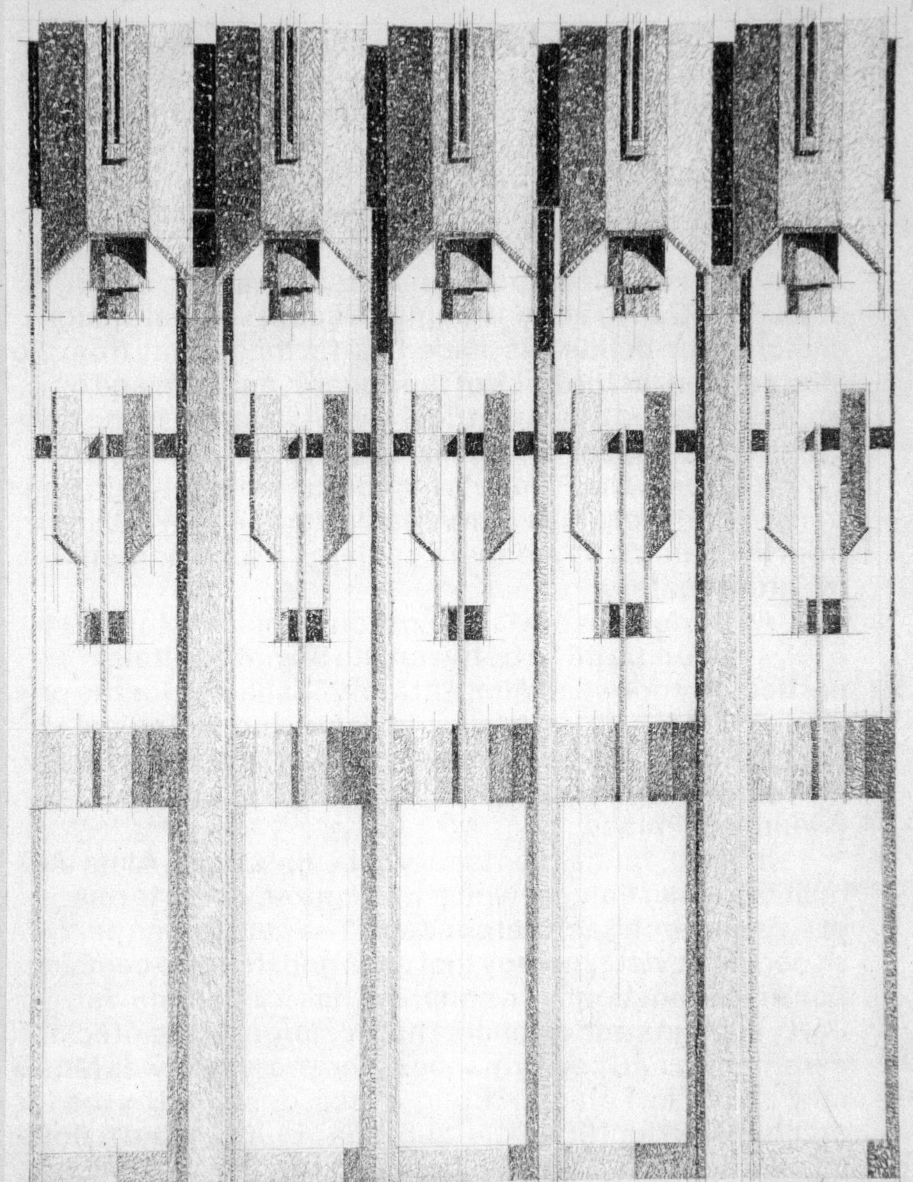

Evgenii Rozanov, façade detail, drawing, second half of the 1970s

HIGHLIGHTS

The Peoples' Friendship Palace is the largest modernist congress and concert hall in Tashkent. It was designed by the architects E. Rozanov, V. Shestopalov, E. Shumov, E. Sukhanova and L. Berezovskaia, and was built from the second half of the 1970s to 1981.

The building stands on the southern bifurcation of Furkat Street, the primary north–south urban axis, with the State Circus at the opposite northern end. The urban position within the city strongly affected several design choices. The building is placed the furthest away from the intersection, at the back of the square, and is raised on a podium. It has a symmetrical layout, aligned to the central axis of Peoples' Friendship Square, coinciding with Furkat Street. The Palace's façade is seemingly light and transparent, yet plays with variable degrees of visibility from the outside by means of panjara-like sunscreens of different scales.

As Boris Chukhovich points out in his text (pp. 504–513), the competition between the Soviet capitals, particularly between Alma-Ata and Tashkent, for the primacy in architecture in terms of scale, technological advancement or spectacularity was an important factor in determining the design criteria for the Peoples' Friendship Palace.

In 1970, for the centenary of Lenin's birth, Alma-Ata built the Lenin Palace, which was impressive in terms of size and architectural concept. The palace was part of a specific Soviet typology that emerged from the combination of the functions of a congress hall for Communist Party summits and a concert hall for large-scale official ceremonies and performances. The prototype was Moscow's Kremlin Palace of Congresses, designed by the architect Mikhail Posokhin and built in 1961. In the following two decades, many Soviet capitals followed Moscow examples and erected similar buildings. These were required to be representative of Soviet power, hence the symmetry, monumental scale, abundant décor and requirement for varying degrees of privacy.

The Lenin Palace in Alma-Ata was much praised at the time of its completion, receiving the State Prize of the USSR in 1971. The Peoples' Friendship Palace in Tashkent, a city that was in competition with Alma-Ata, had to surpass its precedent in scale (a 4,100-seat auditorium, as opposed to 3,000) and in sumptuousness. It is enclosed by a modular yet articulated façade, which blends modernity and tradition (as a result of careful studies by the architects[1]). The honeycomb elements crowning the building recall Islamic muqarnas,[2] and panjara-like elements screen the lower part of the façade. However, while some shapes are evocative of tradition, the extensive and repetitive use of prefab concrete and glazing refers clearly to modernist logic.

The interior of the Palace is impressive in terms of size and decoration, which is uncommon for most public buildings of that era. The sixteen-meter, full-height foyer consists of a spectacular environment on three levels that is airy and bright. The attentive choice of finish materials (pavements, wall claddings, ceilings, doors, handrails), the grand chandeliers, the artworks embellishing the space and their impeccable execution reflect a desire for grandeur and contribute to the uniqueness of this spectacular building. The large 4,100-seat congress/concert hall also has a rather original design.

For its distinctive urban presence, grand appearance, high-quality decorations and finishes, and high level of integrity and authenticity, the Peoples' Friendship Palace deserves to be carefully preserved.

STATE OF REPAIR SCORE:

● 4 – The building is in perfect (or near perfect) condition

The Peoples' Friendship Palace demonstrates a good state of repair owing to constant maintenance, as well as to the 2018 renovations, which mostly concerned the building's façades.

Protection status: The building is listed and protected according to Decision No. 846 of the Cabinet of Ministers, October 4, 2019.

Main criticalities: A few minor issues have been identified with particular reference to the auditorium lighting: some of the ceiling's integrated lights no longer work. Others have been replaced using different color temperature bulbs (the originals were all warm). The result is a rather unpleasant mixture of cold and warm lights.

Possible risks: No particular risks have been identified.

1 Elena Sukhanova and Vladimir Krichevskii, "Dvorets Druzhby narodov SSSR im. V.I. Lenina v Tashkente [The V.I. Lenin Peoples' Friendship Palace in Tashkent]," *Stroitel'stvo i arkhitektura Uzbekistana* [*Construction and Architecture of Uzbekistan*], no. 8, 1981, 18.

2 Boris Chukhovich, *Alerte Héritage* website (https://archalert.net/).

INTEGRITY SCORE:

- Exterior: 4 – The building has retained all the elements necessary to express its significance and is in a good state of repair
- Interior: 4 – The building has retained all the elements necessary to express its significance and is in a good state of repair

The Peoples' Friendship Palace has fully retained its architectural, functional and urban integrity. The renovations carried out in 2018 (exterior) and 2021–2022 (interior) did not impact the integrity of the building, as the main features of the square and its relationship with the building were retained. Moreover, as the building is the venue for large-scale national and international events in Tashkent, maintenance is constant.

AUTHENTICITY SCORE:

- Exterior: 4 – Only minor repairs and conservation activities have been carried out on the building
- Interior: 4 – Only minor repairs and conservation activities have been carried out on the building

Given that no major interventions have been carried out since the construction of the building, its level of authenticity is good. Maintenance and renovations have been respectful of the form and design, and of the material and substance of the building as well.

1989

View of the south façade and fountains, 1984–1985

View of the south façade, 2022

Detail of an entrance door in the north façade, 1988–1989

Detail of an entrance door in the north façade, 2022

1990s

2024

View of the foyer

View of the foyer, 2024

Main auditorium

Main auditorium, 2021

Buffet with ceramic decorations by Aleksandr Kedrin

Banquet hall with ceramic decorations, 2024

LEVEL 1 – MAXIMUM LEVEL OF INTEREST
(No transformations allowed; conservation activities required)

URBAN LEVEL

No new buildings are to be constructed on Peoples' Friendship Square.

The height of the buildings on Peoples' Friendship Square should remain unaltered.

Bunyodkor Square should maintain its axial development, acting as the link between Furkat Street and the entrance to the Palace.

ARCHITECTURAL LEVEL

EXTERIOR

The volume, height, perimeter and shape of the building should remain unaltered in order to preserve its original symmetry and proportions.

The Palace is located at the far end of a north south axis and was designed to be the end point of the axis. This characteristic should be retained, keeping the building on a raised level and avoiding moving its main entrances.

The water fountains on the south side of the building should be preserved because of their compositional relationship with the building.

The façades are undoubtedly the most iconic feature of the Peoples' Friendship Palace. They should not be modified.

INTERIOR

The foyer is the most interesting space in the building and should remain as is. Its vertical articulation and spatiality are to be retained, avoiding the addition of any partitions or new volumes.

The general layout and spatiality of the auditorium should be maintained, avoiding adding horizontal or vertical partitions and preserving the dynamic design of the balconies.

The banquet halls and café should be preserved, avoiding any partitions.

LEVEL 2 – MEDIUM LEVEL OF INTEREST

(Elements included in the second level can be moderately transformed following approval by a designated committee[1])

URBAN LEVEL

Any changes to the façades of the buildings on Peoples' Friendship (Bunyodkor) Square should be submitted to the designated committee for approval.

The construction of any new buildings within the northern part of Alisher Navoi Park (outside the 300-meter buffer zone from the south façade of the Palace) should be submitted to the designated committee for approval.

In order not to affect the visual connection between the Peoples' Friendship Palace and the Circus:

- Any changes to this section of Furkat Street should be subject to approval by the designated committee.
- The eave height of the buildings on Furkat Street can be modified only with the approval of the designated committee.

ARCHITECTURAL LEVEL

EXTERIOR

Any changes to the general layout of the Peoples' Friendship Square are to be subject to approval by the designated committee.

INTERIOR

Any modifications concerning other parts of the building (other than the auditorium, foyer and banquet halls) should be submitted to the designated committee for approval.

DETAIL LEVEL

EXTERIOR

Changes to the cladding (and finishes) of the building's podium should be submitted to the designated committee for approval.

INTERIOR

Replacement of finishes and equipment in the auditorium should be subject to approval by the designated committee.

Upgrading of the escalators should be subject to approval by the designated committee.

1 An international committee of heritage preservation experts to be appointed.

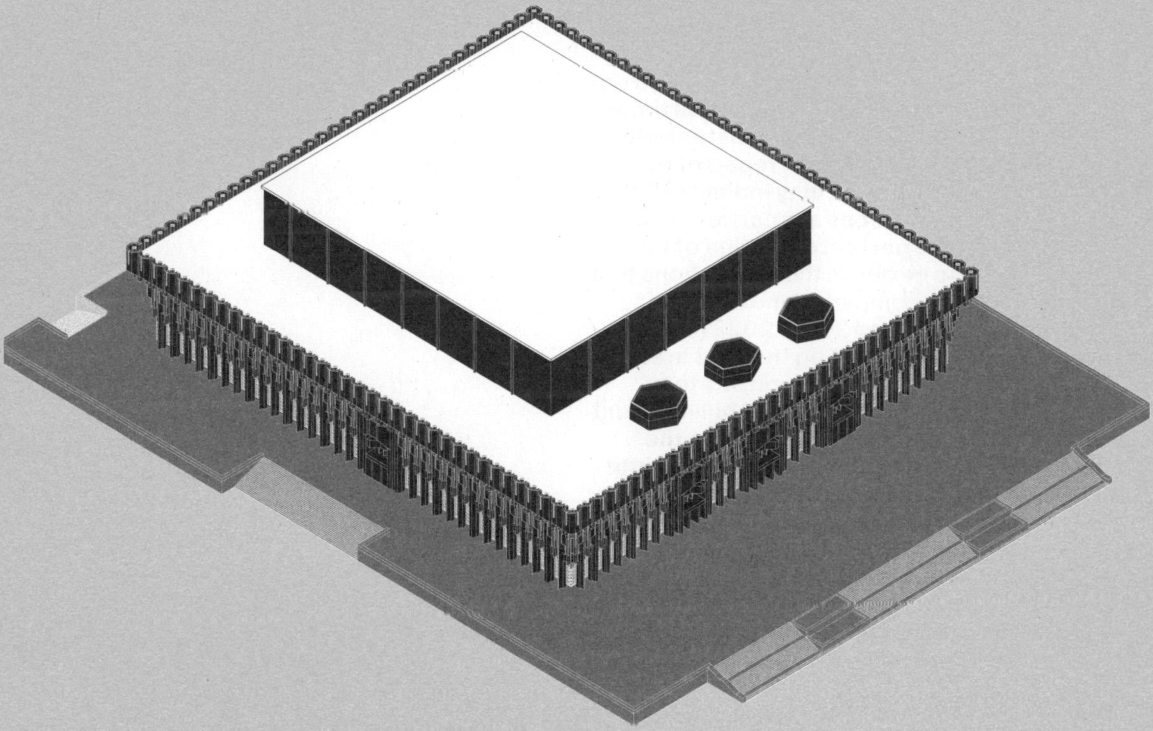

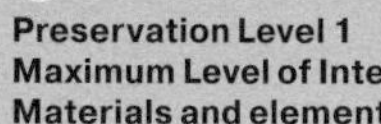

Preservation Level 1
Maximum Level of Interest
Materials and elements to be preserved

Preservation Level 2
Medium Level of Interest
Materials and elements to be preserved

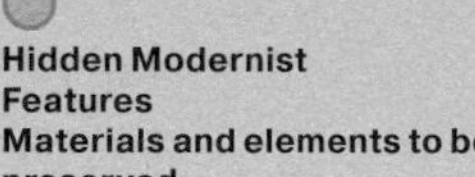

Hidden Modernist Features
Materials and elements to be preserved

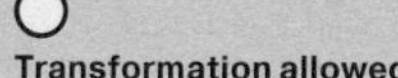

Transformation allowed

Preservation Strategy

The Peoples' Friendship Palace was built from the second half of the 1970s to 1981. Boris Chukhovich suggests that the Palace was intended as a "reaction" to the success of the Lenin Palace built in 1970 in Alma-Ata. In order to compete with this impressive architecture, the Peoples' Friendship Palace had to be grand, in terms of both dimensions and architectural concept. The size and capacity of the Palace are indeed impressive, and the quality of the spaces and finish materials gives it a rather majestic appearance. The location of the building within the city further raises its importance, assigning it a distinctive urban role.

As no major transformations have occurred since its inauguration, the Peoples' Friendship Palace retains a good level of integrity and authenticity. While the layout of the square in front of the building has been modified several times, the Palace itself is almost fully consistent with the original design. The state of repair of the building is also good, which may indicate that maintenance interventions are carried out regularly. However, the perfect condition of the building could also be due to the renovations that took place in 2018 (complete renovation of the exterior façades) and 2021–2022 (a series of interior upgrades, including the café area).

With regard to the preservation strategy, given the good state of repair of the building and its consistency with the original design, the main recommendation concerns future maintenance. Both inspections and maintenance activities should be scheduled on a regular basis in order to ensure the proper conservation of the Palace and thus its persistence through time. Particular attention should be paid to the prefabricated elements decorating the façades, the finish materials, the chandeliers and the ceramic artworks spread throughout the building.

To foster the aforementioned conservation activities, a plan of inspection and maintenance should be developed. To this end, it would be helpful to calculate a maintenance budget and designate a person in charge, who will control the implementation of maintenance activities.

Two further actions could be carried out in order to improve the quality of the indoor spaces. The first involves signage, which is not particularly coherent with the style of the building. It is advisable to replace existing signs with newly designed ones that are more in line with the Palace's architectural language.

The second action concerns artificial lighting. A mixture of cold and warm lights can be seen in both the foyer and the auditorium. The homogenization of light color could improve the overall experience of the incredible spaces inside the Palace.

Interior view from the foyer mezzanine toward the façade

Lenin Museum (State Museum of the History of Uzbekistan)

Building position and address: 3 Sharaf Rashidov Avenue, Tashkent

0 0.5 1km

The city district within which the Lenin Museum was constructed was a transit route almost from the moment that the "new city" was founded on the left bank of the Ankhor Canal, located between centers of city life such as Cathedral Square, which was in front of the White House of the governor-general of Turkestan, and the Voskresensky Bazaar (also known as the Saturday or Sunday Bazaar). During the tsarist period it was bordered by Romanovskaia, Peterburgskaia, Uratiubinskaia and Samarkandskaia streets, which were later renamed Lenin Street (Buyuk Turon), Leningradskaia Street (Matbuotchilar), Pravdy Vostoka Street (Bukhoro) and Lenin Avenue (Sharaf Rashidov Avenue). This was the location for Filipp Iupatov's circus (1914), Pharmacy No. 1 and the Iskra Cinema, which were integrated into this single-story district that was mostly built before 1917.

In the Soviet period Cathedral Square remained the main administrative square in Tashkent. First the House of Government (1931) was constructed there and then the buildings of the Council of Ministers and various ministries (1968–1972). The Voskresensky Bazaar made way for a square, Theater Square, with the Navoi Opera and Ballet Theater (1957) constructed in the east part and the Tashkent Hotel (1959) in the west. The stimulus for the transformation of the district between the two squares was the Tashkent earthquake (1966), which destroyed the circus and pharmacy, after which the area was demolished. A temporary circus tent was erected until a conceptual solution could be devised.

The first versions of the development plan for the center of Tashkent in the 1960s left a park zone between the Pioneer Palace (the former palace of Grand Duke Nikolai Konstantinovich Romanov) and the

Tashkent Hotel. The volume of the Lenin Museum first appeared in its place on the model of 1968. The architects took into account the hinge position between Lenin and Theater squares and tried to create a volume that would look good from both sides, thus determining its symmetrical and centric form. After 1974 only one more element appeared within this ensemble, although it was an extremely important one. The House of Publishers was constructed near the Lenin Museum, forming an integrated whole that may have been the most reproduced, most iconic image of Tashkent in the 1970s and 1980s.

ACTORS	Architects:	Evgenii Rozanov, Vladislav Shestopalov, Iu. Boldychev	
	Engineers:	V. Krichevskii, I. Lentochnikov	
	Artists:	Nikolai Tomskii, N. Krymskoi, E. Nuraliev, A. Shakirov, N. Ibragimov, Makhmud Usmanov, Kadyrjan Khaidarov, V. Ionin, Vladimir Zamkov	
	Institute:	Central Scientific Research and Experimental Project Institute for Entertainment and Sport Facilities (TsNIIEP)	
DATES	Design period:	1968–1969	
	Construction period:	1968–1970	
	Inauguration date:	April 17, 1970	
	Later interventions:	1992; 1995; 1999; 2000; 2022; 2024: façade works	
USE	Current use:	Museum	
	Suitability of current use:	The architectural spaces are still suitable for exhibition use. An upgrade is, however, needed to ensure a more adequate and contemporary use of the museum. Currently installed lighting and temperature control are not appropriate for museum use.	
	Space utilization:	The building is fully used. No unused/underused spaces were detected.	
DIMENSIONS	Number of floors:	Basement + 4 floors	
	Length:	61.0 m	
	Width:	57.1 m	
	Height:	26.3 m	
	Gross floor area:	First floor	2,566.0 m²
		Entrance (second) floor	1,098.0 m²
		Typical exhibition floor	1,202.0 m²
	Gross floor area (total):		9,028.0 m²

Main dimensions of the Lenin Museum
General axonometric view

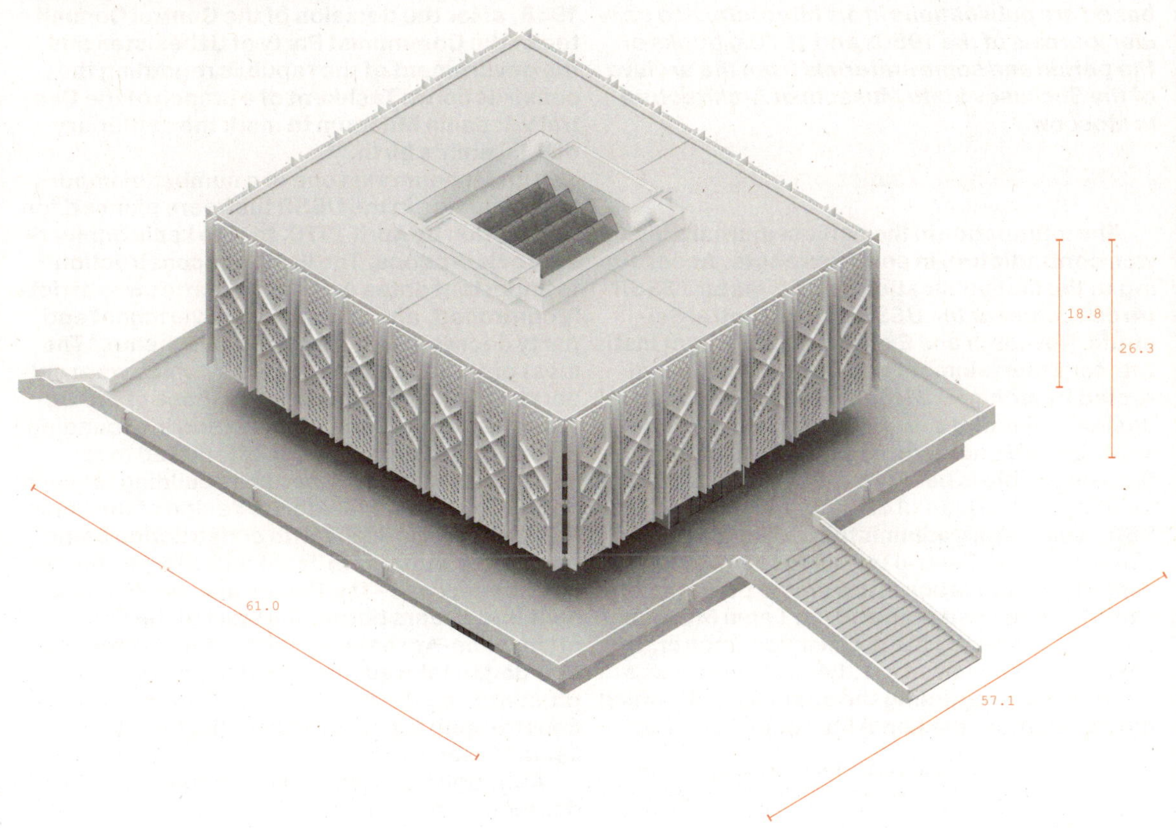

Lenin Museum

The main sources on which this description is based are publications in architectural and popular journals of the 1960s and 1970s, books of the period and some materials from the archive of the Shchusev State Museum of Architecture in Moscow.

The Decision and Choice of Location for Construction

The information in the earliest journal articles was contradictory in some respects. According to the first publication in *Arkhitektura SSSR* (*Architecture of the USSR*), "the Central Scientific Research and Experimental Project Institute for Entertainment and Sport Facilities, directed by architect B. Mezentsev, developed a design project for the central square in Tashkent, Lenin Square, on which a large architectural ensemble is being formed, to include the building of the Council of Ministers of the Uzbek SSR, a multistory administrative building and a branch of the Central Lenin Museum."[1] However, the combination into a single project of the Lenin Square ensemble and the Lenin Museum is not supported by the archive documents. The square was conceived in 1964, and there was a final decision regarding the space in 1965 which did not mention the Lenin Museum.[2] Even so, the architects noted in an Uzbekistan journal in 1970 that "the design of the museum began in 1968, after the decision of the Central Committee of the Communist Party of Uzbekistan and the government of the republic regarding the construction in Tashkent of a branch of the Central V.I. Lenin Museum to mark the centenary of V.I. Lenin's birth."[3]

The Museum was one of a number of important buildings in the USSR that were planned for completion by April 1970, for the Lenin anniversary celebrations. The linking of construction to important dates and anniversaries was strictly controlled, and at least five government and party decrees were issued on this theme.[4] The most prestigious anniversaries, which were celebrated on a grand scale, were those of the October Revolution, Lenin's birth and the founding of the USSR. Each republic attempted to receive funding for a major public building for such dates. Thus, in Alma-Ata the design of the Lenin Palace began in 1967, with construction being completed in 1970. In Tashkent, a large cinema and concert hall—the Palace of Arts—had been built three years before the start of the design of the Alma-Ata palace, and the local authorities decided to take advantage of the possibilities presented by the anniversary in another way, by constructing a local branch of the Central Lenin Museum.

Although the Tashkent earthquake of 1966 damaged a number of buildings between the Tashkent Hotel and Leningradskaia Street,

1 "Zdanie muzeia V.I. Lenina v Tashkente [The Building of the V.I. Lenin Museum in Tashkent]," *Arkhitektura SSSR* [*Architecture of the USSR*], no. 12, 1969, 30.

2 "Protokol No. 52 sovmestnogo zasedaniia Gosstroia UzSSR i Arkhitekturno-stroitel'nogo Soveta Arkhitekturno-planirovochnogo upravleniia Tashgorispolkoma ot 27 iulia 1964 goda. L. 66–70 [Protocol No. 52 of the Joint Meeting of Gosstroi UzSSR and the Architecture and Construction Committee of the Architecture and Planning Directorate of Tashkent City Executive Committee of July 27, 1964. Sheets 66–70]," *Protokoly arkhitekturnoi komissii i ekspertnye kommissii po proektam i smetam, 20 iiunia 1964 – 22 iiulia 1964* [*Protocols of the Architectural Commission and Expert Commissions on Projects and Budgets, June 20–July 22, 1964*], Tashkent City Archive, fund 36, list 1, item 1235, on 162 sheets.

In 1966, during development of the design for the landscaping of the square, the buildings which were planned for the ensemble included the Palace of Congresses (Supreme Soviet – *author's note*), the Central Committee of the Komsomol and the Navoi Library, with no mention of the Lenin Museum. "Ekspertnoe zakliucheniia po arkhitekturno-planirovochnoi chasti rabochikh chertezhei proekta zastroiki i blagoustroistva ploshchadi im. V.I. Lenina v gorode Tashkente [Expert Conclusion on the Architectural and Planning Parts of the Working Drawings for the Project for Construction and Landscaping of V.I. Lenin Square in the City of Tashkent]," *Protokoly zasedanii arkhitekturnoi komissii i ekspertnye kommissii po proektam i smetam stroitel'stva za No. 99, No. 101a, 100, 101, 104, 10 oktiabria 1966 – 20 oktiabria 1966* [*Protocols of Meetings of the Architectural Commission and Expert Commissions on Projects and Budgets No. 99, No. 101a, 100, 101, 104, October 10–20, 1966*]," Tashkent City Archive, fund 36, list 1, item 1332, on 115 sheets, page 3, sheet 86.

3 Evgenii Rozanov, Vladimir Krichevskii, T. Melik-Arakelian, "Muzei V.I. Lenina v Tashkente [The Lenin Museum in Tashkent]," *Stroitel'stvo i arkhitektura Uzbekistana* [*Construction and Architecture of Uzbekistan*], no. 4, 1970, 24.

4 Decrees: Sovnarkoma SSSR ot 1 dekabria 1925 goda "O poriadke razresheniia prazdnovaniia iubileev" [Sovnarkom USSR of December 1, 1925, "On the Order of Permission for Celebrating Anniversaries"], Sovnarkoma SSSR ot 20 aprelia 1926 goda "O raz"iasnenii Postanovleniia SNK SSSR ot 1 dekabria 1925 goda o poriadke razresheniia prazdnovaniia iubileev" [Sovnarkom USSR of April 20, 1926, "On Clarification of the Decree of Sovnarkom USSR of December 1, 1925, on the Order of Permission for Celebrating Anniversaries"], Sovnarkoma SSSR i TsK VKP(b) ot 10 aprelia 1941 goda "O poriadke prazdnovaniia iubileev" [Sovnarkom USSR and Central Committee of the Communist Party (Bolsheviks) of April 10, 1941, "On the Order of Celebrating Anniversaries"], TsK KPSS i Soveta Ministrov SSSR ot 10 maia 1965 goda "O poriadke prazdnovaniia iubileev" [Central Committee of the Communist Party of the Soviet Union and the Council of Ministers of the USSR of May 10, 1965, "On the Order of Celebrating Anniversaries"], TsK KPSS i Soveta Ministrov SSSR "O navedenii poriadka v prazdnovanii iubileev" ot 12 dekabria 1958 [Central Committee of the Communist Party of the USSR and the Council of Ministers of the USSR, "On Putting in Order the Celebration of Anniversaries" of December 12, 1958].

including the Tashkent Circus and Pharmacy No. 1, the site for the future museum was not determined by the disaster. On the first models of the center of Tashkent, dated 1964–1967, the space between the former Romanov palace and the Tashkent Hotel was designated a green zone. Before the decision to create the Museum, the idea of doing so had not been on the urban planning agenda for Tashkent. However, after the government decree the search for a site became urgent, as only two years and three months remained until the anniversary date. The architects and builders were placed in a difficult situation. They had to make a rapid start, yet the urban planning and, more importantly, the ideological significance of the building required a considered design solution and high-quality construction. In fact, the architects managed to find approaches that satisfied the state client, city residents and the architectural community. The Museum was designed and built surprisingly quickly and incorporated innovative technologies and aesthetic solutions. The quality of construction ensured that it remains one of the most attractive and best-preserved modernist buildings in Tashkent even today.

The Ideological Cult and Architectural Typology

The typological originality of Lenin museums in the Soviet Union has not yet been fully explored. These buildings were erected as part of what was an almost religious cult of Lenin, but they also took on the status of research centers and were a field of experimental museology. This combination of innovative and long-established features was also typical of the Tashkent museum. The prototype for such buildings had already begun to form. In 1967 the Moscow Central Scientific Research and Experimental Project Institute for Entertainment and Sport Facilities[5] began designing a Lenin memorial for Ul'ianovsk. A similar building was commissioned by the Uzbekistan authorities, and the team of architects that designed the complex in Ul'ianovsk was, at this time, completing the design of the buildings for Tashkent's main square.

The Lenin Museum was designed opposite the Lenin Pioneer Palace, at the intersection of Lenin Street and Leningradskaia Street, which adjoined Lenin Square, where a monument to Lenin was being constructed. The endless repetition of the same name in a single area of the city regenerated the republic's main square as a cult location, a status that had been lost when the Transfiguration Cathedral was demolished in 1932. Initially this place had been named Cathedral Square. The association between communism and religious ideas and ethics was often stressed by Marxists themselves, beginning with Engels, who drew parallels between the communist movement and early Christianity.[6] However, the "cult" of Lenin was polymorphous, and besides the monotheistic roots one can also see elements of paganism. Most of the Soviet modernist Lenin museums, starting with the one in Tashkent, were designed like "temples" placed on a high podium, the main "sanctuary" of which was the room with the statue of Lenin dominating the space. "The portrait statue of V.I. Lenin," wrote Evgenii Rozanov, one of the architects of the Museum, "is the main compositional aspect of the Tashkent museum. Installed in the central hall, it can be seen from various exhibition levels and creates a sense of Lenin's image pervading the space of the museum."[7] It is likely that the architects inherited the placement of the sculpture, which was visible from different levels of the internal space, from ancient Greek temples. There, after the pronaos (entrance area), the space would lead to the naos, or sanctuary, where the sculpture of the god to whom the temple was dedicated, such as Zeus in the Temple of Zeus at Olympus and Athena at the Parthenon, was located. The main figurative elements of the interior were connected either with demonstrating the mythological deeds of the god or showing the rituals and cults associated with them. The role of the entrance hall in the Lenin Museum was structurally similar to the naos and was mostly of a ritual nature.[8] Flowers were laid at the statue on memorial dates or during important public events, and social coming-of-age rituals were organized here, such as being accepted into the Young Pioneers or the Komsomol. As in a Greek temple, the architecture of the entrance hall and the placement of the sculpture envisaged a particular lighting effect: a skylight installed above directed light at the statue and produced an effect known to ancient and medieval architects, who used the sun's rays to create liminal spaces between the materiality of the temple and the "transcendental world." This technique, used by the architects of the Tashkent museum, was later developed and strengthened in Kyiv, where a special

5 The Central Scientific Research and Experimental Project Institute for Entertainment and Sport Facilities was established not long before this, in January 1964, by decree of Gosstroi USSR (source: https://rgantd.kaisa.ru/object/158341598). Lenin Square and the Lenin Museum were among the institute's first buildings.

6 Frederick Engels, "On the History of Early Christianity," in Karl Marx, Frederick Engels, *Collected Works*, vol. 27 (London: Lawrence & Wishart, 2010), 445–469.

7 Evgenii Rozanov and Vladimir Reviakin, *Arkhitektura muzeev V.I. Lenina* [*The Architecture of V.I. Lenin Museums*] (Moscow: Stroiizdat, 1986), 85.

8 In a more literal, classicist tone the idea of the Greek temple was the basis for the Lincoln Memorial, designed by Henry Bacon and erected in Washington, DC, in 1922.

Visualization of the Parthenon, Athens

Lenin Museum, view of the central foyer, 1972

optical concentrator was installed in the entrance hall skylight, directing the flow of light at the sculpture.

Unlike in a temple, where the naos was the culmination of the ceremony, the entrance hall of the Lenin Museum was intended to be, as one of the architects wrote, "a solemn overture to viewing the museum."[9] The scenes from the life of Lenin that were presented in Soviet Lenin museums were also, of course, associated with icons depicting the lives of the saints and showing the main stages of their life and their deeds. However, the Tashkent museum had its own character, and the display was more akin to Soviet museology experiments of the 1920s than to orthodox church iconography. Unlike Moscow and Ul'ianovsk,[10] Tashkent was not linked to the life of Lenin and had no authentic exhibits of the sort usually displayed in such museums. Accordingly, the institution was to become a laboratory of the new museography. As well as specially made copies of the armored car on which Lenin gave his speech on returning to Russia in 1917, his suit with bullet holes from the 1918 attempt on Lenin's life by Fanny Kaplan and Lenin's desk lamp with a green shade, a model of the cruiser *Aurora* and other items, the museum focused on demonstrating "Lenin's precepts brought to life in Uzbekistan and all of the republics of the Soviet East" (from the speech of Sharaf Rashidov, First Secretary of the Communist Party of Uzbekistan, at the opening of the museum[11]). The display reflected the following themes: "Lenin and the East," "Lenin and the peoples of Turkestan," "Great October and the establishment of Soviet power in Turkestan," "The triumph of the Leninist national policies of the Communist Party in the republics of Central Asia" and others. Ignoring the fantastical and made-up scenes of the meeting of Lenin and peasant messengers in Uzbekistan, one can state that the museum showed the history of Uzbekistan through the lens of Soviet ideology and focused on subjects typical of the Marxist understanding of history, such as class struggle, the destruction of the global imperialist system, attempts to construct a new social order, the interaction of cultures of the Soviet peoples, the modernization of the country and the emancipation of its residents, the increasing role of women and so on.

The display was open, but even so it was spatially structured. Evgenii Rozanov wrote: "Themes are designated by volumetric compositions, or symbols. The main theme of the Feb-

9 Rozanov and Reviakin, *Arkhitektura muzeev V.I. Lenina* [*The Architecture of V.I. Lenin Museums*], 83.

10 Ul'ianovsk (Simbirsk until 1924) was Lenin's birthplace.

11 V. Kostyria, "Glavnaia os' respubliki [The Main Axis of the Republic]," *Ogonëk*, no. 27, 1970, 4.

ruary Revolution is expressed by a model of the two-headed eagle, the coat of arms of the autocracy, which is pierced by rifle bayonets. The model is placed on a low podium in the middle of the space of this section. Against the calm background of stands with a documentary display, this material symbol, with its sharp, barbed silhouette, creates tension, a feeling of anxiety, and also focuses the attention of the viewer on the theme of the new section."[12] The architects attempted to create a universal space in which the exhibition design would allow visitors to move freely from subject to subject without losing their overall orientation in the space. The exhibition models, which were a little over two meters high, left the main space of the museum (where the height of each floor was five meters), free and full of light. This simplified navigation and made it a comfortable experience. The museum's light-bearing qualities, which began with façade walls that allowed in the sun's rays through perforated solar protection grilles, were also reflected in exhibition stands made mainly of perforated metal with invisible illumination from above. Thus, the city could be seen through the walls and the neighboring exhibition spaces through the perforated stands. The lower parts of the modules were at a 45° angle, which allowed for an undistorted perspective while looking at the exhibits.

The main exhibit was the museum building itself. It was conceived, according to the journal *Arkhitektura SSSR* (*Architecture of the USSR*), "as a monument to Lenin on Uzbek land,"[13] as a symbol of the new Uzbekistan, which means that the design was required to be not only technically innovative but also aesthetically specific. Together, these two qualities would provide evidence of the social and cultural fruitfulness of Lenin's policies in the East. Designed as a museum exhibit, the building not only demonstrated the contradictions of the direction that the architecture of Uzbekistan would take in the 1970s and 1980s but also became the main trigger for this change.

The Aesthetic Solution

The new direction was related to a turn toward tradition. As Evgenii Rozanov wrote later, "while working on the museum in Tashkent the authors may have subconsciously been driven by a desire to express the idea of the architectural monument to V.I. Lenin based on the historical development of architectural schemes that expressed the greatest human ideals. They aimed to embody this idea of a centric plan and a static volume, while developing the composition with contemporary means of architectural expression based on national traditional principles of form-making and industrial production of those elements of the building that played the most active role in its visual character."[14] Accordingly, assuming that the "national tradition" of Uzbekistan involved centric and static buildings, the Moscow architects decided to recreate a typical Central Asian building using modernist means.

In commenting on their building, the architects tried to develop their statements regarding the historical architecture of Uzbekistan. In particular, they wrote: "The forms that distinguish the architecture of Central Asia from that of any other part of the world were created over centuries. This distinction has deep forms in the historically created conditions of life, in the climatic particularities of this land, in the sharp receptivity of the Uzbek people to the beautiful." They continued, "the distinguishing factor of the compositional structure of the best architectural monuments of Samarkand, Bukhara and other ancient cities of Uzbekistan is the interconnection between exact, simple mathematical forms and the extremely rich ornamented surface of those forms."[15] This approach reflected the Moscow architects' remote understanding of the nature of the region in which they, by force of circumstance, were working. Otherwise, it would not be possible to qualify "simple mathematical forms" as applied to the architectural tradition of Central Asia, which was extremely developed and nuanced in plastic and geometric terms. It is likely that these words expressed long-standing attempts to extrapolate onto the contemporary architecture of Central Asia certain general ideas regarding so-called Islamic architecture. In particular, in the comment regarding "simple mathematical forms" with "ornamented surfaces" there is a hint of lapidary walls covered with geometric patterns. The architects could not have failed to understand the latent relationship between the lapidary parallelepiped decorated with a pattern that they designed and the religious architecture of Islam, although naturally in the Soviet period they did not refer to it.

The main distinguishing feature of the architectural image of the museum was "solar protection grilles similar to panjara."[16] Their use was read as an attempt by the architects to create

12 Rozanov and Reviakin, *Arkhitektura muzeev V.I. Lenina* [*The Architecture of V.I. Lenin Museums*], 84.

13 "Zdaniia muzeia V.I. Lenina v Tashkente [The Building of the V.I. Lenin Museum in Tashkent]," 30.

14 Rozanov and Reviakin, *Arkhitektura muzeev V.I. Lenina* [*The Architecture of V.I. Lenin Museums*], 87.

15 Rozanov et al., "Muzei V.I. Lenina v Tashkente [The Lenin Museum in Tashkent]," 27.

16 "Zdanie muzeia V.I. Lenina v Tashkente [The Building of the V.I. Lenin Museum in Tashkent]," 31.

Lenin Museum, exhibition view, 1970s

Lenin Museum construction site, anchoring of the prefabricated panels onto the structure

a specifically national building. However, the declarations and actual meanings did not always correlate. In terms of the creation of a visual link between the interior and the exterior, the grille was indeed like a panjara, allowing in some light and revealing fragments of surrounding buildings when looking out from the museum. The illuminated interior also looked spectacular in the evening when seen from the city square. But the solar protection function was only justified on the south, west and east sides of the museum, something that immediately prompted a reaction among Tashkent architects. "Specialists disagree," wrote architectural historian Elena Sarkisiants, "about the architectural solution for the branch of the Central V.I. Lenin Museum, where the proportions and pattern of the grilles are not bad but the urban planning position and centric composition of the building have forced the architects to use identical equipment on all façades, and this is contradictory in terms of the functional logic of the solar protection."[17]

As a formal technique, the ornamental development of the façade was based on ideas of the decorative and ornamental character of the traditional architecture of Central Asia. Although the role of arabesques in the architecture of Islamic countries was extremely significant, the presumption that geometrical ornament dominated in Central Asian architecture in the broad sense had orientalist roots, since, firstly, not all Islamic architecture used such decoration, secondly, not all of the historic architecture of Central Asia was Islamic in origin and thirdly, the correlation of the architecture of Soviet Uzbekistan and Islamic tradition involved an internal conflict, since the Lenin Museum display was anti-religious. The architects tried to smooth over this conflict. In their texts ornament was part of progressive folk heritage. However, regardless of the architects' comments, the assigning to the museum of the communist leader the characteristics of a cult building full of "icons" and "relics," and with a geometric pattern around the perimeter, indicated a change in direction for Tashkent modernism. Tashkent architects, including those who did not approve of historical reminiscences in contemporary architecture, mostly liked the Lenin Museum. Even Richard Bleze, who often criticized Moscow colleagues for their decorative approaches, used the Lenin Museum as an example of "relatively successful work" that "organically integrated into a number of iconic buildings."[18] Perceived as a success, the museum paved the way for a new aesthetic which gradually gained consensus and was accepted more easily by architectural experts and critics.

It is entirely possible that the successful solution came to the architects as a result of them escaping the boundaries of their own rhetorical postulates. Notwithstanding the declarations about the attempt to create a static and centric building, it ended up more dynamic and lighter than most Lenin museums in the USSR.

The first thing that came to mind when looking at the building was a typical modernist struggle with mass. The imposing marble parallelepiped "floated in the air." Its only visible support was a deep-set glass foyer. This created a well-known dynamic effect, canceling out the weight of the concrete structures and Gazgan marble facing. In order to appreciate such dynamism, it is sufficient to compare the Tashkent Lenin Museum with the Tashkent State Museum of Arts (1967–1974), conceived at the same time, and with the Lenin Museum constructed in Frunze fifteen years later. Whereas these buildings really were associated with absolute stasis and incorporated memorial connotations, the Tashkent Lenin Museum was distinguished by its lightness and airiness, which linked it to the dynamic and transparent architecture of the 1960s. The retreat from cubic proportions and the extended nature of the side façades, and even the light effects that appeared in the evening, created an original dynamic.

The laws of nature also seemed to be disrupted in the interior, where there was an air-conditioning and recirculation system, something unprecedented in the USSR at that time. In spaces invisible to the public above the suspended ceilings there were air-distributing ducts that allowed the sunny side of the building to be cooled and the temperature of other parts of the building to be maintained. The aluminum ceiling tiles served as radiators: in winter their temperature was kept at 44°C and in summer it lowered to 18.5°C. The unusual and technically progressive character of the building could be felt even in the restrooms, which had elements of automation. There were also special air-collecting systems in the upper part of the building and used-air expulsion channels underground, linked to shafts at surface level. The source of cold air was a central cooling station built in 1967 under Lenin Square. This way, the museum was an integral part of the administrative complex not only in the ideological sense but also in terms of engineering. The technical elements of the design were the best possible in the Soviet

17 Elena Sarkisiants, "Estetika solntsezashchity v arkhitekture Tashkente [The Aesthetics of Sun Protection in Tashkent's Architecture]," *Arkhitektura SSSR* [*Architecture of the USSR*], no. 3, 1979, 47.

18 Richard Bleze, "Nash gorod [Our City]," *Arkhitektura i stroitel'stvo Uzbekistana* [*Architecture and Construction of Uzbekistan*], no. 9, 1987, 4.

construction industry and justified the vitrine function of this "building-exhibit."

During the design process the architects focused particularly on monumental art. They proposed placing on the north façade a bas-relief with a portrait of Lenin in profile. This plan, which is recorded in photographs of the model, was not realized. Meanwhile, a completely different type of art was developed during the detailed design of the façade. It involved traditional wood carving, which K. Khaidarov, a craftsman from Kokand, used to create three wide doors for the main entrance. The carved theme continued in the interior, in the cinema/lecture hall, where the work was done by N. Ibragimov, and on the staircase pylon walls, which were decorated with ganch (plaster) carving by Makhmud Usmanov.

The possibility of using traditional carving in a modernist building had been frequently discussed by architectural theorists since the early 1960s. Some specialists of the older generation criticized Tashkent architects' use of elements of Western art. Their disapproval was directly linked to the demands of official aesthetics. If in architecture modernism was permitted and even encouraged from the Khrushchëv reforms to the end of the Soviet era, in visual art it was not. The centuries-old tradition of Islamic art in Central Asia was fundamentally nonfigurative and reference to it could be considered a positive development of the forms of "national art." Architectural science suggested that modernist architects examine the possibilities of local tradition when they needed to develop a space artistically without the use of figurative images. "Rather than using architectural and decorative means borrowed from the arsenal of hostile abstract art, it is much more expedient to employ the models of national decoration," wrote Viktor Dmitriev and Vladimir Nil'sen.[19] Lazar' Rempel' went further: "For Tashkent, as for Central Asia as a whole, we do not want a pastiche in eastern style but an architecture that is totally modern, that uses contemporary methods to interpret the best planning, structural and spatial principles of local architecture, especially of folk or vernacular design. Of course, national motifs of traditional decoration can significantly liven up contemporary architectural forms. We need fresh, original motifs for relief terra-cotta, tiles, mosaic and other types of traditional national decoration."[20]

In a building as ideologically important as the Lenin Museum, the architects could not avoid large-format works typical of Soviet monumental art. As already noted, in the Large Hall visitors were greeted by a six-meter vertical statue of Lenin by Nikolai Tomskii. Behind the sculpture was a mosaic panel (Vladimir Zamkov and V. Ionin), which was a conventional depiction of the revolutionary past and the contemporary labor of Soviet Uzbekistan's collective farm workers, workers and intelligentsia. This panel developed the theme of the building-exhibit and was a foretaste of the exhibition, which comprised the same subjects. Its integration into the display was underlined by the lack of clear borders: the panel seemed to envelop the floors of the hall and continued onto the walls of the exhibition spaces.

After the Collapse of the USSR

After the collapse of the USSR the Lenin Museum was transformed almost unchanged into the State Museum of the History of Uzbekistan. The sculpture of Lenin was removed from the hall, as was the mosaic panel that showed the achievements of Leninism. However, soon the artist Bakhodyr Dzhalalov re-established the hall's original sacred meanings by creating the fresco *Beneath the Vault of Eternity* for the frontal wall. It was commissioned by the government of Uzbekistan in 1995. The first sketch of the fresco that Dzhalalov made showed the most important figures in Central Asian history. Timur featured in the lower part, and below him the artist Kamal ud-Din Behzad, the poet Alisher Navoi, the astronomer Mirzo Ulugbek, the founder of the Great Mongol dynasty and chronicler Babur, and many other well-known figures from medieval Central Asia. Above Timur's head, in the geometrical center of the composition, was the Quran. In the upper part were objects from the pre-Islamic civilization of Central Asia: artifacts from Dalverzin Tepe and Nisa; ancient nomadic, Hindu and Zoroastrian cosmogonic symbols and so on. The fresco was designed along a vertical chronological axis: first came ancient cosmogony, then pre-Islamic civilizations, then the Quran, the age of Timur and the Timurids. The same vertical axis included the banner of Timur's state, a light blue flag with three white circles. Seven years later the artist confirmed the chronological principle of his composition, "a cosmic object in the form of an hourglass floating in time and space."[21] The sketch of the fresco was accepted by the authorities after one element was changed. In the final version, president of Uzbekistan Is-

19 V. M. Dmitriev and V. A. Nil'sen, "O napravlennosti v sovremennoi arkhitekture Uzbekistana [On the Direction of Uzbekistan's Contemporary Architecture]," *Obshchestvennye nauki v Uzbekistane* [*Social Sciences in Uzbekistan*], no. 12, 1962, 19.

20 Lazar' Rempel', "Plastika, dekor i novyi stil' [Plasticity, Décor and the New Style]," in *Iskusstvo Srednego Vostoka* [*Art of the Middle East*] (Moscow: Sovetskii khudozhnik, 1978), 261.

21 Bakhodyr Dzhalalov, *Pod svodom vechnosti* [*Beneath the Vault of Eternity*] (Tashkent, 2002), 26.

lam Karimov appeared in place of Timur's banner at the point of the golden ratio. In front of him was a small sphere, the Independence Monument. However, seven years after the grand inauguration of the fresco it was erased by presidential decree and replaced by a gold-framed realistic landscape.

Regardless of the modifications, the building's original façades are relatively well preserved, and it is one of the most important buildings of the 1960s to 1980s in Tashkent, representing a key stage of its evolution in the search for the conjugation of modernist language and historical heritage.

ARCHITECT EVGENII ROZANOV

Place and year of birth:
Moscow, 1925

Place and year of death:
Moscow, 2006

Education:
1945–1951, Moscow Architectural Institute

Evgenii Rozanov was one of the most awarded Soviet and Russian architects. He graduated in 1951 from Moscow Architectural Institute. He worked at the Central Scientific Research and Experimental Project Institute for Entertainment and Sport Facilities from its foundation in 1964 until 1985. He designed numerous buildings in various cities of the USSR, and in Tashkent, as well as designing the Lenin Museum, he led the architectural team that designed the complex on Lenin Square and the Peoples' Friendship Palace. He was awarded the state prizes of Uzbekistan and the USSR a number of times and received the titles Honored Architect of the RSFSR (1977) and People's Architect of the USSR (1983). From 1985 to 1993 he worked as First Deputy Chairman and then Chairman of the State Committee for Civil Engineering and Architecture of Gosstroi USSR (after 1991, Gosstroi Russia). He was a Corresponding Member (1979) and then a Member (1983) of the Academy of Arts of the USSR. He was the Academic Secretary of the Architecture Department of the Academy of Arts of the USSR (1988–2002; after 1991, Academy of Arts of the Russian Federation) and the Vice-President of the Academy of Arts of the Russian Federation (1997–2006). He was a Member of the Russian Academy of Architecture (1992) and President of the International Academy of Architecture.

INSTITUTIONAL FRAMEWORK

Central Scientific Research and Experimental Project Institute for Entertainment and Sport Facilities (TsNIIEP)

PRIORITIES

The Central Scientific Research and Experimental Project Institute for Entertainment and Sport Facilities was created in 1964. The profile of this Moscow institution, which was focused on sport and entertainment, did not initially include the design of administrative buildings. Nevertheless, it was a team from this institute that took part in the competition for the development of Lenin Square in Tashkent and received this important commission. It was followed by two more projects: in 1968 the institute was entrusted with designing the Lenin Museum, and in 1970 the Peoples' Friendship Palace.

Basement floor plan
Original condition

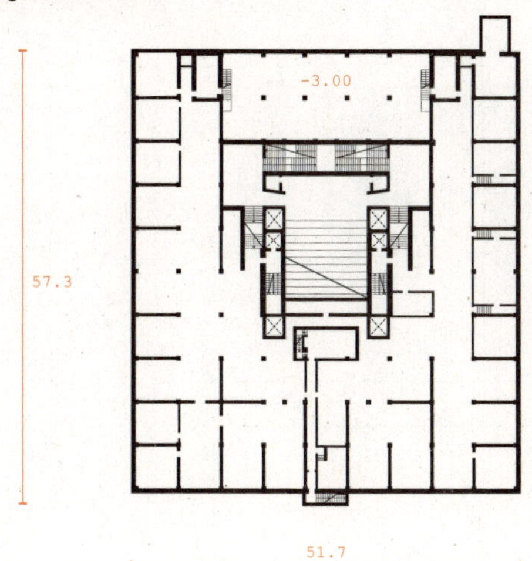

1st floor plan
Original condition

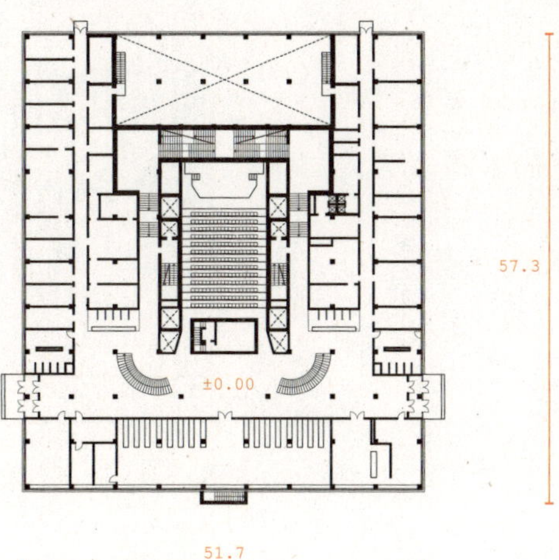

2nd floor plan
Original condition

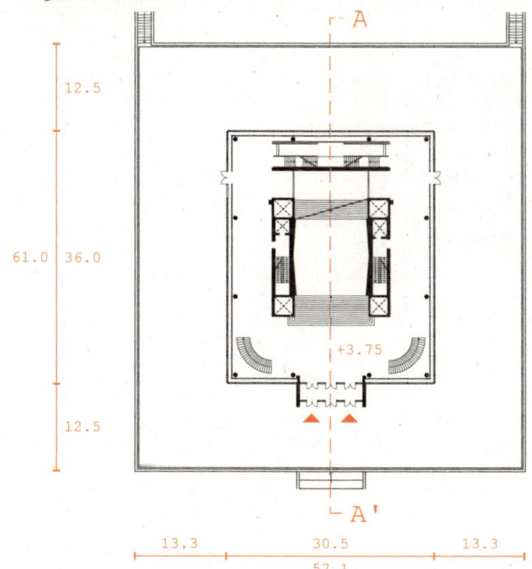

3rd floor plan
Original condition

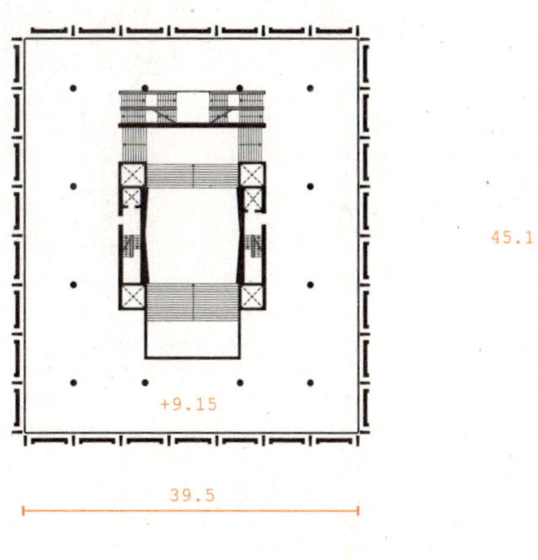

4th floor plan
Original condition

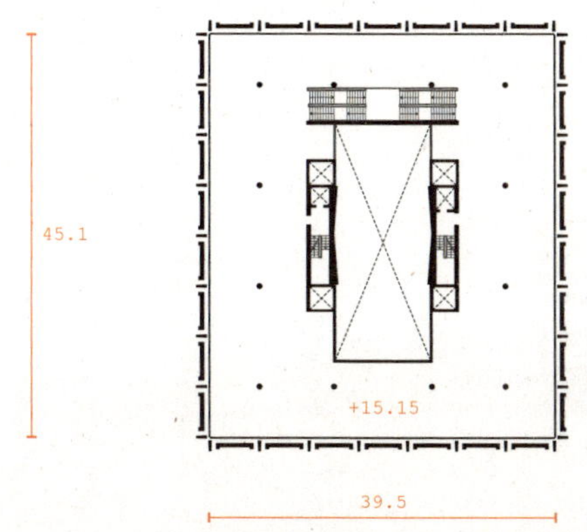

Roof plan
Original condition

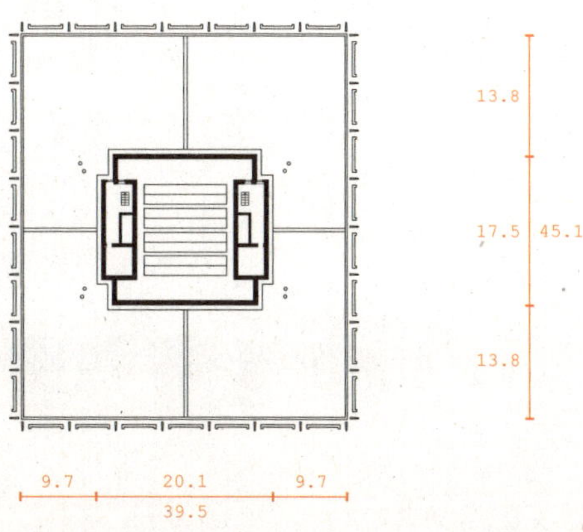

0 5 10m

North-east elevation
Original condition

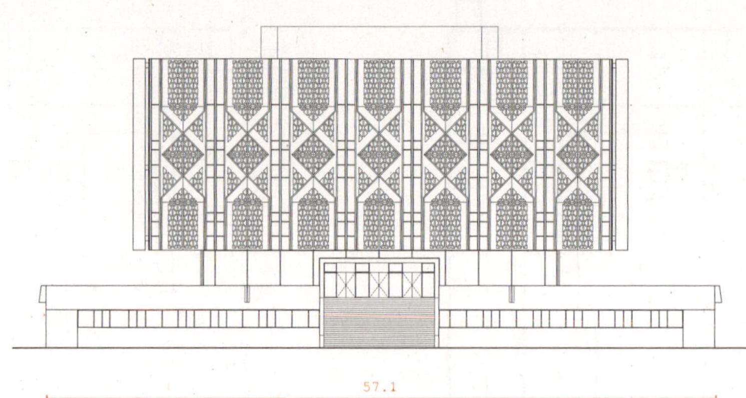

South-west elevation
Original condition

Perspective view
Original condition

North-west elevation
Original condition

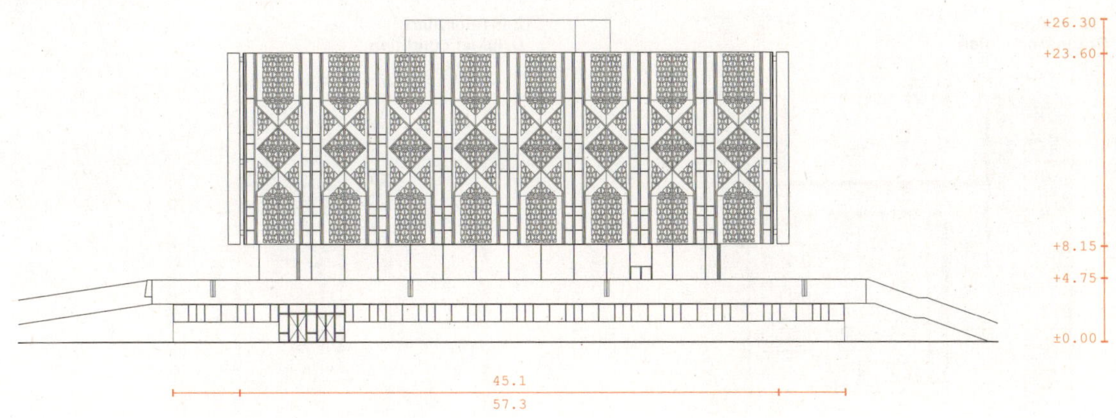

South-east elevation
Original condition

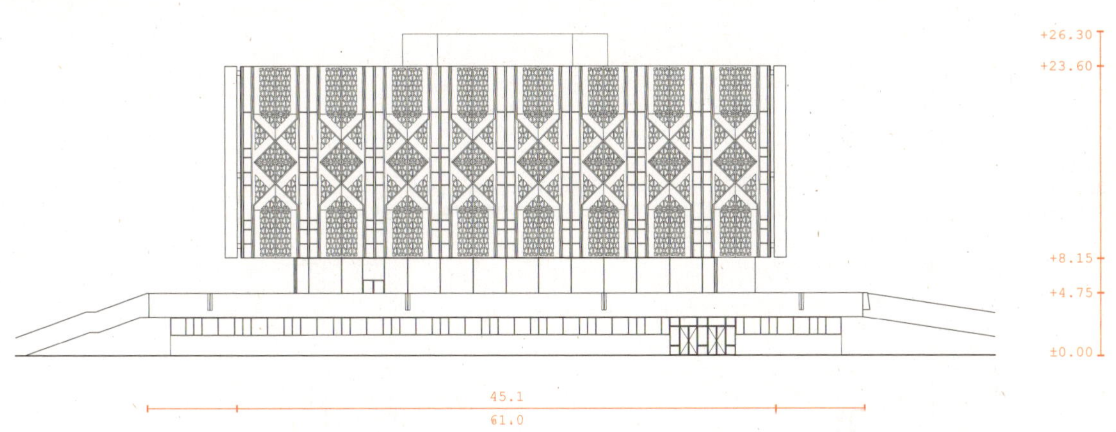

Longitudinal section AA'
Original condition

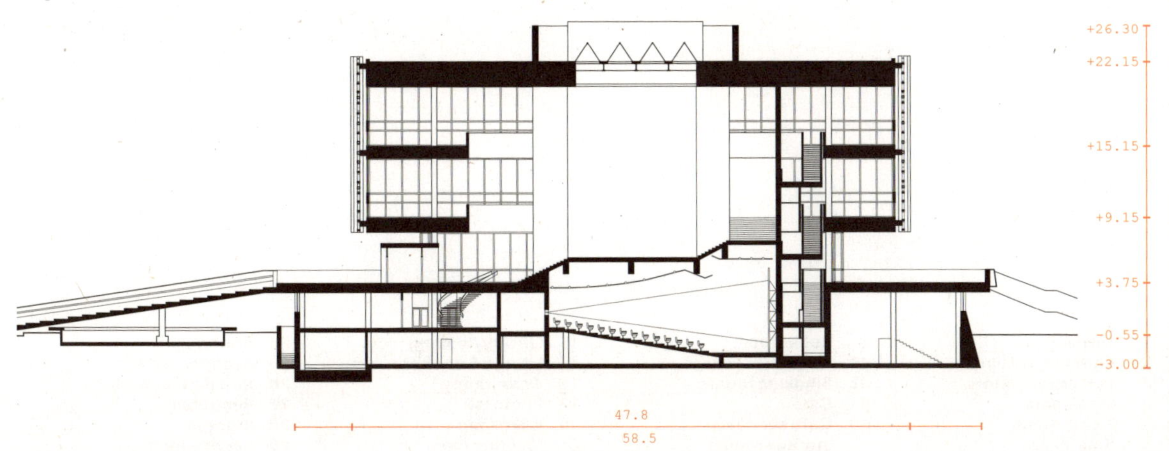

1970

1st floor plan
Original condition

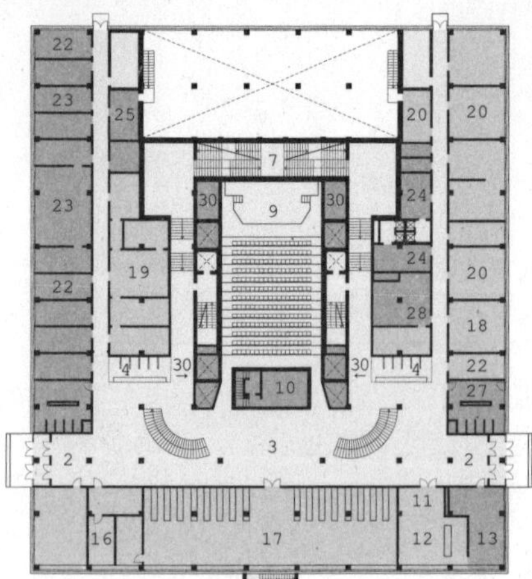

2nd floor plan
Original condition

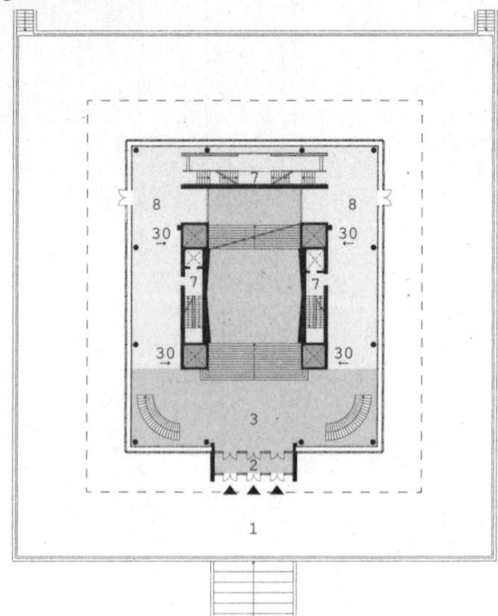

3rd floor plan
Original condition

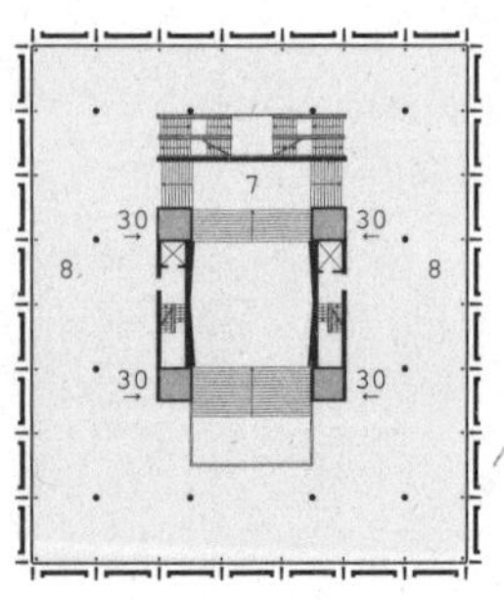

4th floor plan
Original condition

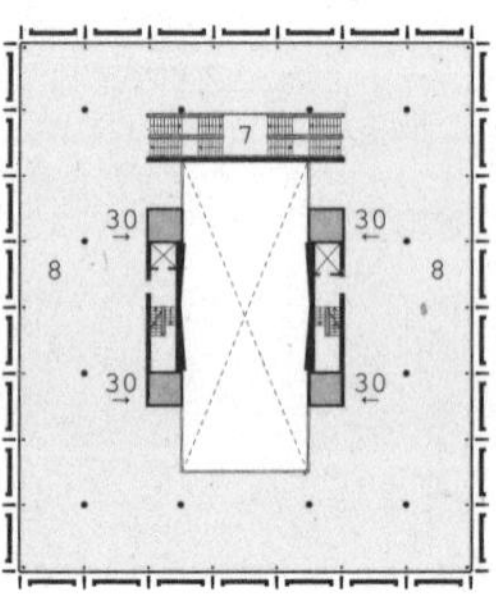

1	Terrace
2	Entrance vestibule
3	Vestibule, visitors
4	Cloakroom
5	Ticket office
6	Kids' Area
7	Circulation, visitors
8	Exhibition hall
9	Auditorium
10	Projection room
11	Smoking room
12	Café
13	Café service, storage rooms
14	Archive
15	Exhibit and art storage
16	Library Reading room
17	Library & book storage
18	Typography
19	Photo lab
20	Workshop
21	Meeting room
22	Museum staff offices
23	Administration
24	Staff room
25	Security room
26	Circulation, workers
27	Restroom
28	Storage
29	Service room
30	Technical area

2022

1st floor plan
Current condition

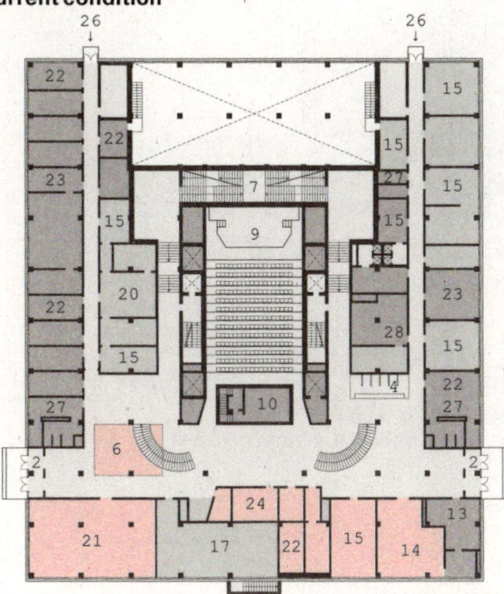

2nd floor plan
Current condition

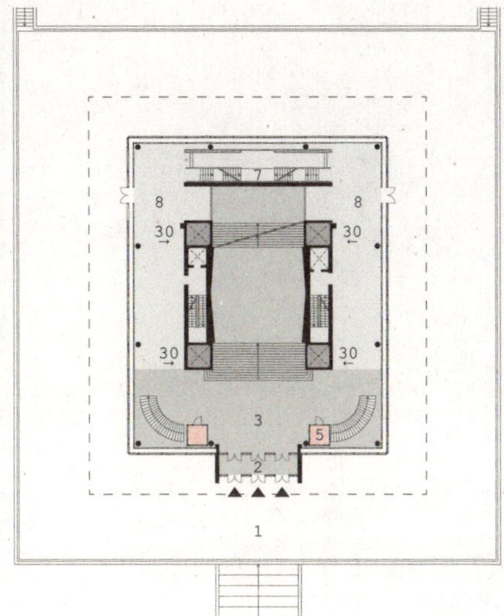

3rd floor plan
Current condition

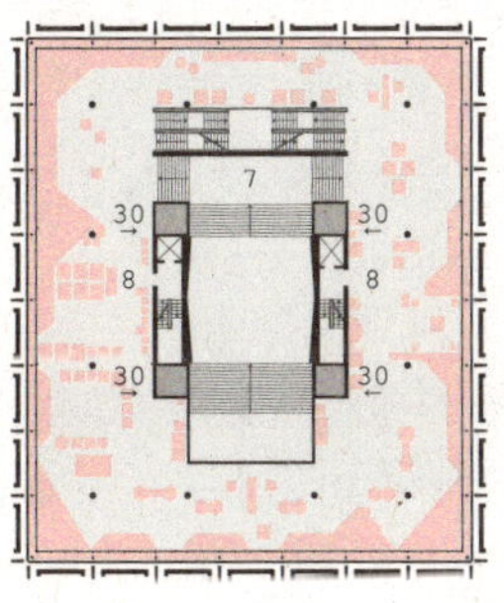

4th floor plan
Current condition

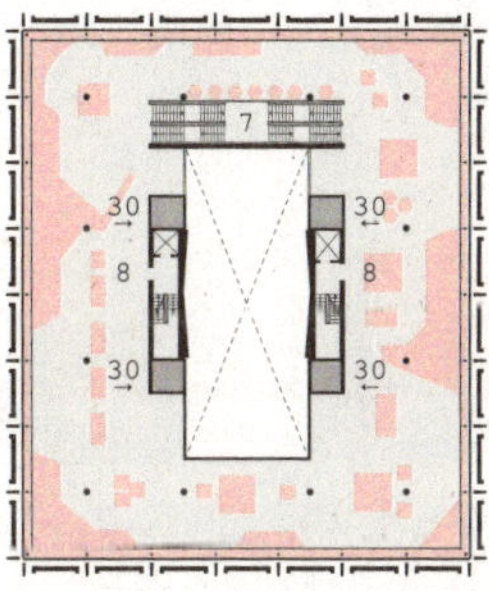

- Exhibition/lecture hall
- Public/workshop
- Administrative/service and technical
- Change of function

0 5 10m

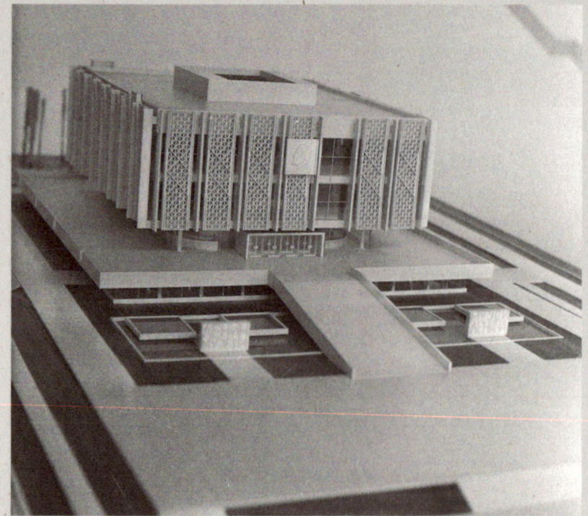

Model of the 1969 design proposal for the Lenin Museum

View of the north façade of the Lenin Museum, 1970s

Steel structure of the Lenin Museum

Lenin Museum site toward completion of construction

Views of the exhibition in the Lenin Museum, 1970s

Detail of the façade, 1977

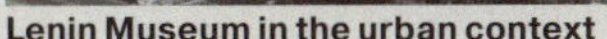

Lenin Museum in the urban context

View of the south-west façade, 2023

View of the south-east façade, main entrance, 2021

North-west corner of the building, view of the House of Publishers, 2023

North-west façade, 2023

Elevated terrace on the entrance floor, 2021

Skylight of the central atrium, 2022

View of the central atrium

Suspended staircase connecting the first and second floors, 2021

Entrance hall, 2021

Conference room located on the first floor, 2022

Exhibition view on the second floor, 2021

Exhibition on the third floor, 2022

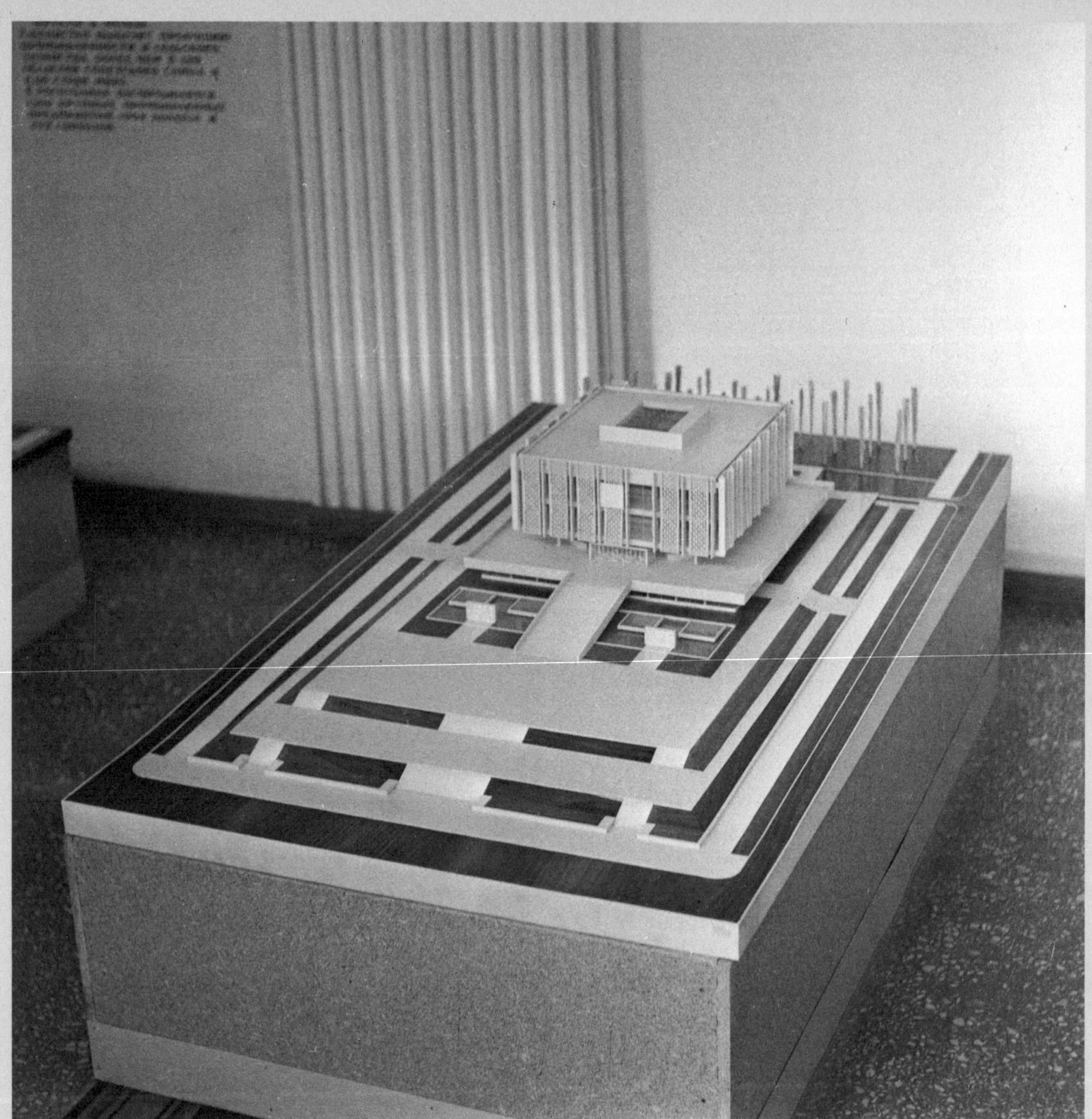

Model of the 1969 design proposal for the Lenin Museum

Lenin Museum, façade drawing, 1968

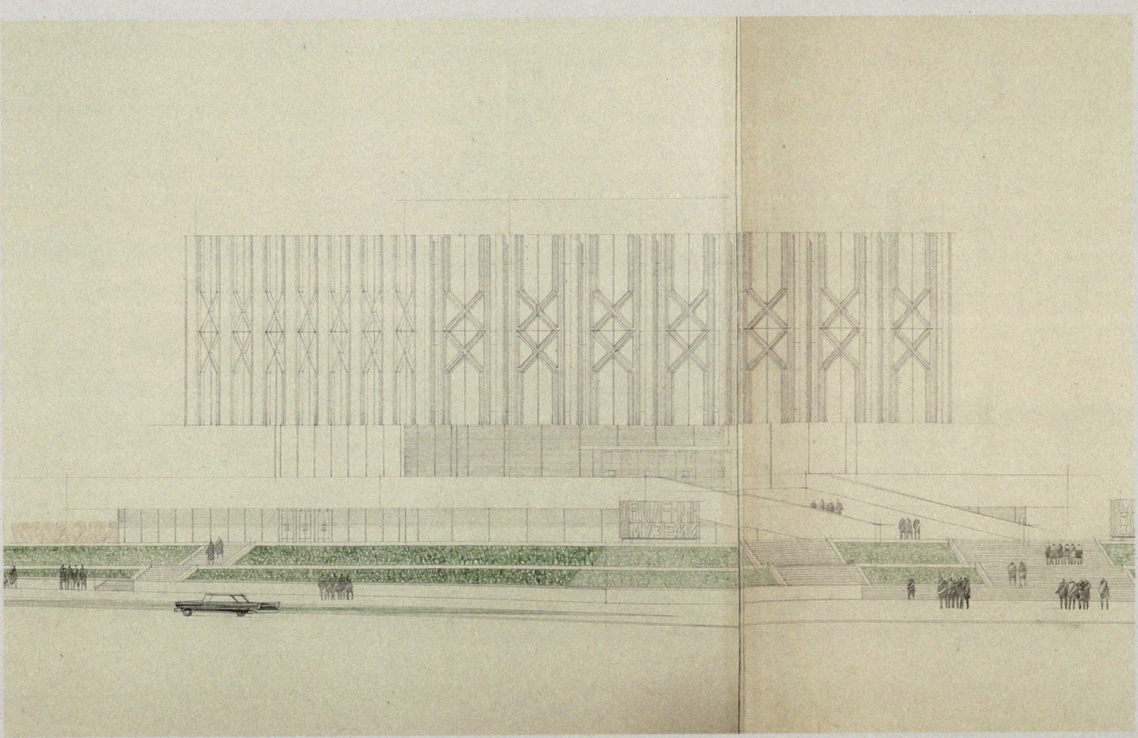

Lenin Museum, façade drawing, 1968

Atrium, design proposal drawing

Atrium, design proposal drawing

Exhibition view, design proposal collage

Exhibition view, design proposal collage

Exhibition view, design proposal collage

	Tashkent	Ul'ianovsk	Central Lenin Museum, Moscow	Central Lenin Museum, Moscow	Central Lenin Museum, Moscow
	Lenin's 100th birthday		Competition Round 1 17 projects submitted in total [closed competition]	Competition Round 2 13 projects submitted in total [closed competition] One winner selected	Competition Open Round 178 projects submitted in total [open competition] Joint first-second prizes awarded to three teams
	1970	1970	1970	1971	1972
Lenin statue in the atrium					
Monumental art					
Exhibition view					
General view					
Atrium section					
Plan 	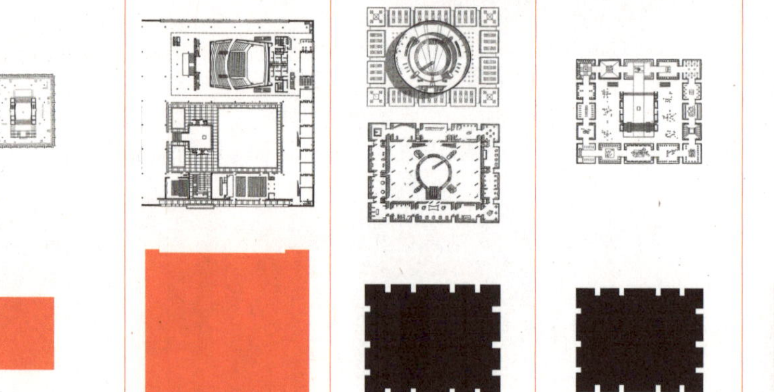				

1870	Birth of V.I. Lenin
1917	October Revolution
1924	Death of V.I. Lenin
1930	Opening of Lenin Mausoleum in Moscow
1936	Opening of the Central Lenin Museum in Moscow

Completion Dates of Pre-modernist Lenin Museums

1937	Leningrad
1938	Kyiv
1938	Tbilisi
1941	Ul'ianovsk
1950	Lviv
1960	Baku

Kyiv	Frunze (Bishkek)	Kazan'	Gorki Leninskie	Krasnoyarsk	Samara (Kuibyshev)
			70th anniversary of the October Revolution		Independence of Uzbekistan (1991)
1982	1984	1987	1987	1987	1989

Exterior perspective view, main façade, original condition

Façade system
Axonometric diagram

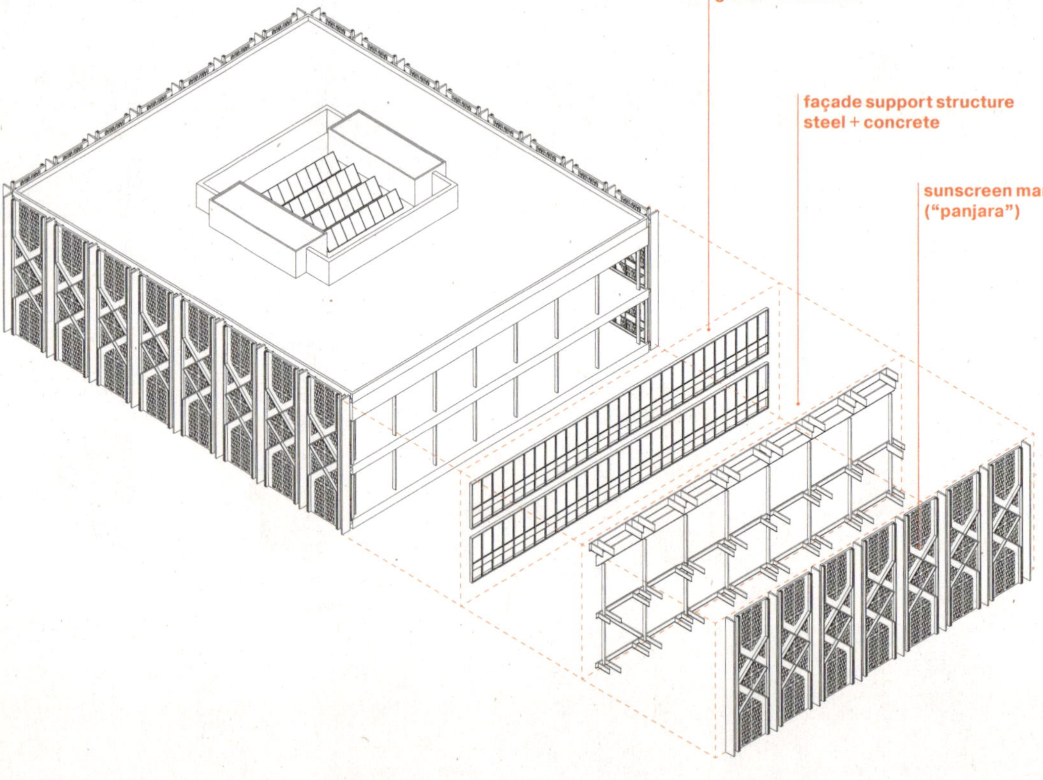

façade glazing
glass + aluminum

façade support structure
steel + concrete

sunscreen marble panels
("panjara")

Façade anchoring system
Axonometric scheme

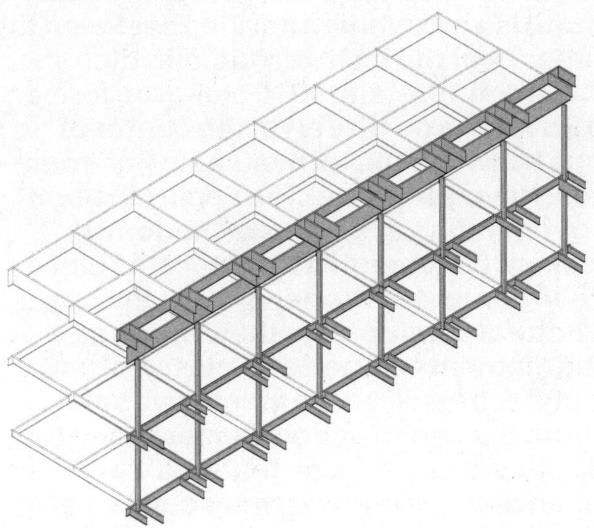

Sunscreen façade panel
Elevation

Sunscreen façade panels, identification of modules
Axonometric scheme

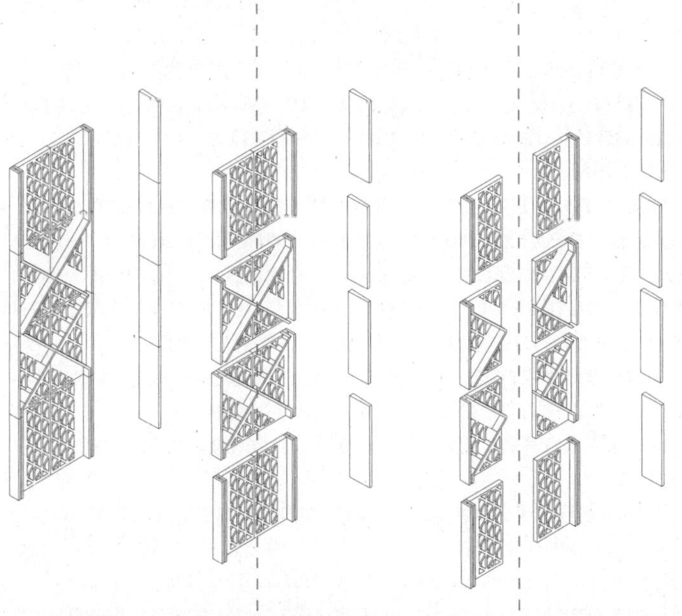

Sunscreen façade panel
Section showing the panel anchoring detail to the steel structure

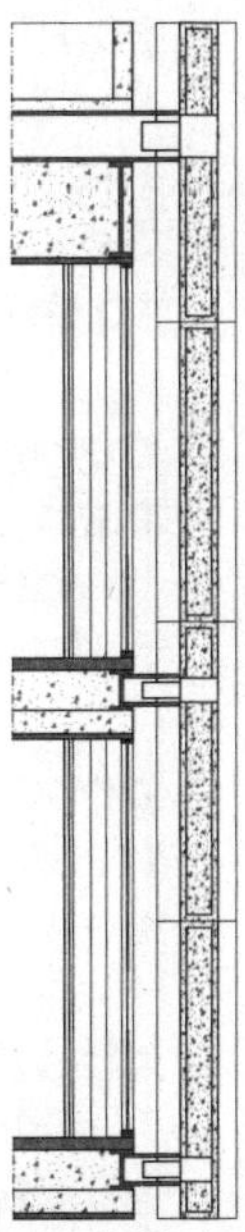

HIGHLIGHTS

The Lenin Museum (since 1992 the State Museum of the History of Uzbekistan) is an exhibition pavilion designed to celebrate the centenary of the birth of Vladimir Il'ich Lenin. It was built between 1968 and 1970 along the former Lenin Street (now Buyuk Turon Street) in the center of Tashkent, as a hinge between the former Lenin (Independence) and Theater (Navoi) squares. The Lenin Museum is one of the most outstanding examples of modernist architecture in Tashkent because of its impeccable placement within the urban context of the new part of the city and its pure architectural concept, synthesizing in an original manner the elements of modern, classical and traditional architecture, as well as the innovative solutions adopted for both the construction elements and the façade. Moreover, since most of these features were then applied to other Lenin museums in the wider context of the USSR, the Lenin Museum proved to be a prototype, as well as an icon symbolizing Tashkent's status as capital.

The museum is now included in the list of protected buildings of Uzbekistan according to Decision No. 846 of the Cabinet of Ministers, October 4, 2019.

Several features make it a building of international relevance:

The authorship of renowned architect Evgenii Rozanov, one of the leading architects at Moscow's Central Scientific Research and Experimental Project Institute for Entertainment and Sport Facilities (TsNIIEP), whose projects were crucial in defining unique building types for Soviet cultural and leisure institutions that are specific to the former USSR.

The primary role the building plays in the urban design of the area next to the former Lenin Square, and, in turn, the impact of the urban position on its architectural layout: an ornamental cube that is nearly identical from all sides and visually permeable toward/from the city.

The spatial typology—a pure volume seemingly suspended, floating over a podium, with a central space inside it, like the naos of an ancient temple, protecting the central statue.

The architectural language, combining modernism, classicism and local tradition: classical as a result of the building's central composition and symmetry; modernist due to the effect of suspension provided by the recessed glass façade at the entrance level; addressing tradition through prefabricated panjara panels on the façade.

Temporal primacy, along with the complex in Ul'ianovsk (1969–1974), among the museums dedicated to

Lenin in the USSR, which is testimony to Tashkent's importance among other capitals of the Soviet Union.

Temporal primacy in relation to other modernist museums in Tashkent (e.g. the State Museum of Arts and the Union of Artists Exhibition Hall) that were built slightly later than the Lenin Museum. These museums adopted very similar spatial solutions.

The innovative mixed structure of the building in steel and reinforced concrete was defined in response to geological and seismic conditions, and because of the short time available for its construction.[1] All main structural elements above ground are in steel, while some parts were built with prefabricated units. Among them, "for the first time in construction practice, prefabricated reinforced concrete elements were used to produce sunshades" suspended from the roof slab on the four sides of the volume. A special feature of the building is the water-filled roof, made to reduce the heat of solar radiation, which is extremely high in Tashkent.[2] A 1970 article in the journal *Stroitel'stvo i arkhitektura Uzbekistana* (*Construction and Architecture of Uzbekistan*) also praises the museum's air-conditioning and climate system as pioneering and innovative for the use of the radiant slab.

STATE OF REPAIR
SCORE:

● 3 – The building shows localized deterioration patterns which do not affect its stability

Protection status:	The building is listed according to Decision No. 846 of the Cabinet of Ministers, October 4, 2019.
Main criticalities:	The main problems are related to the marble cladding of the façade. The obsolescence of the mechanical, electrical and plumbing systems Is a critical issue for the museum.
Possible risks:	A risk is the deterioration of the building due to lack of maintenance and deterioration of the collection in relation to the lack of thermal control.

INTEGRITY
SCORE:

● Exterior: 4 – The building has retained all the elements necessary to express its significance and is in a good state of repair

1 Evgenii Rozanov, Vladimir Krichevskii, T. Melik-Arakelian, "Muzei V.I. Lenina v Tashkente [The Lenin Museum in Tashkent]," *Stroitel'stvo i arkhitektura Uzbekistana* [*Construction and Architecture of Uzbekistan*], no. 4, 1970, 28–29.

2 Ibid., 30.

Interior: 2 – Transformations to the building and its surroundings have caused the loss of some of the elements necessary to express its significance

A distinction must be made between the building as a whole and the interiors.

Despite a few changes, the building and its façade were able to maintain their main features and intended architectural concept.

In contrast, much of the interior artistic apparatus has been lost as a result of the interventions following the fall of the Soviet Union and the transformation of the exhibition space to accommodate the State Museum of the History of Uzbekistan in 1992.

Originally, the permanent museum exhibition was on the third and fourth floors and was organized in chronological order, implying a fixed direction for the museum narrative. As described in Boris Chukhovich's text (pp. 544–551), the Tashkent archives had no original objects or manuscripts relating to Lenin's life because he had never visited Central Asia. For this reason, Chukhovich defined this museum as "a laboratory of the new museography," which focused on demonstrating "Lenin's precepts brought to life in Uzbekistan and all of the republics of the Soviet East" (from the speech of Sharaf Rashidov, First Secretary of the Communist Party of Uzbekistan, at the opening of the museum).

An essential feature of the original design was its clear distinction from architecture. Light vitrines functioned as theatrical and educational devices that did not obstruct the visibility of the main exhibit, the building. This important quality has been compromised by later transformations. The lightness and transparency of the exhibition installations, as well as the presence of natural light and views toward the city in the gallery space, have been lost. Newly added interior walls block the views toward the façade and embed a dense collection of objects and texts inside rather conventional displays, canceling the distinction between the building and the exhibition design.

The wooden decoration inside the building was carved by folk craftspeople of Uzbekistan and is relatively well preserved. The door panels of the main entrance were executed by a master from Kokand, K. Khaidarov, while master N. Ibragimov carved the wooden elements for the Large Hall and craftsmen A. Shakirov and E. Nuraliev worked on the partition walls in ornamental wood.

In the central atrium, a monument to Lenin by Nikolai Tomskii and the large mosaic *We Are Building Communism* by V. Zamkov and V. Ionin were removed in 1992 when the museum became the State Museum of the History of Uzbekistan. A fresco by Bakhodyr Dzhalalov, *Beneath the Vault of Eternity*, which featured numerous historical figures from Central Asia's past, as well as President Karimov, was installed in place of the mosaic in 1995 and then removed in 2008.

Some of the original decorative elements, such as the wooden doors and the ganch wall along the stair, have been preserved.

AUTHENTICITY SCORE:

- Exterior: 4 – Only minor repairs and conservation activities have been carried out on the building
- Interior: 2 – The building has been subjected to localized but significant modifications

Although several changes have occurred since its construction, the building retains a good level of authenticity. In particular, the exterior appearance of the building is very coherent with the original design, notwithstanding a general upgrade of the building in 2000.

A few changes are visible from the outside. A heavy architrave has been added above the entrance volume with wooden doors. It physically anchors the main volume, which originally floated above the entrance block. Another change is the replacement of the aluminum cladding of the underside of the main volume with alucobond panels and the cladding of the technical volume on the roof with alucobond.

There are two fundamental changes inside the building. The first concerns the addition of false interior walls that prevent access to the original façade, blocking out all the natural light.

The second change concerns the central atrium. After the demise of the USSR, the Lenin statue was removed, and the original mosaic was covered by a fresco (by Bakhodyr Dzhalalov) in 1995. In 2002, the fresco was removed and replaced with the painting that is present today.

There were additional changes to the first-floor layout, modifying the configuration of the former library area, which in turn has affected the windows.

The newly added exhibition partition blocks the view toward the central atrium from the gallery space on the fourth floor.

All ceilings have been re-clad with Armstrong panels, replacing the original aluminum panels and the lighting elements.

1970

2022

Main entrance of the Lenin Museum after the inauguration, 1970

Main entrance of the State Museum of the History of Uzbekistan, 2022

Museum atrium, 1970

Museum atrium, 2022

1970s	2022
 Exhibition view, 1970s	 Exhibition view, 2022
 Exhibition view and first-floor interior, 1970s	 Exhibition view and first-floor interior, 2022

LEVEL 1 – MAXIMUM LEVEL OF INTEREST
(No transformations allowed; conservation activities required)

URBAN LEVEL
No modifications are allowed within the street block. The perimeter of the block must not be transformed. The street grid inside the block must not be changed. No new building is possible inside the street block.

ARCHITECTURAL LEVEL
EXTERIOR
All the external stone-clad and glazed volumes of the original façade must be integrally preserved. In particular:

- the podium;
- the volume hosting the museum.

INTERIOR
The original spatial relationship between the exhibition galleries and the full-height central atrium must be preserved.

All the distribution architectural elements (like staircases) must be preserved.

DETAIL LEVEL
EXTERIOR
The elements characteristic of the exterior of the building must not be changed. In particular:

- the window frames and the main door of the entrance floor, as well as the stone portal around the door;
- the stone-clad sunshade panels;
- the aluminum and glass façade behind the sunshade panels.

INTERIOR
The skylight in the center of the volume must be carefully preserved.

LEVEL 2 – MEDIUM LEVEL OF INTEREST
(Elements included in the second level can be moderately transformed following approval by a designated committee[1])

1 An international committee of heritage preservation experts to be appointed.

URBAN LEVEL

For the urban blocks adjacent to the Lenin Museum, any volumetric modification of existing buildings and any new construction may only be carried out after approval by the designated committee.

ARCHITECTURAL LEVEL
INTERIOR

Any internal division of exhibition gallery spaces must be subject to approval by the designated committee.

DETAIL LEVEL
EXTERIOR

The alucobond cladding of the technical volume over the roof can be replaced with the approval of the designated committee.

INTERIOR

The architectural layout consisting of the main atrium with skylight and the staircases must be strictly protected. Any changes to the decorations and furniture must be submitted to the designated committee for approval.

HIDDEN MODERNIST FEATURES

The visual connection between the interior and the street through the transparent façade and the stone brise-soleil was the key aspect of the original architectural concept. This visual connection is now blocked by the false walls surrounding the perimeter of the exhibition spaces on the third and fourth floors. Restoration work aiming to reinstate the original visual connection to the exterior is strongly recommended.

Also, the aluminum ceiling underneath the floating volume of the galleries should be restored and remain visible, if still in place.

Lenin Museum at night, 1970s

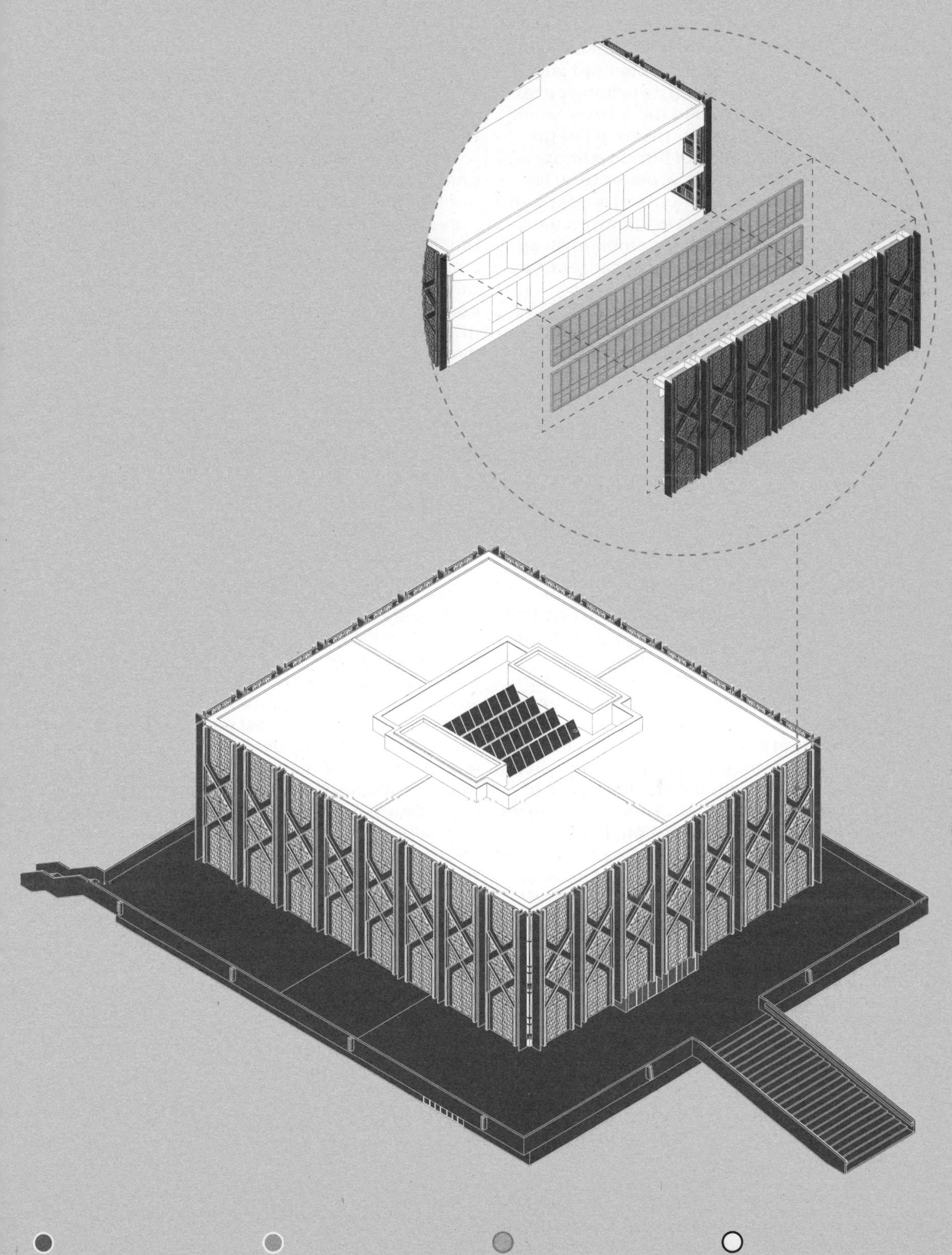

Preservation Level 1
Maximum Level of Interest
Materials and elements to be preserved

Preservation Level 2
Medium Level of Interest
Materials and elements to be preserved

Hidden Modernist Features
Materials and elements to be preserved

Transformation allowed

Preservation Strategy

The relevance of the former Lenin Museum (State Museum of the History of Uzbekistan) lies both in its elegant architectural concept and in its placement within Tashkent's urban context. The museum is located along the former Lenin Street (Buyuk Turon Street), the heart of the "new city" and the location of the most important governmental buildings. Its architectural language blends together elements of modern and traditional architecture in an original manner, and its spatial organization, resembling an ancient temple, conveys a degree of sacredness to the building.

Inaugurated over fifty years ago (1970), the building has largely retained its original features, although some minor or reversible changes have occurred. The most significant change concerns the loss of the transparency of the façade. The interventions in 2000 and the renewed exhibition design resulted in the installation of opaque panels along the internal perimeter of the building, completely blocking the view toward the outside, as well as incoming and outgoing light. The original transparency, a clear tribute to the Modern Movement, was essential to the overall significance of the museum on a conceptual and architectural level. The preservation strategy thus aims to reinstate this currently hidden feature, re-establishing visual connections and original lighting.

To this end, the proposed strategy encompasses four main preservation actions, summarized below.

The first action deals with the reinstatement of the lost transparency of the building envelope. The opaque panels positioned on the inside of the glazing must be removed. This operation entails the redesign of the exhibition. Furthermore, due to aging, the existing glazing is not in good condition: dirt and dust have collected on the windows, gaskets are in disrepair and several glass panels are cracked. To address this issue, two different options are proposed:

- Option 1
  The existing glass panels could be retained, replacing only the cracked and damaged ones. The new panels should have the same visual impact as the originals (color, size thickness). In this case, in order to improve the thermal performance of the envelope, additional, detached glazing should be added on the interior side, next to the existing glazing.
- Option 2
  All of the existing glass panels and frames could be replaced. The new frames should be thicker than the originals in order to contain double glazing, which will improve the thermal performance of the building.

A second action involves the repair of the façade's marble cladding, which is cracked and partly missing. Any broken tiles should be replaced using new tiles of the same material, size and color. Cracked tiles will be repaired using marble glue to give a homogeneous appearance to the whole.

The thin diagonal elements on the panjara panels are only clad on the front side, while the upper and lower sides are plastered, using a gray shade that matches the general coloring of the façades. Due to aging and weather exposure, the plaster is now starting to peel off, exposing the joints between the prefabricated concrete panels and the marble tiles. This situation is potentially dangerous and should be fixed by adding a new layer of plaster.

Some of the façade's prefabricated panels are missing the top flashing and are therefore exposed to rainwater. To avoid future damage, new flashing should be installed where needed.

Finally, all façades will be cleaned in order to remove deposits and discoloration. The result of the cleaning should approximate the original color of the building.

The third proposed action concerns general maintenance and local repairs, both on the inside and outside of the building. Particular attention should be paid to the full-height atrium, the main stair system and the central skylight, which is in a poor state of repair. The supporting metal structure is widely oxidized and, as a consequence, the glass panels have been stained by rainwater carrying rust particles. To repair the metal structure, rust will need to be mechanically removed. It is advisable to perform a thorough inspection in order to detect any relevant reduction in the section of metal elements. If no criticalities are identified, it is possible to proceed by applying a proper anti-rust oil to the entire supporting structure. Finally, the metal elements can be varnished. The glass panels can be removed in order to be cleaned from dust deposits and stains and will be put back in place afterward. While performing these operations it is advisable to maintain and upgrade the roof's waterproofing layer.

Finally, as highlighted by the preliminary monitoring of humidity and temperature parameters, the building would benefit from a general upgrade of the mechanical, electrical and plumbing systems, which will guarantee a better indoor climate. This fourth action will improve both the preservation of exhibited items and the experience of museum visitors.

State Museum of the History of Uzbekistan, exhibition floor view, with façade transparency reinstated
Strategy visualization

State Museum of the History of Uzbekistan, exterior view of the café on the podium
Strategy visualization

Adaptation Strategy

The State Museum of the History of Uzbekistan is a hub for scholarship and inspiration, but also, and quite fundamentally, it is an institution that inquires into how history is interpreted and shown. It shapes awareness about historical interpretations of past events and helps visitors to make personal, meaningful connections between history and the present.

Contemporary historical museums are shifting away from big linear narratives toward a multiplicity of "histories" or "stories" that include voices previously denied the opportunity to speak. Documents and archives have become important tools and concepts around which interpretations of the past are built.

The territory of today's Uzbekistan has a long and complex past, with many important stories still to be uncovered. We propose rethinking the exhibition strategy at the State Museum of the History of Uzbekistan, moving away from a permanent exhibition structured according to a single thread (from prehistory to the present) toward a more open-ended and pluralist concept of narration of the past: three or four temporary thematic exhibitions per year (built around materials from state and private archives in Tashkent) that research, interpret and expose different histories of Tashkent and Uzbekistan.

With such a setup, the two 1,300-square-meter floors of the museum (third and fourth) are deemed sufficient to accommodate the exhibition program, while the first and second floors can be fully focused on public amenities and education. The first floor would be primarily dedicated to education. Its redesign aims to unify the space, making it more clear, ordered and transparent. The second floor, corresponding to the main entrance, will include the information desk, ticket office, a welcome area, a bookshop and a spacious café spilling out onto a shaded terrace. The design of these areas would involve subdued tones, but would be clearly contemporary and distinct from the original architecture of the building.

The exhibition space will become more open and transparent toward both the city (through the opening of the original façade) and the central atrium. An upgrade of the façade system, either by inserting the profile for double glazing or by installing a second layer of glass on the interior, will ensure good performance in terms of climate. A system of retractable curtains will provide additional screening against the sun.

A flexible system of lighting will be installed, which will enable shifting to or combining ambient or spot lighting.

The mechanical, electrical and plumbing systems will undergo a substantial upgrade to match contemporary museum standards.

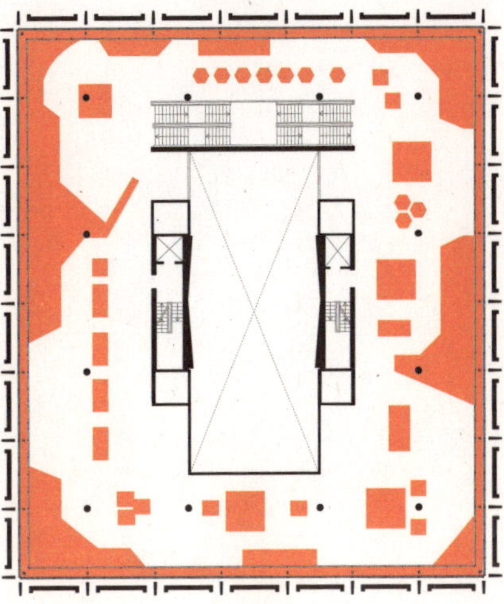

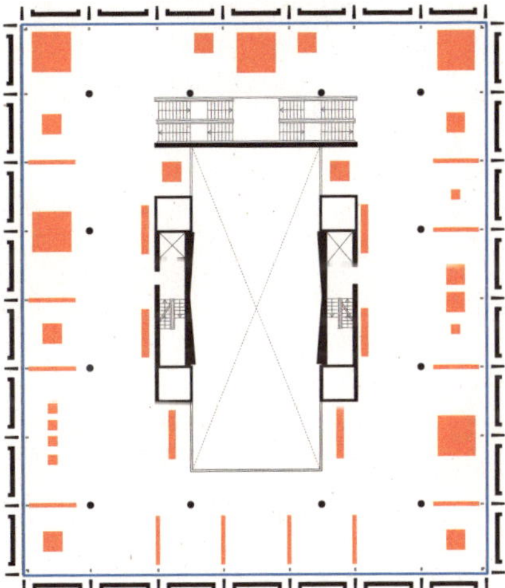

Top: Current exhibition floor plan
Bottom: Strategy proposal to open up the plan and clear the façade

Exhibition Hall of the Union of Artists

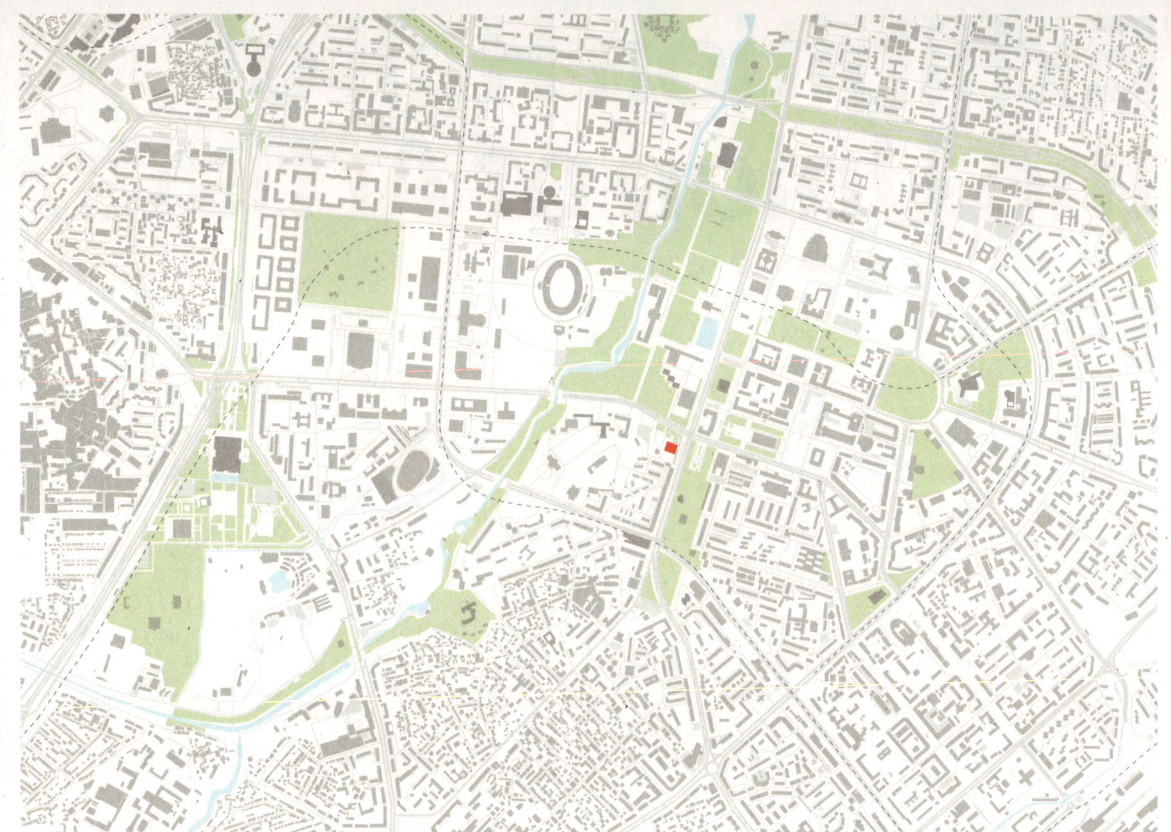

Building position and address: 40 Sharaf Rashidov Avenue, Tashkent

0 0.5 1km

Historically, the territory on which the Union of Artists Exhibition Hall was constructed adjoined the Tashkent fortress, erected immediately after the taking of Tashkent and Turkestan by the Russian Empire. For a long time, this territory was a park zone. Free space was required around the fortress in order to better defend it in case of military incidents. In the Soviet period buildings appeared here, but they were much less dense than in neighboring districts. After the 1966 earthquake they were demolished as part of an ambitious plan to rebuild the center of Tashkent, designed by the Tashgiprogor Institute. Based on the intersection of two important axes, Lenin Avenue (Sharaf Rashidov Avenue, which joins the boulevard) and Uzbekistanskaia Street (Islam Karimov Street), and also visible from Theater Square, the site of the Exhibition Hall was intended to become a transit accent.

Main dimensions of the Exhibition Hall of the Union of Artists
General axonometric view

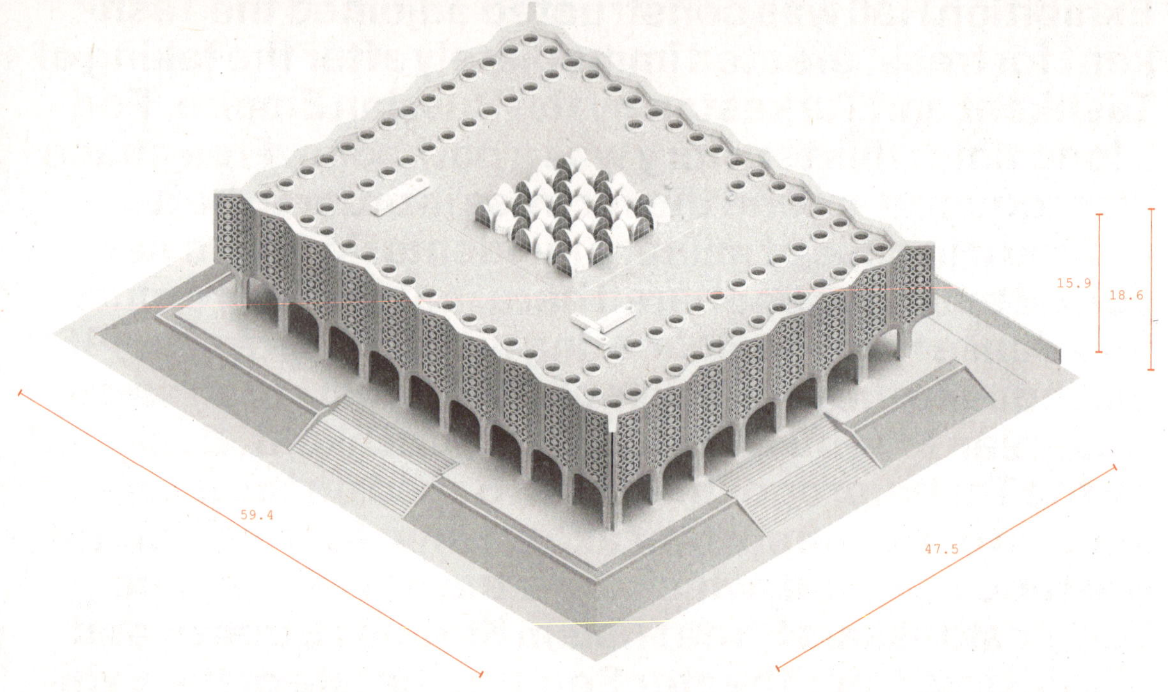

ACTORS	Architects:	Rafael' Khairutdinov, Farkhad Tursunov, B. Mel'nikov, Takhir Sadykov, F. Devlikamova	
	Engineers:	E. Tasman, E. Platzman	
	Artists:	N. Bandzeladze, V. Degtiarev, A. Dzhiashvili, Irena Lipene	
	Institute:	TashNIiPIgenplan (Tashgenplan)	
DATES	Design period:	1969–1974	
	Construction period:	1972–1974	
	Inauguration date:	1974	
	Later interventions:	An underground club was built, demolishing the original café design (date unknown).	
USE	Current use:	Exhibition hall	
	Original use:	Exhibition hall	
	Suitability of current use:	The Union of Artists was conceived as an exhibition hall and still serves the same purpose. However, while the architectural quality and flexibility of the building are well suited for its use, the technical solutions are obsolete and do not meet current standards. In particular, the lighting and climate control system could be improved. Moreover, the exhibition hall could benefit (even in terms of revenue) from additional visitors' facilities, which are currently completely lacking.	
	Space utilization:	The building is fully used. No unused/underused spaces were detected.	
DIMENSIONS	Number of floors:	Basement + 2 floors	
	Length:	59.4 m	
	Width:	47.5 m	
	Height:	15.9 m	
	Gross floor area:	First floor	1,314.0 m²
		Exhibition (second) floor	1,958.0 m²
	Gross floor area (total):		4,855.0 m²

Exhibition Hall of the Union of Artists

This research is based on numerous documents related to the design and construction of the Exhibition Hall of the Union of Artists of Uzbekistan and also to the life of its creators. They include explanatory notes, working drawings and correspondence from the archive of TashNIiPIgenplan Institute (Tashgenplan/Toshkentboshplan LITI) and also materials about the lead architect on the project, Rafael' Khairutdinov, from the archive of Tashgiprogor and his personal archive, the most important items from which are his wife Firuza Khairutdinova's memoirs and drawings from the early period of the Union of Artists design. Of additional interest among other sources is a short description of the Union of Artists in the manuscripts of the Institute of Art History, prepared for the inclusion of the building in the Corpus of Monuments of Uzbekistan.

An Innovative Typology

Until the mid-1960s not a single contemporary building was constructed in the USSR for visual arts museums[1] and not a single space for temporary art exhibitions. At best, artists showed their new works in existing museums, but because of their limited space, routine artistic life flowed into cultural clubs, theater foyers and so on, in other words, outside the professional context. Such "art for the masses" was one of the ideas of the early avant-garde, according to which art was no longer an object of admiration for a narrow elite society and should leave the space of salons and museums and dissolve into the thick of life itself.[2] However, from the 1930s there was a parallel process of gradual isolation of the Soviet art scene. Within it, hierarchical communities now became more important, having the right to apartments in "houses of artists," specially equipped studios, separate sanatoriums, etc. In the 1960s this elitist trend prevailed over the avant-garde and there was now a need for specialist exhibition halls belonging to unions of artists. Evidence of the new stage of institutional evolution was the launch in 1960 of the design of the Central House of Artists on Krymskii Val in Moscow. However, this gigantic building could not be a signpost for the Tashkent architects in terms of size (exhibitions in Uzbekistan did not require so much space), chronology (construction of the Central House of Artists was completed in 1979) or aesthetics, since the Union of Artists of the USSR a priori required a building that would be inclusive for artists from all of the Soviet republics and would therefore demonstrate extreme stylistic neutrality. However, in the late 1960s the situation began to change. In 1967 the first contemporary Soviet hall, the Palace of Art Exhibitions, opened in Vilnius. It was a strictly contemporary building in the spirit of Baltic modernism, in which today's specialists see regional links with the modernist buildings of Scandinavia. Inspired by the Lithuanian precedent, unions of artists in other republics began lobbying for the construction of their own exhibition spaces. In 1968 designs for an exhibition hall in Ashkhabad (constructed in 1979) and the Palace of Arts in Minsk (constructed in 1963) appeared. Local exhibition halls also appeared in the capitals of Armenia and Kazakhstan: in Yerevan as the Museum of Contemporary Art, which initially functioned as a gallery, and in Alma-Ata as a multifunctional seven-story building for the Union of Artists with studios and exhibition spaces. All of these buildings featured asceticism and modernist severity, although during construction the Ashkhabad hall "mutated" toward a more Brutalist baroqueness of concrete walls with sculptural forms. In Tashkent in the late 1960s the question also began to arise regarding building a special space for art exhibitions, although aesthetically this project gradually turned a different way from all of the previous and parallel Soviet analogues.

1 See the text on the State Museum of the History of Uzbekistan in this volume, pp. 544–551.

2 See Boris Groys, "Bor'ba protiv muzeia ili demonstratsiia iskusstva v totalitarnom prostranstve [The Struggle Against the Museum, or the Demonstration of Art in the Totalitarian Space]," in *Sovetskoe bogatstvo: stat'i o kul'ture, literature i kino* [*Soviet Riches: Essays on Culture, Literature and Cinema*], ed. Marina Balina, Evgenii Dobrenko and Iurii Murashov (St. Petersburg: Akademicheskii proekt, 2002), 37–51.

The Beginning of Design

The decision to build a new exhibition hall in Tashkent involved both the republican authorities and the Union of Artists of Uzbekistan, but it is not certain who took the initiative. It was probably the Union of Artists. After the 1966 earthquake, which destroyed the old building of the Museum of Arts of Uzbekistan, artists were deprived of a specialist exhibition space. The decision was not taken immediately. For a long period, there was talk in Tashkent of the construction of a common House of Creative Unions for professionals in different arts who had suddenly lost their headquarters.[3] However, this idea, regardless of Sharaf Rashidov's personal interest in it, was not realized, and at the end of the 1960s the heads of the creative unions of the republic began to act independently. The extant protocol of the administration of the Union of Artists of August 27, 1970, noted: "The project is developed in accordance with the Decree of the Central Committee of the Communist Party of Uzbekistan and the Council of Ministers of the Uzbek SSR based on the design brief

3 Ibid.

provided by the Union of Artists of the Uzbek SSR and the permission of Gosstroi of the Uzbek SSR for individual design."[4] Another document confirmed the date of the release of the architecture and planning brief, April 19, 1969.[5] As shown by the remainder of the documentation, the Union of Artists played an active role in the discussion of the building and making decisions.

The design brief was given to the recently formed Tashgenplan Institute, which had a mandate for creating the general plan of the city, the detailed plan of the center of Tashkent and the design of unique buildings in the center. However, there was institutional failure, as indicated by the memoirs of architect Rafael' Khairutdinov's widow, Firuza Khairutdinova: "The initial design was created by the Tashgenplan Institute in 1970, but their project was not approved by the Council of the Architecture and Planning Administration because of its incompatibility with the stated function and its inexpressive façade."[6] She would go on to record the following turn of events: "When he heard about this, Khairutdinov, on his own initiative, worked at home day and night and within a week had created his own version of the project with a large model of the building. He showed it to the artists, and they liked his proposal."[7] Having received a project they liked, the leaders of the Union of Artists decide to obtain approval for it from the republican leadership. Firuza Khairutdinova's manuscript sheds light on what happened next: "The Chairman [of the board] of the Union of Artists, Rakhim Akhmedov, organized a meeting between the architect and the First Secretary of the Central Committee of the Communist Party of Uzbekistan, Sharaf Rashidov, who carefully examined the project and approved it, allocating additional funds and taking personal control of construction."[8]

This episode reveals the key role played in the decision about the fate of the project by two nonarchitectural figures who had their own ideas about how Uzbek culture should develop: artist Rakhim Akhmedov and writer Sharaf Rashidov (before his Party career Rashidov was a journalist, editor of the influential newspaper *Kzyl Uzbekiston* and chairman of the Union of Writers of Uzbekistan). They had similar personal and artistic fates. From impoverished backgrounds, they both fought in World War II and then, having received professional educations, became adepts of socialist realism. Yet whereas Rakhim Akhmedov was unable to move beyond the conventions of the academic impressionist manner he had learned in studios from the 1930s to the 1950s, as chairman of the Union of Artists he supported those who referenced the style of the medieval and ancient art of Central Asia, such as Chingiz Akhmarov, Dzhavlon Umarbekov, Bakhodyr Dzhalalov and others. Sharaf Rashidov's preference for "Eastern" and "national" elements in architecture is well known. In the case of the Exhibition Hall there was no need for him to impose anything on anyone, since the proposed project matched his values. This explains how Rafael' Khairutdinov, who worked at Tashgiprogor, was appointed to lead a design project run by the Tashgenplan Institute. Rashidov instructed them to award him the work, while leaving the institutional management of the project to Tashgenplan. This decision brought into the circle of those responsible for the project Tashgenplan director Farkhad Tursunov, who would later become co-author.

4 "Protokol No. 372 zasedaniia pravleniia Soiuza khudozhnikov UzSSR, 27 avgusta 1970 [Protocol No. 372 of the meeting of the administration of the Union of Artists of the Uzbek SSR, August 27, 1970]," *Vystavochnyi pavil'on Soiuza khudozhnikov UzSSR: Kratkaia annotatsiia proektnykh reshenii [Exhibition Pavilion of the Union of Artists of the Uzbek SSR: A Short Annotation of the Project Solutions]*, Tashkent, 1975, Toshkentboshplan LITI Archive, archive no. 20, file 2.

5 Ibid.

6 Firuza Khairutdinova, "O zhizni i tvorchestve arkh. Khairutdinova, ostavivshego zametnyi sled v arkhitekture Tashkenta [On the Life and Work of Architect Khairutdinov, Who Made a Significant Mark on the Architecture of Toshkentboshplan]." Manuscript kindly provided by the author.

7 Ibid. During a meeting with Boris Chukhovich in February 2022, Firuza Khairutdinova explained that the speed of completion of the design was due to the fact that she, a qualified architect, had helped her husband do the technical work on modeling.

8 Firuza Khairutdinova, "O zhizni i tvorchestve arkh. Khairutdinova, ostavivshego zametnyi sled v arkhitekture Tashkenta [On the Life and Work of Architect Khairutdinov, Who Made a Significant Mark on the Architecture of Tashkent]."

The Evolution of the Project

The project developed independently by Rafael' Khairutdinov at his own risk was, as a whole, approved. It involved a two-story parallelepiped, with the main façade facing Uzbekistanskaia Street (Islam Karimov Street) and placed on a broad stylobate with grand staircases. The building was surrounded by an arcade with a pedestrian gallery at the ground-floor level, which offered views of the surrounding buildings: the main square complex, TsUM, the Tashkent Hotel and Lenin Boulevard. The arcade became the main expressive façade element and was conceived as a folded structure with slits in the form of arches, with a geometry typical of traditional Islamic architecture. The halves of the arches did not meet, instead being placed at a specific distance. This disconnectedness created a sensation of lightness and even postmodernist play, excluding not only the "keystone" but also the possibility of the elements being supported by each other.

Rafael' Khairutdinov's idea was unusual and comprised an architectural manifesto: the aesthetics of the International Style were rejected in favor of historical quotation restored to the contemporary field of the new architecture. The trigger for this process was another building, the Blue Domes Café, which was located nearby. As Rafael' Khairutdinov wrote, "taking into account the proximity of Lenin Boulevard and its buildings, which utilize contemporary national forms, the architecture of the exhibition pavilion is designed with the plastic connection with that environment in mind."[9] Until the late 1960s nothing of the sort existed in the architecture of Uzbekistan, being limited to the use in new buildings of turquoise ceramic tiles and sun-protection grilles associated with the traditional panjara. There may have been a single source of inspiration for both the Blue Domes Café and the Exhibition Hall—the Iran Pavilion[10] at Expo 67 in Montreal, which received extensive press coverage in the USSR. Above the tables in the café on the first floor of the Iran Pavilion were "blue domes," and the first floor of the façade was designed as an arcade connotatively associated with the monuments of Isfahan and Tabriz. This was only one of the decorative elements surrounding the façade of the pavilion. Rafael' Khairutdinov's solution was more laconic: the arcade of the Exhibition Hall defined the entire external appearance of the building. If the architect was inspired not by the Iran

Top: Blue Domes Café
Bottom: Exhibition Hall of the Union of Artists

Top: Iran Pavilion at Expo 67 in Montreal, 1967
Bottom: Restaurant in the Iran Pavilion at Expo 67 in Montreal, 1967

9 Ibid.
10 "Poiasnitel'naia zapiska. Tekhnicheskii proekt. Vystavochnyi pavil'on Soiuza khudozhnikov UzSSR, tom III [Explanatory Note. Technical Project. Exhibition Pavilion of the Union of Architects of the Uzbek SSR, volume 3]," Toshkentboshplan LITI Archive, no. 20/2.1, on 62 sheets, sheet 6.

Pavilion but by the historical arcades of Iran, then he significantly altered their morphological function. The medieval arcades of Iranian cities almost always faced a courtyard or garden, creating an internal square of a separate building or space, as in Imam Square in Isfahan and the numerous internal arcades of the Tabriz Bazaar. The pedestrian gallery proposed by Rafael' Khairutdinov was attached to the external rather than the internal perimeter of the building and in this sense was more reminiscent of the arcade of the Doge's Palace, which faces the city and opens up its picturesque perspectives through the arches. In this way the architect's concept was more complex and composite than appeared at first glance.

The composite character of the architectural language of the Exhibition Hall was more precisely articulated in the initial sketch, which differed from the finished building in several important ways. Firstly, the arches were flat and not ornamented. The architect proposed decorating the internal wall of the pedestrian gallery under the arcade using terra-cotta bas-reliefs on themes linked to the art and past of Central Asia. Accordingly, the "Islamic arches" were combined with figurative bas-reliefs that are not typical of the Islamic tradition. It may be that the architect, like many artists in Uzbekistan in the late 1960s and 1970s, was inspired by the archeological discoveries of ancient sculpture of Bactria and the Kushan Empire on the territory of the republic, however, his sketch was more akin to the pre-Islamic tradition of Iran or other Middle Eastern civilizations. This concept was not realized.

According to Firuza Khairutdinova's memoirs, Sharaf Rashidov, who appreciated the regional references in the project, recommended that the architecture include a decorative pattern instead of the wall-mounted bas-reliefs, and also that the flat arches be decorated. The architect accepted the proposal as far as the walls of the portico were concerned. The sketch of the façade of the Exhibition Hall from the Khairutdinov family archive shows that the thematic bas-reliefs were replaced by a vegetal pattern based on the arabesques of Samarkand or Isfahan. At some point Director of Tashgenplan Farkhad Tursunov, a confirmed co-author of the project, developed the ornamentation of the arches based on a cotton boll motif. As he was a subordinate in the work hierarchy, Rafael' Khairutdinov agreed with the version proposed by Tursunov and after this the proposed façade came closer to the building that exists today.

The cotton boll motif was a mixed Soviet version of the Islamic vegetal arabesque. Whereas the latter was associated in the religious consciousness with the Garden of Eden, cotton, which began to be extensively cultivated across Central Asia only after Russian conquest in the 1860s and 1870s, gradually became a symbol of the national identity of Uzbekistan, as the main agricultural product in the republic within the logic of the "socialist division of labor." The cotton boll as a symbol of the Uzbek economy was included in all three versions of the coat of arms of the Uzbek Soviet Socialist Republic (1925, 1937 and 1947) and was a constant in city posters and other propaganda produced in Uzbekistan. It was often used as a decoration for architecture of the Stalin period, beginning with the Uzbekistan Pavilion at the Stalin Exhibition of National Economic Achievements (1938) in Moscow, and was then transferred to modernist buildings (for example, it decorated the sun-protection grille of the Tashkent Circus). Accordingly, Tursunov's input to the appearance of the Exhibition Hall had a dual meaning and was in this sense no less composite than Khairutdinov's concept. From a distance the geometrically vegetal pattern of the arcade of the Exhibition Hall was reminiscent of traditional arabesques, and from close up it turned into a conventional Soviet symbol that could be clearly read within the existing state ideology. This solution suited everyone: the republican authorities, who encouraged the search for national identity in the art and architecture of Uzbekistan; the Union of Artists, which had entered a period of so-called "national romanticism" with its interest in the ancient and medieval roots of Uzbek culture; and at least some in the architectural community, who were attempting to rehabilitate ornament after a decade of modernist asceticism.

The planning solution of the Exhibition Hall is yet more evidence of the composite character of the building, the decorated façades of which were associated with picturesque images of the Middle Ages and the plans and interiors of which remained neutral and minimalist. The scenography for visiting the complex and the floor plans were largely reminiscent of one of the first modernist museums, constructed to a design by Philip Johnson, the Munson-Williams-Proctor Museum of Art (1960). In Tashkent, the rectangularly configured building, with sides of 52 × 42 meters and a height of 15 meters,[11] was almost symmetrical and strictly oriented to the cardinal directions, with the main entrance from the north side, which offered a view of Lenin Square. The pedestrian gallery under the arcade offered two additional entrances: from the east into the art salon, which could also, if required, open in the direction of the central sculpture hall, and from the west into the additional sculpture and drawing hall, which was connected to the central double-height space. To the right

11 Ibid., sheet 4.

and left of the central entrance were staircases leading to the second floor. The first exhibition floor was 5.6 meters high, which allowed the inclusion on the mezzanine floor of offices for the administration, guides and other Exhibition Hall staff.[12] The administrative block of the Union of Artists occupied the first and second floors of the south part of the building. This is where the management, reviewers, accountants, human resources department and others were located. From the foyer one could descend to the Vernissage Restaurant, which was in the west part of the basement, as well as to the cloakroom, the restrooms, the stores and the engineering spaces (the ventilation system room and others). Another important element of the building was the vertical block with service areas and an elevator that operated from the basement to the first and second stories for the transportation of heavy artifacts. This segment of the Exhibition Hall was hidden behind the wall of the main atrium and additional walls on the second floor.

Like the authors of the State Museum of Arts, which opened at the same time as the Exhibition Hall, Khairutdinov aimed to create neutral daylight in every exhibition space. However, if the halls in the State Museum of Arts were illuminated thanks to their semitransparent matte walls, in the exhibition space of the Union of Artists light penetrated through skylights. A double-height hall with an area of 224 square meters, with a stepped recess in the floor, reminiscent of an impluvium, only without water, was conceived as the dominant space of the interior and intended for exhibiting sculpture. Around it on the second floor was an enfilade featuring the main exhibition spaces (1,836 square meters[13]). In the free space, with the option of placing stands in various places, the architects proposed exhibiting painting and decorative and applied art. In future, exhibition practices would diverge strongly from this concept. The architects' zoning was rejected and painting, sculpture, works on paper and decorative and applied art were presented in all of the spaces based on the content of specific exhibitions. After almost half a century of use one can confirm the universal character of the exhibition spaces, which allow for a range of installations of objects based on curators' concepts.

All of the exhibition spaces were to have natural light. In order to provide this the architect used two types of skylights. Two rows of zenith skylights measuring 1.5 × 1.5 meters distributed diffused sunlight into the halls on the second floor. The central two-story atrium was illuminated with the help of original skylights that were one of the main visual and technological highlights of the building. These were fifty petal-shaped elements installed in pairs, mirroring each other in relation to the center of the ceiling space. The horizontal projection of the dormers, as seen from the hall, is semicircular. The pairs of dormers, oriented north–south or west–east, create an expressive play of cold and warm tones. This effect, based on the play of pure geometric form, demonstrates the connection between the project and the ideas of "high modernism."

Technological Innovations

The function of the dormers was not limited to illumination. They were also part of the measures that protected the building from overheating in the sun. When open on summer days they offered vertical ventilation of the hall, like the shipang[14] which was developed in traditional Central Asian architecture. Generally speaking, even regarding a deeply technical question like protection from overheating, Rafael' Khairutdinov preferred to rely on the techniques of traditional architecture. The building did not include artificial ventilation or air-conditioning. The pedestrian gallery under the arcade was an effective means of protecting the first-floor spaces from the sun's rays: the first floor was only sunlit during the cold morning hours and in daytime it was protected by the deep shade of the arcade. Another effective means of heat protection was the build-up and composition of the wall. As well as the aesthetic effect of the play of shadow, the folded arcade consisted of sun-protection panels placed at an angle to each other. In absorbing the main heating load, the exterior wall of the arcade did not transmit the hot air inside the building as it was double and the cavity was ventilated. Firuza Khairutdinova, who had written her dissertation on the physics of construction and helped her husband with the calculations, noted that "thanks to the lowering of the heat load in summer the thickness of the walls, which were made of light expanded clay aggregate concrete, [...] could be only 18 centimeters thick, as per winter requirements (for summer temperatures the required thickness was 28 centimeters)."[15] Accordingly, in summer the exhibition spaces were well ventilated and protected from overheating without the use of additional energy.

12 Ibid., sheet 5.
13 Firuza Khairutdinova, "O zhizni i tvorchestve arkh. Khairutdinova, ostavivshego zametnyi sled v arkhitekture Tashkenta [On the Life and Work of Architect Khairutdinov, Who Made a Significant Mark on the Architecture of Tashkent]."
14 This technique involved the cooling effect of the natural vertical ventilation of the halls.
15 Firuza Khairutdinova, "O zhizni i tvorchestve arkh. Khairutdinova, ostavivshego zametnyi sled v arkhitekture Tashkenta [On the Life and Work of Architect Khairutdinov, Who Made a Significant Mark on the Architecture of Tashkent]," 2.

The Soviet tradition of dedicating the construction of unique buildings to ideological dates interfered with the construction of the Exhibition Hall, as the authorities insisted that the architects complete the building by the fiftieth anniversary of the founding of the Uzbek SSR and the Communist Party of the republic, which was due to be celebrated on October 20, 1974. This requirement led to serious changes to the technology of construction and the content of the project. In particular, the builders demanded that the designers replace the "monolithic reinforced concrete structure with a structure of prefabricated elements."[16] The point of the technological changes was the maximal simplification of construction thanks to the use of a larger number of factory-produced standard details and the assembling of ready-made items on-site. Later the authors described the changes in the organization of production as follows: "According to the initial project, for the external wall it was necessary to produce 304 reinforced concrete panels comprising twenty-one standard sizes. As a result of additional development with Tashgenplan the panels were redesigned in expanded clay aggregate concrete and enlarged, and the number of items was reduced to 144 and standard sizes to twelve."[17] Even the most artistic works—the mosaic of the wall in the gallery and the decorative surfaces of the arch—were maximally industrialized, as a result of which the mosaic design was changed to something homogeneous that could be easily produced on standard panels in the factory. The same applied to the external wall panels of the arcade. After they had been clad with Gazgan marble and glazed ceramic tiles over a decorative textured layer made of white cement and white sand, they were transported to the site ready for installation. According to the explanatory note, "the surface ornamented in national style was actually three-dimensional, in two planes and not flat, which heightened the expressiveness of the ornament."[18] These and many other techniques for unifying and industrializing the work allowed the number of man-days on-site to be reduced to 3,000.[19] As a result, the building "was handed over in October 1974, i.e. construction was completed in twenty-three months rather than twenty-seven,"[20] and without exceeding the budget. The acceptance committee noted the high quality of the work. Almost half a century later one can confirm this: the façade of the Exhibition Hall remains one of the most authentically preserved monuments of Tashkent modernism.

The Reception of the Building

The artists received a building that matched their values, but the history of the Exhibition Hall after the completion of construction demonstrates a split among architects regarding its evaluation. From 1974 the building, with its memorable individual appearance, was often featured in books and articles about the architecture of Uzbekistan and became a "visiting card" for Tashkent comparable to the Uzbekistan Hotel, the Panoramic Cinema, the Blue Domes Café and other buildings. However, it was also often judged for the uncritical and formal use of architectural heritage. While some Moscow architects were happy to propose decorativist solutions in "national Uzbek style," others were extremely critical of them. Feliks Novikov wrote: "The main sign of national belonging was the ornamental motifs introduced to the building as obtrusive sun-protection grilles or various patterns distributed across walls, floors and ceilings made from marble, ceramic, ganch plasterwork and so on. In this way it is not difficult to turn even the Parthenon into an Uzbek building. One only needs to apply typical national ornament to the tympanum of the fronton and the metopes."[21] One of the main figures in the national architectural hierarchy, Deputy Chairman of the State Committee for Civil Engineering and Architecture of the USSR Nikolai Baranov, said that the Exhibition Hall "reflected the archaic nature of the Middle Ages."[22] The fact that Tashkent architects were also critical of Khairutdinov's building can be seen in the sociological survey of 1981 conducted among colleagues by the historians and architectural theorists Iosif Notkin and Shukur Askarov. The Exhibition Hall was ranked ninth of eleven buildings by architects from UzNIIPgradostroitel'stva, tenth by those from TashZNIIEP, sixth by those from Tashgenplan and ninth by those from Tashgiprogor. In their summary the authors wrote the following: "Respondents preferred the use of heritage elements in the interior, even where they are rather coarse and somewhat tasteless (the Circus) to their use superficially on façades, even where it is done extremely professionally (Union of

16 Document (the first page of which is missing) signed by chairman L. Briskin and secretary A. Mullabaev, *Vystavochnyi pavil'on Soiuza khudozhnikov UzSSR: Kratkaia annotatsiia proektnykh reshenii* [*Exhibition Pavilion of the Union of Artists of the Uzbek SSR: A Short Annotation of the Project Solutions*], Tashkent, 1975, Toshkentboshplan LITI Archive, archive no. 20, file 2.2.
17 Ibid.
18 Ibid., 4.
19 Ibid.

20 Ibid., 7.
21 Feliks Novikov, "Pravda i lozh' arkhitekturnyoi formy [Truth and Lies of Architectural Form]," *Dekorativnoe iskusstvo SSSR* [*Decorative Art of the USSR*], no. 5, 1978, 12.
22 Ibid.

View of the Union of Artists Exhibition Hall from Lenin Avenue (Sharaf Rashidov Avenue since 1992)

View of the central atrium and surrounding exhibition spaces

Artists Exhibition Hall)."[23] One can, however, state that both Moscow and Tashkent critics of the project read it exclusively externally, focusing on the decorative details of the façade and ignoring Khairutdinov's innovations in terms of the volumetric organization of space based on solutions from the Central Asian tradition. In other words, they fell into the trap of lack of attention to the content side of national heritage, something of which they accused the author.

Over time the interior of the Exhibition Hall underwent several waves of decoration. Firstly, in the late 1970s, the wall of the two-story atrium was decorated with carved ganch plasterwork. Next ganch covered the ceiling of the entrance part of the foyer. In the early 2000s the simple wooden handrails of the staircases were replaced with decorative rails with geometrized ornamentation. There were other changes: the zenith skylights above the exhibition spaces of the second floor were closed off (now only artificial light is used) and the deeper part of the atrium was leveled with the first floor. The Vernissage Restaurant closed. Today there is another restaurant there which is closed for renovation. In the first two decades of the twenty-first century the Academy of Arts, which was now the owner of the building, made several attempts to expand the space at the expense of the pedestrian gallery. Until his death in 2015, Rafael' Khairutdinov opposed these attempts and tried to produce plans for the adaptation of the building to the new conditions without radical changes to its planning and external appearance.

23 Iosif Notkin and Shukur Askarov, "O kachestve arkhitektury [On the Quality of Architecture]," *Stroitel'stvo i arkhitektura Uzbekistana* [*Construction and Architecture of Uzbekistan*], no. 4, 1981, 9.

ARCHITECT RAFAEL' KHAIRUTDINOV

Place and year of birth:
Tashkent, 1932
Place and year of death:
Tashkent, 2015
Education:
1952–1957, Architecture Department of Central Asia Polytechnic Institute (SazPI)

At the beginning of his career Rafael' Khairutdinov spent six years (1957–1963) at Uzgosproekt, after which he moved to Tashgiprogor. Here he immediately joined a notable group of architects who, in particular, won the 1964 competition for the city center, in which urban planners from Moscow, Leningrad and Baku also took part. From then on, the architect was a member of various teams. He was a universal type of architect and worked on a variety of creative briefs.

In 1970 Khairutdinov moved to Tashgenplan and began work on the design of the Union of Artists Exhibition Hall. Upon completing that project, he returned to Tashgiprogor, where he designed a series of buildings, some never built. His design for the House of Services with a sewing factory for 240 workers (1974) within a complex of existing buildings that included the Sharq Hotel (1912) was unusual for the Tashkent context. Upon examining his four versions, which had analogues in Moscow, Warsaw and Tashkent (1. Complete reconstruction of the façades of the old building and modernizing of all façades; 2. Copying and completing the unfinished composition; 3. Stylization and copying the old building; 4. Working in contrast with neighbors), the authors rejected all of them. The decision was as follows: "to create volumes that blend into one another through tactical reciprocal inclusion of elements of architectural décor, the articulation of the surfaces using a similar rhythm and through the identity of the color scheme of the material." The sketches for this unbuilt construction demonstrate a desire to create "contextually sensitive modernism," taking into account the historic fabric.[1]

A decision was taken to integrate the contemporary volume with the historic hotel by using a rhythm matching the existing building to break up the modernist walls and by cladding them with materials which harmonized with the old plaster.

Buildings constructed by Khairutdinov include the House of Forestry Workers (early 1980s), the House of Cinema (1982) and the Ben'kov Art College (1985).

1 Rafael' Khairutdinov, "Kompleks ob" ektov bytovogo obsluzhivaniia" [Complex of Household Service Facilities]," *Stroitel'stvo i arkhitektura Uzbekistana* [*Construction and Architecture of Uzbekistan*], no. 3, 1974, 42.

INSTITUTIONAL FRAMEWORK

TashNIIPlgenplan (Tashgenplan)

CADRE

Tashgenplan separated from Tashgiprogor in 1969 and its mandate was to work on the general plan of Tashkent, the detailed plan of the city center and unique buildings situated in the central district. Accordingly, the first group of designers was formed during the split from Tashgiprogor. The first director of the institute was Farkhad Tursunov, who graduated from the Architecture Department of the Central Asia Polytechnic Institute (SazPI) in 1957 and then rapidly progressed up the career ladder from assistant in one of the university departments to deputy chief architect of Tashkent and director of Tashgenplan (1969). He had a serious influence on the creative platform of the institute.

Once at Tashgenplan architects regularly changed their creative priorities and trajectories, adhering to the requirements of the director, which explains the specific nature of the buildings designed here. Iurii Khaldeev was one of a number of institute leaders who worked here from the beginning, and architects such as Vil' Muratov, Rafael' Khairutdinov and Nuzet Zaidov also ended up at the institute temporarily. As a rule, the director invited them to join, attracting candidates with the opportunity to work on unique buildings in the city center. Rafael' Khairutdinov was commissioned to design the Union of Artists Exhibition Hall, Nuzet Zaidov (and team) the Lenin Pioneer Palace, Vil' Muratov the Blue Domes Café, and Iurii Khaldeev Lenin Boulevard and the Gor'kii Theater (Turkestan Palace). In the late 2010s Iurii Khaldeev, recalling Tursunov, stressed that he had the most sophisticated taste among the parvenus in the hierarchy of architectural functionaries, a taste Khaldeev referred to as "Muscovite." Ironically, this European reference says a lot about the readiness of Moscow architects to create "Uzbek national architecture." In the mid-1970s a research department appeared at Tashgenplan, headed by Margarita Lifanovskaia (and the institute was renamed TashNIiPlgenplan). Under her leadership the general plan was developed, and various research was conducted on the city and the Tashkent agglomeration. This work, and her department, was fairly autonomous, since the directors of the institute were more interested in unique buildings, the planning of the city center and monumental heritage.

Almost all of the buildings designed at Tashgenplan demonstrated a characteristic historicist approach. The evolution of the appearance of the Gor'kii Theater is typical: an initially expressive, Brutalist project gradually accumulated orientalist decorations (panjara, stalactites, arabesques, etc.). This difference can also be seen in buildings by the same architects, who at Tashgiprogor worked in a neutral modernist language and, moving temporarily to Tashgenplan, sharply altered their creative orientation, saturating projects with orientalist forms associated with "national architecture." Such are the differences between Rafael' Khairutdinov's Union of Artists and House of Cinema and Nuzet Zaidov's Lenin Pioneer Palace and KGB building.

Basement floor plan
Original condition

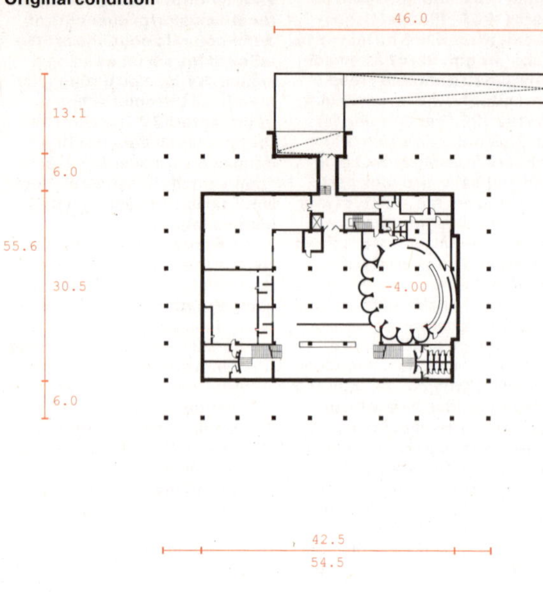

1st floor plan
Original condition

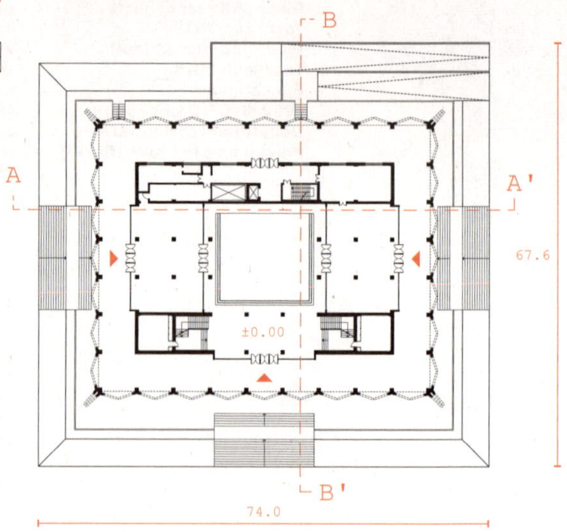

Mezzanine floor plan
Original condition

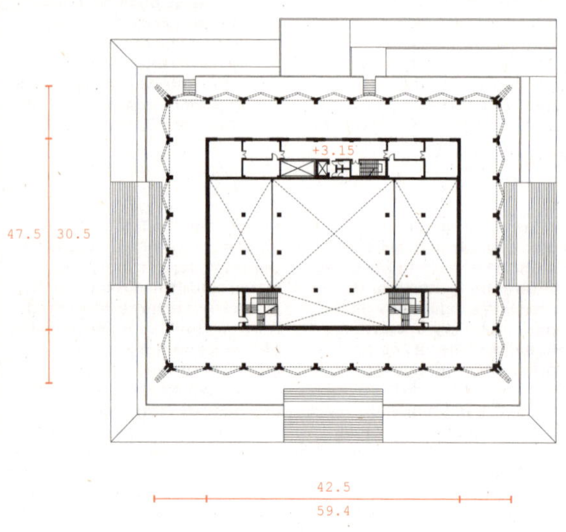

2nd floor plan
Original condition

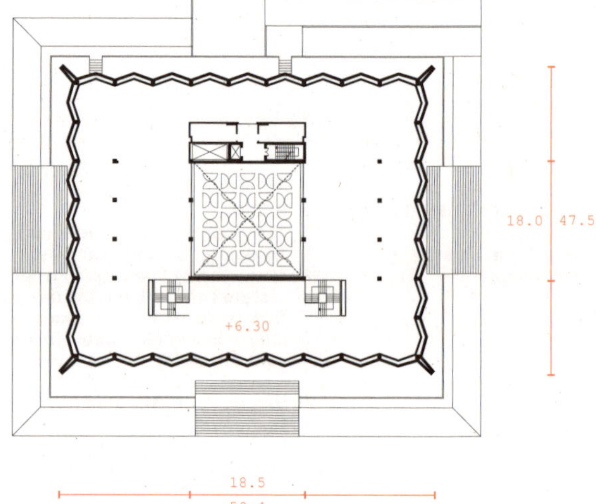

0 5 10m

South-east axonometric view
Original condition

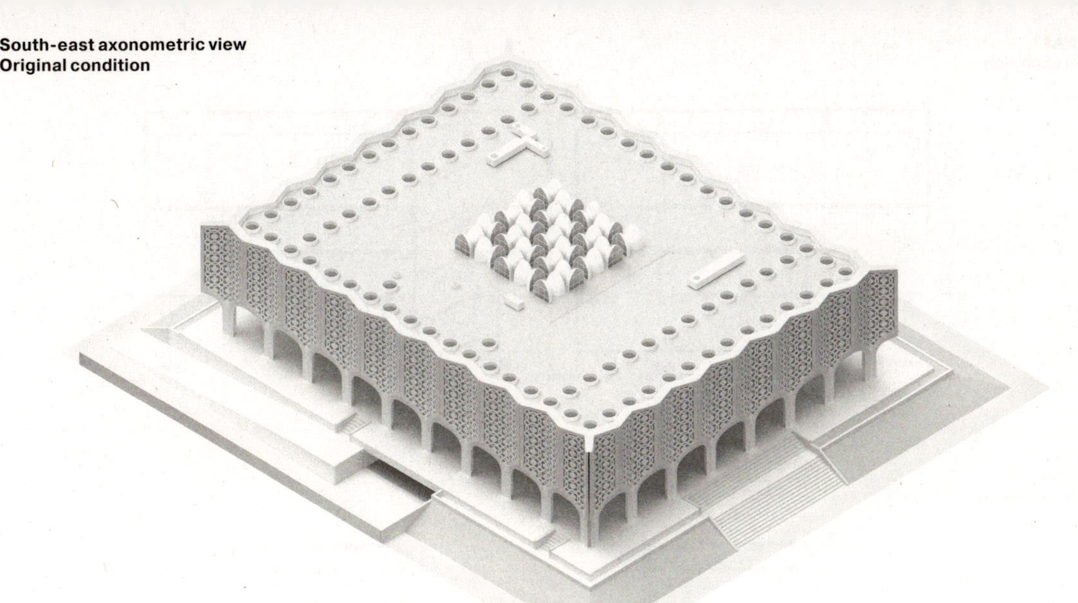

North elevation
Original condition

South elevation
Original condition

0 5 10m

Section AA'
Original condition

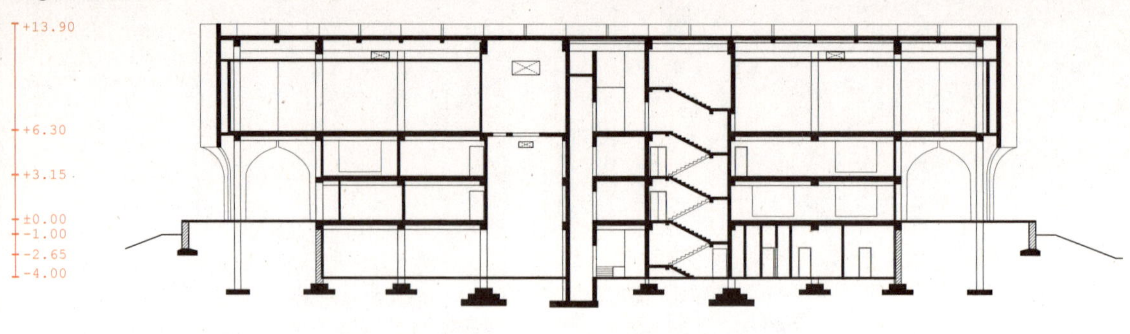

Section BB'
Original condition

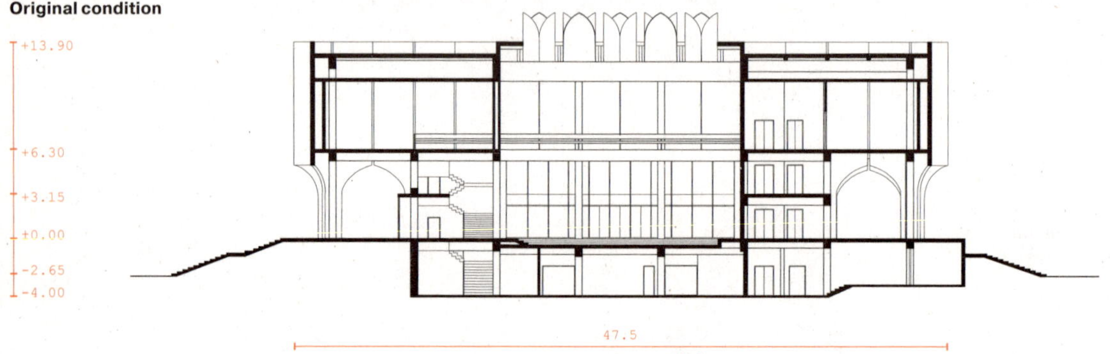

East elevation
Original condition

West elevation
Original condition

0 5 10m

North façade, main entrance
Original condition

View from north-east
Original condition

1974

Basement floor plan
Original condition

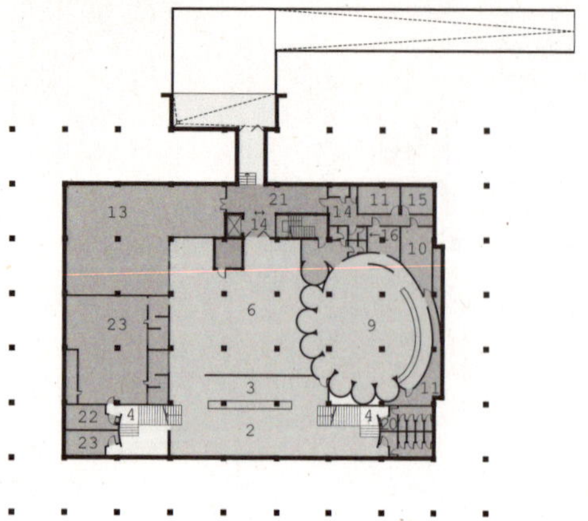

1st floor plan
Original condition

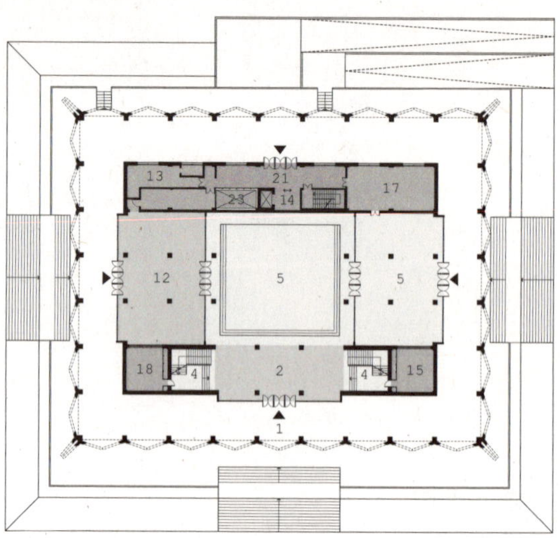

Mezzanine floor plan
Original condition

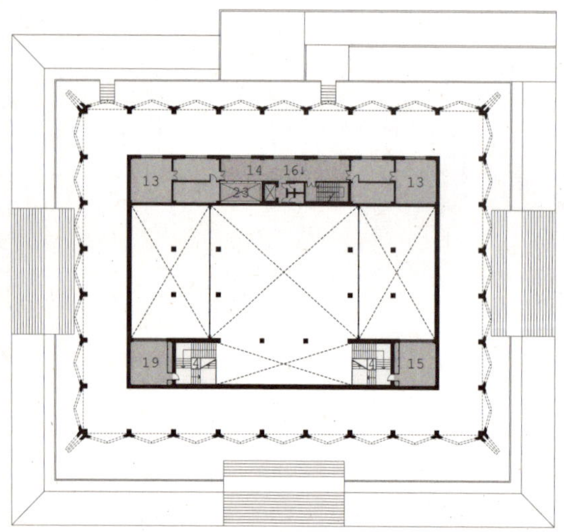

2nd floor plan
Original condition

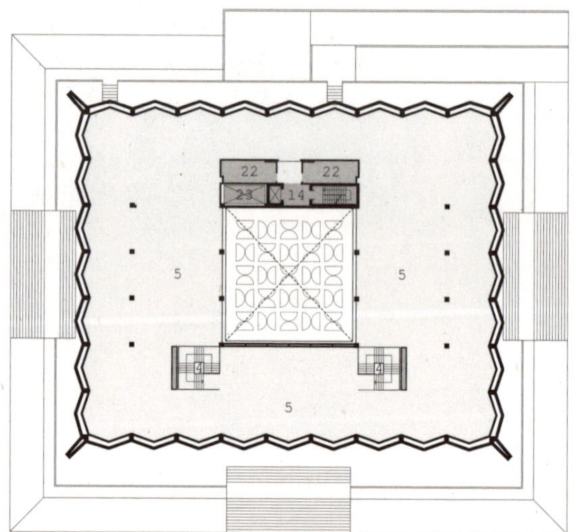

1	Terrace	9	Café	18	Tour guide office
2	Vestibule	10	Café service room	19	Fire station/guard office
3	Cloakroom	11	Café storage	20	Restroom
4	Circulation, visitors	12	Art salon	21	Loading/packing area
5	Exhibition space	13	Art salon storage	22	Storage
6	Exhibition storage	14	Circulation, workers	23	Technical area
7	Art materials shop	15	Administration and offices	24	Roof
8	Commercial space (karaoke bar)	16	Staff restroom		
		17	Restoration workshop		

2022

Basement floor plan
Current condition

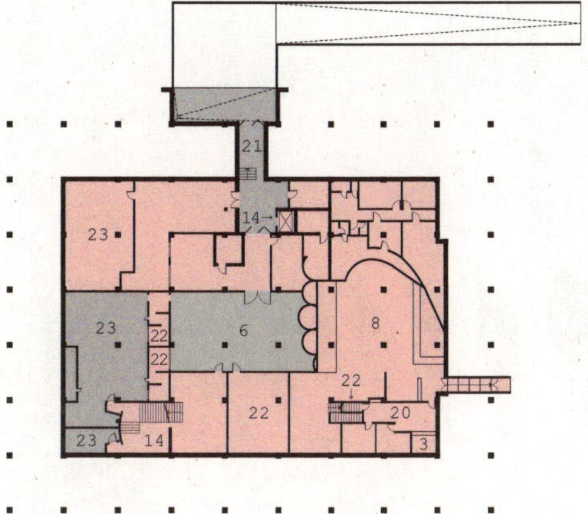

1st floor plan
Current condition

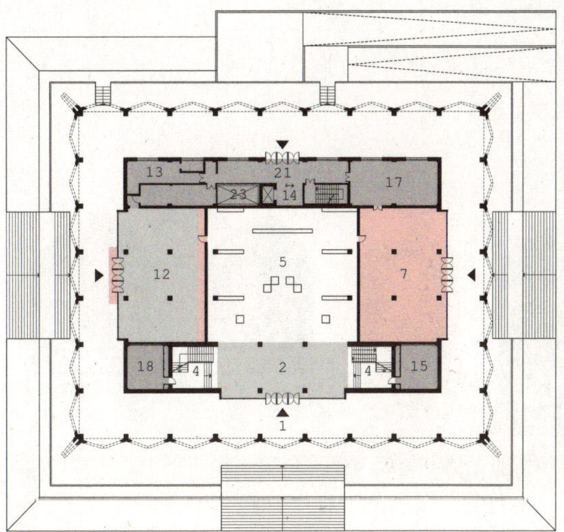

Mezzanine floor plan
Current condition

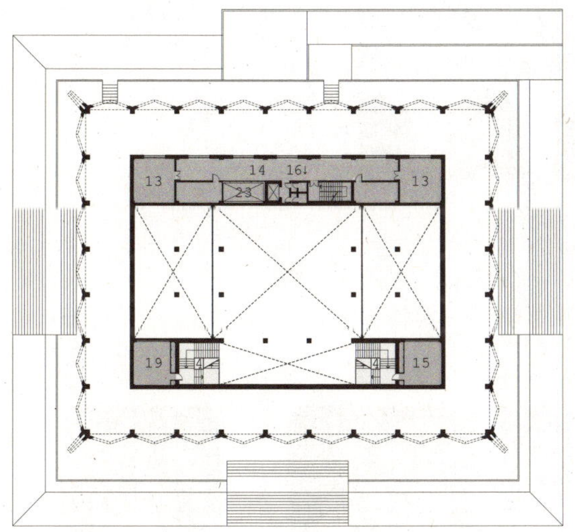

2nd floor plan
Current condition

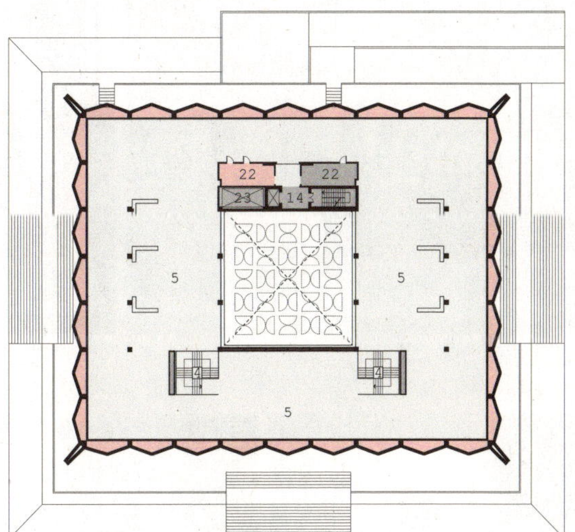

Exhibition
Public
Administrative / service and technical
Change of function

0 5 10m

View of the north-east corner, 1978

View of the north-east corner, 1982

Main entrance to the building, 1980

East entrance to the building, 1977–1978

Sculpture located at the south-east corner of the building, 1979

Sculptures in front of the east entrance of the building, 1979

East arcade

East arcade

East arcade, 1980

Views of the central atrium and exhibition spaces

Skylight providing zenith light to the central hall

North-east corner of the Union of Artists Exhibition Hall, 2022

Façade details, 2022

Front arcade of the building, 2021

View of the park in front of the building from the arcade, 2021

Arcade on the south side of the building, 2021

View of the central atrium and exhibition spaces on the first and second floors, 2022

Detail of the skylight providing zenith light to the central atrium, 2022

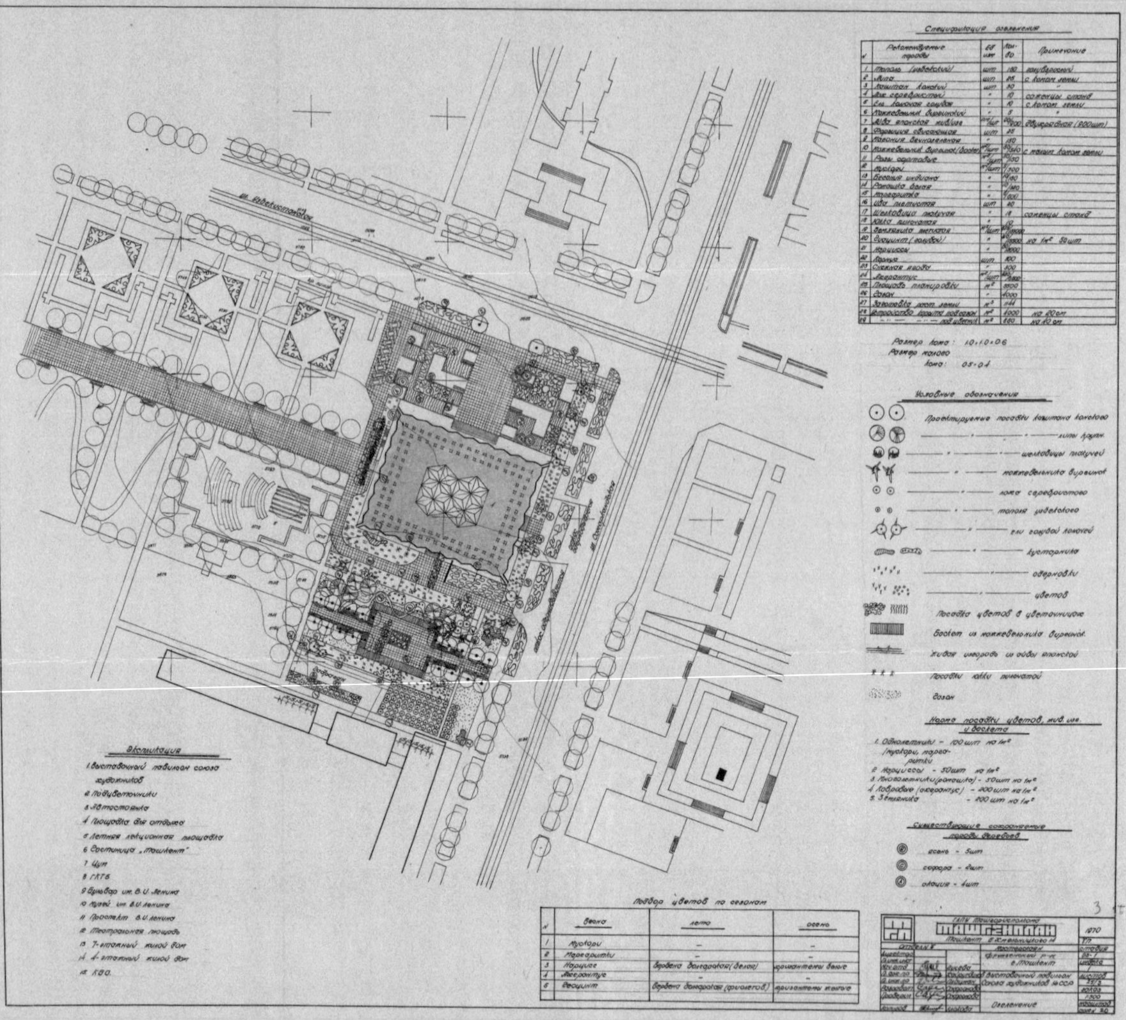

Urban layout for the Union of Artists Exhibition Hall, design proposal, 1970

Design proposal for the Exhibition Hall, drawing of the main façade

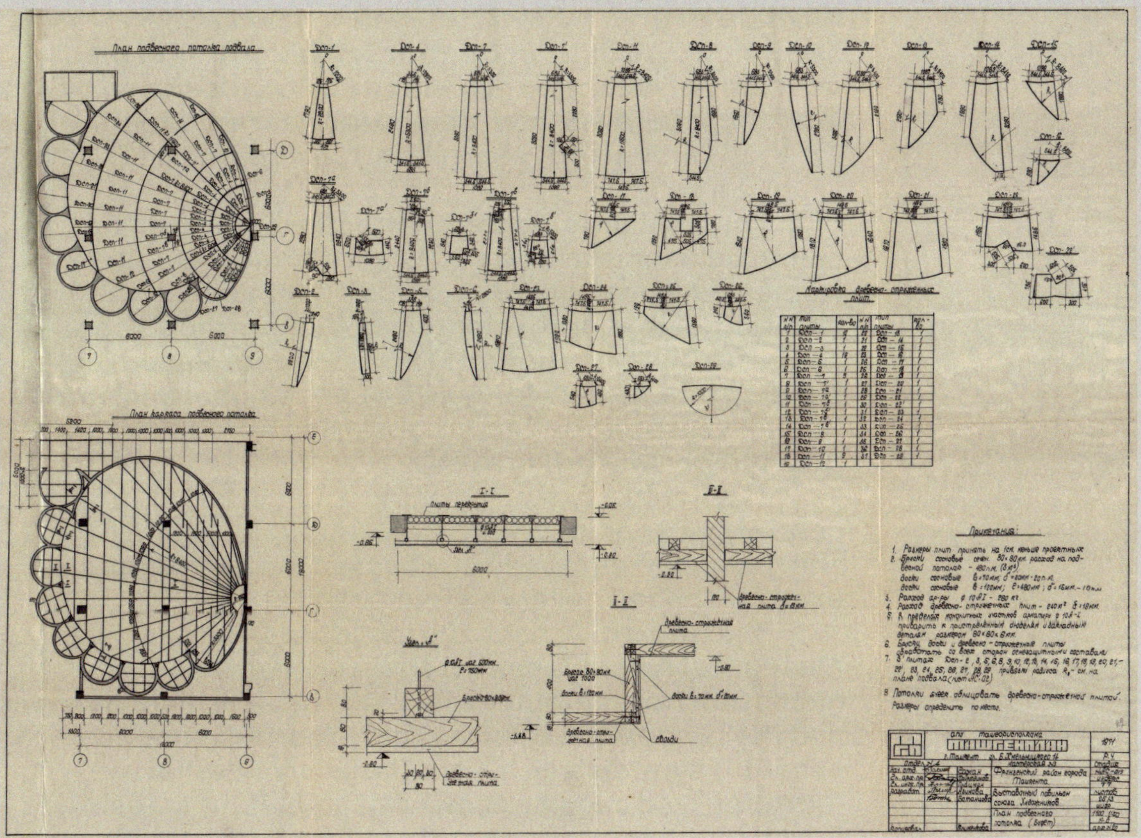

Detail drawings, study of the curvatures for the basement, 1971

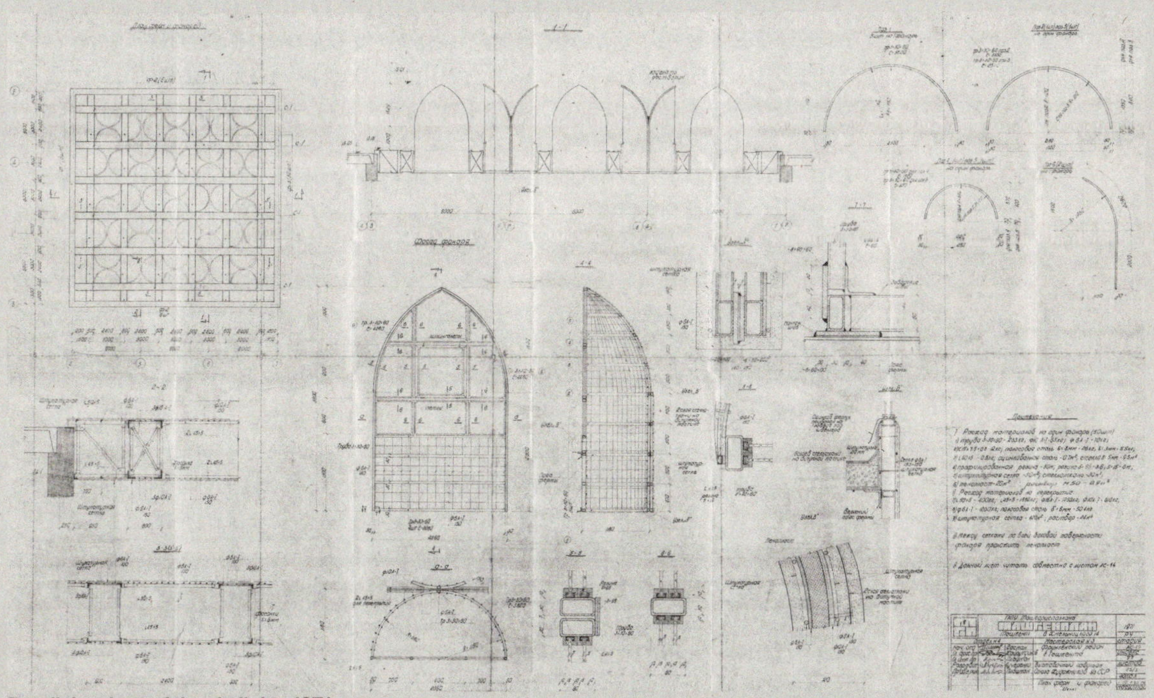

Detail drawings of the skylight, 1971

HIGHLIGHTS

The Union of Artists (or Central Exhibition Hall of the Academy of Arts) is an exhibition pavilion designed by the architects Rafael' Khairutdinov (project architect), Farkhad Tursunov, B. Mel'nikov, T. Sadykov, and F. Devlikamova and built between 1972 and 1974.

The pavilion is located at the intersection of the former Uzbekistanskaia Street (Islam Karimov Street) and former Lenin Avenue (Sharaf Rashidov Avenue), the institutional north–south oriented axis where most representative buildings line up. The architects placed the building on a podium to make it appear higher and be fully visible on two sides, thus emphasizing the convergence of two important urban axes.

The double symmetry of the volume derives from the central plan, composed around a multiple-height atrium. The ground-level façade is recessed inward to create an exterior shaded gallery on four sides.

The Union of Artists, the Lenin Museum and the State Museum of Arts in Tashkent share similar design elements, such as the central plan, the multiple-height atrium and the suspended volume. The three museums successfully synthesized the spatial principles that were "in the ether" and became somewhat ubiquitous across the Soviet republics in the years to follow. The Lenin Museum was the first tangible manifestation of this in Tashkent.

Archival drawings suggest the Union of Artists was intended as a "pavilion in the park," connected to the surrounding green areas, which began to be developed in the 1980s.

Exhibitions would exceed the perimeter of the building and expand into the nearby gardens, the continuity highlighted by the transparency of the glazing on the three entrances (to the north, west and east).

Despite the recent loss of transparency, the building has retained its main architectural qualities, both outside and in. Pointed arches around the perimeter of the pavilion at the entrance level are a reference to traditional architecture, although they are playfully broken by a panel gap in the position of the keystone. The pleated façades are made of prefabricated panels decorated with geometrical and floral motifs (with stylized cotton bolls) on a light-blue mosaic background.

The building has mostly kept the original interior layout, dominated by the central full-height atrium lit by a series of semicircular skylights in the center. However, the skylights above the upper level galleries have been closed.

The pavilion and the garden initially housed several works of monumental art. Irena Lipene, a sculptor known for her work with glass, extensively decorated the café in the basement: curved seating niches arranged as flower petals around the central space of the café were separated by glass partitions designed by Lipene. Today, her works are lost, although a few cylindrical walls are still hidden in the storage areas of the basement.

The Union of Artists pavilion marked an important step in the development of Tashkent architecture, suggesting a more subtle and unexpected declination of historical references within the modernist vocabulary. For its architectural quality and good level of both authenticity and integrity, it must be preserved.

STATE OF REPAIR SCORE:

- 3 – The building shows localized deterioration patterns which do not affect its stability

Overall, the state of repair of the Union of Artists is satisfactory. However, due to an overall lack of maintenance, the building is in need of minor repairs. In particular, during the on-site inspection it was possible to observe water infiltration, soiling, and the absence or detachment of cladding materials.

Protection status:	The building is listed according to Decision No. 846 of the Cabinet of Ministers, October 4, 2019.
Main criticalities:	Obsolescence of technical systems; lack of visitors' facilities; lack of regular maintenance; low quality of exhibitions
Possible risks:	A continued and prolonged lack of maintenance could lead to more severe damage, and therefore to the need for major repairs, with repercussions for the levels of authenticity and integrity of the building.

INTEGRITY SCORE:

- Exterior: 4 – The building has retained all the elements necessary to express its significance and is in a good state of repair
- Interior: 3 – The building has retained all the elements necessary to express its significance but is in a poor state of repair

Overall, the level of integrity of the Union of Artists pavilion is satisfactory.

Despite a few changes having occurred on the inside, the building was able to maintain its main features and intended architectural concept.

The replacement of the glazed walls with solid walls at the first-floor level has weakened the relationship between the building and its urban surroundings, which is, however, still evident from the outside.

The general state of repair is satisfactory, although minor repairs and better maintenance are required.

AUTHENTICITY SCORE:

- Exterior: 4 – Only minor repairs and conservation activities have been carried out on the building
- Interior: 3 – The building has been subjected to slight changes and replacements

Although several changes have occurred since its construction, the building retains a good level of authenticity.

In particular, the outside appearance of the building is very coherent with the original design and has probably only been subjected to minor repairs (as also confirmed by the mediocre state of repair of the façades).

A few more changes are visible on the inside, where the glazed walls enclosing the atrium on the ground floor have been replaced with solid walls, completely changing the perception of the space and erasing the visual connection with the urban context.

Further changes can be found in the finishes and, in particular, in the addition of ganch plaster decoration to the full-height wall of the atrium and in the eclectic wooden parapets that replaced the original plain ones.

The café located in the basement is the part of the building that has been transformed the most. The unique round niches decorated by glass artist Irena Lipene have been dismantled and few people now recall their presence in the building.

1974–1982

Union of Artists Exhibition Hall, 1974

Union of Artists Exhibition Hall, 1982

2024

Union of Artists Exhibition Hall, 2022

Union of Artists Exhibition Hall, 2024

1974

2021

Central atrium and exhibition spaces, 1974

Central atrium and exhibition spaces, 2021

Skylight in the atrium, 1974

Skylight in the atrium, 2021

LEVEL 1 – MAXIMUM LEVEL OF INTEREST
(No transformations allowed; conservation activities required)

URBAN LEVEL

No new buildings should be added on the Union of Artists' block or on the green areas of the facing blocks (to the north and to the east).

ARCHITECTURAL LEVEL

EXTERIOR

The volume, height, symmetry and general proportions of the building should not be modified.

The pleated façades, together with the pointed arches of the arcade, are characteristic and increase the plasticity of the pavilion. They should remain unaltered in any future intervention.

In order not to subvert the original relationship between the building and its immediate surroundings, the three entrances (north, west and east) should be retained.

The small green areas surrounding the pavilion are to be maintained.

The dimensions of the arcade running around the four sides of the building should not be modified. The porch should retain its width, length and height. It cannot be glazed or modified.

The arcade should remain a continuous space. No partitions are to be added.

INTERIOR

The overall architectural layout should remain unaltered and, in particular:

- the full-height central atrium should remain undivided and retain its current proportions;
- the exhibition space developing around the atrium on the first floor should remain continuous;
- no permanent partitions are to be added;
- the atrium should remain permeable and should be visible from the exhibition space on the first floor. No enclosing walls should thus be added on the perimeter of the atrium.

DETAIL LEVEL
EXTERIOR

The prefabricated decorated panels on the exterior façades of the pavilion are to be carefully preserved as they are.

The mosaic cladding the arcade's walls should be preserved.

The fountain situated on the west side of the building should be retained.

INTERIOR

Within the full-height central atrium, the following features should be kept as they are:

- the skylight;
- the finishes (flooring, columns and slab thickness cladding).

LEVEL 2 – MEDIUM LEVEL OF INTEREST

(Elements included in the second level can be moderately transformed following approval by a designated committee[1])

ARCHITECTURAL LEVEL
EXTERIOR

Any changes in the layout of the green areas surrounding the Union of Artists pavilion should be subject to approval by the designated committee.

INTERIOR

Transformations regarding the interior of the pavilion (including administrative areas) are to be submitted to the designated committee for approval.

DETAIL LEVEL
INTERIOR

Any replacements or changes concerning the finishes and lighting system of the exhibition area should be approved by the designated committee.

1 An international committee of heritage preservation experts to be appointed.

HIDDEN MODERNIST FEATURES

The original design of the Union of Artists was characterized by a visual continuity between the indoor and outdoor exhibition spaces. In particular, the east and west atrium walls were once glazed, whereas today they are opaque (drywall). Through this feature, the original design also stressed the urban relevance of the pavilion, which stood at the intersection of important urban axes and formed the arrival point of the pedestrian routes along them. In this sense, the transparency of the two lateral entrances also underlined its role of a converging point.

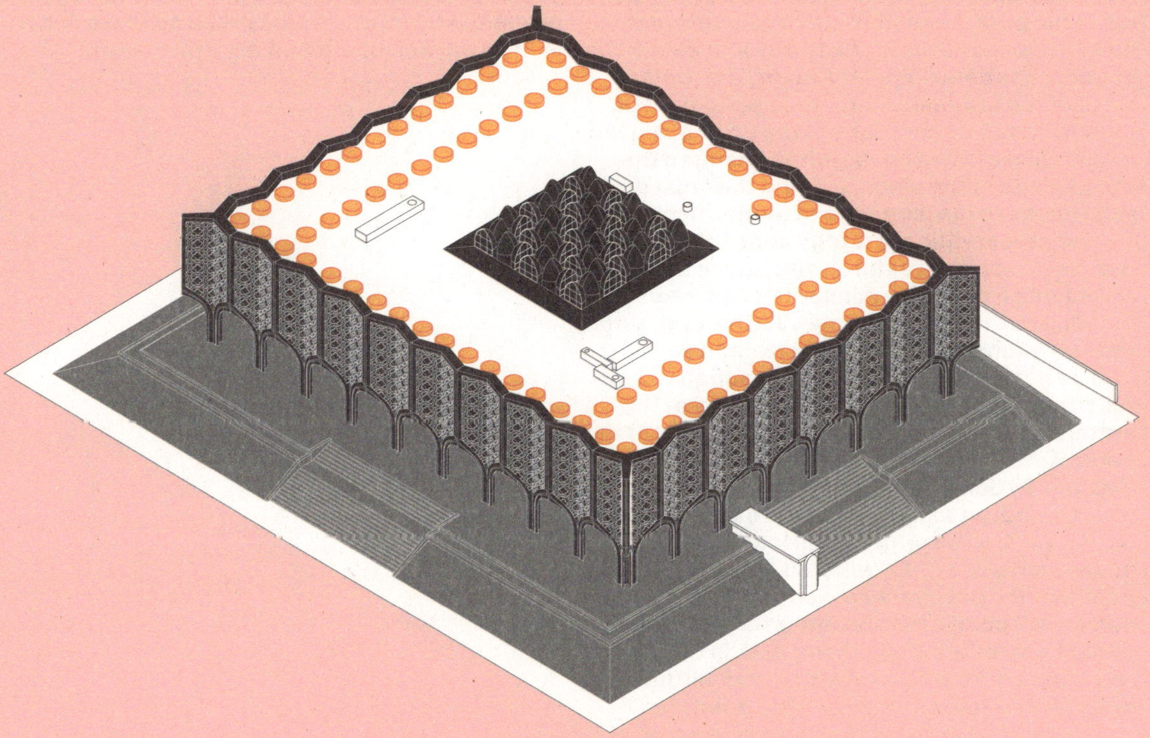

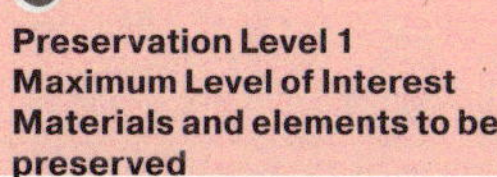

Preservation Level 1
Maximum Level of Interest
Materials and elements to be preserved

Preservation Level 2
Medium Level of Interest
Materials and elements to be preserved

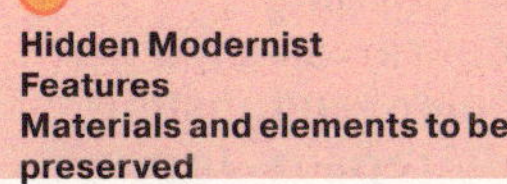

Hidden Modernist Features
Materials and elements to be preserved

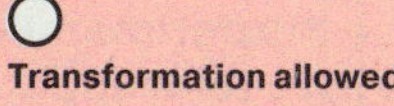

Transformation allowed

Preservation Strategy

The former Exhibition Hall of the Union of Artists, completed in 1974, blends tradition and modernity. The significance of this pavilion lies in its spatial organization—a central-plan building developed around a full-height central atrium—in the particular use of natural lighting, and in its façades, which are enriched by prefabricated mosaic panels. The location of the building amplifies its significance: the pavilion was built along the former Lenin Avenue, where most representative buildings lined up.

Since its inauguration, the building has been subjected to several transformations, particularly in the interior. The most relevant changes concern the entrance level and the basement, where the original layout and glass decorations by Irena Lipene have been almost completely lost. Although the building still has access on three sides, the glazing of the east and west atrium walls was replaced with opaque cladding. As a consequence, the original idea of a "pavilion in the park," highlighting the visual continuity between the indoor and outdoor exhibition spaces, has been lost. Moreover, the replacement of the original railing, the application of ganch plaster decorations in the atrium and the installation of false ceilings has changed the atmosphere of the place, erasing the most direct references to the language of modernism.

The preservation strategy aims to partly recover these lost features and, in particular, to re-establish the visual connection between the building and its surroundings. To this end, three preservation actions have been planned.

The first and most substantial action will entail the demolition of the walls located at the entrance level (on the east and west walls of the central atrium) and their replacement with glazing. By doing so, it will be possible to reconnect the indoor exhibition to the outdoor gardens, which were originally intended to also house works of art. As underlined by its elevated position, the pavilion was also the intersection and arrival point of important urban axes and pedestrian routes along them, and, in this sense, reopening the two lateral entrances will uncover its former role as a converging point.

The second action aims to reverse some of the minor changes which occurred in the exhibition space. More specifically, the chiseled wooden parapets should be replaced with new railings that are more coherent with the original design. The false ceiling should also be replaced. The new solution will integrate a more suitable lighting system, possibly including natural light provided by the round skylights located on the perimeter of the building.

Finally, a third action should involve the general maintenance of the building, suggesting cleaning operations and local repairs. In particular, the façade of the pavilion will be cleaned and repainted with whitewash where needed. Missing mosaic and marble tiles will be replaced.

As for the interior, close attention should be paid to the atrium skylight, which is one of the most appealing features of the building. Since signs of water infiltration are currently visible on the ceiling, it is advisable to check the skylight windows for possible damage and to improve their watertightness. Once the problem is fixed, it will be possible to whitewash the ceiling as well as the niches housing the skylight windows.

Moreover, it is highly recommended to conduct a series of surveys in order to assess the structural condition and state of repair of the building and to obtain a chemical and physical characterization of the main building materials. This will enable evaluation of the compatibility between the building materials and the materials to be used during conservation interventions.

Once this information is obtained, it will be possible to develop a more detailed and comprehensive project, which could be tested on a limited portion of the building (pilot site).

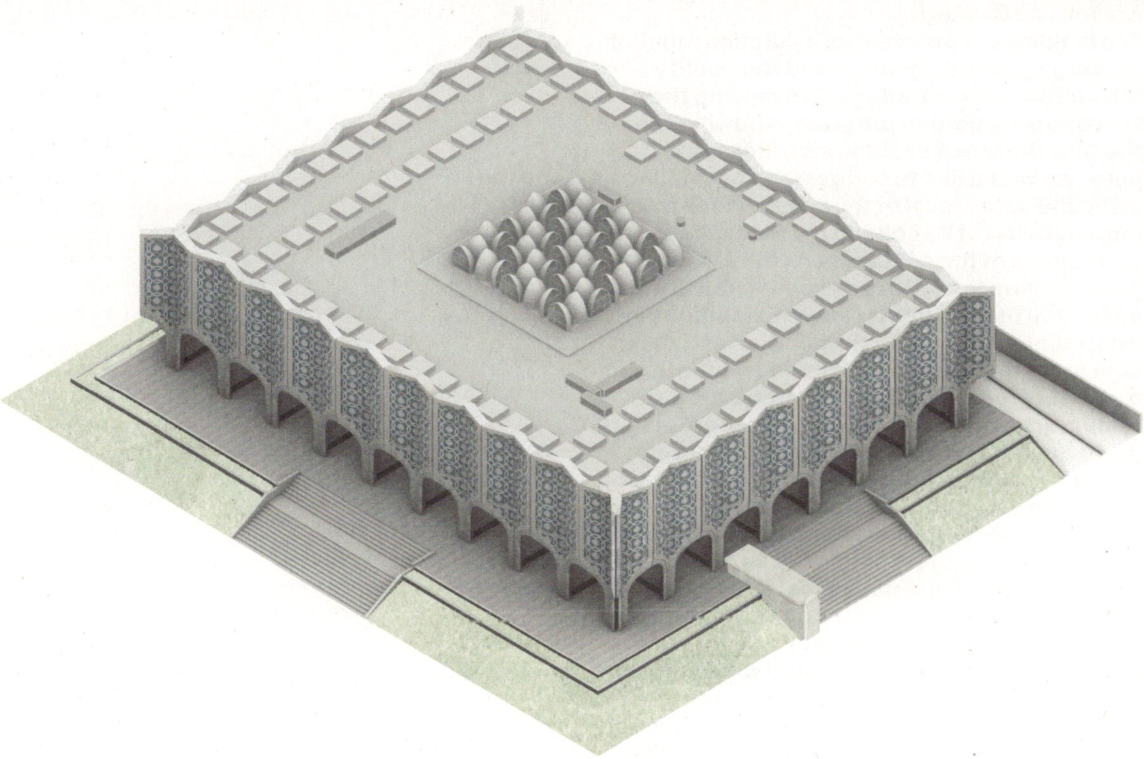

Exhibition Hall of the Union of Artists,
axonometric view of the preservation proposal

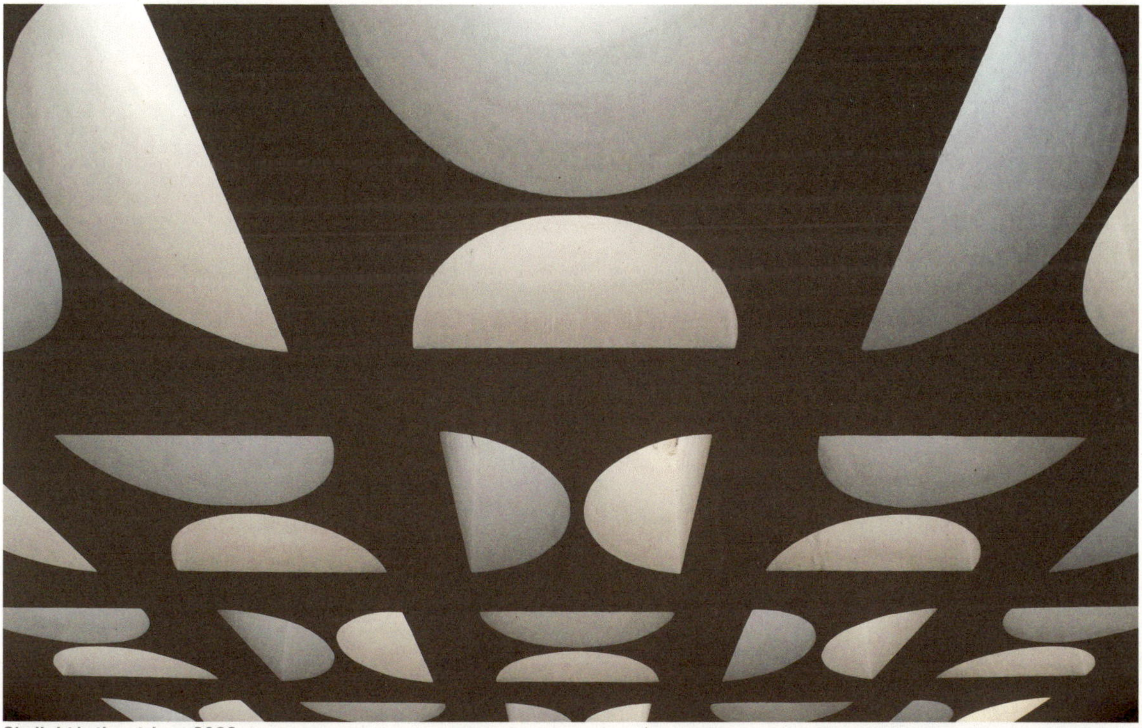

Skylight in the atrium, 2022

Adaptation Strategy

The building will maintain its exhibition function, although given its location and the quality of the architecture we suggest reviewing the content of the exhibition program. Knowing that the Directorate of Exhibitions office is located here, we would like to suggest the possibility of using the upper level of the pavilion for a rotating exhibition of its collection. Given the quality and volume of the collection (several local experts confirm this), it is possible to transform the collection of the Directorate of Exhibitions into a permanent (or rotating) exhibition of Uzbekistan art of the second half of the twentieth century. The ground level would accommodate temporary exhibitions by contemporary artists.

To further enhance the identity of this institution, we suggest dedicating part of the basement to artists' workshops for collective use, equipping them with advanced technical resources to produce and reproduce works of art. This would become a distinctive feature of the pavilion. As in Lafayette Anticipations in Paris, this production activity would have a degree of visibility from the central atrium and would enter into visual dialogue with the exhibition areas.

To activate the basement level, we suggest reopening the café and providing more elegant access to it from the small square to the west of the building.

Exhibition Hall of the Union of Artists, view of the central atrium
Strategy visualization

Sun Heliocomplex

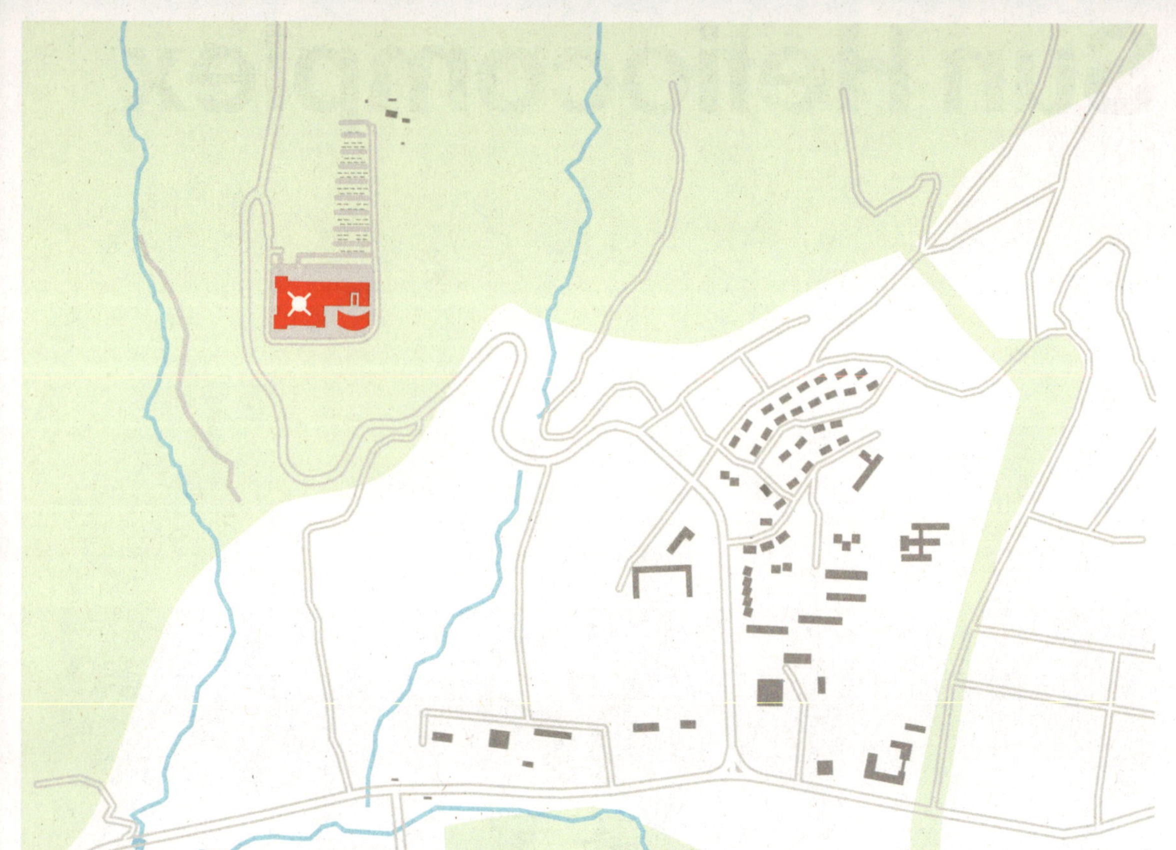

Building position and address: 102226, Tashkent Region, Parkent district, "Sun" settlement

0 0.5 1km

According to the original technological requirements, the site for the Sun Heliocomplex was to be in a place that featured clean air and the least number of cloudy days per year. This predetermined the choice of the foothills of Parkent, a small city located to the east of the Tashkent agglomeration. The direction of the wind, which mainly came down from the mountains, excluded industrial pollution of the air, which would have made the work of the mirrors and solar furnace less effective. One of the advantages of the chosen site was the rock at the base of the hill, which supported the stability of the construction. Historically, there were no settlements in this area, but the project was addressed on multiple levels, and in parallel with construction of the Heliocomplex a small microdistrict for workers was designed, incorporating minimal infrastructure: a kindergarten, a school, and buildings for everyday needs. According to contemporaries, this part of the work was initially planned as "possible," but Sadyk Azimov insisted and Minister of Defense of the USSR Dmitrii Ustinov agreed that the construction project needed to provide normal living conditions for an organization that would become a flagship for the industrial development of the republic.[1]

1 Timur Salimov, "Kak akademik S.A. Azimov otkazalsia ot zvaniia general-leitenanta [How Academician S.A. Azimov Rejected the Rank of Lieutenant General]," *NuzUz*, May 31, 2022, https://nuz.uz/2022/05/31/kak-akademik-s-a-azimov-otkazalsya-ot-zvaniya-general-lejtenanta/.

Main dimensions of the Sun Heliocomplex
General axonometric view

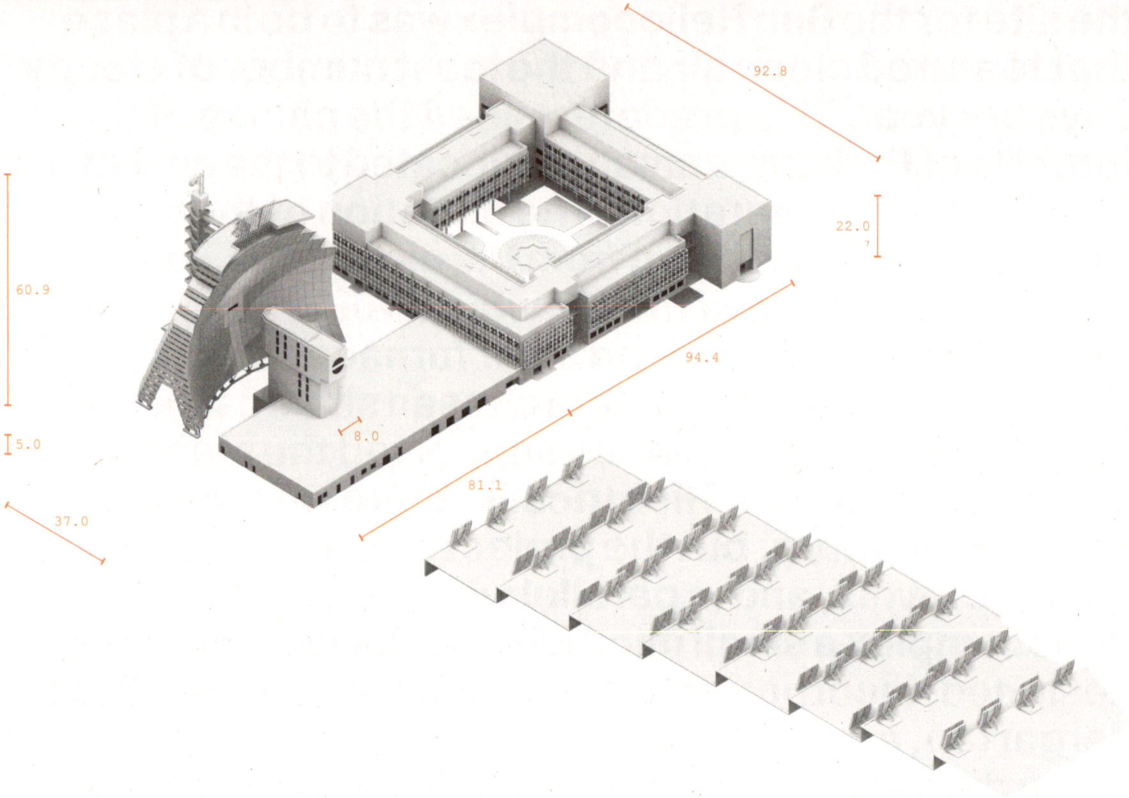

Sun Heliocomplex, detail of façade with lightweight sunshading structure

ACTORS	**Architect:**	**Viktor Zakharov**	
	Engineers:	**E. Makeev, E. Shmakin**	
	Artist:	**Irena Lipene**	
	Institute:	**Postbox A-1158 Project Institute**	
DATES	**Design period:**	**1981–1983**	
	Construction period:	**1981–1987**	
	Inauguration date:	**1987**	
	Later interventions:	**2021–2023: Interior upgrade of one of the laboratory wings. 2024: Reconstruction of administrative building.**	
USE	**Current use:**	**• Development/production of carbon fiber • Development/production of highly pure oxide materials that cannot be obtained by other methods • Development/production of high-voltage converters • Testing thermal insulation materials for aviation and space technology • Development of materials and products from engineered ceramics (for mechanical engineering and energy applications) • Development of innovative materials resistant to high temperatures, including ceramic and thermal insulation materials for electrical power plants • Development of composite materials and coatings • Development of solar heat receivers and storage**	
	Original use:	**• Production of highly pure oxide materials that cannot be obtained by other methods • Testing materials for exposure to extreme solar radiation • 90% – testing materials for spacecraft and military equipment • 10 % – study of new materials**	
	Suitability of current use:	**The building is partially unused, but remains suitable for the intended purpose.**	
	Space utilization:	**Most of the space seems to be underutilized, and the rooms have a high vacancy rate.**	
DIMENSIONS	**Number of floors:**	**Courtyard building**	**Basement + 4 floors**
		Auxiliary building	**Basement + 1 floor**
		Process tower	**Basement + 7 floors**
		Paraboloid concentrator	**22 floors**
	Length:	**Courtyard building**	**94.4 m**
		Auxiliary building	**81.1 m**
		Process tower	**28.0 m**
		Paraboloid concentrator	**57.0 m**
	Width:	**Courtyard building**	**92.8 m**
		Auxiliary building	**37.0 m**
		Process tower	**8.0 m**
		Paraboloid concentrator	**35.0 m**
	Height:	**Courtyard building**	**22.0 m**
		Auxiliary building	**5.0 m**
		Process tower	**28.0 m**
		Paraboloid concentrator	**60.9 m**
	Gross floor area: (first floor)	**Courtyard building**	**3,947.0 m²**
		Auxiliary building	**2,975.0 m²**
		Process tower	**186.0 m²**
	Gross floor area: (total concentrator excluded)		**24,300.0 m²**

Sun Heliocomplex

This text is based on documents found in the archive of the Solntse (Sun) Heliocomplex scientific and production center and texts from architectural journals of the 1980s. Unfortunately, the archives did not include explanatory notes and working correspondence, which could have clarified numerous important aspects of the creation of the complex.

The Heliocomplex and Its Prototype

In the Soviet history of the Sun Heliocomplex, which was built in Parkent in the foothills of the Tien Shan, there are two subjects that are not covered. Soviet publications stressed the pioneering nature of this project. For example, its author, architect Viktor Zakharov, wrote: "The Sun Scientific Production Metallurgical Heliocomplex is the first serious step in exploring solar energy." Its construction "involved many technical solutions that were global innovations" and "the unique structures of the concentrator and the complex of heliotechnical structures with a tracking system are unique in the national economy and have qualitatively new technical features" without "analogues in the USSR or abroad."[1] The description of the history of the use of solar energy by humans published in *Arkhitektura SSSR* (*Architecture of the USSR*) began with anecdotal artifacts from the time of Amenhotep,[2] and did not fail to mention the distorted mirrors with which Archimedes allegedly set fire to the Roman fleet. However, the authors were silent about the existence of a direct prototype of the technological complex in Parkent, the solar furnace in Odeillo in the eastern Pyrenees in France. In fact, it was at the Odeillo complex (1962–1968) that they developed the technology not only for the concentrator, which can focus reflections of the sun's rays on a single point via a system of external mirrors, but also for the furnace, which enabled solar energy to be employed for various scientific and industrial experiments.

The second area of silence involves the initial intention behind the complex. The French heliocomplex at Odeillo was largely focused on two issues: the transformation of solar energy into electricity and the production of new heat-resistant materials and particularly pure metals, thanks to the very high temperatures of around 3,500°C. The complex in Parkent, conceived during the Cold War, was the Soviet answer to the West and, of course, was oriented primarily toward the requirements of the military-industrial complex and the space industry. Although publicly, general phrases were offered about the need for ecologically clean production and renewable sources of energy, the complex was originally devised as a strategic military enterprise and was constructed based on a special decree of the Politburo of the Central Committee of the Communist Party of the Soviet Union, which was, de facto, the supreme executive organ in the USSR.[3] This is confirmed by the specific nature of the organization behind the design, the Postbox A-1158 Project Institute, which was part of the system of military enterprises that concealed their purpose using an anonymous "postbox" number. The institute designed buildings for the nuclear industry, a strategic sector of defense and the economy. The military-industrial purpose of the Heliocomplex in Parkent is also confirmed by what it mainly produced and tested. This included refractory metals and heatproof panels required to construct the Soviet Buran space shuttle and the most powerful Soviet rocket, *Energiia*, the dual purpose of which—exploring space and offering a military counterweight to the USA—was widely known in the 1980s.

Even so, one should not underestimate the role of Uzbekistan's academic and scientific context. In the USSR the military-industrial complex was an outpost of modernization in many spheres. It was supported by the structures and institutes of the Academies of Sciences of the Soviet republics, which were interested in national projects and financing for the promotion of their own research. In particular, Tashkent's Physics and Technical Institute (FTI) of the Academy of Sciences of Uzbekistan, founded in 1943, focused on research in the field of nuclear physics and solar energy. Accordingly, Moscow's and Tashkent's interests combined in the establishment and construction of an experimental base in the form of a unique solar furnace. The Tashkent FTI became the coordinator of the development and construction of the complex. The significance of the initiative, and the role of republican research centers in the distribution of solar technologies, can be confirmed by another fact. According to Tashkent architect Vladimir Sutiagin, after the announcement that a heliocomplex would be built near Tashkent, the director of the Turkmen Sun Research and Production Association from Ashkhabad contacted the design bureau for scien-

1 Viktor Zakharov and Irena Lipene, "Nauchno-proizvodstvennyi metallurgicheskii geliokompleks 'Solntse' [The Sun Scientific Production Metallurgical Heliocomplex]," *Arkhitektura i stroitel'stvo Uzbekistana* [*Architecture and Construction of Uzbekistan*], no. 1, 1988, 16.

2 "Geliokompleks 'Solntse' [The Sun Heliocomplex]," *Arkhitektura SSSR* [*Architecture of the USSR*], nos. 3–4, 1988, 37.

3 Timur Salimov, "Kak akademik S.A. Azimov otkazalsia ot zvaniia general-leitenanta [How Academician S. A. Azimov Rejected the Rank of Lieutenant General]," *NuzUz*, May 31, 2022, https://nuz.uz/2022/05/31/kak-akademik-s-a-azimov-otkazalsya-ot-zvaniya-general-lejtenanta/.

Large solar furnace and heliostats in Odeillo, eastern Pyrenees, France

View of the heliostats and parabolic concentrator, Parkent, Uzbekistan, 2022

tific institutes with a commission for the design of a heliocomplex for Turkmenistan. The project got as far as working drawings but was not built, as the collapse of the USSR redirected the Turkmen economy toward the exploitation of natural resources.

Neither the reproduction in Parkent of the technological scheme of the Odeillo center nor the linking of the building with the Soviet military-industrial complex detracts from the research, production and architectural merits of the Sun Heliocomplex, which was the last large-scale Soviet scientific production project to be built in Uzbekistan. In addition, in terms of architecture I believe that the construction in Parkent featured a purer architectural concept, a more expressive form, a more complex architectural appearance and wider social aims than its French prototype. Without rejecting scientific pragmatism, the authors of the Parkent complex did not limit themselves to utilitarianism. In fact, and this is clear from their texts, they aimed to find a plastic equivalent of their futurological inquiries and their understanding of architecture as a medium for modernizing society. Their explanatory comments include both general aesthetic thoughts "about form and content" and a focus on the viewer's perception that could decode the aesthetic and emotional information with abstract architectural form.

The Overall Project Solution of 1981

The documents located do not indicate when the commission was formulated and at what point it was sent to the designers for development. However, the album with photographs of the plans, façades and perspectives of the building issued by Postbox A-1158 in 1981 proves that by this time the project had been developed in detail and the foundation stone had been laid (the last page of the album marks this event, which took place in the presence of the President of the Academy of Sciences of the USSR, Anatolii Aleksandrov).

The whole complex has five structural components, comprising a field with 62 heliostats, the concentrator, a technological tower, the main building and various service buildings. To summarize, the technological process consists of the following: the heliostats, which are fitted with special turning and inclining mechanisms, direct the sun's rays to a parabolic mirror concentrator that is strictly oriented on a north–south axis; it then redirects the sunlight to the focus point of the furnace in the technological tower, which is 40 cm in diameter. The temperature in the focus point can reach 3,000°C, which enables thermal sessions for making superpure and refractory metals and also heatproof materials. The particular nature of the solutions selected by the authors of the Uzbekistan complex can be clearly seen in comparison with the French prototype. Three main components are similar: a field with heliostats, a concentrator on the north–south axis with an identical geometric form and a technological tower in front of it with a helioreceiver, on the surface of which the sun's rays cross and components melt. However, the structural and compositional solutions of the construction of the concentrator are in two cases completely different.

In France the structure on which the mirrors of the concentrator are fixed forms part of a single whole with the construction that serves as office and service space for staff. As a consequence, the T-shaped building, the north façade of which is a concave surface with segmented edges, from the south looks like an ordinary, box-shaped office building flanked by similar but narrower eight-story blocks. This arrangement means that the curved structure of the concentrator can be hidden under the roof and walls, enabling it to be better preserved. However, here the space of the working areas is limited by the geometry of the concentrator, which makes the complex at Odeillo much less spacious than its Parkent "twin." From the point of view of composition, the French combination of two completely different façades into a single volume seems less expressive than the spatial division of the concentrator and the service block in Parkent. Finally, the French architects' decision to install continuous glazing on the south façade, which is subject to direct sunlight throughout the day in the hottest region of France, is difficult to explain.

In Parkent the concentrator is a separate and constructively more complex building. Its north façade is a parabolic surface limited by a rectangular segment with "pixel" accretions on its upper part. This surface is clad with mirrored elements or facets that are 45 × 45 cm, and each is attached to the base by a device that enables them to be aligned. There is an elevator to all levels of the concentrator that leads to the service galleries. In the description in the journal *Arkhitektura SSSR* (*Architecture of the USSR*) the structural basis of the concentrator is presented as "made of a system of joined pairs of counter-inclined trusses of different heights that are fixed in tiers using horizontally connected trusses. Each pair of counter-inclined trusses is shifted in plan relative to those adja-

View from inside the parabolic concentrator in Parkent, 2021

cent in such a way that the supporting elements of the trusses are placed in plan on two parallel parabolas. The overall rigidity and stability of the building is due to the fact that the metal framework of the concentrator is connected to two foundation slabs made from monolithic reinforced concrete that are placed on the rocky base."[4] The south façade and side walls of the concentrator are in fact sunscreens that protect the load-bearing structure from direct sunlight which, over time, could lead to deformation of the metal. The form of the sunscreen repeated the dynamic forms of the load-bearing structure and emphasized the conical outline of the inclined trusses, which gave the composition tension and completeness. In working with the complex surface of the external screen the authors also included elements of epigraphy. The yellow panels "depict" concentric circles on the screen, reflecting the motif of the bypass circle of the helioreceiver that is located at the top of the technological tower.

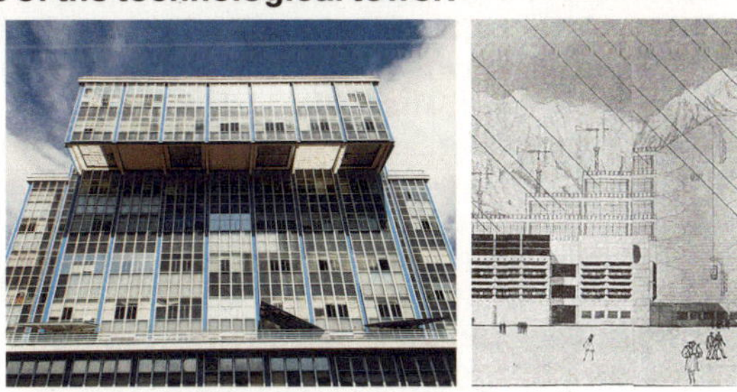

Left: Back (administrative block) of the parabolic concentrator in Odeillo
Right: Back of the parabolic concentrator in Parkent

The Main Building

The main building has its own planning logic, as it is physically detached from the concentrator. It comprises four compartments grouped around an internal courtyard. On the east and west sides are two three-story laboratory blocks, on the north a three-story laboratory and production block and on the south a four-story administrative block. The technical floors, which stretch along the entire perimeter of the building, have a ventilated roof that reduces the amount of solar heating. The architects also developed an innovative approach to sun protection for the windows and walls. Previous experiments in Uzbekistan used a suspended concrete grille like a panjara, which had gradually become a commonplace and then a hackneyed technique of Tashkent architecture. The concrete panjara had a number of drawbacks: its significant weight, which led to greatly increased expenditure on load-bearing structures; the excessively sharp boundaries between light and shade, which hampered work within the building, and the blocking of the view of the city from within the building. The authors of the Heliocomplex took a different route. They developed a light metal structure that worked whether installed vertically or horizontally. Semitransparent glass sun-protection screens were attached to it. This long quote by the author of the project shows how seriously he took both the physical and psychological comfort of employees when developing the sun protection:

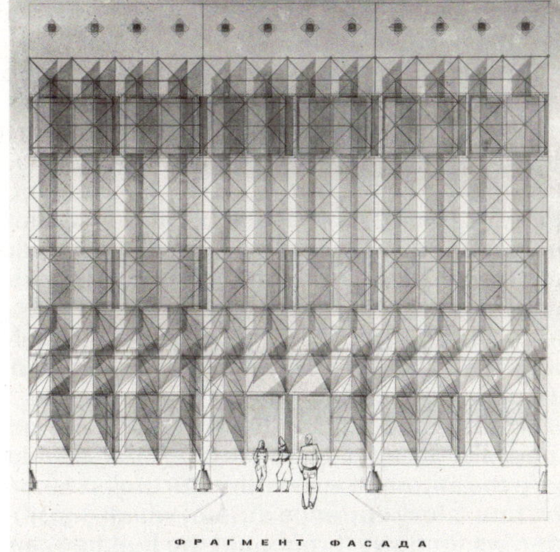

Sun Heliocomplex, detail of the façade of the administrative block with lightweight sunshading structure

"Simultaneous protection from overheating and insolation, which is unresolved in similar devices, is achieved because the sun protection has been created using a light spatial structure cantilevering from the building. It generates a vertical air flow that prevents the transfer of the warm air from the sun-protection device to the façade of the building. [...] The screens are installed at an angle to the façade of the building and should reflect 80 percent of the solar radiation from their surface. Only 20 percent hits the façade of the building, which does not create any discomfort inside the space or heat the envelope of the building itself. Since the screens are made from sun-protecting and heat-reflecting glass that can retard and reflect direct solar radiation and are transparent elements, the link between the internal space of the building and the external environment is not broken, which improves the psychological climate inside. [...] In future the screen panels can be equipped with solar batteries with photo-electric transformers of solar energy, and connected to the consumer."[5]

4 "Geliokompleks 'Solntse' [The Sun Heliocomplex]," 38.

5 Viktor Zakharov and Irena Lipene, "Nauchno-proizvodstvennyi metallurgicheskii geliokompleks 'Solntse' [The Sun Scientific Production Metallurgical Heliocomplex]," 17.

In aiming for comfortable ventilation, the architects placed a pedestrian gallery along the perimeter of three wings in the internal courtyard and a sloping pergola in the west part. The large openings for vehicle access on two sides of the courtyard supported the flow of air and did not allow the space to overheat. Trees were planted in the courtyard, and at the center was a pool with a fountain that comprised a rest area for staff.

The façades of the main block were laconically designed, with an emphasis on horizontals that did not distract from the sculptural form of the concentrator. In addition, the disruption of the horizontal rhythm using openwork sun protection with its rhythmic vertical details and the light-and-shadow accents in the entrance area of the administrative block ensured that the surface did not appear monotonous. Another complex but unifying element of the façades was formed by the articulated vertical blocks of staircases, which clearly structured the volumetric composition. Thanks to them, the multilayered structure of the main building could be clearly read from each side.

Among the particularly carefully developed spaces of the administrative block one should note the entrance area with its Brutalist façade, the four-story entrance atrium, which distributed visitor flows throughout the building, and the 450-seat conference hall situated above the foyer. Each of these elements was painstakingly conceived and had visual meanings as well as utilitarian aims. The planning of the conference hall was original: using its corner position the architects placed it at 45° to the main and side façades. In the project the hall was surrounded by walls with a decorative arcade, but in the end they became simpler, without decorative historical elements. The galleries, which led from the main atrium to various floors, were also spectacular. They were adjoined by a canteen, a buffet, a library with reading rooms, administrative spaces, and corridors that led to the laboratory spaces.

Monumental Art

The Heliocomplex architects aimed to create a symbolically loaded work of architecture by including the resources of monumental art. Having used epigraphy in the composition of the façades of the concentrator and the technological tower,[6] they involved decorative glass artist Irena Lipene, for whom the Heliocomplex would be the last and possibly the largest project created in Uzbekistan. After a series of distinguished experiments in the interiors of the Iubileinyi Palace of Sport, the Panoramic Cinema, Rashidov's Delegation House, the Uzbekistan Hotel, the Tashkent TV Tower and other buildings, Irena Lipene became a true co-author of the main interior spaces of the Parkent complex: the entrance atrium, the conference hall, its foyer and the staircases, where her art objects were placed. The artist developed a number of spatial compositions on astronomical themes for the interiors of the complex: *Hymn to the Sun* (atrium of the complex), *Parade of Planets* (staircase of the main building), *Milky Way* (conference hall) and *Moon* (conference hall foyer). They can be called abstract decorative sculptures made up of numerous elements, mainly three-dimensional sulfide glass, but also metal and in some cases light bulbs. The astronomical associations of *Parade of Planets*, *Milky Way* and particularly *Moon* may seem to be mere poetic metaphors, but nevertheless one can detect an echo of the Soviet cosmism of the 1960s, filled with faith in the creative potential of humankind. The initial iconography of cosmic subjects in Soviet monumental art of the 1960s and 1970s was completely different, as the titanic figure of the "conqueror of the cosmos" was invariably at the forefront. This might be a cosmonaut (for example, Iurii Gagarin) or a scientist/thinker (such as Konstantin Tsiolkovskii or Sergei Korolëv), but also perhaps an ordinary person posing a Promethean challenge to the cosmos. Tashkent architecture did not escape this "cosmology." It can be seen in Arnol'd Gan's bas-relief in the initial design for the Panoramic Cinema (1961), two monuments to Iurii Gagarin,[7] the sculptural composition on Cosmonauts Square[8] and the frescoes at Cosmonauts Avenue metro station.[9] In comparing them with the version of "cosmism" presented in the Heliocomplex, it can be seen that the titanic figure of the human creator has disappeared. The visual solution proposed by Irena Lipene and Viktor Zakharov is dominated by a meditative deliberation on the immensity of the world and of cosmic forces. Here one feels the energy of the flaming protuberances in the composition *Hymn to the Sun*, the distant light of *Milky Way*, the coldness and ephemerality of *Moon* and, finally, the unity of the macro- and micro-worlds in *Parade of Planets*, where "macroplanets" made of glass elements and metal "atoms" with "microparticles" revolving around them are threaded onto a single axis.

6 This refers to the concentric circles picked out on the south façade of the concentrator using yellow enclosure panels. The authors of the project called them "epigraphy," apparently referring to the poster-like nature of the graphic technique used.

7 1969, an obelisk with a depiction of Gagarin; 1979, sculptor Grigorii Postnikov, architect Sabir Adylov.

8 1982, sculptor Iakov Shapiro, architect Iurii Miroshnichenko.

9 1984, artist Arnol'd Gan, architects Sergo Sutiagin and Sergei Sokolov.

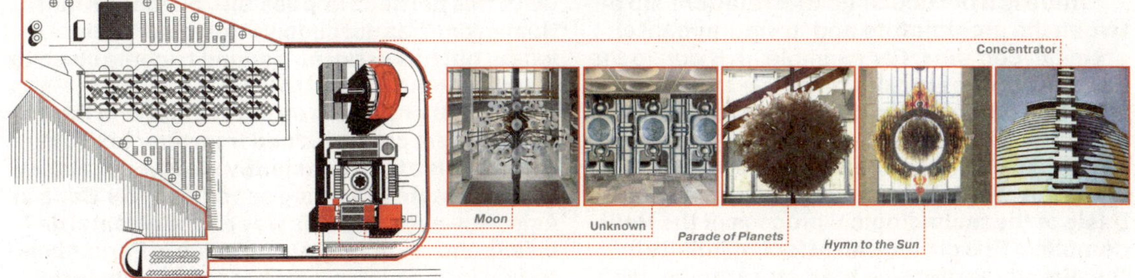

Sun Heliocomplex, monumental art

Hymn to the Sun by Irena Lipene, entrance hall of the administrative block, 2021

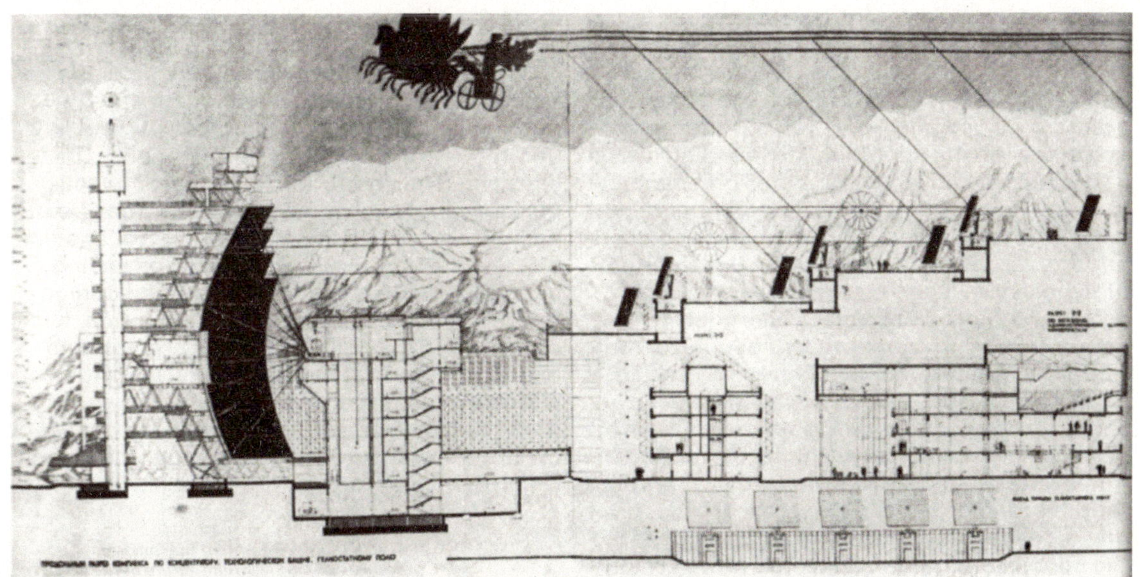
Section of the heliostatic field and the technological tower

There is a particular unique relationship between the architecture and the monumental art in the complex. For example, in *Hymn to the Sun* the art does not decorate the architecture; instead, it becomes part of its visual language. The composition is installed in the entrance space of the atrium, the side walls of which are clad with mirror tiles, a material that is the basis of the technological process of the Heliocomplex. This creates an effect of infinity in the already impressive four-story space, with an endless number of "suns" reflected in it. The polished dark granite floor amplifies the effect of reflection, which can be associated with the theme of "anti-worlds," introduced into late Soviet culture by the poetry of Andrei Voznesenskii and Vladimir Vysotskii. Similar subjects, organic for the Soviet technical and artistic intelligentsia of the 1960s and 1970s, visualize the particular spiritual world and values of the authors of the complex and the people who worked there.

The Natural and Cultural Contexts

The links between the Heliocomplex and the natural and cultural contexts were of particular interest to the architects. The conditions set by the nature of the Parkent foothills complicated the development of practical solutions but made the requirements obvious. Workers at the complex had to be protected from solar radiation and overheating, and the building, in addition to the requirements to adhere to norms of seismic stability and the conditions of a harsh continental climate, had to fit into the natural landscape. Finding solutions for solar protection has been mentioned above, and as far as integration of the complex into the landscape is concerned, this was a clear success for the architects. They selected a rocky foundation and placed the building on it in such a way that from a distance it becomes an attractive orientation point. During the approach, the building grows into a gigantic and almost "alien" complex that both contrasts with and complements the natural surroundings. This expressive combination was positively received by the architects of Uzbekistan. One of the republic's leading architects, Sergo Sutiagin, generously commented: "For me (and I'm sure not only for me), when I hear the words 'Sun Complex' I see an expressive silhouette of a herald of 'cosmic architecture,' a silhouette that appears in such a poetic and fantastic way, without disrupting the primordial silence and harmony of the Parkent foothills, and prompts philosophical reflections on the reality of the unreal, the possibility of the impossible... In introducing a new harmony to this romantic natural environment (can one introduce something without harming nature?) that elevates humans through their involvement (with this perhaps impossible, but actual fact), Humankind has not simply interfered in this silence, but has used pure sound to come close to it and become related to it."[10]

The authors' focus on interaction with the cultural context can be judged from their texts. In their articles they constantly stressed that they tried to create a building specifically for Central Asia. However, and this was a fundamental decision, they refused to reproduce in Parkent historical forms typical of the local architectural tradition. "We attempted to create contemporary architecture," they wrote, "taking into account national traditions while focusing not on superficial expressions of national artistic culture but on its deep, established and still living features, the maintenance of proportions, the preferred color scheme and other national 'ways of seeing' the surrounding world, since the basis of solving the problems of the development of national forms is tradition in unity with contemporary technology."[11]

However, not all of the authors' statements about the project should be taken literally. For example, they wrote: "The interest in historical national cultural values, which has strengthened in recent years under the influence of postmodernism, began to grow into an interest in a deep understanding of our own heritage in the field of construction and architecture, a striving for our regional, national, human architecture that has an individual insularity, is proportional to humans and preserves the established environment—this forms the second direction in the architecture of the Heliocomplex."[12] These ideas seem to be a strained interpretation, since they do not match the project itself. Perhaps only the arrangement of the internal courtyard of the main building is based on the regional historical tradition, but it is also typical of the Middle East and North African countries and India, meaning that any emphasis on "national architecture" is erroneous. The lines about "a deep understanding of *our own heritage*" by Moscow architects who had been commissioned to design something for a region far from Russia look extremely unconvincing, especially since the complex does not demonstrate any concrete steps in this direction. It is obvious that the architects were prompted to express such ideas by the discursive context of late Soviet aesthetics, with its imperatives of creating "national form." A verbal gap between the architects' words and their modernist work, which eased the perception of the innovative

10 Sergo Sutiagin, Review of the Sun Complex, *Arkhitektura SSSR* [*Architecture of the USSR*], nos. 3–4, 1988, 41.
11 "Geliokompleks 'Solntse' [The Sun Heliocomplex]," 39.
12 Ibid., 37.

building in the local and even the Moscow context, was inevitable. In Uzbekistan it was necessary to create "Uzbek national architecture," and the architects' explanatory texts confirmed their adherence to this convention.

Public Perception

Until construction began in the foothills of the Tien Shan, this secret building remained invisible to the Tashkent and global public. However, the design project was sent to the III World Biennale of Architecture Interarch-85 in Sofia, where it was awarded the International Academy of Architecture medal. Construction of the complex was completed in 1987. At that point the building was awarded a gold medal at the II All-Union Review and Competition as best project of the year. It was received with great enthusiasm in Moscow and Tashkent, where laudatory materials appeared in journals, and there were news reports and programs on television. The Union of Architects of Uzbekistan organized several special trips for specialists to visit the innovative building.

However, despite the general approval of the architects' concept, critical notes regarding the quality of construction and the choice of materials sometimes appeared in professional reviews. In particular, Tashkent architect Vladislav Rusanov included the following thoughts in his review: "It did not prove possible to raise the building to high contemporary levels in every aspect. The low ceilings of the corridors of the staff/administrative block, which are a result of the use of the standard anti-seismic series IIS-04, are covered with low-quality, locally produced Akmigran tiles. The metal details for fixing the elegant elements of the sun protection are crude, and painted in a way that does not match the design. The sawn marble of the retaining walls of the heliostatic floor has been unsuccessfully replaced with polished marble. It is a shame that they have used low-quality aluminum window frames and internal doors sourced from the local construction industry. This is the annoying cost of contemporary construction."[13] Nevertheless, architects and architecture and art historians unconditionally approved of Irena Lipene's installations. Everyone who wrote about the complex noted them, and art historian Gul'sara Babadzhanova wrote an entire article about them.[14]

13 Vladislav Rusanov, Review of the Sun Complex, *Arkhitektura SSSR* [*Architecture of the USSR*], nos. 3–4, 1988, 42–43.
14 Gul'sara Babadzhanova, "Tema kosmosa v stekle [The Theme of the Cosmos in Glass]," *Arkhitektura i stroitel'stvo Uzbekistana* [*Architecture and Construction of Uzbekistan*], no. 1, 1988, 23–24.

ARCHITECT
VIKTOR ZAKHAROV

Chief Architect at Minatom (Federal Agency for Atomic Energy), Russia
Place and year of birth:
Moscow, 1949
Year of death:
2021
Education:
Moscow Architectural Institute

Due to the secret nature of the organization in which Viktor Zakharov worked there was no information about his creative biography and education in open sources. Paradoxically, the secret was revealed with the help of the processes of sacralization and new religiosity that characterize every layer of the state apparatus in Russia today, including its scientific and industrial institutions. In particular, the Ministry of Atomic Energy of the Russian Federation, in parallel with its activities focused on the military and civilian use of atomic energy, was actively involved in the construction in Russia of Orthodox churches. Zakharov's name can be found in reports on the completion of construction of such projects. From those publications we can establish that today the architect has the title Honored Architect of Russia and that his later buildings completely departed from the modernist language of the 1980s.[1]

1 "Novyi khram v Pleskovo vozveden po proektu V.V. Zakharova, sozdavshego arkhitekturnyi proekt khrama na Stroginskom bul'vare v Moskve [A New Church in Pleskovo Built to a Design by V.V. Zakharov, Who Designed the Church on Stroginsky Boulevard in Moscow]," *Fedmp.ru*, January 5, 2019, https://www.fedmp.ru/news/novyj-hram-v-pleskovo-vozveden-po-proektu-v-v-zaharova-sozdavshego-arhitekturnyj-proekt-hrama-na-stroginskom-bulvare-v-moskve/.

ARTIST
IRENA LIPENE

Place and date of birth:
Kaunas (Lithuania), December 25, 1939
Place and date of death:
Vilnius (Lithuania), September 6, 2016
Education:
Graduated in 1965 from Vilnius Art Institute

From 1966 to 1985 Irena Lipene lived and worked in Tashkent, after which she returned to Lithuania. In Tashkent she was a teacher in the local theatrical and art institute (1966–1974) and for the rest of the time she worked in an artistic enterprise. She may have been the sole monumental artist in Uzbekistan who worked consistently in the genre of abstract art. It was only in one of her first buildings, the Iubileinyi Palace of Sport (1970), that she produced a decorative glass work with figurative images of sportswomen on ice. Later she preferred to work with abstract forms, which may be explained by her personal aesthetic values, since such works were not only subject to censure but were also significantly less well paid than figurative art. Other notable works by the artist include the stained glass in the Delegation House of the Central Committee of the Uzbekistan Communist Party (1975) and the three-dimensional installation in the Tashkent TV Tower.

INSTITUTIONAL FRAMEWORK

Postbox A-1158 Project Institute (today, GSPI)

CADRE
Information is secret.

PRIORITIES
Construction of buildings for the Ministry of the Atomic Industry of the USSR. An institute on the federal level. Worked on commissions for the Ministry of Defense Industry and the Academy of Sciences of the USSR.

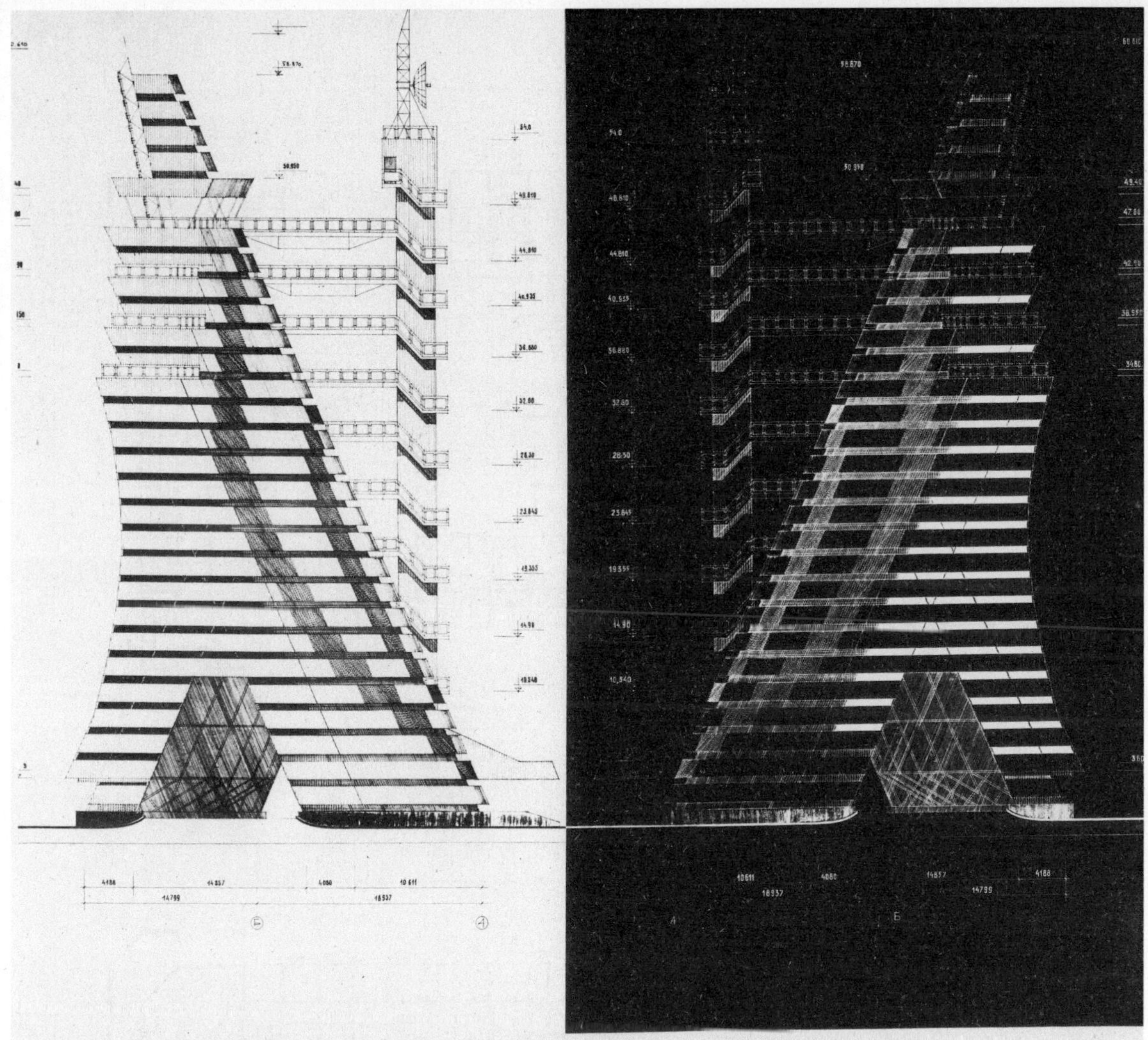

ЗАПАДНЫЙ И ВОСТОЧНЫЙ ФАСАДЫ
КОНЦЕНТРАТОРА

Sun Heliocomplex, west and east façades of the parabolic concentrator

1st floor plan
Original condition

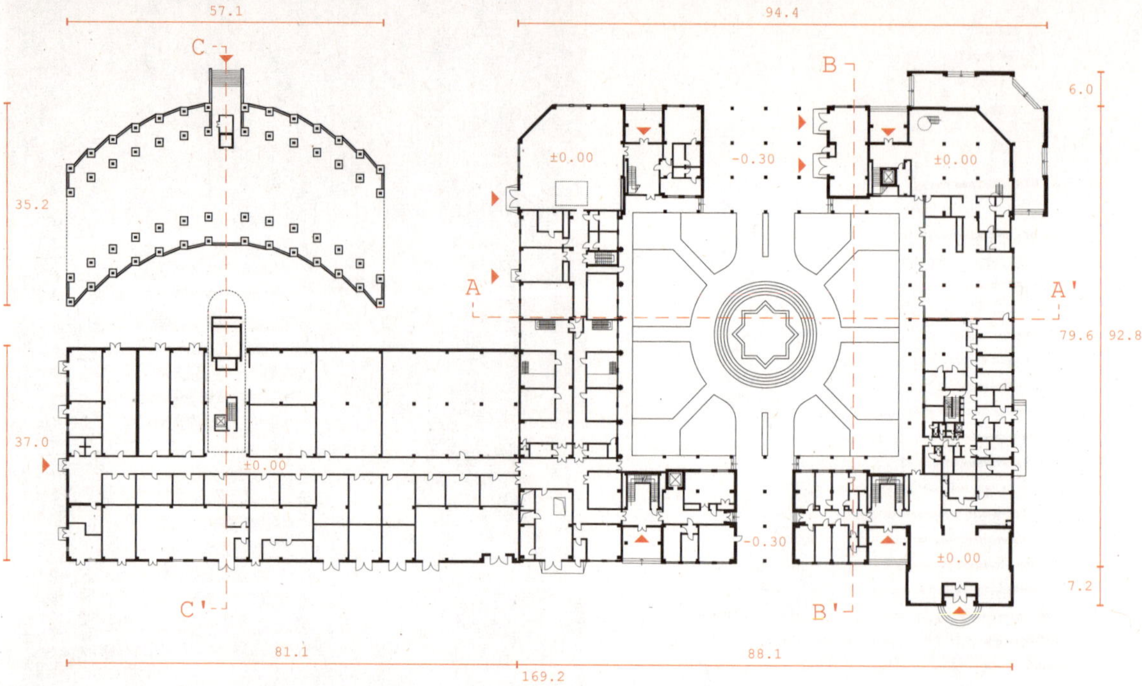

2nd floor plan
Original condition

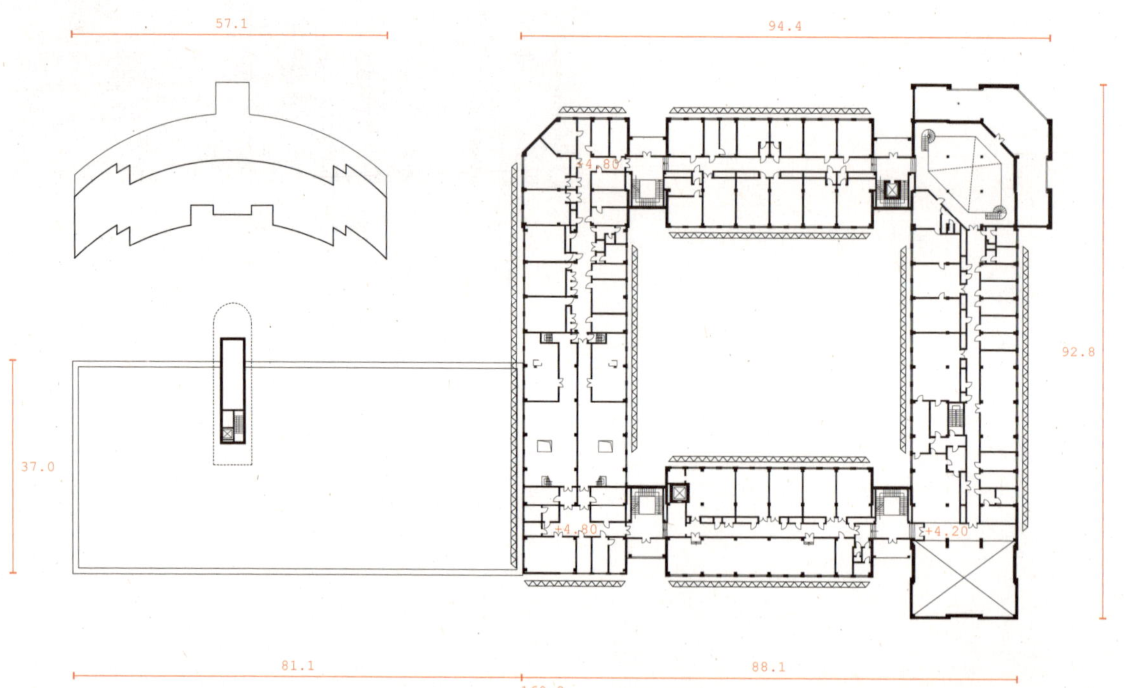

0 5 10 20m

3rd floor plan
Original condition

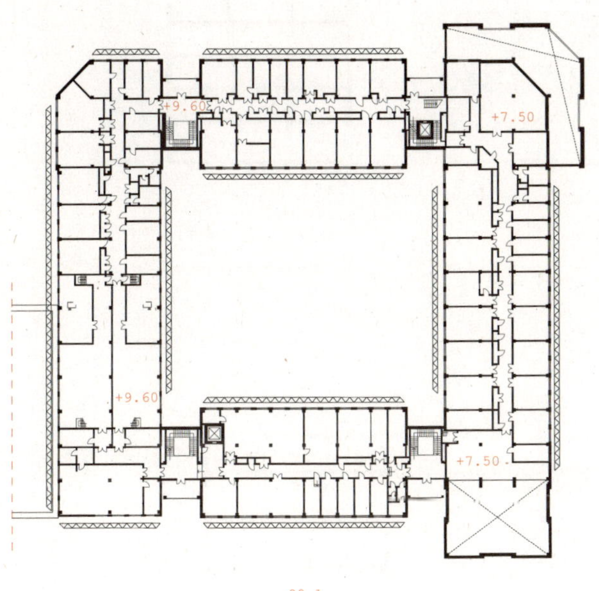

4th floor plan
Original condition

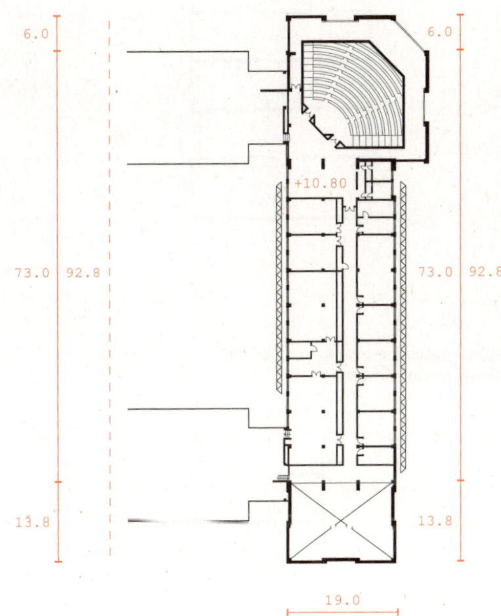

Concentrator, section CC'
Original condition

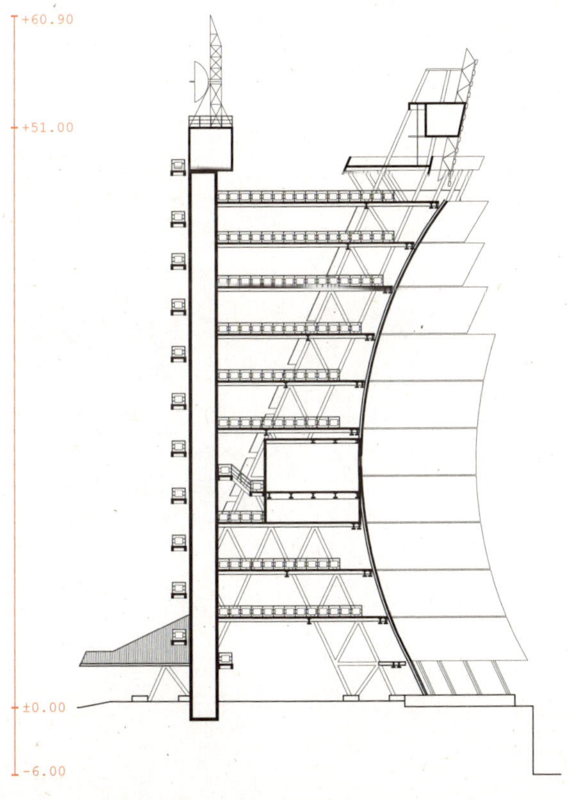

Process tower, section CC'
Original condition

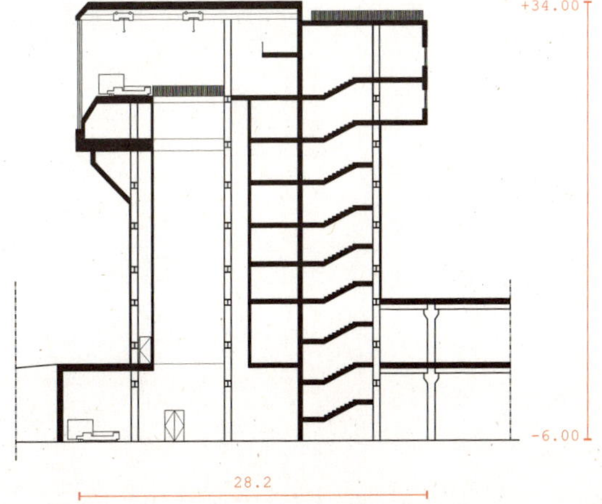

Administrative block, section AA'
Original condition

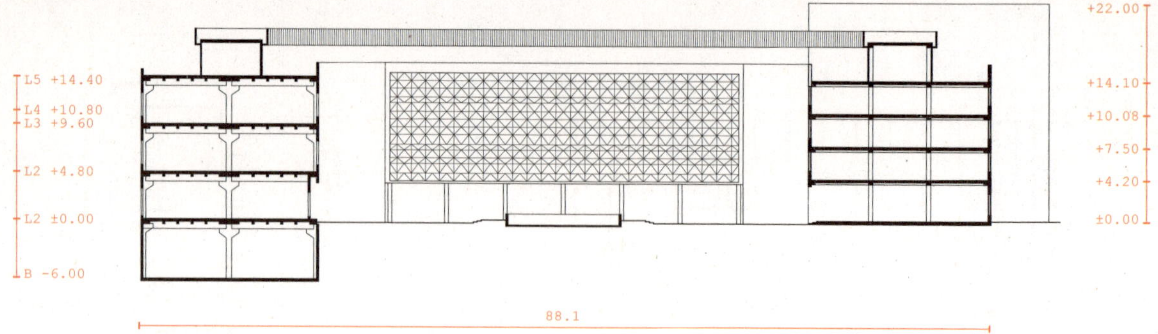

Administrative block, section BB'
Original condition

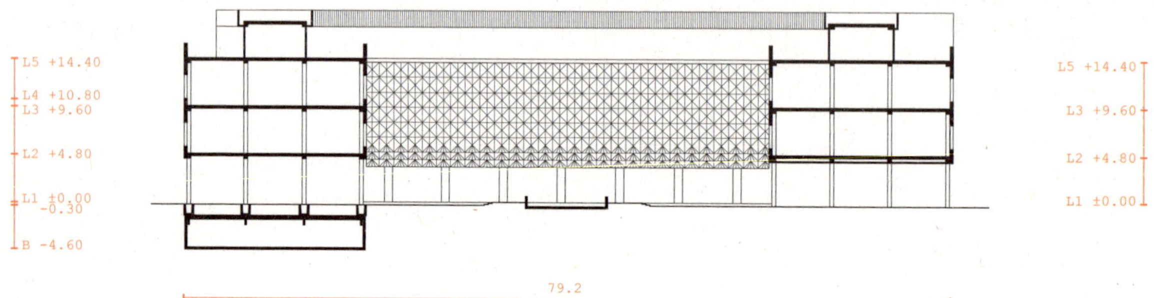

Administrative block, perspective view of the courtyard
Original condition

0 5 15m

North-east axonometric view
Original condition

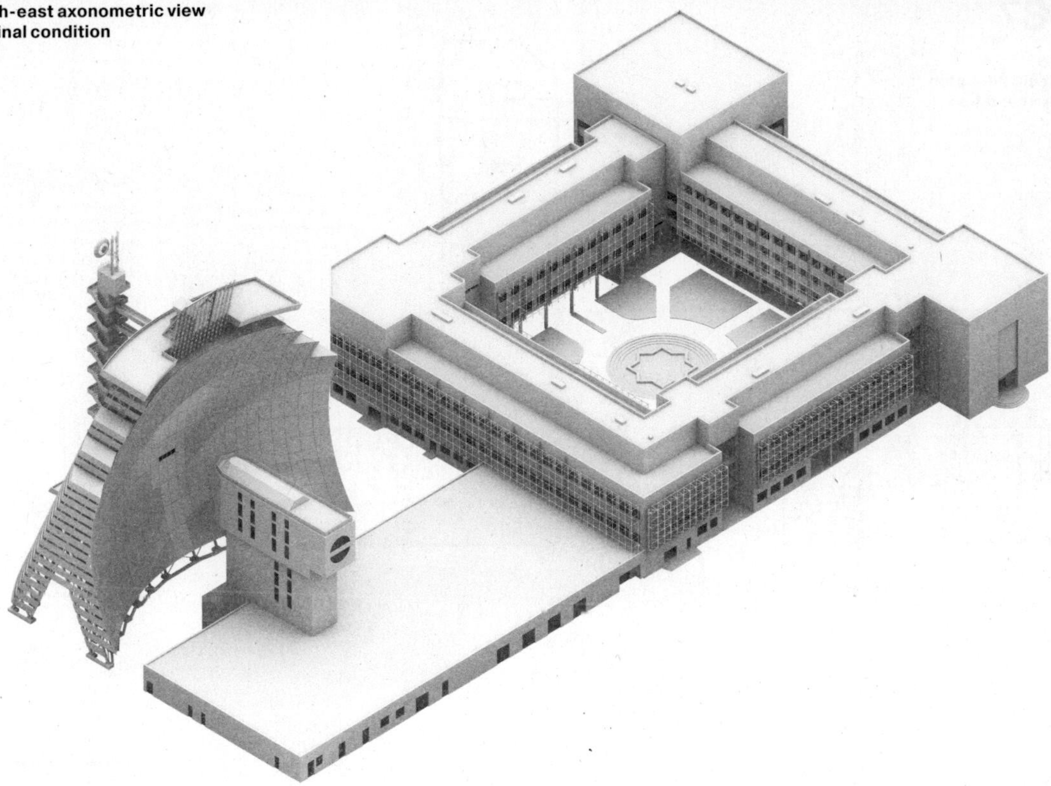

South-east axonometric view
Original condition

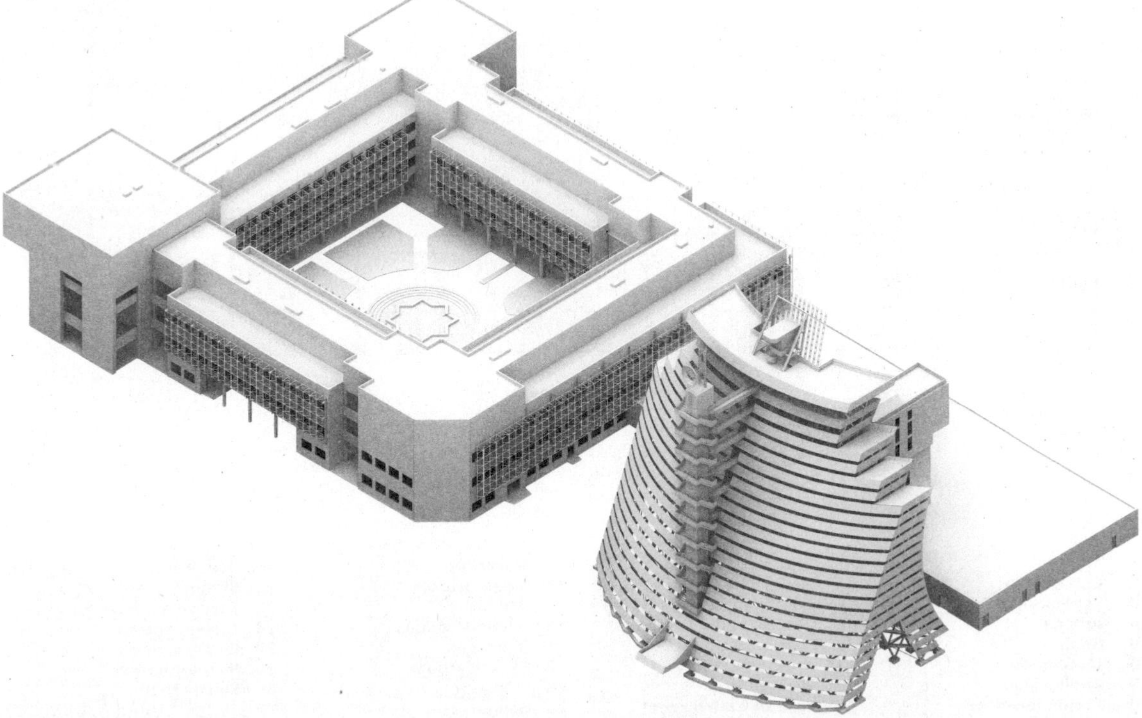

1987

Basement floor plan
Original condition

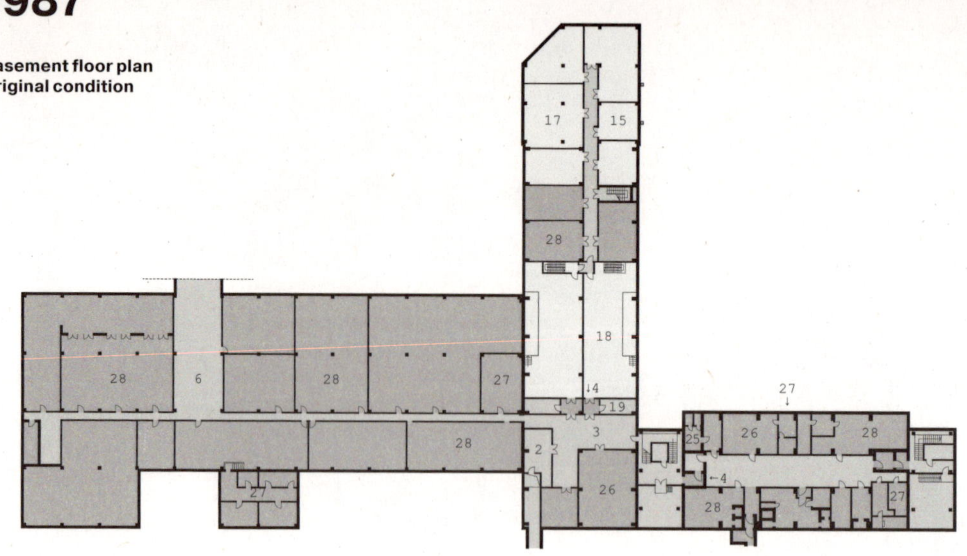

1st floor plan
Original condition

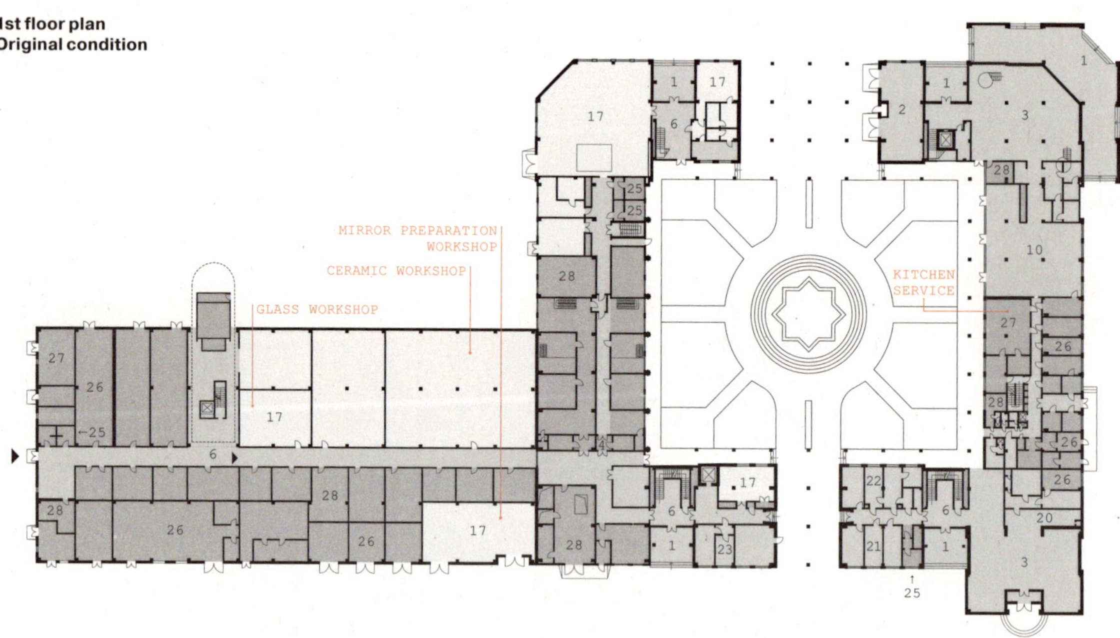

1 Terrace
2 Entrance
3 Vestibule
4 Airlock
5 Shop
6 Circulation
7 Auditorium
8 Projection room
9 Smoking room
10 Dining hall
11 Exhibition hall
12 Library reading room
13 Book storage
14 Photo laboratory
15 Research lab
16 Research lab for rent
17 Workshop
18 Meeting room
19 Offices
20 Administration
21 Staff room
22 Security room
23 First aid
24 Sauna
25 Restroom
26 Storage
27 Service room
28 Technical area
29 Empty spaces
30 No information
31 Sun furnace

2022

Basement floor plan
Current condition

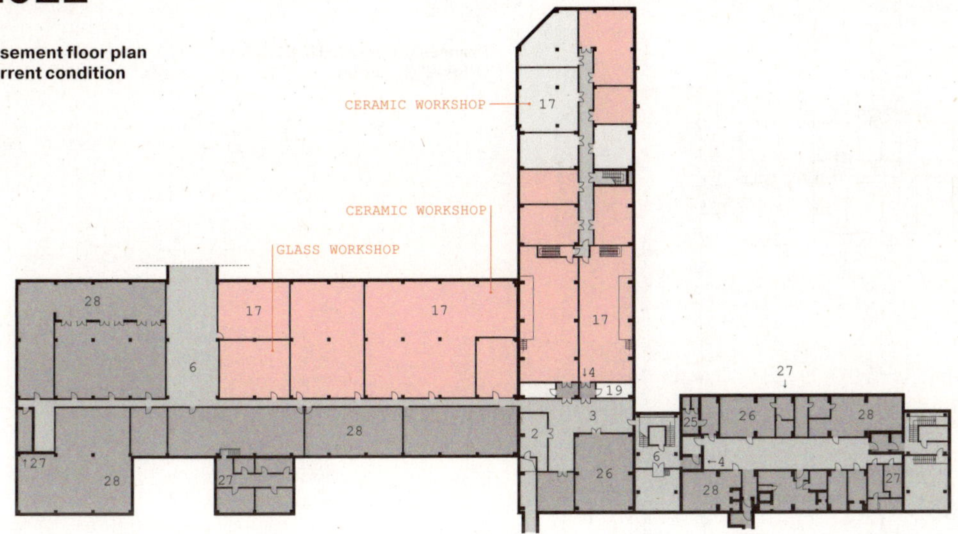

1st floor plan
Current condition

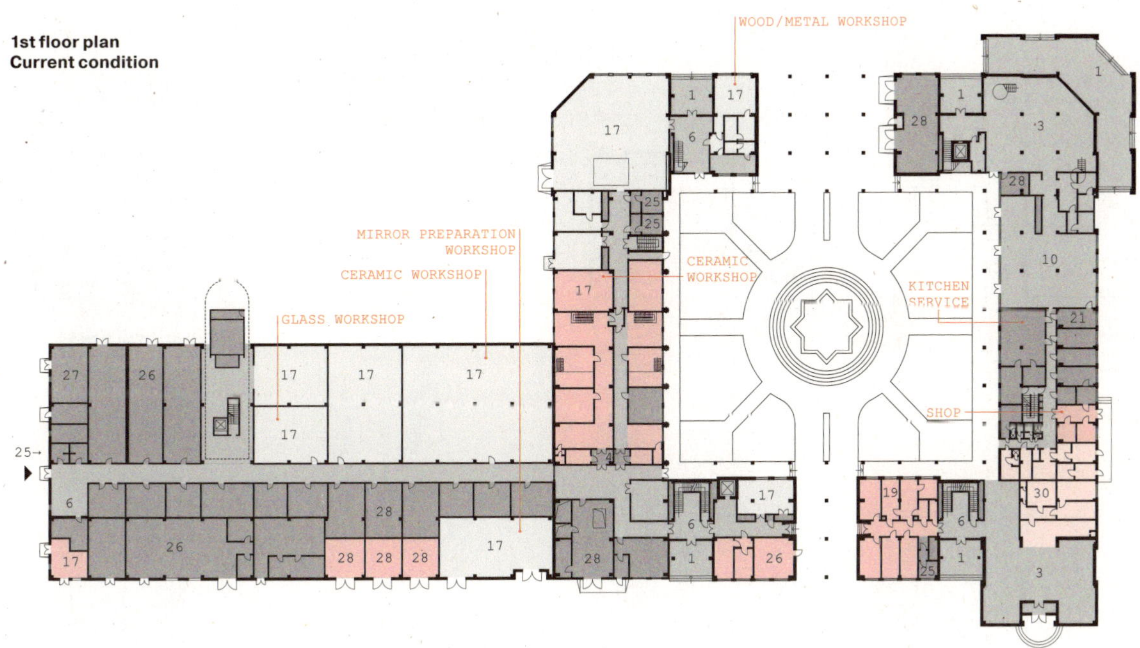

Sun furnace/workshop/laboratory
Public/administrative
Technical
Change of function

0 5 15m

1987

2nd floor plan
Original condition

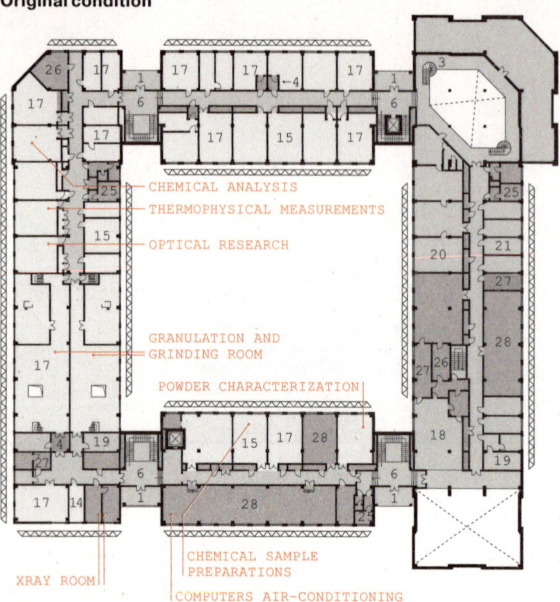

Process tower plan H +20.75m
Original condition

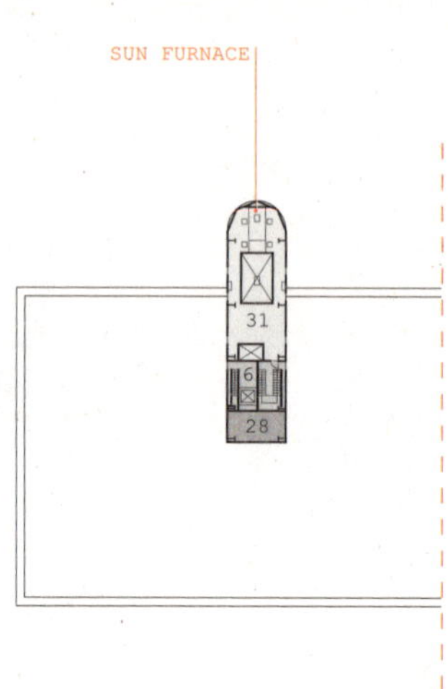

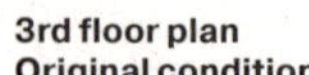

3rd floor plan
Original condition

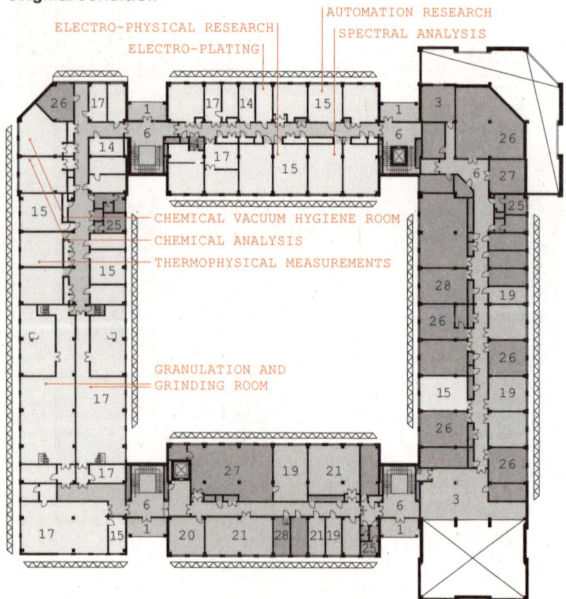

Process tower plan H +24.05m
Original condition

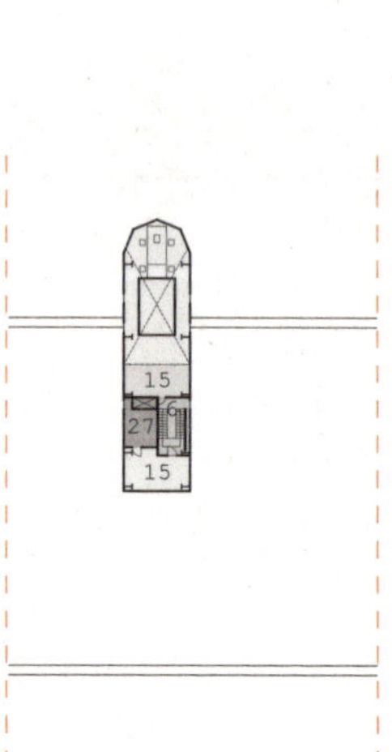

4th floor plan
Original condition

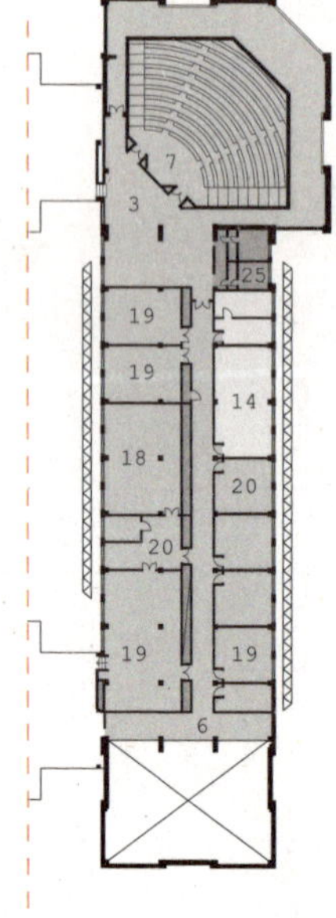

1 Terrace
2 Entrance
3 Vestibule
4 Airlock
5 Shop
6 Circulation
7 Auditorium
8 Projection room
9 Smoking room
10 Dining hall
11 Exhibition hall
12 Library reading room
13 Book storage
14 Photo laboratory
15 Research lab
16 Research lab for rent
17 Workshop
18 Meeting room
19 Offices
20 Administration
21 Staff room
22 Security room
23 First aid
24 Sauna
25 Restroom
26 Storage
27 Service room
28 Technical area
29 Empty spaces
30 No information
31 Sun furnace

2022

2nd floor plan
Current condition

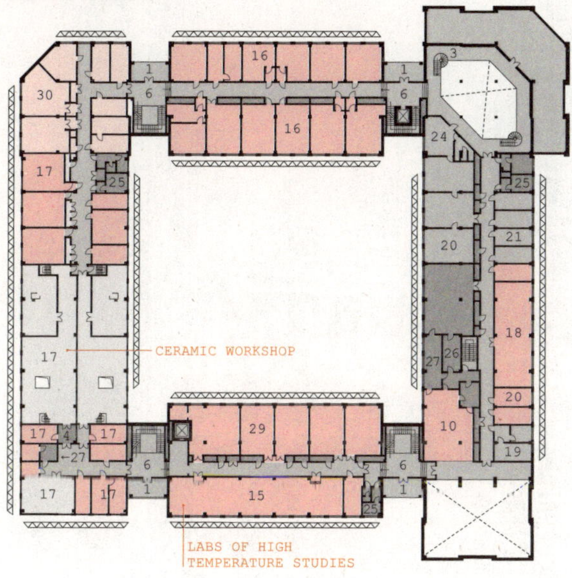

Process tower plan H +20.75m
Current condition

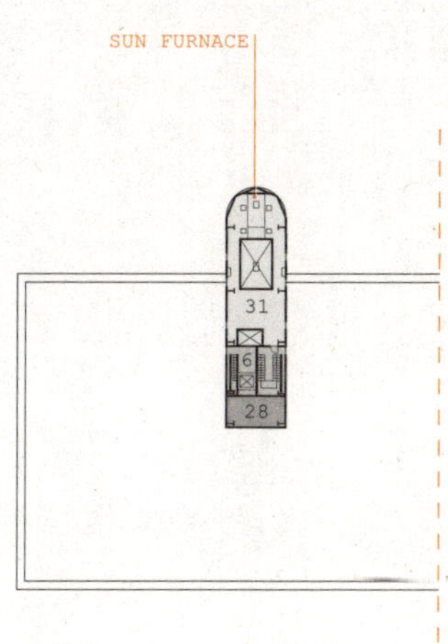

3rd floor plan
Current condition

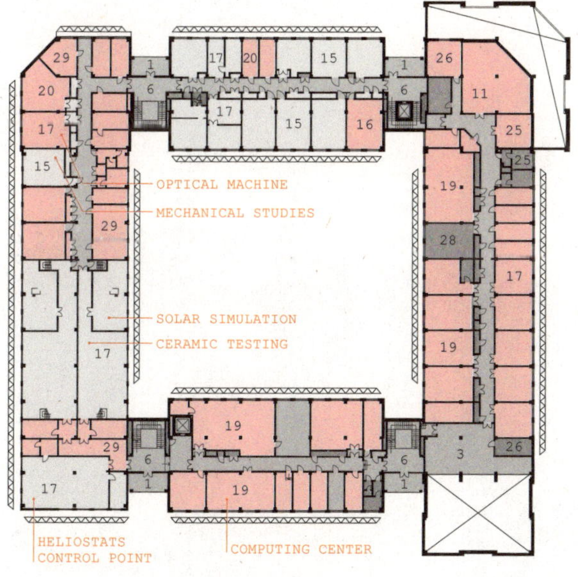

Process tower plan H +24.05m
Current condition

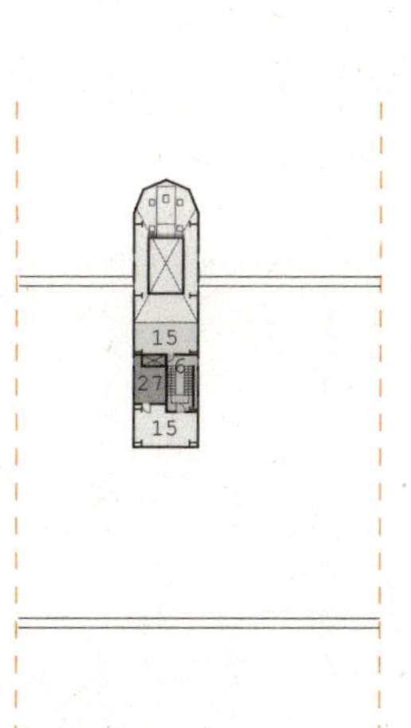

4th floor plan
Current condition

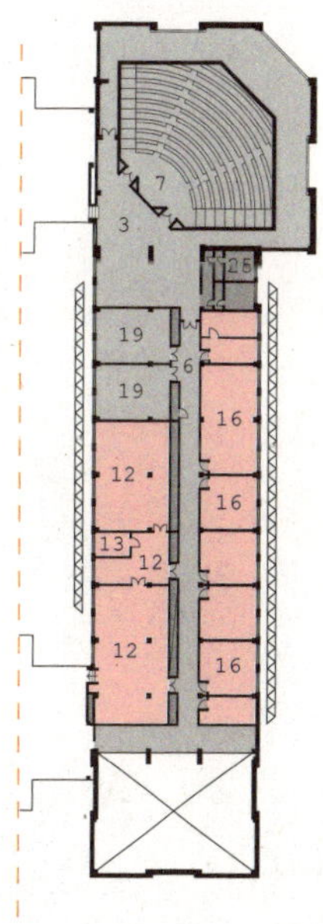

Sun furnace/workshop/laboratory
Public/administrative
Technical
Change of function

0 5 15m

Sun Heliocomplex during construction

General view of the Sun Heliocomplex

View of the administrative block and parabolic concentrator

North façade of the parabolic concentrator

South-west façade of the parabolic concentrator

View from the south-east; arrival road

South façade of the parabolic concentrator

Laboratory block, lightweight sunshading system

South-east façade, 2021

North façade of the parabolic concentrator, 2021

Heliostatic field, general view, 2021

View of the heliostatic field and the parabolic concentrator, 2021

Small solar concentrator on the heliostatic field, 2021

Equipment on the roof of the concentrator, 2021

Auto-reflection mark, a device for heliostat mirror alignment, located on the roof of the concentrator, 2021

Technological tower, 2021

Technological tower, 2021

View of the focal point (furnace) inside the technological tower, 2021

View toward the heliostatic field from the technological tower, 2021

Technological tower equipment, 2021

Outdoor experimental area equipment, 2021

View toward the focal point of the technological tower from the control room in the concentrator, 2021

Administrative block courtyard, 2021

Administrative block courtyard, 2021

Hymn to the Sun by Irena Lipene, entrance hall of the administrative block, 2021

Parade of Planets by Irena Lipene, staircase of the administrative block, 2021

Model of the complex

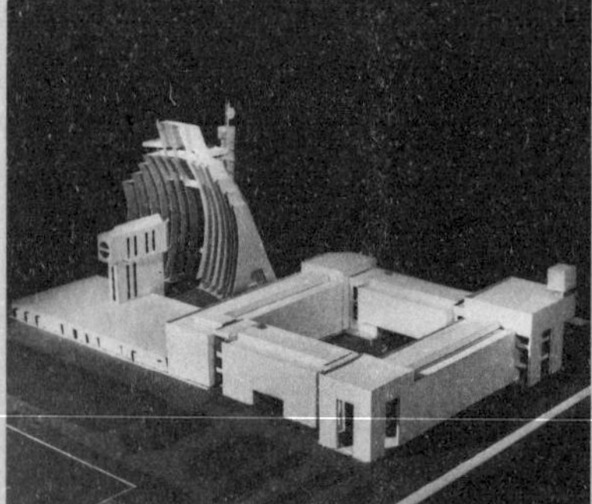

Model of the complex

Model of a single heliostat

Functional zoning and circulation

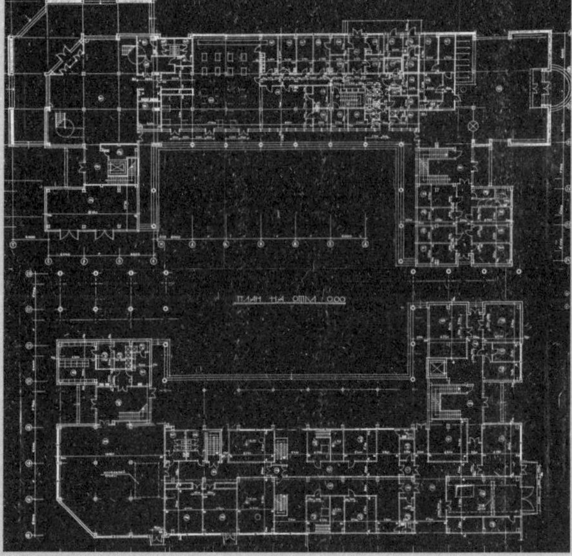

Administrative block, first-floor plan

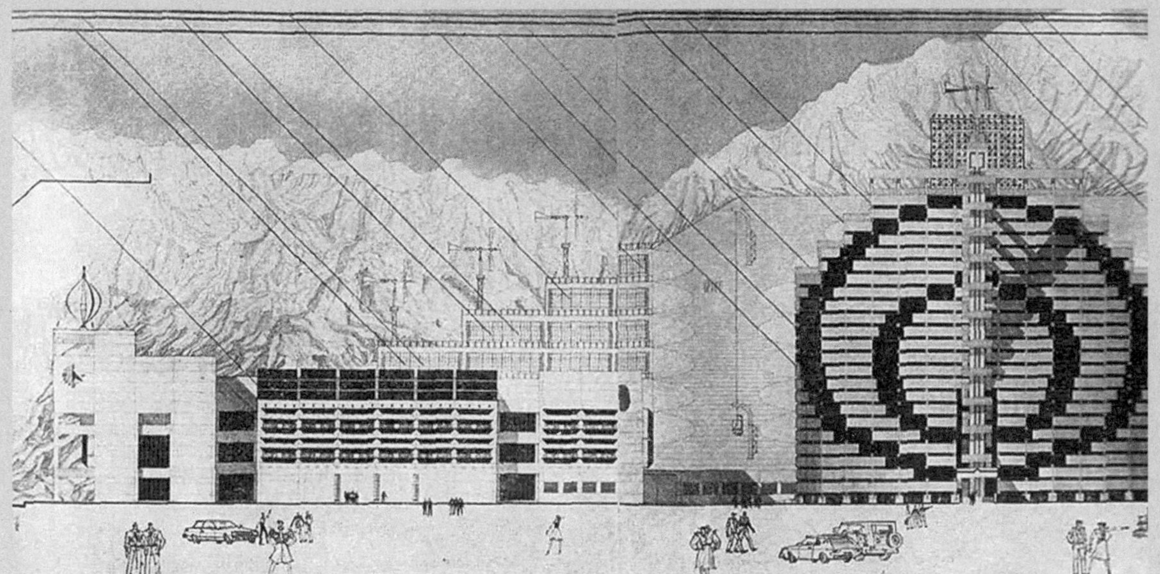

Panoramic view of the Sun Heliocomplex, sketch of the south façade

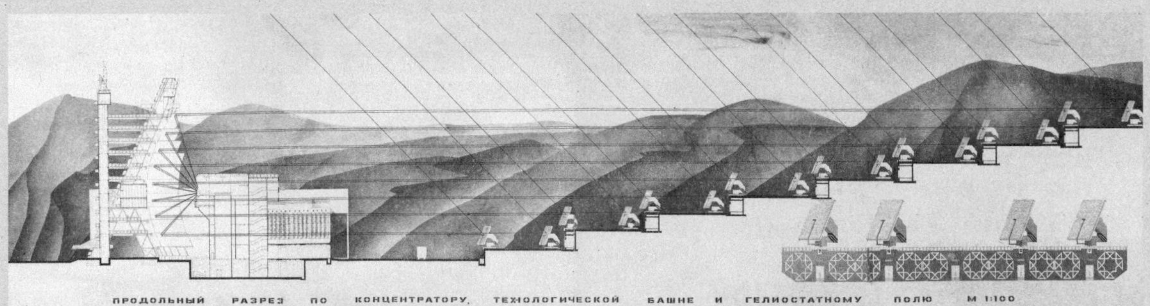

Longitudinal section of the parabolic concentrator, technological tower and heliostatic field

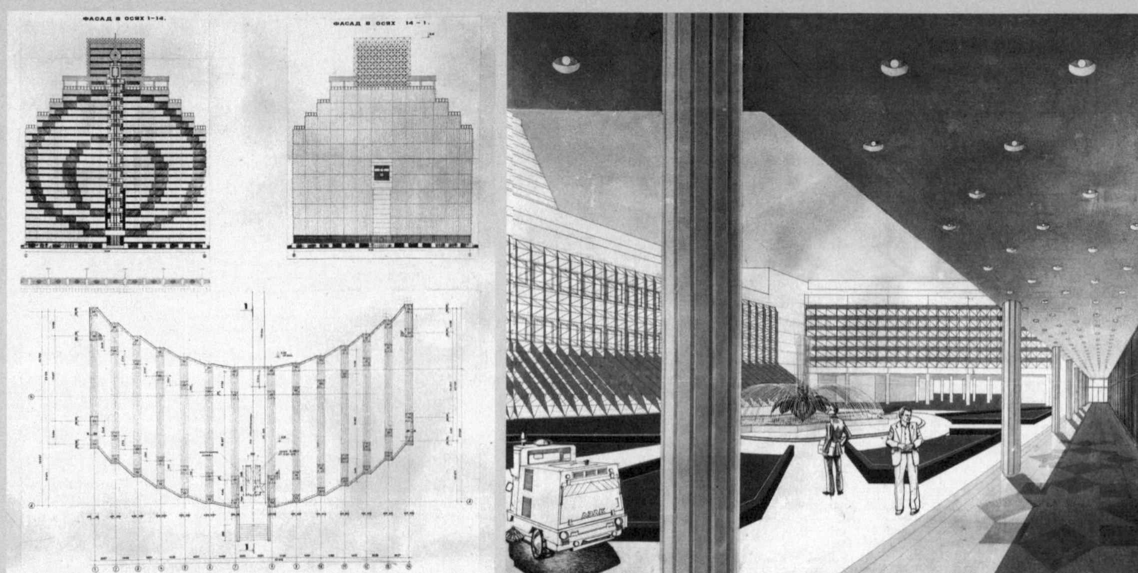

Parabolic concentrator, plan and south and north façades

Administrative block, perspective view of the courtyard

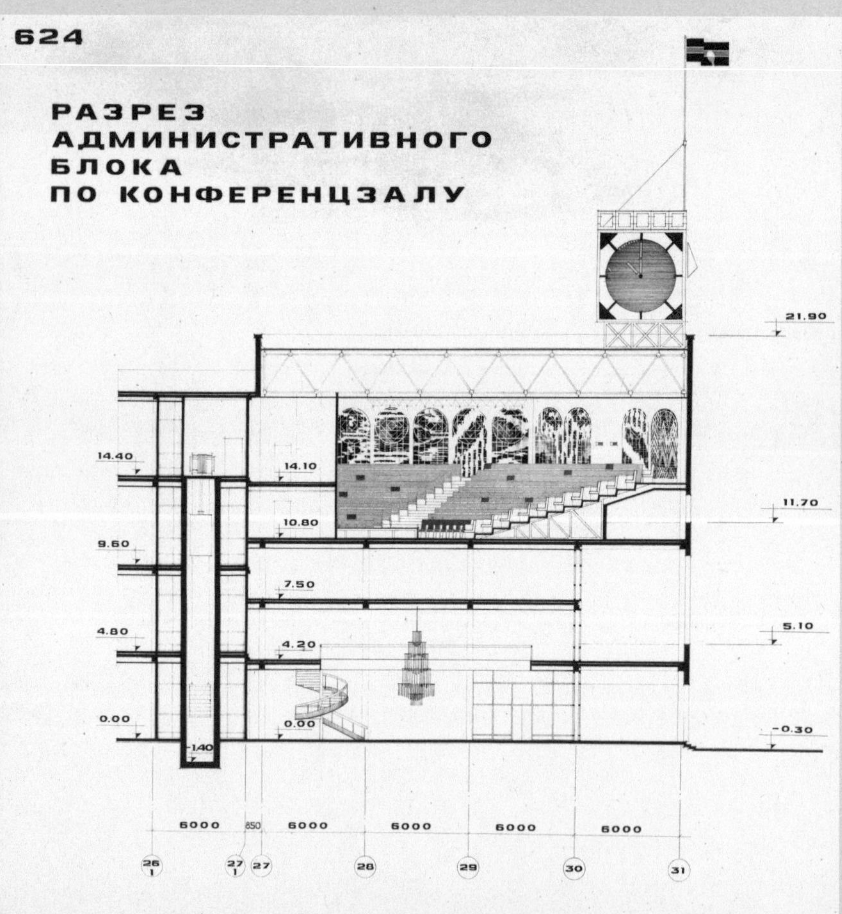

Administrative block, section of the conference hall

Administrative block, perspective view of the meeting room

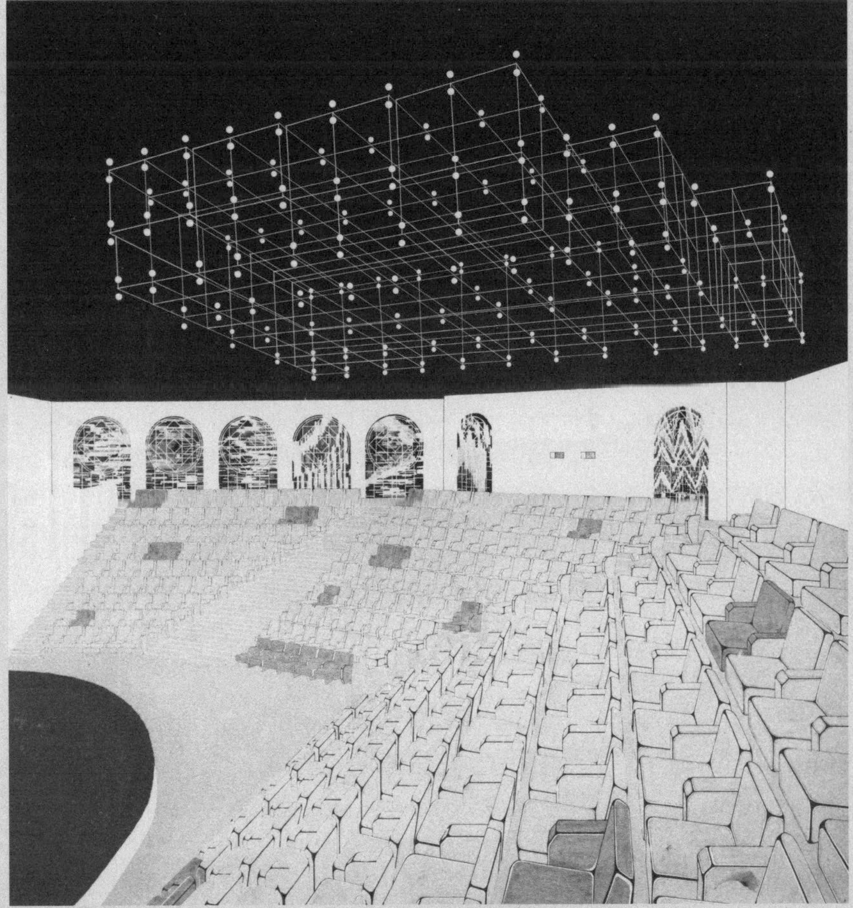

Administrative block, perspective view of the conference hall

HIGHLIGHTS

The Sun Heliocomplex is a set of buildings containing a solar furnace and research complex. It was designed by Moscow architect Viktor Zakharov, working for the classified institute Postbox A-1158, and built between 1981 and 1987 in the mountain area of Parkent, 30 km east of Tashkent.

The building was awarded a gold medal by the Union of Architects of the USSR in 1987 and recognized as the year's best project in the All-Union competition.

The Sun Heliocomplex is an outstanding monument of Soviet modernism and is worthy of international recognition for three reasons:

- it is a unique functional and architectural typology, testifying to the high level of Soviet scientific research;
- the project relies on a unique connection between the architecture, the arid landscape and the dry climate, which is crucial to making such a solar-based heating process possible;
- it is a valuable synthesis between architecture and monumental art, thanks to Irena Lipene's works. Therefore, a conservation strategy should be proposed.

FUNCTION

The complex consists of five functional parts:

1) Heliostatic field – a terraced hill with sixty-two solar mirrors (with a sun tracking system)
2) Concentrator – a large paraboloid shield covered with mirrors oriented toward the solar furnace
3) Furnace – a technical or process tower containing the focal point, where all solar energy is directed
4) Laboratories directly connected to the furnace
5) Courtyard building for laboratories and administration offices

The heliostats on the hill reflect the solar radiation toward the concentrator, which, in turn, directs it toward the focal point of the furnace. There, a sample can be melted or heated to very high temperatures close to 3,000°C. This method, deploying clean sun energy without additional gases, enables the production of particularly pure oxide materials that cannot be made otherwise, and the testing of materials' resistance to intense solar radiation.

MONUMENTALITY

The solar furnace of Parkent is one of only two examples of such infrastructure worldwide, the other being in Odeillo, in the eastern French Pyrenees, built between 1962 and 1968.

Unlike its French precedent, the Parkent center consists of several buildings, each hosting a single technical or administrative function. The Odeillo furnace was studied by Soviet scientists and engineers, who decided that, given the location, the seismic risk and the capacity of the Soviet construction industry, it would be impossible to replicate the combination of the laboratory/office block and the concentrator in a single volume, as in France. Accordingly, each of the five elements of the complex was built as an independent structure, forming a sequence reminiscent of the mechanization of modern architecture, to quote Giedion.

The isolation of the concentrator on the crest of a hill and the tapering shape of its sides, which was dictated by structural requirements, produce a strong sense of monumentality that is absent in Odeillo.

The celebration of science through architecture was common among many Soviet scientific institutes, unlike their European, considerably more utilitarian counterparts, though here it appears to be mainly a result of technical constraints.

LANDSCAPE AND CLIMATE

The complex has a strong relationship with the landscape and the climate as a consequence of its placement and architectural design. This relationship is visible in the prominent horizontality of the compound, a consequence of the choice to break it into several buildings that are well integrated into the landscape. The giant curve of the paraboloid concentrator, decorated with a "solar" motif on the sunshading screen, is the only exceptional element and is visible from afar.

The constant search for vantage points toward the surrounding mountains through the passages on the first floor or through the sunshades with their slender metal structure and transparent panels highlights this focus.

ART AND ARCHITECTURE

The installation created by Irena Lipene represents a high point in the modernist search for a "synthesis of the arts." Lipene made four works of monumental art for the Sun Heliocomplex, each inspired by the universe: *Milky Way*, *Hymn to the Sun*, *Moon* and *Parade of Planets*.

Hymn to the Sun is a gigantic glass chandelier in the central atrium composed of "rays" in red, yellow, amber, orange and golden glass that symbolize the warmth of the sun. The work, together with the hall's interiors, is reflected in full-height mirrors on two sides, duplicating itself to infinity.

Milky Way, which was created for the conference hall, is embedded in the stepped structure of the acoustic ceiling and consists of three rows of ornamental glass parallel to the auditorium's seats, filtering the artificial lighting.

Moon is a metal and glass spatial composition placed in the middle of the secondary foyer. Vertical stainless-steel elements connect the floor and the ceiling. The center of the composition, formed by fused glass spheres and white glass lamps arranged at the ends of bent steel tubes, is marked by two red half spheres, representing the moon itself.

Parade of Planets is a composition of metal and pink and purple frosted-glass spheres that resemble a sequence of planets vertically lined up from bottom to top in a luminous staircase atrium.

STATE OF REPAIR
SCORE:

- 2 – The building shows severe localized damage and/or diffused and extended deterioration patterns. It is, however, still possible to use it.

Protection status:	The building is listed according to Resolution No. 227 of the Cabinet of Ministers, April 22, 2024.
Main criticalities:	Lack of maintenance, poor state of repair, partial nonuse of spaces.
Possible risks:	The building risks undergoing significant transformations.

INTEGRITY
SCORE:

- Exterior: 3 – The building has retained all the elements necessary to express its significance but is in a poor state of repair
- Interior: 2 – Transformations to the building and its surroundings have caused the loss of some of the elements necessary to express its significance

The Sun Heliocomplex retains its integrity both architecturally and artistically. The architecture has not undergone significant transformations and accordingly its relationship to the landscape has not changed.

The original decorations and finishes are intact and contribute to the significance of the building. However, the complex is not fully used today because of a lack of funding and the serious level of obsolescence of parts of the building.

AUTHENTICITY SCORE:

- Exterior: 4 – Only minor repairs and conservation activities have been carried out on the building
- Interior: 3 – The building has been subjected to slight changes and replacements

The building shows a good level of authenticity: no major interventions have been carried out since construction.

The careful choice of materials is still clearly visible, as the original building materials are still in place, as are the original four sculptures by Irena Lipene.

The elegant glass and metal sunscreens on the outer façades of the administration building and in the courtyard have been dismantled.

1987 2022

South façade of the parabolic concentrator, 1987

South façade of the parabolic concentrator, 2022

General view of the Sun Heliocomplex from the mountain, 1987

General view of the Sun Heliocomplex from the mountain, 2022

1987 2022

South-east façade of the parabolic concentrator, 1987

South-east façade of the parabolic concentrator, 2021

North façade of the parabolic concentrator, 1987

North façade of the parabolic concentrator, 2022

LEVEL 1 – MAXIMUM LEVEL OF INTEREST
(No transformations allowed; conservation activities required)

ADMINISTRATIVE/LABORATORY BUILDING
ARCHITECTURAL LEVEL
EXTERIOR

All four façades, characterized by their pronounced horizontality and simple design, should be preserved as they are.

All four façades of the inner courtyard and the steel windbreak systems are to be preserved as they are.

The spatial relationships between the courtyard and the building must be preserved.

The arcades on the first floor ensure a constant relationship with the landscape and should be preserved as they are.

INTERIOR

The spatiality of the main spaces must be preserved. It is not possible to build partition walls or ceilings in the following spaces:

- the main foyer;
- the secondary foyer;
- the conference hall;
- the exhibition hall;
- the canteen space on the first floor;
- the terrace linked to the secondary foyer.

DETAIL LEVEL
EXTERIOR

The following exterior elements must be preserved:

- the marble cladding;
- the three-dimensional elements that constitute the structure of the sunshades and windbreaks of the courtyard façades;
- the glass panels of the sunshade system;
- the fountain in the courtyard, with original cladding;
- the columns, with original cladding.

INTERIOR

In the main foyer, the following elements must be preserved:

- the marble flooring;
- the marble cladding;
- the mirror cladding;
- the lamps;
- the glass chandelier *Hymn to the Sun* by Irena Lipene.

In the secondary foyer and adjacent terrace, the following elements must be preserved:

- the marble flooring;
- the marble cladding;
- the lamps;
- the original handrails;
- the staircases with their structure, finishes and handrails;
- the glass and steel installation *Moon* by Irena Lipene.

In the conference hall, the following elements must be preserved:

- the parquet flooring;
- the marble cladding;
- the glass sculpture *Milky Way* by Irena Lipene.

In the canteen, the following elements must be preserved:

- the marble flooring;
- the marble cladding;
- the ceramic wall and cladding.

In the main staircase, the following elements must be preserved:

- the artwork *Parade of Planets* by Irena Lipene.

AUXILIARY BUILDINGS

ARCHITECTURAL LEVEL

EXTERIOR

- The perimeter and the eave height of the buildings must be preserved.

LEVEL 2 – MEDIUM LEVEL OF INTEREST

(Elements included in the second level can be moderately transformed following approval by a designated committee[1])

1 An international committee of heritage preservation experts to be appointed.

URBAN LEVEL

The construction of a new volume in the surrounding area of the complex must be subject to approval by the designated committee.

ADMINISTRATIVE/LABORATORY BUILDING

ARCHITECTURAL LEVEL

INTERIOR

Any modifications to other parts of the building (besides the main foyer, the secondary foyer, the conference hall and the canteen spaces) should be submitted to the designated committee for approval.

DETAIL LEVEL

EXTERIOR

Any changes to the façades involving the color of the plaster or the replacement of window frames or glazing must be subject to approval by the designated committee.

INTERIOR

The replacement of finishings in other parts of the building (besides the main foyer, the secondary foyer, the conference hall and the canteen spaces) should be submitted to the designated committee for approval.

PROCESS TOWER – THE FURNACE

ARCHITECTURAL LEVEL

EXTERIOR

Any changes to the façades of the buildings must be subject to approval by the designated committee.

INTERIOR

Any changes to the internal spaces of the buildings must be subject to approval by the designated committee.

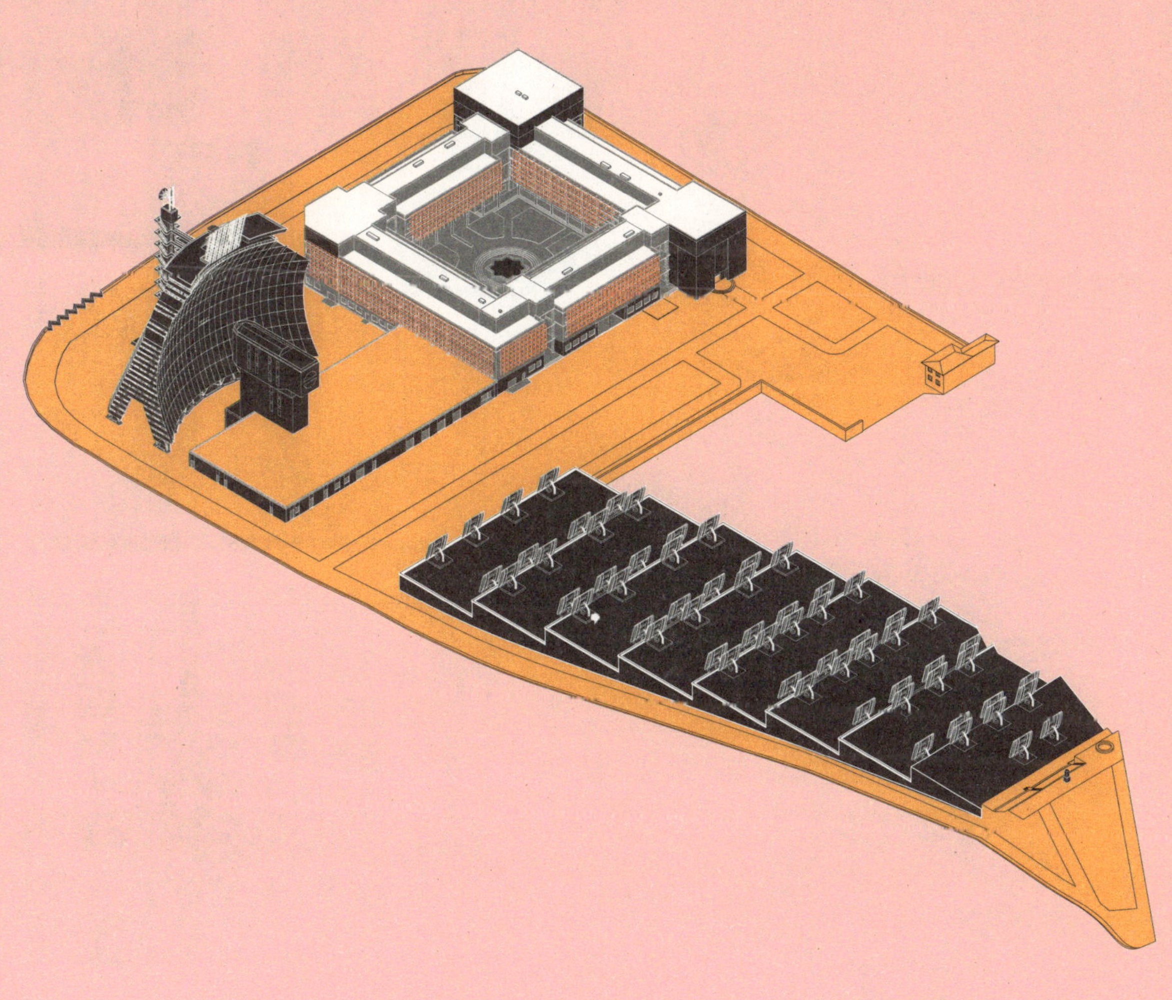

Preservation Level 1
Maximum Level of Interest
Materials and elements to be preserved

Preservation Level 2
Medium Level of Interest
Materials and elements to be preserved

Hidden Modernist Features
Materials and elements to be preserved

Transformation allowed

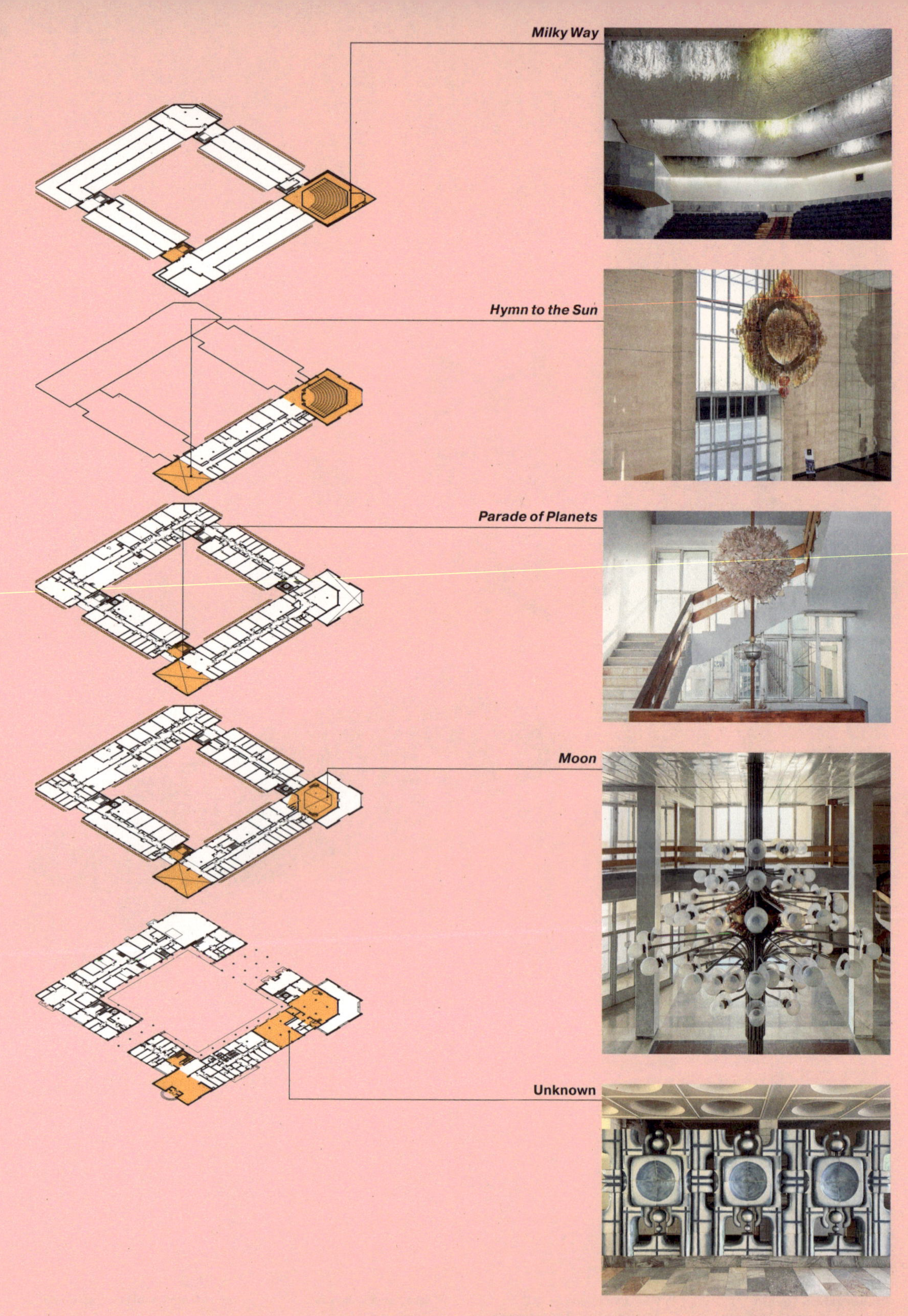
Milky Way
Hymn to the Sun
Parade of Planets
Moon
Unknown

Preservation Strategy

The Sun Heliocomplex is a group of buildings constructed between 1981 and 1987 to house a solar furnace and research center. Its significance is largely related to its uniqueness, since there are only two structures of this kind in the world: in France and Uzbekistan. The location of the Heliocomplex—on the deserted crest of a hill near Parkent—was used by the architects as an opportunity for a monumental arrangement of the two mirrored functional bodies: the heliostatic field and the concentrator.

Distinctive works of art are organically placed within the spaces of the administrative and laboratory building and are coherent with the modernist motto of a "synthesis of the arts." They include four glass sculptures by Irena Lipene (*Hymn to the Sun*, *Milky Way*, *Moon*, *Parade of Planets*) and a ceramic artwork in the canteen.

Over the years the complex has not been subjected to major changes and retains most of its original features and its significance. The overall maintenance of the buildings could, however, be improved. While minimum upkeep is regularly carried out to guarantee the functioning of the solar furnace, repairs that are not strictly necessary and repairs to secondary structures are often postponed.

The aim of the Heliocomplex preservation strategy is thus to provide local repairs and improve maintenance activities, so that the whole complex will be able to endure and retain its integrity and authenticity as much as possible. The main issues to be addressed are listed below.

The Concentrator and the Heliostatic Field

The steel structure supporting the reflecting surfaces shows diffused oxidation. If not treated, this situation could result in damage in the long run. The first preservation action thus entails the mechanical removal of rust from the steel elements and their subsequent coating with proper rust-preventive oils. Finally, the steel structures should be varnished. This process will need to be repeated regularly, both to guarantee the preservation of the building and to improve its appearance.

The replacement and cleaning of mirrors is being done consistently, as it affects the correct functioning of the furnace. In this case, the suggestion is to continue to take all the necessary measures to keep the complex working.

Finally, vertical connections within the concentrator should be improved, making it possible to safely reach the top of the building both for functional and touristic purposes.

The Office Buildings

The most widespread problem concerns the finishes of the façades and the interior spaces, which are suffering from aging and poor maintenance. The stone cladding has cracks and missing tiles, the false ceilings are detaching from their supports and layers of paint are starting to peel off. These issues can easily be fixed by replacing the broken or missing elements and repainting wall surfaces where needed.

Improvements to the roof waterproofing and drainage system are recommended, as water infiltration can be seen on the buildings' façades.

Particular attention should be paid to the steel and glass sunshades protecting the façades of the courtyard, which were mostly removed and should be reinstated, while upgrading the fixing system and the glazing performance in screening the sun. Their presence is an important feature and adds interest to the otherwise monotonous façades.

In the interior, a general upgrade is required in terms of technical services and building finishes.

Finally, it is of critical importance to ensure the preservation of the existing works of art and to keep them in their intended positions.

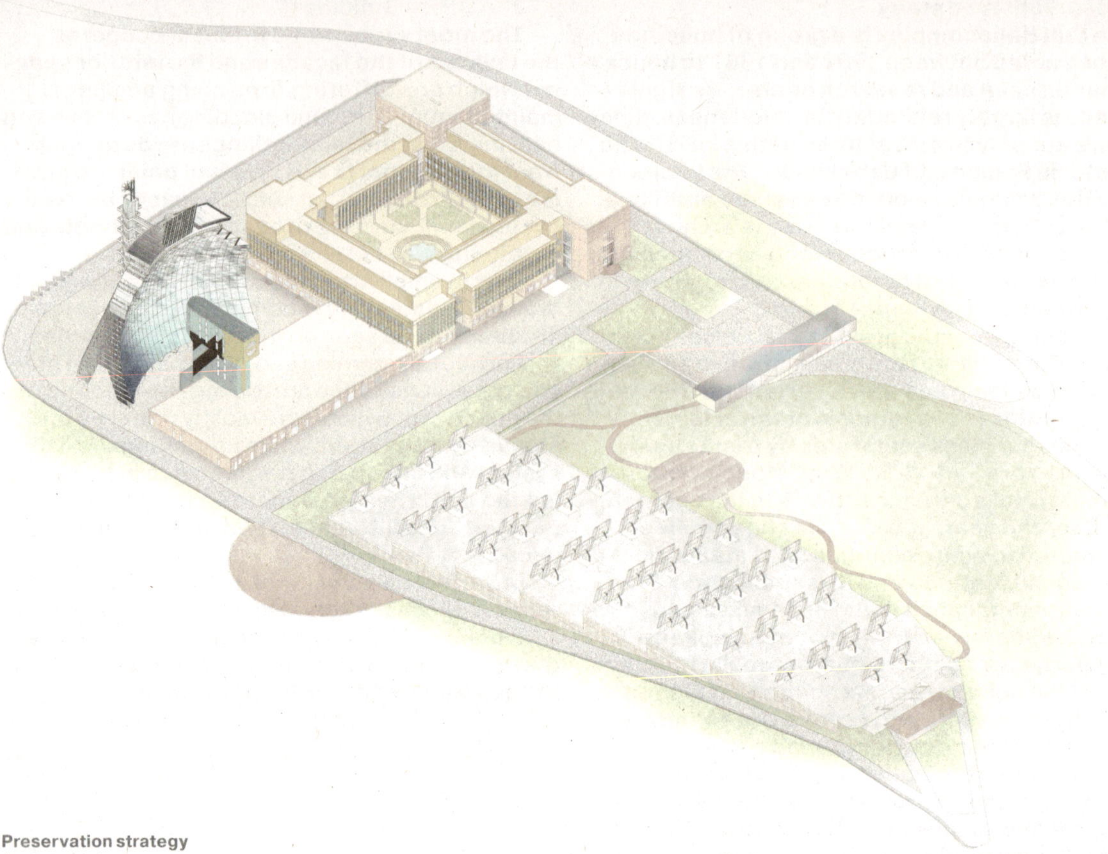

Preservation strategy
Axonometric view

View from the courtyard
Strategy visualization

Adaptation Strategy

The Sun Heliocompex is currently run by two organizations, the FTI (Physics and Technical Institute, Tashkent) and the IMS (Institute of Material Science, Parkent). The two institutes use the complex simultaneously, with various intensities and for different research purposes. While IMS staff are present at the complex on a daily basis, FTI staff come to the furnace specifically to run experiments. The administration and laboratory building is partially unused, which is a consequence of organizational, financial and bureaucratic issues. It is not in the scope of our project to determine the actual cause of the partial vacancy, but we believe it is important to find ways (through financing or collaborative projects) to establish an appropriate scientific research use of these premises.

In recent years this originally secret complex has opened to the public, with the intention of generating additional income. Regular guided tours are organized by IMS staff, but tourists may also enter the grounds and wander freely, even within the concentrator. Of course, the individual discovery of such a mysterious site is a truly unique and unforgettable experience, but it does imply safety problems and interference with scientific research.

Our adaptation strategy focuses on the separation of flows and the organization of the visitor experience. We propose to create a clear path around the complex, an open-air museum marked by educational and leisure "stations" that are accessible without guidance. The sightseeing experience starts at the visitor center, designed in place of the existing gate building. Here, visitors can buy tickets, visit the bookshop, attend a lecture or visit the exhibition on the history of the complex and ongoing research. The path will be equipped with outdoor educational/exhibition facilities, a small café at the top of the heliostatic hill, and picnic area in the orchard. We propose transforming one building under the heliostats into an additional education lab, open to the public.

As there are several vacant buildings under the heliostats, another interesting option is to create an artists' residence to promote collaborative projects in art and technology. Similar experiments have already taken place at CERN (Switzerland) and in other international laboratories.

Guided tours through the different buildings of the complex would remain an important component of the visitor experience.

While the path/stations should have a simple design so as to not interfere with the monumentality of the complex, the visitor center can be designed as a minimalist abstract building with expressive openings facing the concentrator.

View toward the concentrator across the garden next to the heliostatic field
Strategy visualization

View toward the heliostatic field and the visitor center
Strategy visualization

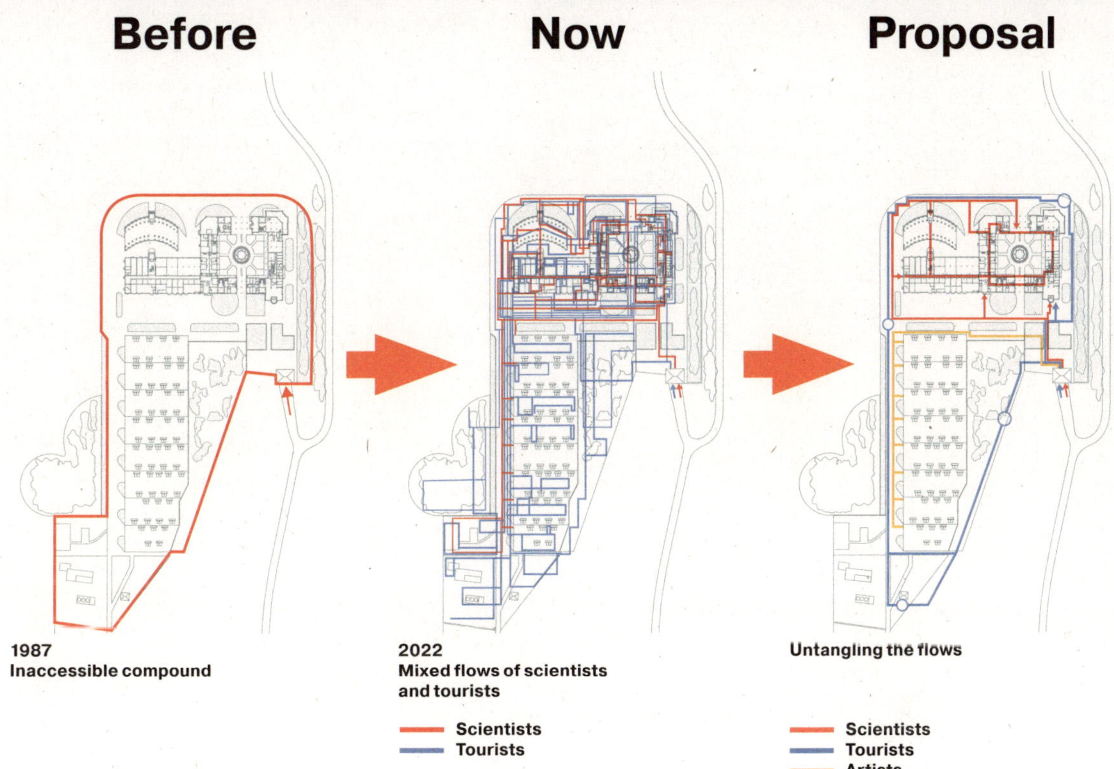

Concept diagram illustrating the initial, current and potential condition of people's flows through the center.

The complex, originally secret, has been opened to the public in recent years with the intention of generating additional income. This resulted in a superimposition of workers' and visitors' flows of movement.

Therefore, the proposal suggests separating the flows by means of additional visitor infrastructure located at the perimeter of the complex and redefining its edge.

Zhemchug Residential Building

Building position and address: 77 Buyuk Turon Street, Mirobod district, Tashkent

Historically, the location of the Zhemchug residential complex was connected to the so-called Turkmen Market, a small bazaar that appeared at the end of the nineteenth century across the road from the future building on a square at the intersection of several roads. At that time this peripheral zone adjoined the first districts of the rectangular grid of streets of "new" Tashkent on one side, and on the other faced more open plots that were used for gardens and barracks. In particular, further down Sapernaia Street (Mirobod), where Zhemchug is located, were the sappers' barracks. In the Soviet period the district became largely residential and single-story, but from the beginning of the 1960s it was subject to intensive redevelopment. The first modernist square in Tashkent was set out further south on Sapernaia Street. This was the location of the Rossiia Hotel, the House of Fashion and the Aeroflot office, which had cash desks and the so-called aerostation, from where checked-in passengers could catch a bus straight to their plane. Soon after the approval of the new project for the detailed urban planning of the center of Tashkent and the construction of Lenin Boulevard, the Turkmen Market was demolished and the site was allocated to a large cultural and educational building. In the district bordered by Sapernaia Street (Mirobod), Shota Rustaveli Street and Cosmonauts Avenue (Afrosiyob) they began to build standard nine- and fourteen-story apartment blocks of various types. The decision was taken to build Zhemchug before the bend of Cosmonauts Avenue and Sapernaia Street, where it became a high-rise accent working with a number of urban perspectives, primarily on the north–south access of the boulevard and also the high-speed road that was Cosmonauts Avenue.

Main dimensions of the Zhemchug building
General axonometric view

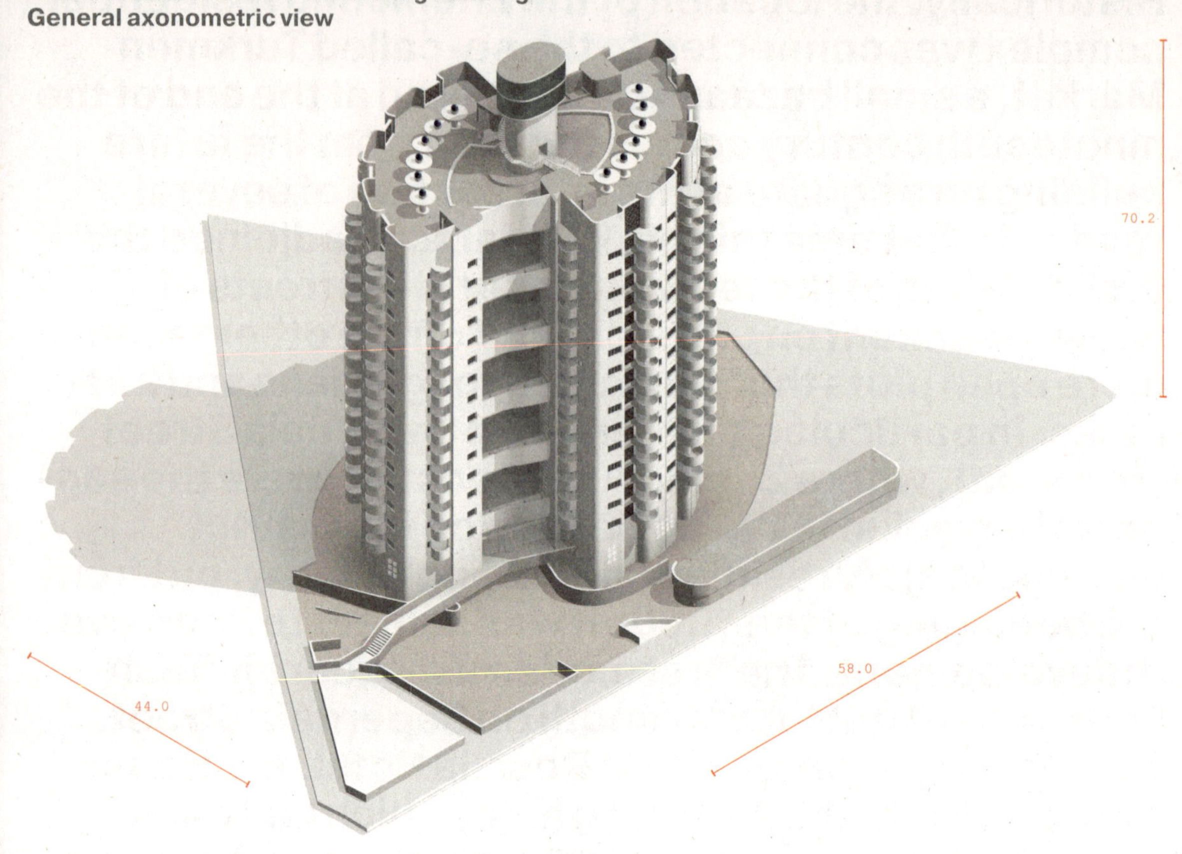

ACTORS	Architects:	Ofeliia Aidinova, G. Golubeva, E. Shatalov	
	Engineers:	P. Levin, Ia. Aradovskii	
	Artists:	Robert Avakian	
	Institute:	TashZNIIEP	
DATES	Design period:	1972–1984	
	Construction period:	1975 (?)–1985	
	Inauguration date:	1985	
	Later interventions:	Continuous small-scale interventions by residents.	
USE	Current use:	Mixed use, primarily residential	
		Entrance floor:	Entrance lobby, storage, rented spaces
		First floor:	Commercial, offices, youth hub
		Upper floors:	Residential
		Rooftop:	Rented
	Original use:	Mixed use	
		Entrance floor:	Entrance lobby
		First floor:	Commercial
		Upper floors:	Residential
		Rooftop:	Public, all residents had access to the roof level
	Suitability of current use:	The building is well suited for its current use, which is the same use for which it was designed and built. The obsolescence of the technical systems (heating, electric, water) is an issue that requires a rapid solution, as it could worsen the overall quality of life of residents and thus reduce the suitability for residential use.	
	Space utilization:	The building appears to be mostly in use, as the majority of residential and commercial units are occupied. However, the central courtyards, which were originally intended as common gathering spaces, are often empty.	
DIMENSIONS	Number of floors:	Basement + entrance floor + 1 commercial floor + 15 residential floors + 2 technical floors + roof	
	Length:	58.0 m	
	Width:	44.0 m	
	Height:	70.2 m	
	Gross floor area:	Entrance floor	1,388.0 m²
		Commercial (first) floor	1,297.0 m²
		Courtyard floors	1,395.0 m²
		Balcony floors	860.0 m²
	Gross floor area (total):		20,264.0 m²
	Number of apartments:	2-room	60
		3-room	30
		4-room	30
		Total	120

Zhemchug: An Experimental Sixteen-Story Residential Building

There are few sources recording the history of the design and construction of the experimental sixteen-story residential building that would later be named Zhemchug (The Pearl), after a shop on the first floor. They comprise the working drawings, which were preserved by the building management organization, fragmentary publications in journals in the 1970s and 1980s, documents and reminiscences about architect Ofeliia Aidinova which were shared with us by her niece Marina Ivanian and indirect recollections by specialists Zlata Chebotareva and Vladimir Narubanskii, who worked at TashZNIIEP. Other important documents include historical photographs of the construction of Zhemchug from the personal archive of Timur Karimov. Unfortunately, most of the documentation, including explanatory correspondence, working correspondence and the original design drawings, particularly the initial sketches, was lost when the archive of TashZNIIEP, where Aidinova worked, was destroyed. Another complicating factor for historical research was the fact that in the architect's lifetime there was not a single special publication of the sort which usually marks the construction of unique buildings.

"A Vertical Mahalla"

The first problem that a historian of the Zhemchug building has to solve is to determine when the design process started. Among the extant documents the project drawings are dated 1976–1984. In the corner stamps of the drawings, the building was called "An experimental sixteen-story residential building on Lenin Street in Tashkent." The dates of production of the project documentation and the link to Lenin Street are important, since there is an indication of an earlier initial design date and the probable intention to construct the building in a different urban context. The journal *Arkhitektura i stroitel'stvo Uzbekistana* (*Architecture and Construction of Uzbekistan*), reporting on the national review of the best projects of 1985, gave the design dates of Ofeliia Aidinova's experimental residential building as 1972–1976.[1] This contemporary publication can be trusted, as the architect never refuted the information. An architectural model of the city center from the mid-1970s, which was long exhibited at the Union of Architects of Uzbekistan, also indicates an earlier origin of the project.[2] According to this model the residential building was situated at the intersection of Cosmonauts Avenue (Afrosiyob) and Abay Street (Almazar), where the sports complex Humo Arena stands today. This proves that there was a period during the design phase that matches the dates in the architectural journal but is not recorded in the extant working drawings.

The question of the date is important for the following reason. The Moscow architect Andrei Kosinskii, who would become an extremely influential figure in the architectural life of Tashkent in the late 1960s and 1970s, was open to the ideas of Tashkent architects and to integrating them into his own projects, especially given the collective character of architectural design in the USSR as a whole and in Uzbekistan in particular. Even so, it often happened that Kosinskii so closely identified with the borrowed and redeveloped material that he was inclined to announce others' ideas as his own.[3] In particular, his design for the Kalkauz microdistrict featured sixteen-story housing towers with shared suspended courtyards every three floors of the building. Designed for the Sibzar district of the "old city," Kalkauz developed the theme of contemporary residential accommodation that retained the spirit and lifestyle of the traditional Uzbek mahalla. This made the project one of the best-known manifestations of Tashkent modernism of the 1970s, even though it was never built. Kalkauz was designed in 1974–1978, and the construction of Zhemchug was completed in 1985. If not for this indirect evidence, it would be natural to assume that Aidinova was inspired by Kosinskii's project, which was heavily promoted in all of the architectural journals. However, the new facts show the opposite: for Kalkauz, Kosinskii borrowed designs for contemporary industrial housing, matching the local cultural traditions and climate that already existed within the practice of Tashkent architects.

The development of a contemporary architectural image and the organization of industrial housing suited to the context of Uzbekistan originated in the 1920s. In 1926 Moisei Ginzburg wrote the manifesto article "National Architecture of the Peoples of the USSR," which greatly influenced Soviet architects' relationship to the historic architecture of Central Asia. The theorist of constructivism insisted that the contemporary architect working in Central Asia would have to deal with the "dead East" and the

1 "Piatyi Vsesoiuznyi smotr luchshikh arkhitekturnykh proizvedenii 1985 goda [Fifth All-Union Review of the Best Architectural Works of 1985]," *Arkhitektura i stroitel'stvo Uzbekistana* [*Architecture and Construction of Uzbekistan*], no. 12, 1986, 20.

2 The model was accidentally captured in a 1984 image in which Tulkinoi Kadyrova, Chair of the Union of Architects of Uzbekistan, was photographed in front of a model of the Chorsu Bazaar.

3 See the text on the Chorsu Bazaar in this volume, pp. 723–730.

Vertical gardens on residential buildings

Residential building, District Ts-27, 1974

"living East." As an example of the "dead East" Ginzburg cited the Ulugbek Madrasa in Samarkand. He said of that building: "The mosque of Ulugbek is the culmination of a once powerful but now absolutely dead historical period in Uzbekistan. It is a grave monument that concludes the period of national development for Muslims, a period of authoritarian oriental tyrants and the apogee of Islamism, which enslaved the vital, active power of working Muslims. Its forms are able only to reflect the atavistic national idea of the East."[4] Ginzburg contrasted the "dead East" with the residential unit. "There is," he wrote, "a typical residential unit—the oriental kishlak, aul or city—that is the launch point for the development of a new national culture of the East."[5] Ginzburg's idea inspired several generations of architects working in Central Asia to study the planning, functional organization and climatic features of the traditional accommodation of local peoples. It was assumed that established techniques of organizing space and combating the negative features of the continental climate could provide the key to creating a living environment that matched the cultural, social and climatic conditions of Uzbekistan.

Besides the basic residential unit—a house with an internal courtyard—architects were interested in the structure of a larger residential setting, the so-called mahalla, which was a district community that served as the basis of social life in the traditional Central Asian city. The initial intentions of Soviet architects in the 1930s were translated into attempts to destroy the mahalla way of life, which they associated with the "Middle Ages," but from the 1950s there was an increased acceptance of this phenomenon. To some, like, for example, the chief architect of Tashkent, Mitkhat Bulatov, the mahalla and its collective self-management was a prototype of the future communist society.[6] Others suggested that even if the mahalla was an anachronism, it was important to approach it tactfully, without destroying existing forms of cultural behavior.[7] And a third group attempted to demonstrate the universality of this type of housing for every modern country. The researcher Zlata Chebotareva wrote: "Does this type of construction deserve the epithets 'feudal,' 'reactionary,' 'unsuitable for the contemporary way of life'? Hardly! Evidence of the weakness of such reproaches is provided by the extensive use in contemporary urban planning of 'Arab-type' buildings in countries for which they are not historical and traditional and, moreover, where this type of building is not a climatic requirement, such as in England, West Germany and others."[8]

One of the main research themes at TashZNIIEP in the late 1960s and 1970s was industrial housing that was suitable for integration into the built environment of the "old city." One result of this work was the idea to create an outdoor space for several apartments. Subsequently, the architects of Tashgiprogor (Tashkent State Urban Project Institute), inspired by TashZNIIEP's suggestions, developed a design for an experimental four-story building with open loggias that operated for several apartments in a two-story block (District Ts-27, 1974). The solution proposed by Ofeliia Aidinova was more radical. It involved the creation of a sixteen-story "vertical mahalla" in which three-story sections of apartments had their own courtyards where neighbors could organize various forms of communal life: family and general celebrations, sport and games, children's play areas, etc.

Planning and Plastic Solutions

The experimental character of Aidinova's building primarily involved new construction technology, the application and profitability of which needed to be tested in practice. As a counterbalance to prefabricated housing—the elements for which were produced by house-building factories (*domostroitel'nye kombinaty*, or DSK) so that, after delivery, they could be put together on the building site—many Tashkent architects looked to the possibilities of industrial production of monolithic reinforced concrete housing constructed using "sliding formwork." This would avoid the need for DSK and the expensive transportation of elements for construction. Monolithic walls and ceilings were assembled on-site by pouring concrete into the formwork casing, and after the concrete was dry the formwork was moved to the next floor, and so the cycle repeated. In addition, "sliding formwork" offered new opportunities for creating varied plastic forms, which meant that housing could be adapted to cultural traditions and specific urban planning situations.

4 Moisei Ginzburg, "Natsional'naia arkhitektura narodov SSSR [National Architecture of the Peoples of the USSR]," *Sovremennaia arkhitektura* [*Contemporary Architecture*], nos. 5–6, 1926, 113.

5 Ibid.

6 Paul Stronski, *Tashkent: Forging a Soviet City, 1930–1966* (Pittsburgh: University of Pittsburgh Press, 2010), 151.

7 See the interview with Andrei Kosinskii in the documentary *Poisk i traditsii* [*Search and Traditions*], directed by A. Grishko (Uchebnaia kinostudiia VGIK, 1975).

8 Zlata Chebotareva, "V zashchitu plotnoi maloetazhnoi zastroiki [In Defense of Dense, Low-Rise Construction]," *Stroitel'stvo i arkhitektura Uzbekistana* [*Construction and Architecture of Uzbekistan*], no. 11, 1974, 18.

Ofeliia Aidinova's focus was mainly on the plastic nature of concrete. This choice was logical given her earlier creative journey, marked by the Samarkand (1966) and Bukhoro (1976) hotels, which were inspired by the Brutalist movement. The plan of a typical floor of the sixteen-story building was made up of arcs of two ellipsoidal quadrants with an empty space between them. The quadrants were placed symmetrically in relation to the center of an imaginary ellipse, where the towers with the elevator shafts were situated. The exit from the elevator shaft led to two internal transit galleries which provided access to both wings of the building, as well as to an emergency staircase and a garbage chute. The galleries provided access to the apartments and were a backdrop for the kitchen and bathroom windows. The external rim of the quadrant was formed by the rounded bay windows of the living rooms and round balconies, the regular rhythm of which was reminiscent of petals on vertical "stems." Vertically, the sixteen-story building was divided into three parts:

- the bottom part, incorporating the basement, the entrance level, the commercial level with a shop, and a technical floor;
- the middle part, incorporating five residential three-story blocks with a "suspended courtyard" for shared use by block residents;
- the top part, incorporating a technical floor, the roof, with a swimming pool and shaded spaces under flat sun "umbrellas," and the elevator tower with a two-story ring of light that was illuminated in the evening.

In each quadrant there were two two-room apartments, one three-room apartment and one four-room apartment. The specific theme that linked Aidinova's experimental building with the exploration of her colleagues at TashZNIIEP was the summer space in the apartments, which was reminiscent of the traditional Uzbek iwan.[9] Specialists in the architecture of Uzbekistan always believed that the structural specificity of the traditional Uzbek house was an "outdoor space within the volume of the building."[10] Architects aimed to introduce this principle into the organization of apartments within multistory buildings. At a certain point, they began to consider ordinary terraces, which had been designed for the majority of residential buildings in Tashkent since the time of standard constructions, to be "insufficiently Uzbek." Accordingly, attempts were made to push the terrace further into the living space, so that it was not an appendage to the life of the family but its natural center. In particular, the new type of iwan was incorporated in experimental buildings that were constructed using "sliding formwork," based on designs by Savelii Rozenblium and Ofeliia Aidinova. The iwan was used in both cases, and sliding windows meant that in cold weather it could be transformed into a multifunctional space and left open in summer.[11] The iwans in Aidinova's building conceptually divided the "external" space of the apartment from the "internal." The external part included the kitchen and living room and the internal part the bedrooms. This division reproduced another principle of the organization of traditional Uzbek and Tajik houses, the split into two parts: one part was accessible for guests and the other was only for family members. In this way the "mahalla courtyard" of the three-story section was supplemented by an iwan and the zoning of the apartments, in which the domestic traditions of the "old city" could be observed if desired. The shaded and well-ventilated iwan served as a cooler recreation zone on hot days, of which there are around 200 a year in Uzbekistan. The open side of the iwan featured solar shading made of bent sheet metal decorated with a typical modernist motif of a single repeating figure from various angles.

Another notable feature of the planning of the apartments was the unusual passages between spaces. The wall between the living room and the iwan had a wide doorway where it was originally planned to use sliding doors. The entrance from the iwan to the sleeping block was also intended to have a sliding door, however the doorway here was to have been standard size. In the four-room apartments one of the bedrooms was a connecting room and was made slightly more private thanks to a sliding screen. On the round balconies accessed via the iwan there was space for two chairs and a small table, like on the semicircular balcony attached to the bedrooms of the four-room apartments.

One of the TashZNIIEP themes reflected in the design of Zhemchug was the multifunctional "building-complex" that matched the demographic structure of Uzbek society, with its large families and requirement for a wide range of social services. As in the 1920s, architects understood the social block as a multifaceted question. It involved collective housework, food

9 In the architecture of the Middle East an iwan is a space surrounded by a wall on three sides and open from the fourth side.

10 Zlata Chebotareva, *Udobstvo, pol'za, krasota: Zhilaia sreda gorodov Srednei Azii* [*Comfort, Use, Beauty: The Residential Environment in the Cities of Central Asia*] (Tashkent: Izdatel'stvo literatury i iskusstva imeni Gafura Guliama, 1990), 29.

11 "16-etazhnyi zhiloi dom iz monolitnogo zhelezobetona v ob"emno-perestavnoi opalubke po ul. B. Khmel'nitskogo [A 16-Story Residential Building Made from Monolithic Reinforced Concrete Using Sliding Formwork, Located on B. Khmelnitsky Street]," *Arkhitektura i stroitel'stvo Uzbekistana* [*Architecture and Construction of Uzbekistan*], nos. 2–3, 1986, 19.

Zhemchug residential building during construction

Savelii Rozenblium's residential building, constructed using sliding formwork

preparation, childcare and leisure.[12] From this research, Aidinova borrowed elements of the social block for her project. On the ground floor there was to be a space for a self-service laundry and on the roof the plan was to create a communal space for all residents: a sunbathing area, a pool and recreation zones. The entire roof was to have been equipped with corrugated concrete canopies, which were then substituted with shading "umbrellas" and a pool. As well as the shared spaces of the five atria, residents could use the roof for various children's activities and also to relax. Here, you could swim, sunbathe and chat. This unique building in the center of the city was also intended as a place for the inhabitants of Tashkent, and for this reason it was planned from the very beginning to open a jewellery shop here, which gave the building its name.

Internal Contradictions of the Project

The first discrepancy in the project was noticed during construction. The experiment with perfecting the new technology of quick and cheap industrial construction without relying on the house-building factories had the opposite effect. Construction was completed in 1985 and took at least six years.[13] The cost was many times greater than that of a standard residential building with the same number of apartments. Ofeliia Aidinova's friends and relatives recall that she was on-site for the entire construction period, and it was only thanks to her energy that the building was successfully constructed. However, this method of organizing the construction process could not become routine. According to the architects Rafail Takhtaganov and Vladimir Narubanskii, who worked at TashZNIIEP in the 1970s, the Tashkent construction industry was unable to quickly and efficiently erect such complex buildings. For example, the concrete that would otherwise have been produced on-site or brought there in cement mixers was delivered in the boxes of dump trucks, poured out onto pallets and then transferred (often using shovels) into special containers and lifted by crane in order to be poured into the forms. A large amount of material was lost during construction, and the road from the concrete factory to the building was covered in lumps of concrete that had leaked from the dump trucks. A more technological idea for constructing a modular monolithic building was developed by Savelii Rozenblium, and several such buildings were constructed along the city's main arteries. Nevertheless, they were not economically viable, something specialists were unanimous about in the late 1980s.[14]

Another type of contradiction concerned the use of the building. Initially it was to be constructed at the intersection of Cosmonauts Avenue (Afrosiyob) and Abaya Street (Almazar), where the sports complex Humo Arena now stands. The distance from this location to today's Zhemchug is a little over a kilometer, but there was a fundamental difference in the urban planning context. The building, planned for a site within the "old city" district of Beshagach, was intended for residents of traditional mahallas. In moving a building created for the "old city" to the center of "European Tashkent," the planners were unlikely to have recognized the social consequences that this would entail. The recipients of apartments in the center of "new Tashkent" were government officials, workers at major factories and representatives of other privileged groups who largely depended on the state and were not accustomed to organizing within lower-class residential communities. Thus, the project missed the target group for which this innovative type of housing had apparently been developed and accommodated a different group that did not share the values for which the striking and expensive spaces for collective use were created. For this reason, those social practices which would have confirmed the validity of Aidinova's assumptions did not appear here in the Soviet period. According to long-term residents, the noise of children playing in the atria tended to irritate the inhabitants and the space was never used as intended. The roof was also unused for a long period of time. In contrast, the collective spaces equipped for the predicted emergence of a community of residents were gradually taken over by a general wave of individual isolation and the battle for privacy. In some places, parts of the internal galleries were cordoned off. The open balconies, which provided the opportunity for communication with neighbors, were glazed in and curtained off. This process increased after the collapse of the USSR. All of the apartments were privatized and one of the first businessmen in the republic leased the roof of the building,

12 Svetlana Moiseeva, "Osobennost' razvitiia sistemy kul'turno-bytovogo obsluzhivaniia naseleniia gorodov Uzbekistana [Features of the Development of a System for Serving the Cultural and Daily Needs of the Population of Uzbekistan's Cities]," *Stroitel'stvo i arkhitektura Uzbekistana* [*Construction and Architecture of Uzbekistan*], no. 8, 1970, 24.

13 The exact date when construction began is unknown, but it may have started in 1976–1978, during the design stage, which was a common construction practice in Tashkent.

14 Mansur Shagaev and Ol'ga Marakanova, *Osobennosti ob"emno-planirovochnykh reshenii monolitnykh zhilykh domov dlia gorodskogo stroitel'stva v raionakh s sukhim zharkim klimatom: Obzornaia informatsiia* [*Features of Volume Planning Solutions for Monolithic Residential Buildings for Urban Construction in Regions with a Dry, Hot Climate: Survey Information*] (Moscow: VNII teorii arkhitektury i gradostroitel'stva, 1989), 44.

where he organized special events for an invited audience. Today, communication among the resulting community of residents differs little from that within an ordinary group of owners in an average condominium, focusing on domestic questions and solving building management issues. One can therefore state that this social experiment, as part of which the residents of the mahalla could reproduce the features of their "collective daily life" in a new type of socialist property which was collective but not faceless state housing, was not justified. However, the energy of the architect's initial, utopian idea of modeling a community through architecture did not entirely disappear. It remains in the city's mythology, constantly generating narratives of "an unusual building" where residents live "in another way." Zhemchug is often visited by popular bloggers and people make video clips, write reports and take photographs, always underlining and often exaggerating the collective element of the residents' everyday life and leisure activities. These fictional tales, where the "suspended courtyards" are a place of noisy games, traditional celebrations and fashionable parties, produce a surreal history of the building that shows life "not as it is but how it could and should have been."

Konstantin Mel'nikov, Palace of Culture for Tashkent, second version, 1933

An Aesthetic Solution

Regardless of the questionable qualities of this technological and social experiment, Zhemchug was immediately perceived by Soviet architects as a unique work of architecture. On completion of construction, the design team, made up of project director Ofeliia Aidinova, lead engineer P. Levin, engineer-technologist Ia. Aradovskii and architects G. Golubeva and E. Shatalov, was awarded the gold medal and diploma of the Union of Architects of the USSR and also the main prize of the All-Union Review of the best projects of 1985. According to the jury, "the prize was awarded for an innovative approach in two areas: 1) For masterful use of the possibilities of monolithic concrete. 2) For the creation of a new type of housing that aimed to increase comfort in multistory accommodation by solving sociological problems of contact between residents in the building based on the techniques and forms of the traditional housing of Uzbekistan."[15] Although the second element of praise was given in advance, since at the end of construction it was not yet possible to judge how "sociological problems of contact between residents" had been solved, the main motive driving the organizing committee of the prize was, in my view, not noted. This was the aesthetic solution, unique for residential architecture and, possibly, the most expressive modernist housing complex built in the USSR since the Constructivist experiments of the 1920s.

There is no direct or indirect prototype of Aidinova's building. There are parallels (and these are not obligatory) with only a few historical "hints." For example, for the Palace of Culture (1933) in Tashkent, which was never built, Konstantin Mel'nikov suggested decorating the façade of the semicircular building with petal-like balconies with flat umbrella canopies over them. Mel'nikov also loved dynamic plans that were symmetrically constructed around the vertical axis rather than smooth surfaces. However, such parallels drawn from the past were not literal, and therefore the idea that Aidinova adapted a model developed by another architect for her own project is unlikely to have any basis in fact.

It is important to note that Aidinova's building was a child of its time, the final stage of the Brutalist movement. Brutalism went through a number of phases. Beginning with coarse, unfinished and geometrically imperfect surfaces, it became an increasingly subtle medium as the technology and tools developed. Soviet architects aimed to follow Western technologies, but they were extremely limited in how they could use them. Sometimes they were helped by craftspeople. The incredible quality of the concrete finish at the Karl Marx Library in Ashkhabad was a result of the creative partnership between architect Abdula Akhmedov and form-maker Mushegh Danieliants, who was a true co-author of the building. Ofeliia Aidinova was born in 1927 in Tashkent, but her parents had been forced to flee to Russian Turkestan during the Armenian Genocide in 1915, and Ofeliia maintained a strong link to Armenian architecture and architects her whole life. There is no doubt that she

15 "Piatyi Vsesoiuznyi smotr luchshikh arkhitekturnykh proizvedenii 1985 goda [Fifth All-Union Review of the Best Architectural Works of 1985]," 18.

followed developments in the architecture of Soviet Armenia, where radical modernism and Brutalism, especially after the erection of the modernist Armenian Genocide Memorial at Tsitsernakaberd in Yerevan, became for a time an element of the national identity of Armenian architecture.[16] In her work in Uzbekistan she never moved outside strict Brutalism, but Zhemchug was an achievement of plastic virtuosity. The sculptural look of the building, the rhythmic development of its vertical structure with the help of high atria, the complex play of volume of each element, as of the atrium ceilings, which have an industrial three-dimensionality thanks to large, cylindrical caissons, or the staircases with rhythmic horizontal slits that give the vertical flatness of the walls and the entire building a new scale thanks to the proportion and rhythm — all of this made Zhemchug an unusually complex construction which incorporated numerous motifs, counterpoints and plastic themes. However, while finding in the project the opportunity to reveal the wide-ranging possibilities of concrete as a medium, the architect also had to confront the reality of the archaic construction industry of Uzbekistan. Her version of Brutalism, compared to the refined models of architecture in Ashkhabad or Yerevan, returned to the Brutalist movement's origins in the 1950s, to the unfinished and unpolished element of concrete. Tashkent builders did not have the requisite technologies to create even surfaces with ideal forms, but their work gave Brutalism its original meanings: concrete is by nature a coarse material; its expressive power is linked to its plasticity, its unpredictability and the energy of a heavy mass. Moreover, this rudimentary plastered and painted concrete was more easily associated with the sloping irregularity of the duvals (traditional walls) in Tashkent's "old city," and the latent parallels with the Soviet avant-garde and Yerevan modernism were reworked into forms and connotations specific to Tashkent. From the point of view of architectural form, these qualities place Aidinova's building in an exclusive typological niche. It has no direct predecessors in world architecture and no notable sequels in the local context.

16 Karen Balian, *Memorial Egern* [*The Yeghern Memorial*] (Moscow: Tatlin, 2015); Boris Chukhovich, "Yeghern Memorial: Erevan," in *The Empire Strikes Back? A Traveling Academy through the Post-Soviet Cityscape*, ed. Michaela Geboltsberger and Georg Schöllhammer (Vienna: Tranzit.at, 2017), 71–76.

ARCHITECT
OFELIIA AIDINOVA

Place and year of birth:
Tashkent, 1927
Place and year of death:
Tashkent, 2007
Education:
1945–1950, Architecture Department of Central Asia Polytechnic Institute (SazPI)

Having graduated from the Architecture Department of SazPI, in 1950 Ofeliia Aidinova began to work at the Selkhozproekt Institute, where she created plans of village settlements and designs for standard houses for collective farm workers. The routine nature of this work did not prevent her from winning, three years later, together with Savelii Rozenblium, a prestigious competition for the reconstruction of the House of Government in Tashkent. Winning the competition enabled her to move to Uzgosproekt, however until 1963 she continued to work mainly on villages, creating standard designs for residential buildings of various capacities for the city and the village and also a new type of architectural construction, a home for elderly people, one part of which was intended for autonomous residents and the other for those who required constant care.

The two Intourist hotels built by Aidinova in Samarkand (1967, design 1965) and Bukhara (1976) are similar to the Hotel Ashkhabad designed by Abdula Akhmedov in Ashkhabad (1967, design 1964) and to the design for a standard hotel created at TashZNIIEP in the mid-1960s by F. Levinshtein. The Samarkand hotel was more severe and Brutalist, and the Bukhara one more decorative, with a carefully developed plan that included an iwan entrance and a picturesque courtyard. When presenting the hotels, the architect stressed their correlation with the local context. For example, in describing the façade of the Samarkand hotel with its "cell-like structure of summer spaces attached to the rooms" (i.e. terraces), she noted that it "takes into account the proximity of one of the most important Uzbek architectural monuments, the Gur-i Amir Mausoleum." She described the entrance block as "a deep entrance niche/iwan." From another paragraph it also follows that the interaction with the historic environment was devised using the principle of contrast: "The energetic, light volumes of the hotel should provide a pleasant contrast to Samarkand's architectural monuments, which are faced with glazed tiles."[1]

Aidinova simultaneously took part in competitions and developed experimental and standard housing. In 1968 she and Rozenblium submitted a competition project for the Puppet Theater, although it is not clear who was responsible for the fantasy forms of the design. In future the portfolios of both architects would include buildings with free planning of spaces that used the plastic possibilities of concrete.

The design phase of Aidinova's main building, the sixteen-story Zhemchug residential building on Cosmonauts Avenue, began in 1972, and construction was completed in 1985. Soon after, she retired.

1 Ofeliia Aidinova, "Gostinitsa 'Inturist' v Samarkande ['Inturist' Hotel in Samarkand]," *Stroitel'stvo i arkhitektura Uzbekistana* [*Construction and Architecture of Uzbekistan*], no. 6, 1965, 22.

INSTITUTIONAL FRAMEWORK

TashZNIIEP

CADRE

When TashZNIIEP was formed in 1963, its staff came from two institutions, the department of standard design of Uzgosproekt, which was reformed as the design department of TashZNIIEP, and the disbanded Scientific Research Institute for Construction of the Academy of Construction and Architecture of the USSR in Tashkent, which became the research department of TashZNIIEP. Three hundred and fourteen staff worked in the new institute, including eleven holders of Ph.D.s in architecture.

PRIORITIES

The work of the research department covered many types of design and construction activity. Specialists studied the issues of construction in seismic zones, air-conditioning, sun protection, the technology of economical manufacture of objects made from concrete and other construction materials, questions of climate, the cultural specificity of a given population, etc. The scientific approach to design was conditioned by the technocratic image of the institute and influenced the thought processes of the architects who worked there. Here there was minimal emphasis (insofar as it was possible in the USSR) on the imperative of "national form," and architects aimed to use research to create standard environments and unique buildings that were suitable for the Central Asian climate and the culture of the peoples who lived there. The zonal nature of the institute, which designed for the entire Central Asian region, not just for Uzbekistan, also helped architects to move the accent away from "national form" toward regional specificity.

Ofeliia Aidinova, Samarkand Hotel, Samarkand

Ofeliia Aidinova, Bukhara Hotel, Bukhara

Basement floor plan
Original condition

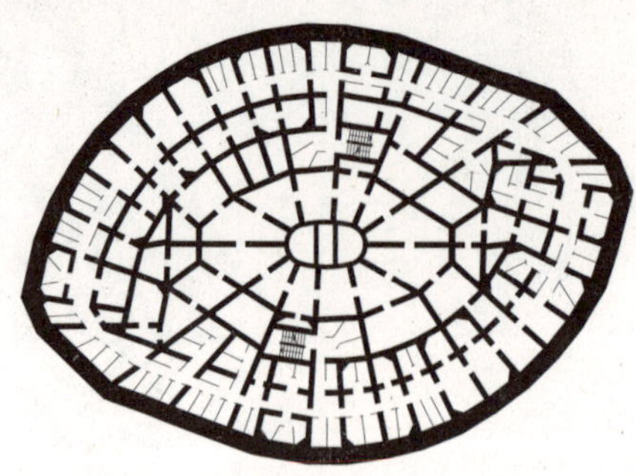

Entrance level floor plan
Original condition

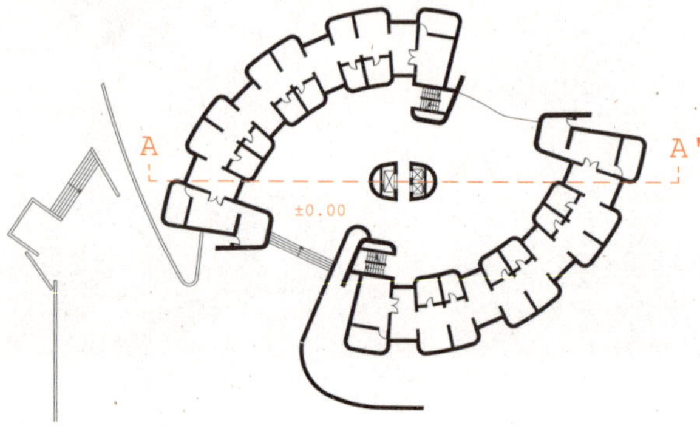

1st floor plan – Commercial
Original condition

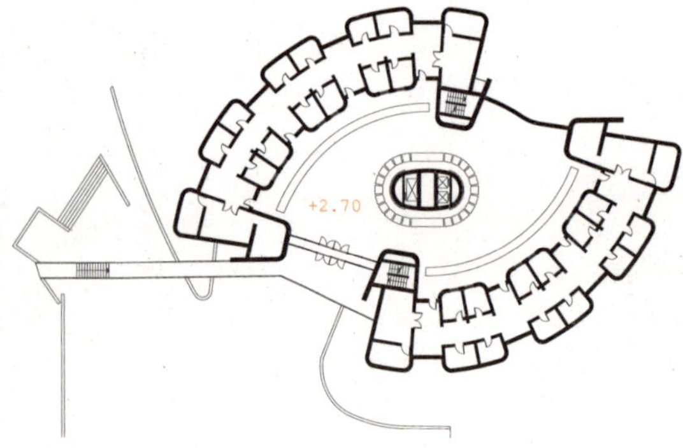

Lower technical floor plan
Original condition

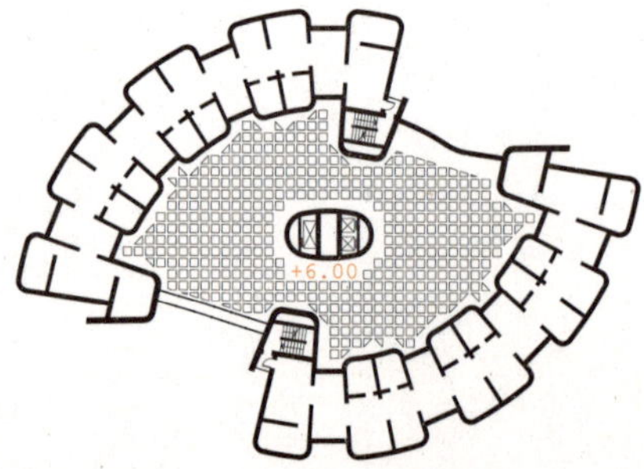

2nd floor plan (typical) – Recreation hall
Original condition

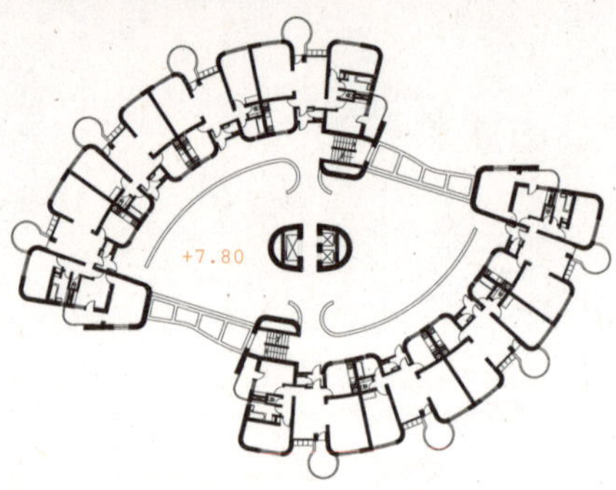

3rd floor plan (typical) – Recreation hall
Original condition

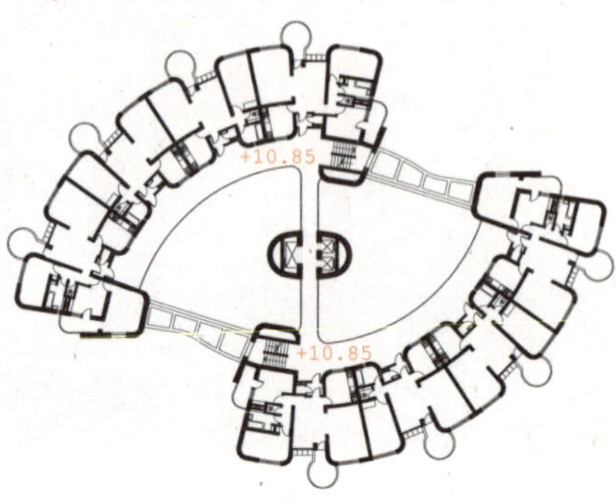

4th floor plan (typical) – Balcony
Original condition

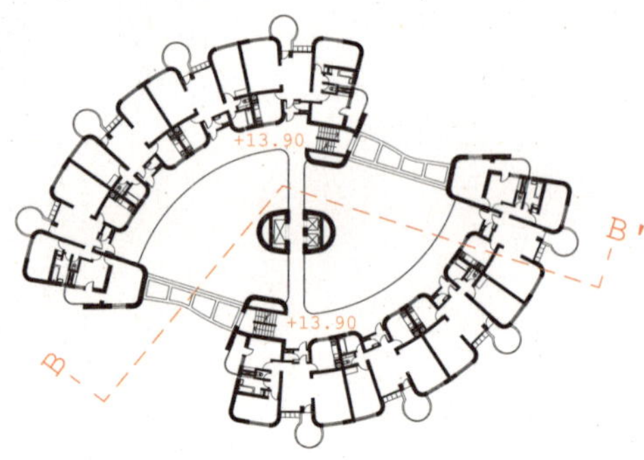

Rooftop terrace plan
Original condition

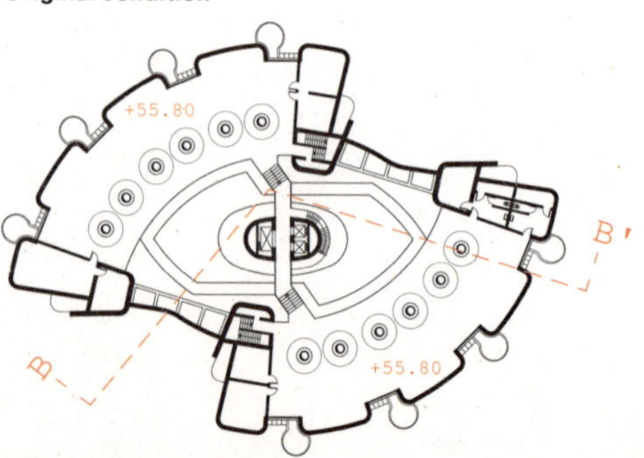

0 5 10m

Exploded axonometric view
Original condition

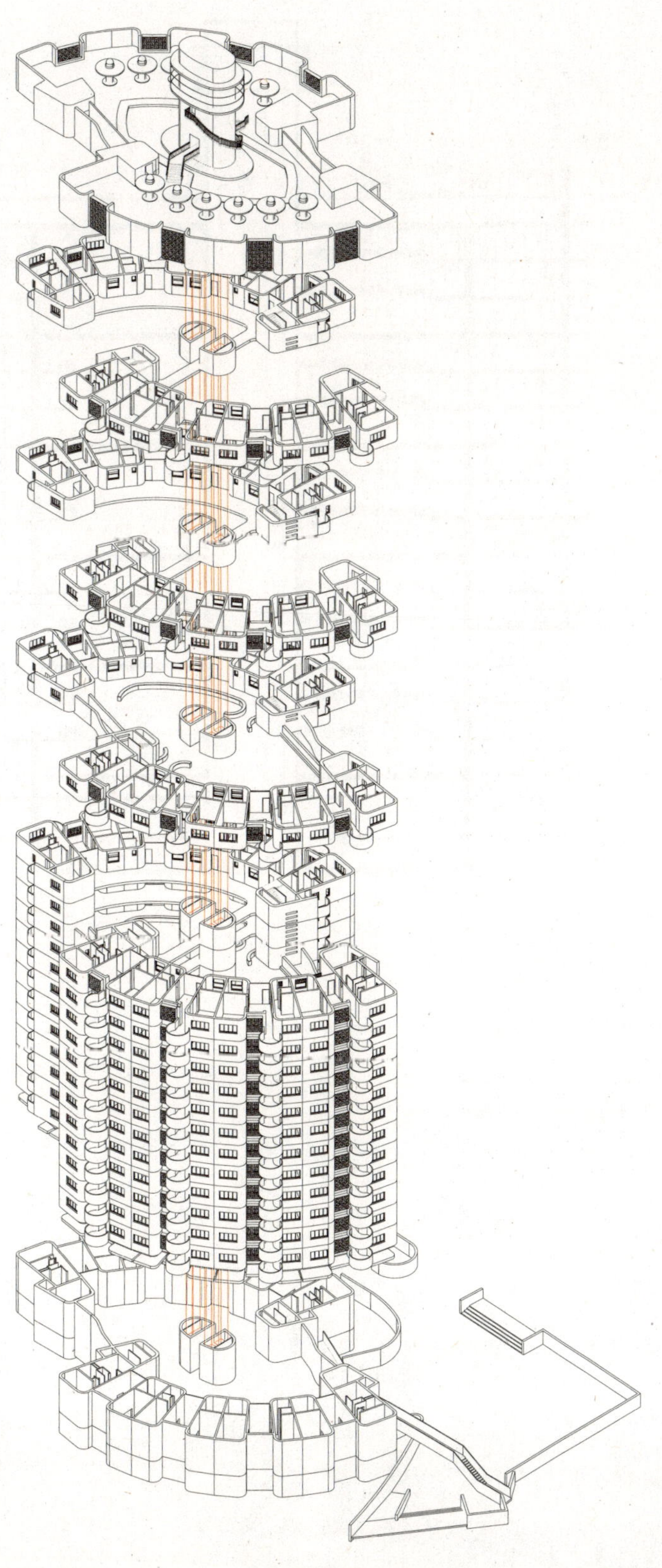

Section AA'
Original condition

+70.15
+58.65
+53.55
+44.40
+35.25
+26.10
+16.95
+7.80
+6.00
+2.70
+0.00

8.6
54.2
19.4

Typical residential block composition, interior perspective view

0 5 10m

Roof level, section BB'
Original condition

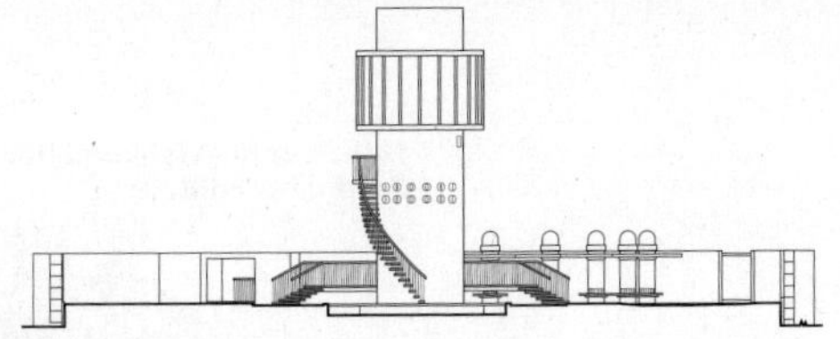

Typical residential block composition, section BB'
Original condition

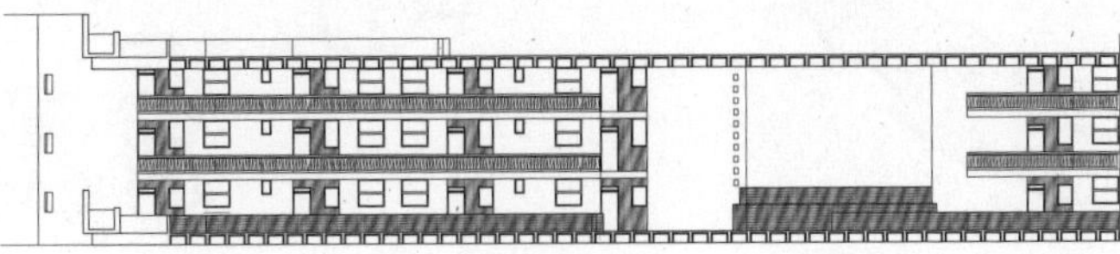

Roof level, axonometric view
Original condition

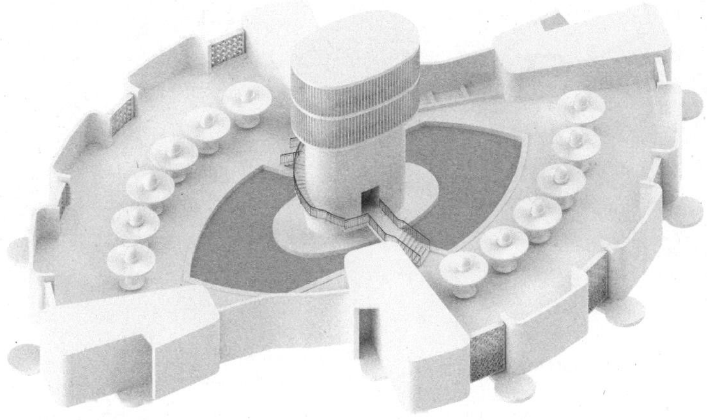

Typical residential block composition, axonometric view
Original condition

0 5 10m

1985

Entrance floor plan
Original condition

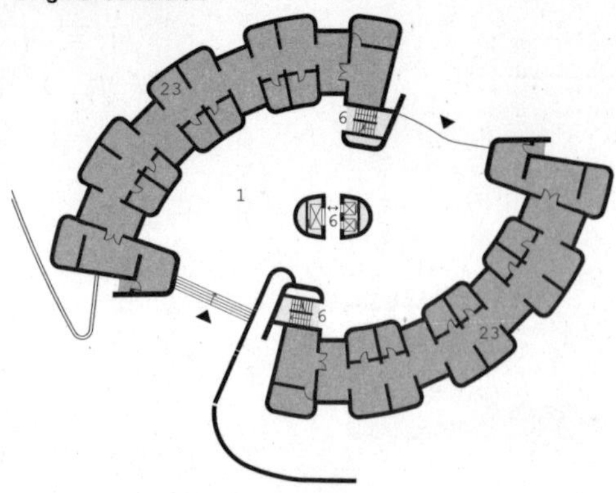

12th floor plan (second floor of typical residential block)
Original condition

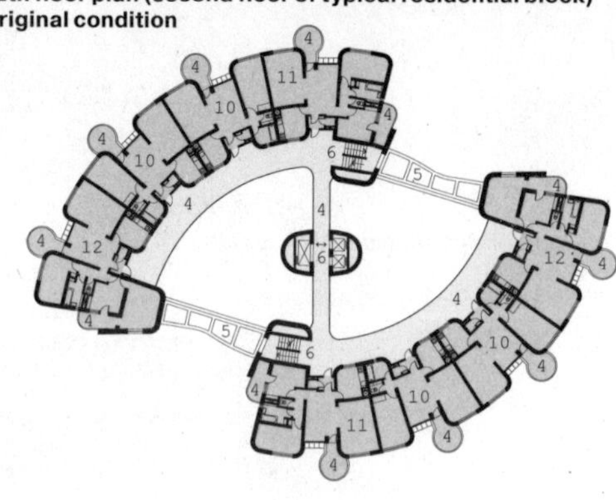

1st floor plan (commercial)
Original condition

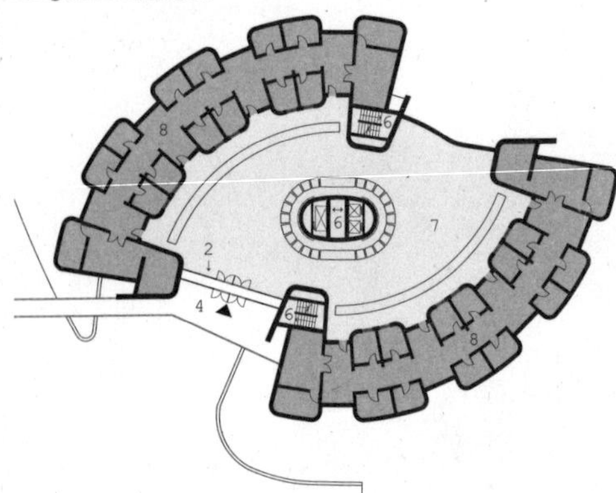

13th floor plan (third floor of typical residential block)
Original condition

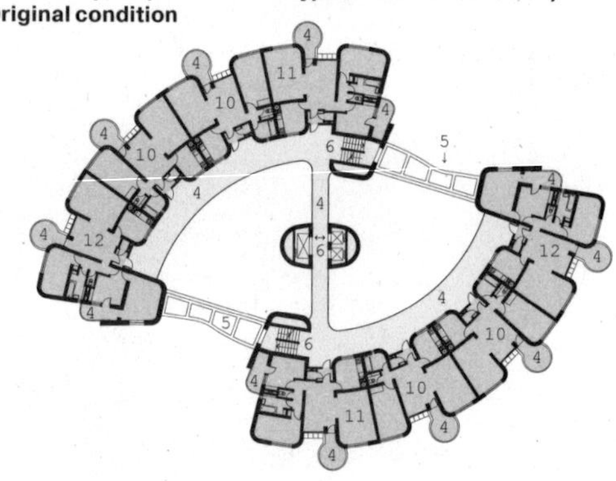

11th floor plan (first floor of typical residential block)
Original condition

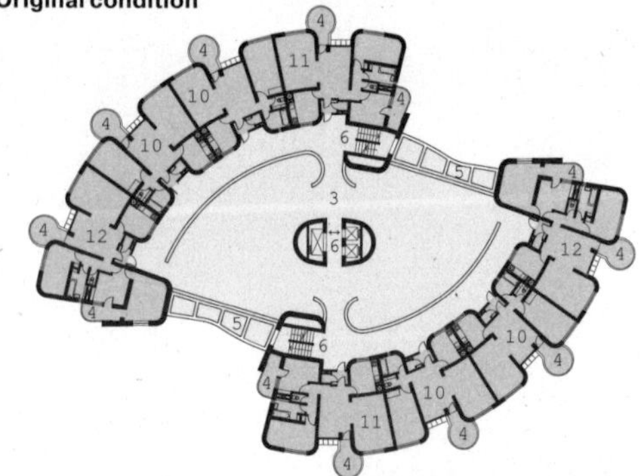

Roof terrace
Original condition

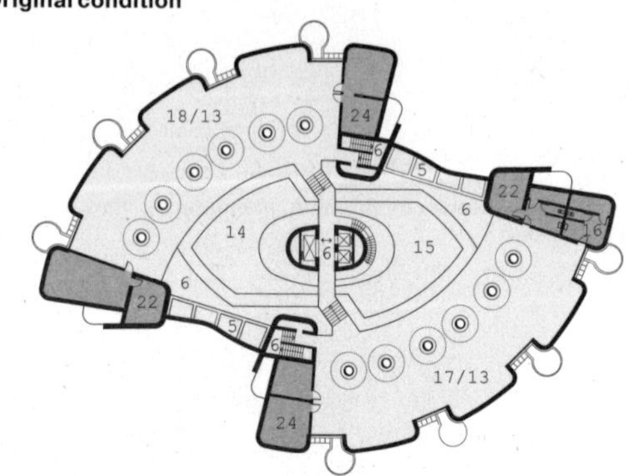

1	Entrance hall	8	Jewellery shop service room	14	Pool for children	21	Security room
2	Airlock	9	Rental space	15	Fish pool	22	Storage
3	Recreation	10	2-room apartment	16	Restroom	23	Service room
4	Terrace/balcony	11	3-room apartment	17	Open-air gym	24	Technical area
5	Vegetation	12	4-room apartment	18	Relaxation zone	25	Offices
6	Circulation	13	Multifunctional roof	19	Conference room		
7	Jewellery salesroom			20	Kitchen		

2022

Entrance floor plan
Current condition

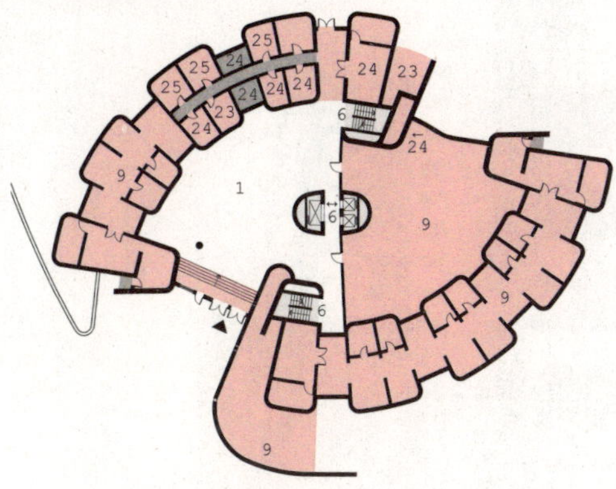

1st floor plan (commercial)
Current condition

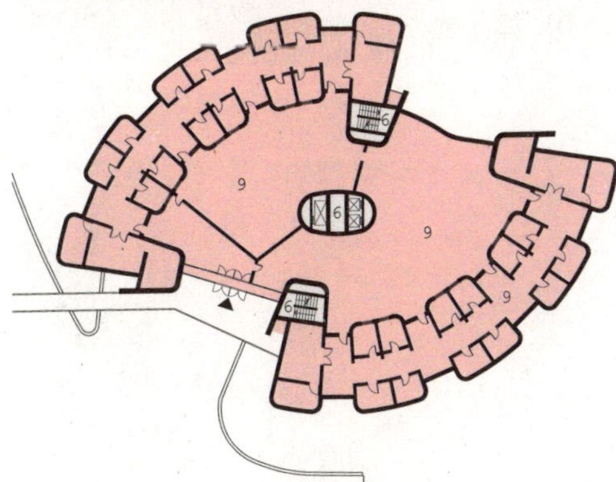

11th floor plan (first floor of typical residential block)
Current condition

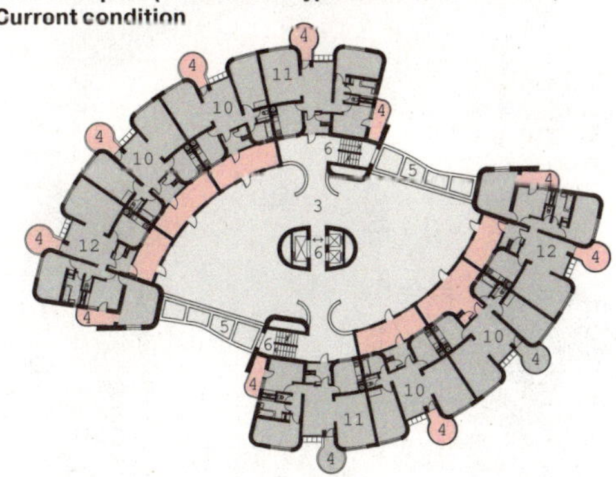

12th floor plan (second floor of typical residential block)
Current condition

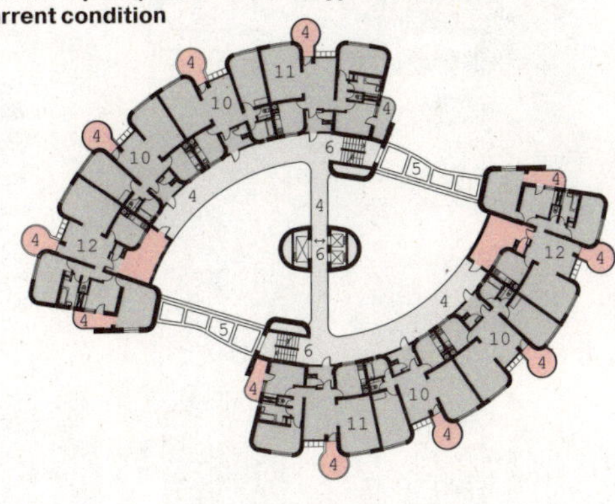

13th floor plan (third floor of typical residential block)
Current condition

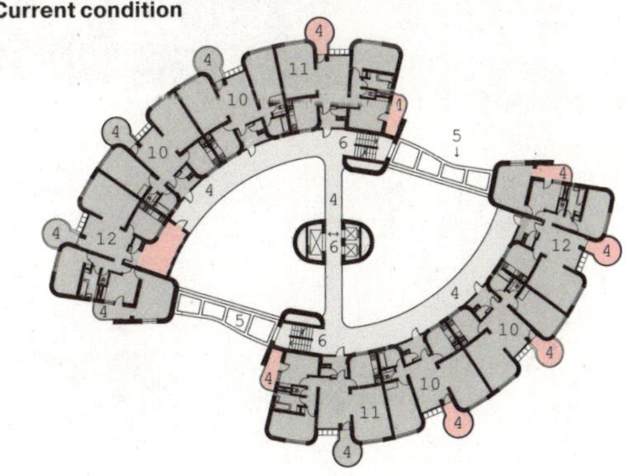

Roof terrace
Current condition

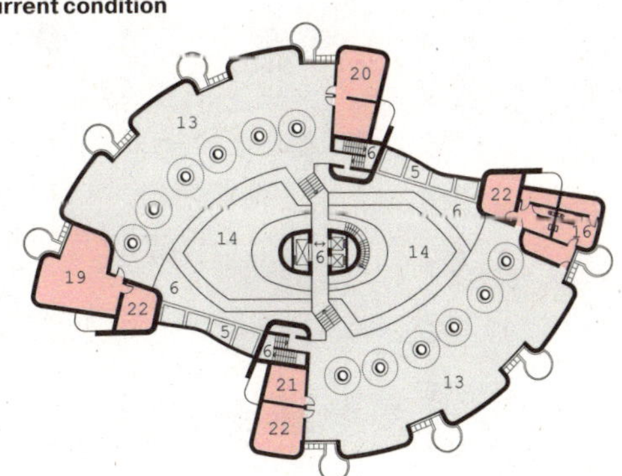

2-room apartment, original layout

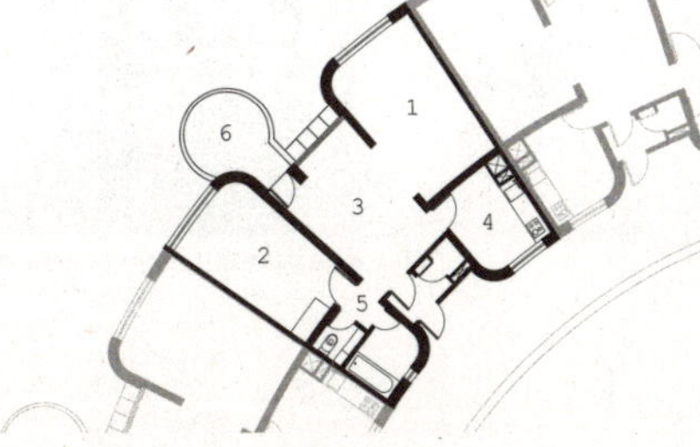

0 5 10m

1	Living room
2	Bedroom
3	Iwan
4	Kitchen
5	Bathroom
6	Balcony

- Public areas
- Apartments
- Service and technical
- Change of function

0 5 10m

Zhemchug residential building during construction

Zhemchug residential building during construction

Children playing in an inner courtyard, 1987

Façade detail, 1987

View of a common courtyard

Inner courtyard activities

Children playing in an inner courtyard, 1987

Detail of common courtyard furniture

View of the rooftop

West façade, 2023

North-west façade, 2022

West façade, 2021

Sculptures on the façade, 2022

Interior view of the entrance floor, 2022

Internal courtyard, 2023

View of a common courtyard, 2021

View of a common courtyard, 2021

View of a common courtyard, 2021

Lighthouse, 2021

Rooftop sunshade grid, 2021

View of the rooftop, 2021

Model of the preliminary design for Zhemchug, 1975

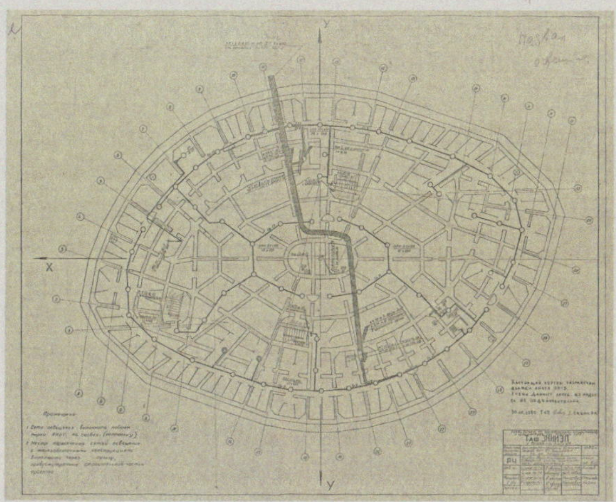
Basement: wiring diagram and systems, 1980

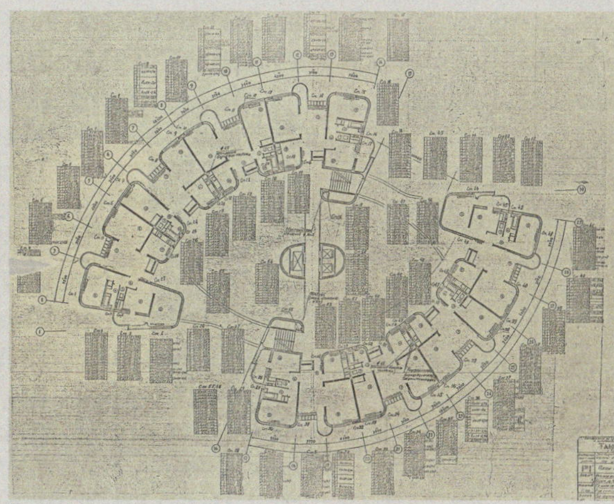
Typical floor plan, 1978

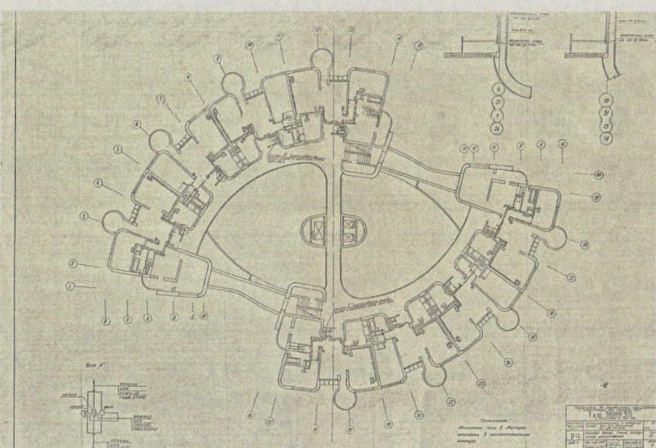
Typical floor: wiring diagram, 1978

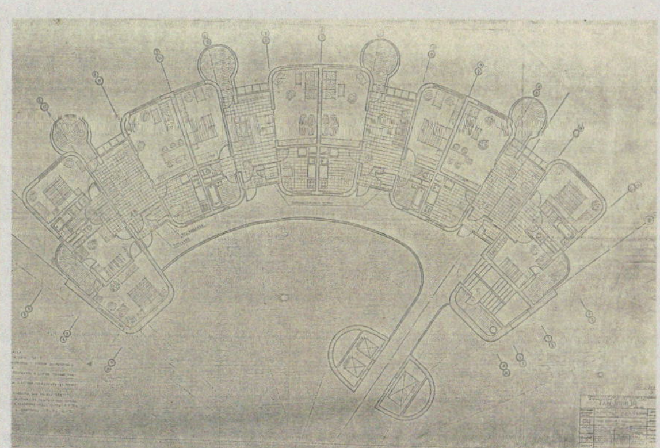
Layout of the apartments with furnishings, 1978

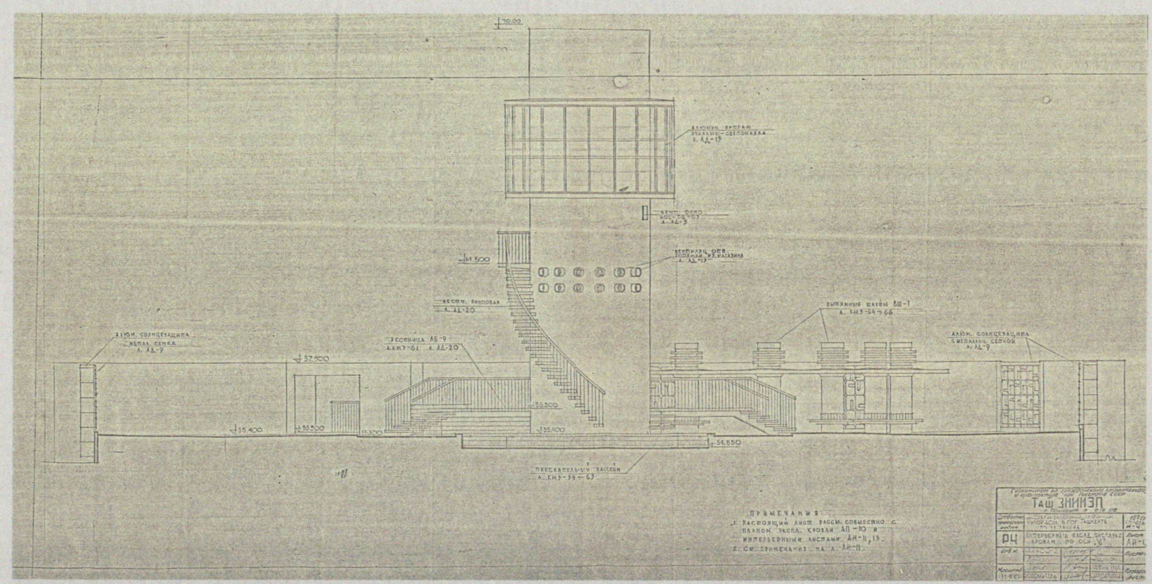
Section of the rooftop, April 1978

HIGHLIGHTS

Zhemchug (The Pearl) is a sixteen-story residential building in Tashkent. Its design was completed in 1984, and in 1986 it was awarded the gold medal as the best building in the USSR by the Union of Soviet Architects. The design team was led by Ofeliia Aidinova and included G. Golubeva and E. Shatalov. The building is on the list of protected buildings of Uzbekistan according to Decision No. 846 of the Cabinet of Ministers, October 4, 2019.

Zhemchug is a highly experimental building, in which the traditional single-story housing typical of Central Asia, the mahalla, is reinterpreted through modern architecture. The innovative construction method, based on the use of monolithic concrete and sliding formwork, liberated the architect from the rigid constraints of prefabrication. Thanks to this highly experimental character, as well as its urban placement, Zhemchug is a unique modernist building and therefore requires a strategy of conservation and technical improvement. It is also important to mention that it is one of the few modernist buildings where design was led by a woman.

Construction was completed in 1985 on a plot of land bordered by Sapernaia Street (Mirobod), Shota Rustaveli Street and Cosmonauts Avenue (Afrosiyob). Such an urban position, in combination with the building's height, guaranteed the higher floors an excellent panoramic view of the city and made Zhemchug an important reference point on the Tashkent skyline.

The architectural layout of the building was inspired by the traditional mahalla, the spirit and quality of which the architects interpreted in a contemporary manner in the common spaces and the apartment layout. The complex was conceived as a "vertical mahalla" or, as Philipp Meuser phrased it, as "a modern response to the traditional community-oriented collective co-existence of the Uzbek people."[1] In order to maintain the minute neighborhood scale within a large tower, five spacious suspended courtyards were created, one every three floors. These courtyards, conceived as common outdoor spaces for residents, have a truly unique quality: they organize three floors of curvilinear balconies, giving access to the apartments on one side and opening up to the city through large triple-height openings on the other. The coexistence of the smaller mahalla scale next to the massive scale of a high-rise, with inevitable components such as cores and stairs, as well as the presence of an additional filter—the courtyard—between the apartment and the exterior

1 Philipp Meuser, *Seismic Modernism: Architecture and Housing in Soviet Tashkent* (Berlin: DOM Publishers, 2016), 236.

is what makes Zhemchug truly unique. The informal mixture of urban furniture and domestic details conveys the idea of a public, yet familiar space, like in a traditional neighborhood.

The beautiful rooftop with a pool was originally intended as a children's playground. It has a distinctive elevator tower, designed as an expressive lighthouse.

The experimental approach applied to the architectural design was also translated into the construction technique. Zhemchug was one of the first high-rise buildings in Tashkent to be entirely constructed using sliding formwork methodology. Architect Ofeliia Aidinova tested this technique, in parallel with Savelii Rozenblium, as an alternative to the widespread prefabricated concrete or mixed solutions, creating a fully monolithic concrete structure. The application of sliding formwork to monolithic construction was calculated to be less expensive and faster, allowing for taller buildings that would exceed the nine-story limitation of standard prefabrication. Moreover, it provided more formal freedom to use organic shapes. History showed that the cost and the speed did not work out as efficiently as planned, but the quality of the result remains outstanding even today and is worth preserving.

STATE OF REPAIR
SCORE:

2 – The building shows significant localized damage and/or diffused and extended deterioration patterns. It is, however, still possible to use it.

Overall, the state of repair of the building is satisfactory, even though maintenance interventions should be improved. In particular, the lack of a set of shared rules concerning upkeep activities has resulted in a general lack of homogeneity in the façade's appearance. The main issues, however, concern the technical systems, which are obsolete and malfunctioning.

Protection status:	The building is listed and protected according to Decision No. 846 of the Cabinet of Ministers, October 4, 2019.
Main criticalities:	In nearly forty years of existence, the building has never been subject to major renovations. The lack of maintenance has led to a few criticalities, which mostly concern the technical systems. In particular, the heating system, electrical system and water supply system are frequently out of order or unusable. The pool located on the rooftop is also causing

problems, as the water is leaking. The lack of maintenance is mostly due to a lack of funds, because the residents cannot afford the expenses and the local administration does not seem particularly interested in the conservation of the building. Another critical aspect is the lack of common rules for intervention and maintenance, which has enabled Zhemchug's inhabitants to freely adjust the apartments to their needs, with rather uneven outcomes.

Possible risks: The spontaneous interventions made by Zhemchug's residents, which include the demolition of internal walls, the opening of new doors and the enclosing of balconies. All this might have negative repercussions on the structural behavior of the building.

Uncontrolled transformation has also significantly changed the appearance of the building from its original condition. If this situation was to persist, further irreversible damage could be done with negative impacts in terms of authenticity and integrity and, therefore, with a decrease in the overall value of the building. Additionally, the lack of maintenance and upkeep might lead to further decay and technical obsolescence, driving away current residents.

INTEGRITY
SCORE:

- Exterior: 4 – The building has retained all the elements necessary to express its significance and is in a good state of repair
- Interior: 3 – The building has retained all the elements necessary to express its significance but is in a poor state of repair

AUTHENTICITY
SCORE:

- Exterior: 3 – The building has been subjected to slight changes and replacements
- Interior: 2 – The building has been subjected to localized but significant modifications

Due to the fact that no major interventions have been carried out on the building since its construction, we can state that its level of authenticity is satisfactory. Nonetheless, widespread spontaneous adjustments made by residents, for maintenance reasons and to make the apartments more suitable for personal needs, have modified some of the original features.

In particular, the round balconies on the external façades have been enclosed to increase the habitable indoor space. Many original windows have been replaced and sunscreens removed, resulting in a rather heterogeneous appearance.

Changes also occurred within the suspended courtyards, where curved wooden partitions marking the access to the apartments have been replaced by brick or other walls, pushing the separation outward to gain more living space. Internal partitions have also been modified, with possible repercussions for the building's structural and seismic safety.

The ground floor was originally enclosed by large glazed openings, which have now been blocked with opaque walls. A portion of the foyer at the ground level has been subdivided into smaller areas for rent.

Finally, the entire building was originally painted white. The use of a single color highlighted the sculptural qualities of the volume. Recently, the color scheme has been modified, combining light beige for the façade and ocher red for the balconies. Nonetheless, from the outside the building is still fairly close to its original appearance.

1987

2022

First floor, 1980s (video still)

First floor, 2021

Zhemchug's balconies, 1987

Zhemchug's balconies, 2022

1980s

2022

Entrance to the apartments, 1980s (video still)

Entrance to the apartments, 2022

General view of one of the courtyards, 1980s

General view of one of the courtyards, 2022

1986

Zhemchug as seen from a building in front, 1985/1986

2022

Zhemchug as seen from a building in front, 2022

Rooftop chimneys (kitchen ventilation outlets and pool shades), 1980s

Rooftop chimneys (kitchen ventilation outlets and pool shades), 2022

LEVEL 1 – MAXIMUM LEVEL OF INTEREST
(No transformations allowed; conservation activities required)

URBAN LEVEL

Today there are no high-rise buildings within a 500-meter radius of Zhemchug, which ensures its visibility as a landmark and guarantees an undisturbed view from the building toward the city. This visual relationship should be retained, avoiding constructing high-rise buildings in the surrounding area.

ARCHITECTURAL LEVEL
EXTERIOR

The volume, shape and height of the building should remain unchanged.

The general layout of the façade of the building should be maintained, with particular reference to:

- the eight vertical sets of round balconies, which, where still open, should not be closed;
- the large courtyard openings toward the city, which bring light to the internal courtyards and relate them to the external context;
- the shape, dimensions and number of the existing windows.

The rooftop should be preserved as is, as a continuous space with no volume additions or partitions significantly modifying the appearance or proportions of the elements.

The system of entrances to the building on different levels, guaranteeing access to both the first (entrance) and second (commercial) floors, should be retained.

INTERIOR

Spatial proportions within the building, as well as the mutual relationship between different parts of it, should be retained: a vertical connection at the core, common courtyards, and apartment units on the outer perimeter.

The oval shape and dimensions of the central core should not be modified.

No partitions should be added within the courtyards, to guarantee the spatial continuity from which the design concept originated. The original low curved walls located on the ground level of each courtyard should be preserved.

The façades overlooking the internal courtyards should retain key architectural elements, with particular reference to the suspended pathways and balconies giving access to the apartments on the upper levels.

The planters adjacent to the courtyard's large openings toward the city should be maintained.

DETAIL LEVEL
EXTERIOR

The lantern, chimneys and pool located on the rooftop should be retained.

Where still existing, the sunscreens on the windows of the iwan rooms and the analogous decorations on the parapets of the rooftop should be preserved.

The decorative flower elements located on the lower portion of the façades should remain untouched.

INTERIOR

The courtyards' coffered ceilings should be kept as they are.

The original rough plaster, largely spread throughout the building, emphasizing the materiality of the building and recalling its monolithic nature, should be retained, where still existing.

All original handrails should be preserved.

The entrance hall's original pavement should be preserved.

LEVEL 2 – MEDIUM LEVEL OF INTEREST

(Elements included in the second level can be moderately transformed following approval by a designated committee[1])

ARCHITECTURAL LEVEL
INTERIOR

Any transformation concerning the architectural layout of the apartments should be submitted to the designated committee for approval.

DETAIL LEVEL
EXTERIOR

Replacement of elements (doors, windows) or finishes of the exterior façades should be planned according to a common set of rules and subject to approval by the designated committee.

Replacement of or changes to the rooftop's finishes should be submitted to the designated committee for approval.

1 An international committee of heritage preservation experts to be appointed.

INTERIOR

Replacement of elements (doors, windows) or finishes of the internal courtyards' façades should be planned according to a common set of rules and subject to approval by the designated committee.

Replacement of or changes to the courtyards' finishes should be submitted to the designated committee for approval.

HIDDEN MODERNIST FEATURES

According to the original design, the exterior of the building, in particular the structural shafts, was finished using whitewashed concrete plaster, which underlined the monolithic and organic nature of this modernist architecture. Today, the façade has been painted in beige shades, causing the building to lose its sculptural appearance.

A second hidden modernist feature can be recognized in the round cantilevering balconies, which were originally intended to be open. The simple shape of these elements, as well as the light-and-shadow effects they created on the façade, was clearly an element of modernist design. In recent decades, most residents have chosen to glaze the balconies, hiding this important feature of Zhemchug.

Preservation Level 1
Maximum Level of Interest
Materials and elements to be preserved

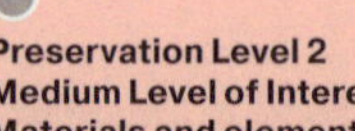

Preservation Level 2
Medium Level of Interest
Materials and elements to be preserved

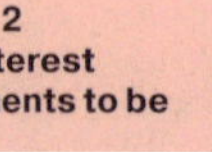

Hidden Modernist Features
Materials and elements to be preserved

Transformation allowed

Preservation Strategy

Among Tashkent modernist buildings, Zhemchug is clearly the most experimental. Architect Ofeliia Aidinova and her team experimented with socio-cultural aspects of spatial organization and construction technology when designing this residential high-rise. In her attempt to create a "vertical mahalla," Aidinova set aside the rigid schemes of prefabricated construction, suggesting a monolithic structure, which, while allowing for organic shapes, was also intended to be less expensive and better performing in terms of seismic resistance. The experimental character of this building makes it unique and worth preserving, as also acknowledged by the Uzbekistan Ministry of Culture, which, in 2019, added it to the list of protected buildings.

Over the last forty years, Zhemchug has undergone several transformations which concerned both the outside and the inside of the building. While the changes to the exterior façade are less significant and mostly reversible, the changes which occurred in the interior courtyards are more relevant and permanent. Zhemchug residents appropriated the building by modifying and decorating the apartment façades facing the interior courtyards according to their personal taste. Some of them expanded their homes, occupying the perimetral portions of the courtyards. Such interventions have heavily modified the original appearance of the courtyards, but, at the same time, have also proven the partial success of the "vertical mahalla" concept. We could assert that changes to the inside of the building can be read as a sign of the vitality of Zhemchug, and thus as a valuable transformation worth keeping.

The preservation strategy developed for Zhemchug proposes a dual approach, reflecting the different levels of transformation of the inside and outside of the building. For the exterior façade, the aim is to revert most changes in order to obtain an overall appearance that is close to the original. While the changes which occurred in the suspended courtyards and apartments are accepted, the most significant remaining architectural features of the original construction, which have retained a fairly satisfactory level of authenticity, will be protected.

The preservation strategy includes the following actions for the exterior façade of the building.

The first action concerns the finishes and the color of the façade. According to the original design, the exterior of the building, in particular the structural shafts, was finished using whitewashed concrete plaster, which underlined the monolithic nature and organic shape of the building. Today, it is multicolored: the vertical concrete shafts have been painted in a peach or beige shade, while the basement and round balconies have been painted in ocher red. Since such changes largely reduce the readability of the original architectural concept, the proposal is to repaint the façades in white, reinstating the original sculpted appearance of the building.

The second action deals with the round balconies, which were originally completely open and are now mostly glazed. With their clean lines and light-and-shadow effects, the balconies can undoubtedly be considered a modernist feature of Aidinova's design. However, they did not have a merely stylistic purpose, as they were also intended to provide natural ventilation to the apartments, thus mitigating the continental climate conditions. Today, the vast majority of these balconies have been enclosed and annexed to the apartments. Although they are not a significant addition in terms of dimensions, they are valued by residents, who have created comfortable niches or little sanctuaries in these spaces. Therefore, instead of reinstating the original design by removing the glazing, the team proposes replacing the spontaneous infills with ad hoc designed folding windows, which will be visually light and highly transparent. This action guarantees homogeneity, a better readability of the original design and the possibility of making use of the original ventilation system.

The third action to be performed on the exterior façades involves the outdoor air-conditioning units. Since their presence is not coherent with the original design, it is suggested that they be moved from their current position and located behind the existing metal "panjara." Where the screens are missing, a new, similar-looking panjara will be installed. This way it is possible to guarantee a comfortable interior climate for Zhemchug residents, without significantly altering the original appearance.

As mentioned, the approach to the interior courtyard of the building is different from the one suggested for the outside. In particular, spontaneous changes made by residents of the building are recognized as a relevant part of Zhemchug's identity and will therefore be retained, accepting future transformations of finishes of the courtyard façades. Further changes in terms of square meterage will not be allowed.

While finish materials and colors will continue to change, a few significant elements should remain the same over time: the circulation system (balconies and passages), central shaft, coffered ceiling and concrete planters are to be preserved as they are, both in terms of form and finishes. In particular, with regard to the circulation system, the following aspects should be considered:

- the continuous lines traced by the slabs of the suspended pathways should remain white and in plain sight;

- the handrails of the suspended pathways are original and should be preserved;
- the low curved walls, outlining the routes on the courtyards' main floors, should be preserved.

While the described strategy will help control the transformations of the building in years to come, the preservation strategy also proposes three main actions to be performed in the immediate future in order to guarantee the material preservation of the building.

The first action concerns the pool located on the rooftop, which is currently causing leakages and subsequent decay of the reinforced concrete structure. The impermeabilization layer of the pool needs to be replaced in order to act on the cause of the problem. It will then be possible to repair the damage observed on the concrete slab by passivating the rebars and integrating the missing portions of rebar cover.

The second action concerns the first level. In 1985, the first-floor lobby of Zhemchug was separated from the exterior by transparent glazing. Thus, it appeared that the heavy volume of the building was suspended above the foyer and rested on the concrete cores. Today, this continuity between the inside and outside is lost because the entrance has been sealed off by an opaque wall. It is suggested that a new glass wall with good thermal properties be installed in order to make the entrance and foyer area consistent with the original design intent.

The third action regards the general repairs, cleaning and maintenance operations to be carried out on the building, including the rooftop. This includes upgrading the water system, the sewage system, the heating system, the electrical system and the elevators. Additionally, the outdoor areas immediately adjacent to the building require an upgrade.

Preservation Checklist

In order to implement the proposed preservation strategy a few aspects will need to be clarified and/or further developed. It is important to conduct a series of surveys to assess the structural condition of the building. In particular, attention should be focused on the roof slab, which may have been damaged by water infiltration from the pool, and on the basement, where structural elements have also been damaged by moisture.

The malfunctioning and outdatedness of the technical systems also requires a survey, which will help identify the main criticalities and support the development of a project for their upgrade. Since the building is listed, the project will need to be approved by the ministry in charge before implementation.

Some of the actions proposed by the preservation strategy will need to be developed to reach an executive level of detail. In particular, this will need to be done for the balcony glazing and for the reinstatement of the original panjara, which will encase the air-conditioning units. The designed solutions could be tested on a single apartment or a limited number of apartments (pilot site) before being extended to the whole building. In this case, preliminary approval should be obtained from the ministry in charge.

Based on the ministry's opinion and the outcome of the pilot site, it will be possible to make final adjustments to the project and to execute it. A plan of inspection and maintenance should be developed and implemented after the interventions in order to guarantee better preservation and functioning of the building. To this end, it will be essential to calculate a budget for maintenance and to designate a person in charge who will control the implementation of maintenance activities.

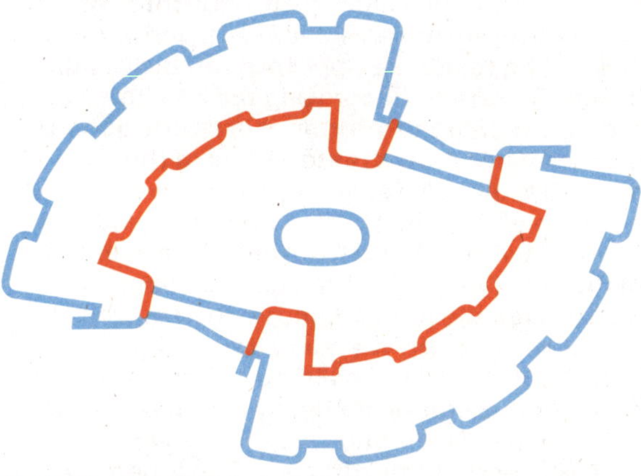

Highlighting the original
Preservation of change

Axonometric view illustrating the result of the preservation actions: the building regains its sculptural and monolithic appearance.

Strategy

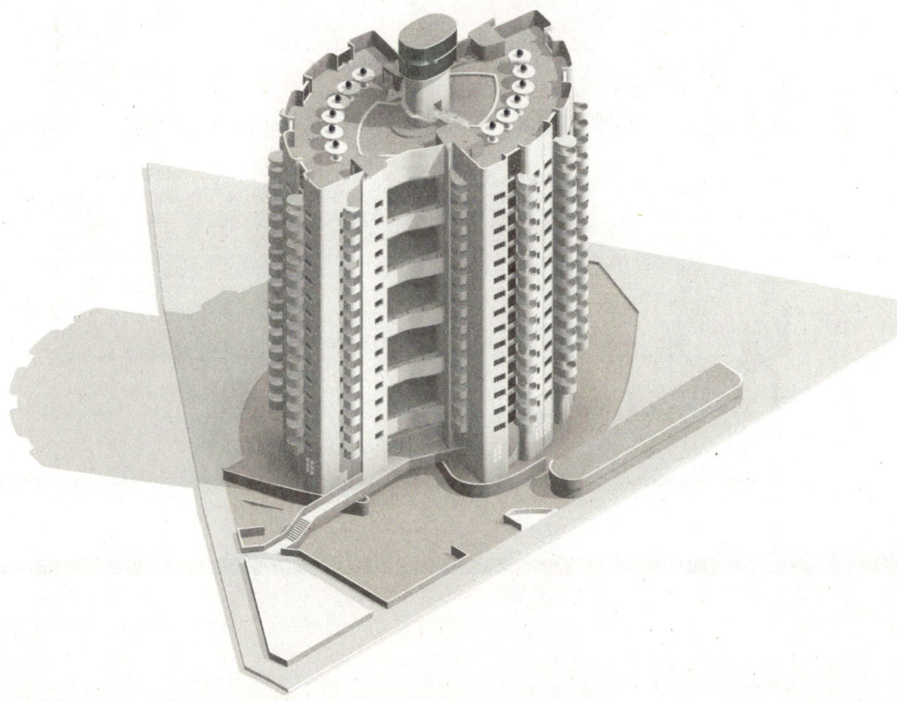

Unfolded elevation, visualization of original inner façade (1985)

Inner façade mapping, reflecting current situation (2022)

Chorsu Bazaar

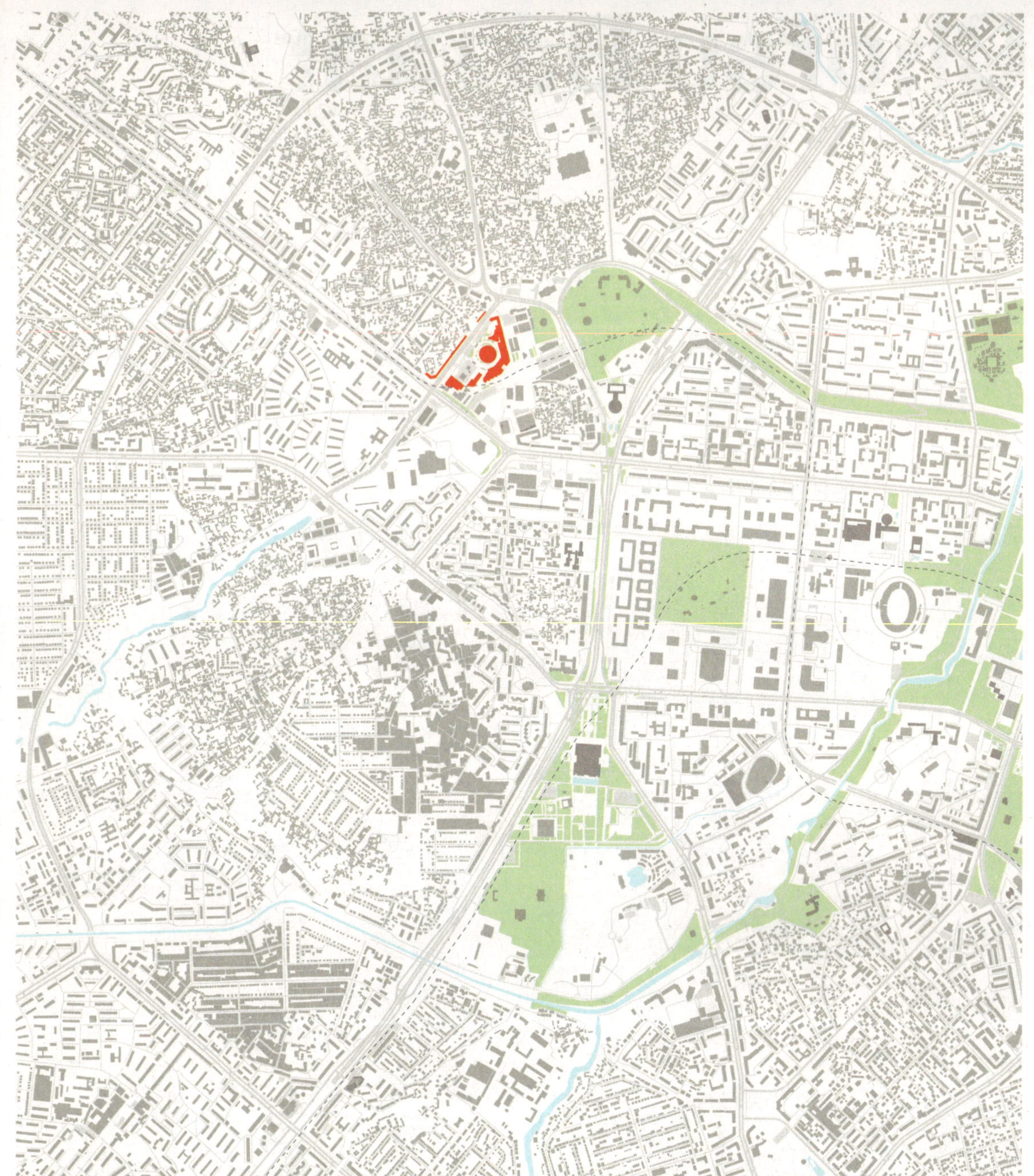
Building position and address: Beruni Street, Tashkent

0 0.5 1km

In speaking about the historical cartography of the Chorsu Bazaar it is necessary to differentiate the actual site on which the complex was built in the 1980s and 1990s from the urban nucleus of the Chorsu bazaar, which had a key significance for the development of Tashkent in the medieval, tsarist and Soviet periods. As a whole, Chorsu was the nucleus where the four main districts of the medieval city met: Kukcha, Sibzar, Sheikhantaur and Beshagach. This site was characterized by centuries-long evolution and the remains of various urban layers. The buildings of the Chorsu Bazaar that appeared in the 1980s and 1990s are on the site of the former Chorsu mahalla, which was located at a boundary point between the Kukcha and Beshagach districts and adjoined the western part of the historical Chorsu bazaar.

Medieval Chorsu was a complex urban area combining trading, cult and town square functions. Spatially it developed from north to south, with a narrow strip in the middle part. Registan Square and the Beklyarbek Madrasa were located in the upper part, and in the lower part, since the sixteenth century, there had been a mosque and two madrasas, Kukeldash and Hodja Akhrar. Between them there were two trading rows. According to research by Abdumannop Ziiaev, materials from an inspection of the Chorsu bazaar in 1866–1867 identified twenty-five trading rows and sixteen caravanserais, which were hotels for merchants and suppliers of goods to the market.[1] The tsarist administration of Turkestan preferred not to get involved in the life of the "old city," and the only European urban planning insertion of that period in the district that directly adjoins the Chorsu complex is the depot of the Belgian company Tashkent

1 Abdumannop Ziiaev, *Tashkent II: XVII–nachalo XX* veka [*Tashkent II: 17th–Early 20th Century*] (Tashkent: San"at, 2009), 187.

Tram, built in 1901. This policy of noninterference was completely reconsidered in the Soviet period. Having set the political goal of "uniting old and new Tashkent" and aiming to destroy the traditional way of life, the Soviet authorities introduced new types of buildings and activities into the "old" city center. Here they built a stadium, laid out a park and opened a theater. Simultaneously, the authorities tried to nullify Chorsu's role as the center of religious life. Most of the religious buildings were closed and the Beklyarbek Madrasa was destroyed so that its territory and the adjacent Registan Square could be used for a new urban space for meetings that would soon be called Kalinin Square.[2] There was a no less dramatic collision with trading activities, which were seen through the prism of Marxism as a form of receiving surplus value.

According to the first Soviet general plan (1929–1932), by Aleksandr Sil'chenkov, the "old city" of Tashkent was to be demolished. The markets were to make way for planned enterprises for the supply, preparation and distribution of food. However, by the second half of the 1930s the relationship to the "old city" on the whole and to bazaars in particular was more realistic. Nevertheless, over time, and especially during World War II, all of the buildings in Chorsu became increasingly dilapidated. For this reason, in the mid-1950s the bazaar was rebuilt. Most of the old structures were demolished and new trading rows made of temporary and nondurable materials appeared, as did a Central Market Pavilion, designed in Stalinist style. From this point work began on the restoration and reconstruction of the remaining religious buildings, particularly the Kukeldash Madrasa, which was rebuilt in the mid-1950s. The first mod-

2 Ibid., 18.

ernist structures appeared in the district a little later: the Gulistan Restaurant (1967, architect: L. Komissar) was built on Kalinin Square, the Tashgiprogor and Sredazgiprovodkhlopok institutes (early 1960s) framed the perimeter of Navoi Street and projects were designed for GUM (1966–1971) and the Chorsu Hotel (1975–1982). To the south of the territory of the future new Chorsu Bazaar, the National Steam Baths was built to a design by Andrei Kosinskii (1973–1977), distinguished by its expressive orientalist character.

The idea to extend the market by demolishing the mahalla to the west of the old market that had been reconstructed in the mid-1950s and was already in poor condition appeared in a version of the detailed plan for the center of Tashkent in 1974. There are several versions with an approximate sketch of this market, but throughout the 1970s the planners could not decide the direction of development. Kosinskii's team proposed that it be developed to the north. After Kosinskii left for Moscow in 1978, the location for the new market was confirmed as being to the west of the old one, and in 1980 architects began developing the layout and shape, which were influenced by the fantasy and semi-orientalist projects of the 1960s and 1970s.

Main dimensions of the Chorsu Bazaar
General axonometric view

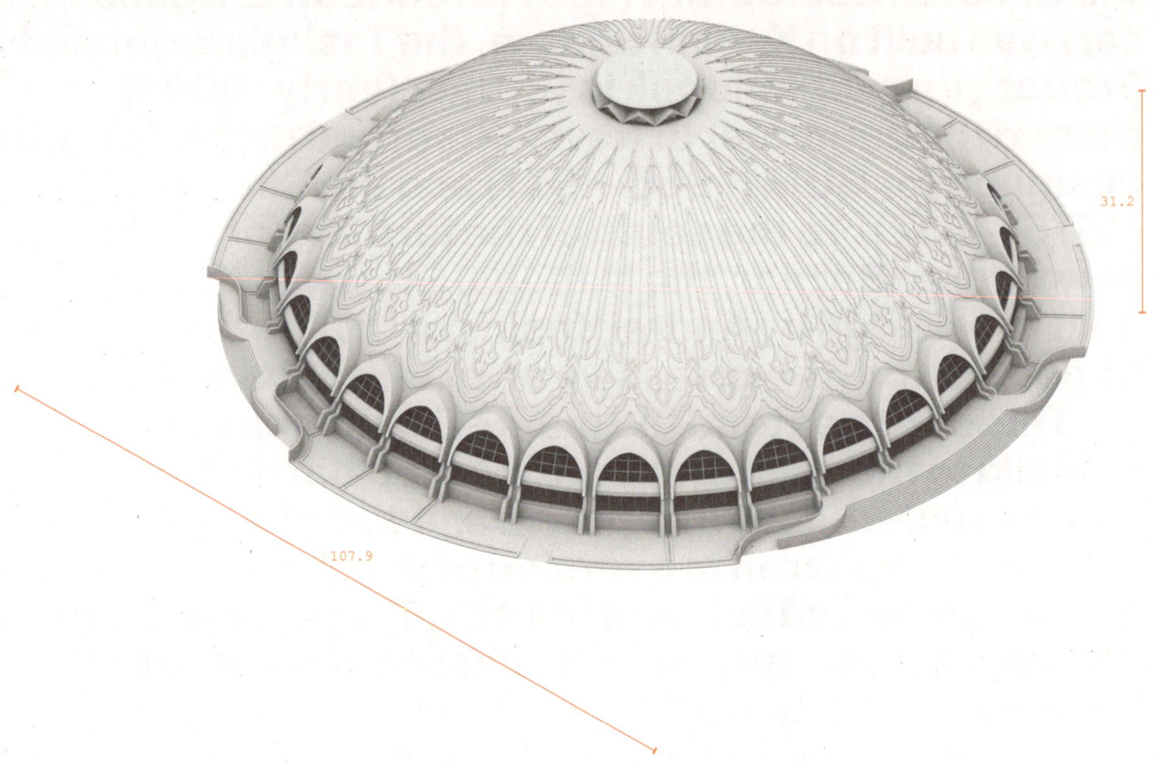

ACTORS	**Architects:**	**Vladimir Azimov, Sabir Adylov**
	Engineers:	**I. Kirilets, K. Li, F. Sivintseva, N. Namednina, G. Belfer, L. Katukova**
	Institute:	**Tashgiprogor**
DATES	**Design period:**	**1980–1986**
	Construction period:	**1983–1990**
	Inauguration date:	**1990**
	Later interventions:	**1990–1994: Placement of mosaics on secondary domes' extrados.**
USE	**Current use:**	**Wholesale, retail, and fruit and vegetable market**
	Original use:	**Wholesale, retail, and fruit and vegetable market**
	Suitability of current use:	**The main dome, as well as the whole area of Chorsu Bazaar, designed to house the district market, is well suited for the current use. However, since the building has not been renovated since its inauguration, it would be appropriate to adapt the spaces to current hygiene standards and renew the technical systems.**
	Space utilization:	**The building is fully used. There do not appear to be any vacancies or underused spaces.**
DIMENSIONS	**Number of floors:**	**Basement + 1 floor + mezzanine**
	Main dome diameter:	**107.9 m**
	Height:	**31.2 m**
	Gross floor area (first floor):	**6,076.0 m²**
	Gross floor area (total):	**14,790.0 m²**

Chorsu Bazaar

The documentary basis of this research is comprised of archive materials from the Tashgiprogor Institute and the recollections of architects involved in the design. There were, however, some serious lacunae. For instance, the Tashgiprogor archive does not contain the project description and working correspondence. There were no extensive historical publications about the market, but it was occasionally mentioned in the professional and popular press in general and subject-based materials.

The Chorsu Bazaar (initially named the October Market) is the largest building in Tashkent to be designed in the 1980s. Alongside the Turkestan Palace it was chronologically and stylistically the last building of Tashkent modernism that directly preceded the wave of neo-eclectic architecture of the 1990s and early 2000s.

The Genealogy of the Project

The need to extend the market had been recognized in 1974, during work on the detailed plan of the center of Tashkent. As a result, the architects reserved a plot for it on the site of an old mahalla that adjoined Beruni Street. According to Iurii Miroshnichenko,[1] in the late 1970s he worked on the project for the extension of the October Market together with architect Evgenii Kaleshov. However, Tashkent Chief Architect Sabir Adylov saw their work at the end of the decade, after which the project was assigned to architect Vladimir Azimov, whose position at Tashgiprogor had gradually strengthened. From then on, the project was led by Azimov, who became the head architect at the institute, and his main co-author was named as Adylov. Their project differed in spatial and compositional terms from that proposed by Miroshnichenko.

The architectural community developed a stable narrative regarding the genealogy of the appearance of this large domed building. It states that Vladimir Azimov borrowed the colored dome from Moscow architect Andrei Kosinskii, who arrived in Tashkent in 1966, after the earthquake. In 1969 Kosinskii led a team that developed a design for the center of Chilanzar district, where trading domes covered with multicolored ceramic played an important role.[2] The causal relationship between the unbuilt Chilanzar project and the Chorsu Bazaar dome, which was developed a decade later, can be seen in publications by the German scholar Jens Jordan[3] and in the thoughts of Iurii Miroshnichenko during one of his meetings with Boris Chukhovich, the author of this text, in 2021. This relationship, in my view, requires critical reconsideration.

Azimov was one of the graduate students who, in 1969, worked with Kosinskii on the design for the center of Chilanzar, which would become a landmark in the evolution of Tashkent architecture toward exotic attractiveness. Like many of Kosinskii's students, such as Leonid Nefedov, Aleksandr Dizik and G. Chernov, Azimov was inspired by the prophetic figure of the Moscow architect who had arrived in Uzbekistan to help reconstruct Tashkent. Architect Vladimir Narubanskii noted how Kosinskii influenced his students: "We got lucky with him. He was a brilliant personality, ambitious, just right for a teacher. He called on students to see in the architectural heritage of the East not only the external appearance but also life itself, the way of life, the construction and organization of spaces, living environments."[4] A practicing architect with an entertaining way of speaking and a memorable drawing technique, Kosinskii was extremely influential among students, many of whom aimed to join Tashgiprogor after graduating so as to continue their career under him. Having arrived in Tashkent, Kosinskii spent much time walking in the "old city" and visiting traditional teahouses there. Later, as he often related, he was the one who opened the eyes of Tashkent architects to exploring the local architectural tradition. However, these stories should be taken with a pinch of salt. An eccentric with a fertile imagination, Kosinskii sincerely believed in his pioneering role and mission, but historical facts disprove many of his legends. For example, he spoke more than once about how he had drawn attention to the cooling of traditional homes using the free vertical flow of air, however, this phenomenon, known as shipang in traditional architecture, was being discussed orally and in the professional press long before Kosinskii arrived in Uzbekistan.[5]

1 In the late 1970s Iurii Miroshnichenko was the head architect at Tashgiprogor. Boris Chukhovich recorded his story about the October Market in October 2021.

2 Andrei Kosinskii and Iurii Miroshnichenko, "Proekt tsentra raiona Chilanzar v Tashkente [Project for the Center of Chilanzar District in Tashkent]," *Arkhitektura SSSR* [*Architecture of the USSR*], no. 2, 1970; Abdulla Babakhanov, "Uspekhi molodykh zodchik Uzbekistana [Successes of Young Architects of Uzbekistan]," *Stroitel'stvo i arkhitektura Uzbekistana* [*Construction and Architecture of Uzbekistan*], no. 7, 1970; Andrei Kosinskii, "Tashkent. Chilanzar. Tsentr [Tashkent. Chilanzar. Center]," *Stroitel'stvo i arkhitektura Uzbekistana* [*Construction and Architecture of Uzbekistan*], no. 6, 1971.

3 Jens Jordan, "Ugroza razrusheniia pamiatnika 'Chorsu bazar' i ego okrestnostei [Heritage Building Chorsu Threatened with Destruction]," *Gazeta.Uz*, November 23, 2018, https://www.gazeta.uz/ru/2018/11/23/chorsu/ (accessed May 19, 2022).

4 From Vladimir Narubanskii's letter to Boris Chukhovich dated December 21, 2021.

5 Viktor Dmitriev, "O vozmozhnosti ispol'zovaniia priema shipang v sovremennoi praktike [On the Possibility of Using the Shipang Technique in Contemporary Practice]," *Stroitel'stvo i arkhitektura Uzbekistana* [*Construction and Architecture of Uzbekistan*], no. 1, 1961.

In fact, Andrei Kosinskii was not the first person to develop the idea of the monumental modernist dome for the design of the new bazaar in Tashkent. Two years before work began on the center of Chilanzar, graduate student Iurii Garamov from the architecture faculty of Tashkent Polytechnic Institute, who was working under Abdulla Babakhanov and Leonid Karash, proposed a design for a market that was stunning in plastic terms, with a dome eighty-six meters in diameter and twenty-eight meters high.[6] Garamov's dome was not decorated with arabesques, but was surrounded by a ring of vaults with surfaces of the second order reminiscent of the cells of Félix Candela, who was popular in the 1960s. In terms of composition, it seemed that the student was inspired by the trading domes of medieval Bukhara, which featured a high central dome below which was a system of small domes that removed part of the thrust and served as additional market space for traders. Garamov's graduation project became well-known in Tashkent and in the USSR, receiving second prize in the All-Union Review of Diploma Works of Architectural Institutes of the Soviet Union, which took place in 1967 in Tbilisi. As a teacher in the architectural faculty, Andrei Kosinskii, who was Azimov's boss, could not have missed it.

However, we can state that an indirect predecessor of Garamov's dome was the covered market in Sidi Bel Abbès in Algeria (1955, architect: Marcel Mauri), which featured a reinforced concrete dome encircled by two-tier shops. The fact that Garamov knew about the Algerian project is confirmed by his 1972 article "Architecture of Covered Markets in Hot Climatic Conditions (International Experience)." Here Garamov made a point of stressing that "the circulation of masses of air inside the market occurs thanks to an oculus at the top of the dome. As a result, heat is removed from the internal surfaces of the structure by convection and there is exchange of air in the trading hall and cooling of the building at night."[7] This idea was the basis of Kosinskii's domes in the designs for the Chilanzar project and the dome of the Chorsu Bazaar. Marcel Mauri's market had its own, nontrivial origin. He was clearly inspired by the dome of the Pantheon, a fact underlined by the circular form and the caissons that lightened the structure. References to the Roman roots of Algeria's cultural heritage, which are tangibly embodied in the ancient sites of Timgad and Djémila, were often reproduced in the discourses of the French colonial administration and society. This, according to many, was the historical "basis" for the right of France, as the heir to the "Roman world," to lay claim to this region.[8] The focus on the link with Roman antiquity became part of the rituals of life of the French colonists and at times concerned architecture. Even in the nineteenth century, one of French Algeria's public figures, Jules du Pré de Saint-Maur, selected stones from Roman ruins as material for the altar of the chapel at Arbal, which were filled with the symbolism of cultural complicity.[9] The same idea of the link to "Roman ancestors" was replicated in the dome of the market constructed by Mauri in the town that would become the citadel of the foreign legion[10] and the stage for a number of dramatic events marking the last phase of "French" Algeria's existence.

Trade and public center of Chilanzar district, Tashkent, sketch by Andrei Kosinskii, 1970

Iurii Garamov was unlikely to have been interested in the finer points of the political opposition in the French colonies of the 1950s. When beginning work on his design for a covered market in Tashkent he was seeking analogues in countries with hot climates, and in Mauri's

6 Abdulla Babakhanov, "Za vysokoe kachestvo podgotovki arkhitektorov [For High-Quality Preparation of Architects]," *Stroitel'stvo i arkhitektura Uzbekistana* [*Construction and Architecture of Uzbekistan*], no. 4, 1968, 23–25.

7 Iurii Garamov, "Arkhitektura krytykh rynkov v usloviiakh zharkogo klimata (zarubezhnyi opyt) [Architecture of Covered Markets in Hot Climatic Conditions (International Experience)]," *Stroitel'stvo i arkhitektura Uzbekistana* [*Construction and Architecture of Uzbekistan*], no. 4, 1972, 32.

8 Pierre Mannoni, *Les Français d'Algérie: vie, mœurs, mentalité de la conquête des Territoires du Sud à l'indépendance* (Paris: Éditions L'Harmattan, 1993), 15; Jean-François Guilhaume, *Les mythes fondateurs de l'Algérie française* (Paris: Éditions L'Harmattan, 1993).

9 Marc Baroli, *La vie quotidienne des Français en Algérie: 1830–1914* (Paris: Hachette, 1967), 167.

10 Jean Michon, "Sidi-bel-Abbès: capitale legionnaire," *Guerres mondiales et conflits contemporains*, no. 1, 2010.

Sketch of the entrance area of Chorsu Bazaar by lead architect Vladimir Azimov

Andrei Kosinskii (project lead), Iurii Miroshnichenko, Irina Demchinskaia, et al., perspective of Bogdan Khmel'nitskii (Bobur) Street, 1970–1972

project he saw a successful use of caissons as skylights to illuminate the internal space of the market and also the natural ventilation of the building using the oculus in the dome. In this dome, and later in the dome of the Chorsu Bazaar, there is a similar oculus, which demonstrated its effectiveness at ventilating and cooling the space underneath. As far as lighting is concerned, in Garamov's and then Azimov's projects light entered not only through the oculus but also through a system of arches, which were circular in Garamov's design and pointed in the Chorsu Bazaar. However, Garamov, following Mauri's logic, proposed also lighting the dome using a belt of windows at a height of 10–12 meters, which would have made the space much lighter than the windowless Chorsu dome.

The evolution of the projects by Mauri, Garamov and Azimov can be used to illustrate what has been known in the humanities since the 1990s as "cultural transfer."[11] When Marcel Mauri's models were transferred to the Uzbek context, their orientation toward Roman antiquity completely disappeared and the spirit of the Pantheon made way for local inspirations. The nature of the commentaries also changed. For both Garamov and Azimov the oculus also suggested the free flow of air, however, in discussing this Uzbek architects did not recall the project of their French colleague, but a traditional Uzbek architectural feature known as a shipang, which, in the 1960s, modernist architects tried to adapt to the new architecture of Uzbekistan.

The trading domes in the design for the center of Chilanzar were significantly different from those in Garamov's project. Unlike the latter, they formed a rhizomatic structure of domes, the vertically stretched outlines of which did not have historical connotations other than, possibly, the turquoise mosaic covering of the external shell, which was reminiscent of the domes of Samarkand. However, Kosinskii avoided traditional decoration and made the illumination of the domes open using circular portholes. In this respect his fantastical project is much closer to contemporary buildings by, for instance, Jean Nouvel than to the severe buildings of Tashkent modernism. However, the link with Iurii Garamov's project can still be seen, since the domes were built up with rhizomatic vaults in the spirit of Candela.[12]

When analyzing the Chorsu Bazaar, which was designed by Azimov's group, we can state that there is a genealogical connection to both Garamov's and Kosinskii's projects. Azimov's central dome is undoubtedly inspired by Garamov's. The similarity could be seen not only in the form of the bi-centered lancet profile and the arrangement of the skylight intended for vertical ventilation of the building but also in the physical dimensions: the height and diameter of the finished market matched to the meter (28 × 86) the graduation project of 1967. Since Garamov's project was tied to the center of Chilanzar, the exact match of its dimensions with the finished Chorsu Bazaar cannot be explained by the specific nature of the site. This means that when beginning work on the design of the dome, Azimov's team based their work on the 1967 graduation project, significantly reworking it. The links between the Chorsu Bazaar and the design for the center of Chilanzar are less substantial. From the latter the finished complex inherited only the additional small domes covered with blue mosaic ceramic and the rhizomatic covered structures that were present on the initial model but never built.

Comparing the dimensions of Garamov's graduation project and the finished Chorsu Bazaar with Marcel Mauri's dome, there is an impressive difference in size. The Algerian magazine *Écho de l'Oranie* wrote in November 1999 that Mauri's dome was one of the largest in the world (in the article its diameter of 41 meters is compared to the dome of St. Peter's in Rome or Constantinople's Hagia Sophia, at 41 and 31 meters respectively),[13] yet the diameter of the Tashkent building was more than twice that of all the examples mentioned. The remarkable tectonics of the structure, which is revealed visually in the interior of the Chorsu Bazaar dome, is perhaps the most valuable element of the building.

11 See Michel Espagne, *Les transferts culturels franco-allemands* (Paris: Presses universitaires de France, 1999).

12 In discussion with Boris Chukhovich, Iurii Miroshnichenko, Kosinskii's co-author on the project for the center of Chilanzar, recalled that on seeing these vaults, Kosinskii immediately named them "candels."

13 "L'une des plus grandes coupoles du monde," *Écho de l'Oranie*, no. 265, November 1999.

Model of Chorsu Bazaar dome with ornamental decoration

Marcel Mauri, covered market in Sidi Bel Abbès, Algeria, 1955

Iu. Garamov, Chilanzar Market, façade, 1967

Iu. Garamov, Chilanzar Market, interior, 1967

The main difference between the finished project and its genealogical predecessors is the extensive ornamentation of the external vaults of the dome. The architects were clearly influenced by Timurid architecture and attempted to reproduce on the dome the vegetal ornament that decorated the ribs of medieval domes. However, the transfer of arabesques to the hypertrophied scale of the Tashkent market prompted associations not with historical architecture but with the subject of traditional Central Asian ceramics, with piyala drinking bowls that are decorated with similar patterns. The return to such decoration marked a U-turn by Tashkent's architects. After the decorative Stalinist epoch they went through a stage of conscious asceticism (late 1950s–early 1960s), firmly rejecting "architectural excesses," then began to modify a number of forms drawn from vernacular vocabulary (second half of the 1960s), then approved the return of traditional forms in terms of direct citations (Blue Domes Café, the arcade of the Union of Artists) and finally began to recreate the forms of the past using contemporary materials, imitating traditional ornaments and vernacular materials. So, the reinforced concrete domes of the Chorsu Bazaar were covered with ornamentation using a ceramic cladding that imitated traditional medieval architecture. The "large dome" of the market contained a formal contradiction between the decorative "ceramic" façade and the interior, the aesthetic of which was created by the geometric plasticity of metal structures. Accordingly, the complex initially represented a transitional form between modernism and the historicist trends that prevailed in the 1990s. The Pantheon, which reminded the French colonists of the Roman past of the Maghreb, was transformed by Tashkent architects into a Central Asian dome that embodied the values of the culture of Uzbekistan at the end of the Soviet epoch.

The Transformation of the Market after the Launch of Construction

Tashkent's architectural historians often had difficulty naming the period when the Chorsu Bazaar was constructed. Their various readings had an objective cause. Documents in the Tashgiprogor archive show that the design of the market occurred in two stages. The initial stage coincided with the end of the so-called era of stagnation, 1980–1984, taking place against a background of deepening stagnation of the Soviet economy, at a time when the number of building projects halted due to lack of money was growing. Construction of the market began in 1983 (a photo from the Republic of Uzbekistan Documentary Film and Photo Archive dated January 20, 1984, records the installation of the first structures of the main dome), but, typically for that time, there were lengthy stoppages. The structure of the large dome was in place by 1989–1990 and work then began on its ornamentation. However, the years that had passed since the launch of construction were a time of historic global transformations that affected Soviet society and the state. After a number of attempts to reform the socialist economy, the government opened the floodgates for private companies. Soviet enterprises began to move toward new economic principles, and entrepreneurs opened private cooperative manufacturing businesses. There were early signs that private property would be legitimized. The market building, which had been designed within a planned economy and initially named in honor of the October Socialist Revolution, could not remain the same in a market economy. As a result, between 1989 and 1993 there was a new stage of designing various pavilions in the complex, including the reconstruction of some completed parts. The cylindrical hotel disappeared from the model of the project. All that remained was the circular canopy of the nearby trading pavilion. In the early 1990s the market was supplemented with new and even more decorative stalls, trading rows and pavilions, the style and materials of which were increasingly less consonant with the original constructions. Over the following decades there were changes to the use of the market. Most of the open spaces, which had been created in the early 1980s to allow a better view of the imposing dome and a perspective of the complex against the background of the "old city," were gradually built upon. The Brutalist-style rhizomatic structures of the 1984 model were created using crude prefabricated structures. New retail spaces appeared on the approaches from Beruni Street. From the Sakichmon Street side a series of kiosks appeared, which obscured the view of the dome, and then in 2008 this approach was cleared and a colonnade marking the entrance to the territory was installed at the accepted boundary of the market. Today the market is a palimpsest in which the structures of the initial project can be identified by their monumental form and the use of durable materials.

Despite the fact that the orientalist/decorativist trend was dominant in architectural life in the 1980s, the reaction of the professional community to the finished Chorsu Bazaar was mixed. Elena Kriukova, historian of Uzbekistan's contemporary architecture, wrote: "The attempt to place Tashkent's old city market under a single dome can hardly be called an achievement, although it seems that its grandiose form matches the famous tim and tok domes.[14] The market, which had once picturesquely spread through the neighboring alleys and craftsmen's areas, could not be subordinated to a strict, compact circle. Despite the enormous capacity of the internal space, trading inevitably moved outside, under canopies, and even at the height of the season there were quite a few free stalls under the dome. This is a clear example of a formalistic approach to heritage, when an external form is borrowed in place of deep and fundamental principles. In fact, the principle here is more like Russian models of compact covered markets."[15] However, the critical opinions of specialists were of little interest. The collapse of the USSR led to the collapse of the architectural community. The tastes of the clients who came to the fore had been formed during late socialism and they required more decoration and historical quotations.

However, even if the Chorsu Bazaar was the last step of Tashkent architects toward the eclecticism of the 1990s and early 2000s, it remained a modernist building thanks to its monumentality and the integrity of its forms. Its positioning within the nucleus of the "old city," which required the demolition of a historic mahalla, also reproduced the initial inertia of modernism, which strove to replace tradition and the old order. The paradoxical nature of this gesture is that this replacement was accompanied by a decorative reference to "tradition."

14 Toks and tims are traditional domed buildings that were constructed at the intersection of streets in the Emirate of Bukhara and served as retail spaces.

15 Elena Kriukova, "Arkhitektura obshchestvennykh zdanii Uzbekistana (1970–1995 gg.) [Architecture of Public Buildings in Uzbekistan (1970–1995)]," manuscript, Archive of the Institute of Art History of the Academy of Sciences of Uzbekistan, IA (M), K-85, no. 1398, 20–21.

Construction of Chorsu Bazaar, 1984

Construction of Chorsu Bazaar, 1984

Main dome of Chorsu Bazaar, 1996

ARCHITECT
VLADIMIR AZIMOV

Place and year of birth:
Most likely Tashkent, 1945

Education:
1964–1969, Architecture Department of Tashkent Polytechnic Institute

Vladimir Azimov was the lead architect on the Chorsu Bazaar project and the director of the studio that designed it. He graduated from the architectural faculty of Tashkent Polytechnic Institute in 1969. His graduate project was part of the center of Chilanzar, which was integrated into the main project which was then being designed at the Tashgiprogor Institute under the supervision of Andrei Kosinskii and Iurii Miroshnichenko. Vladimir Azimov's creative trajectory would go on to develop under the influence of Kosinskii, whose studio he joined after graduation. When Iurii Miroshnichenko left to take up the post of deputy chief architect of Tashkent at GlavAPU, the Main Architecture and Planning Administration, Azimov became the head architect at Tashgiprogor, a post he would hold for around a decade.

INSTITUTIONAL FRAMEWORK

Tashgiprogor

CADRE

Tashgiprogor was the architectural "hub" of Tashkent. In terms of numbers, it was the largest institution, and architects could move here if there were employment problems at other organizations. After the 1966 earthquake Tashgiprogor was "invaded" by architects from Moscow and other cities of the USSR who had come to work on the reconstruction of Uzbekistan's capital. By the 1980s, within Tashgiprogor there were eight studios responsible for the design of the eight urban planning districts of Tashkent that surrounded the center of the city. Accordingly, the institute's architects not only designed unique buildings but also had to think at the level of the city, the district, the microdistrict and the street. Among the protagonists at the institute were the architects Vladimir Spivak, Genrikh Aleksandrovich, Vil' Muratov, Rafael' Khairutdinov (during the design of the Union of Artists Exhibition Hall he moved to Tashgenplan) and Iurii Miroshnichenko, who, with great freedom and lightness of touch, included historical quotations and inspiration in their buildings. The collective image and concept of the institute's architects was also influenced by the twelve-year presence there of Andrei Kosinskii, a Moscow architect who introduced new ideas and solutions to Tashkent architecture that were linked to the architectural heritage of Central Asia. It is known that the leadership of UzNIIPgradostroitel'stva did not approve of Kosinskii's work. At Tashgiprogor the attitude to him was more complicated, but a certain part of the institute formed under Kosinskii's influence, not least because he combined design work with teaching at Tashkent Polytechnic Institute, from where many of his former students came to Tashgiprogor.

PRIORITIES

1960s: use of the techniques and vocabulary of contemporary architecture, primacy of plastic solutions over rectangular geometry. From the late 1960s there was a swing toward the development of "oriental modernism," the return of historical quotations, the study and use in new buildings of the "appropriateness" and know-how of folk architecture.

Typical buildings: 1960s: Chilanzar Shopping Center, Iubileinyi Palace of Sport, Chilanzar Center by Andrei Kosinskii (not built), Gor'kii Theater by Iurii Khaldeev (the fourth and most orientalist version of which was built as the Turkestan Palace in the early 1990s). From the late 1960s: Blue Domes Café, Circus, Zarafshan Restaurant, House of Cinema, Moscow Hotel (Chorsu), Chorsu Bazaar.

1st floor plan
Original condition

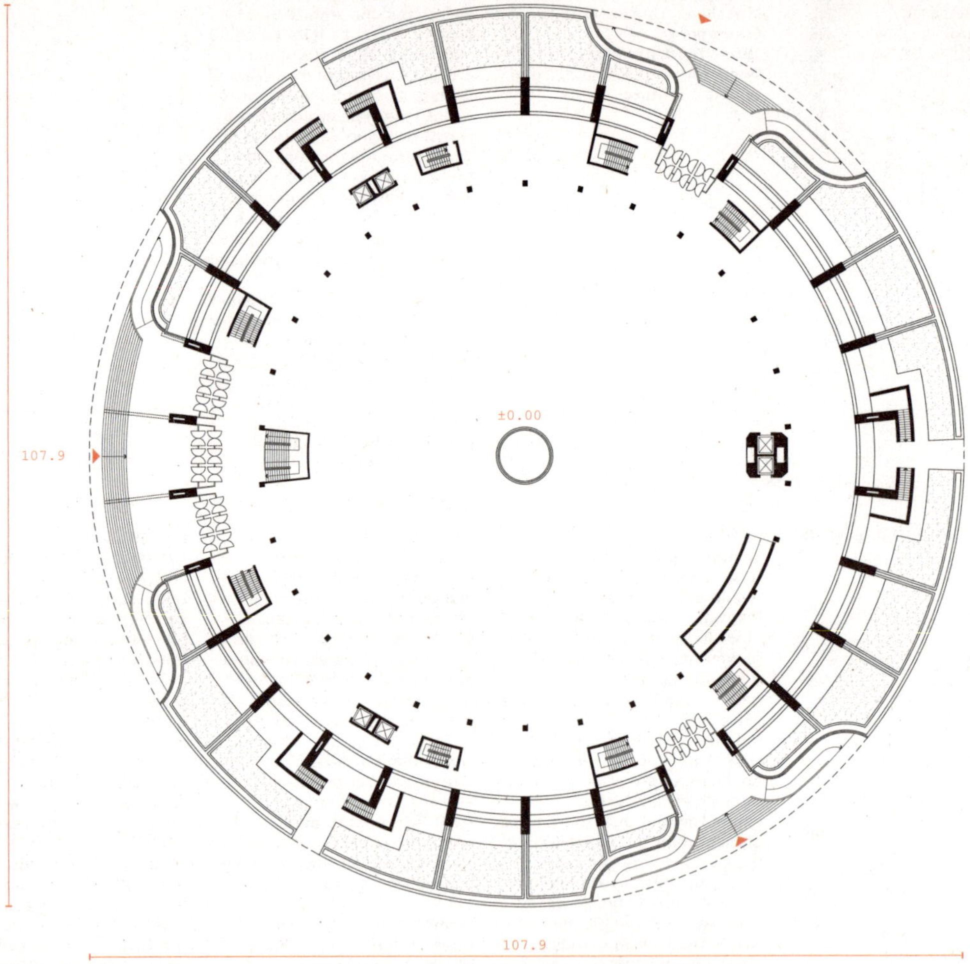

±0.00

107.9

107.9

Entrance view
Original condition

0 5 15m

Mezzanine floor plan
Original condition

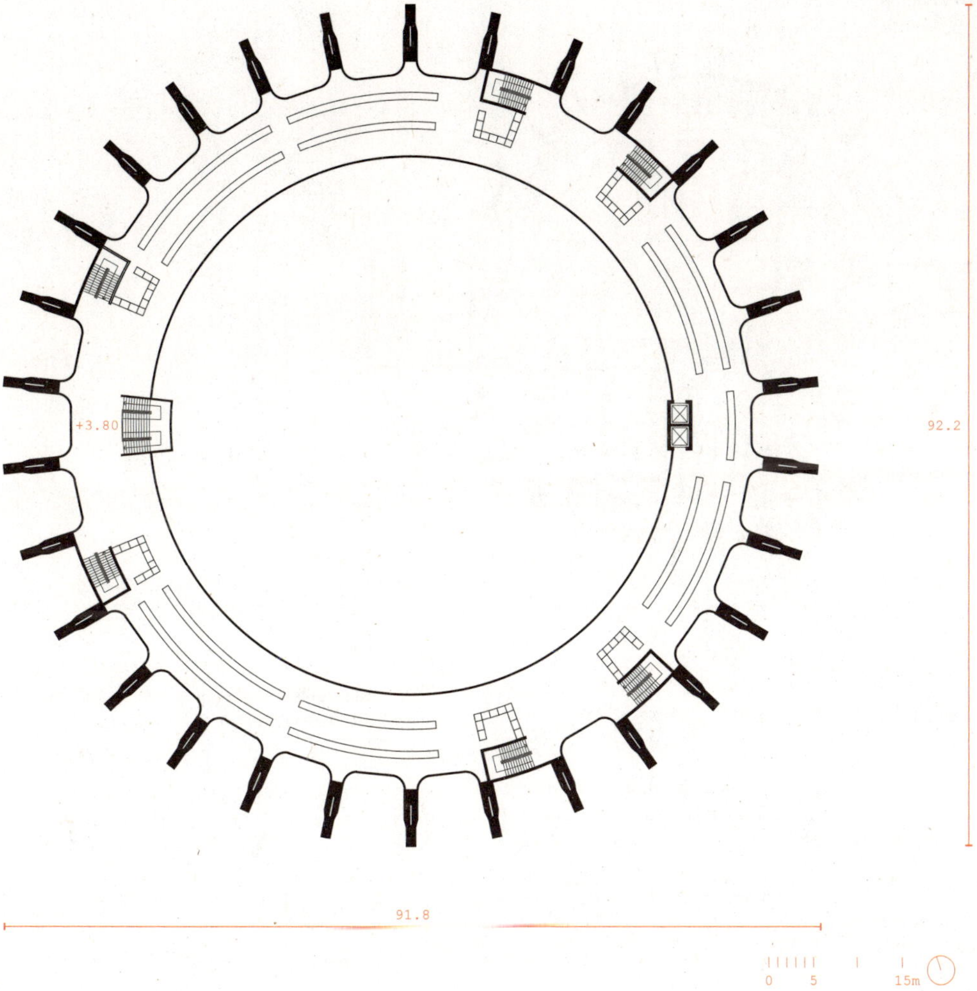

+3.80
92.2
91.8
0 5 15m

Elevation / section
Original condition

+31.20
+3.80
±0.00
-1.07
-5.50
90.6
0 5 15m

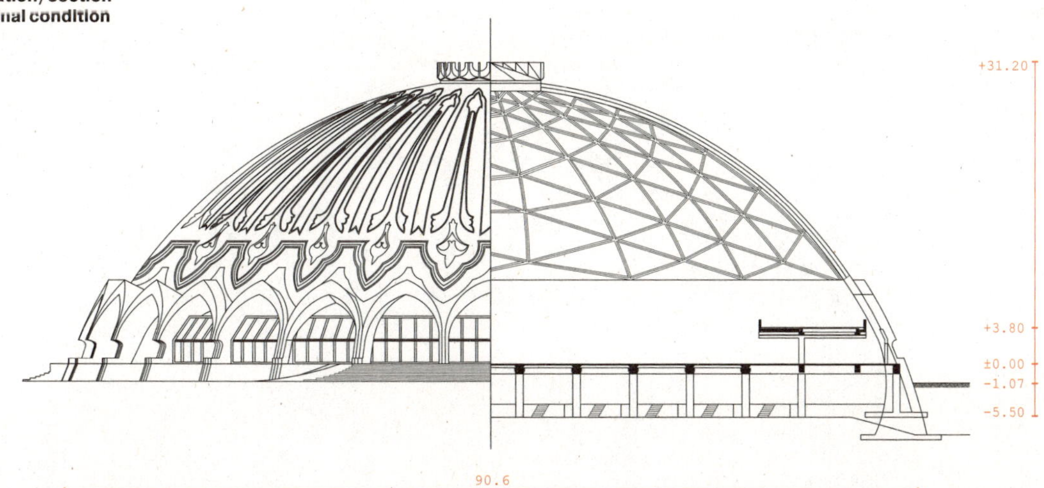

1990

- Commercial / public
- Food service / administrative
- Service and technical
- Change of function

Basement floor plan
Original condition

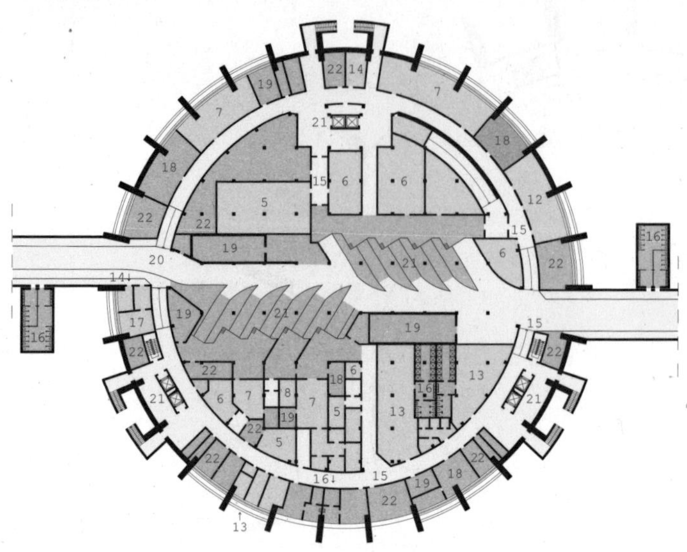

1st floor plan
Original condition

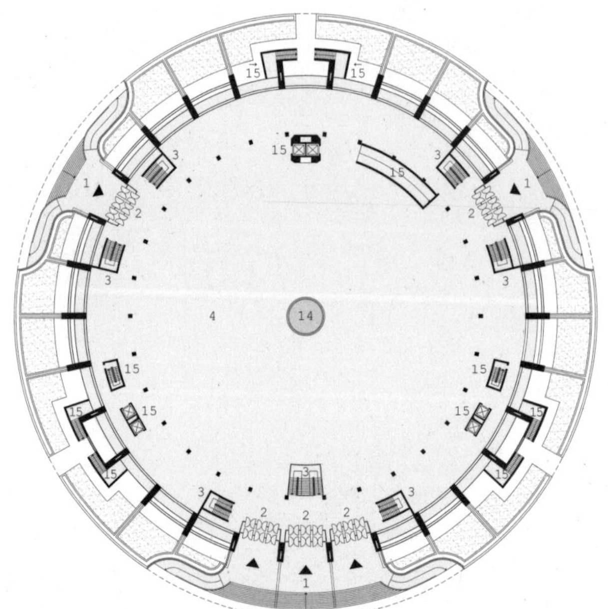

Mezzanine floor plan
Original condition

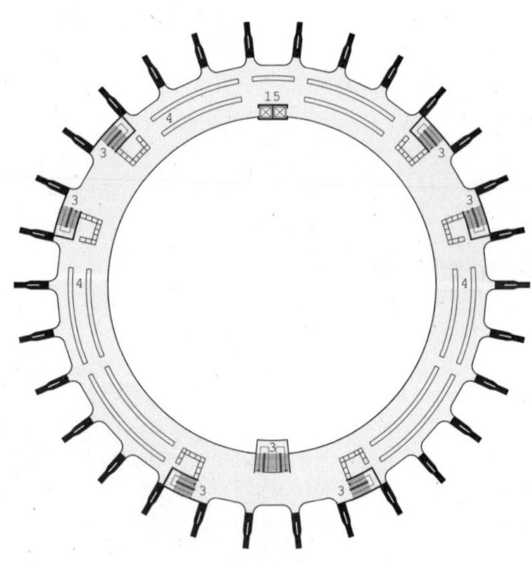

2022

Basement floor plan
Current condition

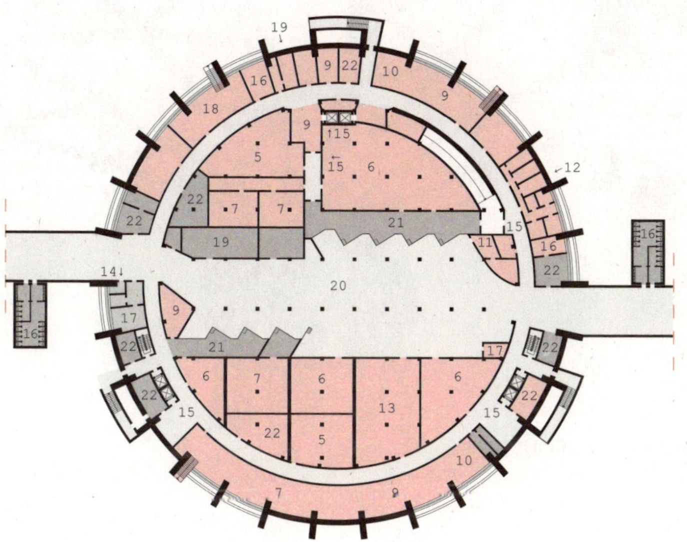

1	Terrace
2	Vestibule
3	Circulation, visitors
4	Commercial
5	Cold food storage
6	Food storage
7	Meat preparation room
8	Food confiscation storage
9	Café
10	Weighing room
11	Doctor's office
12	Laboratory
13	Staff room
14	Control room
15	Circulation, workers
16	Restroom
17	Security room
18	Storage
19	Service room
20	Car path
21	Loading
22	Technical area

1st floor plan
Current condition

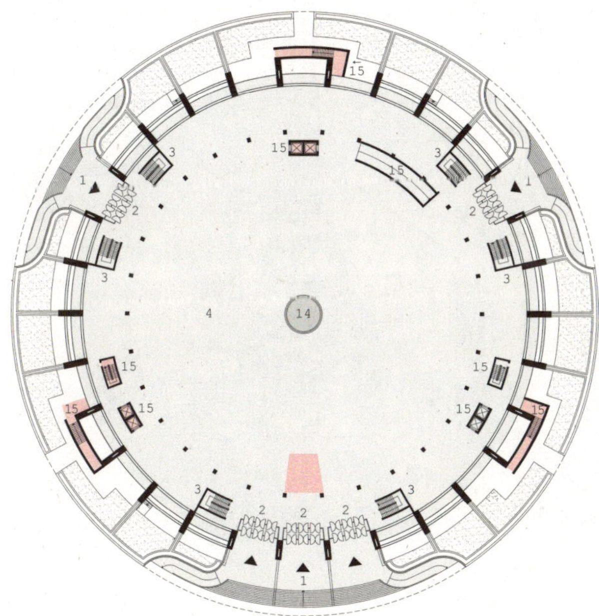

Mezzanine floor plan
Current condition

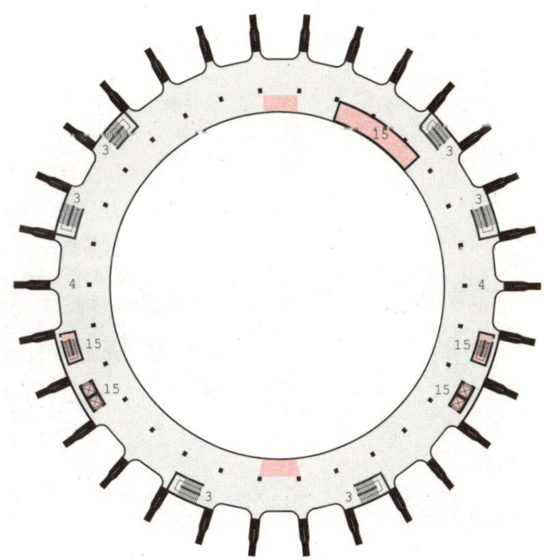

0 5 15m

Urban model of a 1980s proposal for the development of the Chorsu Bazaar area

Construction of the dome structure

Chorsu Bazaar, bird's-eye view, 1994–1996

Tiling of the extrados of the main dome, 1990

Views of the area surrounding the main dome, with temporary and permanent facilities, 1994

Interior of the main dome, 1994

Interior of the main dome, 1996

Main and secondary domes of Chorsu Bazaar, 2023

Main dome of Chorsu Bazaar, 2023

Surrounding market structures, 2023

Interior of the main domo, 2022

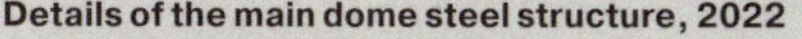

Details of the main dome steel structure, 2022

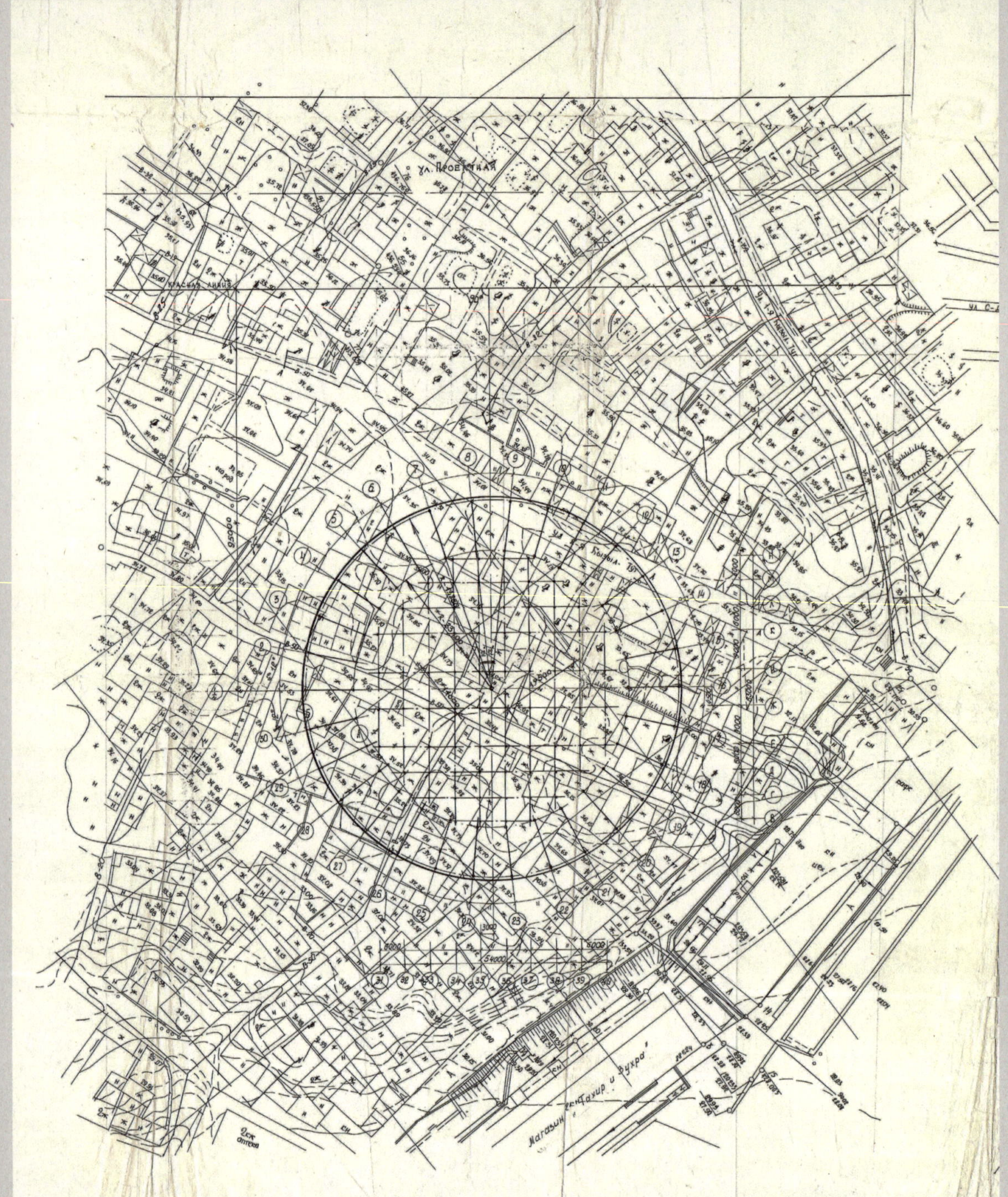

Preliminary plan of Chorsu Bazaar site, 1981

Chorsu Bazaar, main dome façade proposal, mid-1980s

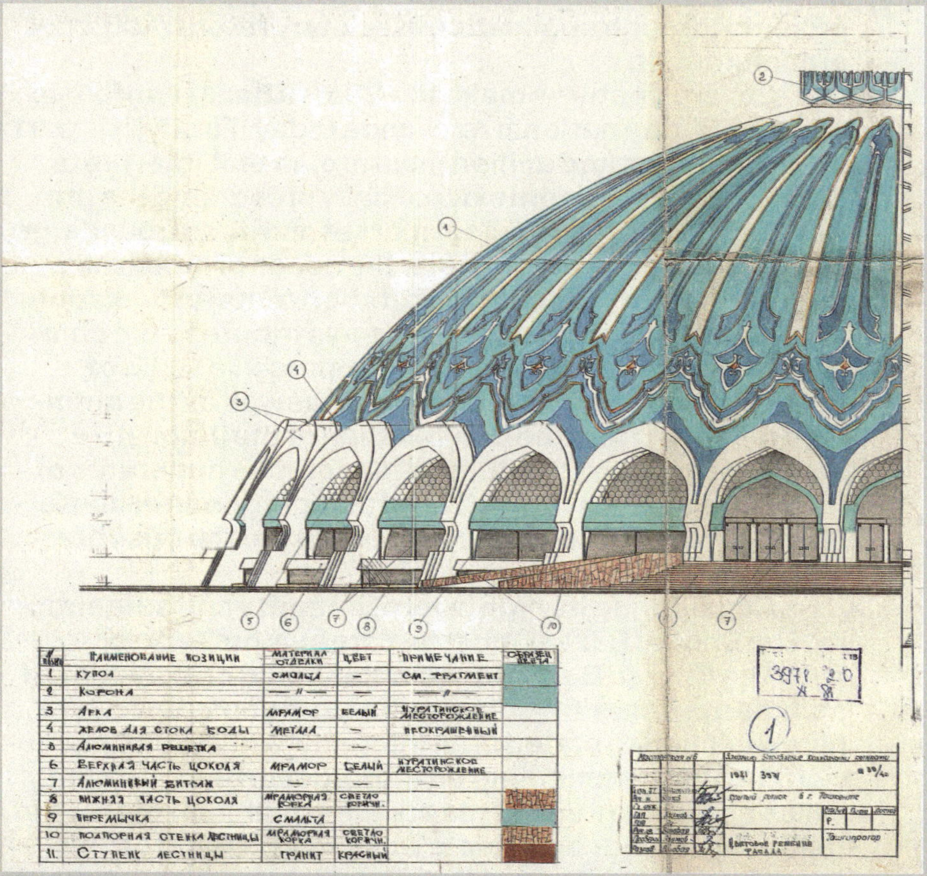

№ позиц.	Наименование позиции	Материал отделки	Цвет	Примечание	Образец цвета
1	Купол	смальта	—	См. фрагмент	
2	Корона	— " —	—	— " —	
3	Арка	мрамор	белый	Нуратинское месторождение	
4	Желоб для стока воды	металл	—	неокрашенный	
5	Алюминиевая решетка	—	—	—	
6	Верхняя часть цоколя	мрамор	белый	Нуратинское месторождение	
7	Алюминиевый витраж	—	—	—	
8	Нижняя часть цоколя	мраморная корка	светло корич.		
9	Перемычка	смальта			
10	Подпорная стенка лестницы	мраморная корка	светло корич.		
11.	Ступени лестницы	гранит	красный		

Chorsu Bazaar, main dome finish materials, 1981

HIGHLIGHTS

"For the Soviet authorities, the bazaar was as much a relic of the past as the church, and since neither could be fully eradicated they had to be reframed as museums. This explains why the market building resembles both a temple and a museum."[1]

The Chorsu Bazaar ensemble was built between 1983 and 1990 on Sakichmon Street, in an urban block where the oldest bazaar of Tashkent was historically located, hence the origin of the name. It was around the ancient Chorsu bazaar that one of the oldest districts in Tashkent was formed.

The market is among the most representative buildings of the second generation of Soviet modernism in Tashkent. From the mid-1970s, buildings constructed according to modernist principles combined the rationalist dogmas of functionality, composition and form with the historicist notion of the local context, expressed in projects through application of reinterpreted traditional ornamentation.

Several features make the Chorsu Bazaar an iconic building of international relevance today. Firstly, it is part of an ambitious and unified masterplan that interprets a complex layered context, partially preserving the pre-existing areas of the ancient market and its surroundings, and finding a balance between the needs of modernization and memory. Secondly, in its horizontal articulation, this modernist urban ensemble pays tribute to the complexity of an ancient bazaar. the impressive scale of the dome and its good proportions, as well as the antinomy resulting from the combination of the innovative structure and the "traditional" decorative apparatus of the cladding, are synthesized in a single gesture, conferring a sense of ordered monumentality to the busy life of the market.

Considering its high level of integrity and authenticity, the Chorsu Bazaar must be carefully preserved.

The Chorsu Bazaar ensemble should be considered a single systematic whole with its surroundings. As Iurii Miroshnichenko stated in an interview with Boris Chukhovich in 2021, commenting on the larger urban block that includes the market and the adjacent mahalla, the idea of the Tashgiprogor architects was to form a kind of "historical reserve" of one of the oldest quarters of Tashkent. In this sense, the new market must be seen in a symbiotic relationship with the nearby old market, the adjacent

1 Anna Bronovitskaya, Nikolay Malinin and Yuri Palmin, *Alma-Ata: A Guide to Soviet Modernist Architecture 1955–1991* (Prague: Artguide Editions, 2022), 166.

Gulbazar mahalla, the Kukeldash Madrasa, and the Jami Mosque. This historic ensemble is encircled by other modernist buildings which also became an important part of the urban composition of the area. These include the Tashkent Circus and the Chorsu Hotel (and previously the bath complex by Andrei Kosinskii, which was demolished in the early 2000s).

The Chorsu Bazaar evokes the main characteristics of the ancient bazaar: different architectural elements are disposed on a large partially sunken podium, and are connected to the surroundings by a system of ramps and stairs. On top of the podium, in addition to the main dome, seven smaller cupolas and undulating canopies organize the different areas of the market. Today, these include commercial premises, small canteens, shops, storage and craftsmen's workshops, whereas previously there were also mosques, baths and caravanserais.

The general plan of the 1980s for this area included a hotel building in the northern part of the Chorsu Bazaar that was never built.

The main market pavilion is the most iconic element of the ensemble. The idea of the dome appears to have different inspirations, according to various sources, and overall can be considered a result of the cultural appropriation of a range of international references over time.

Besides an occasional association with Palazzetto dello Sport in Rome (1956–1957) by Pier Luigi Nervi and Annibale Vitellozzi, which must have been known by Tashkent architects, a careful analysis by Boris Chukhovich led to an unexpected and rather interesting precedent: a market in Sidi Bel Abbès in Algeria, designed by French architect Marcel Mauri. The Algerian dome is also surrounded by a series of undulating canopies, similar to the ones in Tashkent. This latter precedent was published in 1974 in *Construction and Architecture of Uzbekistan* and must have been seen by the authors. However, the diameter of the Chorsu Bazaar dome is much larger than the Italian and Algerian ones and, unlike both references, it has a steel structure, collaborating with the reinforced concrete of the lower part. It was a great challenge to create a large span (of nearly 90 meters) for a public building in a seismic location such as Tashkent, and this justified the use of steel (exceptional for the Soviet construction industry).

The blue tiles covering the main vault and the rhizomatic secondary cupolas were probably inspired by an unrealized project by Moscow architect Andrei Kosinskii for the center of Chilanzar district. The overall composition of these cupolas and the consistency of their color and ornamentation create a strong visual connection to the main dome, hence making them an inseparable and valuable part of the entire ensemble.

STATE OF REPAIR SCORE:

- 3 – The building shows localized deterioration patterns which do not affect its stability

The overall state of repair of the Chorsu Bazaar's main dome is satisfactory, although ordinary maintenance should be improved.

Protection status:	The building is listed according to Resolution No. 227 of the Cabinet of Ministers, April 22, 2024.
Main criticalities:	The Chorsu Bazaar, some thirty years after its opening, has not undergone any major renovation. Due to extensive use, there are some worn and obsolete parts.
Possible risks:	The deterioration of the building owing to lack of maintenance. The same risk concerns the surrounding structures.

INTEGRITY SCORE:

- Exterior: 4 – The building has retained all the elements necessary to express its significance and is in a good state of repair
- Interior: 4 – The building has retained all the elements necessary to express its significance and is in a good state of repair

The Chorsu Market retains its architectural integrity both as an individual building and as an urban ensemble.

Most of the original decorations and building materials are still intact and convey the significance of the building.

AUTHENTICITY SCORE:

- Exterior: 3 – The building has been subjected to slight changes and replacements
- Interior: 4 – Only minor repairs and conservation activities have been carried out on the building

The building shows a fairly good level of authenticity: while the upper part of the main dome is nearly intact, both inside and outside, the lower parts around the first floor and mezzanine have undergone partial transformations. The window frames and their positions have been altered and the stone cladding around the basement has been changed, as have the openings toward the basement level.

Additionally, some of the smaller pavilions appear to have been subject to façade interventions for which very little historical documentation is available. The tiles covering the seven domes are original.

1996

Main dome windows, 1996

2021

Main dome windows, 2021

1996–2011

Chorsu Bazaar, secondary structures, 1996

Main dome interior, 2011

2023

Chorsu Bazaar, secondary structures, 2023

Main dome interior, 2022

LEVEL 1 – MAXIMUM LEVEL OF INTEREST
(No transformations allowed; conservation activities required)

The first level includes the most unique and authentic features of the building and its related urban context. Such elements should be carefully preserved, avoiding even slight transformations.

URBAN LEVEL

The perimeter of the urban block must not be transformed.

The height of the existing buildings inside the block must not be increased.

ARCHITECTURAL LEVEL
(refers to the macrobuilding)

The vertical articulation of the market block, which develops on different levels, should be retained.

The volumetric ratio between built and unbuilt spaces must not be altered.

The underground driveways and aboveground pedestrian paths must not be modified.

ARCHITECTURAL LEVEL
(refers to the main dome)

EXTERIOR

The architectural composition of the main façade, consisting of the tile-decorated dome with the skylight above, the pointed concrete arches below and the podium, must be carefully preserved.

INTERIOR

Subdivision of the internal spaces is not allowed. In particular, the relation between the first floor and the mezzanine must be preserved, as must the distribution architectural elements (foyers, stairs) and double-height spaces in the proximity of the façade.

DETAIL LEVEL
(refers to the main dome)

EXTERIOR

The tiles decorating the extrados, which are inspired by local ornamental motifs (in terms of colors and technique), must be carefully preserved.

The sequence of pointed arches running around the perimeter of the dome must not be transformed.

The zenith skylight on top of the dome must not be transformed.

INTERIOR

The reticular steel structure visible on the dome's intrados must be preserved and kept in plain sight.

The original finishes must be preserved, in particular:

- the entrance level and mezzanine floors;
- the balustrades of the mezzanine, toward the central void and the façade;
- the metal panels between the structural elements of the roof.

ARCHITECTURAL LEVEL
(refers to other domes)
EXTERIOR

The volume and structure must be preserved.

INTERIOR

Subdivision of the internal spaces is not allowed.

DETAIL LEVEL
(refers to other domes)
EXTERIOR

The mosaic/tile decorations on the extrados should be carefully preserved.

ARCHITECTURAL LEVEL
(refers to the galleries)

The ratio between the galleries must be preserved. They must not be enclosed to form a closed structure (building), and should remain open.

LEVEL 2 – MEDIUM LEVEL OF INTEREST
(Elements included in the second level can be moderately transformed following approval by a designated committee[1])

URBAN LEVEL

It is only possible to add new buildings or structures below a certain height (to be defined) within the block, following the scheme presented here and with the approval of the designated committee.

To ensure the visibility of the main building from the adjacent streets and to retain the existing proportions between the buildings in the market area and those located on its borders and surroundings:

- any new constructions along the streets enclosing the block of the market must be subject to approval by the designated committee;

1 An international committee of heritage preservation experts to be appointed.

- any transformations to the existing buildings located along the streets enclosing the block of the market should be submitted to the designated committee for approval.

ARCHITECTURAL LEVEL
(refers to the macrobuilding)
The undulating canopies must remain as open spaces; they cannot be transformed into enclosed buildings. Any changes to these canopies must be subject to approval by the designated committee.

DETAIL LEVEL
(refers to the main dome)
EXTERIOR
The cladding of the podium and the upper windowsills can be replaced, pending the approval of the designated committee.
The lower windowsills (added after the market opened) can be eliminated or clad, pending the approval of the designated committee.

INTERIOR
The alucobond cladding of the ring beams under the dome can be replaced with the approval of the designated committee.

ARCHITECTURAL LEVEL
(refers to the covered outdoor market stalls)
Any changes to the outdoor market stalls covered with undulating metal canopies should be evaluated and approved by the designated committee.

HIDDEN MODERNIST FEATURES

The infrastructure plinth, which connects the retail areas and contains the wholesale market, truck circulation, parking, storage spaces and small cafés and shops, is hidden below ground. It unifies the complex into a single urban entity and optimizes the functioning of the indoor and outdoor facilities above ground.

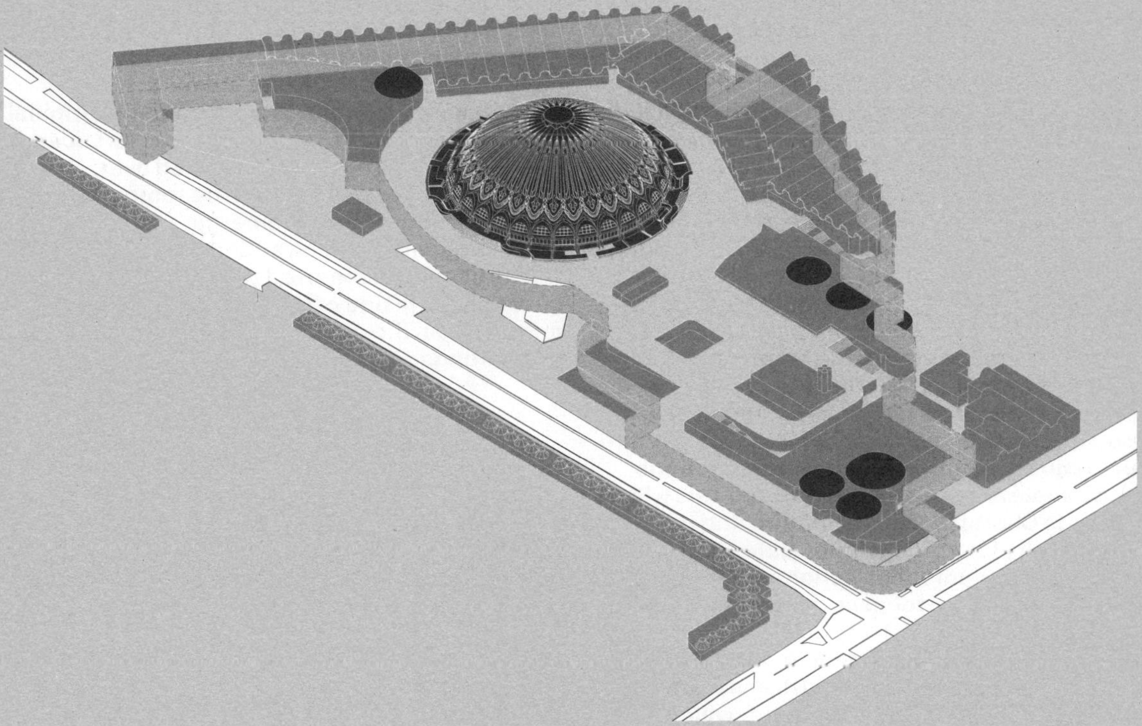

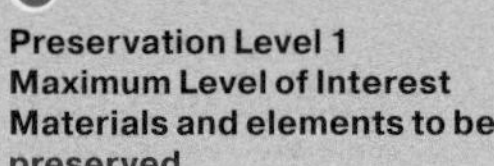

Preservation Level 1
Maximum Level of Interest
Materials and elements to be preserved

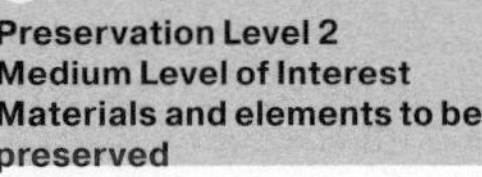

Preservation Level 2
Medium Level of Interest
Materials and elements to be preserved

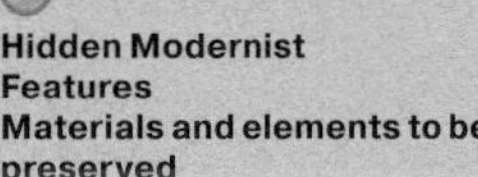

Hidden Modernist Features
Materials and elements to be preserved

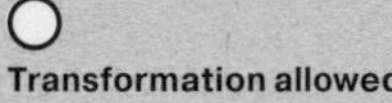

Transformation allowed

Preservation Strategy

The Chorsu Bazaar is among the most representative buildings of Tashkent modernism. Designed in the 1980s, it is characterized by a striking combination of advanced (for the time) structural solutions and references to local ornamental motifs widely used by architects since the 1970s. The bazaar was built between 1983 and 1990 on Sakichmon Street on a site where a mahalla used to stand, next to the area that housed the most ancient bazaar in Tashkent (from which the building takes its name). The significance of the market complex lies in several aspects: it is part of an ambitious and unique urban plan; its articulated design reflects the complexity of the ancient bazaar, and its architectural quality (especially of the main dome) combines tradition and innovation by using a modern structure embellished with traditional ornamentation.

The market complex retains most of its original features. However, given the generalized lack of maintenance and the extensive use of the pavilions, today some parts are worn and there are obsolete elements. In particular, the main criticalities are: obsolescence of technical installations, cracking and detaching of claddings, peeling of plaster, water infiltration and consequent damage to the structural system.

The main immediate objective of the preservation strategy is to provide local repairs and possible upgrades regarding technological aspects. However, in the long run, the goal is to prevent the development of further decay and damage by performing regular inspections and simple maintenance activities. This will enable the Chorsu Bazaar to endure and retain its integrity for as long as possible. To this end, three main preservation actions are proposed.

The first action focuses on the assessment and repair of the most relevant criticalities of the main dome. In particular, concrete elements (pillars, beams and buttresses) show widespread presence of moisture, which, if not treated, could result in even more severe damage (rebar oxidation and consequent expulsion of the concrete cover). The structural conditions of the main dome thus need to be verified through accurate inspections and, eventually, through diagnostic tests. After this evaluation, the decayed elements should be cleaned, leveled to obtain a smooth surface and finally coated with white paint.

The second action addresses the issue of sunshades. Although during the design phase some panjara were planned to screen the large windows from the sun, no sunshade system was actually installed. Vendors have creatively solved the problem by hanging banners and fabrics on the windows. While this solution might somewhat improve the climate, it is certainly not optimal in terms of architectural quality and the fabrics end up hiding part of the beautiful dome. These temporary sunshade systems should therefore be removed and replaced with a more suitable shading solution. The opportunity to change the windows should also be considered, given their poor water resistance and thermal performance. The replacement of existing gaskets and the sealing of the frames is highly recommended, so as to avoid further water infiltration from the windows.

Finally, a third action is devoted to maintenance activities, such as local repair and general cleaning. Close attention needs to be paid to the mosaics at the domes' extrados, where tiles easily detach due to the irregularities of the underlying support. Inspections should thus be frequently planned, and missing tiles replaced with new ones. The coat of paint on the arches of the main dome is starting to peel off. Painted surfaces should be cleaned, leveled and repainted in white, according to the original design. Mosaic tiles located in the interstices between arches have been painted over. The existing layer of paint should be removed in order for the mosaic to re-emerge. Additionally, the alucobond cladding added to the market pavilions should be removed (e.g. the alucobond cover on the inside of the ring beam of the main dome and on the outside of the ring beams of the secondary domes).

Next Steps

In order to implement the proposed preservation strategy a few aspects will need to be clarified and/or further developed.

It will be helpful to conduct a survey in order to assess the structural condition of the building. In particular, attention should be focused on the basement floor, where load-bearing elements are the most damaged. The main dome's buttresses and the joint between the steel dome and its supporting ring beam should also be checked.

The design of the shading solution to be installed on the windows of the main dome should be developed to an executive level of detail. The project will need to be approved by the ministry in charge before implementation.

Once this information is obtained, it will be possible to develop a more detailed and comprehensive project, which could be tested on a limited portion of the building (pilot site). During the pilot site different materials and techniques will be tried out with the aim of identifying the most suitable ones. At this point it will be possible to make last adjustments to the project and to execute it.

After the intervention, a management plan should be developed for the whole market complex. It should provide indications about the

proper frequency of inspections and ordinary maintenance. In order for the plan to actually be implemented, a budget should be set and a person designated to oversee the conservation activities.

Chorsu Market, section diagram

Adaptation Strategy

In the last twenty years, many markets in Europe and Asia that are similar in scale and offer to the Chorsu Bazaar have been modernized to meet contemporary retail trends and security and hygiene standards.

Since 2013, the European Union's URBACT program has promoted and coordinated modernization of markets in Spain, England, Italy, Hungary and other countries, as markets are considered to have huge potential for sustainable development of the surrounding neighborhoods and cities as a whole.

URBACT claims that markets are a key development tool to stimulate urban regeneration, sustainable development, employment and urban entrepreneurship.

Not only are markets seen as an opportunity to improve the quality of the urban space, they are also considered an attraction for the local population and tourists. La Boqueria in Barcelona and Victor Hugo Market in Toulouse acquaint visitors with local customs and products: food, handicrafts and gastronomy. The market is seen as an outdoor "museum" of urban culture, sustaining and promoting local crafts and gastronomy.

In the past food was bought in crowded and lively markets, where the visitor had direct contact with products and could touch, taste and smell them. Today, due to the profusion of supermarkets and new hygiene standards, such close contact with food is impossible in many parts of the world. Markets started attracting fewer people in the postwar period as supermarkets developed, which was prompted by new technologies in the service industry. (For example, the invention of the barcode in the early 1950s enabled the speeding up of the payment process.) These inventions did not spread to markets, making them less effective within the system of global retail.

It is interesting how, after the recent modernization, most European markets have lost a significant degree of authenticity, becoming more standardized, over-gentrified and similar to supermarkets. For example, Moscow's Danilovskii and Usachevskii markets, Rotterdam's Markthal, or the Florence market.

In Tashkent, the situation appears different. The re-evaluation of markets as instruments for urban regeneration has not yet taken place. They still function largely as in the past and have not been gentrified. This is also the case for the Chorsu Bazaar. We see enormous potential in this delay as a way to avoid the mistakes made elsewhere.

Our adaptation proposal focuses on two aspects:

1. Improving the infrastructure of existing market structures to make the retail/support areas more organized in terms of basic hygiene, without any further significant transformation. This would preserve the level of authenticity of the existing market, while supplying sellers with tools to improve the work environment (washing stations, storage areas, differentiated garbage disposal). Additionally, the plinth level of the market needs to be reorganized and upgraded to maintain a basic safety level.
2. The proposed intervention on the urban scale around the market plinth aims to reinforce the potential of the market and reactivate and requalify the surrounding area. We propose to address the car parking issue, one of the most pressing problems in this neighborhood, by transforming a single-level parking area in front of the former Chorsu Hotel into a three-level parking lot (with one or two levels below ground), thereby supplying the same number of parking spaces as currently provided by all ground-level parking areas within the urban block. The proposed structure would remain invisible from outside and merge seamlessly with the adjacent mahalla, which is topographically higher than the parking site. The compact parking lot would liberate space for a system of green public spaces that start on the roof of the parking structure, continue past the madrasa and the mosque, cross the strip above the metro and connect to the park around the House of Children's Creativity.

The strip itself is intended as the main object of intervention. Now, liberated from cars at ground level, it can be transformed into a mixed-use public space, a boulevard or promenade (as was intended in the city center masterplan of 1984) connecting important public venues in the city. This boulevard, encompassing the metro exit, would accommodate small cafés and restaurants with fresh food, a generous green area (to mitigate the heat), leisure areas, playgrounds and sports infrastructure. The commercial and real estate areas directly adjacent to this public boulevard would be upgraded and restructured.

We believe that inserting well-organized public space and rethinking its immediate surroundings can help to preserve the market with its plinth and the adjacent Gulbazar mahalla, finding a balance between preservation of history and current needs.

Chorsu Market proposal
Preservation strategy scheme

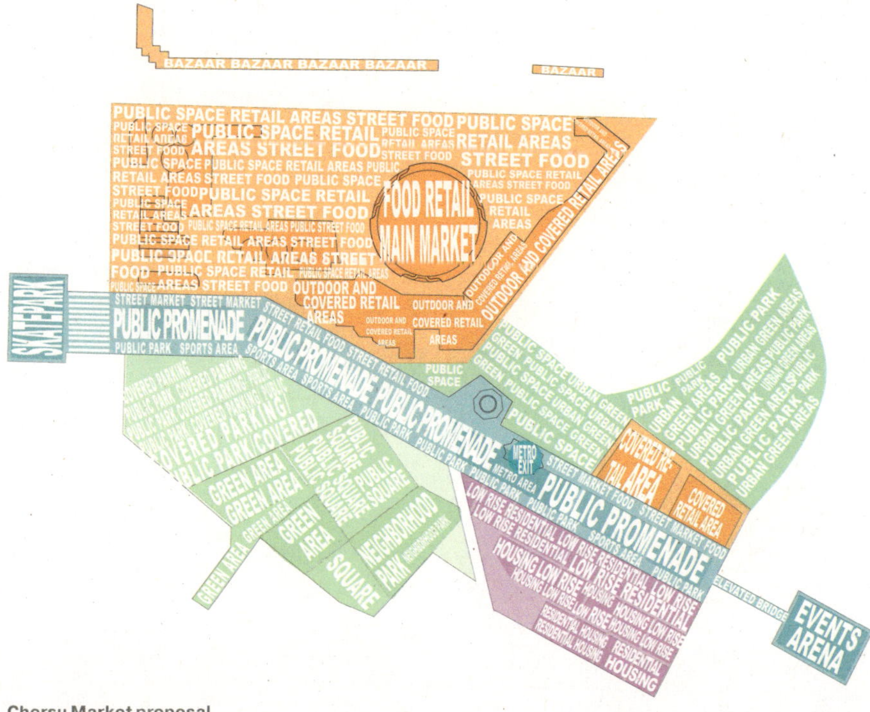

Chorsu Market proposal
Program distribution scheme

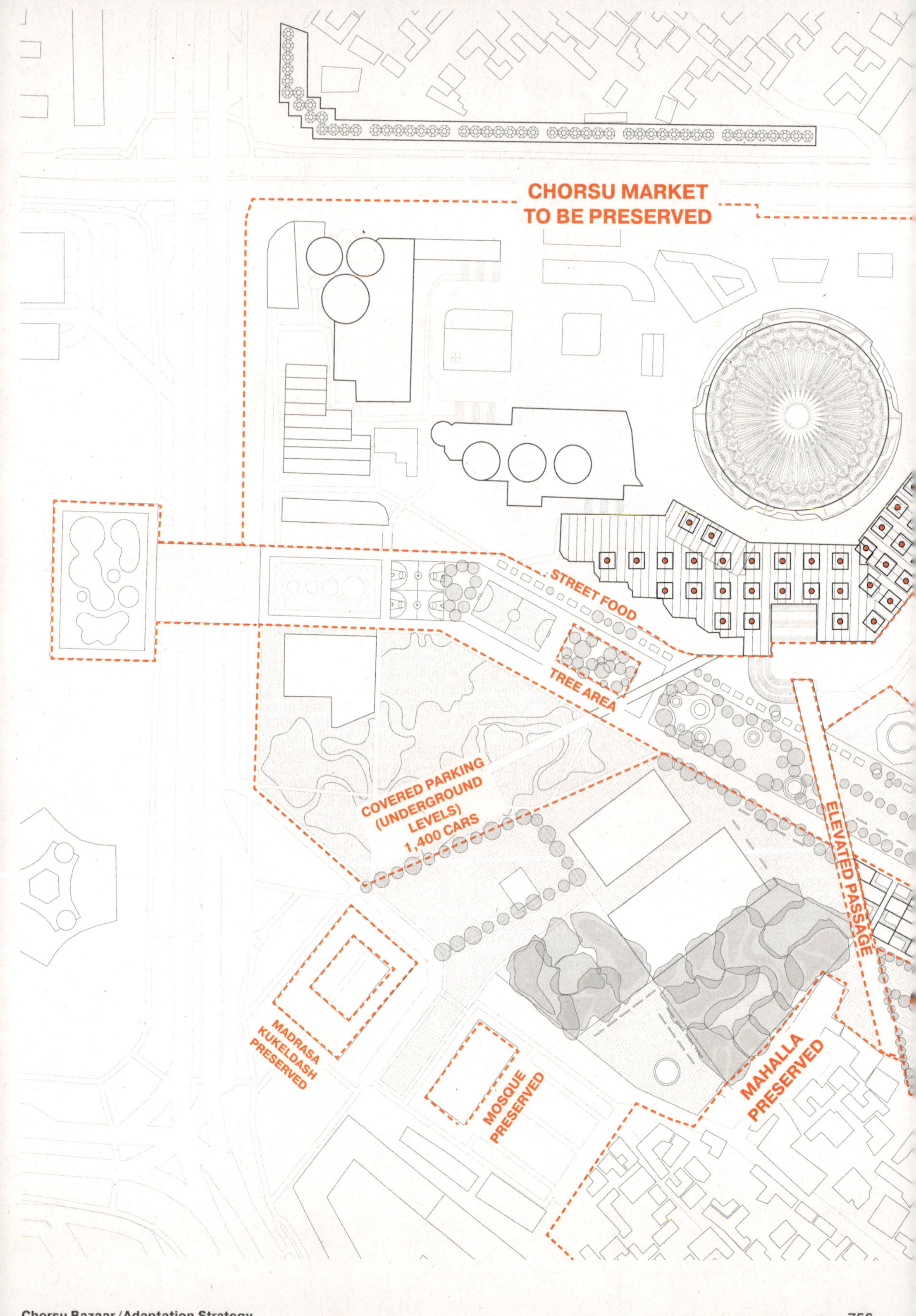
CHORSU MARKET
TO BE PRESERVED
STREET FOOD
TREE AREA
COVERED PARKING
(UNDERGROUND
LEVELS)
1,400 CARS
ELEVATED PASSAGE
MADRASA
KUKELDASH
PRESERVED
MOSQUE
PRESERVED
MAHALLA
PRESERVED

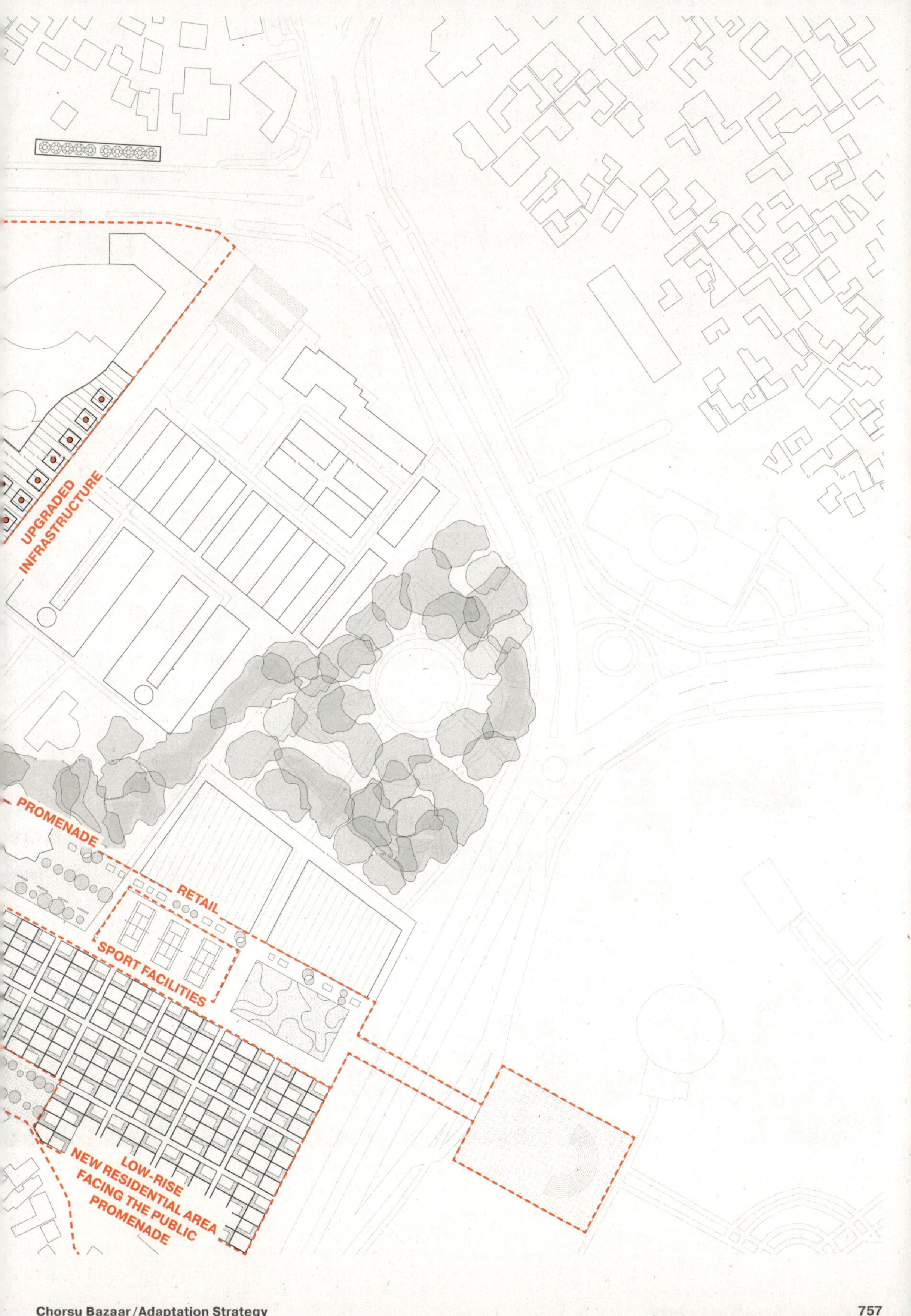
UPGRADED
INFRASTRUCTURE
PROMENADE
RETAIL
SPORT FACILITIES
LOW-RISE
NEW RESIDENTIAL AREA
FACING THE PUBLIC
PROMENADE

State Museum of Arts

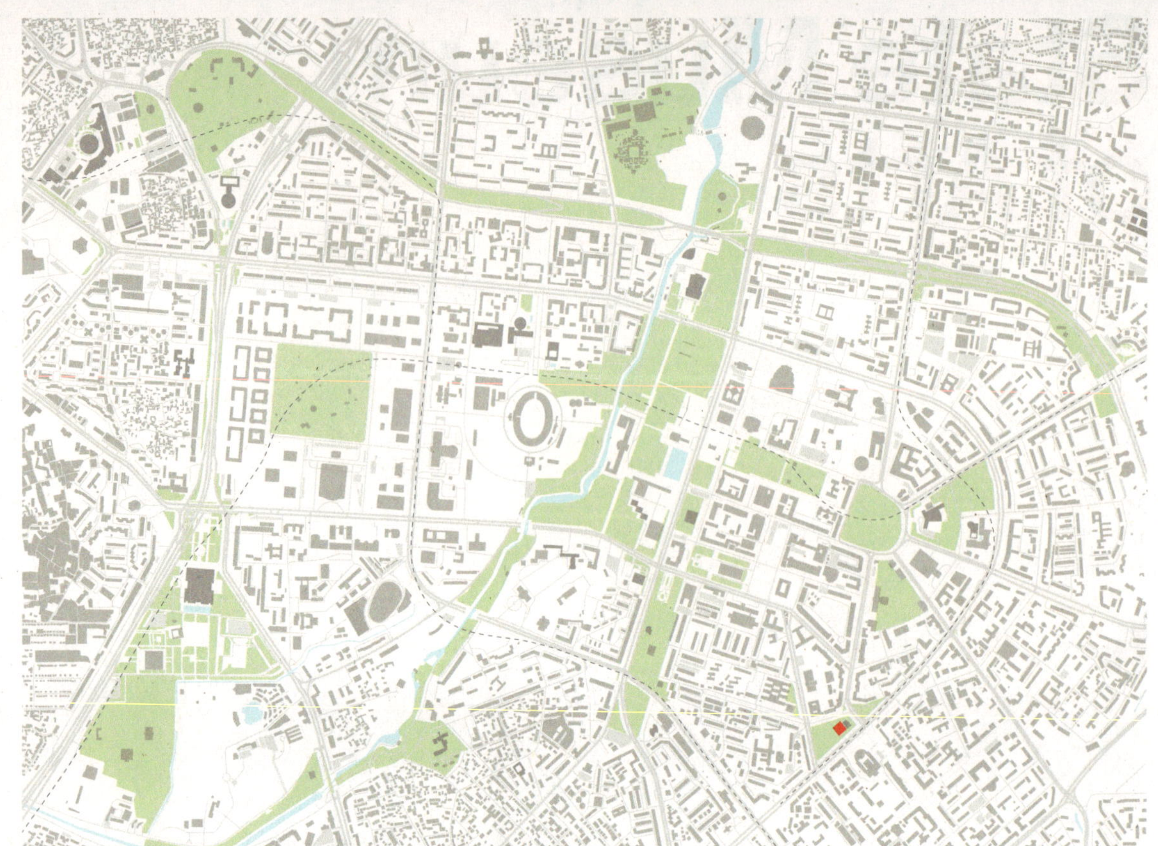

Building position and address: 16 Amir Temur Avenue, Mirobod district, Tashkent

0 0.5 1km

The site where the Museum of Arts is located has undergone several changes in its 150-year history. Initially it was part of a park zone between the city railway station and the main market square (the future Theater Square) of "new" Tashkent. Nearby were barracks of various military units that reported to the tsarist administration of Turkestan, and within the zone, which soon began to be called Aleksandrovskii Square, a theater soon appeared. Then the theater was demolished, but the People's House was built nearby and stood until 1966. The proximity of the military barracks influenced the fate of the square after the revolution of 1917. At first, in 1918, the sappers executed in the Tashkent Fort after the 1912 uprising were buried here. Then, in 1919, during the Civil War in Turkestan, when there was an anti-Soviet uprising led by Konstantin Osipov, the leaders of the Central Executive Committee of the Turkestan Soviet Republic (TurTsIK) were invited to a "meeting" in the barracks, where they were shot. After Osipov's uprising was suppressed, the leaders were buried in the former Aleksandrovskii Square, which was renamed Communards' Square. The memorial was expanded from time to time and became the main communist necropolis in Uzbekistan. In 1923 Mikhail Kafanov, who played an important role in the early history of the Communist Party of Uzbekistan, was buried there (at that point the location was renamed Kafanov Square), followed by the first chairman of the presidium of the Central Executive Committee of Uzbekistan, Iuldash Akhunbabaev (1943); the first Uzbek general, Sabir Rakhimov (1945); and others. In 1970 a 20-meter obelisk was placed on the mass grave of the Turkestan commissars. It was in this context that the Museum of Arts appeared. Its severe forms were an appropriate response to the specific prehistory of the park, which for the whole Soviet period had been used for mourning and memorial ceremonies.

After the collapse of the USSR the significance of a number of the official Soviet burials was reconsidered and the Turkestan commissars were reinterred elsewhere. In 2008 a monument to the Uzbek poetess Zulfiya was erected in the park, but nine years later it was moved to another location. In 2019, a bust of the Belarusian writer Iakub Kolas, who lived in Tashkent during the war, was erected here. The memorial connotations of the park remain relevant to Tashkent residents today.

Main dimensions of the Museum of Arts
General axonometric view

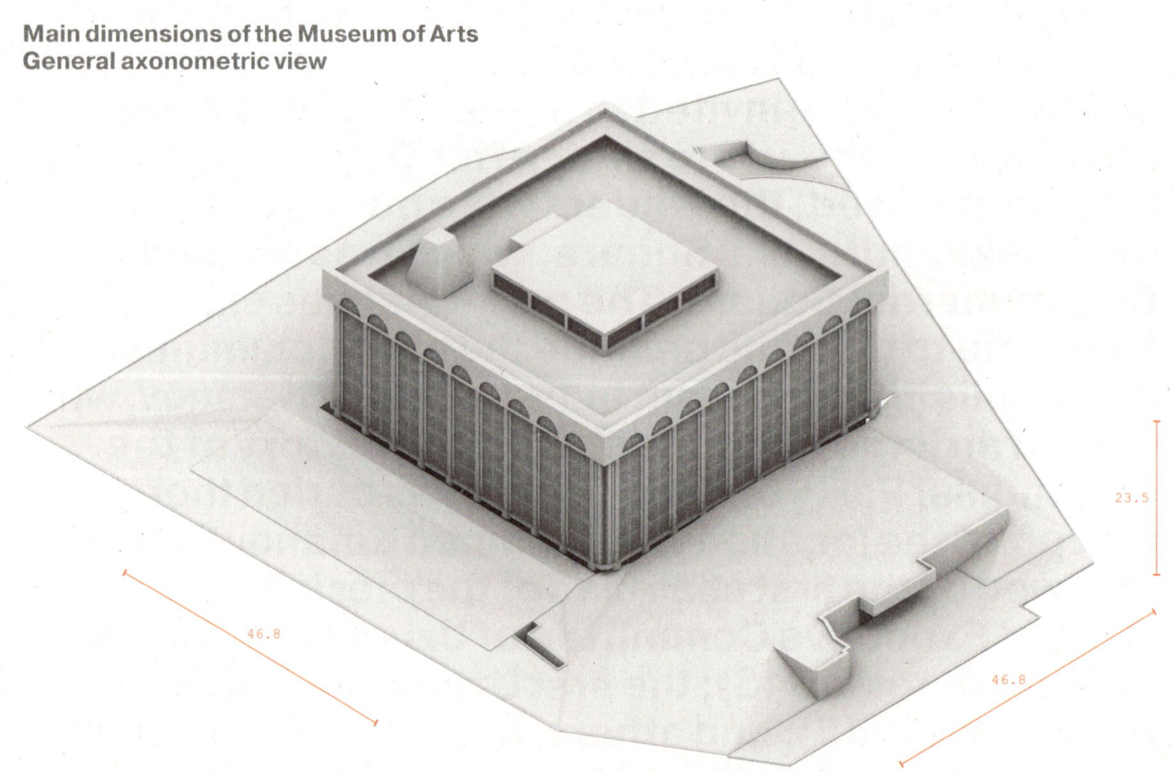

ACTORS	**Architects:**	**Savelii Rozenblium, Iskander Abdulov, Anatolii Nikiforov**	
	Engineers:	**G. Chibriakov, E. Gainulin**	
	Artist:	**Makhmud Usmanov**	
	Institute:	**TashZNIIEP**	
DATES	**Design period:**	**1963–early 1970s**	
	Construction period:	**December 2, 1967–1974**	
	Inauguration date:	**April 30, 1974**	
Later interventions:	**1994:**	**Project for the renovation of the plumbing and heating systems.**	
	1997:	**Reinforcement, intervention and partial replacement of some structural elements.**	
	Early 2000s:	**Renewal intervention: original façade is partly removed and then covered by a new alucobond façade, positioned about 80 cm away from the existing one.**	
	2017, December 11:	**Approval of the reconstruction and expansion program for the State Museum of Arts of Uzbekistan (Decree No. 975 of the Cabinet of Ministers of the Republic of Uzbekistan).**	
	2018, August:	**Geological surveys to study the geological, lithological and hydrogeological conditions of the soil to support the seismic evaluation of the building.**	
	2019:	**The Museum of Arts is closed for renovations.**	
	2020:	**Instrumental analyses are performed on the building by "O'zgashkliti" Duk (sclerometer, shock impulse, thermal imaging, thermohydrometer).**	
	2023:	**Interior upgrade of the first floor and entrance area.**	
USE	**Current use:**	**Museum**	
	Original use:	**Museum**	
	Suitability of current use:	**The building was designed to house a museum and, as such, shows good spatial quality and flexibility. These features are essential in any museum of the past or present. Nonetheless, the concept of the museum and the exhibition have changed over time, and in its current state the Museum of Arts does not meet contemporary requirements in terms of both technical performance and visitor amenities. In particular, the current lighting system is poorly suited to the museum's collection. The lack of a monitoring system to control microclimate parameters is also an issue, affecting both the efficient preservation of exhibited artworks and the comfort of museum visitors. Finally, visitor facilities are undersized and of poor quality: there is no café, proper cloakroom or reception, and the bookshop is a temporary stand in the middle of the entrance hallway. Storage facilities and museum workshops are insufficient and in bad condition. Office spaces require an upgrade.**	
	Space utilization:	**The building is fully used. No unused / underused spaces were detected.**	
DIMENSIONS	**Number of floors:**	**Basement + 4 floors + roof**	
	Length:	**46.8 m**	
	Width:	**46.8 m**	
	Height:	**23.5 m**	
	Gross floor area:	**Entrance (first) floor**	**2,491.0 m^2**
		Typical exhibition floor	**2,222.0 m^2**
	Gross floor area (total):		**12,549.0 m^2**

State Museum of Arts

***The sources for this text are documents relating to the design of the Museum of Arts dated 1967–1968 and 1971, construction photographs dated 1972 in the Republic of Uzbekistan Documentary Film and Photo Archive and the Museum of Arts, and journal articles from the period of design and construction. A short description of the Museum was found at the Institute of Art History, where, in the 1980s, lists of buildings were prepared for the republican* Corpus of Monuments.**

History of the Museum

The State Museum of Arts of Uzbekistan is the oldest art museum in Central Asia and one of the largest museums in Uzbekistan. It was founded in 1918 based on the collection of Prince Nikolai Romanov. The Museum holds archeological collections of ancient artefacts found on the territory of the republic; folk and applied art of Central Asia; Western European and Russian art of the fifteenth to the twentieth century; and Uzbek art of the twentieth and twenty-first centuries. The most important areas of the collection are Kushan sculpture of the first to the third century and the art of Uzbekistan of the 1920s and 1930s. Unlike the Nukus Museum, whose collection, despite its variety, was formed entirely thanks to the efforts of Igor' Savitskii, the collections of the State Museum of Arts are largely autonomous and ended up under one roof due to various historical circumstances.

The People's House (built in 1915), which housed the Museum of Arts from 1935 to 1966

Since it was founded, the museum has moved several times. From 1918 to 1935 it was located in the former palace of Prince Nikolai Romanov, which housed the initial collection. For a time, the museum was located in a former factory kitchen. In 1948 this collection was transferred to the so-called People's House, which had been constructed in 1912 in the south-east of the "new city." Before the State Museum of Arts moved there, the People's House had functioned as a Soviet house of culture, offering various activities for children and adults, lectures, a library with a reading room and children's plays. The relocation of the museum to a prerevolutionary building was a standard Soviet practice in the first decades of the USSR's existence. New museums were not constructed at that time due to the large number of good quality private buildings that became museum spaces after nationalization. However, by the early 1960s the former People's House was in poor condition and no longer met the needs of the State Museum of Arts. Consequently, the Ministry of Culture raised the question of reconstructing and expanding the museum.

The Ministry had its own design team, but it invited architect Savelii Rozenblium from the Uzgosproekt Institute to lead the project. A design for the reconstruction of the People's House and the construction of a new annex was developed by Rozenblium in 1963. No original sketches or working drawings of this project have been preserved, but an idea of its character is given in an article published in the newspaper *Pravda Vostoka* (*Truth of the East*) in 1989, during the architect's lifetime. According to the author, Rozenblium's addition to the People's House almost completely matched the museum building constructed in the 1970s but was designed as an "additional exhibition pavilion."[1] This indicates that even in the early 1960s Tashkent architects were prepared to work with the historical context, not erasing previous layers but instead adding modernist structures to the existing urban fabric. An expert commission demanded a number of modifications and corrections, after which the project was approved.[2] However, the history of the building took a different turn. On April 26, 1966, the People's House was seriously damaged in the Tashkent earthquake. Experts assessed the damage as irreparable; the collection was moved to a temporary location and the decision was taken to demolish the building and construct a new museum on the site. There was no competition. The Ministry of Culture was apparently happy with Rozenblium's previous work and the commission was given to TashZNIIEP, where the architect was now employed. Rozen-

1 A. Klimova, "Spasti muzei: poka ne vospitaem potrebnost' v kul'ture, nichego ne izmenitsia [Saving the Museum: Until We Develop a Requirement for Culture Nothing Will Change]," *Pravda Vostoka* [*Truth of the East*], August 22, 1989, 4.

2 "Zakliuchenie ekspertizy po smetnoi dokumentatsii k proektnomu zadaniiu pristroiki i rekonstruktsii zdaniia Gosudarstvennogo muzeia iskusstv v gor. Tashkente ot 3 dekabria 1963 g. [Conclusion of the Expert Commission on the Budget Documentation for the Project Brief for the Extension and Reconstruction of the State Museum of Arts in Tashkent, dated December 3, 1963]," *Ekspertnye zakliucheniia po proektnym zadaniiam i smetam* [*Expert Conclusions on Project Briefs and Budgets*] August 16, 1963–January 27, 1964, Tashkent City Archive, fund 36, list 1, item 1217, on 160 sheets, 64–69.

blium began work with his studio colleagues Iskander Abdulov and Anatolii Nikiforov. The initial design stage took place in 1967 and 1968, although as can be seen from a text in the journal *Stroitel'stvo i arkhitektura Uzbekistana* (*Construction and Architecture of Uzbekistan*) published in late 1967, by that stage the main decisions had already been taken.[3] There was a simple reason for such speed: the basis of the project, developed by Rozenblium, had existed since 1963.

Planning Scheme

When work began, the Tashkent architects did not have access to established prototypes of art museums, since the actual building type for a modernist museum was still at the experimental development stage. The scenography of museums created as part of the Modern Movement could be divided into two types: prescribed and open. It might seem that Le Corbusier's idea of a permanently expanding museum, which he formulated in the design for the World Museum of the Mundaneum in Geneva (1929) and defined in the National Museum of Western Art in Tokyo (1959), is an illustration of a linear scenography. However, this is not quite the case. Le Corbusier's museum spaces, constructed around a spiral, implied the possibility of viewing the adjoining spaces and the transversal trajectory between them. Their scenography did not predetermine the visitor's every movement between the entrance and the exit. The strictly linear route around the first modernist building of MoMA (Philip L. Goodwin and Edward D. Stone, 1939) was conceived by museum director Alfred Barr, who aimed to create an exhibition "following the development of modern art in a clear logical sequence."[4] It may seem that Frank Lloyd Wright's Solomon R. Guggenheim Museum (1958) correlated with Le Corbusier's spiral, but in fact it strictly regulated a linear route for visitors, and for obvious reasons: an endless museum is unthinkable on Manhattan Island. Like Wright, Philip Johnson organized both of his main museums—the Munson-Williams-Proctor Museum of Art in New York (1960) and the Sheldon Memorial Art Gallery in Lincoln, Nebraska (1963)—around an impressive internal hall, but these two halls played different roles. In the former the hall was an atrium situated at the center of the exhibition space, and in the latter it directed the flow of visitors between the two wings of the museum. In both cases, the space created by Johnson allowed for a limited variation of visitor routes within the circular movement around each floor. In 1968 Ludwig Mies van der Rohe and Lina Bo Bardi constructed two museums (he designed the Neue Nationalgalerie in Berlin and she the São Paulo Museum of Art) in open plan that did not limit the viewing route. Both of these museums appeared after Tashkent's State Museum of Arts, and we do not know whether the Tashkent team had access to the designs before construction was completed.

In terms of overall layout, the State Museum of Arts was closest to that proposed by Philip Johnson at the Munson-Williams-Proctor Museum of Art. Like him, Rozenblium, Abdulov and Nikiforov placed an atrium at the center of the plan with a circular route around it on each floor, after which visitors went upstairs to the next level. Placing staircases at both sides of the main pylon allowed for separation of visitor flows, while the open space of the atrium left the entire exhibition in the viewer's field of vision. This gave them the option to go to any point without circumnavigating each floor. On completion of construction, the museum curators assigned the movement upward a chronological character: in the atrium there were examples of traditional applied art, followed by a presentation of Western European art of the past, and it was only then that the visitor ascended to the floors showing Uzbek art of the twentieth century. This scenario, as it is not difficult to establish today, did not escape the postcolonial trap in which many museums found themselves, exhibiting traditional applied art at the beginning of the visitor trajectory even though it is sometimes produced simultaneously with contemporary art.

The staff and transport block was an important element of the planning, comprising stairs and an elevator that moved employees and exhibits through the museum, from the storage rooms in the basement to the top floor and roof, to which there was a staff staircase. Situated deep within the south-east part of the exhibition space, this block was integrated into the system of intersecting spaces and was not visible to visitors. Only the plastic element on the roof, designed in the spirit of Le Corbusier's late works, indicated to the general public the existence of a staff nucleus within the design.

The Architectural Image

In the architectural typology of the late eighteenth and nineteenth centuries, art museums were not separate from other museum repositories, which took on the character of a new type of city temple: "a temple of knowledge," "a temple of history," "a temple of the arts" (one might recall Étienne-Louis Boullée's concept of the "Museum," in the center of

3 Savelii Rozenblium, "Muzei iskusstv v Tashkente [The Museum of Arts in Tashkent]," *Stroitel'stvo i arkhitektura Uzbekistana* [*Construction and Architecture of Uzbekistan*], no. 12, 1967.

4 Quoted in Christoph Grunenberg, "The Modern Art Museum," in *Contemporary Cultures of Display*, ed. Emma Barker (New Haven & London: Yale University Press, 1999), 36.

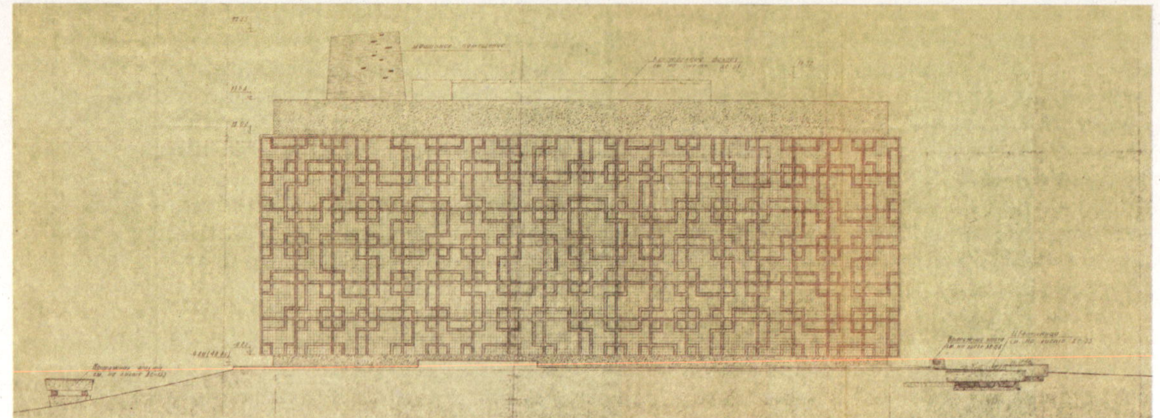
Version of façade, drawing, 1967

Version of entrance solution, sketch, 1967

which was a church with sculptures of famous people). The *art* museum was only defined as a specific type of building in the 1950s. There is a well-known phrase from a letter by Hilla von Rebay, director of the Solomon R. Guggenheim Museum, who defined the architect's task as follows: "I want a temple of spirit, a monument."[5] To construct a "monument" meant to create a "work of art," and this gave rise to an internal conflict that can be seen in the construction of contemporary art museums to this day. In relation to this issue, Philip Johnson wrote: "Today the Museum building stands as a community symbol like the church or courthouse of the last century. The architect must therefore create, inside and out, a symbolic structure which the community can refer to with some pride. This symbolic function of the museum however sometimes runs counter to its function as a home for the fine arts. This problem for the architect is compounded."[6] In creating a "symbolic structure" the architect has the means not only to amplify the resonance of the collection but also to dampen it. The narcissism of the "monument" should, paradoxically, harmonize with its ability to fade into the background, leaving the foreground to the artifacts in the museum; the simplified logic of the "white cube"; or the more nuanced interaction of the building and the works, as can be seen in the Palazzo Grassi (Tadao Ando, 2006), Milan's Fondazione Prada (Rem Koolhaas, Federico Pompignoli, 2015), the Garage Museum of Contemporary Art in Moscow (Rem Koolhaas, Ekaterina Golovatyuk, 2015), the Bourse de Commerce (Tadao Ando, 2020) and others.

The modernist museum of the 1950s and 1960s did not yet function as a machine for urban leisure and entertainment, something that radically changed the structure of the museums of our century, which now include outdoor spaces and recreation areas, cafés and restaurants, gift shops, exclusive art boutiques, book shops, libraries, agoras for public discussions, etc. Its functional and visual link to the temple remained definitive, but the first modernist museums also reflected the elitist insularity of the new institutions. Buildings like the Solomon R. Guggenheim Museum in New York and the National Museum of Western Art in Tokyo gave off a sense of inaccessibility thanks to their windowless walls and Brutalist materials, not to mention Marcel Breuer's Whitney Museum in New York (1966), the severe form of which is reminiscent of a fort. This trend was reflected in Rozenblium's team's design project.

There were no modernist art museums in the USSR when TashZNIIEP was awarded the design commission, but the situation with historical museums was different. In 1967 the Museum of Cosmonautics was launched in Kaluga and in 1968 the Erebuni and Sardarapat museums opened in Yerevan. Whereas the former featured futuristic forms associated with conquering space, the latter two museums established the memorial trend in Soviet modernism, which led to a national romanticism and renewed interest in the architectural heritage of the Soviet republics. The initial design for the State Museum of Arts in 1967 was at the intersection of these vectors. It featured maximally severe rationalist forms. The half cube placed on a raised, grassy area had hardly any façade details. The external volume incorporated four identical walls and a Brutalist entrance created using several concrete plates. The lapidary geometric form blended successfully into the urban fabric: the building geometry integrated five street axes, at the intersection of which it was situated. In contrast, the detailing of the museum façades was not neutral. The translucent glass brick façade panels were decorated with ceramic inserts, the pattern of which, from a distance, was reminiscent of Kufic script. They connotatively linked the museum walls, which were made of innovative materials, with the tradition of windowless walls of Samarkand madrasas and mosques, with their developed geometricized epigraphy. In accenting this historical association, Rozenblium pointed to the color of the ceramic inserts: "The glass brick façade panels incorporated glazed majolica tiles that formed a national pattern of dark blue and turquoise."[7] In the 1960s such ceramic tiles were one of the few indicators of the link between the new architecture and historical tradition. They formed part of the portal of the new Tashkent railway station (1961) and the buildings of the Council of Ministers, the Central Committee of the Komsomol of Uzbekistan (1969) and others.

In the 1967 project the interior of the building was designed in Brutalist style and loaded with church-like connotations. Having crossed the buffer portal of the entrance with its slits, which was reminiscent of Le Corbusier's Ronchamp Chapel, the visitor found themselves in a low corridor that the architect referred to as "three-naved." The "naves" led to the main atrium, which opened out suddenly and dramatically, like a cathedral transept. Rozenblium underlined the contrast between the "low vestibule" and the cubic hall. The slightly vertically

5 Quoted in Julie V. Iovine and Ezra Stoller, *Guggenheim New York/Guggenheim Bilbao* (Princeton: Princeton Architectural Press, 1999), 2.

6 Philip Johnson, "Architect's Statement," in Norman A. Geske and Henry Russell Hitchcock, *The Sheldon Memorial Art Gallery, University of Nebraska, Lincoln* (Lincoln: Sheldon Museum of Art, 1963).

7 Savelii Rozenblium, "Muzei iskusstv v Tashkente [The Museum of Arts in Tashkent]," 28.

extended proportion of the hall (18 × 18 × 19 meters) enhanced the effect of moving from the preparatory liminal space of a horizontal ship to the "altar" space, guiding the visitor's view upwards. The passage from the horizontal space to the atrium was marked by a scenographic asceticism. On the way nothing distracted or amused the visitor. There was no café, restaurant or library, nor even a basic area for people to relax. A visit to the museum was conceived as an exalted pilgrimage, not leisure or entertainment. This is similar to the sense that Johnson attempted to instill in the visitor in his museum experiments of the early 1960s: "The symbolic function of the Sheldon Gallery is fulfilled, I feel, not only by the 'classical' exterior of the travertine but by the great hall, which orients the visitor as well as elevating his spirits. People enjoy pictures more after they have been 'elevated' by big foyers. The home-for-picture functions occur in separated areas grouped around the great hall."[8]

Soviet architects did not think about the tribulation of going up via long flights of stairs, although Wright had provided an example of a solution, programming visitors' ascent using elevators, followed by a leisurely descent along the ramps of his spiral. The main staircase in the atrium, which invited visitor-pilgrims to make the ascent, brought diagonals into the orthogonal space. The mathematical proportions and geometrical vibration of this space, the play of rhythms of the staircases, the complex plotting of the railings on each floor and the alternating rectangular "balcony" projections for the recreation zones gave rise to numerous associations. One could see work with the metaphysics of "empty spaces" and the polysemic character of the material, linking the interior of the museum to the modernist architecture of Japan but also to the 1960s and 1970s work of Italian architect Carlo Scarpa, whose Tomba Brion, constructed at the same time as the Museum, incorporated a number of similar themes: a complex pattern of concrete textures, sculpting of the space using concrete parallelepipeds, and so on.

The Construction and Evolution of the Project

The foundation of the new building was laid on December 2, 1967, but the design process did not stop there. Breaks in construction allowed the architects to refine and modify some solutions. The finished building bears witness to the evolution of their intentions.

Some of the changes related to materials. The Brutalist concrete surfaces, the main expressive element of which in the initial project was the texture of the formwork, were retained only in the vestibule space. The external entrance pylons were faced with gray granite. The theme of gray stone was developed intensively in the interior. The load-bearing columns were clad with polished slabs of gray Nurata marble. The chipped edges of this type of marble slab were used to create the textured cladding for the main pylon in the atrium and the stairwells, as well as the balconies of the three floors, marking the edge of the multistory atrium. The successful choice of marble, along with its durability and the high quality of the work, ensured the preservation of the original aesthetic properties for this part of the museum. As a result, the interior of the atrium and the detailing of the balconies and railings are even today the main attractive element of the building as a whole. The side of the balconies facing the exhibition space is finished with rose Gazgan marble slabs, and the floors, which were initially intended to be covered with a synthetic material that would reduce footstep noise, were laid with parquet.

As well as being a project institute, TashZNIIEP undertook research, and there was a special laboratory for testing new materials. It seems very likely that the experiments conducted here influenced the change in the material of the external walls. Instead of glass blocks the architects decided to use off-white "stevite" to achieve even illumination. Stevite was made of hermetically sealed glass surfaces, between which was a light-dispersing layer of glass fiber unwoven cloth. Thanks to its properties, the museum spaces had an even, dispersed light that did not produce sharp reflections, and in the evening and at night the transparent walls of the museum produced the effect of a shining crystal. However, the main difference from the design was the pattern of the external walls. The edges of the cube, which were to have featured glass blocks with ceramic ornamentation, were replaced by walls with curved corners that softened the strict geometry. The "Kufic" development of the walls gave way to a modernist rhythm of protruding square lucarnes featuring light-dispersing panels. The main part of the façade was faced with sheets of anodized aluminum. As a result, the museum façade lost its orientalist connotations but took on new meanings that connected it to contemporary art, the launch point of which—the "zero of form," as Kazimir Malevich put it—had been associated with the square since the Suprematist revolution. Having become the basis of the façade, this theme moved into the interior. The square openings for ventilation in the pylon, incorporating an air duct, were combined into a hermetic sign created from a combination of three squares.

8 Philip Johnson, "Architect's Statement."

The precursor of the architectural team's new version of the façade is the Beinecke Rare Book and Manuscript Library at Yale University, which was constructed in 1963 and designed by future Pritzker Prize winner Gordon Bunshaft. Photographs of the Beinecke Library were published in the catalogue *Architecture of the USA*, which was distributed at the Seventh American Exhibition in the USSR, a hugely popular event that took place in 1965. This catalogue could be found on the desks of many Soviet architects in the late 1960s and, of course, was known to the authors of the State Museum of Arts. A quote from Savelii Rozenblium when presenting the finished museum helps to confirm that the team was inspired by Bunshaft's masterpiece: "All of this creates a memorable image of the building as a forged jewel box."[9] Rozenblium's turn of phrase is a clear repetition of a comment in the catalogue *Architecture of the USA* about the Beinecke Library: "It is a building within a building, [...] like a crystal jewel box for semiprecious stones."[10] However, the historical evolution of the design demonstrates that Bunshaft's building was not the trigger for creating the museum's overall architectural concept. The initial façades were not linked to the library at Yale and the museum plans were the opposite. In the Beinecke Library the main constituent element of the interior was the bookshelves, which metonymically formed a *building with a building*, whereas in the Tashkent museum it formed around the empty space of the atrium.

The preference for a more geometrical and minimalist solution rather than traditional interior patterns can be seen in the context of the early 1970s as something subversive, since at this time Tashkent's architects tended to orientalize artistic language. If in the late 1960s they rejected the use of decorative "national" elements, after the construction of the Lenin Museum, the Blue Domes Café and the Ministry buildings on Lenin Square, criticism was gradually replaced by acceptance. The design of the Union of Artists Exhibition Hall, which was typologically similar to the State Museum of Arts, was a good example: if in the first design sketches (1971) the arcade of the façade comprised a play of brutal, flat elements that was embellished with a figurative relief on the wall of the pedestrian gallery, in the finished building the arches were decorated with vegetal ornament and the gallery wall with a geometric pattern. The Tashkent Circus underwent a similar metamorphosis. Whereas in the first sketches of the mid-1960s it was reminiscent of a Brutalist spaceship decorated with "portholes," the actual building featured extensive use of traditional ornament. Another example is the Gor'kii Russian Drama Theater (constructed as the Turkestan Palace), for which the 1967 design sketches used Brutalist forms and asymmetric composition. In the 1970s it became "overgrown" with panjara latticework and then stalactites.

The State Museum of Arts evolved in the opposite direction. The initial version included ornamentally developed walls, which were precursors of what would begin to occur in Uzbek architecture within a few years. However, by 1974, when oriental motifs had become embedded in the modernist architecture of Tashkent, the museum emerged as a more severe and stylistically neutral building. The only concession to decorativeness was the painted carving on the ganch plaster of the wall in the small conference room, which was created by master craftsman Makhmud Usmanov. One should note that this "swimming against the tide" by Rozenblium's team reflected the architectural doctrine at TashZNIIEP, where the main buildings—the Zhemchug sixteen-story residential building, the Palace of Aviation Constructors, the Intourist Culture and Information Center, the VodGeo Scientific Research Institute and others—were, until the mid-1980s, untouched by the fashion for orientalist decorativeness.

Compositionally, the design of the Tashkent Museum of Arts comprised two cubic volumes. The first, with an 18-meter-long edge, formed the volume of the three-story main atrium, around which the exhibition spaces were grouped. The second cube, half of which was made up of underground stories (and even so was referred to as a cube by the architects in the accompanying materials), formed the façade of the building. Naturally, this clean, minimalist form invited associations with the early-twentieth-century avant-gardes, and primarily with Suprematism, whose leaders aimed to create a new plastic language based on primary geometric figures. This connotation was reinforced by the rows of Suprematist squares with which the external walls were faced and the black squares that formed an enigmatic symbol on the pylon in the atrium. These forms generated their own meanings and associations, while being connected to the artistic context and creating a spatial environment for it.

By the late 1980s many elements of the building had aged or lost their aesthetic properties. The poor quality of construction led to moist ingress into the offices of the research departments and the art storage rooms, which were located in semibasement and basement spaces. The technical equipment installed in the early

9 Savelii Rozenblium, "Unikal'nye zdaniia [Unique Buildings]," *Stroitel'stvo i arkhitektura Uzbekistana* [*Construction and Architecture of Uzbekistan*], no. 12, 1974, 20.

10 *Arkhitektura SShA: Katalog vystavki v SSSR* [*Architecture of the USA: Catalogue of the Exhibition in the USSR*], 1965, 49.

1970s fell into disrepair.[11] In the early 1990s a correspondent from *Pravda Vostoka* (*Truth of the East*) noted that the walls in the basement had begun to "be covered with mold," "the plaster had crumbled," "part of the external window glazing had been damaged and lost its hermetic seal," "of two air-conditioning units only one was working," "in the rain the roof turned into a 'swimming pool' and water got into the exhibition halls."[12] In addition, aging affected the color and form of the aluminum sheets cladding the façade (they warped due to frequent changes of temperature). In the late 1980s and early 1990s people began to criticize the aesthetic of the Museum. A journalist from *Pravda Vostoka* (*Truth of the East*) named the People's House, which had been destroyed by the earthquake, the most beautiful building in which the museum had been housed and also suggested that "Italian sculpture or, for example, antique furniture does not look good" against the milky glass façade in the background.[13] Also, the initial aesthetics of the Museum were in conflict with the architecture of the 1990s, with its accent on historical forms such as pointed arches and blue domes, its imitation of order systems and so on. The established practice of the time involved substitution of elements rather than undertaking a serious and considered preservation and adaptation of the building. Hence, the elevations that incorporated stevite squares were covered with a new matte glazing articulated by decorative columns with arches. Even so, the interior of the Museum largely retained its initial look and original décor.

State Museum of Arts entrance façade, 1974–1976

Beinecke Rare Book and Manuscript Library, Yale University, USA

11 A. Klimova, "Spasti muzei: poka ne vospitaem potrebnost' v kul'ture, nichego ne izmenitsia [Saving the Museum: Until We Develop a Requirement for Culture Nothing Will Change]."
12 S. Velichkin, "Shedevry v opasnosti [Masterpieces in Danger]," *Pravda Vostoka* [*Truth of the East*], August 8, 1992, 4.
13 A. Klimova, "Spasti muzei: poka ne vospitaem potrebnost' v kul'ture, nichego ne izmenitsia [Saving the Museum: Until We Develop a Requirement for Culture Nothing Will Change]."

ARCHITECT
SAVELII ROZENBLIUM

Place and year of birth:
Odesa, 1926 (evacuated to Tashkent in 1941)

Place and year of death:
Israel, after 2004

Education:
1944–1949 (approximately), Architecture Department of Central Asia Polytechnic Institute (SazPI)

After graduating, the architect began working in the Stalinist era and seemingly already stood out among his colleagues. This is evidenced by the fact that he won the competition for the reconstruction of Tashkent's main administrative building in 1953, when he was twenty-seven and the other architect, Ofeliia Aidinova, was twenty-six. Their design involved enclosing the central part of the Constructivist complex with a colonnade with a stylized "oriental" order and constructing a ministerial dining room in the right wing of the building. The entrance lobby space, staircases and main halls of the building were reconstructed, while the winter garden, which had existed since thetime of Governor-General of Turkestan Konstantin von Kaufmann (1880s), was preserved. After Khrushchëv's reform of architecture and construction in 1955, Rozenblium would no longer use historical citations and stylizations.

Until 1963 the architect worked at Uzgosproekt and then moved to the new organization TashZNIIEP, where he was primarily involved in creating and adapting standard designs for cinemas (the Moscow Cinema in Tashkent, Tselinnyi Cinema in Alma-Ata). As well as his ability to find clear functional solutions, he also demonstrated a talent for designing unique spatial and figurative forms, playing with complex surfaces and textures. An example is his competition project for the Puppet Theater of 1968, designed in collaboration with Ofeliia Aidinova. He produced a similar design for the Planetarium and House of Knowledge in Dushanbe (approved by the government of the Tajik SSR in 1975, but never built).

Rozenblium spent a great deal of time developing so-called "house-complexes," which comprised a search for modern social equivalents of the residential districts of "old" Tashkent, with intricate mahalla-type social connections between residents. At TashZNIIEP this search took place from two positions: Il'ia Merport's team proposed combining various types of accommodation in the "house-complex," whereas Rozenblium's team sought a solution in the rhizomatic spatial organization of multistory residential buildings. In the end, the institute team devised a hybrid of these two approaches and developed a joint project that was, in fact, never built.

In the early 1970s, together with Zlata Chebotareva, he focused on another important theme, the development of industrial low-rise, compact housing using the planning merits of vernacular architecture. At that time Andrei Kosinskii was working in this area, and later Iosif Notkin. Moving temporarily to Tashgiprogor (Tashkent State Urban Project Institute), he also proposed and built a series of multistory concrete residential buildings erected using sliding formwork. This project was notable for the number of possible versions of the building plan based on varying a limited number of modules. This area of modernist architecture never failed to inspire Tashkent's architects, who were keen to find more economical and expedient formulas for variety in the tough conditions of industrial building production. Journals of the time also help to establish that during his work at Tashgiprogor, Rozenblium designed the sixteen-story, 228-apartment building on A. Kakhkhar Street, which was constructed by raising floors; was a member of the design team for the microdistrict Sergeli-8; and designed the Exhibition of National Economic Achievements (VDNKh) for the Karakalpakskaia ASSR, which was never built.

Unfortunately, despite Rozenblium's significance and his own interest in writing texts about architecture, no one wrote about him during his lifetime. He is one of the least studied protagonists of Tashkent modernism.

INSTITUTIONAL FRAMEWORK

TashZNIIEP

CADRE

When TashZNIIEP was formed in 1963, its staff came from two institutions, the department of standard design of Uzgosproekt, which was reformed as the design department of TashZNIIEP, and the disbanded Scientific Research Institute for Construction of the Academy of Construction and Architecture of the USSR in Tashkent, which became the research department of TashZNIIEP. Three hundred and fourteen staff worked in the new institute, including eleven holders of Ph.D.s in architecture.

PRIORITIES

The work of the research department covered many types of design and construction activity. Specialists studied the issues of construction in seismic zones, air-conditioning, sun protection, the technology of economical manufacture of objects made from concrete and other construction materials, questions of climate, the cultural specificity of a given population, etc. The scientific approach to design was conditioned by the technocratic image of the institute and influenced the thought processes of the architects who worked there. Here there was minimal emphasis (insofar as it was possible in the USSR) on the imperative of "national form," and architects aimed to use research to create standard environments and unique buildings that were suitable for the Central Asian climate and the culture of the peoples who lived there. The zonal nature of the institute, which designed for the entire Central Asian region, not just for Uzbekistan, also helped architects to move the accent away from "national form" toward regional specificity.

Basement floor plan
Original condition

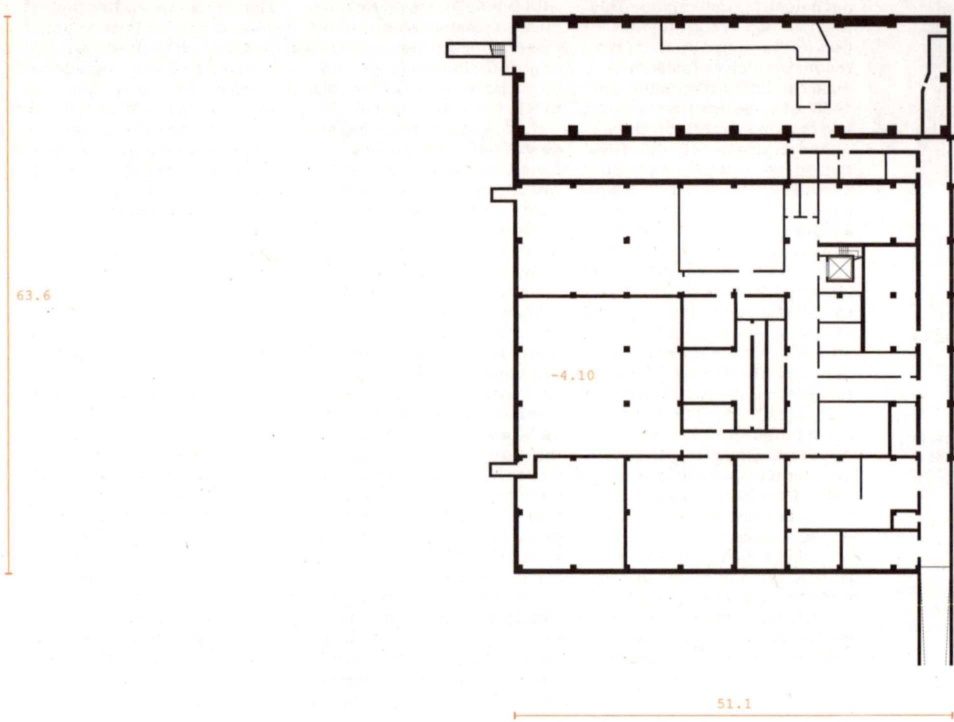

1st floor plan
Original condition

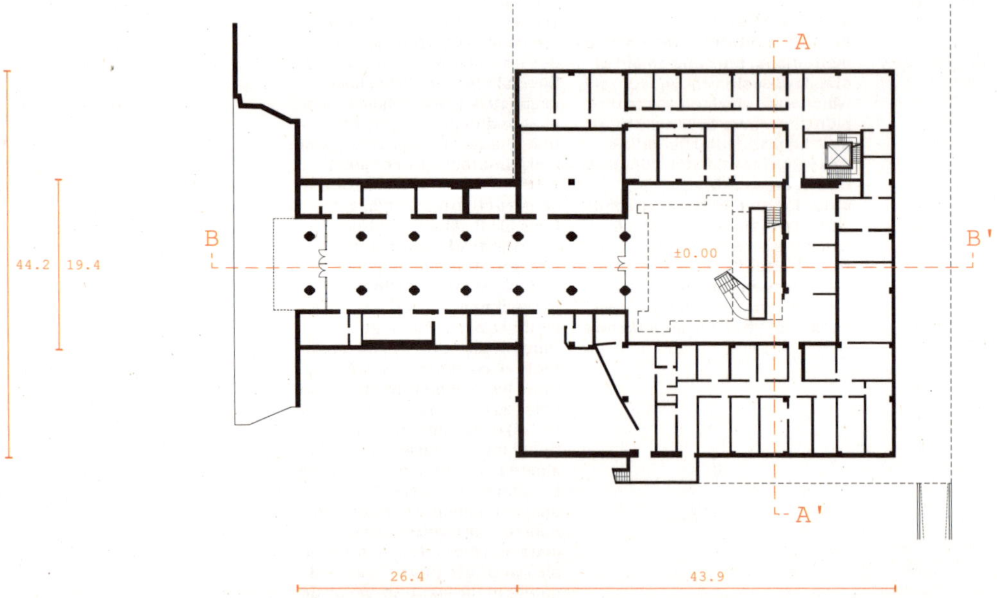

2nd floor plan
Original condition

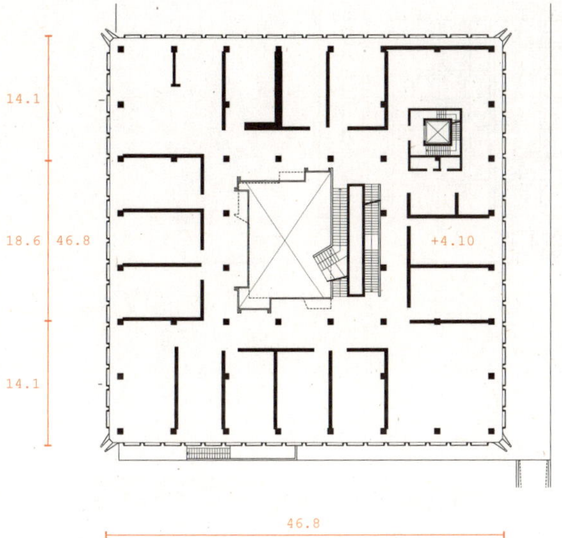

3rd floor plan
Original condition

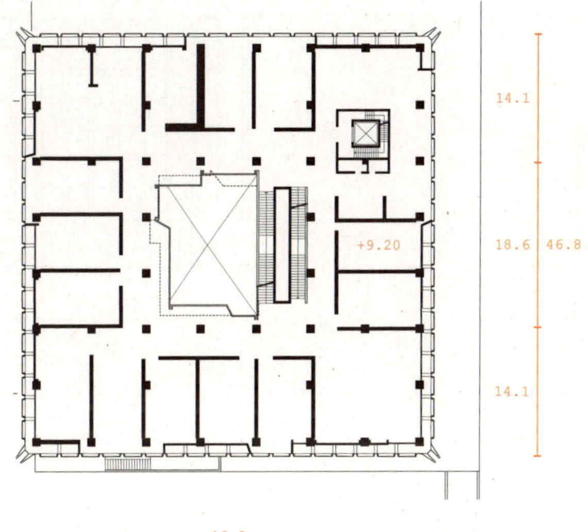

4th floor plan
Original condition

14.1
18.6 46.8
+14.30
14.1
46.8

Roof plan
Original condition

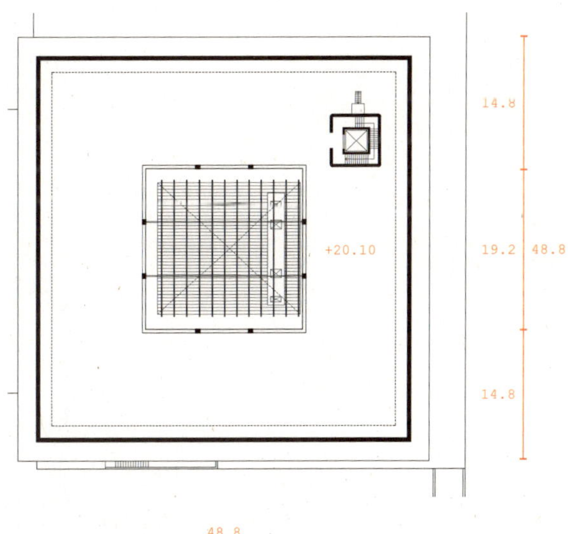

0 5 10m

North-east elevation
Original condition

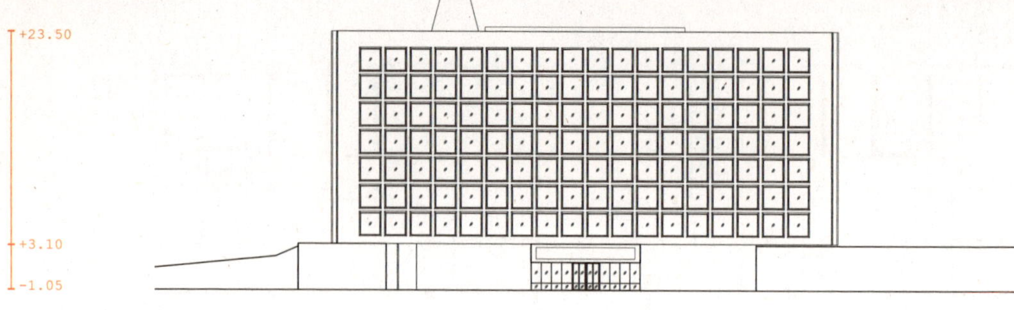

South-west elevation
Original condition

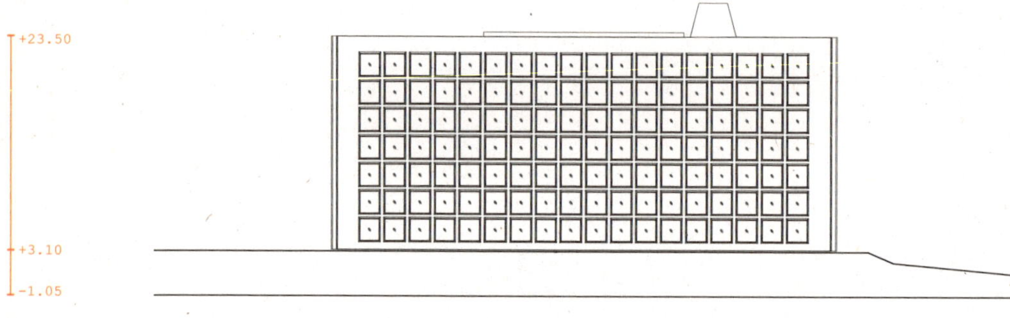

North axonometric view
Original condition

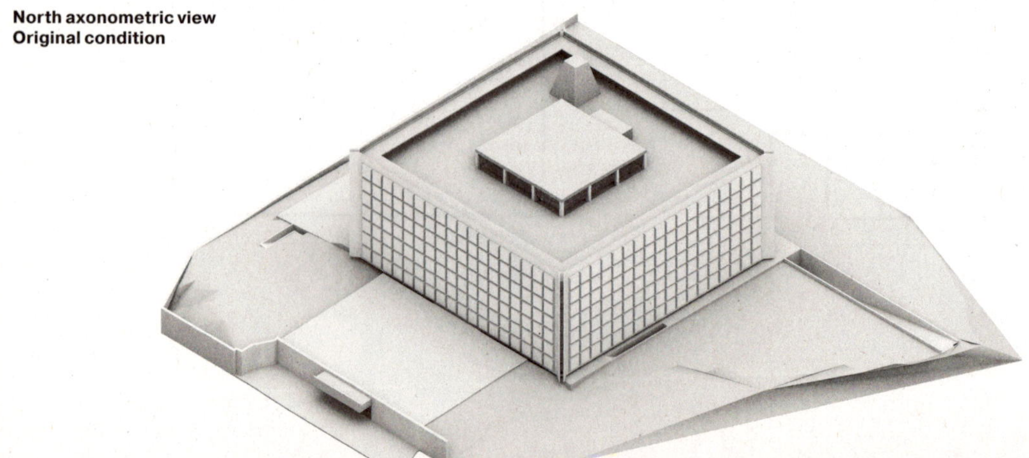

0 5 10m

Section AA'
Original condition

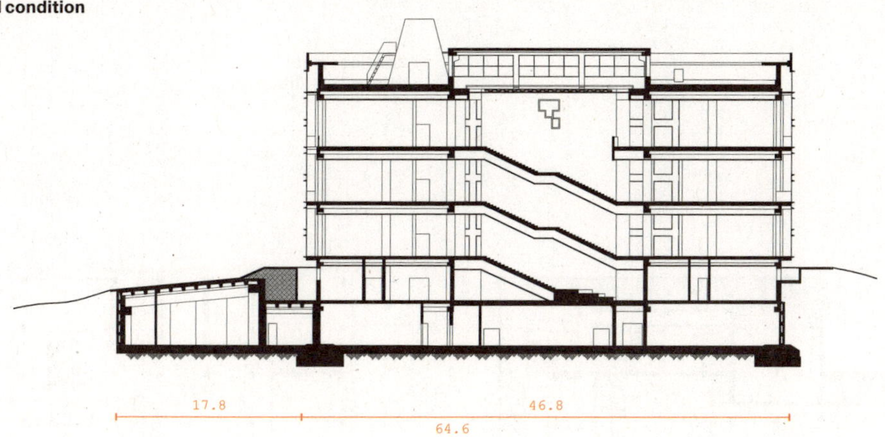

Section BB'
Original condition

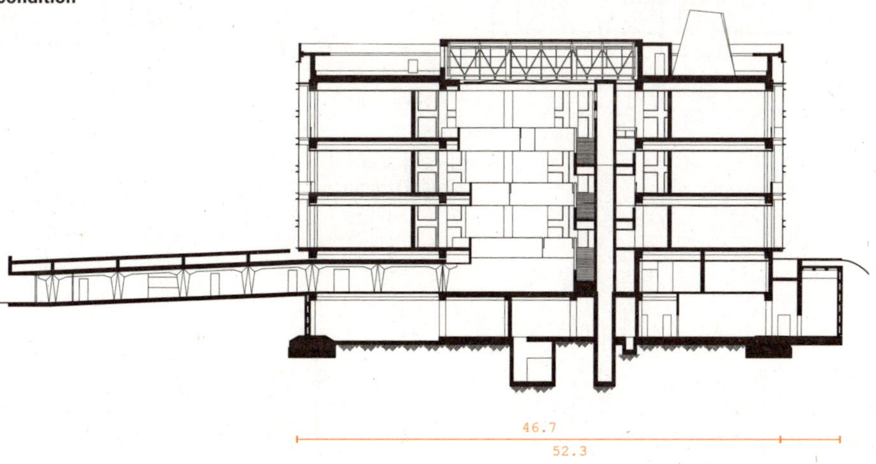

Exterior perspective views
Original condition

0 5 10m

1974

1st floor plan
Original condition

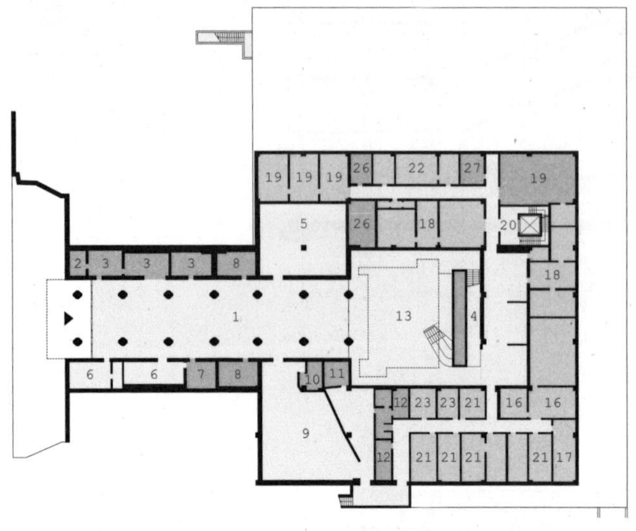

2nd floor plan
Original condition

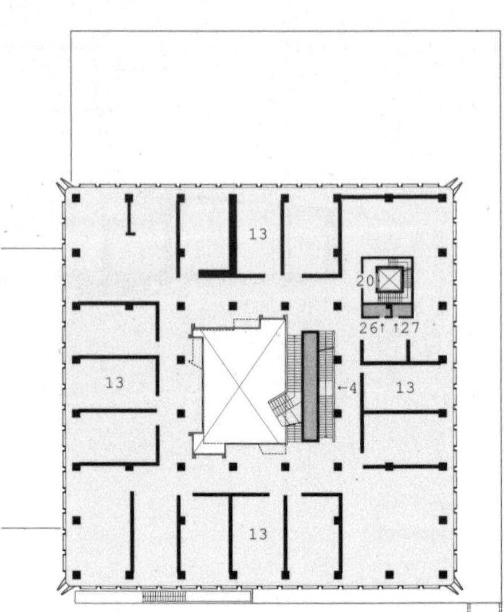

3rd floor plan
Original condition

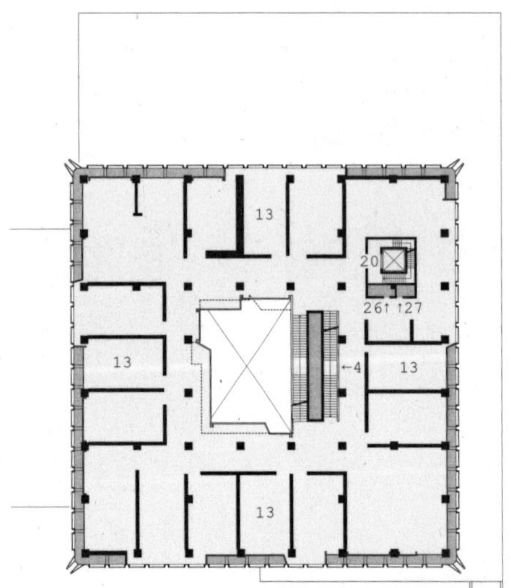

4th floor plan
Original condition

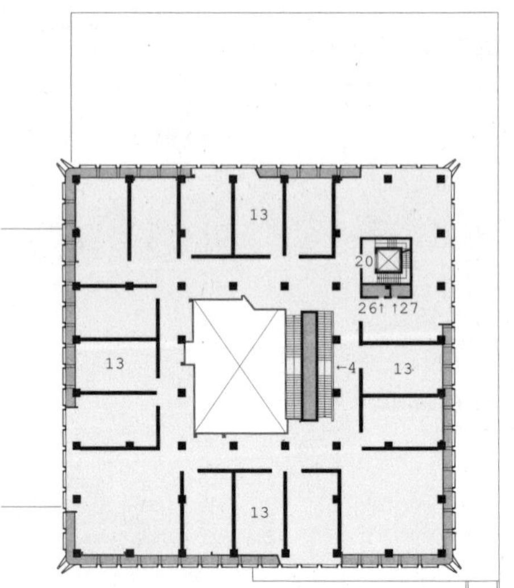

1 Vestibule
2 Ticket office
3 Cloakroom
4 Circulation, visitors
5 Museum shop
6 Café
7 Café service rooms
8 Bathrooms
9 Lecture hall
10 Storage, lecture material
11 Film library
12 Technical lecture hall
13 Exhibition space
14 Museum storage
15 Meeting room
16 Library & book storage
17 Photo library
18 Photo lab
19 Workshop
20 Circulation, workers
21 Museum workers' offices
22 Administration
23 Staff room
24 Security room
25 Storage
26 Service room
27 Technical area
28 Empty space

2022

1st floor plan
Current condition

2nd floor plan
Current condition

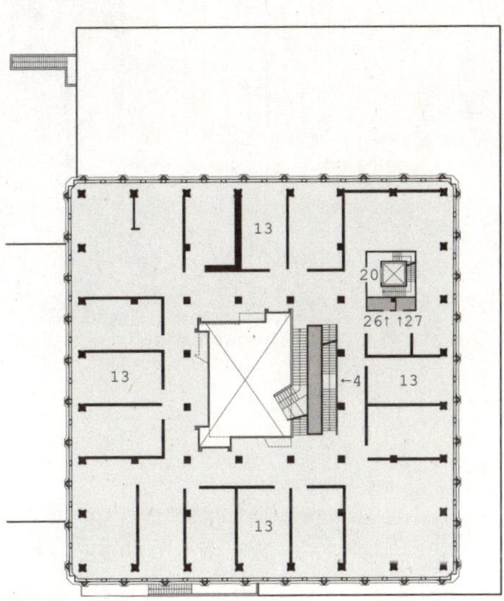

3rd floor plan
Current condition

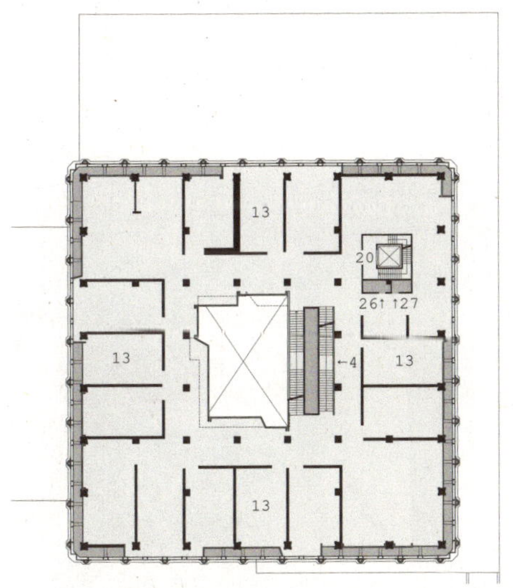

4th floor plan
Current condition

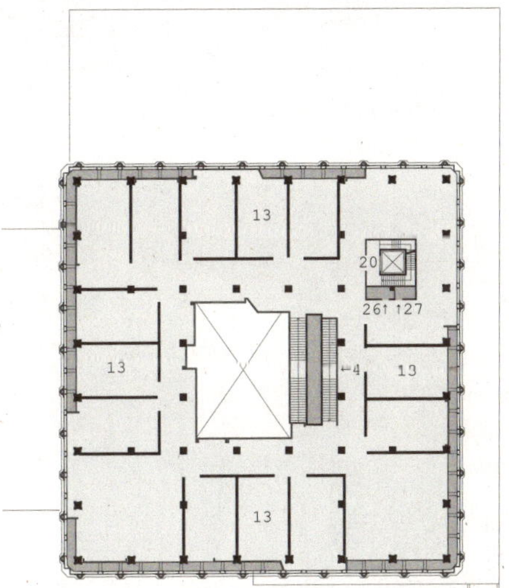

Exhibition/public
Administrative/laboratories
Service and technical
Change of function

0 5 10m

State Museum of Arts construction site

Detail of the construction of one of the corners

General view of the State Museum of Arts

Museum entrance

Aerial view of the museum, 1970s/1980s

Exterior view of the museum

State Museum of Arts, 1980s

Exhibition spaces

Exhibition spaces, 1980s

Full-height atrium, 1982

State Museum of Arts façade, daytime, 2022

West corner of the State Museum of Arts, nighttime, 2023

Atrium skylight, 2022

Façade details, 2022

View of the atrium, fourth floor, 2021

View of the stairs in the atrium, 2021

View of the stairs in the atrium, 2021

View of the third-floor exhibition space from the atrium, 2021

Exhibition views, 2022

Project version model

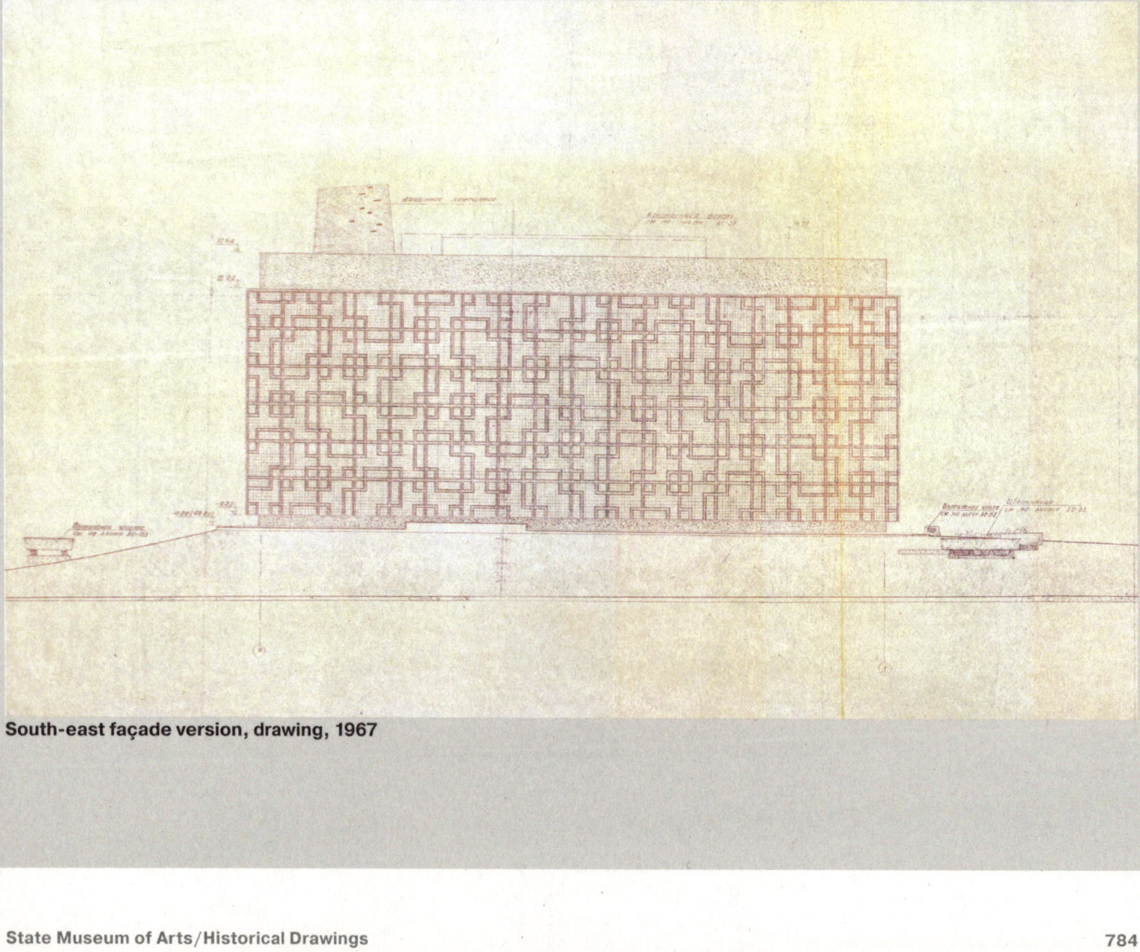

South-east façade version, drawing, 1967

South-west façade version, drawing, 1967

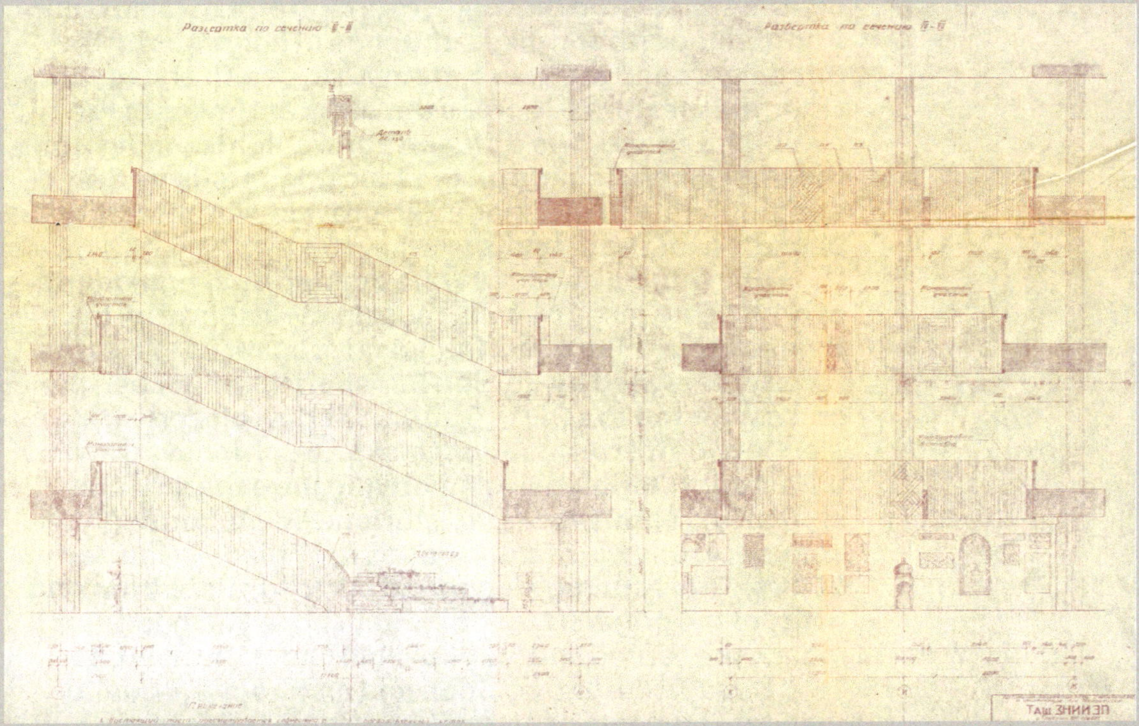

Full-height atrium elevation, 1967

HIGHLIGHTS

The State Museum of Arts of Uzbekistan is an exhibition pavilion designed and built between 1963 and 1974 in the south-eastern part of the city, at the intersection between the former Proletarskaia Street (Amir Temur Avenue) and the former Shota Rustaveli Street (Shakhrisabz Street).

Conceived by the architects S. Rozenblium, I. Abdulov and A. Nikiforov, at the time of its construction the Museum was probably the most abstract building in Tashkent. Its original design, based on austere geometric proportioning, evoked both the symbolism of Suprematism with its main icon, the square, and the mathematic rigor of Islamic architecture (whose starting point was the cubic transcendence of the Kaaba). This unique quality of re-elaborating key symbols of the historical culture of the region and of universal modernist art made this project eminently suitable for the main "temple of arts" of the capital of Uzbekistan.

The cold materials of the original façade and the rigor of the cubic volume, floating over a green carpeted hill, were elegantly softened by curved ribs at the corners of the envelope, and were further contrasted in the interior by the textured natural gray stone finish of the central staircase in the four-story high atrium (also cubic). A continuous ribbon-like sequence of handrails on the three floors and the stairs, framing the central void, provided a visual thread across the different levels of the exhibition space. The diffused natural light coming from the translucent façade on the four sides conferred additional subtlety to the space and provided an abstract backdrop for the exhibits.

The original façades were defined by a regular grid of protruding milky panels, most likely inspired by the Beinecke Rare Book and Manuscript Library at Yale University, designed by Gordon Bunshaft in 1963. Each panel corresponded to a 220 × 220 cm window glazed with stevite to better diffuse light inside. Such innovative and untested material, fully embodying the experimental spirit of modernism, soon deteriorated. Accordingly, a complete renewal of the façades took place in the early 2000s. The resulting alucobond enclosure lacks the originality of the original façade, which, however, has been mostly preserved and is still visible under the new one.

Due to its urban position and architectural quality the State Museum of Arts of Uzbekistan is one of the most significant and pure modernist buildings in Tashkent. Moreover, it is an outstanding example of a modernist masterpiece, with the potential for international relevance, where recent transformations have hidden but not canceled its most clearly modernist feature, the façade. Therefore, as well as preservation, a restoration strategy should be applied.

STATE OF REPAIR SCORE:

- 3 – The building shows localized deterioration patterns which do not affect its stability

Overall, the building is in a satisfactory state of repair. The most severe damage has been caused by recent sampling and diagnostic tests which have not been appropriately repaired. A few cracks were identified on the ground floor, but they appear to be consistent with the normal aging of the building and are not excessively worrying. Finally, the windows are outdated and inefficient, as they provide a low level of thermal insulation.

Protection status:	The building is listed according to Resolution No. 227 of the Cabinet of Ministers, April 22, 2024.
Main criticalities:	The building embodies an outdated concept of a museum and does not fulfill current technical requirements (e.g. lighting, ventilation, microclimate monitoring). Visitor facilities are lacking and, where they do exist, below contemporary standards. Recent diagnostic tests carried out on the building's load-bearing structure caused damage that has not been adequately repaired. The building does not fully meet current seismic requirements.
Possible risks:	A risk for a part of the basement area is related to seismic regulations. Because of the most recent updates to the national standards, some of the Museum's structural elements have ceased to fulfill the seismic requirements.

INTEGRITY SCORE:

- Exterior: 1 – The building has lost most of the elements necessary to express its significance
- Interior: 3 – The building has retained all the elements necessary to express its significance but is in a poor state of repair

The architectural integrity of the Museum has been largely compromised by the complete renewal of the façades in the early 2000s. As a result, the building lost its original exterior appearance, which was one of its most significant features, as well as a strong means of conveying the design concept, focusing on geometry and proportions.

Despite this major change, the building was able to retain its integrity as an urban ensemble, maintaining the dialogue with the surrounding green area, which is complementary to the Museum.

The Museum interiors also show a good level of integrity. Little has changed since construction and the main valuable features of the architectural concept remain unaltered.

AUTHENTICITY SCORE:

- Exterior: 1 – The building has been subjected to major interventions which resulted in an overall transformation
- Interior: 3 – The building has been subjected to slight changes and replacements

Since its construction, the Museum has undergone several maintenance interventions, which have concerned both the functionality and the appearance of the building. A clear distinction should be made between the interior and exterior of the building, as they retain very different levels of authenticity.

The most relevant and evident transformation concerns the façade of the Museum, which was completely altered in the early 2000s. The original envelope was partly dismantled and covered by new alucobond and glass finishes of a rather eclectic composition, completely revolutionizing the appearance of the building. However, a close inspection of the façade system revealed that, although covered, most structural elements of the original design are still in place.

As for the interior of the building, no relevant changes were observed. Most of the repairs focused on maintenance or substitution of technical systems (heating and plumbing) and on structural reinforcement. The installation of the new façade also slightly affected the façade's appearance in the interior. While the application of the opaque glass maintained the original idea of diffused lighting, the new glass panes were moved inward, thus annulling the intended protrusion of the inner space toward the outside.

1974–1980s

Main façade of the State Museum of Arts, 1974–1976

Main façade of the State Museum of Arts, 2022

Lecture hall, 1974

Lecture hall, 2022

Exhibition space, 1980s

Exhibition space, 2022

1982

Full-height atrium, 1982

2022

Full-height atrium, 2022

LEVEL 1 – MAXIMUM LEVEL OF INTEREST
(No transformations allowed; conservation activities required)

URBAN LEVEL

The Museum of Arts stands in a park (Iakub Kolas Park) which occupies an urban block (delimited by Taras Shevchenko Street, Shakhrisabz Street, Amir Temur Avenue and Iakub Kolas Street). According to the original design concept, no other buildings are located on this plot and this feature should be carefully retained. No new volumes should therefore be added within the boundaries of the park surrounding the Museum.

ARCHITECTURAL LEVEL
EXTERIOR

The half-cubic volume and general proportions of the museum should be preserved as they are, avoiding any additions that might change the composition defined by the architects. The clean and simple proportions of this building, as well as the half-cubic shape, represent one of its most evident and valuable features.

INTERIOR

The overall architectural layout of the building should be retained, with particular reference to the full-height central atrium giving access to all the exhibition floors. The atrium should be maintained as is, avoiding any new permanent partition and keeping the zenith lighting provided by the existing skylight.

The contrast between the low height of the entrance corridor and the full-height atrium is also a distinctive feature of the building and is important to retain.

The idea of the milky glazed (or analogous to stevite) façade should be kept in order to retain the lighting intended in the original design concept, though the actual position of the glass might be reverted to the original position. Also, the rhythm of the interior façade structure, organized in 220 × 220 cm squares, is original and should not be changed.

DETAIL LEVEL
EXTERIOR

The stone cladding applied on the retaining walls at the entrance of the building is original and should be preserved.

INTERIOR

The pillars supporting the ceiling of the entrance hallway should retain their shape and section.

The ganch decorations applied to the walls of the conference room on the ground floor should be preserved.

The use of dark, rough stone gives a sculptural appearance to the atrium and increases the contrast with the bright exhibition rooms. This feature should be carefully preserved.

The zenith skylight of the central atrium should be kept as is, retaining the alternating of light and shadow created by the pleated metallic sheets composing it.

The parapets of the atrium and stairs should be retained because of their dynamic design.

The following finishings should also be maintained:

- the marble pavement of the central atrium;
- the cladding of bearing pillars;
- the stone and marble cladding of the parapets and of the wall supporting the stairs.

LEVEL 2 – MEDIUM LEVEL OF INTEREST

(Elements included in the second level can be moderately transformed following approval by a designated committee[1])

URBAN LEVEL

The park surrounding the Museum of Arts is closely connected to the building and its perception. The area should thus be kept as a green space and any transformations should be submitted to the designated committee for approval.

ARCHITECTURAL LEVEL

INTERIOR

Transformations regarding the entrance hall should be submitted to the designated committee.

Transformations concerning the lecture hall on the ground level should be subject to approval by the designated committee.

Any change to the exhibition spaces should be submitted to the designated committee.

1 An international committee of heritage preservation experts to be appointed.

HIDDEN MODERNIST FEATURES

The exterior appearance of the Museum of Arts has undergone a significant transformation since its construction. Some of its modernist features are still present, although hidden by the most recent additions.

In particular, the original façade of the building, which was one of its most iconic and qualifying characteristics, still partly exists behind the new alucobond and glass façade. Although the original stevite panels were removed, the square steel grid of the original façade and the metallic profiles holding the glass panels are still in place. The entrance to the building has also undergone some reversible changes. In particular, the glass wall where the door is located was originally further back. In the original layout, the design was cleaner, more dynamic and markedly modernist.

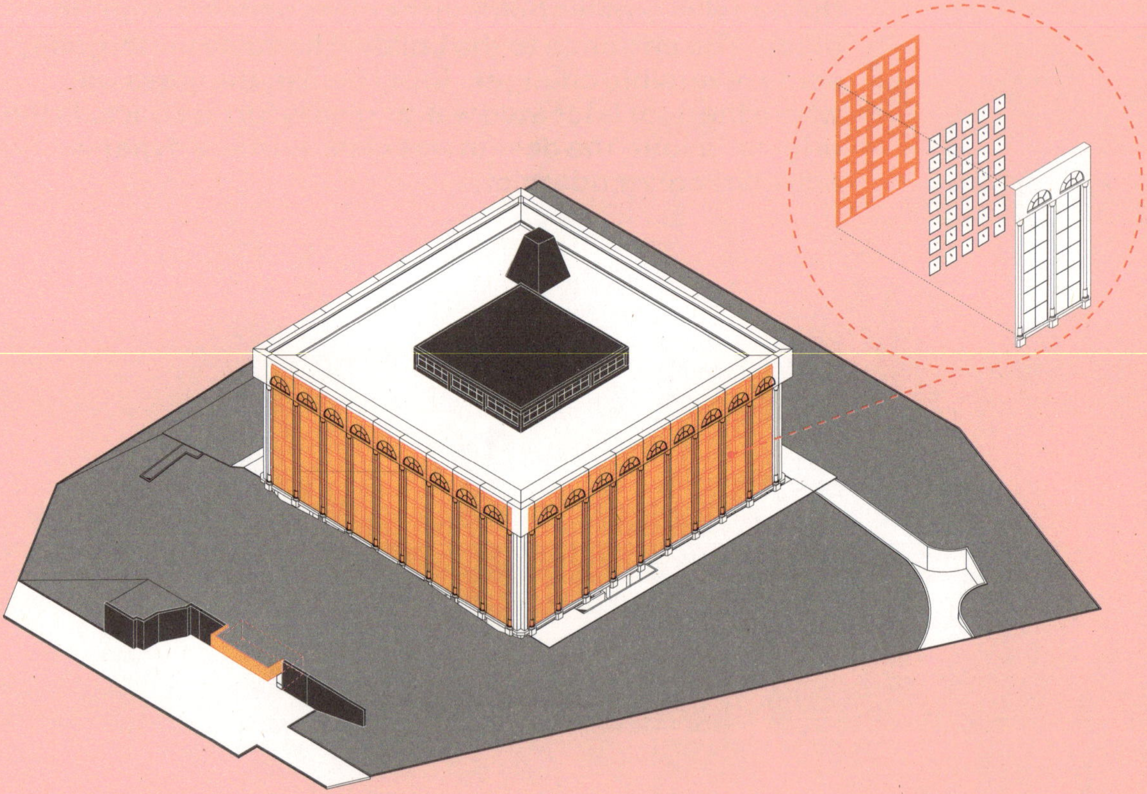

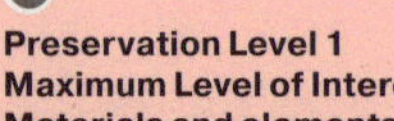

Preservation Level 1
Maximum Level of Interest
Materials and elements to be preserved

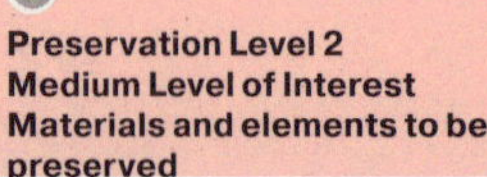

Preservation Level 2
Medium Level of Interest
Materials and elements to be preserved

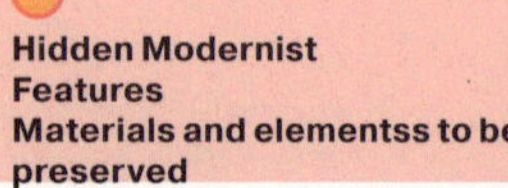

Hidden Modernist Features
Materials and elementss to be preserved

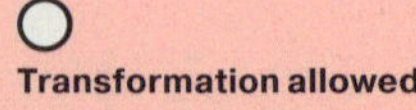

Transformation allowed

Preservation Strategy

At the time of its construction, the Museum of Arts was undoubtedly the most abstract building in Tashkent. Its precise geometric proportions, based on the geometric figure of the square, synthesized the historical culture of the region and the language of global modernism, making this architecture extremely relevant. In step with the experiments of modern architecture, the façades of the Museum were built employing a new and experimental material, stevite, which did not pass the test of time, meaning the building was destined for a cortical remake.

In the early 2000s the original façade was partly dismantled and covered with a new layer, the design of which is completely unrelated to the geometry proposed in the original concept. While this change only slightly affected the interior of the building, it completely undermined the exterior appearance, erasing (or, rather, hiding) the initial design. As confirmed by on-site inspections, the original square grid structure of the façade is still intact and can be uncovered and integrated in order to reinstate the intended appearance of this iconic monument.

To address this issue, as well as other less significant points, the preservation strategy encompasses four main actions, briefly summarized as follows.

The first and most significant action concerns the façade of the building, which has been completely transformed, compromising the architectural identity of the Museum. The original façade will be restored, maintaining the existing metal frame and integrating new and better performing materials. In this process, the first step will be the dismantling of the current façade, which will enable an evaluation of the state of repair of the underlying metal grid. After carrying out the necessary repairs, the structure will be insulated and clad with a new aluminum finish, and new translucent panels will be installed to close the thermal envelope. The proposal is to use a system of innovative panels which guarantee better control of incoming light, improving the quality of both indoor climate conditions and the exhibition space. These can be dimmable (smart glass) panels and/or photovoltaic translucent panels. This solution will thus have a double output: it will restore the original appearance of the building, which largely determined the architectural and cultural value of the Museum, and will ensure a better overall visitor experience and conservation of artworks.

A second preservation action will focus on the entrance to the Museum, which has also been modified over the years, destroying its most markedly modernist features. Originally, the glazed entrance was situated behind the first row of pillars. The latter stood outside, and, together with the cantilevering canopy, provided a small entrance portico characterized by a dramatic contrast of light and shadow. Furthermore, the front of the canopy has been edged with alucobond elements, hiding the sharp, clean lines of the original design. As with the strategy adopted for the façades, we aim to uncover the original design of the Museum entrance, restoring its architectural qualities. The current glazing will be replaced with nonreflecting glazing and pushed backward to its original position. The alucobond cladding currently outlining the cantilevering canopy will be removed.[1]

The third preservation action aims to repair the damage caused by recent structural surveys. In order to test and assess the resistance of the concrete several samples were taken, leaving large gaps in the load-bearing monolithic pillars. Although some of the gaps have already been patched up, it is recommended to verify whether the repairs were adequately made, taking into account the structural relevance of the considered elements.

Finally, a fourth action will involve general cleaning, ordinary maintenance and local repairs.

State Museum of Arts, view from the park, strategy visualization

State Museum of Arts, exhibition floor view, strategy visualization

1 This action was implemented in 2023, while the book was being prepared. For the sake of consistency with the photographs and to avoid similar installations in the future, we chose to maintain this paragraph in the strategy description.

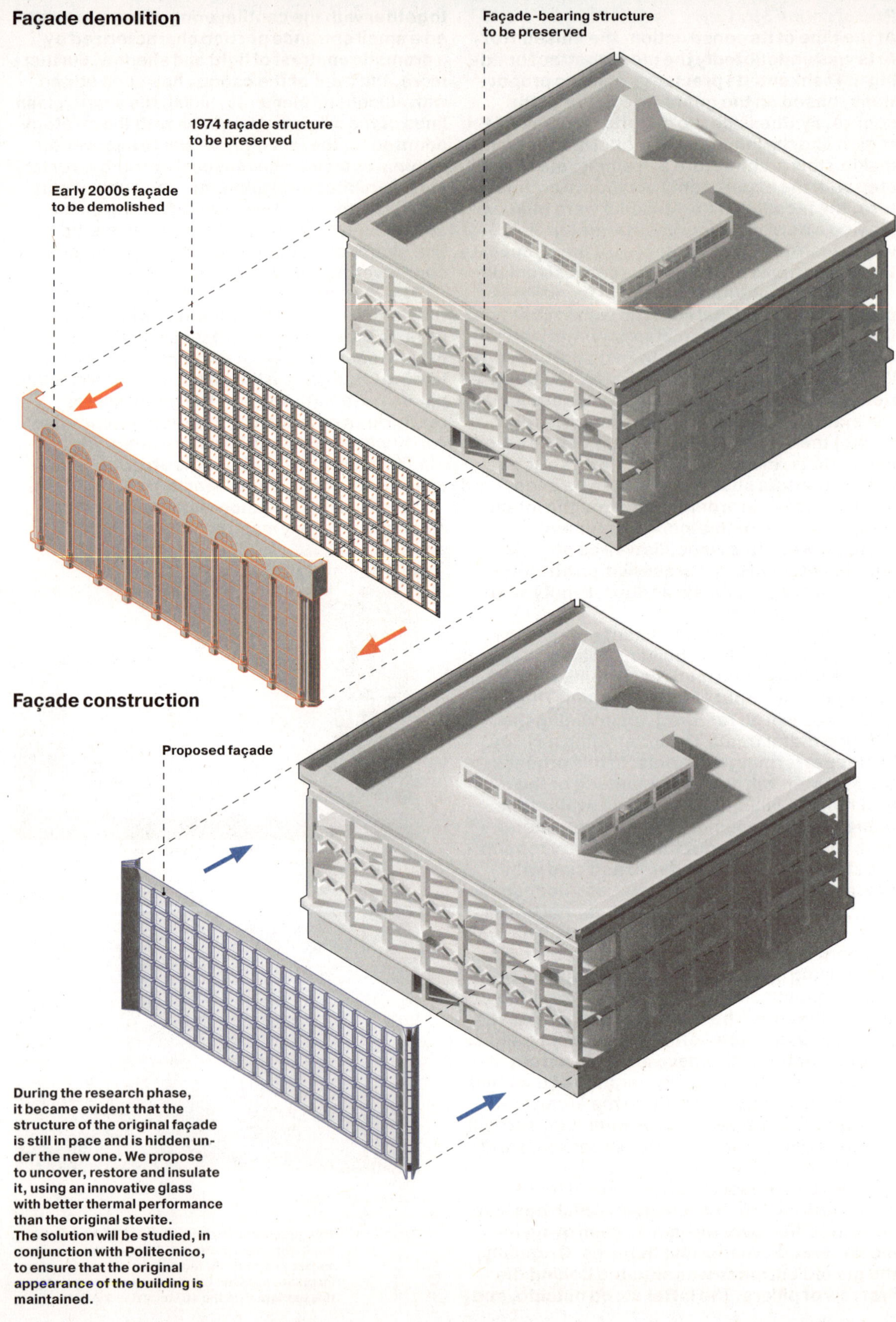

During the research phase, it became evident that the structure of the original façade is still in pace and is hidden under the new one. We propose to uncover, restore and insulate it, using an innovative glass with better thermal performance than the original stevite. The solution will be studied, in conjunction with Politecnico, to ensure that the original appearance of the building is maintained.

Today **Proposal**

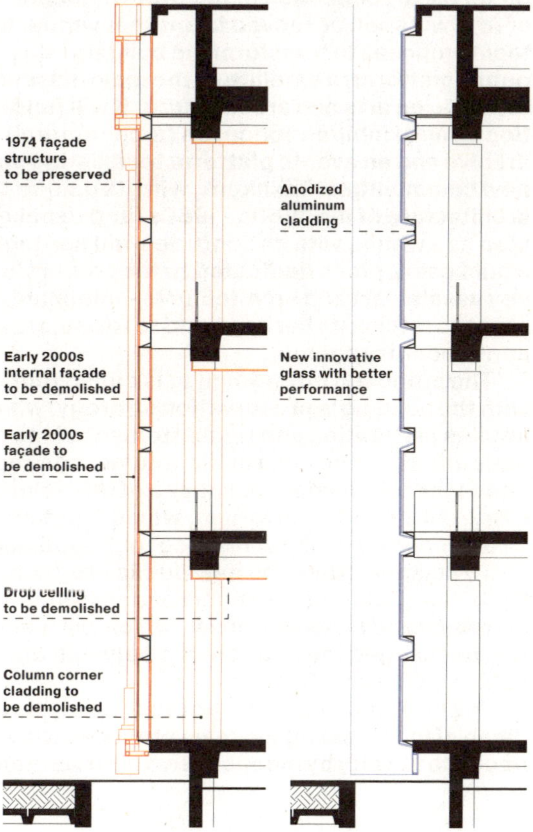

Today **Proposal**

1974 façade structure to be preserved

Early 2000s internal façade to be demolished

Early 2000s façade to be demolished

Drop ceiling to be demolished

Column corner cladding to be demolished

Anodized aluminum cladding

New innovative glass with better performance

Past

Corner of the façade, 1974

Future

Project proposal for the façade

Adaptation Strategy

Since the art collection of the State Museum of Arts will soon be moved to another venue, the team proposes to transform the building into a public platform, a satellite of the main museum, focusing on arts and architecture. It will function as an exhibition space, an (architectural) archive and an events platform for existing and new communities. Tashkent, with its unique architecture of the 1960s–1980s, and Uzbekistan as a whole, with its centuries-old heritage, would gain a place dedicated to the country's key assets—art and architecture—combined, a place to rethink its heritage and to formulate a contemporary agenda.

The proposed programming is consistent with the building's preservation strategy, which implies restoration and reinstatement of the appearance of the main cubic volume, floating above the hill. Inside, the spaces of this volume, centered around a tall atrium, would function as a temporary exhibition space, or Kunsthalle.

To accommodate the new public program, the building will undergo a partial transformation at ground and basement level, which will maintain unchanged the relationship between the cubic volume and the hill.

To counteract the hermetic (and "lonely") condition of the Museum, the team proposes to connect it to the city by means of two interventions.

At the urban scale, Iakub Kolas Street, which separates the park from the adjacent urban block to the north, will be transformed into a limited traffic zone, reducing and reorganizing the car parking areas and repaving and creating a more comfortable shaded environment for pedestrians. This way, the Museum and the park are not isolated by traffic on four sides and are easily accessible on foot. Iakub Kolas Street will also be designed as an element of the "cultural trail."

At the architectural scale, the first floor of the building will be transformed into a spacious public platform that contains a café, bookshop, educational rooms and auditoria and opens directly to Iakub Kolas Park. The basement will accommodate the archive and consultation areas, alongside modernized technical zones and storage.

A café/restaurant will be placed on the roof.

While the upper cubic volume is preserved, partially restoring and partially reinterpreting Savelii Rozenblium's original design, the lower volume (under the hill) will undergo a more significant transformation to provide the Museum with a contemporary public space. A vast flexible-use floor, connected to the park, will house educational and leisure programs for visitors and researchers.

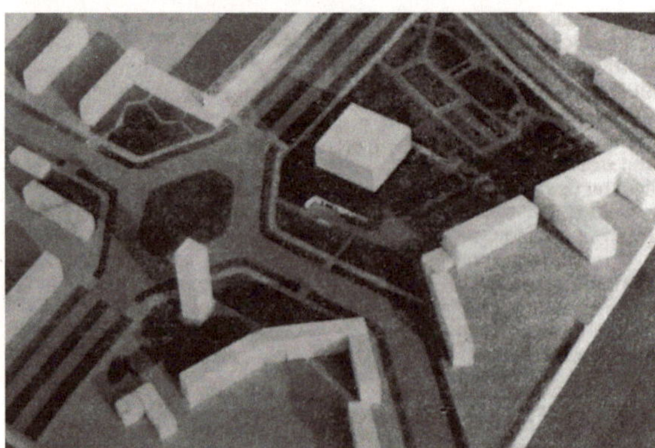

Option for an urban planning solution for the block around the State Museum of Arts, conceptual layout, 1967

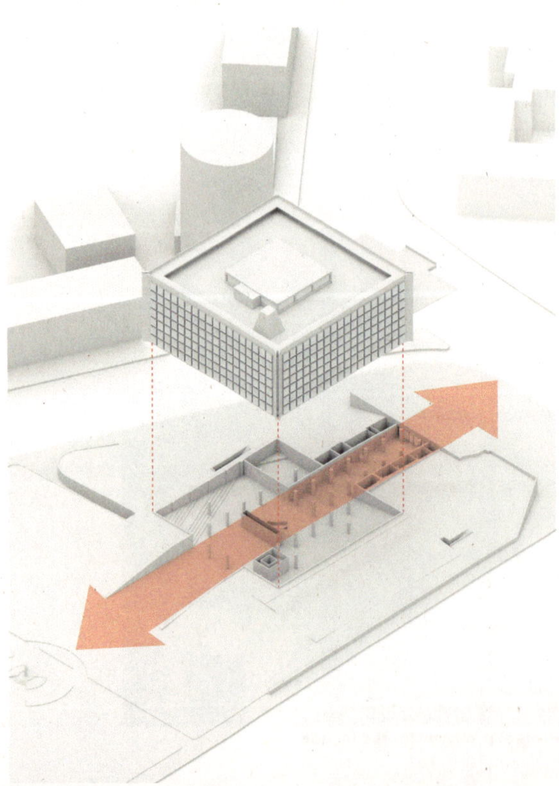

Ground floor connectivity

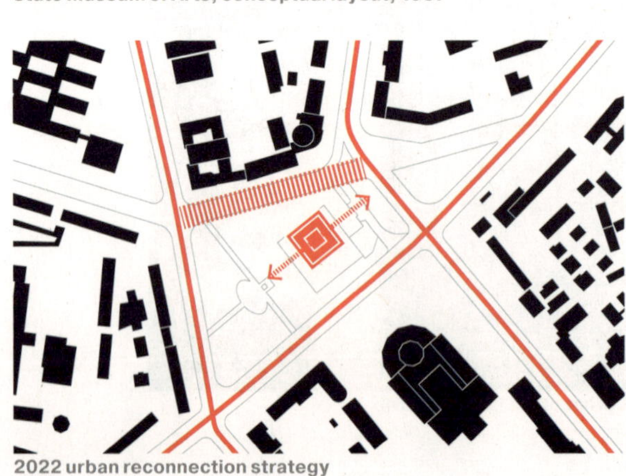

2022 urban reconnection strategy

View of the public ground floor

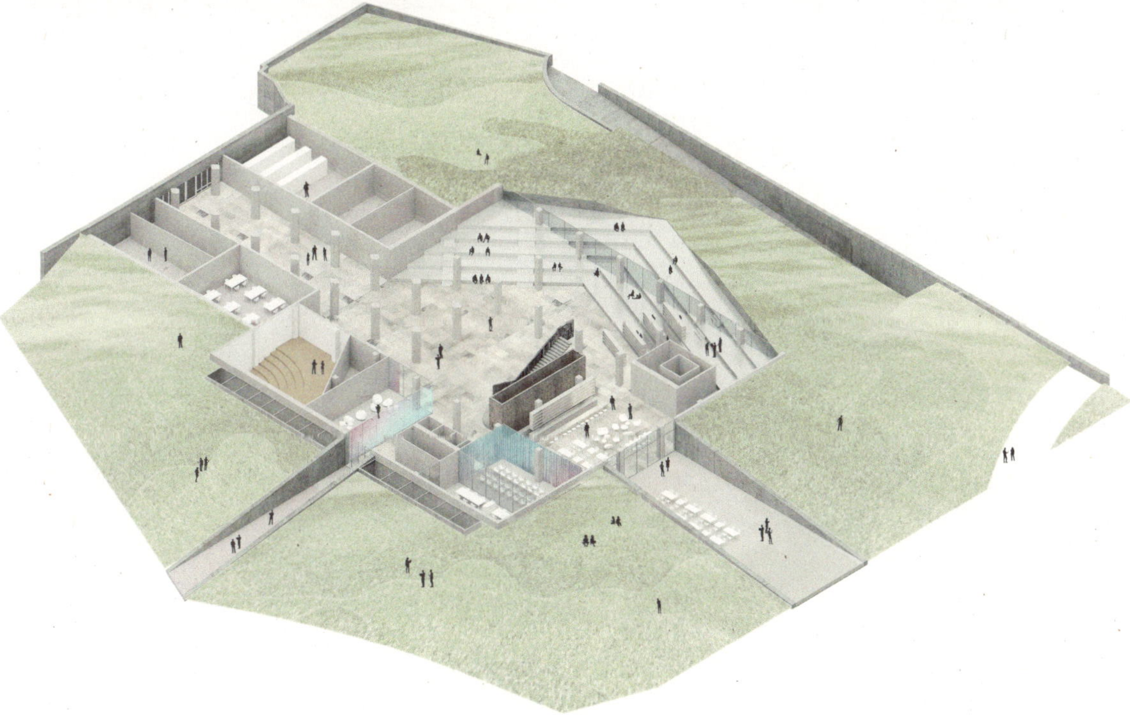

Public ground floor axonometric scheme

The Circus

Building position and address: 1 Sebzar Street, Tashkent

0 0.5 1km

The historical territory of today's Khadra Square, the north part of which is closed off by the Circus, was situated at the eastern side of the city center formed by the Chorsu Bazaar and the Gulbazar Mahalla. Without immersing ourselves in medieval history one should nevertheless say that radical changes to this territory took part during the Soviet period. First, the structure of the traditional mahallas on the western side of Khadra underwent serious change, with Pushkin Park being laid out and a sport stadium constructed. The first Uzbek theater also appeared there, known as the Khamza (the so-called People's House, 1928). The next stage of development of the square occurred in the late 1930s when work began on constructing Navoi Street, which linked the eastern and western parts of Tashkent. Khadra Square appeared on the street from the direction of the "old city." In the 1940s and early 1950s a fountain was erected here, and the hostel of the Mining Technical College was constructed on the right. By the time the design of the Circus began, Navoi Street had already been constructed as far as Akhunbabaev Square (Chorsu Hotel), but Furkat Street, which would later connect Khadra to the Peoples' Friendship Square, had not yet been planned in detail. By the late 1960s the urban planning significance of the square, which was located at the intersection of Navoi Street, Furkat Street, Hamza Street (Zarkainar) and Ahmad Donish Street (Sebzar), had finally been established, and the Circus became the main element of this complex city junction.

Main dimensions of the State Circus
General axonometric view

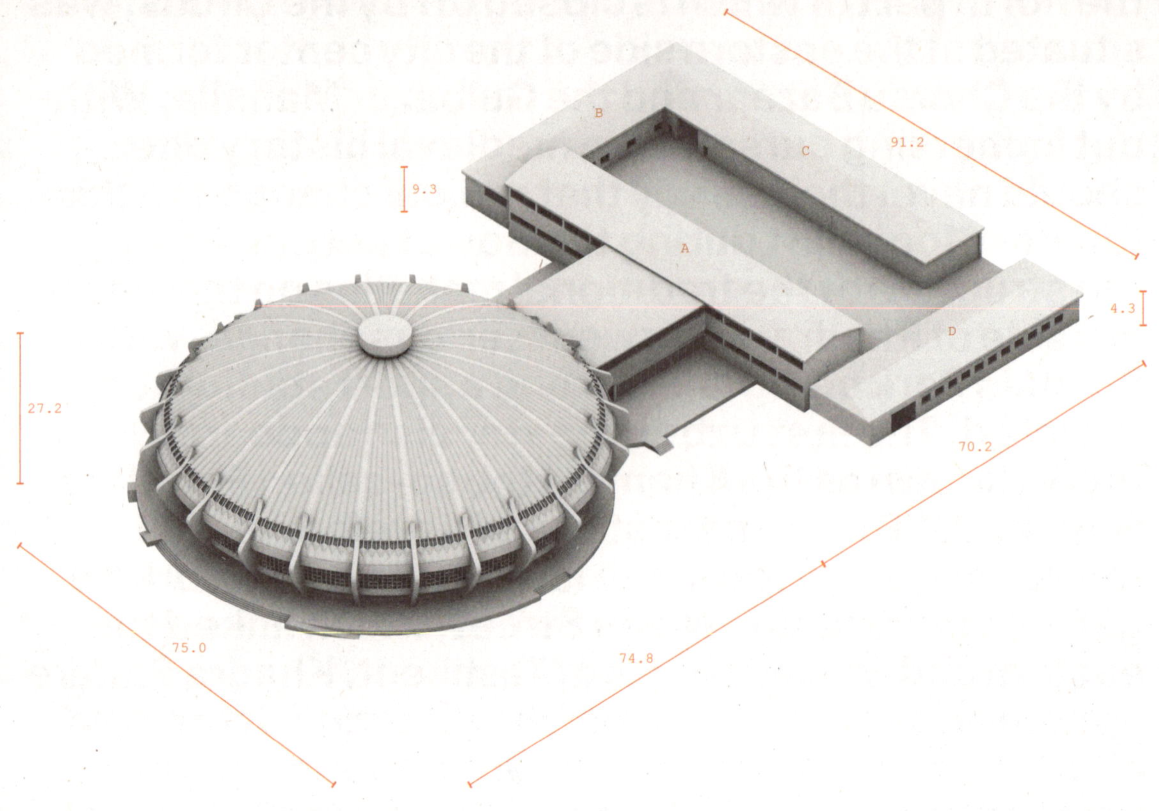

ACTORS	**Architects:**	**Genrikh Aleksandrovich, Gennadii Masiagin**
	Engineers:	**Semen Berkovich, Radik Muftakhov, Iu. Kalinin**
	Institute:	**Tashgiprogor**
DATES	**Design period:**	**1962–1970**
	Construction period:	**1965–1975 (interrupted by the earthquake)**
	Inauguration date:	**1975**
	Later interventions:	**After independence: Façade of upper foyer shifted outward. New finishes on the ceiling and ribs in the lobby and on the upper level.**
USE	**Current use:**	**Circus**
	Original use:	**Circus**
	Suitability of current use:	**The building was designed to house the State Circus, so the architecture is still fit for purpose. However, considering the contemporary concept and functioning of circuses, the lack of adequate workshop and storage spaces and rehearsal rooms is noted. Furthermore, the spaces for animals are inadequate, and the idea of the presence of animals at the circus should be re-evaluated.**
	Space utilization:	**Full utilization. There is a lack of functional spaces.**
DIMENSIONS	**Number of floors:**	**Pavilion — Basement + 4 floors Courtyard building — 2 floors (A,B,C), 1 floor (D)**

Length:	Pavilion	74.8 m
	Courtyard building	70.2 m
Dome diameter:		75.0 m
Width:	Pavilion	75.0 m
	Courtyard building	91.2 m
Height:	Pavilion	27.2 m
	Courtyard building	9.3 m (A,B,C), 4.3 m (D)
Gross floor area (first floor):	Pavilion	3,256.0 m²
	Courtyard building	3,170.0 m²
Gross floor area (total):		19,450.0 m²

The Circus

A relatively large number of documentary sources were found when researching the Tashkent Circus. These are, firstly, working drawings and sketches of 1965–1970 from the archive of Tashgiprogor; secondly, working documents from the period of design and decision-making, one of the most important of which is the record of the discussion of the project in March 1969; texts about the Circus in architectural journals of the 1970s; photographs taken during construction from the Republic of Uzbekistan Documentary Film and Photo Archive; and others. These documents allow us to make a considered judgment of the key stages of the design process, but they are not sufficient for a detailed understanding of the initial stage of design (1962–1964) and a number of aspects of the completed building.

The Problem of Dates and the Urban Planning Context

The first working drawings of the Circus in the Tashgiprogor archive date to March 1965. However, according to later memories of lead architect Genrikh Aleksandrovich, his team received the design commission in 1962 and then, in 1964, after consideration by Gosstroi USSR and other Moscow institutions, it was confirmed. Construction began in 1965 but was interrupted by the 1966 earthquake.[1] Documents in the Tashkent City Archive do not contradict these dates. According to them, the decision on design and construction of the Circus was recorded in a special resolution of the Central Committee of the Communist Party of Uzbekistan and the Council of Ministers of the Uzbek SSR dated August 16, 1962. Responsibility for the project was handed to Tashgiprogor. The institute was instructed to complete the development of the project plan in the first quarter of 1963 and the working drawings by September 1 of that year. In January 1963 Tashgiprogor tried to get a decision from the city authorities about a plot for construction, without which it was impossible to begin work on the project.[2]

The existing documents also show that in May and June 1964, disagreements remained between Tashkent and Moscow regarding the number of spectators that could be accommodated in the new Circus. In a resolution of May 21, 1964, the Council of Ministers of the USSR confirmed a capacity of 3,000 seats; then Director of Gosstroi Nikolai Baranov reduced this figure to 2,000, with Chief Architect of Tashkent Aleksandr Iakushev requesting that the capacity be raised to 2,750.[3] This indicates that by May 1964 only the schematic plan of the project had been developed, and that the site was already selected.

All of these details confirm that the launch of design of the Circus occurred before the All-Union competition of 1964 for the center of Tashkent, which reshaped the urban planning scale of the whole space into nuclei of the "new" and "old" city. The logic of constructing the Circus on Komsomolskaia Square (Khadra Square) was different, yet in some ways similar,

1 Genrikh Aleksandrovich, "Schast'e v professii [Happiness in the Profession]," *Arkhitektura i stroitel'stvo Uzbekistana* [*Architecture and Construction of Uzbekistan*], no. 10, 1988, 28–29.

2 Oleg Rushikovskii, "Pis'mo (no. 84) presedateliu ispolkoma Tashgorsoveta tov. Nishanovu R.N. i nachal'niku APU Tashgorispolkoma Iakushevu A.V. ot 21 ianvaria 1963 goda [Letter (no. 84) to Chairman of the Executive Committee of Tashkent City Council Comrade R.N. Nishanov and Director of the Architecture and Planning Administration of Tashkent City Executive Committee A.V. Iakushev dated January 21, 1963," *Perepiska s gosuchrezhdeniiami o stroitel'stve, proektirovanii i blagoustroistve g. Tashkenta* [*Correspondence with State Organizations about the Construction, Design and Landscaping of Tashkent*], Tashkent City Archive, fund 36, list 2, item 738, on 140 sheets, 100.

3 "Telegramma A. Iakusheva N. Baranovu ot 19 iiunia 1964 goda [Telegram from A. Iakushev to N. Baranov dated June 19, 1964]," *Rasporiazheniia po APU za 1964 god: O proketirovanii i stroitel'stve gostinitsy i tsirka v Tashkente, 27.02.1964–27.12.1964* [*Resolutions of the Architecture and Planning Administration for 1964: On the Design and Construction of a Hotel and a Circus in Tashkent, February 27–December 27, 1964*], Tashkent City Archive, fund 36, list 2, item 146, on 24 sheets, 15.

to the history of the Panoramic Cinema. The idea was to develop Navoi Street, which was conceived as the main artery connecting "new" Tashkent and the "old city" nucleus between Chorsu and Khadra squares. Here, the techniques of traditional European urban planning were employed, with perimeter construction and "pocket" squares that made the spatial appearance of the grand avenue more varied and expressive. By 1962 Khadra Square was already partially formed. From the eastern side it was faced by the monumental façade of the five-story hostel of Tashkent Mining Technical College, from the west by single-story buildings behind which there was a working prerevolutionary tram depot. In the center of the square was a fountain and pool. Accordingly, as with the Panoramic Cinema, it was necessary to incorporate a new modernist building into the historical environment.

Cultural Context

The siting of the Circus in the nucleus of the "old city" combined at least two themes. One concerns the history of circus buildings in Tashkent. Many specialists long believed that circus was a European art form imported to Central Asia under the tsarist administration and then developed by the Soviet authorities. Before the 1917 revolution two circuses did appear almost simultaneously in "new" Tashkent: Georgii Tsintsadze's Coliseum (1912) and Filipp Iupatov's circus (1914), which was built on the same street. This was a venue for touring companies, which were popular in the city. In the Soviet period the circus had its own troupe, and when Iupatov's theater was destroyed in the Tashkent earthquake it was replaced by a circus tent that was initially erected in the same place and then moved slightly north. Accordingly, the first four versions of the Tashkent circus appeared in the same part of the city, within a radius of 350 meters.

Meanwhile, the local circus tradition was long-standing and varied. Although they were not linked together and not part of a professional guild of circus people, in medieval Central Asia there were professional performers (acrobats, tightrope walkers, equilibrists, trapeze artists, jugglers, illusionists, fakirs and animal trainers, as well as clowns and jesters) who made a living playing on the street, and there were national games in the form of equestrian sporting contests.[4] From the second half of the nineteenth century these national collectives adopted the experience of touring circuses. The choice of the "old city" for the construction of the Circus is evidence that the architects and planners understood that circus was not just a "European" art form and would also be popular among residents of traditional mahallas.

The Circus in the USSR: Standard Designs for Unique Buildings

Whereas in the West in the 1960s and 1970s circuses continued to function in old buildings or in tents, the Soviet state, which supported established circus troupes and the entire circus infrastructure as an art form, decided that it was necessary to construct specially equipped, contemporary buildings for them. One issue of the journal *Arkhitektura SSSR* (*Architecture of the USSR*) for 1972 is dedicated to the work of Moscow's Mezentsev Central Scientific Research and Experimental Project Institute for Entertainment and Sport Facilities (TsNIIEP). In an article on circuses, architect I. Chipiga reported on the opening of twenty new circuses and the construction of circuses based on the institute's designs in twenty-seven cities of the USSR.[5] The range of buildings featured reveals the following palette of possibilities open to clients and architects. At the lowest level of complexity were standard designs developed at Moscow's TsNIIEP, which required nothing more than to be placed within local conditions. Chipiga also stated that of the twenty-seven Soviet circuses erected in 1972, sixteen were based on a single design developed for the northern regions of Russia.[6] More complicated projects required adaptation to the conditions in a particular city. For example, the circuses in Ashkhabad, Dushanbe and Alma-Ata were initially intended to be built based on a single design, but adaptations meant either that the only things they had in common were the main structural details and overall massing or that, despite being based on standard designs and construction methods, they were unrecognizable. Finally, the most interesting circus buildings were those with a capacity greater than the standard 2,000 seats. Permission for their design and approval of the project had to come from Gosstroi in Moscow.

Genrikh Aleksandrovich gave a summary of the project approval process in Moscow. "Everyone know S.V. Ivanov, whose quibbling was based on a desire to remove the commission from us and give it to the Muscovites. We young architects had the unexpected support of the director of the department, N. Smirnov, whose words I still recall today: 'To make a tiger out of a hare you have to feed it meat.' We were the

4 For more information on local forms of circus art see Pulatzhan Tashkenbaev, *Tsirkovoe iskusstvo v Uzbekistane vo vtoroi polovine XIX–nachale XX vv.* [*Circus Art in Uzbekistan in the Late Nineteenth and Early Twentieth Centuries*] (Candidate of Art History diss., Tashkent, 1993).

5 I. Chipiga, "Tsirki [Circuses]," *Arkhitektura SSSR* [*Architecture of the USSR*], no. 7, 1972, 28.

6 Ibid.

Kazan Circus, 1967; architects: U. Alparov, V. Panova, G. Pichuev

hares."[7] Relating a similar story about the approval of the design of the famous circus in Kazan, architect Daniil Efimov explained how difficult this task was: "At that time it was almost impossible for regional design organizations to receive permission for the development of an individual design for a public building that was significant at the city level. Moscow kept a tight rein on the monopolistic right of the capital's design institutions to create individual projects, allowing those from other cities to work only with standard designs which had at some point been created at the center."[8] Accordingly, in the 1960s architects from outside the capital rarely had the opportunity to design a nonstandard circus, and exclusions were explained as due to either force of circumstances or the innovative potential of the project. This was largely the case with Tashkent. The appearance of the Tashkent Circus was not only strikingly individual but also specific to its urban context.

Since in the 1960s circuses were designed en masse, their overall planning layout quickly became rather diffused. It involved the combination of a central, circular domed structure with a service block in the form of a square with an internal courtyard. The service block incorporated spaces with a broad variety of functions. Some segments, such as the areas for housing animals, required strict isolation, and there were major differences between the spaces needed for big cats, large animals (elephants, horses, etc.), monkeys and small animals. A food preparation area was normally located nearby. Other structural parts of the service block included the administrative spaces, areas for making and storing sets and costumes, places for the preparation and consumption of food, a garage and an additional rehearsal space. All of these varied areas had functions which were difficult to combine and were a focus of the architects' efforts to make them as inconspicuous as possible. The impressive central structure with a foyer, performance hall and a high, domed roof was always at the forefront.

7 Genrikh Aleksandrovich, "Schast'e v professii [Happiness in the Profession]."

8 Daniil Efimov, "Put' letaiushchei tarelki [The Path of the Flying Saucer]," *Zhurnal Kazan'* [*Kazan Magazine*], May 30, 2019, http://kazan-journal.ru/news/kazan-i-kazantsyi/put-letayushchey-tarelki.

The Initial Solution

Design of the Tashkent Circus began in 1962, simultaneously with the design of the building of the Central Committee of the Communist Party of Uzbekistan. If the construction process had not been delayed, Tashkent would have had one more example of early-1960s architecture which may have been no less distinctive than the Panoramic Cinema. However, in the Soviet setting the Circus was clearly a lower priority than the Central Committee, and the process was delayed. In the late 1960s and early 1970s public demands of architecture changed significantly, and as a result the finished Circus was of interest for the fact that it reflected the main landmarks of the aesthetic and cultural evolution of this fifteen-year period. We will take a look at the main stages.

Genrikh Aleksandrovich's first sketches showed a building with a "space aesthetic," which was typical of the early 1960s. In this respect it was not unique. Buildings clearly inspired by themes of space and spacecraft left their mark on the history of Soviet architecture, from the Museum of Cosmonautics in Kaluga (1961–1967) and the Ostankino TV Tower

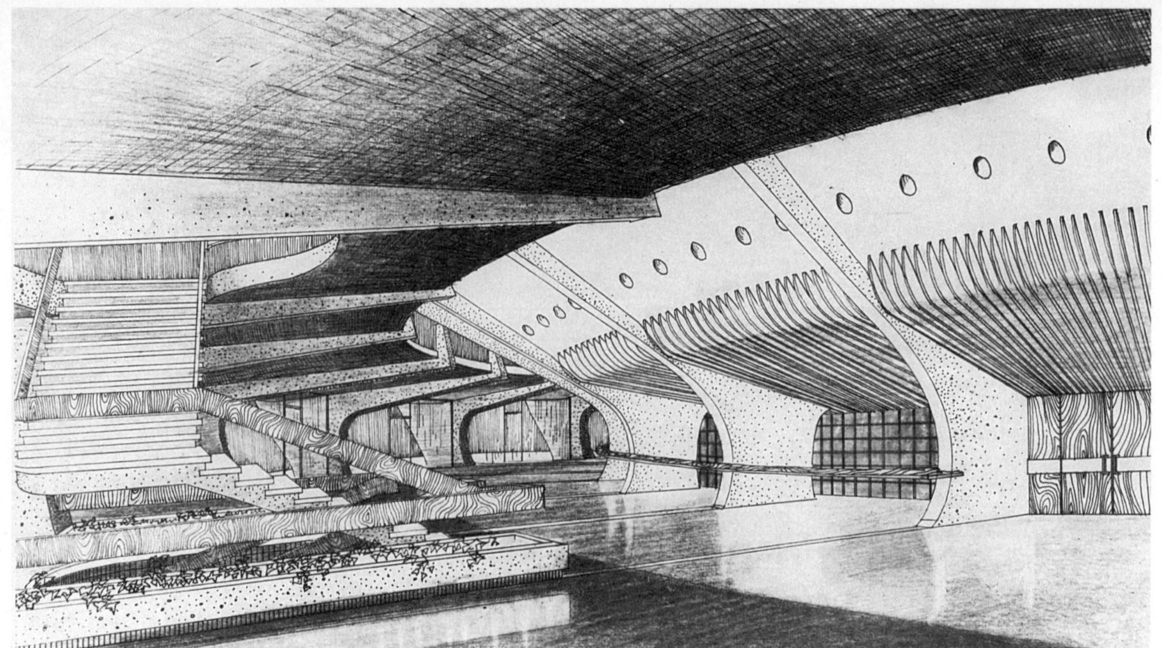

Tashkent Circus foyer, drawing, 1963–1969

(1960–1967) to the Institute of Scientific and Technical Information in Kyiv (1964–1971) and the Sun Heliocomplex in Parkent (1981–1987). This real feature of Soviet architecture should not be confused with the later exoticizing approach to the cultural "otherness" of Soviet buildings developed by some Western scholars and photographers such as Frédéric Chaubin[9] and taken up by Russian specialists who, jumping at these ideas, enthusiastically identified "cosmic" forms in any atypical Soviet building, even those playing with historical styles such as the Union of Artists Exhibition Hall or the Lenin Museum in Tashkent.[10] Although the themes and genres of circus art might seem to have no connection to outer space, the atmosphere of the first years of spaceflight influenced them. A number of circus buildings took a form inspired by flying saucers, starting with the abovementioned circus in Kazan, which literally illustrated this idea, and ending with the numerous Soviet circuses that either were actually inspired by the UFOs that had gripped the public imagination or were perceived in that way by critics and journalists. The space theme combined successfully with the spirit of the Modern Movement. Embodying the break for other worlds by the inhabitants of Earth, it minimalized national differences and confirmed the universal planetary identity of the new architecture. Genrikh Aleksandrovich's initial, early 1960s sketches for the Tashkent Circus were undoubtedly part of this wave, and since they were created almost simultaneously with the design of the circus in Kazan, they significantly anticipated and formed it. However, from the very beginning the Tashkent project had a number of special features.

In defining the evolution of Soviet architecture many people justifiably contrast the lightness and transparency of buildings of the early and mid-1960s with the Brutalist metaphysics and philosophy that would triumph later. The morphology of circus buildings, which made a raised circular performance hall with a dome and an encircling foyer almost unavoidable, inspired architects to play with one of modernism's favorite themes, "the abolition of mass." As a result, the foyers of most Soviet circuses featured continuous glazing, above which a "flying saucer" hung as if weightless. Transparent foyers were created not only for circuses in the northern and central latitudes of the USSR, where insolation was considered a good thing, but also in cities such as Ashkhabad and Dushanbe, i.e. in hotter and sunnier parts of the country. Aleksandrovich's design, on the contrary, originally excluded both lightness and transparency. The architecture was not aiming for the effect of weightlessness. The building was more reminiscent of a powerful sculptural form fixed to the slope of the relief from Eski Juva Square to Khadra. The foyer, which was spa-

9 See Frédéric Chaubin, *CCCP: Cosmic Communist Constructions Photographed* (Cologne: Taschen, 2010).

10 V. G. Ivanov, *Arkhitektura, vdokhnovlennaia kosmosom: Obraz budushchego v pozdnesovetskoi arkhitekture* [*Architecture Inspired by Space: The Image of the Future in Late Soviet Architecture*] (St. Petersburg: Borei Art, 2017).

cious and sculptural, faced the city with the projecting ribs of the massive concrete frames on which the dome was placed. This muscular framework physically revealed the strength of the structure and the mass of the building. If it was a "flying saucer," then it was securely berthed. In accentuating the "mooring" place, the architect proposed a witty and expressive treatment of the ticket office block. Usually placed inside the building, in the main volume of the standard circus, the ticket office block was removed to the western part of the complex and, thanks to the relief, situated in the semi-basement part of the building. Having bought tickets, viewers could go up to the first-floor level via a semicircular staircase that was developed using the rhythm of four transverse vertical pylons. They played the role of cores that visually fixed the connection between the sloping form of the "ship" and the "mooring."

As the main sides of the foyer—east, south and west—were subject to sunlight, the architect developed one of Tashkent's most elegant sun-protection grilles. Deciding not to quote the sun protection of the Latin American and European modernists, he explored more complex geometric motifs based on Kufic epigraphy. Together with the heavyweight form of the concrete, the geometric design of the sun protection gave the building a clearly southern and, in connotative terms, "old city" spirit. Since the Circus was to be a direct neighbor of Chorsu, the architect considered it necessary to create a building which, in terms of its weighted materiality, would match the historical environment.

Even so, the sketches of the Circus did not lose their "cosmic sound." As well as the clearly readable forms of the "ship," the space references were supplemented by the plastic nature of the foyer with its rhythmically placed circular "portholes," which reinforced the perception of the building as a "space station." Here, as in the cabin of a spacecraft, there were no elements of a post and beam system, with the structure appearing to experience not vertical loads but the multidirectional loads of the cosmos. The foyer had two levels. Its circular gallery adjoined the external perimeter, and "bridges" from it led to the performance hall. These elements also reinforced the visual perception of the building as an imposing spaceship with special transit and recreational zones connected by the central, domed performance hall.

In terms of structure the main block comprised twenty-four radial reinforced concrete frames that were rigidly connected to each other. This helped them to support the thrust of the dome rising above them, which was formed of radial metal half trusses embedded in the central drum. The profile of the reinforced concrete frames was designed so that they could form the supports for the amphitheater of the main performance hall and the gallery of the second floor, as well as the dome. This freed up space for the foyer, as there were no vertical supports "messing up" the space of the first and second floors.

From the functional point of view the Circus was conceived as a universal building that could be a venue for public meetings, concerts and other events in addition to circus performances. As well as the traditional staff areas in the "gods" of the performance hall,[11] this was also the location for several projection rooms, a commentary box, a radio and TV control room, a newsreel control room and so on. The architect explained his concept for film projection and lighting as follows: "In the middle and upper levels of the amphitheater there are lighting platforms for spotlights. In the upper zone the lighting boxes are combined with film projection spaces for screenings. Using them, special films accompanying the circus performance can be shown simultaneously on seven screens around the perimeter of the performance hall."[12] By the late 1960s architects were already considering the use of various media in the space, providing the opportunity to heighten the effects of one art form by using others.

The planning of the spectators' block completely correlated with its centric structure. Entry to the performance hall was from three sides, the east, west and south. Even though the south side incorporated fountains and a grand staircase and there were more doors, the entrances were relatively equal, which justified the form of the circular foyer and the location of the ticket offices to the west of the "main" entrance. For the convenience of spectators there was a cloakroom in the basement and a buffet on the second level. There were broad staircases between the levels of the foyer, and access to the performance hall from the second floor was via "bridges." The exterior pedestrian gallery on the second level, which offered views of the city through the sun-protection grille, was an original element of the foyer layout not found in other Soviet circuses. As well as having an entertainment function it also had a climatic logic, improving the sun protection of the foyer. The performance hall was symmetrical. As well as the lower and upper levels of the amphitheater, on the northern side there was a performers' entrance to the circus ring, above which there was a space for the circus orchestra.

11 This refers to the light projection room, the conductor and orchestra's room, the sound amplification room and the recording studio.

12 Genrikh Aleksandrovich, "Zdanie Tashkentskogo gosudarstvennogo tsirka [The Building of the Tashkent State Circus]," *Stroitel'stvo i arkhitektura Uzbekistana* [*Construction and Architecture of Uzbekistan*], no. 4, 1971, 28.

Tashkent State Circus construction site

The service block was designed in a way traditional for 1960s circuses. It was a square with one- and two-story structures around an internal courtyard. Adjacent to the main performance hall was a performers' area, while garages and storage areas were situated in the north part of the service block, stables in the west part, and an administrative area in the east part. The performers' area was the most complex in terms of organization. Here, separated by a corridor, on one side were staff areas such as the horse trainer's room, the saddler's room, the first aid station, the animals' kitchen and cold room and a space for monkeys, and on the other side were large living areas for big cats and large and small animals, the veterinary clinic, the isolation ward and auxiliary areas and a canteen for staff. The problematic element in this plan was the location of an additional rehearsal space at the point where the service block met the main performance hall. This meant that special conditions applied to rehearsals: for example, the big cats had to enter the ring through the additional space, which required supplementary safety measures. In some other Soviet circuses (for instance, in Alma-Ata) the rehearsal space was isolated. This made the process of preparation easier and gave performers more freedom.

Redevelopment of the Project in 1968–1969

Construction began in 1965 and was frozen in 1966. In the meantime, the design was significantly redeveloped. The working drawings that remain at Tashgiprogor were produced in 1968 and 1969. The detailed project was sent to the administration of the Union of Architects of Uzbekistan for discussion. The extant record of the meeting which took place on March 18, 1969, noted the revision of a number of aesthetic priorities.

There were twenty-three people at the meeting, including architectural civil servants and leading architects of different generations. Regarding the aesthetic logic, the speakers mainly focused on four problematic areas of the design: the lack of a "grand entrance," the "ship" form of the design, the lack of attributes of "national architecture" and the color of the dome, which had by that time become turquoise. Leonid Karash noted that "the dome is a traditional color and this is good."[13] Architect Palieva did not agree: "The color of the dome is confusing. The colored dome has the look of a roof and is not perceived as a single volume. If the entire building was white, it would be perceived as a unified whole."[14] Karash was against this: "The idea of using white plaster is less typical of Uzbekistan and the white will soon turn dusty gray. Like the Tashkent Hotel. A texture should be selected where the color will not change, at least in the next five years."[15]

The majority considered the absence of a grand entrance to be undesirable. Although the foyer of the building had a circular belt form, the segments of which were equal, Aleksandrovich's colleagues did not like the fact that "the main entrance is not emphasized," while "the entrance to the ticket office vestibule is heavily emphasized and gives the impression that this is the main entrance" (Gennadii Korobovtsev).[16]

Another irritant in the late 1960s was the "spaceship theme." A. Petrosov put it this way:

13 "Protokol no. 1 rasshirennogo zasedaniia sektsii 'individual'nykh proektov i inter'erov' Pravleniia SA UzSSR, g. Tashkent, 18 marta 1969 [Protocol No. 1 of the Expanded Meeting of the Section of 'Individual Projects and Interiors' of the Administration of the Union of Architects of the Uzbek SSR, Tashkent, March 18, 1969]," *Soiuz arkhitektorov UzSSR: Tvorcheskie sektsii; Materialy deiatel'nosti sektsii individual'nogo proektirovaniia i inter'erov* [*Union of Architects of the UzSSR: Creative Sections; Materials on the Activities of the Section of Individual Projects and Interiors*], National Archive of the Republic of Uzbekistan, fund 2532, list 2, item 89, on 12 sheets, 3.
14 Ibid., 5.
15 Ibid., 3–4.
16 Ibid. 4.

Circus façade, version of the project, 1963–1969

"The entrance to the circus is crushed; the architecture is heavy and oppressive. The spaceship form is a very heavy form."[17] Korobovtsev disagreed, referencing the international context: "I do not agree that the circus is heavy. If we observe the direction of world architecture, we will see that forms have increased in weight. This trend in architecture is reflected very well by the authors."[18] But the main object of criticism was something different. Konstantin Babievskii expressed his doubts the most clearly: "National architecture is completely absent in the interior. The spaceship form is dominant, and the ceiling looks very plain. The rich material possibilities of national architecture should be used in the interior."[19]

As a result, the requirements of the resolution of the meeting included the following:

- It is necessary to include elements of national architecture in the interior.
- It is necessary to emphasize the main entrance and somewhat tone down the entrance to the ticket office vestibule.
- White should be considered as a color for the dome.

The resolution did not include the requirement to reject the "spaceship" aesthetic, but it was implicit, since this aesthetic was in clear opposition to "national architecture." Accordingly, the artistic solution of 1964 began to be perceived critically by the architectural community five years later. The subsequent metamorphoses can be traced by comparing the finished building with the working drawings of 1968–1969.

The Evolution of the Project and the Construction Process

In describing the building under construction, the architect tried to remove the now inappropriate associations with space aesthetics. "The external outline of the building," he wrote, "is reminiscent of the mount of a signet ring, the core of which is a dome."[20] This image was developed in the skylights of the service gallery on the third floor: they were supplemented with a belt with a ribbed pattern. The sun-protection grilles were encrusted with cotton bolls, which had become a symbol of Soviet Uzbekistan. The materials also changed. If in the project of 1968–1969 the main façade material was whitewashed plaster,[21] in the concluding stage of design and construction it was decided to clad the reinforced concrete ribs with marble. Gazgan and Nurata marble was laid in a color scheme that moved from dark gray at the bottom of the building to white and then pink at the top. The attachment of the stone slabs to the bends in the ribs was fragile and the broken pieces produced a domino effect which meant that a material that had seemed durable began to degrade a decade after the completion of construction. The vault of the dome was left light gray. In order to develop a "jewellery-like" connotation, a decorative drum was added at the top. It may have been designed in order to place illuminated advertising, which was one of the demands of the discussion of 1969,[22] but instead of advertising, the word "Circus" appeared on the south side. The architect did not do anything to accentuate the central entrance.

The most radical transformations took place in the interior. The image of a space station made way for a celebratory, palace-like feeling. Whereas initially the main expressive motif of the foyer was the interflowing plastic forms of

17 Ibid.
18 Ibid.
19 Ibid.

20 Genrikh Aleksandrovich, "Zdanie Tashkentskogo gosudarstvennogo tsirka [The Building of the Tashkent State Circus]."
21 "Tsirk na 3000 mest v gorode Tashkente: Zrelishchnyi korpus; Otdelochnye raboty [A Circus with 3,000 Seats in Tashkent: Spectators' Block; Finishing Works]," Technical Archive of Tashgiprogor, project 22.2.4, list 6 (unclear), July 4, 1968.
22 The wish expressed by Leonid Karash was number one in the list of requirements of the resolution of the Union of Architects. See "Protokol no. 1... [Protocol No. 1...]," 5.

the vaults, staircases and bridges, in the finished building the main element was the décor, which was made up of heterogeneous ornamentation. From the project of 1968–1969 the foyer inherited the geometric black-and-white floor pattern of white marble and black gabbro. The entrances to the performance hall at the level of the second-floor "bridges" were decorated with concentric oval arches with traditional ganch plaster carving. Similar ganch arabesques appeared on the ribs of the reinforced concrete ribs and the vaults that filled the space between the ribs from the performance-hall side. Circular rosettes replaced the previous "portholes." The sides of the reinforced concrete ribs were clad with polished rose Gazgan marble that differed in color from the black-and-white floor. On the first-floor level the designers added ceramic panels that were neither thematically nor stylistically connected: here one can see circus performers, circus animals, abstract geometric patterns, heritage buildings and contemporary buildings of Uzbekistan's cities. On the second floor, stained glass windows were installed at the level of the sun-protection grilles, meaning that on looking through them a person could see three layers of ornament: the original sun-protection grille with Kufic motifs, the cotton bolls encrusted on it and the pattern of the stained glass, which had its own logic.

Consequently, on completion of construction the initial image could be seen in the external appearance of the Circus—the form of the flying saucer was too active to be completely canceled out—as could the subsequent layers formed by the intermediate solutions of 1968–1969 and the historicist decoration of the early 1970s, which was evidence of a change in aesthetic priorities. It is interesting that the same professional quorum that, at the end of the 1960s, effectively forced the architect to change the initial concept by giving it "national features" would later be critical of their "crude and somewhat tasteless" execution.[23] On the whole, in the early 1980s the Circus was a favorite of the Tashkent architectural community. Specialists from UzNIIPgradostroitel'stva and Tashgenplan put it in an honorable fifth place, those from Tashgiprogor put it in fourth/fifth, and TashZNIIEP specialists placed it eighth. This perception changed in the twenty-first century, with the interior of the Circus being perceived very positively, on a level with the Navoi Theater. A Russian author who, for obvious reasons, wished to demonstrate the importance of Moscow's input to Tashkent architecture, wrote: "The interiors of the foyer were influenced by those of the Alisher Navoi Theater, which was constructed in 1947 in Tashkent by the architect of the Lenin Museum in Moscow, Academician A.V. Shchusev. This theatrical building became a classic of the Soviet period in the history of the architecture of Uzbekistan as its décor made active use of folk crafts that had been preserved in the republic. As in the interiors of the Navoi Theater, the circus interiors employed encrustation, wood and alabaster carving, and patterned floors."[24]

The Contemporary Situation

Over time many elements of the Circus have become dilapidated. The marble cladding of the external surfaces of the frames was completely removed. Today in its place there is crudely painted concrete and plastic banners. The wooden railings in the foyer, which remained from the mid-1960s project, were replaced with marble, and their balusters are reminiscent of the aesthetic of a house of culture of the Stalinist decades. The external pedestrian gallery of the foyer was removed and the façade of the second floor was moved right up to the sun-protection grilles. This made it impossible to clean them regularly and prevented foyer visitors from going out to get some fresh air. The Circus dome was painted bright turquoise. The physical wear and tear of the building means that the problems and their solutions require urgent discussion.

23 Iosif Notkin and Shukur Askarov, "O kachestve arkhitektury [On the Quality of Architecture]," *Stroitel'stvo i arkhitektura Uzbekistana* [*Construction and Architecture of Uzbekistan*], no. 4, 1981, 9.

24 V. G. Ivanov, *Arkhitektura, vdokhnovlennaia kosmosom: Obraz budushchego v pozdnesovetskoi arkhitekture* [*Architecture Inspired by Space: The Image of the Future in Late Soviet Architecture*], 101.

ARCHITECT GENRIKH ALEKSANDROVICH

Place and year of birth:
Odesa, 1928 (evacuated to Tashkent in 1941)

Place and year of death:
Israel, 2008

Education:
1945–1950, Architecture Department of Central Asia Polytechnic Institute (SazPI)

Genrikh Aleksandrovich studied and began working before Khrushchëv's reform of construction. He recalled that among his teachers were architects and historians with conservative views and his main student impressions were linked to the eighteenth- and nineteenth-century palaces and public buildings of St. Petersburg.

After graduating from SazPI he worked in Ashkhabad for ten years. Two years before he arrived in the city there was a catastrophic earthquake (1948) that was much stronger and more destructive than the one in Tashkent. Since it was necessary to reconstruct Ashkhabad almost from the ground up, for the young architect this period was a school of practical design. He may have constructed more buildings here than he would later create for Tashkent. In Ashkhabad the architect demonstrated flexibility, adapting his projects to a rapidly changing time. Whereas the republican public prosecutor's building (1950–1951) was typical of the Stalinist epoch, with characteristic elements such as an entrance portal decorated with an arch and pilasters with stylized capitals, after 1953 the style of his buildings began to change. The main block of Ashkhabad University (with architect M. Kamyshnikov) is constructed in a more minimalist manner: here the portal is produced in the most laconic forms, recalling the architecture of 1930s Germany, and the new aerostation is the last dash of "Soviet Art Deco," with nonstandard plastic elements supporting the cornice and a portal with stylized columns with an original profile that is a platform for a viewing terrace. Here we can already see the architect's interest in original forms expanding beyond the usual rectangular volumes. There were also unbuilt projects—the Museum of Arts and the Turkmenistan Sanatorium in Kislovodsk. During his time in Kislovodsk the architect was impressed by the sanatorium constructed there in the 1930s by Moisei Ginzburg with the involvement of Ivan Leonidov. He recalled that on returning to Tashkent (1960) he was already prepared to work on mass industrial housing and to shift to a platform of contemporary architecture.

His first significant building, the Circus (1962–1975), showed that Genrikh Aleksandrovich was attracted to a more expressive, plastic, Brutalist and futuristic visuality than that typified by the functionalist buildings of the UzNIIPgradostroitel'stva Institute of the time. Aleksandrovich's design differed from those for the numerous other Soviet circuses of that period mainly due to the absence of a circular glass entrance hall. Due to the local climate the architects preferred to surround the foyer with massive sun protection. The structural part of the project also has an original design. In many Soviet circuses the load-bearing structures were hidden within the building. This allowed architects to play with the well-known modernist theme of "weightless mass." In Tashkent the load-bearing radial reinforced concrete frames became one of the expressive elements of the volume, giving the Circus a heavyweight, Brutalist feel. Simultaneously, cosmic motifs, which were fashionable in the 1960s, were also present. The main volume took the form of a flying saucer and in the interior there were circular "portholes" that made the building look like a space station. With their developed plasticity, the interiors were severe: here concrete and wooden surfaces were neighbors, and there was no decoration of any sort. However, the construction of the Circus was disrupted by the Tashkent earthquake, and when it was relaunched in the 1970s the architect had to modify his project to incorporate the requirements of the new ideological epoch. The concrete surfaces of the interior were covered with ganch plaster carving, the concrete frames of the façades were clad with marble and the Brutalist sun protection was "enriched" with cotton boll motifs. In addition, the interiors were decorated with mosaics of questionable quality. This is how a single building became a meeting (and crossing) place of two opposing aesthetic approaches.

The Tashkent House of Knowledge is another important Tashgiprogor building of the 1960s where Genrikh Aleksandrovich was involved in the design. Like the Circus, construction of the House of Knowledge began before the earthquake and was completed later, in 1968. Regardless of the rectangular contour, the building was distinguished by a memorable plasticity thanks to the sun-protection grilles, the deep shadows under the protruding volume of the foyer and the exceptional mosaic by Moscow artists Leonid Polishchuk and Svetlana Shcherbinina, which covered all of the walls of the three-story foyer.

Another example of the Brutalist plasticity of the 1960s is the Iubileinyi Palace of Sport, which was completed by 1970 under the supervision of Genrikh Aleksandrovich. The building looked dynamic and light thanks to the horizontal, asymmetric planning and one of the favorite modernist motifs of the 1960s, "the struggle with mass." The architect had this to say about it: "The main volume of the auditorium has original, bent contours. The form of the volume of the auditorium emerges from its functional construction as an amphitheater with a large roof span. The contour line of the amphitheater in the volume passes through the first floor. This can particularly be seen in the evening, when the building is lit. The illuminated volume of the auditorium is easily visible through the glass of the foyer and appears to float in the night sky."[1] In this way the concrete volume "rested" on the belt of the glazed foyer and visually lost its materiality.

Later buildings by the architect—the Post Office and the Road Transport Institute—which were designed in the early 1970s and built in the early 1980s, retained elements of Brutalist plasticity. Aleksandrovich did not resort to deliberate decoration in "national style," reverting to the symmetrical compositions that were typical of his 1950s buildings in Ashkhabad.

1 Genrikh Aleksandrovich, "Zdanie Tashkentskogo gosudarstvennogo tsirka [The Building of the Tashkent State Circus]," *Stroitel'stvo i arkhitektura Uzbekistana* [*Construction and Architecture of Uzbekistan*], no. 4, 1971, 23.

INSTITUTIONAL FRAMEWORK

Tashgiprogor

CADRE

Tashgiprogor was the architectural "hub" of Tashkent. In terms of numbers, it was the largest institution, and architects could move here if there were employment problems at other organizations. After the 1966 earthquake Tashgiprogor was "invaded" by architects from Moscow and other cities of the USSR who had come to work on the reconstruction of Uzbekistan's capital. By the 1980s, within Tashgiprogor there were eight studios responsible for the design of the eight urban planning districts of Tashkent that surrounded the center of the city. Accordingly, the institute's architects not only designed unique buildings but also had to think at the level of the city, the district, the microdistrict and the street. Among the protagonists at the institute were the architects Vladimir Spivak, Genrikh Aleksandrovich, Vil' Muratov, Rafael' Khairutdinov (during the design of the Union of Artists Exhibition Hall he moved to Tashgenplan) and Iurii Miroshnichenko, who, with great freedom and lightness of touch, included historical quotations and inspiration in their buildings. The collective image and concept of the institute's architects was also influenced by the twelve-year presence there of Andrei Kosinskii, a Moscow architect who introduced new ideas and solutions to Tashkent architecture that were linked to the architectural heritage of Central Asia. It is known that the leadership of UzNIIPgradostroitel'stva did not approve of Kosinskii's work. At Tashgiprogor the attitude to him was more complicated, but a certain part of the institute formed under Kosinskii's influence, not least because he combined design work with teaching at Tashkent Polytechnic Institute, from where many of his former students came to Tashgiprogor.

PRIORITIES

1960s: use of the techniques and vocabulary of contemporary architecture, primacy of plastic solutions over rectangular geometry. From the late 1960s there was a swing toward the development of "oriental modernism," the return of historical quotations, the study and use in new buildings of the "appropriateness" and know-how of folk architecture.

Typical buildings: 1960s: Chilanzar Shopping Center, Iubileinyi Palace of Sport, Chilanzar Center by Andrei Kosinskii (not built), Gor'kii Theater by Iurii Khaldeev (the fourth and most orientalist version of which was built as the Turkestan Palace in the early 1990s). From the late 1960s: Blue Domes Café, Circus, Zarafshan Restaurant, House of Cinema, Moscow Hotel (Chorsu), Chorsu Bazaar.

Left: Central Committee of the Komsomol of Uzbekistan, Institute of Art Studies, and Sports Committee (partially visible); right: Central Committee of the Komsomol of Uzbekistan; architects: Mariia Kondakova and Leon Adamov Tashgiprogor, 1972

Both images: Institute of Pectoral Surgery; architects: Ol'ga Gaazenkopf, Aleksei Asanov and A. Tuniiants Tashgiprogor, 1975–1980

Basement plan
Original condition

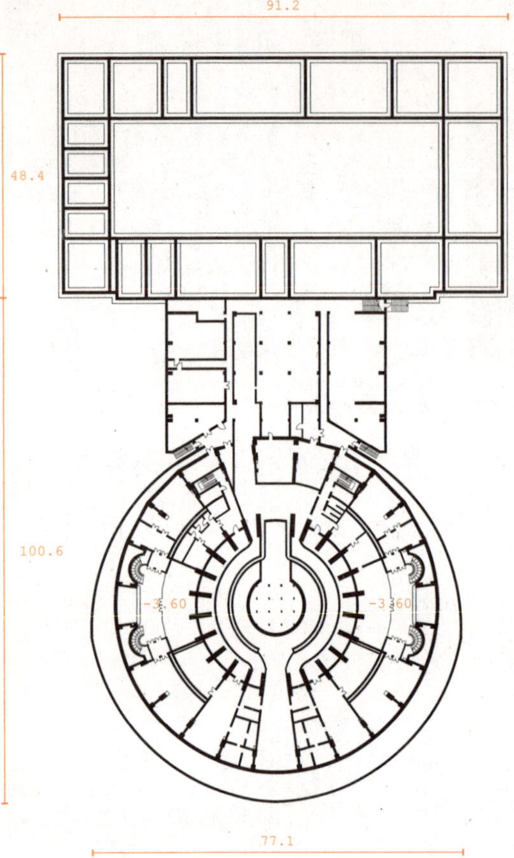

1st floor plan
Original condition

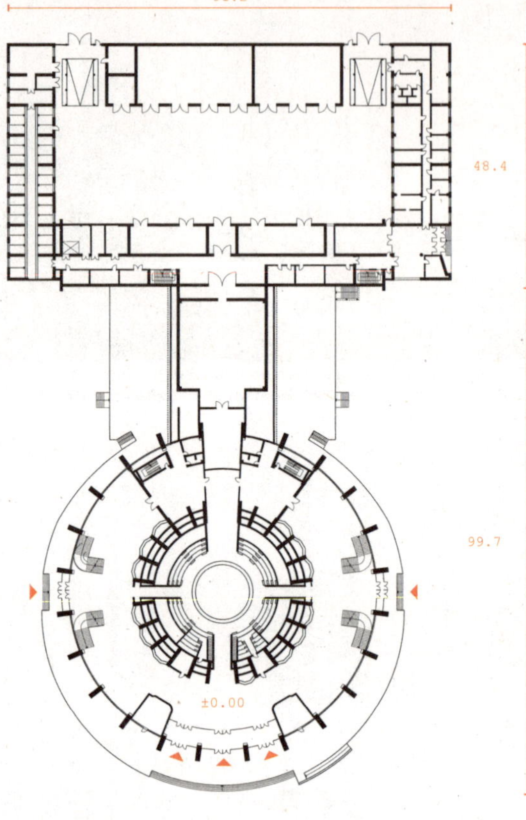

Exterior view
Original condition

2nd floor plan
Original condition

65.8
8.5
25.6
12.4
23.7
74.8
+3.75
75.0

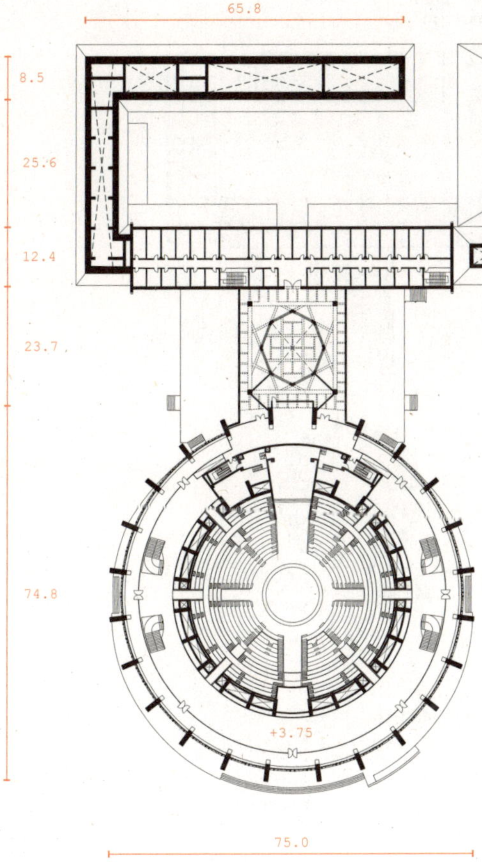

3rd floor plan
Original condition

46.5
23.7
A
A'
74.8
+10.00
75.0
0 5 10 20m

Section AA'
Original condition

+27.17
+25.45
+10.00
+3.75
±0.00
-3.60
-6.30
0 5 10m

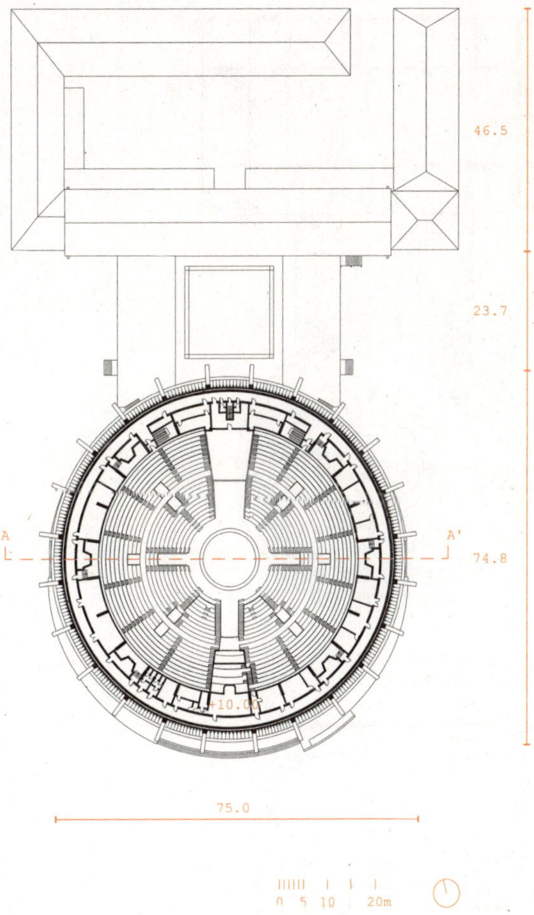

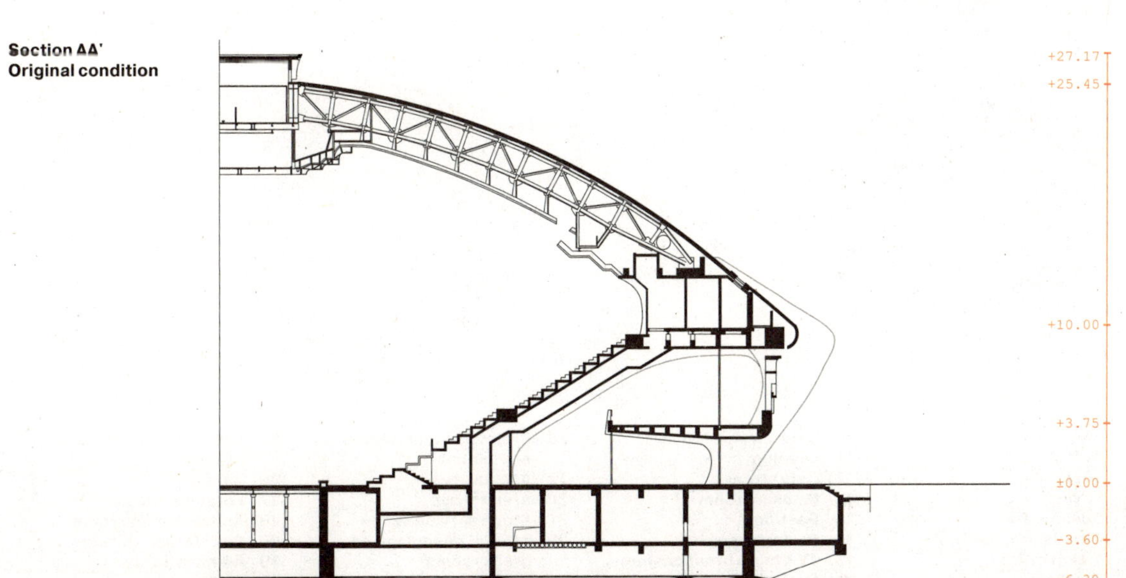

1975

Basement floor plan
Original condition

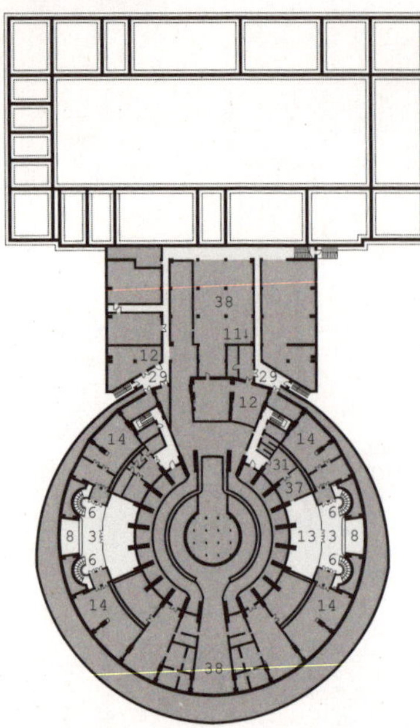

1st floor plan
Original condition

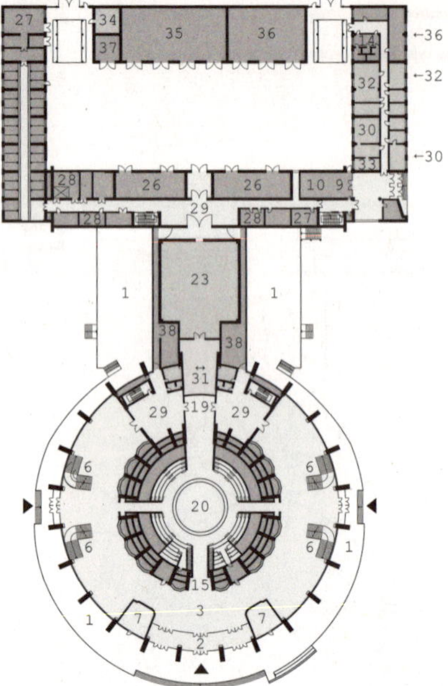

2nd floor plan
Original condition

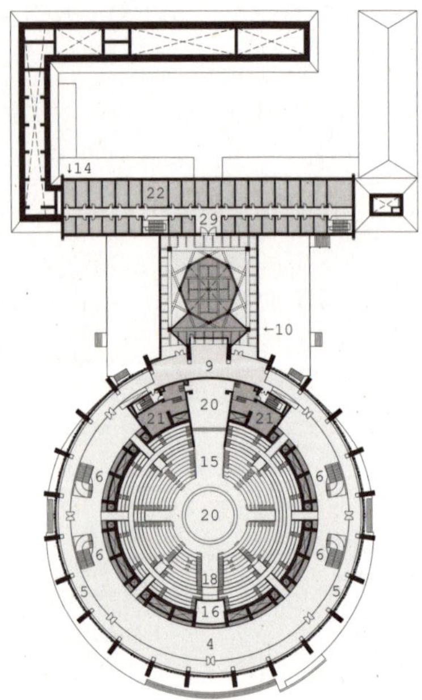

3rd floor plan
Original condition

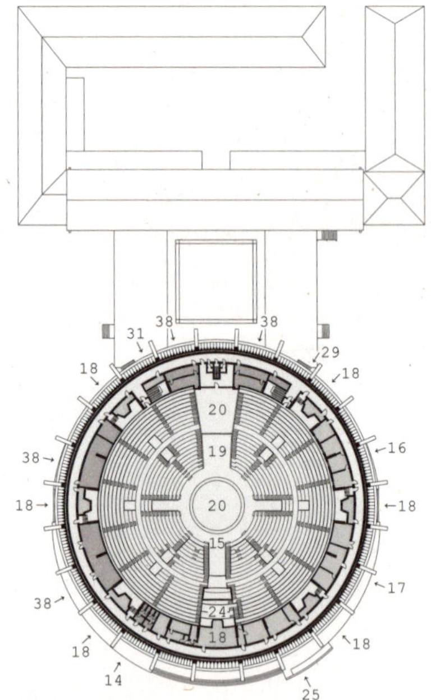

1 Terrace
2 Airlock
3 Vestibule
4 Foyer
5 Summer foyer
6 Circulation, visitors
7 Ticket office
8 Cloakroom
9 Café
10 Café service rooms
11 Loading
12 Café storage
13 Smoking room
14 Restroom
15 Performance hall
16 TV & radio broadcasting
17 Recording studio
18 Projection and cinema equipment
19 Artists' exit
20 Arena stage
21 Stage service space
22 Artists' changing and break rooms
23 Rehearsal room
24 Orchestra
25 Orchestra service and storage
26 Animals
27 Forage storage
28 Animal service room
29 Circulation, workers
30 Administration
31 Staff room
32 Workshop

2022

Basement floor plan
Current condition

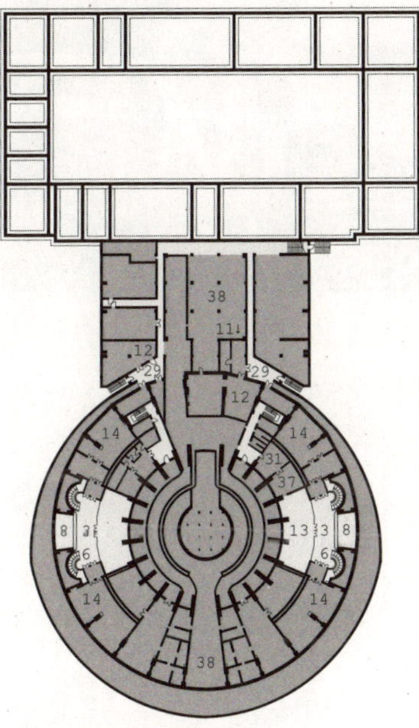

1st floor plan
Current condition

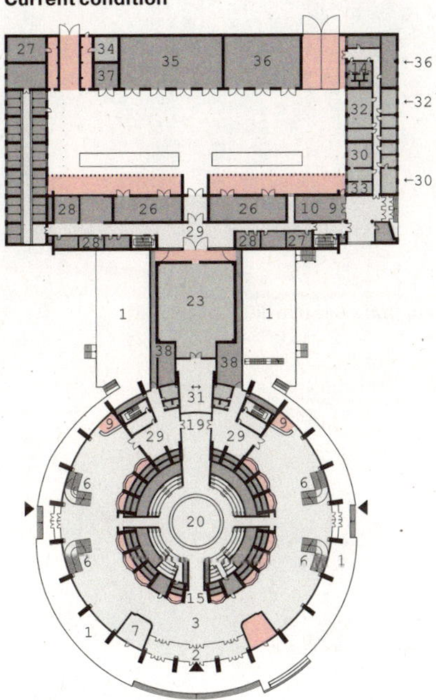

2nd floor plan
Current condition

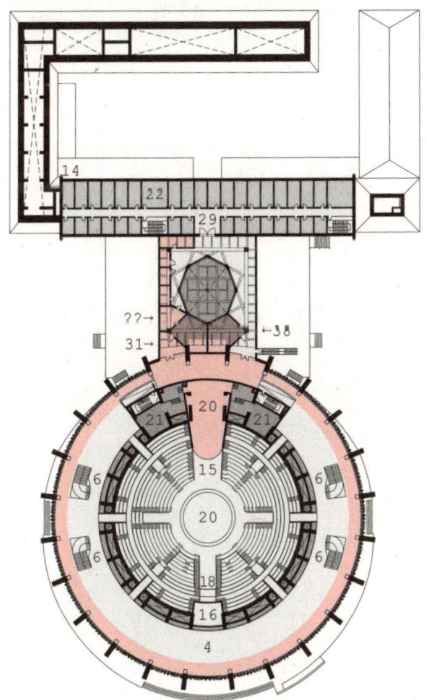

3rd floor plan
Current condition

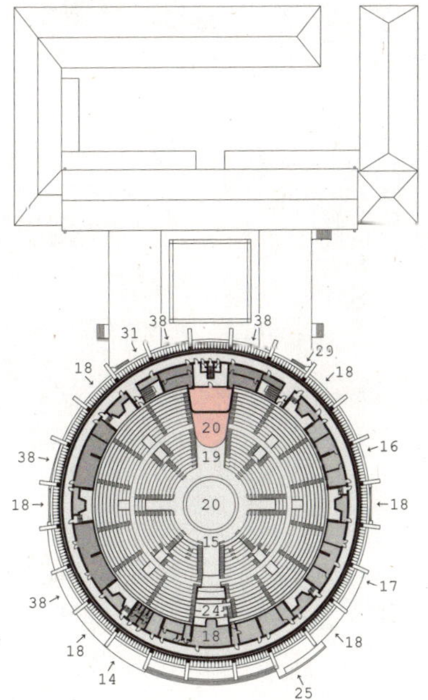

33	Children's nursery
34	Security room
35	Garage
36	Warehouse and storage
37	Service room
38	Technical area

- Performance hall/public
- Artists' space/administration
- Animals/service and technical
- Change of function

0 5 10 20m

Model of the Tashkent State Circus, 1963–1967

State Circus construction site

State Circus construction site

Structural concrete ribs during construction

General view, 1986

View of the State Circus from Khadra Square, 1982

State Circus, bird's-eye view

Detail of the panjara and the load-bearing ribs of the façade, 1970s

Foyer viewed from the first floor

Entrance to the performance hall from the first floor, 1970s

Performance hall, 1970s

Circular pavilion of the State Circus, 2023

Façade details of the circular pavilion, 2022

Interior details of the circular pavilion gallery, 2022

State Circus foyer, 2022

Details of foyer ceiling mosaics, 2022

Performance hall, 2022

Performance hall ceiling detail, 2022

Rehearsal room, 2022

Left: exterior of the rehearsal block; middle: view of the rehearsal block and the circular pavilion; right: distribution corridor to animal areas, 2022

Façade version, 1963–1969

Circus with 3,000 seats in Tashkent: circular pavilion, architectural section, 1968

Façade version, 1963–1969

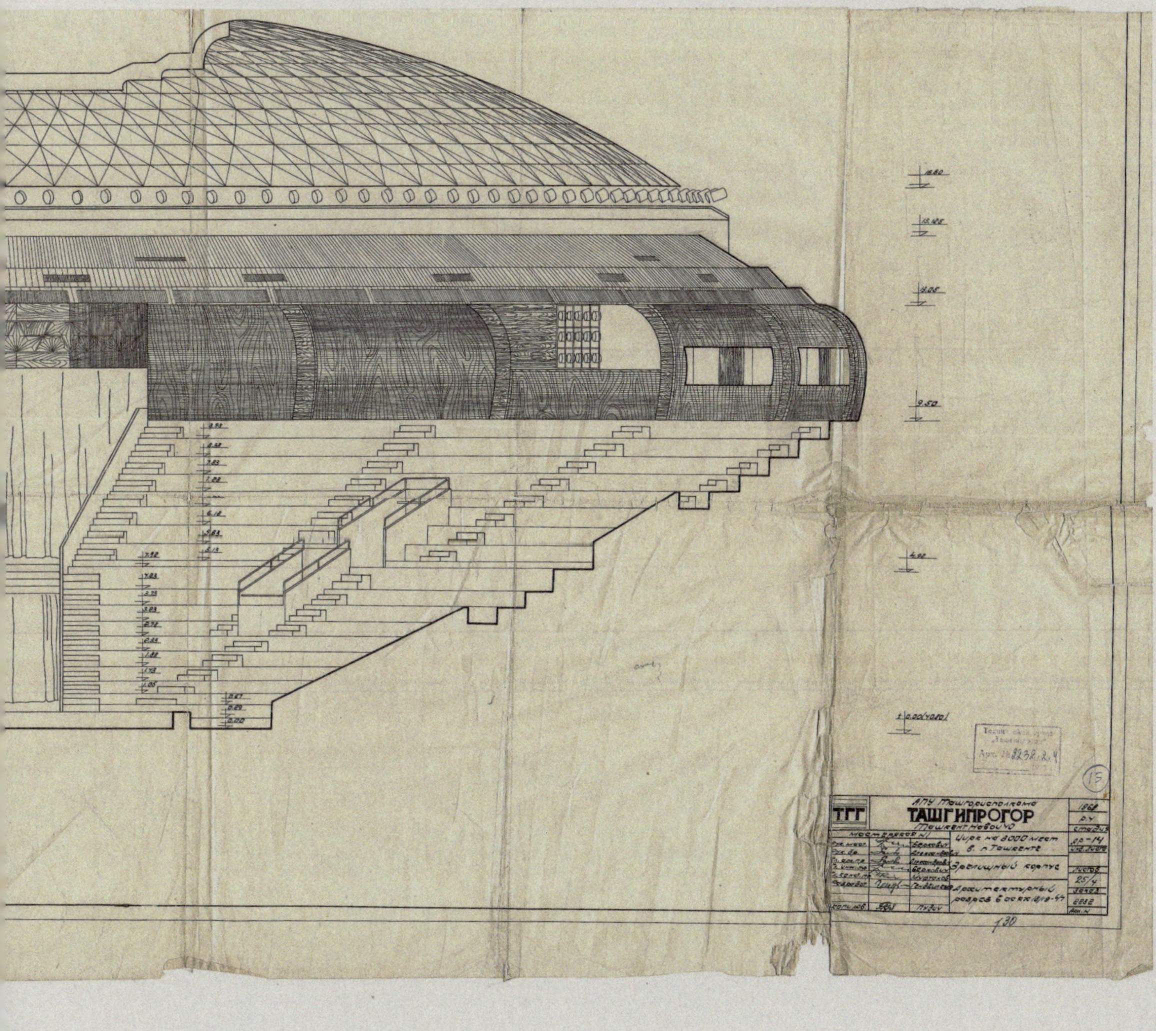

ТГГ
АПУ Ташгорисполкома
ТАШГИПРОГОР
Цирк на 3000 мест в г. Ташкенте
Зрелищный корпус

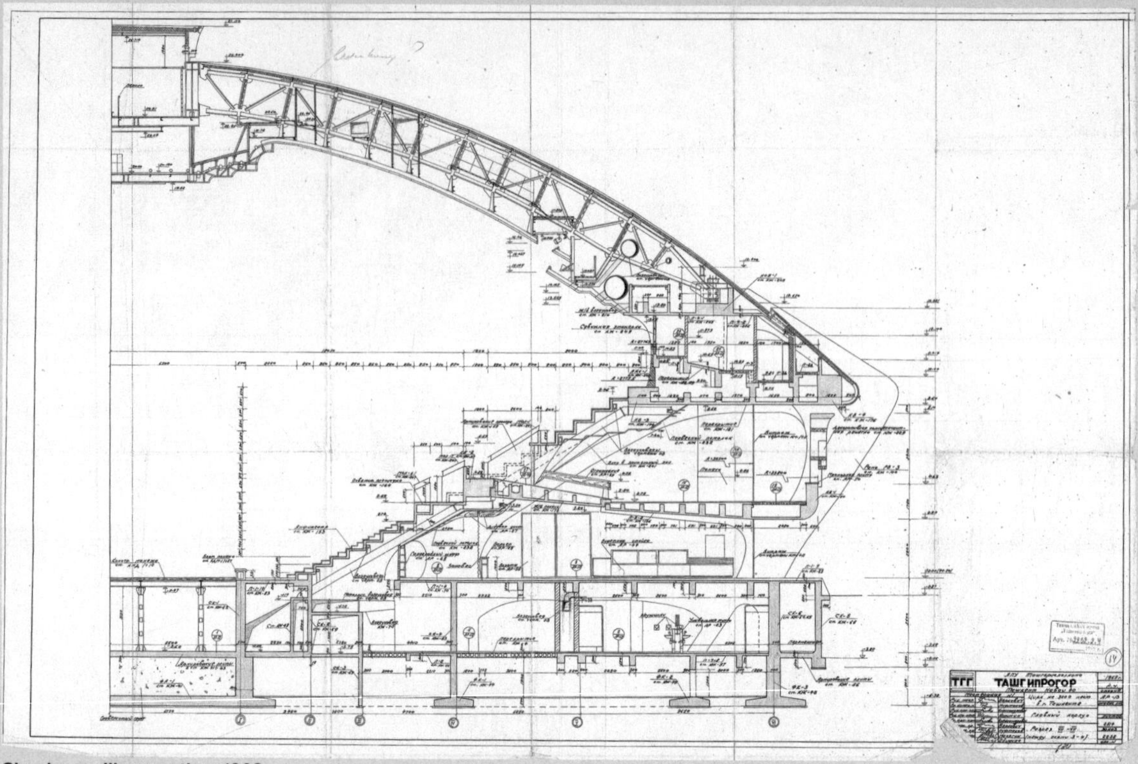

Circular pavilion, section, 1968

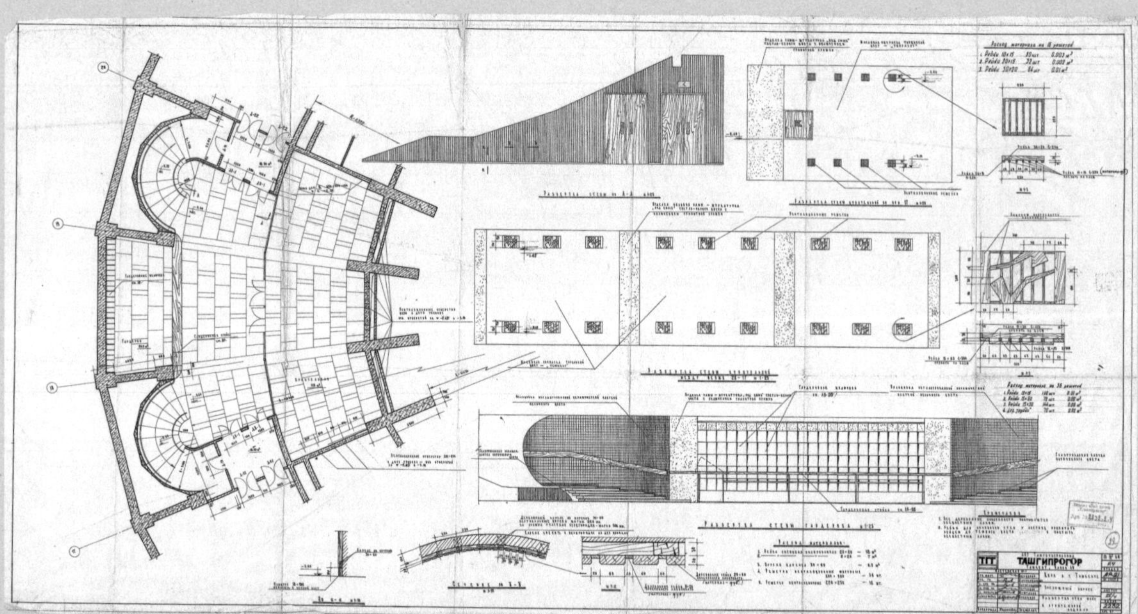

Details of the paneling for the lobby and smoking room in the basement, circular pavilion, 1968

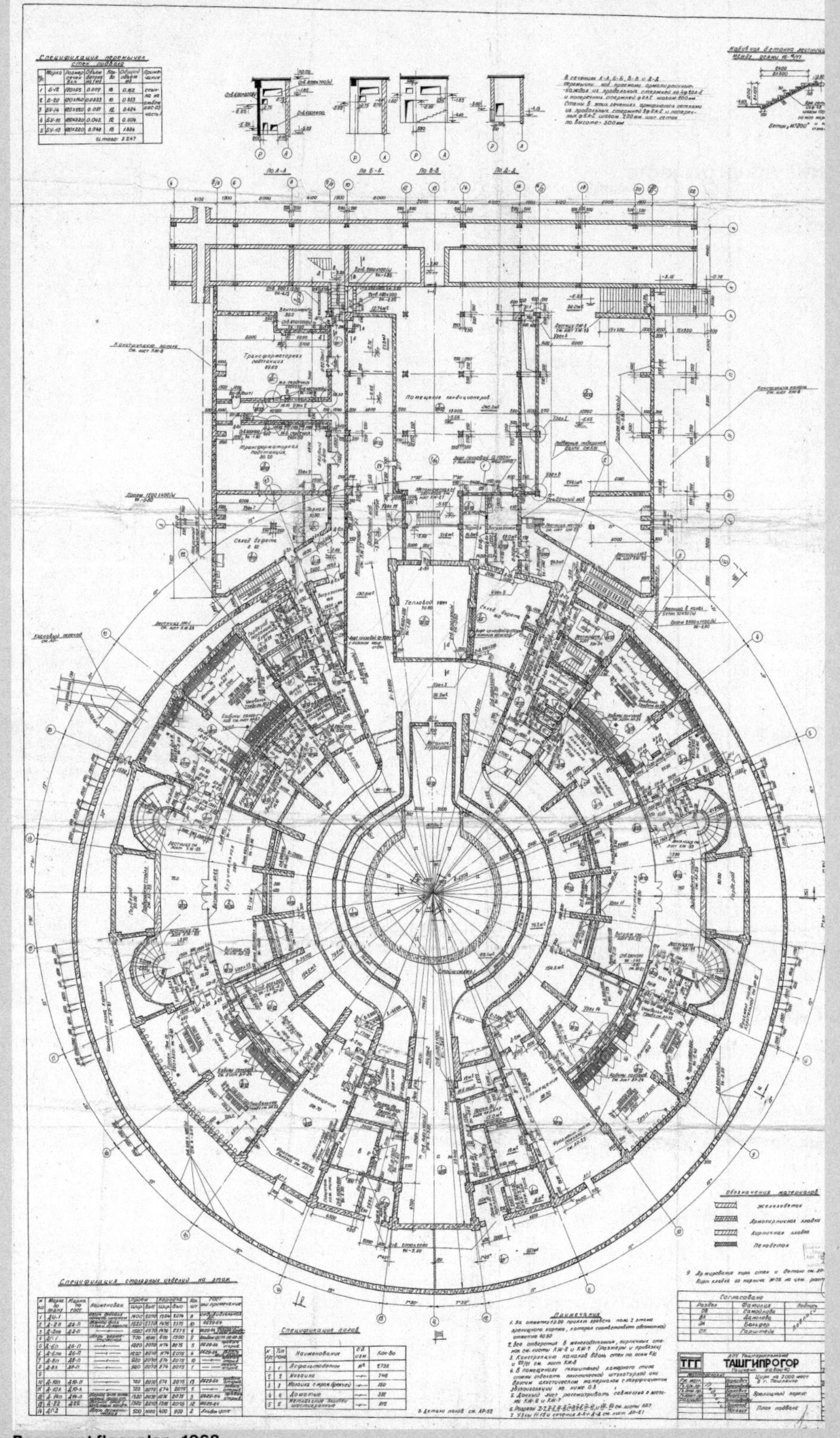

Basement floor plan, 1968

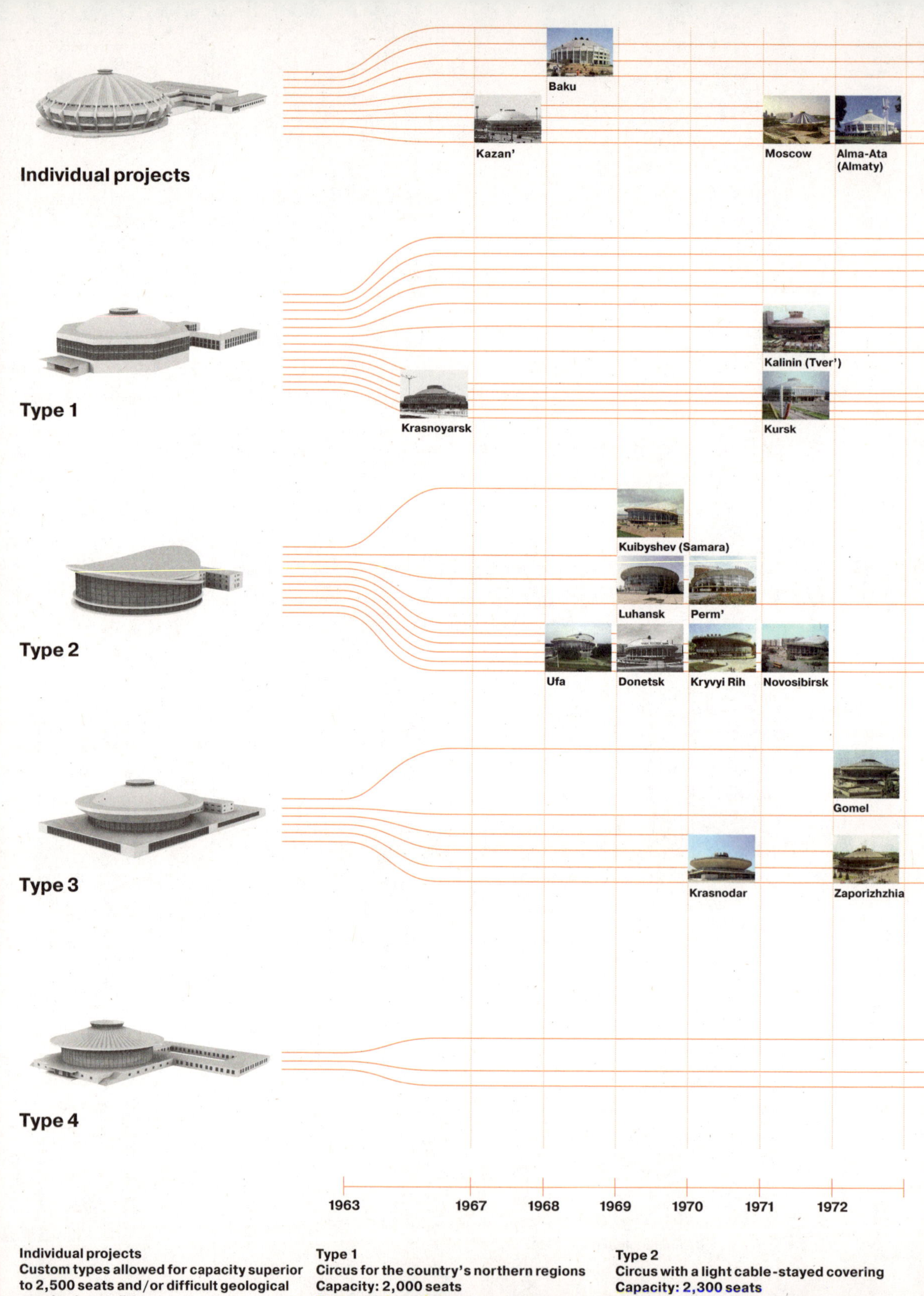

Individual projects
Custom types allowed for capacity superior to 2,500 seats and/or difficult geological or seismic conditions

Type 1
Circus for the country's northern regions
Capacity: 2,000 seats
Octagon-shaped structure, designed to withstand heavy snow and wind loads

Type 2
Circus with a light cable-stayed covering
Capacity: 2,300 seats
A unique suspended cable-stayed shell made of ultra-thin reinforced concrete in the form of a hyperbolic paraboloid

Type 3
Circus for the country's southern regions
Capacity: 2,000 seats
A rectangular stylobate with the amphitheater disc placed on top; in southern regions, the roof could be accessed by visitors

Type 4
Circus for the republics of Central Asia
Capacity: 2,000 seats
Circus layout to withstand seismic stress and rapid visitor egress strategy

HIGHLIGHTS

The State Circus of Tashkent was completed in 1975 in an important urban position on Khadra Square, at the intersection of two of the capital's major roads, Furkat Street and Navoi Street. It is among the largest circuses built in the USSR, with a seating capacity of 3,000 people. Its design history is a unique case, since, unlike many other Soviet circuses of the postwar period, it was not designed according to a standard type provided by Moscow. Instead, a custom project, developed by a Tashgiprogor team, elaborated a tailored response to the functional requirements of a local circus and to the geological, seismic and climatic constraints.

Therefore, the State Circus of Tashkent deserves to be carefully preserved for its symbolic role as a hinge in the capital's urban development, for its essential social function and for its unique architectural and construction characteristics.

The Tashkent Circus was designed by Tashgiprogor Workshop no. 1 under the direction of architects Genrikh Aleksandrovich and G. Masiagin between 1962 and the beginning of the 1970s. It is one of the few remaining Soviet modernist buildings in Tashkent for which design began before the 1966 earthquake, although it was inaugurated a decade later.

The Circus is of crucial importance for the urban context for the following reasons:

- the relationship it establishes with the square and the surrounding area, and with the other modernist buildings, such as the Chorsu Bazaar, the Chorsu Hotel (currently in disuse) and the Peoples' Friendship Palace;
- its strategic urban position at the top of an important axis (Furkat Street), at the opposite end of which the Peoples' Friendship Palace is located. Khadra Square, where the Circus stands, originally marked the edge of the "old city."

At the time of its design, the building was the second largest circus in the Soviet Union (after the circus on Vernadskii Avenue in Moscow): it had a capacity of 3,000 people, whereas the average capacity of standard Soviet circuses was around 2,000.

The large scale posed a great structural challenge, considering the geological conditions of the soil and the seismic conditions of the area. Of particular interest is the structure of the main pavilion, characterized by the mixed use of steel and reinforced concrete. The twenty-four monolithic reinforced concrete ribs, marking the rhythm of the façade, support the lighter steel truss structure of the 74-meter-diameter dome that covers the main performance hall and the two levels of circular foyer around it. An elegant concrete sunshading device encloses the upper level of the foyer, forming a suspended ring, while the lower foyer is recessed and wrapped by a transparent glass façade.

Next to the main circular volume, a lower rectangular block containing the rehearsal, administration and other support spaces completes the complex on the northern side facing the park.

STATE OF REPAIR

SCORE:

- 2 – The building shows severe localized damage and/or diffused and extended deterioration patterns. It is, however, still possible to use it.

Protection status:	Protected. The building is listed and protected according to Decision No. 846 of the Cabinet of Ministers, October 4, 2019.
Main criticalities:	Due to extensive use of the building structure, there are some worn areas.
Possible risks:	The main risk is the deterioration of the building owing to lack of maintenance.

INTEGRITY

SCORE:

- Exterior: 3 – The building has retained all the elements necessary to express its significance but is in a poor state of repair
- Interior: 3 – The building has retained all the elements necessary to express its significance but is in a poor state of repair

The Circus building still fulfills the purpose for which it was designed, though parts of it have become obsolete and insufficient for operational needs. It retains its architectural integrity both as an individual building and as an urban ensemble.

The building was able to maintain a tight relationship with its surroundings, highlighted by precise and perceptible alignments with other buildings.

Internally, most spaces remain preserved, although some parts of the foyer have been compromised, such as the balustrades, the glass façade on the first floor, the cladding of the ribs and the ceiling. Some changes have also occurred externally. The stone cladding of the ribs was removed and substituted with plaster. The roof was painted blue, instead of the original gray.

AUTHENTICITY SCORE:

- Exterior: 3 – The building has been subjected to slight changes and replacements
- Interior: 3 – The building has been subjected to slight changes and replacements

The building shows a satisfactory level of authenticity.

The large public square on which the building stands has not undergone any interventions and its appearance conforms to the design of the 1970s. Even the main urban grid on which the building fits has not changed much since the 1980s.

At the turn of the 1980s and during the 1990s partial interventions were carried out, slightly compromising the authenticity of the original design. On this occasion, the façade of the upper foyer was moved outward, the balustrades substituted and new decorations added to the ceiling and ribs, replacing the original cladding. No other major interventions have been carried out since.

1982

View of the façade, 1982

View of the façade, 2022

Foyer viewed from the first floor

Foyer viewed from the first floor, 2022

Entrance to the performance hall from the first floor, 1970s

Entrance to the performance hall from the first floor, 2022

1983

Performance hall, 1983

2022

Performance hall, 2022

LEVEL 1 – MAXIMUM LEVEL OF INTEREST
(No transformations allowed; conservation activities required)

URBAN LEVEL

The perimeter of Khadra Square must not be transformed.

Inside the perimeter of Khadra Square it is not possible to construct new buildings.

The façade perimeter and roof eaves height of the buildings facing the square must not be changed.

ARCHITECTURAL LEVEL
EXTERIOR

The façade of the circular pavilion, characterized by the rhythm of the concrete ribs and the sun-protection system, and the pleated surface of the dome must not be transformed.

The volume and structure of the rehearsal block connecting the pavilion with the service building must not be transformed.

The volume of the two-level portion of the administrative building must not be modified.

INTERIOR

Internal subdivision of the spaces inside the main circular volume is not allowed. In particular, the performance hall, the rehearsal hall and the foyer on both levels must remain in the original configuration and retain the distribution architectural elements, such as stairs, landings and so on.

DETAIL LEVEL
EXTERIOR

The elements characterizing the exterior of the building must not be changed. In particular:

- the concrete ribs, including their stone cladding (the circular band corresponding to a perimetral beam above the sunshades should be clad in stone);
- the position of the window frames on the first floor;
- the concrete sunshading devices around the upper foyer;
- all roof elements, including windows and cladding;
- the truss structure of the roof.

INTERIOR

The original finishes of the interiors must be preserved. In particular:

- the original floor of the foyer on both levels;
- the mosaic and ceramic works of monumental art on the walls;
- the ceiling of the performance hall.

LEVEL 2 – MEDIUM LEVEL OF INTEREST

(Elements included in the second level can be moderately transformed following approval by a designated committee[1])

URBAN LEVEL

Any new construction within the urban block should be evaluated and approved by the designated committee.

The square design and finishes can be upgraded. All design choices to be subject to approval by the designated committee.

To not affect the visual connection between the Peoples' Friendship Palace and the Circus:

- any changes to this section of Furkat Street should be subject to approval by the designated committee;
- the eave height of the buildings on Furkat Street can be modified only with the approval of the designated committee.

ARCHITECTURAL LEVEL
EXTERIOR

The façades of the block connecting the pavilion with the courtyard building can be moderately transformed following approval by the designated committee.

The footprint of the single-level parts of the service block should be maintained.

The overall maximum height of the administrative block can be modified, but should not exceed its current maximum height at any point.

All decisions to be subject to approval by the committee.

DETAIL LEVEL
INTERIOR

All foyer finishes modified after 1975, such as the ceiling cladding, the balustrades and the rib coverings, can be replaced following approval by the designated committee.

1 An international committee of heritage preservation experts to be appointed.

HIDDEN MODERNIST FEATURES

Among the modernist features of the building, as intended in its original design, were the proportions of the courtyard volumes, the design of the façades and the relationship between solid and voids. These characteristics have been compromised by the interventions carried out in recent decades. In particular, the replacement of the flat roof with a pitched roof has altered the height of the blocks and thus their reciprocal proportions.

Hidden by the new roof, but still present, is the pergola that marks the entrance to the courtyard from the back. This reinforced concrete grid, which establishes continuity between the two wings of the courtyard building, represents an interesting hidden modernist feature.

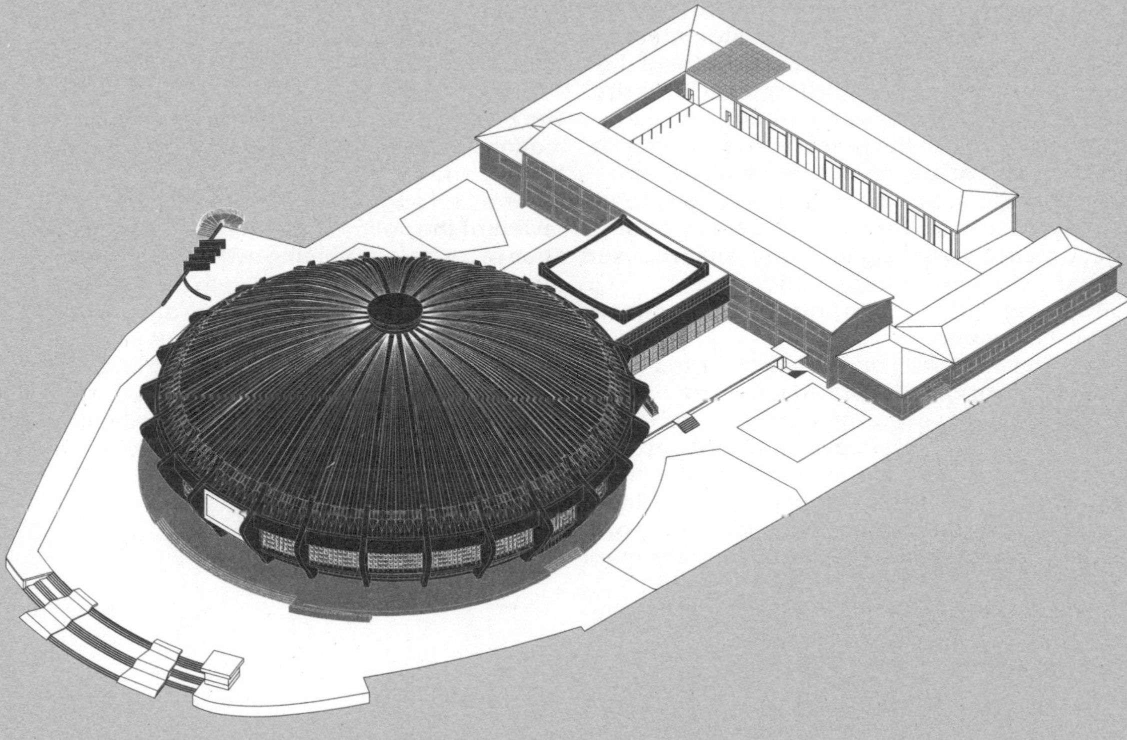

Preservation Level 1
Maximum Level of Interest
Materials and elements to be preserved

Preservation Level 2
Medium Level of Interest
Materials and elements to be preserved

Hidden Modernist Features
Materials and elements to be preserved

Transformation allowed

Preservation Strategy

The State Circus is an outstanding modernist building in Tashkent.

Its design does not belong to a standardized type, as it is one of the few so-called "individual" circus projects.

Though the building was inaugurated in 1975, the design phase started in 1962. The circus is located in a strategic position at the top of two of the capital's major roads, Furkat Street and Navoi Street, connecting the "new" and the "old" city. The building's position was decided before the 1964 masterplan. It was the second largest circus in the Soviet Union, with a planned capacity of 3,000 people, whereas the average capacity of Soviet circuses was about 2,000 people. The building was constructed with unique structural features to address the seismic risk, such as a combination of reinforced concrete ribs and a lighter steel lattice structure for the dome.

Unfortunately, although the Circus retains its architectural integrity, both as a single building and as an urban ensemble, some of its features have been compromised by later interventions. More specifically, while the exterior of the dome pavilion retains a high degree of integrity, inside most of the finishes have been replaced.

The main goal of the preservation strategy is to restore where reasonable the original condition of the iconic dome pavilion and to emphasize the modernist features of the service volume, which has been significantly compromised by post-inauguration interventions.

To this end, three main preservation actions will be implemented.

The first action will bring back selected elements of the original design of the dome pavilion and highlight several modernist features of the service block. This implies the removal of the video screen over the main entrance and the removal of the panels covering the marble finish of the ribs, in order to make the appearance of the dome closer to the original. (Where the marble finish has been lost, it can be reinstated.) It is also suggested that the original color of the dome be restored.

With regard to the interior space, this action implies the demolition of the most recent additions in the lobby and the foyer, which are inconsistent with the original design and of poor architectural quality. In particular, the elements to be removed are the lobby and foyer cladding and 1990s interventions such as the ceiling cladding, the flooring on the first floor and the balustrades. It is also planned to move the glass façade to its original location, inward from the current façade. From historical photos and archive drawings, it is possible to understand the precise location and configuration of the original glazing. Restoring it would solve a series of technical and maintenance issues, including façade cleaning. Additionally, it would create shaded and ventilated galleries on the perimeter of the main building and reinstate the original modernist image of continuity between interior and exterior. Roof waterproofing of the dome should be revised and repaired, particularly at the joint with the façade system.

For the service building, this action implies replacing the pitched roof with a flat roof that is adequately insulated, which will be more coherent with the original design of the volumes and will also solve several problems related to roof leakage.

The second action will entail maintenance activities, such as local repairs and cleaning of the façades, with particular reference to the dome pavilion, but also to the panjara of the courtyard building and other elements of the original project. These actions will guarantee longer conservation of those original features that remain.

Finally, it is recommended to check all issues related to the obsolescence of the technical systems and to intervene where necessary with a project for new systems.

Adaptation Strategy

The State Circus adaptation strategy aims to modernize this infrastructure, both organizationally and conceptually.

As a first suggestion, we recommend a review of the policy of animal use and consideration of new programming without animal performances, or reducing them to the minimum.

While the main dome building and the rehearsal block primarily require preservation and maintenance activities as described above, the service block needs to be fully modernized and reprogrammed. In our view, this implies creating contemporary rehearsal areas, training areas, offices and a hotel.

Suggested program distribution

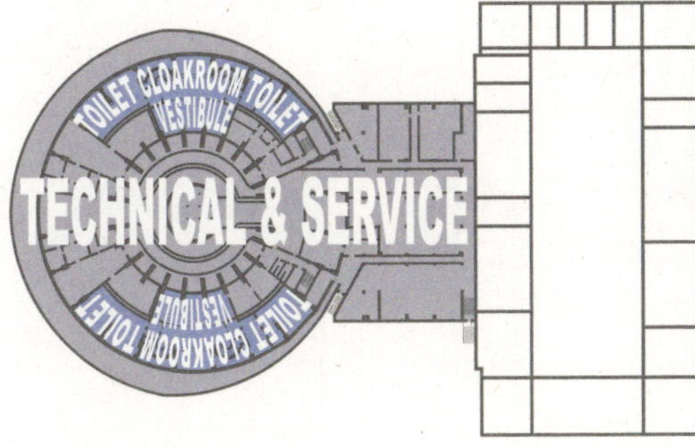

Basement

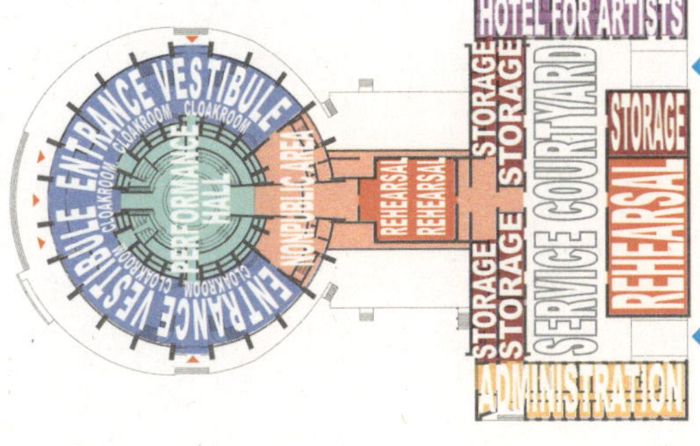

First floor

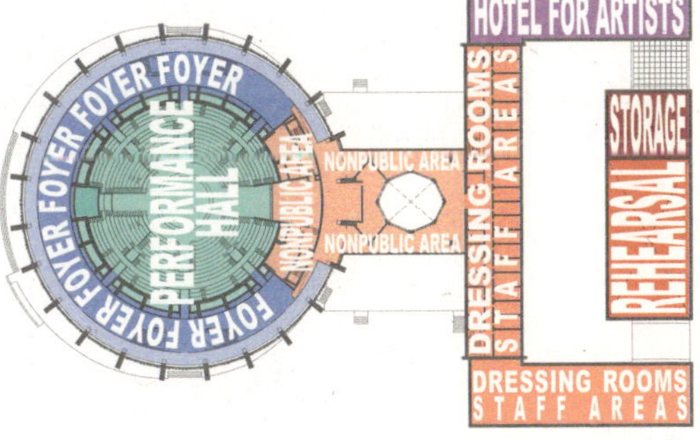

Second floor

Third floor

Strategy visualization
Restored foyer of the State Circus

House of Youth (Shodlik Hotel and Ilkhom Theater)

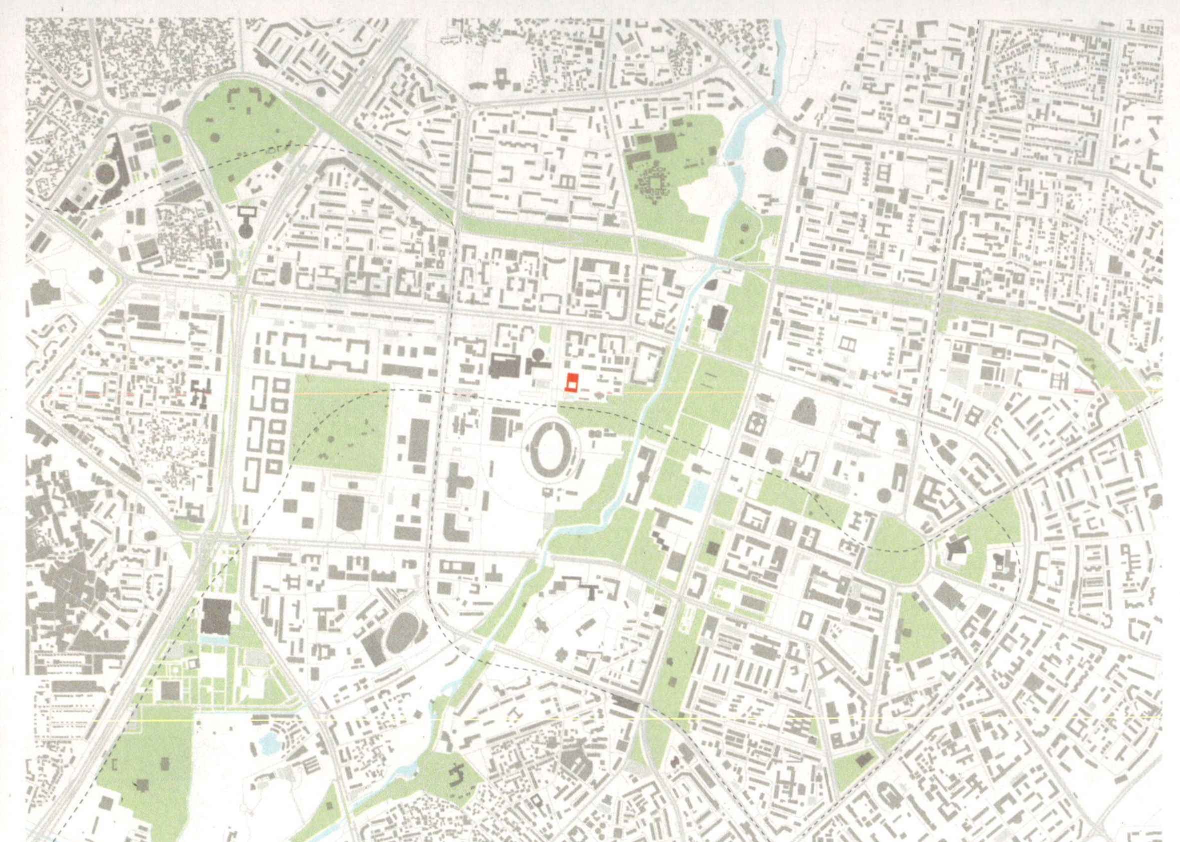

Building position and address: 5 Pakhtakorskaia Street, Tashkent

0 0.5 1km

The urban planning history of the site on which the House of Youth was built begins in the Middle Ages, but this had no effect on Richard Bleze's project. More importantly, from 1937 each general plan of Tashkent included for this space either a large green zone or a central square with a wide avenue. Of particular relevance for the future development of the site were the development of Navoi Street, which became the main transport artery between the "new" and "old" cities, the completion of Pakhtakor Stadium (1956), the construction of the Panoramic Cinema (Palace of Arts, 1964) and the approval of the project for the new center of Tashkent (1964), the main idea of which involved the creation of a central pedestrian green boulevard between Revolution and Khadra squares. These factors predetermined the urban position of the House of Youth. Its southern façade overlooked the green esplanade and Pakhtakor Stadium, while the western façade overlooked Pakhtakorskaia Street and the Panoramic Cinema.

Main dimensions of the House of Youth
General axonometric view

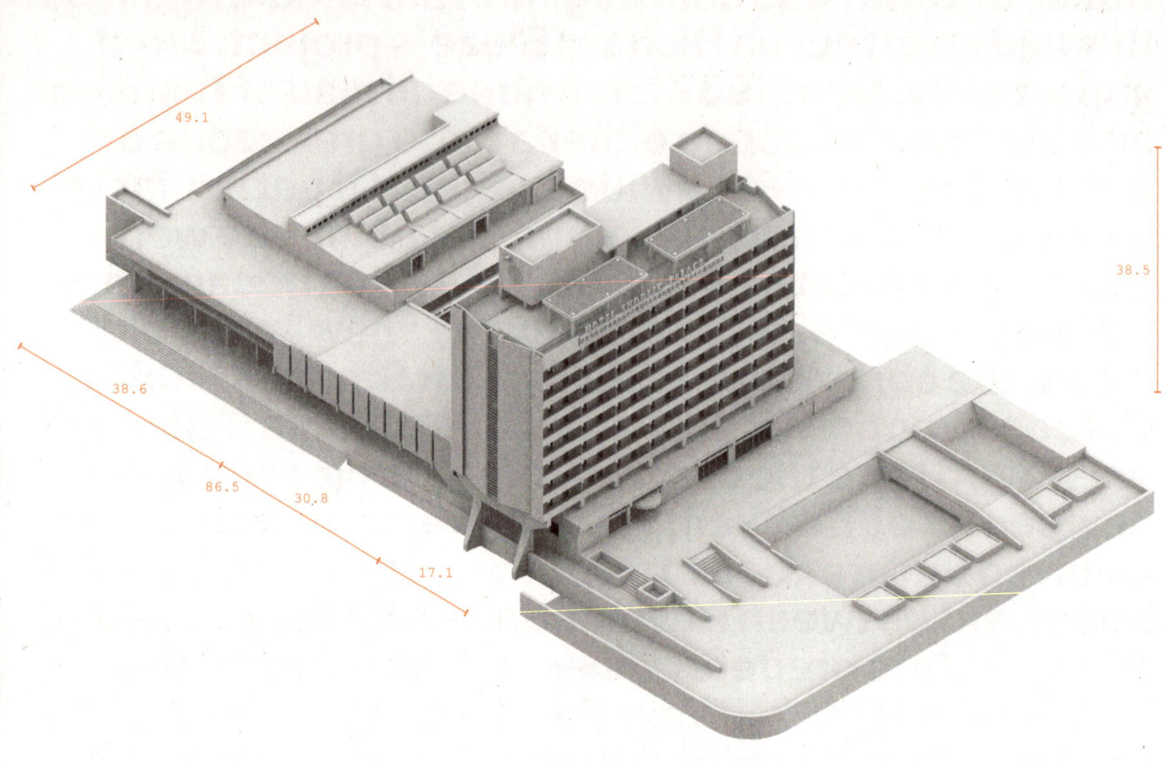

ACTORS	**Architects:**	**Richard Bleze, N. Gorbenko, Aleksandr Blinov, Larisa Khristich, Aleksandr Kuranov**
	Engineers:	**E. Patlis, O. Braverman, L. Arnautova, Farkhad Ganeev**
	Institute:	**Uzgosproekt**
DATES	**Design period:**	**1965–1971 (?)**
	Construction period:	**1967–1975**
	Inauguration date:	**1975**
	Later interventions:	**1976–1977: Public block. Interventions in courtyard spaces, adaptation of the basement and foyer for the theater's requirements. 1996: Fire in the restaurant. 1996–1997: Renovation of the entire building by the German owner. Date unknown: Change of the hotel façade.**
USE	**Current use:**	**Hotel and theater**
	Original use:	**House of Youth (hotel, wedding palace, café, teahouse, Komsomol museum, restaurant, library, club, gym spaces, administrative spaces)**
	Suitability of current use:	**The hotel building is suitable for its current use. However, as it has been around twenty-five years since the last renovation works (1997), the building does not guarantee high performance standards and some technical systems**

		and common spaces are now obsolete. Other than the foyer and the basement, the public block was extensively damaged by the 1996 fire. The part that burned down is currently unsuitable for any type of use.		
	Space utilization:	Within the hotel most spaces are currently used, although the occupancy rate is not high. As for the theater block, damage as a result of the 1996 fire was never repaired and a large part of the building (second and third floor) is currently unused.		
DIMENSIONS	Number of floors:	Public block	Basement + 3 floors	
		Hotel building	2 basement levels + 9 floors + roof	
	Length:	Public block	49.1 m	
		Hotel building	49.1 m	
	Width:	Public block	38.6 m	
		Hotel building	17.1 m	
	Height:	Public block	14.2 m	
		Hotel building	38.5 m	
	Gross floor area:	Public block (first floor)		1,453.0 m²
		Hotel building (first floor)		1,545.0 m²
		Hotel building (typical floor)		600.0 m²
	Gross floor area (total):			14,051.0 m²
	Number of hotel rooms:	Original design	134	
		Current state	102	

House of Youth

The documentary basis of this essay is heterogeneous. At the Uzgosproekt/UzNIIPgradostroitel'stva Institute (O'zshaharsozlik LITI), which was responsible for design and construction of the Tashkent House of Youth, only selected documentation remained by 2021, related particularly to the period of 1976–1977, when the building was already constructed but required the re-equipping of various spaces in order to accommodate the Studio of Creative Youth, which would play a fateful role in the birth and development of the Ilkhom Theater. However, the owner of the former House of Youth (now the Shodlik Hotel) retains documents relating to several stages of the design of the building, from 1967 to 1974, during which period the design evolved. The Tashkent City Archive also preserves a number of documents and, in particular, the transcript of a discussion in 1966 regarding the initial version of the design. An article by architect Richard Bleze, published in early 1966, explains in detail the basic ideas behind the project. Documents which are important for tracing the evolution of the building include those held in Tashkent's Ilkhom Theater and the reminiscences of architects who worked with Richard Bleze (particularly Aleksandr Kuranov and Rem Adylov) and other Tashkent architects in the 1960s and 1970s.

Typology

The typological model of the house of youth in the USSR was a cultural, sport, hotel and entertainment center that combined the functions of a hotel, a hobby club, a sport complex and a creative cluster. Organizations with a similar name, Maison des Jeunes et de la Culture, had existed in France since the 1950s, but there they were intended for the socialization and education of deprived young people in municipalities dominated by the socialists and communists. The Soviet houses of youth were not intended for the young people of the city outskirts. They were much more elitist institutions which aimed to develop creative and sporting initiatives for youth organizations and to promote youth tourism. There was also a hidden purpose: in order to more effectively supervise Soviet young people who showed the most initiative, the KGB created organizations under its control that offered creative, sporting and tourist activities for groups of young people, thus creating suitable conditions for effective "operational work."

The timing of the appearance of "houses of youth" is also significant. Within Stalinist culture, as Vladimir Paperny wrote, "the idea of a youth event could not even exist. This culture attempted to underline the absence of age," and if "it defined particular ages then these were the older person and the baby."[1] The change came with the World Festival of Youth and Students, which took place in 1957 in Moscow. It prompted a wave of designs for special buildings for young people. The symmetrical and static Stalinist "palaces of culture," with their archaic cultivation of the "classic," were replaced by youth cafés and houses of youth in which the dynamic and asymmetrical International Style was reflected.

Two types of Soviet houses (palaces) of youth were built: with a hotel for youth tourism (Yerevan, Tashkent, Leningrad) and without (Tselinograd, Donetsk, Sverdlovsk and others). The direct prototype of the Tashkent House of Youth was its predecessor in Yerevan, the first sketches for which appeared in 1957 and where the foundation was laid a decade later. The complex included a fourteen-story hotel, a wedding hall, a 1,200-seat concert hall, exhibition spaces, a museum, swimming pools, restaurants, bars and a café.[2] The building had an imposing and brutal external appearance, situated on a steep Yerevan slope and conceived to be a highlight of the city skyline. Construction of the Yerevan and Tashkent buildings began almost simultaneously, but the design in Tashkent was somewhat delayed compared to Yerevan, and we can therefore assume that the Tashkent architects took into account the experience of their colleagues.

The First Stage of Design

A letter from the head of the Central Committee of the Komsomol of Uzbekistan to the chief architect of Tashkent of February 15, 1966, stated that the secretariat of the main Komsomol organization in the republic had considered and confirmed the project brief for the House of Youth developed by the Uzgosproekt Institute. On January 28, 1966, these materials had been presented to the Central Committee of the Communist Party of Uzbekistan, where the presidium "considered and approved the project brief for the House of Youth and its construction in Tashkent."[3]

From this we can state that:

- the overall details of the project were established and developed before 1966;
- the client was the Central Committee of the Komsomol of Uzbekistan;
- the project was first approved by the party organizations, after which the Komsomol only had to confirm it.

Judging by the absence of references to a design competition, the commission was sent directly to the Uzgosproekt Institute, where it was assigned to architect Richard Bleze's team. Design may have begun late in 1964. This is indicated by the planning solution. The south façade of the House of Youth faced a green pedestrian boulevard/esplanade connecting the "new" and "old" cities that did not yet exist but was present on the urban plans from the middle of 1964. Bleze confirmed the connection: "According to the general plan for the reconstruction of Tashkent, the site for the construction of the House of Youth is at the intersection of Pakhtakorskaia Street and the planned central pedestrian boulevard, as dictated by the design for the center of the city. [...] In order to meet the urban planning brief the authors, while preserving the idea of the construction along the boulevard, aimed to integrate the new building into the square that appeared between the Palace of Arts and Pakhtakor Stadium."[4] In this way the new building was oriented toward the future new green axis, which was the main idea of the new general plan for the center of Tashkent.

Typologically, Bleze's initial concept was close to the Yerevan prototype. The Tashkent House of Youth had space for a ten-story hotel with 344 beds, a 240-seat youth café/restaurant, a bar for 100 people and a teahouse for 50.[5] The building included a beauty salon, a dance hall, club spaces for interest groups, a universal auditorium for 900 people under a pyramidal vault[6] and a House of Weddings. In order to meet the requirements of the brief, on the third floor, above the restaurant, the architects located a Komsomol museum, but this was canceled due to a lack of exhibits and replaced by a library

1 Vladimir Paperny, *Kul'tura Dva* [*Culture Two*] (Moscow: NLO, 2016), https://kniga-online.com/books/dokumentalnye-knigi/publicism/page-23-216562-vladimir-papernyi-kultura-dva.html (accessed January 30, 2024).

2 Karen Balian, *Artur Tarkhanian, Spartak Khachikian, Grach'ia Pogosian* (Moscow: Tatlin, 2021), 44.

3 "Pis'mo Upravliaiushchego delami TsK LKSM Uzbekistana Mamadzhanova nachal'niku APU Tashgorispolkoma Aleksandru Iakushevu [Letter from Head of the Central Committee of the Komsomol of Uzbekistan Mamadzhanov to the Head of the Architecture and Planning Administration of Tashkent City Executive Committee Aleksandr Iakushev]," Protokoly zasedanii arkhitekturnoi komissii i ekspertnye zakliucheniia po proektam i smetam stroitel'stva za No. 9–28. Nachato 31.01.1966, okoncheno 10 marta 1966 [Protocols of Meetings of the Architectural Council and Expert Opinions on Projects and Construction Budgets, Nos. 9–28. Opened January 31, 1966, closed March 10, 1966], Tashkent City Archive, fund 36, list 1, item 1322, on 154 sheets, 140.

4 Richard Bleze and E. Patlis, "Dom molodezhi v Tashkente [The House of Youth in Tashkent]," *Stroitel'stvo i arkhitektura Uzbekistana* [*Construction and Architecture of Uzbekistan*], no. 5, 1966, 21.

5 Ibid., 22.

6 A similar complex in terms of structure, the Palace of Youth, was designed in the late 1960s in Leningrad. Construction began in 1969 and was completed in 1978, two years later than its Tashkent analogue.

Inner courtyard and teahouse, sketch, 1965–1966

Inner courtyard, view toward the hotel, sketch, 1965–1966

with book storage and a reading room with auxiliary spaces.[7] However, unlike the Yerevan project, the authors of Tashkent's House of Youth also envisaged a developed sports block with gymnastics, basketball and volleyball halls and a swimming pool.[8] A decorative pool with a waterfall and a carefully developed relief on the first level were intended to create a comfortable micro-oasis in the internal courtyard, which served as a distributive area between the various spaces of the complex.

The sports block was located in the north flank of the building. The architects planned an entranceway from the direction of the boulevard/esplanade that would lead over the foundation, between the high-rise block and the pyramid of the universal auditorium. It led to the main staircase, which linked the "basement, vestibule, café and foyer of the auditorium, the floor of club spaces and the terrace for which a summer cinema auditorium was designed."[9] Between the hotel block and the restaurant on the second level the architects placed a dance floor and a "space for meetings with foreign delegations and for press conferences."[10] The building was conceived comprehensively: here Tashkent's youth could have fun, be creative and take part in sport and even, judging by the programming of the building, politics. Visitors to the capital of Uzbekistan could learn about the life of young Tashkent. The plans of the standard floor of the high-rise hotel block incorporated single and double hotel rooms from the south side and five-bed rooms from the north. In line with tradition the reception and service spaces were located on the first floor of the hotel. The roof of the hotel was to be used as a café with a bar and a dance floor. Here there was also a viewing area which looked down on the green esplanade of the center that spread from Revolution Square to Chorsu Square. From the construction point of view the high-rise block was to have a reinforced concrete structure with suspended wall panels and the horizontal block was to have a prefabricated monolithic reinforced concrete structure.[11]

Even at the height of the Thaw no one had revoked the aesthetic imperative of "national form." In the project explanations the authors stressed the planning principle of grouping spaces "around a spacious internal courtyard that is divided functionally into zones and shaded by the high-rise block of the hotel (a technique borrowed from national architecture)."[12] Bleze described the main building as "a multilayered volume with suspended sun-protection grilles and sculptural end walls and an adjoining two- or three-story block of public buildings," the west façade of which used "suspended solid expanded clay and concrete panels and latticed panels with Uzbek ornamentation."[13] "The finishing of the building," the architect continued, "employed elements of national architecture such as Uzbek decoration in the design of the sun-protection grilles, figurative use of brick and natural stone and extensive use of greenery and water features."[14] The architect appears to have overused traditional references, which his colleagues soon pointed out.

At the beginning of March 1966, the initial design project for the House of Youth was discussed by Tashkent's leading architects at a meeting of the Council of the Architecture and Planning Administration. The main expert was Il'ia Merport (who held a Ph.D. in architecture and was deputy director of research at the TashZNIIEP Institute) and the debate included lead architects at Tashgiprogor Leon Adamov, Genrikh Aleksandrovich and Iurii Khaldeev, lead architect at Uzgosproekt Vladimir Berezin and Chief Architect of Tashkent Aleksandr Iakushev. As a result, the proposed project was agreed, but with a series of comments that the architects were to take into account in further developing it. Firstly, they had to simplify the project to build it in two phases, as the city was unable to construct a complex with such varied functions at one time (in Yerevan the same scenario developed, and the construction of the House of Youth took place in two stages). Secondly, the Council criticized the design of the façades,

7 "Dom molodezhi v Tashkente [The House of Youth in Tashkent]," *Svod pamiatnikov istorii i kul'tury Uzbekistana* [*Corpus of Monuments of History and Culture of Uzbekistan*], vol. 2, *Tashkent: Pamiatniki khudozhestvennoi kul'tury (arkhitektury i monumental'nogo iskusstva) Tashkenta* [*Tashkent: Monuments of Artistic Culture (Architecture and Monumental Art) of Tashkent*, Archive of the Institute of Art Studies of the Academy of Sciences of the Republic of Uzbekistan, IA. S48, no. 1253.

8 Ibid., 134.

9 Richard Bleze and E. Patlis, "Dom molodezhi v Tashkente [The House of Youth in Tashkent]," 23.

10 Ibid.

11 "Dom molodezhi v Tashkente [The House of Youth in Tashkent]," *Svod pamiatnikov istorii i kul'tury Uzbekistana* [*Corpus of Monuments of History and Culture of Uzbekistan*].

12 Richard Bleze and E. Patlis, "Dom molodezhi v Tashkente [The House of Youth in Tashkent]," 23.

13 "Protokol no. 21 zasedaniia rabochego apparata arkhitekturnoi komissii Upravleniia po delam stroitel'stva i arkhitektury Tashgorispolkoma ot 3 marta 1966 goda [Protocol No. 21 of the Meeting of the Working Group of the Architectural Council of the Construction and Architecture Administration of Tashkent City Executive Committee dated March 3, 1966]," Protokoly zasedanii arkhitekturnoi komissii i ekspertnye zakliucheniia po proektam i smetam stroitel'stva za No. 9–28. Nachato 31.01.1966, okoncheno 10 marta 1966 [Protocols of Meetings of the Architectural Council and Expert Opinions on Projects and Construction Budgets. Opened January 31, 1966, closed March 10, 1966], Tashkent City Archive, fund 36, list 1, item 1322, on 154 sheets, 135.

14 Ibid.

especially the west side, considering them to be too verbose. It recommended: "When developing the façades of the building it is necessary to achieve architectural and compositional unity by using simpler and architecturally more expressive techniques that provide the opportunity to avoid multiple themes and fractionality, especially on the façade on Pakhtakorskaia Street, where it is necessary to reject sun-protection devices that are complicated in terms of pattern and form, and also to find a more appropriate form of support for the multistory building of the hotel."[15] This requirement by the expert group demonstrates that in the mid-1960s it was still necessary to be careful when working with elements perceived as "national." The architects simply touched on the possibility of encrusting the modernist architecture with them and not all of the proposed versions were seen as acceptable by the professional community. Thirdly, the Council stated that since "the dominant building on the square is the Palace of Arts, it is necessary to rework the pyramidal volume of the auditorium into a simpler and more laconic form with a separate vestibule and foyer that does not conflict with the Palace of Arts."[16] This extremely important requirement demonstrated the Council of the Architecture and Planning Administration's role as an urban planning center that coordinated the efforts of the numerous project institutes in Tashkent. The Council also recommended altering several elements of the roof, making the line of the canopy more sculptural and simultaneously simplifying the outline of the volumes.

Façade of the House of Youth in Yerevan (variant dated 1966); architects: Artur Tarkhanian, Spartak Khachikian, Hrachia Pogosian, Martin Zakharian

House of Youth in Yerevan, Armenia, 1966–1967; architects: Artur Tarkhanian, Spartak Khachikian, Hrachia Pogosian, Martin Zakharian

The Evolution of the Project

The Tashkent earthquake, which occurred six weeks after the meeting of the Council of the Architecture and Planning Administration, had a serious influence on everything connected to construction in the city. Design of the House of Youth continued sporadically from 1967 to 1971 and construction began on schedule at the end of 1967. It is clear that the architect took into account all of the Council's requirements. The planning of the project was reorganized so that it could be built in two stages. Bleze produced a number of variations of the pyramidal volume, but the problem would solve itself in the end since the second stage of construction, which included the universal auditorium, was never realized. The façade on Pakhtakorskaia Street was simplified, which meant that the building was better integrated into a context in which the Palace of Arts dominated. The more sculptural end walls and pilotis for the high-rise block became a visual feature of the House of Youth. Thanks to them it had an individuality and wholeness. Construction was completed in 1975. The architects tried to vary the construction materials in the external and internal finishing. In particular they used labradorite, Nurata and Gazgan marble, brown tuff, pink coquina, travertine, wood and aluminum. The banqueting hall included elements of traditional folk decoration: ceramic, majolica, chased metal and ganch plasterwork.[17] In the pool on the boulevard side a sculpture named *The Meeting* (sculptor: Iurii Kiselev) was installed, which depicted a seated couple in traditional Uzbek clothing.

The fact that the completed building was less expressive than the initial sketches can be explained by more than just the earthquake. At this

15 "Protokol no. 21... [Protocol No. 21...]," 137.
16 Ibid.

17 "Dom molodezhi v Tashkente [The House of Youth in Tashkent]," *Svod pamiatnikov istorii i kul'tury Uzbekistana* [*Corpus of Monuments of History and Culture of Uzbekistan*].

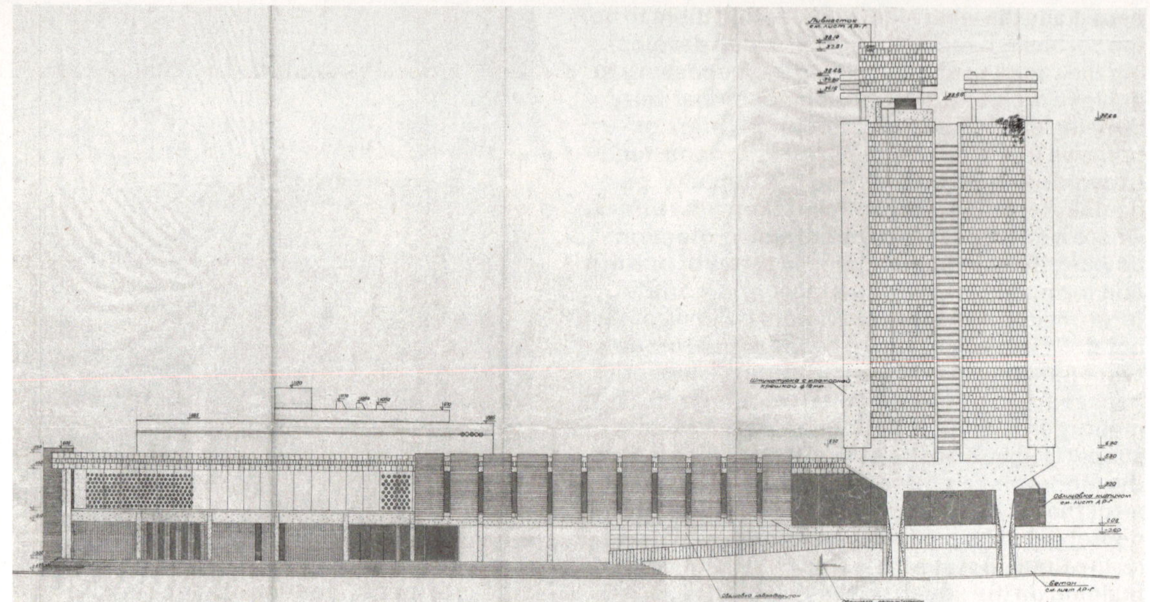
Façade from Pakhtakorskaia Street, 1967

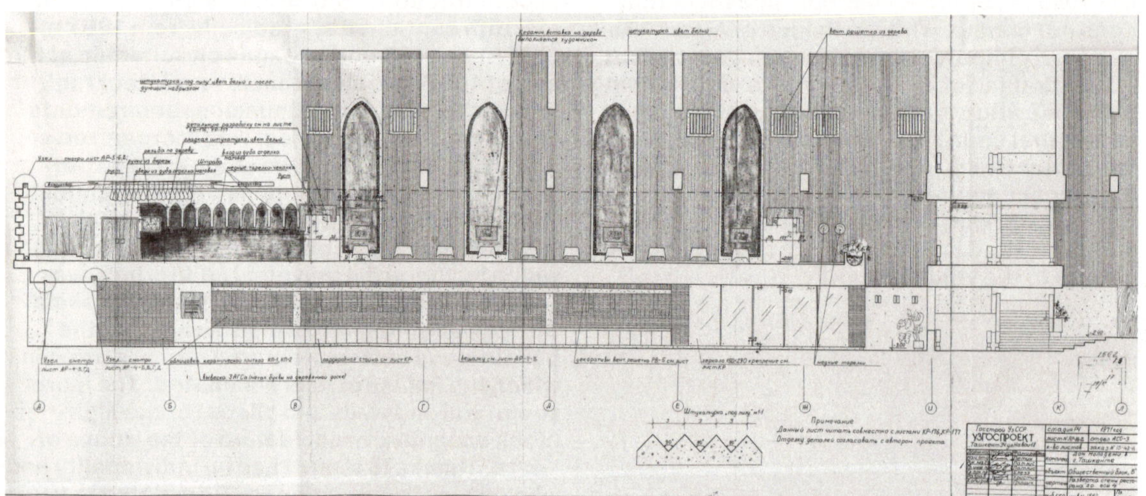
Finishes of interiors of public block B, 1971

Ilkhom Theater, 2022

time the visionary program of the Thaw was being gently edged out by the pragmatics of "perfecting socialism," and the curtailment of Kosygin's economic reforms led to the minimization of expenditure on social and cultural buildings. Even in the late 1970s the architects still hoped that construction of the second stage was imminent. The information text about the completed House of Youth published in the journal *Stroitel'stvo i arkhitektura Uzbekistana* (*Construction and Architecture of Uzbekistan*) in 1978 noted that the building comprised three blocks: "a 350-bed hotel [...]; a public block incorporating [...] a club for creative youth with a bar, a sports hall 18 × 36 m, a swimming pool 10 × 25 m, an art studio, a record library, a discotheque, a club for technical youth and technical areas; a universal auditorium incorporating a multipurpose hall for 750 people [...]."[18] The author of the text had clearly used outdated information from a decade earlier. The swimming pool, sports hall, universal auditorium and the pool with waterfall designed to decorate the internal courtyard were never built. However, he included additional clarification about the "club for creative youth." This important theme is explored in more detail below.

A Change of Fortune

When the building was handed over to the clients in 1976 the bureaucratic nature of Soviet economics and social life almost played a cruel trick on the House of Youth. The club and interest group activities organized in spaces specially designed for them did not take off. The change of fortune for the cultural block and the complex as a whole occurred when young director Mark Weil had the idea to use the House of Youth as a haven for his Ilkhom Theater, which he had organized without the involvement of Gosplan. As a result, this was the venue for one of the most original Soviet theater collectives of the late stagnation period. His link to the building was often described anecdotally, almost like the unexpected birth of the messiah in a manger or, to be more exact, in the space of a restaurant's vegetable storage. However, the director's notes contained more mature associations with this architecture of the Thaw period, which had outlived its time and was now in palpable conflict with reality: "In the 1970s we were probably unified by only one thing, the desire to express the views of our generation and to tell the truth as we understood it. However, where my contemporaries in the West fought against bourgeois society [...], I seemed to inhabit a happy world where I was not prosperous but was free from the power of money and open to new ideas. My generation no longer believed in these ideological dogmas. In our productions the hero was a product of our society who lived by the standards of a dual morality where he thought one thing, said another (what he was supposed to say) and did something else."[19] These words can easily be applied to the architectural generation of the 1970s and 1980s. Formally, the architectural modernism of the 1960s, unlike the avant-garde trends in visual art and literature of those years, was not only not subject to official criticism but was also supported by the authorities right up to the collapse of the USSR (this paradox was regularly articulated by Feliks Novikov, the famous Moscow architect, who stated that the "architectural thaw" did not end with Khrushchëv's exit from the scene, nor after Soviet forces invaded Czechoslovakia, but continued to the end of the Soviet period). However, from the social point of view the projects of the 1970s and 1980s gradually lost their focus on experimentation and the construction of the future, making way for aims of a memorial, regional and metaphysical nature. The building of the "new society" was replaced with the aim of providing more comfort. The social aspects of Soviet modernism were increasingly emasculated and replaced by the requirement for "professionalism." Richard Bleze's oeuvre completely reflected this evolution. The architect worked consistently to perfect the modernist lexicon. Regardless of their organic integration into the urban context his buildings contained increasingly few historical allusions. However, the finished House of Youth differed markedly from his first project of the Thaw period, which reflected Soviet dreams of the new, "universally developed" person.

Links appeared between the theater and the building that could not have been predicted earlier: when the architects began work on the design, Mark Weil had not yet started school, while during construction he was a student at Tashkent Theater and Art Institute. The theater—and consequently the theater space in the basement and then the foyer of the ground level—had its own history. First, Ilkhom became the most popular theater in Tashkent, and then it was recognized outside the borders of the republic, both nationally and internationally. A community of artists, musicians and dancers formed around Ilkhom, then a theater studio appeared, which functioned as an educational institution, and a foyer that was an exhibition space. After the collapse of the USSR the theater succeeded in adapting to market economics.

18 A. Ganiev, "UzNIIPgradostroitel'stva za 50 let (1928–1978 gg.) [50 Years of UzNIIPgradostroitel'stva]," *Stroitel'stvo i arkhitektura Uzbekistana* [*Construction and Architecture of Uzbekistan*], no. 10, 1978, 8.

19 Mark Weil, "Neizvestnyi izvestnyi 'Ilkhom' [The Unknown Famous Ilkhom]," *Fergana News*, February 17, 2010, https://www.fergananews.com/articles/6474.

It was always the focus of attention of foreign embassies and foundations, and even after the tragic death of the founder (2007) it retained its original functions and continued to play the role of a unifying cluster for the artistic life of the city. This is somewhat reminiscent of the fate of the Leningrad Palace of Youth. Having been perceived as a modernist "lump of glass" during construction, in the next decade the Leningrad Palace of Youth became a cult building in the city as the venue for festivals of the Leningrad rock club involving Viktor Tsoi, Sergei Kurëkhin and other figures who had emerged from underground youth culture. The Tashkent House of Youth differs from this example in that it did not become a mere episode in the history of the city but even today continues to form the arts agenda.

In 1976–1977 Bleze's group adapted the basement and the foyer for the theater. The reconstruction included the theater studio, the cloakroom next to the bar, the spaces of the House of Weddings, the restaurant toilets and the internal courtyard.[20] It involved refining the planning using additional partitions and fitting out the new spaces with materials suitable for their functions. For the theater studio the architects suggested "the installation of an amphitheater for seats and a demountable stage, acoustic cladding of the ceiling and walls, replanning of the sound and light boxes and decoration of the space with art objects."[21] From this point the theater auditorium had a transformable stage and seating. The seats could be arranged as a standard parterre from the north side of the auditorium, as a semicircle from the east and north and also on the second level from the south (the space was used in this way in one of the longest running productions at the theater, *A Respectable Wedding*, where the stage was located in the center of the auditorium). During this period the walls were clad with light-colored decorative brick (which was later painted black). The work in the other reconstructed spaces was also decorative in nature. The cloakroom next to the bar "incorporated an additional partition made from plaster slabs, the walls were clad with wood, an emblem was made of forged copper, and decorative light fittings and mirrors were installed."[22] Overall, it should be noted that the theater gradually swallowed up the basement rooms that, in the initial design, were intended for various creative groups. The Studio of Creative Youth, established by administrative order, was to be a meeting place for representatives of various arts. Experience showed that such meetings took place organically in the theater, which became a space for artists and musicians and even for architects. Art exhibitions would take place in the ground-level foyer for the next few decades.

In the post-perestroika period the House of Youth was privatized and various spaces changed hands a number of times, making the chronology of ownership difficult to establish. The high-rise part was transformed into a city hotel (the Shodlik Hotel), but many of its spaces, excluding the vestibule, retained their original plan and some details. However, the overblown (in comparison with the requirements of an average hotel) cultural and catering block was vulnerable. The foyer where exhibitions took place and the spaces of the Ilkhom Theater were reequipped several times, but the spaces above them remained "ownerless" and became very dilapidated. The House of Weddings was moved from the complex and the library and reading rooms no longer exist. New solutions have been in development since the early 2020s. It is important that they benefit both the owner of the building and the theater, while revealing the merits of Bleze's team's original design.

20 "Tekhno-rabochii proekt: pererabotka Doma molodezhi v g. Tashkente v KTM (Klub tvorcheskoi molodezhi). Tom 1. Kniga 1-1. Svodnaia poiasnitel'naia zapiska. Tashkent, 1977 [Technical Working Design: Remodeling of the House of Youth in Tashkent in the Club of Creative Youth, volume 1, book 1-1, Tashkent, 1977]," O'zshaharsozlik LITI Archive, fund (1562) 35, inv. no. 5, items 8, 4.
21 Ibid.
22 Ibid.

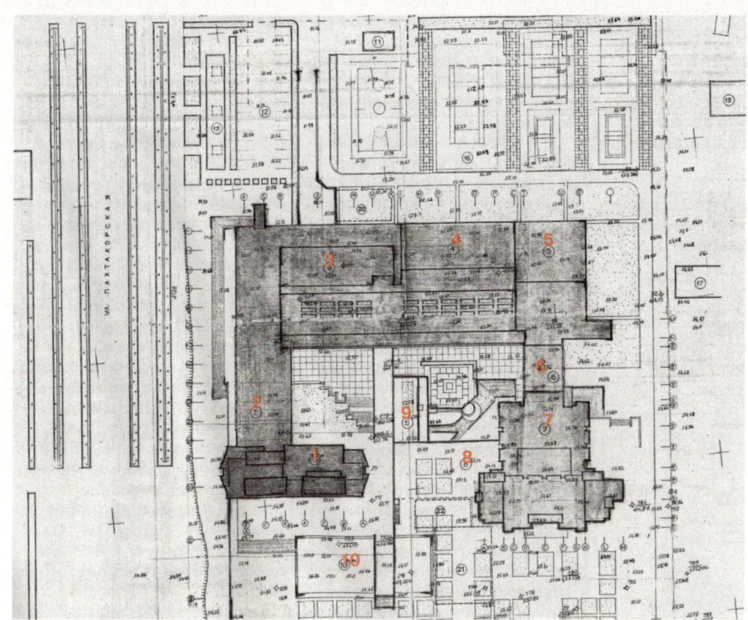

General plan scheme, 1972

1 Hotel – block A
2 Passageway – block B
3 Restaurant – block V
4 Sports block – block G
5 Swimming pool – block D
6 Foyer/passage – block E
7 Universal hall – block Zh
8 Teahouse bar – block K
9 Internal courtyard of teahouse
10 Pool no. 1 – Fountain

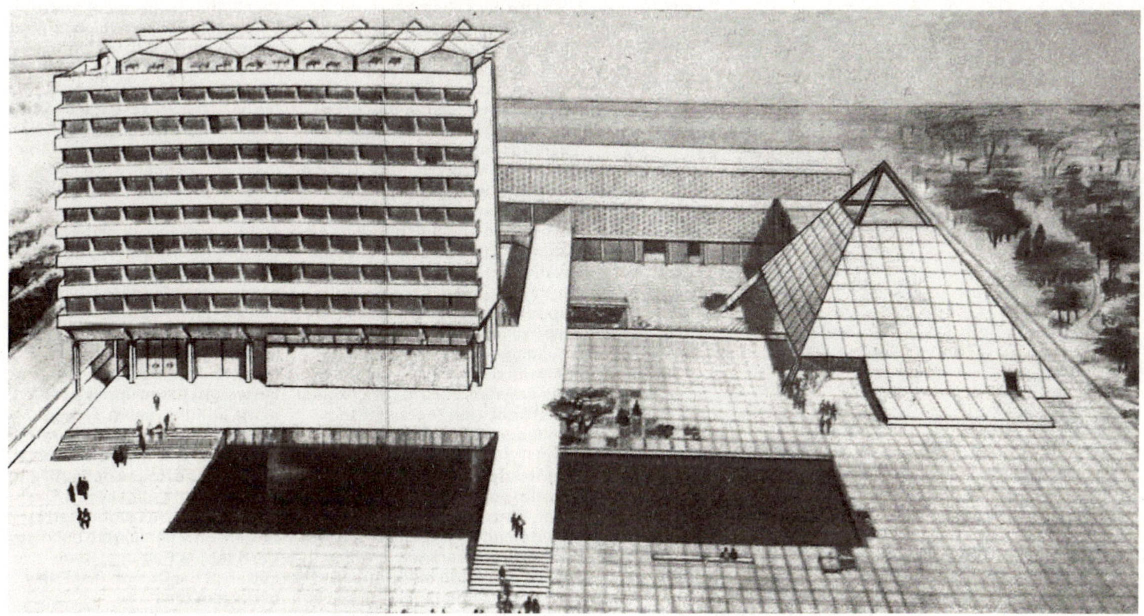

House of Youth, project sketch, 1965–1966

ARCHITECT
RICHARD BLEZE

Place and year of birth:
Tashkent, 1936
Place and year of death:
Sosnovy Bor, Leningrad Region, Russia, 2002
Education:
1955–1961, Architecture Department of Central Asia Polytechnic Institute (SazPI)

Richard Bleze's first practical experience as a young architect was under Vladimir Berezin, on the project for the Central Committee of the Communist Party of Uzbekistan.

His first independent work—the "Intourist Hotel," but in fact the out-of-town hotel of the Central Committee of the Communist Party of Uzbekistan in the village of Durmen—re-elaborated the already established architectural language of the 1960s characteristic, in particular, of administrative buildings: glass façades from the north, sun protection from the south, open asymmetrical planning and the functional division of volumes and blocks.

His second large independent project was the House of Youth (1965–1975). After this Richard Bleze designed the House of Publishers (1970–1974), one of the iconic structures of "modernist Tashkent." While maintaining the functionality of the layout, he integrated it into the urban context, bringing together numerous fragments of the city center: Theater Square with Lenin Square, Lenin Boulevard with the Tashkent Hotel and Theater Square, the lower and upper parts of Lenin Square with the Lenin Museum. The large number of images in which the House of Publishers features together with the Lenin Museum demonstrates that they were perceived as a single ensemble. Incidentally, the House of Publishers was designed after the Lenin Museum was constructed and was an urban planning response to its appearance. The House of Publishers, possibly more than other buildings of the time, bore the imprint of the futurist ideas of the previous decade. While most Tashkent architects, like their colleagues from Central Asia and the Caucasus, were already seriously interested in the memorial possibilities of modernism, Bleze aimed to create a contemporary, technicist building, the appearance of which was connected to the epoch of electronic communications. In particular, he wrote: "The illuminated newspaper/advertisement, which occupies a leading position in the night-time lighting of the city, plays a major role in creating the image of the building. The universal, four-color running light display fully meets three basic requirements: attracting attention; compact, intelligible and comprehensible information; topicality."[1] Flashing advertising was also designed for the west and south surfaces of the elevator tower. The vertical volume was crowned by "a sculptural symbol of contemporary information," the stainless steel "teletype antenna of the Uzbek Telegraphic Agency," which remained a decorative element.

These details aside, the project incorporated features of 1970s architecture, with its Brutalist forms, and also a certain historicism. The upper cubic volume of the clock was nuanced with a belt of geometric patterns that referenced the ribs of the Lenin Museum and the twenty-story tower of the Ministries Building. The walkway to the neighboring publishing block, constructed in the Stalin period, was softened by circular arches. Critics of the time, who were influenced by the imperatives of Soviet aesthetics with its slogan of "national form," post-factum attributed the sun-protection grille to this imperative, as well as the unusual pattern of the balconies of the upper floors, in which they saw "stalactites." However, evidence accessible today indicates that, on the contrary, Bleze did not adhere to Sharaf Rashidov's insistent requests to make the building more decorative.

Bleze's last large building in Tashkent was the uncompleted Computing Center, which formed a single entity with the three-story Gosplan building. Flanking Lenin Square from the north, the building was distinguished by well-composed sun protection and Brutalist plastic forms. The rhythmic verticals were coordinated with the project for the National Library (Sergo Sutiagin), which was designed for the neighboring site, yet both buildings may have been influenced by the Robarts Library at the University of Toronto. Unlike in the Toronto complex, Bleze would develop the theme of "modernist entablement," adding weight to the upper part of the building using a sculptural finishing element (separate aspects of this theme can be traced in the House of Youth and the House of Publishers). The same theme was embodied in Bleze's final completed building, the Bukhara Regional Committee of the Communist Party of Uzbekistan.

Bleze, unlike Sergo Sutiagin, was rarely written about, but he occasionally described his own projects. In his commentary on the project for the center of Tashkent (mid-1980s), which was symptomatically named "Our City," Bleze defined what he did not like about Tashkent architecture, and today these lines can be seen as a demand for a strictly contextual approach that avoids the traps of representativity, orientalism and scholastic "model thinking."

"A negative example in building practice in Tashkent is the solution for Lenin Square, with its 'Niemeyer-like' quality of architecture, as interpreted by Moscow architects, where they failed to connect the enormous space of the square with the high-rise parameters of the buildings. In short, the main rule of architecture—harmony—is broken. In addition, the interpretation of national architectural techniques is cosmetic. There are relatively successful buildings in the practice of that group of authors. These include the branch of the Central Lenin Museum and the Peoples' Friendship Cinema and Concert Hall. However, where the museum integrated organically into a series of iconic structures, the cinema and concert hall did not form an ensemble with the neighboring buildings on the hypertrophied square, which prompts contradictory opinions about the quality of this work."[2]

1 Richard Bleze, "Redaktsionnyi-izdatel'skii korpus kompleksa izdatel'stva TsK KP Uzbekistana [The Editorial and Publishing Block of the Publishers' Complex of the Central Committee of the Communist Party of Uzbekistan]," *Stroitel'stvo i arkhitektura Uzbekistana* [*Construction and Architecture of Uzbekistan*], no. 1, 1972, 21.

2 Richard Bleze, "Nash gorod [Our City]," *Arkhitektura i stroitel'stvo Uzbekistana* [*Architecture and Construction of Uzbekistan*], no. 9, 1987, 4.

INSTITUTIONAL FRAMEWORK

Uzgosproekt / UzNIIPgradostroitel'stva

CADRE

The history of Uzgosproekt since the early 1960s was defined by the arrival of Vladimir Berezin, Sergo Sutiagin, Richard Bleze and Dmitrii Shuvaev, who quickly became the heads of the design studios. Having learned to cooperate in designing the major projects of the first half of the 1960s—building of the Central Committee of the Communist Party of Uzbekistan and the Panoramic Cinema—they had compatible views on architecture and formed architectural groups that shared their values.

PRIORITIES

Use of techniques and vocabulary of modern architecture, rejection of historicism and formal quotations, evolution from simple and transparent volumes in the 1960s to more complex Brutalist forms in the 1970s and 1980s, functionalism of the plan which determined the volume solution. Representative buildings: Central Committee of Communist Party of Uzbekistan, Panoramic Cinema, House of Publishers, Navoi Library (not built), Computing Center (not completed), State Planning Committee, Music and Drama Theater and Literature Museum in Kokand, Cosmonauts Avenue metro station, theaters in Nukus, Karshi and Urgench, Namangan and Bukhara Party Committees.

Basement floor plan
Original condition

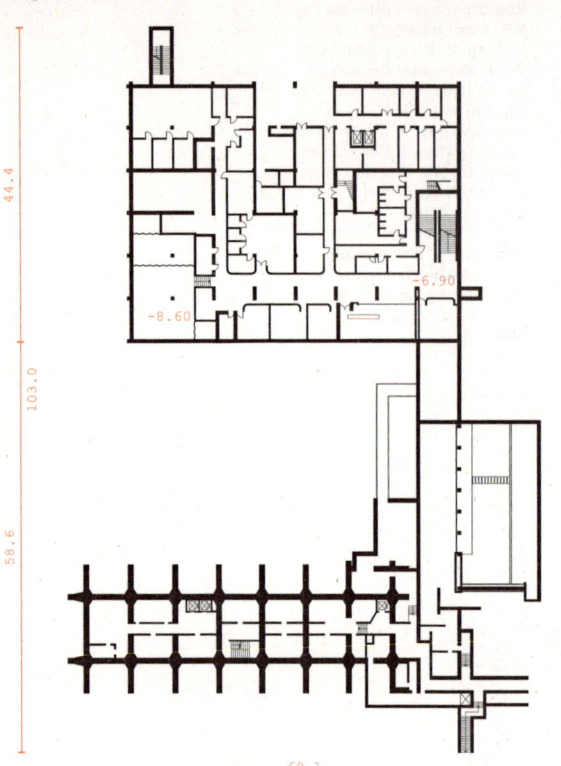

1st floor plan
Original condition

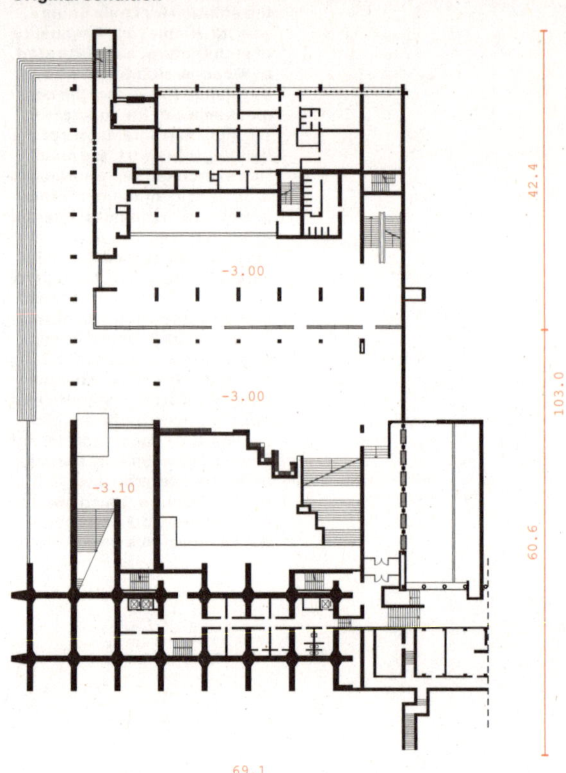

2nd floor plan
Original condition

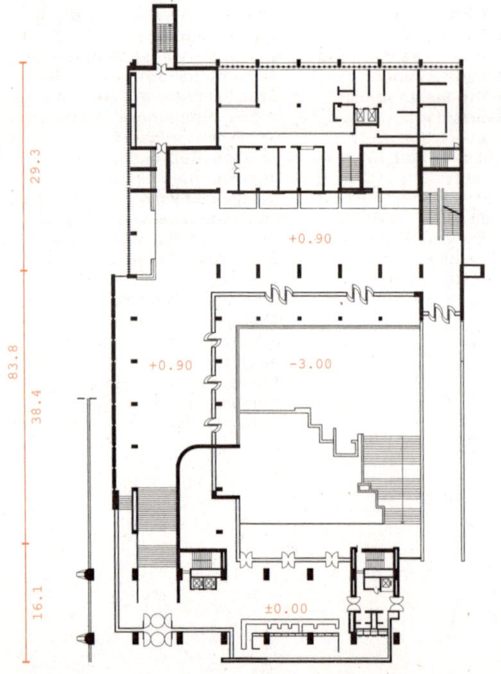

3rd floor plan
Original condition

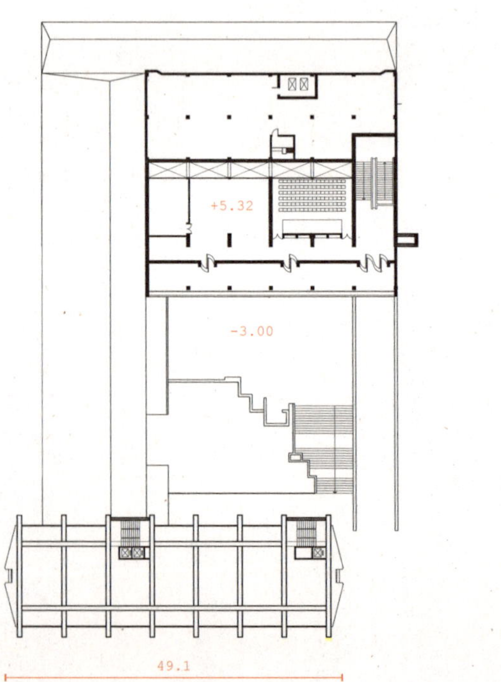

0 5 15m

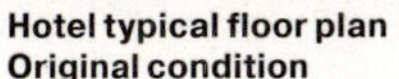

Hotel typical floor plan
Original condition

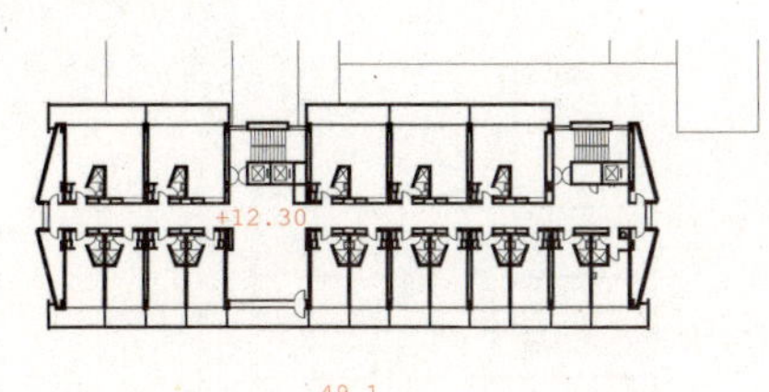

Hotel rooftop plan
Original condition

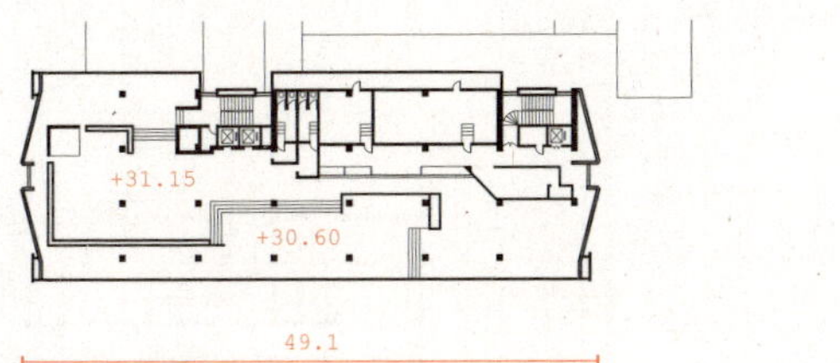

West elevation
Original condition

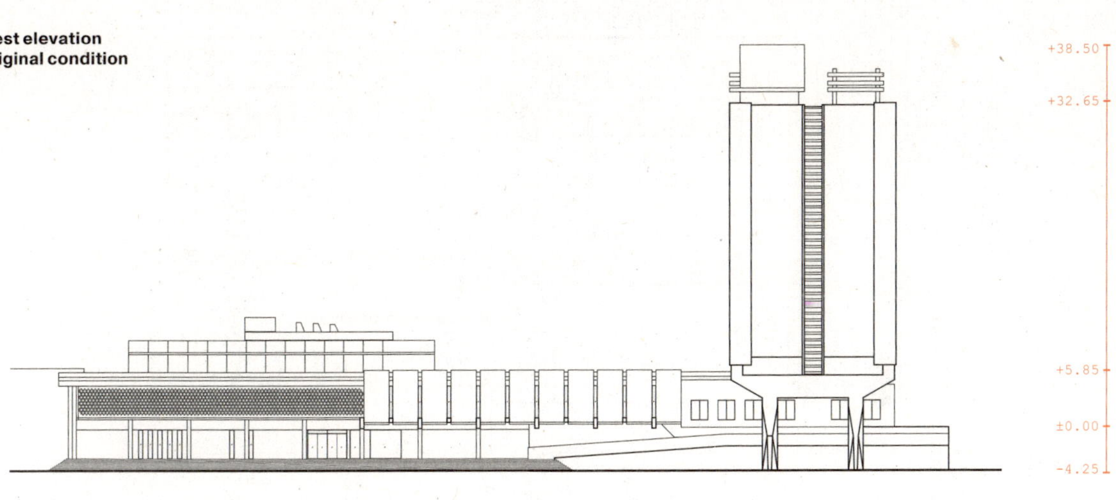

North-west axonometric view

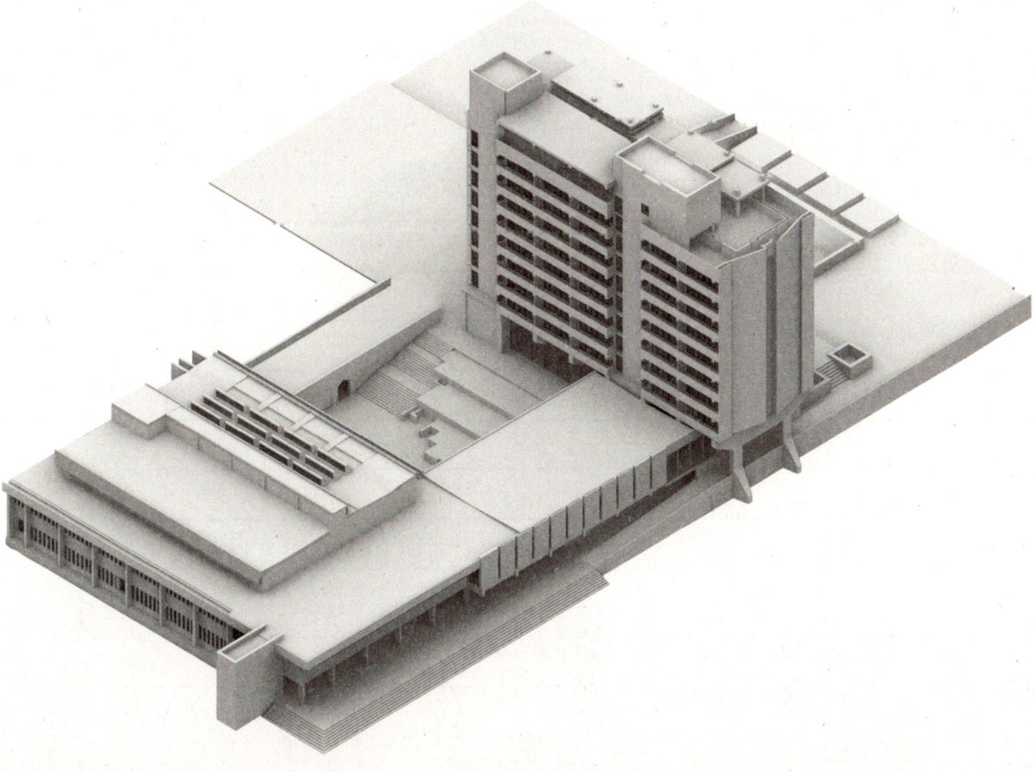

0 5 15m

North elevation
Original condition

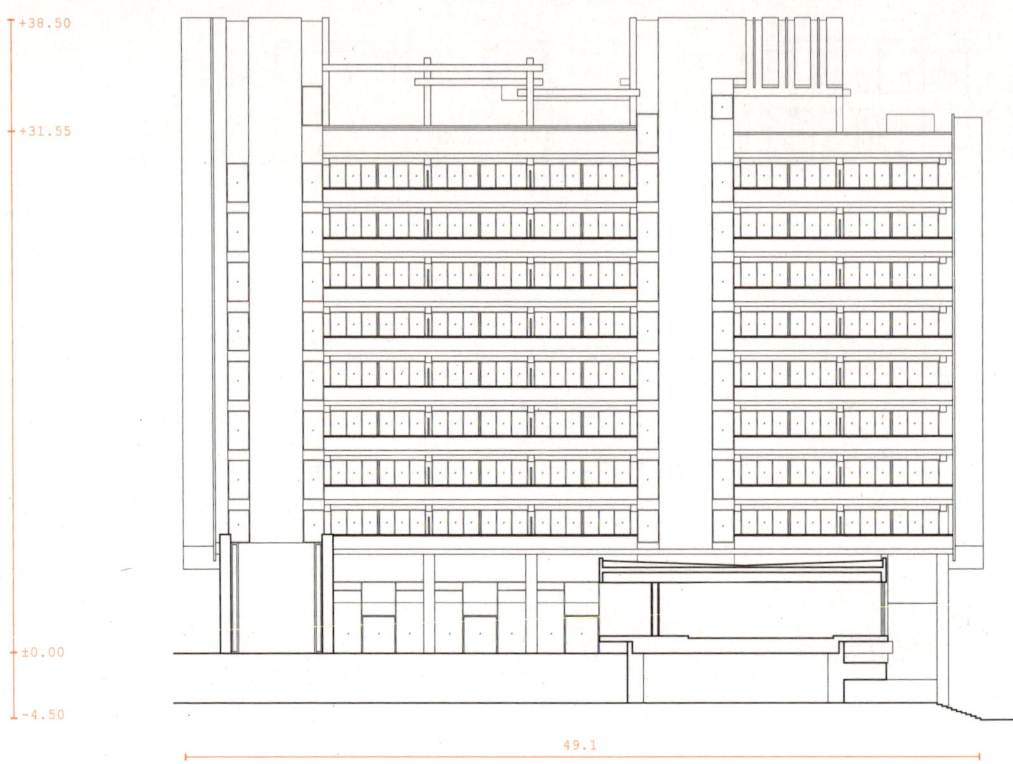

South elevation
Original condition

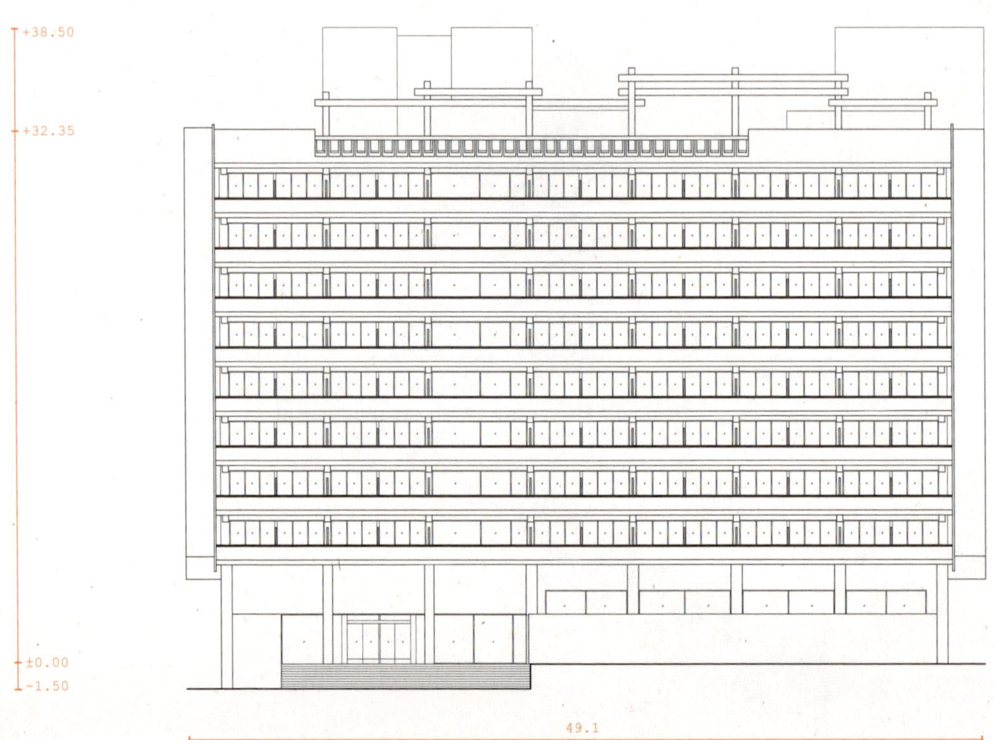

(E1) Interior elevation of the second floor of public block lunch hall
Original condition

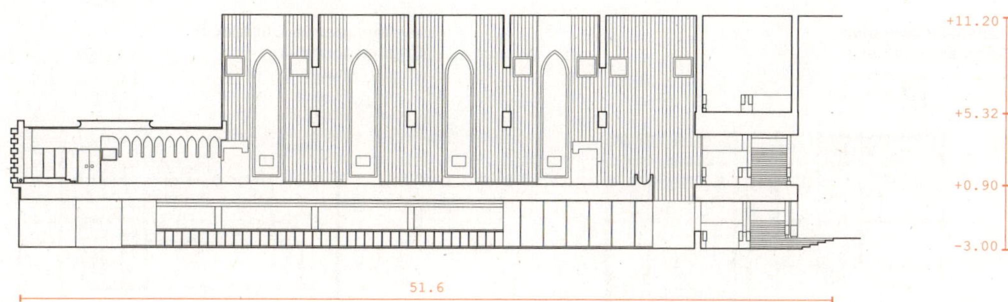

(E2) Eastern elevation of the teahouse block
Original condition

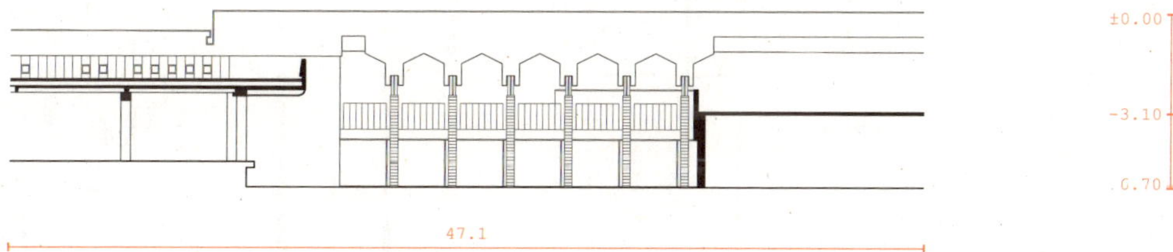

Section AA' – passageway
Original condition

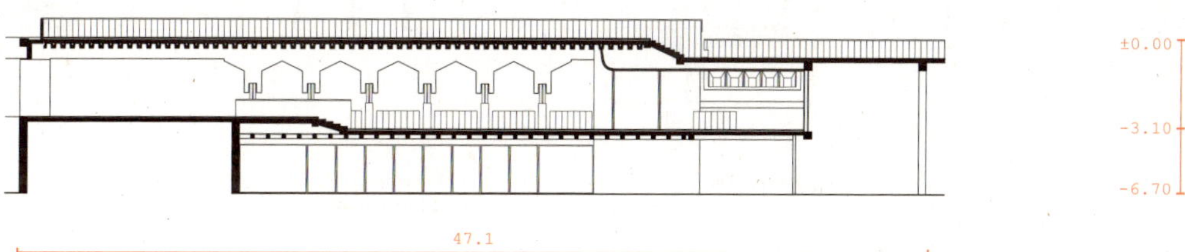

Exterior view from Pakhtakorskaia Street
Original condition

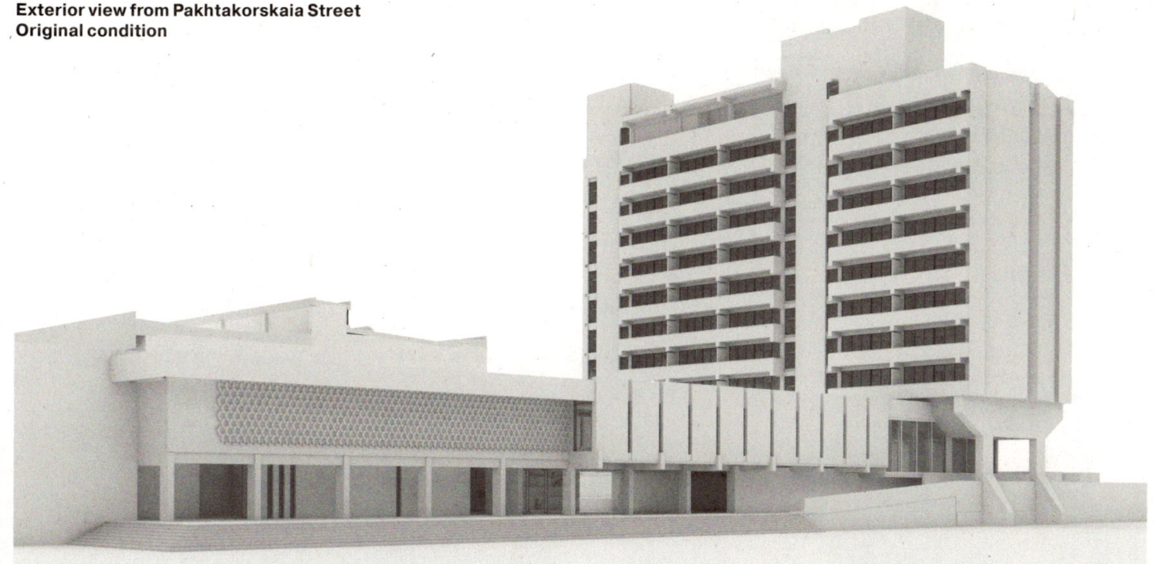

0 5 10m

1975

Basement floor plan
Original condition

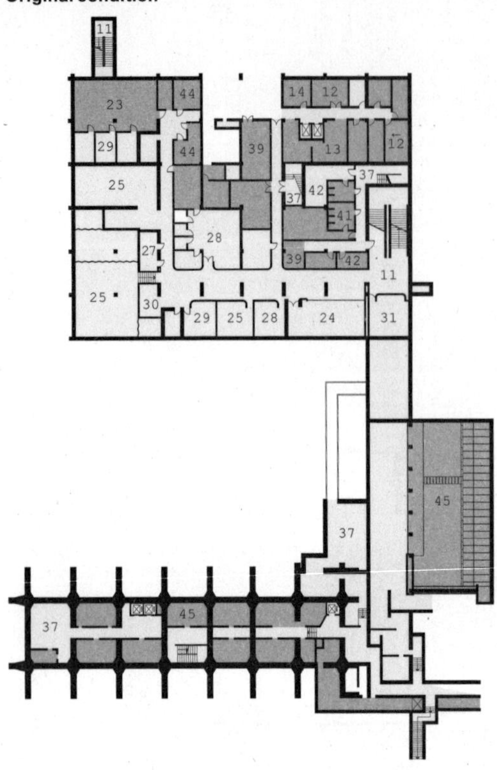

1st floor plan (public block)
Original condition

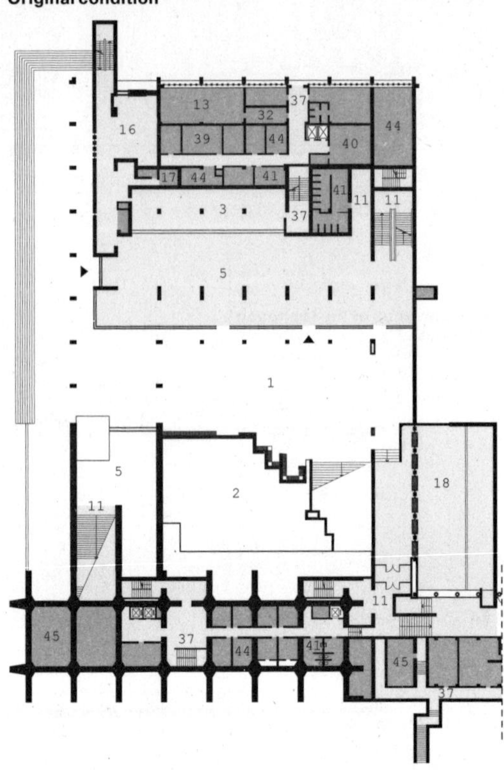

2nd floor (public block) and 1st floor (hotel) plan
Original condition

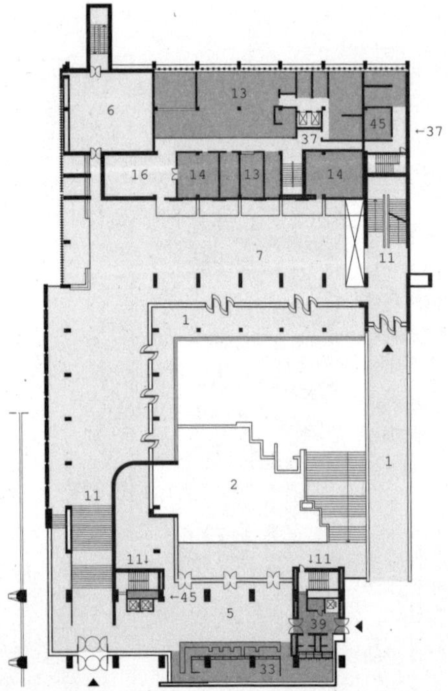

3rd floor (public block) and technical floor (hotel) plan
Original condition

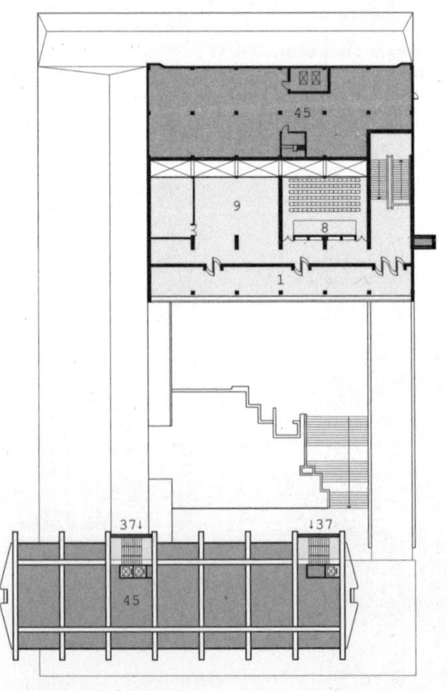

2022

Basement floor plan
Current condition

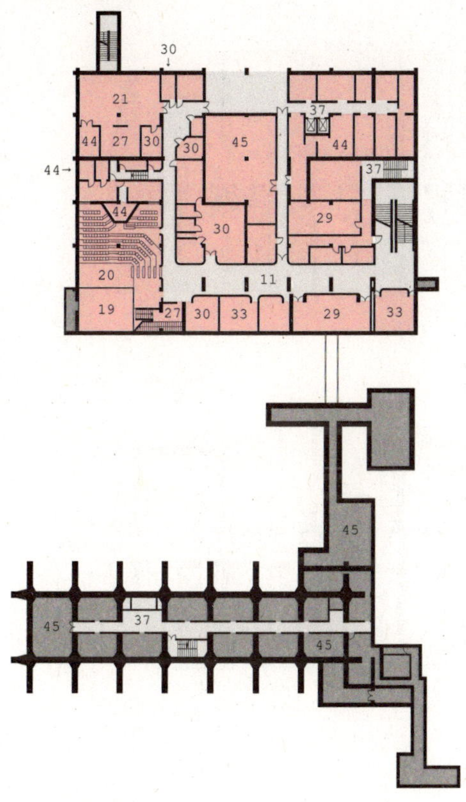

1st floor plan (public block)
Current condition

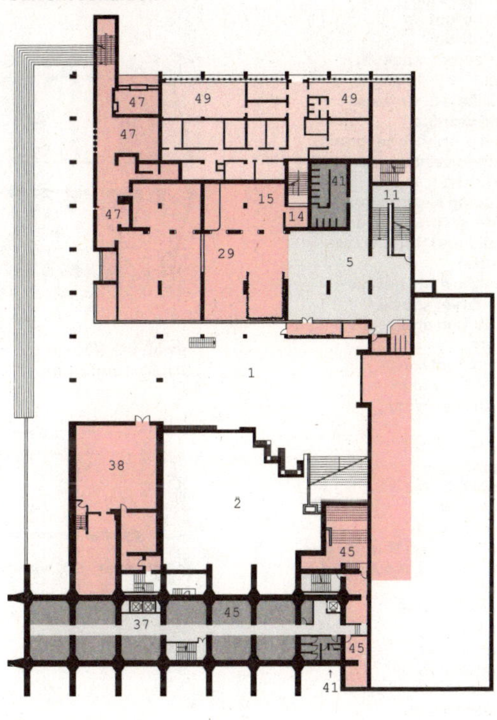

2nd floor (public block) and 1st floor (hotel) plan
Current condition

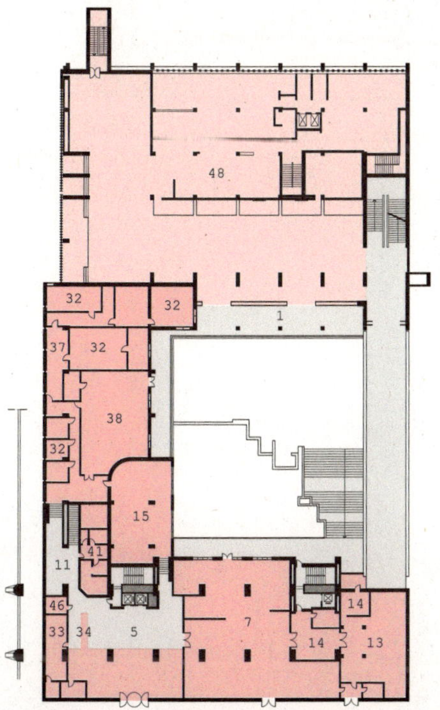

3rd floor (public block) and technical floor (hotel) plan
Current condition

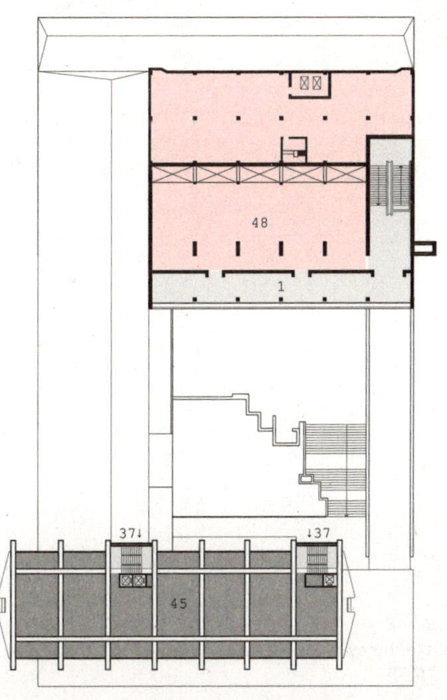

1 Terrace, balcony
2 Vegetation
3 Cloakroom
4 Airlock
5 Vestibule
6 Banquet hall
7 Restaurant
8 Auditorium
9 Komsomol museum
10 Gym
11 Circulation, visitors
12 Food storage
13 Food preparation rooms
14 Kitchen service rooms
15 Bar, buffet
16 Wedding registration hall
17 Bride's/Groom's room
18 Chaikhana (teahouse)
19 Theater
20 Transformable stage
21 Rehearsal space
22 Exhibition and event space
23 Equipment room
24 DOSAF car club
25 Exhibition room
26 Film lab
27 Sound control / recording
28 Photo lab
29 Workshop
30 Artists' room
31 Room for sports competition trainers and judges
32 Office
33 Administration
34 Reception
35 Double room
36 Quintuple room
37 Circulation, workers
38 Meeting room / conference
39 Service room
40 Changing rooms
41 Restroom
42 Massage room
43 Dance floor
44 Storage
45 Technical area
46 Security room
47 Rented spaces
48 Burned spaces
49 Empty spaces

1975

Hotel: Typical floor plan (floors 3–7)
Original condition

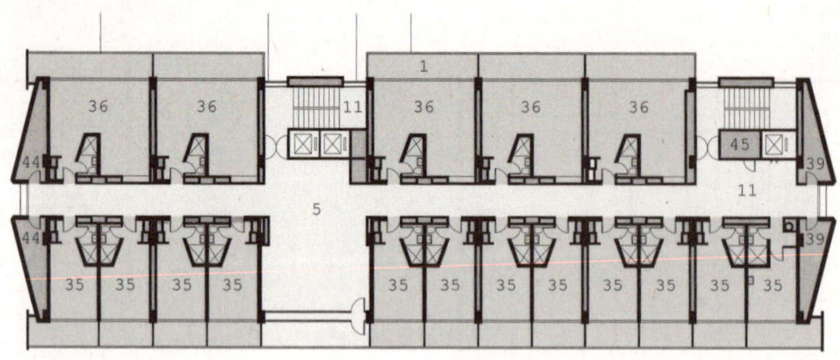

Hotel: 8th floor plan
Original condition

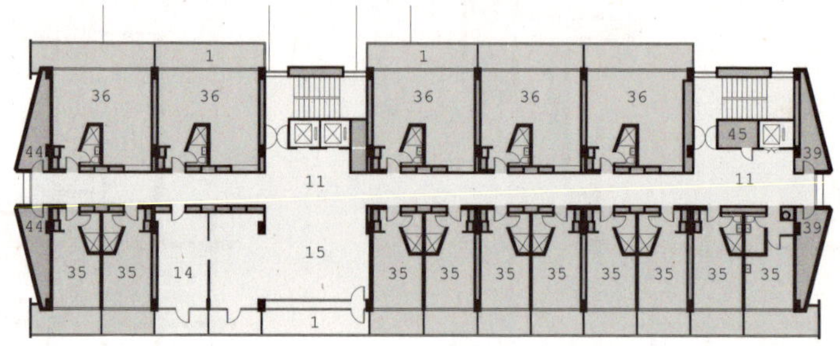

Hotel: Rooftop plan
Original condition

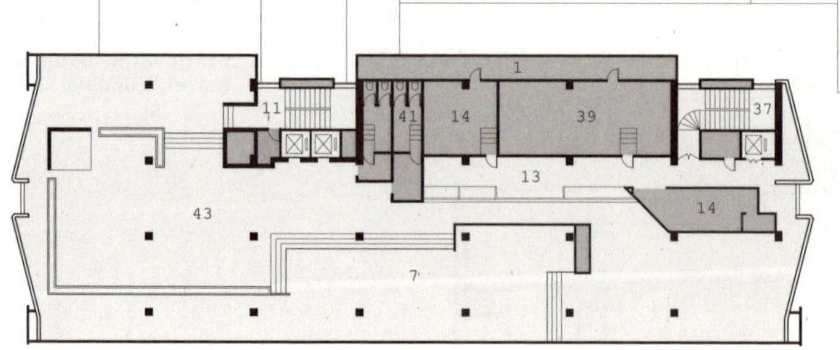

Public
Hotel rooms
Service and technical
Change of function

2022

Hotel: 3rd floor plan
Current condition

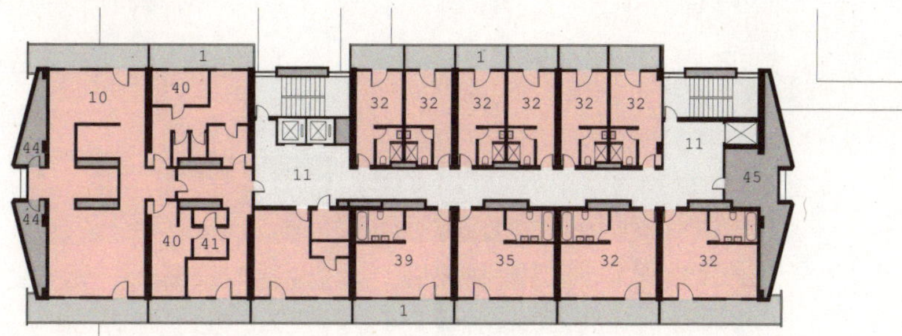

Hotel: Typical floor plan (floors 4–7)
Current condition

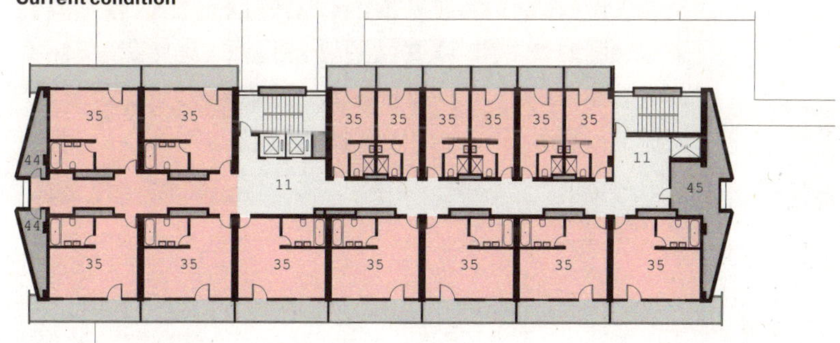

Hotel: 8th floor plan
Current condition

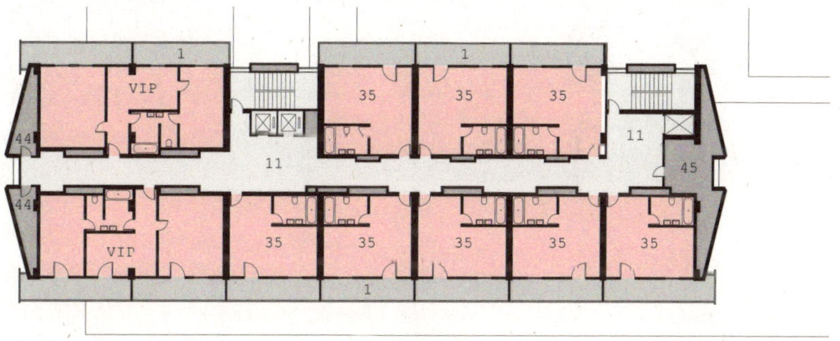

Hotel: Rooftop plan
Current condition

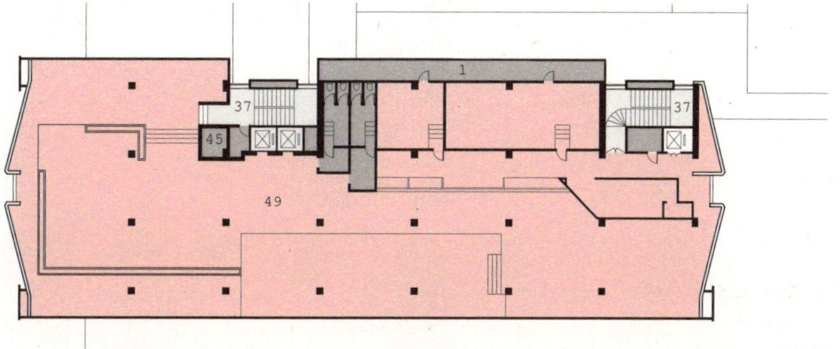

0 5 10m

The House of Youth during construction, view from Pakhtakor Stadium, 1969

South façade of the House of Youth

Entrance to the public block from Pakhtakorskaia Street, 1978

A wedding seen from Pakhtakorskaia Street, 1982

North façade of the hotel, view from the courtyard, 1980

Iurii Kiselev, *The Meeting*, currently located in front of the building, but originally in the courtyard, 1980–1985

Access to the courtyard from Pakhtakorskaia Street, 1980–1985

South façade of the Shodlik Hotel, 2021

Stairs to the courtyard from Pakhtakorskaia Street, north-west façade, 2021

Façade details, 2021

Connection between the hotel and the public block seen from Pakhtakorskaia Street, 2021

Connection between the hotel and the public block seen from the internal courtyard, 2021

Interior views of the public block, 2021

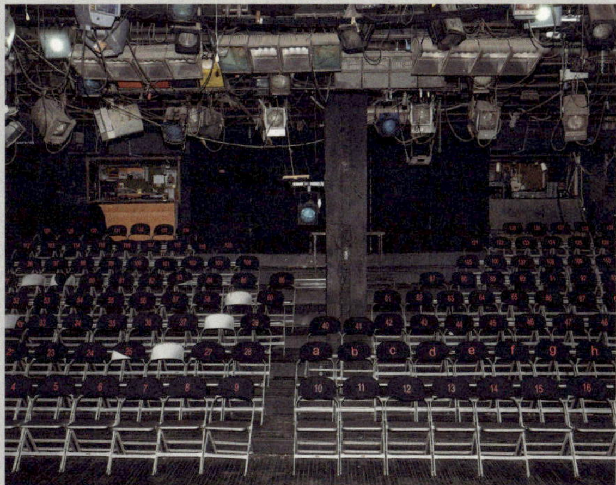

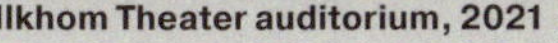

Ilkhom Theater auditorium, 2021

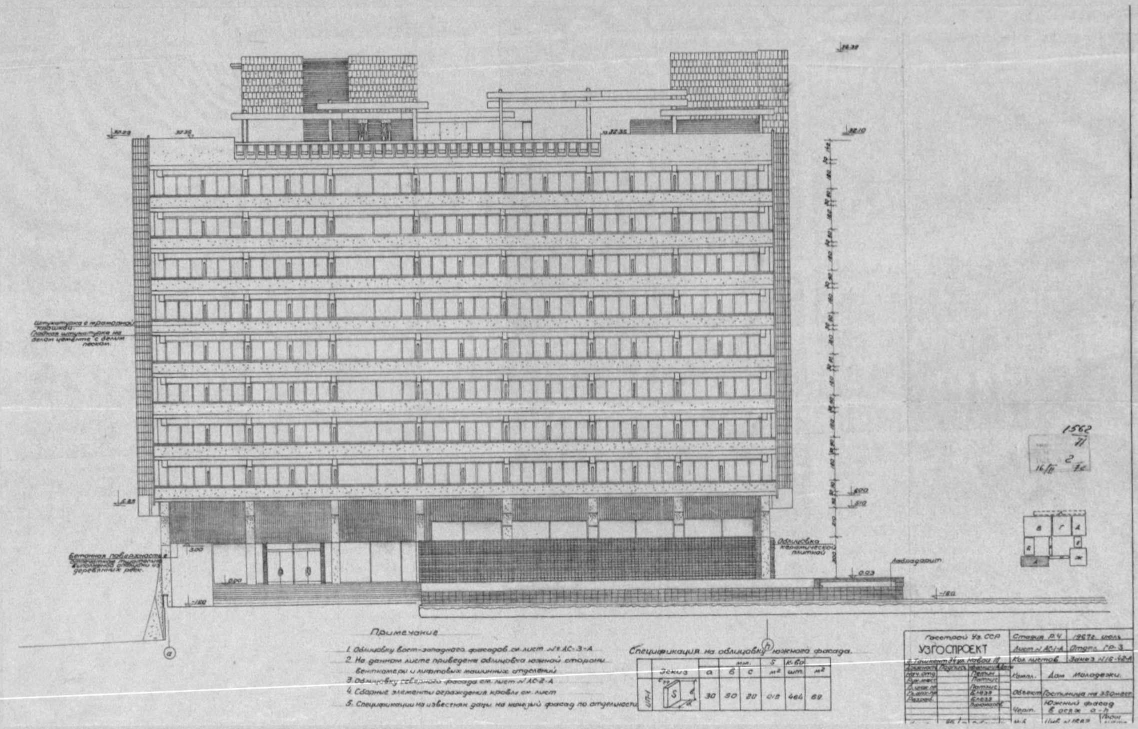

House of Youth, south façade of the hotel, 1967

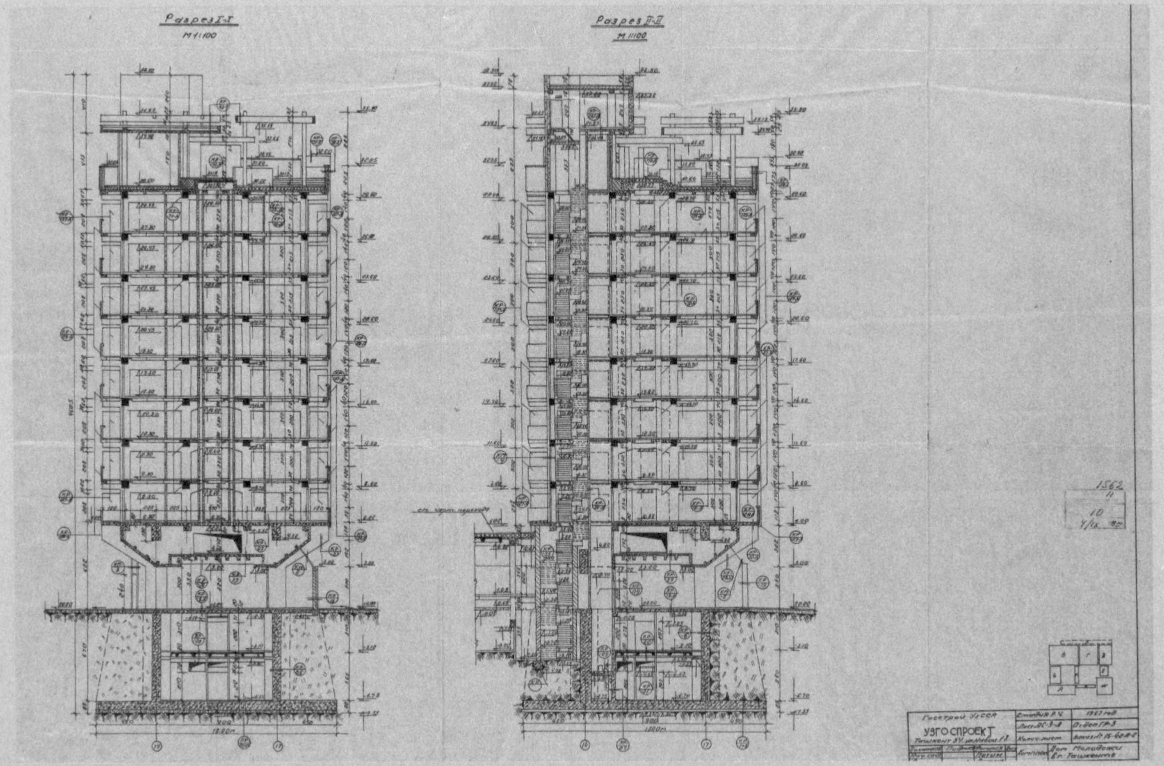

House of Youth, hotel sections, 1967

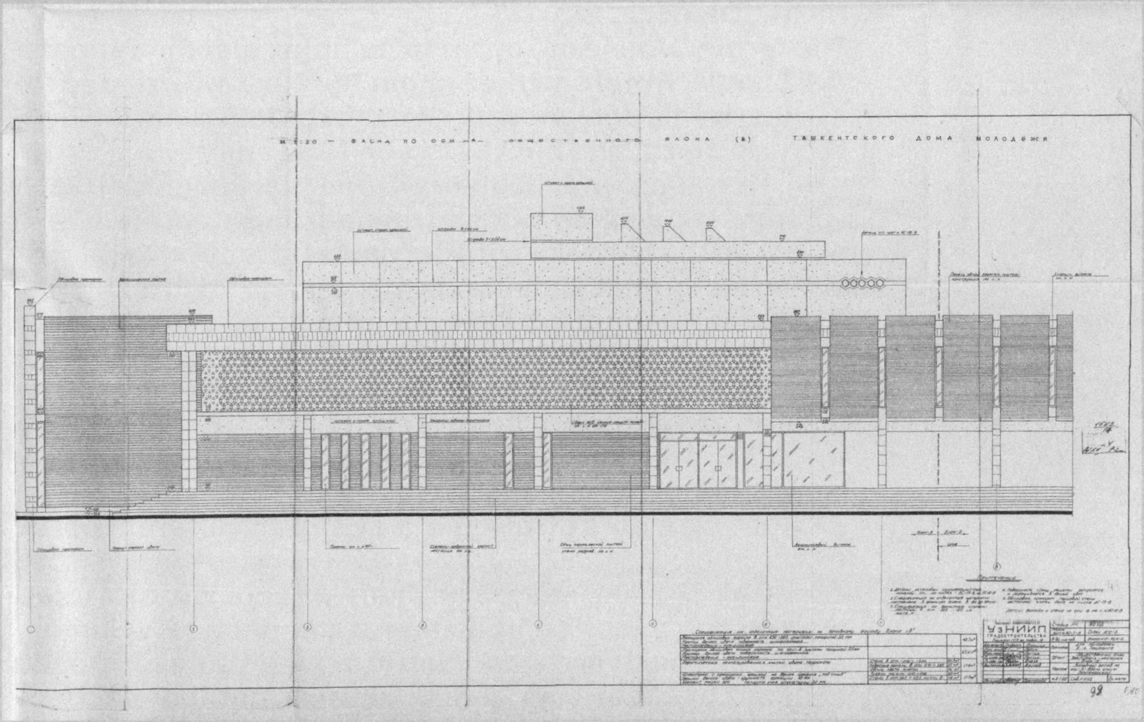

House of Youth, public block, west elevation, 1972

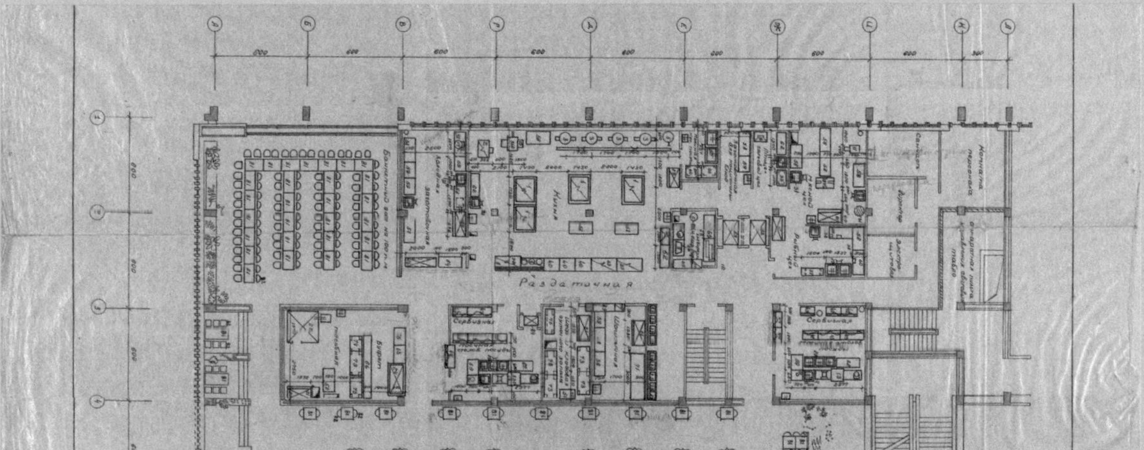

House of Youth, public block, café plan, 1967

HIGHLIGHTS

The former House of Youth is a complex that today hosts the Shodlik Hotel and the Ilkhom Theater, with related facilities. It was designed by an Uzgosproekt team led by Richard Bleze, and built between 1967 and 1975.

The complex articulates a repertoire of modernist volumes in a well-composed manner and is carefully placed in the context, with particular attention to the adjacent Panoramic Cinema, TV Center and Pakhtakor Stadium. This high-quality urban ensemble, shaped over a period between the late 1950s and the mid-1970s on the territory of the former "old city," took into account the masterplan proposal for a green esplanade connecting the old and the new parts of Tashkent. (Conceived in the early 1960s, the esplanade was never completed, although fragments of its logic are visible in different parts of the city.)

On a building scale, the complex consists of an elaborate yet balanced composition of architectural volumes and open courtyards resulting in a system of good quality spaces connected by raised walkways, outdoor pools and decoration in the form of sculptures and fountains. The tall volume of the hotel placed on the southern side of the complex casts a shadow on and protects from heat the terraced courtyard around which the lower volume of the public block is organized. The House of Youth is actually only half of the project originally developed by Bleze.

The upper part of the hotel design is rather sober and rational, with the only concession to expressiveness being a sequence of Brutalist concrete pylons connected into portals by massive beams at the height of the recessed technical floor.

The public block is connected to the hotel tower by a bridge. Given the block's depth, its design is rather inventive in bringing natural light inside: it includes a series of multiple-level skylights and perforated prefab concrete panels with ornamental geometric designs.

The open-air pool in front of the hotel was part of a centralized air-conditioning system.

The Ilkhom Theater was founded by Mark Weil in 1976 in a room in the basement of the public block, and expanded over the years to occupy most of the underground level and the first level. Ilkhom was the only nongovernmental theater in the Soviet Union, with truly radical programming that was well known beyond the boundaries of the republic of Uzbekistan. The theater has continued to function since the death of Weil in 2007, and is a fundamental and identity-shaping component of the complex.

Today, the complex shows a nonuniform state of preservation and authenticity due to a succession of different owners and as a consequence of a fire damaging the public block.

STATE OF REPAIR SCORE:

- Overall: 2 – The building shows severe localized damage and/or diffused and extended deterioration patterns. It is, however, still possible to use it.
- Hotel building: 3 – The building shows localized deterioration patterns which do not affect its stability
- Public block: 2 – The building shows severe localized damage and/or diffused and extended deterioration patterns. It is, however, still possible to use it.

Protection status: The building is listed according to Resolution No. 227 of the Cabinet of Ministers, April 22, 2024.

Main criticalities: In the last twenty-five years the building has not undergone major renovations. The lack of maintenance has led to a few criticalities which mostly concern the technical systems. The part of the public building that burned down has never been repaired and is now unusable.

INTEGRITY SCORE:

EXTERIOR

- Overall: 2 – Transformations to the building and its surroundings have caused the loss of some of the elements necessary to express its significance
- Hotel building: 2 – Transformations to the building and its surroundings have caused the loss of some of the elements necessary to express its significance
- Public block: 3 – The building has retained all the elements necessary to express its significance but is in a poor state of repair

INTERIOR

- Overall: 1 – The building has lost most of the elements necessary to express its significance
- Hotel building: 1 – The building has lost most of the elements necessary to express its significance
- Public block: 1 – The building has lost most of the elements necessary to express its significance

The exterior of the volume housing the hotel demonstrates a mediocre state of integrity, since the architectural interventions of the 1990s made partial changes to the façades. The state of integrity of the interior is worse, as it has been completely renovated. Nevertheless, the building retains its original use.

The volume hosting the theater was seriously damaged by a fire in 1996 and the top two floors have never been restored.

The whole complex maintains a tight relationship with its surroundings, underlined by precise and perceptible alignments.

AUTHENTICITY SCORE: EXTERIOR

- Overall: 3 – The building has been subjected to slight changes and replacements
- Hotel building: 2 – The building has been subjected to localized but significant modifications
- Public building: 3 – The building has been subjected to slight changes and replacements

INTERIOR

- Overall: 1 – The building has been subjected to major interventions which resulted in an overall transformation
- Hotel building: 1 – The building has been subjected to major interventions which resulted in an overall transformation
- Public building: 1 – The building has been subjected to major interventions which resulted in an overall transformation

The volume that hosts the hotel underwent changes during the intervention in 1996–1997. The volume of the building has not been modified in the upper part, but both the elevations and the plans have changed since the original project.

- The roof structure has been altered.
- The ground floor housing the lobby has been modified, hiding significant parts of the structural system.
- The balconies of all rooms have been modified and parts of windows have been bricked up.
- The windows in the staircase have been changed.
- On the north façade of the hotel, partition walls were added to the balconies, whereas on the south façade some of the original partitions of the balconies were removed.
- The color of the building has changed.
- The single rooms on the main façade were modified into doubles, eliminating partition walls.

Open spaces have also undergone transformations.

1980s

House of Youth, south façade of the hotel, 1980s

2021

South façade of the Shodlik Hotel, 2021

1978

House of Youth, north façade of the hotel and east façade of the public block seen from Pakhtakorskaia Street, 1978

2021

North façade of the hotel and east façade of the public block seen from Pakhtakorskaia Street, 2021

LEVEL 1 – MAXIMUM LEVEL OF INTEREST
(No transformations allowed; conservation activities required)

The first level includes the most unique and authentic features of the building and its related urban context. Such elements should be carefully preserved, avoiding even slight transformations.

URBAN LEVEL

The volumetric relationship between the buildings and open spaces in the urban ensemble—including the House of Youth, the Panoramic Cinema and the TV Center—must not be transformed. To be more precise:

- the eave height of the buildings on Pakhtakorskaia Street must not be changed;
- no new buildings should be added to the urban block housing the TV Center and the Panoramic Cinema;
- the green areas around Pakhtakor Stadium should remain for park use;
- within the urban block housing the TV Center and the Panoramic Cinema, the perimeter and eave height of the existing buildings must not be transformed.

ARCHITECTURAL LEVEL
EXTERIOR

- The spatial relationships between the spaces and volumes composing the original massing—the entrance courtyard, the hotel volume, the internal courtyard, and the public volume—must be preserved as they were originally designed.
- The façade on Pakhtakorskaia Street (west façade), characterized by a harmonious combination of the various elements (the hotel and theater block, the street, the access ramp), should be preserved as it is.

DETAIL LEVEL
EXTERIOR

- The solar-shading system consisting of prefabricated concrete panels with ornamental geometric designs must be preserved.
- The concrete structure characterizing the first floor of the hotel—which is also visible on the west façade—cannot be transformed.

INTERIOR

- The stone-clad walls of the theater's staircase building, visible on the floors destroyed by the fire, must be preserved.

LEVEL 2 – MEDIUM LEVEL OF INTEREST

(Elements included in the second level can be moderately transformed following approval by a designated committee[1])

URBAN LEVEL

- The construction of new buildings on the block of the House of Youth must be subject to approval by the designated committee.
- Any changes concerning the height of the existing buildings located on the urban block of the House of Youth should be submitted to the designated committee for approval.

ARCHITECTURAL LEVEL

EXTERIOR

- Any changes concerning the façades of the hotel (with the exception of the façade on Pakhtakorskaia Street, which is subject to Level 1) should be subject to approval by the designated committee.
- Any changes concerning the façades of the theater volume (with the exception of the façade on Pakhtakorskaia Street, which is subject to Level 1) should be subject to approval by the designated committee.

INTERIOR

- Any changes concerning the first floor of the hotel should be submitted to the designated committee for approval.
- Any changes within the theater volume should be subject to approval by the designated committee.

DETAIL LEVEL

EXTERIOR

Any changes to the elements characterizing the courtyards—the original walkways, the outdoor pool, the sculpture in the pool—must be submitted to the designated committee for approval.

INTERIOR

Any changes to the theater auditorium should be subject to approval by the designated committee.

1 An international committee of heritage preservation experts to be appointed.

HIDDEN MODERNIST FEATURES

Two striking modernist features of the Shodlik Hotel / Ilkhom Theater project are the large reinforced concrete pillars that characterize the first floor of the hotel and the transparency and visibility between the open space in front of the hotel and the courtyard between the two volumes. The 1996–1997 interventions compromised this feature by constructing an opaque new lobby volume on the first floor of the hotel.

Restoration work aimed at highlighting the original condition is strongly recommended.

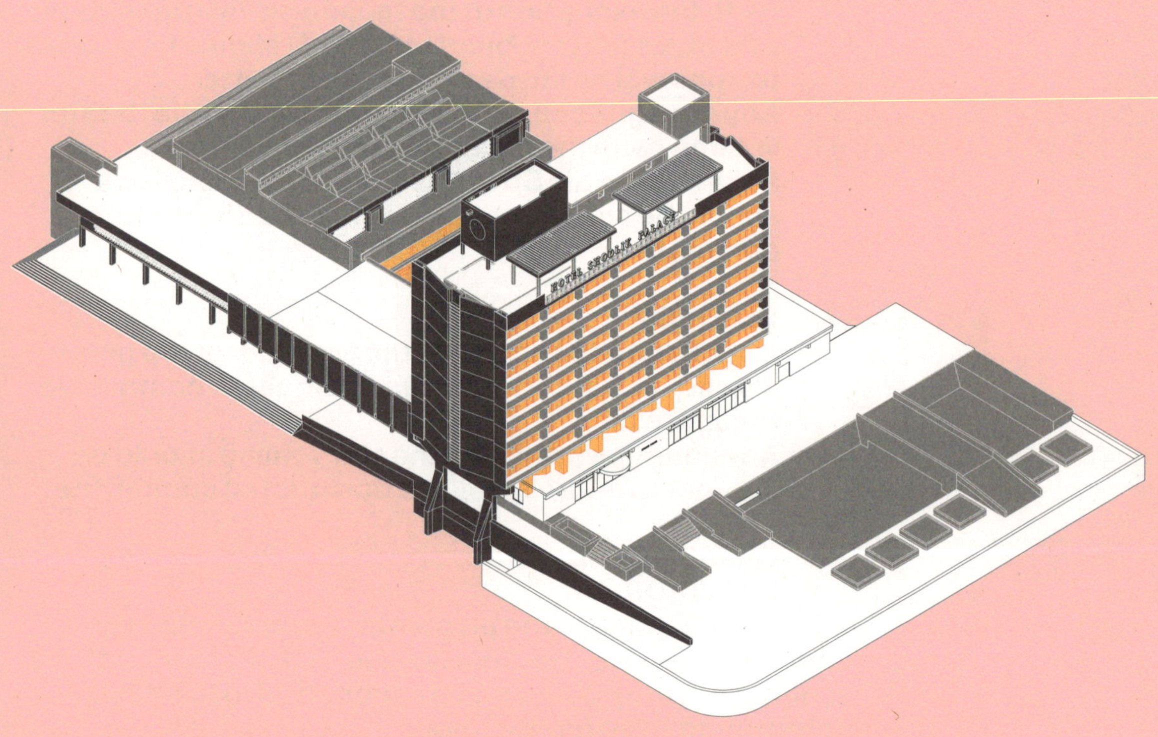

Preservation Level 1
Maximum Level of Interest
Materials and elements to be preserved

Preservation Level 2
Medium Level of Interest
Materials and elements to be preserved

Hidden Modernist Features
Materials and elements to be preserved

Transformation allowed

Preservation Strategy

Built between 1967 and 1975, the former House of Youth was a busy venue, loved by the inhabitants of Tashkent and visited by guests of the capital. Its position within the unrealized green esplanade and its proximity to iconic buildings such as the Panoramic Cinema and, later, the TV Center influenced its design, leading to a well-balanced and rational composition. Its sober appearance possesses attributes typical of the architectural language of the Modern Movement, placing the Ilkhom/Shodlik complex on the map of Tashkent modernist heritage.

Over time, the former House of Youth has been subjected to several transformations, both architecturally and programmatically. Due to substantial renovations and a destructive fire that occurred at the end of the twentieth century, the original interiors of both the hotel and the public block have been mostly lost. The façades, on the other hand, are still in place in spite of aging and a few modifications.

The purpose of the preservation strategy is thus twofold: to guarantee the conservation of the most valuable features of the building and, where possible, to restore its original appearance, with particular reference to its modernist character.

The preservation strategy includes seven main actions, which are briefly described here.

The first action concerns the high-rise building of the Shodlik Hotel, the main modernist feature of which—the pilotis—is mostly hidden. In fact, the sequence of Brutalist concrete pylons supporting the structure of the hotel was originally in plain sight and the perimeter of the entrance hall was completely glazed. However, to relocate the hotel restaurant after the fire, the entrance hall was expanded and as a result concealed the expressive structure. It is suggested to revert this intervention, finding a more fitting space for the restaurant, demolishing the volumes that were added at the first-floor level and, finally, bringing the pylons back into sight.

The second action also regards the Shodlik Hotel and, in particular, the openings on its north and south façades, the dimensions of which were reduced following the 1996–1997 renovations. The original design had a nearly full glazed façade on all levels. However, the poor thermal efficiency of the original glass and the need to adapt the rooms to more contemporary standards resulted in the replacement of the original windows and a significant reduction of glass surfaces. The strategy presented here proposes expanding the current openings in order to recreate the original transparency, taking into account substantial improvements in glass thermal performance. Moreover, full glazing is typical of modernist architecture and thus represents an important feature to bring back in order to enhance the design of this building and its compliance with the original intent of the architect.

The third action calls for the hotel's façades to be repaired where needed and painted over using appropriate white tones (instead of the current orange ones), in accordance with the original design.

The façade on Pakhtakorskaia Street, facing the Panoramic Cinema, is also extremely interesting and should be preserved and enhanced. Hence, the fourth preservation action aims to improve the current condition of this façade by removing the existing billboards, making local repairs, completing a general cleaning and adding a fresh layer of paint, to be chosen in accordance with the original design.

The fifth action concerns an interesting element on this façade: the honeycomb prefabricated concrete panels, which were meant to protect the building from excessive sunlight and heat. Today, many of the glass panes are missing and should be replaced in order to maintain a comfortable climate in the building. The honeycomb was adopted on one of the courtyard's façades, and here also it will be necessary to intervene by replacing the missing panes and fixing the existing ones.

The sixth action concerns the courtyard, which is an intimate space located at the center of the building. The courtyard's façades will be cleaned, repaired and repainted. Particular attention will be paid to the balustrade on the first floor of both the hotel and the public block, which has been modified since its construction in the 1970s and should now be returned to its original appearance.

The seventh and last action relates to the skylights located on the roof of the public block, which are currently in a state of neglect. The temporary covers that have been added to protect the skylights will be removed in order to assess the state of repair of the underlying concrete skylights. It will then be possible to carry out the necessary repairs and to install new glass windows to reinstate the original natural lighting.

The Ilkhom Theater is one of the few parts of the public block which was not damaged by the 1996 fire and has thus retained its original use. The fame of this theater—a truly rare case of a nongovernmental theater in the USSR—exceeded the boundaries of the Uzbek SSR, and later Uzbekistan. Moreover, and most importantly, the theater is an identity-shaping component of the complex and should thus be preserved. To this end, a general upgrade of spaces and some local repairs need to be carried out. To improve future conservation, it is recommended to plan regular inspections and maintenance operations.

Next Steps

In order to implement the proposed preservation strategy a few aspects will need to be clarified and further developed. The very first step will be to conduct a structural survey in order to assess the conditions of the building. This is absolutely essential for the public block, given that the damage caused by the 1996 fire was never assessed and further damage may have been caused by the latest fire (2022). Before implementing any project, the residual resistance of the structure should be evaluated to decide whether any strengthening interventions are needed.

The second step should focus on the inspection of technical systems. This will help identify the main criticalities and, especially in the case of the public block, support design decisions.

Once this information is obtained it will be possible to develop a more detailed and comprehensive project, which could be tested on a limited part of the building (pilot site) to assess materials and techniques.

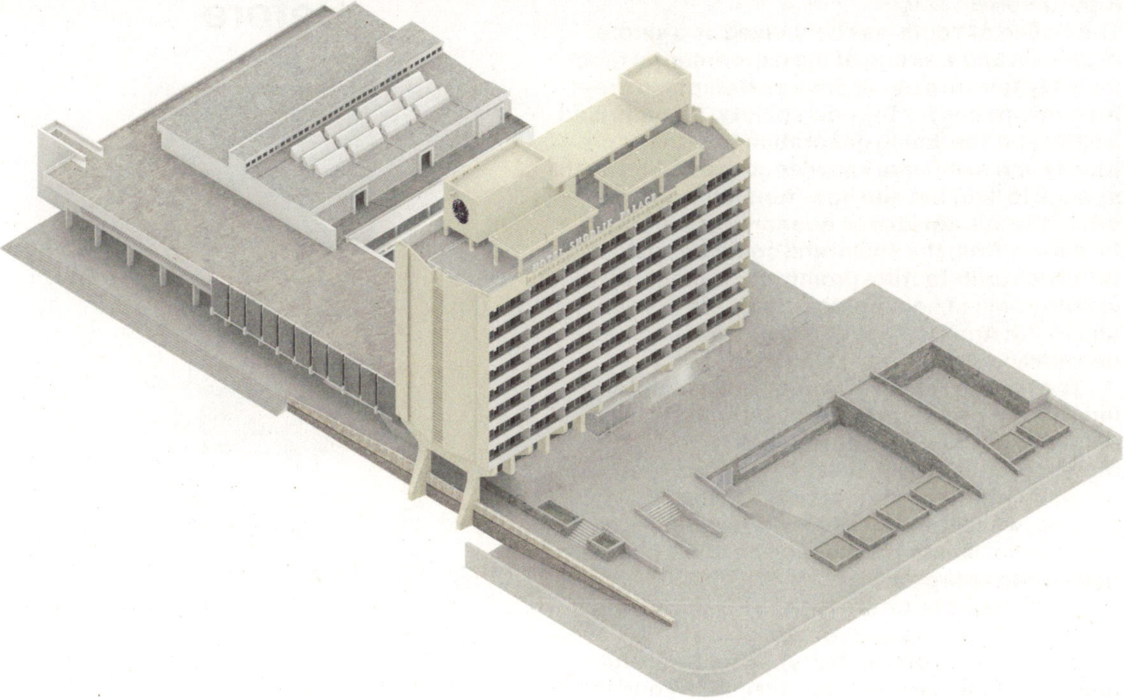

Axonometric view illustrating the result of the preservation actions: the complex regains its original coherence while the performance of the building is upgraded.

View from Pakhtakorskaia Street
Strategy visualization

Adaptation Strategy

The House of Youth was conceived as a single organism and was one of the experimental functional types born out of Soviet attempts to create new spaces for the new society. It comprised a space for the young generation to develop creatively and exchange knowledge, combined with spaces to live, eat and have fun. Although the era of the market-driven economy has dictated a turn away from the social and collective values that such architecture promoted, today, with the visible crisis of neoliberal attitudes in Europe and North America, we can claim that such values are acquiring a new relevance.

The former House of Youth, while maintaining a single owner, progressively split into two separate entities. The hotel block (Shodlik) continues to function with a reduced capacity after the pandemic and without using all the available spaces, while the public block is partially occupied by the Ilkhom Theater and partially abandoned due to fire damage.

We propose to return to the idea of a single entity, a contemporary version of the House of Youth (or House of Creativity). After a careful analysis of the current room availability and the pipeline of upcoming hotels in Tashkent (saturated with four- and five-star hotels), as well as an evaluation of Shodlik's structural constraints, we propose converting the hotel tower into a four-star apart-hotel. The rooms will include a small kitchen and basic home appliances. There is very little accommodation like this on offer in Tashkent, yet the demand for long-term accommodation is quite high.

The public block would work in sync with the apart-hotel: besides preserving the Ilkhom Theater at the basement and the first level, other areas could be leased to an innovative coworking company targeting youth, start-ups and creative industries. Additionally, the café and restaurant areas can be included to create full synergy between the different activities. The House of Youth would make it possible to live, work and have cultural and leisure experiences within one complex. The economic model would allow the owner to cover expenses for the Ilkhom Theater utilities.

The interior of the public block combines the original features of the 1970s building with contemporary design: raw concrete surfaces contrast with warm and cool material finishes, such as wood and aluminum. The hotel interior should be fully upgraded to create an innovative interior that speaks to both the history of the building and its contemporary potential.

Before

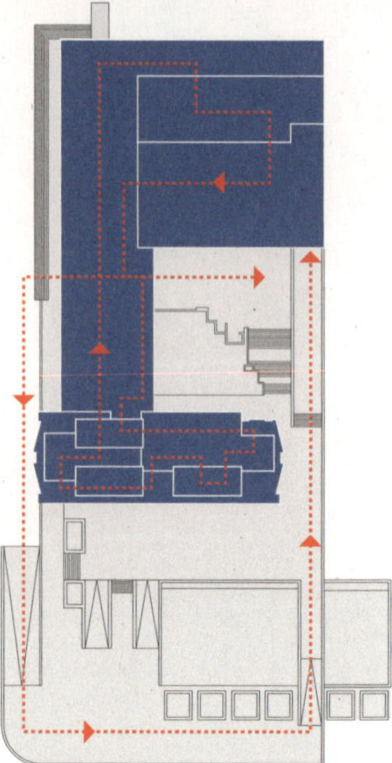

House of Youth

Now

Theater
Hotel
Abandoned

Proposal: Single Organism

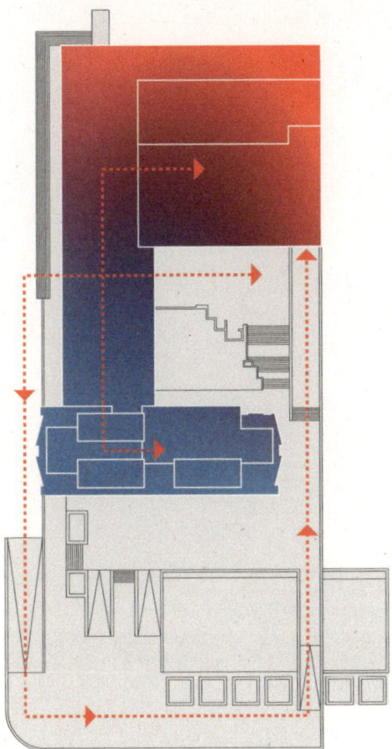

Theater
Coworking for youth, start-ups and creative industries
Public space
Café
Apart-hotel

Activated internal courtyard
Strategy visualization

Uzbekistan Hotel

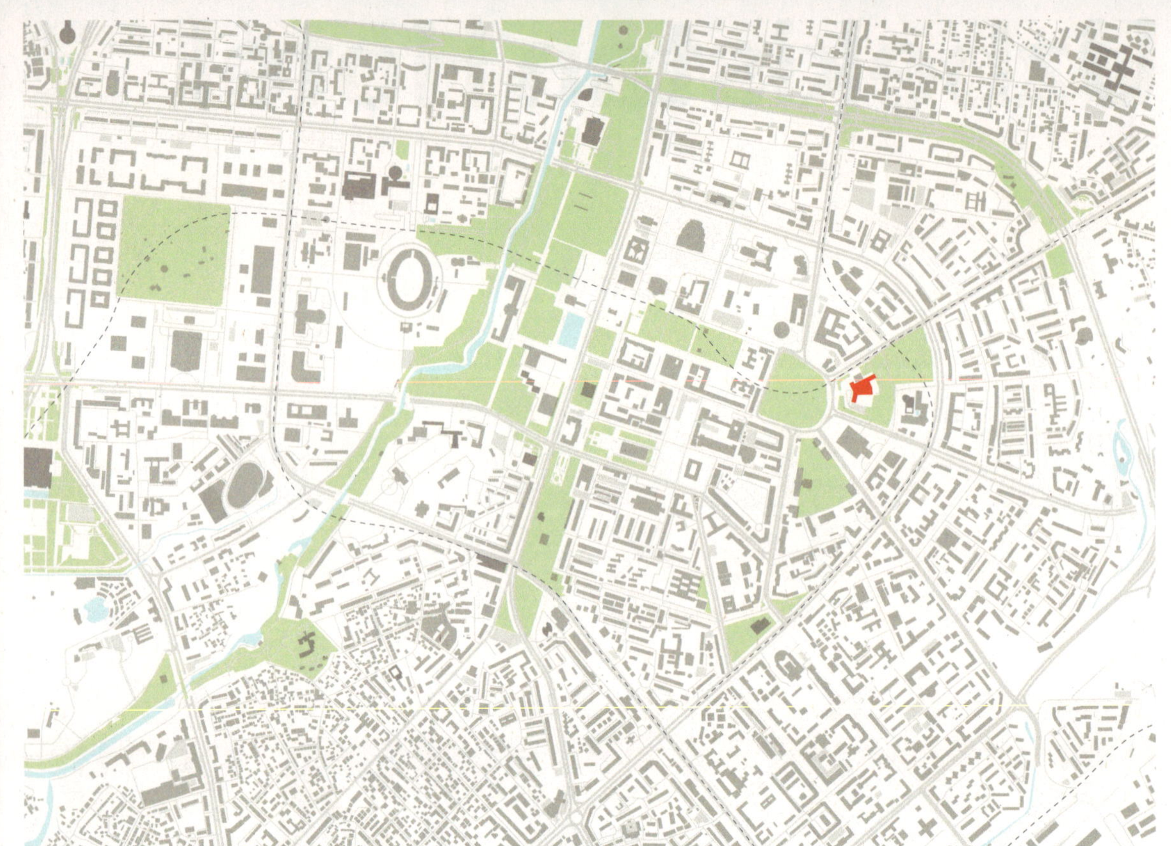

Building position and address: 45 Mirzamakhmud Musakhanov Street, Tashkent

0 0.5 1km

Unlike the first urban nucleus of "new" Tashkent, which appeared around the house of the governor-general (later Lenin Square) and always played the role of an administrative center, the second nucleus, which formed around the central square and was always multifunctional, was focused on various forms of urban leisure. Historically this alternative nucleus appeared after 1870, when A. Makarov proposed laying his radial plan of development of the city over the original rectangular grid established under the direction of M. Kolesnikov. Half of this space, which was adjacent to Kaufmanskii Avenue (Salarskaia Street/Karl Marx Street/Sayilgoh), was set aside for "government buildings" and the other, which faced Pushkinskaia Street, for gardens. By 1890 the entire space of the district was arranged into around ten plots with single-story buildings that faced the perimeter of the streets. By this time the square and the nearby City Garden functioned as public city parks. The first monuments to the Russian conquest were erected in the square and the City Garden was the location for initial forms of urban public life, with the first summer cinemas established there in the early twentieth century. Exhibitions organized by the Turkestan government took place in both the square and the City Garden, which made their spaces considerably more politicized than the dacha of the governor-general and parks belonging to Prince Nikolai Romanov. However, their ideologization did not prevent residents from appropriating the space for their own needs: as a place of leisure and for various cultural events and entertainment. A number of governmental, commercial, educational and cultural institutions appeared in the neighborhood, as in the center of any city.

The ideological significance of the square was preserved in the Soviet era. Here, one after another, monuments related to whatever moment the state was experiencing were raised. They included Lenin, Stalin and Marx monuments. Simultaneously, the square remained an attractive place for walks. It was the end point for Tashkent residents' favorite evening promenade along Karl Marx Street (known as "Broadway" by the stilyagi, members of the "stylish" youth counterculture of the postwar period). The space of the City Garden, renamed Gor'kii Park of Culture and Leisure by the Soviet authorities, was an equally ambivalent space. Here, an obelisk in memory of the revolutionary events was erected, and in 1947 the Tashkent Chimes were constructed. The park was also home to children's fairground rides and two summer cinemas.

After the new, detailed plan of the city center was approved in 1965, the district to the east of the square was demolished to make way for an urban vertical that would mark the beginning of the green city esplanade. A multistory hotel for tourists, which provided rooms with a view of the city center and a neighborhood ideal for walks, was a functional match for the site, for which reason there was never any disagreement among urbanists. In addition, when the Soviet era came to an end a large new hotel was built behind the Uzbekistan Hotel on land originally slated for a theater or cinema. Openness to the world required new spaces for accommodating tourists and visitors.

Main dimensions of the Uzbekistan Hotel
General axonometric view

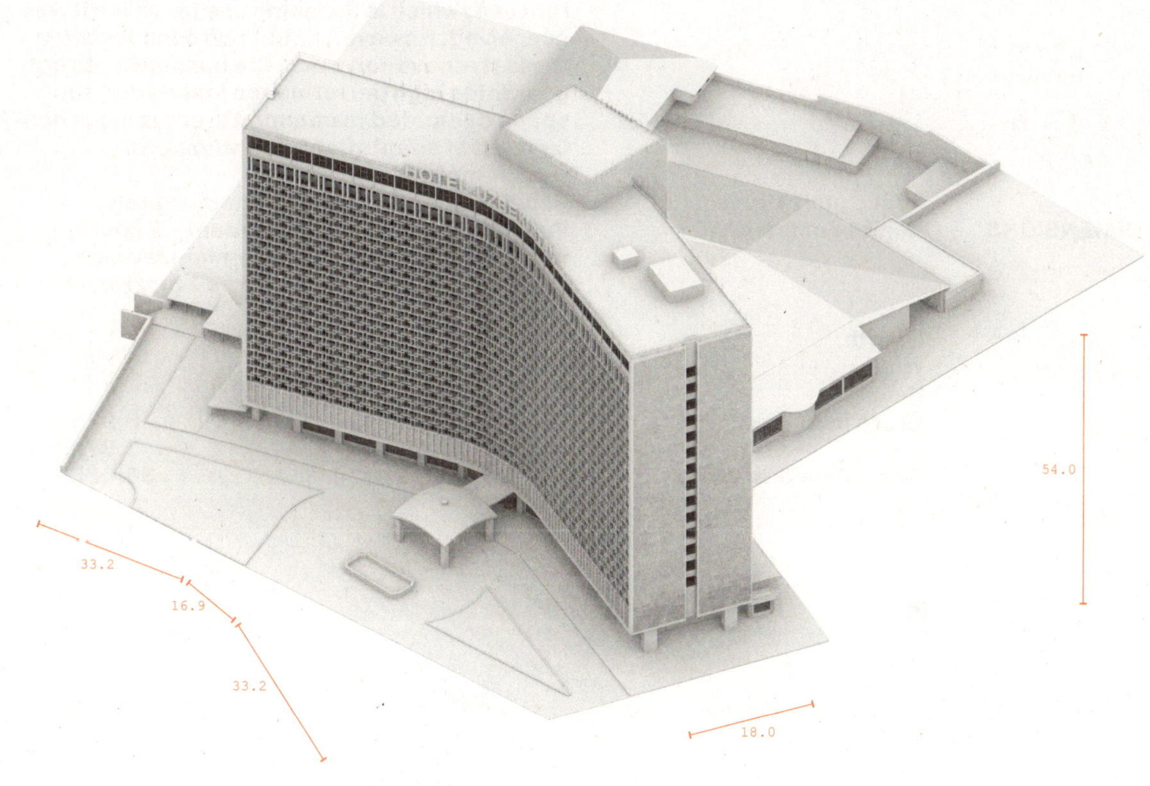

ACTORS	**Architects:**	**Il'ia Merport, Liudmila Ershova, Viacheslav Rashchupkin, Vladimir Narubanskii**
	Engineers:	**Lev Gorlitskii, Vadim Starosel'tsev, Vadim Burdman**
	Artists:	**Makhmud Usmanov, Irena Lipene, Vladimir Chub, Iurii Strel'nikov, S. Bondareva**
	Institute:	**TashZNIIEP**
DATES	**Design period:**	**1963(?)–1974**
	Construction period:	**1969–1974**
	Inauguration date:	**1974**
	Later interventions:	**1997:** **Renewal of the interiors of the left wing of the hotel by a Malaysian company.** **2000:** **A new canopy in front of the main entrance and reconstruction of the lobby by a Turkish company. Also, the first-floor windows were moved toward the outside and became flush with the upper façade to enlarge the internal space. A gift shop was attached to the lobby.** **2005:** **Renewal of the entire right wing of the hotel by a local company.** **2000s:** **Demolition of the pool.**

USE	**Current use:**	**Hotel, restaurant**	
	Original use:	**Hotel, restaurant, banquet hall, swimming pool**	
	Suitability of current use:	**The hotel building is partly suitable for its current use, which is the same use for which it was conceived. However, about two decades after the last renovation work, the building does not guarantee high performance standards. The space dedicated to common areas is in particular need of adaptation to contemporary requirements.**	
	Space utilization:	**Uzbekistan Hotel is used almost entirely.**	
DIMENSIONS	**Number of floors:**	**Public block**	**Basement + 2 floors**
		Hotel building	**2 basement levels + 16 floors + mezzanine + roof**
	Length:	**81.0 m**	
	Width:	**18.0 m**	
	Height:	**54.0 m**	
	Gross floor area:	**Entrance (first) floor**	**6,965.0 m²**
		Typical hotel floor	**1,375.0 m²**
	Gross floor area (total):		**36,685.0 m²**

Uzbekistan Hotel

The main documentary sources reflecting the process of creating the Uzbekistan Hotel have not been preserved. When the Tashkent Zonal Scientific Research Institute for Experimental and Standard Design (TashZNIIEP) was restructured in the 2000s, its valuable archive was almost completely and irreplaceably lost. For this reason, today the history of the design and construction of the hotel can only be partly reconstructed based on documents in the Tashkent City Archive, where the protocols of many discussions at the Main Architecture and Planning Administration (GlavAPU) are kept; articles in architectural journals of the 1960s and 1970s; historical photographs from the Republic of Uzbekistan Documentary Film and Photo Archive; and evidence from specialists who were involved in the design and construction.

Background

The hotel business in Tashkent was always a mirror, reflecting the role the city had in the country and the world. In the 1910 city directory of Tashkent there were eleven hotels listed in the new part of the city and one in the old part, plus various caravanserais.[1] However, when private property was eliminated the number of hotels was reduced, as was the number of foreign tourists (and tourists as a whole). Official visitors could be accommodated at the National Hotel, built in 1912 and renamed Tashkent and then Sharq. Other levels of visitors were served by the several small hotels that remained. Ordinary guests of the city were expected to find rooms to rent in the institutional sector or from individuals. During World War II Tashkent became a very important city, as it was the temporary location for dozens of industrial enterprises that needed to receive specialists and partners from other cities. Responding to this requirement, the Council of People's Commissars of the Uzbek SSR and the Central Committee of the Communist Party of Uzbekistan issued a decree on the construction of a hotel with 250 rooms, which would be located on the east part of Red Square.[2] They returned to this issue in 1945, although the project would only become a reality thirteen years later in the form of the Tashkent Hotel, which was built on Theater Square, south of the original site. But times had changed. After the death of Stalin the USSR rapidly opened up to foreign tourism, and Tashkent was particularly attractive for delegations from "developing countries" which, after the worldwide collapse of the colonial system, wished to see the "Soviet East" with their own eyes. Plus, the construction quality of the Tashkent Hotel left a lot to be desired. After two years of operation the building was subject to deformation, and the problem of its dangerous condition had to be resolved at the level of the State Committee for Construction and Architecture and the government of the republic.[3] Accordingly, in 1960 the government of the republic issued a decree on the construction of three more hotels with a total of 1,016 beds, as well as another hotel for the Aeroflot system. The former included two Intourist hotels with 380 and 400 beds. However, soon afterward the city commission decided to construct a single hotel with 780 beds and locate it on Kirov Street (Zarafshan), opposite the Navoi Theater.[4] This idea would eventually result in the design for the Uzbekistan Hotel.

1 *Adres-spravochnik Turkestanskogo kraia s illiustratsiiami, kalendarem na 1910 g., kartoi kraia i ob"iavleniiami [Address Book of Turkestan Krai with Illustrations, a Calendar for 1910, a Map of the Area and Announcements]* (Tashkent: V.M. Il'in Printing House, 1910), 110.

2 "Pis'mo Predsedatelia Tashgorispolkoma Khusainova i nachal'nika upravleniia po delam arkhitektury pri SNK UzSSR Dzhakhangirova Predsedateliu Soveta narodnykh kommissarov UzSSR Abdurakhmanovu, ot 31 iiulia 1945 g. [Letter from Chairman of the Tashkent City Executive Committee Khusainov and Director of Architectural Affairs of the Council of People's Commissars of the Uzbek SSR Dzhakhangirov to Chairman of the Council of People's Commissars of the Uzbek SSR Abdurakhmanov, dated July 31, 1945]," *Plan i perepiska po Tsentral'noi gostinitse v g. Tashkente na 250 nomerov [Plan and Correspondence Regarding the Tsentral'naia Hotel in Tashkent with 250 Rooms*, April 21–July 31, 1945], Tashkent City Archive, fund 36, list 1, item 993, on 25 sheets, 25.

3 The documents note that after two years of operation "the finishes in many of the more important parts fell away and the plumbing began to leak onto the lower floors." See "Pis'mo Predsedatelia Gosstroia Uzbekskoi SSR L. Pozharova Predsedateliu Soveta Ministrov Uzbekskoi SSR A. Alimovu ot 31 iiulia 1960 goda [Letter from Chairman of Gosstroi of the Uzbek SSR L. Pozharov to Chairman of the Council of Ministers of the Uzbek SSR A. Alimov of July 31, 1960]," *Proekty postanovleniia Soveta ministrov UzSSR i Tashgorispolkoma, prikazy i protokoly Goskomiteta i Gosstroia SSSR i UzSSR i perepiska rekonstruktsii i stroitel'stva g. Tashkenta [Drafts of Resolutions of the Council of Ministers of the Uzbek SSR and Tashkent City Executive Committee, Decrees and Protocols of the State Committee and Gosstroi USSR and Gosstroi Uzbekistan and Correspondence on Reconstruction and Building in Tashkent]*, Tashkent City Archive, fund 36, list 2, item 111a, on 120 sheets, 57/1.

4 "Protokol kommissii po vyboru ploshchadki dlia stroitel'stva gostinitsy 'Inturist' v Tashkente, ot 28 marta 1960 goda [Protocol of the Selection Committee for the Site for the Construction of the Intourist Hotel in Tashkent dated March 28, 1960]," *Rasporiazheniia po APU, protokoly soveshanii kommissii po vyboru ploshchadki dlia stroitel'stva (gost.) 'Inturista' v Tashkente [Instructions on Architecture and Planning Conditions, Protocols of Meetings of the Selection Committee for the Site for the Construction of the Intourist (Hotel) in Tashkent]*, January 10–December 25, 1960, Tashkent City Archive, fund 36, list 2, item 114, on 55 sheets, 15.

The Genealogy of the Image

The exact point at which design of the hotel began has not been documented. There was no competition. Zlata Chebotareva, who in 1963 was working at the Uzgosproekt Institute, saw a model of the hotel on architect Viacheslav Rashchupkin's desk in that year.[5] Also in 1963, TashZNIIEP was founded as a result of the reform of the department of standardized design at Uzgosproekt, and the new organization was commissioned to design the hotel. Another indicator that design work began early is a document in which Tashkent Chief Architect Aleksandr Iakushev addressed the designers, asking them to ensure that the design of the hotel conformed to the project for the center of Tashkent which was then being developed by Tashgiprogor, the Tashkent State Urban Project Institute ("The development by your institute of the aforementioned buildings must not be done without coordinating with the masterplan for the city center."[6]). This means that work on the hotel was ongoing either before the launch of the project for the center of Tashkent or in parallel with it.[7] The program for the development of the city center was sent out on November 13, 1963, and the Intourist Hotel was mentioned in the list of buildings to be preserved and of projects approved for construction.[8] Based on these facts it can be assumed that the initial project for the hotel already existed in model form in 1963, and it is probable that it was planned for the existing location or nearby.

These details are important for an understanding of the genealogy of the appearance of the hotel because previously there were some hasty conclusions on this matter. In particular, Anna Bronovitskaia and Nikolai Malinin, authors of a book about modernism in Alma-Ata who rightly noted the architectural rivalry between the Kazakh and Uzbek capitals, saw the influence of Alma-Ata in the Uzbekistan Hotel. "Tashkent," they wrote, "was Alma-Ata's main competitor [...]. Though generally considered the fourth most influential Soviet city, as well as the construction capital of Central Asia, it often seemed a few steps behind Alma-Ata in terms of architecture. In response to the Zhetysu Hotel (1959), Tashkent built the Rossiia Hotel (1965) with a very similar grid around the windows. When the Alma-Ata Hotel (1967) came along with its gently bending form, Tashkent's Uzbekistan Hotel (1974) would also bend, with the addition of ornamental sun barriers across the façade."[9] If we consider the dates of the beginning of the design stage rather than the completion of

5 According to Zlata Chebotareva, she also saw Il'ia Merport visiting Viacheslav Rashchupkin's office to discuss this project. Soon these two names would be among the first in the architectural team, but in the Tashkent City Archive there are documents in which Rashchupkin alone is named lead architect. See, for example, "Zakliuchenie ekspertizy po smetnoi dokumentatsii k proektnomu zadaniiu stroitel'stva gostinitsy 'Inturist' na 750 mest v g. Tashkente [Conclusion of the Expert Commission on the Budget Documents of the Project Plan for the Construction of the 750-Bed Intourist Hotel in Tashkent]," *Protokoly zasedanii arkhitekturnoi komissii i ekspertnye zakliucheniia po proektnym smetam* [*Protocols of Meetings of the Architectural Commission and Expert Conclusions on Project Budgets*], February 17–March 25, 1965, Tashkent City Archive, fund 36, list 1, item 1277, on 170 sheets, 80.

6 "Pis'mo glavnogo arkhitektora Tashkenta A. Iakusheva direktoru TashZNIIEPa A. Petrosovu ot 24 sentiabria 1964 goda [Letter from Chief Architect of Tashkent A. Iakushev to Director of TashZNIIEP A. Petrosov dated September 24, 1964]," *Perepiska s gosuchrezhdeniiami o proektirovanii i stroitel'stve, 2 iiulia–30 sentiabria 1964 g.* [*Correspondence with State Organizations on Design and Construction, July 2–September 30, 1964*], Tashkent City Archive, fund 36, list 2, item 763, on135 sheets, 12.

7 Leon Adamov's expert opinion of the hotel design, dated March 17, 1965, noted that "the design of the Intourist Hotel in Tashkent was produced by the TashZNIIEP Institute based on a decision by the Council of Ministers of the USSR of April 16, 1964," and "the initial data was provided by the design commission of the Directorate for Foreign Tourism of the Council of Ministers of the USSR, no. Shch-60 dated January 13, 1965, the architecture and planning plan of the Architecture and Planning Administration of Tashkent City Executive Committee, no. 2 dated August 22, 1964, permission for individual design from the State Committee for Civil Engineering and Architecture of Gosstroi SSSR, no. 3-1676 dated August 19, 1964, and also the project sketch of the center of Tashkent." (Leon Adamov, "Zakliuchenie po proektnomu zadaniiu gostinitsy 'Inturist' na 750 mest v g. Tashkente [Conclusion on the Project Plan for the Intourist Hotel with 750 Beds in Tashkent]," *Protokoly zasedanii arkhitekturnoi komissii i ekspertnye zakliucheniia po proektnym smetam* [*Protocols of Meetings of the Architectural Commission and Expert Conclusions on Project Budgets*], February 17–March 25, 1965, Tashkent City Archive, fund 36, list 1, item 1277, on 170 sheets, 106.) However, in view of what was stated it appears that work began earlier and was later given a new impulse by the aforementioned decrees, commissions and instructions.

8 "Programma zakrytogo konkursa na razrabotku eskiznogo proekta planirovki i zastroiki tsentra g. Tashkenta Prilozhenie k prikazu Gosstroia SSSR ot 13 noiabria 1963 goda, no. 300 [Program for a Closed Competition for the Development of a Design Sketch of the Layout and Construction of the Center of Tashkent: Appendix to the Decree of Gosstroi USSR dated November 13, 1963, no. 300]," *Postanovleniia TsK KP Uzbekistana i Soveta ministrov UzSSR o stroitel'stve vystavki, posviashchenooi 40-letiiu UzSSR i stroitel'stva v g. Tashkente, 5 ianvaria–20 dekabria 1963* [*Resolutions of the Central Committee of the Communist Party of Uzbekistan and the Council of Ministers of the Uzbek SSR on the Construction of an Exhibition to Mark the 40th Anniversary of the Uzbek SSR and Construction in Tashkent, January 5–December 20, 1963*], Tashkent City Archive, fund 36, list 2, item 134, on 76 sheets, 17.

9 Anna Bronovitskaya, Nikolay Malinin and Yuri Palmin, *Alma-Ata: A Guide to Soviet Modernist Architecture 1955–1991* (Prague: Artguide Editions, 2022), 194.

construction, the logic of the Moscow specialists' argument is disrupted, since the overall design of the Uzbekistan Hotel was finished in 1963, four years before the Alma-Ata Hotel appeared. We must also take into account that in the 1960s "book-like buildings" were tested on a number of occasions and were particularly popular in the USSR. After publication of the design for Kalininskii Avenue in Moscow, where such "books" appeared for the first time (this version, which was not the first, dates to late 1963), they were further developed not only by professional architects such as Natan Osterman's team for the design of the House for the New Way of Life in Moscow (1965–1971) but also for numerous student projects across the Soviet Union.[10] However, there was a special trigger for the migration of this form to Tashkent: the modernist architecture of Havana.

Unlike Europe and the USSR, where the genesis of modernism was closely tied to social projects and, particularly, the construction of industrial, cheap housing for workers, Havana modernism during Fulgencio Batista's second term in power after the 1952 coup was the style of the fashionable life of the country's elite. The main waterfront of the Cuban capital soon saw the construction of luxury hotels in severe modernist forms (Havana Hilton, 1958; Havana Riviera, designed like an open book, 1957; and others) and, after the passing in 1952 of the new law on condominiums, multistory housing also appeared. The FOCSA Building (1954–1956) was one of the highest and most striking of the new residential complexes. Constructed in the form of an open book with a curved central section, this twenty-nine-story galleried building offered the residents of its 364 apartments a sea view. On the opposite side there was a tower containing the elevators, at the top of which there were offices and restaurants. The whole complex was situated on a horizontal podium made up of several floors that housed a club, office space, a swimming pool, a restaurant, a theater and even two radio stations. The proportions and functional plan of the FOCSA Building are strongly reminiscent of the building which, seven years later, would begin to appear in the sketches and working drawings of the Tashkent architects.

The cultural transfer through which Soviet architects could be inspired by the architecture of an "ideologically alien" political system was possible because of the following context. On January 1, 1959, Batista's regime fell, and the dictator left Cuba. The revolutionaries seized power and their leader, Fidel Castro, while looking for a convenient office, made the modernist Havana Hilton his headquarters. Che Guevara stayed here, and in future the hotel would house Cuba's most important guests, such as Salvador Allende, Valentina Tereshkova and famous chess players and sportspeople. Soviet guests visited Cuba often in the early 1960s. In February 1961 Khrushchëv's first deputy, Anastas Mikoian, arrived; in July 1961 Iurii Gagarin made his first foreign trip here; and in May 1962 the leader of Uzbekistan, Sharaf Rashidov, visited Havana as part of a Soviet delegation. Many of these visits were widely publicized in the media, accompanied by striking photography. As a result, Havana's modernist waterfront began to be perceived as "the face of socialist Cuba," despite being constructed in the previous decade. As far as the Uzbekistan Hotel is concerned, it would be inaccurate to suggest a direct borrowing. We can only note the compositional and planning similarities, especially since the functions and urban planning role of the Tashkent hotel were significantly different from those of Havana's FOCSA Building. In addition, when transported to Tashkent the "building-book" form was supplemented with a spectacular and memorable element that was not on any of the prototypes: a sun-protection grille across the western façade, which became an iconic image of the capital of Uzbekistan.

Urban Function

The selected visual solution was organically in sync with the aim that the planners had defined for the hotel complex when they situated it on Revolution Square at the boundary of the eastern nucleus of the green esplanade. Its spatial designation was as a visual closure of the esplanade and a representation of the opening in the western direction, in the direction of Chorsu, the center of the "old city." Since the eastern boundary of the square was semicircular, the high-rise "book" was situated on its axis on all models of the center of Tashkent after 1965. However, its angle in relation to the square changed. On the 1965 model the architects attempted to combine the uncombinable, orienting the hotel on an axis parallel to Karl Marx Street, which disorganized the space of the district in which it was located. Then the hotel was placed on the median axis between Pushkinskaia and Karl Marx streets in the direction of the center of the square, which provided a more natural solution.

The sun-protection grille also had particular urban planning significance. The problem was that the initial height of the hotel, which the architects tried to extend to twenty stories in the sketches, was insufficient to "contain" the

10 See M. Basko, Design for a Residential Complex, Kyiv Art Institute, 1964 (*Arkhitektura SSSR* [*Architecture of the USSR*], no. 5, 1965, 53); V. Kovalev, Design for the Radio Electronics National Research Institute, Moscow Architectural Institute, 1965 (*Arkhitektura SSSR* [*Architecture of the USSR*], no. 6, 1966, 9); and others.

FOCSA Building, Havana

“Book-like buildings” in Moscow

surrounding space until the next high-rise dominant, the Ministries Building on Lenin Square. The sun-protection grille, which was broken up into a number of horizontal cells per floor, visually heightened the building. However, in the initial design options the architects proposed enriching the form of the sun protection by combining small and large cells, creating a larger pattern. They later rejected this decorative excess, selecting the more severe version we see today. The homogeneous grid-like surface certainly creates an impressive monumental effect.

Model of the Uzbekistan Hotel

The Evolution of the Project

The documentation of the expert commissions and discussions of the hotel's design in spring 1965 show the differences between the initial project and the finished building. The architects moved away from the original commission for a sixteen-story building and proposed a twenty-story hotel. They were motivated by a wish to create a vertical that would be in dialogue with the Ministries Building on Lenin Square. However, as the expert commission noted, in absolute terms the twenty-story hotel was still 14.2 meters lower than the Ministries Building due to the drop in relief from Lenin Square to Revolution Square and the stories being different heights.[11] Both the architects and the engineers noted that a twenty-story building was the maximum economical height in the USSR for reinforced concrete structures. Due to the increased weight, above this height it was cheaper to build using steel frame structures, plus the national calculation did not take into account that Tashkent is located in a seismic zone. The discussion of 1965 did not produce a final decision, but after the 1966 earthquake the architects and engineers took a more cautious approach. The completed building has seventeen stories and was built using a metal structure.

Initially the composition of the complex comprised two volumes: a twenty-story vertical volume and a single-story horizontal one, with a functional division into an accommodation block and a block for eating and leisure. The expert commission recommended that the single-story block have two floors, which was accepted. In other cases, the architects stood firm regarding their proposals, the experts' critique notwithstanding. Their rejection may sometimes have been for technical reasons. For example, the architects ignored the experts' request that they provide a strip for electronic advertising at the top level (this type of element would appear nine years later on the House of Publishers building). However, some recommendations were rejected for creative reasons. The experts noted that "the main entrance is not particularly successful. The hypertrophied supports and beams are not only out of proportion to the size of a person, but they cancel out the scale of the first floor. The main entrance is unattractive; it does not welcome visitors but repels them. Here this approach should be rejected, since the supporting elements cannot be significantly lightened. It appears necessary to shift the high-rise volume to the east along the platform, leaving only the cantilevered part of the block above the entrance. In this way there will be an interesting solution not only for the entrance. The vestibule will become deeper, and parts of the courtyards will belong not only to the restaurant and café but also to the hotel's common spaces."[12] The main entrance remained unmarked on the façade. The architects likely decided that the "book" shape was sufficient for guests to intuitively move in a centripetal direction and end up there.

The new version of the project included a seventeen-story building and a two-story rear block, although the latter was divided into three relatively autonomous subparts that incorporated seismic stitches: the restaurant block, the

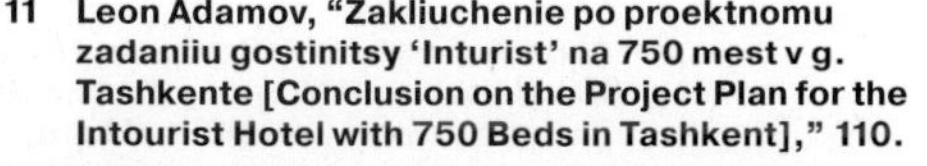

11 Leon Adamov, "Zakliuchenie po proektnomu zadaniiu gostinitsy 'Inturist' na 750 mest v g. Tashkente [Conclusion on the Project Plan for the Intourist Hotel with 750 Beds in Tashkent]," 110.

12 Ibid., 111–112.

kitchen and utility block and the café block. The two-story part was developed in more detail. As E. Gainulin wrote, "the one- and two-story part adjoining the high-rise part forms an internal courtyard with a gallery and outdoor seating for cafés. Around the free space of the courtyard is a 450-seat restaurant, a 250-seat café, an express café for 40 people, a banqueting hall for 100 people, and a 100-seat bar. In the courtyard, above the smooth surface of the pools, there is a teahouse. Couches in the form of cantilevered platforms hang over the pool. The use of sliding panels (glass in aluminum frames) in the enclosure structures allows visual communication of all the spaces with the internal courtyard. The descent from the gallery to the courtyard is via a spiral staircase made of monolithic concrete. A sun-protection grille is arranged over the internal courtyard."[13] Since in his journal article of 1975 Feruz Ashrafi repeated this paragraph almost word for word,[14] this part of the project must have been built more or less as described. One can also confirm that in 1967 the area with the swimming pool had not yet appeared in the south-eastern part of the project.

Gainulin's article also shows that in 1967 there was no intention to face the end façades of the high-rise block with Gazgan marble.[15] Apparently the architects initially proposed constructing them in the same materials as the elevator block tower, which was located in the eastern part of the complex, but in the early 1970s they decided to replace concrete with marble. This solution was typical for many projects of the time. One might mention the replacement of the concrete texture of the portal of the Museum of Arts (1974) with gray granite, of the concrete surface of the pylons of the Circus (1976) with marble cladding and so on. The side walls of the Uzbekistan Hotel were particularly carefully developed. Here the builders created a fading effect, facing the lower part of the surface with dark marble and then moving through neutral, intermediary light layers to the use of delicate rose-white shades at the top. The quality of the application was also outstanding. Unlike the many cases where marble cladding on façades came away or was damaged, the end walls of the Uzbekistan Hotel retain their original appearance even today.

Further modifications can be judged from articles in the journal *Stroitel'stvo i arkhitektura Uzbekistana* (*Construction and Architecture of Uzbekistan*) in 1975 and 1977, photographs of the 1970s and 1980s and the building itself, in which many layers of the 1970s are still clearly visible. The hotel opened in 1974. The most significant change was the increase in capacity: designed for 750 beds in the 1960s, the hotel could actually accommodate 930 people. The sun-protection grilles on the western façade were made with aluminum instead of concrete, and a swimming pool with a spectacular cantilevered canopy was added to the two-story block. The pool was not incorporated within the original perimeter of the building but outside it, in a space that faced the corner of Karl Marx Street (Sayilgoh) and Khorezmskaia Street (Istiklol). The high-rise part of the hotel was constructed using a metal structure and the underground part, a two-story basement with walls and ceilings, was made of monolithic reinforced concrete with "a solid reinforced concrete foundation slab on a specially compressed base with waterproofing." The "lower part used a monolithic reinforced concrete frame on a pillar foundation."[16] The specification of the cladding of the load-bearing pylons of the first floor was adjusted. The black, polished gabbro visually slimmed these massive elements and almost disappeared against the background of the window frames. Thus, the building seemed to be lighter and more dynamic.

The last stage of design and construction of the hotel was linked to the inclusion in the interior of monumental art made using a range of techniques, media and means of expression. In the internal spaces of the vestibule and the passageway between the restaurant and the café the wall was decorated with traditional ganch plaster carving. The artists were Makhmud Usmanov and a group of craftspeople under his supervision. The three-dimensional abstract stained glass wall in the bar was produced by artist Irena Lipene. In the hotel restaurant artists Vladimir Chub and Iurii Strel'nikov created the figurative fresco *Fruits of the Earth*, which depicted Uzbek "types": elderly people in a teahouse, a young couple planting a tree and so

13 E. Gainulin, "17-etazhnaia gostinitsa 'Inturist' na 750 mest v Tashkente [The 17-Story, 750-Bed Intourist Hotel in Tashkent]," *Stroitel'stvo i arkhitektura Uzbekistana* [*Construction and Architecture of Uzbekistan*], no. 7, 1967, 22.

14 "The hotel consists of two parts, a high-rise section with bedrooms and an adjoining two-story block housing the public catering group (a 350-seat restaurant, a banqueting hall for 100, a 250-seat café, a 40-seat express café and a bar for 100). The public catering block that adjoins the high-rise volume forms an internal courtyard with a water feature and a green gallery. In the courtyard, above the surface of pools with fountains, there is a teahouse. Couches in the form of cantilevered slabs hang over the pool." Feruz Ashrafi and R. Kontorer, "Gostinitsa Uzbekistan na 930 mest v Tashkente [The 930-Bed Uzbekistan Hotel in Tashkent]," *Stroitel'stvo i arkhitektura Uzbekistana* [*Construction and Architecture of Uzbekistan*], no. 7, 1975, 29.

15 E. Gainulin, "17-etazhnaia gostinitsa 'Inturist' na 750 mest v Tashkente [The 17-Story, 750-Bed Intourist Hotel in Tashkent]," 23.

16 Feruz Ashrafi and R. Kontorer, "Gostinitsa Uzbekistan na 930 mest v Tashkente [The 930-Bed Uzbekistan Hotel in Tashkent]," 29.

Volume of the hotel swimming pool

on. A monumental mosaic panel decorated the second floor of the hotel's internal courtyard and also the supporting wall of the circular staircase leading to the second floor. All of these monumental works were lost as a result of various reconstructions of the hotel between the 1990s and the 2010s.

After the Completion of Construction

Once constructed, the Uzbekistan Hotel became the main Intourist hub and accommodated the vast majority of foreign tourists who arrived in Tashkent. It was particularly crowded during the week of the Tashkent International Film Festival of Asia, Africa and Latin America and other international forums and conferences that occasionally took place in the capital of Uzbekistan. Thanks to its organic placement near the square and its memorable external appearance, the hotel became one of the most popular buildings of Tashkent modernism and often featured in films and popular photo books about Tashkent. In a 1981 sociological survey of Tashkent architects, specialists from UzNIIPgradostroitel'stva nominated it the third most significant modernist building in Tashkent, and their colleagues from TashZNIIEP, TashNIiPIgenplan and Tashgiproqor put it in second place.[17]

Today we can confirm the loss of many elements of the external and internal structure of the building. The pool was demolished, and the two-story catering block was radically redesigned, as a result of which the building lost its internal, ventilated courtyard. An entrance area with a decorated vault on four columns was added to the lobby. The black gabbro was replaced with brown tiles, which were used to face both the columns and the space between them. The free space underneath the high-rise part was closed off due to the extension of the vestibule. The lobby and the internal decoration of the restaurant and café were almost entirely remodeled in the eclectic style of the 2000s and 2010s. Even so, the façades of the high-rise block retained their original look, and in the urban planning sense the building continues to play the role of a modernist emblem of Tashkent.

17 Iosif Notkin and Shukur Askarov, "O kachestve arkhitektury [On the Quality of Architecture]," *Stroitel'stvo i arkhitektura Uzbekistana* [*Construction and Architecture of Uzbekistan*], no. 4, 1981, 9.

Meeting the hotel's architects and engineers. From left to right: Vladimir Minakov (client from Intourist), architects Il'ia Merport and Liudmila Ershova, chief project engineer Lev Gorlitskii, Anatolii Podlipnov (architect, but not of this building), engineer Vadim Starosel'tsev

ARCHITECT
IL'IA MERPORT

Place and year of birth:
Tashkent, 1917
Place and year of death:
Boston (USA), 2004
Education:
1934–1940, Architecture Department of Central Asia Polytechnic Institute (SazPI)

One of the pioneers of standardized design in Uzbekistan and an architect-researcher. A veteran of World War II, after the war Merport was one of the architects involved in the reconstruction of Kyiv.

From 1946 to 1958 he worked at various design organizations in Tashkent and as a result of career development he became director of Tashgorproekt. In the Stalinist period he designed the Teahouse of Honored Elders (Tashkent, 1947), a residential building on Proletarskaia Street in Tashkent (1950) and a series of standard buildings in the Golodnaia Steppe. The second building of the Tashkent airport was constructed between 1953 and 1958 based on a design by Merport and Mariia Kondakova (the first building, in Constructivist style, was erected in the 1930s). It was distinguished by its unusual use of style, which differed from the development of orientalist motifs typical of that period, being more like an example of late Soviet Art Deco. The open galleries on the second floor and the open, shaded courtyards in place of waiting rooms are evidence of a search for local specificity in a building which could accommodate numerous people on hot summer days.

Merport was the author of more than fifty academic texts, mostly on the typology of housing in dry, hot climates. In 1959 he became director of the residential sector of the Tashkent Construction Research Institute. He defended his dissertation and in 1963 was appointed deputy academic director of TashZNIIEP.

INSTITUTIONAL FRAMEWORK

TashZNIIEP

CADRE

When TashZNIIEP was formed in 1963, its staff came from two institutions, the department of standard design of Uzgosproekt, which was reformed as the design department of TashZNIIEP, and the disbanded Scientific Research Institute for Construction of the Academy of Construction and Architecture of the USSR in Tashkent, which became the research department of TashZNIIEP. Three hundred and fourteen staff worked in the new institute, including eleven holders of Ph.D.s in architecture.

PRIORITIES

The work of the research department covered many types of design and construction activity. Specialists studied the issues of construction in seismic zones, air-conditioning, sun protection, the technology of economical manufacture of objects made from concrete and other construction materials, questions of climate, the cultural specificity of a given population, etc. The scientific approach to design was conditioned by the technocratic image of the institute and influenced the thought processes of the architects who worked there. Here there was minimal emphasis (insofar as it was possible in the USSR) on the imperative of "national form," and architects aimed to use research to create standard environments and unique buildings that were suitable for the Central Asian climate and the culture of the peoples who lived there. The zonal nature of the institute, which designed for the entire Central Asian region, not just for Uzbekistan, also helped architects to move the accent away from "national form" toward regional specificity.

Basement floor (hotel) and 1st floor (public block) plan
Original condition

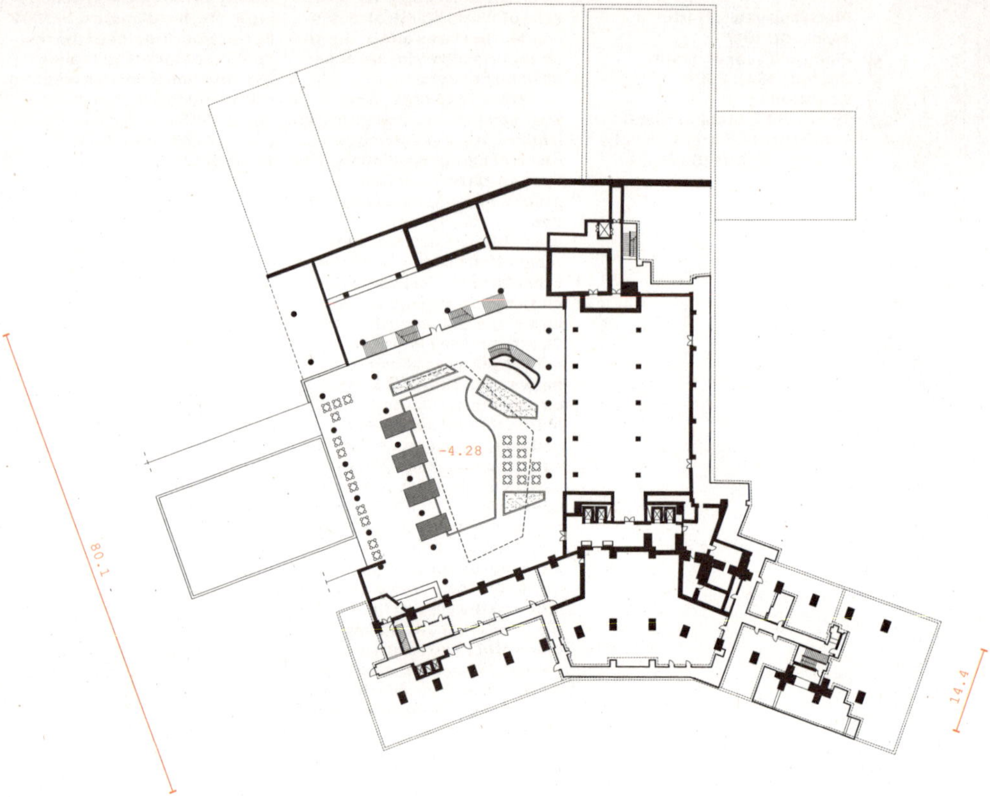

-4.28

80.1

14.4

West elevation, main entrance of the Uzbekistan Hotel
Original condition

1st floor (hotel) and 2nd floor (public block) plan
Original condition

74.5
±0.00
14.4
0 5 15 20m

Typical floor plan
Original condition

16.9
18.0
33.2
33.2
0 5 15m

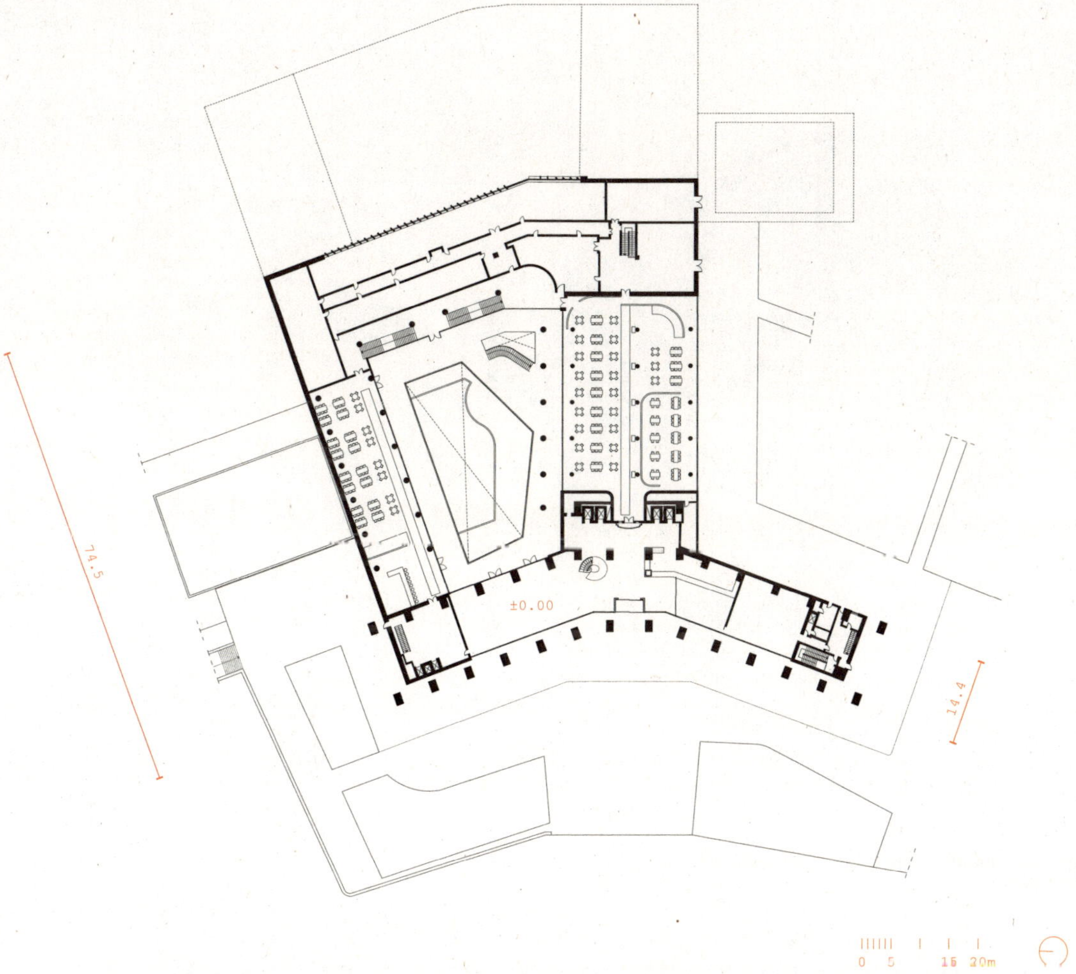

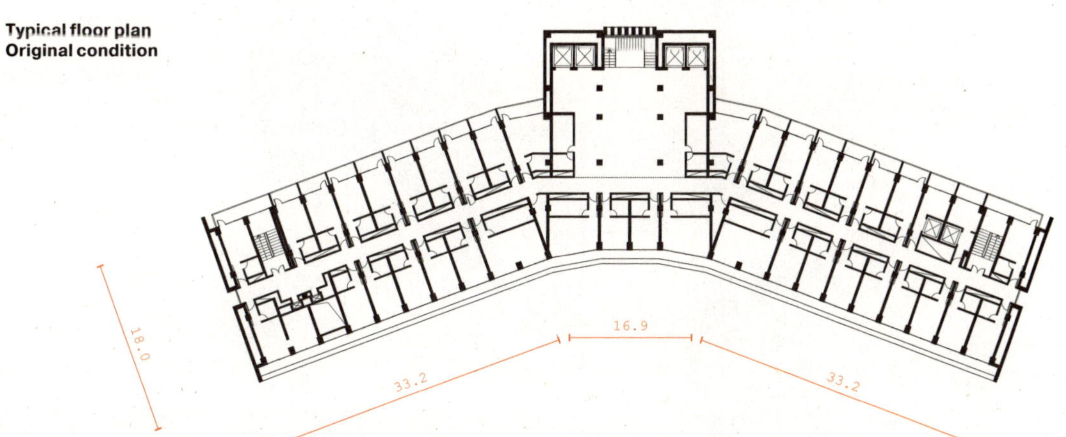

South-west axonometric view
Original condition

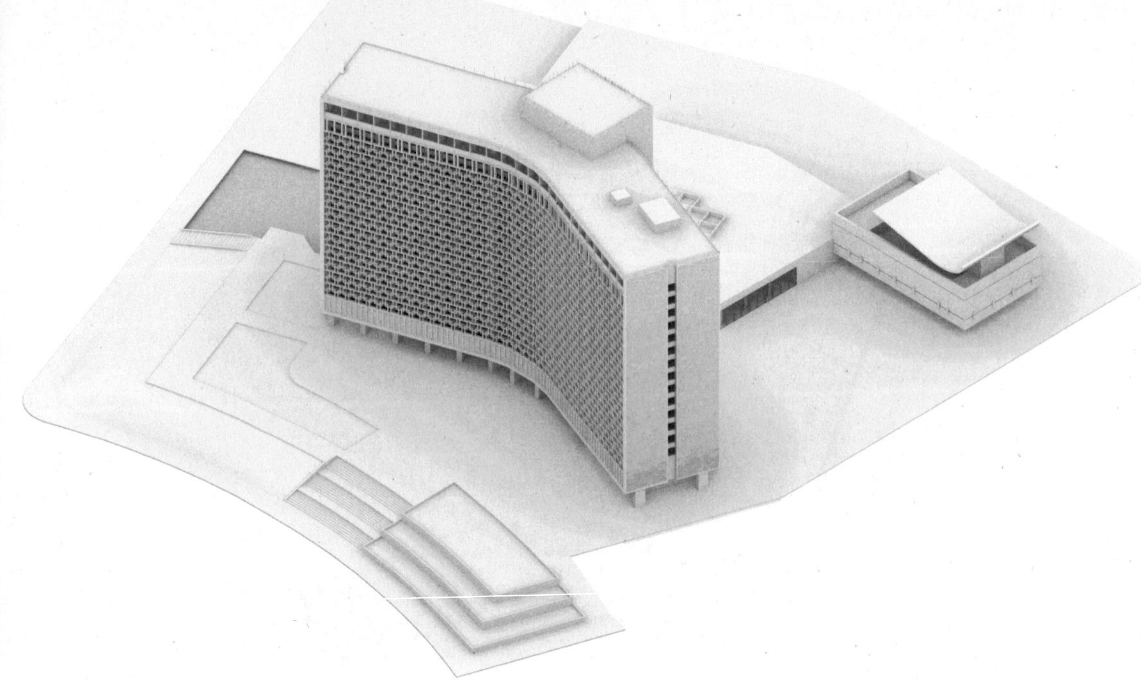

North-west axonometric view
Original condition

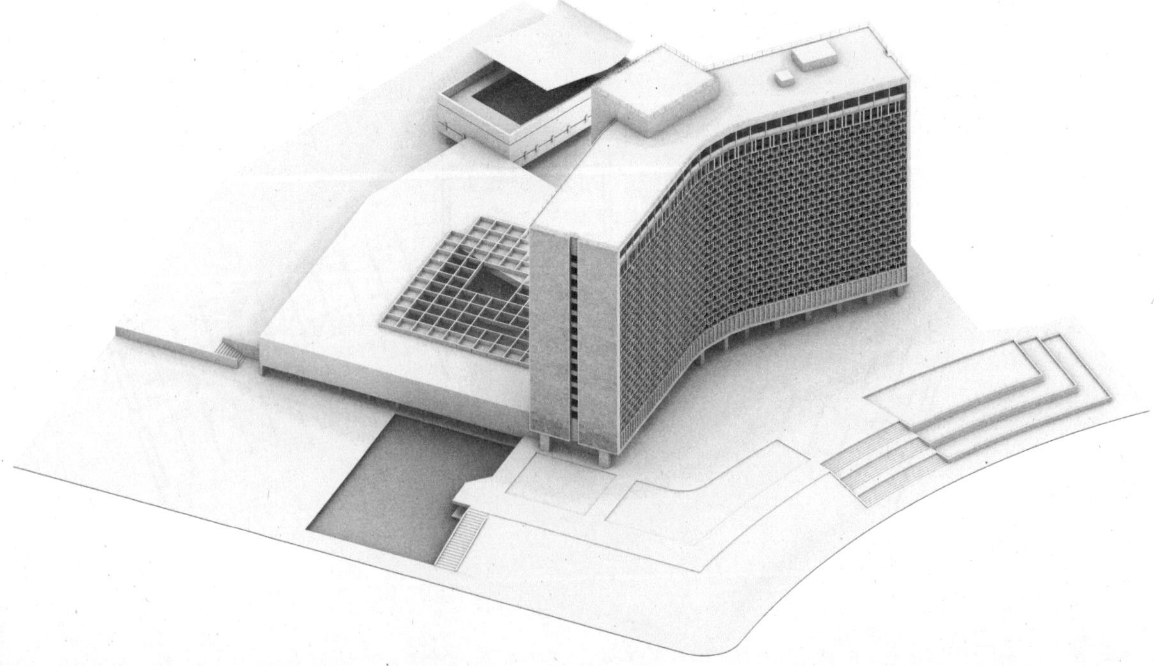

North-east axonometric view
Original condition

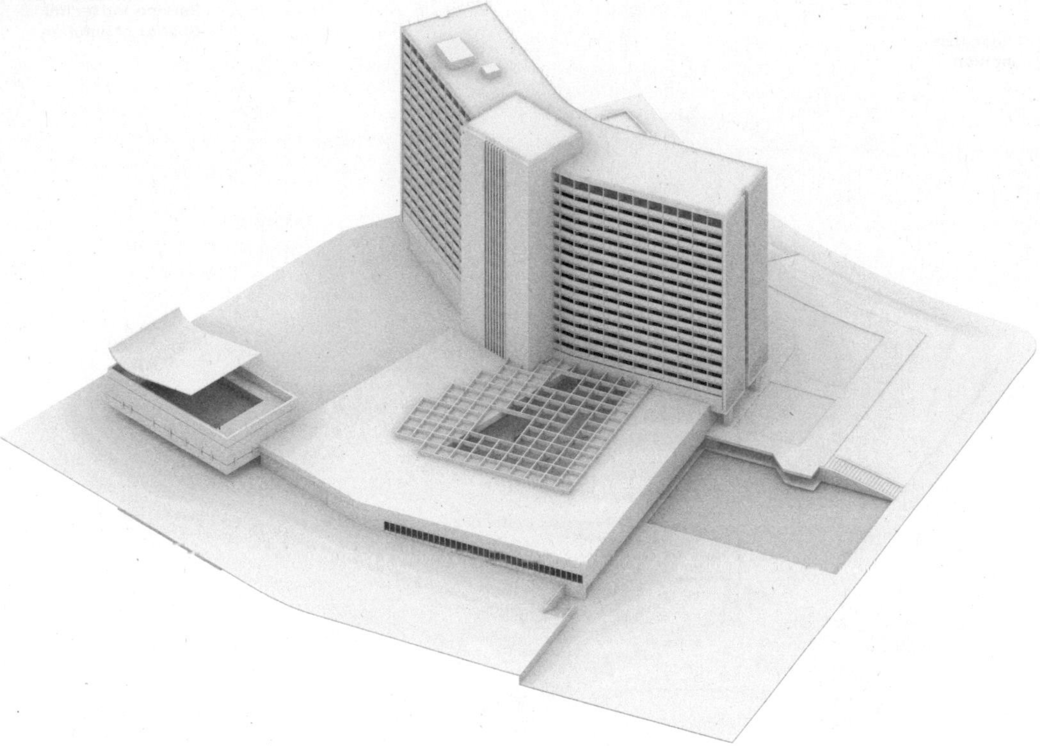

South-west perspective view
Original condition

1974

Public/restaurant
Hotel rooms
Service and technical
Change of function

Basement floor plan
Original condition

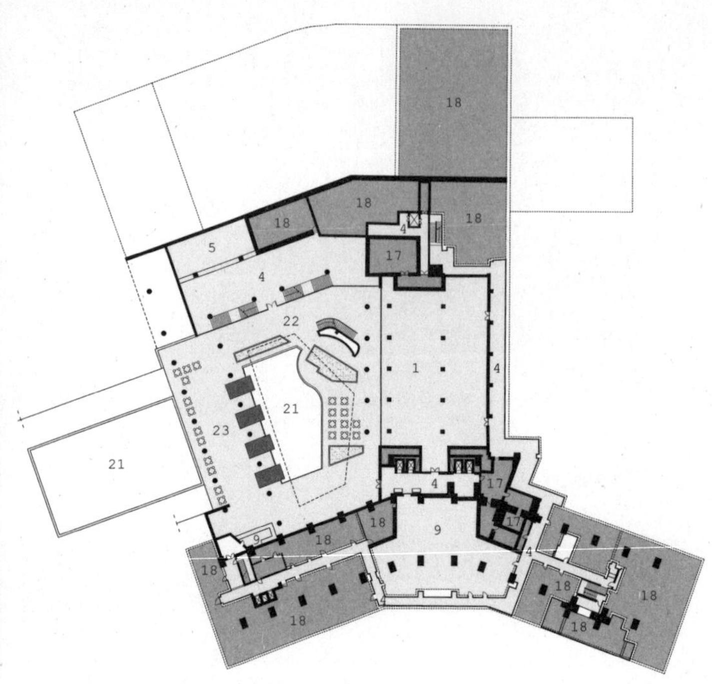

Hotel: 1st floor plan
Original condition

Typical hotel floor plan
Original condition

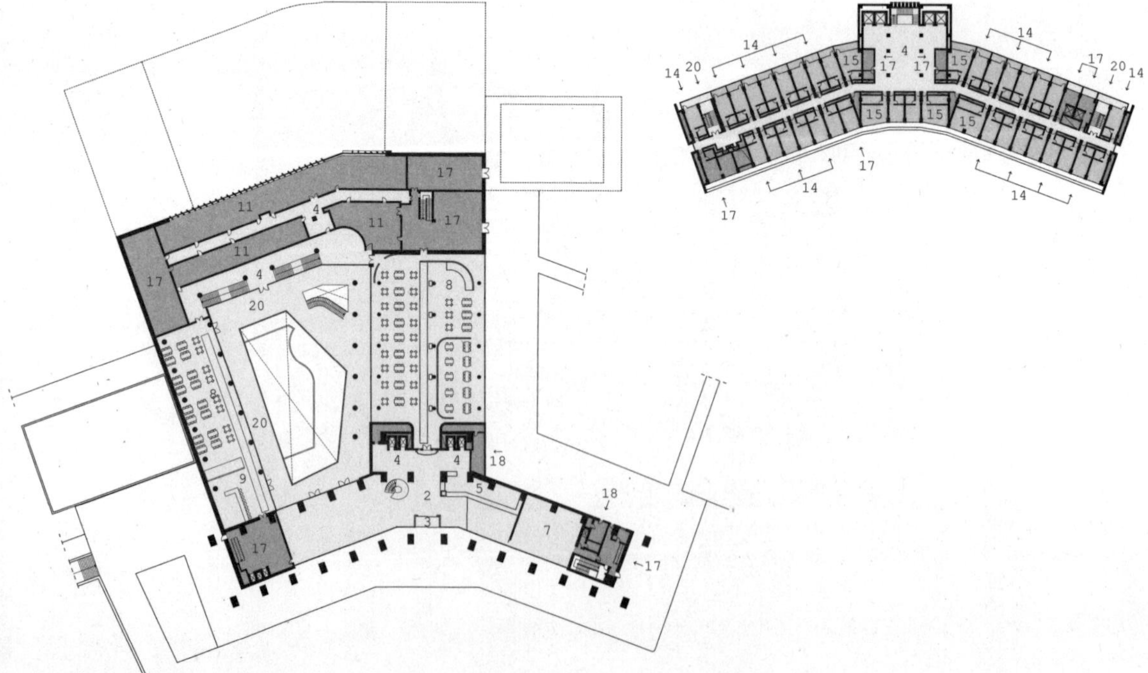

2022

1	Banquet hall
2	Vestibule
3	Airlock
4	Circulation
5	Cloakroom
6	Conference hall
7	Reception
8	Restaurant
9	Bar
10	Bika Club restaurant
11	Kitchen
12	Souvenir shop
13	Single room
14	Double room
15	Family room
16	Office
17	Service space
18	Technical space
19	Entrance canopy
20	Balcony
21	Pool/fountain
22	Internal courtyard
23	Chaikhana (teahouse)

Basement floor plan
Current condition

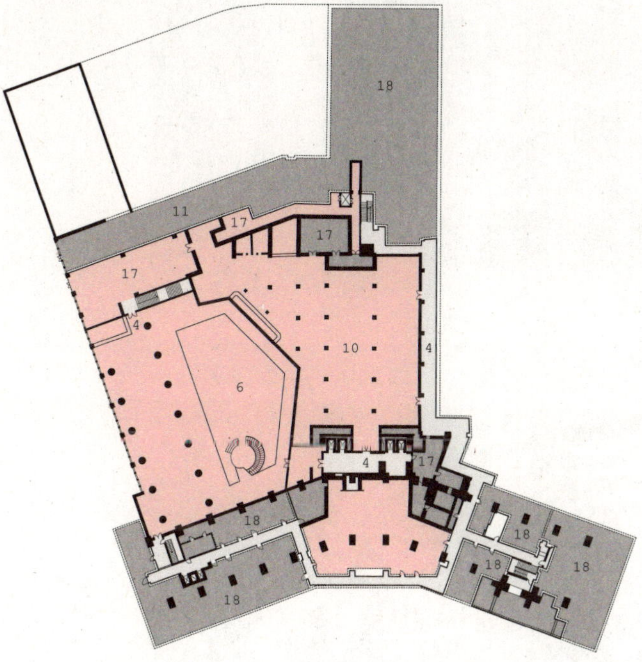

Hotel: 1st floor plan
Current condition

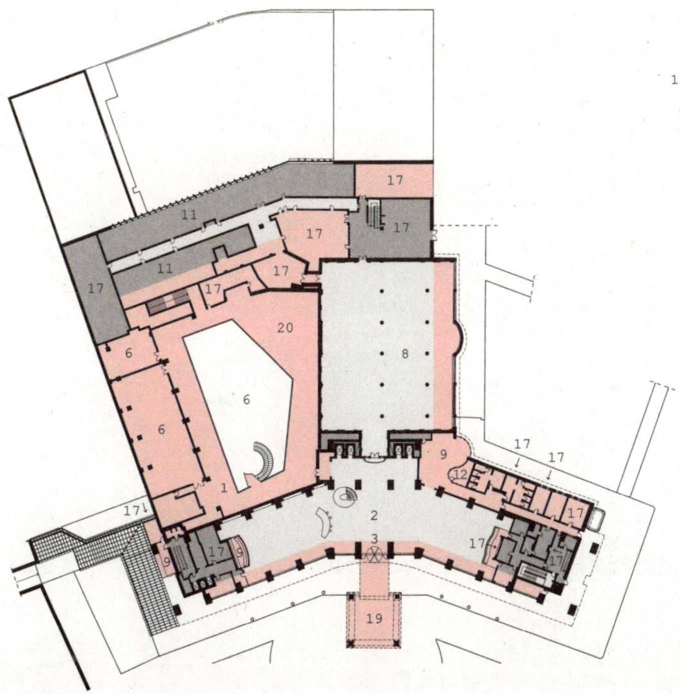

Typical hotel floor plan
Current condition

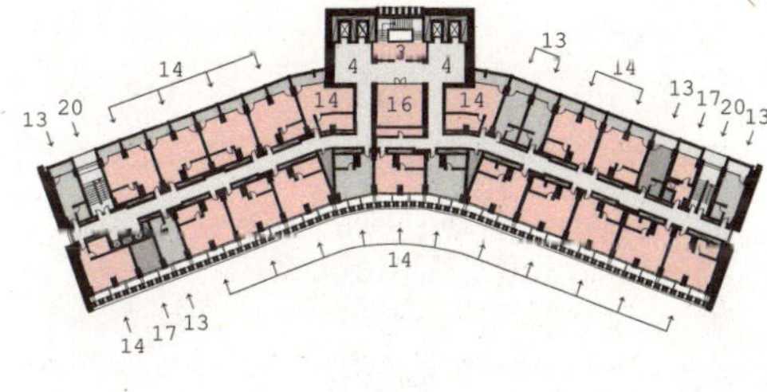

0 5 15m

Construction of the Uzbekistan Hotel, steel structure, west façade

Construction of the Uzbekistan Hotel, west façade

Il'ia Merport (lead architect) and Lev Gorlitskii (chief engineer), south façade of the Uzbekistan Hotel and swimming pool building, 1976

Construction of the building

West façade of the Uzbekistan Hotel, 1979

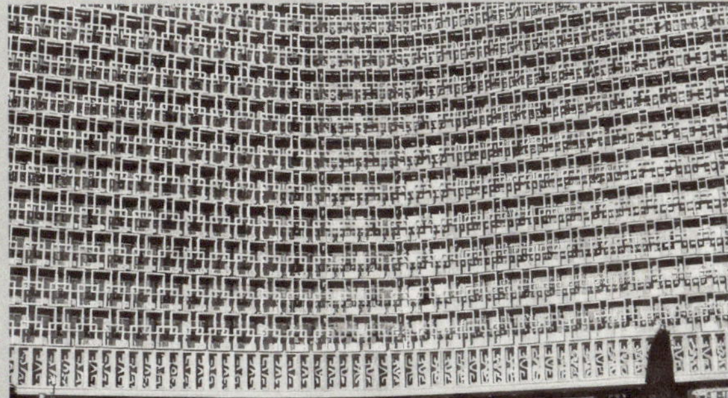

Main entrance, west façade, 1970–1980

East façade of the hotel and swimming pool building, 1974

East façade of the hotel and swimming pool building, 1974

Teahouse on the first floor of the two-story block

Restaurant in the two-story block

Restaurant in the two-story block

West façade, 2022

Corner of the west and south façades, 2022

Detail of cladding on the south and north façades, 2022

Detail of sunshading on the west façade, 2022

East façade, 2022

Close-ups of sunshading on the west façade, view from the interior, 2022

Staircase block on the east façade, 2022

Corridor on the third floor of the hotel, 2022

Model of the building

Uzbekistan Hotel, restaurant sketch, 1967

Uzbekistan Hotel, exterior sketch, 1967

Uzbekistan Hotel, interior sketch, 1967

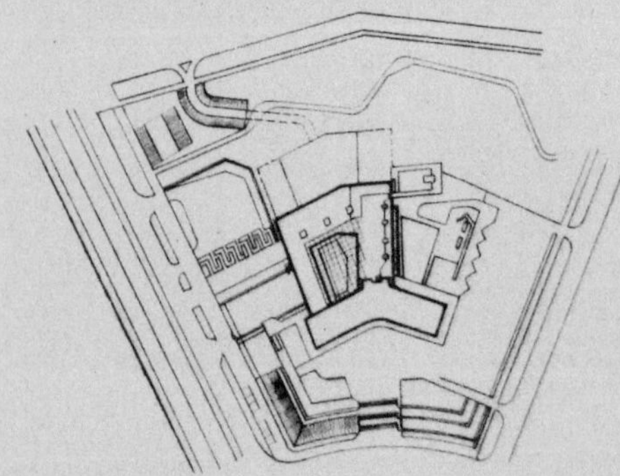
General planimetry

Plan of the inner courtyard

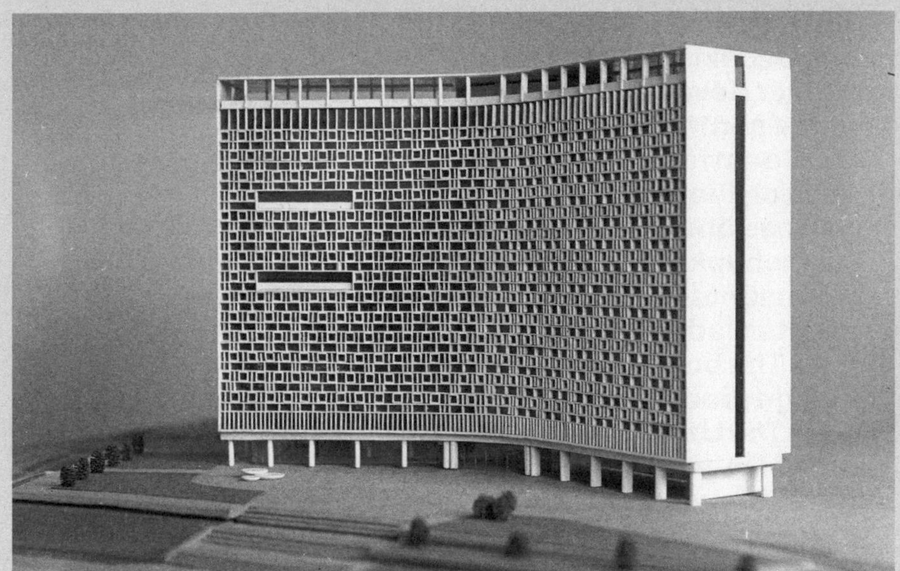
Model of the building

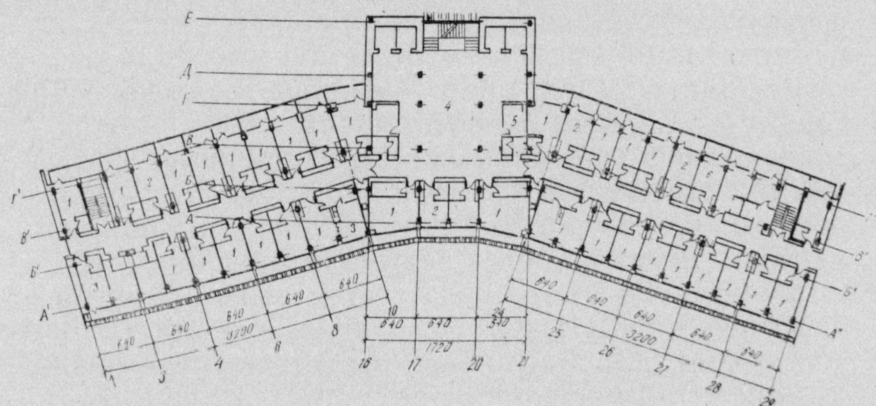
Typical floor plan with measurements

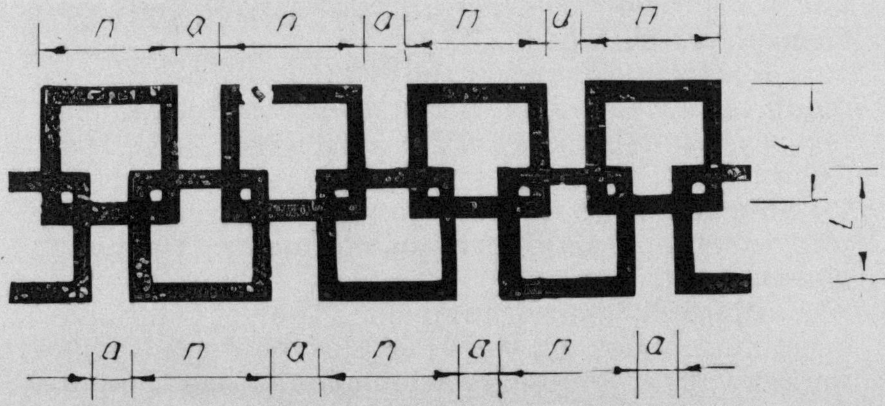
West façade sunshading grid, drawing with measurements, 1974

HIGHLIGHTS

The Uzbekistan Hotel is a high-rise building located on the former Revolution Square (now Amir Temur Square), one of the central squares of the "new" city. It was designed by a team from the TashZNIIEP project institute led by architect Il'ia Merport. The team included a number of other professionals: architects Liudmila Ershova, Viacheslav Rashchupkin and Vladimir Narubanskii; engineers Vadim Starosel'tsev, Lev Gorlitskii and Vadim Burdman; and artists Vladimir Chub, Irena Lipene and S. Bondareva.

The building was inaugurated in 1974, although the design process began in 1963, before the earthquake.

The Uzbekistan Hotel is one of the most iconic examples of modernist architecture in Tashkent, due to a well-chosen placement on the urban plot and the elegant curved shape, full-height sunshading screen on the façade facing the square and, finally, construction technology that was innovative for the time.

The hotel was one of the first tall modernist buildings in this part of the "new city." The architects tried to coordinate the hotel's position with the only other high-rise (at the time) on Lenin Square, the Ministries Building. The volume is composed of two architectural blocks: a tall slab containing the hotel rooms and a low plinth with restaurant services, banquet halls and a pool. The curved profile of the slab follows the rounded shape of the square, softening the monumental scale of the building. The hotel's height offers generous views of Tashkent from the upper levels and it is also a very visible landmark. The horizontal block, attached to the slab at the two lower levels, was once centered around a cozy courtyard with a retractable roof for shade. This volume balanced the overall massing of the hotel, creating an articulated composition from the side of the park, in contrast with the laconicism of the main façade.

This façade has made the building an icon of Soviet modernism, combining its "open book" shape with the panjara-inspired texture of the sunshading. Placed on the western elevation, the interwoven second skin protects the hotel rooms from the sun's rays by interpreting a traditional separation device using modernist language and materials.

A third highlight is the advanced nature of the construction technology, which includes the steel structure, the innovative prefabrication techniques (used during construction to speed up the process and guarantee seismic safety, including special elevators and cranes) and the finishes.

Finally, the hotel once represented a valuable synthesis between monumental art and architecture, as numerous works were made by important artists and artisans of the time. Sadly, this aspect has since been lost.

STATE OF REPAIR SCORE:

- 3 – The building shows localized deterioration patterns which do not affect its stability

Protection status: The building is listed and protected according to Resolution No. 227 of the Cabinet of Ministers, April 22, 2024.

Main criticalities: Due to the extensive use of the building structure, there are some worn parts.

Possible risks: The main risk is the deterioration of the building owing to lack of maintenance.

INTEGRITY SCORE:

- Exterior: 2 — Transformations to the building and its surroundings have caused the loss of some of the elements necessary to express its significance
- Interior: 1 — The building has lost most of the elements necessary to express its significance

The integrity of the building is partially lost due to major interventions which have occurred over the years. The part of the low block housing restaurant services and the pool was demolished, modifying the overall architectural perception of the building. The façade glazing at the first-floor level has been rebuilt in a position different from the original.

The original interiors, such as the hotel rooms, the foyer, the café, the restaurant and amenities, were mostly renewed, with the exception of the corridors and hotel rooms on the third floor. Also, the artworks that embellished the interiors have been lost, including the stained glass wall titled *Day and Night* by Irena Lipene and the relief painting *Fruits of the Earth* by Vladimir Chub.

AUTHENTICITY SCORE:

- Exterior: 2 – The building has been subjected to localized but significant modifications
- Interior: 1 – The building has been subjected to major interventions which resulted in an overall transformation

Since its construction, the hotel has undergone several interventions to both the functionality and the appearance of the building. A distinction should, however, be made between the interior and the exterior of the building, as they retain different levels of authenticity.

On the exterior of the building, the transformation of the volume behind the hotel, with the demolition of the swimming pool, undermined the overall authenticity.

Furthermore, some small elements such as the canopy in front of the main façade were added. The low volume housing the restaurant and other services was also transformed.

The interior of the building has been completely transformed. All of the decorative apparatus, which was a highlight of the project, has been lost, and the finishes have been completely replaced.

1983

2022

West façade of the hotel, 1975

West façade of the hotel, 2022

West façade of the hotel, 1982

West façade of the hotel, 2022

North façade of the two-story block, 1983

North façade of the two-story block, 2022

1977

2022

East façade of the hotel, 1974

East façade of the hotel, 2022

Main lobby, 1977

Main lobby, 2022

Bar on the first floor, 1975

Bar on the first floor, 2022

LEVEL 1 – MAXIMUM LEVEL OF INTEREST
(No transformations allowed; conservation activities required)

URBAN LEVEL

The boundaries of the urban block where the hotel Uzbekistan is located must not be altered.

Inside the perimeter of Amir Temur Square it is not possible to add new buildings.

The façade perimeter and roof eaves height of the buildings facing Mustaqillik Avenue must not be changed.

The façade perimeter and roof eaves height of the buildings facing Taraqqiyot Street must not be changed.

ARCHITECTURAL LEVEL
EXTERIOR

The front façade of the hotel volume, including the ornamental sunshading system, must not be transformed.

The lateral façades of the hotel volume with the stone cladding characterized by the color gradient from bottom to top must not be transformed.

The back façade of the high-rise block should not be transformed.

The overall exterior volume of the building must not be modified.

INTERIOR

The distribution corridors on the third floor and the staircase on the east façade, which are the only original architectural elements in terms of their dimensions and finishes, should be preserved as they are.

DETAIL LEVEL
EXTERIOR

The elements characterizing the exterior of the building must not be changed. In particular:

- the concrete sunshading grilles;
- the stone-clad sunshading panels;
- all of the concrete panels on the main façade;
- the stone cladding.

INTERIOR

The original cladding and furniture of the third-floor corridors must be preserved.

The original cladding of the main staircase volume on the east façade of the hotel must be preserved.

In particular:

- the marble covering of the steps;
- the balustrades.

LEVEL 2 – MEDIUM LEVEL OF INTEREST
(Elements included in the second level can be moderately transformed following approval by a designated committee[1])

URBAN LEVEL

Any new construction within the urban block or changes to the architectural layout of the urban block should be submitted to the designated committee for approval.

ARCHITECTURAL LEVEL
EXTERIOR

The façades of the low volume at the back containing the restaurants can be replaced with committee approval.

INTERIOR

Transformations of the space of the foyer can only occur if approved by the designated committee.

Transformations of the hotel rooms can only occur if approved by the designated committee.

Transformations of the panoramic deck on the top floor of the hotel can only occur if approved by the designated committee.

Transformations of the restaurant spaces can only occur if approved by the designated committee.

DETAIL LEVEL
INTERIOR

Windows and doors, particularly where original, may only be replaced with the approval of the designated committee.

HIDDEN MODERNIST FEATURES

Like many modernist buildings, the Uzbekistan Hotel was meant to "float" above the ground, appearing as a massive block suspended on relatively thin pillars. To obtain such an effect, the glazed façade of the ground floor was pushed back from the building outline, leaving only the dark freestanding pillars along the perimeter. However, for functional reasons in 2000 the entrance hall was enlarged, pushing the glazing outward to incorporate the pillars and creating a continuous façade, which completely erased the "floating" effect.

The "dematerialization" of the building also concerned the top floor, which originally housed open galleries. The presence of such terraces enhanced the

1 An international committee of heritage preservation experts to be appointed.

modernist language of the building, producing further contrasts of solids and voids.

A further hidden modernist feature can be recognized in the former courtyard, which was located on the plinth on the east side of the hotel. Suspended on pilotis, this additional volume provided a certain level of permeability to the building, connecting it to its urban surroundings, much like other modernist buildings in Tashkent (e.g. the Zarafshan Restaurant built in 1974).

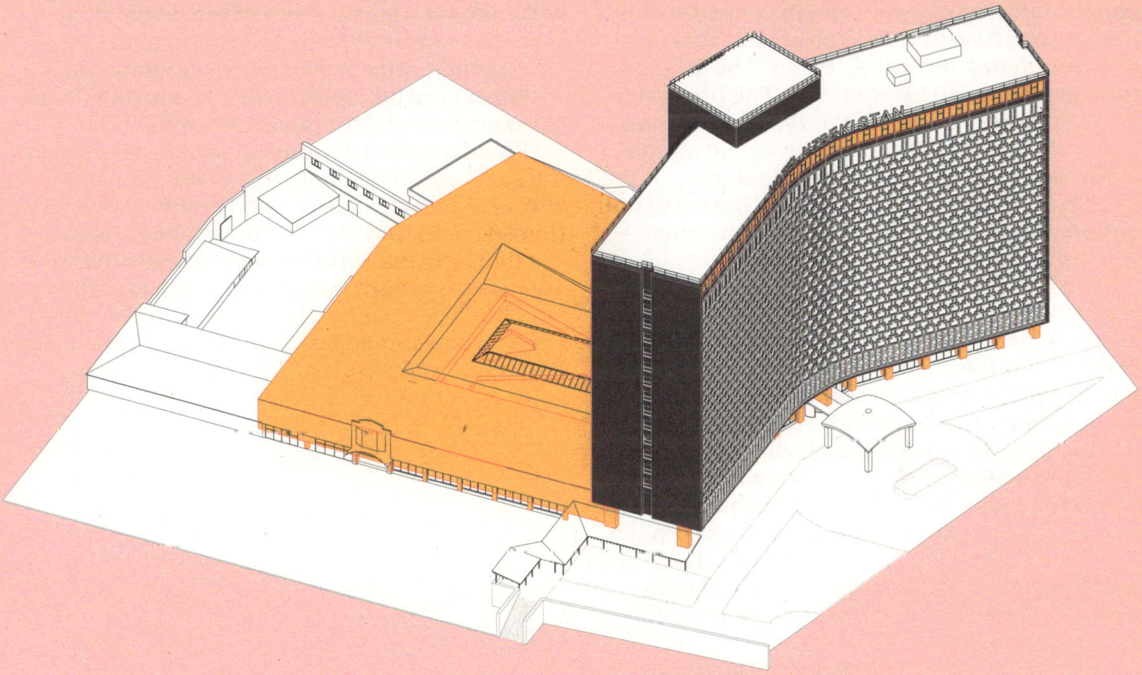

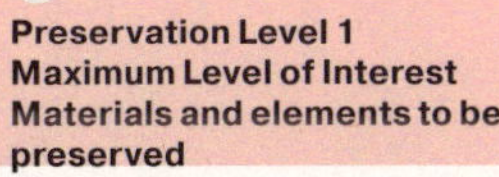

Preservation Level 1
Maximum Level of Interest
Materials and elements to be preserved

Preservation Level 2
Medium Level of Interest
Materials and elements to be preserved

Hidden Modernist Features
Materials and elements to be preserved

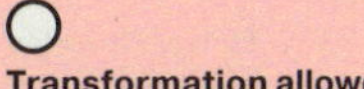

Transformation allowed

Preservation Strategy

Because of its prominence within the urban landscape and its architectural design, today the Uzbekistan Hotel is one of the most iconic and well-known modernist buildings in Tashkent. Inaugurated in 1974, the hotel was built using the most advanced technologies. Its artistic relevance was originally reinforced by a number of works of monumental art in the interior, created by important artists and artisans of the time.

Since then, the hotel has changed considerably, both inside and out. The original features that openly declared its affiliation to modernism have been partially erased and of the ones that are left, some are now partially hidden or compromised. The preservation strategy developed for the Uzbekistan Hotel aims to reveal those features, restoring, as far as possible, the original appearance and architectural quality of the building from the outside.

While the interiors of the hotel have been completely transformed and the artworks lost, the façades have retained an acceptable level of authenticity and integrity, and the changes that occurred can be reversed. The preservation actions hereby proposed will thus enhance the modernist character of this iconic monument, uncovering its intended design.

The strategy includes six main preservation actions which will mostly focus on the main—and most iconic—façade of the hotel.

The first action is aimed at reinstating the original "floating" effect of the building, which was lost in the renovation works that occurred in 2000. For functional reasons, the original glazing on the first floor was pushed outward to incorporate the pillars and create a continuous façade. By moving the glazing back to its original position, it would be possible to restore this effect, which is crucial for the modernist character of the hotel. Additionally, the heavy portico that was built in front of the hotel to protect the drop-off area in case of rain should be demolished and replaced with a more suitable solution.

The second action focuses on the removal of the LED tubes that were attached to the main façade to project advertisements at night. The vertical extension of these elements interferes with the geometric pattern of the sunshade lattice, the most recognizable and original feature of the building. It is thus advisable to dismantle the LED tubes, together with the metallic profiles supporting them, and expose the original design of the main façade.[1]

To the serve the same purpose, a third action proposes a general reorganization of the gap between the sun lattice (panjara) and the actual façade, which currently houses the technical equipment, with cables and pipes in disarray. The reorganization of this interstitial space and the removal of the equipment will greatly improve the appearance of the façade, while also providing a pleasant view from the inside toward the exterior.

The fourth action concerns the top level of the hotel, which originally hosted open galleries on the east and west façades. The galleries were glazed during reconstruction work to create more space for hotel facilities (bar, gym, restaurants). Reopening the former terraces will contribute to restoring the modernist language, composed of contrasts of solids and voids.

A fifth action will involve the reopening of the former courtyard, located on the plinth on the east side of the hotel. Once again, this operation will uncover a lost feature of the original design: the permeability which used to connect the building with its urban surroundings via a wide covered passage toward the former Pushkinskaia Street (Mustaqillik Avenue).

Finally, a sixth action concerns all the external surfaces of the high-rise building, which will be cleaned, repaired and painted where required using the original colors and design. Particular attention will be paid to the cladded surfaces (panjara, north and south façades), which will be checked for possible detaching tiles. These should be properly reattached or, if damaged, replaced with new ones.

1 This action was implemented in 2024, while the book was being prepared. For the sake of consistency with the photographs and to avoid similar installations in the future, we chose to maintain this paragraph in the strategy description.

West façade of the hotel, 1994

West façade, main entrance
Strategy visualization

Adaptation Strategy

While preserving the Uzbekistan Hotel as the most iconic modernist building in Tashkent, the project needs to ensure that the functionality and commercial sustainability of the hotel is proportionate to its architectural significance.

Taking into account the importance of the site of the hotel on Amir Temur Square, a careful analysis of the current room availability and the pipeline of expected hotel openings until 2026 has been conducted, with the conclusion that a four- or five-star hotel would be commercially justified in this location.

To achieve such a rating an interior refurbishment is necessary (compatible with the Statement of Significance and the preservation strategy). Room sizes have to be increased and diversified, and additional hotel facilities included. A unique contemporary interior design is a crucial element to distinguish the Uzbekistan Hotel from others on the market (and to compensate for the contained ceiling height of the original building).

As well as targeting business and leisure travelers for short stays, the hotel should once more become an attractive destination for the residents of Tashkent. This role was fulfilled by the large two-story high plinth in the original 1974 building. Originally, the plinth contained a variety of restaurants, cafés and chaikhanas (traditional teahouses) organized around a courtyard with a shallow pool in the middle and a large shading device over it. The courtyard was directly accessible from Pushkinskaia Street via a broad covered passage. The proposal reinstates the public plinth (instead of the existing introverted volume that includes an overscaled restaurant and a very large events hall). In the absence of historical drawings, the research team has reconstructed the volume of the courtyard and its shape from available photographs and sketches, with the intention of implementing it as contemporary architecture imbued with the memory of the original place.

The functionality of the public plinth will be updated to meet the needs of present-day Tashkent. Rather than inserting a food court, along with cafés and restaurants it includes a spa (with a pool), a medium-size business center and a retail area (with designer shops, bookshops, etc.). These programs would not be managed by the hotel but would be leased to independent tenants (companies/start-ups).

The swimming pool was an important feature of the original complex, though it was not part of the original design intent. The proposed strategy contemplates the realization of the swimming pool, either as a volume or as an outdoor pool at ground level, depending on the further development of the design.

The park behind the hotel should be upgraded and connected to the programs of the plinth.

The reopened terrace on the seventeenth floor will accommodate a high-end restaurant with spectacular views of Tashkent and the surrounding mountains.

While the hotel caters to tourists, the plinth should belong to the residents of Tashkent. Therefore, instead of being a closed, anonymous and inaccessible block, the openness and accessibility that were so crucial to the original 1974 design should be reinstated.

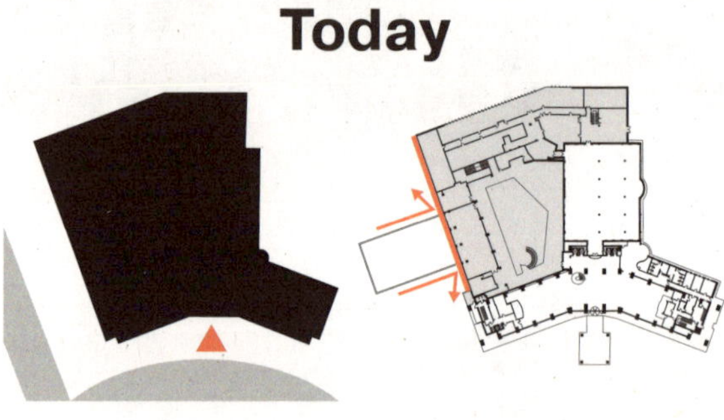

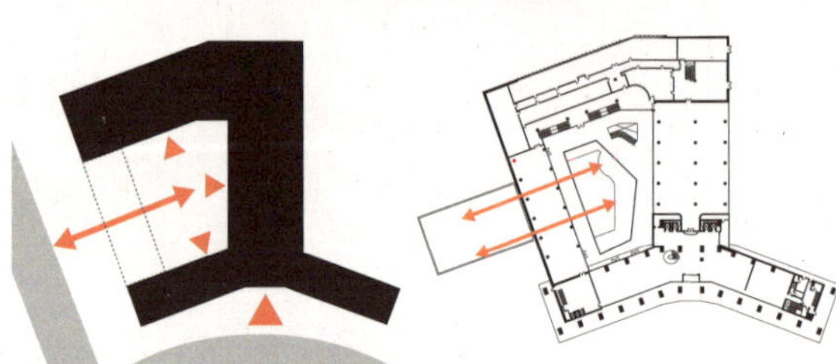

Today

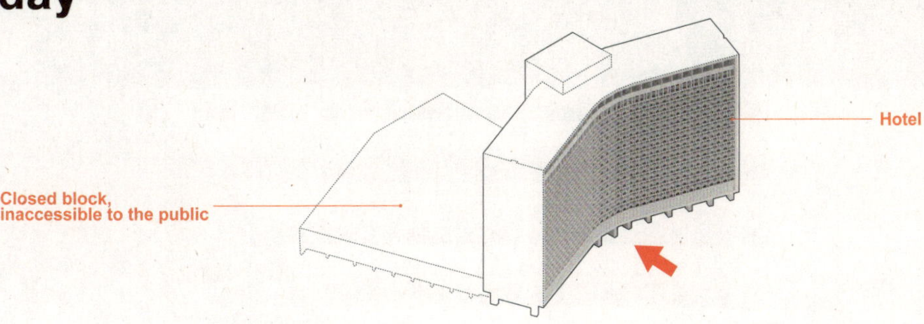

Potential

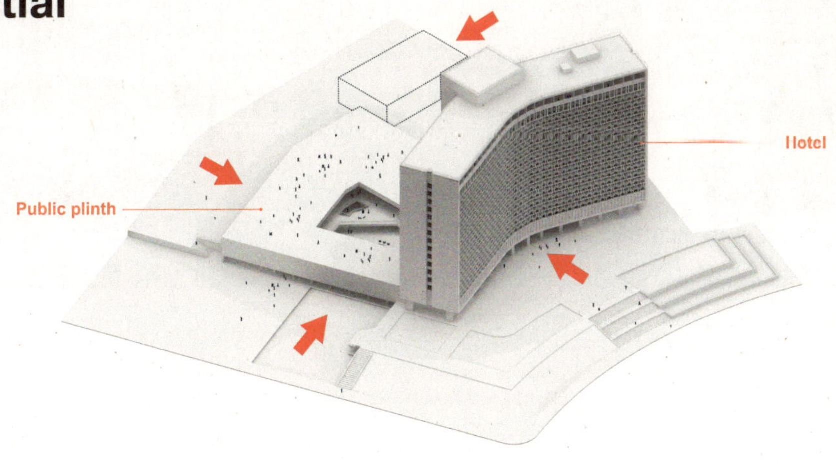

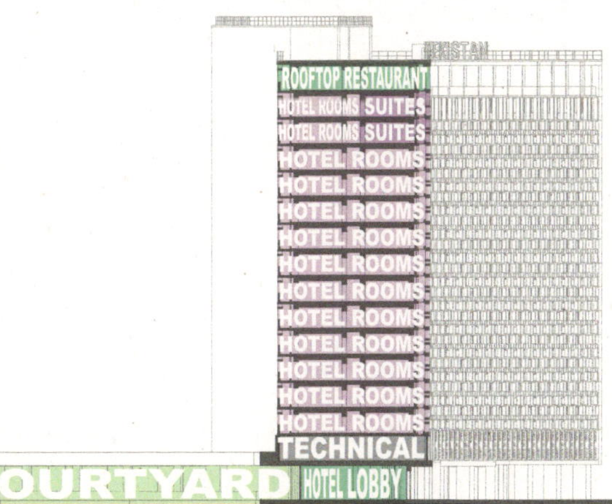

Programmatic section, potential

Internal courtyard as an urban space, view toward the hotel volume
Strategy visualization

Internal courtyard reconnected to the city
Strategy visualization

Appendix

Bibliography

Books and Articles

- "16-etazhnyi zhiloi dom iz monolitnogo zhelezobetona v ob"emno-perestavnoi opalubke po ul. B. Khmel'nitskogo [A Sixteen-Story Residential Building Made from Monolithic Reinforced Concrete Using Sliding Formwork, Located on B. Khmel'nitskii Street]." *Arkhitektura i stroitel'stvo Uzbekistana [Architecture and Construction of Uzbekistan]*, nos. 2–3 (1986): 19.
- "1973 Law of the Union of Soviet Socialist Republics: On the Protection and Use of Historic and Cultural Monuments." *Future Anterior: Journal of Historic Preservation, History, Theory, and Criticism* 5, no. 1 (2008): 74–80.
- Aalto, Alvar. *Arkhitektura i gumanizm [Architecture and Humanism]*. Moscow: Progress, 1978.
- Adamov, Leon. "TashNIiPIgenplanu – 20 let [TashNIiPIgenplan Is 20]." *Arkhitektura i stroitel'stvo Uzbekistana [Architecture and Construction of Uzbekistan]*, no. 9 (1989): 1–2.
- *Adres-spravochnik Turkestanskogo kraia s illiustratsiiami, kalendarem na 1910 g., kartoi kraia i ob'iavleniiami [Address Book of Turkestan Krai with Illustrations, a Calendar for 1910, a Map of the Area and Announcements]*. Tashkent: V.M. Il'in Printing House, 1910.
- Aleksandrovich, Genrikh. "Zdanie Tashkentskogo gosudarstvennogo tsirka [The Building of the Tashkent State Circus]." *Stroitel'stvo i arkhitektura Uzbekistana [Construction and Architecture of Uzbekistan]*, no. 4 (1971): 25–28.
- Aleksandrovich, Genrikh. "Shagi v budushchee [Steps into the Future]." *Stroitel'stvo i arkhitektura Uzbekistana [Construction and Architecture of Uzbekistan]*, no. 3 (1974): 21.
- Aleksandrovich, Genrikh. "Schast'e v professii [Happiness in the Profession]." *Arkhitektura i stroitel'stvo Uzbekistana [Architecture and Construction of Uzbekistan]*, no. 10 (1988): 26–29.
- Alomar, Gabriel, F. Sorlin and Piero Gazzola. *Protective Inventory of the European Cultural Heritage, Criteria and Methods for the Use of the Index Card I.E.C.H.* Strasbourg: Council of Europe, 2016.
- Altintaş Kaptan, Meriç, Aslihan Ünlü and Uta Pottgiesser. "Connecting the Dots: A Global Exploration of Local Docomomo Inventories." *Docomomo Journal* 69, no. 2 (December 2023): 76–85.
- Anderson, Richard. "The USSR's 1948 Instructions for the Identification, Registration, Maintenance, and Restoration of Architectural Monuments under State Protection." *Future Anterior: Journal of Historic Preservation, History, Theory, and Criticism* 5, no. 1 (2008): 64–72.
- Anderson, Richard. *Russia: Modern Architectures in History*. Chicago: University of Chicago Press, 2015.
- Applebaum, Rachel. "The Friendship Project: Socialist Internationalism in the Soviet Union and Czechoslovakia in the 1950s and 1960s." *Slavic Review* 74, no. 3 (2015): 484–507.
- Arkhangel'skii, Valentin, and Gennadii Korobovtsev. "I etap: 1929–1941; 'Zarozhdenie,' SAKhIPI–SASI–SAII [I. Stage: 1929–1941; 'The Origin,' SaKhIPI–SASI–SAII]." *Arkhitektura i stroitel'stvo Uzbekistana [Architecture and Construction of Uzbekistan]*, no. 7 (1990): 1–3.
- "Arkhitektor Andrei Kosinskii: 'Ia do sikh por ne znaiu, chto takoe khoroshii vkus' (chast' III) [Architect Andrei Kosinskii: 'Even Now I Don't Know What Good Taste Is']." *Fergana News*, August 1, 2006. https://www.fergananews.com/articles/4524.
- *Arkhitektura SShA: Katalog vystavki v SSSR [Architecture of the USA: Catalogue of the Exhibition in the USSR]*, 1965.
- Artem'ev, Vladimir. "Pamiatnik epokhi v sovremennoi zastroike [A Historical Monument in a Contemporary Neighborhood]." *Arkhitektura i stroitel'stvo Uzbekistana [Architecture and Construction of Uzbekistan]*, no. 4 (1990): 28–30.
- Asamov, Kh. "Tvorcheskii put' TashZNIIEP za 10 let [The Creative Path of TashZNIIEP over 10 Years]." *Stroitel'stvo i arkhitektura Uzbekistana [Construction and Architecture of Uzbekistan]*, no. 12 (1974): 1–4.
- Asamov, Kh., and Il'ia Merport. "Perspektiva i puti razvitiia vysotnogo domostroeniia v Tashkente [Prospects and Development Paths of High-Rise Construction in Tashkent]." *Stroitel'stvo i arkhitektura Uzbekistana [Construction and Architecture of Uzbekistan]*, no. 6 (1975): 1–5.
- Asanov, Aleksei. "Pamiatnik arkhitektury i ego okhrannaia zona [The Architectural Monument and Its Protected Area]." *Stroitel'stvo i arkhitektura Uzbekistana [Construction and Architecture of Uzbekistan]*, no. 3 (1969): 20–23.
- Asanov, Aleksei. "V tvorcheskom poiske [In Creative Pursuit]." *Stroitel'stvo i arkhitektura Uzbekistana [Construction and Architecture of Uzbekistan]*, no. 3 (1974): 14.
- Ashrafi, Feruz, and Roman Kontorer. "Gostinitsa Uzbekistan na 930 mest v Tashkente [The 930-bed Uzbekistan Hotel in Tashkent]." *Stroitel'stvo i arkhitektura Uzbekistana [Construction and Architecture of Uzbekistan]*, no. 7 (1975): 24–29.
- Askarov, Shukur. "Pervyi proekt pereplanirovki Tashkenta [The First Project for Replanning Tashkent]." *Arkhitektura i stroitel'stvo Uzbekistana [Architecture and Construction of Uzbekistan]*, no. 7 (1973): 33–36.
- Askarov, Shukur. "Okhrana pamiatnikov – na uroven' sovremennykh gradostroitel'nykh trebovanii [Protection of Monuments – According to Modern Urban Planning Requirements]." *Stroitel'stvo i arkhitektura Uzbekistana [Construction and Architecture of Uzbekistan]*, no. 11 (1975): 30–32.
- Askarov, Shukur. "Krizis khudozhestvennogo [Crisis of the Artistic]." *Arkhitektura i stroitel'stvo Uzbekistana [Architecture and Construction of Uzbekistan]*, no. 2 (1988): 12–13.
- Askarov, Shukur. *Genezis arkhitektury Uzbekistana [The Genesis of the Architecture of Uzbekistan]*. Tashkent: Izdatel'stvo San'at, 2014.
- Avermaete, Tom, Serhat Karakayali and Marlon von Osten, eds. *Colonial Modern: Aesthetics of the Past, Rebellions for the Future*. London: Black Dog Publishing, 2010.
- Aveta, Claudia. "Piero Gazzola: Restauro dei monumenti e conservazione dei centri storici e del paesaggio." Ph.D. diss., Università degli Studi di Napoli Federico II, 2005.
- *The Awakened East: A Report by Soviet Journalists on the Visit of N. S. Khrushchov to India, Burma, Indonesia and Afghanistan*. Moscow: Foreign Languages Publishing House, 1960.
- Azimov, A. "Zdanie Kairoskogo radio- i teletsentra [The Building of the Cairo Radio and TV Center]." *Stroitel'stvo i arkhitektura Uzbekistana [Construction and Architecture of Uzbekistan]*, no. 7 (1969): 42–44.
- Azimov, A. "Nekotorye tendentsii v sovremennom gradostroitel'stve Arabskoi respubliki Egipet [Some Trends in the Contemporary Urban Planning of the Arab Republic of Egypt]." *Stroitel'stvo i arkhitektura Uzbekistana [Construction and Architecture of Uzbekistan]*, no. 10 (1972): 32–38.
- Azimov, A. "Simvol druzhby narodov [A Symbol of Peoples' Friendship]." *Vechernii Tashkent [Evening Tashkent]*, no. 106, May 12, 1978.
- Babadzhanova, Gul'sara. "Khudozhnik i metro [The Artist and the Metro]." *Arkhitektura i stroitel'stvo Uzbekistana [Architecture and Construction of Uzbekistan]*, no. 6 (1985): 17–23.
- Babadzhanova, Gul'sara. "Tema kosmosa v stekle [The Theme of the Cosmos in Glass]." *Arkhitektura i stroitel'stvo Uzbekistana [Architecture and Construction of Uzbekistan]*, no. 1 (1988): 23–24.
- Babakhanov, Abdulla. "Za vysokoe kachestvo podgotovki arkhitektorov [For High Quality Preparation of Architects]." *Stroitel'stvo i arkhitektura Uzbekistana [Construction and Architecture of Uzbekistan]*, no. 4 (1968): 23–25.
- Babakhanov, Abdulla. "Uspekhi molodykh zodchikh Uzbekistana [Successes of Young Architects of Uzbekistan]." *Stroitel'stvo i arkhitektura Uzbekistana [Construction and Architecture of Uzbekistan]*, no. 7 (1970): 23–29.
- Babievskii, Konstantin, Konstantin Kriukov and Khamza Ubaidullaev. "Arkhitekturnoe obrazovanie v Uzbekistane [Architectural Education in Uzbekistan]." *Stroitel'stvo i arkhitektura Uzbekistana [Construction and Architecture of Uzbekistan]*, no. 12 (1972): 16–18.
- Babievskii, Konstantin, and Khamza Ubaidullaev. "Uzbekskaia arkhitekturnaia shkola [The Uzbek Architectural School]." *Stroitel'stvo i arkhitektura Uzbekistana [Construction and Architecture of Uzbekistan]*, no. 12 (1979): 1–7.
- "Badiiy akademiya Markaziy ko'rgazmalar zalida yong'in sodir bo'ldi [A Fire Occurred in the Central Exhibition Hall of the Academy of Arts]." *Gazeta.uz*, December 30, 2018. https://www.gazeta.uz/oz/2018/12/30/yongin/.
- Balian, Karen. *Memorial Egern [The Yeghern Memorial]*. Moscow: Tatlin, 2015.
- Balian, Karen. *Artur Tarkhanian, Spartak Khachikian, Grach'ia Pogosian*. Moscow: Tatlin, 2021.
- Bardian, Feodosii. *Sovetskii tsirk na piati kontinentakh [The Soviet Circus on Five Continents]*. Moscow: Iskusstvo, 1977.
- Barkhin, Mikhail. "O khudozhestvennom obraze v sovetskoi arkhitekture [On the Artistic Image in Soviet Architecture]." *Arkhitektura SSSR [Architecture of the USSR]*, no. 5 (1972): 34–38.
- Baroli, Marc. *La vie quotidienne des Français en Algérie: 1830–1914*. Paris: Hachette, 1967.
- Baydarov, E. "Analysis of the Preservation of Historical and Cultural Heritage in Uzbekistan." *Eurasian Research Institute Weekly E-Bulletin*, no. 98 (2017).
- Belfer, G. A. "Osveshchenie Tashkentskogo tsirka [Lighting of the Tashkent Circus]." *Stroitel'stvo i arkhitektura Uzbekistana [Construction and Architecture of Uzbekistan]*, no. 4 (1971): 29–32.

- Bell, James. "Redefining National Identity in Uzbekistan: Symbolic Tensions in Tashkent's Official Public Landscape." *Ecumene* 6, no. 2 (1999): 183–213.
- Belmonte, Carmen. *A Difficult Heritage: The Afterlives of Fascist-Era Art and Architecture*. Cinisello Balsamo: Silvana Editoriale, 2023.
- Benevolo, Leonardo. *Storia dell'Architettura Moderna*. Bari: Laterza, 2010.
- Bernshtein, David, et al., eds. *Arkhitektura Zapada: Kniga 3; Protivorechiia i poiski 60–70-kh godov [Architecture of the West: Book 3; Contradictions and Explorations of the 1960s and 1970s]*. Moscow: Stroiizdat, 1983.
- Bleze, Richard. "Redaktsionnyi-izdatel'skii korpus kompleksa izdatel'stva TsK KP Uzbekistana [The Editorial and Publishing Block of the Publishers' Complex of the Central Committee of the Communist Party of Uzbekistan]." *Stroitel'stvo i arkhitektura Uzbekistana [Construction and Architecture of Uzbekistan]*, no. 1 (1972): 20–24.
- Bleze, Richard. "Nash gorod [Our City]." *Arkhitektura i stroitel'stvo Uzbekistana [Architecture and Construction of Uzbekistan]*, no. 9 (1987): 4–5.
- Bleze, Richard, and E. Patlis. "Dom molodezhi v Tashkente [The House of Youth in Tashkent]." *Stroitel'stvo i arkhitektura Uzbekistana [Construction and Architecture of Uzbekistan]*, no. 5 (1966): 21–25.
- Bocharov, Iurii, and Nikolai Gulianitskii. *Arkhitektura SSSR, 1917–1987 [Architecture of the USSR, 1917–1987]*. Moscow: Stroiizdat, 1987.
- Boni, Giacomo. "Il catasto dei monumenti in Italia." *Archivio Storico dell'Arte* 4, (November–December 1891): 417–424.
- Boschi, Ruggero, and Pietro Segala. *Codici per la conservazione del patrimonio storico: Cento anni di riflessioni, "grida" e carte*. Florence: Nardini Editore, 2006.
- Bronovitskaia, Anna, and Nikolai Malinin. *Alma-Ata: Arkhitektura sovetskogo modernizma 1955–1991; Spravochnik-putevoditel' [Alma-Ata: A Guide to Soviet Modernist Architecture 1955–1991]*. Moscow: Garage Museum of Contemporary Art, 2018.
- Bronovitskaia, Anna, and Nikolai Malinin. *Leningrad: Arkhitektura sovetskogo modernizma 1955–1991. Spravochnik-putevoditel' [Leningrad: A Guide to Soviet Modernist Architecture 1955–1991]*. Moscow: Garage Museum of Contemporary Art, 2021.
- Bronovitskaya, Anna, Nikolay Malinin and Yuri Palmin. *Moscow: A Guide to Soviet Modernist Architecture 1955–1991*. Prague: Artguide Editions, 2019.
- Bronovitskaya, Anna, Nikolay Malinin and Yuri Palmin. *Alma-Ata: A Guide to Soviet Modernist Architecture 1955–1991*. Prague: Artguide Editions, 2022.
- Budantseva, Tatyana. "Avant-Garde Between East and West: Modern Architecture and Town Planning in the Urals, 1920–1930s." Ph.D. diss., TU Delft, 2007.
- Bulatov, Mitkhat. "Osobennosti i printsipy progressivnogo resheniia planirovki i zastroiki goroda Tashkenta [Features and Principles of Progressive Solutions for the Planning and Construction of the City of Tashkent]." In *Akademiia stroitel'stva i arkhitektury SSSR: Nauchno-issledovatel'skii institut raionnoi planirovki i gradostroitel'stva [Academy of Construction and Architecture of the USSR, Scientific Research Institute for Regional Planning and Urban Planning]*. Moscow/Tashkent: Central State Archive, 1960.
- Bulatov, Mitkhat, and Tulkinoi Kadyrova. *Tashkent*. Leningrad: Avrora, 1977.
- "Bul'var im. V. I. Lenina [V. I. Lenin Boulevard]." *Stroitel'stvo i arkhitektura Uzbekistana [Construction and Architecture of Uzbekistan]*, no. 7 (1974): 11.
- Bykov, V., and Iu. Khripunov. "Tipy kinoteatrov s universal'noi proektsiei [Types of Cinemas with Universal Projection]." *Arkhitektura SSSR [Architecture of the USSR]*, no. 9 (1959): 24–37.
- Bylinkin, Nikolai, and Aleksandr Riabushin, eds. *Sovremennaia sovetskaia arkhitektura, 1955–1980 [Contemporary Soviet Architecture, 1955–1980]*. Moscow: Stroiizdat, 1985.
- Cagiano De Azevedo, Elena, and Roberta Geremia Nucci. *Riflessioni sulla tutela: Temi, problemi, esperienze*. Florence: Polistampa, 2010.
- Candilis, Georges. *Stat' arkhitektorom [Becoming an Architect]*. Moscow: Stroiizdat, 1979.
- Carbonara, Giovanni. "Il restauro come problema di metodo." *Parametro*, no. 266: 21–55.
- Castillo, Greg. "Soviet Orientalism: Socialist Realism and Built Traditions." *Traditional Dwellings and Settlements Review* 8, no. 2 (1997): 33–47.
- Ceccarelli, Paolo. *La costruzione della città sovietica 1929–31*. Padua: Marsilio, 1970.
- Chaubin, Frédéric. *CCCP: Cosmic Communist Constructions Photographed*. Cologne: Taschen, 2011.
- Chebotareva, Zlata. "V zashchitu plotnoi maloetazhnoi zastroiki [In Defense of Dense, Low-Rise Construction]." *Stroitel'stvo i arkhitektura Uzbekistana [Construction and Architecture of Uzbekistan]*, no. 11 (1974): 14–18.
- Chebotareva, Zlata. *Udobstvo, pol'za, krasota: Zhilaia sreda gorodov Srednei Azii [Comfort, Use, Beauty: The Residential Environment in the Cities of Central Asia]*. Tashkent: Izdatel'stvo literatury i iskusstva imeni Gafura Guliama, 1990.
- Chepko, E. "Krupnopanel'noe domostroenie vo Frantsii [Large Panel House Building in France]." *Stroitel'stvo i arkhitektura Uzbekistana [Construction and Architecture of Uzbekistan]*, no. 6 (1961): 27–31.
- Chipiga, I. "Tsirki [Circuses]." *Arkhitektura SSSR [Architecture of the USSR]*, no. 7 (1972): 28–29.
- Christ, Emanuel, Christoph Gantenbein and Victoria Easton. *Typology*. Zurich: Park Books, 2012.
- Chukhovich, Boris. "Building the 'Living East.'" In *Soviet Modernism 1955–1991: Unknown History*, edited by Katharina Ritter, Ekaterina Shapiro-Obermair and Alexandra Wachter, 214–231. Vienna: Park Books, 2012.
- Chukhovich, Boris. "Local Modernism and Global Orientalism: Building the 'Soviet Orient.'" In "19th Vienna Architecture Congress: Soviet Modernism 1955–1991; Unknown Stories." Special issue, *Hintergrund* 54 (2013): 31–39.
- Chukhovich, Boris. "Orientalist Modes of Modernism in Architecture: Colonial/Postcolonial/Soviet." In *Orientalism from the Margins: Perspectives from India and Russia*, edited by Philippe Bornet and Svetlana Gorshenina, 263–293. Lausanne: PUL, 2014.
- Chukhovich, Boris. "Arkhitekturnyi brutalizm v Tsentral'noi Azii [Architectural Brutalism in Central Asia]." *Fergana News*, October 13, 2017. https://www.fergananews.com/articles/9586.
- Chukhovich, Boris. "Palace of Arts." In *SOS Brutalism: A Global Survey*, edited by Oliver Elser, Philip Kurz and Peter Cachola Schmal, 236–237. Berlin: Park Books, 2017.
- Chukhovich, Boris. "Yeghern Memorial: Erevan." In *The Empire Strikes Back? A Traveling Academy through the Post-Soviet Cityscape*, edited by Michaela Geboltsberger and Georg Schöllhammer, 71–76. Vienna: Tranzit.at, 2017.
- Chukhovich, Boris. "Zapovednik (k arkheologii muzeeifitsirovaniia v gradostroitel'stve Uzbekistana) [The Cultural Reserve (Toward an Archeology of Museification in the Urban Planning of Uzbekistan)]." *CAAN*, January 9, 2019. https://www.caa-network.org/archives/14980.
- Chukhovich, Boris. "Architectural Modernism and 'Old Tashkent': The Long History of a Brief Encounter." In *Mahalla: Urban Rural Living*, exhibition catalogue of the Uzbekistan National Pavilion at the 17th Venice Architecture Biennale, 70–79. Tashkent/Bolzano: Longo, 2021.
- Cohen, Jean-Louis. "Soviet Legal Documents on the Preservation of Monuments." *Future Anterior: Journal of Historic Preservation, History, Theory, and Criticism* 5, no. 1 (2008): 62–63.
- Collins, Peter. *Changing Ideals in Modern Architecture, 1750–1950*. 2nd ed. Montreal and Kingston: McGill-Queen's University Press, 1998.
- *Conservation Management Plans: A Guide*. London: Heritage Lottery Fund, 2002.
- Conte, Roberto, and Stefano Perego. *Soviet Asia: Soviet Modernist Architecture in Central Asia*. London: Fuel Design & Publishing, 2019.
- Cooper, Nicholas. *Guide to Recording Historic Buildings*. London: ICOMOS, 1990.
- Cosgrove, Denis E. *Social Formation and Symbolic Landscape*. London: Croom Helm, 1984.
- Council of Europe. *Preservation and Rehabilitation of Groups and Areas of Buildings of Historical or Artistic Interest: Protective Inventory of the European Cultural Heritage (I.E.C.H.) Based on the Palma Recommendation; Criteria and Methods for the Use of the Index Card I.E.C.H.* Strasbourg: Council of Europe, 1968.
- Council of Europe. *Architectural Heritage: Inventory and Documentation Methods in Europe; Proceedings of the Nantes Colloquy*. Strasbourg: Council of Europe, 1998.
- Council of Europe. *Guidance on Inventory and Documentation of the Cultural Heritage*. Strasbourg: Council of Europe, 2009.
- Crews, Robert. "Civilization in the City: Architecture, Urbanism and the Colonization of Tashkent." In *Architecture of Russian Identity*, edited by James Cracraft and Daniel Rowland, 117–132. Ithaca: Cornell University Press, 2003.
- De Magistris, Alessandro. "Reconstructing a Socialist Capital: Moscow and the General Plan of 1935." In *The Twentieth Century Urban Experience*, edited by Robert Freestone, 87–104. Mendrisio: Mendrisio University Press, 1998.
- Del Curto, Davide, and Sofia Celli. "The Treachery of Images: Redefining the Structural System of Havana's National Art Schools." *Sustainability* 13, no. 7 (2021): 3767–3801.
- Dmitriev, Viktor. "O vozmozhnosti ispol'zovaniia priema shipang v sovre-

mennoi praktike [On the Possibility of Using the Shipang Technique in Contemporary Practice]." *Stroitel'stvo i arkhitektura Uzbekistana* [*Construction and Architecture of Uzbekistan*], no. 1 (1961): 15–18.

- Dmitriev, Viktor, and Vladimir Nil'sen. "O napravlennosti v sovremennoi arkhitektury Uzbekistana [On the Direction of Uzbekistan's Modern Architecture]." *Obshchestvennye nauki v Uzbekistane* [*Social Sciences in Uzbekistan*], no. 12 (1962): 14–19.
- "Dom molodezhi v Tashkente [House of Youth in Tashkent]." *Stroitel'stvo i arkhitektura Uzbekistana* [*Construction and Architecture of Uzbekistan*], no. 5 (1966): 21–24.
- Durand, Jean-Nicolas-Louis. *Recueil et parallèle des édifices de tout genre anciens et modernes, remarquables par leur beauté, par leur grandeur ou par leur singularité, et dessinés sur une même échelle*. Paris, 1801.
- Durand, Jean-Nicolas-Louis. *Précis des leçons d'architecture données à l'École polytechnique*. Paris: Chez l'Auteur et Bernard, 1825.
- Durth, Werner, and Winfried Nerdinger. *Nicht vergessen... Architektur und Städtebau der 30er/40er Jahre: Ergebnisse der Fachtagung in München, 26–28 November 1993*. Bonn: Deutsches Nationalkomitee für Denkmalschutz, 1994.
- "Dvorets Druzhby narodov imeni V.I. Lenina v Tashkente [V.I. Lenin Peoples' Friendship Palace in Tashkent]," *Arkhitektura SSSR* [*Architecture of the USSR*], nos. 3–4 (1983): 86–89.
- Dzhalalov, Bakhodyr. *Pod svodom vechnosti* [*Beneath the Vault of Eternity*]. Tashkent, 2002.
- Efimov, Daniil. "Put' letaiushchei tarelki [The Path of the Flying Saucer]." *Zhurnal Kazan'* [*Kazan Magazine*], May 30, 2019. http://kazan-journal.ru/news/kazan-i-kazantsyi/put-letayushchey-tarelki.
- Egorov, Iu. N. "VDNKh: vchera, segodnia zavtra; K 20-letiiu Vystavki dostizhenii narodnogo khoziaistva Uzbekskoi SSR [VDNKh: Yesterday, Today, Tomorrow; Marking the 20th Anniversary of the Exhibition of National Economic Achievements of the Uzbek SSR]." *Arkhitektura i stroitel'stvo Uzbekistana* [*Architecture and Construction of Uzbekistan*], no. 10 (1985): 17–23.
- Espagne, Michel. *Les transferts culturels franco-allemands*. Paris: Presses universitaires de France, 1999.
- Evelev, John. *Picturesque Literature and the Transformation of the American Landscape: 1835–1874*. Oxford: Oxford University Press, 2021.
- Faizullaev, R., and Ia. Mansurov. "Tashkentskii metropoliten im. V.I. Lenina [The Tashkent V.I. Lenin Metro]." *Arkhitektura i stroitel'stvo Uzbekistana* [*Architecture and Construction of Uzbekistan*], no. 5 (1982): 19–23.
- Fedorov, Nikolai. "Vopros o bratstve, ili rodstve, o prichinakh nebratskogo, nerodstvennogo, t.e. nemirnogo, sostoianiia mira i o sredstvakh k vosstanovleniiu rodstva: Zapiska ot neuchenykh k uchenym, dukhovnym i svetskim, k veruiushchim i neveruiushchim [The Question of Brotherhood or Kinship, of the Reasons for the Unbrotherly, Unkindred or Unpeaceful State of the World, and of the Means for the Restoration of Kinship]." In Nikolai Fedorov, *Sochineniia* [*Writings*], vol. 4 (Moscow: Progress, 1995).
- Ferdman, Iurii. "Novye zdaniia i sooruzheniia televideniia i radio [New Buildings and Structures for Television and Radio]." *Arkhitektura SSSR* [*Architecture of the USSR*], no. 11 (1980): 45–51.
- Ferrari, Oreste. "La catalogazione: Innovazione di un processo permanente." In *Memorabilia: il futuro della memoria; Beni ambientali, architettonici, archeologici, artistici e storici in Italia*, edited by Francesco Perego, 327–332. Bari: Laterza, 1987.
- "Figures de l'orientalisme en architecture." Special issue, *Revue du monde musulman et de la Méditerranée*, nos. 73–74 (1994).
- Fineleib, Aleksandr, and Eval'd Lennesh-midt. "Novoe administrativnoe zdanie stolitsy [The New Administrative Building of the Capital]." *Stroitel'stvo i arkhitektura Uzbekistana* [*Construction and Architecture of Uzbekistan*], no. 3 (1965): 25–30.
- Gainulin, Ernest. "17-etazhnaia gostinitsa 'Inturist' na 750 mest v Tashkente [The 17-Story, 750-Bed Intourist Hotel in Tashkent]." *Stroitel'stvo i arkhitektura Uzbekistana* [*Construction and Architecture of Uzbekistan*], no. 7 (1967): 21–24.
- Ganiev, Aziz. "UzNIIPgradostroitel'stva za 50 let (1928–1978 gg.) [50 Years of UzNIIPgradostroitel'stva (1928–1978)]." *Stroitel'stvo i arkhitektura Uzbekistana* [*Construction and Architecture of Uzbekistan*], no. 10 (1978): 1–11.
- Gantner, Eszter, Corinne Geering and Paul Vickers. *Heritage under Socialism: Preservation in Eastern and Central Europe, 1945–1991*. Oxford: Berghahn Books, 2021.
- Garamov, Iurii. "Arkhitektura krytykh rynkov v usloviiakh zharkogo klimata (zarubezhnyi opyt) [Architecture of Covered Markets in Hot Climatic Conditions (International Experience)]." *Stroitel'stvo i arkhitektura Uzbekistana* [*Construction and Architecture of Uzbekistan*], no. 4 (1972): 30–36.
- Gausa, Manuel, and Marta Cervelló. *Barcelona: Modern Architecture Guide*. Barcelona: Actar Publishers, 2013.
- Gazzola, Piero. "La responsabilità dello storico di fronte ai problemi della tutela del volto delle antiche città." *Bulletin C.I.H.A*, year II (April–September 1967): 3–4.
- Gazzola, Piero. "Per un inventario globale." *Costruzioni Casabella*, no. 314 (1967): 44.
- Gazzola, Piero. *L'inventario di protezione del patrimonio culturale: Settore dei beni immobili: IPCE scopo e norme di esecuzione*. Verona, 1970.
- Gazzola, Piero, and Loris A. Fontana. *Analisi culturale del territorio: Il centro storico urbano*. Padua: Marsilio, 1973.
- "Geliokompleks 'Solntse' [The Sun Heliocomplex]." *Arkhitektura SSSR* [*Architecture of the USSR*], nos. 3–4 (1988): 36–39.
- Germann, Georg. *Gothic Revival in Europe and Britain: Sources, Influences and Ideas*. London: Lund Humphries, 1972.
- Geske, Norman A., and Henry Russell Hitchcock. *The Sheldon Memorial Art Gallery, University of Nebraska, Lincoln*. Lincoln: Sheldon Museum of Art, 1963.
- Ginzburg, Moisei. "Natsional'naia arkhitektura narodov SSSR [The National Architecture of the Peoples of the USSR]." *Sovremennaia arkhitektura* [*Contemporary Architecture*], nos. 5–6 (1926): 113–114.
- Ginzburg, Moisei. "Konstruktivizm v arkhitekture [Constructivism in Architecture]." *Sovremennaia arkhitektura* [*Contemporary Architecture*], no. 5 (1928): 143–145.
- Giovannoni, Gustavo. "Per un inventario ragionato dei monumenti italiani." *Bollettino del Centro Nazionale di Studi di Storia dell'Architettura—Sezione di Roma* XXI, no. 2 (February 1943): 4–5.
- Glendinning, Miles. *Mass Housing: Modern Architecture and State Power—A Global History*. London: Bloomsbury, 2021.
- Golosov, Il'ia. *Soviet Cities New and Renewed*. Moscow: Foreign Languages Publishing House, 1939.
- Gorshenina, Svetlana. *Asie centrale: L'invention des frontières et l'héritage russo-soviétique*. Paris: CNRS Éditions, 2012.
- Graf, Franz, and Giulia Marino. "Concerning the Research 'Material History of the Built Environment and the Conservation Project' (2008–2020), Methodology and Results." In *History of Construction Cultures: Proceedings of the 7th International Congress on Construction History (7ICCH), July 12–16, 2021, Lisbon, Portugal*, edited by João Mascarenhas-Mateus, Ana Paula Pires, Manuel Marques Caiado and Ivo Veiga, 780–786. Abingdon-on-Thames: Taylor & Francis Group, 2021.
- Grama, Emanuela. *Socialist Heritage: Politics of Past and Present in Romania*. Bloomington: Indiana University Press, 2019.
- Gropius, Walter. *Granitsy arkhitektury* [*The Scope of Total Architecture*]. Moscow: Iskusstvo, 1971.
- Groys, Boris. "Bor'ba protiv muzeia ili demonstratsiia iskusstva v totalitarnom prostranstve [The Struggle Against the Museum, or the Demonstration of Art in the Totalitarian Space]." In *Sovetskoe bogatstvo: stat'i o kul'ture, literature i kino* [*Soviet Riches: Essays on Culture, Literature and Cinema*], edited by Marina Balina, Evgeny Dobrenko and Iurii Murashov, 37–51. St. Petersburg: Akademicheskii proekt, 2002.
- Grunenberg, Christoph. "The Modern Art Museum." In *Contemporary Cultures of Display*, edited by Emma Barker, 26–48. New Haven and London: Yale University Press, 1999.
- Guilhaume, Jean-François. *Les mythes fondateurs de l'Algérie française*. Paris: Editions L'Harmattan, 1993.
- Guliam, Gafur. "Slava Leninu, Partii slavu poiu [Glory to Lenin, Glory to the Party I Sing]." *Ogonёk*, no. 9 (February 27, 1959): 4.
- Gulianitskii, Nikolai. "O prostranstvennoi kompozitsii obshchegorodskogo tsentra Tashkenta [On the Spatial Composition of the City Center of Tashkent]." *Arkhitektura SSSR* [*Architecture of the USSR*], no. 3 (1973): 12–19.
- Gutnov, Aleksei, and Il'ia Lezhava. "Estetika goroda (predposylki sovershenstvovaniia khudozhestvennogo oblika sovremennykh gorodov) [Aesthetics of the City (Preconditions for the Improvement of the Artistic Image of Contemporary Cities)]." *Zodchestvo* [*Architecture*], no. 2 (21).
- Haugen, Arne. *The Establishment of National Republics in Soviet Central Asia*. New York: Palgrave Macmillan, 2003.
- Hennecke, Stefanie. "Der Volkspark für die Gesundung von Geist und Körper: Das ideologische Spannungsfeld einer bürgerlichen Reformbewegung zwischen Emanzipation und Disziplinierung des Volkes." In *Gärten und Parks als Lebens- und Erlebnisraum: Funktions- und nutzungsgeschichtliche Aspekte der Gartenkunst*

in Früher Neuzeit und Moderne, edited by Stefan Schweizer, 151–165. Worms: Wernersche Verlagsanstalt, 2008.

- Herford, Frank. *CCCP Underground: Metro Stations of the Soviet Era*. Salenstein: Benteli, 2021.
- Iakushenko, Ol'ga. "Sovetskaia arkhitektura i Zapad: otkrytie i assimiliatsiia zapadnogo opyta v sovetskoi arkhitekture kontsa 1950-kh-1960-kh godov [Soviet Architecture and the West: The Discovery and Assimilation of Western Experience in Soviet Architecture of the Late 1950s and 1960s]." *Laboratorium* 8, no. 2 (2016): 76–102.
- Iasnyi, G. "Leniniana zodchikh [Architectural Leniniana]." *Arkhitektura SSSR [Architecture of the USSR]*, no. 7 (1972): 6–7.
- Ibragimov, S. "Stroitel'stvo v Iaponii [Construction in Japan]." *Stroitel'stvo i arkhitektura Uzbekistana [Construction and Architecture of Uzbekistan]*, no. 3 (1967): 17–26.
- Ibragimov, S. "Stroitel'stvo zhilykh i grazhdanskikh zdanii v Kanade [Construction of Residential and Civil Buildings in Canada]." *Stroitel'stvo i arkhitektura Uzbekistana [Construction and Architecture of Uzbekistan]*, no. 4 (1968): 44–48.
- Ikonnikov, Andrei. *Sovremennaia arkhitektura Anglii: planirovka gorodov i zhilishchnoe stroitel'stvo [The Contemporary Architecture of England: Urban Planning and Housing Construction]*. Leningrad: Gosizd. literatury po stroitel'stvu, arkhitektury i stroitel'nym materialam, 1958.
- Ikonnikov, Andrei. *Novaia arkhitektura Finliandii [The New Architecture of Finland]*. Moscow: Stroiizdat, 1971.
- Ikonnikov, Andrei. *Arkhitektura goroda: esteticheskie problemy kompozitsii [The Architecture of the City: Aesthetic Problems of Composition]*. Moscow: Stroiizdat, 1972.
- Ikonnikov, Andrei. *Sovremennaia arkhitektira Shvetsii [The Contemporary Architecture of Sweden]*. Moscow: Stroiizdat, 1978.
- Ikonnikov, Andrei. *Arkhitektura SShA: Arkhitektura v sisteme burzhuaznoi kul'tury [The Architecture of the USA: Architecture in the System of Bourgeois Culture]*. Moscow: Iskusstvo, 1979.
- Ikonnikov, Andrei, et al., eds. *Arkhitektura Zapada: Kniga 2; Sotsial'nye i deologicheskie problemy [Architecture of the West: Book 2; Social and Ideological Problems]*. Moscow: Stroiizdat, 1975.
- Iovine, Julie V., and Ezra Stoller. *Guggenheim New York/Guggenheim Bilbao*. Princeton: Princeton Architectural Press, 1999.
- Ishankhodjaev, A., and S. Dzhumabaev. "Tashkent Subway Today and in the Future." *Science of Europe*, no. 72 (2021): 55–59.
- Israilov, Isak. "Uzbekskii nauchno-issledovatel'skii i proektnyi institute po gradostroitel'stvu i ego razvitie [The Uzbek Scientific Research Institute for Urban Planning and Its Development]." *Stroitel'stvo i arkhitektura Uzbekistana [Construction and Architecture of Uzbekistan]*, no. 1 (1974): 34–42.
- Iuga, Liliana. *Reshaping the Historic City under Socialism: State Preservation, Urban Planning and the Economy of Scarcity in Romania (1955–1977)*. Vienna: Central European University (CEU), 2016.
- Ivanov, Vladimir. *Arkhitektura, vdokhnovlennaia kosmosom: Obraz budushchego v pozdnesovetskoi arkhitekture [Architecture Inspired by Space: The Image of the Future in Late Soviet Architecture]*. St. Petersburg: Borei Art, 2017.
- Jones, Kay Bea, and Stephanie Pilat, eds. *The Routledge Companion to Italian Fascist Architecture: Reception and Legacy*. Abingdon-on-Thames: Routledge, 2021.
- Jordan, Jens. "Ugroza razrusheniia pamiatnika 'Chorsu bazar' i ego okrestnostei [Heritage Building Chorsu Threatened with Destruction]." *Gazeta.uz*, November 23, 2018. https://www.gazeta.uz/ru/2018/11/23/chorsu/.
- Jordan, Jens Werner, Hans-Rudolf Meier and Thomas Will, eds. *Baudenkmale in Taschkent: Beiträge zu einer Denkmaltopographie*. Dresden: Thelem, 2022.
- Kadyrova, Tulkinoi. *Sovremennaia arkhitektura Uzbekistana [Contemporary Architecture of Uzbekistan]*. Tashkent: Izdatel'stvo literatury i iskusstva im. Gafura Guliama, 1974.
- Kadyrova, Tulkinoi. *Arkhitektura tsentra Tashkenta [The Architecture of the Center of Tashkent]*. Tashkent: Izdatel'stvo literatury i iskusstva imeni Gafura Guliama, 1976.
- Kadyrova, Tulkinoi. *Arkhitektura sovetskogo Uzbekistana [Architecture of Soviet Uzbekistan]*. Moscow: Stroiizdat, 1987.
- Kadyrova, Tulkinoi, and Svetlana Moiseeva. "Molodye zodchie Uzbekistana [Young Architects of Uzbekistan]." *Arkhitektura SSSR [Architecture of the USSR]*, no. 9 (1969): 33–36.
- Kadyrova, Tulkinoi, Konstantin Babievskii and Farkhad Tursunov. *Arkhitektura sovetskogo Uzbekistana [Architecture of Soviet Uzbekistan]*. Moscow: Stroiizdat, 1972.
- Kadyrova, Tulkinoi, and Iosif Notkin. "Samobytnost' – v splave traditsii i novatorstva [Singularity – in the Blend of Tradition and Innovation]." *Arkhitektura SSSR [Architecture of the USSR]*, no. 9 (1974): 17–20.
- Kadyrova, Tulkinoi, and M. Abidzhanova. "Arkhitekturno-prostranstvennyj zamysel i ego realizatsiia v nature [The Architectural and Spatial Plan and Its Realization in Nature]." *Stroitel'stvo i arkhitektura Uzbekistana [Construction and Architecture of Uzbekistan]*, no. 5 (1977): 27–33.
- "Kakim byt' tsentru Tashkenta? [How Should the Center of Tashkent Be?]." *Pravda Vostoka [Truth of the East]*, May 19, 1968: 1.
- Katernoga, Musii. "Kievskii gosudarstvennyi khudozhestvennyi institute [Kyiv State Art Institute]." *Arkhitektura SSSR [Architecture of the USSR]*, no. 5 (1965): 51–53.
- Katsnel'son, Raisa. *Sovremennaia arkhitektura Italii [The Contemporary Architecture of Italy]*. Moscow: Stroiizdat, 1983.
- Kerr, James Semple. *The Conservation Plan*. 7th ed. Australia ICOMOS, 2013.
- Kesting, Piney. "Tashkent's Underground: Masterpieces." *AramcoWorld* 71, no. 4 (July–August 2020): 10–19. https://www.aramcoworld.com/Compilations/2020/July-August-2020/Tashkent-s-Underground-Masterpieces.
- Khalid, Adeeb. *Making Uzbekistan: Nation, Empire, and Revolution in the Early USSR*. Ithaca and London: Cornell University Press, 2015.
- Khan-Magomedov, Selim. "Natsional'noe i internatsional'noe v sovremennoi arkhitekture [The National and International in Modern Architecture]." In *Internatsional'noe i natsional'noe v iskusstve [The International and National in Art]*, 200–274. Moscow: Nauka, 1974.
- Khan-Magomedov, Selim, Raisa Katsnel'son and Anatolii Strigalev, eds. *Arkhitektura Zapada: Kniga 1; Mastera i techeniia [Architecture of the West: Book 1; Masters and Trends]*. Moscow: Stroiizdat, 1972.
- Kim, V. "V poiskakh natsional'nogo svoeobraziia: Na primere arkhitekturnoi praktiki Uzbekistana [In Search of National Identity: The Example of Architectural Practice in Uzbekistan]," *Arkhitektura SSSR [Architecture of the USSR]*, no. 1 (1982): 29–34.
- Kirasirova, Masha. "Building Anti-Colonial Utopia: The Politics of Space in Soviet Tashkent in the 'Long 1960s.'" In *The Routledge Handbook of the Global Sixties: Between Protest and Nation-Building*, edited by Jian Chen, Martin Klimke, Masha Kirasirova, Mary Nolan, Marilyn Young and Joanna Waley-Cohen, 53–66. Abingdon and New York: Routledge, 2018.
- Kirichenko, Evgeniia. *Arkhitekturnye teorii XIX veka v Rossii [Nineteenth-Century Architectural Theories in Russia]*. Moscow: Iskusstvo, 1986.
- Kirilova, Irina. "Istoriko-arkhitekturnoe nasledie v sovremennoi gorodskoi srede [Historical and Architectural Heritage in the Contemporary Urban Environment]." *Arkhitektura i stroitel'stvo Uzbekistana [Architecture and Construction of Uzbekistan]*, no. 9 (1989): 15–16.
- Klinova, Alla. "Spasti muzei: poka ne vospitaem potrebnost' v kul'ture, nichego ne izmenitsia [Saving the Museum: Until We Develop a Requirement for Culture Nothing Will Change]." *Pravda Vostoka [Truth of the East]*, August 22, 1989: 4.
- Knoepfli, Albert. *Inventories of Artistic Architectural and Cultural Heritage in European Countries: Present State and the Need for Their Promotion*. Strasbourg: Council of Europe, 1985.
- Koolhaas, Rem. *Elements of Architecture*. Cologne: Taschen, 2018.
- Kopp, Anatole. *Ville et révolution: architecture et urbanisme soviétiques des années vingt*. Paris: Édition Anthropos, 1967.
- Kopp, Anatole. *Città e Rivoluzione: Architettura e urbanistica sovietiche degli anni Venti*. Milan: Feltrinelli, 1987.
- Korobovtsev, Gennadii. "Tashkent: 'Staryi' gorod, kakim tebe byt'? [Tashkent: 'Old' City, What Should You Be Like?]." *Arkhitektura i stroitel'stvo Uzbekistana [Architecture and Construction of Uzbekistan]*, no. 10 (1971): 19–26.
- Korobovtsev, Gennadii. "Arkhitektura Tashkentskogo metropolitena: obratnaia sviaz' [The Architecture of the Tashkent Metro: Feedback]." *Stroitel'stvo i arkhitektura Uzbekistana [Construction and Architecture of Uzbekistan]*, no. 2 (1988): 5–8.
- Korobovtsev, Gennadii. "Sotsiologiia programmy 'Dom dlia naroda' [The Sociology of the Program 'Housing for the People']." *Arkhitektura i stroitel'stvo Uzbekistana [Architecture and Construction of Uzbekistan]*, no. 3 (1988): 4–7.
- Korovin, M. "Tashkentskii metropoliten [The Tashkent Metro]." *Stroitel'stvo i arkhitektura Uzbekistana [Construction and Architecture of Uzbekistan]*, no. 9 (1969): 1–4.
- Kosinskii, Andrei. "Tashkent: Chilanzar; Tsentr [Tashkent: Chilanzar; Center]."

Stroitel'stvo i arkhitektura Uzbekistana [*Construction and Architecture of Uzbekistan*], no. 6 (1971): 18–28.
- Kosinskii, Andrei. "Poisk obraza magistrali (zastroika ul. Bogdana Khmel'nitskogo) [The Search for an Image of the Arterial Road (The Construction of Bogdan Khmel'nitskii Street)]." *Stroitel'stvo i arkhitektura Uzbekistana* [*Construction and Architecture of Uzbekistan*], no. 3 (1974): 25–31.
- Kosinskii, Andrei. "V chem zhe pravda arkhitektury? [What Is the Truth of Architecture?]," *Dekorativnoe iskusstvo* [*Decorative Art*], no. 6 (1979): 31–34.
- Kosinskii, Andrei, and Iurii Miroshnichenko. "Proekt tsentra raiona Chilanzar v Tashkente [Project for the Center of Chilanzar District in Tashkent]," *Arkhitektura SSSR* [*Architecture of the USSR*], no. 2 (1970): 52–56.
- Kostyria, V. "Glavnaia os' respubliki [The Main Axis of the Republic]." *Ogonëk*, no. 27 (1970): 24–25.
- "Kritika konstruktivizma [A Critique of Constructivism]." *Sovremennaia arkhitektura* [*Contemporary Architecture*], no. 1 (1928): 1–2, 6, 10, 12, 14.
- Kriukov, Konstantin. "Dom tvorcheskikh soiuzov Uzbekistana [The House of Creative Unions of Uzbekistan]." *Stroitel'stvo i arkhitektura Uzbekistana* [*Construction and Architecture of Uzbekistan*], no. 1 (1968): 20–25.
- Kultermann, Udo, ed. *Kenzo Tange: 1949–1969*. Moscow: Stroiizdat, 1978.
- Kuriazov, T. *Chelovek s utonchennym golosom* [*A Person with a Refined Voice*]. Tashkent: Turon-Iqbol, 2015.
- Kuznetsov, Aleksandr. "Rekonstruktsiia stolitsy Uzbekistana [Reconstruction of the Capital of Uzbekistan]." *Arkhitektura SSSR* [*Architecture of the USSR*], no. 7 (1939): 6–15.
- "L'une des plus grandes coupoles du monde." *Écho de l'Oranie*, no. 265 (November 1999). http://www.echo-deloranie.com/medias/files/265-coupole-sba.pdf.
- Latour, Alessandra. *Mosca 1890–2000*. Rome: Edizioni Kappa, 2008.
- Le Corbusier. *Arkhitektura XX veka* [*Architecture of the 20th Century*]. Moscow: Progress, 1970.
- Le Corbusier. *Modulor: MOD 1: MOD 2* [*The Modulor: Modulor 2*]. Moscow: Stroiizdat, 1976.
- Legostaeva, Ol'ga. "Proektirovanie kompleksa VDNKh Uzbekskoi SSR [Designing the VDNKh Complex of the Uzbek SSR]." *Stroitel'stvo i arkhitektura Uzbekistana* [*Construction and Architecture of Uzbekistan*], no. 3 (1974): 39–43.
- Liernur, Jorge. "Orientalism and Modern Architecture: The Debate on the Flat Roof." *Ra. Revista de Arquitectura*, June 2010: 61–78.
- Lodder, Christina. "Lenin's Plan of Monumental Propaganda." *Sbornik: Study Group on the Russian Revolution*, nos. 6–7 (1981): 67–82.
- Lowenthal, David. *The Past Is a Foreign Country*. Cambridge: Cambridge University Press, 1985.
- Macdonald, Susan. "Conserving the Modern in the Twenty-First Century." In *Modern Architectures: The Rise of a Heritage*, edited by Maristella Casciato and Emilie D' Orgeix, 149–156. Wavre: Mardaga, 2012.
- Macdonald, Susan. "Conserving Modern Heritage: The Work of the J. Paul Getty Trust." In *Conserving 20th-Century Architecture*, edited by Maria Paola Borgarino and Davide Del Curto, 31–33. Switzerland: Springer Nature, 2023.
- MacKenzie, David. "Tashkent: Past and Present." *The Russian Review* 28, no. 2 (1969): 207–216.
- Madgazin, R. "Organizatsiia rabot po montazhu metallokonstruktsii pokrytiia zritel'nogo zala panoramnogo kinoteatra v Tashkente [Organization of Work on the Installation of Metal Structures Covering the Auditorium of the Panoramic Cinema in Tashkent]." *Stroitel'stvo i arkhitektura Srednei Azii* [*Construction and Architecture of Central Asia*], no. 11 (1964): 38–40.
- Mairesse, François, and Renata F. Peters, eds. *What Is the Essence of Conservation? Materials for a Discussion: Papers from the ICOM-CC and ICOFOM Session at the 25th General Conference Held in Kyoto, 4 September 2019*. Paris: ICOFOM, 2019.
- Manfredi, Carlo, ed. *Le politiche di tutela del patrimonio costruito: Modelli a confronto in Europa*. Milan: Mimesis, 2017.
- Man'kovskaia, Liia. "O rabote sektsii istorii arkhitektury, restavratsii i okhrany pamiatnikov (1967–1971 gg.) [On the Work of the Section on the History of Architecture, Restoration and Protection of Monuments (1967–1971)]." *Stroitel'stvo i arkhitektura Uzbekistana* [*Construction and Architecture of Uzbekistan*], no. 8 (1971): 20–21.
- Mannoni, Pierre. *Les Français d'Algérie: vie, mœurs, mentalité de la conquête des Territoires du Sud à l'indépendance*. Paris: Editions L'Harmattan, 1993.
- Marini Clarelli, Maria Vittoria. "Il censimento oggi." Oral presentation delivered at the conference *Ereditare il Presente: Conoscenza, tutela e valorizzazione dell'architettura italiana dal 1945 ad oggi*, Rome, October 11–12, 2022.
- Martin, Terry. *The Affirmative Action Empire: Nations and Nationalism in the Soviet Union, 1923–1939*. Ithaca and London: Cornell University Press, 2001.
- Martin, Timothy D. "Robert Smithson and the Anglo-American Picturesque." In *Anglo-American Exchange in Postwar Sculpture: 1945–1975*, edited by Rebecca Peabody, 164–174. Los Angeles: J. Paul Getty Museum, 2011.
- Matchanov, N. "Okhranu i restavraciiu pamiatnikov istorii i kul'tury – na nauchnuiu osnovu [The Conservation and Restoration of Monuments of History and Culture Based on Scientific Principles]." *Stroitel'stvo i arkhitektura Uzbekistana* [*Construction and Architecture of Uzbekistan*], no. 1 (1978): 1–4.
- Meriggi, Maurizio. "Un 'Viaggio in Oriente.'" In Moisei Ginzburg, *Arte e Architettura Tatara in Crimea*, 5–29. Pisa: Pisa University Press, 2022.
- Meurs, Paul, and Maria Theresia Antoinette Van Thoor, eds. *Sanatorium Zonnestraal: History and Restoration of a Modern Monument*. Rotterdam: Nai Publishers, 2010.
- Meuser, Philipp, ed. *Architekturführer: Taschkent*. Berlin: DOM Publishers, 2012.
- Meuser, Philipp. *Zwischen Stalin und Glasnost: Sowjetische Architektur 1960–1990*. Berlin: DOM Publishers, 2013.
- Meuser, Philipp. *Seismic Modernism: Architecture and Housing in Soviet Tashkent*. Berlin: DOM Publishers, 2016.
- Meuser, Philipp, Jörn Börner and Caroline Uhlig. *Die Ästhetik der Platte: Wohnungsbau in der Sowjetunion zwischen Stalin und Glasnost*. Berlin: DOM Publishers, 2015.
- Meuser, Philipp, and Dimitrij Zadorin. *Towards a Typology of Soviet Mass Housing: Prefabrication in the USSR, 1955–1991*. Berlin: DOM Publishers, 2015.
- Michon, Jean. "Sidi-bel-Abbès: capitale légionnaire." *Guerres mondiales et conflits contemporains*, no. 1 (2010): 25–38.
- Migotto, Andrea, and Martino Tattara, eds. *Contested Legacies: Critical Perspectives on Postwar Modern Housing*. Leuven: Leuven University Press, 2023.
- Mirkina, L. "Arkhitektor O.P. Aidinova (tvorcheskii portret) [Architect O.P. Aidinova (A Creative Portrait)]." *Stroitel'stvo i arkhitektura Uzbekistana* [*Construction and Architecture of Uzbekistan*], no. 6 (1978): 28–29.
- Miroshnichenko, Iurii, and Gennadii Korobovtsev. "Tvorcheskaia napravlennost' v razvitii arkhitektury zhilishcha Uzbekistana [Creative Direction in the Development of Residential Architecture in Uzbekistan]." *Arkhitektura i stroitel'stvo Uzbekistana* [*Architecture and Construction of Uzbekistan*], nos. 2–3 (1986): 52–58.
- Miyake, Riichi, Shin Muramatsu and Masayuki Fuchigami. *581 Architects in the World*. Tokyo: Toto, 1995.
- Moiseeva, Svetlana. "Angliia: traditsii i sovremennost' [England: Traditions and Modernity]." *Stroitel'stvo i arkhitektura Uzbekistana* [*Construction and Architecture of Uzbekistan*], no. 11 (1965): 41–46.
- Moiseeva, Svetlana. "Osobennost' razvitiia sistemy kul'turno-bytovogo obsluzhivaniia naseleniia gorodov Uzbekistana [Features of the Development of a System for Serving the Cultural and Daily Needs of the Population of Uzbekistan's Cities]." *Stroitel'stvo i arkhitektura Uzbekistana* [*Construction and Architecture of Uzbekistan*], no. 8 (1970): 23–29.
- Moneo, Rafael. "On Typology." *Oppositions*, no. 13 (Summer 1978): 22–45.
- Müller-Wille, W. *Stadt und Umland im südlichen Sowjet-Mittelasien*. Wiesbaden: Steiner, 1978.
- "Muzei V.I. Lenina v Tashkente [The Lenin Museum in Tashkent]" (photograph). *Arkhitektura SSSR* [*Architecture of the USSR*], no. 12 (1972): 18.
- "Nasha anketa [Our Questionnaire]." *Arkhitektura i stroitel'stvo Uzbekistana* [*Architecture and Construction of Uzbekistan*], nos. 2–3 (1986): 6–11.
- Nashchokina, Mariia. "Antichnoe nasledie v arkhitekture pozdnego russkogo klassitsizma [Antique Heritage in the Architecture of Late Russian Classicism]." In *Russkii klassitsizm vtoroi poloviny XVIII–nachala XIX veka* [*Russian Classicism of the Second Half of the Eighteenth and Early Nineteenth Centuries*], 184–234. Moscow: Izobrazitel'noe iskusstvo, 1994.
- "Nazvanie 'Druzhba narodov' vernut dvortsu i stantsii metro [The Name 'Peoples' Friendship' Will Be Returned to the Palace and Metro Station]." *Gazeta.uz*, April 27, 2018. https://www.gazeta.uz/ru/2018/04/27/friendship/.
- Negri Arnoldi, Francesco. "La catalogazione del patrimonio artistico in Italia, storia e attualità." *Musei e Galleria d'Italia*, no. 43 (1971): 3–33.
- Negri Arnoldi, Francesco. "La catalogazione del patrimonio artistico in Italia, sviluppi e prospettive." *Musei e Galleria d'Italia*, no. 57 (1975): 9–36.

- Nicoloso, Paolo. *Mussolini, Architect: Propaganda and Urban Landscape in Fascist Italy*. Translated by Sylvia Notini. Toronto: University of Toronto Press, 2022.
- Niemeyer, Oscar. *Moi opyt stroitel'stva Braziliia* [*Minha experiência em Brasília*]. Moscow: Izdatel'stvo inostrannoi literatury, 1963.
- Niemeyer, Oscar. *Arkhitektura i obshchestvo* [*Architecture and Society*]. Moscow: Progress, 1975.
- Nil'sen, Vladimir. "Spetsifika diplomnogo proektirovaniia u architektorov-restavratorov v TashPI [The Specifics of Diploma Projects for the Architect-Restorers at TashPI]." *Stroitel'stvo i arkhitektura Uzbekistana* [*Construction and Architecture of Uzbekistan*], no. 11 (1978): 8–12.
- Nil'sen, Vladimir. *U istokov sovremennogo gradostroitel'stva Uzbekistana (XIX – nachalo XX vekov)* [*The Sources of Contemporary Urban Construction of Uzbekistan (19th–Early 20th Century)*]. Tashkent: Izdatel'stvo literatury i iskusstva imeni Gafura Guliama, 1988.
- Notkin, Iosif, and Shukur Askarov. "O kachestve arkhitektury [On the Quality of Architecture]." *Stroitel'stvo i arkhitektura Uzbekistana* [*Construction and Architecture of Uzbekistan*], no. 4 (1981): 7–9.
- Novikov, Feliks. "Pravda i lozh' arkhitekturnoi formy [Truth and Lies of Architectural Form]," *Dekorativnoe iskusstvo SSSR* [*Decorative Art of the USSR*], no. 5 (1978): 10–13.
- Novikov, Feliks, and Vladimir Belogolovskii. *Sovetskii modernizm: 1955–1985* [*Soviet Modernism: 1955–1985*]. Moscow: Tatlin, 2010.
- *Ocharovan toboi, Uzbekistan* [*Enchanted by You, Uzbekistan*]. Tashkent: Gos. izd. Uzbekskoi SSR, 1964.
- Otto, Frei. *Visiachie pokrytiia: ikh formy i konstruktsii* [*Tensile Structures*]. Moscow: Gosizd. literatury po stroitel'stvu, arkhitektury i stroitel'nym materialam, 1960.
- Ovsyannikova, Elena, and Vladimir Shukhov. "Phenomenon of the Russian Avant-Garde: Moscow Architectural School of the 1920s." *Docomomo Journal*, no. 49, 2013.
- "Palais des arts, Tachkent, Ouzbékistan." *L'Architecture d'Aujourd'hui*, no. 147 (1970): 52–53.
- Paperny, Vladimir. *Kul'tura Dva* [*Culture Two*]. Moscow: NLO, 2016.
- "Parizhane o Tashkente [Parisians on Tashkent]." *Pravda Vostoka* [*Truth of the East*], February 2, 1960: 4.
- Pasternak, Aleksandr. "Puti k standartu [Ways Toward a Standard]." *Sovremennaia arkhitektura* [*Contemporary Architecture*], no. 2 (1927): 54–64.
- "Piatyi Vsesoiuznyi smotr luchshikh arkhiteurnykh proizvedenii 1985 goda [Fifth All-Union Review of the Best Architectural Works of 1985]." *Arkhitektura i stroitel'stvo Uzbekistana* [*Architecture and Construction of Uzbekistan*], no. 12 (1986): 18–22.
- Polupanov, Stefan. "Zal zasedanii Verkhovnogo soveta Uzbekskoi SSR [The Conference Hall of the Supreme Soviet of the Uzbek SSR]." *Arkhitektura SSSR* [*Architecture of the USSR*], no. 12 (1940): 50–52.
- Pommier, Édouard. *L'invenzione dell'arte nell'Italia del Rinascimento*. Turin: Einaudi, 2007.
- Pugachenkova, Galina. "K sozdaniiu regional'noi initsiativnoi gruppy respublik Srednei Azii Sovetskogo komiteta ICOMOSa [Toward the Creation of a Regional Initiative Group of the Central Asian Republics in the Soviet Committee of ICOMOS]." *Arkhitektura i stroitel'stvo Uzbekistana* [*Architecture and Construction of Uzbekistan*], no. 6 (1982): 31–33.
- Pugachenkova, Galina, and Lazar Rempel'. *Istoriia iskusstv Uzbekistana s drevneishikh vremen do serediny deviatnadtsatogo veka* [*The History of the Arts of Uzbekistan from Ancient Times to the Mid-Nineteenth Century*]. Moscow: Iskusstvo, 1965.
- Pugachenkova, Galina, and Liia Man'kovskaia. "Mezhrespublikanskaia zonal'naia konferentsiia sredneaziatskoi regional'noi gruppy Komiteta ICOMOSa [Inter-Republic Conference of the Central Asian Regional Group of the ICOMOS Committee]." *Arkhitektura i stroitel'stvo Uzbekistana* [*Architecture and Construction of Uzbekistan*], no. 5 (1984): 1–10.
- Quatremère de Quincy, Antoine. *Encyclopédie méthodique: Architecture*. Vol. 3. Paris: Chez Mme veuve Agasse, 1825.
- Quatremère de Quincy, Antoine. *Dictionnaire historique d'architecture: comprenant dans son plan les notions historiques, descriptives, archéologiques, théoriques, didactiques et pratiques de cet art*. Paris: Librairie d'Adrien le Clere et Cie, 1832.
- Raab, N. "The Tashkent Earthquake of 1966: The Advantages and Disadvantages of a Natural Tragedy." *Jahrbücher für Geschichte Osteuropas* 62, no. 2 (2014): 273–294.
- Raab, N. *All Shook Up: The Shifting Soviet Response to Catastrophes, 1917–1991*. Montreal/Kingston: McGill-Queen's University Press, 2017.
- Ravshanovich, Kh. S., K. A. Xurramoviich and A. N. Inomovich. "The Problem of Protection and Use of Architectural Reserves of Historical Cities of Uzbekistan." *IJDIAS* 1, no. 5 (2021): 1220–1223.
- Reap, James K., et al.. *Preserving the Silk Road: Cultural Heritage Legislation in 5 Central Asian Countries*. Samarkand: International Institute for Central Asian Studies, 2024.
- Reinik, Wessel. "Altern und ewige Jugend: Restauration und Authentizität." *Daidalos*, no. 56 (June 1995): 96–106.
- Rempel', Lazar, et al. *Iskusstvo sovetskogo Uzbekistana, 1917–1972* [*The Art of Soviet Uzbekistan, 1917–1972*]. Moscow: Sovetskii khudozhnik, 1976.
- Reviakin, Vladimir. "Muzei: Vystavki [The Museum: Exhibitions]." *Arkhitektura SSSR* [*Architecture of the USSR*], no. 7 (1972): 41–43.
- Riabushin, Aleksandr. *Novye gorizonty arkhitekturnogo tvorchestva: 1970–1980-e gody* [*New Horizons of Architectural Creativity: 1970s–1980s*]. Moscow: Stroiizdat, 1990.
- Ritter, Katharina, Ekaterina Shapiro-Obermair and Alexandra Wachter, eds. *Soviet Modernism 1955–1991: Unknown History*. Vienna: Park Books, 2012.
- Rodríguez, Eduardo Luis. *The Havana Guide: Modern Architecture 1925–1965*. Princeton: Princeton Architectural Press, 2000.
- Rossi, Aldo. *L'architettura della città*. Padua: Marsilio, 1966.
- Rossi, Aldo. *The Architecture of the City*. Cambridge: MIT Press, 1982.
- Roy, Olivier. *La Nouvelle Asie centrale ou la Fabrication des nations*. Paris: Éditions du Seuil, 1997.
- Rozanov, Evgenii, Vladimir Krichevskii and Telemak Melik-Arakelian. "Muzei V.I. Lenina v Tashkente [The Lenin Museum in Tashkent]." *Stroitel'stvo i arkhitektura Uzbekistana* [*Construction and Architecture of Uzbekistan*], no. 4 (1970): 24–31.
- Rozanov, Evgenii, and Vladimir Reviakin. *Arkhitektura muzeev V.I. Lenina* [*The Architecture of V.I. Lenin Museums*]. Moscow: Stroiizdat, 1986.
- Rozenblium, Savelii. "Muzei iskusstv v Tashkente [The Museum of Arts in Tashkent]." *Stroitel'stvo i arkhitektura Uzbekistana* [*Construction and Architecture of Uzbekistan*], no. 12 (1967): 24–28.
- Rozenblium, Savelii. "Unikal'nye zdaniia [Unique Buildings]." *Stroitel'stvo i arkhitektura Uzbekistana* [*Construction and Architecture of Uzbekistan*], no. 12 (1974): 19–22.
- Rusanov, Vladislav. Review of the Sun Complex. *Arkhitektura SSSR* [*Architecture of the USSR*], nos. 3–4 (1988): 42–43.
- Rusanov, Vladislav. "Novyi radioteletsentr [New Radio and Telecenter]." In *Arkhitektura Uzbekistana, Al'manach* [*Architecture of Uzbekistan, Almanac*], 40–47. Tashkent: Izdatel'stvo literatury i iskusstva imeni Gafura Guliama, 1989.
- Russi, Nicola. *Background: Il progetto del vuoto*. Macerata: Quodlibet Studio, 2019.
- Sahadeo, Jeff. *Russian Colonial Society in Tashkent, 1865–1923*. Bloomington: Indiana University Press, 2007.
- Said, Edward W. *L'orientalisme: L'Orient créé par l'Occident*. Paris: Éditions du Seuil, 1980.
- Salimov, Timur. "Kak akademik S.A. Azimov otkazalsia ot zvaniia general-leitenanta [How Academician S.A. Azimov Rejected the Rank of Lieutenant General]." *NuzUz*, May 31, 2022. https://nuz.uz/2022/05/31/kak-akademik-s-a-azimov-otkazalsya-ot-zvaniya-general-lejtenanta/.
- Sarkisiants, Elena. "Tvorcheskie poiski i slozhenie obraza kinokontsertnogo zala v Tashkente [Creative Explorations and the Coming Together of the Image of the Cinema and Concert Hall in Tashkent]." *Stroitel'stvo i arkhitektura Uzbekistana* [*Construction and Architecture of Uzbekistan*], no. 10 (1977): 18–22.
- Sarkisiants, Elena. "Estetika solntsezashchity v arkhitekture Tashkenta [The Aesthetics of Sun Protection in Tashkent's Architecture]." *Arkhitektura SSSR* [*Architecture of the USSR*], no. 3 (1979): 44–49.
- Schubert, Karsten. *Museo: Storia di un'idea; dalla Rivoluzione Francese a oggi*. Milan: il Saggiatore, 2004.
- Semënov, Vladimir. "Poselki dlia predpriiatii, evakuirovannykh v Sredniiu Aziiu [Settlements for Enterprises Evacuated to Central Asia]." *Arkhitektura SSSR* [*Architecture of the USSR*], no. 1 (1942): 17–21.
- "Seryi 'Zhemchug' Tashkenta [The Gray 'Pearl' of Tashkent]." *Fergana News*, June 22, 2020. https://fergana.news/photos/118962/.
- Shagaev, Mansur, and Ol'ga Marakanova. *Osobennosti ob"emno-planirovochnykh reshenii monolitnykh zhilykh domov dlia gorodskogo stroitel'stva v raionakh s sukhim zharkim klimatom: Obzornaia informatsiia* [*Features of Volume Planning Solutions for Monolithic Residential Buildings for Urban Construction in Regions with a Dry, Hot Climate: Survey Information*]. Moscow: VNII teorii arkhitektury i gradostroitel'stva, 1989.

- Shakhov, A. “Gradostroitel’stvo Sovetskogo Uzbekistana [Urban Planning in Soviet Uzbekistan].” *Arkhitektura SSSR [Architecture of the USSR]*, no. 9 (1974): 11–16.
- Shaw, Charles. “The Gur-i Amir Mausoleum and the Soviet Politics of Preservation.” *Future Anterior: Journal of Historic Preservation, History, Theory, and Criticism* 8, no. 1 (2011): 42–63.
- Shvetsov, A. “Arkhitektura tsirkov [Circus Architecture].” *Arkhitektura SSSR [Architecture of the USSR]*, no. 8 (1976): 39–43.
- Smithson, Alison, and Peter Smithson. *The Charged Void: Urbanism*. New York: Monacelli Press, 2005.
- Smithson, Robert. “Frederick Law Olmsted and the Dialectical Landscape.” *Art Forum*, no. 11 (February 1973): 62–68.
- Sokolov, Sergei. “O problemakh proektirovaniia metropolitena [On the Problems of Designing the Metro].” *Arkhitektura i stroitel’stvo Uzbekistana [Architecture and Construction of Uzbekistan]*, no. 2 (1988): 16–17.
- Soloviev, N.K., et al. *Sovremennaia arkhitektura Frantsii [The Contemporary Architecture of France]*. Moscow: Stroiizdat, 1981.
- Speitkamp, Winfried. *Die Verwaltung der Geschichte: Denkmalpflege und Staat in Deutschland 1871–1933*. Göttingen: Vandenhoeck & Ruprecht, 1996.
- Speroni, Mario. *La tutela dei beni culturali negli stati italiani preunitari*. Milan: Giuffrè, 1988.
- Spivak, Vladimir. “Gostinitsa ‘Moskva’ v Tashkente [The Moscow Hotel in Tashkent].” *Arkhitektura i stroitel’stvo Uzbekistana [Architecture and Construction of Uzbekistan]*, no. 2 (1983): 15–23.
- “Stalo izvestno, kak budet vygliadet’ posle rekonstruktsii obnovlennaia ploshchad’ ‘Druzhby narodov’ [It Is Now Known How the Renovated Peoples’ Friendship Square Will Look After Reconstruction].” *podrobno.uz*, July 12, 2018. https://podrobno.uz/cat/obchestvo/stalo-izvestno-kak-budet-vyglyadet/.
- Stronski, Paul. *Tashkent: Forging a Soviet City, 1930–1966*. Pittsburgh: University of Pittsburgh Press, 2010.
- Sukhanova, Elena, and Vladimir Krichevskii. “Dvorets Druzhby narodov SSSR im. V.I. Lenina v Tashkente [The V.I. Lenin Peoples’ Friendship Palace in Tashkent].” *Stroitel’stvo i arkhitektura Uzbekistana [Construction and Architecture of Uzbekistan]*, no. 8 (1981): 18–24.
- Sutiagin, Sergo. “Dvorets iskusstv v Tashkente [The Palace of Arts in Tashkent].” *Stroitel’stvo i arkhitektura Uzbekistana* [Construction and Architecture of Uzbekistan], no. 6 (1977): 24–27.
- Sutiagin, Sergo. Review of the Sun Complex. *Arkhitektura SSSR [Architecture of the USSR]*, nos. 3–4 (1988): 41.
- Sutiagin, Sergo. “Vladimir Vladimirovich Berezin (stranitsy tvorchestva) [Vladimir Vladimirovich Berezin (Pages of Creativity)].” *O’zbekiston Arxitektura va Qurilishi [Construction and Architecture of Uzbekistan]*, no. 1 (2001): 57–60.
- Sutiagin, Sergo, and Aleksandr Braslavskii. “Dvorets iskusstv v Tashkente [The Palace of Arts in Tashkent].” *Arkhitektura SSSR [Architecture of the USSR]*, no. 11 (1965): 7–12.
- Suzdal’tseva, A. “Beton i sintez iskusstv v arkhitekture [Concrete and the Synthesis of Arts in Architecture].” *Arkhitektura SSSR [Architecture of the USSR]*, no. 5 (1976): 52–55.
- Tange, Kenzo. *Arkhitektura Iaponii [The Architecture of Japan]*. Moscow: Progress, 1978.
- Tankhel’son, A. “Samyi bol’shoi v Srednei Azii [The Largest in Central Asia].” *Pravda Vostoka [Truth of the East]*, no. 13 (January 16, 1977): 4.
- Tashkenbaev, Pulatzhan. *Tsirkovoe iskusstvo v Uzbekistane vo vtoroi polovine XIX–nachale XX vv. [Circus Art in Uzbekistan in the Late Nineteenth and Early Twentieth Centuries]*. Ph.D. diss., Tashkent, 1993.
- *Tashkent: Entsiklopediia [Tashkent: An Encyclopedia]*. Tashkent: Glavnaia redaktsiia Uzbekskoi sovetskoi entsiklopedii, 1984.
- Tits, Aleksei, ed. *Osnovy arkhitekturnoi kompozitsii i proektirovaniia [The Foundations of Architectural Composition and Design]*. Kyiv: Vishcha shkola, 1978.
- Tkachenko, I. “Rekonstruktsiia stolitsy Uzbekistana [Reconstruction of the Capital of Uzbekistan].” *Arkhitektura SSSR [Architecture of the USSR]*, no. 10 (1969): 17–23.
- Turgunov, T. “Gosudarstvennyi muzei iskusstv Uzbekskoi SSR [State Museum of Arts of Uzbek SSR].” *Stroitel’stvo i arkhitektura Uzbekistana [Construction and Architecture of Uzbekistan]*, no. 10 (1981): 18–22.
- Tursunov, Farkhad. “Arkhitekturnyi oblik gorodov Uzbekistana [The Architectural Appearance of Cities in Uzbekistan].” *Arkhitektura SSSR [Architecture of the USSR]*, no. 11 (1977): 26–32.
- Tursunov, Farkhad. “Ideino-khudozhestvennye problemy formirovaniia tsentra goroda [Ideological and Artistic Issues in Forming the City Center].” *Arkhitektura SSSR [Architecture of the USSR]*, no. 2 (1982): 21–25.
- Ubaidullaev, Khamza, and Valentin Arkhangel’skii. “III etap: 1945–1989; ‘Stanovlenie,’ SAII–SazPI–TashPI–SamGASI [III. Stage: 1945–1989; ‘Formation,’ SAII–SazPI–TashPI–SamGASI].” *Arkhitektura i stroitel’stvo Uzbekistana [Architecture and Construction of Uzbekistan]*, no. 7 (1990): 8–10.
- Umarov, Abdulkhai. “Monumental’no-dekorativnoe iskusstvo Uzbekistana [Monumental-Decorative Art of Uzbekistan],” *Sovetskoe monumental’noe iskusstvo [Soviet Monumental Art]*, no. 74 (1976): 57–61.
- Umarov, Abdulkhai. “Preemstvennost’ traditsii v sovremennom monumental’nom iskusstve Uzbekistana [Continuity of Tradition in Contemporary Monumental Art in Uzbekistan].” *Stroitel’stvo i arkhitektura Uzbekistana [Construction and Architecture of Uzbekistan]*, no. 4 (1978): 30–35.
- Valiev, Rustam, Tulkinoi Kadyrova and Abdulkhai Umarov. *Arkhitektor i vremia [The Architect and Time]*. Tashkent: Izdatel’stvo Gafura Guliama, 1982.
- Vanke, Aleksandr, Iurii Puretskii, A. Stazaeva and Aleksandr Iakushev. *General’nyi plan razvitiia Tashkenta [General Plan for the Development of Tashkent]*. Tashkent: Izdatel’stvo TsK KP Uzbekistana, 1967.
- Veimarn, Boris. *Istoriia iskusstva narodov SSSR: iskusstvo narodov SSSR 1960–1977 [History of Art of the Peoples of the USSR: Art of the Peoples of the USSR 1960–1977]*. Moscow: Izobrazitel’noe iskusstvo, 1984.
- Velichkin, S. “Shedevry v opasnosti [Masterpieces in Danger].” *Pravda Vostoka [Truth of the East]*, August 8, 1992: 4.
- Vercelloni, Virgilio. *Atlante storico dell’idea europea di città ideale*. Milan: Jaca Book, 1994.
- Vileikis, O., E. Escalante Carrillo, S. Allayarov and A. Feyzulayev. “Documentation for Preservation: Methodology and a GIS Database of Three World Heritage Cities in Uzbekistan.” In *ICOMOS/ISPRS International Scientific Committee on Heritage Documentation (CIPA): 26th International CIPA Symposium – Digital Workflows for Heritage Conservation*, edited by J. Hayes, C. Ouimet, M. Santana Quintero, S. Fai and L. Smith, 311–318. ICOMOS, 2017.
- Villasana, D., and S. Hiltner. “Peer Inside Tashkent’s Art-Filled (and Long-Shrouded) Subway.” *The New York Times*, November 20, 2019. https://www.nytimes.com/2019/11/20/travel/tashkent-uzbekistan-subway.html.
- Vinken, Gerhard. *Zones of Tradition—Places of Identity*. Bielefeld: De Gruyter, 2021.
- Vitruve. *Les dix livres d’architecture, corrigez et traduits en françois avec des notes et des figures*. Translated by Claude Perrault. Paris: Chez Jean Baptiste Coignard, 1673.
- Volynskii, Leonid. “Doroga k novoi zemle [The Road to a New Land].” *Novyi mir [New World]*, no. 12 (1961): 118–160.
- Voronina, Veronika. *Narodnye traditsii arkhitektury Uzbekistana [Folk Traditions of Architecture in Uzbekistan]*. Moscow: Arkhitektury i gradostroitel’stva, 1951.
- Voronina, Veronika. “Klimat i arkhitektura Severnoi Afriki [The Climate and Architecture of North Africa],” *Stroitel’stvo i arkhitektura Uzbekistana [Construction and Architecture of Uzbekistan]*, no. 8 (1966), 46–52.
- Voronina, Veronika. “Villy Severnoi Afriki [Villas of North Africa],” *Stroitel’stvo i arkhitektura Uzbekistana [Construction and Architecture of Uzbekistan]*, no. 3 (1975): 46–50.
- Voronina, Veronika. “Iz istorii gorodov sovremennogo Alzhira [From the History of Cities of Contemporary Algeria].” *Stroitel’stvo i arkhitektura Uzbekistana [Construction and Architecture of Uzbekistan]*, no. 8 (1977): 27–28.
- Voslensky, Mikhail. *Nomenklatura: The Ruling Class in the Soviet Union*. Translated by E. Mosbacher. 2nd ed. London: Overseas Publications Interchange Ltd, 1990.
- Vronskaya, Alla. “The Utopia of Personality: Moisei Ginzburg’s Project for the Moscow Park of Culture and Leisure.” *Quaestio Rossica*, no. 4 (2015): 40–56.
- *Vseobshchaia istoriia arkhitektury [General History of Architecture]*. Vol. 12, part 1. Moscow: Stroiizdat, 1975.
- Weil, Mark. “The Unknown Infamous Ilkhom: An Attempt to Survey the History of the Ilkhom Theater for Those Who Don’t Have the Slightest Idea About It.” In *Neizvestnyi izvestnyi “Il’khom”: Teatr Marka Vailia [The Unknown Famous Ilkhom: Mark Weil Theater]*, 18–24. Tashkent, 2003.
- Weise, Kai, Shristina Shrestha and Anie Joshi, eds. *Inventory of 19th and 20th Century Architectural and Industrial Heritage of Nepal*. ICOMOS Nepal, 2020.
- Wolf, Garett C. “Reproducing Tashkent: Reconceptualising Transition from the Socialist City to the Post-Socialist City.” Ph.D. diss., University of Manchester, 2019.

- *The Workshop 2008 for Protection of Cultural Heritage at Tashkent in Uzbekistan*. Cultural Heritage Protection Cooperation Office, Asia/Pacific Cultural Centre for UNESCO, 2009.
- Yafasov, A. Ya., and V. A. Akimov. "Tectonic Factor in the Formation of the Radon Fields in the Atmosphere of the Tashkent Subway." *Atomic Energy*, no. 90 (2001): 130–136.
- Zakharov, Viktor, and Irena Lipene. "Nauchno-proizvodstvennyi metallurgicheskii geliokompleks 'Solntse' [The Sun Scientific Production Metallurgical Heliocomplex]." *Arkhitektura i stroitel'stvo Uzbekistana* [*Architecture and Construction of Uzbekistan*], no. 1 (1988): 15–22.
- Zakhidov, Pulat. "Organizatsiia okhrannykh zon pamiatnikov [Organization of Protection Zones of Monuments]." *Stroitel'stvo i arkhitektura Uzbekistana* [*Construction and Architecture of Uzbekistan*], no. 10 (1968): 29–30.
- Zakhidov, Pulat. "Nekotorye voprosy okhrany pamiatnikov Uzbekistana [Questions Regarding the Preservation of Monuments in Uzbekistan]." *Stroitel'stvo i arkhitektura Uzbekistana* [*Construction and Architecture of Uzbekistan*], no. 11 (1971): 28–31.
- Zakhidov, Pulat. "Okhrana pamiatnikov – zadacha gradostroitel'naia [The Preservation of Monuments Is an Urban Planning Task]." *Stroitel'stvo i arkhitektura Uzbekistana* [*Construction and Architecture of Uzbekistan*], no. 11 (1978): 1–3.
- "Zdanie muzeia V.I. Lenina v Tashkente [The Building of the V.I. Lenin Museum in Tashkent]." *Arkhitektura SSSR* [*Architecture of the USSR*], no. 12 (1969): 30–32.
- Ziiaev, Abdumannop. *Tashkent II: XVII–nachalo XX veka [Tashkent II: 17th–Early 20th Century*]. Tashkent: San'at, 2009.
- Ziiaev, Abdumannop. *Tashkent: V trekh chastiakh; Chast' III, XX – nachalo XXI veka* [*Tashkent: In Three Parts; Part III, 20th–Early 21st Century*]. Tashkent: Izdatel'stvo San'at, 2009.

Laws, Decrees and Resolutions

These are presented in chronological order. Dates in the English translations follow American usage: month, day, year.

- Postanovlenie TsK KPSS i Soveta Ministrov SSSR "O dal'neishem razvitii i uluchshenii obshchestvennogo pitaniia" [Decree of the Central Committee of the CPSU and the Council of Ministers of the USSR "On the Further Development and Improvement of Public Catering"]. *Sobranie postanovlenii pravitel'stva SSSR za 1959 g.* [*Collection of Decrees of the Government of the USSR for 1959*], Nos. 1–20. Moscow: Gosiurizdat, n.d.: 66–72.
- Postanovlenie Soveta Ministrov SSSR 21 fevralia 1967 g. "Ob osnovnykh printsipakh general'nogo plana razvitiia g. Tashkenta" [Resolution of the Council of Ministers of the USSR of February 21, 1967, "On the Fundamental Principles of the Tashkent General Development Plan"].
- Zakon SSSR ot 29.10.1976, ot 21.09.1983, "Ob okhrane i ispol'zovanii pamiatnikov istorii i kul'tury" [Law of the USSR "On the Protection and Use of Historical and Cultural Monuments," 10.29.1976, 09.21.1983].
- Postanovlenie Soveta Ministrov Uzbekskoi SSR, ot 24.02.1979 g. No. 149, "O merakh po dal'neishemu sovershenstvovaniiu upravleniia okhranoi i restavratsiei pamiatnikov material'noi kul'tury respubliki" [Resolution of the Council of Ministers of the Uzbek SSR "On Measures to Further Improve the Management of the Protection and Restoration of Monuments of Tangible Cultural Significance of the Republic," No. 149, 02.24.1979].
- Zakon SSSR ot 21.09.1983, "Ob okhrane i ispol'zovanii pamiatnikov istorii i kul'tury" [Law of the USSR "On the Protection and Use of Historical and Cultural Monuments," No. 1002-X, 09.21.1983].
- "Ustav obshchestva okhrany pamyatnikov istorii i kul'tury Uzbekistana [Charter of the Society for the Protection of Historical and Material Cultural Monuments of Uzbekistan]," 1986.
- Zakon Respubliki Uzbekistan, ot 30.08.2001 g. No. 269-II, "Ob okhrane i ispol'zovanii ob"ektov kul'turnogo naslediia. I. Obshchie polozheniia" [Law of the Republic of Uzbekistan "On the Protection and Use of Objects of Cultural Heritage," No. 269-II, 08.30.2001].
- Postanovlenie Kabineta Ministrov Respubliki Uzbekistan, ot 29.07.2002 g. No. 269, "O merakh po dal'neishemu sovershenstvovaniiu okhrany i ispol'zovaniiu ob"ektov kul'turnogo naslediia" [Resolution of the Cabinet of Ministers of the Republic of Uzbekistan "On Measures to Enhance the Protection and Use of Cultural Heritage Objects," No. 269, 07.29.2002].
- Zakon Respubliki Uzbekistan, ot 09.10.2009 g. No. ZRU-228, "O vnesenii izmenenii v zakon Respubliki Uzbekistan 'ob okhrane i ispol'zovanii ob"ektov kul'turnogo naslediia'" [Law of the Republic of Uzbekistan "On Amendments to the Law of the Republic of Uzbekistan 'On the Protection and Use of Cultural Heritage Objects,'" No. ZRU-288, 10.09.2009].
- Postanovlenie Kabineta Ministrov Respubliki Uzbekistan, ot 30.03.2019 g. No. 265 "Ob utverzhdenii normativno-pravovykh aktov po ispol'zovaniiu i okhrane ob"ektov material'nogo kul'turnogo nasledіia" [Resolution of the Cabinet of Ministers of the Republic of Uzbekistan "On Approval of the Regulations on the Use and Protection of Objects of Tangible Cultural Heritage and the Organization of the Activities of the Department of Cultural Heritage under the Ministry of Culture of Uzbekistan," No. 265, 03.30.2019].
- Postanovlenie Kabineta Ministrov Respubliki Uzbekistan, ot 04.10.2019 g. No. 846 "Ob utverzhdenii natsional'nogo perechnia ob"ektov nedvizhimosti material'nogo kul'turnogo nasledіia" [Resolution of the Cabinet of Ministers of the Republic of Uzbekistan "On Approval of the National List of Real Estate Objects of Tangible Cultural Heritage," No. 846, 10.04.2019].
- Ukaz Prezidenta Respubliki Uzbekistan, ot 06.04.2021 g. No. UP-6199, "O merakh po dal'neishemu sovershenstvovaniiu sistemy gosudarstvennogo upravleniia v sferakh turizma, sporta i kul'turnogo nasledіia" [Decree of the Republic of Uzbekistan "On Measures to Further Improve the Public Administration System in the Fields of Tourism, Sports and Cultural Heritage," No. UP-6199, 04.06.2021].
- Postanovlenie Prezidenta Respubliki Uzbekistan, ot 19.06.2021 g. No. PP-5150, "O merakh po organizatsii deiatel'nosti agentstva kul'turnogo nasledіia pri ministerstve turizma i sporta Respubliki Uzbekistan, a takzhe innovatsionnomu razvitiiu sfery" [Resolution of the Republic of Uzbekistan "On Measures for the Organization of Activities of the Agency of Cultural Heritage under the Ministry of Tourism and Sport of the Republic of Uzbekistan, and also to Innovative Development of the Field," No. PP-5150, 06.19.2021].
- Postanovlenie Kabineta Ministrov Respubliki Uzbekistan, ot 25.03.2024 g. No. 154, "O vnesenii dopolnenii v natsional'nyi perechen' ob"ektov nedvizhimosti material'nogo kul'turnogo nasledіia" [Resolution of the Cabinet of Ministers of the Republic of Uzbekistan "On Making Additions to the National List of Real Estate Objects of Tangible Cultural Heritage," No. 154, 03.25.2024].
- Postanovlenie Kabineta Ministrov Respubliki Uzbekistan, ot 22.04.2024 g. No. 227, "O vnesenii izmenenii i dopolnenii v natsional'nyi perechen' nedvizhimogo imushchestva, ob"ektov material'nogo kul'turnogo nasledіia" [Resolution of the Cabinet of Ministers of the Republic of Uzbekistan "On Introducing Amendments and Additions to the National Register of Intangible Property of Tangible Cultural Heritage," No. 227, 04.22.2024].
- Postanovlenie Kabineta Ministrov Respubliki Uzbekistan, ot 20.05.2024 g. No. 295, "O merakh po dal'neishemu sovershenstvovaniiu deiatel'nosti nauchno-ekspertnogo soveta agentstva kul'turnogo nasledіia Respubliki Uzbekistan" [Resolution of the Cabinet of Ministers of the Republic of Uzbekistan "On Measures to Further Improve the Activities of the Scientific and Expert Council of the Cultural Heritage Agency of the Republic of Uzbekistan," No. 295, 05.20.2024].

Websites

- ACDF Tashkent Modernism: https://www.tashkentmodernism.uz/
- Alerte Héritage: https://archalert.net/
- "Behind the Architecture: The State Museum of Arts of Uzbekistan," Google Arts & Culture: https://artsandculture.google.com/story/behind-the-architecture-the-state-museum-of-arts-of-uzbekistan/5gJSNi-CvAW4LQ
- "Friendship of People's Palace: Tashkent, Uzbekistan," Divisare: https://divisare.com/projects/307036-uta-gelbke-friendship-of-people-s-palace-tashkent-uzbekistan
- Institute of Materials Science of Uzbekistan Academy of Sciences: https://imssolar.uz/en/
- Pis'ma o Tashkente [Essay on Tashkent]: https://mytashkent.uz/
- "Mahalla – Urban Rural Living," Google Arts & Culture: https://artsandculture.google.com/story/zgUxn90I5CRP2Q
- Retro View of Mankind's Habitat: https://pastvu.com/
- Soviet Modernism 1955–1991: http://wiki.azw.at/sovietmodernism_database/home.php?l=deu
- State Museum of the History of Uzbekistan: https://www.history-museum.uz/
- "Tashkent Modernist Architecture: Modernity and Tradition in Central Asia," Tentative List, UNESCO World Heritage Convention: https://whc.unesco.org/en/tentativelists/6708/
- Tashkent Retrospective: https://dzen.ru/tashkent
- Zhemchug: https://hiddenarchitecture.net/zhemchug/

Archives

- Adamov, Leon. "Zakliuchenie po proektnomu zadaniu gostinitsy 'Inturist' na 750 mest v g. Tashkente [Conclusion on the Project Plan for the Intourist Hotel with 750 Beds in Tashkent]," *Protokoly zasedanii arkhitekturnoi komissii i ekspertnye zakliucheniia po proektnym smetam* [*Protocols of Meetings of the Architectural Commission and Expert Conclusions on Project Budgets*], February 17–March 25, 1965. Tashkent City Archive, fund 36, list 1, item 1277, 170 sheets.
- Arkhiteturno-planirovochnoe zadanie no. 143 ot 19 aprelia 1969 goda [Architecture and Planning Brief No. 143, dated April 19, 1969]," *Vystavochnyi pavil'on Soiuza khudozhnikov UzSSR: Kratkaia annotatsiia proektnykh reshenii* [*Exhibition Pavilion of the Union of Artists of the Uzbek SSR: A Short Annotation of the Project Solutions*], Tashkent, 1975, page 2. Toshkentboshplan LITI Archive, archive no. 20, file 2.
- Bleze, Richard, "Ekspertnoe zakliuchenie na proekt kompleksnoi rekonstruktsii kinokontsertnogo zala Dvortsa iskusstv v g. Tashkente [Expert Opinion on the Project for the Complex Reconstruction of the Cinema and Concert Hall of the Palace of Arts in Tashkent]," 1 (March 4, 1974). O'zshaharsozlik LITI Archive, file 1397.
- Document (the first page of which is missing) signed by the chairman L. Briskin and the secretary A. Mullabaev, *Vystavochnyi pavil'on Soiuza khudozhnikov UzSSR: Kratkaia annotatsiia proektnykh reshenii* [*Exhibition Pavilion of the Union of Artists of the Uzbek SSR: A Short Annotation of the Project Solutions*], Tashkent, 1975. Toshkentboshplan LITI Archive, archive no. 20, file 2.
- "Ekspertnoe zakliuchenie po arkhitekturno-planirovochnoi chasti rabochikh chertezhei proekta zastroiki i blagoustroistva ploshchadi im. V.I. Lenina v gorode Tashkente [Expert Conclusion on the Architectural and Planning Parts of the Working Drawings for the Project for Construction and Landscaping of V.I. Lenin Square in the City of Tashkent]," *Protokoly zasedanii arkhitekturnoi komissii i ekspertnye zakliucheniia po proektam i smetam stroitel'stva za No. 99, No. 101a, 100, 101, 104, 10 oktiabria 1966–20 oktiabria 1966* [*Protocols of Meetings of the Architectural Commission and Expert Commissions on Projects and Budgets No. 99, No. 101a, 100, 101, 104, October 10–20, 1966*]." Tashkent City Archive, fund 36, list 1, item 1332, 115 sheets.
- Executive Committee of Tashkent City Council of Workers' Deputies, Main Architecture and Planning Administration, GlavAPU. Tashkent City Archive, fund 36, list 1, 119 sheets.
- Khairutdinova, Firuza. "O zhizni i tvorchestve arkh. Khairutdinova, ostavivshego zametnyi sled v arkhitekture Tashkenta [On the Life and Work of Architect Khairutdinov, Who Made a Significant Mark on the Architecture of Tashkent]." Manuscript kindly provided to Boris Chukhovich.
- Kriukova, Elena. "Arkhitektura obshchestvennykh zdanii Uzbekistana (1970–1995 gg.) [Architecture of Public Buildings in Uzbekistan (1970–1995)]," manuscript. Archive of the Institute of Art History of the Academy of Sciences of Uzbekistan, IA (M), K-85, no. 1398, 157 sheets.
- Kriukova, Elena. *Osnovnye etapy razvitiia arkhitekturnoi kritiki v Uzbekistane* [*Fundamental Stages of the Development of Architectural Criticism in Uzbekistan*], manuscript, 1997. Archive of the Institute of Art History of the Academy of Sciences of Uzbekistan, IA (M), K-77, no. 1466, 78 sheets.
- "Pis'mo direktora Dvortsa iskusstv N. Vaslieva glavnomu inzheneru Uzenergosbyta Akhmedovu [Letter from N. Vasliev, Director of the Palace of Arts, to Akhmedov, Chief Engineer of Uzenergosbyt]," O'zshaharsozlik LITI Archive, file 1397.
- "Pis'mo glavnogo arkhitektora Tashkenta A. Iakusheva direktoru TashZNIIEPa A. Petrosovu ot 24 sentiabria 1964 goda [Letter from Chief Architect of Tashkent A. Iakushev to Director of TashZNIIEP A. Petrosov, dated September 24, 1964]," *Perepiska s gosuchrezhdeniami o proektirovanii i stroitel'stve, 2 iiulia–30 sentiabria 1964 g.* [*Correspondence with State Organizations on Design and Construction, July 2–September 30, 1964*], Tashkent City Archive, fund 36, list 2, item 763, 135 sheets.
- "Pis'mo Predsedatelia Gosstroia Uzbekskoi SSR L. Pozharova Predsedateliu Soveta Ministrov Uzbekskoi SSR A. Alimovu ot 31 iiulia 1960 goda [Letter from Chairman of Gosstroi of the Uzbek SSR L. Pozharov to Chairman of the Council of Ministers of the Uzbek SSR A. Alimov of July 31, 1960]," *Proekty postanovlenii Soveta ministrov UzSSR i Tashgorispolkoma, prikazy i protokoly Goskomiteta i Gosstroia SSSR i UzSSR i perepiska o rekonstruktsii i stroitel'stva g. Tashkenta* [*Drafts of Resolutions of the Council of Ministers of the Uzbek SSR and Tashkent City Executive Committee, Decrees and Protocols of the State Committee and Gosstroi USSR and Gosstroi Uzbekistan and Correspondence on Reconstruction and Building in Tashkent*], Tashkent City Archive, fund 36, list 2, item 111a, on 120 sheets.
- "Pis'mo Predsedatelia Tashgorispolkoma Khusainova i nachal'nika upravleniia po delam arkhitektury pri SNK UzSSR Dzhakhangirova Predsedateliu Soveta narodnykh kommissarov UzSSR Abdurakhmanovu, ot 31 iiulia 1945 g. [Letter from Chairman of the Tashkent City Executive Committee Khusainov and Director of Architectural Affairs of the Council of People's Commissars of the Uzbek SSR Dzhakhangirov to Chairman of the Council of People's Commissars of the Uzbek SSR Abdurakhmanov, dated July 31, 1945]," *Plan i perepiska po Tsentral'noi gostinitse v g. Tashkente na 250 nomerov* [*Plan and Correspondence Regarding the Tsentral'naia Hotel in Tashkent with 250 Rooms*]," April 21–July 31, 1945. Tashkent City Archive, fund 36, list 1, item 993, 25 sheets.
- "Pis'mo Upravliaiushchego delami TsK LKSM Uzbekistana Mamadzhanova nachal'niku APU Tashgorispolkoma Aleksandru Iakushevu [Letter from Head of the Central Committee of the Komsomol of Uzbekistan Mamadzhanov to the head of the Architecture and Planning Administration of Tashkent City Executive Committee Aleksandr Iakushev]," *Protokoly zasedanii arkhitekturnoi komissii i ekspertnye zakliucheniia po proektam i smetam stroitel'stva za No. 9–28. Nachato 31.01.1966, okoncheno 10 marta 1966* [*Protocols of Meetings of the Architectural

Council and Expert Opinions on Projects and Construction Budgets. Opened January 31, 1966, closed March 10, 1966]. Tashkent City Archive, fund 36, list 1, item 1322, 154 sheets.

- "Poiasnitel'naia zapiska: Tekhnicheskii proekt; Vystavochnyi pavil'on Soiuza khudozhnikov UzSSR, tom III [Explanatory Note: Technical Project; Exhibition Pavilion of the Union of Architects of the Uzbek SSR, volume 3." Toshkentboshplan LITI Archive, no. 20/2.1, 62 sheets.
- "Programma zakrytogo konkursa na razrabotku eskiznogo proekta planirovki i zastroiki tsentra g. Tashkenta: Prilozhenie k prikazu Gosstroia SSSR ot 13 noiabria 1963 goda, no. 300 [Program for a Closed Competition for the Development of a Design Sketch of the Layout and Construction of the Center of Tashkent: Appendix to the Decree of Gosstroi USSR, dated November 13, 1963, no. 300]," *Postanovleniia TsK KP Uzbekistana i Soveta ministrov UzSSR o stroitel'stve vystavki, posviashchenoi 40-letiiu UzSSR, i stroitel'stva v g. Tashkente, 5 ianvaria–20 dekabria 1963* [*Resolutions of the Central Committee of the Communist Party of Uzbekistan and the Council of Ministers of the Uzbek SSR on the Construction of an Exhibition to Mark the 40th Anniversary of the Uzbek SSR and Construction in Tashkent, January 5–December 20, 1963*]. Tashkent City Archive, fund 36, list 2, item 134, 76 sheets.
- "Programmnoe zadanie na proektirovanie panoramnogo kinoteatra s universal'nym zalom na 2500 mest v gorode Tashkente [Program Brief for the Design of a Panoramic Cinema with a Universal Auditorium with 2,500 Seats in the City of Tashkent]," Stenogramma obsuzhdeniia proektov panoramnogo kinoteatra pri Soiuze arkhitektorov UzSSR, 20 fevralia 1961 [Transcription of a Discussion of Designs for a Panoramic Cinema at the Union of Architects of the Uzbek SSR, February 20, 1961]. National Archive of the Republic of Uzbekistan, fund 2352, list 1, item 258, 119 sheets.
- "Protokol kommissii po vyboru ploshchadki dlia stroitel'stva gostinitsy 'Inturist' v Tashkente, ot 28 marta 1960 goda [Protocol of the Selection Committee for the Site for the Construction of the Intourist Hotel in Tashkent, dated March 28, 1960]," *Rasporiazheniia po APU, protokoly soveshanii kommissii po vyboru ploshchadki dlia stroitel'stva (gost.) 'Inturista' v Tashkente* [*Instructions on Architecture and Planning Conditions, Protocols of Meetings of the Selection Committee for the Site for the Construction of the Intourist (Hotel) in Tashkent*], January 10–December 25, 1960. Tashkent City Archive, fund 36, list 2, item 114, 55 sheets.
- "Protokol No. 1 rasshirennogo zasedaniia sektsii 'individual'nykh proektov i inter'erov' Pravleniia SA UzSSR, g. Tashkent, 18 marta 1969 [Protocol No. 1 of the Expanded Meeting of the Section of 'Individual Projects and Interiors' of the Administration of the Union of Architects of the Uzbek SSR, Tashkent, March 18, 1969]," *Soiuz arkhitektorov UzSSR: Tvorcheskie sektsii; Materialy deiatel'nosti sektsii individual'nogo proektirovaniia i inter'erov* [*Union of Architects of the UzSSR: Creative Sections; Materials on the Activities of the Section of Individual Projects and Interiors*]. National Archive of the Republic of Uzbekistan, fund 2532, list 2, item 89, 12 sheets.
- "Protokol No. 21 zasedaniia rabochego apparata arkhitekturnoi komissii Upravleniia po delam stroitel'stva i arkhitektury Tashgorispolkoma ot 3 marta 1966 goda [Protocol No. 21 of the Meeting of the Working Group of the Architectural Council of the Construction and Architecture Administration of Tashkent City Executive Committee, dated March 3, 1966]," *Protokoly zasedanii arkhitekturnoi komissii i ekspertnye zakliucheniia po proektam i smetam stroitel'stva za No. 9–28. Nachato 31.01.1966, okoncheno 10 marta 1966* [*Protocols of Meetings of the Architectural Council and Expert Opinions on Projects and Construction Budgets. Opened January 31, 1966, closed March 10, 1966*]. Tashkent City Archive, fund 36, list 1, item 1322, 154 sheets.
- "Protokol No. 52 sovmestnogo zasedaniia Gosstroia UzSSR i Arkhitekturno-stroitel'nogo Soveta Arkhitekturno-planirovochnogo upravleniia Tashgorispolkoma ot 27 iulia 1964 goda. L. 66–70 [Protocol No. 52 of the Joint Meeting of Gosstroi of the UzSSR and the Architecture and Construction Committee of the Architecture and Planning Directorate of Tashkent City Executive Committee, July 27, 1964. Sheets 66–70]," *Protokoly arkhitekturnoi komissii i ekspertnye kommissii po proektam I smetam, 20 iiuniia 1964–22 iiuliia 1964* [*Protocols of the Architectural Commission and Expert Commissions on Projects and Budgets, June 20–July 22, 1964*]. Tashkent City Archive, fund 36, list 1, item 1235, 162 sheets.
- "Protokol No. 372 zasedaniia pravleniia Soiuza khudozhnikov UzSSR, 27 avgusta 1970 [Protocol No. 372 of the meeting of the administration of the Union of Artists of the Uzbek SSR, August 27, 1970]," *Vystavochnyi pavil'on Soiuza khudozhnikov UzSSR: Kratkaia annotatsiia proektnykh reshenii* [*Exhibition Pavilion of the Union of Artists of the Uzbek SSR: A Short Annotation of the Project Solutions*], Tashkent, 1975. Toshkentboshplan LITI Archive, archive no. 20, file 2.
- "Protokol soveshchaniia pri Zamestitele Predsedatelia Gosstroia UzSSR tov. Sarkisovoi R.A., ot 10 sentiabria 1974, po voprosu kapital'nogo remonta i rekonstruktsii Dvortsa iskusstv v g. Tashkente, Pis'mo UzNIIPgradostroitel'stva – UPO UVD Tashgorispolkoma za No.ASO-4-180 ot 29 iiuliia 1974 goda, Pis'ma MVD UzSSR i UzNIIPgradostroitel'stva ot 16 marta 1972 goda, 25 i 29 marta 1975 goda, 18 iiuniia 1975; UzNIIPgradostroitel'stva – Gosstroiu UzSSR ot 20 marta 1975 goda; i dr. [Protocol of a Meeting with the Vice Chairman of Gosstroi of the Uzbek SSR Comrade Sarkisova R.A. of September 10, 1974; On the Question of Major Renovation and Reconstruction of the Palace of Arts in Tashkent, Letter from UzNIIPgradostroitel'stva to UPO UVD Tashgorispolkoma, No.ASO-4-180, July 29, 1974, Letters of the Ministry of Internal Affairs of the Uzbek SSR and UzNIIPgradostroitel'stva, March 16, 1972, March 25 and 29, 1975, June 18, 1975; From UzNIIPgradostroitel'stva to Gosstroi of the Uzbek SSR, March 20, 1975; etc.]." O'zshaharsozlik LITI Archive, file 1397.
- Rushkovskii, Oleg. "Pis'mo (no. 84) predsedateliu ispolkoma Tashgorsoveta tov. Nishanovu R.N. i nachal'niku APU Tashgorispolkoma Iakushevu A.V. ot 21 ianvaria 1963 goda [Letter (no. 84) to Chairman of the Executive Committee of Tashkent City Council Comrade R.N. Nishanov and Director of the Architecture and Planning Administration of Tashkent City Executive Committee A.V. Iakushev, dated January 21, 1963," *Perepiska s gosuchrezhdeniiami o stroitel'stve, proektirovanii i blagoustroistve g. Tashkenta* [*Correspondence with State Organizations about the Construction, Design and Landscaping of Tashkent*]. Tashkent City Archive, fund 36, list 2, item 738, 140 sheets.
- Stenogramma obsuzhdeniia proektov panoramnogo kinoteatra pri Soiuze arkhitektorov UzSSR, 20 fevralia 1961 [Transcription of a Discussion of Designs for a Panoramic Cinema at the Union of Architects of the Uzbek SSR, February 20, 1961]. National Archive of the Republic of Uzbekistan, fund 2352, list 1, item 258, 119 sheets.
- Sutiagin, Sergo. "Dvorets iskusstv [The Palace of Arts]" (manuscript of memoirs), personal archive of Karine Sutiagina, 20 sheets.
- *Svod pamiatnikov istorii i kul'tury Uzbekistana* [*Corpus of Monuments of History and Culture of Uzbekistan*], vol. 2, *Tashkent: Pamiatniki khudozhestvennoi kul'tury (arkhitektury i monumental'nogo iskusstva) Tashkenta* [*Tashkent: Monuments of Artistic Culture (Architecture and Monumental Art) of Tashkent*]. Archive of the Institute of Art Studies of the Academy of Sciences of the Republic of Uzbekistan, IA. S48, no. 1253.
- Tashkent City Archive, fund 35, list 2, sheet 5.
- "Tekhno-rabochii proekt: pererabotka Doma molodezhi v g. Tashkente v KTM (Klub tvorcheskoi molodezhi). Tom 1. Kniga 1-1. Svodnaia poiasnitel'naia zapiska. Tashkent, 1977 [Technical Working Design: Remodeling of the House of Youth in Tashkent in the Club of Creative Youth, volume 1, book 1-1, Tashkent, 1977]," O'Zshaharsozlik LITI Archive, fund (1562) 35, inv. no. 5, item 8.
- "Telegramma A. Iakusheva N. Baranovu ot 19 iiunia 1964 goda [Telegram from A. Iakushev to N. Baranov, dated June 19, 1964]," *Rasporiazheniia po APU za 1964 god: O proketirovanii i stroitel'stve gostinitsy i tsirka v Tashkente, 27.02.1964–27.12.1964* [*Resolutions of the Architecture and Planning Administration for 1964: On the Design and Construction of a Hotel and a Circus in Tashkent, February 27–December 27, 1964*], Tashkent City Archive, fund 36, list 2, item 146, 24 sheets, 15.
- "Tsirk na 3000 mest v gorode Tashkente: Zrelishchnyi korpus; Otdelochnye raboty [A Circus with 3,000 Seats in Tashkent: Spectators' Block; Finishing Works]." Tashgiprogor Technical Archive, file 22.2.4, list 6 (unclear), July 4, 1968.
- "Zakliuchenie ekspertizy po smetnoi dokumentatsii k proektnomu zadaniiu pristroiki i rekonstruktsii zdaniia Gosudarstvennogo muzeia iskusstv v gor. Tashkente ot 3 dekabria 1963 g. [Conclusion of the Expert Commission on the Budget Documentation for the Project Brief for the Extension and Reconstruction of the State Museum of Arts in Tashkent, dated December 3, 1963]," *Ekspertnye zakliucheniia po proektnym*

zadaniiam i smetam [Expert Conclusions on Project Briefs and Budgets], August 16, 1963–January 27, 1964. Tashkent City Archive, fund 36, list 1, item 1217, 160 sheets.

- "Zakliuchenie ekspertizy po smetnoi dokumentatsii k proektnomu zadaniiu stroitel'stva gostinitsy 'Inturist' na 750 mest v g. Tashkente [Conclusion of the Expert Commission on the Budget Documents of the Project Plan for the Construction of the 750-Bed Intourist Hotel in Tashkent]," *Protokoly zasedanii arkhitekturnoi komissii i ekspertnye zakliucheniia po proektnym smetam [Protocols of Meetings of the Architectural Commission and Expert Conclusions on Project Budgets]*, February 17–March 25, 1965. Tashkent City Archive, fund 36, list 1, item 1277, 170 sheets.
- "Zapiska ob organizatsii stroitel'stva vystavochnogo pavil'ona Soiuza khudozhnikov Uzbekistana [Note on the Organization of Construction of the Exhibition Pavilion of the Union of Artists of Uzbekistan]," *Vystavochnyi pavil'on Soiuza khudozhnikov UzSSR: Kratkaia annotatsiia proektnykh reshenii [Exhibition Pavilion of the Union of Artists of the Uzbek SSR: A Short Annotation of the Project Solutions]*, Tashkent, 1975. Toshkentboshplan LITI Archive, archive no. 20, file 2.

Image Sources

Images are listed from top left to bottom right.

All 2D and 3D drawings, diagrams and schemes published in the book were prepared by and are courtesy of GRACE.

We have made every effort to identify all relevant rights holders. In those instances where we have not been able to locate and/or notify the rights holder(s), we ask that they contact the editors or publisher. Any omissions will be corrected in subsequent editions.

Foreword		
12	1–2	Jean-Louis Cohen archive
Interview		
38	1	OMA/AMO
41	1	OMA/AMO
43	1	Photo: GRACE
44	1	Jean-Louis Cohen archive
46	1	OMA
50	1–6	OMA
51	1	OMA

Before Modernism

60 1 Library of Congress. https://www.loc.gov/item/2006626074/
2 Library of Congress. https://www.loc.gov/item/83690086/

61 1 Boris Chukhovich archive

63 1 Tashkent Retrospective https://www.facebook.com/tashkentretrospective/posts/738111126376170/
2 Marjani Foundation

65 1 Abdumannop Ziiaev, *Tashkent: V trekh chastiakh; Chast' III, XX – nachalo XXI veka* (Tashkent: Izdatel'stvo San'at, 2009), 9
2 Abdumannop Ziiaev, *Tashkent: V trekh chastiakh; Chast' III, XX – nachalo XXI veka* (Tashkent: Izdatel'stvo San'at, 2009), 19

66 1 Album *Tashkent: General Reconstruction Project* (Moscow: Mosoblproekt, 1937–1938) Iurii Miroshnichenko archive Scan - Architecture and Design Studio SAD
2 *Stroitel'stvo i arkhitektura Uzbekistana*, no.7, 1974, 33–36
3–4 State Museum of Arts of Uzbekistan

67 1 Photo: Boris Chukhovich, 2022

68 1 Mitkhat Bulatov, "Osobennosti i printsipy progressivnogo resheniia planirovki i zastroiki goroda Tashkenta," in *Akademiia stroitel'stva i arkhitektury SSSR: Nauchno-issledovatel'skii institut raionnoi planirovki i gradostritel'stva* (Moscow/Tashkent: Central State Archive, 1960)

69 1 Republic of Uzbekistan Documentary Film and Photo Archive, 1-21877
2 Republic of Uzbekistan Documentary Film and Photo Archive, 1-21878

70 1 Tulkinoi Kadyrova, *Arkhitektura sovetskogo Uzbekistana* (Moscow: Stroiizdat, 1987), 135
2 Aleksandr Vanke, Iurii Puretskii, et al. *General'nyi plan razvitiia Tashkenta* (Tashkent, 1967)
3 Boris Chukhovich archive

71 1–2 Toshkentboshplan LITI Archive

Earthquake as Alibi

74 1–2 Valentin A. Arkhangel'skii, ed., *Tashkent – gorod bratstva* (Tashkent: Izd. CK KP Uzbekistana, 1969)

75 1 Valentin A. Arkhangel'skii, ed., *Tashkent – gorod bratstva* (Tashkent: Izd. CK KP Uzbekistana, 1969)
2 Philipp Meuser, *Seismic Modernism: Architecture and Housing in Soviet Tashkent* (Berlin: DOM Publishers, 2016)

76 1–2 Aleksandr Vanke, Iurii Puretskii, et al. *General'nyi plan razvitiia Tashkenta* (Tashkent, 1967)

77 1 *Arkhitektura SSSR*, no. 5, 1969.
2 Aleksandr Vanke, Iurii Puretskii, et al. *General'nyi plan razvitiia Tashkenta* (Tashkent, 1967)

79 1 Republic of Uzbekistan Documentary Film and Photo Archive, 0-106089

80 1 *Krokodil*, no. 29, 1967

81 1 Aleksandr Vanke, Iurii Puretskii, et al. *General'nyi plan razvitiia Tashkenta* (Tashkent, 1967)

82 1 Republic of Uzbekistan Documentary Film and Photo Archive, 1-45156

83 1 Republic of Uzbekistan Documentary Film and Photo Archive, 0-103601

84 1–2 Toshkentboshplan LITI Archive

86 1 G.C. Wolf, "Reproducing Tashkent: Reconceptualising Transition from the Socialist City to the Post-Socialist City," Ph.D. thesis, University of Manchester, 2019

Institutional History

89 1 *Arkhitektura i stroitel'stvo Uzbekistana*, no.7, 1990, 8-9

90 1 Boris Chukhovich archive

93 1 Karine Sutiagina archive
2 *L'architecture d'Aujourd'hui*, no. 2, 1972

94 1 Oscar Niemeyer, *Moi opyt stroitel'stva Braziliia* (Moscow: Inostrannaia literatura, 1963)
2 Le Corbusier, *Arkhitektura XX veka* (Moscow: Progress, 1977)
3 Frei Otto, *Visiachie konstruktsii* (Moscow: Gosstroiizdat, 1960)
4 Georges Candilis, *Stat' arkhitektorom* (Moscow: Stroiizdat, 1979)
5 Catalogue of the exhibition *Arkhitektura SShA*, 1965

97 1 *Deutsche Architektur*, no.3, 1966, 142–143
2 Karine Sutiagina archive

99 1–2 Firuza Khairutdinova archive

100 1 Photo: Efim Iuditskii, 1964

101 1 Unknown author from Uzgosproekt

102 1 Sharaf Rashidov Foundation
2 Andrei Kosinskii archive

103 1 Andrei Kosinskii archive

105 1 Sharaf Rashidov Foundation

Standardization and Hybrid Typologies

107 1 Aldo Rossi, *L'Architettura della citta'*, 1966
2 Andrei Ikonnikov, *Arkhitektura goroda*, 1972

109 1–2 Jean-Nicolas-Louis Durand *Recueil et parallèle des édifices de tout genre anciens et modernes, remarquables par leur beauté, par leur grandeur, ou par leur singularité, et dessinés sur une même échelle*, 1801. Universitätsbibliothek Heidelberg: https://doi.org/10.11588/diglit.1608

110 1–6 Graphics: GRACE

113 1–6 http://kaluga-history.ru/soviet-covered-markets/
7 Photo: B. Mindelia Postcard, Cherkasy Market, 1961–1970
8 Photo: V. Falin
9 V.G. Zabolotny State Scientific Architectural and Construction Library Archive, Kyiv, Ukraine
10 https://moniacs.kh.ua/kruglyj-rynok/
11 Photo: Kamila Banks Anastasiia Fedorova, "Come Undone: A Last Glimpse Inside a Soviet-Era Dagestani Bazaar," *NEW EAST DIGITAL ARCHIVE*, 2016
12 https://pastvu.com/p/446777

114 1 Photo: Xenïa Antunes Wikipedia Commons
2 Boris Mezentsev, Boris Zaritskii, Evgenii Rozanov, "Proekt administrativnogo tzentra Tashkenta," *Arkhitektura SSSR*, no.9, 1965, 16
3 Collection of CCA, 344868
4 Republic of Uzbekistan Documentary Film and Photo Archive, 0-134860

117 1 Photo: Igor Palmin
2 Photo: V. Sobrovin *Belgorod - The City of the First Firework*, postcard collection
3 Photo: R. Iakimenko Postcard © USSR Ministry of Communications, 1987
4 Vitalii Samogorov, et al., Kosmicheskii Kuibyshev (Moscow: Tatlin, 2016)

118 1 Graphics and research: GRACE

119 1 Graphics and research: GRACE

121 1 Graphics and research: GRACE

122 1 Graphics and research: GRACE

124 1 Postcard
2 *Through the Ancient Cities of Uzbekistan (Tashkent, Samarkand, Shakhrisabz, Bukhara, Khiva)*, 1988
3 CC – Wikimedia Commons
4 Veronika Voronina, *Narodnye traditsii arkhitektury Uzbekistana [Vernacular traditions of architecture of Uzbekistan]* (Moscow: Gosudarstvennoe izdatel'stvo arkhitektury i gradostroitel'stva, 1951), 48
5 C.N. Trueman Roman Houses https://www.historylearningsite.co.uk/ancient-rome/roman-houses/

Modernism as Orientalism

127 1 Republic of Uzbekistan Documentary Film and Photo Archive, 0-99959

128 1 Republic of Uzbekistan Documentary Film and Photo Archive, 1-24694

129 1 Marjani Foundation

131 1–3 State Museum of Arts of Uzbekistan
4 Shchusev State Architecture Museum Archive, P Ia 14046
5 Shchusev State Architecture Museum Archive, P Ia 14057

133 1–2 Photo: GRACE

134 1 Research: GRACE, Boris Chukhovich Graphics: Linda van Deursen

136 1 Photo: Usmanov, 1971 Republic of Uzbekistan Documentary Film and Photo Archive

137 1 Vil' Muratov archive
2 Photo: Aleksei Naroditskii

138 1 Shchusev State Architecture Museum Archive, P Ia 14047

139 1 Photo: A. Vainshtein Republic of Uzbekistan Documentary Film and Photo Archive, 1-52726
2 Photo: GRACE

Protection Inventory for Modernist Heritage

187 1 1875, Paris: Capital of the 19th Century. Brown Digital Repository. Brown University Library. https://repository.library.brown.edu/studio/item/bdr:86734/).

188 1 Bibliothèque nationale de France gallica.bnf.fr/

189 1 Wikimedia Commons; photo: Cassowary Colorizations

191 1 Wikimedia Commons
2 Wikimedia Commons; image from the Horta Museum collection
3 Wikimedia Commons; author Kris Roderburg; image provided by Rijksdienst voor het Cultureel Erfgoed

193 1 Frédéric Chaubin *CCCP: Cosmic Communist Constructions Photographed* (Cologne: Taschen, 2011)
2 *Soviet Modernism: 1955–1991/ Unknown History* (Vienna: Park Books, 2012)

194 1 Collage: GRACE Archival photo: https://mytashkent.uz/2019/06/19/dom-znanij-3/ Current photo: Open sources
2 Collage: GRACE Archival photo: Farkhad Tursunov archive Current photo: Denis Davydov
3 Collage: GRACE Archival photo: Republic of Uzbekistan Documentary Film and Photo Archive, 1-46653 Current photo: Aziza Rakhmatova

195 1 Collage: GRACE Archival photo: Sergo Sutiagin family archive Current photo: Denis Davydov
2 Collage: GRACE Archival photo: Republic of Uzbekistan Documentary Film and Photo Archive, 0-127352 Current photo: GRACE
3 Collage: GRACE Archival photo: https://pastvu.com/_p/a/v/k/y/vkyr6cyn2modzh4nlq.jpg Current photo: GRACE

196 1 Research: GRACE, Boris Chukhovich Graphics: Linda van Deursen

201 1 Graphics: GRACE and Politecnico di Milano (PoliMi hereafter)

202 1 Graphics: GRACE

Modernist Palimpsest

207 1–2 https://www.gazeta.uz/ru/2021/05/20/ancient-maps/

208 1 *Sovremennaia Arkhitektura*, no.5, 1929, 172

209 1 Shchusev State Architecture Museum Archive

2 *Stroitel'stvo Moskvy*, no.1, 1930, 19

210 1 Stroitel'stvo i arkhitektura Uzbekistana, no.7, 1974, 33–36

211 1 Boris Chukhovich archive

213 1 https://rpa.org/work/reports/regional-plan-of-new-york-and-its-environs

214 1 Toshkentboshplan LITI Archive

215 1 Toshkentboshplan LITI Archive

216 1–2 Laboratorio Permanente

219 1 State Museum of Arts of Uzbekistan

220 1 Laboratorio Permanente

Addressing the Future of Tashkent Modernism

223 1 *Tashkent: A Modernist Capital* (New York: Rizzoli, 2025), cover

225 1 Research: GRACE, Boris Chukhovich, PoliMi
Graphics: GRACE

226 1 Research: GRACE, Boris Chukhovich, PoliMi
Graphics: GRACE

228 1 Research: GRACE, Boris Chukhovich, PoliMi
Graphics: GRACE

Visual Essay

236–419 Armin Linke

Panoramic Cinema

425 1 Sergo Sutiagin family archive
432 1 Iurii Khaldeev archive
434 1–4 Sergo Sutiagin family archive
435 1 Sergo Sutiagin family archive
2 Frei Otto, *Visiachie pokrytiia: ikh formy i konstruktsii* (Moscow: State Publisher of Literature on Construction, Architecture and Construction Materials, 1960), 105
437 1–2 Sergo Sutiagin family archive
438 1 Sergo Sutiagin family archive
441 1–2 Sergo Sutiagin family archive
442 1 Ekaterina Berezina archive
443 1 *Arkhitektura SSSR*, no. 12, 1983, 30
450 1 Sergo Sutiagin family archive
2 Photo: Boris Kaufman https://www.instagram.com/p/Clje8gxJvxB
3 Photo: Aleksei Varfolomeev https://www.instagram.com/p/COLI-MTZplbV/
4–5 Sergo Sutiagin family archive
451 1–5 Sergo Sutiagin family archive
452 1–4 Photo: Armin Linke
453 1–5 Photo: Armin Linke
454 1–5 Sergo Sutiagin family archive
6 O'zshaharsozlik LITI Archive, 1397/55, inv. no.7
455 1 O'zshaharsozlik LITI Archive 1397/15, inv. no.18
2 Sergo Sutiagin family archive
460 1 Photo: Efim Iuditskii, 1964
2 Photo: GRACE
3 Sergo Sutiagin family archive
4 Photo: GRACE
5 Sergo Sutiagin family archive
6 Photo: GRACE
461 1 Sergo Sutiagin family archive
2 Photo: GRACE
3 Sergo Sutiagin family archive
4 Photo: PoliMi
466 1 Sergo Sutiagin family archive
2 Copyright: GRACE
Visualization: SUN

Cosmonauts Avenue Metro Station

469 1 Photo: GRACE
472 1 Photo: A. Belenkii
477 1–2 Sergo Sutiagin family archive
478 1 Sergo Sutiagin family archive
2 *Arkhitektura i stroitel'stvo Uzbekistana*, no. 5, 1982, 19
480 1 Photo: GRACE
482 1 *Arkhitectura SSSR*, no. 12, 1983, 30
484 1–2 https://dzen.ru/a/Xb3wmwKNaACuUqBd
3 Sergo Sutiagin family archive
485 1–3 Sergo Sutiagin family archive
486 1 Google maps
2 Photo: GRACE
3–4 Photo: Armin Linke
487 1–4 Photo: Armin Linke
488 1–2 Sergo Sutiagin family archive
489 1 Sergo Sutiagin family archive
2 Sergei Romanov archive
492 1 Soviet Visuals https://www.facebook.com/photo?fbid=1440106839388889&-set=pcb.1440107079388865
2 Sergo Sutiagin family archive
493 1 Photo: Armin Linke
2 Photo: GRACE

Peoples' Friendship Palace

499 1 Photo: Rashit Zagidoullin https://pastvu.com/p/674678
506 1 *Stroitel'stvo i arkhitektura Uzbekistana*, no. 10, 1977, 18
2 *Through the Ancient Cities of Uzbekistan (Tashkent, Samarkand, Shakhrisabz, Bukhara, Khiva)*, 1988
510 1 *Arkhitektura SSSR*, 1983, nos. 3–4, p.86
512 1 *Arkhitektura SSSR*, nos. 3–4, 1983, 89
514 1 https://www.rah.ru/the_academy_today/the_members_of_the_academie/member.php?ID=51337
2 Photo courtesy of Elena Sukhanova
515 1 Tulkinoi Kadyrova, *Arkhitektura sovetskogo Uzbekistana* (Moskva: Stroiizdat, 1987), 155
522 1 Republic of Uzbekistan Documentary Film and Photo Archive, 0-116520
2 Republic of Uzbekistan Documentary Film and Photo Archive, 0-116758
3 Republic of Uzbekistan Documentary Film and Photo Archive, 1-50417
4 Republic of Uzbekistan Documentary Film and Photo Archive, 0-119190
5 *Arkhitektura i stroitel'stvo Uzbekistana*, no. 8, 1983, 28
523 1 Galina Pugachenkova, *Pamiatniki iskusstva Sovetskogo Soiuza: Sredniaia Aziia* (Moscow: Iskusstvo, 1983)
2 Photo: Vsevolod Tarasevich RIA Novosti — https://riamediabank.ru/media/5605384.html
3 *Arkhitektura SSSR*, nos. 3–4, 1983
4 https://archalert.net/objects/getObject/18/#photos
5 https://archalert.net/objects/getObject/18/#photos
6 *Tashkent–2000* (Tashkent: Uzbekistan Publishing House, 1983)
524 1–6 Photo: Armin Linke
525 1–4 Photo: Armin Linke
5 Photo: PoliMi
526 1 *Stroitel'stvo i arkhitektura Uzbekistana*, no. 10, 1977, 20
2 *Arkhitektura SSSR*, no. 10, 1978, 24
3 *Arkhitektura SSSR*, nos. 3–4, 1983, 87
527 1 Shchusev State Museum of Architecture Archive, Pla-12197
531 1 *Through the Ancient Cities of Uzbekistan (Tashkent, Samarkand, Shakhrisabz, Bukhara, Khiva)*, 1988
2 Photo: GRACE
3 *Arkhitektura SSSR*, 1983, nos.3–4, p.86
4 Photo: GRACE
532 1 https://archalert.net/objects/getObject/18/#photos
2 Photo: GRACE
3 https://archalert.net/objects/getObject/18/#photos
4 Photo: GRACE
5 *Tulkinoi Kadyrova, Arkhitektura Sovetskogo Uzbekistana* (Moscow: Stroiizdat, 1987), 267
6 Photo: GRACE
537 1 Photo: Armin Linke

Lenin Museum

539 1 Sharaf Rashidov Foundation
546 1 Neomam Studios / My Voucher Codes https://www.esquire.com/it/lifestyle/viaggi/g21549034/rovine-aspetto-originario/?slide=2
2 Postcard. *Tashkent, Lenin Memorial Museum*, interior Aurora Art Publishers no. 450
548 1 Republic of Uzbekistan Documentary Film and Photo Archive, 1-37512
2 Republic of Uzbekistan Documentary Film and Photo Archive, 0-86138
552 1 Source: https://www.rah.ru/the_academy_today/the_members_of_the_academie/member.php?ID=51337
558 1 Republic of Uzbekistan Documentary Film and Photo Archive, 1-34197
2 https://archalert.net/objects/getObject/15/#photos
3 Republic of Uzbekistan Documentary Film and Photo Archive, 1-35653
4 Republic of Uzbekistan Documentary Film and Photo Archive, 1-55473
5 Republic of Uzbekistan Documentary Film and Photo Archive, 1-37339
6 Republic of Uzbekistan Documentary Film and Photo Archive, 1-37337
559 1 *Stroitel'stvo i arkhitektura Uzbekistana*, no. 3, 1978, 25
2–3 Farkhad Tursunov archive
560 1–5 Photo: Armin Linke
6 Photo: PoliMi
561 1–3 Photo: Armin Linke
4 Photo: PoliMi
5 Photo: Armin Linke
6 Photo: PoliMi
562 1 Republic of Uzbekistan Documentary Film and Photo Archive, 1-34196
563 1 Shchusev State Architecture Museum Archive, KLof 5158-108
2 Shchusev State Architecture Museum Archive, KLof 5158 - 107
564 1–3 Sharaf Rashidov Foundation
565 1–2 Sharaf Rashidov Foundation
566 1 Research and graphics: GRACE
574 1 *Evgenii Rozanov and Vladimir Revlakin, Arkhitektura muzeev V.I. Lenina* (Moscow: Stroiizdat, 1986), 57
2 Photo: GRACE
3 *Tashkent* (Planeta Publishing House, 1982)
Photo: A. Markelov and R. Ozerskii
4 Photo: PoliMi
575 1 Republic of Uzbekistan Documentary Film and Photo Archive, 1-37337
2 Photo: PoliMi
3 Republic of Uzbekistan Documentary Film and Photo Archive, 0-39205
4 Photo: GRACE
578 1 Republic of Uzbekistan Documentary Film and Photo Archive, 1-37518
581 1 Copyright: GRACE
Visualization: SUN
582 1 Copyright: GRACE
Visualization: SUN

Exhibition Hall of the Union of Artists

585 1 Photo: Iu. Dorogavtsev https://pastvu.com/p/1450673
591 1 https://dzen.ru/a/Wi5wszx-Q95OFNA10
2 Farkhad Tursunov archive
3 Bibliothèque et Archives nationales du Québec, Fonds Euclide Sicotte — https://numerique.banq.qc.ca/patrimoine/details/52327/3426780?docref=x5oIPNcrC6fRmqSR7kPCQg
4 Library and Archives Canada RG71, Box number: TCS 00868; Item no. (creator): 8311; Item ID number: 4916895
595 1 Source unknown
2 Farkhad Tursunov archive
597 1 Firuza Khairutdinova archive
604 1 Photo: Iu. Dorogavtsev (scan of photo from personal archive) https://pastvu.com/p/1450673
2 Tashkent Entsiklopediia, 1983
3 *Stroitel'stvo i arkhitektura Uzbekistana*, no.4, 1980, 21
4 *Stroitel'stvo i arkhitektura Uzbekistana*, no.4, 1980
5 *Stroitel'stvo i arkhitektura Uzbekistana*, no.6, 1979, 20
6 Farkhad Tursunov archive
605 1–2 Farkhad Tursunov archive
3 *Stroitel'stvo i arkhitektura Uzbekistana*, no.4, 1980, 21
4–7 Farkhad Tursunov archive
606 1–3 Photo: Armin Linke
4–6 Photo: PoliMi
607 1–2 Photo: Armin Linke
608 1 Toshkentboshplan LITI Archive
2 *Stroitel'stvo i arkhitektura Uzbekistana*, no.7, 1974, 22–23
609 1–2 Toshkentboshplan LITI Archive
613 1 https://mytashkent.uz/2019/03/11/vystavochnyj-zal-akademii-hudozhestv/
2 Photo: GRACE
3 *Tashkent: Entsiklopediia* (Tashkent: Glavnaia redaktsiia Uzbekskoi sovetskoi entsiklopedii, 1984), 67
4 Photo: GRACE
614 1 Farkhad Tursunov archive
2 Photo: GRACE
3 Farkhad Tursunov archive
4 Photo: GRACE
619 1 Photo: Armin Linke
621 1 Copyright: GRACE
Visualization: SUN

Sun Heliocomplex

623 1 *Arkhitektura SSSR*, nos. 3–4, 1988, 2
626 1 *Sun Research and Production Complex. Basic Architectural and Planning Solutions*, PO Box A-1158, Moscow, 1981
629 1 *Emmanuel Guillot et al, "Some Details of the Third Rejuvenation of the 1000 kW Solar Furnace in Odeillo: Extreme Performance Heliostats,"* conference paper, 2017
2 Photo: GRACE
630 1 Photo: Armin Linke
631 1 Photo: Alastair Philip Wiper https://alastairphilipwiper.com/blog/worlds-largest-solar-furnace-france
2 *Arkhitektura SSSR*, no. 3–4, 1988, 2
3 *Sun Research and Production Complex. Basic Architectural and Planning Solutions*, PO Box A-1158, Moscow, 1981
633 1 Research and graphics: Grace
2 Photo: Armin Linke
3 *Arkhitektura SSSR*, nos. 3–4, 1988, 40–41
636 1 Open source photograph
2 https://mytashkent.uz/2019/03/26/hudozhnik-irena-lipene/
637 1 *Sun Research and Production Complex. Basic Architectural and Planning Solutions*, PO Box A-1158, Moscow, 1981
646 1 Republic of Uzbekistan Documentary Film and Photo Archive, 0-131457
2 *Arkhitektura SSSR*, nos. 3–4, 1988, 40
647 1–3 *Arkhitektura SSSR*, nos. 3–4, 1988, 40–41
4 *Arkhitektura SSSR*, nos. 3–4, 1988, cover
5 *Arkhitektura SSSR*, nos. 3–4, 1988, 2
6 *Arkhitektura SSSR*, nos. 3–4, 1988, 40–41
648 1–2 Photo: Armin Linke
649 1–5 Photo: Armin Linke
650 1–6 Photo: Armin Linke
651 1–6 Photo: Armin Linke
652 1–8 *Sun Research and Production Complex. Basic Architectural and Planning Solutions*, PO Box A-1158, Moscow, 1981
653 1 *Arkhitektura SSSR*, nos. 3–4, 1988, 39
2 *Sun Research and Production Complex. Basic Architectural and Planning Solutions*, PO Box A-1158, Moscow, 1981
654 1–3 *Sun Research and Production Complex. Basic Architectural and Planning Solutions*, PO Box A-1158, Moscow, 1981
655 1–2 *Sun Research and Production Complex. Basic Architectural and Planning Solutions*, PO Box A-1158, Moscow, 1981
660 1 *Arkhitektura SSSR*, nos. 3–4, 1988, 2
2 Photo: GRACE
3 Arkhitektura SSSR, nos. 3–4, 1988, 40–41
4 Photo: GRACE
661 1 *Arkhitektura SSSR*, nos. 3–4, 1988, cover
2 Photo: Armin Linke
3 Arkhitektura SSSR, nos. 3–4, 1988, 40–41
4 Photo: GRACE
666 1 Photo: GRACE
2–3 Photo: Armin Linke
4–5 Photo: GRACE
668 1 Copyright: GRACE
Visualization: SUN
670 1–2 Copyright: GRACE
Visualization: SUN

Zhemchug Residential Building

673 1 Photo: Vladimir Telegin *Arkhitektura i stroitel'stvo Uzbekistana*, nos. 2–3, 1986, 35

679 1 Boris Chukhovich archive
2 Institute of Modernism archive

682 1 Temur Karimov archive
2 *Arkhitektura i stroitel'stvo Uzbekistana*, nos. 2–3, 1986, 56

684 1 Frederick Starr, *Melnikov: Solo Architect in a Mass Society* (Princeton: Princeton University Press, 1978), 191

686 1 Marina Ivanian archive

687 1–2 *Stroitel'stvo i arkhitektura Uzbekistana*, no. 6, 1978, 29

694 1–3 Temur Karimov archive
4 Photo: Vladimir Kovrein

695 1 Photo: Vladimir Kovrein https://archalert.net/objects/getObject/30/#photos
2 https://archalert.net/objects/getObject/30/#photos
3 Source unknown
4 Photo: Vladimir Kovrein
5 Arkhitektura i stroitel'stvo Uzbekistana, no. 12, 1986, 22
6 https://archalert.net/objects/getObject/30/

696 1–2 Photo: Armin Linke
3 Photo: Grace
4–6 Photo: Armin Linke

697 1–6 Photo: Armin Linke

698 1 *Stroitel'stvo i arkhitektura Uzbekistana*, no. 6, 1975, 2

699 1–5 Zhemchug Residents' Committee Archive

704 1 *So far, the only one*, Fragment from the newsreel *Stroitel'stvo i arkhitektura*, no 1, Tashkent, 1988
2 Photo: PoliMi
3 Photo: Vladimir Kovrein https://archalert.net/objects/getObject/30/#photos
4 Photo: GRACE

705 1 *So far, the only one*, Fragment from the newsreel *Stroitel'stvo i arkhitektura*, no 1, Tashkent, 1988
2 Photo: GRACE
3 https://archalert.net/objects/getObject/30/#photos
4 Photo: GRACE

706 1 https://pastvu.com/_p/a/v/k/y/vkyr6cyn2modzh4nlq.jpg
2 Photo: GRACE
3 https://archalert.net/objects/getObject/30/#photos
4 Photo: GRACE

714 1 Research and graphics: Gianluca Maggio, GRACE

715 1 Research and graphics: Gianluca Maggio, GRACE

Chorsu Bazaar

717 1 https://www.tripadvisor.ru/LocationPhotoDirectLink-g293968-d317881-i186765003-Chorsu_Bazaar-Tashkent_Tashkent_Province.html

724 1 https://a-s-kosinskiy.livejournal.com/

725 1 *Arkhitektura i stroitel'stvo Uzbekistana*, no. 8, 1987, 20
2 Shchusev State Museum of Architecture Archive, P Ia-14057

727 1 Republic of Uzbekistan Documentary Film and Photo Archive, 1-52726

728 1 https://archipostalecarte.blogspot.com/2013/03/si-belles-halles-sidi-bel-abbes.html
2 *Stroitel'stvo i Arkhitektura Uzbekitana*, no.4, 1968, 24
3 *Stroitel'stvo i Arkhitektura Uzbekitana*, no.4, 1968, 25

730 1 Republic of Uzbekistan Documentary Film and Photo Archive, 1-52723
2 Republic of Uzbekistan Documentary Film and Photo Archive, 1-52727
3 Photo: Iio Akitoshi https://dzen.ru/a/X4YCvzlAR2xmlHwH

731 1 Source unknown

736 1 *Arkhitektura i stroitel'stvo Uzbekistana*, no. 8, 1987, 22
2 Republic of Uzbekistan Documentary Film and Photo Archive, 1-52727
3 https://www.facebook.com/tashkentretrospective/photos/a.476188385901780/932252456962035/?type=3&theater

737 1 Photo: Ernst Kluge https://pastvu.com/p/1073399
2 https://cronobook.com/en/pic/fbee6f53-2dd7-41f9-b8b6-7ca0d938a919
3–5 Photo: Tongariki-https://4travel.jp/travelogue/10436110?fbclid=IwAR1SCw348Wo5dr4I-f9cxYe8b-5qIdS5oI9Pm_k6ViNOkRvSd56zAi_ztjSk
6 Photo: Iio Akitoshi, https://dzen.ru/a/X4YCvzlAR2xmlHwH

738 1–2 Photo: Armin Linke

739 1–4 Photo: Armin Linke

740 1 Tashgiprogor Institute Archive, 3971/1.1, sheet 2

741 1 Tulkinoi Kadyrova, *Arkhitektura sovetskogo Uzbekistana* (Moskva: Stroiizdat, 1987), 245
2 Tashgiprogor Institute Archive, 3971/2.0, sheet 1

746 1 Photo: Iio Akitoshi https://dzen.ru/a/X4YCvzlAR2xmlHwH
2 Photo: PoliMi

747 1 Photo: Iio Akitoshi https://dzen.ru/a/X4YCvzlAR2xmlHwH
2 Photo: Armin Linke
3 Frédéric Chaubin, *CCCP: Cosmic Communist Constructions Photographed* (Cologne: Taschen, 2011)
4 Photo: GRACE

758 1 Copyright: GRACE Visualization: SUN

State Museum of Arts

761 1 Farkhad Tursunov archive

766 1 pastvu.com

768 1 State Museum of Arts of Uzbekistan Archive
2 *Stroitel'stvo i arkhitektura Uzbekistana*, no. 12, 1967, 26

772 1 Photo: V. Stukalov *Tashkent* (Leningrad: Aurora Art Publishers, 1977), ill. 35
2 https://commons.wikimedia.org/wiki/File:Beinecke-Rare-Book-Manuscript-Library-Yale-University-Hewitt-Quadrangle-New-Haven-Connecticut-Apr-2014-a.jpg

773 1 Marina Ivanian archive

780 1 Republic of Uzbekistan Documentary Film and Photo Archive, 0-95750
2 Republic of Uzbekistan Documentary Film and Photo Archive, 0-95748
3 Republic of Uzbekistan Documentary Film and Photo Archive, 0-103174
4 Republic of Uzbekistan Documentary Film and Photo Archive, 0-103297
5 Photo: Aleksei Varfolomeev Soviet postcards, 1980

781 1 Republic of Uzbekistan Documentary Film and Photo Archive, 0-102640
2 Farkhad Tursunov archive
3 Republic of Uzbekistan Documentary Film and Photo Archive
4–5 *Stroitel'stvo i arkhitektura Uzbekistana*, no. 10, 1981, 21
6 *Tashkent* (Planeta Publishing House, 1982)

782 1 Photo: Armin Linke
2 Photo: GRACE
3 Photo: Armin Linke
4 Photo: GRACE
5 Photo: Armin Linke

783 1–5 Photo: Armin Linke

784 1–2 State Museum of Arts of Uzbekistan Archive

785 1–2 State Museum of Arts of Uzbekistan Archive

789 1 Photo: V. Stukalov *Tashkent* (Leningrad: Aurora Art Publishers, 1977), ill. 35
2 Photo: PoliMi
3 *Stroitel'stvo i arkhitektura Uzbekistana*, no. 12, 1974, 20
4 Photo: PoliMi
5 *Stroitel'stvo i arkhitektura Uzbekistana*, no. 10, 1981, 21
6 Photo: PoliMi

790 1 *Tashkent* (Planeta Publishing House, 1982)
2 Photo: GRACE

795 1–2 Copyright: GRACE Visualization: SUN

798 1 *Stroitel'stvo i arkhitektura Uzbekistana*, no. 12, 1967, 24

799 1 Copyright: GRACE Visualization: SUN

The Circus

801 1 Photo: Aleksei Varfolomeev RIA Novosti — https://riamediabank.ru/media/449349.html
807 1 https://kazan-circus.ru/istoriya-kazanskogo-tsirka
808 1 State Circus Archive
810 1 Republic of Uzbekistan Documentary Film and Photo Archive, 1-100836
2 Republic of Uzbekistan Documentary Film and Photo Archive, 1-55834
811 1 State Circus Archive
813 1 Iurii Miroshnichenko archive
815 1 *Tashkent* (Leningrad: Aurora, 1977)
2 Republic of Uzbekistan Documentary Film and Photo Archive, 1-33850
3 https://mytashkent.uz/2020/04/23/grudnaya-hirurgiya/
4 Iurii Miroshnichenko archive
820 1 State Circus Archive
2 *General Plan for the Development of Tashkent* (Tashkent: Central Committee of the Communist Party of Uzbekistan Pusblishing House, 1967), 15
3 Republic of Uzbekistan Documentary Film and Photo Archive, 0-102958
4 Republic of Uzbekistan Documentary Film and Photo Archive, 0-100376
5 Republic of Uzbekistan Documentary Film and Photo Archive, 1-45479
821 1 Photo: Nabi Utarbekov https://archalert.net/objects/getObject/5/#photos
2 Photo: Aleksei Varfolomeev RIA Novosti — https://riamediabank.ru/media/449349.html
3 *Tashkent guidebook*, 1981 https://mytashkent.uz/2017/01/21/tri-panoramnye-fotografii-1980-god/
4 Tulkinoi Kadyrova, *Arkhitektura sovetskogo Uzbekistana* (Moscow: Stroiizdat, 1987), 256
5 Photo from a Soviet magazine of late 1970s
6 *Stroitel'stvo i arkhitektura Uzbekistana*, no. 3, 1978, 26
7 *Stroitel'stvo i arkhitektura Uzbekistana*, no. 3, 1978
822 1–4 Photo: Armin Linke
5 Photo: PoliMi
823 1–3 Photo: Armin Linke
4–6 Photo: GRACE
824 1 State Circus Archive
2 Tashgiprogor Institute Archive, 2232/2.4, sheet 15
825 1 State Circus Archive
826 1 Tashgiprogor Institute Archive, 2232/2.4, sheet 14
2 Tashgiprogor Institute Archive, 2232/2.4, sheet 1
827 1 Tashgiprogor Institute Archive, 2232/2.4, sheet 22
828 1 Research: GRACE, Boris Chukhovich
Graphics: GRACE
833 1 Photo: A.V. Brukhanskii
2 Photo: GRACE
3 Photo from a Soviet magazine of the second half of the 1970s
4 Photo: GRACE
5 *Stroitel'stvo i arkhitektura Uzbekistana*, no. 3, 1978, 26
6 Photo: GRACE
834 1 *Stroitel'stvo i arkhitektura Uzbekistana*, no. 3, 1978
2 Photo: GRACE
839 1 Copyright: GRACE
Visualization: SUN

House of Youth

841 1 https://dzen.ru/a/XpQg_570X1UNNBly
847 1 *Stroitel'stvo i arkhitektura Uzbekistana*, no. 5, 1966, 22–23
2 *Stroitel'stvo i arkhitektura Uzbekistana*, no. 5, 1966, 24
849 1 Karen Belian, *Artur Tarkhanian, Spartak Khachikian, Grach'ia Pogosian* (Moscow: Tatlin, 2012), 45
2 Karen Belian, *Artur Tarkhanian, Spartak Khachikian, Grach'ia Pogosian* (Moscow: Tatlin, 2012), 46
850 1 O'zshaharsozlik LITI Archive
2 O'zshaharsozlik LITI Archive, 1562/18, sheet 17
3 Photo: Armin Linke
853 1 O'zshaharsozlik LITI Archive, 1562/4, sheet 2
2 *Stroitel'stvo i arkhitektura Uzbekistana*, no.5, 1966, 21
854 1 https://mytashkent.uz/2018/04/25/bleze-rihard-vladimirovich/
864 1 Photo: Boyar Sandor *Tashkent Retrospective* facebook.com/tashkentretrospective
2 Republic of Uzbekistan Documentary Film and Photo Archive, 1-46792
3 Republic of Uzbekistan Documentary Film and Photo Archive, 0-103824
865 1 *Tashkent Retrospective*, author unknown
2 *Arkhitektura i stroitel'stvo Uzbekistana*, no. 11, 1982, 21
3 Photo: N.Vasil'kin From a set of postcards with views of Tashkent, Gafur Guliam Publishing House, 1980
4 https://pastvu.com/p/940082
5 https://pastvu.com/p/1034412
866 1–4 Photo: Armin Linke
867 1–6 Photo: Armin Linke
868 1 O'zshaharsozlik LITI Archive, 1562/71, sheet 2
2 O'zshaharsozlik LITI Archive, 1562/71, sheet 10
869 1 O'zshaharsozlik LITI Archive, 1562/17, sheet 4
2 O'zshaharsozlik LITI Archive, 1562/71, sheet 34
874 1 Republic of Uzbekistan Documentary Film and Photo Archive, 1-46792
2 Photo: GRACE
875 1 *Tashkent Retrospective*, author unknown
2 Photo: GRACE
881 1 Copyright: GRACE
Visualization: SUN
883 1 Copyright: GRACE
Visualization: SUN

Uzbekistan Hotel

885 1 gazeta.uz
894 1 https://en.wikipedia.org/wiki/FOCSA_Building
2 https://x.com/oxytan1/status/1532022166170087424
895 1 *Stroitel'stvo i arkhitektura Uzbekistana*, no. 7, 1967, 21
897 1 *Stroitel'stvo i arkhitektura Uzbekistana*, no. 1, 1975, 28
899 1 *Stroitel'stvo i arkhitektura Uzbekistana*, no. 7, 1967
906 1 Republic of Uzbekistan Documentary Film and Photo Archive, 1-39554
2 Republic of Uzbekistan Documentary Film and Photo Archive, 0-101400
3 Republic of Uzbekistan Documentary Film and Photo Archive, 1-39553
4 Republic of Uzbekistan Documentary Film and Photo Archive, 0-110191
5 Republic of Uzbekistan Documentary Film and Photo Archive, 1-46681
907 1 https://pastvu.com/p/995932
2 Photo: Dmitrii Bal'termants https://mytashkent.uz/wp-content/uploads/2015/02/ban2-800x560.jpg
3 Photo: V. Stukalov *Tashkent* (Leningrad: Aurora Art Publishers, 1977), ill. 2
4 Source unknown
5–7 Uzbekistan Hotel archive
908 1 Photo: GRACE
2–3 Photo: Armin Linke
909 1–6 Photo: Armin Linke
910 1 *Stroitel'stvo i arkhitektura Uzbekistana*, no. 7, 1967, 24
2 Republic of Uzbekistan Documentary Film and Photo Archive, 1-27775
3 *Stroitel'stvo i arkhitektura Uzbekistana*, no. 7, 1967, 22
4 *Stroitel'stvo i arkhitektura Uzbekistana*, no. 7, 1967, 23
5 *Stroitel'stvo i arkhitektura Uzbekistana*, no. 7, 1967, 22
6 *Stroitel'stvo i arkhitektura Uzbekistana*, no. 5, 1977, 27
7 *Stroitel'stvo i arkhitektura Uzbekistana*, no. 5, 1977, 28
911 1 Republic of Uzbekistan Documentary Film and Photo Archive, 1-27776
2 *Stroitel'stvo i arkhitektura Uzbekistana*, no. 5, 1977, 31
3 Philipp Meuser, *Die Ästhetik der Platte* (Berlin: DOM, 2015)
915 1 https://pastvu.com
2 Photo: PoliMi
3 Photo: Ilario Olivi https://www.facebook.com/photo?fbid=543639692332135&set=a.193372167358891
4 Photo: PoliMi
5 https://pastvu.com/p/1329167
6 Photo: PoliMi
916 1 Photo: V. Stukalov *Tashkent* (Leningrad: Aurora Art Publishers, 1977), ill. 2
2 Photo: PoliMi
3 *Stroitel'stvo i arkhitektura Uzbekistana*, no. 1, 1975, 30–31
4 Photo: PoliMi
5 *Stroitel'stvo i arkhitektura Uzbekistana*, no. 1, 1975, 27
6 Photo: PoliMi
921 1 Photo: Tongariki
2 Copyright: GRACE
Visualization: SUN
924 1 Copyright: GRACE
Visualization: SUN
925 1 Copyright: GRACE
Visualization: SUN

Buildings Analyzed in the Tashkent Modernism XX/XXI Project *Red text indicates that a condensed version of the respective Building Monograph is included in this volume.*	Listed and Protected	Visual Essay by Armin Linke	Statement of Significance	Preservation/ Adaptation Strategy
Panoramic Cinema	2019	p. 372	p. 456	p. 465
Central Committee of the Communist Party of Uzbekistan	2019		•	
Central Department Store (TsUM)				
House of Knowledge				
Institute of Oriental Studies				
Museum of Applied Arts	2019	p. 326	•	•
Council of Ministers				
Lenin Museum	2019	p. 344	p. 570	p. 580
Blue Domes Café	2019		•	
Tashkent University campus				
Institute of Art Studies		p. 340	•	
Ministries Building				
Residential buildings on Bogdan Khmel'nitskii Street		p. 286		
Zarafshan Restaurant				
State Museum of Arts	2024	p. 296	p. 786	p. 795
Exhibition Hall of the Union of Artists	2019	p. 334	p. 610	p. 618
Uzbekistan Hotel	2024	p. 290	p. 912	p. 920
House of Publishers			•	
Institute of Pectoral Surgery	2024	p. 418	•	
Delegation House of the Central Committee of the Uzbekistan Communist Party	2024	p. 330	•	•
Circus	2019	p. 394	p. 830	p. 838
House of Youth	2024	p. 364	p. 870	p. 879
Samarkand Teahouse				
Tashkent Institute of Irrigation and Agricultural Melioration (TIIMSKh)		p. 256		
TV Center	2024	p. 384	•	
Palace of Aviation Constructors	2024	p. 262	•	
Peoples' Friendship Palace	2019	p. 406	p. 528	p. 536
Chorsu Hotel				
Cosmonauts Avenue metro station	2024	p. 304	p. 490	p. 497
TV Tower	2019	p. 276	•	
Zhemchug residential building	2019	p. 308	p. 700	p. 711
Ben'kov Art College				
Republican House of Tourism		p. 288	•	
Sun Heliocomplex	2024	p. 236	p. 656	p. 667
Chorsu Bazaar	2024	p. 414	p. 742	p. 752
Turkestan Palace		p. 356		
Turkestan Arena	2024	p. 360	•	•